BRITISH NAVAL INTELLIGENCE

To Nicholas,

Who has contributed so
much to the history of
the Royal Navy in this
period.

With best wishes,

Andy B

October 2020.

To all who contributed to British naval intelligence
through the twentieth century

'Not by rambling operations, or naval duels, are wars decided, but
by force massed and handled in skilful combination.'
A T Mahan, *Sea Power in its Relations to the War of 1812*

BRITISH NAVAL INTELLIGENCE THROUGH THE TWENTIETH CENTURY

ANDREW BOYD

FOREWORD BY ANDREW LAMBERT

Seaforth
PUBLISHING

Copyright © Andrew Boyd 2020
First published in Great Britain in 2020 by
Seaforth Publishing,
A division of Pen & Sword Books Ltd,
47 Church Street,
Barnsley S70 2AS

www.seaforthpublishing.com

British Library Cataloguing in Publication Data
A catalogue record for this book is available from the British Library

ISBN 978 1 5267 3659 8 (HARDBACK)
ISBN 978 1 5267 3660 4 (EPUB)
ISBN 978 1 5267 3661 1 (KINDLE)

Pen & Sword Books Limited incorporates the imprints of Atlas,
Archaeology, Aviation, Discovery, Family History, Fiction, History,
Maritime, Military, Military Classics, Politics, Select, Transport, True
Crime, Air World, Frontline Publishing, Leo Cooper, Remember When,
Seaforth Publishing, The Praetorian Press, Wharncliffe Local History,
Wharncliffe Transport, Wharncliffe True Crime and White Owl

Maps by Peter Wilkinson, diagrams by Stephen Dent
Typeset by Mac Style

Printed and bound in the UK by CPI Group (UK) Ltd,
Croydon, CR0 4YY

Contents

List of Maps and Diagrams

List of Illustrations

The plate sections are between pages 296–297 and 552–553.

Admiral of the Fleet Sir John Fisher in 1915

Captain Sir Mansfield Cumming, first Chief of the Secret Intelligence
Service

The secret agent Hector Bywater in 1909

Captain William Reginald Hall in 1914, before becoming Director of
Naval Intelligence

Sir Alfred Ewing, head of Room 40, in 1915

Thüringen firing on *Black Prince* – Jutland night action

A E W Mason in 1915, Hall's most important agent

Nigel de Grey, Room 40 cryptographer

Sir William Wiseman, Secret Intelligence Service representative in America,
1915–1918

Alastair Denniston, Head of the Government Code and Cipher School,
in 1939

Alfred Dillwyn 'Dilly' Knox, leader of the British Enigma attack in the
late 1930s

The Secret Intelligence Service agent TR16's report on the Battle of Jutland

Rear Admiral Sir Hugh Sinclair, Chief of the Secret Intelligence Service,
1923–1939

Vice Admiral Sir William James, Deputy Chief of Naval Staff, in 1936

Vice Admiral John Godfrey, Director of Naval Intelligence, in 1942

Sidney Cotton, architect of British aerial photographic reconnaissance in the Second World War

Commander Ian Fleming, staff officer to Director of Naval Intelligence

Frank Birch, head of Bletchley's naval section from 1939

Mavis Lever, who made a crucial break into Italian naval Enigma

Hugh Foss, architect of successive attacks on Japanese naval attaché systems

John Tiltman, a dominant figure in British-American SIGINT for sixty years

Room 39 wartime morning meeting

Commander Rodger Winn, head of the Admiralty submarine tracking room, 1941–1945

Captain Alan Hillgarth as naval attaché in Madrid

Aerial photograph of the German battlecruiser *Scharnhorst* at Kiel, June 1942

Sinking of *Scharnhorst*, 26 December 1943

Rear Admiral Edmund Rushbrooke, Director of Naval Intelligence, 1942–1946

Vice Admiral Katsuo Abe, senior Japanese naval attaché in Europe, at Bergen, January 1944

The British UKUSA team, Harry Hinsley, Edward Travis and John Tiltman, in 1945

Rear Admiral Norman Denning on appointment as Director of Naval Intelligence in 1958

HM Submarine *Courageous* in the early 1970s

Moscow ABM site, 1967

British Chevaline Polaris warhead, early 1980s

Soviet Delta IV SSBN

Foreword

British naval intelligence is a familiar subject, but it has long stood in need of a coherent, consistent and, above all, reliable overview, connecting the capture of Napoleon's signal codes with Cold War satellite-based systems, one that emphasises the underlying need for improved understanding to inform decision-making. Andrew Boyd has closed that gap: this book is at once a comprehensive and sophisticated re-examination of a fascinating subject, an opportunity to emphasise the place of intelligence in the wider work of navies, in peace and war, and to stress the critical role of naval power in British policy. Furthermore, it is not a history of the Royal Navy's intelligence activity, but of the naval focus of the entire national intelligence gathering and processing effort, and the ways in which intelligence has informed all aspects of naval activity, from planning and mobilisation to specific operations and tactical methods.

Andrew Boyd's previous book, *The Royal Navy in Eastern Waters: The Linchpin of Victory 1935–1942* (2017), demonstrated a mastery of detail, incisive analysis and fresh thinking, which overturned accepted wisdom on a major aspect of the Second World War. *British Naval Intelligence* tackles a different subject, providing the vital long-term perspective, demonstrating how intelligence activity evolved to reflect the technologies of war and communication, the security climate, and the shift from peace to war. It was always linked to diplomacy, naval policy, operations and strategic planning. It is also a profoundly human story: individuals matter, especially those with the ability to improve the process and pass on their expertise. None escape a fresh analysis.

Naval intelligence has long excited popular interest, from Edwardian invasion scares to Ian Fleming's Commander James Bond RN, who, we are reminded, worked for MI6, not naval intelligence. However, this book demonstrates Fleming's work in the Second World War was far more important than the exploits of his literary creation, even if names and characters were redeployed from wartime fact to post-war fiction.

Fleming's fiction worked because it contained a critical element of reality, drawing from his wartime roles. In recent years, the publication of official histories and the release of substantial archival evidence has opened new approaches, which have made 'intelligence history' into an academic specialisation. This book exploits these new resources and fresh research, in a landmark text that will be the base line for future research. A field littered with controversy, and a significant amount of nonsense, has been accorded elegant, incisive analysis, one that dissects old myths and exposes suspect arguments. Famous tales of ignorant naval officers misunderstanding critical information provided by Room 40 during the First World War are dissected and discredited, before examining alternative, intelligence-led choices. Shifting the 1914–18 focus from Jutland to economic warfare and the peace process emphasises long-term trends, and the larger national role of naval intelligence. Britain needed to keep control of the seas, and preserve the ability to use that control to attack the economies of military rivals, because it relied on maritime strategy, not military power. The Navy has always been the right arm of the British state.

For all the headlines, intelligence did not 'win the war', and was rarely 'decisive': it enabled, supported and facilitated, and its importance was most obvious when it was lacking. 'Ultra' did not win the Battle of the Atlantic, but it did make a major contribution, best understood in the ebb and flow of events. Across this book there are repeating patterns, emphasising how a long-term mastery of context and the ability to anticipate hostile moves produced spectacular results. A series of crippling air and submarine attacks on large German warships from mid 1941 onward, including the very specific minelaying effort at the end of the Channel Dash, reduced a major threat to Atlantic shipping, releasing Royal Navy units for critical offensive operations in other theatres.

Better intelligence informed and enabled decision-making, at all levels, but the product was only as good as the questions that had been posed, and the skill of the analysts who processed the evidence. Above all, this approach emphasises something fundamental: highly capable professional organisations, like the Royal Navy, necessarily ask better questions of their intelligence organisations. Such organisations can refine and focus their efforts. The contrasting naval intelligence operations of Britain and Germany in the world wars reflected something more than technical proficiency. An ingrained maritime culture, willingness to ignore the party line, and listen to outsiders enabled British intelligence to defeat a powerful, but monolithic enemy. It is no accident that lawyers and historians feature throughout the book, for the ability to develop a case that is more than simply the sum of the facts has always been critical, while the benefit of past experience captured and processed to educate and inform future action was recognised by the Victorians.

Despite the occasional spectacular failure, British naval intelligence consistently outperformed rivals, enemies and allies, finding the human resources and innovative solutions to address new problems, taking on board new technologies, and welcoming allied input. The picture that emerges is of a nation that focused its intelligence efforts on the oceans, mobilised extraordinary resources, human and material, and made excellent use of sources that were not 'secret'. If there is a British way of acquiring and assessing intelligence, one that is strikingly outward-facing, with a distinctly naval character, then Andrew Boyd has written its history.

Andrew Lambert
Laughton Professor of Naval History,
King's College, London

Acknowledgements

I am indebted to numerous fellow historians who helped me tackle the challenges posed by this book which took me into areas and periods where my initial knowledge was limited.

Although most of their core work is now more than fifty years old, I have once again found that Arthur Marder and Stephen Roskill still provide an essential foundation to the history of the Royal Navy in the first half of the twentieth century. Nor could I easily have progressed without the pioneering contributions on British naval intelligence and its place in the wider intelligence community provided by Patrick Beesly, Donald McLachlan, Christopher Andrew, Keith Jeffery and, above all, the magisterial Second World War study by Harry Hinsley.

Professor Andrew Lambert not only kindly wrote the foreword, but his work has been an inspiration and model to which I can only aspire.

I owe particular thanks to Professor Derek Law and to Dr Anthony Wells who both read the entire text and offered much valuable comment and advice. Anthony produced the first comprehensive appraisal of British naval intelligence over the period 1880–1945 in his doctoral thesis completed almost fifty years ago under the guidance of Harry Hinsley, and has the distinction of having held major posts in both the British and American naval intelligence communities. I am also grateful for support and encouragement from Professors Saul David, Eric Grove, Peter Hennessy and Daniel Todman, and from Iain Mathewson. Tony Insall kindly shared his manuscript for *Secret Alliances*, which proved an excellent guide to British intelligence operations in Norway 1940–45, and Edward Hampshire helped in accessing Naval Historical Branch archives.

The study of British intelligence history has been transformed by the steady release of official British and American intelligence records over the last twenty-five years, yielding superb primary source material of which earlier historians could only dream. I have benefited not only from direct access to this material, but the outstanding research which others have done on it over the last two decades. Without their contributions I could not have plotted a sensible course through the mass of intelligence related information now available. I have especially valued the work of John Ferris, Ralph Erskine and Michael Smith. In tackling the Cold War period, I am indebted to the records available in the CIA digital library, which cover ground not yet available anywhere else.

I am again grateful for the outstanding service provided by the holders of relevant archives, in particular The National Archives at Kew, the Churchill Archives Centre at Cambridge, the British Library, the National Maritime Museum at Greenwich, and the Imperial War Museum.

It has again been a joy to work with Julian Mannering at Seaforth publishing. He has not only provided constant encouragement and outstanding support and advice, but has somehow tolerated and accommodated repeated requests for both greater length and more time. I also thank Stephanie Rudgard-Redsell for her excellent and sensitive editing, and her seemingly endless encyclopaedic knowledge of all matters naval.

Finally, I must thank my daughter Isabelle for all her help with maps and photographs, but the most important person of all has been my wife Ginette. She has once again not only endured my historical obsessions, but provided constant encouragement and support and deployed her fine editorial judgement.

Abbreviations

ABC-1	American British Staff Conference No 1
ABM	Anti-Ballistic Missile
ACCHAN	Allied Command Channel
ACINT	Acoustic Intelligence
ACNS	Assistant Chief of Naval Staff
AGI	Auxiliary Gatherer of Intelligence
AMWIS	Air Ministry Weekly Intelligence Survey
ARL	Admiralty Research Laboratory
ASD	Anti-Submarine Division (1916–1918)
ASDIC	Anti-Submarine Detection Investigation Committee
ASW	Anti-Submarine Warfare
BSC	British Security Co-ordination
CAS	Chief of Air Staff
CDS	Chief of the Defence Staff
CIA	Central Intelligence Agency
CIC	Combined Intelligence Committee
CIGS	Chief of the Imperial General Staff
C-in-C	Commander-in-Chief
CIU	Central Interpretation Unit
CNA	Centre for Naval Analyses
CNO	Chief of Naval Operations in the US Navy
COMINT	Communications Intelligence – intercept and analysis of communications passed by cable, wire, radio or other electronic means
COS	Chiefs of Staff
CSDIC	Combined Service Detailed Interrogation Centre
DCNS	Deputy Chief of Naval Staff
DGI	Director General Intelligence
DIA	Defence Intelligence Agency
DID	Director of Intelligence Division (1912–1917)
DIS	Defence Intelligence Staff

DMI	Director of Military Intelligence
DNI	Director of Naval Intelligence
DRC	Defence Requirements Committee
EASTLANT	NATO Command Eastern Atlantic
ELINT	Electronic Intelligence – intercept and analysis of non-communications transmissions
EW	Electronic Warfare
FECB	Far East Combined Bureau
FSL	First Sea Lord and Chief of Naval Staff
GC&CS	Government Code & Cipher School
GCHQ	Government Communications Headquarters, and successor to GC&CS
HTP	High Test Peroxide or Hydrogen Peroxide
ID	Intelligence Division (1912–1917)
IIC	Industrial Intelligence Centre
IJN	Imperial Japanese Navy
IJAAF	Imperial Japanese Army Air Force
IJNAF	Imperial Japanese Naval Air Force
IMINT	Imagery Intelligence
ISIS	Inter-services Information Series
IS (O)	Intelligence Section (Operations)
ISTD	Inter-services Topographical Department
IUSS	Integrated Undersea Surveillance System
JIB	Joint Intelligence Bureau
JIC	Joint Intelligence Committee
JN25	Japanese Navy Cipher
JPC	Joint Planning Committee
JPS	Joint Planning Staff
LOFAR	Low-Frequency Array
LRMP	Long-Range Maritime Patrol Aircraft
MIRV	Multiple Independent Re-entry Vehicle
NATO	North Atlantic Treaty Organisation
NEI	Netherlands East Indies
NID	Naval Intelligence Department (1887–1912), Naval Intelligence Division (1917–1965)
NRO	National Reconnaissance Office (US)
NSA	National Security Agency (US)
OIC	Operational Intelligence Centre
ONI	(United States) Office of Naval Intelligence
OSINT	Open Source Intelligence
OSS	Office of Strategic Services
PCO	Passport Control Organisation or Officer
PDU	Photographic Development Unit
PIU	Photographic Interpretation Unit

PM	Prime Minister
PNIO	Pacific Naval Intelligence Organisation
POW	Prisoner of War
PPAG	Polaris Performance Analysis Group
PR	Photographic Reconnaissance
PRU	Photographic Reconnaissance Unit
RAF	Royal Air Force
RESC	Restriction of Enemy Supplies Committee
RN	Royal Navy
RNAS	Royal Naval Air Service
SIGINT	Signals Intelligence – includes both COMINT and ELINT
SIS	Secret Intelligence Service
SNCP	Special Naval Collection Programme
SOE	Special Operations Executive
SONAR	Sound Navigation and Ranging
SOSUS	Sound Surveillance System
SURTASS	Surveillance Towed Array Sensor System
SSBN	Nuclear Ballistic Missile Submarine
SSGN	Nuclear Cruise Missile Submarine
SSN	Nuclear Attack Submarine
SSK	Conventional Submarine
TCH	Trade Clearing House
USN	US Navy
VCNS	Vice Chief of Naval Staff
WIR	Weekly Intelligence Report
WTID	War Trade Intelligence Department
WTSD	War Trade Statistical Department

Additional abbreviations used in references

ADM	Admiralty
AIR	Air Ministry
AT	Admiralty Telegram
CAB	Cabinet Office
CCA	Churchill College Archives, Cambridge
FO	Foreign Office
IWM	Imperial War Museum
JM	Japanese Monograph
MM	*Mariner's Mirror*
NHB	Naval Historical Branch
NMM	National Maritime Museum, Greenwich
PREM	Premier
TNA	The National Archives
UCI	University of California Irvine Libraries
WO	War Office

Introduction

The idea that secret services express a nation's subconscious resonates powerfully in Britain, where 'secret services' and 'intelligence' have special prominence in the national image projected across the twentieth century.[1] Any list of items chosen to symbolise Britain over this period might well include Bletchley Park and James Bond. The popular image of intelligence has inevitably influenced historians, who in turn have helped cultivate it.

Most of those examining Britain's journey across the last century now recognise that intelligence was an important, sometimes crucial, element in the operation of the British state, as it confronted threats to national survival through two world wars and the Cold War that followed. But even if Britain's historians have recognised the importance of intelligence, coverage and interest remain selective, especially in popular accounts. Specific sources receive too much attention, while the fragmentary nature of much intelligence and the complementary role of secret, diplomatic and open-source information is insufficiently stressed. Personalities are favoured over institutions. The big picture is frequently lost behind colourful, exciting, but often inaccurate 'spy stories' and one-off operations which glamorise the collection of intelligence, and neglect its assessment, and real operational and policy impact. Wars inevitably draw more attention than peacetime, where perceived intelligence failures and weakness are emphasised, while achievements are overlooked. The civilian intelligence agencies and their role, only gradually and reluctantly acknowledged by British governments in the 1980s, are a source of endless fascination, although too often with imperfect understanding. The contribution of the more overt military agencies is underestimated.

These themes are evident in the story of British naval intelligence from its modern origins in the 1880s. Popular histories and more specialist works have focused quite narrowly on the role of Room 40 and the birth of radio intercept and codebreaking in the First World War, and that of Enigma-based 'Special Intelligence' or 'Ultra' from Bletchley Park, and its particular contribution to the Battle of the Atlantic, in the Second. These contributions were important and deserve the scrutiny they have received. However, beyond them, with occasional notable exceptions, lies a void in both coverage and understanding. The importance of the Naval Intelligence Department (NID) to Royal Navy policy and planning in the decade before the First World War is increasingly acknowledged, but accounts have posed as many questions as answers over the quality and use of intelligence itself.[2] The interwar Naval Intelligence Division, as it was now renamed, is still invariably dismissed as a moribund institution, starved of money and people, contributing little of value to understanding and managing the rising Axis threats. The security demands of the Cold War, particularly in the important area of submarine operations, meant that historical scrutiny of post-1945 naval intelligence was negligible, until some records and first-hand testimony appeared in the last two decades. Despite important recent contributions, the picture here remains incomplete.[3]

Furthermore, while greater attention has been given to the role of naval intelligence in the two world wars, there are important gaps here too. Accounts of the First World War have emphasised the contribution of intelligence to fleet operations, primarily in the North Sea, but neglected its role in orchestrating the blockade against Germany and in countering the U-boat challenge. The focus on Bletchley Park in the Second World War overshadows the contributions from aerial photographic reconnaissance and human sources, including prisoners of war. Neither the sheer range of naval intelligence activity in these two wars, nor its ultimate strategic and operational value have been adequately addressed. There are also geographic imbalances, with coverage heavily weighted to the home and Atlantic theatres at the expense of the Mediterranean and the East.[4]

This limited coverage and, perhaps, limited interest in the story of British naval intelligence is surprising. From the eighteenth century, the Royal Navy and the maritime supremacy it achieved was widely regarded, with good reason, as the ultimate guarantor for the security and prosperity of the British nation and its empire. It symbolised British power and what it meant to be British. This belief, broadly endorsed without question by the ruling institutions of the British state, ensured the Royal Navy remained the largest and most widely deployed navy until 1942. Most modern historians accept that naval power was the critical factor in enabling Britain's survival and ultimate victory in the two world wars. While 1945 brought rapid decline, the Royal Navy still ranked third in size for the rest of the twentieth century, and in submarine warfare, especially in the second half of the Cold War, it achieved influence and impact for Britain far exceeding the resources expended in this area. The way intelligence created, supported and sustained this British naval power across the century deserves more scrutiny.

One obvious reason naval intelligence has been neglected is that any history confined to NID and the naval elements of its successor, the Defence Intelligence Staff (DIS), lacks the excitement and mystery and 'marketability' surrounding the activities of the Secret Intelligence Service (SIS) or Bletchley Park. With some important exceptions, NID in its successive incarnations did not run secret agents, nor did it often engage in the dramatic and daring operations associated with the Special Operations Executive (SOE). NID and DIS did run impressive covert technical programmes, sometimes involving drama and risk comparable to anything undertaken by SIS or SOE. Nevertheless, outside wartime, NID and DIS are usually portrayed as pedestrian, bureaucratic and even ineffective organisations, primarily processors of information collected by others, rather than collectors in their own right.[5] Even the writer Ian Fleming, staff officer to the wartime Director of Naval Intelligence (DNI) Vice Admiral John Godfrey, widely seen as the model for his fictional 'M', placed his action hero James Bond in MI6 rather than NID (although he did give him naval provenance with the rank of commander).

However, the story of modern British naval intelligence is more than the story of NID or DIS. The achievements of naval intelligence rested on contributions from all the different agencies which came together over the twentieth century to form the British intelligence community. Equally important, the requirements and processes and, to a significant extent, the traditions and values of naval intelligence created and then shaped that wider community. Those secret services at the heart of the British subconscious have a naval heritage.

The Royal Navy did not invent British Signals Intelligence (SIGINT) nor was the Admiralty's Room 40 the single dominant SIGINT organisation of the First World War. However, it was the DNI from 1914, Captain Reginald 'Blinker' Hall, who recognised the contribution SIGINT could make to strategic and political, as well as naval, intelligence. It was the Royal Navy from 1917, after many vicissitudes, which pioneered the integration of SIGINT with intelligence from other sources to deliver real-time operational effect. It was also the demands of the naval blockade which caused a separate agency, the War Trade Intelligence Department (WTID), to develop techniques for collecting and analysing communications data on an industrial scale. In these ways, British naval intelligence laid the foundations for modern SIGINT. The internet and modern social media now present SIGINT opportunities and challenges far beyond anything dreamt of by Hall and his colleagues. Yet many of the techniques and concepts in use today in the British Government Communication Headquarters (GCHQ) or the American National Security Agency (NSA), including emphasis on metadata and traffic analysis for counter-terrorist work, can be traced back to ideas first pioneered by Room 40 and WTID.

The first two chiefs of SIS (also known as MI6), Captain Mansfield Cumming (1909–1923) and Rear Admiral Sir Hugh 'Quex' Sinclair (1923–1939), were naval officers, Sinclair moving to SIS after succeeding Hall as DNI. Their naval background influenced the enduring values of SIS, and Cumming's provenance ensured that the Admiralty was the primary customer of the early service.[6] This helped guarantee SIS remained an inter-governmental service and avoided falling under the sway of the War Office. Sinclair also took control of Britain's first dedicated SIGINT agency, the Government Code and Cipher School (GC&CS), formed in 1919 after the First World War through the fusion of Room 40 and its military intelligence counterpart. Sinclair's nurturing of GC&CS through the difficult interwar years, when it was vulnerable to both political whim and financial stringency, reflected his awareness of the achievements of Room 40 and the structures, processes and values created around it. This was the context for providing the new GC&CS home at Bletchley Park in 1938, the infusion of new talent from civilian life and, ultimately, by drawing on the lessons of 1914–18, the creation of the mass SIGINT organisation that gave Britain such a valuable asset in the new war.

British naval intelligence in the First World War produced two principal and enduring lessons. These were valuable to the Royal Navy, but have proved time and again universally relevant to the successful practice of intelligence anywhere. The first is the value of including iconoclasts and free-thinkers drawn from a wide range of backgrounds in intelligence services, and encouraging challenge to conventional ideas and established practices. Reconciling such freedom with adequate political and financial accountability and security – let alone the hierarchy and discipline necessary to a fighting service – is difficult. The balance between fostering creativity and innovation without at best impairing operational efficiency, and at worst promoting organisational anarchy, is a fine one. It was perhaps most striking in Bletchley Park, where one member later recalled 'the mixture of efficiency with which the most important secrets of the war were uncovered' with its 'chaotic mad-hatter-tea-party insouciance'.[7] Hall got this balance right as DNI from 1914–19, and those who worked for and with him ensured his organisation and values were replicated on a wider scale in Britain's naval intelligence operation from 1939. The success of Hall and his legacy poses fascinating questions. Was the Royal

Navy of 1914 more open to intelligence, organisational, and cultural innovation than generally assumed? If so, why? Why did the Admiralty of the late 1930s similarly remain open to intelligence innovation? Was it primarily awareness of the previous wartime successes? Or did wider institutional and cultural influences allow senior admirals in 1940 to defer to the expertise of a 21-year-old Cambridge history undergraduate, Harry Hinsley?[8]

The second lesson was effective co-ordination – the decisive operational advantage gained by drawing together relevant intelligence from all sources and collocating it with own and enemy movements to produce a single, integrated operational picture. The Admiralty was reaching towards this concept from the autumn of 1917. The structures were still imperfect by the time of the armistice, although most advanced in the submarine tracking room, and they largely lapsed once the war ended. However, there was enough understanding among the remaining naval intelligence specialists in both NID and the new GC&CS and, even more important, the rising generation of senior naval officers in the 1930s, to ensure that the 1918 concepts could be resurrected and rapidly developed from 1937.[9] By the outbreak of war in 1939, the Admiralty Operational Intelligence Centre (OIC) surpassed the far-sighted vision held by some in 1918. The new OIC was an integral part of NID, but enjoyed the full support of senior naval staff. It received intelligence feeds directly from all parts of the British intelligence community, with especially close links to GC&CS, and combined this with all the information available to the operational sections of the Admiralty. Importantly, it had authority not only to communicate freely across the Admiralty, but also with naval commanders at sea and with other government departments.[10] The OIC was a visionary concept, not replicated on anything approaching the same level by either the other British services, or by any other country. Over the war, it set a standard for what could be achieved with an integrated intelligence picture, only occasionally replicated, and rarely surpassed, anywhere over the rest of the twentieth century. The OIC model remains visible in British and American structures created to deal with the new terrorism threats in the wake of 9/11, notably the British Joint Terrorism Analysis Centre (JTAC).

Another key aspect of the overall British intelligence story across the twentieth century is the intelligence relationship with the United States, increasingly important as the century progressed. This again originated with naval needs and capabilities, which played an enduring role in shaping it. NID initiated the formal exchange of intelligence with its US Navy counterpart after American entry into the war in 1917, although

Hall had developed important American contacts well before this, facilitating his management of the Zimmermann telegram operation. Formal relations ended after the war, as the two navies entered a period of suspicion and rivalry lasting into the 1930s. Intelligence-sharing then cautiously resumed in 1938, when the Admiralty decided to treat the Americans 'exceptionally'. Initially driven by shared perceptions of the growing threat from Japan in the Far East, relations expanded rapidly with the outbreak of the European war in September 1939. By 1940, the trust established through the naval intelligence exchanges stimulated a wider relationship, drawing in the other services and, importantly, GC&CS. The close British-American SIGINT relationship, later enshrined in the first post-war 1946 UKUSA agreement, began with an American visit to Bletchley Park in February 1941, where the Americans shared their successful breaking of the Japanese Purple diplomatic cipher, and the British reciprocated with briefing on the German Enigma. However, it was shared naval interests that dominated the intelligence agenda for the next two years, and substantially influenced structures and attitudes which shaped the wider intelligence relationship for the next fifty. The partnership that evolved through those years comprised multiple strands, but Britain consistently made naval contributions that outweighed the far smaller resources she deployed.

This contribution of British naval intelligence in the second half of the twentieth century, dominated by the Cold War, has received limited attention from historians. It has mainly featured as a by-product in studies focused elsewhere, either addressing the work of SIS, GCHQ, or the Security Service (MI5), or accounts of the naval aspects of specific conflicts, notably the Falklands War in 1982. This is partly because for the first fifteen years of the Cold War (1947–62) the naval threat from the Soviet Union is invariably presented as a distant third to the strategic nuclear threat from aircraft and land-based missiles, and the conventional land threat in central Europe. Until recently, reference to naval intelligence in this period was invariably confined to an embarrassing high-profile failure (the Commander Crabb incident in Portsmouth harbour in 1956) and damaging Soviet intelligence penetrations (the Portland spy ring and the Vassal case). The void in historical coverage after the early 1960s, only now receiving some, if selective, study, has reflected the limited release of government records (at least in Britain), and admirable silence by participants in Cold War intelligence activity, which mirrors the attitude of the previous Bletchley Park generation.

So there is an important and wider story to tell here too. The British intelligence community played a bigger part in understanding and countering Soviet naval power through the Cold War than has so far been recognised. Although some aspects of this role, notably submarine-based intelligence collection in the Barents Sea, have received increasing attention, this is only one part of a complex picture with many interlocking strands. Little note has been taken of the crucial naval insights provided by Colonel Oleg Penkovsky, the Soviet agent jointly run by SIS and the American Central Intelligence Agency (CIA) in the early 1960s. The closeness and importance of the British-American relationship in aerial photographic and imagery intelligence, which parallels the SIGINT relationship, how and why it developed as it did and its role in Cold War naval intelligence, is likewise rarely mentioned. In order properly to understand British policy and strategy through the Cold War, British-American relations over the last seventy-five years, the history and credibility of the British nuclear deterrent, or the nature of the British intelligence community today, it is essential to include this naval intelligence dimension.

Furthermore, the Soviet threat during the Cold War was never an exclusive preoccupation for British naval intelligence. The retreat from empire and its residual responsibilities was a significant focus for the Royal Navy until the 1970s. One-third of its frontline strength was deployed east of Suez in the 1960s, and the confrontation with Indonesia over its claim to Malaysia had the potential to become a major naval war. The year 1982 brought the Falklands War and the requirement to build a major intelligence capability against Argentina, almost from scratch. Naval intelligence has also contributed to modern needs in unexpected ways. The geographic studies of Iraq originally produced by NID in the 1920s proved invaluable to American and British planners in the second Iraq war in 2003.

Finally, before readers continue this book, it is essential to clarify what it means by 'intelligence'. In recent years this has become a much used, and abused, term. Two important questions are: how does 'intelligence' differ from 'information'; and does intelligence have to derive from secret sources? References to 'diplomatic intelligence' or to 'open-source intelligence' are increasingly common. Evidently, these categories do not derive from 'secret sources', a term also requiring definition. There is no standard answer to these questions. In this book, 'intelligence' is defined as information that met two criteria. First, it was information collected to meet requirements bearing on the security or well-being of the British state set by servants of the British state. Secondly, the same information required protection from parties hostile to the British state. It is these joint needs for *discrimination* and *protection* that define 'intelligence' across the period covered. Information relating to British national interests provided in confidence by a trusted contact to a British ambassador or naval attaché does, indeed, still represent intelligence. Although not collected by an intelligence agency deploying covert means, the information meets a requirement and requires protection, using a 'confidential' or even 'secret' classification. Similarly, the intercepted bearing of a U-boat transmission and/or the plain-language content of that transmission by a Royal Navy corvette during the Battle of the Atlantic also counts as intelligence, even though no secret agency was involved. The point is that the information acquired by the corvette met a state requirement, while the effectiveness of the intercept technique, and even its very existence, required protection too.

Much of the intelligence described in this book, and often the most important categories, nevertheless comprises that derived by 'secret sources'. Intelligence from secret sources, or 'secret intelligence', requires the discrimination defined above, but takes the protection under which it is collected and processed to a new level. Britain developed secret intelligence capabilities across the period covered by this book (and into the present day) to penetrate the most protected areas of hostile states (or other parties of interest), and obtain, against their wishes, information they did not want Britain or others to know. To be successful, such British intelligence activities – direction, collection and processing – must be concealed from hostile states and others. If British knowledge or the British hand in obtaining it was revealed, the target power would take action to mitigate its information loss, undermining the value of the British intelligence effort. While most British secret intelligence activity described in this book was aimed at understanding the intentions and capabilities of hostile naval powers, it also sometimes aimed to exert covert influence over the policies and actions of hostile states and parties to British advantage. In short, therefore, through secret intelligence activity, the British state aimed to achieve understanding of, and exert influence over, hostile states and others, not possible through overt political or diplomatic activity.[11]

Intelligence has limitations. The former United States Defence Secretary, Donald Rumsfeld, was much mocked for his 'known unknowns', but he expressed an important point. In principle, intelligence can uncover many of an enemy's secrets. The enemy's order of battle may not be known, but it is knowable. The enemy's intentions may not be known, but they too are knowable, although they may change for many reasons. But there are also 'mysteries' which are essentially unknowable. What a leader truly believes, or how that leader and his colleagues would react under extreme pressure, such as a nuclear confrontation, cannot be known, but can only be judged. Judgement is, therefore, often an important element in understanding and using intelligence. It should still be informed by the best available information, which often includes secret intelligence, but it has to accommodate both secrets and mysteries, and it cannot offer certainty.[12]

Clearly, a book like this one involves difficult choices over structure and content. The most important decision was to set the period covered from the foundation of a modern Naval Intelligence Department in the 1880s, with a single-chapter introduction placing this in the context of developments earlier in the nineteenth century, through to the natural breakpoint provided by the end of the Cold War in 1989. The intelligence requirements faced by Britain after this date were very different from the Cold War, and the specific naval aspects more limited. The thirty years up to the present day need to be treated as a whole, rather than artificially broken in the year 2000, and authoritative government records for this period are lacking. Having defined beginning and end points, doing proper justice to the naval intelligence story in a single-volume history across these hundred years, including two global wars and a long, armed confrontation, has proved challenging. The book aims to cover the developments and achievements that were most important, to explain not only how intelligence was collected but why, and with what result. I have tried to avoid sterile bureaucratic history, and to give some feel for key personalities who shaped events. However, in the space available, it cannot be comprehensive. To put this problem in context, Professor Sir Harry Hinsley's definitive multi-volume *British Intelligence in the Second World War* devoted space equivalent to this book solely to the naval intelligence aspects of his conflict, and he omitted the Far East theatre. Similar space could easily be devoted to the First World War and Cold War, let alone the various peacetime periods. A deliberate choice, therefore, has been not to repeat detailed accounts of intelligence operations and events already well covered elsewhere. For example, the book gives only limited space to the Zimmermann telegram affair in 1917 and concentrates solely on aspects that are new or deserve more emphasis, and it does not describe the famous Operation Mincemeat in 1943 at all. Likewise, it avoids much detail on the technicalities of Enigma. Whether the story that follows suffers from those omissions, readers must now judge.

PART I

The Foundation of Modern Naval Intelligence

1

Beginnings 1800–1882

The Admiralty only took the first hesitant steps towards forming a dedicated department for collecting and assessing intelligence to support the Royal Navy in the early 1880s. That did not mean the value of intelligence in achieving British naval objectives was previously unrecognised. The need for information advantage, advance knowledge of the intentions, strength and capability of hostile naval forces, had always existed, and intelligence in the widest sense of the term played at least some part in most naval conflicts from the dawn of a recognisable Royal Navy. However, even the global naval challenges Britain faced during the Napoleonic Wars from 1793–1815 did not cause the Admiralty to create any lasting organisation to identify naval intelligence requirements and collect against them within a systematic framework. Through these wars and the bulk of the Victorian period, naval intelligence was essentially a devolved, informal and unstructured business, heavily dependent on individual initiative. Fleet or squadron commanders received an operational directive which might include initial background information and any subsequent political or military insights on enemy forces available in London. But it was then left to frontline naval commanders and local British diplomatic representatives to seek any information to help achieve their objectives.[1]

Despite this lack of any central naval intelligence organisation, by the start of the French war in 1793 there were significant established capabilities within the wider British state both for collecting intelligence and conducting other covert operations. These capabilities shaped intelligence structures and attitudes towards the business of intelligence in the future. The first and most important was money. There had long been government funding allocated for 'secret services', and from 1797 this became subject to annual vote by Parliament. This secret fund could

3

be accessed by the principal secretaries of state for home and foreign affairs and by the first commissioner of the Admiralty and secretary of state for war. They in turn approved requests for covert funding from British officials, civil or military, home or overseas. Prior to 1900, the 'secret service vote' never funded any established intelligence service. It was used for political and diplomatic bribery, funding propaganda, paying part-time informants, and undertaking any other secret operations by freelance agents. During the Napoleonic wars, annual expenditure under this vote regularly exceeded £100,000, with a peak of £172,830 in 1805 (just over one per cent of the naval vote that year), and the bulk of this wartime secret funding focused on activity directed at the French naval threat. After 1815 the secret vote declined sharply and by the late nineteenth century, largely now under Foreign Office control, it was often less than £30,000. Its lasting significance was to give British governments an enduring financial mechanism to support secret intelligence activity. It provided the means to fund secret agencies from 1909 through most of the twentieth century with minimal oversight. In different form, it continues to this day.[2]

Another important capability in the embryonic secret state was the Post Office. By the late eighteenth century, on behalf of the government, this ran a comprehensive and increasingly sophisticated organisation for delivering official and private correspondence, not only within the United Kingdom and British territories overseas, but also into many parts of Europe. This organisation was a fruitful source of intelligence from its wide-ranging network of officials, and through the covert interception and opening of mail. By 1800, the Post Office 'secret office', managing interception and located within the Foreign Office, employed a staff of ten (alongside an official Foreign Office strength in London that year of about twenty personnel), which during the war years concentrated mainly on foreign, especially diplomatic, correspondence. Supporting the secret office was a small Deciphering Branch, controlled by the Foreign Office and funded by the secret vote, and for over 120 years run by the family of its founder Edward Willes, a bishop of Bath and Wells. In addition to attacking foreign ciphers, it also produced ciphers for British use. Unfortunately, Willes's descendants lacked his cryptographic aptitude and the quality of the service declined steadily after his death in 1773, contributing less value through the Napoleonic wars than it should have.[3] Post Office interception had petered out and the Deciphering Branch closed by 1850. This reflected increased political sensitivity to exposure of interception and the use of private couriers for carrying high-value diplomatic correspondence. Nevertheless, the capabilities resumed in different form, largely under Admiralty initiative, in the First World War.[4]

A third asset, of more specific value to the Admiralty, was Lloyd's of London, which by 1800 was the greatest centre of marine insurance in the world, covering risks approaching £100 million (about 25 per cent of British GDP). The success of the Lloyd's operation depended on a unique system of global maritime intelligence. It recorded shipping arrivals and departures on a worldwide basis, and received all relevant news of political, naval and military significance from its extensive network of agents. All of this intelligence was potentially available to the Admiralty, which in turn passed on naval information judged useful to Lloyd's and its customers, including details of convoy sailings. Lloyd's also worked closely with the Post Office, which accorded Lloyd's special privileges in distributing its shipping newspaper *Lloyd's List* and communicating with its agents.[5]

These state capabilities demonstrate that the Admiralty did not seek or receive intelligence in isolation. The offices of the three secretaries of state for home and colonies, war, and the foreign department all sought intelligence to meet their specific requirements. Each also sometimes commissioned reporting at the request of the Admiralty to meet Admiralty requirements. Thus Evan Nepean, the undersecretary at the Home Office from 1782–94, who ran an extensive espionage network, deployed agents to cover French naval activity at Toulon, Brest and on the Normandy coast in 1784–5. (Nepean's subsequent career included stints as undersecretary for war in 1794, secretary to the Board of Admiralty from 1795–1804 and chief secretary for Ireland 1804–5, thus covering every major intelligence role in the British state.) Along with the Admiralty, each of these offices shared information they judged relevant to another department. Anything involving Ireland went to the Home Office, which passed it on to the Irish government in Dublin, while anything involving activity at sea was copied to the Admiralty. Such information was also usually passed with an assessment of its reliability. Significant reports from any department were shared with relevant minsters, and often with the Cabinet.[6]

In the period 1750–1850, and crucially through the global conflict with Napoleonic France, the Admiralty could therefore draw on significant intelligence assets. There was money to finance intelligence collection, support from the assets controlled by other departments, the prospect of at least some strategic political and military intelligence through Post Office interception, and a constantly updated global picture of maritime movements from Lloyd's. However, the central Admiralty organisation in this period was tiny, perhaps sixty staff in 1800 from the political head, the First Lord, through to the most junior clerk. There was no dedicated intelligence staff and, indeed, no war planning staff at all.

In the absence of such a staff, the focal point for intelligence was the First Lord, along with his senior civil servant, the first (or principal) secretary to the Board of Admiralty. They received any intelligence available in London, including that from London-controlled secret agents, embassy and consular networks, the foreign press, debriefing of merchant ship captains, as well as the sources already described. They used the secret vote to commission collection operations directly or, more often, to support collection by frontline naval commanders or British representatives overseas. Both the Admiralty directly and fleet commanders ordered reconnaissance operations by Royal Navy vessels to assess the naval strength and support facilities of enemy countries, actual or potential, in peacetime as well as wartime. Both commissioned Royal Navy officers, either active or unemployed who had suitable language skills and aptitude, to visit hostile countries on intelligence missions. Examples were Captain Philippe d'Auvergne, who commanded a squadron of small ships based in Jersey and maintained surveillance of the French Atlantic ports from the 1780s through the Napoleonic wars, until retiring as a rear admiral in 1812;[7] Captain Sir William Sidney Smith, who participated in nefarious clandestine operations for nearly twenty years from 1793;[8] Captain Leake of the Royal Artillery, deployed by the Admiralty in the eastern Mediterranean in the early 1800s;[9] and Lieutenant Henry Wood, deployed by Vice Admiral Sir Horatio Nelson, when Commander-in-Chief Mediterranean, to reconnoitre the Black Sea in 1804.[10] Both the Admiralty and local commanders used paid informants of variable quality who were judged to have relevant and useful access. Occasionally, these were long-standing and of enduring value. A Dutch woman, Margrete Wolters, based in Rotterdam, ran a network directed at French and Spanish naval activity from the Seven Years War through to the late 1780s.[11] Finally, although the Admiralty possessed no dedicated intelligence office or assessment staff, the clerks to the principal secretary compiled a classified index by geographical area into which every piece of intelligence was inserted. Relevant information about sources, including payment, was carefully recorded.[12]

The unstructured and dispersed nature of British naval intelligence over the century from 1750 makes it difficult to judge its strategic impact. There were specific operations during the Napoleonic wars where it had a critical effect, notably during Napoleon Bonaparte's expedition to Egypt, which culminated in the dramatic victory by Nelson at the Nile on 1 August 1798. The intelligence record here demonstrates both success and failure, and beautifully illustrates how naval intelligence was acquired and assessed in this period. It also emphasises the limitations posed by the slow communications of the time, and imperfect co-ordination between different departments in London. The Admiralty was too slow to bring order to an admittedly confused intelligence picture from multiple sources and identify Egypt as Napoleon's target, although there was sufficient evidence in London by the end of April. The final direction Nelson received was that Napoleon would strike in the Mediterranean at any of Spain, Naples or conceivably the Levant, which was of limited help. On the positive side, the intelligence did persuade the Admiralty to send powerful reinforcements to join him. Nelson's ultimate success came from his faith in the judgement of John Udney, the British consul in Leghorn (now Livorno), who convinced him to focus on Egypt. He possibly also exploited the fortuitous capture of a map of Aboukir Bay, where the French fleet had anchored. Had Nelson known earlier of the growing evidence in London pointing to Egypt, he might have caught Napoleon's crowded transports at sea, winning an even more decisive victory, and probably ending Napoleon's prospects.[13] Perhaps conscious of this missed opportunity, Nelson devoted much effort to improving the Mediterranean intelligence network in his later period in overall command there from 1803–05.[14]

Other examples of intelligence-led success include the victory over the Spanish at St Vincent in 1797, exploiting excellent local sources acquired by the Royal Navy commander, Vice Admiral Sir John Jervis,[15] and the successful interception of a Spanish treasure fleet in 1804, a good instance of London ordering decisive action in response to intelligence from a local commander.[16] Intelligence was a significant factor in Nelson's pursuit of the French fleet to the West Indies in early summer 1805 and overall British judgements that the French navy was conducting a series of feints to cover an invasion.[17] Intelligence from naval sources also made an important contribution to British Army operations in the Peninsular War from 1808–13.[18] Finally, there are striking examples in this period of the Royal Navy using intelligence, not always successfully, to alleviate the logistic wear and tear involved in maintaining a close observational blockade off enemy ports, an operational challenge it would face again one hundred years later.[19]

Two other capabilities important to the evolution of naval intelligence arrived in this period. The first was the creation of the visual shutter telegraph system, which enabled simple messages to be transmitted from the Admiralty through line-of-sight relay stations to select naval bases and other key sites. A line to Portsmouth opened in 1796, enabling messages to pass in fifteen minutes, and one to Plymouth in 1808. These landlines were complemented by coastal signal stations, which by 1800 covered much of the south and east coasts from Land's End to Berwick. Intelligence could thus be transmitted in almost real time from London to any naval unit in line of sight along the coast, and then relayed on by fast frigate.[20] Of more lasting importance was the *General Code of Signals*, invented by Rear Admiral Sir Home Riggs Popham and adopted by the Admiralty from 1803. Popham provided a new flag-signalling system using twenty-four flags and eleven special indicators. The flags conveyed a message through a number, translated by sender and recipient using a double-entry codebook, but by using the indicators the flags also represented letters in order to spell out unusual words. In its final form, Popham's system offered over 250,000 different signals and was used by the Royal Navy with minimal change for the next two hundred years. By using a telescope, complex messages could now be sent and received at extreme visibility range. Intelligence could, therefore, be transmitted at sea, and exploited operationally more effectively and efficiently. It particularly helped the conduct of blockade operations.[21] The concept of an alphanumeric double-entry codebook remained applicable in the age of radio, opening up far-reaching intelligence opportunities covered later.

In 1815 Britain emerged from the Napoleonic wars as the pre-eminent global power and for the next two generations, by most measures, its lead increased. By 1875, its population rose by 67 per cent, but GDP per capita still doubled in real terms.[22] By 1860, with 2 per cent of the world's population, Britain's share of manufacturing output was 20 per cent, with a higher share of the most modern industries, and it was still increasing; it produced 50 per cent of iron, coal and lignite, and consumed five times the energy of its nearest rival. It controlled one-fifth of world trade and two-fifths of that in manufactured goods. Britain possessed one-third of the world's merchant marine, a share that reached around half by the early twentieth century.[23] Britain was carrier for the world and Lloyd's of London insured this shipping. After Waterloo, the pound sterling became the preferred currency for almost all international trade and commercial transactions. This economic power generated huge surpluses, much of which was invested overseas. British overseas investment was just £10 million in 1815 (or 1.85 per cent of GDP), but £1 billion by 1875 (75 per cent), £2.5 billion by 1900 (126 per cent), and £4 billion by 1914 (158 per cent).

The foundations for achieving this global economic power were in place before the French wars began in 1793, and were intimately linked with naval power. In 1793 British pre-eminence at sea was still contested and had been found wanting in the American war for independence. In 1815 the Royal Navy emerged in undisputed command of the oceans.[24] This maritime supremacy was the critical factor that converted British economic potential into actuality. For the rest of the nineteenth century and beyond, it remained a symbiotic relationship. Naval dominance, in the 'long lee of Trafalgar', enabled British global economic power to flourish without check or interference. Economic wealth and industrial strength, especially in the maritime sector, where by the 1870s Britain produced 80 per cent of oceangoing shipping, ensured Britain could see off any potential naval challenger with ease.

For at least sixty years after 1815, there was no credible threat to Britain's maritime security. The only serious challengers at sea were France and Russia, and the Admiralty, reflecting government policy established in 1817, nominally maintained a 'two-power' standard of strength for the Royal Navy, to match a Franco-Russian combination, a standard which remained in force for the rest of the century.[25] Only France presented a plausible threat to the British homeland and there were war scares every decade or so, fed especially by competing interests in the Mediterranean. It is doubtful British political leaders ever saw a major conflict with France, let alone invasion, as an imminent, rather than theoretical, possibility. However, the belief that steam power had effectively 'bridged' the Channel and could facilitate a surprise French attack had traction for a while, creating sufficient nervousness by the late 1850s for the government to invest heavily in new fortifications to protect major ports.[26] There is an argument that the French navy proved better at identifying and exploiting technological innovation in the mid-nineteenth century with its early adoption of steam power for major war vessels in the 1840s and the building of the first iron-clad warship, *Gloire*, in 1858, providing potential 'seriously to rival and even surpass' the Royal Navy through the 1860s.[27] However, despite bouts of Admiralty anxiety, the French never found the political will or the sustained resources to mount a credible challenge to British naval supremacy. This was partly because French initiatives always drew a rapid and overwhelming response. The French might innovate, but the British rapidly bettered their designs and, with superior economic and industrial strength and greater shipbuilding resources, could always comfortably out-build France. Above all, there was the rock-solid political and public consensus in Britain that a superior fleet to the Royal Navy would not be tolerated.[28]

Throughout the century, the primary British concern over Russia was that she would exploit the weakening Ottoman Empire to achieve a dominant position in the eastern Mediterranean. Russian ambitions here were checked by her defeat in the Crimean War 1854–56 by Britain and France in alliance with the Ottomans. However, the Ottoman Empire remained vulnerable, and the security of the eastern Mediterranean became more important to Britain with the opening of the Suez Canal in 1869. The potential threat posed by a powerful Russian fleet in the Black Sea to Britain's primary route to the East, especially if it combined with a hostile France, thus remained a key factor in British strategic calculations. In 1877 Russia again went to war with Turkey, and her control of Constantinople and the Dardanelles, and therefore safe exit to the Mediterranean, looked imminent. The Russian threat in the Mediterranean was also complicated in the final decades of the century by the growing land threat she posed to India, and her more limited naval threat to British interests in the Far East.

While the potential threats from France and Russia caused occasional concern through the middle decades of the century, they never seriously undermined British confidence in her maritime dominance. There was, therefore, little incentive for the Admiralty to develop or improve its naval intelligence operation. For over two generations, it not only failed to build on the intelligence successes achieved against Napoleon, but several capabilities atrophied. In peacetime, money was tighter and both the naval and secret votes declined sharply. Within fifteen years, both were around a third of their 1815 level. By the 1850s, the Foreign Office had become a larger and more professional operation, but professionalising diplomatic work provoked deliberate distancing from any covert activity, such as use of foreign paid informants, which might bring embarrassment. The Deciphering Branch was closed in 1844, ending diplomatic codebreaking for seventy years.[29] The Admiralty even found it difficult to persuade the Foreign Office to continue routine naval returns from consular officials at overseas ports.[30] The War Office also let intelligence-gathering decline. It later acknowledged that 'secret service work' was largely forgotten after 1815, and that neither Britain nor France had any useful information during the Crimean campaign.[31]

This bleak picture of mid-century naval intelligence capability requires perspective. Admiralty tracking of foreign naval strengths was neither consistent nor comprehensive, and the details issued to the fleet were often out of date. Given the tiny number of professional naval officers in the Admiralty at this time, it could hardly be otherwise. However, the standard reporting through Foreign Office, and sometimes War Office, sources was sufficient to alert the Admiralty to any foreign naval developments of potential concern. The Admiralty also still commissioned authoritative intelligence when it mattered, as demonstrated in an assessment of relative

British and French naval strength produced in July 1858, when concern over developing French capability was reaching its height. This drew on a detailed report commissioned from Colonel Edward Claremont, military commissioner at the Paris embassy, who visited most of the important French naval centres, with impressive results.[32]

There were also positive developments, with important implications for the future, in this period. The first was the introduction of the telegraphic cable, invented by Samuel Morse in 1837. The Admiralty established cable links between London and the key naval bases in the 1840s, replacing the visual shutter system; the first cross-channel link was achieved in 1851, and the first permanent transatlantic link in 1866. The initial impetus for developing a global cable network was commercial, but by 1870 the British government had recognised the strategic value of an empire network based on submarine cables, and the first line to India was laid that year. These imperial cables were routed so as to be entirely under British control, and with Royal Navy supremacy they were immune to interference in wartime.[33] The completion of this British network meant government messages, including diplomatic and military intelligence, could be communicated to all parts of the empire within hours and with high security. During the Napoleonic war, Admiralty messages often took many weeks just to reach the western Mediterranean. The telegraphic cable did not in itself stimulate the Admiralty to create a new intelligence organisation, but it offered greater potential if and when one appeared. It was ironic that the Foreign Office terminated its deciphering capability just when a much richer source of traffic for interception was about to be created.

A second followed the creation of a Royal Navy Hydrographic Office under Alexander Dalrymple in 1795. This was firmly established by the end of the war, but in the following decade the Admiralty endorsed a worldwide chart system. The driver behind this was the rapid upsurge in world trade and the belief that wherever British ships traded, the Royal Navy must protect them. Wherever either went, they needed charts to navigate safely. This global charting effort began in the 1820s, and was overseen for twenty-five years by the greatest of all Hydrographers, Francis Beaufort. He could draw on a vast Admiralty archive of maritime information which had developed since the mid eighteenth century. Over this period, every Royal Navy vessel not only kept a log, but also a 'remark book' which recorded information on the waters and coasts visited. The standard remark book, which was forwarded to the Admiralty, contained entries on depth soundings, suitable anchorages, sources of fresh water, wood and provisions, potential landing places, details of fortifications and any other relevant intelligence. The books frequently included sketches of coasts with significant landmarks and points of interest.[34] By the mid 1850s, the Admiralty Chart series was truly worldwide, with two thousand charts covering every sea. These were backed by a system for updating them, and by supporting publications, such as sailing directions and tide tables.[35] The main impetus was undoubtedly commercial, but there were important intelligence implications. It facilitated the global mobility of the Royal Navy, but it also created a global database of maritime information which could be exploited to military advantage in the future. The survey process also created a new network of global contacts exploitable for wider intelligence purposes. Two excellent examples of the application of intelligence collected by the Hydrographic Office are a detailed assessment prepared in December 1861 for a Royal Navy blockade of the United States eastern seaboard in the event of conflict provoked by the American Civil War,[36] and the advice given during the confrontation with Russia in 1878 that the Russian forts at Kronstadt and Sveaborg were too strong to be reduced by bombardment.[37] Hydrographic and geographic information became an intimate part of the future Naval Intelligence Division and its successor through the twentieth century.

The final development was the creation of the naval attaché. Naval and military attachés were serving officers posted to embassies as specialist military advisers and commentators on military affairs. The War Office began posting attachés in the mid 1850s, beginning with Paris, and the Admiralty followed suit with the appointment of a single naval attaché to Paris in 1860.[38] While the army appointed attachés to specific capitals of interest, gradually building a network across Europe, the Admiralty approach was different. In 1871, at Foreign Office suggestion, they abolished their single attaché post in Paris to create a travelling attaché. Instead of a single officer permanently based in a country, an officer would visit all countries in Europe that possessed a navy of interest to Britain. This concept of the itinerant attaché, with a second officer soon appointed to share the workload, inevitably made it harder to acquire deep expertise on a specific country. Nor could a visitor hope to build the personal relationships of trust that might deliver valuable information.[39] The intelligence value the Admiralty got from its attachés before 1900 was therefore more limited than it could have been with a small additional investment. However, the itinerant attaché reporting on the French and Russian navies, the two that mattered in the final decades of the nineteenth century, was still of good quality and influential. While not ideal, the itinerant concept could also be developed in the future, exploiting the army model for comparison. Meanwhile, the reporting from itinerant attachés drove a demand for some section within the Admiralty to process their reports and to provide direction. Their existence, therefore, contributed to emerging pressure for a more structured approach to intelligence.

If Britain was confident it could command the oceans in the decades before 1860, the remainder of the century proved more challenging. This was not because either France or Russia became notably more hostile. Nor was there increased prospect of a Franco-Russian naval alliance actively directed at Britain. Nor was it likely that Britain might lack the political will, the financial and industrial resources, or the technical capability, to maintain a comfortable two-power standard, if this seemed appropriate. The challenge was rather the unprecedented rate at which naval technology was changing, and how this interacted with Britain's rapidly changing geo-strategic situation.

By the 1860s, Britain's share of world trade was peaking at 25 per cent. Thereafter, it slowly declined, but it was still 17 per cent, well above its nearest rivals, in 1900. This trade brought great wealth, but it also reflected growing dependence on the import of food and raw materials to feed the fast-growing population and industrialisation. In the 1830s, over 90 per cent of food consumed was home-produced. By 1900, nearly half Britain's grain and meat was imported. The proportion of raw materials imported by this date was higher, around 80 per cent in many key categories. Britain's dependence on seaborne imports was greater than that of other major powers, who could more easily exploit the rapid improvement and greater diversity in land communications brought by the railways. Britain was, therefore, uniquely vulnerable to disruption of her sea communications. As Admiral Sir John Fisher, the future First Sea Lord declared: 'It's not invasion we have to fear if our Navy's beaten, it's starvation.'[40]

If an attack on Britain's seaborne trade was an existential threat, the Admiralty had to assess what form an attack would take in practice, and how to counter it. Through the 1870s and into the early 1880s, it faced a complex mix of problems here, for which it was ill-equipped in policy and strategy development, and therefore struggled to address.[41] Britain remained the pre-eminent maritime power, but over the decades since 1815, in structure and organisation, in deployment and mindset, the Royal Navy had steadily assumed the characteristics of a global maritime police force. It was well-suited to protecting expanding British trade and newly acquired territory from local and small-scale threats, and for executing special tasks like anti-slavery. It was less prepared for conflict with a major naval power. This was not a matter of overall resources, where it held its decisive lead, but these resources had become widely dispersed. In a rapidly changing strategic environment, the Royal Navy had to balance concentration against the main fleet of a potential enemy with adequate protection for its increasingly vulnerable trade routes.

In the Napoleonic wars Britain had secured its sea communications by blockading enemy fleets in harbour and by convoying essential merchant traffic under naval escort against isolated raiders. New technology challenged both concepts. The introduction of the marine multiple-stage high-power steam engine from 1880 transformed the reliability, mobility and speed of warships and merchant traffic within a decade. It was more difficult to maintain a long-term blockade, certainly at any distance, with steam-powered warships requiring constant re-coaling. Meanwhile, the blockaded fleet could exploit greater mobility and was no longer dependent on the weather in attempting a breakout. The introduction of the mine, the torpedo and long-range coastal artillery further compounded the problems of close blockade. Convoying fast steamships against raiders, potentially operating on a global scale, posed similar technical and logistic challenges. At the grand strategy level, the Suez Canal, which cut the distance from London to Bombay by 50 per cent, promised to be transformative. By the early 1880s, new fast steamers could reach China without re-coaling, one-third of British merchant tonnage was passing through the canal annually, and three-quarters of overall canal traffic was British. The security of the eastern Mediterranean, therefore, became ever more important to Britain.

If the Admiralty was to find answers to these challenges, it required new thinking, new structures to translate this thinking into practical plans and, not least, a new approach to intelligence collection and assessment. New thinking about naval warfare gained attention from the mid 1870s, but from outside an uninterested Admiralty. Two figures were influential. The first was Captain John Colomb, a retired Royal Marine officer, who was well-connected, wrote and lectured widely on strategic and naval topics, and later promoted his ideas further as a Member of Parliament. He emphasised the importance of good intelligence on the naval policies and capabilities of foreign powers. He also stressed the protection of commerce and the effective blockade of enemy ports. The second was Sir John Knox Laughton, an influential naval educator and historian, who argued that the study of history provided an essential foundation for the development of modern naval strategy, and the doctrines and capabilities to deliver it. There were also reform-minded senior naval officers, notably Admiral Sir Geoffrey Phipps Hornby, commander of the Mediterranean Fleet in the late 1870s; his contemporary Admiral Sir Astley Cooper Key; and Vice Admiral Philip Colomb, elder brother of John, friend of Key, inventor of the Navy's new signal system and, in time, also a notable historian.

These reformers began a debate and gathered supporters, but the Russian attack on Turkey in 1877 proved a more decisive catalyst for change. By early 1878, the Russians were encamped outside Constantinople, potentially able to command the Dardanelles, renounce previous treaty commitments, and move naval forces into the Mediterranean as desired, an intolerable prospect for Britain. In a brilliant demonstration of flexible sea power and seamanship, perhaps a model for what some hoped might be achieved by the more famous operation undertaken in 1915, the Royal Navy Mediterranean fleet under Hornby transited the Dardanelles in February to threaten the flank of the Russian army, forcing their withdrawal and an acceptable diplomatic solution. This appeared a perfect outcome, but events in the background were more worrying. A Russian cruiser squadron, apparently ideally suited to commerce-raiding, had deployed from the Baltic to the American eastern seaboard without Admiralty knowledge. Russian shipping agents had also attempted to hire fast steamers from British companies as auxiliary cruisers, with the Admiralty only alerted thanks to patriotic company staff. Meanwhile, plans to exert pressure on Russia in the Baltic revealed failings in mobilisation and further intelligence gaps. This created a perception, rapidly exploited by Admiralty critics, of potential Royal Navy over-stretch, poor planning, inadequate intelligence unable to illuminate Russian objectives and capability, and, above all, the prospect of a dangerous attack on Britain's trade for which it was unprepared.[42] Some of these concerns were over-stated. The Russian navy lacked the capability to sustain a serious attack on Britain's trade and despite the specific intelligence failings, the Admiralty was adequately briefed on real Russian strength and its limitations from attaché reports and other sources. Nevertheless, political perceptions mattered, and the perceived lackadaisical Admiralty approach to intelligence-gathering was challenged.

The first attempt at subsequent intelligence reform came from W H Smith, the First Lord appointed under the incoming government of Benjamin Disraeli in 1879. He adopted the suggestion of the naval attachés that one of them should return to London and, along with the clerk already maintaining confidential papers on foreign navies, establish a small intelligence section at the Admiralty. An intelligence section was also favoured by Hornby and Key, designated commander of the Baltic operations planned the previous year. The new section would concentrate on the naval policies and dispositions of foreign navies as advocated by Colomb. It would also examine coastal fortifications and arsenals, and the distribution of foreign commercial shipping. Reallocating existing manpower would avoid having additional expenditure opposed by the Treasury. Smith met resistance from both the naval and civil leadership in the Admiralty, who feared his initiative would undermine their existing authority and powers, and incur unnecessary expense. Crucially, Key lost enthusiasm after he was appointed First Naval Lord, apparently now worried that an intelligence section would become an independent power base outside his control.[43]

However, the concerns raised by the Russian actions in 1878 also produced an inter-departmental committee under the retired Admiral Sir Alexander Milne to examine the possible consequences of a war with Russia on Britain's maritime trade and commerce. Milne had been First Naval Lord from 1866–68 and again from 1872–76. Along with Hornby, he had consistently highlighted the rapidly changing strategic environment and specifically the defence of trade in the new steam era. As early as 1858, when serving as Third Naval Lord, Milne had advised the then prime minister, Lord Palmerston, that the French threat to ships carrying industrial materials as they approached home waters was almost as serious as the danger of invasion, anticipating Fisher by several decades.[44] Milne's committee triggered a more wide-ranging investigation of the defence of Britain's commerce and possessions overseas by a Royal Commission under Lord Carnarvon, with Milne a member.

The Carnarvon Commission produced three linked reports by 1882. For the first time, it formally and publicly defined the dramatic growth in global seaborne trade, the unique importance of this trade to Britain, and the role of the Royal Navy in protecting it. It also identified key factors that underpinned the security of Britain's trade, overseas refuelling bases under British control, use of the Suez Canal, availability of cable communications, the role of marine insurance and, not least, the importance of good intelligence to provide warning of possible threats and allow countermeasures. The commission examined how hostile powers might disrupt British trade, emphasising the use of commerce raiders modelled on those used in the American Civil War. A key finding here was that modern commercial shipping practices, the speed of new steamships, and the flexible routing allowed by cable communications rendered the traditional protected convoy in wartime undesirable and ineffective. This conclusion cast a long shadow up to and through the First World War. Overall, the Carnarvon Commission exposed Admiralty failure to address new threats to British maritime security and established a policy agenda that framed Royal Navy thinking through to 1914.[45]

The Carnarvon Commission recommendation that the Admiralty create a naval intelligence department as a matter of urgency did not guarantee it would happen. Political commitment for naval reform from the new administration of William Gladstone, especially if it implied additional expenditure, was lukewarm. Key remained reluctant and Evan MacGregor, the Admiralty Secretary and senior civil servant who currently oversaw intelligence matters, was determined that naval officers should not gain decisive influence in this area. Several developments overcame Admiralty resistance. Lord Northbrook, Gladstone's new First Lord, was closely involved in the creation of the army's Intelligence Branch (IB) ten years previously while serving as undersecretary in the War Office. Northbrook inevitably focused on the lack of any naval equivalent. He was also lobbied by Major General Charles Gordon (later Gordon of Khartoum) who stressed that valuable information was often available to the Admiralty from ships and consuls, but not properly exploited. 'Next to having no information is the having information and keeping it shut up.'[46] Northbrook therefore reviewed the ideas of his predecessor W H Smith and sought advice from Key. The latter now agreed that it was desirable to establish a new system for collecting and recording information on the capabilities of foreign naval powers. He resurrected Smith's proposal of withdrawing one of the travelling attachés to head a new intelligence section, supported by a senior clerk from Military Branch.[47] Northbrook was reluctant to cut an attaché, but saw no prospect of Treasury funding for an additional naval post. Meanwhile, further evidence that current intelligence arrangements were inadequate emerged during preparations for the bombardment of Alexandria in July 1882.

It was Captain George Tryon, appointed Naval Secretary in 1882, who found the right formula to get an intelligence section started. Tryon later achieved notoriety as Commander-in-Chief Mediterranean in 1893, when his disastrous error caused the loss of his flagship *Victoria* and his own death following collision with *Camperdown*. But he was also a notable innovator and reformer, a confidant of Hornby, with the energy, determination and political skills to achieve change. With the approval of Northbrook, Tryon orchestrated a process through the autumn of 1882 which created a Foreign Intelligence Committee by the end of the year, charged with examining existing intelligence arrangements and records, and implementing improvements. Key presided over this committee with a naval officer appointed on a temporary basis to provide expert support and implement its decisions, and a secretary, G H Hoste, drawn from the Military Branch. This was a masterly exercise in political and bureaucratic management by Tryon. Key felt he remained in control.

MacGregor was mollified by Tryon insisting that the new committee would not usurp his existing intelligence responsibilities, and ensuring the committee was administered by the Military Branch under his supervision. This made sense, because all correspondence to and from the Admiralty, including intelligence material, flowed through MacGregor's secretariat. Furthermore, the implication that the committee was temporary reassured MacGregor and his civilian secretariat staff that this unwelcome injection of naval officers in their domain was to provide professional advice for a limited period before civilian control was restored. It also avoided the need for Treasury approval for Key's expert assistant, since this was a temporary appointment. The committee was accordingly established by Board minute on 5 December 1882, tasked 'to classify, collate and index information that would be required for naval operations.'[48] The Treasury was only briefed on the committee in February 1884. They were advised that a body intended to be temporary had demonstrated the need for a small permanent intelligence staff similar to that in the War Office, for which funding was now sought. To encourage Treasury approval, Northbrook now reluctantly agreed to dispense temporarily with one attaché.[49]

The expert naval assistant selected by Tryon to support Key on the Foreign Intelligence Committee was Commander William Henry Hall, soon promoted to acting captain.[50] Although nominally Key's assistant, Hall was effectively the personification of the committee throughout its short life before becoming the first Director of Naval Intelligence (DNI) in 1887. He was the first of three generations of the Hall family to have a prominent role in the evolution of British naval intelligence. (His son Reginald, already mentioned in the Introduction, became DNI in 1914, perhaps the greatest of all holders of the post, while his grandson Richard had a central role in the Battle of the Atlantic in the Second World War.) Following Treasury approval placing the committee on a permanent footing, Hall was joined in early 1884 by one Royal Marine officer, two clerks and a copyist, and later acquired a naval officer as deputy, also at captain rank.[51] Hall proved an inspired choice. He came with a reputation for intelligence and energy, and with a fanatical work ethic. He was also well connected with officers pushing for reform, both present and future. As a gunnery specialist he had served in the gunnery training ship *Excellent* with an elite group, including Key, Laughton, Fisher, and two influential future admirals, Sir Arthur Hood, First Naval Lord from 1885, and Sir Cyprian Bridge. Less foreseeable were his strategic insight and his political shrewdness. He proved a master at getting an archaic Admiralty structure to work for him. His great achievement was to take the potentially awkward arrangement negotiated by Tryon and within a few years create an intelligence and planning capability recognised by most members of the Board of Admiralty as indispensable. 'Few men have wielded influence so effectively, yet so unobtrusively.'[52] Hall's guiding principle was the objective identified by the Carnarvon Commission. The Royal Navy did not exist to provide 'local protection to seaports or harbours', but rather for 'blockading the ports of an enemy, destroying his trade, attacking his possessions, dealing with his ships at sea', and 'preventing an attack in great force against any special place.' This vision set the Navy's agenda through to 1914. It was one entirely familiar to its leaders in the Napoleonic wars.[53]

2

The Creation of a Naval Intelligence
Department 1882–1905

The term Foreign Intelligence Committee soon proved misleading, as Tryon had anticipated. Key provided general direction to Hall and quickly came to appreciate the value of his contribution, but his role as president was nominal, as was that of Hoste. For practical purposes, Hall enjoyed complete autonomy and ran a distinct intelligence 'section' or 'department', terms which were soon widely used inside and outside the Admiralty, not least by Northbrook. The foundation of a modern Naval Intelligence Department ought therefore to date from 1882, rather than 1887 when the term was formally adopted with a new directive. Nevertheless, it is true that the creation of the Foreign Intelligence Committee did not initially alter existing responsibilities for collecting intelligence. It did not have the staff or funds, or a mandate to create new sources. If it had not existed, the intelligence arriving at the Admiralty during the 1880s would probably have been much the same. That is also true for a significant number of the finished intelligence publications distributed within the Admiralty, to the fleets, and to other government departments.

Initially, the main value of the Foreign Intelligence Committee lay in bringing order to existing information and ensuring its effective exploitation. It also brought professional scrutiny and analysis to new reporting arriving from the attachés, the Foreign Office, frontline commanders, and the Hydrographic Office. Its position here was enhanced in August 1885, when the Board confirmed that it was responsible for recording and disseminating information on foreign warships previously handled by the Controller's department.[1] The implications of any new intelligence for Britain's naval position were therefore now better assessed and understood. This structured and disciplined exploitation of all available intelligence was an essential prerequisite to effective war planning. Hall and his team were the first body of naval officers in the Admiralty without administrative responsibilities. By its nature, Hall's section was bound to become forward-looking. As it got into its stride, it increasingly had to decide what information to collect, which required judgements about future needs. Given the right leadership, it would inevitably acquire some planning responsibilities and therefore some of the characteristics of a naval staff, even if that was exactly what Key had wished to avoid.[2] Furthermore, once Hall proved his value beyond a narrow intelligence remit, even Key could not resist passing him additional tasks. In late 1884 he asked Hall to report on problems in mobilising the reserve fleet. This led to mobilisation becoming a responsibility of the Foreign Intelligence Committee's successor.[3]

The Foreign Intelligence Committee took over the preparation and publication of finished intelligence reports from the Military Branch, but used the same style and format. In some cases, it continued a report series it inherited with little change. The last report issued under the Military Branch in February 1883 covered 'Foreign Ports and Anchorages' for the Mediterranean Station, part of a Geographical Index Series drawing primarily on information from the hydrographic service. The first Foreign Intelligence Committee report was 'Naval Dockyard Ports, Italy', issued in March 1883. The second continued the geographic series and covered 'Baltic and North Sea Channels'. During its first year, the committee issued a further seven reports, including the mercantile marine of France, Germany, Spain and Italy respectively, and south-coast defences of France. These reports evidently drew on information already available in the Admiralty.[4] Reports in the second year began to break new ground, notably with a series on the capability of potential enemies and allies in the Far East theatre. All these reports were detailed and well-presented, demonstrating that Hall was determined to make them useful and relevant to his customers.[5]

In 1884 W T Stead, the influential editor of the *Pall Mall Gazette*, dismissed Hall as a 'mere compiler of information, a contemporary gazetteer in breeches'. There was still 'no intelligence department at the Admiralty' worthy of the name.[6] The Foreign Intelligence Committee made itself indispensable and proved Stead wrong by adding significant value to assessments of the Royal Navy's two main potential opponents, France and Russia. The primary source of intelligence on both countries which the committee inherited was the two itinerant naval attachés, although to help fund Hall's team one of these was temporarily placed on a part-time basis.[7] Despite their wide geographic brief, the quality of reporting the attachés provided by the early 1880s was high, reflecting good access to key decision-makers. They kept the Admiralty well informed on French and Russian deployable strength and building plans, and contributed regular insights on deep technical issues relating to ship construction, armour distribution, gun design and propellants, and the development of new weapons, such as torpedoes. Their surviving reports invariably show a sharp eye for innovation.[8] In addition to the other sources of information on foreign navies previously mentioned, Hall and his team had the time and expertise to explore and exploit the growing number of specialist periodicals dealing with naval topics. Some foreign publications contained useful insights on equipment and tactics from serving officers, which complemented attaché reporting.[9]

During the 1870s, France was preoccupied by the consequences of her defeat in the Franco-Prussian war at the beginning of the decade. Her dominant concern was the land threat from a united Germany, with the French navy starved of funds and unable to pose a new challenge to Britain. An ambitious construction programme did get underway after 1876, laying down fifteen first-class armoured vessels by the end of the decade, which the incoming Northbrook administration in 1880 felt obliged to counter with a substantial new British building programme.[10] However, when the Foreign Intelligence Committee arrived at the end of 1882, the Admiralty already had considerable evidence, primarily through the attachés, that the French programme was faltering. This reflected erratic budgeting, insufficient shipbuilding capacity exacerbated by pervasive inefficiency, and constant design changes which lengthened delivery time. Hall and his team rapidly confirmed that the French navy faced fundamental problems, including new budget cuts of over 20 per cent from 1883–85, and that the relative balance between the two navies was steadily shifting in Britain's favour. In December 1884, Key reflected Hall's assessment to Hornby:

> We now have twenty-seven ironclads in commission. The French have eleven. We could commission thirteen more in a month. I cannot find that the French have more than two ready and one of these has her boilers condemned (*Richelieu*). Many of our ships are of obsolete types – so are many of theirs. Moreover being of wood, theirs cannot last long. I would have no fear whatever with Russia and France now, so far as our navy is concerned.[11]

Northbrook conveyed this picture in more detail to his Conservative party successor, Lord George Hamilton, in July 1885, commending Hall's overall contribution.[12]

Admiralty confidence, endorsed by Hall, that Britain retained a decisive lead over France was challenged during 1884 in a savage press campaign waged by Stead and other commentators. They indicted the Admiralty for allowing the decline of the Royal Navy as a fighting force and potentially letting it fall behind France. Hall provided Northbrook and Key with authoritative information to refute Stead's charges, which were wildly exaggerated and probably drew on information from disgruntled serving officers, including Fisher. However, the campaign provoked sufficient public and political pressure to force the government to allocate the Navy an additional £3.1 million, over 25 per cent of the 1884 naval budget.[13]

It was probably Stead's attack that encouraged Hall to submit a paper to the Board of Admiralty in late September 1884, defining how a naval war with France should be conducted. This was his first foray into war planning, as opposed to intelligence assessment. His analysis combined applied naval history, influenced by Laughton, with modern strategic analysis. Hall identified two main options for the Royal Navy. The first was a defensive strategy. This required the deployment of squadrons to defend Britain's sea lanes and the introduction of convoys to defend merchant shipping from attack by French raiders. Effort would also go into protecting naval and commercial ports at home, and vital bases and territories overseas, from French attack. Hall argued that Britain lacked the naval resources for this policy. There were too many points to defend. More important, contrary to the traditions of the Royal Navy, it would cede the initiative to France. He preferred an offensive strategy. This would eliminate all enemy units on deployment at the start of hostilities; aggressively blockade enemy ports rendering its main naval forces useless; and reduce enemy bases, coaling stations and commercial ports through bombardment. This strategy would force France to focus on its own vulnerabilities rather than exploiting opportunities against Britain. Hall understood that his offensive objectives could not be achieved simultaneously. Initial priorities were, therefore, to eliminate enemy forces and bases overseas, while maintaining sufficient strength at home to deter any major enemy sortie.[14]

Hall believed that a close blockade of the main French naval bases was impossible with current British resources. Given the logistical requirements of supporting steam-powered fleets, the Royal Navy lacked the numbers to guarantee superiority outside each enemy base. Furthermore, a close blockading fleet would be vulnerable to torpedo attack from small enemy craft, especially at night. Countering the torpedo threat was possible, but required new types of protection vessel in considerable numbers. Hall therefore advocated a more distant 'watching' blockade until these problems could be resolved, raising issues that dominated Royal Navy strategic thinking for the next thirty years.[15] From 1885, blockade options were regularly tested in exercises, and blockade became a persistent driver of intelligence requirements.[16] In updated form, Hall's offensive vision was broadly that adopted by Britain against Germany in 1914.

Hall's paper coincided with the rise of a new school of thought in the French navy known as the *Jeune Ecole*. This advocated an asymmetric naval strategy aimed primarily at Britain. It combined fast commerce-raiders to destroy Britain's trade with the use of torpedo vessels to defeat a blockading fleet. It therefore targeted two of the most important British vulnerabilities identified by Hall and posed important questions for the Foreign Intelligence Committee. Understanding the impact of *Jeune Ecole* became especially important after the appointment of its main advocate, Vice Admiral Theophile Aube, as minister of marine in January 1886. Aube helpfully set out his views to the British naval attaché, Captain Henry Kane, the following month, asserting that 'no blockade will now prevent fast ships putting to sea, and that it is therefore impossible for any nation to make herself "Mistress of the Seas" in the way Britain was after Trafalgar, however strong she maybe in ironclads'.[17]

Hall noted that this reflected Aube's views in various French periodicals, and he was not surprised that the French now virtually suspended their ironclad programme to meet the new *Jeune Ecole* priorities of cruisers and torpedo craft. He and his staff followed the new construction programme closely, as well as the experimental deployment of torpedo craft in naval exercises. By the end of 1886 the Foreign Intelligence Committee estimated that the French navy possessed eighteen first-class torpedo craft, with fifty-one under construction, and thirty-nine second-class. However, they also observed that Aube's request for funding of another 100 torpedo craft over the next four years was rejected. Meanwhile, Hall's team had rapidly acquired authoritative reports, again primarily from French periodicals, demonstrating that the torpedo craft had performed poorly in the 1886 French navy annual manoeuvres. In August that year, Captain Reginald Custance, currently Hall's assistant director but also a future DNI, produced a detailed analysis of the origins and progress of *Jeune Ecole*, drawing on information dating back to 1872. He identified the operational tests that it must pass and drew on eyewitness accounts of the recent exercises from French naval officers, who publicly expressed doubts over the torpedo boat and its suitability for fleet operations. The limitations of the anti-blockade element of *Jeune Ecole* were further exposed in the 1887 annual manoeuvres, during which the French government fell and Aube left office after just fifteen months.

His departure left the French navy in chaos. The *Jeune Ecole* concept lacked credibility, creating now deep divisions over future strategy and force planning. The financial position was dire and the building programme disrupted. Kane and his successor Captain Sir Cecil Domville kept the Foreign Intelligence Committee and its successor department well sighted on all these developments. For the remainder of the decade, the intelligence picture, in contrast to further flurries of alarmist press reporting, gave the Admiralty absolute confidence that the French navy posed no credible threat to Britain for the foreseeable future.[18]

Despite the absence of immediate threat, the issues raised by *Jeune Ecole*, like Hall's proposals for an offensive strategy, were of lasting importance. The French did not have the political commitment, the military leadership and vision, or the resources to make *Jeune Ecole* a viable option. Above all, the technology was not yet good enough. But the basic theme that a weaker naval power could fight a successful naval war through long-range commerce-raiding and asymmetric action against a dominant battle-fleet remained extant. France, and then Germany, continued to pursue this idea, although it required the submarine to turn it to decisive strategic effect. For the Royal Navy, *Jeune Ecole* thinking was an enduring threat to its maritime security but it also offered opportunities, explored with determination when Fisher achieved power at the start of the next century.

The Russian navy in the early 1880s was much smaller than that of France and, given its geographical location, posed a more limited threat. Its main challenges were to the security of the eastern Mediterranean and the potential to raid British sea communications. The picture the Foreign Intelligence Committee inherited, again drawn primarily from attaché reporting, was one of chronic weakness. In 1881 Captain Lewis Beaumont reported on the Baltic and described two 'belted' frigates under construction, which worried the Admiralty as potential commerce-raiders. Beaumont's overall assessment was dismissive: 'neither the personnel nor material of the Russian navy is in a satisfactory or effective condition. So far as I have been able to ascertain there is not one powerful or effective ship in the whole navy.'[19]

In 1884 a visit by Kane to the annual manoeuvres of the Russian Baltic Fleet, their primary naval force, reinforced British perceptions of a backward and ineffective navy. Kane was especially insightful on the state of Russian tactics, which he found primitive and poorly executed. Importantly, the exercises were predominantly defensive, a conclusion confirmed by subsequent reporting, including an article written by a senior Russian naval officer, forwarded to Hall by the Foreign Office. In 1887 attaché reports on a visit to the Black Sea and the dockyards of

Nickolaieff and Sevastopol were equally scathing. Throughout the life of the Foreign Intelligence Committee, therefore, the information reaching Hall was of a navy comprising poor-quality ships, poorly manned and supported, defensively orientated with primitive tactics, and thus posing little threat. Few, if any, Russian ships seemed capable of extended ocean operations. Hall was aware that Russian naval expenditure increased sharply across the decade, keeping at 50 per cent of the British level, but there was little evidence, even by the end of the decade, that this had significantly improved overall capability. Hall reassured a concerned Foreign Office on the status of three new ironclads building at the Black Sea dockyards in the late 1880s. They would be slow to build and the Black Sea Fleet was in a deplorable state. It was barely capable of coping with the Turkish navy, which lacked modern vessels and was hardly efficient.[20]

This consistent intelligence coverage was important given the imminent risk of war with Russia in 1885, provoked by a dispute in Afghanistan known as the Panjdeh incident. Hall confidently advised the Admiralty leadership that the Russian naval threat to Britain was minimal. In March that year he also submitted a paper to the Board of Admiralty on how a war with Russia might be conducted. This was spurred by the Panjdeh dispute, but complemented his paper on France the previous September. As with France, Hall dismissed any attempt to defend the entirety of British sea communications against Russian raiders, which he anticipated would be high-endurance, armed merchant ships of good speed, rather than navy cruisers. He again advocated an offensive strategy based on deploying a powerful squadron to blockade the entrance to the Gulf of Finland. Smaller squadrons would then hunt down and destroy any ships already at large, or which eluded the blockade. Hall advised against bombarding the key Russian bases of Kronstadt and Sveaborg which he judged too well defended.[21]

Hall's papers on France and Russia initiated a coherent strategic vision for the way in which Britain should use her naval power to defend the United Kingdom home territory, her growing empire, and her global trading interests. Hall established the principle of confining enemy forces to port, restricting access to the open sea, as the most effective and economic means of preventing invasion and securing British commerce. It would be the over-arching theme in British naval policy for the next seventy years, even if practical execution often proved complicated.[22]

The Panjdeh incident and the prospect of war with Russia in 1885 boosted press claims of naval weakness and lack of preparedness. Although the Admiralty was confident the Russian navy posed little threat, the crisis challenged the effectiveness of mobilisation plans, which Key had tasked

Hall to examine. It fell to the new Board constituted under the incoming administration of Lord Salisbury to deal with any genuine weaknesses in war-readiness, as well as the wider political and press criticisms of the Admiralty initiated by Stead. Hamilton, Northbrook's successor as First Lord, was a competent administrator, conservative by temperament, focused on fiscal restraint, but willing to contemplate careful and evolutionary reform. With one notable exception, he appointed a board in his image. His appointee as First Naval Lord in succession to Key was Admiral Sir Arthur Hood. Hood was well known to Laughton, who regarded him as measured and conscientious, but lacking the energy and creativity to deal with a period of dramatic naval change. Laughton feared his efforts would focus on 'preventing advance becoming too rapid'. The exception in this conservative board was the Junior Naval Lord, Captain Lord Charles Beresford, who possessed energy, imagination and vision in abundance, albeit not always balanced by tact and judgement, and arrived with a strong operational record and reputation. Although a serving naval officer, he was also an MP, which was permitted at this time, and enjoyed the patronage of Salisbury and the Prince of Wales, which explained his appointment in mid 1886. This patronage, along with his independent income and political status, gave him the confidence to pursue an independent agenda.

Beresford quickly made himself patron of the Foreign Intelligence Committee, although this was outside his remit. In October, barely two months after his arrival, he sent a memorandum to Board colleagues. He argued that the committee should become a formal Admiralty department responsible for mobilisation and war preparations, areas where he claimed Britain lagged behind other powers, as well as collection, analysis and dissemination of foreign naval intelligence. He showed his memorandum to Salisbury and probably leaked it to Stead's *Pall Mall Gazette*. Hood was already contemplating giving the Foreign Intelligence Committee responsibility for mobilisation, a natural extension of Key's earlier initiative, but preferred this to happen incrementally. Hamilton, keenly aware of the political consequences of Beresford's actions, insisted that Hall submit proposals on the future of the Foreign Intelligence Committee immediately. Hall seized the opportunity to make an ambitious but well-argued pitch, amply confirming both his vision and mastery of Admiralty politics. Predictably, based on the experience of the last four years, he advocated a larger department with responsibility not just for mobilisation and foreign naval intelligence, but also strategy development. Reflecting his appreciations on France and Russia, Hall argued that preparations for war required the intelligence function to take responsibility for developing the naval strategy appropriate for various contingencies, and the accompanying allocation of naval forces.

Hamilton and Hood were impressed by both Hall and his report. Hall had worked under Hood at HMS *Excellent* and had been commended to Hamilton by Northbrook. His recommendations were therefore approved with minor changes, and Hall was appointed to head the new department for two years. The creation of an intelligence department would probably still have happened without Beresford's intervention, but it would have taken longer and Hall might have achieved less influence. The scope of the new department would probably then have been more limited, and excluded a war-planning remit.[23]

The Board issued formal Instructions for the Director of Naval Intelligence in January 1887. These effectively commissioned the new Naval Intelligence Department (NID), although negotiations with the Treasury over funding continued until August.[24] The instructions defined the duties of the department, its objectives, and its initial organisation and staff. Its functions were to be 'purely advisory', not 'administrative', and its focus was 'preparation for war'. NID would be supervised by the First Naval Lord, but DNI would deal directly with other naval lords where their interests were involved. Its duties were:

- to collect and assess all maritime information of use in war;
- to prepare and maintain a mobilisation plan;
- to prepare 'plans of naval campaign' (ie war plans) as directed;
- to advise on all preparations necessary for war but not to advocate any policy on shipbuilding or armaments unless asked.

Its primary role was to obtain and record 'complete knowledge' of the naval resources of foreign powers and their ability to conduct a naval war, keeping frontline commanders briefed as directed. It would maintain information on distribution and condition of foreign warships, active and reserve; distribution of foreign and British merchant vessels; status of foreign coastal defences and the security of British coaling stations; personnel of foreign navies available for mobilisation in war; British reserve strength in ships and personnel available for mobilisation. The department would have two separate sections, Intelligence and Mobilisation, each headed by an assistant director of captain rank reporting to the DNI. The first incumbents were Captain J Eardley-Wilmot for Intelligence and Custance for Mobilisation. Intelligence Section was authorised to have two additional naval officers, three Royal Marine officers and five support staff. Mobilisation Section was smaller. All significant papers produced by

NID would go to the First Naval Lord and Secretary. DNI would report monthly to the Board and was granted direct access to the War Office intelligence departments.[25]

These Board instructions not only marked the formal beginning of a distinct naval intelligence department but were a substantial step towards the creation of a de facto naval staff.[26] Hall would have preferred to have a third section dedicated to planning, and he later broached more ambitious ideas for a naval staff with the power and authority of the German general staff. But whatever the limitations of the new arrangement, the Admiralty now had a planning capability, and establishing a clear link between intelligence and war planning could only be helpful. The role and responsibilities established for NID in 1887 lasted the next twenty-five years with limited change, but it took a further five years before the Admiralty created a full-scale planning department in its own right, and then only under the pressures of existential war.

In its first year, NID produced around thirty published reports which, although consistent with the new DNI instructions, broadly followed the topics and the format adopted under the Foreign Intelligence Committee. Not surprisingly, the reports concentrated on France and Russia, but Germany received significant attention, and Turkey, Austria, Italy and Holland were also covered. The primary source remained the two roving attachés, and the reports were read closely by Hood and Hamilton. Updated lists of all foreign warships in commission and reserve and building were provided, together with their specifications and photographs where available. Reflecting the concerns raised by *Jeune Ecole*, there was a new book covering all foreign torpedo craft. For France, topics included the status of specific ports and coastal defences, Mediterranean annual naval manoeuvres, and administration and personnel. Outside the Admiralty, reports were usually copied to relevant overseas commanders, key shore establishments such as *Excellent* and *Vernon*, the Royal Naval College, and sometimes ambassadors. Overall, given the limited staff available to Hall, this 1887 output was an impressive beginning.[27]

One report broke significant new ground with important policy impact. This was a 'comparative statement of the Navies of Great Britain, France and Russia in 1887 and 1890, along with 'a comparison of the relative forces available in home waters in 1890'. The final version of the report issued in May 1888 did more than list comparative numerical strengths.[28] It placed these strengths in the context of the strategic goals pursued by Britain and her most likely enemies. It also examined the global distribution of comparative forces in detail. Hall, as author, argued that Royal Navy strength must reflect both the naval policy it adopted and the strength and disposition of its probable enemies. He considered the worst case of France and Russia acting together against Britain. Not surprisingly he advocated the 'offensive' British strategy based on flexible blockade, as recommended in his two earlier papers examining the prosecution of a war against France or Russia. He reiterated the historical precedents for this strategy, but underlined one major change from previous conflicts. While underlining Britain's new vulnerability to trade disruption, especially of food supplies, he insisted that convoying was no longer practical, given the scale of resources now needed to protect Britain's global trade routes.

Hall's figures showed that Britain was likely to retain a small lead in both battleships and cruisers over the combined forces of France and Russia at the end of 1890. Following comments from the Director of Naval Construction, Sir William White, he acknowledged that the raw figures probably understated the Royal Navy advantage, since many French second- and third-class units had wooden hulls, reducing their remaining lifespan and operational effectiveness. (The figures also showed that for sloops, the Royal Navy advantage should improve substantially, compensating for a small deterioration in the balance for gunboats and torpedo craft.) However, Hall concluded that the British advantage was dangerously misleading for two reasons. First, the Royal Navy had a higher proportion of its strength deployed overseas than France (in the case of cruisers, almost a half, compared to a fifth). Secondly, the challenge of emerging threats such as the torpedo and the demands of refuelling meant effective blockade required superior strength over enemy forces at each of his bases. Hall suggested the superiority required was 25 per cent for battleships and 33 per cent for cruisers. Existing Royal Navy strength could not achieve this. He identified a deficit of thirteen battleships (all classes), thirty-eight cruisers (all classes) and thirty-two torpedo craft. If, as a consequence of this shortfall, the French defeated a weaker Royal Navy home squadron off one of their bases, this might enable them to combine their forces and outmatch any British response.[29]

Although he did not use the term, Hall was arguing here for a risk-based measure of Royal Navy strength, rather than one based on purely numerical comparison with the strength of foreign naval powers. As noted earlier, Britain had adopted a two-power standard for Royal Navy strength in 1817, meaning numerical equivalence to the next two strongest naval powers. Despite the connotations of Hall's conclusions, this concept of the numerical standard, albeit with changing ratios, was shortly established in parliamentary legislation and remained the main arbiter of Royal Navy strength until 1939. The numerical standard was primarily, and most easily, applied to comparative battleship strength.

(The term 'battleship' was adopted for large armoured warships in 1887, replacing 'ironclad'. From 1906, battleships and battlecruisers were jointly classified as 'capital ships'.[30]) The Royal Navy generally sought flexibility in comparing other categories, often arguing it had absolute as well as comparative requirements here. Hall's point, not lost on future Royal Navy leaders, was that a numerical standard was not necessarily sufficient for Britain's naval security. Range of geographic commitments, force distribution, and relative vulnerability to trade disruption all mattered too. So did relative fighting quality, as well as numbers. A modern definition of risk would consider threat, comprising intent and capability (in which numbers would be a significant but not necessarily decisive factor), the probability of the threat taking effect, and the impact it might achieve, or damage it might inflict.[31] Good intelligence was essential to ensuring an agreed standard of strength, but even more important to a sensible assessment of risk.

In his new role, Hall could legitimately question whether, in a war against an alliance of France and Russia, and with current Royal Navy commitments and deployment, simple numerical equality with their combined navies guaranteed control of home waters and adequate protection of trade in all circumstances. However, his report posed a worst-case risk without subjecting it to full analysis, or applying important qualifications reflecting good intelligence. As Hall well knew, attaché reports had consistently noted the difficulty both the French and Russian navies had in meeting building targets. They had also stressed wider material deficiencies and poor dockyard support, preventing maximum force generation for war. Finally, they had highlighted lack of an agreed war strategy and, for Russia, low fighting quality. White had also cautioned Hall not to overstate French strength. Furthermore, while Hall emphasised the problem Britain as a single power faced in covering multiple enemy forces and bases, he did not adequately stress the equivalent constraints faced by the other side, or the possibility Britain might have allies.

Given a free hand, it is unlikely Hall's report would have persuaded either Hamilton or Hood to alter the existing Royal Navy building programme, let alone promote a major shift in naval policy. Their relaxed response to excitable but erroneous press reports of French mobilisation at Toulon in January 1888 confirmed their confidence that the French navy was in a poor state and unable to challenge Britain.[32] Hamilton's priority was financial restraint. Hood lacked the critical thinking and strategic vision to promote radical measures. However, by the time Hall issued the final version of his report in May 1888, the Admiralty was facing a new round of attacks from press and naval commentators and in political circles. The primary catalyst and the most influential player in shaping subsequent events was again Beresford, who had resigned as Junior Lord in January. The immediate trigger was salary limitations imposed on NID, which, Beresford argued, undermined the effectiveness of an intelligence capability essential to creating a modern naval policy with the right forces to support it. Beresford's resignation freed him to conduct a high-profile campaign, to which he enlisted the recently retired Admiral Hornby. Beresford's case was that the Admiralty had no credible strategy for a future naval war, above all trade protection, and that present Royal Navy strength was inadequate for the global commitments it would face in dealing with one major power, let alone two. He castigated the Admiralty for relying on numerical equivalence with France and Russia, rather than confronting underlying strategic realities. In making these arguments, Beresford denied he was reflecting Hall's paper, claiming it had not been shared with him. In response, Hamilton robustly defended existing Admiralty policy, insisting that there was no significant change in the naval balance, and that Britain retained a comfortable margin of superiority over France and Russia combined.

Beresford and Hornby were better at mobilising political and press scrutiny of naval policy, and creating political unease in the Salisbury administration, than articulating what their new naval strategy meant in practice. However, through the first half of 1888 they received powerful backing from the long-standing naval commentator John Colomb, now an MP, and his colleague in parliament, Captain Penrose Fitzgerald. These brought intellectual weight and historical perspective. Also important was the contribution of John's elder brother Philip, now a vice admiral on the retired list, working with Laughton on naval history and strategy. Philip Colomb had delivered two important lectures at the Royal United Services Institute the previous year promoting the continuing relevance of convoying and the value of offensive blockade. He distinguished different types of blockade: 'sealing up' (traditional close blockade to prevent enemy movement); 'masking' (tempting the enemy out so as to be surprised by a superior force); and 'observation' (keeping a distant watch to permit later interception).[33] These concepts shaped the blockade debate in several navies over the next twenty-five years. Colomb now took his arguments further, reinforcing the case for an offensive blockade strategy, similar to that advocated by Hall, and using this to determine desired Royal Navy strength. The influence he exerted both inside and outside the Navy, and the resulting press coverage he attracted, markedly increased the political pressure for more ambitious naval investment.

Such was the interest in blockade generated by Colomb and Hall that the 1888 annual manoeuvres focused on key questions they had raised. The decision to explore blockade preceded Hall's comparison paper and the formal conclusions from the exercise were not available until well into 1889. The exercise did not, therefore, influence the fierce debate currently underway. However, the exercise umpires confirmed Hall's argument that a successful blockading force required significant superiority, proposing that for battleships this should be four to three, rather than Hall's 25 per cent.[34] This conclusion gained weight with further exercises, and became a compelling argument for a strong Royal Navy building programme through the 1890s.

The result of the intense naval lobbying through the first half of 1888 was that in July the Cabinet asked Hood what force he required 'under certain eventualities'. They posed three questions: the force required in a war with France to secure the United Kingdom from invasion or bombardment along with the overseas bases of Gibraltar and Malta; the force needed for protection of trade routes and overseas coaling stations; and the force required in a naval war without allies against a combination of France and Russia, including protection of Constantinople. Hood drew on Hall's May paper to press for a significant increase in Royal Navy strength and an enhanced building programme. The Cabinet agreed Hood's requirements, and in May 1889 a five-year, £21.5 million investment programme and long-term commitment to a two-power standard were confirmed in a Naval Defence Act, the first and last time Royal Navy strength was subject to Act of Parliament.[35] Despite its new constitutional status, this two-power standard was open to different interpretations, and more a political device than an effective strategic concept. It allowed the government to appease the navalist lobby, while retaining significant freedom in framing the balance of naval power.[36]

Nevertheless, following the 1889 Act the Royal Navy pursued a substantial investment programme through the 1890s into the new century. Britain aimed to secure her trade and empire by massively out-building her potential naval rivals. In numerical terms she was successful. Britain comfortably matched the combined battleship output of the next two naval powers, France and Russia, who remained the primary threat in this period. In the 1890s she laid down thirty-six first-class battleships, compared to just eleven by France.[37] She also built double the number of cruisers compared to France and Russia, reflecting the new emphasis on trade protection. Qualitatively, with occasional exceptions, Britain also outmatched her rivals. British battleships were larger, better armed, and better designed. Cruisers were, at least, competitive. Superior British economic and shipbuilding resources ensured she could respond to any perceived challenge much more quickly than her rivals. But this naval investment was expensive. In the fifteen years 1889–1904, the cost of a battleship doubled and that of a first-class cruiser increased fivefold. The pace of technical change meant faster depreciation.[38] Annual British naval expenditure tripled to £34 million and manpower doubled to 122,500. Inevitably, this brought demands for economy.

In theory, this huge naval effort provided unprecedented security against opponents that the Royal Navy had generally judged inferior in fighting quality. Nevertheless, through the 1890s successive Royal Navy leaders worried that they had not found adequate answers to a sustained attack on Britain's trade. NID correctly assessed that this was the preferred French policy and would also be the focus of a Franco-Russian alliance. This decade saw the final abandonment of convoy for protecting merchant shipping in wartime. Instead, cruisers would patrol defined sea lanes and guard vulnerable choke-points. This defensive deployment had to consider attack by widely dispersed small cruisers (the most economical option for an enemy), by concentrated squadrons of such vessels, or large armoured cruisers (a more expensive option but more certain to deliver results). It produced some innovative thinking, including the idea of deploying 'powerful cruisers at the end of a telegraph wire' to deal with raiders and the use of large, fast, long-range passenger liners as auxiliaries.[39] The former idea contributed to the birth of the battlecruiser concept, a term which the Royal Navy began to apply to its new armoured cruisers procured from the early 1890s onward. These were not just to undertake trade protection, but potentially to operate in direct support of the battlefleet. This thinking would shortly be taken further by Fisher. Meanwhile, German use of the latter preoccupied the Admiralty in the first decade of the next century.

Another concern was Royal Navy vulnerability to tactical innovation facilitated through rapidly changing technology. The immediate threat here was the fast evolving capability of the surface torpedo vessel, the one warship category where combined Franco-Russian numbers significantly exceeded the Royal Navy. NID expected France to use these against coastal merchant traffic in the Channel and North Sea, to pick off British blockading units and to attack British ports.[40] There was a rather odd belief that British ports were especially vulnerable to such attack, while French ports were not.[41] The antidote promoted by Fisher was the torpedo boat destroyer, which by 1900 had substantially countered the surface torpedo threat, at least in open waters.[42] But by this time the submarine had appeared, posing a more dangerous means of delivering a torpedo attack.

The biggest worry was that, consistent with the findings of the 1888 manoeuvres, a two-power margin was not enough for an offensive blockade strategy against multiple enemy bases. This decade saw a growing conviction that traditional close blockade was no longer feasible, and it was effectively abandoned for Colomb's alternatives of 'masking' or 'observing'. Achieving consensus on a credible new strategy took longer.[43] The lack of a convincing alternative to close blockade posed a particular challenge in the Mediterranean, as Turkey became more antagonistic to Britain in the mid 1890s. This meant that the Russian Black Sea Fleet might freely transit the Dardanelles, challenging British control of the eastern Mediterranean and threatening the vital artery to the eastern empire. In the worst-case scenario of war with France and Russia, even a two-power margin would not guarantee the security of a 3500-mile front from the English Channel and the French Atlantic bases across both ends of the Mediterranean.[44]

NID contributed limited hard intelligence to illuminate these perceived problems. This was not a lack of the right sources and methods, but rather that precise answers did not exist. Britain's potential opponents were struggling with all these questions too. There were plenty of theoretical ideas for targeting Britain at sea, but little realistic war planning. What NID could and did provide was good intelligence on evolving French and Russian capabilities, and on any informal strategic debates offering clues to how those capabilities might then be deployed in war. The main intelligence insights here continued to come from the attachés. Until 1900, these still operated on a travelling basis, but thereafter permanent posts were established and the network grew steadily. The growing attaché network also benefited from the appointment of a dedicated intelligence officer to the staff of Commander-in-Chief Mediterranean in 1893 and the China Fleet in 1900.[45]

Over the five years from 1895, attaché reporting on Russia was regular and authoritative, by 1900 convincing NID that the threat from the Russian navy was minimal. That year Custance, now a rear admiral and DNI, concluded that the Russian navy was 'an artificial production incapable of standing up against a prolonged struggle at sea'. Building capacity and dockyard support would not sustain a credible operational fleet 'manned by officers and men who are little at sea' and 'dislike going afloat'.[46] Russian performance against Japan soon amply confirmed that judgement. Through the late 1890s, attaché reports similarly exposed the weaknesses of the French navy. The overriding priority given to the land threat from Germany constrained its available budget, making it difficult to compete with Britain under any circumstances. However, limited resources were rendered more ineffective by inability to define a credible strategy and sustain it over time. Throughout the decade and beyond, France vacillated between a strategy of trade warfare drawing on the principles of *Jeune Ecole*, and building a battle-fleet capable of confronting, and hopefully beating, a major Royal Navy force. This vacillation was compounded by frequent changes of government, producing a stop–start effect on building programmes and endless changes in design. The French, therefore, produced multiple sample warship designs, rather than the homogenous classes of the Royal Navy.[47] By 1900 Custance felt earlier fears of a Franco-Russian union in the Mediterranean had evaporated, and that a French attack on trade could be easily countered.[48]

There was one important exception to this more relaxed view of the Franco-Russian threat that the Admiralty had reached by 1900. This was the Far East theatre, where Russia had significantly expanded its fleet, established a major base at Port Arthur, and appeared set on dominating northern China. By 1901 the Royal Navy was significantly outnumbered by the combined Russian and French naval forces in the Pacific, and reinforcement on the far side of the world meant carrying undesirable risk elsewhere. Britain, therefore, faced at least a theoretical threat to its major commercial stake in China, to Hong Kong, and even Singapore, when Russian land expansion was pressing on the boundaries of its Indian empire. The solution was an alliance with Japan, also concerned with Russian ambitions, signed in January 1902. Japan now had a significant modern navy, much of it built by Britain and closely modelled on the Royal Navy. Their combined forces comfortably outmatched the Dual Alliance. The Anglo-Japanese alliance secured Britain's interests in the Far East for the next twenty years, and heralded the beginning of a major redistribution of the Royal Navy from widespread global deployment to concentration in home waters.

The alliance also provided an early and important intelligence windfall when the Russo-Japanese war broke out in February 1904. The war lasted eighteen months, ending in decisive victory for Japan, and featured the first conflict at sea between major powers deploying the full range of naval capability since 1815. Both navies were equipped with modern vessels and weaponry and, on paper, enjoyed similar strength, although Japan had initial superiority within the theatre. There were two major naval battles, with the second at Tsushima comparable to Trafalgar in scale and impact. The war also demonstrated the effectiveness of mining and torpedoes, and provided new evidence on the challenges of blockade and commerce-raiding. It was thus the first big test of the revolutionary changes in technology and tactics over the previous quarter-century.

Despite initial Japanese reluctance, the Admiralty deployed two senior Royal Navy officers at sea with the Japanese fleet, in addition to the attachés accredited to Tokyo.[49] Reports from these officers were comprehensive and of high quality, and the eyewitness accounts of the various actions, especially Tsushima, gave NID and its customers unique insights into the reality of modern naval warfare.[50] How far these insights influenced or changed subsequent Admiralty policy on either equipment or tactics is harder to assess. The apparent lessons of the war were often contradictory. They encouraged new thinking, notably the potential of offensive mining, but did not stop the Admiralty persisting with policies that would be found wanting ten years later.[51]

The end of the Russo-Japanese war in 1905 is a good point to take stock of British naval intelligence. NID had existed almost twenty years and, in several respects, this year marked a paradigm strategic shift in British naval policy. The Russian navy had been removed as a credible fighting force for the foreseeable future. The Royal Navy enjoyed crushing superiority over a French navy beset with problems, lacking a credible doctrine, falling behind in warship design, and chronically under-resourced. In addition, the prospect of French enmity was fading, following the friendship agreements initiated with Britain under the Entente Cordiale in 1904. The Admiralty now looked increasingly at Germany as the most important potential naval threat. The year 1906 was the last one in which France spent more on naval construction than Germany: a year later German expenditure was 13 per cent higher. It was also the first year since the 1889 Naval Defence Act that British expenditure on new construction fell below the combined total of the next two naval powers (now France and Germany).[52] Meanwhile, the arrival of Fisher as First Sea Lord[53] and the laying down of the new battleship *Dreadnought* presaged a revolution in naval power and its application.

NID, under the leadership of Captain Charles Ottley as DNI, now comprised four divisions. The original Intelligence and Mobilisation divisions were accompanied by two further divisions, a War Division created in 1900 to take on the strategic planning element of the DNI brief, and a Trade Division established two years later, reflecting the growing importance of commerce protection. NID's responsibilities had reached their zenith.[54] In the coming years they were gradually reduced under successive Admiralty reforms to create a department focused solely on intelligence.

Each NID division was headed by a Royal Navy officer of captain rank and between them they had a further nineteen junior naval or Royal Marine officers. Intelligence was the largest division with ten officers, twice the strength agreed at NID's creation.[55] Also under the direction of NID was the network of naval attachés. This had expanded steadily since 1900 with dedicated posts accredited to each of the major naval powers, France, Russia and Germany, but also the United States and Japan.[56] Many attachés had postings to NID, either before or after deployment overseas, enhancing the effectiveness of the NID intelligence operation. Ottley served periods as attaché in Washington, Tokyo and St Petersburg from 1900–1902.[57] From the early 1890s, NID had also promoted the appointment of a dedicated intelligence officer on the staff of fleet and independent squadron commanders. These intelligence officers, frequently drawn from the Royal Marines, received and distributed reports from NID, but also recruited naval assistants, and exploited local agent networks to collect information on its behalf. Captain Maurice Hankey, Royal Marines, acted as an informal intelligence officer to the Rear Admiral Mediterranean Fleet in 1899, and then served as a coastal defence specialist in NID 1902–06, before returning as the official Mediterranean Fleet Intelligence Officer from 1907–09.[58] He was immensely able and enjoyed the patronage of Fisher, who first noticed him in the Mediterranean, and then brought him into his planning team as First Sea Lord. He succeeded Ottley as Secretary to the Committee of Imperial Defence in 1912, holding this post until 1938, also becoming the first Cabinet Secretary in 1916, aged just thirty-nine. He was thus a dominant influence on British national security for nearly three decades. Hankey's early career demonstrates that by the late nineteenth century the role of intelligence was accorded higher status within the Royal Navy than often suggested, and drew talented officers. The status of DNI in the Admiralty had also increased steadily since the days of Hall. Officers selected for the post were invariably rising stars of their generation. Most went on to achieve flag rank, and they included one future First Sea Lord, Prince Louis of Battenberg, DNI from 1902–05.

NID had produced nearly eight hundred reports since January 1887. There was now a smooth, well-established system for distribution to customers ashore and afloat, and for updating reports and withdrawing material no longer relevant. About half were edited and published versions of reports originating from the naval attachés. The remainder were prepared and issued by NID staff. A handful derived from commanders-in-chief or, occasionally, from information collected by a more junior officer.[59] With one significant exception, none of the regular NID sources over this period qualified as covert or secret. The attachés produced much high-quality material, but operated within a strictly diplomatic framework. Frontline commanders exploited a variety of contacts within their respective theatres and took the opportunity to observe foreign warships with a professional eye, but few used regular paid sources. Otherwise, NID drew heavily on what would now be described as open-source intelligence. It was assiduous in scrutinising professional journals and the mainstream press across all countries of interest. In 1907 it subscribed to over thirty French language publications and over ten German.[60]

The significant exception to this pattern was an arrangement negotiated by Fisher as Commander-in-Chief Mediterranean 1899–1902 with the Eastern Telegraph Company, whereby it agreed to share cable traffic of intelligence interest passing through its Mediterranean relay stations with Mediterranean Fleet command at Malta. Fisher was an avid user of this source during his tenure, claiming later also to have acquired the keys to most foreign ciphers. It made him especially receptive to the opportunities of cable and radio intercept which opened up in 1914. So highly did Fisher rate the ability of W H Cottrell, the Eastern manager at Syra in the Aegean, to cover and interpret French cable traffic in the eastern Mediterranean that he sought to reward him financially from the secret service fund.[61] Fisher was the first Royal Navy commander to spot the potential of an integrated picture drawing on intelligence from cable, the new medium of radio, and more traditional consular and human sources, where his network rivalled that of Nelson a century earlier. He persuaded the Foreign Office to allow consuls in the Mediterranean to communicate with him directly on foreign warship movements, enhanced their contribution by assiduously fostering personal relationships with them, and provided secure communications to enable information to be immediately telegraphed to Malta. He negotiated with Sir Nicholas O'Conor, the British ambassador in Constantinople, for the speedy transmission of intelligence from the Black Sea, and persuaded the governor of Malta to intercept the mail of the Russian consul during the South African war.[62] To gather intelligence on the French, Fisher cultivated Martyn Gurney, Consul General at Marseilles. He admired Gurney's 'zeal, ability, activity and great knowledge of naval matters', first evident when he was vice consul at Spezia, and later nominated him for a knighthood. Gurney appointed Norman Haag as acting vice consul at Toulon to assist him, reporting to Fisher that Haag was 'lying low, making friends and keeping his eyes open'. Haag subsequently received an allowance from the secret service vote and established direct contact with NID. While much of his information derived from open sources, some was acquired more covertly. In 1902 he provided a confidential report on French submarine construction, which Fisher forwarded to the newly appointed Inspecting Captain of Submarine Boats, Reginald Bacon.[63]

Fisher's experience of communications intercept, linked to his wider network of sources, led him to create a strategic plot of the Mediterranean in his Admiralty House headquarters in Malta, displaying present and predicted enemy warship movements. This plot helped him address his primary challenge as Mediterranean commander. He potentially faced three hostile fleets, the French at Brest and Toulon, and the Russians in the Black Sea. He was superior to any one of these, but not to a combination of all three. By locating each of them with confidence and predicting their movements, he could defeat them in detail. In creating this plot, drawing on intelligence from multiple sources delivered through cable, with intercept promising to become the most important, Fisher became the father of what, a century later, would be termed 'network-centric warfare'.[64]

Once back in London, Fisher promoted the establishment of overseas intelligence centres to feed an integrated intelligence picture displayed in an Admiralty war room. The first two intelligence centres opened at Gibraltar and Malta in 1903, and three more followed at Colombo, Singapore and Hong Kong in November 1904. Prior to the establishment of these centres, embassies, consulates and colonial officials addressed information of naval interest direct to the local naval commander. This risked delay if the commander was at sea, or his immediate whereabouts unknown. NID issued consuls in certain foreign ports with ciphers from 1902, probably at the instigation of Fisher, but this risked provoking suspicion from local authorities and was therefore disliked by the Foreign Office. Before 1914 the intelligence centres were modest affairs, comprising one officer and a tiny support team. However, by providing a clearing house where intelligence could be rapidly assessed and passed on to commanders, they rapidly demonstrated value, becoming a building block for a more elaborate system when war came in 1914.[65] As First Sea Lord, Fisher explored visionary ideas for exploiting this new global intelligence to change the nature of naval warfare.

With this Mediterranean exception, NID's dependence otherwise on diplomatic and open sources meant it remained better sighted on the capability of foreign navies than their underlying intentions towards Britain or their detailed war plans, both of which were naturally closely protected. Not all readers were admirers of its reports. In November 1904 Commander Herbert Richmond, soon to become naval assistant to Fisher as First Sea Lord, before going on to found the *Naval Review* professional journal, and eventually to reach full admiral, dismissed NID as 'merely a collector of notes on various subjects', providing 'badly written and dull blue books'. It published the 'results of naval attachés' work and a hundred other things – all of value but generally so dully produced that most people take no trouble to read them'.[66]

Many NID reports were dull. Even the best intelligence can make heavy reading, particularly specialised topics not immediately relevant to the reader. Nevertheless, despite this failing and, more important, the lack of genuine secret sources, the quality and power of the information base NID had established by 1905 should not be underestimated. A scan across the reports issued demonstrates that its knowledge of the fighting power of possible opponents was comprehensive, and its assessments of the naval risk they posed to Britain invariably balanced and realistic. Following his service in NID, Hankey judged foreign intelligence 'far better than could have been expected from so small a staff and expenditure'.[67] The rise of Germany now promised new challenges, while new technology would transform the intelligence business.

3

Defining a Rising German Threat 1905–1909

The traditional view of the Anglo-German naval rivalry from the start of the twentieth century to the outbreak of war in 1914 saw the German naval threat as a dominant influence on British strategic policy, shaping attitudes within the political and naval leadership, driving the *Dreadnought* revolution, and primarily focused on a future Trafalgar-type clash between battle-fleets in the North Sea.[1] Subsequent assessments questioned both the primacy of the German threat, and the real motives of the reforms and innovations championed by Admiral of the Fleet Sir John Fisher as First Sea Lord 1904–10, by deploying three main arguments.[2] First, that financial retrenchment and technological opportunity were more important drivers for reform and change in the Royal Navy over the first decade of the twentieth century than a perceived threat from Germany. Secondly, that Fisher harboured more radical ideas for harnessing new technology to secure British naval supremacy at reduced cost than previously recognised. He favoured flotilla defence by torpedo craft and submarines to secure the United Kingdom from invasion, rather than fleets of expensive capital ships. He also planned to secure Britain's global interests and its vital trade routes with large, fast, heavily gunned armoured cruisers, or 'battlecruisers', directed to threatened areas by a new global communications system, a strategy of manoeuvre warfare in the open sea. Finally, as the German threat became more apparent, Fisher initiated a strategy to exploit Britain's financial dominance to achieve the rapid collapse of the German economy, 'a British Schlieffen Plan', rather than relying on the long attrition of a traditional blockade.[3]

These arguments have, in turn, provoked challenge, so that British naval policy in the decade before the First World War remains contested ground, with the significance of economic warfare to both British and German strategy especially controversial.[4] Given the potential importance of this debate to the origins and progress of the First World War, it attracted surprisingly little attention during the recent centennial commemorations and the arguments have stayed within a narrow academic audience.[5] They need not necessarily be mutually exclusive. The Admiralty, like any military organisation, prepared for various contingencies and possible enemies. Officers held different views or changed their position over time. Fisher exerted huge influence through the period 1900–1914, but was only First Sea Lord for one-third of it and out of office for another third. He was also famously inconsistent on many key points of policy. Finally, in deploying evidence to support a particular historical argument, the wholesale destruction of Admiralty records covering this period dictates caution. Little can be said with complete certainty, but so far the more traditional interpretation has stood the test of time and been supplemented, rather than displaced.[6]

The portrayal of British naval intelligence in shaping British perceptions of the German naval threat and influencing the policy response has been selective. This partly reflects the limited number of intelligence records surviving from this period. But where intelligence reports do exist, they have often been deployed in arguments without adequately explaining what they said, from where and how they originated, and how representative they were. There has been no comprehensive overview of British naval intelligence in the decade before 1914, or its coverage of the rising German threat.[7] Yet intelligence is crucial to a convincing assessment of pre-1914 British naval policy. Especially important is how far it illuminated the rationale behind German naval policy and Germany's likely priorities in a naval war with Britain.[8] The viability of a Fisher-sponsored flotilla-defence strategy to defend home waters depended on an effective central communications system able to direct its flotilla elements, but also whether adequate intelligence of enemy movements was achievable. 'Vectoring' battlecruisers as a precision strike force likewise depended on whether a global intelligence warning system was a credible prospect at this time.[9] The viability of a British blockade strategy and more ambitious plans for rapid collapse of the German economy required detailed understanding of that economy and its vulnerabilities. Intelligence was important at the tactical level too. Whether Admiral Sir John Jellicoe planned during the first part of the war to engage the German battle-fleet using rapid and concentrated fire at medium range must take account of NID intelligence acquired on German gunnery capability and tactics, and how Jellicoe interpreted this.[10]

This broader picture of the role of intelligence also matters because the overall British achievement on the German naval target before 1914 was creditable, and deserves more recognition. As Captain Reginald Hall, who became DID in November 1914, acknowledged: 'Before the war some very wonderful results were obtained by men who seldom enough could be rewarded for their long years of patient and unobtrusive and sometimes most dangerous work.'[11] Finally, the decade before 1914 was important too, because it marked the first steps in creating the wider intelligence community which would operate alongside NID and its army counterpart. There were other developments, notably the rapid changes in communications technology and networks, which would have a profound impact on the intelligence business across the rest of the twentieth century.

The initial significance of the German naval threat to Britain may be disputed. But there is agreement that it began in 1897 when the newly appointed State Secretary at the Imperial Navy Office, Admiral Alfred von Tirpitz, persuaded Kaiser Wilhelm II that for Germany to achieve her desired status as a world power with an overseas empire, a substantial battle-fleet was required as insurance against Britain, her most dangerous potential opponent at sea.[12] In a war against a dominant sea power such as Britain, Germany was vulnerable to close blockade, which could destroy her economy within a year. Germany, therefore, required a deterrent fleet large enough that even victory by a superior British fleet would risk losses sufficient to undermine its continuing command of the sea. Tirpitz calculated that a 'risk fleet', two-thirds the size of the Royal Navy, would have sufficient strategic value to justify building it. The programme to build such a fleet began with the two Navy Laws of 1898 and 1900.[13]

The Admiralty recognised this new naval threat earlier than is often suggested.[14] NID was quick to spot that Germany might exploit Anglo-French tensions provoked by the Fashoda incident in 1898.[15] The implications of German naval expansion were addressed by Custance as DNI in December 1900. He anticipated that Germany would overtake Russia to become the third naval power from 1906, and he judged the German navy more effective. British building plans must reflect this.[16] The following year he noted that Fisher as Commander-in-Chief Mediterranean was a powerful advocate for his fleet, but the needs of the Home Fleet also required attention, given the formidable German force developing in the North Sea.[17] Recognition of rising German naval power provoked the appointment of the first naval attaché to Berlin, Commander Arthur Ewart, in November 1900.[18] Custance was initially a lone voice in the Admiralty in his concerns about Germany, which the First Lord, the Earl of Selborne, insisted should not distract from the primary threat posed by France and Russia.[19] By early 1902, Selborne's attitude shifted and he increasingly questioned the German build-up and underlying

German intentions. Reporting from Ewart, now promoted to captain, to NID that German naval expansion was unquestionably directed at Britain was influential.[20] So was lobbying by Selborne's political deputy, the Parliamentary and Financial Secretary Hugh Arnold-Forster, who consistently emphasised the German threat, especially to trade.[21] That spring, NID War Division began rudimentary studies of what a naval conflict with Germany would entail.[22] It examined German exercises, including those testing defences at the mouth of the Elbe and at Kiel.[23]

In October 1902 Selborne advised the Cabinet that the new German navy was undoubtedly aimed at a future war with Britain, a view shared by the ambassador in Berlin, Sir Frank Lascelles.[24] At present rate of construction, Germany could have twenty-six battleships available in the North Sea by 1907.[25] Selborne's position reflected a further powerfully argued assessment circulated the previous month by Arnold-Forster, following a trip to Germany which included visits to Kiel and Wilhelmshaven.[26] Arnold-Forster received strong support from the Director of Naval Construction, Sir Philip Watts, who felt Royal Navy dispositions must adjust to this threat.[27] Political support for Selborne's view of Germany was more limited. Few Cabinet colleagues yet viewed her as a serious threat and, importantly, the First Sea Lord, Admiral Lord Walter Kerr, was also sceptical.[28] Nevertheless, during 1902 Selborne initiated the purchase of land for a major naval base opposite Germany on the east coast at Rosyth, and the Admiralty confirmed its development as an operational base for a potential war with Germany the following year.[29] The Russo-Japanese war heightened Admiralty concerns over German naval intentions. German supply of coal, using Hamburg-Amerika Line merchant ships, to the Russian Baltic Fleet transiting to the Far East demonstrated that the German navy was developing a global logistic support and intelligence network.[30] Such support, along with the Kaiser's pledge to protect Russia's exit from the Baltic, suggested direct German intervention against Britain's ally Japan was possible.[31]

Growing British anxiety over a substantial German battle-fleet in the North Sea was exacerbated by another German threat emerging in parallel. This was German ability to conduct a trade war by exploiting its merchant fleet, the world's second largest. The prospect of a French attack on British trade using armoured cruisers had been an enduring Admiralty concern through the 1890s. In 1901 NID warned the Board of Admiralty that Germany might pursue a variant of this strategy, encouraging and subsidising German shipping companies to build fast merchant vessels suitable for conversion into armed raiders for global deployment against Britain in wartime. The following year NID focused specifically on

Germany's fast transatlantic liners, of which she had three, with a fourth building. These had the speed (over 23 knots) and endurance once armed to hunt down any British merchant ship, while easily evading pursuit by British warships, which had lower sustained speed and range. They thus posed a more dangerous threat than French armoured cruisers. Selborne was sufficiently anxious to alert the Cabinet in July 1902. Apart from the specifics of the threat, his memorandum was the first Cabinet paper to identify a future war with Germany as a realistic possibility. Selborne argued that building a 'special cruiser' to counter the problem of the German liners would be prohibitively expensive, weak in fighting power compared to a battleship, and unsuitable for general naval use. Instead, he proposed subsidising British merchant cruisers to match the German ships, but improve on their speed.[32]

Under the tenure of Prince Louis of Battenberg as DNI from late 1902 to 1905, this auxiliary raider threat, with the liners to the fore, was a continuing obsession. Until 1906 NID's assessment of the German trade threat was deductive, based on analysis of German capability. It had no hard intelligence of German plans or intentions.[33] However, its deductive assessment was broadly correct. The German navy was indeed planning to use armed merchant raiders against Britain. The fast liners had been selected as especially suitable and had received deck strengthening and fittings ready for gun mounting when required. Significant work had also been done by 1906 on where raiders would be deployed.[34]

Fisher recognised the potential naval threat posed by Germany on taking office in October 1904. As early as 1901, while Commander-in-Chief Mediterranean, he speculated that Britain's long-term interests aligned better with France than Germany, where he saw increasing scope for hostility.[35] As Second Sea Lord 1902–03, he knew of the concerns raised by Selborne and Arnold-Forster as well as NID. Before appointing him, Selborne insisted that NID war planning must consider every possible threat, including 'Germany singly or in any combination'.[36] This does not mean Fisher yet saw Germany as the Royal Navy's first or inevitable enemy, nor was Germany initially the primary driver of his modernisation agenda.[37] The Russo-Japanese war made the prospect of British conflict with Russia and therefore potentially France, as Russia's ally, as high as ever. The Russian Baltic Fleet's sinking of Hull trawlers the day after Fisher's arrival as First Sea Lord indeed made war with Russia appear imminent although, even at this point, Fisher saw Germany as an important instigator of tension.[38] German logistic support during the Baltic Fleet transit heightened his suspicions. Two weeks later, Battenberg advised him that conflict with Russia and Germany now looked more probable than with Russia and France, and that the rapid growth of the German fleet at Kiel made this a more formidable proposition. Battenberg proposed substantially strengthening the Home Fleet at the expense of the Mediterranean, which Fisher agreed.[39] From this point, maintaining a fleet superior to Germany in the North Sea became a central tenet of Admiralty policy.[40] Meanwhile, Selborne stressed the worst-case possibility of German intervention against Britain while she was engaged in a still undecided war with France and Russia. Insurance against this risk required a margin beyond the two-power standard.[41]

For Fisher, the rising German naval threat complicated Britain's strategic choices, but his immediate preoccupations were finance and technology. He arrived in office aware that the naval budget was under pressure. Annual naval expenditure at £37 million in 1904/5 was now nearly 15 per cent of overall government spending and as a proportion of GDP it had doubled in fifteen years to 1.8 per cent. Without transformational change the rate of increase would continue.[42] Judged by patterns later in the century, peacetime expenditure of 1.8 per cent was not excessive (overall British defence expenditure was 6.2 per cent in 1960 and never fell below 4 per cent throughout the Cold War), but at this time it was politically unsustainable. Fisher's most pressing priority, therefore, was to make the Royal Navy more effective at lower cost. He believed new technology could achieve this, but recognised that this was developing at an unprecedented rate, posing opportunities and threats which the Royal Navy must manage successfully, irrespective of budgetary advantage.

That does not imply Fisher pursued modernisation to transform Royal Navy capability independently from any specific threat, whether from Germany or elsewhere.[43] Isolating capability from the context in which it might be used is a false distinction. Fisher certainly saw innovation and reform as a means to ensure continuing British maritime supremacy at more acceptable cost. He achieved this. Over the five years of his tenure, the new force structure he commissioned, along with modern communications, fleet redeployment and reorganisation, and personnel reforms bequeathed his successor a more capable Navy, while achieving savings of 11 per cent on the 1904/5 budget baseline. However, modernisation and reform was shaped by the evolving naval threat and the intelligence which illuminated it.

Fisher's focus on Germany intensified across 1905, the first full year of his tenure. His perception of her changed from that of 'dangerous meddler' to primary naval enemy. That does not mean that by the end of 1905 the German threat now dictated Admiralty policy. The revised fleet deployments in 1904/5, with their greater concentration in home waters, were designed, at least initially, as much for flexibility in countering France and Russia as dealing with Germany. The new perception of Germany partly reflected the changed status of France and Russia. Relations with France warmed considerably during 1905, while Tsushima removed Russia as a naval threat for the foreseeable future. This left Germany by default as Britain's only naval challenger. However, Germany's own actions hardened suspicions about her long-term ambitions. Her provocative interference in Morocco not only risked war with France, but suggested intent to acquire naval bases on the African Atlantic coast, which the Admiralty judged a serious threat to British maritime security.[44] The year, therefore, saw further reinforcement of the Home Fleet, now renamed the Channel Fleet, partly achieved through withdrawing capital ships from the Far East, and significant planning for a German war. This included the feasibility of blockading Germany's North Sea ports, early thoughts on attacking her economy by strangling her overseas trade, and discussion with the army regarding amphibious operations on the Baltic coast.[45] On several occasions, Fisher also spoke in typically trenchant terms within British leadership circles of the desirability of a pre-emptive strike to 'Copenhagen' the German fleet at Kiel. Some of these comments were picked up in Germany, strengthening Tirpitz's support.[46] Meanwhile, the possibility that Germany could exploit its naval strength to mount an invasion of the United Kingdom, or at least a major raid, or to conduct a pre-emptive 'bolt from the blue' torpedo strike on the British fleet was studied by NID and investigated in a Naval War College exercise in autumn 1906. Captain Philip Dumas, the Berlin naval attaché, judged such an operation unlikely, but stressed Britain had no current means of obtaining timely warning of secret German planning.[47] Others in government had similar thoughts, stimulating the creation of new intelligence capabilities.

The first initiative promoted by the Admiralty was ensuring an adequate consular network based in German and Danish ports to report on naval developments and movements, following the Mediterranean model. Fisher's direct influence here was evident in the transfer of Norman Haag, who, the Foreign Office noted, was 'specially clever at obtaining information on naval matters', from Toulon to Bremerhaven, and an attempt to move Martyn Gurney in Hamburg. Foreign Office support for this new network, patently aimed at intelligence-gathering with minimal commercial justification, was reluctant. They feared raising German suspicion, stressing the Consular Service were 'not intended to act as spies'. They constrained some Admiralty ambitions, but the Foreign Secretary, Sir Edward Grey, broadly endorsed the naval requirement and the consular intelligence service developed rapidly through 1907. That summer, the Consul General in Hamburg, Sir William Ward, confirmed that the primary role of the new vice consuls now installed at Bremerhaven (Haag), Emden and Hamburg was naval reporting. This covered German warship construction, troop movements, coastal defences, mine, torpedo and submarine development, and any aeronautical matters. He also mentioned 'private agents' at Rendsburg and Cuxhaven. Most of what this network collected came from open sources, visual observation, conversation with business and professional contacts, and scrutiny of the local press. Much was mundane, but it helped to build an overall picture of emerging German capability, and it extended the reach of the naval attaché. However, there was some genuinely covert work, such as photography of coastal fortifications produced by Haag and funded from the secret vote. Arrangements were also made for secure communication with London, occasionally through the post using cipher, but preferably by passing reports by 'safe hand' through the captains of British merchant ships heading to the United Kingdom. Consuls also visited NID when back in London.[48]

While the Admiralty assessed the potential German naval threat and considered its response, there was an important development in the British government's management of defence and security. The Committee of Imperial Defence (CID) had been created in December 1902 under the government of Arthur Balfour, replacing the Defence Committee introduced by the Salisbury administration in 1895, which had proved ineffective. Its primary purpose was to provide the Cabinet with 'information and expert advice required for shaping national policy in war' and making 'necessary preparations in peace'. It was chaired by the prime minister, and key members comprised the chancellor, the foreign and home secretaries, and the political and professional heads of the Navy and army. The committee took a while to bed down, but improved with the establishment of a permanent secretariat in 1904. Initially, it was an advisory body for the prime minster and Cabinet, but it steadily acquired a more formal and proactive role in shaping national security strategy. Prior to 1914 it was the only forum which obliged the Admiralty and War Office to collaborate in threat assessments and war planning, and it was where intelligence and planning interacted within a national policy framework. In contrast to the War Office, the Admiralty was a passive participant in the committee's early years, and during the first half of Fisher's tenure it was often downright obstructive. This reflected Fisher's obsessive secretiveness and suspicion of any forum that might interfere in naval affairs, his ingrained hostility to the War Office, and his personal dislike of the committee's first secretary, Sir George Clarke, a retired army officer. His attitude moderated somewhat when Ottley became secretary in 1907, but it required the arrival of Winston Churchill as First Lord in 1911 for the Admiralty to exercise influence in the committee commensurate with its weight and importance.[49] Admiralty passivity is demonstrated by the fact that over the period 1902–14 the War Office sponsored nearly three times as many papers.[50]

The dreadnought battleship and the battlecruiser formed the core of the force restructuring central to Fisher's modernisation programme. Building *Dreadnought* was controversial. Fisher supporters insisted it was a necessary step-change, vital to secure Britain's position. Critics argued that by rendering previous battleships obsolete it surrendered Britain's lead and allowed Germany to catch up. Debate over the balance of advantage, Fisher's true motives, and whether his primary interest always lay with the battlecruiser and its development has raged ever since. Fisher did not invent the concept of a battleship with a uniform heavy armament. The Admiralty considered a design featuring this as early as 1902.[51] It was an inevitable evolution as gun technology improved, with the prospect of longer-range engagement. However, for Fisher, uniform heavy armament was part of a wider technology package embracing turbine power for higher speed and endurance, advanced fire control, and long-range radio communication. Combining these technical advances in a revolutionary overall design promised a more effective capital ship force at lower cost. Quality would replace quantity at overall force level, while manpower costs for individual ships would be lower, something the US Navy also recognised.[52]

Fisher knew that other navies had similar intentions. By late 1904 the Admiralty had 'secret information' that both the Russians and the Japanese had decided their future battleships should have 12in guns and a speed of 20 knots. The US Navy was also planning a ship with twelve guns above 10in and no others apart from 3in quick-firing anti-torpedo guns.[53] In the nineteenth century the Royal Navy let France innovate, confident that Britain, with greater industrial resources, could rapidly copy and improve on such innovation and out-build France too. Fisher's view was different. He believed that Britain's competitive advantage in shipbuilding and related naval industries made the Royal Navy uniquely well-placed to embrace the opportunities of new technology. It need not fear change, because it could replace ships more quickly than anyone else. He accordingly advocated 'plunging' ahead with innovation to put competitor navies off balance. Once your rival is committed to a design, you 'plunge' with one '50 per cent better', knowing that 'your rapid shipbuilding and command of money' will provide a vessel fit to fight as soon as your rival. For Fisher, *Dreadnought* offered a decisive shift in fighting power and improved cost-effectiveness. But intelligence determined the timing and speed with which he pushed her forward. If others had similar ambitions, maintaining Royal Navy superiority required 'plunging' pre-emption.[54]

While there are several Admiralty references to 'secret information' regarding a *Dreadnought*-type competitor, no intelligence report has survived.[55] The information probably derived from the respective attachés in St Petersburg and Tokyo, and in the case of the United States, initially from open sources. For both Japan and the United States, the information was correct. Japan completed plans for the battleship *Aki*, armed with twelve 12in guns and a speed of 20 knots, before the end of 1904 and she was laid down at Kure in March 1905, well before *Dreadnought*. However, *Aki* then encountered financial and technical difficulties and was not completed until 1911.[56] Meanwhile, in early 1905 the United States Congress authorised two *Michigan*-class battleships armed with eight 12in guns in super-firing turrets, an arrangement the Royal Navy did not adopt for some years. But, as with Japan, there were delays in executing the order. Political opposition to the revolutionary design prevented their start until 1907.[57] By 1905, the Admiralty also knew that Germany planned an all-big-gun battleship. *Nassau* was designed contemporaneously with *Dreadnought*, although not laid down until July 1906. Work was then suspended while the Germans clarified *Dreadnought's* specifications.[58] An assessment of *Dreadnought* competitors (including those planned by Germany) was prepared for the Board of Admiralty by the Controller, Captain Henry Jackson, at the beginning of 1906. It was reasonably accurate and incorporated in a review of the Royal Navy's future build programme.[59] This emphasised the inevitability of the dreadnought type and British success in securing early advantage. Britain enjoyed a satisfactory lead over the next two naval powers, Germany and France, although forward projections were less favourable. The combined budget of Germany and France would soon exceed that of Britain.[60]

Fisher's promotion of the battlecruiser concept has provoked even more controversy than *Dreadnought*. The three *Invincible* class, laid down shortly after *Dreadnought*, were another 'plunging' design incorporating a similar technology package, including a uniform 12in gun armament, but sacrificing armour for speed. A definitive rationale for the battlecruisers is elusive, because Fisher was notoriously secretive over his motives, which evolved over time, and because there are gaps in Admiralty records. They were both a reasonable variant of the new

Dreadnought technology package and a logical extension of the large armoured cruisers favoured over the previous decade. Fisher undoubtedly valued speed for delivering decisive effect at a distance, for achieving surprise, and for setting the terms of an engagement. Speed and gun power allied to modern communications therefore made the battlecruiser the ultimate offensive hunter.

As with *Dreadnought*, intelligence contributed to the timing and specifications of the *Invincibles* by presenting an immediate practical requirement, namely the German merchant raider threat. Although intelligence on this was deductive prior to 1906, it still triggered an important British policy response. In line with Selborne's recommendation, the Cabinet agreed to subsidise Cunard in building two large passenger liners, *Mauretania* and *Lusitania*, to be armed as raider-hunting auxiliaries in the event of war. On completion in late 1907, these were the world's largest ships, significantly faster than their German equivalents, both holding the blue riband for the fastest transatlantic crossing. Negotiations with Cunard were complex. The Admiralty recognised that two ships offered only a partial answer to the problem, but a wider subsidy scheme would be expensive, and poor value for money. Battenberg favoured, if size and cost were no object, constructing a large cruiser to take on the role.[61]

This German raider threat encouraged Fisher, on becoming First Sea Lord, rapidly to turn Battenberg's 'possibility' into reality. He had become Second Sea Lord in June 1902, so was in the Admiralty as the Cunard arrangement was negotiated, and was aware of its purpose and limitations. He had closely followed the growth of the German merchant marine and the unique capabilities of its fast liners while still in the Mediterranean.[62] He had long been concerned that Britain was uniquely vulnerable to an attack on its trade routes. He knew Selborne had argued against building a 'special cruiser' to deal with the raider problem, but the arrival of turbine propulsion technology meant that the warship solution desired by Battenberg, expensive and difficult in 1902, looked eminently feasible in 1904. Fisher frequently insisted that the *Invincibles* were aimed at fast merchant raiders, and as a direct replacement for the Cunarders, which he judged a flawed concept.[63] Their specification, great endurance, and ability to sustain high speed of over 25 knots in heavy Atlantic weather support this claim, subsequently confirmed by Admiral Sir Reginald Bacon, the first captain of *Dreadnought* and Fisher's biographer, and Jellicoe, Director of Naval Ordnance when the *Invincibles* were designed.[64]

The *Invincibles* were not only suited to merchant raider hunting. Their speed, endurance and armament made them a uniquely effective and economical means of dealing with the armoured cruisers which had long worried the Admiralty, as *Invincible* and *Inflexible* demonstrated against Admiral Graf von Spee's squadron at the Falklands in 1914. When the *Invincibles* were conceived, the prospect of fighting French armoured cruisers was fading following the Entente, and the Russian threat had evaporated. The Royal Navy also enjoyed a comfortable lead in this category over the combined total for France and Germany.[65] Although no immediate new measures were therefore required to deal with warship raiders, by the end of 1905 the Admiralty learnt that Germany was planning a cruiser armed with four 11in guns, superior to any existing Royal Navy cruiser.[66] If the German fast liner threat had not existed, this would surely have pushed Fisher to build something like the *Invincibles*, although perhaps not as quickly.

Claims that Fisher harboured a consistent vision for the battlecruiser, wanted to prioritise it over the battleship, indeed eventually to supersede it, are less convincing.[67] During his tenure, the Royal Navy laid down twice as many battleships as battlecruisers, and there was a gap of three years between the *Invincibles* and *Indefatigable*, the first of the next class. By the time *Indefatigable* was laid down in February 1909, Germany had two battlecruisers under construction (*Von der Tann* and *Moltke*), with specifications superior to their British counterparts. In addition to rapid long-range projection of overwhelming force against any raider threat to Britain's trade routes, Royal Navy battlecruisers now had to mark Germany's in the North Sea and forestall a possible breakout. The battlecruiser is, therefore, best viewed as necessary for certain specific tasks before technology enabled an effective synthesis of gun power, armour and speed in designs like the abandoned 1921 G3.

Dreadnought battleships and *Invincible*-class battlecruisers were the most visible capability change initiated by Fisher during his first months as First Sea Lord, but were accompanied by another 'plunging' innovation, with the potential to transform naval warfare, and which therefore influenced the future of British naval intelligence. There were three linked elements to his goal: a new global communications network based on the new medium of radio; exploitation of this network to create a global maritime information picture; and, finally, use of this picture for more effective command and control. Fisher's vision here drew on his experience with communications intelligence in the Mediterranean. But almost uniquely among senior naval officers, he recognised the revolutionary impact of radio for naval operations. Conceptually, Fisher was thinking on the right lines, but he overestimated how far his Mediterranean intelligence network, and especially the cable access through Syra, was transferable elsewhere. He was reaching beyond the available technology and his support for those elements that were achievable proved inconsistent. It would be ten years before the Admiralty implemented a more limited version of the operational intelligence centre Fisher envisaged, and then only under the extreme threat of losing the Atlantic trade war in 1917.[68]

Fisher moved quickly on the first element, accelerating the establishment of a dedicated Admiralty radio network. New transmitters at Cleethorpes and Horsea in the United Kingdom, Gibraltar and Malta, and the fitting of warships with new 1.5 kilowatt (kw) transmitters (14kw in battlecruisers), enabled long-range, two-way, ship-to-shore radio communication in the area stretching from Greenland to Aden by the end of 1908. Further afield, the Admiralty still relied primarily on cable, but significantly enhanced communication by establishing transmitters at each naval cable base station. In 1912 it supplemented its long-range capability with three W/T (wireless telegraphy) cruisers, or mobile communication centres, *Defence*, *Europa* and *Vindictive*, fitted with Poulsen equipment with a range of 1200 miles.[69] The Admiralty radio network was enhanced further by exploiting the long-standing co-operation with Lloyd's and their ever-improving global radio network, for which the Admiralty had agreed substantial financial support in 1901.[70] Meanwhile, Royal Navy warships equipped with radio increased from 157 to 435 between 1908 and 1913, including widespread installation in smaller torpedo craft and submarines.[71]

This investment in radio was accompanied by improvements in the collection, processing and exploitation of shipping intelligence, after the creation of the new Trade Division within NID under Captain Edward Inglefield in 1902. Trade protection received a powerful boost the following year from a Royal Commission on the supply of food and raw materials in wartime, which posed searching questions to the Admiralty. Inglefield brought a more systematic approach to the collection of shipping data and presentation of British commercial shipping movements using coloured charts. He used this picture to identify specified wartime routes to keep merchant shipping clear of known threats, communicated with the help of Lloyd's. This 'safe route' policy was endorsed by Ottley as DNI, with broad support from Fisher, but opposed by the Commander-in-Chief Channel, Admiral Sir Arthur Wilson, who insisted that wartime routes would not remain secret and would become a magnet for attack.[72] Fisher accepted Wilson's alternative, proposing that in wartime merchant traffic be diverted away from all normal routes.[73] Inglefield resigned and moved to Lloyd's, although he maintained positive relations with the Admiralty.[74]

Captain Henry Campbell, who took over Trade Division in mid 1906, accordingly abandoned Inglefield's 'safe route' policy, which implied Admiralty direction of shipping, for one of local 'advice and assistance'. If the location of British merchant ships requiring protection and of threatening enemy vessels was known, then British ships could be advised using the latest intelligence to take whatever route seemed safest. Wartime routes would not be fixed, as proposed by both Inglefield and Wilson, but flexible according to threat. To make this policy viable, Campbell proposed a global intelligence-reporting network. This would expand the existing regional intelligence structure, adding new centres staffed by a single retired naval officer, starting with the route to Latin America. Each centre would take responsibility for a defined geographic area and act as clearing house for threat information relevant to shipping within it. They would exploit traditional sources such as local consular networks and shipping agents, but Campbell saw British merchant ships themselves as a key source. The increasing availability of radio and the Admiralty's developing communications network would knit this global network together and facilitate rapid transmission of threat information to and from ships at sea. It would give the Admiralty a better global intelligence picture.[75]

Campbell's proposals got strong support from Captain Edmund Slade, Ottley's successor as DNI, but, for reasons that remain unclear, were consistently blocked by Fisher. It took a further two years before Campbell's intelligence network began to evolve under the sponsorship of Slade's successor, Rear Admiral Alexander Bethell, who faced opposition from the Treasury and the Foreign and India offices. The first three new intelligence centres were established by the end of 1911 at St Vincent in the Cape Verde Islands, Montevideo and Pernambuco.[76] By early 1914, four further centres were added at Shanghai, Cape Town, Kingston and Fremantle, providing a total of twelve by the outbreak of war. Plans for a network of fifteen centres in the United Kingdom to cover home waters and to be mobilised in wartime were also prepared.[77]

Fisher's obstructiveness towards the global intelligence network casts doubt over his real commitment to a navy built around a core of battlecruisers deployed under central direction against threats around the globe. Without a reporting system similar to that proposed by Campbell, long-distance raider hunting was not viable. Even with it, experience a generation later in the Second World War, with far better communications technology and the benefit of aerial reconnaissance, showed it was still immensely difficult. Fisher apparently believed that Lloyd's offered a cheaper and more effective intelligence solution, but he never pursued this. When war began in 1914, the seven new stations established from 1911 proved essential in enabling the Admiralty to maintain effective communication with overseas commanders. Without them the management of global operations would have been more difficult, making Fisher's opposition even more puzzling.[78] Meanwhile, it is clear that Campbell, Slade and Bethell believed the primary role of this global intelligence network was to counter the threat from German merchant raiders, rather than warships. This threat remained a major concern, bolstered by a steady stream of intelligence reports, through to the outbreak of war.[79]

The Admiralty focus on the raider threat was justified by German planning, which became more extensive and sophisticated as NID implemented its global intelligence network. The Germans recognised that their lack of overseas bases was a major constraint in any sustained campaign against Britain's trade routes. Their answer was a network of supply facilities (*Etappen*), established in neutral countries to ensure the availability of coal, essential spare parts and food. An officer was appointed to each *Etappe* area to co-ordinate activities in support of raiders, to mobilise support from German commercial representatives, consuls and residents, and to liaise with naval attachés. Rendezvous points were identified, clear of shipping routes, where supply vessels could safely meet raiders, either warship or merchant. An intelligence system would operate alongside the *Etappen*. One of the most important, dictated by geography and communications, was the Canary Islands.[80]

Despite his opposition to the global intelligence network, Fisher did promote another initiative that would eventually transform the exploitation of intelligence and, indeed, naval warfare. In early 1905 NID began to plot British warships, fleet auxiliaries and colliers, along with the warships and supply vessels of select foreign powers, on a giant global wall chart measuring about 12ft by 6ft in what became known as the War Room, and hence the War Room plot, although as late as 1914 some officers called it the Chart Room. This was located in what was formerly the First Lord's state bedroom on the first floor of Admiralty House. Commercial ship movements judged significant, British and foreign, were also plotted. The plot was maintained in working hours during peacetime with daily updates and, as it became more sophisticated, it presented not only an 'as is' picture, but also predictions of future movements. The latter was helped by monitoring coal stock availability at ports and bases, and the global movement of colliers. During the next few years, the plot was divided into two parts, one covering home waters and the other the rest of the world. The primary plot at the Admiralty was also eventually linked directly with local plots maintained at the regional intelligence centres at Gibraltar, Malta, Colombo, Singapore and Hong Kong.[81] [82]

The War Room plot was visionary for its day and gave the Admiralty an invaluable strategic overview of global maritime operations. But it had limitations. Ships could be accurately located in port if there was someone to report on them with adequate communications. But once at sea, positional information in the first decade of the twentieth century was subject to substantial error.[83] Radio reporting pre-1914 suffered from partial coverage, the limited range and poor reliability of much seaborne radio equipment, and shortage of personnel with the requisite skills.[84] Interception of foreign signals traffic did not yet exist. NID manpower was restricted, constraining the amount of information it could process, and there were limits on what a wall plot could usefully display. Furthermore, NID did not control the transmission of information to and from the Admiralty, which was the responsibility of the Military Branch. Collating and displaying information in real time was therefore more a hypothetical possibility than something routinely achieved. There was a gulf between sources that could theoretically feed the plot (reports from the regional intelligence centres, direct reports to the Admiralty from Royal Navy warships, diplomatic and consular sources, including the attachés, customs and Lloyd's) and those able to do so in practice. The impression sometimes fostered by Fisher and others that the plot showed the location of all warships and merchantmen of interest in real time was exaggerated.[85] Following the outbreak of war in 1914, the flood of incoming information swamped available staff, rendering the plot almost useless in the early months of hostilities.[86]

The pre-1914 plot was, therefore, not sufficient for the Admiralty to exercise central control over British forces in order reliably to intercept those of the enemy. Nor was it, as Fisher perhaps hoped, a solution to the problem of covering multiple enemies over wide geographical spaces with limited resources. The capability of the plot was explored in annual grand manoeuvres from 1909, and Wilson, as First Sea Lord, managed a successful radio interception off Spain in 1910, but consistent and effective tactical control of operations by the Admiralty proved elusive. Nor were obvious issues of demarcation between the Admiralty and fleet commanders addressed. The exercises did highlight important issues in the management of radio communication. They sensitised the Royal Navy to the threat of interception, encouraging radio silence whenever possible, and a preference for visual signals (flags and lights) for short-range tactical communication, in contrast to German and American preference for radio. They also led to innovations such as the 'broadcast' system.[87] The pre-1914 plot is best viewed as an essential first step on a journey by way of the 1917 convoy Chart Room that would ultimately achieve Fisher's vision in the Second World War Operational Intelligence Centre, of which more later.

In January 1907 Ottley, as DNI, reviewing Royal Navy strength against other naval powers, confirmed a continuing comfortable two-power margin. The *Dreadnought* pre-emption strategy had also been successful. *Dreadnought* was in commission, two similar battleships had been laid down and a third ordered, and two more were planned for the 1907/8 programme. Three *Invincible* battlecruisers were under construction. NID knew of no foreign equivalent of either type yet building, although most navies had vessels on order. Britain had therefore secured a comfortable lead, but Ottley feared it was temporary. Germany and France would probably start six ships overall during 1907. Without further orders, Britain's advantage would then reduce to the three *Invincibles*. Britain could not relax her guard. Germany, in particular, was determined to make up lost ground.[88]

Ottley's concern regarding Germany was confirmed by the autumn. Germany laid down four *Nassau*-class *Dreadnought* equivalents between June and August, and ordered her first battlecruiser, *Von Der Tann* (responding to the *Invincibles*) in September. Dumas, the Berlin naval attaché, expected all four *Nassau*s to be commissioned in summer 1910, but the first two ships beat this by six months.[89] The previous year, Dumas assessed that German shipbuilding capacity could potentially rival Britain's for both output and speed of delivery.[90] During 1906, NID also learnt that the primary German armaments company Krupps was investing heavily in new facilities for manufacturing large-calibre naval guns. The source was the managing director of the Coventry Ordnance Works, Herbert Mulliner, who did regular business with Krupps. Mulliner's message, initially passed to the War Office and thence to the Admiralty, was twofold: that Krupps was developing technical capabilities superior to anything in Britain; and that once its investments were complete it would have potential output 'far in excess' of current British capacity.[91] NID briefed the Berlin attaché to seek confirmation. Following a visit in September 1906, he reported that signs of new construction and rebuilding were everywhere visible, suggesting 'more than normal' expansion of the works. A year later, during a further visit, the attaché found his access restricted, but saw immense development work continuing. By July 1908, further updates, including from Mulliner but probably also from an NID source within the Krupps works, persuaded the DNI, now Slade, that when work at Krupps was complete, Germany could achieve a capital-ship building rate of eight or nine ships annually, double present output.[92] This judgement foreshadowed a major change in British building policy the following year.

The trigger for what is known to history as the 1909 'naval scare'[93] was reporting from late summer 1908, initially from Dumas and then his successor as attaché, Captain Herbert Heath, that Germany was accelerating the construction of battleships authorised under their 1909/10 programme. Important confirmation came in October from the British consul in Danzig, stating that an order for one of next year's battleships had gone to the Danzig shipyard Schichau-Werke. A second order had apparently gone to A G Vulkan at Stettin.[94] The first part of the consul's report was correct. Tirpitz later admitted that the contract for the battleship *Oldenburg* was promised to Schichau in autumn 1908.[95] Furthermore, she was laid down on 1 March 1909, a month before the start of the financial year under which she was authorised. The second claim was only partly correct. The battlecruiser *Goeben* was ordered at the same time, but from Blohm & Voss, Hamburg not Stettin, and she was not laid down until August 1909. Slade nevertheless emphasised that these orders came six months prior to budget approval, and about fourteen months before British ships of the corresponding year were allotted. The crucial factor determining build time was the manufacture of heavy guns and mountings. By starting these in advance, Germany could complete her ships in about two years from April of the programme year.[96]

Further confirmation reached the Admiralty in December from the military attaché in Constantinople, Colonel Herbert Conyers Surtees, reporting comments about Krupps by the representative of the rival German armaments firm Erhardt. In recent years, Krupps had purchased enormous quantities of heavy machinery only suitable for 'manufacturing big guns and big naval mountings', far more than needed for existing programmes in Germany. German naval mountings were simpler in construction than British ones and designed for rapid manufacture. It seemed probable that these preparations at Krupps were for 'secretly' preparing 'mountings, ships' plates, ammunition, etc' for rapid creation of a battle-fleet to 'at least, equal the naval strength of England'.[97]

More signs of acceleration came from the managing director of Vickers, Sir Trevor Dawson, following a visit to Germany in February 1909. Dawson had legitimate business interests in Germany, giving significant access to their shipbuilding and armaments industries. However, he was a former Royal Navy officer who retained close contacts with the Admiralty, and was prepared to take intelligence briefs, even using Vickers' own agents on their behalf.[98] He began sending written reports to the Admiralty in September 1906, initially through the new First Lord, Lord Tweedmouth, and then his successor Reginald McKenna, rather than direct to NID. He provided a steady flow of high-quality intelligence through to the outbreak of war in 1914, more than fifty reports across these eight years. In addition to a comprehensive overview of the German and Austrian capital ship programmes, he contributed detailed insights on gunnery progress, the facilities at Krupps, and stockpiling of nickel supplies, on the German submarine programme, and turbine development.[99] He was highly regarded by Fisher, who in early 1915 pressed Churchill to get him appointed as Britain's 'chief buyer' for wartime supplies in the United States.[100]

Dawson provided three separate reports pointing to acceleration over the winter 1908/9 and it remained a regular theme in his coverage over the next fifteen months. Much of his information pointing to acceleration was circumstantial rather than conclusive, but overall he presented a disturbing picture, and his expertise and ability to reach areas barred to Heath made his evidence compelling. Separately, at the end of February Mulliner again underlined to Ottley, now secretary to the CID, the scale of recent expansion at Krupps, and their ability to expand production of heavy naval guns and mountings at short notice. He also judged German heavy guns superior to those of Britain, more durable and more easily handled. Finally, he identified seven German shipyards, each capable of building two battleships per year.[101]

The cumulative impact on the Board of Admiralty and NID of this intelligence regarding acceleration, acquired over six months, was considerable. In January 1909, prior to receiving the contributions from Dawson and Mulliner, the Fourth Sea Lord, Vice Admiral Alfred Winsloe, advised the Controller and Third Sea Lord Rear Admiral Sir Henry Jackson, that by expanding capacity and advancing orders, Germany would complete seventeen dreadnoughts by April 1912 and might even achieve twenty-one. If Britain laid down six ships in the coming year, she would have a margin of eighteen to seventeen by this date, but a powerful group in the Cabinet insisted on a maximum of four. The potential impact of 'acceleration' is evident from comparing Winsloe's figure here for German future build with NID's broadly accurate picture of the German programme at this time. NID assessed that, by April, Germany would have eight battleships (including one 1909/10 ship begun in advance of the financial year) and three battlecruisers (with one 1909/10 ship initiated in advance) under construction, with two further battleships to be commenced shortly.[102] All of these might credibly complete by April 1912 to give thirteen dreadnoughts, although, in the event, NID underestimated German construction time by at least six months. Winsloe's four extra ships would be achieved if the Germans began construction of four 1910/11 ships within the present year, as the Admiralty believed had occurred with two of the 1909/10 ships.

By February, the Board of Admiralty agreed that the acceleration intelligence required a minimum British 1909/10 programme of six capital ships to maintain an adequate safety margin over Germany. This would still fall below the two-power standard notionally in force. McKenna and Fisher proved determined and effective lobbyists in the fierce political battle that followed, and which famously secured eight ships rather than six.[103] Both were persuaded by the intelligence, much of which McKenna shared with senior Cabinet colleagues. McKenna emphasised three points to Prime Minister Henry Asquith and Grey as Foreign Secretary in December: first, 'Germany is anticipating the shipbuilding programme laid down by the law of 1907'; secondly, 'she is doing so secretly'; and finally, 'German capacity to build dreadnoughts is at this moment equal to ours.'[104] Fisher's resolute commitment to a minimum of six ships, and preferably eight (including only two battlecruisers), demonstrated that whatever vision he held for a naval revolution based on torpedo craft and submarines, he would not sacrifice capital ship superiority in the North Sea.

McKenna's three points neatly summarised how the Admiralty assessed the cumulative acceleration intelligence. In two respects, however, this assessment was flawed. Tirpitz had undertaken limited pre-ordering, but this does seem aimed at securing a better contract price and had little, if any, impact on construction start time or duration. More important, despite Admiralty fears, German construction time for capital ships never significantly improved on three years, and was often inferior to that of Britain. The British had four of their eight 1909/10 ships commissioned by April 1912, the Germans only one. However, McKenna's final point was probably right. By 1909, Germany had the potential dreadnought building capacity to match present British capacity. Whether Germany then chose to allocate the necessary resources and forgo other budgetary and military demands was another matter. Nor could she assume British capacity would stand still. Ultimately, the importance of the acceleration intelligence was that it highlighted a genuine risk to adequate British naval superiority. The subsequent debate was over what weight to give that risk. Whatever the merits of the intelligence case, the four extra ships ordered in 1909/10 provided almost the entire margin Britain enjoyed over the German fleet in the first four months of the coming war.[105] Equally important, the British 1909/10 programme triggered a growing conviction among German decision-makers that the Tirpitz risk fleet concept was unachievable at any reasonable cost.

4

The Beginning of an Intelligence Community 1909–1914

Policy judgements relating to the acceleration scare in 1908–09 did not draw on covert sources, although Dawson perhaps operated on the boundary between discreet targeted collection and the genuinely covert. On becoming DNI in October 1907, Slade was disturbed to find NID had no formal secret collection capability.[1] A year later this was beginning to change. Two of Slade's NID officers, Captain Frank Temple[2] and Captain Roy Regnart,[3] both Royal Marines, began visiting Germany in civilian guise, both to liaise with members of the consular network with a view to recruiting paid agents in German ports, and to develop two potentially important secret sources, one in the German Admiralty and the one in the Krupps works referred to earlier. Slade's attempts to exert increasing Admiralty control over the consular network, to promote their involvement in more covert activity, and to establish direct secure communications with the Admiralty, including sending letters with a false name to Slade's home address, provoked a sharp Foreign Office response. The Foreign Office was angered by what it perceived as Admiralty duplicity, but also feared that the activities of the consular system were spiralling out of control, risking severe diplomatic damage. During the first half of 1909, the Foreign Office permanent secretary, Sir Charles Hardinge, imposed strict new ground rules on both the Admiralty and War Office on what information the consuls were permitted to collect and what activities they could legitimately undertake.[4] The Admiralty inevitably judged the Foreign Office attitude obstructive and unhelpful, and it continued seeking consular intelligence assistance in direct contravention of Foreign Office instructions on an occasional basis up to 1914.[5] Nevertheless, NID risked overreaching. A disastrous operation in the Frisian Islands the following year, described in the next chapter, demonstrated that it was playing with fire. It possessed neither the experience nor resources at this time to find and handle secret agents overseas in a secure and deniable way, and on a sustained basis.

As the need for intelligence on the German navy increased, NID supplemented intelligence acquired through the consular network by sponsoring serving officers on reconnaissance trips under 'tourist' cover.[6] It also encouraged frontline units and personnel to exploit port visits or chance encounters to obtain information of interest through visual study of German ships and facilities, or through casual conversation. By 1908 such opportunities for 'overt' collection were more formally orchestrated by NID, with advance briefing on priority needs. In that year, the future DNI Reginald Hall, as captain of the cruiser *Cornwall*, received specific requirements before a visit to Kiel, which he met by contriving an opportunity to take photographs using a concealed cameraman.[7] Hall's targets included the status of the building slips and the progress of the new *Nassau*-class battleship *Posen*.[8] Two of his Royal Marine officers, Lieutenant Vivian Brandon and Captain Bernard Trench, conducted an intelligence reconnaissance ashore, for which they were commended by NID. Their recommendation that the Frisian Islands required more study had unfortunate consequences.[9] By 1914, prior briefing for, and subsequent reporting on, major visits was extensive. Inevitably, much information received comprised details of warship appearance or snippets gleaned in conversation, of limited interest taken in isolation. However, gossip between professional naval officers could still be revealing. A visit to Kiel that year showed that the High Seas Fleet was achieving high levels of sea-time, was regularly exercising in the Iceland area, and was to date achieving inconclusive results with director firing.[10] There was supporting evidence for a major gunnery exercise involving the battleship *Elsass* and cruiser *Blücher* southwest of the Faroes in April 1911, and authoritative intelligence confirmed the lack of a widely deployed director system shortly after the Kiel visit.[11]

By 1908, the War Office had thought rather more about covert intelligence collection than the Admiralty, driven by its experience in the Boer War, where military intelligence performance was initially dire. After that war, the Directorate of Military Intelligence and Mobilisation (broadly analogous to NID) lapsed, but an intelligence section continued within the Directorate of Military Operations. At the core of this was a 'special duties' section responsible for 'secret service' and counter-intelligence, successively known as I.3, MO3 and MO5 which drew on the secret vote to fund its agents and operations. This section considered how a secret service might operate in Europe as early as 1903.[12] In 1907

MO5, under its new head Lieutenant Colonel James Edmonds, with the approval of the Director of Military Operations (DMO), Major General John Spencer Ewart, set out to organise an espionage network in Germany. The impetus for this effort was growing concern that Germany might acquire the capability to mount a sudden 'bolt from the blue' invasion operation against Britain.[13] To execute his German project, Edmonds used a former head of the Metropolitan Police Special Branch, William Melville, recruited to work for MO3 in 1903.[14] Melville had some long-standing German contacts dating from Special Branch days, including Gustav Steinhauer, who in 1901 became head of the British section of the German admiralty's new intelligence service, the Nachrichten-Abteilung, also known as 'N'. He had already sent his assistant, Herbert Dale Long, on covert missions into Germany on behalf of the War Office, beginning in 1904 and including investigation of naval construction.[15] By mid 1909, with the help of Melville and Long, MO5 had four agents, paid through the Foreign Office secret vote, who could contribute on Germany, and one long-standing source based in South Africa. The German sources were an Austrian named Byzewski, who also reported on Russia, designated 'B'; a Belgian, Arsène Marie Verrue designated 'U' or 'V'; Captain Walter Christmas, a former officer of the Royal Danish Navy, designated 'K'; and a British naval journalist, Hector Bywater, based in Germany and known as 'HC'.[16]

Although the Admiralty discounted an invasion operation, Slade favoured any opportunity for better intelligence on Germany and agreed with Edmonds that the intelligence effort here should be collaborative. When Slade left NID in early 1909, he had three or four agents in place, working jointly for the War Office and Admiralty. These were probably Melville and Bywater (who were certainly partially funded from NID by this time), Long, and either Byzewski or Christmas. Slade's 'joint sources' probably excluded sources in the German admiralty and Krupps being developed the previous autumn, and a source based in Rendsburg, talent-spotted by Sir William Ward and subsequently taken on by Temple, who provided him with encrypted communications.[17] Later in 1909, Ward helped Edward Inglefield, now working for Lloyd's, explore on behalf of the Admiralty options for placing an agent to monitor naval movements through the Kiel Canal, although this was not pursued further.[18] Meanwhile, Slade also encouraged Max Schultz, a Southampton-based yacht broker who had a German father and spoke the language fluently, to travel to Germany on business with an intelligence brief.[19] It is doubtful whether by the end of 1909 these initial MO5 and NID agents targeted at Germany delivered much useful intelligence beyond what the attachés and the consular network could achieve.[20] Some of the operations also proved insecure.[21] However, two of these early recruits, Christmas, who was taken over by Regnart, and Bywater, developed into valuable naval sources later.[22] So, more briefly, did Schultz.

This initial experience of targeting Germany, MO5's view of what an effective foreign intelligence collection system required, a belief that all Britain's European rivals were doing better in the intelligence field, and not least the Foreign Office clamping down on the consular network, persuaded the War Office and Admiralty that new intelligence structures were needed. The driving force here was Ewart, with the Admiralty a willing, but initially passive, supporter.[23] Winning political endorsement for new measures was helped by growing concern over German espionage, linked with the regular, well-publicised, if fanciful, 'invasion scares' aired in the press. Ewart persuaded the Secretary of State for War, Richard Haldane, that the CID should form a subcommittee to consider new measures to deal with both the foreign espionage threat and the system for obtaining information from abroad. This was duly established at the end of March 1909. Haldane and Ewart represented the War Office, and McKenna and Bethell, as incoming DNI, the Admiralty. They were joined by the Home Secretary, H J Gladstone, Hardinge for the Foreign Office, the Treasury permanent secretary, and the Commissioner of Police, with Ottley acting as secretary.[24]

The subcommittee reached two main conclusions at the end of July. First, there was a serious threat from German espionage and current arrangements for addressing this were inadequate. Secondly, arrangements for acquiring information on activities in foreign ports and dockyards were also defective, especially for Germany. Both the War Office and Admiralty, perhaps primed by Hardinge, stressed that dealing with foreign spies with information to sell, without a suitable 'intermediary', risked embarrassing the government. The subcommittee accordingly recommended establishing a Secret Service Bureau to:

- act as a cut-out between the Admiralty and War Office and foreign spies with information to sell;
- liaise through the Home Office with the police and, if necessary, deploy agents to identify foreign espionage activity;
- act as an intermediary between the Admiralty and War Office and secret agents employed in foreign countries.[25]

These recommendations were prepared by a small subgroup of Haldane's committee, chaired by Hardinge, which met in April and comprised

Ewart, Bethell, and the Police Commissioner, Sir Edward Henry. In addition to agreeing the role of the Secret Service Bureau (SSB), this group recommended it should include 'two ex-naval and military officers', and be at least partly funded from the secret vote. They also agreed that a retired police officer, clearly Melville, should conduct a reconnaissance visit to Germany to identify potential agents in German ports.[26]

The original terms of reference for the Haldane committee were generic, to consider the espionage threat from all foreign states and all information requirements overseas. In practice, the focus was Germany. This was underlined when the Haldane recommendations were translated into an operational directive for the new SSB in October.[27] Most of the committee's meetings concentrated on the espionage threat, yet two of three SSB recommendations focused on intelligence collection by Britain overseas. This reflected the influence and composition of its subgroup.[28] Hardinge, with his Foreign Office perspective, inevitably looked primarily overseas, but this was also the priority for Ewart and Bethell. Furthermore, Hardinge, determined to avoid further lobbying for proactive use of the consular network for reporting German naval movements, wanted an intelligence system isolated from official government departments.[29] Although Ewart, briefed by Edmonds, dominated discussion in the Haldane committee and provided most of the espionage evidence, with McKenna and Bethell maintaining their more passive role, Admiralty requirements overseas were emphasised in the committee's conclusions. However, it was still Ewart who received primary responsibility for getting the SSB up and running.[30]

The SSB was established over a series of meetings orchestrated by Ewart between August and October. By the end of October it had divided into two distinct agencies, a foreign service, which for the present retained the title SSB, under a naval officer, Commander (later Captain) Mansfield Cumming,[31] and a home security service, soon called the Counter-Espionage Bureau, Special Intelligence Bureau, or MO5(g), under an army officer, Captain Vernon Kell.[32] Of the two, not surprisingly it was Cumming's service that brought the largest contribution to British naval intelligence, both now and in the future. Why Cumming was proposed as the Admiralty's candidate for the emerging secret service is a mystery. He was on the active retired list when Bethell approached him and had been in charge of Portsmouth boom defences for six years, an essential task, but not a job he or anyone else expected to deliver career advancement or even recognition. He had never served in NID and there is no evidence of unofficial intelligence activity. Nor is it apparent how he had demonstrated more general qualities to persuade Bethell and others that he was right for the new role. Yet somebody did spot his potential, because he proved a superb choice. Either Bethell had connections with Cumming now lost to view, or he mentioned his requirement and somebody recommended Cumming. Whatever happened, Cumming amply justified the faith placed in him. He was aged fifty on appointment and might reasonably have anticipated retirement, but approached his new task with energy, enthusiasm and dogged determination. He was undaunted by entirely new challenges for which he had no experience and received scant useful advice. Although he did not flaunt it, he had an adventurous streak and was attracted by new opportunities, embracing both motor racing and flying. He was also willing to take risks, though he judged the stakes shrewdly. He brought two priceless assets to his new role. The first was a remarkably clear vision for what an intelligence organisation could and should achieve. Despite numerous frustrations and constraints in the coming years, he created a service that was modern, forward-looking, and adaptable to changing circumstances, one appropriate to the twentieth century rather than the nineteenth. The second was his gift for handling people and his ability to command confidence and win trust. This applied to the agents he recruited, the officers who worked for him, but also in managing the political and bureaucratic terrain of Whitehall. People respected his judgement, his obvious integrity and liked his steadiness and humour, but understood there was steel there too.

The precise 'constitutional' status and role of the SSB, and therefore its management and accountability, was subject to ambiguity and confusion over at least the next ten years, with key personalities exerting crucial influence over its direction at various points. It has been aptly suggested that, in the early years, 'The War Office thought it controlled the Bureau (i.e. the SSB), the Admiralty thought it controlled Cumming, while the Foreign Office, which paid for it, did not at this stage want too much to do with it'.[33] The War Office indeed regularly insisted that the SSB was ultimately subordinate to DMO and later to the Director of Military Intelligence (DMI) when that post was recreated. It accordingly claimed direction and even a veto over any military work undertaken by Cumming, and it constantly sought to curtail his independence, especially once war began. This reflected Ewart's dominant part in the SSB's creation and the formal responsibility given to him by Haldane's committee. Equally important was the powerful personality of Edmonds' successor at MO5, Lieutenant Colonel George Macdonogh, who took practical charge of implementing the new secret service organisation on Ewart's behalf. Macdonogh proved one of the two outstanding intelligence officers of his generation, the other being the future DNI Reginald Hall. Macdonogh dominated British military intelligence from August 1909 and through the war, becoming DMI in 1916, and ending up a lieutenant general. Like Hall, he was also an astute player of Whitehall politics.[34] Bethell and his successor, Captain Thomas Jackson, generally avoided direct confrontation with Macdonogh, but quietly guarded Cumming's independence and encouraged his natural inclination to give naval requirements priority. Once Hall arrived as DNI in 1914, Cumming was protected by a Whitehall infighter as determined and cunning as Macdonogh, albeit then giving Cumming the new problem of ensuring his independence from Hall.

Meanwhile, it was true that the Foreign Office was initially more detached than the War Office and Admiralty, since it did not at this stage seek to direct SSB tasking or operations. However, funding the SSB almost entirely from the secret vote gave the Foreign Office financial control. SSB financial accountability to the Foreign Office then brought growing political oversight, since the Foreign Secretary inevitably questioned the justification for significant new expenditure.[35] Foreign Office financial control and political influence enabled Cumming to use the Foreign Office as referee in dealing with competing demands from the War Office and Admiralty but, more important, as ultimate guarantor of his independence from either. Without the Foreign Office role provided by the long-standing secret vote and the decision to make a naval officer the first head of the foreign secret service, the SSB might have fallen increasingly under War Office control, especially under the demands of the Western Front in the coming war. Hardinge's formula for managing the SSB was typical British constitutional pragmatism, drawing on existing structures of the state to create something new. In doing so, perhaps more by chance than design, he created a remarkably flexible and adaptable institution that served the British state and, not least, naval intelligence well over the rest of the century.

Most of the SSB's effort, and certainly its most important results prior to the outbreak of war, were on the German naval target. The first substantive naval intelligence acquired by the SSB appears in Cumming's diary for January 1910. He recorded information received from source 'WK' the previous month. This was Melville's recruit Walter Christmas, until now jointly run by MO5 and NID, whom Cumming took over in November.[36] Topics covered were new naval facilities and defences at Heligoland; the speed achieved on trials by *Nassau*, the first *Dreadnought* equivalent, the armoured cruisers *Blücher*, *Scharnhorst* and *Gneisenau*, and a new turbine-powered torpedo boat; and progress on submarine construction.[37] There was enough here for several reports directly relevant to NID requirements, with detail beyond what the naval attaché might acquire. Christmas provided regular reporting of this type from trips to Germany, as well as good coverage from Danish sources of German naval movements in the Skagerrak and Kattegat.

Simultaneously with his first dealings with Christmas, Cumming was probably in contact with Dawson, although whether he was acting here on behalf of Bethell, or now took over the relationship completely, is unclear.[38] A little later he recruited a director of the Sheffield steel firm Davy Brothers, Frederick Fairholme. Fairholme was half-German, spoke the language fluently, and had regular business with Krupp. He was therefore an intelligence source in the mould of Mulliner and Dawson but, under SSB control, more effectively tasked. Fairholme produced the earliest known SSB report, covering the performance of Krupp naval guns.[39] His most important contribution came in early 1911 when he provided detailed reporting on the new Krupp armour-piercing shell, including its ground-breaking fuze.[40]

Another early source for Cumming was the yacht broker Max Schultz, also taken over from NID. During successive visits to Germany, Schultz recruited several sub-sources, some before coming under Cumming's control. Two of these were potentially valuable, a businessman, Ernst von Maack, who provided collateral reporting on German plans for merchant raiders, and had access on U-boat engines, and Karl Hipsich, a marine engineer recommended by von Maack, who worked in the Weser naval shipyard. Cumming mounted a successful operation to recruit Hipsich, who provided important documents, including drawings of the latest battleships. It was probably reporting from von Maack and Hipsich which alerted the Admiralty to German interest in large diesel engines capable of powering German cruisers, and thus giving them the range and endurance for sustained trade war in the Atlantic.[41] Unfortunately, Schultz's network was too complicated and too insecure to escape German attention for long. In March 1911, just two months into Hipsich's career as an agent, the main participants were arrested. Hipsich received a sentence of twelve years, underlining the damage he had done to German interests, Schultz seven, and von Maack three.[42] Schultz served almost all his sentence before escaping in the chaos following Germany's collapse in November 1918 when, as described later, he created a final episode in his intelligence career.[43]

The overall value of the SSB's naval contribution in the first two years of its existence is hard to judge, because so little reporting survives. However, 1911 brought a significant improvement in NID's organisation and assessment of information on the German target. The catalyst was the arrival of Fleet Paymaster Charles Rotter in late April that year, to take charge initially of the section monitoring the movement of foreign warships known as E1 and subsequently of NID's German section, Section 14, later ID14.[44] Rotter had just completed two years in *Dreadnought* as staff intelligence officer to Commander-in-Chief Home Fleet, Admiral Sir William May. May's flag captain throughout most of this period was Herbert Richmond, a man with strong views on war planning, the role of intelligence, and the need for a more professional approach to staff work, all of which influenced Rotter. NID proved an inspired appointment for him. Rotter was a qualified German interpreter and his knowledge of German language and culture was exceptional, broadened by frequent visits to Germany during his leaves, and 'he knew the way German naval officers talked, thought and acted'. Equally important was a natural affinity for intelligence work, and he was a central figure in NID from now until 1923, not least playing a critical part in the birth and development of its signals intelligence capability.[45]

In his neat handwriting, Rotter tabulated every piece of information, whether from open sources, the attachés, or the SSB, for every German warship or submarine and significant merchant vessels. He carefully noted the date and origin for every item received. SSB reports were denoted by the letter 'S' followed by a three figure number. This system, begun in 1911, continued with little change throughout the coming war. NID therefore had an instantly available, constantly updated, and regularly corrected record of the current status of every significant German unit. Rotter's records made it easier for NID to identify important trends in German capability. They enabled better monitoring of the capital ship programme, identifying the slowdown in delivery from early 1913,[46] the evolution and build-up of the German submarine arm, important in shaping Royal Navy blockade policy, and the armed merchant cruiser threat, including the possibility that by 1912 guns were kept on board permanently ready for installation if war broke out.[47] Reporting from the SSB on the armed merchant cruiser threat shaped Admiralty assessments and policy at the highest level, including the CID. It influenced a major War College exercise on Atlantic trade protection in early 1914, informed attitudes in the Trade Division reconstituted that year under Captain Richard Webb, and was on the agenda for a major conference of senior Royal Navy officers planned for the end of July 1914.[48] As noted previously, from 1912 the Admiralty also recognised the potential threat posed by diesel-engined cruisers to Atlantic trade.[49]

Sufficient of Rotter's records survive to indicate the shape of the full system and the quality of the information feeding it. They suggest that the SSB issued about a thousand reports in total, from its foundation up to the outbreak of war.[50] The proportion which comprised naval reporting must be speculative, but from what is known of Cumming's sources a figure of two-thirds seems reasonable. Most of Rotter's references to SSB reports gave the date, subject and a brief description, but some replicated entire reports. For example, S612, dated 16 January 1913, gave a comprehensive update on the status of the submarine programme. Key points were delay in the planned transfer of twelve submarines from Kiel to Wilhelmshaven; poor seaworthiness of the early boats up to *U-14*, rendering them unsuitable for open-water operations; characteristics of *U-16*, including her surface speed on trials (all broadly accurate); and confirmation that six boats were currently under construction at the Germania yard in Kiel, with *U-26* floated out in December (again correct).[51] Where Rotter provided this level of detail it is sometimes possible to identify the source of the report. S612 fits with Hector Bywater.

Bywater was the most important pre-war SSB source on the German navy. He was probably approached by Melville in 1908, was a regular paid agent jointly funded by MO5 and NID from early 1909, and passed by Bethell to Cumming in early 1910.[52] In line with Cumming's often quirky sense of humour, he then received the pseudonym 'HHO' or 'H2O'. Although born to British parents, Bywater spent most of his early life in New York. His consuming passion from boyhood and throughout his life was warships and navies, and at the age of nineteen he convinced the *New York Herald* to take him on as an occasional naval reporter. Four years later in 1907, his elder brother Ulysses persuaded him to join him in Dresden, where Ulysses, who had acquired American citizenship, was United States deputy consul. Bywater seized the opportunity of reporting as a journalist on the rising Imperial German Navy, becoming European naval correspondent for the *Herald*, and writing for prominent British naval outlets such as the *Navy League Journal*, which were widely replayed in national and regional newspapers. He proved a superb linguist, with German soon good enough to pass as a native speaker. This, along with his mastery of naval affairs, brought a wealth of good German contacts.[53] He also became a close friend of J L Garvin, the high-profile editor of the *Observer*. The articles for the *Navy League Journal* brought Bywater to the attention of Fisher, who discussed his status and background with Alan Burgoyne, then Honorary Treasurer of the Navy League, and a prominent naval supporter in Parliament. Fisher probably then drew him to the attention of Slade, who used Melville, or conceivably Regnart, as an intermediary to recruit him. Bywater was undoubtedly the 'splendid spy in Germany', subsequently referred to by Fisher in two letters to Churchill in late 1911.[54]

Within a year of Bywater's transfer to the SSB, he became its most prolific source, and he reported continuously on the German navy until June 1914.[55] With Cumming's approval, he persuaded Ulysses to get him an American passport, giving his place of birth as Boston in order to deflect any German suspicion that he was reporting to the British government.[56] Bywater gave a lightly disguised autobiographical account of his SSB service, published in 1934.[57] Although selective and inevitably incomplete, it conveys the range and nature of the reporting he produced.[58] A measure of Bywater's value was the payment he received, which by early 1912 was £750 per annum (the equivalent of about £75,000 today). This made him Cumming's highest paid agent, 25 per cent more than Cumming received himself, and around 10 per cent of Cumming's overall budget.[59] Few agents in SIS's future history commanded this level of reward. It is possible some of the money went to sub-sources, rather than Bywater himself, but it still suggests he was delivering exceptional results. By early 1913, he was judged by the DNI, Captain Thomas Jackson, who did not offer praise lightly, to be providing 'good stuff'. During 1914, at least one report on German naval gunnery was thought so significant that he was questioned in London by Rear Admiral Reginald Tupper, one of the Royal Navy's most distinguished gunnery specialists, who had previously served in NID.[60]

American cover was used by another agent recruited by Cumming, probably in 1912. This was John Herbert-Spottiswoode (usually abbreviated to Spottiswoode), then aged thirty, who shared Cumming's passion for fast cars and aeroplanes. Importantly, Spottiswoode was also a fluent German speaker and had dealings with Mercedes-Benz, perhaps resulting from a period working for Rolls-Royce. Cumming may have met him through the Royal Aero Club, where they were both members, although possibly he was recommended to Cumming by Charles Rolls, with whom Cumming was also in contact.[61] Cumming suggested Spottiswoode should visit Germany, posing as an Irish-American, and use his language and aviation expertise and contacts to investigate Zeppelin airship construction, a requirement following a report from a technical subcommittee of the CID in July 1912.[62] Spottiswoode later claimed to have worked in a Zeppelin factory and provided the SSB with blueprints for engines which the Admiralty had been unable to acquire commercially.[63] His American cover also allowed him to remain in Germany after the outbreak of war, although he was soon interned before being repatriated following illness. This SSB contribution on the German airship programme was supplemented by regular and comprehensive reporting from the naval attachés,[64] and at least one exploratory visit to Germany by the Admiralty Director of the Air Department, Captain Murray Sueter. This provoked considerable policy debate, including within the CID. By the outbreak of war in 1914, the NID had an excellent picture of German airship strength, capability, and probable operational deployment.[65] This triggered three operations in the first five months of the war against what was believed (correctly) to be the primary naval Zeppelin base at Cuxhaven at the mouth of the Elbe.[66]

In the final eighteen months before the war, Cumming executed a different operation. This followed pressure on the Admiralty from the Foreign Office to release the consuls in Denmark from naval reporting. Although the Foreign Office was more relaxed about allowing a naval intelligence role in Denmark compared to Germany, the consul at Helsingfors, Robert Erskine, transferred to Denmark from Sevastopol at Admiralty request in 1908, had attracted unwelcome attention.[67] Denmark was important to tracking German naval movements between the North Sea and the Baltic. At the end of 1912 Cumming accordingly recruited Walter Archer, a retired civil servant from the Board of Agriculture, along with his son Hugh, a former naval lieutenant and specialist navigator. Given the codenames Sage and Sagette, they were tasked with establishing a network of sub-sources to provide a ship-watching service in Norway and Denmark, countries they knew intimately and where they had credible reasons to travel around using a yacht subsidised by the SSB, and even base there for a period if required. The operation, initially focused on four ports, was expensive and the budget of £1200 per annum (about £120,000 in today's money) was significantly exceeded, provoking acrimonious negotiation between Cumming and the Archers. Despite the difficulties over funding, it was remarkably successful, delivering valuable intelligence up to and throughout the war, amply justifying its cost. It established a model for similar coast-watching networks in both world wars. It was later enhanced when Walter Christmas rejoined the Danish navy to access its reports on the movement of German warships and submarines from the Baltic into the North Sea.[68]

While the establishment of the SSB made an important contribution to naval intelligence on Germany in the years immediately preceding 1914, another intelligence capability, as yet undeveloped, proved even more crucial to Royal Navy prospects in the coming war. This was the intercept of foreign communications by cable or radio later known as signals intelligence, or SIGINT. Britain had important potential advantages here. British companies dominated the cable industry and therefore the global network. Over the forty years from 1870, British strategic planners, in close concert with British companies, had also implemented an empire network, an 'all-red' system routed to ensure that it was immune to foreign disruption. It used either British-controlled territory or maritime routes guaranteed by the Royal Navy. With the 'red' route secure, planning focused on offensive cable-cutting to disrupt the communications of potential enemies in wartime. By 1912, the CID had approved a plan, to be implemented by the Post Office under Admiralty direction, to cut Germany's main international cables running from the island of Borkum to the Azores, to Tenerife and Vigo in Spain. This would isolate Germany from America and its colonies in Africa.[69] In addition to these offensive measures, Britain had regulations and plans, drawing on experience in the South African war, to implement censorship across the entirety of British-controlled cable networks in wartime. The primary motivation for this censorship was defensive, preventing useful information pertaining to Britain or its allies reaching an enemy. Prior to the outbreak of war in 1914, little thought was given to exploiting censorship 'offensively' in the way pioneered by Fisher in the Mediterranean. It was assumed (wrongly as it turned out) that an enemy would not use cables under British control, and it seems that the potential benefits of reading neutral or commercial traffic were not considered either. In the event, cable censorship delivered huge quantities of intelligence across all these areas, of incalculable value to Britain's naval priorities in the coming war.[70]

Britain enjoyed another advantage. The rapidly developing Admiralty radio network and the new overseas intelligence centres provided the potential to monitor foreign radio transmissions for operational benefit. By early 1914, the Admiralty recognised that the benefit of cutting German cables was reducing, because Germany was developing a long-range radio network capable of covering Africa and even the Pacific if combined with intercontinental cables beyond British interference. This radio network was a serious threat, because it would help Germany mount a global attack on British shipping using dispersed raiders, including the armed merchant cruisers the Admiralty so feared and, perhaps in the future, diesel-powered warships. The problem could only be countered by destroying the key radio transmitters or successfully decrypting German naval traffic. By the summer, British army units in the Gold Coast (modern Ghana) had detailed intelligence on the pivotal German radio station at Kamina in neighbouring Togoland, and plans were ready to silence it in the event of war. In parallel, the Admiralty considered afresh what was possible with communications interception.[71]

From 1844, when the Foreign Office Deciphering Branch closed, until the outbreak of war in 1914, there was no formally constituted unit anywhere within the British government dedicated to intercepting foreign communications or exploiting this for intelligence value. That did not mean the British state and its servants entirely abandoned the interception of communications in this seventy-year period or ignored its potential. Intelligence gleaned from the intercept of military and diplomatic traffic featured to a greater or lesser extent in most conflicts in which Britain participated during these years, most importantly during the Boer War. However, such intercept was geared to the needs of a specific conflict, or a local initiative such as Fisher in the Mediterranean, and did not promote any enduring capability in either collection facilities or cryptanalysis. There was one important exception. With the approval of the government of India and India Office, the Indian Army established a small permanent interception bureau in 1906, which achieved considerable success against Russian, Persian and Chinese military and diplomatic traffic. This provided a kernel of expertise when the War Office and Admiralty began to consider the requirements for communications interception in a major European war.[72]

The Royal Navy recognised the potential for intercepting enemy traffic as soon as it began experimenting with radio communication at sea from around 1900. Interception of plain-language radio messages and studying call-signs as a clue to enemy composition and organisation (a rudimentary form of what was later called 'traffic analysis') featured in several fleet exercises before 1914. So did jamming and deception messages. NID began to collect and publish material on foreign naval radio capability and procedures, drawing on open sources and direct observation.[73] It produced a comprehensive survey of the radio assets of foreign countries in June 1914.[74] It also looked for procedural weaknesses it might exploit. In 1904 British warships were instructed to transmit to the Admiralty copies of all foreign radio messages they intercepted. In 1908 the Royal Navy began to collect German radio traffic in a systematic way. By 1912 naval commanders were beginning to appreciate the potential of direction finding (D/F) and more advanced traffic analysis, extracting operational value from the timing and pattern of enemy transmissions.[75] Discussions with Marconi and the Post Office into how they could help with collection and D/F began at this time.[76] Once Rotter took over the German section in NID in 1911, he began to log these German messages and then attempted to decrypt them. Despite attempts to procure a German naval codebook, including purchase of what turned out to be a forgery, he was unsuccessful.[77] This reinforced a conviction prevalent among some senior officers that encrypted German messages would never be read.[78] However, given the threat from a German long-range radio network, others in the Admiralty persevered. In June 1914 an Admiralty committee investigating mechanical cipher systems, which had attracted interest from the Navy and the army for several years, took advice from the chief expert of the Indian Army intercept bureau, Major George Church.[79] Church demonstrated cryptanalytical techniques that could easily break systems which the Admiralty had considered highly secure, thereby demonstrating that gleaning valuable intelligence from encrypted enemy traffic was possible, while also illustrating the importance of defensive cipher security. One of the potential cipher machines investigated by the committee was a design put forward by the Director of Naval Education, Sir Alfred Ewing. Ewing's interest in cryptography led to his selection to head the Admiralty's new SIGINT team, later known as Room 40, following the outbreak of war.[80]

When war came, therefore, the Admiralty had recognised the potential of SIGINT, had systematically collected German radio traffic, and was edging towards establishing a unit similar to the Indian Army's bureau to try and extract intelligence. The 1912 plans for War Room organisation on mobilisation included a section (Section C) to deal with 'intercepted wireless messages'. For reasons explained later, Section C was not implemented and the wartime organisation for signals interception and its relationship to the war staff was different.[81] If this progress appears modest, it was far ahead of the German navy, which prior to the war was largely oblivious to the opportunities posed by SIGINT.[82] The War Office, with MO5 and Macdonogh in the lead, was in a similar position to the Admiralty. It had a better understanding of the process of cryptanalysis than the Admiralty, but prior to hostilities lacked access to German army traffic, or indeed the means to collect it. Both departments were also restricted by a legal bar on cable interception in British Empire territory apart from India. SIGINT, therefore, lagged some years behind intelligence from human sources being pioneered by the SSB.[83]

5

Trafalgar or Economic Warfare 1912–1914

The previous two chapters describe how British intelligence monitored the potential strength and fighting effectiveness of the growing German navy and how this influenced a policy response. Understanding how intelligence shaped British strategy for fighting a naval war with Germany is also important. By the end of 1912, the core elements of the naval strategy with which Britain began the war in August 1914, although not its detailed implementation, were settled. The overriding aim was to cut Germany off from the maritime world by exploiting Britain's geographic position to impose a distant blockade, sealing all Germany's exits from the North Sea. Beyond the blockade line, German warships at large would be eliminated, and German merchant shipping captured or confined to port. British and Allied ships would be barred from trading with Germany, and access by neutral ships controlled where possible. Meanwhile, the Royal Navy would also secure the British coasts from attack and ensure the safe transit of an expeditionary force to France, should this be required. The Admiralty assessed that a distant blockade strategy, combined with severance of cable communications, would severely disrupt the German economy, compromising its capability for waging war. It also judged that, to relieve its situation, Germany would send a force into the North Sea sufficient not only to break up light forces executing the blockade, but to offer general battle with the main British fleet. A distant blockade would ensure such an action took place far from the German coast, in waters advantageous to Britain.[1]

This distant blockade strategy was the end point of a journey begun with Philip Colomb in the late 1880s, although progression from one to the other was far from linear. Despite the long-recognised problems with close blockade, operational and logistic, Admiralty planners revisited this as a preferred option when serious work on a German war began in

1906. Germany was a more difficult target for close blockade than France because she was further away, compounding the problem of sustaining a blockading force on station. Nevertheless, despite the logistical challenge and the risk to a blockading force from modern weaponry, not just torpedoes and mines but, increasingly, submarines, bottling up the bulk of the German fleet in its North Sea ports was an attractive proposition for the Royal Navy. Blockading light forces could wage a war of attrition against their German equivalents and deny them any outlet, while also providing early warning of any sortie by major units of the High Seas Fleet. The fleet would be vulnerable to attack by destroyers and submarines as it exited, and the Royal Navy could position its forces to dictate the terms of any subsequent engagement. Britain would thus retain control of the North Sea, securing its coast against raids and minimising the possibility of significant German forces breaking out into the Atlantic to attack British trade. As late as 1911, Admiralty planners also saw close blockade, along with mining, as the optimum means of countering the growing German submarine force. These defensive naval benefits existed alongside the emerging offensive economic case for blockade, but they were distinct.[2]

Close blockade was abandoned in 1912, not because the naval benefits were perceived as less important, or because execution became technically and tactically impossible; rather, it was because the numerical balance in light forces was changing to Britain's detriment. Britain could no longer guarantee sufficient forces on station to compete with the growing German destroyer and submarine force.[3] Persisting with close blockade, therefore, risked increasing British rather than German attrition, and defeat in detail as the Germans acquired local superiority. Ultimately, the Royal Navy might be sufficiently weakened to give the High Seas Fleet a real chance of victory.[4] The new distant blockade strategy, therefore, aimed to remove the growing operational risks of a close blockade, while preserving maximum economic leverage over Germany. However, such a British retreat in the North Sea raised two fundamental challenges. First, without the operational intelligence provided by close blockade, guaranteeing the security of Britain's long eastern coastline against raids, or even invasion, was more difficult. As Royal Navy commanders recognised, they now faced a 'North Sea problem' which remained unsolved at the start of the war.[5] Secondly, abandoning close blockade meant Britain could no longer impose a commercial blockade under international law. It would have to fall back on a policy of contraband control, with much less effect on the German economy. In purely practical terms, a distant blockade across the long, stormy, northern boundary of the North Sea would also be more challenging to operate. The implications raised by these constraints on the economic pressure Britain could apply had still not been adequately addressed by August 1914.[6]

The two separate motivations for blockade not only made the route to distant blockade at the end of 1912 a complicated one, but ensured that arguments for a more aggressive close blockade strategy to overcome the distant blockade limitations regularly resurfaced during the coming war. The effort devoted to close blockade planning and intelligence operations to support it, throughout the tenures of Fisher and his successor Wilson as First Sea Lord, undermines the proposition that either planned to forsake control of the North Sea for a purely defensive strategy based on protecting Britain's coast with flotillas of light craft.[7]

Both blockade motivations generated intelligence requirements from 1906, and intelligence shaped Admiralty thinking. A possible solution to the problem of sustaining a close blockade of Germany's North Sea ports was to capture a forward operating base, with Borkum in the East Frisian Islands, north of the Ems, the preferred choice. This potential need for a forward base triggered intelligence-gathering operations of variable quality, lasting until at least 1912, since successful capture depended not only on detailed knowledge of German defences, but also local geography. NID accordingly commissioned reporting from the consuls, including covert photography of defences, but also several trips to the German Frisian Islands by serving officers under tourist cover from 1906, including that undertaken by Brandon and Trench during the *Cornwall* visit two years later. This Frisian reporting was closely monitored by Fisher, who strongly favoured the advance base concept.[8] In 1910 Brandon and Trench volunteered for a further, more ambitious, reconnaissance mission, sponsored primarily by NID and planned by Regnart, but with support from the new SSB. Their commitment and sense of adventure were commendable, but the execution was amateur, and the result disaster. Both were arrested as suspect spies, convicted and imprisoned, with significant embarrassment for the British government, since their provenance was obvious. Brandon and Trench were subsequently pardoned and released when King George V visited Germany in May 1913. Both subsequently enjoyed distinguished careers in naval intelligence, serving together as naval interrogators in 1917–18. Trench made an exceptional contribution as an interrogator, especially on U-boats, in both world wars.[9] The episode powerfully underlined the need for a deniable secret service. At least one more major professional reconnaissance was conducted, this time under the full control of the SSB using Bywater, although the vice consul in Emden, William Sinclair, also contributed useful information on the Borkum defences gleaned during family holidays.[10] Churchill as First Lord, albeit with little support from the senior naval leadership, was still promoting the seizure of Borkum in early 1915.[11]

From 1905, spurred by the experience of the Russo-Japanese war, Admiralty planners debated whether close blockade might be facilitated by mining operations and judicious placing of block ships, both on port access routes and the western end of the Kiel Canal. Blocking was ruled out by successive Hydrographers, but variants of mining continued to be explored.[12] Partly from its own exercises, but also intelligence on German experience, the Admiralty recognised that submarines were especially vulnerable when exiting through narrow channels or in shallow inshore waters during their initial transit into the North Sea. While the German submarine force was small, this appeared to tip the balance of advantage towards blockaders compared to the blockaded. From 1906, NID therefore devoted significant effort to gathering relevant hydrographic intelligence to enable Royal Navy light forces to operate in German coastal waters.[13] A variant to close blockade explored in 1908–09 was an observational blockade, conducted further out in the German Bight using the new oil-powered (and therefore longer endurance) destroyers. This generated additional requirements for hydrographic information regarding the difficult inshore waters, including potential safe anchorages. In June and September 1909 the modified torpedo gunboat *Halcyon* therefore conducted covert surveys off the Danish coast near Esbjerg and in the area of Horns Reef.[14]

The balance in light forces and submarines ultimately dictated whether close blockade was viable. Successive naval attachés were accordingly tasked to give high priority to German destroyer and submarine strength, and related building plans. Throughout the decade before the war, their resulting reporting was consistently good. The attachés kept the Admiralty closely briefed on numbers and designs, emphasising the high quality of destroyer personnel, which they rated comparable to the Royal Navy, and giving detailed accounts of tactics deployed during exercises.[15] From 1910 the SSB also focused on the submarine programme, producing regular reporting to complement that of the attachés.

Ottley, as incoming DNI, recognised Germany's vulnerability to an attack on her trade as early as 1905.[16] However, the potential for exploiting this vulnerability for strategic effect first gained attention during the winter of 1906/7 in the committee established by Fisher, under Captain George Ballard with Hankey as secretary, to devise a strategy for a naval war with Germany. This committee concluded that blockading Germany to sever her overseas trade should be central to British naval strategy. If combined with seizure of an offshore island or adjacent

German territory, blockade would force the German fleet to sea. It might also seriously damage the German economy. They reviewed options for close blockade, generating the first intelligence requirements[17] here to assess its feasibility, and for a more distant blockade. They did not claim that blockade alone could deliver decisive results, and offered only general thoughts on its economic effects. Nevertheless, the idea that economic warfare alone might achieve victory over Germany gathered influential supporters from this time. Hankey, Ottley and Slade, who was currently head of the Naval War College and would shortly take over as DNI, were early converts. So, broadly, was Fisher, although as with much else, his commitment was not consistent.[18]

Ottley had already directed Campbell, when the latter took over the Trade Division in 1906, to investigate economic blockade as an offensive weapon against Germany, in addition to his work on trade protection. Campbell studied the subject in depth over the next two years. He examined Germany's import and export statistics, her supply routes, maritime and overland, and how her trade patterns were changing. With Ottley's support, he commissioned detailed reporting from the Berlin naval attaché (Dumas), and Sir Robert Giffen, the distinguished statistician and retired controller general of the Board of Trade.[19] He also examined the report of the royal commission into Britain's food supplies in wartime, chaired by Stewart Murray in 1903, to identify similar potential vulnerabilities in German supply. In July 1908 he concluded that if Germany was denied sea access to food and raw materials, she could not make up the loss by overland routes. Maritime blockade would inflict sufficient damage on her economy and social cohesion, through shortages, inflation and widespread unemployment, to make a war unsustainable.[20]

At the end of that year the concept of conducting economic war against Germany was scrutinised for the first time by the CID. The prime minister convened a subcommittee to review empire military policy, which held three meetings that winter and produced a final report the following July. The subcommittee explored the strategy Britain should adopt if she supported France in a war against Germany. Would naval support alone suffice or would deployment of an expeditionary force to the Continent be required too? The first meeting on 3 December focused on how Germany might conduct an attack on France, and the military options open to Britain if she supported France. Haldane then sought Admiralty advice on how German trade would be affected in such a war, and whether she could withstand being deprived of her imports. Slade, who attended as DNI, along with Fisher and McKenna, promised a paper for the next meeting scheduled two weeks later.

Following the first meeting, McKenna sought reassurance from Ottley, attending as secretary to the CID, that NID had adequately studied the implications of attacking Germany's trade. Ottley confirmed that throughout his own time as DNI, the Admiralty judged that Britain's geographical position and preponderant sea power provided 'a certain and simple means of strangling Germany at sea'. In vivid language, he added that in a protracted war 'the mills of our sea power (though they would grind the German industrial population slowly perhaps) would grind them exceedingly small – grass would sooner or later grow in the streets of Hamburg and widespread dearth and ruin would be inflicted.'[21]

Slade's presentation on 17 December, backed with comprehensive analysis by Campbell and Giffen, defined what naval blockade might achieve. He drew parallels between the British and German economies. Both were increasingly dependent on seaborne supply and, therefore, vulnerable to disruption. Britain's dependence was greater, but so was its ability to maintain supplies owing to its geographical advantage and naval supremacy. It could also draw on its huge merchant fleet and overseas investments to provide additional credit in wartime. Germany was more vulnerable financially. Denied vital imports and unable to export in the face of a British blockade, she would face economic and social distress, and potential bankruptcy. However, Slade emphasised that effective blockade meant preventing Germany trading through neutral countries, notably Holland and Belgium, and he stressed the interdependence of the modern global trading and financial system. Ensuring that Britain did not suffer serious damage from the inevitable economic disruption triggered by a major war would require careful management.

Lord Crewe, Secretary of State for the Colonies, evidently speaking for the subcommittee, stated that Slade had made a convincing case that Germany would suffer greater economic loss in a war than Britain. The committee's final report the following July accordingly concluded that blockade would create a serious economic situation in Germany and the longer a war lasted, the more serious her position would become. However, it stopped short of judging that blockade alone would be decisive and insisted that it could not guarantee that France would withstand a determined German attack. The army general staff should therefore continue planning for an expeditionary force, although whether such a force was deployed, or Britain relied solely on naval means, must be a decision for the government at the time.[22]

Slade's presentation was an important milestone in intelligence history. As he and his fellow advocates readily acknowledged, the concept of economic warfare was not new. Both Britain and France sought decisive economic effect through the destruction or curtailment of their opponent's trade during the Napoleonic wars and each attempted sophisticated strategies.[23] Indeed, it is often argued that blockade against Germany was merely a continuation of the British way of warfare. However, the work of Slade and Campbell, supported by Fisher, Ottley, Hankey and others, broke new ground in several respects. First, they brought detailed measurement and analysis, admittedly partial and imperfect, to the German economy and its susceptibility to attack. Here they initiated an increasingly important subset of the intelligence business over the rest of the century. Secondly, their strategy consciously advocated inflicting suffering on the whole population, implicitly including the women and children of an enemy state, not just its combatants, in order to achieve a decisive strategic outcome. By endorsing this, whether they appreciated it or not, the CID moved Britain towards a policy of total war, where every aspect of a country's military potential became an acceptable target. This concept, too, evolved across the century, ultimately making entire cities an acceptable target for incineration. Finally, the strategy suggested that economic coercion alone might bring decisive results in war, rendering engagement with the enemy's main military forces unnecessary. Again, this idea cast a long shadow over future British thinking, not least the belief in bombing as the decisive weapon of the Second World War.

There were, however, weaknesses in a strategy of economic warfare against Germany, still only partially recognised and understood by the Admiralty and CID. For blockade to work, Britain must prevent Germany establishing alternative supply lines through neutral states on its borders, who would inevitably pursue their own interests. Germany was aware she faced probable blockade and could therefore take countermeasures by planning for domestic substitution and building up stocks. Much also depended on how Britain interpreted international law on commercial blockade, including definitions of contraband and the rights of neutral shipping. Britain potentially weakened its position here, with its initial acceptance of the 1909 Declaration of London, which substantially restricted attacks on commerce. In addition, as Slade had stated, unless the complex interdependencies now inherent in global trade, especially in financial flows, were understood and managed, Britain would suffer collateral damage. Finally, there were powerful commercial voices in Britain with political and institutional influence that preferred to minimise trade disruption, even with an enemy state.[24] Overall, while the Royal Navy could impose a blockade, achieving the economic collapse of Germany would be a complex political and economic operation beyond the Admiralty's remit and resources.

Furthermore, while Fisher enthusiastically promoted the concept of economic warfare, his commitment to practical implementation was erratic, and the changes he oversaw in Admiralty organisation in autumn 1909, including abolition of the Trade Division, were unhelpful. Even worse, his chosen successor Wilson was convinced that economic warfare was a waste of time, because Germany would compensate by trading through neutral powers.[25]

Slade and Trade Division appreciated the risk of leakage through neutral states. In May 1908, when consulted further about German dependence on global markets,[26] Dumas suggested contacting the Consul General at Frankfurt, Sir Francis Oppenheimer, and the consuls at Dusseldorf, Danzig, Stettin and Copenhagen.[27] Oppenheimer was a more important and influential figure than his status as a Consul General, an honorary post, implied. His father was a German Jew and successful businessman, who moved to Britain and acquired British citizenship before moving back to Frankfurt as Consul General. On his death in 1900, his son succeeded him in the post, and over the next few years was increasingly acknowledged as Britain's foremost expert on the German economy. After graduating from Oxford, Oppenheimer was called to the bar, where he was pupil to Sir Rufus Isaacs, the future Lord Reading, Attorney General 1910–13 and later Viceroy of India and Foreign Secretary. Isaacs became a patron and lifelong friend and introduced Oppenheimer as an economic expert to Churchill as President of the Board of Trade and David Lloyd George as Chancellor of the Exchequer.[28]

Slade accordingly asked the Foreign Office for help in assessing how Germany could cope if she were unable to trade through her national ports. What were her alternative sources of food and raw materials and at what extra cost? Could neutral countries, including Russia if not a combatant, make up the difference? Did Antwerp and Rotterdam have the capacity to replace German ports, and could internal communications cope with extra traffic? The consensus from the consuls at Hamburg, Dusseldorf, Amsterdam, Rotterdam and Antwerp was that a blockade would inflict short-term damage, but its ultimate effectiveness was doubtful. Oppenheimer took a year to reply, but his secret assessment finally reached the Admiralty in October 1909. He concluded that a blockade closing Germany's ports would certainly create severe economic disruption in the short term, but he too doubted its effectiveness in a long war. Holland and Belgium with their major North Sea ports (Antwerp and Rotterdam), and Italy and Austria with their Mediterranean ports (Genoa and Trieste) all had the motivation, the capacity and land communications with Germany substantially to compensate for loss of the German ports.

Britain had the option of extending a blockade to cover the neutrals, but the political consequences of doing so would be serious.[29]

Oppenheimer's assessment had more impact in the Foreign Office and Treasury, where it underlined the complexities involved in executing blockade, than in the Admiralty, where its arrival coincided with disruption in NID created by the abolition of Trade Division and other organisational changes.[30] Fisher's departure and the arrival of the unsupportive Wilson followed shortly afterwards. Wilson was not only uninterested in the economic case, but distrusted all planning bodies, let alone anything that hinted at a naval staff, preferring to keep any strategic ideas he had locked firmly in his own head.[31] Even before these changes, Bethell, who replaced Slade as DNI in March, had concluded that the requirements of trade protection and any outstanding work on the impact of offensive blockade no longer justified a dedicated trade division in NID.[32] The result was hiatus and the Admiralty did little further work on the vulnerability of the German economy for at least three years, following the winding up of Trade Division and departure of Campbell. This was a pity, because Oppenheimer had more to offer. In 1912, by which time he had been promoted to commercial attaché for northern Europe, he produced an important study of German planning for 'financial mobilisation' in the event of war.[33] Somebody in the Admiralty, possibly Bethell, evidently did recognise Oppenheimer's potential, because around 1910–11 two attempts were made to recruit him for 'secret service' work, which Oppenheimer rejected.[34]

However, as Admiralty investigations petered out with the changes in NID, the CID secretariat, first under Ottley and then Hankey, both now determined advocates of economic warfare, began turning aspiration into practical strategy. From 1910, they orchestrated a programme of work to present the CID, and ultimately the Cabinet, with a coherent agreed policy and the measures to deliver it. The scale of this effort, involving every relevant government department, remains under-recognised. It was the first cross-government strategic planning initiative, easily comparable to the most complex royal commission of inquiry. There were two main components to the work. A subcommittee, chaired by the Earl of Desart, was established in early 1911 to investigate 'trading with the enemy' in wartime, and Hankey created a 'war book', regularly updated, detailing all measures, constitutional, legal and financial, required for initiating blockade. Desart's committee assumed the Royal Navy would prevent trade bound for German ports and seize all accessible German vessels. His work therefore focused on prohibiting British goods reaching Germany by neutral routes, and preventing Germany circumventing the blockade by exploiting transit via neutral neighbours, such as Holland and Belgium.[35]

The CID approved Desart's report and recommendations on 6 December 1912. It also agreed that in order to maximise economic pressure on Germany, it was essential that Holland and Belgium were either friendly, allowing their trade to be managed to minimise leakage, or definitely hostile, in which case their ports could be blockaded.[36] This meeting has been interpreted as proof that the British government both endorsed an Admiralty strategy of 'economic warfare' against Germany and 'pre-delegated' authority to the Admiralty, in the event of war, to implement measures to 'devastate' the German economy 'in short order'.[37] This would be achieved by the traditional methods of denying maritime passage and seizing ships and cargoes, but also by disrupting Germany's access to the global trading system, insurance, cable communications, banking and finance.[38] In fact, this claim does not easily fit with the record of the meeting or the wider context in which economic warfare was now being addressed. The meeting addressed Desart's report, not the entirety of economic warfare. None of Desart's recommendations promised 'rapid devastation'. They focused on the policies and technical measures required to minimise German trade, notably how Britain should interpret international law and the rights of neutrals, along with the measures required for British and Empire compliance on preventing 'trading with the enemy'. Both Desart and the CID recognised complex issues here, affecting important foreign relationships, as well as costs and benefits for Britain's own economic war potential, on which further deliberation was required. Both were wary of interfering with international financial flows, fearing this would harm Britain as much as Germany. This wariness reflected important and deep-seated attitudes running through the British political and economic establishment. These were partly ideological, a commitment to liberal internationalism, embracing individual and property rights, the rule of law and limits on the use of force, which implied protection of neutrals and civilians. But they also reflected a hard-headed desire to protect Britain's central position in the global economic system and to avoid wrecking it.[39]

Importantly, the 6 December meeting also coincided with the Admiralty's abandonment of close blockade. As noted earlier, without close investment of all German ports, Britain could not invoke a commercial blockade as defined under the international law to which she had committed, although not yet ratified by Parliament, under the Declaration of London in 1909. Britain would therefore be obliged to fall back on the less effective option of contraband control, along with the most coercive approach to neutrals she could implement without unacceptable political cost, or economic damage to her own interests. The Admiralty certainly understood this constraint, although their new distant blockade war plan published shortly after the meeting insisted that this revised variant of blockade would still 'severely disrupt' the German economy.[40] It is unsurprising, therefore, that neither before, during or after the meeting did any senior member of the Admiralty, notably Churchill who attended as First Lord, or Battenberg, present as First Sea Lord designate, claim that blockade would achieve rapid and comprehensive German collapse. There was probably Admiralty consensus that, in line with Ottley's dictum, the distant blockade envisaged at the end of 1912 would still grind the Germans down, but that it would take longer.[41] Furthermore, despite the new war staff created earlier in the year, the Admiralty possessed neither the resources and expertise, nor the planning capacity and detailed economic intelligence, to credibly promote a strategy of more rapid collapse – even assuming political will to set aside the international legal constraints and accept serious damage to relations with neutrals.[42] Nor could such a strategy, had it existed, be controlled and executed by the Admiralty in isolation. By the end of 1912, Hankey not only owned economic warfare as secretary to the CID, but had achieved agreement that a project of this complexity must be addressed under close Cabinet control on a cross-government basis. As for 'pre-delegation', Hankey's war book certainly assigned the Admiralty actions relating to blockade and economic warfare to be implemented in the event of hostilities. But the same applied to half a dozen other departments.[43]

Following endorsement of Desart's report, the impact of blockade on the German economy received little further study over the remaining eighteen months of peace. Neither Hankey nor NID sponsored intelligence effort directed at German plans for countering the economic effects of blockade or potential attitudes within key neutral states. German economic planning would have been a difficult target at this stage. It was delicate territory for the naval attaché to broach, while the still-new SSB lacked the resources and expertise in this field, where its intervention would anyway be fiercely resisted by the Foreign Office. Oppenheimer was best placed to help, but never tasked. Ironically, after reporting on German plans for 'financial mobilisation' in war, he lobbied for the British government to establish a 'technical council' on wartime finance, drawing on the German model, but made no headway.[44] The failure to seek intelligence on German countermeasures was unfortunate, because plans and preparations to meet a British blockade certainly existed. They were far from comprehensive, but there was enough activity after 1912 to warn Britain that many of its key assumptions about the impact of blockade on the German economy were shaky. German research into its economic vulnerability in wartime had begun almost simultaneously with Campbell's work, and Tirpitz predicted the impact of a British blockade with extraordinary accuracy in 1907, even drawing attention to the Royal Commission on Food Supply. Overall, Germany's pre-war thinking on protecting supplies of food and raw materials ensured that it began countering the British blockade imposed from 1914 long before it was effective. The German economy survived the first two years of war without serious difficulty.[45]

Through 1913, therefore, rather than continuing to examine its impact on the German economy, the Admiralty focus was on the purely naval challenges of its distant blockade strategy. Churchill worried about the effectiveness of a distant blockade in containing the German fleet and, specifically, that it left the British east coast too exposed to German raids. As a result, he constantly sought to revisit more offensive options, only to be reminded of harsh resource and tactical realities. Admiralty planners did, however, acknowledge that distant blockade would significantly increase the prospect of neutral leakage, reducing damage to the German economy. A potential solution was to place minefields in the North Sea to prevent neutral shipping reaching German ports, and give Britain better control over access to neutral ports. Preparations to implement this plan were not complete when war broke out, and there were also political reservations to be overcome.[46]

It can be argued that by shifting to distant blockade, which surely implied a policy limited to contraband control, the Admiralty consciously abandoned economic coercion as a decisive war-winning strategy for the lesser goal of provoking the High Seas Fleet to put to sea, where it could be engaged in decisive battle. Distant blockade, therefore, had a purely operational goal, not a grand strategic one. The December 1912 war plan and the amendments incorporated over the next eighteen months fit this interpretation. So does the failure to move forward proactively with blockade planning and related intelligence collection during this final period before the war.[47] But this view poses questions. It was easy to set the goal of provoking a German sortie, harder to make it happen. Why would the Germans take the risk of engaging a superior British fleet, with the prospect of irretrievable losses, unless the distant blockade was imposing unacceptable economic damage, a war-winning weapon which left Germany only the option of a last desperate throw? Pursuing the military goal of a German sortie therefore required the Admiralty to make the distant blockade as coercive as possible. If Germany did sortie in such circumstances and suffered decisive defeat, what then? Presumably Britain would apply a close blockade to complete the destruction of the

German economy? Separating military and strategic goals is thus a false distinction. They were inextricably bound together, as Admiral Sir George Callaghan, commander of the Home Fleet, implied in 1913. Based on the entrances to the North Sea:

> the battlefleet is ready for anything and can act when it is required. If the Germans will not risk a meeting, the fleet dominates the situation and Germany must submit to whatever action we choose in regard to her trade and colonies. If this treatment is more than she can stand, she must come out to fight knowing that the British fleet is superior in strength and possesses the initiative.[48]

Callaghan's assessment proved correct, but not in the way he anticipated. The British blockade which evolved from 1914 did provoke German counteraction, but with U-boats, not the main High Seas Fleet.

If this debate becomes circular, it also assumes greater clarity and consensus within both the Royal Navy leadership and wider government on the execution of economic warfare against Germany than yet existed. There was broad agreement through 1913–14 that cutting, or at least sharply reducing, Germany's Atlantic trade through naval power could inflict enough economic damage to make it difficult for her to sustain a modern war. However, there remained unresolved differences on how long it would take to reduce Germany's fighting capability, and on whether economic action alone could be decisive. The questions raised by the CID in December 1912 on minimising damage to Britain's own war potential, and managing relations with neutrals, remained extant eighteen months later. Royal Navy leaders understood that moving to distant blockade potentially reduced their ability to impose rapid damage on Germany, but knew that within the wider picture this was one of many issues to be resolved. They assumed that war would resolve the questions, and bring harsher interpretation of blockade rules. For them, economic pressure undoubtedly remained the primary way that the Royal Navy could contribute to German defeat. Drawing out the German fleet to its destruction was desirable but secondary, and its containment in port while blockade took effect was acceptable.[49]

Meanwhile, between 1909 and the outbreak of war there were significant changes in Admiralty organisation, affecting the role of NID and therefore the direction and management of intelligence. In May 1909, following his appointment as DNI, Bethell informed Fisher that present arrangements for managing frontline forces and operations on behalf of the First Sea Lord were inadequate. Responsibility for implementing orders from the First Sea Lord was divided between NID and the civilian Military Branch. NID possessed the naval expertise, undertook war planning and advised on force deployment. But the implementation of plans and deployment fell to Military Branch, since NID had no executive authority. NID proposed, but Military Branch disposed, despite lacking appropriate professional expertise. Furthermore, because Military Branch provided all administrative support, NID neither controlled the papers it received, nor the reports it issued. What was required, Bethell argued, was a single professional war staff, with executive authority to both plan and implement under the First Sea Lord's direction. The new staff would be grouped under DNI although a better title, reflecting his new role, might be chief of staff. He should have two divisions: Intelligence which would be little changed, and a War Division which would absorb Trade. Mobilisation Division, which had little relevance to operational management, should come under the Second Sea Lord.[50]

The structure that emerged that autumn reflected some of Bethell's secondary recommendations, but ignored his central message. Trade was indeed merged with War Division, but Mobilisation remained, and nothing was done about executive authority, or the relationship with Military Branch. Even worse, NID was split in two. A new Mobilisation Department was created, which absorbed the expanded War Division. NID therefore lost both status and half its strength, its role reduced to that of the Foreign Intelligence Committee prior to 1887, the collection and collation of intelligence. This was a profound change. In theory, no single officer now co-ordinated work on intelligence, war planning and mobilisation to ensure coherent advice to the First Sea Lord, since DNI and Director Mobilisation were co-equals.[51] In practice, under Wilson's tenure, Bethell as DNI remained the First Sea Lord's primary adviser and retained significant influence over war planning, but the new structure was a mess, further compounded by Wilson's determined opposition to the concept of 'a staff', and general lack of interest in planning.[52]

The appointment of Churchill as First Lord in October 1911 triggered more change. He arrived with instructions from Asquith to reform Admiralty administration, widely perceived as archaic and unable to cope with modern demands, with too much power concentrated in the First Sea Lord. The immediate cause here was Wilson's poor showing at the CID meeting on 23 August called to review war policy. The political perception, powerfully expressed by Haldane, was that the Admiralty required a professional staff similar to the army staff created after the Boer War. Bethell would have argued that NID prior to 1909 had become a de facto staff, that Admiralty war planning under Fisher's tenure compared well with that of the army, and that his proposed reforms were a logical evolution. However, the political perception of Admiralty failure, shaped first by Fisher's bitter dispute with Lord Charles Beresford, while the latter was Commander-in-Chief Channel 1907–09, and then Wilson's performance, was now entrenched. (The Beresford affair ostensibly centred on his determined opposition to key parts of Fisher's reforms and policies, but was exacerbated by complex personal rivalries and culminated in a high-profile CID inquiry and considerable political embarrassment.[53]) Wilson never compromised on his opposition to a formal naval staff, reiterating his views even more forcefully after Churchill's arrival, thereby triggering his replacement by Admiral Sir Francis Bridgeman in November.[54]

The war staff created by Churchill in January 1912, headed by a chief of staff, comprised three divisions, Intelligence, Operations and Mobilisation. The already truncated NID now formally ceased to be a distinct department and became the Intelligence Division (ID). It could be argued that this was merely a reversion to the NID structure inherited by Ottley in 1905. Indeed, when the Trade Division was recreated in 1914, it became identical. Personnel numbers were similar too, with twenty-nine naval officers in the overall war staff in 1914, with fifteen in the new ID, compared to twenty-three in the 1905 NID with its wider remit.[55] The chief of staff reported to the First Sea Lord and became his principal adviser, but was not a member of the Board and still lacked executive authority. His position and responsibilities, therefore, mirrored those of DNI under pre-1909 arrangements. The new structure thus corrected the shambles created in 1909, but otherwise did not advance much down the road marked by Bethell. It met the political requirement for change, but the war staff remained an advisory body, and responsibility for implementing operational decisions remained with Military Branch.[56] Its capabilities were essentially no more than those previously available through NID if properly exploited, and fell short of what was needed to develop and implement effective war plans, especially in the complex area of economic warfare.[57] With the downgrading of DNI, now re-badged as Director Intelligence Division (DID), the profile of intelligence inevitably reduced, although the right personality could compensate. More importantly, it meant intelligence became more detached from operations and planning. This had serious consequences at the start of the coming war.

Perhaps the most important British intelligence success against the German naval target came just at the outbreak of war. Between July and November 1914 ID acquired classified German naval documents relating to gunnery performance. Surviving Admiralty records do not show how

ID acquired the documents, whether they derived from a single source, came as a single batch, or arrived several months apart. The first reference to this material came on 30 September when the Admiralty sent Jellicoe, as Commander-in-Chief Grand Fleet, a German report by the commander of their 1st Battle Squadron, dated 21 April 1914, reporting on 'the third day of the firing practice 1913/14'. Jellicoe circulated it to subordinate flag officers, with instructions to brief ships under their command. He noted the German intention to develop a high rate of fire on acquiring the range, and that salvo spread from heavy guns was small. Since main and secondary armament had fired together, the range in this exercise had probably not exceeded 8000yds. No mention was made of a director system, which was therefore probably not fitted.[58] A few weeks later, the court of inquiry into the operations against the German battlecruiser *Goeben* and cruiser *Breslau* in the Mediterranean, which failed to prevent their escape to Constantinople, confirmed that ID had recent intelligence on German gunnery capability, including information on salvo spread and fire control. The latter depended primarily on range-finding and spotting, although the Germans were apparently now using an equivalent of the British Argo clock. This intelligence was evidently available prior to the outbreak of war. It was separate, therefore, from the 30 September document, although probably from the same source.[59]

In December ID issued the more detailed 'Results of the Firing Practices of Ships and Coast Artillery in the Firing Year 1912–13', compiled at the Imperial Navy Office Berlin in 1914. This secret document of 262 pages covered all categories of firing practice for most of the High Seas Fleet. It included detailed tables for long-range firing under 'easy' and 'difficult' conditions for main and secondary armament of battleships and cruisers, conducted by both day and night. Most of the document had been translated, but to enable rapid circulation parts remained in the original German. An ID preface stated that it had been obtained 'under exceptional circumstances'.[60]

Given the importance in wartime of getting these documents to the fleet as soon as possible, it seems the 30 September gunnery document, the shortest and easiest to translate and process, was not acquired before July at the earliest and more likely after the outbreak of war. The document issued in December would have taken longer to process, but may also have been obtained separately and later.

Where did these documents come from? The ultimate source must have been German, either serving in the navy or a civil servant with access to classified naval information. (Although theoretically there could have been more than one source, the nature of the material suggests a single originator. It also seems doubtful two individuals with access to similar information betrayed it at the same time.) It is most unlikely the naval attaché would have solicited documents of this sensitivity from such a German source or would have accepted them if offered. It is equally improbable they were sent as an unsolicited sealed package either to the British embassy or a British official, since the document markings might identify the sender.

The most credible candidate, therefore, for finding and exploiting a German source is the SSB, and probably Bywater. Bywater's 1934 autobiography suggested that from early 1911 he produced regular reports on German gunnery developments, and notably investigation of long-range firing above 12,000yds. He noted that German capability here was beyond anything previously known, and British experts were initially sceptical. Thereafter, the SSB had 'redoubled its efforts' on German gunnery. 'At some risk, and after the exercise of much ingenuity and endless patience, certain avenues of communication were opened by means of which we hoped to secure the desired intelligence.' Precise details were too sensitive to be disclosed, even in 1934. Significantly, Bywater also referred to obtaining photographs of damage inflicted on obsolete battleships used as targets in a High Seas Fleet firing exercise. These had caused a sensation in ID.[61] A further pointer to Bywater's possible role is the substantial budget allocated to him from 1912 and noted earlier, some of which might have funded a special German source.

If SSB was the source, and Bywater the agent handler on the ground, the challenge of getting material of this sensitivity out of Germany, even in peacetime, was formidable. It was even harder in wartime. The documents were protected items, and the long gunnery report easily identified. The latter could hardly be removed permanently without being missed. The British source acquiring it would therefore probably have access only for a short period, hours or, at most, a few days. The short 30 September document could have been laboriously copied in long-hand, but the only way of rapidly copying the other document was photography. Executing this with the technology available in 1914 was demanding, but Bywater's reference to photography and status as a journalist suggests relevant experience.

Material received before the outbreak of war could in theory have been sent by the naval attaché using the diplomatic bag, but Foreign Office sensitivities would probably have prevented this. Covert exfiltration using a courier under suitable business or other cover was more likely. At the end of July, with war imminent, Cumming got approval from Rear Admiral Henry Oliver, DID since November 1913, to deploy a female agent to Berlin and to pay her £100 for a month's work there. Her role is not known and she did not go because she lacked the right travel papers.[62] The figure of £100 was a substantial sum (about £10,000 today) for a short deployment, which probably involved supporting an existing agent or operation. Cumming and Oliver evidently judged the visit risky, but important. The gunnery documents, especially the long report, justified exceptional effort. Exfiltration after the outbreak of war would probably have been through Holland or Denmark.

Whatever the truth of the source of these documents and Bywater's possible role, there is further tantalising, but inconclusive, evidence pointing to a British agent with access to senior circles in the German navy, probably the naval staff, continuing to operate during the first months of the war. The most compelling pointer is intelligence available in the Admiralty by late December 1914 warning of an attack first by German naval Zeppelins on some east-coast town, and subsequently a combined attack by naval and military airships on London.[63] This intelligence was timely and accurate, did not come from SIGINT, and suggests access to high-level planning.[64] The source here might be the same as the provider of the gunnery documents. Furthermore, in November 1921 a senior German navy officer told the American naval attaché in Berlin that the British Admiralty had received information on German naval movements during the war from an officer in the German admiralty bribed by British secret agents, although the case for a high-level naval source persisting throughout the war is unconvincing.[65] In November 1939 Sir Stuart Menzies, head of the Secret Intelligence Service (the successor to the SSB), was adamant that all attempts to penetrate Germany in the previous war had been a 'complete failure'. As the next chapter demonstrates, this was not literally true, but probably accurately reflected failure to recruit a senior source actually serving within the government or military.[66]

The value of the 1914 gunnery intelligence to Royal Navy commanders should have been considerable. In theory, the authority of these German documents, their direct relevance to the challenges facing Grand Fleet units in any engagement with their High Seas Fleet counterparts, and their timeliness at the very start of the war could hardly be bettered. However, as with any intelligence, the documents had to be interpreted with care. There were apparent contradictions between these documents covering gunnery practice, which demonstrated considerable focus on long-range firing, and German fleet tactical orders recovered by the Russians from the cruiser *Magdeburg*, and which reached NID contemporaneously in mid October. The *Magdeburg* documents suggested a strong preference for an action fought at medium range. By the time Jellicoe and his staff came to assess the German tactical orders issued by ID in January, wartime experience at the Falklands and Dogger Bank engagements cast serious doubt on the medium-range intent. Both these actions had demonstrated German willingness to fight at long range, and their effectiveness in doing so. Jellicoe appears, therefore, not to have placed much weight on the medium-range emphasis. What he took from the gunnery documents, however, was the effort the Germans had put into long-range firing practice and the need for the Grand Fleet to make this a top priority too.[67] As he stated in 1919:

> I knew, perhaps better than most of our officers, how efficient was the gunnery and torpedo work of the High Seas Fleet, and how rapid had been its advance in the year or two before the war. A great increase had been made in the allowance of ammunition for practice. Before the war this was much higher than our own, and there was no doubt in my mind that the German allowance would be well expended. Indeed, we had obtained information which placed this beyond question.[68]

These challenges of interpretation should not detract from the fact that the successful acquisition and exfiltration of these German documents was a major intelligence coup. It is one of the least-known British intelligence achievements of the twentieth century, but one of the more important.

Naval intelligence on the eve of war

The German naval challenge in the decade before 1914 was the first real test of British naval intelligence in its modern form. How well, therefore, had ID as an intelligence department, and its partners elsewhere in government, prepared Britain for the naval war it would fight from August that year? Did ID have adequate understanding of German naval capability and how it would be used? How well did ID intelligence support Admiralty war planning, especially the focus on blockade and economic warfare? Finally, how well had ID prepared the ground for the wider naval intelligence capabilities required in a global war? The pre-1914 performance of NID and ID has recently been summarised as 'lacklustre', reflecting a small, overworked department, inadequate for comprehensive assessment and poorly linked to policy and planning.[69] Set against the picture in this chapter, that judgement looks harsh. Despite the small size of ID (still only sixteen officers and nine clerks in 1914[70]), the limited attaché network, and the tiny resources available to the SSB, there were significant achievements in all three areas defined above. Not surprisingly, there were also important failings.

NID and ID knowledge of the German navy order of battle, its forward building plans,[71] and the strengths and weaknesses of individual ship classes and weapons was always adequate from the start of the Tirpitz programme. This enabled Britain to manage the naval risk posed by Germany, as illustrated in the debates around 'acceleration' in 1909, to retain an adequate lead, and ultimately to win the naval race decisively. By 1914, ID's picture of the German navy was remarkable for its quality and depth, as illustrated in the comprehensive report it circulated at the start of the war.[72] This understanding of German capability informed strategic and tactical planning, whether in the shift to distant blockade or gunnery tactics in a future fleet encounter. The collection and application of intelligence to planning for economic warfare was patchy, but much good work was done, and it helped to illuminate key issues and problems.

The charge, sometimes made, that the Royal Navy leadership consistently ignored good technical intelligence is not convincing.[73] Jellicoe's assessment of the relative merits of British and German capital ships, shared with Churchill in July 1914, showed an excellent grasp of German material capability (evidently drawing on the latest ID intelligence), and no complacency over possible areas of British weakness.[74] There was, equally, no assumption that the Royal Navy necessarily enjoyed an advantage in training and experience, either within the battle-fleet or beyond. ID reported that the High Seas Fleet had spent 'considerably greater' time at sea during the financial year 1912/13 than even the best British squadrons.[75] In early 1914 German expenditure on ammunition for gunnery practice was also judged significantly higher.[76] Jellicoe's rapid response to the excellent intelligence on German gunnery tactics acquired later in the year has been described. The Admiralty did fail to act on the detailed report on the new German armour-piercing shell and advanced Krupp fuze, provided by the SSB from Fairbrother in 1911. As a result, British shells at Jutland were less effective than they should have been. However, the shell story is complex, involving multiple industrial, technical, financial and even tactical issues, and to reduce it to failure to recognise and exploit good intelligence is to over-simplify.[77]

Meanwhile, the investment in intelligence infrastructure from 1909 created a basis for future success. The achievements of the SSB on the German naval target over its first five years of life were remarkable. It surpassed the German naval intelligence effort against Britain, and it outperformed its equivalents in France and Russia which had been in business much longer.[78] It was probably the Admiralty who recommended Cumming for the Companion of the Bath (CB) awarded to him in 1914, a significant honour for his rank, and a mark, therefore, of the importance placed on his contribution.[79] While there was still no formal naval SIGINT organisation when war broke out, arrangements for collecting German traffic on a sustained basis were in place, and there was a growing understanding of what else was needed to deliver operational value. Finally, while much still had to be done to convert theory into reality, Royal Navy leaders had grasped the potential of modern communications to exploit intelligence to create a global strategic picture of Britain's naval operations using the Admiralty War Room and overseas intelligence centres. No other navy was yet thinking in this way. The claim that British naval intelligence capability was poorly placed in 1914 to respond to a wartime environment therefore needs adjustment.[80]

PART II

The First World War: Enduring Lessons

6

Room 40 and the Foundation of Modern SIGINT

Britain's first naval war with Germany began at midnight on 4 August 1914 and lasted four and a quarter years. This book does not attempt a full summary of this conflict, let alone an exhaustive account. It shows how and where British naval intelligence shaped the struggle at sea, and sometimes the wider war, and the impact it achieved. Most mainstream histories that cover the intelligence aspects of Britain's naval war from 1914 to 1918 concentrate on Room 40 and SIGINT. Room 40 is, indeed, a key part of the story, but accounts of its role are often selective and unbalanced, and downplay other sources. Two other aspects of the first modern intelligence war deserve more attention. The first is how naval intelligence influenced, and interacted across, the different levels of war: strategic, operational and tactical. The second is the organisation and management of the intelligence business. In August 1914 the personnel working on British naval intelligence objectives, whether in ID, as attachés, or for the SSB, numbered barely fifty. By the end of the war, a complex British intelligence community was evolving, and those working directly on naval intelligence numbered several thousand.

On the outbreak of war, the Admiralty began implementing the strategy evolved since December 1912 to isolate Germany from the maritime world, and apply economic pressure through distant blockade. By the end of 1914, most of the initial objectives defined for this strategy had been met. The British expeditionary force was successfully conveyed to France without loss. Germany's international communications were severely disrupted. The northern exit from the North Sea was barred to Germany by the Grand Fleet based at Scapa Flow, while transit through the Straits of Dover meant running the gauntlet of multiple light forces and submarines, as well as the Channel Fleet and extensive French forces.

A blockade line was in place from Shetland to Norway. Most German warships located overseas had been destroyed or were being determinedly hunted down. The merchant raiders, so feared by the Admiralty before the war, had posed little threat. This was partly because the intelligence had over-stated both their numbers and readiness, but also because the sudden outbreak of war allowed Germany little time to execute its deployment plans. The few potential raiders located overseas were now mainly bottled up in neutral ports, with little prospect of acquiring the armament or fuel to move against British shipping, although as late as April 1915 Fisher considered placing the battlecruisers *Invincible* and *Indomitable* off New York to guard against forays by the German liners there.[1] The *Etappen* system struggled to support the few raiders that did deploy. Its communications were largely broken, British control of coal supplies was ruthlessly effective, and Royal Navy patrolling pervasive.[2] Finally, the German merchant fleet was almost entirely immobilised, with 1525 ships, comprising 3,873,000 tons, either trapped in German or neutral ports, or secured as British prizes.[3]

However, in these opening months the Royal Navy leadership still faced major problems where the right intelligence could make a critical contribution. Britain could secure the exits to the North Sea, but without a satisfactory alternative to the observational intelligence provided by close blockade, it was harder to ensure control of the North Sea itself. The Grand Fleet based in Scapa Flow, 450 miles from the German Bight, would struggle to respond to a German sortie in time to prevent a major raid on the British coast. The fleet could undertake constant patrolling, but the resulting wear and tear implied unacceptable attrition when the British margin of superiority in capital units was small. Breaking the fleet down into smaller elements to extend coverage risked defeat in detail. Jellicoe correctly assumed that a key German objective was to isolate and destroy an element of the Grand Fleet, possibly the Battlecruiser Force, to reduce or eliminate the British numerical advantage.[4] Effective containment of the High Seas Fleet, therefore, either meant revisiting options for closer observation of German ports, including seizure of an advanced base, or some entirely new warning system. It also required reliable insights into German intentions for their fleet and its evolving capabilities. Meanwhile, within weeks of the war starting, mines and submarines were also taking a toll, and new means of addressing these threats were badly needed. There was also the problem of the Baltic. So long as the High Seas Fleet was intact, Germany could dominate this sea, protect vital war supplies from Sweden and Norway, thus reducing the effectiveness of the British blockade, and deny Britain and France the most practical sea route to

Russia and hence easy delivery of important war material. Finally, as many had predicted, the blockade was proving difficult to manage, both politically and at sea. Without better direction, more resources, and better intelligence on German countermeasures, its impact would be limited. If Britain could not inflict serious damage on the German economy, it could not limit its liability through a predominantly maritime war strategy. It would be forced inexorably towards total war and a major open-ended land commitment on the Continent.[5]

The Admiralty took its first intelligence-related initiative within hours of Britain's declaration of war at midnight on 4 August 1914. In accordance with the long-standing plans approved by the CID,[6] the Post Office cable ship *Alert* dredged up and cut the five German cables which ran from Emden down the Channel to France, Spain, Africa and the Americas. A later operation cut the six cables linking Britain to Germany. The remaining German-controlled cables, running from Monrovia in Liberia to Brazil, and from the Azores to New York, were severed in 1915.[7] Germany was severely inconvenienced, rather than completely isolated, by these cable-cutting operations. It could use long-range radio to communicate with its African colonies and, for a while, a combination of radio and neutral cable lines to reach other areas, notably the Americas. It also negotiated the passage of sensitive messages hidden in the diplomatic traffic of friendly neutrals like Sweden. In the last resort, it had surface mail, although this was vulnerable to interception wherever it crossed seas or territories under the control of Britain or its Allies.[8] The German embassy in Madrid became an important radio centre for routing traffic onward to the Mediterranean and to South America, and to the United States, via the Cadiz to Pernambuco cable. The Admiralty was well aware of the threat posed by the German radio network and, working with the War Office, took immediate steps to silence all accessible German stations, an objective largely achieved within eight weeks. Royal Navy warships eliminated the stations at Dar-es-Salaam in German East Africa and Yap in the Caroline Islands, the principal German relay for the Pacific, within ten days. The most important relay station in the whole German system at Kamina in Togoland was destroyed during the night of 24 August, following a British attack from the Gold Coast. Most others were silenced by the end of September, leaving only stations at Tsingtau in China, captured by the Japanese on 7 November, and Windhoek in German Southwest Africa, which survived until May 1915. Germany's international communications footprint was accordingly further reduced. In due course, it attempted with mixed success to build a new global radio network, using more powerful transmitters based in friendly neutral countries.[9]

Britain did not enjoy exclusivity in cable-cutting. From the start of the war, Germany attempted its own campaign, and devoted significant effort and considerable ingenuity to it for the next four years. Initially, she focused on isolating Russia from its Western allies by severing cables in the Baltic and Black Sea. These operations were successful enough to force Britain to lay two entirely new cables to Russia round the north of Norway. From 1915, Germany then conducted a sustained attack on the cables connecting Britain with neutral countries across the North Sea. At this stage, she avoided attacking transatlantic cables, judging this would harm her own communications as much as those of the Allies. Although virtually every cable to the Continent was cut at some point in the period 1915–17, and some regularly, Britain always had adequate resources and sufficient control of the North Sea to repair the damage. The German campaign, therefore, achieved harassment and disruption, but never completely severed British communications. The most ambitious German operation came in the last year of the war when, after the entry of the United States, Germany judged she had little to lose and much to gain by now attacking the Atlantic cables. As conceived, the plan envisaged cutting every cable within a narrow time window, not only dramatically reducing Allied communication capacity, but placing repair resources under impossible pressure too. Almost all the cutting would be conducted underwater, using specially equipped U-boats, a technique which Germany had mastered over the previous two years. Although many cables were successfully cut, it proved impossible to achieve the comprehensive and simultaneous impact envisaged, but the potential for this operation to alter the balance of advantage at a critical point of the war in spring 1918 was considerable.[10]

Meanwhile, the day after war broke out the DID, Henry Oliver, lunched with Alfred Ewing and asked him to establish a small team to decrypt intercepted German radio messages. Selecting Ewing for this task reflected his known interest in radio technology and machine ciphers, his intellect and academic standing (Oliver wanted 'a big brain'), the trust he enjoyed as Director of Naval Education, and not least his fluent German.[11] Oliver's immediate priority was not German naval traffic in the North Sea, transmitted in the shorter wavelengths and still collected by Rotter's EI section, albeit not on a consistent basis, and without any breakthrough in decryption. It was the strategic, long-wavelength traffic emanating from Nauen near Berlin, the sole means for directing German global maritime operations (including attacks on Britain's trade) once her cables were cut.[12] Oliver's focus on Nauen also reflected expert opinion that only long-wavelength signals would be susceptible to interception from current British sites in wartime.[13] Nauen traffic was collected by the single Admiralty intercept station in the United Kingdom at Stockton and the new British station at Accra in the Gold Coast, ideally located to monitor traffic bound for Kamina. In the four weeks between 29 July, when Nauen switched to government traffic, and Kamina's destruction, around 229 messages passed along this route, most of which were intercepted in Accra and forwarded to the Admiralty.[14] The importance of Madrid was also identified in this period. Traffic was collected with enough messages in plain language to underline its potential.[15]

Ewing rapidly recruited five temporary assistants, primarily individuals with knowledge of German, from the naval colleges. Most became permanent members of the future Room 40, and some later joined the post-war Government Code and Cipher School (GC&CS). The most significant early recruit was Alastair Denniston, a Scot and Olympic hockey player teaching German at the Royal Naval College Osborne, who became the first Head of GC&CS and dominated British SIGINT for the next thirty years.[16] With Oliver's help, Ewing also established a relationship with the War Office, after spotting that some intercepts collected by the Admiralty related to military, not naval, traffic. George Macdonogh, now a brigadier and head of intelligence to the British expeditionary force, had arranged for Brigadier Francis Anderson to establish a small deciphering subsection within MO5, to be known as MO5(e), and before leaving for France agreed with Ewing that their two embryonic units would co-operate. Anderson had a background in cryptanalysis dating from the Boer War, and together with George Church had contributed to the War Office cryptographic manual published in 1911. By the end of August, he had recruited five staff, the same number as Ewing.

Neither Ewing nor Anderson had made any progress on German encrypted traffic by mid September. However, Macdonogh had established contact with the French war ministry's cryptographic bureau before the war under the umbrella of Anglo-French staff talks, and this relationship now paid dividends. In early October the French provided the current key to the main German army cipher and, despite key changes, they enabled MO5(e) to maintain coverage for the rest of the year. Given this French gift, the precarious situation on the Western Front and the decline in long-range traffic from Nauen, as German overseas stations were eliminated, Ewing and Anderson now agreed to focus on military traffic and to exploit this together. Anderson's team probably had more cryptographic understanding at this stage, which no doubt influenced Ewing. Their joint effort made a vital contribution to British survival during the 'race to the sea'.[17] By mid October, their two small units were moving towards a merger.[18] Naval SIGINT did not entirely lapse. Ewing's recruits maintained a watching brief on long-wave naval traffic when they could, and Rotter continued independently to log and work on shorter wave naval signals reaching him from the North Sea, which Ewing's team had so far ignored. Naval SIGINT might now have remained in relative limbo for quite a while, with no dedicated team working on it, as Ewing was drawn inexorably towards MO5(e) and military requirements. However, a series of chance interventions changed everything.

The German navy started the war with three principal codes, and within four months the Admiralty had acquired copies of all of them.[19] Two separate copies of the first were obtained by the Royal Australian Navy barely a week into the war, from the German merchant ships *Griefswald* captured in Fremantle on 10 August, and from *Hobart* off Melbourne on 11 August. This was the *Handelsverkehrsbuch* (HVB). Initially thought to be used by the German Admiralty and warships for communication with merchantmen, it was also widely used within the High Seas Fleet itself, and particularly by submarines and Zeppelins. Of more immediate significance, it was also the codebook used by the German Asiatic Squadron for communicating with its support ships. A copy of the wartime cipher which gave the code an additional encryption layer (super-encryption) was also captured. The Australian Naval Board notified the Admiralty in London the following day, but received no response, obliging them to send a reminder on 7 September, by which time the Australians had captured additional copies from *Prinz Sigismund* and *Wildenfels*. In this second message, embarrassingly for the Admiralty, the Australians advised that they had already broken several German signals, and offered to decrypt any signals the Admiralty cared to send, pending arrival of a copy of the codebook in London. The decryption was done by Dr F Wheatley, an instructor at the Royal Australian Naval College in Geelong, who was a German linguist, a neat parallel, therefore, to Ewing's recruits from the British naval colleges. In failing to recognise the initial Australian report, the Admiralty probably missed an opportunity to gain an earlier insight into the movements of the German Asiatic Squadron across the Pacific, on which Wheatley provided some valuable and unique HVB decrypts until November.[20]

By the time a copy of the HVB reached London in late October, the Admiralty had acquired the more important *Signalbuch der Kaiserlichen Marine* (SKM), the most widely used codebook by the German navy. A copy of this, together with two ciphers and the German navy's squared charts for the North Sea and Baltic, was captured by the Russians from the German light cruiser *Magdeburg*, following a brief engagement on

26 August off the coast of Russian Estonia. The Russians shared their haul, including other valuable papers described later, with their British ally, and the whole package was handed over to Churchill as First Lord on 13 October.[21] The final codebook, the *Verkehrsbuch* (VB), was acquired on 30 November, found in a lead-lined chest dredged up by a British trawler fishing off the Texel. This was correctly jettisoned by the German destroyer *S-119* when, along with three sister vessels, she was sunk in a short, sharp engagement with a Royal Navy force in the North Sea six weeks earlier. Although intended primarily for flag officers, the VB was also used for communication with warships overseas, and with embassies and naval attachés, including the important traffic to Madrid. The chest again contained other valuable documents, the whole catch being christened 'the miraculous draught of fishes'.[22]

Another chance development early in September had important consequences. A friend of Ewing's, Russell Clarke, a barrister by profession, but also an amateur radio enthusiast, informed him that he and a fellow enthusiast, R J Baynton Hippisley, had regularly monitored foreign transmissions before the war, and he was convinced they could intercept interesting German traffic. Clarke approached Ewing because of their personal relationship, rather than because he had or expected to intercept naval traffic specifically. Ewing had already been exploring new options for intercepting German traffic with Marconi and the Post Office, and saw Clarke and Hippisley as another avenue to pursue.[23] He therefore authorised them to recommission their home-based receivers, shut down on the orders of the Post Office, and send any results to the Admiralty. By early October these were sufficiently promising for Ewing to find them a better location than their homes in the West Country. He arranged access to the coastguard station at Hunstanton, which overlooked the Wash and had an existing experimental Post Office radio set and receiver mast. Here Clarke and Hippisley, with a third radio amateur, Leslie Lambert, installed their own equipment and commenced a twenty-four-hour watch. It quickly proved an ideal site for covering traffic from northeast Germany through to Flanders and northern France. However, reflecting collaboration with MO5(e), Ewing instructed them to focus on German army, rather than naval, traffic. This fitted with Hippisley's personal inclination. He was Honorary Lieutenant Colonel of the North Somerset Yeomanry, came from an army family, and had served on a pre-war War Office committee on wireless telegraphy.[24]

On receiving the SKM, the first codebook to reach him, Ewing had the sense to call on Rotter, head of ID14 (Germany), to help exploit it. Rotter knew that signals using the SKM were further enciphered, because the Russians had provided photographic copies of the peacetime cipher and one used for communicating with merchant ships.[25] These suggested that the current cipher was a simple substitution system. Rotter also spotted that the text of the weather signals broadcast from the main German navy transmitter at Norddeich near Emden was sent out in the base code without encryption. However, the weather signal numbers were enciphered in sequence, providing a perfect route into the current cipher table. Study of the base code showed that it was cumbersome, with several major weaknesses. This made it relatively easy for the British team to cope with cipher changes by the Germans, even when these were imposed with increasing frequency, by late 1916 every twenty-four hours. Its complicated structure also dissuaded the Germans from changing the SKM base code. It therefore remained in force until May 1917, and the British had almost complete readability throughout.[26]

Simultaneously with Rotter's breakthrough, Russell Clarke visited Ewing from Hunstanton, and saw Norddeich intercepts waiting to be decrypted. He claimed that he could intercept 'hundreds' of such messages daily from Hunstanton on both long and short wavelengths. These would open up the daily activities of the High Seas Fleet, whereas the Norddeich messages were general broadcasts to all ships, and rarely of major operational importance. Ewing was initially loath to divert Hunstanton from its military coverage, but agreed to a weekend trial. This immediately demonstrated that lower frequencies, especially in the 400–800m range, were indeed rich in tactical traffic, and by 12 November a regular flow of intercepts from Hunstanton was available. Almost contemporaneously, an underemployed German army radio unit attached to the 4th Army found it could pick up similar Royal Navy traffic across the Channel. The German navy spotted the potential this offered, and also discovered that British ciphering was vulnerable. A German navy radio-monitoring and SIGINT operation now got underway.[27]

Both Clarke and Hippisley were now formally inducted into ID. Clarke joined Ewing's SIGINT team, while Hippisley, who had the deeper understanding and experience of interception techniques, became a commander in the Royal Navy Volunteer Reserve (RNVR), instructed to establish and operate an interception service under the incoming DID, Captain Reginald 'Blinker' Hall.[28] Although Operations Division was already investigating interception opportunities with Marconi and the Post Office before the Hunstanton trials, this was probably linked with the inquiries begun by Ewing at the start of the war, rather than a separate initiative.[29] What is clear is that a network of sixteen intercept sites in the United Kingdom, each connected to Ewing's team by landline, was constructed under Hippisley's supervision and to his design over the next two years, with about half operational by the end of 1915. Some of these sites were adapted from existing Marconi and Post Office facilities, drawing on their equipment and personnel. Hippisley also established three sites in the Mediterranean, at Malta, and Ancona and Otranto in Italy.[30] The network achieved complete coverage of the North Sea by early 1917, but coverage of the Baltic and Mediterranean was more limited.[31] Meanwhile, the HVB and VB codebooks were rapidly commissioned as well, and on 20 December Ewing informed Fisher, now restored as First Sea Lord, that his team 'could now, confidently and accurately, read all the German naval signals'.[32]

Ewing's claim skated over problems that neither he, nor others briefed on the naval SIGINT successes, yet appreciated. He was correct that by late December the British could potentially read any German naval signal they intercepted. However, processing the intercepts, which were soon arriving in industrial quantities, and identifying whether, how, where and when each might deliver operational value, posed huge problems. So did source protection. If the Germans received any hint their traffic was compromised, all could be quickly lost. More personnel were needed in every area, at collection sites, to handle decryption and translation, and to identify and exploit operational intelligence, but finding people with the right skills was difficult. Those working on decryption often lacked basic naval knowledge, let alone operational awareness. Naval staff receiving decrypted signals did not appreciate the context and limitations under which the decryption teams worked. Designing an effective management system which recognised these issues, and could handle intelligence of this scale and complexity, was challenging, with no precedents to draw on. Not surprisingly, therefore, the organisation established in early November following Rotter's breakthrough into the SKM had weaknesses.

Once the SKM was readable, the team Ewing had gathered since the beginning of August was constituted on a formal basis. Staff working with MO5(e) were withdrawn and permanent accommodation was found at Room 40 in the Old Admiralty Building, close to the Boardroom and First Sea Lord's office. The initial team gathered in Room 40 comprised seven people, including Rotter, who now relinquished his role as head of ID14, where he was replaced by Commander Vivian Brandon, the same Brandon imprisoned by the Germans in 1910 following the disastrous Frisian Islands reconnaissance. These seven were joined by five new recruits by end December, although one of the original seven, Richard, Lord Herschell, moved to become Hall's private secretary.[33] The Admiralty now had a dedicated SIGINT unit, referred to by those in the know until 1917, and history thereafter, as 'Room 40' or 'Room 40 OB'.[34] The sudden suspension of joint working without adequate explanation, owing to the secrecy surrounding the SKM success, was a surprise to MO5(e), provoking some resentment. However, the increasingly close collaboration MO5(e) enjoyed with the French compensated for the withdrawal of Ewing's team, and co-operation continued on an occasional basis. The Admiralty provided MO5(e) with a German cipher key used on the Eastern Front, presumably acquired from the Russians, and one member of the new Room 40, W H Anstie, continued with military work until January. Although the initial close working relationship between Admiralty and War Office SIGINT teams definitely lapsed from early 1915, with each now focused on separate priorities, there was enough contact at senior level to avoid unnecessary duplication, especially over political and diplomatic interception. A more integrated relationship would have brought some added value and gains in efficiency, but it is unlikely major opportunities were missed.[35]

The formal establishment of Room 40 was accompanied by a charter for the unit agreed between Churchill and Hall, as incoming DID, on 8 and 9 November. Oliver replaced Henry Jackson, now a full admiral, as Chief of War Staff. Churchill's charter, co-signed by Fisher, now reappointed First Sea Lord, stated that an officer of the war staff, preferably from ID, should study all decrypted intercepts to assess German movements and intentions and make reports. Original intercepts, along with their decrypts, should be entered in a locked book, with other copies destroyed. The book should be handled only under the direction of the chief of staff. Churchill added that he wanted Sir Alfred Ewing to 'associate himself continuously with this work.' Hall replied that he had consulted Ewing and was appointing Rotter to assess the intercepts. He proposed that once intercepts were decrypted and translated, the original would be securely filed, and the translation only entered in the locked book. Two copies of the translation would then be circulated by hand – one given personally to the chief of staff to exploit operationally, and the other to DID to compare with other intelligence. Sending the book round would cause too much delay and would not avoid copies, given the quantity of intercepts received.[36]

Hall, new to the Admiralty and its current personalities and politics, and faced with a fait accompli, deserves credit for tempering the charter to make it more workable, if still far from ideal. Crucially, he ensured that as DID he had oversight, and therefore influence, over Room 40's work, even if he did not control it. Equally important, this ensured that a second senior naval officer besides the chief of staff could watch for any action required on a decrypt. However, Rotter did not become the 'intelligence analyst'. He was too valuable in overseeing the technical decryption operation, not least because of his exceptional German, and knowledge of German naval terms.[37] Instead, Commander Herbert Hope, who had joined E1 foreign warship tracking section from the War College at the start of the war, was appointed.[38] As a member of ID staff, this was probably Hall's decision, endorsed by Oliver. He proved an inspired choice, superb at extracting the intelligence that mattered from what was soon a mass of material. But he was also one of the rare individuals comfortable operating in different cultures and communicating between them. Thus he commanded the loyalty and respect of the disparate and often eccentric individuals, predominantly from civilian life, forming a steadily expanding Room 40, while retaining the trust and professional confidence of his naval peers and superiors. Promoted to captain on 30 June 1915 on the personal recommendation of Fisher, he became the linchpin of the Room 40 SIGINT operation for the next three years.[39]

Churchill's charter is blamed for creating a disastrous division between producers and users of SIGINT, and for a protective security regime that sharply curtailed its operational exploitation. Room 40, it is argued, did not deliver value commensurate with the quality of the British coverage, falling short as an effective intelligence service for at least two years after its founding. Instead, it became a 'private cryptographic bureau' of the chief of staff. The view that Churchill was more concerned to keep power in his own hands than to protect the SIGINT source, and that his instructions usurped decisions on Admiralty operational organisation belonging to the First Sea Lord, is unduly harsh.[40] Churchill's original 8 November note, co-signed by Fisher, was a joint political and professional naval view of what was required. Crucially, it recognised that circulating raw decrypts was not sufficient, and that analysis, assessment and interpretation was needed. That seems obvious now, but it was not then. Nobody in the Royal Navy, or indeed elsewhere, had previously handled what promised to be a regular flow of high-quality intercepted messages and the intelligence analyst role which Churchill and Fisher were reaching for did not exist. The instruction that the chief of staff should take on the whole burden of exploitation with a single officer, completely isolated from the war staff structure, to support him was, of course, impracticable, and the security arrangements ridiculously cumbersome. However, on 8 November neither Churchill nor Fisher could know how much material would soon be involved.

The charter, despite Hall's adjustments, left open two other points which influenced the management and exploitation of SIGINT over the next two years. It stated, almost as an afterthought, that Ewing was to remain 'associated' with SIGINT work, but left unclear whether he was in formal charge and, if he was, under what remit, and to whom he was accountable. It also envisaged that SIGINT would be managed and conducted in isolation from the existing Intelligence Division which was its logical home. ID remained small at this stage, but it held all the existing records and expertise on the German navy, and received all the incoming reports from other sources, including the SSB. Exploiting SIGINT in isolation from this wider information base reduced the value of both. Hall himself could still draw connections between SIGINT and intelligence from other sources, and would do so with enthusiasm. However, for all his talents, he could not spot everything and, because he was not responsible for Room 40, he focused on specific operational opportunities, rather than wider issues of SIGINT management.

Herbert Hope's appointment might easily not have worked, or at least not for a while. Hall thought he understood what he wanted Hope to do, extract usable intelligence from a stream of intercepted messages produced by cryptographers with limited naval understanding. But he could not give Hope direct access to Room 40 because he did not control it. More important, Hall did not fully appreciate what the Room 40 product would look like, nor had he adequately considered the practicalities of conveying it to operational customers within the constraints set by the charter. Hope was therefore installed in an office in ID, remote from Room 40, where translated decrypts were delivered for his comments, before passing to Hall and Oliver. He had no context for what he saw, could not ask follow-up questions, or offer guidance on priorities. By his own admission, his initial comments verged on the banal, and did his reputation no good with Oliver. He remonstrated with Hall, who recognised the difficulty Hope faced, but was unwilling or unable to change matters. Quite fortuitously, Hope then had a chance encounter with Fisher who, on hearing of the problem, directed that Hope should not only have immediate access to Room 40, but report to him with intercepts on a twice-daily basis. By 16 November, therefore, just over a week after Churchill's directive, Hope was fully indoctrinated. Once he had access to Room 40, the ambiguities surrounding its status and accountability worked to Hope's advantage and he rapidly became its de facto head on a day-to-day basis, albeit also straddled uneasily between two masters, Hall and Ewing.[41]

Ewing remained nominally responsible for Room 40 for the next two years, until becoming Principal of Edinburgh University in October 1916. Assessing the comparative roles and influence of Ewing and Hall in this period is difficult. Hall was one of the greatest intelligence chiefs

Britain has produced. He was a charismatic and inspirational figure, with an unparalleled eye for an operational opportunity and a talent for self-promotion, all qualities evident in his relationship with Room 40. Ewing was a respected and well-connected academic, but cerebral, cautious, and low-key in his personal style and dealings. The two had little in common and found it difficult to work together. Hall resented not controlling an intelligence source that promised endless possibilities. Ewing resented interference on his turf, suspecting correctly that it often took place behind his back. Oliver, while acknowledging Hall's talents, felt he lacked tact in handling Ewing. Eventually, their clashes provoked a major row which Balfour, by then First Lord, ordered Oliver and the Admiralty Secretary, Sir William Graham Greene, to resolve. They succeeded in calming tempers, but did not impose any structural changes.[42] Ewing and Hall continued their battle after the war, each seeking to establish credit for Room 40 and its achievements in various accounts and memoirs, a contest which Hall, the more cunning political operator, largely won.[43]

Ewing's role in the founding of Room 40 is easily underestimated, and he is usually credited with little influence from the end of 1914, following the initial breakthroughs. From this point, he is presented as preoccupied with interests elsewhere, out of touch with Room 40's daily activities and needs, and rarely contributing value although, somewhat inconsistently, his critics primarily blame him, along with Oliver, for Room 40 remaining a 'private cryptographic bureau' through the first half of the war.[44] By contrast, Hall is credited with seeing the full potential of Room 40 from the start, providing the direction it needed through Hope, recruiting talented outsiders to staff it, and taking new initiatives such as the creation of a political section.[45] Hall's dominant place in the Room 40 story reflects his over-arching role in the portrayal of wider British intelligence successes of the First World War, and his compelling and colourful personality. It also reflects the specific contribution of Room 40 to some of Hall's more famous achievements, notably the Zimmermann telegram affair in 1917, described later. This has fostered a popular belief that Room 40 underpinned most of Hall's operations from the earliest months of the war. Reality is more complex. Hall did sometimes exploit Room 40 intelligence to great effect, but its contribution is also frequently exaggerated. Furthermore, it is essential to distinguish between Hall's use of Room 40 intelligence prior to autumn 1916 to assist his operations as DID, and the influence he exerted in this period over Room 40 priorities and organisation.

It is impossible to judge whether Hall or somebody else would have done better than Ewing in getting a SIGINT operation off the ground.

However, Ewing's contribution was important in two respects. His academic network provided an initial team of unusual talent and quality recruits for the rest of the war and for long afterwards. His link with King's College, Cambridge, proved an especially fertile source of cryptographic flair. Two King's fellows recruited in 1915, Dilwyn (Dilly) Knox, classical scholar, papyrologist and linguist, and the historian Frank Birch, played a dominant role in codebreaking through both World Wars. Knox was central to the early attack on the German Enigma machine cipher in the late 1930s, and Birch became the official historian of British SIGINT up to 1945. A third King's recruit, Frank Adcock, after serving Room 40 with distinction, returned to Cambridge to become Professor of Ancient History, and from 1937 a primary talent spotter for Room 40's successor organisation at Bletchley Park. One of the new generation King's recruits was the mathematician Alan Turing, recruited in 1938 and becoming the outstanding cryptographic genius and a major contributor to naval intelligence in the Second World War. That war ultimately saw about one-third of King's fellows brought into Bletchley Park which consequently acquired the nickname 'Little King's'.[46] Hall supplemented the academics with excellent recruits to Room 40 from other walks of life, but without Ewing the Admiralty might have struggled to find the core skills it needed.

Through 1915, Ewing and Hall probably contributed equally to recruitment, raising Room 40 numbers over the year from about ten to thirty.[47] Ewing's science and engineering background and established interest in cryptography also brought together the different technical strands of the SIGINT service, such as the intercept network, more quickly than might have happened otherwise. Ewing's own account of his experience with Room 40 conveys a man who, far from out of touch, remained deeply involved in all its activities at least to the end of 1915, when he began to reduce his commitment. He was in the War Room at the Dogger Bank action, an active participant in decisions regarding the sinking of *Lusitania*, and in Room 40 helping to deal with German cipher changes during at least part of the Jutland battle.[48] In October 1915 he, not Hall, addressed War Office concerns that Admiralty-controlled intercept sites were neglecting army requirements, and through 1916 he continued managing intercept support from both the Post Office and Marconi.[49] Nor is it correct that the political section was a Hall initiative that bypassed Ewing.[50] George Young, the first head of the section, stated that it began under Ewing's instructions in autumn 1915 with the approval of the Board of Admiralty.[51] In September 1916, just a month before Ewing departed, Graham Greene confirmed Board agreement that Young was to remain under Ewing's supervision on the same terms as originally agreed for Room 40, although he was to keep DID informed, and the latter was to manage the link with the Foreign Office.[52] Finally, it is significant that Ewing's contribution to Room 40 won praise from Churchill, Balfour, Fisher, Oliver and Jellicoe, none of whom were inclined to offer it lightly.[53] Oliver, in particular, felt Ewing received inadequate recognition and tried to rectify this at the end of the war.[54]

The specific claim that the limited number of people briefed on Room 40 and its SIGINT product, along with strict limits on its dissemination, hindered effective operational exploitation requires perspective. Those initially briefed within the Admiralty were the First Lord, the First Sea Lord, the Second Sea Lord, the Secretary, Sir Arthur Wilson, who had returned as an adviser on the outbreak of war,[55] the chief of staff, the DID, the Director of Operations Division, his assistant director and three duty captains.[56] Numbers here were broadly comparable to those briefed inside the Admiralty on Enigma-generated Ultra intelligence early in the Second World War, a source of similar sensitivity.[57] Naval personnel briefed outside the Admiralty were Jellicoe, as Commander-in-Chief Grand Fleet; Rear Admiral Charles Madden, his chief of staff; Vice Admiral Sir David Beatty, commanding the Battlecruiser Force; Commodore Roger Keyes, commander Harwich Submarine Flotilla; Commodore Reginald Tyrwhitt, commander Harwich destroyer force; and Rear Admiral Sir Horace Hood, commander Dover Patrol.[58] Again, numbers briefed in the home waters commands are comparable to those first indoctrinated into Ultra. The initial Room 40 SIGINT-indoctrinated group was small, but not exceptionally so for a source of this sensitivity. It included all essential operational decision-takers in the Admiralty and all key commanders in home waters. So long as these personnel understood the origin and quality of the intelligence they received, they could direct operations without revealing the source, although doing so effectively required them to have an adequate planning capability to support them.

Through the rest of the century, numbers briefed on new intelligence sources comparable in value to Room 40, leaving aside the obvious example of Ultra, were similar. Churchill and Fisher recognised, as did their successors, that Room 40 SIGINT was an exceptionally *valuable* source, but also exceptionally *vulnerable*.[59] In November 1914 the value was anticipated rather than proven, but even at this point those in on the secret would have endorsed Oliver's statement to Balfour exactly two years later:

The principal advantage which the possession of the German naval codes gives us is that of security. We can be reasonably certain that

no naval operation can be undertaken by the High Seas Fleet without
our having information about it. Without this knowledge we would
be compelled to keep a large proportion of our scouting forces
constantly at sea, with all the liability of damage by torpedo or mine,
and the consequent wear and tear of personnel and material ...[60]

As to vulnerability, Room 40's success in breaking German traffic soon
revealed weaknesses in the Royal Navy's own cipher systems, which at
the beginning of the war were inferior to those of Germany. Until these
could be addressed, the Admiralty was right to worry. However, in
containing the potential German threat, the British had two advantages,
which endured throughout the war. First, German successes were
broadcast rather too freely through the High Seas Fleet, alerting Room
40 and enabling countermeasures. Secondly, the German navy did not
create a coherent, centralised SIGINT organisation – E-Dienst, analogous
to Room 40 – until spring 1916. Although the importance of all elements
of SIGINT – decryption, D/F and traffic analysis – was recognised from
the start of the war, for almost two years, collection and exploitation
occurred on a devolved basis with a tactical focus. Over the eighteen
months from November 1914, with significant help from German army
units, near-total penetration of simpler codes used by British patrol and
coastal forces was achieved, but there was negligible progress on the more
complex Grand Fleet systems. Furthermore, decentralisation survived the
creation of E-Dienst with day-to-day collection and decryption divided
between three separate centres at Tondern, Bruges and Libau, leaving the
headquarters at Neumünster to provide strategic direction and long-term
research. The benefits brought by the creation of E-Dienst were further
compromised by dual tasking. In addition to attacking British traffic, it
was required to monitor German fleet communications on behalf of the
High Seas Fleet command. This lessened time available on the British
target, hampering the building of expertise, and reducing effectiveness.
By comprehensively breaking German codes so early in the war, and
establishing strong central control with a strategic focus in Room 40,
Britain not only gained decisive operational advantage, but also a
permanent window into German SIGINT activity, reducing Germany's
chance of matching Britain in the information war unless she moved
rapidly to establish a comparable strategic organisation, which she failed
to do until too late.[61]

The British state had never previously had intelligence of such long-
term strategic significance as that provided by Room 40. Yet, as with
Ultra in the later war, one injudicious action, one over-explicit signal could

alert the enemy, causing him to shut everything down. Over time, in both world wars and the Cold War, arrangements were developed for moving the balance between source protection and intelligence exploitation more towards the latter, but in November 1914 everything was new. Oliver believed Churchill had briefed the prime minister on Room 40, but doubted the War Cabinet knew, let alone other ministers. He underestimated how far the circle of knowledge had spread informally, if not officially. The prime minister confided in his daughter Violet Asquith, his mistress Venetia Stanley, and, no doubt, others in his close circle, and was remarkably cavalier in his handling of secret papers.[62] Despite their greater awareness of the vulnerability of SIGINT, senior officers too were often surprisingly lax in private correspondence with others in the indoctrinated group. Henry Jackson, as First Sea Lord from May 1915, frequently referred to the content of 'decrypts' and 'intercepts' in his private letters to Jellicoe.[63]

7

The Initial Exploitation of
Naval SIGINT 1915

Assessing the management of Room 40 SIGINT output during the first part of the war means understanding what early intercepted messages looked like, how many there were, how they were circulated, how action was decided, and how intelligence was then communicated to frontline commanders. Herbert Hope soon recognised that many intercepts provided no operational value (eg routine harbour movements or administration), or were too fragmentary to be useful in isolation. Filtering was required.[1] During working hours, Hope himself chose what decrypts to circulate. At night, the duty watch decided. The priority was to identify major movements by the High Seas Fleet, where two German practices helped. They conducted a comprehensive radio exercise each night, enabling Room 40 to construct a detailed picture of fleet organisation and routines. It could then identify changes which were operationally significant. Ships or squadrons also regularly reported their position at sea using the grid system acquired from *Magdeburg*, which divided the North Sea into six-mile squares. By monitoring the grid, Room 40 could observe movement patterns and identify preferred exit routes from the German bases and probable minefields.[2]

Most decrypted signals were brief, often a single sentence, and rarely more than twenty words. The decrypt as issued was a literal translation. Room 40 allocated a report number in sequence, the German time of origin, and the time of issue by Room 40 following decryption. The gap between German time of origin and issue by Room 40 was generally between thirty and ninety minutes. This reflected the whole cycle comprising acquisition at the remote intercept site, transmission to the Admiralty by dedicated phone line, then logging, decryption and translation in Room 40. In the early months, decrypts were handwritten and initialled by the issuing officer.[3] Hope or the night watch occasionally added a written comment, but this was unusual. There was additional informal communication by Admiralty internal phone or face-to-face meetings, but visits to Room 40 by indoctrinated staff from Operations Division were rare. Until the end of 1916, separate copies of each decrypt, a literal translation of an individual German signal, were circulated to DID, the chief of staff, and Operations Division in locked red boxes to which only indoctrinated personnel had keys.[4] Herbert Hope was available for advice, but analysis, assessing the meaning of a signal, and deciding if action was required rested with the recipients. The only significant evolution to this procedure during the first two years of the war came in February 1916, when a daily SIGINT summary prepared by Hope, also known as the War Diary, was circulated.[5]

During the first six months of its operation, beginning 8 November 1914, Room 40 issued just over 4000 decrypts. This compares with 20,000 by the Battle of Jutland, 54,000 by mid 1918, and perhaps 65,000 by the end of the war.[6] Numbers increased steadily across the period, from ten to twenty per day, rising to over thirty by May 1915, as new intercept sites started to come on stream. Specific German operations generated bursts of traffic in the early months: fifty signals relating to the Scarborough raid of 14–17 December, and over eighty for the Dogger Bank action of 22–26 January.[7] By comparison, six hundred decrypts were issued over the six-day period bracketing Jutland, with nearly three hundred over the two days, 31 May and 1 June.[8]

The first six decrypts associated with the Dogger Bank action, recorded in Hope's log, are typical of the signals Room 40 processed in this period, and illustrate the intelligence value derived from both individual signals and a series of related messages:

1917   22/1 CinC has gone on board DEUTSCHLAND. DEUTSCHLAND will take callsigns of Fleet flagship while he is on board.

1004   23/1 CinC tells AC 1st CS that 1st CS and 2nd SG, 1st FdT and 2 flotillas chosen by AC 1st CS are to reconnoitre the Dogger Bank. They are to leave this evening during the darkness and return during darkness tomorrow.

1101   23/ 1 3rd S/M ½ reports 2nd of 4th gone to 108 epsilon.

1103   23/1 1st FdT (Rostock) ref 1004 from CinC suggests 5th TF, 18th T ½ and 2nd T ½.

1108   23/1 AC 1st CS orders boats ready for sea of 8th TF to assemble at Schillig Roads before 3.30pm.

1154   23/1 AC 1st CS asks that buoy 8 and Alte Jade C may be lighted before dusk and WLS 'A' Jade in position. From 5.45pm to 7 pm outer limits of Jade to be shown for going out.[9]

The 1004 decrypt illustrates how even a short signal could provide strategic intelligence of high value. The 1101 illustrates how Room 40 was now acquiring regular position reports of U-boats using the grid system from *Magdeburg*. The 1154 asking for navigation routes to be lit is a typical warning indicator of operational activity, which Room 40 exploited to good effect on future occasions.

Decrypts following the action were also revealing:

0511   24/1 AC 1st CS says *Seydlitz* must go into floating dock tonight and land about 110 killed. *Kolberg* similarly 2 killed. Requests that *Derfflinger* may go into Wilhelmshaven for urgent repair.

0548   24/1 Aeroplane 202 of Helgoland FS has seen in 52 epsilon a Swedish steamer on a westerly course. In 162 delta two destroyers, unarmoured cruiser and battlecruiser at slow speed.

1030   24/1 *Derfflinger* reports following damage owing to hits below the waterline. (1st) in compartment 9 bunker and passage near 3rd and 4th port stokehold full of water, extent of damage not yet ascertained, armour plate bent ... (3) in starboard part of watertight wing passage bulkhead tunnel injury as far as can be ascertained considerable. Further slight damage to torpedo nets, cables, searchlights, ventilator shafts and cabins. No loss of life.[10]

The 0511 and 1030 messages provided important insight into the real damage suffered by the German force, while the 0548 message showed how the Germans could observe the damaged British battlecruiser *Lion* and report her position.

These sample decrypts before and after the Dogger Bank action were achieved in what were later described as 'halcyon days of British cryptography'. Possession of the SKM codebook made decryption relatively straightforward, and German intent expressed in their opening signals was clear. There was no doubt they were making a sortie or of its timing and direction. Indeed, the future Grand Admiral Erich Raeder, then chief of staff to the commander of the First Scouting Group, Rear

Admiral Franz von Hipper, later acknowledged that the commander-in-chief's signal 1004 of 23 January was a needless gift to British intelligence. Since Hipper's flagship *Seydlitz* was still anchored in the outer harbour, the signal could easily have been transmitted by light.[11] Reporting after the action was similarly clear and detailed. Later in the war, the task became more difficult. When the SKM and the other initial codebooks eventually changed, Room 40 often had laboriously to reconstruct the new one from scratch. Equally important, the Germans became more security-conscious, and by Jutland, signals dealing with major operations gave less information away.[12]

If these raw decrypts typified Room 40 output in this first phase of the war, and with only minor changes up to Jutland, how were they assessed and exploited for British action? The Admiralty had two options. It could follow the traditional policy of operational delegation to fleet commanders, giving them all available intelligence and letting them act as they saw fit within the broad strategic directive they were given. Or it could exploit the unprecedented and almost real-time access to enemy movement and intent provided by Room 40, along with the power of modern communications, to exert greater central control from the Admiralty, Fisher's ambitious vision of 1906. Acute fear of compromising the precious SIGINT source dictated the second option. The Admiralty staff, therefore, assessed the Room 40 decrypts, planned any British response to German moves judged necessary, and then passed sufficient information to enable frontline commanders to implement it. Source protection and the small group indoctrinated into Room 40 meant assessment and planning could not be done in the War Room, or in front of the majority of Operations Division staff. Oliver, Wilson and Captain Thomas Jackson, the Director of Operations Division, therefore scanned decrypts as they appeared on a daily basis. The First Sea Lord (Fisher until May 1915, then Henry Jackson until the end of 1916) also took a close interest. Thirty decrypts a day, the average Room 40 output by May 1915, was a manageable volume for this group to absorb.[13] Most raw decrypts issued were short and self-explanatory, and misunderstandings or obscurities could be resolved through consultation with Herbert Hope. On most days, most decrypts were informative, requiring no action. In many other cases, action required was straightforward, warning of a specific U-boat threat or possible minefield, or implementing a minor route change for high-value traffic, either naval or merchant.

The occasions when the Germans executed a major operation, triggering an alert by Room 40 SIGINT, were few: the Scarborough raid in December 1914; the Dogger Bank the following January; the

Lowestoft raid; and Jutland in 1916 being the main examples in the first half of the war. The practice established during the first two operations, little changed for Jutland, was for Oliver, Wilson and Jackson to gather round a chart of the North Sea in the chief of staff's room, plot the likely German movement and an optimum British interception, and then, following consultation with the First Sea Lord if available, issue necessary instructions to commanders. In effect, therefore, the three operated as intelligence analysts, as well as operational planners. Oliver ordered commanders to prepare for sea as soon as a warning decrypt arrived, and completed plans while the fleets were being readied, issuing any final instructions just before the flagship slipped.[14] During this first phase of the war, including the first period of unrestricted U-boat warfare in 1915, Oliver also plotted all submarine movements and locations acquired through Room 40 on charts in his room, and again decided countermeasures either himself, or in consultation with Wilson and Jackson, and often the First Sea Lord.[15]

The Admiralty restricted transmission of SIGINT-derived intelligence via radio and, whenever possible, essential intelligence was only communicated to commanders by secure landline before they sailed.[16] This was the procedure adopted for countering both the Scarborough raid and Dogger Bank operation.[17] However, during the Dogger Bank engagement some risks were taken. At least two Admiralty signals warning of action against the retiring British battlecruisers, one by U-boats and the other referring to a night destroyer attack, drew explicitly on Room 40 decrypts and were revealing enough potentially to alert the Germans.[18] Following this experience, Oliver recognised the need for procedures to get essential updates to commanders by radio at sea after they had sailed. The Admiralty therefore tried to reduce the risk of German interception by using low-power transmitters at Aberdeen as the Grand Fleet moved south, and to disguise the SIGINT content by careful 'sanitisation' (in modern parlance) of the text to hide any connection with the original German signal on which the intelligence was based. Implying that information derived from direction finding (D/F) was often helpful here. As Ewing later stated:

> No secret was made of the fact that we used directional wireless, to find the position of enemy ships. This gave it a camouflage value as a means of hiding the fact that we were reading their cipher. People were allowed to ascribe to directional wireless the information which had come to us in quite another way. It diverted suspicion from the essential secret.[19]

However, if sanitising was done clumsily or in too summary a form, it either failed to convey sufficient information to be useful, caused confusion, or worse, loss of confidence in the quality of the information. This caused problems at Jutland.[20]

D/F not only provided cover for SIGINT, but brought significant added value. The Admiralty started to explore the possibilities for D/F and traffic analysis with Marconi and the Post Office around 1912, but had made little progress by the start of the war, and possessed no dedicated D/F facilities. The genesis of an extensive and sophisticated wartime naval D/F operation lay with experiments conducted for the army in France by a Marconi engineer, Henry Round, from the end of 1914, with the support of Marconi's director of research, Maurice Wright. Round, commissioned into MO5 at the start of the war with the rank of captain, demonstrated, using equipment he had designed, that it was possible to track German army units, aircraft and Zeppelins by following their transmissions. This ultimately led to a chain of D/F stations along the Western Front. The Admiralty learnt of Round's success in France through Wright, with whom they had worked closely pre-war, and asked him and Round to establish a similar capability for the navy. Initial trials began at the Marconi station at Chelmsford in March, before moving to Lowestoft, which offered better coverage into the North Sea. In May, Oliver informed Jellicoe that a U-boat had been successfully tracked by 'directionals' across the North Sea. (Wright's son Peter was a security service officer after the Second World War and wrote the notorious book *Spycatcher*. He claimed that his father had established a D/F station in Christiania (modern Oslo) in 1915, which operated successfully for several months in a joint operation conducted by ID and the SSB.[21])

These trials justified investment in a network of additional stations, initially sited along the east coast. By the end of 1915, DID had six stations operational, under his direct control, at Birchington, Lowestoft, York, Flamborough Head, Aberdeen and Lerwick. Two of these, Lowestoft and Aberdeen, also performed interception. A substantial additional network, under the control of the Admiral Commanding Reserves, was added over the next year, extending coverage right around the British Isles. Five stations were later established in Ireland directed at the Western Approaches, under Vice Admiral Queenstown.[22] The initial D/F network was independent from Hippisley's intercept network, and he was initially unaware of its existence.[23] It is unclear why the divisions in the control and management of the D/F organisation as it evolved over the winter of 1915/16 occurred. Probably Hall drove the establishment of the initial network, working closely with Round, and planned to keep it under his control, but lacked the resources in ID to administer a bigger network. The wider D/F network soon became intertwined with the interception network, often using the same sites, and with more general radio developments. Relations with Marconi and the Post Office were also complex, and many of their staff were transferred to the Royal Naval Reserve (RNR).[24] Captain William James estimated that when he took over Room 40 in early 1917 there were at least forty supporting radio sites with around eight hundred personnel. Making Admiral Commanding Reserves responsible for administering much of this infrastructure, but under DID's overall strategic direction, made sense.[25]

D/F intercepts, from whatever site, were sent to Room 40, where they were evaluated and then, if appropriate, issued as reports, known as 'directionals', to Operations Division.[26] Once the bulk of the network was producing from spring 1916, this doubled the number of reports issued by Room 40. Eventually, it established a new dedicated section to handle D/F material with its own charts to plot bearings and determine possible 'fixes', and conduct traffic analysis.[27] Traffic analysis, or TA, as it later became known, comprises the study of an opponent's communication networks, radio procedures, call-signs, individual operator identities, and plain-language transmissions to yield operational intelligence. Its potential was spotted pre-war, but it now became a distinct intelligence process. The term traffic analysis was not yet used. Instead, it was called wireless intelligence, or W/T intelligence, or wireless network research.[28]

Histories of Room 40 emphasise the failure to make it 'an intelligence centre as opposed to a cryptographic bureau'. They insist that until important changes were introduced after 1916, the value of Room 40 intelligence was reduced, because the few indoctrinated users often failed properly to understand the decrypts they received, to assess them alongside other available intelligence, or to exploit the wider expertise and knowledge of the Room 40 team. The implication is that the Room 40 staff were too often patronised as mere technicians, with nothing to offer on the conduct of naval operations. Such prejudice was supposedly exacerbated by the failure of some Room 40 staff to follow Royal Navy procedure and custom, or to use correct naval terminology. The blame for the failure to create an 'intelligence centre' is invariably placed on Ewing and Oliver, while Hall is credited with anticipating what was needed, but unable to make it happen before he took over Room 40 in October 1916.[29]

Several aspects of this popular view must be disentangled. It is easy to find weaknesses in the Admiralty's arrangements for handling SIGINT through the hindsight of the structures imposed after 1917, and even more those of the Second World War. Some members of Room 40 claimed they recognised the lack of an adequate system to exploit their intelligence, and to use it proactively, as early as 1915. In their eyes, Room 40 was viewed both by the senior leadership and Operations Division primarily as a warning system for monitoring sorties by the High Seas Fleet, and thus solving the North Sea problem. Herbert Hope believed that excessive anxiety over source protection through fear of losing this warning system made Oliver and Operations Division too conservative. He emphasised the wide knowledge of German practice and insight into their operations which Room 40 accumulated, and could have provided if suitably tasked and resourced. A decrypt giving the co-ordinates of a German minefield might appear, but Room 40 could also identify minefields in the German Bight by studying movement patterns over time. Decrypts revealing a U-boat position or a Zeppelin sortie were valuable, but Room 40 could potentially add information on patrol cycles and the history of individual units. Room 40 was probably also the most authoritative and comprehensive source on current German order of battle. Since SIGINT was not shared with the ID departments studying German order of battle and capability, and senior indoctrinated staff had neither the time nor specialist knowledge to monitor these areas, much valuable information was unused.[30]

Jellicoe claimed that ID estimates he received immediately prior to Jutland exaggerated High Seas Fleet strength, leading him to anticipate twenty-seven or twenty-eight German battleships and six battlecruisers rather than the actual totals of twenty-two and five.[31] Beatty's assumptions and recommendations also reflected an inaccurate picture of German strength.[32] The intelligence here came from ID14, the German section, which covered all aspects of German naval strength, capability, organisation and infrastructure. ID14 estimates of German navy order of battle would have been much improved by Room 40 SIGINT, as illustrated later in the year when Henry Jackson confided in a private letter to Jellicoe that the new battleship *Bayern* was 'going to sea tonight' for the first time.[33]

Whether failure fully to exploit SIGINT was genuinely recognised within Room 40 during its first two years of existence, rather than aired with the benefit of later hindsight is debatable. Most witnesses, including Hope, testified after seeing the value of changes implemented in 1917–18. They downplayed both the importance of source protection, and the strategic and operational advantage achieved during 1915–16 with far fewer resources than were available later.[34]

Separate questions are what an intelligence centre meant in practice, and who should have created it. Critics of Room 40's role, status and performance in the period 1914–16 have not explained whether the Admiralty should have added an analytical wing, presumably composed of naval staff, to the existing cryptographic capability inside Room 40, created a SIGINT analysis section elsewhere in ID or within Operations Division, or created a self-contained, fully fledged operational intelligence centre, comparable to that in the Second World War. Nor do they address how SIGINT would be co-ordinated with intelligence from other sources, while preserving its security. They also fail to acknowledge that the role of Room 40, and its relationship to its Admiralty customers and to ID during this period was not fundamentally different from that of the naval sections of GC&CS at Bletchley Park from 1939 to 1945, even if these operated on a vastly different scale. Furthermore, the isolation of Room 40 from operational decision-making for much of the war, while especially damaging, was not the only problem. The separation of the E1 and E2 tracking sections from the War Room in autumn 1914 meant that even non-SIGINT intelligence was not fully exploited. Although their data was shared with the War Room, this was done primarily through daily updates. There was no real-time plot of own and enemy forces to provide the situational awareness from which to judge new intelligence and make decisions.

This problem was recognised by some in late 1914, before the specific problems with Room 40 became apparent. One of the War Room duty captains, Cecil Staveley, argued that operations and intelligence required integration. Incoming intelligence should be examined, sifted and analysed, and any action proposed by a responsible staff officer with all relevant facts available. He should know the position of his own forces, their operations and prospective movements, the position of the enemy and their anticipated movements, the trade situation, and any other factors influencing the operational environment. (As the war progressed, the position of minefields and cleared routes was an obvious example of the last point, especially in the North Sea.) Since no single officer could monitor intelligence and operations across the globe, Staveley advocated division into separate areas of responsibility. Area staff officers, under the supervision of the chief of war staff, would act as agents for the Admiralty, authorised to guide and direct frontline commanders. This would relieve the chief of staff of much routine business, freeing him to focus on major operational and policy decisions.[35] This was the War Room plot Fisher had wanted ten years earlier, but which had lacked the intelligence inputs to make it viable.

Staveley's ideas were not accepted. Sadly, it took three years of war before in October 1917 Hope's successor, Captain William James, proposed similar arrangements to the new Deputy First Sea Lord, Vice Admiral Sir Rosslyn Wemyss. SIGINT and other relevant intelligence on enemy locations and movements should be assessed and presented, together with the status of own forces, on a plot in a dedicated chart room staffed by indoctrinated personnel. Operations would be planned and directed in this room by cleared members of the war staff, drawing on a complete, constantly updated, picture. James acknowledged that this proposal replicated for fleet operations the concept of the U-boat tracking room ('X' room) established under Trade Division a few months earlier and evolved from E1.[36] Conceptually, this was the model adopted informally by Oliver, Wilson and Jackson when they plotted the Scarborough and Dogger Bank interceptions in the chief of staff's room. But it improved on this by providing the Admiralty's senior planners with a permanent plot, properly staffed, with access to all relevant intelligence, professionally assessed and filtered. In different ways, both Staveley and James were reaching for a dedicated operational intelligence centre, anticipating that established in the Second World War. However, it took another twenty years from James's intervention before, as Deputy Chief of Naval Staff, he finally achieved that goal.

The Staveley/James model seems an obvious step so why was something similar never attempted before 1918? Oliver and Hall were best placed to identify the requirement and to address it. Yet neither did so. It seems that through Jutland to the end of 1916, Oliver, consistent with his note to Balfour and Hope's speculation, did indeed see Room 40 SIGINT primarily as a warning system directed at the main High Seas Fleet, to be protected at all costs. He knew Jellicoe lived in 'mortal terror' Germany would discover British success against its ciphers, which would 'be fatal'.[37] Oliver also evidently felt that, with the support of Wilson and Jackson, he could cope with the existing flow of decrypts and deal adequately with any action arising. He perhaps lacked imagination in failing to see Room 40's wider potential, in not anticipating problems with the management of SIGINT exposed at Jutland, and then not addressing them afterwards. However, the unprecedented range and quality of Room 40's coverage, as it appeared to him, inevitably discouraged change. Through 1916, the decisive information advantage provided by Room 40 still seemed to promise eventual victory at sea. Oliver lacked precedents for organising matters differently and nobody else, including Hall, was pressing new ideas.

Hall's relationship with Room 40 in the first two years of its existence raises most puzzles. As DID, and through the perspective provided by Herbert Hope, he had greater insight into the work of Room 40 than

Oliver. He may have held ambitions for more effective exploitation of SIGINT, its integration with other intelligence sources, especially D/F, over which he had effective control by the end of 1915, and in planning and managing operations. But he did little actively to promote such an agenda prior to Ewing's departure in late 1916, and even then change was slow. Hall hardly features in Admiralty deliberations around Scarborough, the Dogger Bank, and even Jutland. His influence over Room 40 was constrained while Ewing remained in charge, with little prospect of incorporating it in ID. He was also restrained by Churchill's charter and the views of Oliver. But there were still things he could have done. He could have encouraged Hope to produce composite reports and assessed intelligence, as well as decrypts, much earlier, at least from the start of 1916 when D/F intercepts became available in significant quantity. Hope later claimed to have wanted this, and that much value was missed in the first half of the war.[38] Oliver and Operations Division might have resisted, insisting that assessment was entirely their business, but Hall could have persuaded them to test what Room 40 could deliver. He could have given Hope a naval assistant once the latter was promoted, and employed an indoctrinated officer in ID to work with Hope on the links between Room 40 SIGINT and intelligence from other sources. Above all, as his standing in the Admiralty increased, Hall could have exerted influence to push for something like James's dedicated chart room. Indeed, there was nothing to stop Hall establishing this in ID and letting its value speak for itself.

Hall did none of this before Ewing's departure, and when he achieved control of Room 40 his reforms for handling naval SIGINT were gradual and modest. James did not get his integrated intelligence centre before the war ended. There was never systematic sharing of intelligence between different sections of ID. The submarine tracking room, which evolved from the E1 U-boat plot, received some raw SIGINT from autumn 1917, but the rest of the German section only in the last months of the war. Collated SIGINT reports with assessment and comment were not introduced until July 1918.[39] Hall made no reference to 'intelligence reform', or the importance of integrating Room 40 into ID and with Operations Division in planning his later memoirs. Indeed, given their dominant role in the naval war, he devoted surprisingly little space to either operations against the High Seas Fleet or the U-boat campaign. Caution in referring to SIGINT was no doubt a factor here, and Hall wanted colourful stories to attract readers, not a turgid account of ID organisation. Nevertheless, the outline for the memoirs revealed what he thought important and claimed his attention as DID. While he highlighted 'bad intelligence' during the April 1918 High Seas Fleet sortie, he did not suggest this was a problem at

Jutland requiring major organisational change.[40] Claims that Hall would have transformed the management of SIGINT if he had achieved control of Room 40 earlier therefore require caution. They reflect the cult of Hall as all-seeing intelligence genius, as well as aspiration and hindsight by those who later shaped the Room 40 story.

By the start of 1915, Room 40 was providing intelligence beyond that covering major fleet movements in the North Sea, such as Scarborough and the Dogger Bank. The most significant contribution, ever more important as the war progressed, was knowledge of U-boat operations. By January, Room 40 was well informed on the strength and location of the U-boat fleet in home waters and the Western Approaches, and initiated daily returns to Churchill, Fisher, Oliver and Wilson, giving the last known position of each U-boat gleaned from decrypts. Traffic to and from U-boats was extensive out to a range of 300 miles, and relevant signals were intercepted from FdU (Senior Officer U-boats), fleet broadcasts and coastal stations. The quality of this information is demonstrated by a decrypt circulated on 9 March. FdU reported that U-24 was ready for service at Emden, but U-28 was only available for local operations in the Bight; at Wilhelmshaven, U-21, U-22 and U-30 would be operational on 27 March, but availability of U-33 was uncertain; at Kiel, U-32 would be ready on 11 March, and U-19 on 4 April; U-20, U-23, U-27 and U-29 were already deployed on a distant mission. Decrypts also provided some insights into German detection of, and action against, British submarines. Room 40 achieved advance warning of the initiation of unrestricted submarine warfare in designated waters around the United Kingdom, with its interception of a message from Norddeich on 7 February.[41] It also monitored U-boat strength with precision during the year the first unrestricted campaign lasted. U-boat strength at the beginning of 1916 was fifty-four, when the official Admiralty estimate was fifty-five.[42]

Nevertheless, the emphasis on source protection meant analysis and exploitation of U-boat intelligence from SIGINT until the end of 1916 was rudimentary. As happened with High Seas Fleet sorties, Oliver and Wilson plotted any U-boat activity they judged important on the private chart kept in Oliver's room, with Fisher and then Henry Jackson again taking a close interest. This was better than nothing: it enabled some action to protect high-value targets by holding them in port, arranging escorts, or re-routing, and Wilson was apparently good at anticipating U-boat moves, but with the many other demands on their time, they could only maintain a partial picture, and inevitably missed things.[43] However, what most reduced the value of this precious U-boat intelligence was failure to share it with either Trade Division, or E1 and ID14. This had two consequences. First, E1 and ID14 had their own important sources of U-boat intelligence, including D/F reports, which by autumn 1915 were extensive and valuable, sightings by British naval and merchant ships, information from neutrals, reporting from naval attachés, agents deployed by both ID and the SSB, and from prisoner interrogation and captured documents. Linking this intelligence with the SIGINT from Room 40 would have enhanced the value of both, not least maintaining an accurate order of battle. Secondly, as already explained, E1 kept plots located in Room 42A showing the whereabouts of all German warships, including U-boats. By early 1916, E1 issued monthly reports, which reconstructed about two-thirds of Atlantic U-boat patrols with reasonable accuracy. The quality of these reports, which included detailed track charts, improved steadily over the next year.[44] They were valuable in establishing U-boat patterns and overall impact, and identifying potential opportunities for countermeasures. But they could not enable real-time action, and they inevitably had important gaps, including confirmation of precise U-boat identities, which Room 40 SIGINT could have filled. Meanwhile, the wealth of information Room 40 provided on U-boat operations could not be adequately displayed, or readily exploited, on the small-scale private charts used by Oliver and Wilson.[45] If the separate intelligence held by Room 40 and E1 on U-boat activity off southern Ireland at the beginning of May 1915 had been jointly assessed, it might have saved *Lusitania*.

How far the rudimentary SIGINT analysis undertaken by Oliver and Wilson contributed to the twenty U-boats destroyed during 1915 is hard to assess from surviving evidence. It probably contributed, directly or indirectly, to a maximum of five, but more realistically two or three.[46] Although not responsible for countering the U-boat threat, Jellicoe was privy to the intelligence, and recognised current arrangements were inadequate. He pressed the Admiralty, albeit without success, to implement a centralised assessment system, and to appoint an energetic flag officer to direct anti-U-boat operations.[47]

There was a further limitation to U-boat intelligence from the second half of 1915. In May, Germany began deploying U-boats to the Mediterranean, and by September there were fourteen boats there, nine based at Cattaro and Pola in the Adriatic, and five at Constantinople – a quarter of overall U-boat strength. Five large U-boats transited from Germany through the Gibraltar Strait, while the remainder, comprising the smaller UB- and UC-boats, were transferred overland in sections and reassembled at Pola.[48] Room 40 identified the move of most of the larger boats, but once they entered the Mediterranean its coverage was lost. There was no capability to decrypt German naval traffic in this theatre until 1917, and the D/F network, shared with France and Italy, also only worked effectively in the last year of the war. E1 painstakingly reconstructed U-boat patrols in the Mediterranean from late 1915, drawing connections with the Atlantic where possible, but without SIGINT its Mediterranean reports faced the same limitations as their Atlantic counterparts.[49] The Mediterranean proved a happy hunting ground for the U-boats. It was easy to find targets, the weather was better than in the North Sea and Atlantic, there was less risk of diplomatic incidents with the Americans, and the anti-submarine effort suffered from the poorer intelligence, divided responsibility between three Allies, and often second-rate units and personnel.

For Germany, the first U-boat campaign against Allied, predominantly British, trade, broadly unrestricted (sinking on sight rather than observing prize rules) between March and September 1915, then continued in modified form for a further six months, was a strategic failure. There were too few U-boats available, with a maximum of ten but average of seven on patrol, to achieve any decisive effect.[50] British merchant losses at 721,000 tons in 1915, less than 3.5 per cent of British capacity at the start of the war, and offset by captures and requisitions, had negligible effect on the war effort. Hankey summarised the position succinctly for Asquith in April 1916. To date, the Germans had sunk 423 British merchant ships comprising 1,410,000 tons, while there were 424 ships comprising 1,423,000 tons on the stocks.[51] The impact of an additional 250,000 tons of neutral shipping destroyed was distinctly mixed, partly through the negative effect on neutral opinion, but also because a significant proportion of the lost cargo was destined for Germany.[52] By later standards, twenty U-boats was also a high price to pay, although not all of these losses were directly associated with the trade war. However, the real damage incurred by this first campaign lay in the irreparable harm done to Germany's relationship with the United States.

Given the quality of British intelligence on the U-boat threat through 1915 and into 1916, primarily from Room 40 SIGINT, but also the inputs to E1 and ID14, including significant reporting from the SSB from mid 1915, the Admiralty should have asked more searching questions about how this threat could develop in the future, and how it was to be countered. By the time the first unrestricted campaign finally ended under American pressure, following the torpedoing of the French passenger ferry Sussex on 24 March 1916, Hall and Oliver knew that U-boat strength, at some seventy boats, had doubled from that at the start of the campaign a year earlier. They watched it double again by the start of 1917.[53] Furthermore, in January 1916 Hall had decrypts of American diplomatic traffic acquired from the military SIGINT section MO5(e), recently renamed

MI1(b) following the recreation of the Military Intelligence Directorate, which he shared with Hankey.[54] These demonstrated German confidence in achieving decisive leverage against Britain with a submarine blockade. Hankey concluded that Britain faced a 'bitter and relentless submarine campaign', and must take measures to meet it.[55] The reassuring statistics which he subsequently put to Asquith that April did not, therefore, imply complacency, although they were unhelpful in ensuring prime ministerial attention. Hall also had intelligence by February 1916 revealing that the chief of the German general staff, General Erich von Falkenhayn, saw a continuing unrestricted U-boat campaign as decisive to the success of his forthcoming offensive against the French at Verdun. British leaders knew, therefore, that the halt following *Sussex* would be temporary. In September, Hall told Captain Guy Gaunt, the naval attaché in Washington, that he expected a new U-boat offensive in weeks.[56]

Simple arithmetic suggested that if an average of seven boats at sea could sink 750,000 tons (British, Allied and neutral) in the six months April–September 1915, then a new unrestricted campaign with four times the number might sink upwards of 500,000 tons per month. The Mediterranean provided a starker warning. In the last quarter of 1915, an average of four U-boats at sea sank 290,471 tons, a rate one-third greater than achieved across all theatres over the summer.[57] (In fact, the Germans achieved an average of over forty U-boats at sea in the first six months of their 1917 campaign, six times the 1915 number, and sank about 640,000 tons per month.[58]) Furthermore, while Britain built 651,000 tons of new merchant shipping in 1915, a significant reduction on pre-war output, but almost enough to recoup losses that year, production fell to 542,000 tons in 1916, demonstrating a gulf between Hankey's numbers on the stocks and actual completions.[59] Such calculations should have pushed the Admiralty to present a major strategic assessment to the Cabinet by spring 1916, at the latest, identifying the extreme risks inherent in a new campaign against Britain's trade. However, although the naval staff partially acknowledged the risk, a mixture of complacency, bureaucratic inertia, divided responsibility and, above all, a lack of grip by the senior Admiralty leadership meant far too little effort went into anti-U-boat planning until late in the year, when further intelligence warned that a new campaign was imminent.[60]

Room 40 coverage of the German Naval Airship Division also developed rapidly from the beginning of 1915. This coverage was important as an indicator of German naval operations in the North Sea, where the airships provided vital reconnaissance support to the High Seas Fleet, but also because until spring 1916 the Admiralty took primary responsibility for the air defence of the United Kingdom. The Zeppelins used the HVB code, unenciphered, and their radio practices and signals security were bad, even by the generally poor standards of the German navy. They employed simple call-signs, invariably reported take-off and landing, and sent regular position reports, making tracking relatively easy, even before D/F infrastructure was in place, and rendering their operational intentions transparent. Zeppelin traffic was, therefore, easier than other categories for Oliver and Operations Division to assess, and to provide timely warning of raids against the mainland, or implement other appropriate action.[61]

Meanwhile, Room 40 SIGINT helped the Royal Navy eliminate the German navy's few remaining assets overseas. Intercepts of traffic using the VB and HVB codes revealed that the cruiser *Königsberg* was sheltering in the Rufiji river in German East Africa, while her engines were repaired, and also the German efforts to assist her, enabling the destruction of the supply ship *Rubens*.[62] The subsequent and ultimately successful British operations to destroy *Königsberg* involved what was probably the first use of an important new intelligence source, aerial reconnaissance: first to pin down her precise location in the myriad tributaries of the delta, and then, with photography, to assess the damage inflicted by long-range monitor fire.[63] The provision of the HVB codebook by the Australians, and Wheatley's work in solving its related cipher system, provided some insight into Spee's movements, and his options for coaling and supply, although this intelligence was too fragmentary directly to influence the Royal Navy deployment to the Falklands. It did help the cruisers *Glasgow* and *Kent* locate the German light cruiser *Dresden*, the sole survivor of Spee's force, at the Juan Fernandez Islands in mid March. This followed the interception of a signal arranging a rendezvous for *Dresden* with the collier *Gotha*.[64]

SIGINT also contributed to dealing with auxiliary raiders deployed direct from Germany, but with limited results. There were two significant raider deployments, the first from the end of 1915, and the second over the winter of 1916/17. The Germans abandoned the pre-war concept of using large, fast liners, because of the difficulty in providing coal supplies, and adopted more economical small steamers, easier to disguise. The most successful raider, *Möwe*, first deployed at the end of December 1915 for a two-month Atlantic cruise, destroying 57,000 tons of merchant shipping and laying mines which sank the pre-dreadnought battleship *King Edward VII* off Orkney. Room 40 identified her departure, but she skilfully monitored the radio transmissions of the 10th Cruiser Squadron to slip out of the North Sea, and thereafter offered few clues to her movements. The departure of *Greif* in February was also spotted by Room 40, leading to her successful interception and destruction by the armed merchant cruiser *Alcantara*, northeast of Shetland.[65] *Möwe* deployed in November for a longer operation, including the South Atlantic, and sinking 122,000 tons. Room 40 detected she was out, but never pinpointed her, and ID only learnt of her return in March from the SSB source TR16. Simultaneously, *Wolf* embarked on a more ambitious operation lasting eighteen months, reaching the Indian Ocean and sinking 120,000 tons, while avoiding numerous pursuers.[66]

Early in 1915, Room 40 realised that the VB was used by the Germans to encode traffic between Berlin and the naval attachés at Madrid, Washington, Buenos Aires and Peking, and between the German Admiralty and Constantinople.[67] The traffic to Madrid was a rich source for Room 40 throughout the war, because it offered insights into German intelligence and naval activity in the Iberian Peninsula, and Madrid was a communications relay point to the Mediterranean and the Americas. Meanwhile, Room 40's intercept of a Berlin telegram, dated 12 March, to the German inspector general of coast defences at the Dardanelles, suggesting the Turkish defenders were short of ammunition, persuaded Fisher to sanction a naval effort to force the straits five days later.[68] In contrast with the care taken over referring to SIGINT in the North Sea, Churchill and Fisher were explicit in briefing Vice Admiral Sir Sackville Carden, the commander of the Eastern Mediterranean Squadron, on this intelligence.[69] This 12 March decrypt also mentioned that deployment of a German or Austrian submarine to the Dardanelles was being considered. A later VB decrypt at the end of May revealed that *U-21* had arrived at the Austrian base at Cattaro, and listed the location of British battleships based at the Dardanelles. Hall immediately forwarded this information to Commodore Roger Keyes, chief of staff to Vice Admiral John de Robeck, the Dardanelles naval commander, but the warning failed to prevent *U-21* sinking the battleships *Triumph* and *Majestic* a week later.[70]

SIGINT was not the only source of intelligence in the first months of the war which directly helped the Royal Navy assess and counter the High Seas Fleet, and deal with its 'North Sea problem'. German gunnery documents circulated by ID in September and December 1914 were described earlier. In January ID issued a series of reports based on documents acquired from *Magdeburg* and shared by the Russians, and separately from *S119*. The main items were:

(i)   'Manoeuvring Instructions for the Fleet, 1914' classified 'secret' described as a 'draft' (*Entwurf*), dated 3 February 1914, Berlin, printed at the Naval General Staff under the signature of the

Chief of the Naval General Staff, Admiral Hugo Von Pohl. (*Magdeburg*)

(ii)   'Strategical Disposition of Naval Forces, Winter Season, 1913– 1914.' (*Magdeburg*)

(iii) 'Minutes of War Game played on 13 March 1913.' (*Magdeburg*)

(iv)   'German Naval Warfare: Scouting and Guard Duties', 207 pages. (Origin unknown)

(v)   'German Naval Warfare: Destroyer Tactics', 405 pages, divided into two main sections: 'Regulations for Destroyer Exercises' and 'Use of Destroyers'. (Origin unknown)

(vi)   'German Tactical Orders', 19 pages. (Origin unknown but probably *Magdeburg*[71]).

The last three items were issued under ID report numbers 976, 977 and 979 respectively. Two copies of item (i) survive, but not the formal published version, although a version evidently reached Jellicoe in early December, causing him to issue changes to Grand Fleet orders.[72] Items (ii) and (iii) apparently no longer exist.[73]

This was a rich haul of material, especially when added to the high ID intelligence baseline for German navy order of battle and capability in place at the start of the war.[74] It was supplemented by occasional German navy documents provided by the French, starting in early 1915, but continuing through the war.[75]

By the time of the Dogger Bank action, there was no aspect of German tactics or warship or weapon performance which should have surprised Royal Navy commanders. Perhaps no navy was ever better informed of its opponent's strength and capability. Meanwhile, although Room 40 intelligence might have been better exploited, in just three months it had proved its worth as a warning system, and demonstrated that it could provide critical insights into enemy dispositions and intent. It had twice created an opportunity to destroy a significant element of the High Seas Fleet. If decisive success was elusive at the Dogger Bank, that was due more to tactical failings by Vice Admiral Sir David Beatty, commanding the Battlecruiser Force, and his deputy, Rear Admiral Archibald Moore, than shortcomings of intelligence organisation. The year 1915 now showed that, in skilled hands, SIGINT had wider potential. It could contribute not just to the maritime war in other theatres as decrypts from the VB illustrated, but to tightening the blockade, and the delivery of strategic advantage for Britain in areas beyond the naval sphere. Furthermore, while Room 40 was a new and rich contributor of naval intelligence, other sources developed too.

8

The Hall Tradition

The wider intelligence story now underway, and its successes, is inextricably linked with the personality and qualities of Captain William Reginald 'Blinker' Hall, DID from November 1914 and remaining in post for the rest of the war, before retiring from the Royal Navy as a rear admiral, and with a knighthood for war service, in February 1919. Promoted to captain in 1905 at the early age of thirty-five, Hall was long viewed as a rising star destined for high rank.[1] Despite its reduced status from 1912, DID remained a prestigious post and Hall was an obvious potential candidate. He also later claimed a family interest: 'My father created the position of Director of Naval Intelligence, and it was my ambition to sit in his seat'.[2] However, he succeeded Oliver at this time because he became unfit for sea service, obliging him to relinquish command of the battlecruiser *Queen Mary*. Many of the qualities that made him an outstanding intelligence chief were evident in his previous career record. He had abundant drive and energy, was an exceptionally good organiser, and an inspirational leader. James, successively Hall's second in command in *Queen Mary*, head of Room 40 from 1917, and biographer, noted 'a quite remarkable gift for drawing everything that was best from his fellow men'. He was 'the most stimulating man to work for I have ever known', and 'you felt you would do anything, anything at all, to merit his approval'. Unusual among his naval peers was a taste for innovation, an inclination for unconventional thinking, and a marked willingness to take risks. He was a 'gambler', insisting that 'mistakes may be forgiven, but even God himself cannot forgive the hanger-back'. His staff followed with 'blind devotion' the risks he took, 'sure he would win'.[3] They also emphasised his charm, charisma and formidable presence which, with his sharp penetrating eyes, gave him the look of a peregrine falcon. The writer and SSB officer Compton Mackenzie, fixed by Hall's 'horn-rimmed horny eye', felt like 'a nut about to be cracked by a toucan'.[4] Others, perhaps lulled by Hall's kindly and avuncular moments and innate love of mischief, saw a striking physical resemblance to Punch.

Hall discovered a natural affinity for the intelligence world, revelling in the intrigue and adventurism of the 'Great Game', which perfectly fitted his gambler's temperament. He relished the independence he achieved as DID and, untroubled by self-doubt, readily took on responsibility beyond the traditional naval remit of the post, confident that he knew what he was doing and what was required to win the war. Like Cumming, he proved exceptional in exploiting relationships and leveraging them to advantage. He possessed an unusual mix of charm, incisive insight, and ruthlessness in pursuing an opening. He was a formidable interrogator, and his ability to persuade senior interlocutors to take risks they would not normally countenance was legendary. He talked McKenna, the Home Secretary, into approving the illegality of mail interception, and convinced Balfour as Foreign Secretary to give him a free hand in exploiting the Zimmermann telegram, to the irritation of the Foreign Office permanent secretary. The American ambassador Walter Hines Page famously described Hall to President Woodrow Wilson as someone able to look through to 'your immortal soul while he is talking to you', 'a clear case of genius', besides whom 'all other secret service men are amateurs'.[5] Herbert Yardley, the head of the United States Army codebreaking effort, insisted rather fancifully that Hall's mastery of diplomatic intercepts placed him 'next to Lloyd George in power'.[6] In 1941 President Franklin Roosevelt, who as Assistant Secretary of the Navy met Hall in 1917, regaled John Godfrey, Hall's successor as DNI in the Second World War, with the stories Hall had sold him twenty-five years earlier, which Godfrey knew were largely fictitious.[7] Ruth Skrine, Hall's secretary through much of the war, agreed with Jimmy Bone, the London editor of the *Manchester Guardian*, that Hall was 'half Machiavelli and half schoolboy'.[8] The Machiavellian Hall was a compulsive intriguer, prepared to resort to almost any methods to get results, but ruthlessness was moderated by his sheer sense of fun, making him a joy to work with.

Hall's performance as DID was partly shaped by personal attributes previously latent, partly the relatively free hand he enjoyed in recasting the role for global war, and partly his skilful exploitation of Room 40 SIGINT, especially, after 1915, its coverage of political and diplomatic traffic. Godfrey doubted if Hall was aware of his 'great gifts' prior to becoming DID, but once there he lost no time in exploiting them. He recognised that Hall was fortunate in not being constrained by institutional structures developed after 1919, and at the onset of the Second World

War. Within the Admiralty, the naval staff was still in its infancy, with no Plans Division until 1917. Beyond the Admiralty, there was no powerful chiefs of staff structure, no Joint Intelligence Committee, no independent GC&CS to handle SIGINT, no Special Operations Executive (SOE) to take charge of special operations, and no Political Warfare Executive (PWE) handling propaganda and disinformation. Hall could not only move freely across the spaces these controlled in the next war, but in areas such as political SIGINT set the agenda from scratch, confident that nobody else had either knowledge or authority to intervene. Hall, therefore, exploited the opportunities and needs of global war to expand the role of DID outside the naval sphere, achieving a level of political and strategic influence greater than any predecessor, and which would never be possible again. He demonstrated the eternal truth that he who controls the greatest secrets achieves the greatest influence.[9]

Hall's undoubted intelligence achievements and the colourful stories collected around him have ensured him favourable treatment, with many accounts bordering on hagiography. While the eulogies are often justified, aspects of his tenure require scrutiny. His Machiavellian streak extended to dealings with senior naval colleagues, where his behaviour was sometimes, at best, partisan, but at worst disloyal. He conspired to some degree against every First Lord and First Sea Lord he served under during his tenure as DID. Partly for this reason, many were not sorry to see him retire in 1919. Questions relating to his relationship with Ewing, and his passive stance over the operational exploitation of naval SIGINT were aired earlier. It is striking how most accounts of Hall's relationship with Room 40 focus on achievements drawing on the political and diplomatic, rather than naval, traffic. Here too the story is more complicated than often implied. Room 40 coverage in these areas was quite limited until late 1916, and MI1(b) made a more important contribution, including to naval interests, than usually acknowledged. Hall also had strong political views grounded in the right wing of the Conservative Party, becoming a Member of Parliament from 1919 to 1923, and later working for Conservative Central Office, where he was involved in leaking the notorious Zinoviev letter to undermine the Labour government.[10] It is doubtful that he deliberately exploited intelligence for political purposes during his time as DID, as opposed to using unconventional means in pursuit of legitimate government objectives. But the influence he exercised through intelligence relating to Ireland,[11] to Britain's role in the Middle East,[12] and on potential peace initiatives promoted by the United States during the war,[13] raises questions. Finally, the drama and excitement surrounding some of Hall's operations has diverted attention from the results actually achieved. Love of intrigue and delight in a cunning plan sometimes drove him to activity for its own sake.

Hall initiated his first political influence operation barely two months into his tenure. In early January, encouraged by Fisher and Hankey, he contacted three Britons who knew Turkey well, with good high-level contacts in the leadership, including the Grand Vizier, Prince Said Salim, and the minister of the interior, Talaat Pasha. They were Gerald Fitzmaurice, former Chief Dragoman and Oriental Counsellor at the British embassy in Constantinople; George Eady, a building contractor; and Edwin Whittall, a merchant banker. Fisher and Hankey knew Fitzmaurice from their time in the Mediterranean, and he probably recommended the others. Hall instructed the three to negotiate Turkey's withdrawal from the war, which she had joined in October alongside Germany, her resumption of neutrality, and the opening of the Dardanelles to Allied shipping. They would also ideally hand over the German battlecruiser *Goeben*, which had taken refuge in Constantinople in August. In return, Hall authorised them to offer the Turks up to £4 million (about £400 million today). He also arranged financial, logistic and communications support from Cumming. Collecting up-to-date intelligence on Turkish defences was a secondary objective. The trio were delayed getting to the eastern Mediterranean, but met Taalat Pasha's emissary at Dedeagatch on 15 March.[14] Although action to force the Dardanelles had already begun, a deal might still have been achieved but for Hall's inability to guarantee that Constantinople would remain in Turkish hands, since it had been promised to the Russians. Negotiations therefore broke down. This coincided with the receipt of the VB decrypt from Berlin suggesting that the Dardanelles defences were short of ammunition. Convinced that a naval attack could now succeed, Fisher ordered Hall to cease contact with the Turks.

Although unsuccessful, this operation established a pattern for the future, exhibiting classic elements of what became the Hall style. It illustrated his appetite for responsibility and risk. Although Churchill and Fisher instigated the dialogue with the Turks, Hall set the detailed terms and the financial inducement on his own initiative. Negotiations were well underway before he sought their further approval. Both were horrified to learn he had committed a huge sum of money without authority although, as Hall had calculated, they remained content to proceed. Neither the Cabinet nor the Foreign Office was consulted, although Hall kept Hankey in the picture, and the latter possibly informed the prime minister. The use of Cumming and SSB in an executive assistant role also became characteristic.[15]

After the Dardanelles operation ended in disaster, Churchill insisted that a purely naval assault in March could have worked, if pressed with determination. This claim rested heavily on intelligence that the defenders were short of ammunition. Testifying to the Dardanelles Commission in October 1916, Hall provided some support to Churchill. He stated that ID had good intelligence on the fortifications lining the Dardanelles, including the presence of mobile guns and howitzers. This claim depended on recent information from the Russians, since ID's last comprehensive assessment dated from 1907. The Russian information was not necessarily up to date, either, and did not address Turkish or German enhancements once they recognised in February that a British attack was imminent.[16] Inexcusably, ID failed to consult the War Office, which had shared recent intelligence with Operations Division in September 1914.[17] Nevertheless, the intelligence immediately available to Admiralty planners and to Carden in theatre was accurate enough to show that forcing the Dardanelles would be a formidable undertaking. Admiral Sir Henry Jackson, now Admiralty adviser on overseas expeditions, assessed it would put six out of eight ships in a battle squadron out of action, with the remaining two severely damaged.[18]

Hall also insisted in 1916 that intelligence for the defending forces being short of ammunition came from several sources and was authoritative. Apart from the VB decrypt mentioned earlier, which was hardly conclusive (and which he could not quote at the inquiry), his account of these sources, one of which probably reported through the Fitzmaurice trio, was unconvincing. Given Jackson's reservations, it hardly justified Fisher's conviction that a naval assault could now work. Finally, Hall claimed to have direct evidence in mid March that the Ottoman government was about to evacuate Constantinople in the belief that arrival of a British fleet was imminent.[19] Again, his probable source was Fitzmaurice or colleagues. Given what is now known of the defences in March, including the minefields on which the British were less well informed, it is unlikely that a naval assault alone could ever have succeeded. Furthermore, on the basis of what they knew at the time, this should have been the ID assessment too. The famous VB decrypt was tenuous evidence on which to overturn Jackson's view, as Hall should have recognised.[20]

The Dardanelles campaign had another enduring intelligence legacy. It stimulated Hall to adopt a proposal by the geographer Professor Henry Dickson, of University College, Reading, to establish a new section, eventually designated ID32, to research the topography and human geography of theatres of war where the Royal Navy might deploy. The section recruited some of the best academic geographers and cartographers of the day, and was initially based at the Royal Geographical Society premises in Kensington, before moving to Hertford House, Manchester Square. Twenty-seven handbooks (some multi-volume) were produced over the war, providing comprehensive coverage of individual countries, or sometimes whole regions. They covered all physical and human topics relevant to military operations, terrain, ethnology, political administration and economic resources, with particular emphasis on transport infrastructure and communications facilities. There were also manuals covering more specific topics, including a new edition of the *Atlas of the North Sea* prepared for the Hydrographer, as well as shorter 'geographic reports', suitable for attachment to military or political briefing papers, including items for the CID. As the war progressed, ID32 also produced excellent maps, often at short notice, to meet military, and sometimes political, requirements. It based its output purely on scientific research and supplied information to address naval, military, diplomatic or political questions, but did not tackle these itself. The research underpinning its handbooks, their presentation and production were of high quality, and they quickly established a reputation for rigour and accuracy. As a result, from early 1917 its information base was used in initial planning for post-war peace negotiations, although inevitably responsibility for this soon passed to the Foreign Office. The outputs of ID32 were ultimately used and exploited more by the army than the Navy, making it more logical for MI or another War Office department to have owned this capability. However, Dickson's initial approach to the War Office was rebuffed, and it was Hall who saw the need and pressed ahead, creating a base of knowledge improved and extended by his successor in the next war.[21]

The SSB suffered a sharp reduction in the quality of its naval reporting for the first six months of the war. As late as July 1915, Staff Paymaster Ernest Thring, working in E1, claimed the only useful intelligence reaching him came from Russian sources, which in the case of the *Magdeburg* haul was, indeed, hugely valuable.[22] Bywater, the most prolific SSB source, was on leave in England when war broke out, and did not return to Germany. Presumably it was judged that despite his American citizenship, his known British business and family links were too great a risk to his security. Although some important new sources came on stream during 1915, a 1919 review of the SSB's wartime naval output stated that only 260 reports were produced overall during the first three years of the war, probably less than half the output before 1914. This reflected the difficulty of penetrating Germany in wartime, but also weakness in the direction and briefing of naval agents. Better organisation led to a dramatic improvement in output during 1918.[23]

Cumming's life was made difficult until 1916 by the efforts of both the War Office and the Admiralty to restrict his remit, the scope of his operations, and even his independence. The War Office was particularly predatory, and Macdonogh tried hard at one point to make the SSB a branch of the Military Intelligence Directorate (MI), insisting that it should be designated MI1(c) alongside the newly named MI1(b).[24] Hall was more supportive and never questioned the SSB's ultimate independence, but viewed Cumming as a junior partner, and sometimes brutally reminded him of this. Part of the threat to Cumming's independence came from the fact that, once war began, both MI and ID resumed recruiting and running their own agents with enthusiasm. Despite Foreign Office resistance, the military and naval attachés also inevitably adopted a more proactive intelligence role.[25] MI focused primarily on building tactical intelligence networks to provide intelligence on the Western Front and did the same in theatres overseas. However, it readily acquired more strategic sources if opportunity presented, with no automatic assumption these should pass to Cumming. Hall's focus was always more strategic, but he was readier to collaborate with Cumming, albeit on his terms. This resumption of agent-running by MI and ID was inconsistent with the 1909 recommendations of the CID which had created the SSB. But the demands of wartime made it inevitable, and while the SSB was created to distance the hand of the British government and provide deniability, no formal bar had ever been placed on the War Office or Admiralty running their own operations. The Foreign Office could, in theory, discourage such operations, but unless it saw major political risks, it acquiesced in activity judged essential to the war effort. Nevertheless, as the war progressed, it increasingly valued the political and economic intelligence the SSB provided and intervened to protect it. In late 1915 Cumming finally lost patience with War Office interference, and appealed to Sir Arthur Nicolson, the Foreign Office permanent secretary, for his status to be clarified. Nicolson provided what was effectively a new charter for the SSB. Cumming was given sole control of secret agents overseas and was entirely responsible for how 'special information' was acquired. Equally important, the Foreign Office took over full financial control of the SSB from the War Office. Although the War Office and Admiralty continued to run their own agents for the rest of the war, often with scant oversight, Nicolson's charter effectively secured the SSB's future as a distinct independent secret service. Cumming was further strengthened by developing new customers, such as the Ministry of Munitions.[26]

Despite occasional tensions, Hall and Cumming rapidly established a good working relationship, and throughout the war they met almost daily when they were in London. Their common naval background helped, but they also viewed the intelligence business in a similar way, and probably recognised they shared certain character traits. Hall was important to Cumming as one of his key sponsors who could be relied on to keep the War Office at bay. Cumming was important to Hall, not just as a provider of useful naval intelligence, but because he could bring support for the activist, unconventional operations that so appealed to Hall. Hall was also aware of the strength of the SSB's immediate pre-war naval reporting and the prospect that this would resume in the future.[27] In covering the important neutral territories of western Europe, they soon agreed that the SSB would lead in Holland and Scandinavia, while ID would take primary responsibility for the Iberian Peninsula. Reviewing the history of secret intelligence in the First World War twenty-five years later, Hankey noted that the Admiralty had set up a special section to deal with Spain, but that Cumming often had to obtain Foreign Office funds for this, without knowing how they were to be spent.[28]

Cumming opened a station in Rotterdam in September under the shipping businessman Richard Tinsley, who had worked with the Berlin naval attaché before the war, securing him the rank of commander RNR. Tinsley was a pugnacious character, much disliked by MI officers, who suspected, probably rightly, that he engaged in financial chicanery on a substantial scale. Rotterdam became Cumming's most important centre on the Continent, running an extensive network in support of Western Front operations, contributing vital blockade intelligence and, not least, handling high-grade sources across the border in Germany. It also liaised with the Dutch military, who provided some valuable intelligence on Germany, including intercepts of communications from the German legation.[29] Tinsley worked closely with the Consul General in Rotterdam, Ernst Maxse, who throughout the war acquired useful intelligence from long-standing commercial contacts inside Germany. Maxse also maintained regular contact with Hall.[30] In Scandinavia, Cumming had important assets from before the war, notably Walter Christmas in Denmark, and the coast-watching network established by Sage and Sagette. These were handled by Lieutenant Commander Frank Stagg, an ID officer loaned by Hall, and Major Richard Holme, a Royal Artillery officer. Both were fluent in Danish and Norwegian. Stagg remained formally based in ID, working under Brandon in ID14 in Room 39BI, until September 1915, when he transferred permanently to the SSB.[31] For the first nine months of the year, he therefore worked for the SSB on a visiting basis, using an American passport, while Holme was based in the embassy in Copenhagen.[32] Christmas rejoined the Danish navy at the start of the war, and passed the SSB everything the Danes knew about German naval order of battle, movements and blockade-running, until he was betrayed and had to be evacuated to Britain in November 1915.[33] The pre-war independent coast-watching networks were expanded to cover all the exits from the Baltic from both Denmark and Sweden, and along the southern Norwegian coast, and were especially important in covering U-boat movements.[34] Stagg also achieved a productive relationship with the Norwegian navy, and capitalised on this twenty-five years later when he worked on Norway for SOE in the next war. On formal transfer to the SSB, Stagg continued to cover Scandinavia from London, but also acquired responsibility for Russian operations and liaison with ID. However, his visits to Denmark probably ceased from early 1916, after a fraught clash with the Foreign Office over blockade policy, and the position adopted by the commercial attaché, Richard Turner.[35]

As with Holland, Denmark was an ideal base for running agents into Germany. At least one important SSB naval source, designated D15, was reporting from here by the time of Jutland.[36] In May 1916 there was also regular SSB reporting on Zeppelin operations[37] and in the same month a source, designated D10, provided a long and detailed report highlighting shortages caused by the British blockade.[38] The previous autumn there was evidently an agent with access to circles around Crown Prince Rupprecht, then commander of the German 6th Army. It was probably this source who reported suspicion in some German government circles that the Irish nationalist leader, Sir Roger Casement, was working for Britain.[39]

Although, unlike Holland and Scandinavia, Spain was geographically isolated from the central powers, it was strategically important to both sides. For Germany, it was a critical communications link to the wider world, especially the Americas, offered a valuable base for intelligence operations into the Mediterranean and North Africa, could potentially be used to refuel U-boats and support blockade-runners, and provided a vital source of strategic raw materials, notably wolfram, the ore yielding tungsten, a key component of high-quality steel. Germany could also exploit the support of a large expatriate community of seventy thousand. Britain sought to deny these benefits to Germany, but it too depended on Spanish supplies. Two-thirds of its steel production in 1916 used Spanish ores, and almost all its pyrites came from Huelva. It required Spain to remain neutral or tilt towards the Allies. Spanish attitudes to the warring powers were divided. There was significant German sympathy within the royal court, the army, and the conservative Carlists. The Liberal party, led by Alvero de Figueroa, Conde de Romanones, which held power most of the period from 1912 to 1918, and business circles generally supported the Allies.

Hall began with important assets in Spain. There was the VB traffic between Berlin and Madrid, which Room 40 began reading in January 1915, and the Gibraltar intelligence centre, under Major Charles Thoroton, always known as 'Charles the Bold', provided a valuable base independent of the Madrid embassy. Hall also diverted Richard, Lord Herschell, one of Ewing's initial recruits, to become his private secretary soon after becoming DID. Herschell, who had been Lord in Waiting to King George V, moved in European royal circles and was a close friend of King Alfonso XIII and his wife Victoria Eugenie. This link had obvious intelligence potential, and Hall put Herschell in overall charge of Spanish operations. In addition, he recruited the novelist and former Liberal Party Member of Parliament, A E W Mason (best known for *The Four Feathers*), perhaps on the recommendation of Churchill or Fisher, to develop an operational network.[40] Mason was the first of a long line of writers who contributed to British naval intelligence over the next thirty years, including Compton Mackenzie, Alan Hillgarth, Charles Morgan, Graham Greene and Ian Fleming.

SSB operational support for Hall began early. In addition to helping with Eady and Whittall in Turkey, on 9 February Hall asked Cumming to send a man to Santiago and Punta Arenas to assist with the hunt for *Dresden*.[41] On 13 December the Admiralty learnt from Charles Milward, the British consul in Punta Arenas, that *Dresden* had arrived there two days earlier, following the battle off the Falklands, to refuel, and communicate with Germany through the German consul. To avoid internment, *Dresden* left after thirty hours, before she could be intercepted by her British pursuers. There followed a three-month cat-and-mouse game in the desolate coastal waters of southern Chile, with both sides drawing on expatriate support. On 6 January Fisher instructed Milward secretly to acquire copies of *Dresden*'s signals and forward them telegraphically to the Admiralty, authorising him to spend up to £2000. Milward did not respond, probably because the message went astray, and by early February the Admiralty was losing confidence in him, hence Hall's decision to use Cumming.[42] Cumming was also allowed £2000, an enormous sum for him and about one-third of his current annual budget. This investment demonstrates that the Admiralty not only wanted to chase down *Dresden*, but to collect every signal that might provide a 'crib', a plain-language phrase or passage likely to match a given piece of encrypted text, to help Room 40 to break the latest HVB cipher key. Cumming's agent, deployed within two days, probably helped pin down *Dresden*'s whereabouts, although the final interception came after *Glasgow* managed to break the HVB cipher locally.[43]

Cumming's relationship with Hall, in contrast to that with Macdonogh and MI staff, was sufficiently close and trusting for them regularly to exchange personnel where they saw mutual intelligence advantage. Hall therefore passed Cumming Frank Stagg, while Cumming loaned Hector Bywater. Hall's most valuable transfer to Cumming, made in July 1915, was Pierre-Marie Cavrois O'Caffrey, a French Jesuit priest of Irish stock, who offered his services to the commander of the Royal Naval Air Service (RNAS) wing based at Dunkirk, Charles Samson, in September 1914. O'Caffrey rapidly demonstrated remarkable ability to recruit useful sources behind German lines, and Samson got him commissioned as a lieutenant RNR and appointed him unit intelligence officer. When O'Caffrey offered to investigate the Zeppelin bases being established in Belgium, Samson realised he had a source with strategic potential, and over the next few months O'Caffrey was taken over first by the Director of the Royal Navy Air Department, Captain Murray Sueter, who then passed him to Hall.[44] O'Caffrey's reporting on the Zeppelins led to a successful raid by RNAS aircraft on the sheds near Evere in June 1915. His Belgian network also reported on wider naval requirements, notably the results achieved by the Royal Navy's bombardment of Zeebrugge in August, and details of the new Flanders U-boat bases. By the end of August, a year after starting his intelligence work, he had apparently produced 162 reports, many of high quality and often including detailed maps.[45] Hall's decision to pass him to Cumming probably reflected his recognition that O'Caffrey could address requirements beyond the naval sphere. He could rely on Cumming to exploit and fund this wider potential without neglecting naval interests. By the autumn, Cumming had put O'Caffrey in charge of a new SSB air section, which he headed until mid 1917, when he moved to Greece. While aviation reporting from Belgium and German-occupied France dominated O'Caffrey's SSB output, he also contributed on poison gas production, and supported Tinsley in developing agents within Germany.[46]

Although the start of the war was a low point for the SSB's German naval coverage, especially with the loss of Bywater, the outlook changed dramatically in November 1914 when a former German naval engineer officer approached the British legation in The Hague and offered his services as an agent. This was Karl Krüger, designated TR16 by the SSB, and its most important source during the First World War. TR16 produced a steady flow of valuable intelligence on the German navy from early 1915, and continued reporting for twenty years after the war, until he was caught in 1939 and subsequently executed. His original motivation was a desire for revenge on his former service after his court martial for striking a fellow officer who was a relative of the Kaiser. However, as with most agents, once committed to spying, other factors came into play, not least the substantial sums he was paid. Meetings took place monthly, almost all of them in Holland where, with some help from the SSB, he established good business cover. Over his long career, he proved highly disciplined and professional, never missing a meeting, and writing nothing down until established in a safe house, when he wrote out his reports for his case officer, drawing on his extraordinary photographic memory.[47]

TR16's first known reports date from April 1915 and covered U-boat construction, which featured regularly through the war and again from the mid 1930s. Few aspects of current German naval strength, building progress, and design and development were beyond his reach. He travelled regularly to all the main German ports, where he drew on his own observations, and tapped numerous good contacts. He reported on Zeppelin construction and operations and the long-range guns used for the bombardment of Paris in 1918. He also provided valuable insights on political and economic conditions in Germany. More than fifty of his wartime reports survive, many marked with complimentary comments from Hall and others.[48] A post-war evaluation of his reporting described it as always accurate, up to date, and of the 'very greatest possible value'.[49] His finest wartime coup, his post-Jutland report, is described later.

Meanwhile, over the winter of 1914/15 and the following spring, Hall executed two major coastal surveillance operations, using borrowed yachts in which he installed hand-picked naval crews under civilian cover. The first, conducted by *Sayonara* during December and January, focused on the west coast of Ireland. It followed discussion with Sir Basil Thomson, head of Special Branch at Scotland Yard, regarding intelligence that Sir Roger Casement planned an imminent landing there with German advisers and arms. Casement had travelled to Germany at the end of October to win support for an armed insurrection. Thomson had some insight into Casement's activities from coverage of Irish nationalist exile groups in the United States. More detailed intelligence of his movements and plans came from his Norwegian manservant, Adler (or Eivind) Christensen, who approached the British legation when Casement stopped off in Christiania (modern Oslo), offering his services as an informer in return for payment. The Consul General, Mansfeldt Findlay, promised Christensen, apparently on his own initiative, the huge sum of £5000 (£500,000 today) if he facilitated Casement's capture. At the initial meeting, Christensen provided copies of several incriminating papers, including a cipher message from the German ambassador in Washington, Count Johann von Bernstorff, to the chancellor, Theobald von Bethmann-Hollweg.[50] He returned a month later, tasked by Casement with arranging support in Norway for passage to Ireland, including purchase of a yacht. Between late November and early January, further intelligence passed to Findlay, including letters from Casement to Irish leaders in the United States, indicated a landing on the Irish west coast in January. Casement's group would now cross the North Sea in the Danish coaster *Mjolnir* before meeting a yacht owned by a rich American off Ireland. Casement had charts for the voyage showing the location of British minefields.[51]

Hall wanted *Sayonara* to monitor Casement's two vessels and intercept them, with naval assistance if necessary once they were committed, seizing all participants afloat and ashore. *Sayonara* would also identify possible landing sites for Casement, his Irish republican volunteers and arms shipments, and obtain intelligence on those preparing to receive them. She would pose as the yacht of a wealthy American on a winter cruise, allowing her to impersonate Casement's American yacht if circumstances permitted.[52] She would also watch for U-boats using covert sites along the Irish coast to refuel. Thomson found a Boer War veteran and well-travelled businessman with a gift for languages called Wilfred Howell to pose as the American owner with suitable nationalist sympathies, while Hall recruited Lieutenant F M Simon RNR, who had served with him in *Cornwall* and could also pass as an American, as his skipper. The *Sayonara* team were convincing enough to persuade local Royal Navy units, who had not been briefed by Hall, and senior members of the Loyalist community that they were up to no good. It is unlikely they won the trust of any nationalist supporters, and the primary purpose of the operation was defeated because Casement abandoned this attempt. It remains unclear whether this was because Christensen confessed his treachery to Casement, or the Germans failed to deliver the promised support. Despite Hall's later insistence, it is doubtful there were any useful results.[53]

The *Sayonara* operation was imaginative, well-crafted and expensive. It was also planned, executed and terminated before Hall had been in post three months and while he had other pressing priorities. The primary goal was not speculative but drew on excellent intelligence from sources in Ireland, as well as Christensen.[54] Given the febrile background in Ireland earlier in 1914, senior British ministers found the prospect of a major figure such as Casement arriving with substantial German support alarming.[55] Hall's investment was therefore justifiable. Nevertheless, the operation still defied logic. Ireland was part of the United Kingdom, and British forces could move freely wherever they wished. Given uncertainty over Casement's precise destination, the Royal Navy could provide more effective coastal surveillance than a single yacht, and could better manage an interception. It was true that *Sayonara* might conduct covert monitoring while a British warship would arouse concern. But the chances of achieving this in practice were slim. The prospect of U-boats refuelling in Ireland without drawing immediate British attention was also implausible. The operation did make Hall an integral part of the intelligence operation monitoring Casement and wider Irish extremism. He was copied in on intelligence from Thomson, MO5(g) and War Office sources, and was active in deploying his own assets, later including Room 40. This had important consequences in the run-up to the 1916 Easter rising. Casement papers through 1915–16 underline that relations across Britain's developing intelligence and security community were closer than often suggested. Hall later implied that Room 40 monitored some German diplomatic messages dealing with Casement's visit contemporaneously. That was not the case, although conceivably some messages, in addition to those supplied by Christensen, were acquired through human sources in the United States.[56]

Hall was pleased enough with the *Sayonara* trip to mount a similar operation in the spring of 1915 along the Atlantic coast of Spain using the yacht *Vergemere*, loaned by Commander-in-Chief Portsmouth. This time the skipper and crew (all naval volunteers) presented as British, and the expedition was led by an affable and worldly Anglo-Irish baronet, Sir Hercules Langrishe. Its primary objective was to identify support for German naval operations, such as refuelling of U-boats or blockade-running. A second goal, through lavish entertainment, was to talent-spot useful contacts and potential agents, Spanish or expatriate.[57] The *Vergemere* operation had more justification than that of *Sayonara*. The Royal Navy could not explore neutral Spain's coastal waters, and U-boats did occasionally refuel in Spanish waters from late 1915 onward. Furthermore, by spring 1915, through coverage of the Madrid VB traffic, Room 40 was gaining a good window into German intelligence activity throughout Spain. The *Vergemere* expedition was the first of several operations capitalising on these insights and involving yachts in coastal waters. Cumming acquired two vessels for Hall that spring, *Beryl* and *St George*, for U-boat-hunting, albeit with no useful results.[58] The VB window explains why, in the second half of the year, Hall deployed Mason for an extended period and sent Gerald Kelly (later the painter and President of the Royal Academy, Sir Gerald) to Seville.[59] Only partial records of Hall's Spanish operations survive, and Mason's own accounts often blurred fact and fiction. However, Mason had notable achievements, exposing U-boat use of Cartagena, and badly disrupting the German intelligence organisation in Barcelona and Morocco.[60] In late 1915 or 1916 Hall's Spanish network also established a link, through Thoroton, to the immensely wealthy businessman and financier Juan March. This initiated an enduring and important intelligence relationship, valuable in the First World War, although here he probably dealt with both sides, but more critical for Hall's successors in the Second where March was important in ensuring Spain's neutrality.[61]

The two best-documented Spanish operations occurred in parallel over the winter of 1917/18. Both were complex affairs, which Hall personally directed and orchestrated, with an impact bordering on the strategic. Both depended initially on leads from SIGINT, but exploited different strands of intelligence from multiple sources. They then required the skilled exercise of political and diplomatic influence as well as direct naval action. The first operation was the disruption of a German attempt to smuggle out wolfram known as the *Erri Berro* affair. The supply line was successfully broken, but the attempt to sink the U-boats taking delivery of the wolfram, for onward transport to Germany failed. The other operation sought to counter a German plan to smuggle anthrax and glanders germs through Spain to Argentina to infect animals bound for Britain. This was part of a much wider biological warfare campaign against animals supporting the Allied war effort, including reindeer sledging British arms to Russia through northern Norway, and cattle supplied to Russia from Romania. Countering the Argentine element was only partly achieved, but Hall's disruption of the wider operation was largely successful. Furthermore, following a briefing from Herschell on Germany's biological programme, King Alfonso ordered the expulsion of their ambassador Prince Ratibor. The *Erri Berro* affair had already discredited the naval attaché, who was withdrawn by Berlin. The German embassy's role as an intelligence hub was effectively ended.[62]

9

Hall's Intelligence War in the
United States 1915–1916

From the start of his tenure, another major focus for Hall was the United States. Following the outbreak of war, Britain had two immediate intelligence priorities here: identifying and countering German attempts to sabotage Allied war supplies, and countering German exploitation of individuals and groups based in the United States sponsoring unrest in British Empire territories, notably Ireland and India. During 1915, a third requirement gained traction – American attitudes to the war, and encouraging her support for Britain through covert means. With the partial exception of the first issue, security of Allied supplies through American ports, none of these requirements were the responsibility of the Admiralty and therefore the business of ID. The dominant position that Hall acquired in the intelligence war conducted in and with America partly reflected the British personnel on the ground in the first part of the war, partly Hall's unique eye for an intelligence opportunity, and his ability and willingness then to exploit it to strategic advantage, and partly the privileged insights conferred by Room 40 SIGINT.

Hall's immediate entry into American affairs resulted from the presence of an energetic and effective naval attaché in Washington, the Australian-born 45-year-old Captain Guy Gaunt, who had arrived in June 1914. By contrast, there was no military attaché until 1917, and no SSB presence until late 1915, when Cumming deployed Sir William Wiseman, whose role and achievements are discussed later. Britain had no covert intelligence capability, apart from a Home Office agent at the consulate in New York, monitoring expatriate support for Irish extremist groups with a small secret service fund held by the Consul General Sir Courtney Bennett. There was also a small network established by William Hopkinson, a retired Indian policeman working for the Canadian Department of the

.nterior, watching Indian revolutionary groups on the West Coast of the United States, but this lapsed when Hopkinson was murdered by a Sikh extremist in October 1914.[1]

Prior to his posting, Gaunt had enjoyed a successful but conventional naval career, culminating in command of the battleships *Majestic* and *Thunderer*. As attaché, he displayed other qualities. He was an outgoing and likeable man, and a fine horseman and yachtsman, qualities which won him important and influential American friends. These included Teddy and Franklin Roosevelt, the banker J P Morgan Junior, whose firm dominated American financing of the British war effort and supervised its arms purchases, his partners, Edward Stettinius and Henry Davison, the Secretary of State (from late 1915) Robert Lansing and Colonel Edward House, President Woodrow Wilson's most important adviser on foreign affairs.[2] In October 1915 House accepted Gaunt's offer to provide him with secure communications with the British government. During 1916, Gaunt had around fifty meetings with House, who by the end of that year evidently found Gaunt a more useful contact than the ambassador, Sir Cecil Spring-Rice.[3] But Gaunt was more than a shrewd diplomatic networker. He possessed operational skills that made him a natural for the intelligence world. He was adept at manipulating relationships, ruthless in pursuing his objectives, and could look after himself on the street. In many respects, he was like Hall, making the two natural partners.[4] To support Gaunt, Hall, on the recommendation of Cumming, twice deployed Hector Bywater on visits to New York during 1915, where he posed as a German-American tasked with infiltrating a German sabotage cell in Hoboken, New Jersey.[5]

Soon after the war began, Gaunt was approached by a Czech nationalist, Emanuel Victor Voska, sent by the Czech leader Thomas Masaryk to establish a covert support network from Czech and Slovak exiles in the United States, directed against the Austro-Hungarian empire. Voska, whose extraordinary intelligence career spanned more than three decades, offered the services of this embryonic network to Gaunt. Over the next year, they together planned and executed the infiltration of almost every significant German and Austrian organisation and operation in the United States, yielding a treasure trove of intelligence, comprising operational leads, and valuable military and diplomatic documents.[6] The value of Gaunt's contribution is evident in the award of a CMG in the 1916 New Year Honours, followed by a knighthood and promotion to rear admiral in 1918.[7]

Germany started the war holding significant cards in the United States. Ambassador von Bernstorff had six years of experience, understood

America, and was well-connected. The naval attaché, Captain Karl Boy-
Ed, was popular with the US Navy, had worked closely with Tirpitz, and
had headed Department N, the office of naval intelligence, as had the
ambassador in Mexico, Paul von Hintze. The military attaché, Major
Franz von Papen, was well connected within the German military and
would precede Adolf Hitler as chancellor in 1932. When war began,
both attachés were tasked with undermining the Allied war effort and
lavishly funded for a covert campaign of propaganda and sabotage,
subject to oversight from Bernstorff.[8] They could draw on a substantial
and supportive German community, and the German ships and crews
contained in New York and other ports were an ideal base from which
to mount sabotage operations against British shipping. Irish and Indian
groups based in the United States and committed to violent action
against Britain were receptive to German support. Furthermore, while
the attitudes and values of the Wilson administration and the American
political class were more aligned with the Allies, Wilson was determined
to avoid taking sides, to keep America out and to protect her commercial
and trade interests. Although he privately voiced pro-Entente views early
in the war, and he was appalled by German action towards Belgium, the
tightening British blockade made him more neutral. In 1916, following
British blacklisting of American companies, Wilson told Walter Page, his
ambassador in London, that he now saw the war, not as a liberal crusade
against German aggression, but rather a quarrel to settle economic
rivalries between Germany and England. The Kaiser's U-boats were an
outrage, but British 'navalism' was no less evil, and posed a far greater
challenge for the United States.[9]

During the first half of the war, the German team achieved some
notable successes: the sabotage of numerous British and some American
ships and cargoes, disruption to British war orders in American factories,
and interference with transport to ports. Operations orchestrated by
a special agent of the general staff, a commander in the naval reserve,
Fritz von Rintelen, the notorious 'Dark Invader', during a four-month
stay from April 1915, were especially effective.[10] During that summer,
there were explosions in thirteen outbound Entente ships, and in ten
factories involved in war production for the Allies.[11] Rintelen created the
network responsible for the greatest single feat of German sabotage, the
spectacular destruction in July the following year of a large quantity of
munitions bound for Russia in the 'Black Tom' explosion off New York
harbour, which also killed seven United States citizens.[12] Nevertheless,
the German operations lacked strategic coherence. Their successes came
within a scattergun approach, producing numerous poorly conceived

and insecure operations, which therefore failed. Early failures included two ambitious attempts by von Papen and Hans Tauscher, the Krupps representative for America, to supply arms to revolutionary groups in India, and plans to sabotage one of the main rail routes into Canada, and the Welland Canal linking the Great Lakes with the St Lawrence river.[13] Through 1915, much of Germany's covert campaign was identified by Voska's network and reported to Gaunt, who then worked with Hall to expose it to the American authorities and in the press. Gaunt was effective at winning support from American officials of intermediate rank, notably the head of the New York bomb squad, Thomas Tunney, of Protestant Irish origin with a brother in the Royal Irish Constabulary, and Nicholas Biddle, the deputy police commissioner. His main press contact was John R Rathom, editor of the *Providence Journal*, with good links to the *New York Times*. Rathom was a brilliant, if unscrupulous, journalist, virulently anti-German, and happy to promote any revelations Gaunt and Hall could supply, making him the ideal channel for influence.

The biggest damage to the German campaign in the United States came from two successive operations mounted by Hall, with Gaunt's help, in August 1915. Rintelen had fallen out with the two German attachés, who successfully plotted his recall. Hall, alerted by Gaunt drawing on intelligence from Voska, successfully intercepted Rintelen during his voyage back to Germany under Swiss disguise, and brought him to London for interrogation. Rintelen's admissions, supplemented by papers found in the luggage of his travel companion, the arms trader Andrew Meloy, produced valuable insights into German covert operations in which, not surprisingly, Rintelen readily implicated the attachés. Almost contemporaneously, Voska reported that the Germans were using an American journalist, F J Archibald, as an occasional courier, and Hall had him lifted from his ship at Falmouth barely a fortnight after Rintelen.[14] Less than ten days after his interrogation of Rintelen, Hall provided a selective account to Edward Bell, the second secretary at the American embassy.[15] In addition to extensive evidence of German sabotage operations, Hall revealed that the German general staff had tasked Rintelen with executing regime change in Mexico, despite knowing that this directly contravened American policy and perceived interests.

Bell had arrived in London in September 1913, a few months after Page became ambassador, and with whom he became close. He was an anglophile and his second wife, whom he married in 1914, was British, from an established army family. He was intelligent, with a brilliant intuitive mind, energetic, proactive and immensely personable, all qualities that appealed to Hall. By early 1915, Bell had prime responsibility for embassy relations with the Admiralty, War Office and Scotland Yard, and was also tasked with liaison on intelligence and security matters, making Hall a priority contact.[16] Bell's role reflected the fact that there was no permanent American military presence on the staff of the embassy until Captain William MacDougall was appointed naval attaché in September 1916. Furthermore, the United States Army had no formal military intelligence organisation between 1914–17. The US Navy had an Office of Naval Intelligence (ONI), established contemporaneously with the Foreign Intelligence Committee in 1882, although it only became an independent department in 1915. Despite a good attaché network, its foreign collection capability before 1917 was poorly developed, and even after American entry into the war it focused primarily on monitoring shipping in American waters, on coastal defence, and internal security.[17]

Bell's liaison role became more important and influential at the beginning of 1916, with the establishment of the Bureau of Secret Intelligence (BSI) within the State Department. Its purpose was to act as a clearing house for intelligence relating to the war and its impact on the United States. Although formally accountable to Lansing as Secretary of State, the impetus for the BSI came primarily from House, who ensured it reported to the Counselor, Frank Polk, a lawyer drawn from House's close circle.[18] Leland Harrison, the new head of BSI, was equally close to House, while his deputy, Gordon Auchincloss, was House's son-in-law. The BSI was thus not only an intelligence clearing house, but a parallel foreign service which House could use and direct on behalf of Wilson, independently of Lansing.[19] Although BSI gradually acquired some independent intelligence sources, at this stage its intelligence mainly comprised material shared by foreign military and civilian intelligence agencies. The British were prolific providers, and Bell thus became BSI's most important source.[20]

Bell later described Hall as simply irreplaceable, 'a perfectly marvelous person but the coldest blooded proposition that ever was – he'd cut a man's heart out and hand it back to him'.[21] Hall, for his part, saw Bell as a valuable channel to the American government, one he could manage directly, rather than working through the Foreign Office or Gaunt. By mid 1915, Bell was not only in close and regular contact with Hall, but also Herschell and Hall's personal assistant, Claud Serocold. Bell's report on Rintelen, revealing the sheer scale of German sabotage activity, as well as their interference in Mexico, and directly implicating the attachés, badly damaged Germany's standing within both the Wilson administration and wider political establishment. Lansing was convinced the attachés should be expelled, while the Mexico affair brought important future consequences in 1917.

The 110 documents recovered from Archibald were a rich haul. They included a report from the Austrian ambassador, Konstantin Dumba, describing his role in fomenting strikes among munition workers, as well as uncomplimentary references to senior American officials, seventeen reports from the German embassy, sabotage progress reports from the attachés, and more material relating to Mexico.[22] Hall wanted to share this material with Bell, judging correctly that it would compound the damage done by Rintelen's information. However, the Foreign Office refused approval, fearing adverse repercussions from Archibald's status as an American citizen, and preferring to publish extracts in a parliamentary White Paper. After appealing to Balfour as First Lord without success, Hall disobeyed instructions and briefed Bell anyway, claiming the Americans must have got the information from their own sources in the United States. Wilson agreed to expel the Austrian ambassador, but initially resisted action against the attachés, before acceding at the end of the year to demands from Lansing and a press campaign, partly orchestrated by Gaunt, that they too should go. Hall could not interfere with von Papen as an accredited diplomat on his journey home in January 1916, but searched his luggage, yielding further valuable and incriminating material.[23]

If the German team in the United States had been more careful and selective, avoided damage to American property or action perceived as directly hostile to American interests, and focused on fostering resentment towards the British blockade, they might have achieved more enduring damage to the British war effort. As it was, the steady exposure of their covert campaign was not only a public-relations disaster for the German cause, but eroded their limited political support in the United States, making a shift from neutrality to intervention in support of the Allies more likely.[24] Hall, ably assisted by Gaunt, exploited his opportunities with great skill, and deserves credit for orchestrating a significant strategic defeat on Germany. But the Germans made his life easier.

There is a persistent belief that Room 40 SIGINT played a significant role in countering the German operations in the United States through 1915 and the first half of 1916 through interception of both German and American communications. Similarly, that Room 40 had extensive coverage of German support for the 1916 Easter Rising in Dublin, much of which was orchestrated from the United States. Hall is credited both with creating the Room 40 political section that made this coverage possible, and with selective use of the resulting intelligence to suit his own agenda. In reality, prior to mid 1916, the contribution of Room 40 to German operations in America and the German-Irish connection was limited.[25]

Room 40 only began work on German diplomatic codes and ciphers when George Young's political section, based in Room 47, was established in autumn 1915 at the instigation of Ewing, not Hall. The two codebooks which provided the foundation of Room 40's diplomatic work were captured during a British raid on the German consulate at Bushire on the Persian Gulf coast in early March 1915. The claim that ID, working in collaboration with the SSB, had earlier acquired a German diplomatic codebook in the autumn of 1914 after recruiting an Austrian communicator, Alexander Szek, following German occupation of the main radio station in Brussels, lacks credibility.[26] The fascinating story of the Persian capture, the identity of the codebooks involved, their subsequent exploitation, and the reasons for the obfuscations and confusion in the subsequent histories of Room 40 diplomatic codebreaking and coverage are brilliantly described elsewhere. Some of the more colourful elements in earlier accounts do not stand scrutiny, and Hall's personal role is not as central or romantic as he and his disciples later suggested.[27] The traffic that could be directly decrypted using the two codebooks taken at Bushire (known as 3512 and 89734) was of limited value. However, they gave Young's Room 47 team, with support from Rotter, sufficient insight into the structure of German diplomatic communications to enable them to identify and reconstruct the more important codes. This was a laborious and time-consuming process with the limited staff available, and contributed to Rotter breaking down in August.[28] But by November, Room 47 could read messages between Berlin and Tehran, enabling Britain and its Russian ally to defeat the German attempt to win over Persia at a critical moment in the war.[29] The following May, the political section pioneered the use of Hollerith punched card machines, which greatly speeded cryptographic investigation. This was an innovation of lasting importance, and the producer of the machines, the British Tabulating Machine Company, was closely linked with British codebreaking for the next thirty years, producing electromechanical 'bombes' for Bletchley Park in the next war.[30] With this help, by the summer of 1916 it became possible to read currently a selection of confidential diplomatic correspondence between Berlin, Madrid, Lisbon, Washington, and occasionally other capitals. This contributed to the defeat of German intrigues in Spain, Portugal, Ireland and Morocco, including a series of risings in the latter, and kept the British government sighted on most German diplomatic activity in North America and southwest Europe.[31]

Decrypting German diplomatic traffic was not enough. Room 40 had to collect it, which was not straightforward. After it was denied access to the international cable network by British action at the start of the war, Germany used three options for communicating with the United States. The most important was the service provided by neutral Sweden of including encrypted German messages disguised within its own diplomatic traffic. Adding German traffic on the direct route between Washington and Stockholm aroused British suspicions, and this was halted in early 1915 following complaints from the Foreign Office. Thereafter, Swedish help continued, but the transfer to and from Swedish hands took place between the German embassy and Swedish legation in Buenos Aires. Between Buenos Aires and Stockholm, German messages were secreted within Swedish diplomatic traffic, usually passing along British-controlled cables across the Atlantic and North Sea. This method became known to Room 40 as the 'Swedish roundabout'. A second method used more rarely, with American approval, was the American diplomatic channel between Washington and Berlin via Copenhagen. Bernstorff argued successfully that to provide a negotiating channel for the Americans with his government, they must provide him with communications facilities. The final route was by long-range radio between the German station at Sayville on Long Island and Nauen. Its value was limited, because the American government applied strict censorship and neutrality rules to radio, and prohibited use of encryption.[32]

Since Swedish traffic to and from Buenos Aires passed over British cables, Room 40 could obtain copies from the British cable censor MI8, and then identify and decrypt the German traffic buried within it. However, although puzzled as to how German traffic to and from North America was routed, Room 40 did not identify the 'roundabout' until July 1916, following clues in an intercepted letter from the German minister in Mexico, Heinrich von Eckhardt, revealing continuing Swedish complicity in facilitating German communications. Hall then had Room 40 examine all Swedish traffic acquired by the censor, exposing numerous ciphered German diplomatic messages for Room 40 to attack.[33] Naturally, Room 40 focused first on decrypting current traffic. Only in late autumn did it have capacity to investigate traffic sent before mid 1916.[34]

Meanwhile, it was MI1(b), not Room 40, which worked on American diplomatic traffic, probably achieving its first decrypts by late autumn 1915. It certainly decrypted messages from Colonel Edward House when he arrived in London the following January.[35] MI1(b) turned to diplomatic codes in early 1915, because its access to German army radio traffic, with the notable exception of army airships, largely ceased in late 1914, leaving it with spare capacity to explore the plethora of diplomatic traffic available from the censor.[36] In practice, due to staffing limitations (it still had only ten personnel by autumn 1916, although it quadrupled in size over the following year), MI1(b) concentrated almost exclusively on America through 1915, as the most important neutral power with traffic readily accessible. The following year it extended its effort, successfully attacking Greek, Swiss and Spanish codes, and in 1917 added Danish, Dutch, Swedish, Norwegian, Italian, Japanese and Vatican traffic.[37] By early 1916 there was renewed collaboration between Room 40 and MI1(b), and a de facto, if never precise, division of labour, Room 40 focusing on enemy diplomatic traffic (reflecting its growing insight into German diplomatic codes) and MI1(b) on allies and neutrals. Co-operation strengthened further later in the year, because Room 40 required MI1(b) assistance in locating German messages hidden within American and Swedish traffic, and there was a regular dialogue here between Denniston in Room 40 and Captain Gordon Crocker of MI1(b).[38] A further elaboration in the relationship came in spring 1916, when the War Office took over strategic responsibility for United Kingdom air defence. This coincided with the establishment of a specialist radio interception section by the War Office, known as MI1(e). This eventually had nine stations in the United Kingdom focused primarily on the air threat, seven in France along the Western Front, and further representation in overseas theatres.[39]

The attack on German diplomatic traffic altered the balance of power in the relationship between Ewing and Hall. As noted earlier, it was Ewing who established the Room 40 Political Section, and formally this remained under Ewing's direction for the first year of its life until October 1916, when Ewing moved to Edinburgh. However, with the notable exception of the radio traffic between Berlin and Madrid, most of the important German diplomatic traffic was delivered through cable, and collection here was effectively controlled by Hall, not Ewing. Either it came from MI1(b), in the case of the American traffic, or from MI8, in the case of the Swedish roundabout, or, much more rarely, from the mail censor MI9, all relationships which Hall directed and managed. Hall believed he was better suited to exploit German diplomatic traffic than Ewing, and saw his control over cable as the means to achieve this, circumventing Ewing's formal status. Rather than negotiate Room 40 decryption effort with Ewing, he commissioned this privately, without Ewing's knowledge, using Denniston, Dilly Knox and Nigel de Grey, the last a linguist from the publisher Heinemann spotted by Hall after he joined the RNVR, and supplying them with additional, mainly female, support staff. Hall discussed what had been collected on what routes, what it might reveal, and set the priorities. He then took the product and decided how it should be used.[40]

Prior to the detection of the Swedish roundabout in late summer 1916, the only German diplomatic traffic from North America available to

Room 40 through cable intercept was the small quantity concealed in American traffic, and even here the highest-grade code was not broken before the middle of the year. With one significant exception, Room 40 did not, therefore, read a series of eleven telegrams between Berlin and the German embassy, issued between 10 February and 22 April, relating to German support for the Easter Rising in Ireland on 24 April 1916. The exception was a telegram sent by Bernstorff on 18 February:

> The Irish leader, John Devoy, informs me that rising is to begin in Ireland on Easter Saturday. Please send arms to (arrive at) Limerick, west coast of Ireland between Good Friday and Easter Saturday. To put it off longer is impossible. Let me know if help may be expected from Germany.

The reason Room 40 read this was that, unlike others in the series, it was sent under American cover, included surreptitiously in a telegram concerning *Lusitania* negotiations, which the Americans were therefore willing to facilitate. Since MI1(b) were now reading American traffic, they identified the German telegram and sent it to Room 40. Here Room 40 had a further stroke of luck. They had not yet broken the high-grade code used for the *Lusitania* message, but spotted there was a second message, encrypted in a military *Satzbuch* code. This had become readable through analysis of traffic on the Berlin–Madrid route. Once Room 40 decrypted this message, warning of an Easter rising with possible German support was passed to relevant military authorities by the Director of Military Intelligence, and by the Admiralty to Admiral Queenstown on 23 March, providing, therefore, a month's notice. By itself, this decrypt was too vague to guarantee naval interception of incoming German arms shipments. However, subsequent Room 40 coverage of German naval traffic disclosed that a ship disguised as a tramp steamer would leave Germany for Ireland on 12 April, escorted by two submarines. The ship, *Libau*, posing as the Norwegian *Aud* and carrying a significant quantity of arms, was intercepted by the Royal Navy sloop *Bluebell* near Tralee Bay on 20 April, and scuttled herself while being escorted to Queenstown. The submarine *U-19* then landed Sir Roger Casement with two companions at Tralee the following day, where all three were rapidly apprehended.[41]

Casement was removed to London to be interrogated at Scotland Yard by Thomson, Hall and Frank Hall (no relation), the MI5 officer responsible for Ireland.[42] Hall's presence in this interrogation reflected his close involvement in the Casement affair since late 1914, but Casement's transport by U-boat was a specific and legitimate naval intelligence interest, as was the procurement and activity of *Libau*. So was anything Casement was prepared to admit about his dealings with German officials in the United States, given ID's dominant role there, or insights into German communications that might help Room 40. Thomson also had a justified regard for Hall's abilities as an interrogator. In the event, Casement provided little of value that his interrogators did not already know.[43]

Hall's direction of the British intelligence effort in the United States through 1915–16, his associated contributions to forestalling German operations in Ireland and India, and his early recognition of the intelligence opportunities offered by attacking German diplomatic communications, were significant achievements. They all display Hall's outstanding skills as an intelligence chief, his eye for an opportunity, his intuitive sense for how disparate pieces of information contributed to a bigger picture and, above all, his ability and willingness to exploit intelligence for strategic advantage. If these operations displayed Hall's best qualities, they also fostered a taste for taking personal initiatives and acting outside conventional boundaries. Taking action on intelligence and ensuring it was used to best advantage, especially in wartime, was laudable. However, action in the United States, in Irish affairs, or by exploiting diplomatic decrypts as Room 47 capability here developed, invariably had political consequences. In all these areas, Hall is frequently accused of taking political decisions not only on his own initiative, but in pursuit of his own agenda.[44]

Hall's influence as DID over naval policy and operations was constrained by established Admiralty organisation and structure. He was responsible for collecting and distributing intelligence, but decisions on action fell to others in the war staff. He could withhold or prioritise intelligence, and advise on its reliability, but was always accountable to the Admiralty command chain. Since he did not formally control Room 40 until 1917, he had limited influence over the distribution of naval SIGINT, and no authority over its use. In dealing with intelligence on German sabotage or subversion operations outside the conventional naval sphere, or political intelligence produced by Room 47 from diplomatic decrypts, the constraints on Hall were more limited. Despite Ewing's formal responsibility for Room 47, Hall received copies of everything it produced, and had complete control of its cable-generated intelligence. He could, therefore, largely determine both action and circulation for German political and diplomatic intelligence from intercepts. In theory, he remained accountable for the output of Room 47, through the chief of war staff to the First Sea Lord and First Lord. In practice, they were dependent on what Hall chose to tell them and, given the complexity of operations in these areas, were poorly equipped to challenge him.

There is little evidence that Hall deliberately withheld important intelligence under any category, certainly in the first half of the war. The claim that he did so with Irish-related decrypts prior to the Easter Rising is wrong.[45] However, he was undoubtedly selective in circulating German diplomatic intelligence, often sending summaries, rather than raw decrypts, and deciding which ministers and government officials received material, as he saw fit. The charge that this selectivity reflected political bias, rather than reasonable concern for protecting precious and vulnerable sources, is easy to make, but hard to demonstrate convincingly. Hall undoubtedly had strong political views and prejudices, and was firmly opposed to a compromise peace, making him suspicious of the negotiations undertaken by House during his visits to Europe in early 1916, and again the following winter. Hall looked determinedly for intelligence prejudicial to a House peace agenda, and was selective in choosing who saw what he found.[46] However, there is still no evidence he completely withheld intelligence, and he was invariably careful to protect his position, if material was politically awkward, by briefing Hankey, where Hall would have heartily endorsed the view, ascribed to a future Chief of the Imperial General Staff, General Sir Henry Wilson, 'If you once lose hold of Hanky-Panky, you are done, absolutely done'.[47] Hall probably also received wide discretion in handling sensitive diplomatic intelligence from Balfour, as First Lord from May 1915 to end 1916 and thereafter Foreign Secretary. Hall did disobey instructions over passing the Archibald material to Bell, but felt obliged to consult the Foreign Office and Balfour, even if he did not get the answer he wanted. Discrimination shown by Hall in handling sensitive diplomatic decrypts should also be kept in context. The quantity of material available by autumn 1916, and its vulnerability if the source was compromised, posed unprecedented challenges in managing it. Successive British intelligence chiefs across the rest of the century often faced tricky judgements over handling political intelligence uncomfortable for the government of the day, or factions within a government, and acted in a similar way to Hall.

The single instance during 1915–16 where Hall may justifiably be accused of pursuing a personal political objective is over Casement. Following Casement's conviction, Hall (and probably Thomson too) circulated typewritten copies of extracts from his diaries, giving lurid accounts of his pre-war homosexual lifestyle, to senior members of the British establishment and representatives of the British and American press. Hall's targets here included Bell, since Ambassador Page later acknowledged seeing the extracts. This influence operation was undoubtedly effective in countering appeals for clemency, and Casement was hanged on 3 August.

Hall's action may legitimately be viewed as an abuse of his position, as well as distasteful. However, with Britain now committed to total war, and the Battle of the Somme raging, Hall and other senior security officials were inevitably influenced by the regular (and accurate) reports they had read over two years detailing Casement's determined efforts to enlist German support, and to pressure Irish prisoners of war into what most of those prisoners saw as a betrayal of regiment and country. Determination that Casement should pay the price is understandable, even if the means are less acceptable to a modern audience.[48]

10

Jutland: Intelligence Limitations Exposed

No naval engagement has received more analysis than the Battle of Jutland, lasting from the afternoon of 31 May to the morning of 1 June 1916, the only occasion during the war when the entire Royal Navy Grand Fleet met the German High Seas Fleet, offering the fleeting prospect of a decisive Trafalgar-type engagement. The contribution of intelligence has been studied since the 1960s, but in more detail following release of SIGINT records thirty years later. There is consensus that Room 40 SIGINT was critical in making Jutland possible, but that failings in understanding and managing intelligence were an important, perhaps decisive, factor in closing off prospects of a British victory through interception of the returning German fleet. Nevertheless, important aspects of the intelligence story remain misunderstood or overlooked.

Three points require emphasis. First, the sheer quantity of German signals processed by Room 40 potentially relevant to the operation, around a thousand from the first U-boat deployments in mid May to the last post-action reports on 3 June, and about a hundred and fifty over the combat period from 1430 on 31 May to 0630 the following morning. These numbers far surpassed those for any previous fleet encounter, reflecting the size of the forces engaged and the operational activity they generated. They posed unprecedented analytical demands, since most decrypts were fragments of information which meant little until pieced together and placed in wider context. Furthermore, inevitable inconsistencies with interception and processing meant that decrypted signals issued from Room 40 did not necessarily mirror the sequence of original German transmission. There were many delays and gaps in the SIGINT information picture.

Secondly, SIGINT at Jutland, produced exclusively through Room 40, could only realistically contribute high-level insights at the fleet level of command. It could provide warning of a German sortie, identify the main forces deployed, their broad direction of travel and, therefore, likely objectives through different phases of the operation. But inevitable gaps in coverage, delays in processing, ambiguity in interpretation and, not least, navigational errors embedded in individual enemy signals meant it could rarely add reliably and usefully to the real-time tactical picture, in contrast to immediate visual (and occasionally short-range wireless intercept) reports from fleet units. SIGINT confirmed that the German main force, under the High Seas Fleet commander, Vice Admiral Reinhard Scheer, was moving northwest in close support of Rear Admiral Franz Hipper's battlecruiser force at 1610 on the afternoon of 31 May. It demonstrated that Scheer was heading for Horns Reef from 2130 that evening. But it could not give Jellicoe information quickly enough to be useful about Scheer's movements during his pursuit of Beatty's battlecruiser force in the 'run to the north' from 1700 that afternoon. It could not, therefore, help Jellicoe's battle-fleet deployment decision from 1800. Similarly, it could not immediately inform Jellicoe precisely how, when and where Scheer's large, widely dispersed forces were breaking through the British lines to reach Horns Reef. In both cases, only intelligence from within the fleet could give Jellicoe the real-time tactical picture he needed. Neither the Admiralty team, nor Jellicoe and Beatty, had yet thought enough about what Room 40 SIGINT could reasonably deliver during a full-scale fleet encounter. Thus the Admiralty sent too many dated snapshots giving the position, course and speed of individual German forces, rather than focusing on big-picture intent. Jellicoe invariably found such snapshots unhelpful and frequently wrong, and therefore missed the trend that might have convinced him Scheer was heading for Horns Reef.

The third point is how SIGINT related to other operational information available to the Admiralty, and to Jellicoe and Beatty as fleet commanders. Within the Admiralty, operational traffic to and from the Grand Fleet and other home waters commanders was handled by Operations Division. The whereabouts of own and enemy forces as reported by these commanders were displayed on the home waters plot in the War Room. Separate plots maintained by E1 section in ID recorded German surface warship and U-boat positions and movements respectively. The latter plot was important at Jutland, because most U-boats had been deployed in support of the High Seas Fleet. Although most of E1's information was copied to the main War Room plot, this did not happen in real time, and neither E1 nor the War Room was allowed to display intelligence derived from Room 40 decrypts. However, they did display D/F intelligence, even though this was also filtered through Room 40. As at the Dogger Bank engagement, decrypts of intercepted signals were assessed on the third private plot kept in the chief of staff's room. Indoctrinated personnel could, in theory, move between all three plots, but the geographic separation of E1 made this difficult. However, essential E1 intelligence was copied to the main plot, so Oliver and Thomas Jackson stayed mainly in the War Room, diverting to the private plot to assess incoming SIGINT as required. These two therefore attempted to monitor the largest naval engagement in history, giving information, advice or direction to Jellicoe and Beatty as they judged appropriate, while also acting as SIGINT analysts. This system had just about worked at previous encounters, including the Dogger Bank, where the scenario was simpler, forces engaged were limited, and the quantity of SIGINT far smaller. On this occasion, by the time the main fleets sighted each other late afternoon on 31 May, they were completely swamped. It is easy to blame the Admiralty leadership for not anticipating this, but their successors in the late twentieth century, with infinitely better technology, might have struggled with the intelligence demands of a Jutland.

Jellicoe also had an operational plot at Jutland, a concept proposed by his flag captain, Captain Frederick Dreyer. Essentially it was a chart, distinct from the navigational chart, for presenting own and enemy positions and projected movements to help with situational awareness. It was therefore a small-scale equivalent of the Admiralty War Room plot. The idea of keeping such a plot at sea, unique to the Royal Navy, was still in its infancy and had not yet been tested in exercises. Jutland would demonstrate two crucial points: it required good reporting of positional information, own and enemy, by subordinate units; and also good navigation. At Jutland, both were lacking. An important evolution introduced afterwards was that ships reported all positions relative to the flagship, rather than relying on their own estimated geographical position. The plot gave Jellicoe a potential means of better exploiting Room 40 intelligence sent by the Admiralty, but it appears little, if any, SIGINT data was displayed, and it was used mainly for plotting torpedo countermeasures. The weaknesses in fleet plotting exposed at Jutland nevertheless drove experiment and innovation during the rest of the war, leading to significant investment and training in the 1930s, and a transformation in Royal Navy attitudes to night-fighting.[1]

The scene was set for Jutland in early 1916 when Oliver and other senior members of the war staff assessed that intelligence coverage of German naval capability, intentions and movements established over the previous eighteen months offered potential new solutions to the North Sea problem, perhaps enabling a decisive victory over the High Seas Fleet. The critical intelligence asset was Room 40 SIGINT, which had now demonstrated that it could reliably warn of German fleet sorties, identify their targets, provide some tracking of movements, and help ID keep an accurate order of battle. It also offered occasional insights into wider German strategic plans, and how they viewed British intent. Meanwhile, the D/F network coming on stream promised more accurate monitoring of German movements, while SSB reporting provided additional insights into present and future German strength and capability, and sometimes intentions. Oliver accordingly reassessed the North Sea position at the beginning of April. The Royal Navy now enjoyed a battle-fleet advantage of thirty dreadnought battleships and ten battlecruisers, compared to German figures of eighteen and five.[2] British ships were more heavily armed, and the numerical lead would continue growing over the next year. The minimal advantage that worried Jellicoe in autumn 1914 had become overwhelming dominance. There was a similar lead in armoured cruisers, but Germany retained slightly greater destroyer strength available for the North Sea.

Given British superiority, Oliver judged it unsurprising the Germans should avoid a fleet action. Yet the Grand Fleet and other British forces remained tied down, imposing considerable logistic strain. With the bulk of the Grand Fleet based at Scapa Flow, 450 miles from the Heligoland Bight, the Germans had a day's start for executing operations south of the Humber. Even if the time of their exit was known, they could reach the east coast, spend six hours there, and return safely. Successful interception required the Grand Fleet to deploy on the possibility of a German sortie before it was confirmed. This would fail if the sortie was anticipated by more than one day, because the Grand Fleet must return to refuel. Even with the current intelligence advantage, prospects of successful interception were therefore minimal, unless the High Seas Fleet deliberately sought action, or attempted a northern breakout into the Atlantic. Meanwhile, the Germans could inflict serious damage on the east and south coasts, and potentially cross-channel traffic, with relative impunity.

Basing the Grand Fleet further south posed problems. Neither the Forth nor the Humber could take the whole fleet. Dividing the fleet between them sacrificed the concentration valued by Jellicoe, and risked one part being defeated by a superior force, although this part might still inflict considerable damage, leaving the other part intact and superior to the residual German fleet. Without more forward deployment, even if it meant division, decisive victory seemed impossible. Oliver therefore proposed basing three-quarters of the fleet in the Forth, a force numerically superior and with greater hitting power over the maximum High Seas Fleet, with the remainder retained at Scapa as a reserve. East-coast defence would be boosted with older pre-dreadnought squadrons based in the Humber and Thames.

Closer deployment of the bulk of the Grand Fleet resurrected ideas for offensive operations to lure the Germans out into a trap. Belief that Scheer, the new commander of the High Seas Fleet, would be more aggressive than his predecessor was influential here.[3] So was SIGINT demonstrating that the Germans were alert to opportunities to strike at British forces near the Bight. The lure, whether air assault from a seaplane carrier, surface bombardment or minelaying operation, would draw Hipper's battlecruisers into an engagement with Beatty. If Beatty received the new, fast, 5th Battle Squadron of five *Queen Elizabeths*, the speed and hitting power of his combined force would destroy Hipper before the main German battle-fleet intervened. They, in turn, could be trapped by more rapid deployment of the Grand Fleet, exploiting SIGINT to get between the Germans and their bases. Ideally, this concept would be executed when the Germans were known to be planning a sortie, and conducted in poor weather, denying them Zeppelin surveillance.[4]

There were flaws in such ideas, and Jellicoe was accordingly receptive but cautious. The distance gain from basing the Grand Fleet at the Forth had to be weighed against its vulnerability to submarines and mines and its limited space. Beatty relished the possibility of a larger detached force under his command and lobbied hard for the 5th Battle Squadron. Jellicoe worried this would encourage recklessness. He was willing to explore new options for luring the High Seas Fleet into a trap. An air attack against the Zeppelin sheds at Tondern, combined with minelaying in the Bight, was mounted in early May, but the Germans did not take the bait.[5] A more complex operation involving deployment of cruisers in the Skaggerak was planned for early June, but forestalled by the German sortie leading to Jutland.[6] The British naval leadership, Henry Jackson and Oliver in the Admiralty, and Jellicoe and Beatty in the fleet, were right that Britain's intelligence advantage could be used to better strategic effect, but distance and fleet distribution were not the only problems. They all underestimated the limitations of SIGINT and its exploitation within current handling arrangements. Meanwhile, the German raid on Lowestoft at the end of April, a variant of the 1914 Scarborough operation, albeit poorly executed with meagre results, underlined the threat to the southern North Sea and the impossibility of effective Grand Fleet intervention here, despite another good Room 40 intelligence performance. A conference at Rosyth on 12 May therefore agreed that the Forth must replace Scapa as primary fleet base, but left interim redeployment options unresolved, and it took two more years to complete the move to the Forth.[7]

Within three weeks of this Rosyth meeting, several of these ideas for exploiting intelligence advantage within a new deployment pattern were subjected to the ultimate test of the long-sought engagement between the two fleets. SIGINT gave the Grand Fleet the advance deployment advantage Oliver judged ideal. Beatty had temporarily been allocated the 5th Battle Squadron and had the opportunity to trap Hipper with a superior force. Later, he withdrew under protection of the 5th, again rather as Oliver anticipated. With better management, SIGINT might have enabled Jellicoe to trap the retreating High Seas Fleet as Oliver hoped.

Unlike the Dogger Bank, no single decrypted German signal during preparations for the Jutland operation defined its objective. There was also less warning of the forces to be deployed, and their departure times. Instead, there was an accumulation of evidence, beginning with U-boat deployments from mid May, of something unusual underway, confirmed by a signal on 29 May bringing the fleet to 'special readiness'.[8] Late morning the following day, the High Seas Fleet was ordered to assemble in the Jade outer roads by 2100. A further signal followed which Room 40 translated as: 'Reckon on the proceeding out of our own forces on May 31st and June 1st'. On decrypting these two signals, the Admiralty advised Jellicoe that a sortie was imminent, and at 1730 ordered the Grand Fleet to sail to intercept. The signals used a new codebook variant which Room 40 had not fully reconstructed, creating uncertainty over whether the second signal referred to 'own' or 'enemy' forces, before the former was chosen. When it acquired the full codebook in August 1918, Room 40 learnt that it should have read 'enemy forces', provoking Hall to exclaim that the Grand Fleet had therefore sailed on the basis of a false translation.[9] The error meant Jellicoe cleared Scapa two and a half hours before Hipper's battlecruisers left the Jade.[10] Without it, the Admiralty and Jellicoe might have delayed until a flurry of intercepts from late afternoon confirmed that the High Seas Fleet would sail in the early hours of the next morning for an operation designated GG 2490.[11] By the time these were decrypted and assessed, Jellicoe would not have left until after midnight, losing his time advantage. Room 40 did not know that GG 2490 involved an attack on shipping near the Skaggerak designed to lure a portion of the British fleet into an ambush.[12]

These late-afternoon intercepts on 30 May suggested that the whole High Seas Fleet would sortie in the early hours of the following morning, but Room 40 could not provide Scheer's detailed sailing orders, or confirmation of his departure. The relevant signals were intercepted, but in a new cipher not broken until next afternoon, by which time the fleets were in action.[13] By 0900 on 31 May, the only new intelligence relevant to the German sortie showed that aerial reconnaissance was not available, and that two U-boats had reported sighting substantial British forces, including battleships, at sea.[14] Without further news of Scheer's movements, by late morning the Admiralty faced a dilemma, since Jellicoe would expect an update. At 1230, they signalled: 'No definite news of enemy. They made all preparations for sailing this morning. It was thought fleet had sailed but directional wireless places flagship in Jade at 1110 GMT. Apparently they have been unable to carry out air reconnaissance which has delayed them.'

This signal is part of Jutland folklore. The placing of the flagship still in port is notoriously blamed on Thomas Jackson,[15] Director of Operations Division, who allegedly stormed angrily into Room 40, peremptorily demanding to know where D/F placed 'DK', the normal German flagship call-sign. (The monitoring of DK by Room 40 is a good example of traffic analysis.) Informed DK was still in the Jade, Jackson left without being reminded that this was not a conclusive indicator of the flagship's location. It was customary to shift DK to the Wilhelmshaven wireless station on sailing, and adopt a different call-sign, deliberately concealing that the commander-in-chief was at sea.[16] The implication is that Room 40 was confident Scheer had departed according to plan, with Jackson's behaviour illustrating the patronising attitude of the naval staff towards Room 40 on operational matters, and their general ignorance of SIGINT capabilities, underlining the lack of a proper intelligence centre.[17]

The traditional picture of Jackson taking ill-informed action on his own initiative originates with the newly arrived Room 40 cryptographer William Clarke, and lacks credibility. Jackson was not the blustering fool usually painted, but a highly intelligent officer, well-informed on modern radio and SIGINT. Claims that he denigrated Room 40 and its intelligence, despite reading about fifty reports daily and experiencing the SIGINT contribution at Scarborough, the Dogger Bank and Lowestoft, and to the ongoing U-boat war, look unlikely. As DID in 1913, Jackson had not dismissed the contribution of civilians, praising Bywater's reporting. Clarke's suggestion of a cultural gulf between the naval staff and Room 40 does not fit with most contemporary accounts, which have Room 40 accorded admiration and respect.[18]

Furthermore, before taking any decision, Jackson would have got approval from the First Sea Lord and Oliver, who, with a fleet action imminent, were all gathered in the War Room, anxiously waiting for the picture to clarify. They knew from Ewing and Herbert Hope that Room 40 were trying to break traffic in a new cipher.[19] There was no evidence of Scheer not sailing in accord with the previous day's decrypts, but absence of aerial surveillance and warnings of British heavy ships at sea might have provoked delay. Scheer later acknowledged that the U-boat warnings made him wonder if 'the enemy has taken note of our departure', but he judged this unlikely and decided to continue the operation.[20] By late morning, with no further intercept intelligence, it was logical for Jackson, either on his own initiative or at the behest of the First Sea Lord and Oliver, to seek a directional fix. The subsequent exchange on DK in Room 40 perhaps began as Clarke claimed. But it seems inherently implausible that none of those present explained the call-sign issue, or that Hope was not consulted. Furthermore, in denouncing Jackson for ignorantly asking the wrong question about DK, Clarke was disingenuous about Room 40's knowledge of the call-sign shift. Room 40 knew the Germans had made the shift in earlier sorties. The previous afternoon the Germans had ordered the same shift for this operation as part of the sailing orders. But Room 40 had still not decrypted these when Jackson posed his question. Precedent therefore demonstrated that the presence of DK in the Jade did not prove Scheer was still there. But Clarke's account conveniently ignored that Room 40 could not confirm to Jackson that Scheer had sailed and that, as Hope's war diary confirms, the first indications that the High Seas Fleet was at sea did not arrive until 1430, two hours after the Admiralty's signal to Jellicoe.[21]

Whatever the truth of the DK exchange, the resulting signal was issued with the authority of the First Sea Lord and Oliver. It represented an Admiralty assessment, not Jackson's personal interpretation. While the Admiralty owed Jellicoe an update, neither of them faced any immediate operational decision. Jellicoe could keep heading south without adverse consequences. If Scheer had sailed to plan, Jellicoe would be well positioned to intercept. If he had delayed or cancelled, no harm was done. The Admiralty problem in assessing Scheer's movements was therefore different from that faced by Admiral of the Fleet Sir Dudley Pound with *Tirpitz* and PQ 17 a generation later, with a comparable incomplete SIGINT picture. Both were situations where 'absence of evidence is not evidence of absence', but Pound had to choose between two actions, each carrying significant risk.

The Admiralty would have done better to raise the possibility with Jellicoe that Scheer had delayed but then left matters open, suspending judgement until there was more information. Nevertheless, their 1230 signal did not significantly affect Jellicoe's progress southward or the dynamics of the forthcoming fleet-to-fleet encounter.[22] It might, therefore, not have mattered, merely registering as an embarrassing footnote to Jutland, if it had not been the first in a series of signals that steadily undermined Jellicoe's confidence in Admiralty intelligence, with unfortunate consequences.

During the combat phase of Jutland, Room 40 could potentially help with three requirements: locating the main body of the High Seas Fleet for Jellicoe during the battlecruiser action between 1545–1800; locating the High Seas Fleet after Scheer disengaged from Jellicoe the second and final time at 1930; and identifying the route and timing of Scheer's escape home. During the battlecruiser action, Room 40 intercepted two German signals giving the position of their 'main force' at 1609 and 1630. Both positions were forwarded to Jellicoe, the first reaching him at 1700 and the second at 1753. The first was the more accurate and potentially useful, stating: 'At 4.9pm enemy battlefleet Lat 56.27N Long 6.18E. Course NW. 15 knots'. Although based on a grid reading, Room 40's interpretation of Scheer's position was accurate. Had Jellicoe applied dead reckoning to this 1609 position using this course and speed, he would have had an excellent 1700 location for the battleship *König* leading the German 3rd Battle Squadron. This squadron was then engaging Beatty's remaining battlecruisers, and about to switch fire to the approaching 5th Battle Squadron, still running south. Scheer's flagship *Friedrich der Grosse* was about five miles due south of *König*.[23] For understandable reasons, Jellicoe disregarded this Admiralty input, which probably never reached the flagship plot. The position was nearly an hour old, it might be based on D/F of doubtful accuracy, while course and speed could also be estimates and change at any time.[24] Meanwhile, within the last twenty minutes he had six reports from British ships claiming to have the High Seas Fleet in view, and which he expected to be reliable. The second 1630 German position was accurate enough to validate the earlier one, but when it reached Jellicoe at 1753 it was nearly ninety minutes out of date, and with Beatty emerging out of the mist and smoke at this time, evidently under fire, there were other things to worry about. It is doubtful Jellicoe even saw it. With hindsight, the 1609 decrypt was the best fix Jellicoe received on Scheer and his movements until the arrival of Beatty's force, for the navigational accuracy, visual estimates and communication of those British units and commanders in contact with the High Seas Fleet between 1630 and 1800 proved atrocious.[25]

When Scheer disengaged at 1930, Jellicoe knew that he had retreated westward, and skirmishing over the next hour, especially involving Beatty's battlecruisers, established the southern extremity of the High Seas Fleet by nightfall at 2100. For the next six hours, Jellicoe steered just east of south at 17 knots, confident that he was keeping Scheer to the west and cut off from his two obvious routes home. At 2100 the

High Seas Fleet was indeed spread between southwest and northwest of the main body of the Grand Fleet, at an average range of eight miles. However, soon afterwards, Scheer turned southeast at 16 knots, heading for the Horns Reef route home. This put him on a converging course to Jellicoe, but slightly slower, and meant his main body passed through the northern part of the Grand Fleet between 2330 and 0030.[26] When Jellicoe turned north at 0245 on 1 June, Scheer was safely past the Grand Fleet, some twenty-eight miles northeast, and fast approaching the mine-strewn waters south of Horns Reef, where interception was impossible.[27] In order to cut the High Seas Fleet off by daybreak at 0330, Jellicoe had to identify Scheer's rough track and intent by 0200 at the latest, and turn the Grand Fleet east as Scheer crossed level with the midpoint line of Horns Reef.[28] Here Jellicoe was let down badly by his subordinate commanders and individual ships in the northern part of his force. Their reporting during a series of short-range, often savage, actions, as the High Seas Fleet pushed through, was woeful and, despite the darkness and mist, inexcusable.[29] Unfortunately, the performance of the Admiralty team drawing on Room 40 was no better.

The minimum time between German transmission of a signal and an Admiralty summary reaching Jellicoe during Jutland was fifty minutes. The signal had to be intercepted at a listening site, forwarded by landline to the Admiralty, decrypted and translated by Room 40, and passed to Operations Division. Oliver, Jackson or one of their indoctrinated staff had to assess its operational value, possibly plot it on the private chart, consider source protection, and draft a suitable message for Jellicoe. Inevitably, this cycle often took longer. If 0200 was the latest time Jellicoe could turn east in order successfully to intercept Scheer, the Admiralty had to provide sufficient intelligence by this time to convince Jellicoe where the High Seas Fleet was located, that they had already crossed his track heading southeast for Horns Reef, and that he must proceed east at maximum speed. Allowing for processing time, only German traffic originating before 0100 could inform his decision. How did the Admiralty perform, and could they have done better?

The Admiralty sent Jellicoe only three signals conveying Room 40 intelligence on the status of the High Seas Fleet between 1930 and the 0200 deadline. The first provided a position for the rear ship in the German main force, transmitted by the cruiser *Regensburg* at 2100 and forwarded to Jellicoe at 2158, who received it at 2223. The wording of the outgoing signal was sanitised to make the information consistent with D/F, with all reference to the German originator excluded. Unfortunately, the position quoted by *Regensburg* was wrong, placing the rear ship ten miles south of its true position, and the same distance southwest of the Grand Fleet main body. Jellicoe knew this was not credible, because his 3rd Light Cruiser Squadron was in the area at the time. He concluded it was a poor D/F fix and it further undermined his confidence in Admiralty information. The second signal sent by the Admiralty at 2241 stated that the High Seas Fleet had been ordered home at 2116, and was now steering southeast at 16 knots with the battlecruisers to the rear. This potentially indicated Horns Reef as Scheer's destination but, from Jellicoe's perspective, the course given was a single snapshot, now ninety minutes out of date, and it lacked a credible starting point.[30] The Admiralty's presentation of this signal was unfortunate, because it combined two separate decrypts which had Scheer on a southeast course at both 2114 and 2146. The Admiralty could have made this clear without risk of compromise, since a series of D/F fixes pointing southeast was credible. The information might then have received more attention from Jellicoe and his staff. Finally, at 0148 the Admiralty provided a position, course and speed for the damaged *Lützow*, adding that all U-boats were being rushed to an attacking position, and that one German 'flotilla' (unspecified) was returning round the Skaw.[31] The information conveyed in these three signals was not remotely sufficient to persuade Jellicoe to turn east, confident that Scheer was taking the Horns Reef route. They also only added marginally to the picture available from his own forces, had the fleeting sightings and engagements with the High Seas Fleet to his north been properly reported.

However, these three Admiralty signals were a small part of the intelligence acquired by Room 40, and passed to Operations Division (OD) between 2100 and 0130 (the latest time for getting information to Jellicoe by 0200), and omitted numerous indications of Scheer's progress and intent during this period. There were about fifty decrypts in this period of which the Admiralty drew on only five in their three reports to Jellicoe (numbers 1, 3, 4, 5 and 14 below).[32] The most valuable were:[33]

	German Time of Origin	Content	Time passed to OD
1	2100	*Regensburg* position etc	2125
2	2106	Request for air reconnaissance of Horns Reef	2210
3	2114	Main body course and speed	2155
4	2129	High Seas Fleet disposition for night passage	2155
5	2146	Main body course	2210
6	2150	Position of *Lützow* and four destroyers at 2130	2330

	German Time of Origin	Content	Time Passed to OD
7	2232	Main body course	2315
8	2232	Confirmation of rendezvous at Horns Reef 0400	2315
9	2302	Confirmation course southeast to Horns Reef	
10	2306	Position of main fleet at 2300	2350
11	2330	Battleship *Westfalen* steering southeast	
12	2336	C-in-C confirms course southeast	
13	2339	C-in-C confirms course southeast	
14	0017	Position of *Lützow* at midnight	0100
15	0031	Position of 2nd Scouting Group	0105
16	0033	Light cruiser *Rostock* torpedoed, position given	
17	0043	Position for main body at 0030	0120
18	0048	Light cruiser *Elbing* cannot manoeuvre, position given	
19	0103	Position of head of main body at 0100	0125

Exploiting this information, the Admiralty might have sent further signals at:

- 2359, drawing on 2,7 and 8, emphasising that at 2230 Scheer was steering southeast for Horns Reef;
- 0030, drawing on 9 and 10, giving main body position at 2300 and confirming course then remained southeast to Horns Reef;
- 0100, drawing on 12 and 13, main body still steering southeast;
- 0200, drawing on 17 and 19, positions of main body at 0030 and 0100.

Whatever his doubts about the reliability of earlier Admiralty reports, Jellicoe would hardly have ignored such a consistent stream of intelligence. It would also have caused him to investigate developments astern of him (see the map on page 176).

Why did the Admiralty fail to act on this excellent Room 40 reporting? The perceived overriding need to protect the SIGINT source undoubtedly caused indoctrinated personnel, from the First Sea Lord downward, to minimise traffic and avoid references, such as aerial reconnaissance of Horns Reef, that could not credibly come from D/F.[34] But signals could easily have been drafted to get the core intelligence to Jellicoe, without

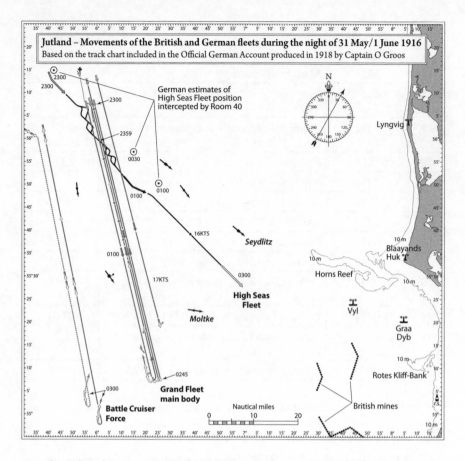

Jutland – Movements of the British and German fleets during the night of 31 May/1 June 1916
Based on the track chart included in the Official German Account produced in 1918 by Captain O Groos

German estimates of
High Seas Fleet position
intercepted by Room 40

Lyngvig

Seydlitz

Blaayands
Huk

Horns Reef

High Seas
Fleet

Vyl

Moltke

Graa
Dyb

Rotes Kliff-Bank

Grand Fleet
main body

Battle Cruiser
Force

British mines

Nautical miles
0   10   20

much risk of compromise by using phrases such as 'all directionals consistently point to Horns Reef', etc. It appears that the small indoctrinated team in Operations Division struggled to absorb the sheer quantity of decrypts and identify what was important. Furthermore, the Admiralty had limited knowledge of Jellicoe's movements and intent, and perhaps assumed (not unreasonably) that he knew more than he did from his own local fleet reporting. The First Sea Lord subsequently told Jellicoe that he was reluctant to intervene based on fragments of information.[35] Fatigue was a factor too.

However, allowing for the 'fog of war', the judgement that Operations Division displayed 'criminal neglect' in not sharing this intelligence seems fair.[36] Operations Division was brilliantly served by the small Room 40 night watch, but failed to use what it received to give Jellicoe the chance of dealing with Scheer at daybreak. Jellicoe inevitably felt aggrieved when he later discovered how much intelligence he was denied, insisting it would undoubtedly have caused him to turn east towards Horns Reef.[37] Whether this would have led to a significant engagement, let alone a decisive victory, is more doubtful. The Grand Fleet was little damaged, had superior numbers and firepower and, approaching from the west, would have the advantage of the light. Scheer's strung out and badly mauled fleet was in no state to fight another battle. But Jellicoe's battle-fleet was separated from the bulk of his destroyer force, and visibility was poor that morning, a maximum of four miles, and half this near Horns Reef. Finding the Germans at all would have been challenging, let alone manoeuvring for an optimum tactical position. In a short-range action, complicated by difficult navigation and the threat of torpedo attack from destroyers and submarines, a series of brief inconclusive engagements was likely.[38] Weather rather than SIGINT was therefore ultimately more important in defining the limits of the possible on the morning of 1 June. For all the attention it has understandably received, the 'criminal neglect' by Operations Division perhaps made little difference.

As the High Seas Fleet completed its escape, Room 40 obtained valuable intelligence on German losses and damage. Around one hundred and fifty decrypts were issued between 0600 and 2359 on 1 June. These revealed that the brand new *Lützow*, Hipper's flagship, had definitely sunk, as had the pre-dreadnought battleship *Pommern*, the light cruisers *Rostock*, *Elbing* and *Frauenlob*, and the destroyer *S-35*.[39] They also showed that, of the battlecruisers, *Seydlitz* was in a sinking condition, while *Moltke* and *Derfflinger* were seriously damaged, as were the battleships *König* and *Ostfriesland*, and many other vessels. At 1600 that afternoon Jackson, still unaware of the major British losses, wrote to Jellicoe, passing on these intelligence highlights and congratulating him on what appeared a significant victory. He also stressed source protection, warning that the Germans suspected their traffic was compromised. They had changed their cipher on leaving harbour, and although Ewing and Rotter had worked on this all night, their sailing orders could not be decrypted until the afternoon of 31 May.[40]

Meanwhile, Hankey, who learnt of British losses before seeing any intelligence, initially assessed Jutland a 'terrible disappointment', with the Germans 'superior to us in fighting power'. By 3 June, briefed by Hall, he was less gloomy, stating that 'secret information' showed that the Germans 'got a tremendous hammering – more than admitted'.[41] Hall also asked Cumming to obtain collateral. On 2 June the SSB in London accordingly briefed its Rotterdam and Copenhagen stations that 'reliable information' on damage suffered by the German fleet was 'urgently required'. Tinsley briefed TR16 next day, and between 3 and 20 June he visited ten German dockyards. Meanwhile, D15, controlled by Copenhagen, visited Wilhelmshaven and reported back on 19 June, describing damage to major units and providing an accurate breakdown of German casualties. He added that *Seydlitz* had survived, that the new battleship *Bayern* had completed fitting-out, but the new battlecruiser *Hindenburg* would not be ready before end September. Although the main elements of the report were correct, it was let down by significant errors.[42] By contrast, TR16's comprehensive five-page report, delivered on 27 June, was described by Hall as 100 per cent. He too demonstrated that, overall, the Germans had sustained much more serious damage than admitted, with eight capital ships out of service for three months.[43]

Although Room 40 and the SSB did well in establishing German damage, and demonstrating that in material terms the outcome of Jutland was more balanced than the Royal Navy initially feared, British naval intelligence missed a more important prize. It gained no insight into Scheer's report on the battle, delivered to the Kaiser on 4 July. This showed that D15 and TR16 overestimated the time required for the High Seas Fleet to return to full strength. With the exception of *Seydlitz* and *Derfflinger*, Scheer expected to have his full nominal strength available again by mid August. However, his core message was that even the most successful outcome of a future fleet action would not force Britain out of the war, or even break her blockade. Both geography and the balance of naval forces were too much in Britain's favour. German victory could only be achieved within a reasonable timescale by destroying the British economy by using the U-boats against British trade. For the German navy, therefore, Jutland was a turning point. There was brief euphoria over the losses inflicted on the British battlecruisers, but Scheer knew he had come too close to annihilation for comfort. The High Seas Fleet made three more sorties in the war, in August and October 1916 and April 1918, but it was more reluctant to run risks. Inactivity gradually eroded its morale and competence, exacerbated by the steady shift of resources to the U-boat effort. In theory, as Hankey believed, that left the Grand Fleet in control of the North Sea, encapsulated succinctly in the oft-quoted American newspaper headline – 'The German fleet has assaulted its jailor but is still in jail'.[44] In reality, the exercise of control proved more complicated.

As both sides assessed the implications of Jutland, the war was reaching its halfway point. In two years, British naval intelligence had vastly extended its capabilities and reach. The outstanding achievement was the creation of Room 40 SIGINT, directed first at naval communications, but now increasingly at diplomatic traffic too. As described in the next chapter, there had been a parallel effort against open-source communications by other departments in support of the blockade. Taking MI1(b) into account, Britain had moved from negligible SIGINT capability in August

1914 to a position where, by autumn 1916, it was easily the dominant SIGINT power, a position it held for the next thirty years. As Jutland confirmed, Room 40's primary value in the first half of the war was strategic. SIGINT denied the German navy surprise. It largely eliminated the always slim prospect of it winning the naval war through a 'whittling' strategy, provoking a portion of the Grand Fleet into action against larger but hidden forces, or luring it into a submarine trap.[45] Room 40 naval SIGINT not only made distant blockade practicable – it effectively restored most of the traditional naval advantages of close blockade, solving the Royal Navy's North Sea problem, at least for surface operations. The Royal Navy had yet to find convincing answers to the U-boat challenge, but SIGINT would clearly be a major part of the solution. Nevertheless, despite the enormous value offered by SIGINT, Jutland had revealed significant weakness in intelligence management, and it would be a while before this was properly addressed.

In other areas too, naval intelligence had come of age. ID now had fifty staff, divided almost equally between naval personnel and civilians, and three times its size at the start of the war.[46] It had demonstrated that it could collect and use intelligence on a global basis, exploiting the attachés, Hall's independent agents such as Mason, the network of overseas intelligence centres established by Bethell, which had now doubled in size, and the support of the SSB. SSB too was developing, becoming a genuinely global operator with 1024 staff and agents on its strength by October 1916. Its largest effort was concentrated in Holland and Belgium, followed by Scandinavia. But it now had networks in southern Europe, the Balkans, the Near East, Russia, South America and the United States. Its headquarters staff had risen to sixty, ten times the number in 1914.[47] With TR16, it had demonstrated that it could run high-value naval penetrations of the main enemy in wartime. With the outcome of the war finely balanced, there were now new challenges.

11

Blockade: The Under-recognised Intelligence Triumph

As the third year of the war got underway, neither side had achieved decisive advantage, while the costs, human, material and financial, rose relentlessly. All the combatants were experiencing serious political, social and economic strain, with Russia and Austria–Hungary showing the first signs of potential collapse. In the west, Germany's great assault on Verdun had failed, but had crippled the offensive power of the French army. Britain's attack on the Somme had also failed to break through, but had exhausted German forces not deployed at Verdun. In the east, Russia's Brusilov offensive in Galicia had almost broken Austria–Hungary and with the accession of Romania to the Entente, the ability of the central powers to sustain the war was briefly in doubt. Germany stabilised the Eastern Front by the end of the year, but at the price of adopting a defensive position in the west for the foreseeable future.

All the main combatants had elements which favoured exploring mediation. However, Britain and Germany, as leaders of the opposing alliances, both ultimately embraced a policy of escalation. Both saw a change of leadership. Lloyd George replaced Asquith as prime minister, heading a coalition committed to a decisive outcome, ' a fight to the finish'. In Germany, Field Marshal Paul von Hindenburg replaced Falkenhayn as chief of the general staff, with General Erich Ludendorff as his chief of staff and quartermaster general. These two not only took over the Supreme Command, *Oberste Heeresleitung* (OHL), but rapidly became the de facto German leaders, exerting direction over Chancellor Bethmann-Hollweg, and reducing the Kaiser to an essentially symbolic role. Lloyd George believed that by mobilising for total war, exploiting American resources and tightening the blockade, the Entente could grind Germany down. Hindenburg and Ludendorff believed that holding in the west could buy sufficient time to mobilise fresh fighting power and rejuvenate the German army. Crucially, they also judged that Germany's survival required countering American support of the Entente by severing the Atlantic supply lines. They were content to let Bethmann-Hollweg explore mediation if this bought further time, and demonstrated commitment to a purely defensive war, but they would then unleash the U-boats.

As Britain's Somme offensive drew to a close, and Germany prepared its defensive position on the Western Front, Britain accordingly faced three interconnected strategic challenges that winter. First was the renewal of the U-boat offensive, which resumed in restricted form in September. Depending on how Germany assessed American attitudes, Britain recognised that it would evolve into an all-out unrestricted campaign, with limited warning and waged with far greater resources than in 1915. The second was the prospect that Germany would exploit President Woodrow Wilson's ambition to broker a compromise 'peace without victory'. The risk was that by appearing to acquiesce in American arbitration, Germany could encourage Wilson to coerce the Entente powers into a settlement to Germany's advantage. The final challenge was the blockade. Hankey's vision for economic warfare had encountered many vicissitudes since August 1914, but two years on, Britain now had the structures, the resources and the intelligence to make the blockade an effective grinding agent. By the end of the year, it was inflicting serious damage on Germany's economy and social cohesion, but in tightening the blockade, Britain risked the goodwill and support of important parts of the American political establishment, notably Wilson himself. If Wilson denied Britain new lines of credit, it would be difficult to continue the war, let alone achieve a successful outcome.[1] British naval intelligence was critical in helping the British government and its Entente partners navigate these challenges. It also delivered a coup, perhaps the single greatest intelligence success of the twentieth century, that helped ensure United States entry into the war on the Allied side, thereby rendering their eventual victory almost certain.

While the U-boat threat became the dominant focus of the naval war from late 1916, the High Seas Fleet remained an important intelligence target. In part, this was because a capable and intact fleet always posed the threat of raids on the British coast, or to trade in the North Sea and beyond. But the presence of the High Seas Fleet was also essential to the U-boat campaign. It made the U-boats less vulnerable to British countermeasures, preventing the Royal Navy intercepting U-boats near their bases, and rendering offensive mining in the Bight impracticable.

Scheer himself admitted that without the support of capital ships the submarine fleet would soon have been blocked in. The High Seas Fleet also denied Britain access to the Baltic, making it impossible to use this route to supply Russia, a factor that might have prevented her collapse in 1917, or to cut off vital German supplies from Sweden. Finally, the status of the High Seas Fleet determined the strength of the Grand Fleet, including its destroyers and other light forces. Without the continuing threat it posed, significant numbers of destroyers would have been released to counter the U-boats and support convoy operations.[2] The indecisive outcome of Jutland, therefore, had lasting strategic consequences for the naval war. Beyond the North Sea, intelligence operations in the Mediterranean also became more important from 1916.

Scheer's doubts in the wake of Jutland that a decisive fleet victory was possible did not prevent a major sortie on 18/19 August. This involved the full High Seas Fleet with the exception of the battlecruisers *Derfflinger* and *Seydlitz*, still under repair, but with the addition of the newly completed battleship *Bayern*. The plan was essentially the original concept for the Jutland operation, a bombardment of Sunderland, designed to create an opportunity to isolate and destroy a significant British force. However, there was a more sophisticated 'combined arms' dimension to this sortie than its predecessors. Extensive Zeppelin reconnaissance would help achieve the desired interception, while providing early warning of Grand Fleet intervention. Such intervention would also be countered by carefully placed U-boat traps, which Scheer hoped could achieve significant attrition.

Once again, Room 40 performed well, providing twelve hours' warning of Scheer's departure. This enabled the Grand Fleet to deploy, along with the Harwich Force and extra submarines. Both fleets suffered early casualties to submarine attack, the British losing two light cruisers and the Germans damage to the battleship *Westfalen*. This caused Jellicoe temporarily to halt his progress south, while Scheer was lured towards the Harwich Force by a faulty Zeppelin report. These diversions prevented the fleets meeting, before Scheer, alerted to the Grand Fleet's presence, beat a hasty retreat.[3]

Although the sortie produced no engagement between surface forces, Jellicoe, backed by Beatty, drew stark conclusions, reluctantly endorsed by the Admiralty. The British were alert to a German combined arms threat, 'bait plus Zeppelins plus submarines', but the U-boat successes were a shock, demonstrating that even fast-manoeuvring warships were now at risk. The loss of the two cruisers underlined Jellicoe's long-standing fears of submarine traps, which he judged now dominated German thinking.

The ever-increasing mining operations by both sides in the North Sea were a further threat, constraining deployment options and making traps potentially more effective. Jellicoe did not believe he had sufficient destroyers to protect his fleet in the new circumstances, and agreed with the Admiralty that the Grand Fleet would now only deploy south of the line between the Farne Islands and Horns Reef in 'exceptional circumstances'. These included an attempt at invasion, a clear opportunity to engage the High Seas Fleet in daylight in an area where the Grand Fleet was not disadvantaged, or possibly a major German attack on the Thames, or through the Dover straits. They did not include raids on east-coast ports, where timely interception was unlikely.

All this had important intelligence implications. British monitoring of Scheer's movements through decrypts and D/F worked better than at Jutland, supplemented by some good submarine reporting, exploiting the fitting of more powerful Poulsen 3kw radios. However, this August sortie gave warning that the British information advantage was reducing. German radio discipline was better and their own SIGINT operation, which had already made a useful contribution at Jutland, more effective. Room 40 feared that the Germans would soon tighten up on their harbour transmissions, which were critical to early warning of fleet movements and German intent. The Admiralty had agreed with Jellicoe that in future, when it directed the Grand Fleet to sail in response to an anticipated German sortie, it would state the degree of urgency, although without SIGINT insights this would be difficult. British submarine surveillance of the Bight accordingly became a critical backstop. As William James stated many years later: 'These wonderful modern inventions, the plane, wireless cryptography, *may* assist, but *nothing* can give the same *assurance* as the "frigate" off the enemy's coast'.[4] The Zeppelin problem also spurred British investment in air capability, which proceeded on a wider front, and with greater resources than Germany could muster. From the end of the year, Zeppelins were increasingly vulnerable to British countermeasures, while British aerial surveillance provided further insurance against a German surprise.[5]

Scheer took more positives from the August operation than Jellicoe, and anticipated further operations exploiting the lessons learnt, to make Zeppelin and U-boat support more effective. However, before he was ready to try again, the Admiralstab decided on 6 October to resume commerce warfare, albeit initially under prize rules. This left Scheer with too few U-boats to risk a long-range strike on the British east coast, and he resorted to a more limited operation on 18 October against North Sea shipping, hoping to lure out Beatty's battlecruisers. Room 40 gave the

Admiralty five hours' warning, and the Grand Fleet was alerted but, in accordance with the new policy, did not sail. Scheer was unsettled by early attacks on two of his cruisers by the British submarine screen in the Bight, and then by intercepts suggesting the British knew he was at sea. With the weather deteriorating, he decided potential benefits did not justify the risk of continuing, and aborted the operation. It was the last High Seas Fleet sortie for eighteen months. If Scheer harboured any illusions about the risk of operating without a strong Zeppelin and U-boat reconnaissance screen, they were dispelled in early November, when two battleships were damaged by a British submarine during an operation to recover two returning U-boats stranded off Jutland.[6]

Overall, the August and October sorties made both sides at least temporarily more risk averse. Both Jellicoe, and Beatty when he took over as commander-in-chief in December, agreed that the primary role of the Grand Fleet was to underpin the British blockade. Germany could not open the sea routes for her trade without defeating the Grand Fleet, only possible by first reducing British superiority through mines or submarine attack, or successfully trapping a portion of the fleet. Destruction of the High Seas Fleet remained eminently desirable, but neither was willing to risk attrition in bringing this about. Through the winter, the destroyer shortage worsened, owing to the demands of the new U-boat offensive, constraining fleet mobility. Scheer had a parallel goal, supporting Germany's counter-blockade through the U-boats, and a similar mobility constraint: lack of U-boats for protecting his fleet during a sortie. The primary role of the High Seas Fleet, therefore, became protection of the U-boat bases and their immediate approaches. Beatty appreciated this, arguing during the armistice negotiations that surrender of the High Seas Fleet surface units was more important than the U-boats. Remove the power of the High Seas Fleet, and 'the submarine menace would completely collapse'.[7] The threat posed by the High Seas Fleet also limited release of destroyers from the Grand Fleet for the anti-submarine war. Scheer would not risk attrition from the superior Grand Fleet prejudicing this overriding goal. By the end of 1916, the prospects of a major fleet encounter were thus minimal, with both sides committed to a cautious 'fleet in being' policy. The naval war now focused on the execution of the two blockades. Each side sought to tighten their own, while limiting that of their opponent. For both, this also implied a significant shift in resources and manpower away from the main fleets.[8] It also brought major changes to the management of British naval intelligence. The intelligence operation to support the British blockade had already seen considerable innovation, but the problems in exploiting Room 40 intelligence exposed at Jutland were not addressed until well into 1917.

Despite the cross-government preparations supervised by Hankey, Britain entered the war in 1914 with the differing views over the scope of economic action against Germany, and how it would be applied, partially unresolved. Three measures commanded consensus within the British government: the removal of German merchant shipping from the seas; banning British ships from entering enemy ports; and imposing severe restrictions on British-controlled trade with Germany. Theoretically, these measures alone reduced German trade by 80 per cent. However, as long foreseen, they did not prevent Germany shifting its trade to neutral ships and ports, exploiting land sources of supply, or conniving covertly with willing suppliers. The Admiralty's commitment to a policy of distant blockade was also an important constraint, both practically and legally. Practical implementation required effective scrutiny of all commercial traffic bound for northern European ports passing north and south of the United Kingdom. Sealing the Dover strait and imposing an inspection regime requiring vessels to call at the Downs or Falmouth was relatively straightforward. Neutral acquiescence here was ensured by declaring the North Sea a war zone, and obliging them to seek advice on safe routes through British and German minefields.[9] However, operating an effective northern blockade line between Shetland and Norway by the 10th Cruiser Squadron, equipped initially with old, ill-suited vessels, in winter weather was demanding. Determined blockade-runners could generally avoid interception, although there were few of these, and most were subsequently identified, making further use in blockade avoidance difficult. But even vessels prepared to accept inspection were often missed. Perhaps 20 per cent of vessels on this northern route passed unexamined in the first nine months of the war, although the proportion was steadily reducing.[10]

Legally, Britain had to decide whether to abide by the Declaration of London. If she did, and declared a distant blockade, it was restricted to a policy of contraband control, though definitions of contraband were open to interpretation. If she ignored the Declaration and ruthlessly asserted belligerent rights, it risked a damaging clash with neutral powers, above all the United States, determined to exercise its right to freedom of the seas. Leaving aside the arguments for respecting international law which persisted after the outbreak of war, there were more hard-nosed reasons to uphold the Declaration. Britain and her allies needed material and financial support from the United States, and could not risk reprisals following a dispute over neutral rights. Nor did she want to encourage the

United States to become an enthusiastic and determined supplier of war materials to Germany, perhaps even placing German merchant vessels trapped in American ports under the American flag. There was also a convincing case that a co-operative, rather than coercive, relationship with the northern neutrals – Holland, Denmark and Norway – would best meet British interests, minimising German trade diversion through their territories, while safeguarding their important supplies to Britain.[11] Finally, if Britain abandoned the constraints of international law, Germany would too, resorting to indiscriminate mining and submarine warfare. Many felt all-out trade war would be deeply damaging and therefore not in Britain's interests, even if she eventually won it.

For a Liberal government this combination of ideology and realpolitik, promoted by Edward Grey and the Foreign Office, but commanding broad support in the Cabinet, including from Churchill, was compelling. For the first nine months of the war, therefore, British policy was to observe the Declaration of London 'so far as may be practicable'. This meant that only a limited list of war goods was proscribed, while many valuable raw materials and much food passed without hindrance along neutral routes. Although Britain steadily extended her definition of contraband to reduce neutral 'leakage', she was constrained by the need to appease the United States. During this period, the combination of British restraint and Germany's pre-war mitigation planning meant the blockade had limited impact on the German economy. It worsened Germany's terms of trade and reduced its exports, but imports continued near pre-war levels, and vital war materials such as copper and cotton, largely acquired from the United States pre-war, still reached Germany via neutral sources. American shipments of copper to Italy, Scandinavia and Switzerland quadrupled.[12]

Navigating the political, economic, legal and practical issues to reach a coherent and effective blockade policy was initially further complicated by divided responsibility and conflicting agendas across different Whitehall departments, by lack of specialist expertise, and by inadequate and poorly shared intelligence. Nevertheless, through 1915 important new intelligence and enforcement arrangements steadily developed. Better intelligence illuminated the weaknesses of a blockade conducted under Declaration terms, hardening political attitudes. It enabled British contraband control measures to be better targeted and circumvention, including that by British exporters, to be closed off. By the summer, Britain was using intelligence to deny bunkering facilities to neutral shippers who failed to accept British blockade rules, including her definitions of contraband.[13] Intelligence-driven enforcement enabled an ever-tighter blockade, as political constraints were removed, the latter spurred by the arrival of coalition government in May, with the appointment of Balfour to the Admiralty, and Lord Robert Cecil as undersecretary of state overseeing the Contraband Department in the Foreign Office.[14] The Contraband Department under the Foreign Office's foremost German expert and future permanent secretary, Sir Eyre Crowe, was one of two organisations critical to managing a blockade, which over the first year of the war remained essentially confined to contraband control. It directed blockade policy and action to prevent the passage of contraband items through an interdepartmental Contraband Control Committee.

The other vital organisation was the Admiralty Trade Division, headed by Richard Webb until October 1917. This was the most important repository of blockade intelligence within the government, and primary evidential source for decisions of the Contraband Committee until late 1915.[15] Its main sources were reports from British and Allied naval attachés, warships and merchant vessels, diplomatic reports, commercial sources such as Lloyd's, intercepted correspondence from cable, mail or radio, and agent reports from the SSB. Once cable censorship got underway, it was evident that this would be the most important and prolific source of blockade intelligence, but a new system was required to store and retrieve a potential deluge of information. A new database, the Neutral and Enemy Trade Index, or Admiralty Index, was accordingly established on 25 October 1914, the term 'index' reflecting its comprehensive card index system (the initial order for thirty thousand cards was viewed with 'a mixture of amusement and dismay'). Initially, it was hoped the NET Index could be operated by just two clerks, but by early 1917 it had evolved into a database, now managed by the War Trade Intelligence Department, requiring thirty clerks who handled up to three thousand cables per day.[16] From the beginning, the NET Index was intended to identify patterns and trends, and focused on suppliers, cargoes and recipients as much as ships. As it progressed, it underpinned a 'statutory black list' of British individuals and organisations known to be trading with the enemy and subject therefore to criminal prosecution, and a 'general black list' for foreign individuals and organisations believed to have dealings with the enemy. Its reports were channelled through a second interdepartmental committee, the Restriction of Enemy Supplies Committee (RESC), chaired by Sir Francis Hopwood.[17]

Through 1915, the collection of trade intelligence from sources overseas, above all from North America, improved significantly. The Foreign Office re-tasked consular staff in North America to collect shipping and cargo data, and from the spring, daily reports on transatlantic traffic were collated and despatched by the Washington embassy, becoming increasingly reliable and comprehensive. The consulate in New York, because of its size and importance, reported separately to London, and was supplemented by a separate shipping intelligence network run by Guy Gaunt. Britain also received considerable help from Canada in gathering this shipping intelligence in the United States. Canadian agents visiting American ports attracted less attention, and any exposure of their role was less damaging, since it avoided inflaming anti-British sentiment.[18] All this material was copied to the naval intelligence centres at Halifax, St John's, Kingston Jamaica, and Bermuda, all covering the eastern Atlantic seaboard, and Esquimalt, covering the Pacific coast. These drew appropriate connections with information from local sources. Immediate action on this North American intelligence rested with the Contraband Committee, with Trade Division applying analysis and assessment through the RESC.[19]

Only fragmentary references to blockade-related intelligence from the SSB have survived, but sufficient to demonstrate that it was useful. In early 1915 Ronald Campbell, the private secretary to Sir Arthur Nicolson, congratulated Cumming on the excellence of his 'commercial intelligence'. The following year, Frank Stagg boasted to Sir Samuel Hoare, the future politician and First Lord, who was about to become the main SSB representative in Russia, that SSB was creating a global commercial intelligence system. By the end of 1916, the SSB was issuing a weekly digest on economic conditions in Germany and by November 1917, it had a distinct economics section with similar status to its naval and military sections.[20]

These early arrangements for monitoring the blockade pioneered by the Foreign Office and Admiralty delivered some important results in the first year of the war, given the limited resources deployed. At their best, they combined strategic insight with effective action by the Contraband Committee. They also revealed the extent of import leakage into Germany, including important items originating from British sources. By mid 1915, Whitehall judged that the penalties imposed on the German economy were growing, but there was little impact on her fighting capability.[21] Meanwhile, there was frustration that British strategy lacked clarity and grip, and was hampered by poor co-ordination across the multiple departments and committees now involved. A review prepared for the prime minister in July by Edwin Montagu, the Financial Secretary, confirmed that the present management of the blockade was indeed 'confused and chaotic', and he pressed the case for a single responsible minister.[22] A further problem was that the quantity of trade intelligence now available completely swamped the analytical capacity in Trade Division, despite the innovation of the NET Index.[23]

Fortunately, major investment in intelligence organisation and capacity was already underway. At the beginning of the year, Hankey had focused on information management as the key to a more effective blockade strategy. He emphasised to the CID that improvements to intelligence organisation, and additional resources, were required to make limited contraband control effective, let alone support more comprehensive blockade measures. As the world's primary financial and trade centre, London was awash with commercial intelligence relevant to the blockade, but it must be collected and shared systematically. In addition, the censorship offices established to monitor communications with Germany, cable, radio and postal, promised to become a rich source on blockade avoidance activity. In January 1915 the collection of communications intelligence (COMINT) from these sources was divided between the War Office and the Admiralty. In accordance with plans agreed pre-war and incorporated in Hankey's War Book, the War Office established a new department, MI8, on the outbreak of war, under a chief cable censor, Colonel Arthur Churchill, to scrutinise all cable traffic accessible to Britain, home and overseas. In parallel, the Admiralty established a naval censorship office in Room 37OB under retired Commodore Douglas Brownrigg, to monitor radio communications. This reflected the Admiralty's long-standing links with Marconi. In practice, most private radio traffic was soon halted, and within a year all radio stations were under effective Admiralty control. However, initially no arrangements were made for extending postal censorship, and for the first months of the war only a tiny proportion of mail, that judged to pose a direct espionage threat, was scrutinised by MO5 officers.

The initial censorship arrangements were directed purely at defensive security, but it was soon apparent that monitoring private and commercial communications offered far wider intelligence potential, although exploiting this would need a huge lift in resources.[24] Hankey therefore advocated a central clearing house, staffed by a professional secretariat, to collect, process and distribute blockade intelligence. The outcome was the creation of the Trade Clearing House (TCH), headed by T H Penson, administered by a new War Trade Department in the Treasury under Lord Emmott which absorbed a Committee on Trade with the Enemy, established at the start of the war. The censors would continue their monitoring role as before, albeit in the case of cable and postal with much increased staff, but would be guided by the TCH on information of blockade interest, and deliver it accordingly.[25]

Hall later claimed to have first identified the important contribution that mail censorship could make to blockade intelligence, after illegally establishing an intercept unit to operate in parallel with the small MO5 team under Colonel George Cockerill. He further claimed that when he and Cockerill were confronted by the Home Secretary over his unauthorised interference with the mail, he persuaded both McKenna, and subsequently the prime minister, that not only should monitoring continue, but that it should be subsumed in a new War Trade Intelligence Department. Hall's account is colourful, but probably exaggerates his role and is embroidered by hindsight. The term War Trade Intelligence Department did not exist until early 1916, and Hall's account omits any reference to the exploitation of cable traffic, where intercepts of interest were already regularly forwarded from MI8 to Brownrigg, and thence to Richard Webb in Trade Division to be incorporated in the NET Index. It is more credible that Hall discussed the need for a new blockade intelligence organisation with Hankey, which would explain why Hankey anticipated that the TCH would come under Admiralty control.[26] It is also possible that T11 section within Trade Division under Commander Leverton Harris, tasked with 'commercial and financial questions' and 'scrutiny of intercepted telegrams', was established with Hall's encouragement in March 1915. However, with the founding of the TCH this would have been a logical step for Webb to take.[27] While there are questions over Hall's influence in the founding of the TCH, there is little doubt that he and Cockerill were successful in persuading McKenna to approve an expanded mail intercept team. By the new year this had 170 staff, and in April it was formally constituted as a distinct War Office department MI9, working alongside MI8.[28] As with MI8, intelligence of interest to the Admiralty was then delivered via Brownrigg's team.

The TCH opened on 1 February 1915 with thirty staff, more than twice the number working on trade intelligence in Admiralty Trade Division, where the relevant sections (T1, T8 and T11) then had twelve staff.[29] Emmott defined three roles for the new organisation: collect trade information from all possible sources, including all government departments; collate information to enable executive action in support of the blockade; and produce reports and recommendations on the operation of the blockade. From early on, as Hankey anticipated, the TCH exploited the power of COMINT from MI8 and MI9. Cable was the more important of the two. Britain used its command of the transatlantic cable system to ensure that all private messages sent across the Atlantic went in plain language, or a few approved commercial codes of which Britain had copies. By mid 1915, the TCH was reading most of these messages, although copies continued to go to the naval censors and thence to Trade Division and to MO5. From early 1916 it read virtually all of them. These

COMINT intercepts were valuable in themselves, but also enhanced the contribution of material from other sources. Crucially, unlike Trade Division, the TCH had the capacity to process and analyse the vast haul of intercepts and cross-reference it alongside other information.

Building the TCH analytical capability, and making the resulting intelligence relevant and actionable, took time, and for its first nine months it operated in parallel to Trade Division, with the NET Index still the primary database for recording and processing cable traffic. However, TCH products, for both confidential analysis within government and for external influence, soon gained distinct authority and legitimacy. By mid 1915, it was issuing regular publications, such as the *Contraband Herald* warning potential suppliers to Germany that their activities would not escape British scrutiny. A typical issue of the *Herald*, published weekly, comprised ten pages. It made extensive use of both open-source and cable intercepts, where the latter did not compromise sensitive sources. It aimed to show that the blockade was working, and that British coverage of transgressors was ubiquitous.[30] The Foreign Office deployed such material to influence the American government through diplomatic channels, and it played a significant role in shaping the Anglo-American relationship through 1916. Meanwhile, Gaunt used it to great effect in his more covert propaganda operations in the United States.[31] By late autumn, having expanded to 150 staff, the TCH had superseded Trade Division as the primary intelligence authority on the blockade, and in early 1916 the NET Index, other unique records in Trade Division, and some of its staff were transferred to avoid duplication.[32]

The contribution of COMINT and the maturing of the TCH transformed the operation of the blockade, but also its potential. By the end of 1915, Britain had an intelligence system able to enforce the strictest form of blockade feasible in diplomatic terms. The inexorable logic driving all major combatants towards policies of total war inevitably led Britain to depart from Declaration terms and tighten its blockade. Conservative members of the coalition, aware of reports from Jellicoe highlighting the scale of leakage, favoured such tightening, and the improving intelligence emphasised the limited impact of present measures. A comprehensive assessment, drawing on multiple sources, of the economic situation in Germany by the highly regarded British Consul General in Budapest, William Max Müller, delivered in January 1916, was especially influential. He saw no prospect that present blockade measures would materially diminish German military power, and judged food supplies were adequate until the next harvest. Furthermore, he argued that even more 'grinding' economic pressure would have only limited impact, unless accompanied by military success. Nevertheless, pursued in parallel to a determined military effort, blockade could still make an important contribution to Germany's defeat.[33]

What was feasible diplomatically changed markedly in the last half of 1915, primarily because of Germany's first unrestricted U-boat campaign, but also its sabotage operations in the United States. Britain's distant blockade conducted on Declaration terms had forced Germany to pay an economic premium by trading through neutrals, but had neither permanently reduced imports, nor yet successfully denied Germany any essential war commodity. Counter-attacking with U-boats in a campaign bound to be judged illegal, and arguably criminal, under international law only made sense if Germany could inflict significant economic or military damage on Britain. Such damage was not possible with the resources available to her in 1915. Germany gained nothing, but incurred the hostility of the United States and other neutrals, especially with high profile incidents like *Lusitania*, and gave Britain the excuse to abandon the Declaration of London and adopt a rigorous definition of belligerent rights. The British shift was still risky, and relations with the United States over blockade policy were distinctly tetchy throughout 1915–16, but especially the first months of 1916, when an embargo on the export of munitions to Britain seemed possible.[34] Nevertheless, although Grey was not always robust, Britain exploited different factions in Washington with considerable skill, helped by MI1(b)'s coverage of American diplomatic traffic. In the battle for economic advantage, Germany's U-boat decision was a profound strategic error.[35]

As 1916 opened, three factors were therefore transforming the effectiveness of the blockade: political determination to pursue it more aggressively; the intelligence capability to make this possible; and new concepts of enforcement. This new effectiveness was enhanced by organisational changes. Drawing on Montagu's earlier recommendations, blockade policy, its implementation, and the intelligence operation to support it were concentrated in the Foreign Office, within a new Ministry of Blockade under Lord Robert Cecil. Although Cecil nominally reported to Grey, a Foreign Secretary temperamentally disposed to appease American and other neutral sensitivities where possible, he had a seat in the Cabinet giving him and his ministry considerable independence. The Contraband Department formed his policy staff, he acquired the Trading with the Enemy Department from the Home Office, and operational oversight of all other committees and organisations across government, connected to the blockade. The TCH, still under Penson, became the War Trade Intelligence Department (WTID) supported by the separate War

Trade Statistical Department (WTSD) under R E Harwood. Both remained part of the War Trade Department in the Treasury for administrative purposes, but Cecil had effective operational direction. Leverton Harris moved from the Admiralty to become his parliamentary secretary, and supervised a new finance section, tasked primarily with denying credit to banks operating in neutral territory that might be accessed by enemy states. Vice Admiral Sir Dudley de Chair, former commander of the 10th Cruiser Squadron, the northern blockade force, became naval adviser. Once the Ministry of Blockade was fully established, the Foreign Office directly controlled all government bodies involved in applying economic pressure on the enemy, and did so with increasing effect until 1919.[36]

Cecil immediately promoted rationing to restrict the imports of neutrals to their normal, established peacetime requirements. This concept had been aired as far back as 1912, when Lloyd George raised it in the CID at the end of that year.[37] The principle of rationing was cautiously endorsed by the government following the outbreak of war, and some agreements were in place, notably in Holland, where Francis Oppenheimer negotiated a joint clearing house called the Netherlands Overseas Trust under which, in return for certain concessions, Dutch companies voluntarily agreed not to re-export contraband items to Germany. However, rationing was now implemented rigorously through 1916, with formal embargoes laid on shipments of a wide range of commodities to the northern neutrals judged in excess of their domestic requirements.[38] Here, the WTSD was critical, since statistical intelligence and quantitative analysis were essential to make rationing work.[39] The stick of rationing was accompanied by the carrot of purchasing neutral production surpluses, especially agricultural items, on favourable terms. Three other enforcement measures were extended: the Navicert system, the Black Lists, and bunkering control. Under the first, American exporters submitted advance notice of all shipments to Scandinavia, receiving Letters of Assurance if these were approved, allowing the cargo then to pass without detention. The Black Lists were extended and better targeted, not just to deny the enemy goods from any sources under British or Allied control, but also to deny the assistance of British banks, accepting houses and underwriters to neutral firms engaged in enemy trade. Harris's new financial section, which opened in May 1916, significantly improved the power of the Black List system. Bunkering control meant exploiting Britain's near-monopoly of global coal supplies for maritime transport, to coerce shipping companies into compliance with British blockade regulations. Failure to follow the inspection regime meant denial of future coal supplies.[40]

Blockade always ultimately rested on British sea power, the ability of the globally deployed Royal Navy substantially to define the terms of all maritime movement, and specifically to interdict any maritime traffic containing goods that might reach Germany. But from 1916, blockade was not primarily enforced by far-off, storm-tossed ships. It was mainly enforced by intelligence officers and lawyers. Intelligence, above all COMINT, became the critical weapon, providing knowledge, evidence and means for leverage. Through 1916, the WTID created a more sophisticated and wide-ranging intelligence assessment capability than any other institution or country had achieved up to this time. Indeed, it possibly ranks as the finest intelligence assessment body of the twentieth century. It was a remarkable performance, involving collection from multiple sources across the globe, technical intercept on a vast scale, and an unprecedented effort in data processing and analysis, extraordinarily sophisticated given the constraints posed by the manual systems of the day. By the end of the year it had around two hundred staff, rising to nearly three hundred and fifty by the end of the war, many of them women, who also occupied some of the more senior posts. The COMINT operation at the heart of WTID's effort was prodigious. By the end of the war, British censors had examined 80 million cables, of which 11 million were sent to government departments for action, 25 million wireless messages, and perhaps one billion letters. This censorship operation began with ten staff in 1914, but had over eight hundred in mid 1918.[41]

WTID intelligence told Britain when specific firms were trying to break the blockade, often triggering the use of other sources (including detectives hired from agencies like Pinkertons, as well as the more conventional consuls) to gather further information. Such collateral was then shared with foreign authorities, justifying British action against their nationals as necessary retaliation to the German U-boat campaign, and without jeopardising the precious COMINT source. All ships sailing to Europe were inspected at British control points, either on the western side of the Atlantic, or at the choke-points north and south of the United Kingdom. Here, cargo, crew and passengers were scrutinised through physical means and intelligence. If contraband was suspected, the blockade was enforced by the Treasury Solicitor's Department before the Probate, Divorce and Admiralty Division of the High Court of Justice, a British national court enforcing international law. This accepted secret intelligence (especially intercepted correspondence) as evidence, and had tough procedures. Vessels and cargoes without the right clearance through the Navicert system could be held for months, disrupting shipping schedules and destroying profitability.

All potential traders, including neutral suppliers and shippers, wished to avoid these risks. The more they saw the power of British surveillance and Britain's ability to use this to deliver punishment by blacklisting, confiscation under the rationing system, or denial of coal supplies, the more they accepted British rules of blockade. By the end of 1916, 75 per cent of neutral ships entering or leaving the North Sea called voluntarily at British inspection points and most were adopting the Navicert system and other mechanisms that facilitated legitimate traders. Of the remaining 25 per cent, four-fifths were intercepted, leaving a mere 5 per cent of successful evaders.[42] By April 1917, when the United States entered the war, it was practically impossible for any vessel to undertake a voyage to northern Europe without British approval, and if any tried, it was soon discovered. Hall assessed there had been no serious attempt to run the blockade after autumn 1916, and that remaining evaders were unimportant, comprising mainly small schooners passing between Iceland and Denmark. It was also now easier to capture any offending vessel at her port of loading or unloading than to intercept her in the open sea.[43] At the end of August 1917, the United States War Trade Board introduced a licensing system, which effectively eliminated any residual neutral leakage through Holland and Scandinavia, ending remaining German imports from the west. Naval force to back up the blockade was now superfluous, and the 10th Cruiser Squadron was withdrawn at the end of the year.[44] In earlier wars, naval blockade was more battleaxe than scalpel, damaging relations with firms and states in a counterproductive fashion. In this war, effective intelligence helped Britain apply it with accuracy. The ultimate contribution of the blockade to Germany's defeat remains debatable, but intelligence was fundamental to its application, minimising the damage to Britain while maximising that on the enemy.[45]

The Admiralty intelligence operation conducted through ID and Room 40, and the Ministry of Blockade operation conducted through WTID, as they operated at the end of 1916, present important contrasts. Each supported one of the two main elements of the naval war against Germany, elements rooted in the strategic debates before 1914. ID and Room 40 focused on control of the North Sea, the threat posed by the High Seas Fleet and, increasingly, the U-boat campaign. WTID supported the naval blockade. For each, the most valuable and prolific source was COMINT, but each drew on multiple other sources, often the same ones, the SSB, the naval attachés, and diplomatic reporting. The number of staff each employed in their primary target areas was similar.[46] But there were two crucial differences. The most obvious was the treatment of COMINT: compartmentalised and, at best, partially exploited within the Admiralty structure; fully integrated and professionally assessed in WTID. This reflected a wider contrast between the two organisations. The culture within ID and Room 40, promoted by Hall, was creative, intuitive and opportunistic, and encouraged initiative. WTID pursued a more systematic approach to the intelligence business, emphasising co-ordination, cross-checking and analytical rigour. It is not clear how closely Hall monitored WTID's handling of COMINT and its approach to assessment, but there were lessons that could have reformed the Admiralty's management of intelligence earlier, and more effectively.

The combination of rationing and the intelligence-driven approach possible with the maturing of the WTID transformed the impact of the blockade across 1916, and Germany suffered badly. Imports from the United States by the northern neutrals plunged, down in most cases between a half and two-thirds, affecting both raw materials and food supplies. Shortage of key commodities such as copper hit industrial production, with direct impact on vital war outputs.[47] GDP for 1916 was down almost one-fifth compared to 1913, and remained static for the rest of the war.[48] Lack of fertiliser hit domestic food production, compounded by a poor harvest, causing widespread shortages in the notorious Turnip Winter of 1916/17, when for a few months food supplies only supported about half the average pre-war calorific norm. Food availability recovered somewhat during summer 1917, but imports fell a further half to two-thirds by mid 1918. Apart from the 1916/17 winter, Germany theoretically had enough food to give the population a nutritionally adequate, if unappetising, diet. However, this assumes average consumption with efficient and fair distribution. In practice, poor management and distribution, especially to urban areas, and inequalities across society meant some groups suffered disproportionately, while the daily choice for most was grim and monotonous. Perhaps few genuinely starved, but many were badly undernourished and susceptible to illness, while morale plummeted and social tensions increased.[49]

By autumn 1916, the British leadership had enough indications of growing problems in Germany to be confident that Ottley's long-ago promise for the 'mills of our sea power' was now becoming a reality. At the end of October, the WTID recognised that German industry faced growing shortages of raw materials. War production had so far held up well, but present output was not sustainable. Food supplies were falling and stocks acquired in Romania would have limited impact.[50] The difficult food situation in Germany that autumn was underlined in reports to Washington from the American chargé d'affaires in Berlin, Joseph Grew, which were intercepted by MI1(b) and passed to Hall.[51]

In a wide-ranging review of the war, prepared for Lloyd George as incoming prime minister on 8 December, Hankey stated that economic pressure on the enemy was so 'admirably handled' by the Foreign Office, that he could only suggest continuing the present policy, while losing no opportunity to 'turn the screw', depriving Germany of munitions and food.[52]

12

Counter-blockade: Struggling with the U-boat Threat 1916–1917

Intelligence warning of a new U-boat offensive

Britain was not aware that Scheer's Jutland despatch to the Kaiser on 4 July had recommended an all-out U-boat assault on Britain's supply lines. Nor did she obtain intelligence on the conference held at Pless Castle on 31 August, when the German political and military leadership reviewed the case for resuming unrestricted U-boat warfare. Admiral Henning von Holtzendorff, chief of the German naval staff, argued that Germany was on the defensive, the Entente had greater resources, the blockade was becoming more oppressive, and time was not on Germany's side. The U-boats gave Germany the means to force Britain out of the war within months. Negative impact on neutral powers could be managed. Without this step, he feared *finis Germaniae.* His view was endorsed by his military colleagues, including Hindenburg and Ludendorff, but opposed by Bethmann-Hollweg and other civilian ministers present. The latter group doubted the U-boat offensive would deliver decisive results in any acceptable timescale, and feared the impact on neutral opinion, with American intervention against Germany probable. At this point, Bethmann-Hollweg was politically strong enough to rule against Holtzendorff, although all present knew a decision was merely deferred.[1]

However, in late September Britain gained important insights into German thinking from SIGINT, suggesting that early resumption of unrestricted U-boat warfare was probable. An intercepted telegram from Bethmann-Hollweg to Bernstorff in Washington, dated 25 September, was revealing. Since neither side could anticipate an early breakthrough on land, Germany was preparing for a ruthless submarine assault on Britain as its primary enemy. This would force Britain to the peace table in months, but also reduce her supplies of munitions, thus relieving pressure on the Somme. Nevertheless, Germany was prepared to hold back if President Wilson planned an early peace initiative. Bernstorff was tasked to establish, preferably through Colonel House, if this was likely. Bethmann-Hollweg stressed the need for Wilson to move quickly. A lengthening war was not in Germany's interest. She must push soon for a decisive result.[2]

There was important collateral for German thinking in American diplomatic reporting from Berlin at the end of September and beginning of October. This confirmed that Germany was anxious to explore peace terms and sought American help in achieving this, but it was vital any American initiative did not appear to come at German instigation.[3] Meanwhile, the American naval attaché had reliable information from the German admiralty that planning for 'early resumption of submarine warfare in violation of neutral rights' was underway, and that the admiralty now anticipated political support.[4] But there was also confirmation that Germany would temporarily suspend submarine action to avoid embarrassing the president, should he undertake a peace initiative.[5] These telegrams were almost certainly intercepted by MI1(b), but no decrypts of this particular series appear to have survived. There are surviving MI1(b) decrypts of American reporting from Berlin in December, showing that the German desire to exploit American mediation before resorting to unrestricted U-boat warfare remained extant.[6] American reporting was authoritative, not only because of their mediation role, but because both the Berlin ambassador, James Gerard, and his deputy Joseph Grew were well-connected and perceptive observers. Their relationship with Count Adolph Montgelas, the official responsible for the United States and Mexico in the German foreign office, was especially important. Montgelas had served in Washington and had an American wife. For personal and political reasons, he feared American intervention alongside the Entente, making him bitterly opposed to unrestricted U-boat warfare, a topic on which he spoke candidly. Ironically, he was one of the authors of the Zimmermann telegram, contributing, therefore, to the American entry he was desperate to avoid.[7] His brother, Maximilian, was an army general, who later in the war became an important source of intelligence on German leadership thinking for both the Americans and the British.[8]

Bethmann-Hollweg's telegram to Bernstorff made a powerful impression on Hall, causing him to inform Gaunt in Washington that the Germans might start their submarine offensive 'within the next few weeks', after one final attempt 'to secure an armistice'.[9] Hall had other indicators beyond diplomatic decrypts. Room 40 coverage of U-boat operations remained excellent – better than it had ever been. The increased number of boats, improved radio equipment, and the demands of more distant operations increased the volume of U-boat traffic, helping Room 40's task. All departures and arrivals for U-boats continued to be broadcast, but boats were also more talkative during deployment. Outward-bound U-boats through the English Channel reported the route they had taken and problems encountered. Intelligence on British shipping was broadcast, as were operational updates from returning boats. The D/F system was now more extensive and efficient, often compensating for any delays in decryption. There were limitations in exploiting U-boat traffic. U-boats used radio freely near their bases, but less during transit and in their operational areas, making tracking intermittent.[10] Nevertheless, Room 40 had an accurate picture of U-boat strength and overall deployment patterns, with considerable insight into individual operational patrols.[11]

The quality and limitations of Room 40's U-boat coverage are demonstrated in ID reports from January 1918, which included a breakdown of U-boats commissioned and lost, month by month, throughout the war up to the end of 1917.[12] ID figures for monthly U-boat losses during the war up to this date correlate closely with post-war assessments.[13] With one important exception, ID estimates for new U-boats commissioned were also accurate. The exception was the spurt in commissioning of UC minelaying U-boats in the last quarter of 1916, ready for the unrestricted campaign. ID credited Germany with twenty fewer UC boats at the end of December 1916 than she had nominally commissioned by this date, although all were identified and added to German strength by the end of the next quarter. This meant that while total U-boat output in 1916 and 1917 was respectively 107 and eighty-five, the British figures reversed these, crediting Germany with eighty-seven and 107 for these years.[14] At one level, this was a minor issue of statistical presentation and did not matter. By the end of March, official German U-boat strength was 150 and the British put it at 153. However, when linked with other indicators, for a while it fuelled British fears that monthly U-boat output was rising significantly, when in reality it had already peaked and showed a small reduction across 1917.

The ID estimates of January 1918 do not reveal sources. Some of their data came from British reports following engagements with U-boats, from TR16 and other secret agents, from prisoner interrogation and from captured documents, including some acquired from dives on sunken U-boats from 1916 onward. However, the detailed monthly accounting also reflected comprehensive SIGINT coverage, which detected the first operational appearance of each new U-boat, its type, and probable yard of origin, and monitored it until it went silent, indicating its potential loss. Producing this accounting in tabular form required considerable analytical effort, only available when Room 40 SIGINT was shared with select ID sections from late summer 1917. The quality of U-boat SIGINT collected did not change much between late 1916 and late 1917. Room 40, therefore, had the data to produce similar tables in 1916, if it had received the direction and possessed the management and organisation to do so. Furthermore, even if they could not yet produce precise tabular records, Room 40 could still provide a detailed picture of U-boat strength, capability and deployment over the winter of 1916/17, if asked the right questions.

By early autumn, Room 40 knew, and informed Hall, that the U-boat fleet was re-equipping and undergoing intensive training and preparation. In early October they monitored a trial voyage by *U-53* to the United States eastern seaboard. In November they intercepted a telegram from Bernstorff to Eckhardt in Mexico using a code known as 13040, asking him to explore the prospects of obtaining a U-boat base there. Ability to read Washington–Mexico traffic in 13040 shortly became more significant.[15] There were also signs that the Germans were collecting information to help them assess the impact of an unrestricted campaign on British shipping resources.[16] Henry Jackson described the latest diplomatic decrypts to Jellicoe on 19 October. Germany was threatening President Wilson with a new U-boat campaign (here Jackson noted that 'one U-boat', *U-53*, was currently returning from a patrol off the American coast, while two more were ready to deploy), while flattering him with calls to take on the role of mediator. Meanwhile, the Americans were being difficult over war finance. Britain was monitoring these developments through 'secret sources', but managing the relationship with the United States would be difficult.[17]

Diplomatic and naval SIGINT together enabled Hall to monitor the evolution of German U-boat strategy and its interaction with American policy and politics for the rest of the year, the latter helped by his regular meetings with Edward Bell. He assessed correctly that Wilson's personal position, and American opinion, generally still remained determinedly neutral and resolutely opposed to intervention.[18] He was undoubtedly selective in choosing who saw specific reports, but Hankey, Balfour and Jackson probably saw everything. The evidence that he deliberately held back intelligence on the peace negotiations from the Foreign Office and ministers is scanty. American intercepts were under MI1(b)'s control, and were certainly seen by Lloyd George, first as Secretary for War, and then as prime minister. The diplomatic decrypts available through the last months of 1916 and beginning of 1917 provided sufficient insight into the diplomatic manoeuvres and underlying intentions of Germany and the United States to avoid undesirable concessions, or alienating President Wilson as his peace initiative unfolded. The British viewed Wilson as naive, even hostile, and susceptible to German manipulation, but the decrypts gave them confidence Germany would not offer concrete proposals for negotiation. So long as they were patient, therefore, sooner or later the Germans would resort to the U-boats, provoking a confrontation with the United States which Britain could exploit. In the event, the Zimmermann telegram, of which more shortly, accelerated this confrontation.[19]

There were limitations to this SIGINT coverage. It revealed the intent to move to an unrestricted campaign and the broad rationale behind it. The Zimmermann telegram also gave two weeks' notice of the precise start date on 1 February. However, just as Britain had no direct knowledge of the Pless conference at the end of August, she obtained no intelligence on Holtzendorff's famous memorandum of 22 December, presenting the case for unrestricted warfare, or the OHL conference on 9 January, when the German leadership decided to proceed, convinced they could now coerce Britain into ending the war. Britain was not, therefore, aware that the Germans planned a dramatic step-change in sinkings to 600,000 tons of shipping per month for five months to break 'England's backbone', before American intervention achieved any useful effect.[20] She also lacked coverage of the differences between the political and military leadership, although the American diplomatic decrypts provided some insight here. Naval SIGINT ensured those indoctrinated into Room 40 had an accurate picture of current U-boat strength and deployment but, as noted earlier, predicting future building rate and capacity for a sustained campaign was more difficult.

British preparations for a new unrestricted campaign

From Bethmann-Hollweg's telegram to Bernstorff at the end of September, Britain therefore had four months to prepare for the unrestricted campaign which began on 1 February 1917. How did the Admiralty and Cabinet use this intelligence warning? Did they recognise the risk they faced? What preparations were made? While the prospect of unrestricted warfare was disturbing, two more immediate factors gave the U-boat threat renewed priority during October and November. The first was the resumption at the beginning of September, after a long summer lull, of restricted warfare under prize rules in home waters. U-boat sinkings rose 50 per cent in that month on the average for the first eight months of the year, and in October they tripled. Tonnage lost in the last four months of 1916 was double that for the first eight months, and by the end of January it was twice that in the seven months of unrestricted warfare in 1915. Significantly, 40 per cent of the losses were in the Mediterranean, where only 20 per cent of the U-boat force was deployed and, with fewer American vessels, prize rules were interpreted more flexibly.[21] Almost all this damage was done by surfaced U-boats, with 80 per cent of victims warned before being sunk, and 75 per cent sunk by deck gun rather than torpedo. The five months to end January cost the Germans just ten U-boats, including one to a mine in the Bosporus, and three to the Russians in the Black Sea.[22] The second factor was the deployment of larger U-boats over a more extended area. SIGINT monitored the rise in U-boat size and numbers, with around 130 available in the frontline by the end of the year, and their deployment as far as the American seaboard.[23] Despite this excellent intelligence, through September into October the Admiralty watched the increased losses and progressive expansion of the submarine danger zone, 'with the anxiety of a physician who studies the steady, unrelenting spread of a harmful symptom'. The philosophically detached Balfour stressed to the War Committee of the Cabinet the need to accept 'palliation', and measures 'to diminish an evil which unfortunately we cannot wholly cure'.[24]

However, the growing U-boat strength, alongside the deteriorating picture in weekly shipping-loss statistics, profoundly influenced Jellicoe by mid October. He recognised that the U-boat threat, rather than a battle with the High Seas Fleet, was now the crux of the naval situation, provoking him to send Balfour a memorandum at the end of the month. Jellicoe's language here was dramatic but, given events the following spring, not unreasonable. The submarine menace was the most pressing issue the Royal Navy faced, and by early next summer, merchant losses, British and neutral, could be severe enough to force the Entente into peace on unfavourable terms.[25] Jellicoe's intervention certainly grabbed attention. Balfour passed his letter to the prime minister, who invited him to address the War Committee on 2 November, while the top Admiralty leadership met the following day. (The War Committee, instituted in late 1915, was the supreme policy-making body for managing the war under the full Cabinet. It was chaired by the prime minister and comprised about half the Cabinet, the First Sea Lord, Chief of the Imperial General Staff, Foreign Office permanent secretary, and other senior military and civilian officials, typically about twenty members in all. Oliver as chief of staff often accompanied the First Sea Lord. Hankey was secretary.)

Jellicoe's representations had less immediate impact than they should have done. At the War Committee, they coincided with parallel assessments on the shipping position from Hankey and the President of the Board of Trade.[26] These warned of adverse trends, notably losses in the Mediterranean and availability of neutral shipping, and showed that, overall, shipping stock was declining. However, they did not convey urgency: indeed, given the U-boat depredations of the coming months, Hankey was complacent, even complimenting the Admiralty on its defensive measures. Close analysis of the statistics available to Hankey, the responsibility of Trade Division, would have revealed that 52 per cent of shipping losses to U-boats in these nine months had occurred in the Mediterranean, where less than a quarter of the current U-boat force was deployed. The average number of boats at sea here was half that during the 1915 unrestricted campaign, yet they sank more than 80 per cent of the tonnage achieved in that campaign, reflecting the greater freedom permitted to Mediterranean U-boats in selecting targets.[27] It was a stark warning of what a new unrestricted campaign would unleash. Without such analysis, it was hard, therefore, for the War Committee to square the statistical picture in Hankey's assessments with Jellicoe's picture of imminent doom.

Poor presentation also weakened Jellicoe's case. His October memorandum lost sight of the wood by meandering through the trees. After asserting that existing anti-U-boat measures were flawed or of declining value, his recommendations looked mundane and muddled. His primary proposal was to form a committee of experts to examine ideas for new weapons, such as an anti-submarine howitzer.[28] At the War Committee, three weaknesses that blighted Jellicoe's forthcoming tenure as First Sea Lord were visible: his inclination to default to detail, rather than concentrate on the big picture; his unwillingness to contribute beyond his own brief; and his tendency to pessimism. The meeting also demonstrated Jellicoe's support for two entrenched Admiralty policies which hampered progress in the coming months – opposition to convoy, and a fixation on arming as many merchant ships as possible with guns. The latter was a reasonable response to present U-boat tactics, but its value would reduce if the Germans resumed unrestricted warfare and shifted to a torpedo-first tactic. Lloyd George was evidently frustrated both by Jellicoe's manner and his arguments, not least on convoy, which he sensed reflected dogma, not reasoned analysis. This suggested that their relationship would not prosper.[29]

Jellicoe's memorandum also triggered a meeting in the Admiralty on 3 November, the day after the War Committee. Those present comprised almost the entire London-based naval leadership, including the four sea lords, Jellicoe, Arthur Wilson, Oliver, Thomas Jackson, Webb, and other key members of the war staff but, surprisingly, not Hall. This was the first time such an eminent group had gathered to address the U-boat problem, and it should have stimulated a full stocktaking of present strategy. There was important (and expensive) investment currently underway: notably, the construction of mine and net barrages across the Dover strait and the Otranto strait, closing off the Adriatic U-boat bases in the Mediterranean; there were plans for bombardment of the U-boat base at Zeebrugge; and the extensive mining and submarine operations against the German egress routes in the Bight deserved review too. There was also the experience gained in diverting merchant traffic away from known U-boat locations, and how this concept might be further developed. Linked with this was the crucial issue of convoy. Opposition to this was solid across the war staff, yet weekly convoys were already successfully run to Holland, and Oliver noted that high-value ships under escort were rarely attacked. There was a potential inconsistency here to be explored. All these issues proved important to countering the U-boat problem over the next two years, yet they were barely mentioned at the meeting itself, although Oliver referred to most of them in subsequent correspondence. Instead, the meeting focused narrowly on the recommendations in Jellicoe's memorandum. The howitzer concept would be investigated, but in place of a committee, there was consensus that a flag officer be appointed to supervise all anti-submarine measures. Remarkably, throughout these exchanges, there was no reference to intelligence, or improving its exploitation which, as time showed, underpinned everything else. Some of those present knew how much Room 40 SIGINT could contribute; some knew what the WTID could offer on shipping movements and statistics; most knew the importance of the growing D/F network.[30]

The Jellicoe-inspired discussions did not provide a coherent policy on the U-boat threat in what proved the dying weeks of the Asquith administration, but they raised its priority and triggered change in the Admiralty leadership. Jackson became convinced he was not the right man to address the new challenge, resulting in Jellicoe's appointment as First Sea Lord at the end of the month. A week later, Lloyd George replaced Asquith as prime minister, Balfour moved to the Foreign Office, and Edward Carson became First Lord. On 2 November the War Committee had at least concluded that the protection of shipping was 'one of the gravest questions facing the Allies'. Two weeks later, Jackson and Oliver pressed it to review the possibility of a land offensive against the submarine bases at Zeebrugge and Ostend.[31] The committee was supportive, with Asquith recording a consensus that 'the submarine constitutes by far the most dangerous menace to the Allies at the present'.[32] The desirability of removing these German bases was a constant theme over the next nine months, and a significant factor in justifying the Passchendaele offensive the following autumn. Hankey, influenced by November shipping statistics, also abandoned any complacency. In his memorandum on war priorities, prepared for Lloyd George as incoming prime minister on 8 December, he ranked the U-boat problem top of the list for attention.[33]

Jellicoe's first major step as First Sea Lord was the creation in mid December of a new Anti-Submarine Division (ASD) under Rear Admiral Alexander Duff, reporting directly to him, with Dreyer as deputy. This was a logical evolution of his original idea of a committee, translated on 3 November into a supervisory flag officer. The ASD was to tackle the U-boat threat as a single problem, bringing all anti-submarine measures previously spread across several departments under its remit. It would become a centre of expertise, control all forces permanently deployed on anti-submarine work, including aircraft, and supervise the development and procurement of all anti-submarine weapons and equipment.[34] Its status under the First Sea Lord effectively gave it executive authority, beginning a process that by the summer transformed the war staff into a true naval staff.[35]

During its first two months of operation, extending into the first weeks of the unrestricted campaign, ASD reviewed existing anti-submarine operations and capabilities, but without any immediate change in policy. No measures were abandoned, even if evidence suggested they were ineffective, as with the Dover barrage, and naval bombardment of the Belgian bases. Room 40 decrypts showed the former was merely an inconvenience, even to larger U-boats, and the latter achieved no lasting damage. There was little attempt to challenge received wisdom (that convoy was unworkable and ineffective), or to anticipate how the U-boat threat might evolve (a shift to torpedo rather than gun attack with unrestricted warfare). Oliver, admittedly not the most objective observer, felt ASD spent too much time reinventing the wheel. Certainly, there was little in the initial ASD approach inconsistent with the views he expressed in the wake of the 3 November discussions.[36]

Room 40 intelligence, in which Duff and key members of his staff were indoctrinated at the insistence of Jellicoe, encouraged this conservative approach. It provided much detailed information on U-boat transit routes and patrol locations in home waters and the Western Approaches. During February and March, the first two months of the unrestricted campaign, Room 40 identified fifty different U-boats at sea here, tracking the majority through the position reports they signalled every few days.[37] It was, therefore, tempting for the incoming team to conclude that the primary problem was failure to sink enough U-boats, and the reason was not the measures so far adopted, but rather inadequate material. Better mines, produced in quantity, would make the transit routes increasingly perilous, while new sensors and weapons for finding and attacking submerged U-boats would make aggressive prosecution by surface hunting groups, exploiting Room 40 location intelligence, viable. In material developments, ASD brought badly needed energy and drive, and sponsored important developments in weapons and sensors that would not have happened otherwise, or not as quickly. It commissioned improved mines in quantity, ultimately based on the excellent H2 (horned) German model, better hydrophones for both surface vessels and submarines, effective depth charges again in adequate numbers, and paravanes. The last was a small, towed underwater glider, primarily used for high-speed sweeping of tethered mines, but when fitted with an explosive charge also a rather crude anti-submarine device. All these took time to arrive (the first H2 mines were not laid until late September[38]), but they were vital facilitators of the integrated anti-submarine strategy that emerged in the second half of 1917.

In assessing that existing measures could deliver with better material, ASD was partly right. Using Room 40 SIGINT to target the transit routes used by U-boats for deploying to and from their Bight and Belgian bases, and then for passage either through the English Channel or north around Scotland, was profitable once effective mines were available. U-boat losses to British mining rose dramatically from two to sixteen between the first and second half of 1917, compared to four losses overall in 1916. Meanwhile British submarines exploiting SIGINT, primarily on these routes, sank six U-boats in 1917, compared to one the previous year. As the new mines arrived, the British adopted a combination in the Bight of offshore fields laid by surface minelayers and inshore fields deployed by 'E'-class submarines. There was a constant battle here between British laying and German sweeping. The proximity of the High Seas Fleet always constrained British access, but laying some fields further offshore, following agreement with Holland and Denmark over an extended Notified Mined Area, increased the burden for German minesweepers, while making them vulnerable to sudden attack from British light forces. Nearly 16,000 mines were laid in the Bight in 1917, claiming six U-boats and thirty-three surface vessels. In 1918, as German resources became more stretched, it was increasingly possible to apply a close blockade to U-boat routes in the Bight. Britain laid 21,000 mines in the Bight that year, and U-boat swept channels were frequently closed for forty-eight hours.

The effectiveness of the Dover barrage depended on both improved mines, and sufficient warship patrolling to oblige U-boats to dive into the minefields. This combination was not achieved until December 1917, after ID drew on documents recovered from *UC-44* off Waterford, Ireland, in September along with other intelligence, including SIGINT, to demonstrate conclusively to the new Director of Plans, Rear Admiral Sir Roger Keyes, how little the existing barrage measures were impeding transit.[39] The intelligence-driven debate over tightening the barrage ultimately triggered the sacking of the Commander-in-Chief Dover, Vice Admiral Sir Reginald Bacon, and his replacement by Keyes. It also contributed to the decision to replace Jellicoe after he resisted moving Bacon. Following implementation of the new barrier measures, twelve U-boats were destroyed here between November and May, and three more before the end of the war. The Flanders U-boats were consequently increasingly reluctant to use this route, and Channel shipping losses fell sharply. ID figures suggest transits of the strait in both directions in February 1918 were just a third of those the previous December.[40] Overall, mining accounted for thirty-five of the U-boats destroyed between 1 July 1917 and the end of the war, about one-third of the total in this period.[41]

It was also reasonable in its first months for ASD energetically to pursue arming of merchant vessels and deploying more Q-ships (vessels with heavy concealed armament to take U-boats by surprise). Over the first half of 1917, it doubled the number of armed merchant vessels to over three thousand, expending considerable war resources with significant diversion from army requirements. Other self-defence measures – zigzagging, dazzle-painting and smokescreens – also received new impetus.[42] While it is not certain how far the Admiralty had studied merchant ship losses by the time ASD was created, the pattern across 1916 was striking. Of 310 armed merchant ships attacked by U-boats that year, sixty-two were sunk by torpedo without warning, but only twelve by gunfire. By contrast, of 302 unarmed merchant ships attacked, thirty were sunk by torpedo, but 205 by gunfire. Under restricted, or prize, rules, arming merchant ships was therefore effective. Even before ASD began their new programme, Holtzendorff acknowledged that this measure would cap the destruction achievable under prize rules. Torpedoing merchant vessels identified as armed, without warning, would merely compensate for a steady decline in destruction by gunfire as more vessels were armed. It would, therefore, be difficult to improve on sinkings achieved in the last quarter of 1916 without resorting to unrestricted warfare.[43] Merchant vessel arming, along with the Q-ship risk, probably therefore encouraged the German shift in policy, although the economic arguments were decisive.[44] Surprisingly, Q-ships still delivered value in the first half of 1917, despite greater enemy alertness, and a theoretical reduction in opportunity once unrestricted warfare began: 180 were deployed, leading to sixty-three engagements and five U-boats sunk, with several others damaged. Thereafter, the decisive German shift to torpedo attack led the Admiralty to abandon the concept.[45]

If ASD's faith in intelligence-led mining proved justified, their hope that better sensors and weapons would enable effective intelligence-led hunting by increased surface patrols in the U-boat operating areas proved illusory. By early January, ASD was transmitting a constant stream of signals conveying U-boat movements and instructing local commanders to deploy forces to intercept.[46] However, they faced two intractable problems. First, the information provided by SIGINT and D/F, although impressive, was neither accurate nor frequent enough to locate a U-boat with the required precision. It was too fragmentary to provide what in the future became known as an ocean-surveillance capability. Secondly, even if a hunting group did reach the right area, a surfaced U-boat would invariably sight a hunting group first and then submerge. Once down, it was virtually undetectable, even by the improved directional hydrophones available from late 1917, in anything other than the calmest sea state, and with the listening vessel stopped and vulnerable. In the early weeks of their tenure, it was understandable for Jellicoe and ASD to believe that if determined research delivered means to find a submerged U-boat a few thousand yards away, then SIGINT and D/F would prove a winning card.[47] Research did deliver the capability to detect a submerged U-boat with the invention of ASDIC (or active sonar) at the very end of the war. But only in the late 1950s would active sonar acquire the range to make prosecution of an intelligence datum by this means alone credible. The improved hydrophones, inspired by the hunting concept, were more useful in inshore waters, and as a submarine-mounted sensor. Hunting also provoked a realistic assessment of the number of depth charges required to attack a U-boat successfully. By the end of 1917, each Royal Navy anti-submarine vessel carried, on average, ten times more depth charges than at the beginning of the year, and they were equipped with throwers, making them more effective. From two U-boats sunk by depth charge in 1916, the number rose to twelve in 1917.[48] Half of these were sunk in inshore areas subject to defensive patrolling, and the remainder by escorts to convoys, after these were introduced in May. While intelligence-led offensive patrolling failed, the new capabilities it fostered were, therefore, still used to good effect.[49]

The stimulus ASD brought to the development and production of new anti-submarine equipment justified its creation. Most projects it initiated were worthwhile, and many ultimately proved critical to countering the U-boat campaign, if not always as originally anticipated. However, it struggled to create an overall strategy, and to demonstrate inside or outside the Admiralty how the various measures it promoted fitted together. Furthermore, many of these measures, including production of new mines and depth charges, would not bear fruit for many months, while new patrol vessels on order would not arrive until 1918. This begged the question of how the growing U-boat threat would be contained in the meantime.

Here, the advice to the War Cabinet from the Admiralty and the new Shipping Controller appointed by Lloyd George, Sir Joseph Maclay, underestimated the impact of unrestricted warfare on shipping losses. (The War Cabinet, which met daily, was the supreme policy body for running the war under Lloyd George. Chaired by the prime minister, the core comprised four or five ministerial members, normally without departmental responsibility. The First Sea Lord, Chief of the Imperial General Staff, and Foreign Office permanent secretary usually attended, but were not formal members. Departmental ministers attended for items within their area of responsibility. It was more streamlined, effective and efficient than Asquith's War Committee. Hankey remained secretary.) As the German campaign opened on 1 February, the Admiralty projected total shipping losses (British, Allied and neutral) of 320,000 tons in January, rising progressively to 420,000 tons in May. The initial predicted loss for the first four months of the unrestricted campaign was 1.5 million tons. These figures assumed a positive impact from arming merchant ships and more efficient anti-submarine measures, balanced by more U-boats operational, more aggressive German mining, and possibly more deployment of surface raiders.[50] Overall, Maclay anticipated a net loss for British-owned shipping of about 2 million tons across 1917. This assumed that average monthly war losses would run at the December 1916 level (the highest on record) plus 25 per cent (reflecting increasing U-boat effectiveness), so about 220,000 tons per month, while new-build would not exceed 750,000 tons. This meant that by the start of 1918, the percentage of imports available for civil supplies, after essential war needs and food staples were met, would be halved.[51]

Actual British Allied and neutral losses over the first four months of the unrestricted campaign were nearly 2.6 million tons, 60 per cent higher than the Admiralty had anticipated, and well over Holtzendorff's target of 600,000 tons per month. Had the Admiralty extrapolated from the Mediterranean losses in the last quarter of 1916, 428,000 tons achieved by 20 per cent of the frontline U-boat force in conditions close to unrestricted warfare, they would have reached an estimate of 2.8 million tons, close to actuality. The validity of the Mediterranean yardstick is underlined, because while 20 per cent of U-boats deployed here produced 40 per cent of overall losses in the last quarter of 1916, once the unrestricted campaign began, the Mediterranean loss rate was proportionately no different to that now achieved in the Atlantic.[52] Admiralty underestimation was also surprising, because simultaneously they overestimated U-boat production, assuming an output of three per week, or an addition of 150 overall during 1917 which, without allowing for losses, would give a strength of 316 by the end of the year.[53] In reality, U-boat output at the end of January was half that rate.

Maclay accompanied his projection for 1917 shipping losses with recommendations for reducing net loss and minimising its impact. These were accepted by the War Cabinet and from 8 February underpinned an overall policy to counter the unrestricted campaign: combat U-boats by all known measures; increase shipping construction; economise on shipping use; restrict imports; and increase domestic production.[54] Although direct action against U-boats, and reducing their access to targets through the introduction of convoy, were essential to threat reduction, the wider measures identified in February and applied with increasing effect over the rest of the war were equally important in making German ambitions unattainable. During 1917, Britain doubled Maclay's expectations for new shipping, with an extra 415,000 tons new-build and over 300,000 tons acquired from Japan. A judicious mixture of incentives and coercion, overseen by Robert Cecil, including seizure of Dutch shipping in Allied waters by asserting belligerent rights, ensured that contrary to German hopes, Britain's access to neutral shipping did not significantly decline.[55] Overall, by mid 1918, adjustments to production and consumption released 6.7 million tons of shipping space.[56] Ironically, although British shipping losses in 1917 at 3,729,631 tons were over 40 per cent higher than Maclay projected in February, the combined effect of all British policy measures across 1917 made his estimate of a 2,050,650-ton net loss for British-controlled shipping remarkably accurate. The reality was 2,266,631 tons. Military demands for shipping, not least American troop movements, did mean these losses brought a reduction in food imports, down 6 per cent on 1916, with a further fall of 4.5 per cent in 1918. This was partly compensated by increased domestic production, but overall food supply was 1.4 per cent below the 1900–1913 average in 1917, and 2.7 per cent below in 1918. This shortfall was managed through food control and rationing measures.[57] It is worth noting that during the second quarter of 1917, the worst period of shipping losses, Britain increased imports of wheat and flour to a wartime maximum of 1.8 million tons.[58]

Nevertheless, as the German campaign got underway in February, the effectiveness of British countermeasures lay in the future, and early

German results were alarming. The underestimation of shipping losses by the Admiralty and the lack of immediate naval countermeasures was evident when Jellicoe briefed the War Cabinet on 21 February. Losses in February would now be at least 425,000 tons (in reality they were 25 per cent higher), but likely to be 'substantially exceeded' in the following months. Faced with this grim prospect, Jellicoe insisted that 'no complete and practicable cure for the submarine menace' was likely, 'short of the destruction of the bases, a military measure of great magnitude'. With no prospect of a cure, the Admiralty offered a list of twelve measures initiated by ASD since its creation. These were a mixture of equipment and operational initiatives, the latter including the destroyer hunting groups, submarine hunting, protected lanes for merchant vessels, air patrols, and Q-ships. These measures lacked any obvious order or priority, and the impression on the War Cabinet was of an Admiralty desperately pressing every button, hoping some would work. Jellicoe, revealing the pessimism that became increasingly evident in the next few months, did not project confidence in their impact. Instead, he emphasised two basic choices: bearing current losses, or reducing maritime supply to overseas theatres, releasing naval escort forces and merchant shipping to home waters. The latter option, along with a land offensive to capture the Flanders U-boat bases, remained Jellicoe's dominant answer to the U-boat threat throughout the first half of the year.[59]

A month later Jellicoe confirmed that the situation was deteriorating. Losses in February were up 50 per cent on the average for October to January, with ships identified as British or Allied now liable to be torpedoed without warning. Although Germany had probably deployed the maximum U-boat effort possible from 1 February, it could not be assumed losses had peaked. Longer days and better weather would help the U-boats, and new intelligence suggested U-boat output could reach fifteen boats per month in this year, compared to an average of eight in 1916. New anti-submarine measures would have limited impact until the second half of the year. Jellicoe therefore expected losses to reach 700,000 tons in June, with some relief thereafter. The key question was the impact such losses would have on capacity to continue the war. There would probably now be a shortfall of 40 per cent in shipping for essential civilian and military requirements between April and August.[60]

The new intelligence on U-boat production came from TR16, reporting monthly via the SSB station in Rotterdam. Information on U-boat construction gathered from his visits to most German yards dominated his output at this stage. Jellicoe's building figures for the War Cabinet derived from a longer report, which suggested output could rise as high as twenty per month. Although TR16 received high praise from ID for his reporting throughout the first half of 1917, his March figures, which he acknowledged were an estimate, were wrong. U-boat production in 1917 averaged just under eight per month, lower than the nine achieved in 1916. This reflected growing shortages of specialist materials and skilled labour (factors noted by TR16). Of fifty-one boats ordered in February and ninety-five in June, only twenty-two were commissioned by the end of the war. A more important error in TR16's April report claimed 357 boats in service with fifty-three losses since 1914. The true strength in April, as Room 40 knew, was about 150 which suggests '3' may have substituted for '1', following an error in translation or decryption. The loss figure was about right.[61]

By the beginning of April, Jellicoe and his staff recognised that hope of containing shipping losses while the new measures sponsored by ASD were developed was failing. Despite Room 40 intelligence, current mining operations were inflicting little damage. Investment in merchant ship self-defence was largely nullified by the new U-boat policy of torpedo attack without warning.[62] Above all, the policy of protecting merchant traffic by patrolling designated lanes and 'cones of approach', where traffic converged to enter Britain's major ports was unravelling.[63] The system had some success while the U-boats operated close inshore. Room 40 intelligence facilitated some traffic diversion to designated fall-back routes, and within limited geographical areas there were sufficient patrol vessels to keep U-boats down. It was ineffective against growing numbers of larger U-boats operating several hundred miles out along the shipping lanes. The area to be protected was too large for available resources, and U-boats could pick favourable locations. Far from offering protection therefore, the patrolled approach cones became magnets for U-boats and a death zone for merchant vessels, with one in every four now leaving the United Kingdom failing to return. U-boat hunting in open-water patrolled areas delivered negligible U-boat losses for huge expenditure of resources, while shipping losses spiralled. Attack had outstripped defence with no relief in sight, and resistance to convoy left the Admiralty with no apparent naval answers to an existential threat.[64] Jellicoe accordingly increasingly emphasised non-naval measures: land attack on the Flanders bases, reduced support to overseas theatres, and building up food stocks at the expense of other imports, to survive the next six months.[65]

Patrolling protected areas could never have solved the 1917 problem with the technology available, but would have been less ineffective had the Admiralty reformed the management of intelligence earlier than it did. It is often suggested that following the problems in exploiting Room

40 intelligence at Jutland, Hall recognised the need to integrate Room 40 into an 'operational intelligence centre' and immediately campaigned accordingly.[66] The evidence for this is tenuous. There were only two changes by the end of 1916. Commander-in-Chief Grand Fleet received by officer courier a copy of Hope's daily war diary, summarising the day's decrypts with any associated comment, and when ASD was created its senior staff were indoctrinated into U-boat decrypts, with Duff authorised to release information and instructions to operational commanders. In advising Jellicoe that he would receive the war diary, Balfour stressed the acute sensitivity of SIGINT, emphasising there could be no relaxation in arrangements to protect it.[67] The indoctrination of Duff and his key staff coincided with the retirement of Wilson, who had previously scrutinised and acted on U-boat decrypts.[68] Consequently, ASD only brought marginally more resource to bear here, none of those indoctrinated were trained analysts, and all had other demands on their time. At the beginning of the unrestricted campaign, exploitation of U-boat decrypts therefore remained distinctly amateur and selective, with much priceless intelligence going to waste.

Furthermore, as 1917 opened, the bar on contact between Room 40, still a department outside ID, and the two sections within ID dealing with U-boat intelligence, E1 and ID14, remained largely intact. All reports from British, Allied and neutral sources of ships attacked, and of sighting and attacking U-boats came to E1, where they were carefully plotted and recorded. It also received D/F reports through Room 40, and from the summer of 1916 some SIGINT-derived intelligence was allowed to trickle through, without indicating its origin. However, E1 was not briefed on Room 40's core role, and still knew nothing of the huge volume of intelligence acquired from decrypting U-boat radio traffic in complete isolation from the British reports.[69] Room 40 invariably knew the identity of individual U-boats, monitored their departure from, and arrival at, their bases, and frequently gathered progress updates during their patrols. E1 followed their track so far as British reports and D/F revealed. But the two sections were not permitted to pool their information and work together. Likewise, co-operation with ID14 would have enormously helped Room 40 monitor German navy strength and capability, and vice versa, but again this was denied. The ability of E1 and ID14 sections, despite this handicap, nevertheless to construct an impressive picture of U-boat strength and deployment from non-SIGINT sources at this stage of the war is evident in an ID report from the end of October 1916.[70]

The intelligence loss from this divided approach increased during 1916, as ID acquired more intelligence from sunken or captured U-boats and interrogation of U-boat survivors. The most important documentary material recovered from U-boats this year came from Allies. The French obtained a wealth of material from *UB-26*, sunk off Le Havre in shallow water in April. This included charts of German minefields in the North Sea, navigation marks used by U-boats operating out of Belgium, details of British anti-submarine barriers, and orders for U-boats operating in the Channel.[71] The British exploited this intelligence to lay new minefields off the Belgian coast during late April and May, which probably destroyed three U-boats by the end of July.[72] The Italians recovered useful items from *UC-12*, sunk at Taranto in March, including the Austrian *Offsekt* codebook, and details of minelaying equipment and tactics. Understanding her mine-release gear was important, because it proved defective and was probably responsible for seven U-boat losses, including *UC-2*, sunk off Yarmouth and subsequently examined by British divers the previous July.[73] Meanwhile, the British salvaged *UC-5* intact after she ran aground on Shipwash shoal off the Essex coast, and brought her into Harwich. There were few useful documents, but some important intelligence from prisoners and the opportunity to study her construction at leisure was valuable.[74]

If Hall really favoured an operational intelligence centre, or at least enabling Room 40, E1 and ID14 to collaborate, then the arrival of Jellicoe and Carson, along with the creation of ASD, and the almost simultaneous departure of Ewing, surely provided the opportunity to press his case. Given his experience at Jutland and his recent request for access to Room 40 material, Jellicoe would be sympathetic, Carson was unlikely to object, and Duff would see advantage. With these three supportive, objections from Oliver could be overcome. However, there is no evidence Hall ever took such an initiative. Indeed, ID and the contribution of intelligence appear oddly absent as the U-boat situation deteriorated, and the fierce policy debates over convoy got underway. Hall was much preoccupied with managing the Zimmermann telegram through late January and February, but that was hardly an excuse. It seems Hall was ultimately more gripped by the excitement of running operations than driving through organisational change. Matters only advanced with the reorganisation of the naval staff in May, and the parallel initiation of Atlantic convoying. However, E1 and 14 did not get access to Room 40 material until September.[75]

Hankey watched the mounting shipping losses over the first two months of the unrestricted campaign with growing alarm. By the end of March, he shared Jellicoe's view that the situation was fast deteriorating. With one million tons of shipping lost in two months, he feared Britain could yet be beaten at sea. So, perhaps, did Fisher, who wrote to Hankey not entirely in jest: 'Can the Army win the war before the Navy loses it?'[76] Unlike Jellicoe, Hankey placed much of the blame on ineptitude at the Admiralty, and its resistance to new ideas, above all convoying. However, Hankey initially struggled to engage Lloyd George and the War Cabinet. Both displayed surprising equanimity over the U-boat threat until well into April, and were curiously slow to confront the failing Admiralty strategy. They perhaps judged that after a difficult few months, the policy package approved in February would keep losses within manageable limits. No doubt there was also a consensus that Jellicoe and his new Admiralty team deserved time to deliver. Lloyd George met Carson, Jellicoe and Duff over breakfast on 13 February to consider proposals for convoying from Hankey, but for the present deferred to Jellicoe's professional view that it was not feasible.[77] In his daily briefings to the War Cabinet, Jellicoe tended to exaggerate U-boat losses,[78] while Admiralty figures in mid March provided brief reassurance that shipping losses had reached a plateau.[79] Lloyd George himself was preoccupied by securing his vulnerable political position, and negotiating with the French over the Nivelle spring offensive, which involved facing down fierce opposition from the Chief of the Imperial General Staff, General Sir William Robertson, and Field Marshal Sir Douglas Haig, Commander-in-Chief in France. He could not afford a parallel fight with the First Sea Lord. Perhaps reflecting faith in Maclay's shipping reorganisation, he apparently also initially underestimated the damage the U-boats could do to the overall war effort, telling Hankey in late April: 'I have never regarded that matter as seriously as you have'.[80] Meanwhile, German hopes peaked. The Kaiser boasted that if Britain now sought terms, they would be rejected out of hand, and she 'must be made to grovel'.[81]

American intervention and the Zimmermann telegram

Another factor influenced British leadership thinking through February and March: the attitude of the United States, and the prospect of her joining the Entente powers, bringing significant new naval forces to the anti-U-boat campaign. The American government received just one day's formal notice from the Germans of the start of unrestricted warfare which, arriving in the midst of what they believed were continuing peace negotiations, was a shock.[82] The Germans recognised that unleashing the U-boats could provoke American intervention, but calculated Wilson would prevaricate, and that Britain would be forced to sue for peace before the United States affected the military balance. On the first point, they were correct. Wilson broke off diplomatic relations on 3 February, but held off from further action pending direct attacks on American shipping and personnel, and a decisive shift in public opinion. Personally, he remained reluctant to contemplate war, even at the end of March, but ultimately bowed to pressure from his cabinet, Congress and the press.[83]

Hall received almost daily insights into the heart of the American administration through the regular meetings of Gaunt and Sir William Wiseman with Colonel House. Wiseman, in his early thirties, was a baronet who had pursued a pre-war career in journalism, business and finance, including periods working in the United States, Canada and Mexico. He was also an accomplished boxer and occasional playwright. Wounded early in the war, he drew the attention of Cumming, who had served with his father and recruited him into the SSB. Cumming judged him the ideal candidate to establish an SSB station in North America in late 1915, with an initial focus on counter-intelligence (German, Irish and Indian networks), and the security of war supplies. This inevitably brought competition with Gaunt, resulting in turf disputes over the next two years until Gaunt's departure. Wiseman's most important achievement was the rapid access he achieved to senior members of the United States administration, including Frank Polk, who introduced him to House.[84] Here he made an immediate and favourable impression, with House describing him, when they met in December 1916, as 'the most important caller I have had for some time'. He rapidly displaced both the ambassador, Spring-Rice and Gaunt as House's preferred British contact, ideally placed to monitor and influence the political debates in Washington leading up to the American declaration of war on 7 April. By this point he was also in regular contact with Auchincloss, perhaps introduced by House, taking over liaison with BSI at the Washington end.[85] By May at the latest, he was having occasional private meetings with Wilson, and soon Wilson not only regarded him as his primary British contact, but as one of his closest confidants on all matters relating to the war. In late July, the press baron Lord Northcliffe, now Lloyd George's Director of Propaganda, told Churchill, as incoming Minister of Munitions, that Wiseman was the 'only person, English or American, who has access to Wilson and House at all times'.[86]

Throughout 1918, Wiseman provided a stream of high-quality insights from the top of the American administration, reporting both through Cumming and direct to Balfour through his private secretary, Sir Eric Drummond. When, in April, Wiseman sought to clarify his role, Balfour directed that he should be free to do whatever he judged best.[87] Since managing the relationships with House and Wilson now consumed almost all his time, he devolved his intelligence work in New York to his deputy, Captain Norman Thwaites, another invalid from the trenches recruited by Cumming, and a brilliant German speaker. Pre-war, Thwaites had worked for the publisher Joseph Pulitzer and become a close friend of Frank Polk, enabling him to introduce Wiseman and consolidate the British intelligence link to State and BSI.[88] Lloyd George also now made Wiseman special liaison officer in Washington for the War Cabinet.[89] From the naval perspective, Wiseman's reporting was especially important from late summer, when he illuminated Wilson's thinking on how 'freedom of the seas' would be incorporated in a future peace treaty backed by his US Navy 'second to none'. Wiseman's relationship with House[90] was the first of numerous confidential, off-the-record, personal relationships developed by the SSB and its Secret Intelligence Service (SIS) successor with foreign politicians, senior officials and advisers over the rest of the century. Such individuals were not under clandestine British control, but participants in an exchange to mutual advantage of intelligence (in the widest sense of the term), views and ideas outside the constraints of a formal diplomatic relationship. Both sides accepted that what was said was protected, and that neither party would subsequently be held to account.[91]

The evolution of American policy in response to the unrestricted U-boat campaign occurred in parallel with, and was partially shaped by, a British intelligence operation, often described as the single greatest intelligence coup of the twentieth century. This was the interception by Room 40, and subsequent exploitation by Hall, of the telegram sent by the German Foreign Minister Arthur Zimmermann on 16 January to the German ambassador in Mexico, with instructions to approach the Mexican government, proposing an alliance against the United States. The complex story of the origin of this telegram and precisely how it was decrypted and deployed to influence the United States government is described elsewhere.[92] Important inaccuracies in traditional accounts have recently been corrected, but parts of the story will probably remain unknown, because the two primary witnesses, Hall and Nigel de Grey, left selective and deliberately misleading accounts.[93] Nevertheless, key aspects of the affair require emphasis, or additional perspective.

The first point, already noted, is that in unveiling the Mexican plan, the telegram also disclosed 1 February as the start date for unrestricted U-boat warfare. This was itself a critical piece of intelligence, evident in the first partial and imperfect decrypt, delivered to Hall by de Grey on 17 January.[94] Hall's claim that he briefed nobody on the contents for almost three weeks, while he worked on obtaining a complete text and a plan to protect Room 40's role, still widely accepted, is not correct. He certainly briefed Jellicoe, and probably Carson too, on the start of the

U-boat campaign because on 25 January Jellicoe informed Beatty that the Admiralty had 'very secret information' that this would begin on 1 February.[95] Furthermore, it seems probable Hall spoke to Balfour about the entire content of the German telegram (so far as it was comprehensible) by the last week of January, making it likely he also briefed Jellicoe and Carson on the Mexican dimension. In briefing Balfour, Hall was better placed than anyone else in the British government to assess German-Mexican relations because he had until recently had an agent, a Dutchman named Vincent Kraft, within the German embassy in Mexico City.[96]

The next point is that the telegram went first to Bernstorff in Washington for onward transmission to the German embassy in Mexico. Until recently, partly as a result of disinformation spread by Hall and de Grey, it was believed it was transmitted to Washington on multiple routes. In reality, it went solely under the American diplomatic cover negotiated with the State Department, and using a relatively new code 0075, delivered to the German embassy in Washington by the cargo submarine *Deutschland* the previous November.[97] Room 40 only had partial readability of 0075, sufficient to reveal about 70 per cent of Zimmermann's text, albeit covering most of the crucial points, but not enough for perfect transcription.[98] In exploiting the telegram, Hall therefore faced three interconnected challenges: the overriding need to ensure the Germans did not suspect their communications were compromised (in the worst case, raising suspicion about the security of their naval codes); avoiding the political damage if the Americans suspected Britain was reading their traffic too, and losing another important intelligence source if the Americans then changed their codes; and obtaining a complete version of the telegram, important for authenticity and reducing the likelihood that it was dismissed as a British hoax. On the first point, Hall was right to worry. The Germans did examine the security of their codes in the six months following the exposure of Zimmermann's telegram.[99]

Hall's solution was to obtain an encrypted copy of the telegram from the Mexico City telegraph office, following retransmission from the German embassy in Washington. On its Washington–Mexico leg, the telegram was encrypted with the older 13040 codebook, which Room 40 could read, since the German legation in Mexico did not possess 0075. Furthermore, suggesting the telegram had been stolen in Mexico avoided American suspicion that their own communications were being read and, with careful management, also disguised British involvement from the Germans.[100] It remains unclear why Hall delayed nearly three weeks before initiating action to obtain the Mexico copy on 5 February.[101] It made sense to see if the opening of unrestricted U-boat warfare triggered an immediate American declaration of war, rendering exposure of the Zimmermann plan to the Americans unnecessary. But this did not preclude preparatory steps to acquire the telegram received in Mexico, which might differ from that sent to Washington, although, in the event, it did not. The longer the delay in procuring a copy of this version from the telegraph offices in either Mexico or Washington, the greater the risk it might be lost or destroyed. Hall was reluctant on security grounds to brief the Foreign Office before it was essential, and their authorisation was necessary to task Edward Thurstan, the British minister in Mexico City. However, the risk in briefing Sir Charles Hardinge, now back as Foreign Office permanent secretary after serving as Viceroy of India, and his private secretary Ronald Campbell, the two officials whose support was required, was minimal.[102]

Once Hall had a decrypt of the full telegram acquired through Mexico on 19 February, successful but secure exploitation with the Americans relied on two factors: keeping control of the operation in his hands, and using his close relationship with Bell.[103] Balfour, famously, ensured the first.[104] Balfour's willingness to give Hall full autonomy reflected the confidence he had gained in Hall while at the Admiralty, but also his recognition that Hall now had better access into the American administration than anybody else, and unique insights into German-Mexican relations too. Hall's relationships with Bell, but also directly with Walter Page, who was very close to Wilson, were crucial here, but these were not Hall's only means of influence. By February 1917, Hall not only had a relationship of mutual trust with Bell, but understood Bell's status in BSI, and how BSI linked to Frank Polk and Edward House, and thence to Wilson. He recognised that Polk, House and Leland Harrison all had a vested interest in promoting BSI's capabilities, and therefore seizing credit for the Zimmermann telegram. The Washington response to the telegram was, indeed, managed by Polk and House, with Lansing given limited detail on how it had been obtained.[105] Hall monitored American handling of the telegram through MI1(b)'s coverage of exchanges between the State Department and the London embassy.[106] He then continued influencing matters directly through Bell, but also reinforced points to House through Gaunt and Wiseman. Later in the year, House described Hall as 'one of the driving forces of the war'.[107]

Despite the recent adjustments to the Zimmermann story, and the outstanding puzzles and unknowns, Hall's handling of the operation was masterly, and deserves the praise given over the years. A more difficult question is the real influence it exerted on American entry into the war. A fair assessment is that it was important, but not decisive. The unrestricted U-boat campaign was inexorably pushing the country towards intervention, which the majority of Wilson's cabinet saw as inevitable and necessary. The telegram gave the interventionists additional momentum. But opposition to war remained strong, and the telegram did little to shift overall opinion in Congress, press or wider public. Wilson already felt personally betrayed by Germany releasing the U-boats, given the effort he had invested in the peace negotiations. The telegram, with its direct threat to American security, and blatant abuse of the communication privileges he had endorsed, compounded the betrayal, making it difficult to withstand the consensus for intervention within his administration. Even so, it took a month to overcome his deep reluctance to accept intervention, and put the case to Congress. The telegram played only a small part in Wilson's argument here, and it barely featured in the subsequent congressional debate. Overall, it probably brought war forward by just a few weeks. Nevertheless, these weeks were important to Britain in two respects. It avoided a potential collapse in confidence over Britain's ability to keep funding the war, and it ensured an injection of American naval support when the viability of convoy as a solution to the U-boat crisis was still finely balanced.[108]

United States entry into the war left the Swedish roundabout as Germany's only communications link with its representatives in Latin America. At the same time, the region, especially Mexico, became more important as a base for intelligence-gathering and subversion. Hall now worked closely with BSI to identify German activity and, where possible, disrupt or expose it. By the summer, he had collected material damaging to Germany's position in Argentina. He persuaded the Americans to leak select items to the press, judging that breaking the roundabout link was a price worth paying to destroy Germany's position in Argentina, and discredit her in Sweden.[109] The loss of the roundabout spurred German plans to establish a long-range radio link using the station at Ixtapalapa outside Mexico City. ID were first alerted to this by Kraft before his departure at the end of 1916, but in the following months, separate intelligence emerged in Spain of German efforts to acquire high-powered valves known as audion lamps, clearly destined for Mexico. Hall despatched Mason to Mexico, posing as an eccentric butterfly collector, to investigate German intentions and recommend action. Through a combination of ingenuity and skulduggery, and some advice from Marconi, Mason managed to buy up all the audion valves available in Mexico, and destroy those already installed.[110]

13

The Emergence of Operational
Intelligence 1917–1918

The growing shipping crisis recognised by Hankey was finally confronted in late April 1917. Lloyd George at last brought his powerful focus on to both the U-boat threat and the performance of the Admiralty. The War Cabinet took their first comprehensive look at the problem over two meetings on 23 April.[1] They concluded that their picture of the submarine menace and its implications was inadequate, and that the prime minister would visit the Admiralty to investigate further.[2] The immediate trigger for this scrutiny was Jellicoe's report on the appalling shipping loss figures for April, his admission that these would continue for several months and, importantly, his inability to provide convincing answers for how they might eventually be contained.[3] Specifically, Jellicoe's report did not mention convoying, even though he knew Duff and others were now revisiting this option in the Admiralty. He should also have known that convoy had support from Beatty and Rear Admiral William Sims, the new commander of American naval forces in Europe. Pressed by Lloyd George, who had done his own research, including a meeting with Beatty at Rosyth, and informal briefings from junior Admiralty staff,[4] Jellicoe acknowledged convoy was under review, but its adoption was constrained by the limited availability of destroyer escorts. He agreed, however, to report further.[5] Most members of the War Cabinet had probably also read two MI1(b) reports recording American embassy reporting on the U-boat crisis, which drew on the briefings Jellicoe had given Sims. The American reports were bleaker than the direct reports received from Jellicoe, and underlined the depth of the crisis.[6] Matters now moved quickly. Within a week, the Admiralty had agreed internally to commence convoy trials, and within a month comprehensive plans for implementing convoy for all important transatlantic traffic were complete.

The reasons for the Admiralty's entrenched opposition to convoy, the factors that provoked a rethink, and whether political pressure from Lloyd George was decisive in its final adoption have been endlessly rehearsed. A detailed account of the debates is beyond the scope of this book, with its focus on the intelligence war. The arguments against convoy, reaffirmed by Jellicoe and Duff when they arrived in December, fell under three broad headings: logistic, tactical and resources. The logistic arguments related to port congestion, and time wasted in collecting and organising a convoy. The tactical objections primarily focused on increased vulnerability. A convoy was a large target and, once located, a U-boat firing a fan of torpedoes would hit multiple ships. Fast ships would lose their advantage, since the convoy would have to adopt the speed of the slowest. Station-keeping would be difficult, especially at night or in fog, and defensive zigzagging impossible. Finally, but perhaps most important, it was claimed there were not enough long-range destroyer escorts available, given numerous other commitments, especially the protection of the Grand Fleet.[7] On the tactical point there was compelling evidence that should have provoked a rethink, certainly by the end of February, and perhaps earlier. This was the negligible loss suffered by traffic to Holland and for the French coal trade where convoys were used, the point noted by Oliver back in November, but not pursued. Of 3223 vessels convoyed here over the three months February to April (including Scandinavia from April), only eighteen were lost.[8]

Intelligence should have influenced this debate in several critical respects, but it did not do so. First, as already emphasised, there was a wealth of high-quality intelligence available in the Admiralty on U-boat strength, present and future, on how and where boats were deployed, on preferred methods of attack, and on German ability to sustain its campaign. Room 40 SIGINT was the most important source, but there were excellent insights available in sections E1 and ID14 too. If Jellicoe and Duff did not fully appreciate this, it was up to Hall and Oliver to put them right. Yet in late April, five months after arriving at the Admiralty, Jellicoe told Carson that insufficient knowledge made it impossible to make any useful assessment of the U-boat campaign and its prospects in coming months.[9] This was an appalling admission for a First Sea Lord at any time, but given the totality of the intelligence available, it was a disgrace. The successive updates produced by Jellicoe for the War Cabinet during the three months February to April fell far short of the comprehensive professional review of the U-boat campaign required.[10] Increasing War Cabinet frustration was understandable. They deserved a clear picture of how the threat was evolving, and a convincing analysis of possible naval countermeasures, including convoy.

Secondly, during the first half of 1917, Jellicoe over-stated the fighting power of the High Seas Fleet, and its ability to mount raids across the North Sea without risk of timely interception by the Grand Fleet, still concentrated in distant Scapa Flow. He believed much improved Zeppelin reconnaissance also reduced the chances of taking any German force by surprise. Jellicoe even argued that German naval forces in the southern North Sea were superior, and that British control of these waters could not be guaranteed. Some of these concerns were valid. Despite better submarine surveillance, countering any German sortie still depended heavily on adequate warning from Room 40. Improvements in German communications security might eliminate this, a danger underlined by the issue of a new German codebook at the beginning of May, which blacked out Room 40 for a month. Furthermore, the proximity of the Belgian-based destroyers and their good radio security made warning of raids from here especially problematic. Room 40 at least knew the codebook change was coming, and took steps to minimise its operational impact. These included exploring how far traffic analysis could substitute in providing warning. Their detailed understanding of German communications procedures also enabled rapid progress in mastering the new book. Jellicoe, therefore, had a point, but he downplayed the enduring information advantage provided by SIGINT and D/F, and attributed a quality advantage to German warships not supported by available intelligence.[11]

This exaggerated picture of German surface capability had three consequences impacting the British anti-U-boat effort. First, it encouraged conservative, over-defensive and inefficient deployment of naval forces in home waters. Secondly, it discouraged forward operations to hamper U-boat and destroyer deployment by contesting known transit routes to and from their Bight and Belgian bases, and by offensive mining and countering German sweeping. Offensive action to blockade the High Seas Fleet and the U-boats was much discussed between the Admiralty and frontline commanders in late summer, and Beatty did eventually mount a major operation to trap German minesweeping and covering forces in the Bight in November, albeit with limited success.[12] Intelligence was good enough to have done this earlier, then to have executed repeat operations regularly, making them more effective and keeping the Germans off-balance. The final consequence was to cause the Admiralty to push for the construction of large warships, notably battlecruisers, despite the inevitable reduction in merchant shipbuilding capacity, pressure which, fortunately, the War Cabinet resisted.[13] Conservative deployment also helped entrench the belief that convoy was impossible owing to insufficiency of escorts. This does not mean that the Admiralty should have stripped the Grand

Fleet and the forces on the east coast of destroyers. Convoy escorts had to come primarily from the hunting forces in the Western Approach funnels, which were achieving little. But the conservative approach in the North Sea fed resistance to change anywhere. Jellicoe's reluctance to consider innovative deployment options exploiting Room 40 intelligence makes a striking contrast with the ideas aired by Jackson the previous year.[14]

Jellicoe's exaggerated fear of losing control of the southern North Sea also combined with his continued lobbying for a land offensive against the Flanders U-boat bases. Through the early summer Jellicoe pressed for such an operation, eventually telling the War Policy Committee when it reviewed the case for a Flanders offensive on 20 June that it was pointless making plans for 1918 because 'we cannot go on'. Hankey summarised the naval case during these deliberations as follows:

- the difficulty of controlling the Channel in the face of the German Flanders bases;
- although the number and size of U-boats based there was small, they were still a major irritant, not least as covert minelayers;
- the destroyers were a bigger danger, constantly posing the threat of a mass attack on British cross-channel traffic;
- the need to convoy ships to Holland to counter these threats;
- the prospect of diverting scarce naval resources to provide adequate Channel protection if the bases were not eliminated;
- Jellicoe's pessimism over continuing the war without a decisive Flanders success.[15]

Hankey was correct that the Admiralty now saw the destroyers as the most pressing problem, but he understated the U-boat threat. By the summer, there was an average of thirty-five boats in Flanders, about 25 per cent of the overall frontline force, they were inflicting proportionate shipping losses, and their numbers were increasing. Their movements were also more difficult for Room 40 to monitor than those from the German bases. The Flanders boats knew that their predominantly coastal operating areas, the Channel, the Bay of Biscay and Irish Sea, were subject to close D/F surveillance from both British and French sites, and consequently kept radio transmissions to a minimum. The War Policy Committee recognised that eliminating Germany's Flanders bases would not itself reduce either destroyer or U-boat strength, since the forces could be redeployed to Germany. But it would make their operation less efficient, allowing redeployment of Royal Navy forces, and reduce the threat to cross-channel supply lines. While nobody in the committee shared Jellicoe's pessimism over survival into 1918, there was, therefore, consensus that clearing the Belgian coast would be a valuable strategic prize, although Lloyd George and others still felt some gains might be achieved through naval means alone, as indeed was demonstrated with substantial sealing of the Dover straits at the end of the year. Set against the other factors pushing for a Flanders offensive, the final influence of the naval case is hard to judge, but it probably tilted the balance in favour of proceeding.[16]

Meanwhile, a final lost intelligence opportunity was failure to draw on the experience of using SIGINT to divert high-value ships away from a U-boat threat. The Admiralty war staff might have concluded that diversion would be an even more effective tactic with a convoy, where multiple ships could be diverted, including the many vessels lacking radio that could not be contacted when sailing alone. The future success achieved with convoy diversion, initially its most important benefit, seems to have come as a surprise.

Failure to make the best use of intelligence in addressing the U-boat threat reflected the shortcomings in its management already discussed, but also wider problems in Admiralty organisation, not least the lack of a true naval staff with executive responsibility, and the absence of a dedicated planning section. These issues were prominent when the prime minister visited the Admiralty on 30 April, where he was briefed by Carson and Jellicoe, along with Duff and Webb. Traditional accounts of this visit focused heavily on the convoy debate, and whether pressure from Lloyd George was decisive in pushing the Admiralty to change its policy. Such portrayals were often over-dramatic and partisan, with supporters of Lloyd George and Jellicoe offering opposing views.[17] Although recent descriptions of the convoy debate are more balanced, the impression that it was the centrepiece of the visit lingers. In reality, discussion of convoy occupied only a small part of the day, and was non-controversial because the Admiralty had committed to a trial – and Duff told the prime minister he had 'completely altered his view'. How far the Admiralty change of heart was primarily due to professional reassessment or political pressure remains debatable. Both undoubtedly played a part. Professional opinion was shifting, with some encouragement from the new American ally and the prospect of US Navy escorts. Twenty-four American destroyers reached Queenstown by 1 June, a significant contribution, and almost half the available US Navy destroyer strength.[18] But political pressure probably made the Admiralty move more quickly. The continuing emphasis on convoy in accounts of the prime ministerial visit is a pity, because it overshadows both the more important issues discussed, and the sheer power of Lloyd George's scrutiny and analysis.

The visit demonstrates how a political leader with the right skills can bring clarity, order and decision to a complex professional body that has lost its way.[19]

The prime minister returned to the War Cabinet with ten recommendations. Four of these brought enduring value to the conduct of naval intelligence. The first was the reorganisation of the war staff. It was agreed that the First Sea Lord should now become the Chief of Naval Staff, following the model of the Chief of the Imperial General Staff for the army. He would have a Deputy Chief of Naval Staff (DCNS) – for the present, Oliver – to run day-to-day operations on his behalf, and to manage relations between the war staff and the administrative side of the Admiralty. Reporting to the Chief of Naval Staff, alongside his deputy, would be a series of co-equal directors whose responsibilities might include operations, intelligence, trade, and anti-submarine. Director Operations Division, now Rear Admiral George Hope replacing Thomas Jackson, would have the specific task of developing strategic policy and planning on behalf of the First Sea Lord. The Director of Intelligence would provide the information to support his fellow directors. The Director of Trade Division would manage all merchant movements, including convoying. To some extent, this recommendation formalised changes in war staff organisation that Jellicoe had already initiated. However, the discussion with Lloyd George injected clarity and emphasised three critical points: that the naval staff under the First Sea Lord now had executive status; that the First Sea Lord must be freed from routine operational detail to focus on the big picture; and that he must have a team able to deal with policy issues. The structure suggested by Lloyd George inevitably evolved over the rest of the year, but is recognisable in the final wartime organisation implemented in January 1918. The main modifications were the appointment of Duff as an additional Assistant Chief of Naval Staff (ACNS) to oversee all trade protection operations, the creation of a new Mercantile Movements Division to manage convoying alongside Trade Division, and, most important, the establishment of a distinct Plans Division, rather than leaving this function in Operations.[20]

The second recommendation relevant to intelligence was that the Director of Operations should prepare a weekly appreciation of the naval situation for the First Sea Lord and for circulation to the War Cabinet. It should focus particularly on the progress of the submarine campaign and cover not just events and relevant intelligence over the previous week, but include comments and suggestions on future policy. The third recommendation was a programme to fit radio into merchant ships currently without it, along with trained operators. This would facilitate intelligence-led diversion from known threats, and earlier intelligence of shipping losses. The final intelligence recommendation was the establishment of an Admiralty statistical department to collect and analyse data relevant to naval operations, and especially the monitoring of submarine losses. Reports should be shared with the War Cabinet and Shipping Controller, as well as the senior naval staff.

The most significant non-intelligence recommendation was the appointment of a civilian business expert, Sir Eric Geddes, as Controller and Third Sea Lord, to oversee all shipbuilding, and the supply of all naval material and equipment. Geddes was a Scottish railway engineer by background, an energetic, hard-driving and brilliant manager, who had transformed transport and logistics on the Western Front. Lloyd George saw him as a man to get things done, ideally suited to shake up support services in the Admiralty in the short term, but the prime minister probably already saw him as a candidate to replace Carson as First Lord, which he did in July.

The reorganisation of the naval staff and the trialling of Atlantic convoying which followed the prime minister's visit brought rapid changes to the management of intelligence. The most important was the incorporation by the end of May of Room 40 into ID, under the designation ID25. The transfer was accompanied by a change in management. After two and a half years supervising the eclectic team in Room 40, and handling the tricky relations with Oliver and Operations Division, Herbert Hope was exhausted, and desperately wanted a command at sea. To replace him, Hall persuaded Beatty to release Commander William 'Bubbles' James from the staff of the Grand Fleet.[21] Hall was convinced that James, whom he knew well from *Queen Mary*, had the right qualities to take SIGINT into a new era. James was less popular with the old hands of Room 40 than the much-loved Hope, and had limited interest in the minutiae of cryptography. But he was an outstanding leader and manager, with an excellent intuitive grasp for how SIGINT should be exploited for operational effect. His understanding here was probably better than Hall's and, as noted previously, his championship of integrated intelligence was important not just in 1917–18, but in preparing the Royal Navy for the Second World War.

The formal transfer of Room 40 meant that, subject to veto by Jellicoe or Oliver, Hall and James could now manage SIGINT as they chose. However, the integration of SIGINT with other intelligence sources was still a gradual evolution, not fully achieved before the armistice in November 1918. The first step which, followed closely on the creation of ID25, was the establishment of the charting section, under Commander

John Carrington, within Duff's ASD, in 'X' Room on the ground floor of Admiralty House. This followed the decision on 25 June to implement full Atlantic convoying and to create the necessary support organisation. The charting section was responsible for convoy routing, and displayed the position of every convoy, along with every known U-boat location, on a wall chart 6ft by 9ft. For the first time, locations derived from decrypts, and not just D/F, both transferred from the Room 40 complex by pneumatic tube, were plotted regularly and continuously for staff use. E1 was collocated in the same room, so that its cumulative knowledge was instantly available. ('X' Room was originally acquired by Hall for E1, probably in the first months of 1917, and charting section effectively absorbed the E1 plot.[22]) There was an irony here, in that under the 1912 War Room organisation, E1 and E2 were supposed to be fully integrated with the other War Room sections. However, it proved impossible to accommodate all the desired sections within the War Room space, and the intelligence sections were hived off back to ID. Now for U-boats, though not for surface warships, the wheel had come full circle after three years.[23]

Initially, only the head of E1, Fleet Paymaster Ernest Thring, was fully indoctrinated into SIGINT, but the rest of the section received access in September. E1 then worked openly with ID25 on the analysis of U-boat SIGINT, and applied the results with their existing sources to produce an integrated picture for the 'X' Room plot. For security reasons, care was taken not to correct D/F positions sent to forces at sea with subsequent positions acquired from an intercepted U-boat signal, unless there was a marked difference between the two and the U-boat position was judged reliable.[24] Security constraints also still caused occasional confusion, notably insistence that the U-boats on the plot received a contact number (and sometimes multiple numbers), rather than their actual identity. Overall, however, the collaboration with E1 marked a huge step forward.[25]

The start of 1918 saw further improvements in the 'X' Room process. The increasingly seamless relationship between ID25 and E1 was recognised by incorporating E1 in ID25 as ID25B, with the main SIGINT section becoming ID25A, both now under James's supervision, and comprising in total about one hundred staff. ID25A improved its management of D/F by establishing a dedicated section under Lieutenant Commander Frank Tiarks, which included a chart room for plotting directionals. ID25B drew on this to maintain the 'X' Room plot, and was specifically tasked with keeping individual U-boat histories, drawing on all possible sources. ID25B was also authorised to despatch daily summaries of U-boat locations, activities and forecasts of future movements, designated 'Navintels', to distinguish them from executive signals, to frontline commanders.[26] The security constraints on the 'X' Room plot were relaxed, and U-boats were displayed with their U-boat number. Key operational and intelligence staff involved in managing the convoys and directing the anti-U-boat effort met in front of the plot each morning, to review developments in the last twenty-four hours, and address any problems.[27] Duff, as ACNS now commanding all aspects of the anti-U-boat effort, including convoy operations, had 'always at his hand an accurate picture of the situation and can direct his convoys accordingly'.[28]

Headline statistics confirm that the impact of convoying from early summer 1917 was decisive. Of some 84,000 ships convoyed during the final eighteen months of the war, only 257 were sunk, a loss rate of just 0.3 per cent. During the same period, 1500 vessels sailing independently were lost, a rate of nearly 6 per cent. The most important consequence of convoying was that it dramatically reduced the probability of a U-boat finding a target. A forty-ship convoy might occupy a rectangle of ten square miles, but the chances of visually sighting such a moving rectangle in millions of square miles of Atlantic ocean were little greater than for individual ships. The probability of a searching U-boat finding one or more of forty ships sailing independently was thus far higher than finding them in a single group. U-boat commander Karl Dönitz, who commanded Germany's U-boat force in the next war, stated that with the introduction of convoying, the 'oceans at once became bare and empty'. Convoying also meant that anti-submarine forces were concentrated where U-boats had to be in order to achieve any success. U-boats invariably faced escorting warships before they could reach a merchantman, and rarely had time to strike more than one target. They risked detection for every ship they attacked in a convoy, making them more vulnerable to counter-attack. As a result, convoy escorts sank twenty-four of the forty U-boats sunk by surface warships in home waters and the Atlantic after mid 1917, and two-thirds of those in the Mediterranean.[29]

The combination of SIGINT (decrypts and D/F) and 'X'-Room tracking and assessment made the ocean far emptier than it would have been otherwise. The 'X'-Room team under ACNS now had the intelligence, the situational awareness, and the rapid communications to divert a convoy away from any threat. Diverting single ships, even a high-value target, was always problematic, because the Admiralty rarely had their precise location, while many older ships lacked radio. By contrast, the convoy track was known and agreed in advance, while the commodore in command always had radio. In the circumstances of 1917–18, when U-boats almost always operated singly and enjoyed minimal intelligence support from either radio intercept or aerial reconnaissance, intelligence-led evasive routing was critical in keeping convoy losses to a minimum. Apart from diversion, 'X' Room could also alert the convoy escort if a U-boat was in the vicinity, making imminent attack likely.[30]

By the summer, with British shipping losses falling significantly, wiser members of the German leadership, notably Bethmann-Hollweg, recognised that the U-boat campaign was failing and proving a costly mistake. It had brought American intervention, had not broken the British blockade, and showed no sign of crippling Britain's war economy. Criticism of the German admiralty for their conduct of the campaign featured in SSB reporting.[31] The influential politician Matthias Erzberger, who conducted the armistice negotiations for Germany the following year, attacked the campaign in the Reichstag, triggering a peace motion and the resignation of Bethmann-Hollweg. Disillusion with the war contributed to disorder in the High Seas Fleet during late July and August, although harsh discipline and working conditions, poor food, and resentment at officer privileges were factors too. ID did not obtain a comprehensive account of this 1917 mutiny until June the following year, but it was broadly informed of the disturbances and their causes by early October, primarily from the interrogation of prisoners recovered from U-45 and UC-55, both sunk in September, but also neutral sources.[32] As Hall noted, these reports demonstrated that discontent was spreading to the U-boat service. The mutiny and its meaning were widely discussed in British leadership circles in mid October, partly drawing on this intelligence, but also the statement of the German state secretary for the navy, Admiral Eduard von Capelle, to the Reichstag on 9 October, accusing the Social Democratic Party (SDP) of fomenting unrest.[33] Holtzendorff, having underestimated the robustness of the British economy, and overestimated U-boat capability, was slow to accept reality – in late August claiming to an incredulous Crown Prince Rupprecht that the U-boat campaign would still have Britain out of the war by November. Ludendorff harboured similar illusions, and even predicted that the arrival of the Americans would not fundamentally alter the balance against Germany. But despite such optimism, the Supreme Command were increasingly worried by morale at home as a fourth year of war beckoned, and the British blockade now tightened with American help.[34]

The failing U-boat campaign and the disillusion voiced in the Reichstag stimulated new German peace-feelers made separately to Britain and France during September by the new foreign minister, Richard von Kühlmann. These aimed to create divisions between the Allies and undermine popular support for the war, rather than provide a serious basis for negotiation.[35]

The approach to the British came through a Spanish intermediary, and MI1(b) tracked its origin and progress, sharing its coverage with Hall.[36] Balfour asked Hall to summarise intelligence relating to German peace initiatives the previous year.[37] Hall doubted Balfour's robustness, and lobbied Geddes with arguments for dismissing the German approach.[38] The War Cabinet had already instructed Balfour to inform Germany that any approach would be addressed by the Allies together. Kühlmann never responded, and there is no evidence that Geddes influenced government attitudes.[39] Several aspects of Hall's thinking, nevertheless, deserve note: first, his scrutiny of German politics and weaknesses here, which Britain could exploit; secondly, his stress on the continuing threat posed by Germany's U-boats following any negotiated settlement, and the desirability of destroying this capability permanently to ensure Britain's future security, a position reflected in the armistice terms the following year.[40] Finally, his assessment that the German government was using the July naval mutiny to undermine the SDP, the only political force in Germany retaining democratic legitimacy. Hall underlined his lobbying with an intelligence report to Geddes later in the month, reporting fierce opposition to the war in the Reichstag provoked by growing food shortages, and a gloomy assessment given to the Kaiser by the influential shipping magnate Albert Ballin.[41]

Thring was not initially convinced that convoying and intelligence-led diversion was an effective long-term counter to the U-boat threat. In October he argued that, discounting April as an unusually bad month, convoy had not reduced losses, merely stopped them getting higher. He seemed to have a point. Average monthly losses (British, Allied and neutral) due to U-boat action in the third quarter of the year, compared to the average in the first half, excluding April, were only down 11.5 per cent. Thring believed convoying had limited effect on losses, because ships were sunk after leaving convoy on their final journey to port, and that it did not help in sinking submarines. Convoying merely diverted U-boats to where they could be more effective, and were less vulnerable to counter-attack.[42] Thring was correct that introducing convoy in the Western Approaches displaced some U-boats to unescorted shipping in coastal waters, but his core argument was wrong. Wherever convoy was introduced, including to coastal areas, shipping losses immediately dropped and destruction of U-boats by escorts increased. The steady extension of convoying meant that overall shipping losses were down nearly 20 per cent in the fourth quarter compared to the third, with further reductions of about 15 per cent through each quarter of 1918. This steady fall occurred despite a rise of 10 per cent in U-boat strength through 1917. Unfortunately, variants of Thring's argument persisted through 1918 and the interwar period. There was an enduring belief that convoy was defensive. It might contain the submarine threat, but the campaign must be won by sinking decisive numbers of U-boats, requiring offensive tactics, primarily aggressive hunting patrols. Whenever this option was renewed in the last year of the war, results were meagre or non-existent. This continuing debate between hunting patrols and escorts highlighted the lack of an intelligence tool that only matured during the Second World War – operational research, the application of evidence-based analysis to improve operational decisions. Its application to convoying in 1942 was an early success.[43]

The fact that the full benefits of convoying were not yet understood in autumn 1917, and that earlier extension would have enhanced those benefits, did not mean complementary measures lacked value. Thring was correct in emphasising the importance of targeting transit routes and, in concert with Plans Division, promoting defence in depth. At its most ambitious, this envisaged close mining of the Bight and Flanders bases, mine barrages at both exits from the North Sea, backed by extensive patrols, and systematic surveillance of much of the North Sea, but especially the approaches to the two barrages, using aircraft, balloons deployed from destroyers, and warship hunting groups. This operation would be underpinned by improved intelligence of U-boat routes and movements, directed from an enhanced 'X'-Room facility. Attacks on U-boat bases by naval bombardment, aerial bombing, and direct assault would also be pursued.[44] Only parts of this vision were implemented by the end of the war, and of these only some worked. Intelligence-led mining in the Bight was effective during the final year of the war, as was the Dover barrage from December 1917, with ever fewer U-boats risking this route. The northern barrage proved too ambitious owing to geography, resources and logistics, and was complicated by negotiations with the Americans. It was never completed, and accounted for at most two U-boats. By mid 1918, daily available air strength reached three hundred aircraft, a figure not achieved in the next war until 1943. Using them to establish protected lanes, and hunt down U-boats identified by SIGINT, proved no more effective than had surface vessels, and with prevailing technology they were incapable of destroying a U-boat, even if they found one.[45] However, when aircraft or balloons were used in direct support of a convoy, their deterrent effect was critical, rendering the convoy virtually immune from attack. Surface hunting groups, exploiting SIGINT and D/F, were deployed in the North Sea transit routes and off the north coast of Scotland but, still lacking effective underwater search capability, with no greater success than in early 1917. Considerable resources expended here sank just one U-boat. Nevertheless, if sinkings were meagre, forcing U-boats to use the northern exits from the North Sea through closure of the Dover strait made transit longer and more hazardous, reducing time in operational areas.[46]

All forms of direct attack on the U-boat bases, including the high-profile raid on Zeebrugge and Ostend in April 1918, completely failed to interrupt operations. Nevertheless, the intelligence aspects of these April raids deserve attention. The overall intelligence case added valuable perspective to the pre-Passchendaele debate the previous year, and drew on meticulous aerial reconnaissance, the first time this became the primary source for a major strategic naval operation. It explained why eliminating the Flanders bases remained a priority, but also identified important limits on what was achievable through a blocking operation. ID correctly identified thirty-eight U-boats and thirty destroyers based in the Zeebrugge–Ostend–Bruges triangle. It assessed that the U-boat force was responsible for 25–30 per cent of current shipping losses, while the destroyers were a constant threat to the Dover straits. Successful blocking would bottle up the destroyers and any larger U-boats, but could not prevent smaller U-boats escaping through the canals via Antwerp. For the U-boats, despite what the public were led to believe at the time, the maximum achievable goal was, therefore, a reduction in operating efficiency owing to relocation to German ports, and even this was questionable, since most Flanders boats were now deploying northward. Complete elimination of the destroyer threat was more credible, although DCNS stressed this would not allow release of British destroyers from the Dover force, since a threat from the German bases would remain.[47] Aerial reconnaissance and photography was also central to planning the details of the assault, and was used to build models for the assault forces, anticipating the more detailed modelling techniques of the next war.[48] In the event, although the operation was an enormous morale boost for Britain and the Royal Navy at a difficult time, the impact on German operations was negligible, and ID knew this from SIGINT coverage within hours.[49]

Conceptually, the intelligence-led, 'defence in depth' approach that the naval staff sought in 1918 to combat the U-boat threat, even if it could not yet fully articulate it, was on the right lines. Failures were usually a consequence of vision outrunning available technology. Although some lessons would be forgotten in the interwar period, most of the 1918 elements were taken up in the next war when their impact was transformed by better technology and the arrival of the new sensors, radar, sonar and mobile D/F. These made the hunting group a viable concept when deployed in support of convoys.

Although the 'X' Room and its integration with E1 transformed the exploitation of SIGINT and D/F against the U-boats in home waters and the Atlantic, two other sources made an important contribution in the last eighteen months of the war. These were intelligence from the interrogation of U-boat prisoners, and material recovered from sunken U-boats. It is not clear when Hall first established an interrogation unit in ID, but Bernard Trench and Vivian Brandon were serving as interrogators by the end of 1915, based in Admiralty Room 32 BIII, and were probably soon joined by Commander Charles Ennals and Lieutenant Commanders Walter Bagot and Burton Cope.[50] Brandon and Trench headed the unit until the end of the war, and both returned in the same role under Hall's successor in 1939, as did Cope.[51] Like some others in ID, Trench had served with Hall in *Cornwall*. Hall not only had high regard for his qualities, but believed he had been abandoned by the Admiralty over the disastrous 1910 Frisian reconnaissance, and wanted to give him a new opportunity. Both Trench and Brandon had acquired excellent colloquial German during their captivity, they had learnt from their experience on the receiving end of interrogation, and they became highly skilled at drawing information out of their prisoners. The most productive technique, deployed in both wars and with particular effect against U-boat prisoners, was the skilled presentation of 'omniscience', through careful exploitation of previous intelligence, which included judicious use of SIGINT. If the interrogator already knew almost everything about the U-boat arm and its operations, suggesting other prisoners must have talked freely, as well as multiple sources inside Germany, what was the point in holding back? Establishing empathy for the prisoner's condition, along with chattiness about U-boat personalities, nicknames, and the unique atmosphere of submarine life were vital too. The interrogator could offer better treatment or other inducements, although it appears that Trench occasionally resorted to threats and violence too. Trench also made frequent use of stool pigeons in the Second World War, suggesting he probably used this technique in the earlier conflict.[52] In 1917–18 Trench collaborated with MI's prisoner interrogation section MI1(a) to establish a joint service operation based in Cromwell Road, to conduct deeper, long-term interrogation of select U-boat and air prisoners. This included the development of covert eavesdropping with concealed listening devices, and a specially adapted property in Wimbledon was about to be commissioned as the war ended.[53]

Survivors were interrogated from at least a quarter of the 150 U-boats sunk in 1916–18, with composite reports produced for each of these boats. These reports were invariably detailed, often comprising twenty pages of text and diagrams packed with useful information, which could then be cross-checked with other E1 data. For example, the report on *U-48* issued in December 1917, following her stranding on the Goodwins the previous month, included sections on her final patrol and previous patrols; anti-submarine methods; losses of other U-boats; recognition marks for aircraft; personnel, organisation and recruiting for the U-boat service; submarine training; morale in the U-boat service; and the July mutiny in the High Seas Fleet, including the possible murder of Captain Thorbecke of the battleship *König Albert*.[54] The last item illustrates that U-boat prisoners often provided valuable insights beyond their own service. The report issued the previous month from *U-45* survivors included a detailed section on the German battlecruiser fleet drawn from a crew member who had served until late 1916 in *Moltke*.[55] By mid 1918, with U-boat losses mounting, prisoner interrogation detected a significant fall in U-boat morale.[56] Interrogation of prisoners of war, and occasionally German deserters who had escaped to neutral territory, as well as questioning of British escapees, also yielded valuable intelligence on surface warships and raiders, and conditions and morale in the surface fleet. During the first six months of 1917, deserters from three different battleships, *König*, *Friedrich der Grosse* and *Ostfriesland*, one of whom arrived carrying a sample German shell fuze, painted a picture of growing discontent in the High Seas Fleet, owing to inadequate food, harsh discipline, war weariness, and growing doubts over Germany's prospects. Up to twenty personnel had deserted the battlecruiser *Seydlitz* after Jutland, with none recovered. Incidents of sabotage and disobedience were also becoming frequent.[57]

The history of the diving operations on sunken U-boats is coloured by decades of rumour, tall stories and disinformation, the latter enthusiastically propagated by Hall, and encapsulated in the designation 'Tin-Openers'. In reality, naval diving teams appear to have investigated twenty-two U-boats during the war, and entered eleven, with valuable intelligence from about half these, but the majority of successful operations only took place in the last six months of the war. The earliest known dive was on *UC-2* off Yarmouth in mid 1915, the only one conducted that year. She was not entered and there was no intelligence. There were no successful British dives in 1916, but the first limited British recovery of intelligence from a U-boat came from *UC-5* in May, after she grounded on Shipwash Bank and was removed to Harwich. In addition, the French and Italian recoveries from *UB-26* and *UC-12* respectively, described earlier, emphasised to ID the potential value of such operations. Four U-boats were investigated in 1917, but the important intelligence taken from *UC-44* off Dunmore, Ireland, in September that year was the first major British success. Material recovered and subsequently circulated by ID included the briefing given to U-boat captains in January on the commencement of unrestricted warfare; the German picture of British minefields in the Bight as of June; arrangements for escorting U-boats in the Bight; and a copy of German submarine orders.[58] *UC-44*'s demise was probably enabled by intelligence from the French, following their capture of *UC-26* and most of her crew, after she grounded near Cap Gris-Nez in thick fog on 26 July. This intelligence revealed both the regular routine of German minelaying off Irish ports, but also that the Germans were reading British mine clearance signals. Hall, therefore, arranged for a field laid off Waterford in June to be left intact, while signalling that it had been cleared. *UC-44* accordingly began laying a replacement field, triggering one of the earlier mines.[59]

The recoveries from *UC-44* caused Hall to collaborate with Admiralty salvage section in establishing a specialist diving team, dedicated to covert underwater entry operations. This became operational in May 1918, under Commander Guybon Damant, comprising two officers and four divers, led by Warrant Shipwright E C Miller. It was briefed by ID staff on the details of different U-boats and their weapons, and was on standby for any opportunities. Their most important early successes were entries to *UB-33* at the end of May after she was sunk off Dover the previous month, and *UC-11* at the end of June, following her sinking off Harwich a few days earlier. Both produced valuable and timely intelligence, including some cipher and related communications material, special charts identifying transit routes, operational orders, and logbooks.[60] The extensive U-boat losses in the Dover barrage from December 1917 offered a plethora of sites accessible to divers and, in addition to *UB-33*, a further eight boats were investigated here through the summer, but only *UB-109* at the end of August produced high-grade intelligence. Although there were further successful operations in the autumn, the proximity of the armistice meant the intelligence recovered had no useful operational impact. Almost all of these diving operations were technically demanding, highly dangerous, and involved unimaginably difficult working conditions, requiring enormous skill and courage. The results were valuable, but the purely British achievements from sunken U-boats came too late in the war to have the same impact as prisoner interrogations had provided from 1916 onwards.[61]

The first naval weekly appreciation for the War Cabinet requested by Lloyd George at the Admiralty meeting on 30 April covered the week ending 27 May, and they were issued weekly thereafter until the end of the war. This first one opened with a concise summary of current British naval strategy, identifying four strategic goals, two offensive and two defensive:

- protecting the sea communications of British and Allied armies, especially the primary offensive theatre in France;
- eliminating enemy trade to undermine enemy military capability and popular will to fight;
- protecting British and Allied trade;
- preventing invasion and raids directed at the United Kingdom.

These were best achieved through destruction of Germany's High Seas Fleet. The success of the present U-boat offensive partly depended on the latent power of this fleet. It diverted British destroyers from direct protection of trade, and made attack on U-boats close to their bases hazardous. It accordingly suited the High Seas Fleet to adopt a strictly defensive attitude. British strategy must therefore control own and enemy communications, in order to resist enemy pressure and drag out his fighting ships. The Grand Fleet must remain concentrated and alert, but reduce the immobilising power of the High Seas Fleet by deploying destroyers and submarines in patrolling the northern exit of the North Sea, where possible. This would counter further German deployment of fast, armed raiders into the Atlantic, a temptation if she judged the U-boat campaign was flagging.[62]

The appreciations were an undoubted success, giving the War Cabinet and others the key developments they needed and, as Lloyd George intended, were an excellent means of tracking progress in the U-boat campaign and identifying problems. For example, the appreciation for the week ending 3 June 1917 included a detailed map of U-boat distribution in home waters and the Atlantic at midnight on 2/3 June, with twenty-two U-boats and nine UB- and UC-boats listed.[63] Estimates for U-boat losses, drawing mainly on SIGINT, were generally accurate. The appreciations initially over-stated overall German naval strength, assessing U-boat and destroyer numbers about 10 per cent above reality, and insisting that up to four new battlecruisers after *Hindenburg* would soon be available. However, by 5 January 1918, the Admiralty estimate for current U-boat strength of 179 was exactly right, and it tracked gains and losses with precision for the rest of the war.[64] The positive and ultimately decisive impact of convoying on shipping losses was amply demonstrated. The appreciation for 16 February 1918 showed that of 1656 ships convoyed in the first half of that month, only eleven had been lost. It also stressed the increasing contribution of air power to convoy protection, recording nearly one million miles flown in support of anti-submarine operations in the last seven months, with 132 sightings of U-boats and nineteen attacks on convoys prevented.[65]

There is an important qualification to the vital contribution of intelligence to countering the 1917 U-boat campaign and underpinning the success of convoy. British, Allied and neutral shipping losses to U-boats in the Mediterranean in 1916 at 1,045,258 tons were almost 50 per cent of the global total that year, and achieved by an average force of twenty U-boats. In 1917 the Mediterranean share of shipping losses dropped to 25 per cent over the year as a whole, but was closer to 30 per cent in the second half, a level significantly better than the 20 per cent of the overall U-boat force deployed there. Only two U-boats were sunk in the Mediterranean in each of these years, compared to a total of seventy-five in home waters and the Atlantic.[66] Inadequate intelligence and poor exploitation of what was available played a large part in this dismal record. British naval intelligence in the Mediterranean remained for too long on its pre-war basis. This was primarily because, with the notable exception of the first phase of the Gallipoli campaign, the Mediterranean was perceived as a secondary theatre by the Royal Navy. It recognised the importance of trans-Mediterranean communications and the supply lines to the armies in the Middle East and Salonica, but initially was content to let France and Italy take the lead, while it concentrated on the 'real war' elsewhere. Even as the unrestricted U-boat campaign began, there was limited understanding in the Admiralty of what the U-boats had already achieved in the Mediterranean, and how this linked fundamentally with Britain's overall position.

The main intelligence failure, ironic given Fisher's achievements at the beginning of the century, was the delay in creating an effective D/F and SIGINT capability similar to that covering the North Sea. This partly reflected limited specialist personnel and equipment, but also reluctance to share British expertise with allies viewed as untrustworthy. (Hall made little secret of his willingness to lose French and Italian ships, rather than risk compromising SIGINT.) There were no shore-based British intercept sites until 1917, and no British intelligence officer visited the theatre until that year. As a result, Hall and Room 40 were unaware that the French collected considerable quantities of German and Austrian traffic which was relayed to Paris, some of it via Malta. Nor was it appreciated that the French and Italians had made considerable progress on Austrian codes, some of which were already in British hands, but unexploited. Matters improved in the second half of 1917, following an exploratory visit by de Grey. Intelligence centres and intercept sites were commissioned at Brindisi and Otranto and a small joint British-Italian SIGINT unit of seven officers, including de Grey, was established in Rome to work on Austrian ciphers.[67] Malta maintained a pre-war plot analogous to that in the Admiralty War Room, covering Mediterranean naval movements, own and enemy. By autumn 1917, there was also a charting and tracking room displaying U-boat positions and movements, similar to E1 before it evolved into the 'X' Room. It incorporated D/F intelligence from British and Allied stations, intelligence from visual sightings and occasional agent reports, Navintels received from the Admiralty, but no decrypts.[68] Strenuous efforts were also made to identify U-boats transiting to the Mediterranean from their German and Flanders bases and intercept them, especially in the Gibraltar straits. For example, *UB-71* was successfully tracked and sunk east of the straits on 17 April 1918.[69]

Hall summarised Mediterranean intelligence capability, following a visit in early spring 1918.[70] He approved the basic organisation at Malta, but emphasised major limitations in the intelligence sources currently available. D/F between the three Allies remained poorly co-ordinated, with gaps in coverage.[71] It was vital to improve coverage of the area between the main U-boat base at Cattaro and the Otranto straits, where radio traffic was extensive, and boats, especially those outbound, could be identified and tracked. Arrangements for rapid sharing of resulting intelligence between relevant Allied forces to enable operational action also required improvement. North Sea experience was relevant here. Meanwhile, British collection and exploitation of SIGINT was minimal. Even by July 1918, there was no systematic analysis of U-boat call-signs in the Mediterranean.[72] The only British-controlled collection sites were at Otranto and Malta, but the latter still had no decryption capability when Hall visited. Hall advocated a new British centre at Brindisi, to work with the Italians on Adriatic codes and deployment of ID25A specialists to Malta to work on German traffic. There would also be an additional collection site at Ancona.[73] Results would then be shared in sanitised form with the Allies, although the Italian director of naval intelligence later received more detailed indoctrination. On both D/F and SIGINT, Hall now recognised that the British must be proactive in driving change, exploiting experience at home, and lead in promoting Allied co-operation, including bilateral relations between France and Italy.[74]

Hall's improvements produced an adequate Mediterranean intelligence organisation by the armistice, but there was little time left for better D/F and SIGINT to affect the submarine war. U-boat losses in the Mediterranean rose significantly in 1918, with fourteen boats sunk, only just below the loss rate elsewhere. The British intelligence improvements initiated in 1917 no doubt helped, but their impact must be weighed against the contributions from convoy, larger anti-submarine forces, better weaponry, and air patrols in the Otranto straits and other choke-points. Despite growing support problems, the Mediterranean U-boat force, which maintained a nominal 20 per cent of U-boat strength through 1918, inflicted significantly higher shipping losses than its peers elsewhere until the end of the war.[75]

14

1918: Last Acts and *Finis Germaniae*

The integrated intelligence picture applied to the 'X'-Room convoy and U-boat plot did not persuade Operations Division to introduce a similar arrangement for surface operations. Handling of SIGINT here remained similar to the practice at Jutland, and it was not incorporated in the main War Room plot. The lack of an integrated picture contributed to the poor response to German cruiser and destroyer sorties against Scandinavian convoys on 17 October and 12 December 1917, in both cases leading to serious British losses on this vital war route.[1] It also hampered the attack on the German minesweeping forces in the Bight in November. The October convoy attack triggered the forceful representations by James to the new Deputy First Sea Lord, Vice Admiral Sir Rosslyn Wemyss, at the end of October, mentioned in an earlier chapter. James argued that a fleet plot on the 'X'-Room model would have facilitated better decisions, not only over the convoy, but also in preventing the escape of *U-70* after she became stranded on the Goodwin Sands at the end of September.[2] James possibly also reflected the view of the First Lord in early September that ID should be divided into 'Intelligence Affecting Naval Operations' and 'General Intelligence'.[3] If by this, Geddes meant extending the 'X'-Room model to surface operations, it was never taken forward.

Rather than an integrated operational intelligence centre, James had to settle for incremental improvements in the distribution of ID25 intelligence. Commander-in-Chief Grand Fleet continued to receive a daily copy of the ID25 war diary, and new procedures were implemented to alert him to unusual German activity in the Bight. From August 1917, he and other frontline commanders received a weekly update on North Sea minefields and swept channels, displayed on coloured charts, and they were copied all U-boat Navintels. They also now received directionals direct from ID25. In November, in direct response to the October convoy disaster, an improved SIGINT telegram service was introduced for the commander-in-chief, using special codewords and indicators. Where the meaning of an ID25 decrypt was clear, Operations Division immediately transmitted it in paraphrased form. Where there was doubt, the full text of the decrypt was sent, along with an appreciation from Operations Division as to its likely meaning.[4]

The second convoy disaster on 12 December showed that these improvements were inadequate. A week later, Beatty remonstrated with Hall, painting a chaotic picture of the intelligence and instructions he had received from the Admiralty regarding German movements relevant to the convoy. He also too often discovered vital intelligence in the war diary which should have been telegraphed earlier. He feared further German sorties against the convoys, including deployment of heavy ships in bad weather. Early warning was essential. Hall underlined that, under existing arrangements, responsibility for passing special intelligence to the commander-in-chief rested with Director Operations Division, who often felt obliged to consult DCNS, and even the First Sea Lord. Release of intelligence could take three hours, and even then be incomplete.[5] Although Hall did not say so, these failings were further exacerbated because ID14, the primary German intelligence section, was still not fully indoctrinated into SIGINT as was E1. It acquired some access from autumn 1917, but this was gradual, and never complete.[6] The intelligence loss here was partly mitigated, because ID14 U-boat intelligence was shared with E1/ID25B, but it was a major opportunity missed, given that intelligence gleaned from German radio traffic reached its peak in late 1917. ID25 personnel later judged that at this point, the naval staff had 'reliable, continuous and detailed information concerning the enemy such as no belligerent has ever yet possessed'.[7] Yet, as Beatty complained, for surface operations the problems in exploitation demonstrated at Jutland remained, at best, only partially addressed eighteen months later.

Beatty's remonstrations over intelligence reflected wider concerns formally aired with the Admiralty in January. He argued that the massive theoretical superiority enjoyed by the Grand Fleet, now enhanced by American support, was deceptive. Battleship strength was often reduced by a third due to the refit cycle, and regular detachment of a squadron to cover the Scandinavian convoys. Only the three *Lion*-class battlecruisers were competitive with the German battlecruisers, which Beatty believed, incorrectly, now included *Mackensen*, as well as *Hindenburg*. His light forces were eroded by the increasing demands of the mine war in the Bight, and convoy support, constraining fleet mobility. Overall, the Grand Fleet was vulnerable to dispersion, while the High Seas Fleet could exploit this to sortie in full force at its selected moment, either against the east coast or a northern convoy. This would not bring it decisive victory, but could produce an indecisive engagement, or inflict heavier British losses, especially taking account of U-boat traps. The Admiralty accordingly agreed with Beatty that the Grand Fleet should not pursue action at any cost, but aim at containment and harassment. Aggressive offensive operations in the Bight would achieve this goal, and by obliging the Germans to undertake extensive sweeping before a sortie, contribute to intelligence warning.[8]

The German offensive on the Western Front, beginning on 21 March, raised Admiralty fears that the High Seas Fleet might support this with a major raid either on the Thames, or to destroy the Dover barrage and disrupt Channel traffic. To counter this, the Grand Fleet moved to Rosyth. The Admiralty was correct that the High Seas Fleet would act in support of the German army. Scheer sortied on 23 April but went north, aiming to destroy one of the large Scandinavian convoys now running every four days, and possibly trap some of its heavy escort. On this occasion, growing suspicion regarding British SIGINT capability ensured excellent German communications security before departure. This, along with a cipher change, gave ID25A little concrete to work on during Scheer's first twenty-four hours at sea. The submarine surveillance screen also failed. Despite this successful start, two factors destroyed Scheer's prospects of success. German intelligence was poor, there was no convoy to be found, and Scheer could not linger. Worse, the strike force comprising Hipper's battlecruisers was beset by mechanical difficulties, with *Moltke* temporarily immobilised, and later torpedoed. Both factors provoked signals traffic which gave ID25A a good picture of the operation. This was primarily through D/F, although Scheer's order to return was also successfully decrypted, albeit too late for Beatty to intercept. The sortie was the furthest ever taken by the High Seas Fleet, and proved to be its last. Scheer was unlucky, in that deploying a day earlier or later might have netted him a convoy and its escort. But he also ran greater risk than he realised, being unaware that the Grand Fleet was now at Rosyth on his flank.[9]

ID25A's post mortem identified some clues to the operation which were overlooked, notably the 'catchword' transmitted to warn U-boats of a forthcoming sortie, but the long-anticipated improvement in German security demonstrated that the days of easy SIGINT warning were over.[10] Once the Germans did break silence, transmission of reports to Beatty and interaction with Operations Division worked well. Apart from the warning issue, the operation indicated another important intelligence gap, the poor condition of the German fleet. The fleet was accumulating defects which could not be adequately addressed, owing to skill shortages and lack of materials. Poor-quality coal affected speed and range. Lack of sea-time and diversion of quality personnel to the U-boat force also impaired efficiency. These factors posed questions over the true seaworthiness and battle-readiness of the High Seas Fleet, suggesting Beatty's comparative assessment in January was too pessimistic.[11] Certainly, his claim that the new battlecruisers *Repulse* and *Renown* were outmatched by their German equivalents was unjustified. It was difficult for SIGINT to illuminate these issues – most prisoners came from the U-boat force, and SSB agents such as TR16 only offered limited visibility. Concern over the specific threat posed by 'superior' German battlecruisers persisted to the end of the war, and the Admiralty insisted on early completion of the battlecruiser *Hood* as a necessary British response. Perceptions were exacerbated by almost complete absence of intelligence on the specifications of *Mackensen* and her sisters, although the Admiralty correctly suspected they carried a heavier armament. The presence of *Goeben* at Constantinople, which faced no equivalent Allied unit in theatre, was a further worry. *Goeben* was actually unrepairable, following damage received during a brief sortie in January, but ID did not know this.[12]

The ultimate responsibility of Operations Division for final assessment of all intelligence on enemy surface movements, and for deciding what passed to frontline commanders, was reaffirmed six months after Hall's session with Beatty.[13] ID25 issue of directionals, U-boat reports through Navintels, and minefield updates on its own authority raised questions over whether the division of responsibility between ID25 and Operations Division was sufficiently clear. James's improvements, and his collaborative attitude, ensured that this Operations Division primacy worked adequately for the rest of the war, and included better intelligence engagement with Beatty and other frontline commanders.[14] Nevertheless it underlined the obvious anomaly. In ASD, intelligence and operations were now completely integrated with everything relevant displayed on a single plot. By contrast, for surface warfare, intelligence and operations remained distinct, with no integrated plot. History, entrenched attitudes and inertia contributed here. Operations Division was long established and staffed by naval officers with determined views over how operations were conducted. Furthermore, the High Seas Fleet never posed the same existential threat as the U-boats through 1917, inevitably pushing ASD to innovate. Finally, at the midpoint of 1918 the First Sea Lord judged that intelligence was working exceptionally well. He told Hall, now redesignated with the pre-war title DNI,[15] that over the last six weeks he had never lacked intelligence, enabling him to conduct operations he could never have contemplated without it.[16] Given this ringing endorsement, there was no incentive to change.

James's innovations continued in the final months of the war. In July he created a new ID25A section to produce vetted intelligence reports, with analysis and comment in place of unadorned plain decrypts of enemy signals. Another section was established to produce longer occasional reports, based on cumulative and deferred intelligence, exploiting material gathered sometimes in fragmentary form over an extended period. This acknowledged that important intelligence had previously been ignored. Indeed, until autumn 1916 most Baltic traffic collected had been routinely destroyed, despite the fact that this was the primary German area for training and trials, and that many units here were especially garrulous. By autumn 1918, ID25A had therefore evolved four distinct branches: cryptanalysis, the breaking of encrypted enemy radio messages; D/F and traffic analysis; assessment of current enemy movements and intent drawing on all available sources; and the cumulative long-term picture of enemy plans and capability.[17] This whole ID25A effort was underpinned by the elaborate intercept network, home and overseas. In finally integrating in one place four key processes – interception, D/F and traffic analysis, cryptanalysis and interpretation – it marks the true birth of modern SIGINT.[18]

The Admiralty had three intelligence priorities as the war drew to a close. Two were predictable and related to the present conflict: the prospects of a dangerous resurgence in the U-boat campaign if Germany survived through the winter; and a sortie by the High Seas Fleet designed to inflict sufficient damage to improve Germany's negotiating position. The latter might be accompanied by deployment of battlecruiser raiders into the Atlantic, a recurring theme through 1918, especially for the Americans, who feared for their troop convoys.[19] ID were apparently not aware that Hipper had proposed 'cruiser warfare' in the Atlantic with the newest battlecruisers in November 1914, drawing some support from the then High Seas Fleet commander, Admiral Friedrich von Ingenohl. This idea was rejected in favour of U-boat warfare and never resurrected, but it anticipated German practice in the next war.[20] The third priority was the post-war policy of the United States Navy, and the prospect that it aspired to become the pre-eminent maritime power, an issue addressed in a later chapter.

Two related factors drove concern over the future of the U-boat campaign. ID assessed that U-boat strength at the start of 1918 was 160 boats, and that for the first five months of the year losses outweighed gains, taking strength down to 145 at the end of May. However, by September, it judged that fewer sinkings and an increased commissioning rate meant the U-boat force was again growing and would reach 180 by December, more than 10 per cent up on the year. The Admiralty credited reduced U-boat losses to a shift in German tactics towards more distant deployment, and the diversion of offensive anti-submarine forces to escort additional American troop convoys despatched to meet the German spring offensive. Meanwhile, the increased commissioning rate threatened a new offensive, which the Allies might struggle to meet with existing resources.[21] Scheer, who succeeded Holtzendorff as chief of the admiralty staff in August, did promote a big new U-boat programme to the Kaiser the following month, but also admitted that the U-boat force was currently losing the tonnage war, and that prospects for turning this around were bleak.[22] Scheer's thinking did not, however, reach ID, whose assessment reflected statistical analysis rather than intelligence on German intent. Admiralty statistics, based primarily on SIGINT, were now remarkably accurate, but the conclusions drawn were flawed.[23] The Admiralty was correct that in headline terms, U-boat strength was still growing, but the net increase had halved over the first eight months of 1918 compared to 1917 and, adjusting for monthly fluctuations, the loss rate remained steady. The perceived negative shift in the spring did not exist, nor did evidence suggest more offensive hunting would have helped. Importantly, as ID25A should have stressed, increased headline strength had not translated into increased operational availability, with frontline numbers actually down on average on 1917. This suggested the Germans had already reached the limits of what they could sustain. Even as the Admiralty aired its concerns, the Germans were preparing to abandon the Flanders and Adriatic bases, leading to the scuttling of fourteen boats. With improvements to the northern barrage and ever more Allied anti-submarine resources, Scheer was correct in discounting an early shift in Germany's favour.[24]

The judgement that the High Seas Fleet intended a final sortie was correct. Improving Germany's negotiating position was one motive, but for the naval leadership, restoring the navy's credibility and protecting its political position post-war were equally important.[25] ID did not receive advance intelligence of German thinking. However, ID25A monitored the redeployment of the U-boat fleet to the North Sea from 20 October, following German agreement to cease operations against commercial shipping, in return for the opening of negotiations on an armistice. On 23 October the Admiralty warned Beatty that German activity in the North Sea was unusual, with extensive minesweeping underway.[26] Four days later, Rear Admiral Sir Sydney Fremantle, Deputy Chief of Naval

Staff, noted more sweeping done in the last ten days than the previous six weeks, and that a major High Seas Fleet operation seemed imminent. On 29 October Fremantle told Beatty that German intent was probably to lure him southward over a submarine trap, although Hall favoured U-boat penetration of the Forth for a direct attack on the Grand Fleet at Rosyth. Meanwhile, British mining operations were underway to improve the chances of ID25A being alerted to the German exit. Fremantle did not rule out an Atlantic raider operation, but thought it unlikely.[27]

The German sortie was planned for the evening of 29 October, but was abandoned after widespread mutiny, primarily within the capital ships, began in Wilhelmshaven and spread to Kiel by 1 November. By 4 November, revolutionary red flags were flying at all ports. The Admiralty correctly assessed from ID25A decrypts that a sortie was imminent on 29 October, and by 2 November it was confident it had been postponed, but did not know the reason.[28] The postponement caused Hall to abandon what was possibly the first long-range aerial reconnaissance operation over a well-defended, hostile naval base. Overflights of the Heligoland Bight area were to be mounted on three successive days, by aircraft taking off from Belgium and then landing at a covert location in Denmark, where they would be refuelled by SSB agents.[29] This operation was insurance against the failure of ID25A to provide timely warning of a German exit.

ID25A identified the first definite indications of unrest on 4 November, although by then reports were also reaching the Admiralty from neutral sources in Holland and Denmark.[30] By 5 November, decrypts showed the unrest was serious, but Wemyss told Beatty that there was still insufficient information to assess the implications. Some units appeared to be under the control of a soldiers' council, and complete disintegration seemed probable, but a last-ditch sortie by loyal forces was possible.[31] However, over the next two days an abundance of SIGINT, not least from the U-boat force trying to quell the mutineers, demonstrated that the High Seas Fleet had indeed disintegrated.[32] ID had pointers to potential unrest in the German navy from late summer onward from prisoner interrogations and other sources, but had not anticipated the speed and extent of the collapse in discipline.[33] There was one bizarre footnote to the mutiny. The imprisoned SSB agent Max Schultz, who had briefly worked on naval requirements in 1911, was released by the revolutionary council in Hamburg, and despatched as an emissary to discuss British support for a revived Hanseatic League. With the help of the Dutch consul, he reached the SSB station in Rotterdam and ended up briefing Cumming, Macdonogh and the Foreign Office although, predictably, the idea did not prosper.[34]

The First World War in retrospect

Arthur Marder concluded his great history of the Royal Navy in the Fisher era stating that the 'ultimate and decisive results' of the First World War demonstrated the Royal Navy performing 'superbly'. It had been 'completely successful' in its main tasks, ensuring the use of the sea for Allied purposes and depriving the enemy of its use. Distant blockade had ground Germany down, steadily undermining its war effort, demoralising its population and contributing to the revolutionary outbreak which ended military resistance.[35] Fifty years on, such decisive conclusions seem surprising, certainly in Britain, where the conflict is predominantly viewed as a futile tragedy with no clear winners. The British naval contribution has been eclipsed over this period by professional historical debate primarily focused on the Western Front as the decisive theatre, and by national memory fixed firmly on the lot of the common soldier in the trenches. Anyone watching the 2018 centennial commemoration of the armistice might wonder whether the Royal Navy participated in the war at all. When the naval war does get attention, the emphasis is on perceived failures at Jutland, or in the 1917 U-boat campaign, rather than ultimate strategic success. The blockade is rarely emphasised.

If Marder's conclusions are less fashionable, this book underlines their enduring validity, and the essential contribution of British sea power to the outcome of the war. Blockade would not alone have achieved Germany's defeat. But without it, the war would certainly have lasted longer, possibly ending in stalemate. Equally, if Germany had successfully broken the Atlantic supply lines controlled by Britain, the Allies would have been forced into an unsatisfactory negotiated peace. Intelligence, over which Marder had only partial visibility, was more central to this maritime contribution than he appreciated. The more complete picture now available of British intelligence capabilities, and how they interacted with policy, shows that from its beginning, this first great naval war of the twentieth century was intelligence-driven. From the end of 1914, through a mixture of luck, the institutional structures and cultural ingenuity to exploit that luck, and control of global communications infrastructure, British naval intelligence gained decisive information advantage which it never lost.

From the start of the war, naval SIGINT not only gave Britain adequate control over the North Sea, but restored many of the advantages of close blockade, albeit now exercised from a distance. From early 1917, this capability evolved to contain not just the High Seas Fleet, but to make U-boat deployment from German and Flanders ports more difficult and costly. The U-boat threat stimulated far-reaching developments in the integration of intelligence and operations. Although not fully mature at the end of the war, by facilitating evasive routing these substantially increased the effectiveness of convoy, and enabled an all-arms offensive against U-boat transit routes.

The intelligence contribution to the evolution and conduct of the British blockade has received insufficient recognition. Marder judged the blockade critical to Allied success, but did not adequately explain its operation, and hardly referred to it at all from the end of 1916. Most subsequent naval histories acknowledge its importance, but are equally sparing in their treatment, often confined to a description of the 10th Cruiser Squadron and its limitations. Intelligence histories addressing the maritime war focus almost exclusively on Room 40 and naval SIGINT. The role of COMINT and WTID in underpinning the operations of the Ministry of Blockade has been largely overlooked, disappearing into the cracks between different historical disciplines.[36] This omission has distorted views of how the blockade actually worked, and encouraged downplaying of its significance. In delivering strategic advantage, the achievements of WTID were easily as important as those of Room 40. WTID intelligence made the blockade effective, achieving the results anticipated by Ottley ten years earlier, if not in the way he expected. In the sheer scale of its data collection and processing, WTID, more than Room 40, is the real forerunner of modern communications intelligence.[37]

The centrality of intelligence to the naval war drove the growth of NID, now restored to its original title, across the conflict. By the armistice, its Admiralty-based staff numbered 140 officers, just over 40 per cent of the overall naval staff, compared to sixteen in July 1914. About half this total were in ID25.[38] However, this Admiralty element was a small part of the resources now contributing to naval intelligence requirements. NID controlled around fifty intercept and D/F sites, home and overseas, the attaché network, twenty-six overseas intelligence centres, and a further thirty centres in the United Kingdom.[39] It also drew extensively on an evolving intelligence community, notably MI8 and MI9, the SSB, MI1(b) and WTID. Overall, perhaps five thousand people worked on naval intelligence tasks. Much credit for identifying the potential of this wider network and exploiting it so effectively goes to Hall. Marder rightly identified him as one of five outstanding Royal Navy figures of the war 'a genius in his own sphere'.[40] Preserving the essential parts of this vital national capability in the changed circumstances of the post-war world were the next challenge.

PART III

Interwar: Lean Times and New Enemies

15

Post-war Retrenchment and Restructuring

The traditional picture of British naval intelligence between the wars portrays an NID rapidly run down following the armistice and the departure of Hall, starved of funds and quality personnel thereafter, contributing little value until the arrival of Captain John Godfrey as DNI in early 1939 began a renaissance.[1] For NID itself, there is some truth in this picture. However, the story of naval intelligence in this period embraces more than NID. It continued to draw on a wider community of intelligence departments and agencies, which evolved significantly between the wars, becoming closer to what exists today than the structures inherited in 1918. This wider context reveals that naval intelligence prepared Britain better for the challenges it faced at sea from 1939 than traditional accounts allow.

NID strength certainly fell fast, a development Hall recognised as inevitable within days of the armistice.[2] By January 1920, its Admiralty-based staff, excluding ID25, which faced a different future, were just under half the strength at the armistice, and two years later it had halved again. This reduction mirrored that across the rest of the naval staff, and the 1922 strength of seventeen officers and thirty-five civilian support staff was similar to July 1914.[3] It occurred against a background where the Royal Navy was at its zenith, superior in capital ships in mid 1919 to the next four navies combined. It was hard to identify credible naval threats to British Empire security for the foreseeable future. Germany was defeated and disarmed, Russia in chaos, France and Italy recent allies with navies too small to worry about. The only clouds on the horizon arose from the ambitions of the United States and Japan. The former appeared determined to challenge Britain's claim to unique naval supremacy, and anticipated American capital shipbuilding would rapidly erode Britain's lead.[4] Japan was still an ally, but also had ambitious building plans.

They would give her overwhelming superiority in the Far East, although she did not appear an imminent threat. Not surprisingly, therefore, the Treasury sought a substantial peace dividend in the intelligence sphere. Until the mid 1920s it was relentless in seeking cuts, and the challenge for the Admiralty was to ensure these did not eliminate capabilities that had proved essential in the war and might be needed in future.

NID could cope with the smaller peacetime staff in the Admiralty. Although nominal 1922 strength was the same as 1914, its post-war remit focused more narrowly on intelligence, while responsibility for naval SIGINT passed elsewhere. Its function was now to collect, collate and disseminate all information helpful to the Royal Navy in a future conflict, and to assist the naval staff in preparing war plans. It could also accept a reduced peacetime home intelligence network within the United Kingdom comprising District Intelligence Officers (DIOs) at the main naval bases, along with Hull and Liverpool. Preserving adequate overseas representation was more difficult. The Treasury wanted the naval attaché network limited to seven posts (Washington, Paris, Rome, Tokyo, The Hague, Copenhagen and Buenos Aires), although DNI protested that this compared to eight posts pre-war, while the United States currently had twenty, and France and Japan eleven each. It also questioned the continuing relevance of the overseas intelligence centres. The Admiralty insisted the network had proved essential in a global naval war and protecting Empire trade routes. Once lost, it would be difficult to resurrect for a future conflict, and it did not duplicate any other government overseas network, with both the War Office and new Air Ministry relying on it for important requirements. Treasury resistance was softened by getting Canada and Australia to contribute to the costs. The result was approval for a reduced network of thirteen centres in locations almost identical to those of 1914.[5]

Although similar to 1914, the post-war overseas intelligence network was more sophisticated and integrated. It partly reflected ideas proposed by the retired Vice Admiral Henry Campbell for an 'Imperial Intelligence System', an ambitious if unaffordable evolution of the global intelligence network he had advocated as Director of Trade Division from 1906.[6] Modern communications linked operational plots in Malta and, much later, Colombo and Hong Kong, drawing on a wider range of sources, including the SSB (now renamed the Secret Intelligence Service). This enabled the Admiralty to direct a global naval war and counter threats to empire trade routes, whether from surface raiders or submarine, exploiting lessons from the war. It also supported the rapid and flexible deployment of Royal Navy forces to meet new requirements. It divided the world into nine intelligence regions, corresponding to the main overseas commands, each supervised by a DIO. These exploited all possible sources within their areas, especially the consular system and shipping agents, to maintain a regional maritime intelligence picture distributed to local commanders and the Admiralty. Further capacity and flexibility was provided by Supervising Intelligence Officers (SIOs) within the major commands, who doubled as Intelligence Officer Afloat and adviser to the commander-in-chief. The organisation had limitations and was not yet real-time, but brought the Admiralty as controlling centre closer to the global picture sought by Fisher twenty years earlier. However, until the mid 1930s there was a major omission, ruled out on grounds of expense. With the exception of limited facilities at Malta, there were no shore-based D/F stations under Admiralty control overseas.[7]

The Admiralty never contemplated abolishing the post of DNI and merging NID into another part of the naval staff at the end of the war.[8] There are claims that by 1918 Hall had overreached as DNI, deploying intelligence selectively, and occasionally even fabricating it in order to shape government policy in line with his own views. This allegedly provoked the Foreign Office and other departments to press for Hall's removal, and to curtail the role of DNI. Hall also supposedly created enemies within the Admiralty, and lost the support of Wemyss for intriguing against Jellicoe and displaying partisan support for Beatty. The case for any concerted campaign to remove Hall is tenuous, set against numerous accolades he received on retirement, not least from Charles Hardinge, Foreign Office permanent secretary during the last two years of Hall's tenure, and from Wemyss. Many accusations regarding Hall's exploitation of political and diplomatic SIGINT during the final eighteen months of the war also imply that he enjoyed unique access and control over this source. In reality, much of the intelligence he supposedly manipulated was controlled by MI1(b).

Hall's retirement on 3 February 1919 reflected more prosaic factors. The war was over, he had been DID/DNI for over four years and change was due, he was medically unfit for sea, limiting both promotion prospects and the attractiveness of future postings, and he had political ambitions.[9] His successor, Hugh Sinclair, always known as 'Quex', was, like Hall, a former battlecruiser captain before becoming chief of staff in the battlecruiser force, and then briefly Hall's deputy. Hall warmly welcomed the appointment, telling Sinclair that he was 'the only man who can do it'.[10] Hall was correct in judging Sinclair eminently suited for the world of intelligence. He was DNI for only eighteen months, but after serving as Flag Officer Submarines, led two of the civilian intelligence agencies with distinction for the rest of the interwar period.

NID's future was potentially more threatened by the Cabinet decision in February 1922, as part of their economic retrenchment effort, to establish a committee under Sir Alfred Mond to consider amalgamating common services of the Navy, army and air force. Intelligence was one of nine common functions suggested, perhaps encouraged by the model already applied to SIGINT.[11] This idea met strong resistance from all three services, and in early May Mond informed the Cabinet that amalgamation posed difficulties, although economies might be achieved through better 'co-ordination'.[12] Intelligence integration did not proceed further at this time, although inevitably the idea occasionally resurfaced over the next forty years, before it was finally implemented in the 1960s.

By autumn 1922, therefore, NID settled into a size and structure that endured through most of the interwar period. DNI, together with his fellow directors heading the Plans and Operations Divisions, reported to DCNS, but kept the right of direct access to the First Sea Lord.[13] Through Hall's reign, DID/DNI had retained the privileged status of senior director, *primus inter pares* within the naval staff, reflecting DNI's original broad remit and role as confidant to the First Sea Lord. Post-war this status lapsed, and although DNI remained the only director to retain flag rank, Plans became informally the premier division. Reporting to DNI were a deputy director (DDNI), who ran the Admiralty-based organisation, and an assistant director (ADNI), who ran the DIO organisation, home and overseas, and liaison with other government departments including the intelligence agencies. The Admiralty organisation comprised six geographic sections with primary responsibility for British Dominions, Russia, Germany, Italy, United States and Japan respectively, supplemented by sections for coastal reporting and monitoring foreign naval movements, although the last two were cut sharply by the end of the decade.[14] NID also now operated within a more complex, but more integrated, naval staff organisation than existed in 1914, with important implications for how intelligence was used.

Traditional accounts of the interwar NID portray a self-contained organisation laboriously collating routine data from ships, consuls and open sources, before regurgitating it in indigestible reports often out of date and rarely read, a repetition of Herbert Richmond's 1904 complaint. They claim that the Admiralty, along with the War Office and Air Ministry, failed to recognise that intelligence involved more than the collection of factual information, and required professional analysis and assessment to deliver policy and operational value.[15] This underestimates the quality of the reporting NID acquired from covert, diplomatic and attaché sources, and ignores the collegiate way in which the naval staff now exploited information and evolved policy. Even by the armistice, the relatively new Plans Division worked closely with NID, and the relationship tightened as they grappled with post-war challenges. Proposals developed by Director of Plans drew on available intelligence, and were sometimes initiated by it. They were invariably critiqued by DNI before going to DCNS. Plans Division posed questions for NID to address. Where intelligence had technical or industrial implications it was forwarded to the Controller, Director of Naval Construction (DNC) and the specialist divisions such as Gunnery under ACNS. Aspects of this collegiate approach existed pre-war, but by 1918 it was more sophisticated, exploiting the more professional naval staff organisation. Intelligence was a fundamental and constant part of problem-solving and policy development by the staff.[16]

Meanwhile, there were important early developments within the wider British intelligence community, inherited from the war, which affected coverage of naval requirements. In January 1919 the Cabinet established a committee under the Acting Foreign Secretary, Lord George Curzon, to reach recommendations on the future of the various 'secret services' within government.[17] Other key members were the new First Lord, Walter Long, Churchill, now Secretary of State for War and Air, and Ian MacPherson, Chief Secretary for Ireland. The threat from Bolshevik-type domestic subversion, powerfully emphasised by Long, was the key driver of this review, but it also focused on foreign intelligence collection, where the future of SIGINT and the SSB raised important naval interests.[18]

Immediately after the armistice, Major General Sir William Thwaites, who had recently succeeded Macdonogh as DMI, suggested to Hall that MI1(b) and ID25 should unite in a single post-war SIGINT agency as part of a wider joint-intelligence organisation. Hall had his own ideas on new intelligence structures, but agreed in principle to a SIGINT merger, probably calculating that this would best protect what he saw as a critical national, as well as naval, asset. He perhaps also judged that the larger ID25 could dominate the new organisation. Hall, rather than Thwaites, initiated an interdepartmental conference, comprising Admiralty, War Office and Foreign Office, to consider the future of SIGINT on 27 February 1919. Possibly with an eye to securing Treasury funding, this conference placed more emphasis on cipher security, and the desirability of producing future British ciphers on a joint basis, than it did on foreign intelligence collection. Nevertheless, the desirability of maintaining the latter also received strong joint endorsement. The conference recommendations were approved by Curzon's committee on 29 April, which agreed that the new Government Code and Cipher School (GC&CS) would be placed within the Admiralty, but under civilian administration. The decision reflected Admiralty insistence on retaining control of naval SIGINT in wartime, the desirability of locating SIGINT capability within an operational culture, and security requirements.[19] The anodyne term 'school' in the GC&CS title, suggested by the head of the Foreign Office communications department, Courtenay Forbes, underlined for public consumption its defensive role to advise on 'the security of codes and ciphers by all government departments and to assist in their provision'. Its secret directive was 'to study the methods of cipher communications used by foreign powers'.

The Admiralty candidate Alistair Denniston, recommended by William James, was selected in preference to the former MI1(b) chief, Malcolm Hay, to head the new agency, and allowed a permanent staff of twenty-five officers, initially volunteers from ID25 and MI1(b), and forty support staff. Denniston was not a good manager. He was described rather viciously by one colleague 'as possibly fit to manage a small sweet shop in the East End', and his failings here were brutally exposed in the Second World War. However, he had an outstanding strategic vision for what modern SIGINT could achieve, he was prepared to delegate, or at least recognised when not to intervene, and he created an informal environment where eccentric talents and teamwork could flourish.[20] The most important ID25 members joining Denniston were Dilly Knox, William Clarke, Oliver Strachey and Edward Travis. The latter became GC&CS's second head in 1942. Admiralty control over GC&CS was qualified from the start, and did not endure. Importantly, Curzon ensured that the Foreign Office supervised distribution of the information GC&CS produced, arguing that in peacetime the bulk of its work would be political. He insisted that as Acting Foreign Secretary he received all decrypts, and decided what went to the prime minister or other indoctrinated ministers.

In establishing GC&CS, no mention was made of how raw traffic would be collected. Wartime cable censorship ceased in July 1919, and the Admiralty radio intercept network was rapidly dismantled under Treasury pressure. The Curzon committee accordingly ensured that the 1920 revised Official Secrets Act included a clause instructing all cable companies operating within the United Kingdom to hand over copies of all messages within ten days of despatch or receipt. Denniston established a small unit under Henry Maine, one of the MI1(b) recruits, to liaise with the cable companies over the procurement of relevant traffic. Maine executed this task brilliantly, by exercising charm and persuasion more than legal coercion, over the next twenty years. Not content with access limited to London, he arranged with Cable and Wireless to gather traffic from other points in the international network, notably Malta, which proved crucial to intercepting Japanese diplomatic telegrams to Europe, and later Hong Kong.[21] Meanwhile, Sinclair as incoming DNI gained Treasury approval to retain two stations from the Admiralty's wartime radio intercept network at Scarborough and Pembroke, the latter transferring to Flowerdown in Hampshire in 1929. Owing to absence of naval targets, these soon concentrated on foreign diplomatic and commercial radio traffic. In 1921 the War Office commissioned a further intercept station at Chatham, and two years later the Air Ministry established one at Waddington.[22]

Despite Sinclair's support, when GC&CS opened operations in October 1919 at Watergate House off the Strand, it was rapidly clear that there was no interest in the naval material it collected. As a result, naval cryptography effectively ceased between 1920–24.[23] The same was broadly true of military cryptography. With the Treasury looking for cuts, GC&CS might have had a short life. However, from the start, the Foreign Office recognised the high value of diplomatic and political decrypts. Here, GC&CS inherited and extended the coverage of American and neutral traffic achieved by MI1(b) during the war, made rapid progress on French and Japanese traffic which had not been targeted by MI1(b), and began work on the new Soviet codes. The Americans introduced a new 'hatted' diplomatic code, requiring significant new effort, but it was mastered by mid 1921, in time for the Washington Naval Conference.[24] By this time, after eighteen months of operation, GC&CS was issuing an average of 330 diplomatic decrypts per month. Apart from American traffic, the highest volumes were on the Soviet Union, Germany, Greece, Italy and Japan, joined the following year by France and Turkey.[25] Curzon now described GC&CS as 'by far the most important branch of our confidential work', with its deciphered telegrams of foreign governments a 'most valuable source' on their policy and actions, and 'the cheapest means of obtaining secret political information'. He accordingly persuaded Arthur Lee, Long's successor as First Lord, to transfer administrative responsibility from the Admiralty to the Foreign Office, giving the latter full control of GC&CS from April 1922.[26]

The service ministries soon regretted this transfer, fearing that the interdepartmental status of GC&CS was fatally weakened. In late 1923, therefore, a new compromise was arranged. GC&CS was placed under the authority of Sinclair, by now Chief of SIS, the successor to the SSB. Sinclair remained accountable to the Foreign Office, but had sufficient operational independence to satisfy the Admiralty and War Office.[27] Importantly, he provided the leadership, management skills and Whitehall 'savviness' which Denniston lacked, and could set GC&CS work within a wider intelligence perspective. Later, GC&CS also drew critical benefit from SIS's liaison with various foreign services, which it might not have achieved as a separate agency under either the Foreign Office or Admiralty. Following this rearrangement, GC&CS moved to occupy the third and fourth floors of the new SIS headquarters building at Broadway in 1926. By the end of that year it had issued around twenty-five thousand diplomatic decrypts since its creation and it regularly covered all the major European powers and many minor ones, as well as the United States and Japan. It continued doing so for another dozen years, until the increasing deployment of machine ciphers made life more difficult.[28]

It is often suggested that Room 40 created British SIGINT and morphed seamlessly into GC&CS at the end of the war, preparing the ground for Bletchley Park and its contribution to the new Battle of the Atlantic in the next war. The account above shows that the story is more complicated. Despite the prominence given to Hall between 1914–18, MI1(b) was just as important as Room 40 in delivering diplomatic and political SIGINT during the war and, despite the role of Denniston, its legacy was more important in getting GC&CS off the ground and ensuring its survival. It provided about two-thirds of the initial GC&CS staff, and at least two-thirds of initial output drew on previous MI1(b) coverage. It is sobering to reflect, therefore, that the powerful naval SIGINT organisation and pathfinder for integrated operational intelligence overseen by William James in autumn 1918, comprising more than one hundred staff, had dwindled to a tiny handful of personnel just two years later. None of these were employed on naval requirements, and they were instead re-skilling in what had previously been MI1(b) tasks.[29] Nevertheless, the crucial point is that despite the waning of Admiralty interest, the creation of GC&CS, with powerful Foreign Office sponsorship behind it, ensured that a national SIGINT capability survived and ultimately prospered. This was not inevitable. Without strong support from Curzon and Churchill, institutionalised SIGINT might have lapsed, reverting to the position before 1914 at least for a while. The British lead and much unique expertise would then have been lost. In the event, while GC&CS was smaller than the combined ID25 and MI1(b) strength in 1918, with about one hundred staff from the mid 1920s until the mid 1930s, when numbers began to increase, it was still easily as large as the SIGINT organisation possessed by any other power. It was as effective as any competitor, better than most, and perhaps the best for most of the interwar period.[30] It retained the skills and experience to regenerate a specific naval capability when required.

Meanwhile, with the end of the war, the civilian intelligence agencies SSB and MI5 (the name adopted by Kell's security service in January 1916) faced both Treasury cuts, and threats to their very existence from competitive manoeuvring in Whitehall. This potentially risked the SSB contribution to naval requirements. It was, therefore, ironic that Hall was a prime player in this power game. Even before the war ended, he encouraged Sir Basil Thomson to push for a unified domestic intelligence service, integrating Special Branch and MI5, which Thomson would head. Thomson cast this as essential to counter Bolshevik subversion in Britain. This goal reflected Hall's right-wing political prejudices and his poor opinion of Kell. Thomson also enjoyed strong political support from Walter Long, at this stage Colonial Secretary, but soon replacing Geddes as First Lord. Long was convinced that Britain was susceptible to the same revolutionary forces currently gripping Germany and Russia, and constantly lobbied his colleagues, including Lloyd George, for countermeasures. By November, Thomson had extended his ambitions, seeking to become supremo of the whole civilian intelligence community, including the SSB.[31] Meanwhile, in parallel with his SIGINT intervention, Thwaites also proposed a radical reorganisation of MI5 and the SSB. Barely a month into the post of DMI, he too did not lack ambition. His proposal had three main elements: amalgamation of the two agencies into a single Special Intelligence Service; secondment of significant numbers of army, navy and air force officers to the new service to keep it focused on defence requirements; and appointment of a tri-service liaison group to provide direction and oversight. Cumming was appalled, seeing the Thwaites proposal as another thinly disguised attempt at a War Office takeover.[32]

For the next two years, Cumming faced a protracted struggle to protect the independence of his service. Fortunately, his vision for the SSB's post-war role had broad support from the Foreign Office. Cumming impressed on Hardinge, who required little convincing, that only the Foreign Office could supervise intelligence operations overseas, a responsibility especially important in peacetime. He added that while defence requirements remained important, the SSB contribution on political and economic topics was now significant, areas the Admiralty and War Office were not qualified to judge. Finally, Cumming emphasised the desirability of keeping foreign intelligence collection distinct from domestic security. The latter required close liaison with the Home Office and police, involving different political sensitivities and judgements. Although Thwaites persisted with variants of his original proposal, Cumming's arguments were compelling, and it was never likely that the Foreign Office under Curzon would willingly relinquish control over the SSB and its funding to predominantly military influence and oversight. Meanwhile, Thomson overreached in his power bid, steadily alienating potential sympathisers for a more integrated civilian intelligence structure focused primarily on political subversion. The Foreign Office view, therefore, prevailed in Curzon's committee, which commended the SSB's performance in the war, justifying the heavy investment it received to achieve results probably superior to any other power.[33] The SSB and MI5 emerged from these debates with their constitutional status outwardly little changed.

SSB's survival as an independent service did not end Cumming's problems. Throughout the period 1919–23, like NID, he faced remorseless Treasury pressure for cuts. His budget of £90,000 for the financial year 1922/23 was about one-tenth of SSB expenditure in the final year of the war. Although this reduction was dramatic, in real terms it was still roughly five times the 1914 budget, demonstrating ministerial willingness to maintain a substantial foreign intelligence effort, even in a period of comparatively low military threat. It also concealed an important subsidy. It was agreed the SSB would manage visa issue on behalf of the Foreign Office through a network of passport control officers (PCOs). The PCO system provided cover, both defensive and offensive, for most SSB stations overseas. It was a legitimate task, which provided diplomatic protection, and in assessing visa applications, PCOs could conduct investigative work. The Foreign Office paid for the visa service. It did not cover all the network costs, but it meant the SSB got overseas representation at a substantial discount. The continuing value placed on the SSB was underlined by a prime minister's committee on intelligence created in 1921, another evolution in the British secret state. It was chaired by the Treasury permanent secretary and head of the home civil service, Sir Warren Fisher, with Hankey, still Cabinet Secretary, and Sir Eyre Crowe, Hardinge's successor at the Foreign Office, as members. Its initial brief was to reduce secret service expenditure and eliminate overlap between the agencies. In exercising this, it was supportive of the SSB, pressing Cumming on efficiency, but protecting core capabilities with stable, long-term funding. This committee, albeit with slightly expanded membership, managed intelligence agency funding until the 1990s.[34]

Cumming was still in office when he died in June 1923, although Sinclair was nominated to take over as Chief, or 'C', in September. It is not clear why Sinclair was selected. Cumming had established the precedent of a naval officer as 'C', the Admiralty naturally wanted to preserve its influence and, with Kell still heading MI5, its claim on the post dating from 1909 stood. However, the Foreign Office view was decisive. Appointing a service officer showed deference to defence requirements without seriously compromising Foreign Office control, but a naval officer was less likely to display the predatory attitude shown by

Macdonogh and Thwaites. As a former DNI, Sinclair had appropriate intelligence credentials, he was known and liked in Whitehall, and well connected in wider society. Above all, like Cumming, he commanded trust, a factor evident in his relationship with successive Foreign Office permanent secretaries. He was uniquely close to Sir Robert Vansittart, who headed the Foreign Office through most of the 1930s, and described Sinclair as 'a man equal to Blinker Hall in natural genius for the game'.[35]

Cumming himself was pleased by Sinclair's appointment, finding him 'in every way qualified and suitable to take over the service'. Sinclair's selection also demonstrated how far the SSB had advanced under Cumming's tenure. Instead of DNI recommending a comparatively junior officer as 'C', this was now considered a post suitable for a rear admiral, who had himself served as DNI.[36] From this time, the service Sinclair inherited was generally known as the Secret Intelligence Service, or SIS, although the cover term MI1(c) was still occasionally used until 1939, when it was superseded by the new cover term MI6.[37] SIS in 1923 comprised just under two hundred staff, about one-third based at headquarters and the rest deployed in thirty-three stations overseas. Although still predominantly focused on Europe, the war had made it a genuinely global service, and the 1922 financial settlement was sufficient to retain at least a skeletal global footprint in peacetime, capable of future expansion. Intelligence collection or production was organised on a geographic basis, while circulation was handled by four customer-facing sections, II, III and IV covering air, naval and military respectively, and V political. Section I, economic, which had focused primarily on blockade intelligence during the war, was closed, but resurrected in different form later in the decade.[38]

This settlement of SIS's future ensured the continuity of its existing naval reporting and the prospect of effort on new Admiralty requirements, notably Japan. The most important established source remained TR16, whose personal position improved after the war. He created a successful engineering consultancy which, besides lucrative naval contracts, took him into the aviation sector, and eventually election to the board of the federation of German industries.[39] However, with the signing of the Versailles peace treaty and the reduction of the German navy to a minimal level, demand for TR16's reporting looked limited, and he might have fallen victim to financial cuts. His reporting on treaty compliance secured his survival in the short term, but from the mid 1920s he once again became a source of the first rank. This reflected unique access to covert German plans to retain and develop the U-boat expertise and technology denied under Versailles.[40] Few other SIS sources retained from wartime contributed to Admiralty priorities after 1920. Wiseman produced valuable insights into American naval policy during the peace conference, but thereafter his reporting declined rapidly, as House lost influence during the final phase of the Wilson presidency. SIS maintained a station in New York throughout the interwar period, but it never delivered useful reporting for NID on the US Navy, and all intelligence work directed at the United States ended in June 1938.[41]

The SIS operation in Japan got off to an awkward start, and through the 1920s was equally unproductive. The awkwardness arose because the activities of the SIS station, initially opened in Tokyo in 1917 before moving to Yokohama two years later, potentially overlapped with the longer-standing intelligence operations conducted by the consul, Colin Davidson, on behalf of the Indian political intelligence service. Davidson's intelligence was influential, providing early indications of latent Japanese hostility to the British Empire through its support for Indian extremists, which helped persuade the Foreign Office, and especially Curzon, a former viceroy, to argue against renewing the Anglo-Japanese alliance. This had important naval implications at the Washington disarmament conference over the winter 1921/22.[42] By contrast, neither of Cumming's early representatives spoke Japanese, and their understanding of the Japanese environment and political culture was poor. The independent deployment in 1921 of a former deputy director of the Delhi Intelligence Bureau as regional intelligence officer covering the whole Far East area, funded jointly by SIS and the India Office, caused further confusion, and achieved little other than to irritate the Tokyo embassy. The Yokohama station closed in 1923, and in his final months Cumming deployed an officer under business cover to report on Japanese naval and air matters. A network of sources was gradually developed, but over the five years this arrangement lasted it yielded no significant intelligence.[43]

The other area where SIS influenced naval operations immediately post-war was Russia. Allied intervention in Russia, beginning in 1917, initially aimed to keep Russia in the war but following the peace treaty with Germany signed at Brest-Litovsk early the following year, it evolved into collaboration with anti-Bolshevik forces. Prior to the November 1918 armistice, the primary aim was to oblige Germany to retain significant forces in the East, but countering the perceived ideological threat from Communism, by supporting Russian groups committed to destroying the Soviet regime, became increasingly important. In January 1919 a significant Royal Navy squadron was deployed in the Baltic under Rear Admiral Walter Cowan to contain naval forces under Soviet control and protect the emerging independent Baltic states. Through the winter of 1918/19, Cumming mounted a series of successful intelligence gathering operations into Russia, providing the British government with its only reliable insights into the composition and plans of the new Soviet leadership, and the chaotic circumstances of the escalating civil war.[44] In March 1919 NID described Cumming's star agent ST/25, Paul Dukes, as 'the only reliable and regular source of information about happenings in the Baltic Fleet'.[45]

To maintain contact with Dukes, Cumming arranged with DNI, now Sinclair, for the loan of two high-performance motor torpedo boats under the command of Lieutenant Augustus Agar, given the SSB designation ST/34. This was probably the first time a Royal Navy unit was committed to the direct support of an SSB/SIS intelligence operation. Operating with Finnish approval from a base at Terijoki, Agar successfully landed a courier near Petrograd to contact Dukes. Subsequent attempts to exfiltrate Dukes over the next three months all failed, although, fortunately, Dukes then managed to escape overland via Latvia. Meanwhile, between his clandestine tasks, and contrary to Cumming's instructions, but with support from the fire-eating Cowan, on 17 June Agar attacked and sank the Soviet cruiser *Oleg* off Kronstadt, despite losing one of his boats. Two months later he guided a British flotilla in a further attack which sank two battleships and largely eliminated Soviet capability in the Baltic sea. These achievements gained Agar a VC and DSO.[46]

By the end of 1919, British government support for intervention was waning, and Cowan's force could not influence the outcome on land. Beatty, as incoming First Sea Lord, therefore counselled withdrawal of the main Baltic force.[47] He was more concerned by intelligence warnings emphasising the threat a Soviet victory would pose to British interests in the Middle East, especially the security of Persian oilfields, which had vast untapped potential – 75 per cent of Royal Navy mobility now depended on oil, but only 4 per cent of global supplies were under direct British control. Beatty, therefore, lobbied for a more activist policy in the Caspian and Black seas, where he argued British naval support could be effective.[48] His pleas won little traction, and by 1921 it was clear the Soviet regime would inexorably consolidate its grip over all Russian territory. The threat of Communist subversion, stimulated from the new Soviet Union, preoccupied successive British governments and the wider intelligence community through most of the 1920s. The prospect of 'red' revolutionary ideas spreading through the British fleet periodically exercised Royal Navy leaders, encouraged by intelligence of variable quality, not least in initial assessments of the Invergordon mutiny in 1931.[49] While subversion might have the potential to undermine the Royal Navy, the conventional naval threat to British sea power from the new Russia was minimal. Even when fears of subversion reached their height in 1920,[50] the Admiralty and NID were more focused on the challenge posed by the United States and Japan.

16

New Naval Rivals and the Road to the 1921 Washington Conference

With the surrender of the German fleet and its subsequent sinking in Scapa Flow in June 1919, the US Navy and the Imperial Japanese Navy (IJN) became the second and third navies in size after the Royal Navy. Both had a full range of modern capabilities: the Admiralty judged the design of their ships competitive, and respected their professionalism and fighting qualities. American entry into the war brought a close working relationship with the Royal Navy, with a battle squadron deployed to the Grand Fleet and an integrated anti-submarine effort. The Anglo-Japanese alliance created a relationship with the IJN that was collaborative and friendly, if never warm. Britain gained naval security on the eastern boundary of the empire, allowing its forces to concentrate in Europe, and lucrative arms sales. Japan gained essential access to naval technology and materials, facilitating its own naval industrial base. Her first super-dreadnought, the battlecruiser *Kongo*, which on completion in 1913 outmatched her then-British competitors, was designed and built in Britain. Technology transfer enabled Japan to build her sisters and succeeding classes at home. Moreover, the IJN saw the Royal Navy as a model to emulate and much of its training and organisation reflected British practice.[1]

However, Japan adopted a minimalist approach to alliance commitments in the war, except where it gained direct benefit. By its end, relations were increasingly distant, owing to growing British concerns over Japanese ambitions, especially in China, where it made a pre-emptive bid to annex German assets in Shandung (Shandong). Meanwhile, the IJN determinedly fostered independence, and its attitude to Britain became increasingly exploitative.[2] As 1919 opened, Britain's problem was that without current enemies or competitors in Europe, the US Navy and IJN inevitably set the baseline for the post-war Royal Navy in both size and quality. War with either seemed inherently unlikely, certainly in the case of the United States, but the scale and pace of their building programmes still determined whether Britain could remain the dominant naval power. Furthermore, although both navies remained allies, there were growing tensions, both in their respective relations with Britain and with each other, that influenced their future naval policies.

Looking back at the period 1919–21 some twenty years later, Admiral of the Fleet Sir Ernle Chatfield, at the heart of British naval policy-making through the 1920s before becoming First Sea Lord from 1933–38, described war with the United States as 'unthinkable'.[3] Yet during the first half of 1919, Britain's naval leaders not only thought about it, they commissioned war planning, and the theoretical possibility of a naval conflict with the United States lasted for at least the next ten years. Parallel US Navy planning for a war with Britain persisted even longer.[4] The first overt references to war with the United States appeared in Admiralty policy papers drafted in late March by Long and Wemyss in readiness for the forthcoming annual naval estimates.[5] Since the War Cabinet ruled earlier in the month that the United States was not a potential enemy 'for the present', these references were essentially hypothetical, internal mind-clearing to prepare for resisting Treasury cuts.[6] However, they also reflected underlying attitudes within the Admiralty and within political circles, going beyond abstract calculations of relative naval strength.[7]

British concern over American naval policy dated from February 1916, when President Wilson announced that the US Navy should become 'incomparably the greatest in the world'. As a political aspiration, this commanded limited attention in Britain against the context of Jutland and the Somme. Congressional approval for the ambitious 1916 naval programme comprising ten battleships, six battlecruisers and 140 smaller vessels was harder to ignore. Although British observers of congressional debates saw little appetite for aggressive competition with the Royal Navy, by 1921, in modernity and weight of broadside, the American battle-fleet would potentially become superior.[8] American entry into the war as Britain's ally in April 1917 should have put aside or deferred worries over naval competition. Instead, British concerns strengthened, owing to initial American insistence on maintaining the 1916 battle-fleet programme when Britain was desperate to see effort diverted into escort and merchant ship construction in order to meet the U-boat peril, now at its height. Although the battleship programme was suspended in late summer under British pressure, and the Americans commenced a large programme of escorts and merchant hulls, underlying tensions persisted. The British knew the battleship suspension was temporary, and that by mid 1918 the

US Navy Board had reaffirmed commitment to a 'commanding lead in the Pacific' over Japan, along with 'defensive superiority' in the Atlantic. They also identified clear intent by the US Navy leadership to achieve equality with the Royal Navy, with plans for a 70 per cent expansion of the 1916 capital ship programme once it resumed.[9] British concern over a capital ship programme which had no convincing threat justification was then exacerbated during 1918 by resentment that the United States was not pulling its weight in the naval war, and was concentrating on merchant construction in order to dominate maritime commerce in the post-war world. Meanwhile, each country eyed apparent moves by the other to carve out new areas of influence, Britain in Latin-America, and the United States in the Middle East, with growing suspicion.

British assessments of American naval policy through 1918 and during the Paris peace talks the following year were neither based on, nor required, covert sources. Gaunt as naval attaché and his successor, Captain Arthur Snagge, from May 1918, kept the Admiralty well-informed on the political and policy context in Washington, and on American naval programmes and their timing, as did Commander-in-Chief North America and West Indies Admiral Sir William Lowther Grant. Wartime co-operation between the Royal Navy and US Navy promoted sharing of information on battle experience and designs. The future British Director of Naval Construction Stanley Goodall was temporarily assigned to the US Navy in 1917, and his briefing on the new battlecruiser *Hood*, laid down the previous year, convinced both sides that *Hood* was a superior design to the projected American *Lexington*-class battlecruisers, with better protection. Indeed, US Navy constructors judged her as revolutionary in concept as *Dreadnought*, and they radically redesigned the *Lexington*s.[10] Much detail on American naval programmes, and even design specifications, were available from open sources. However, the most valuable insights into American naval policy and prejudices throughout this period came from William Wiseman, drawing on his regular exchanges with House, and less frequent contacts with Wilson.

Wiseman illuminated and, where possible, helped to manage two additional points of conflict which erupted during the autumn of 1918. These were the treatment of the German fleet following its surrender and 'freedom of the seas', the second of the famous 'fourteen points' which Wilson had declared to Congress the previous January as essential to a lasting peace settlement. The first issue concerned the future of the German battle-fleet, since there was broad agreement on eliminating their U-boat capability. Britain wanted this destroyed, reducing the German navy to a small coastal defence force. The Americans favoured Germany retaining a significant capital ship force, perhaps ten ships, as a calculated curb on British ambitions. With a serious European opponent, the British were less likely to pursue policies that challenged American neutral and maritime rights. If sinking the German battle-fleet was undesirable, even worse from the American viewpoint would be distribution among the victors on the basis of war losses, vastly increasing British superiority. The second issue, freedom of the seas, defined as 'absolute freedom of navigation, outside territorial waters, alike in peace and in war', except for closure by international agreement and enforcement, was fundamental for Wilson. In responding to unrestricted U-boat warfare, it was the principle for which the United States had gone to war. However, neither Wilson and many others in the American political establishment, nor the US Navy, had forgotten their deep-seated resentment at the British blockade. By 1916, Wilson viewed British interference at sea as unacceptable as Germany's, albeit with the crucial difference that Britain did not take American lives. Hence his 1916 naval programme, 'Let us build a bigger navy than hers and do what we please!' Britain, for her part, insisted on her right to deny the seas to an enemy. Blockade was an essential weapon, albeit keeping interference with neutral shipping proportionate. As Wemyss stated, the British Empire could not in future wars trust its security to an untested international organisation (Wilson's League of Nations), or surrender the sea supremacy which had never failed it.[11]

Both these points, but especially freedom of the seas, provoked clashes, sometimes brutally expressed. Wiseman warned Eric Drummond, within weeks of Wilson's January declaration, that freedom of the seas could damage the Anglo-American relationship. In October House warned Wiseman that British opposition to freedom of the seas risked bringing down on them 'the dislike of the world'. The United States and others would no longer submit to British control of the seas. The United States could out-build Britain, with 'more money, men and resources'.[12] A week later, House told Lloyd George that Britain would lose on this issue. The latter retorted that Britain would spend its 'last guinea' to keep a navy superior to the United States, or any other power.[13] American determination to pursue naval superiority was apparently underlined at the end of the year by Navy Secretary Josephus Daniels, with effusive support from Wilson, requesting Congress to authorise a repeat of the 1916 programme for 1919.

This mutual suspicion explains why in early 1919 the naval staffs on both sides of the Atlantic contemplated a future Anglo-American naval conflict in internal policy papers. NID advocated resuming a two-power standard, aimed at the United States and France, although

Geddes sensibly demurred.[14] Tensions peaked on 31 March, with fierce clashes between Long and Wemyss on the one hand, and Daniels and the US Navy Chief of Operations, Admiral William Benson, on the other, part of the confrontation known to history as 'the Naval Battle of Paris'.[15] Wemyss challenged US Navy insistence on a peacetime building programme that appeared disproportionate and, therefore, deliberately coercive, especially given the recent British decision to cancel *Hood*'s three sisters.[16] Benson resented British arrogance and their refusal to countenance the United States moving towards naval equality, despite its defensive requirements across two oceans. However, despite intemperate language and talk of war, both parties knew that support within the United States for a big naval programme was fragile and that, while Britain was not yet prepared to say so, it would settle for equality with the United States, although not inferiority. The British naval leadership was well-briefed by their sources in Washington.[17] House, primed by Wiseman, whom he saw almost daily, understood the dynamics within the British government and their likely bottom line. He advised Daniels, prior to the clash with Long and Wemyss, that halting American building after the 1916 programme offered a good compromise, giving the US Navy 75 per cent of nominal British strength, but more modern ships.[18] The rhetoric, and the underlying policy papers from the respective naval leaders, therefore reflected jostling for advantage and protecting budgets, more than serious belief in future conflict.

Meanwhile, the clash between the naval leaders influenced the political mood, underlining the dangers of continued confrontation. Wilson had hoped the threat of a big naval programme would coerce Britain into accepting his peace agenda. Lloyd George countered by making British support for Wilson's League of Nations conditional on naval concessions, including the vexed issue of freedom of the seas. A way forward, again with support from Wiseman, was negotiated between House and Robert Cecil, still Balfour's deputy at the Foreign Office, in the first half of April. In return for Britain supporting the League, Wilson promised both to abandon the projected 1919 building programme and, in a further important concession, to postpone ships from the 1916 programme not yet laid down, pending a lasting, comprehensive Anglo-American naval agreement, although this second undertaking was not kept.[19] Wilson also agreed to abandon specific references to freedom of the seas in the peace treaty, deciding that the issue was satisfactorily addressed under the terms of the League. The Naval Battle of Paris accordingly ended in compromise, with good intelligence on respective underlying goals assisting this outcome.

By apparently capping American naval ambitions, the Paris understanding reduced the requirement for any immediate British response to the resumed 1916 programme, although the refusal of the United States Congress to ratify accession to the League potentially negated House's commitment. However, even if the US Navy persisted with the full 1916 programme, and the Admiralty conceded that it had only laid down three of the ten projected battleships, and none of the battlecruisers by late summer 1919, it would not achieve parity with the Royal Navy before 1924. Given existing British naval dominance, and wartime orders still being completed, the Cabinet therefore adopted a 'wait and see' policy while politics played out in Washington, in August halting all new warship construction until further notice. Meanwhile, in framing future plans, the Admiralty should assume no alteration in the pre-war standard of naval strength without approval, implying Royal Navy equality with next two largest navies, excluding the United States. Finally, all three armed services should base future requirements on the assumption of no major war in the next ten years.[20] This assumption, soon known as the ten-year rule, was repeated annually until 1932.

In October the Admiralty advised the Cabinet that funding constraints had reduced the Royal Navy operational fleet to twenty capital ships. Despite a similar British force in reserve, for practical purposes the US Navy already had parity. This approximate equality would rapidly translate into inferiority if there was no new British construction and the United States maintained its 1916 programme, providing ships superior to all the existing Royal Navy fleet, with the exception of *Hood*. By 1923, Britain would, therefore, become the second naval power, unless there was a diplomatic initiative to limit American building, or the ban on new British construction was lifted within a year. The Admiralty also questioned excluding the US Navy from the established two-power standard. The US Navy could no longer be judged in isolation from other naval powers, as was possible in 1914. It was now determined to assert global influence, with implications for empire trade and security.[21] In particular, the projection of American naval power in the Pacific risked conflict with Japan, raising implications for renewal of the Anglo-Japanese alliance in 1921. The government might prefer to end an alliance which could embroil Britain in a conflict with the United States. But without the treaty, Britain must secure the naval defence of its eastern interests and territories, including Australia, against a substantial IJN, which by 1925 could have sixteen capital ships, all less than twelve years old. Nevertheless, as a determinant of future British naval strength, Japan remained a distant second to American power.[22]

Against this background, the main naval intelligence requirement over the two years from October 1919 was to monitor the pace of the American and Japanese capital shipbuilding programmes, and their respective ship specifications, to enable an appropriate British response. Here, NID continued to rely on overt and diplomatic collection in both target countries, and its primary source remained the Washington and Tokyo attachés. Neither SIS nor GC&CS contributed significantly in this period. The relative openness of American government and press made tracking the US Navy programme easier than that of the IJN. However, although NID obtained accurate data on both the *South Dakota*-class battleships and *Lexington*-class battlecruisers, it still underestimated the pace of the American programme, believing that the *Lexington*s were a year behind the battleships, whereas most were laid down contemporaneously. Arguably, it also underrated the *Colorado* class, the first four battleships of the 1916 programme, classifying them as Class B (a pre-Jutland design), whereas judged by date of construction, their general characteristics and 16in gun armament they were contemporaries of *Hood* and the IJN *Nagato*s, all rated as Class A (post-Jutland).[23]

Japanese protective security, and the reduced role of British designers and suppliers in their warship construction, made it difficult to verify even basic details of displacement, armament and speed for planned IJN ships.[24] NID got the timing and overall scope of their programme commencing in 1920 broadly correct. However, in November that year NID credited the two new *Tosa*-class battleships, laid down in February and July with eight 16in guns – similar to the preceding *Nagato* class – when, in reality, as much larger vessels, they had ten. NID also underestimated their speed by 3 knots.[25] It similarly underestimated the speed of the preceding two *Nagato*s, the first of which was just completing, although otherwise E L Attwood, chief assistant to the Director of Naval Construction, had an accurate account of her specifications when she launched in November 1919.[26] Details of the four new *Amagi* battlecruisers, laid down from December 1920, intended to outclass *Hood* and the American *Lexington*s, were even more sketchy than for the *Tosa*s.[27] Chatfield, now Assistant Chief of Naval Staff, acknowledged that the Admiralty had to finalise its own new battlecruiser design, without knowing equivalent Japanese specifications.[28] Better information from the Tokyo attaché the following July, including the important detail that the *Amagi*s would have ten 16in guns, arrived too late to influence British plans.[29] In 1920 the Japanese parliament, or Diet, approved proposals for four additional battleships and battlecruisers to follow the *Tosa*s and *Amagi*s, creating with the two *Nagato*s an 'eight-eight' fleet. Initial design work proceeded over the next year, and an enhanced armament of ten 18in guns was projected for the battleships.[30] Admiralty plans for an 18in armament for the four N3 battleships proposed for 1922/23 were by now well advanced, although it is unlikely this reflected specific intelligence of Japanese intent, as opposed to anticipation of what they and the Americans might do.

Despite gaps in NID's coverage, its overall picture of the American and Japanese programmes was sufficient for the Admiralty accurately to assess the implications for Britain's naval position, and devise an effective response. In February 1920 Long as First Lord reiterated that naval equality with the United States was the minimum position Britain could accept, and that without agreement to limit future building, it should adopt a one-power standard against the strongest naval power. The Cabinet acquiesced in this, albeit still hoping that American and Japanese building would proceed slowly, allowing British plans to be deferred. However, by late November, the Admiralty assessment was stark. Fourteen of sixteen capital ships planned under Wilson's original 1916 programme were now under construction, and the final two would be laid down shortly. By 1925, therefore, Britain would have a single Class A ship, *Hood*, while the US Navy would have twelve, and Japan eight, with a further eight in build. Unless Britain responded, she risked permanent relegation to third naval power. The minimum acceptable investment to maintain one-power status was four ships in 1921/22, and a further four the following year, giving the Royal Navy nine Class A vessels by the end of 1925. Long and Beatty invoked industrial and political factors to apply further pressure on the Cabinet. The post-war cessation in warship building, especially of heavy ships with their associated specialised guns and armour, threatened rapid loss of industrial capacity. Unless new ships commenced by the end of 1921, it would be impossible to sustain the rate of four per year necessary to catch up with the American and Japanese programmes. Britain risked falling even further behind. The Admiralty also advised against postponing a British programme in order to persuade the Americans to reduce theirs or make cancellations. Even if the Americans cancelled six ships (two not yet laid down and four least advanced), which seemed inconceivable, Britain still required four ships in 1921/22 to balance remaining American numbers, let alone those of Japan. Furthermore, such a large American cancellation, which they could easily afford, could make it politically impossible for Britain to initiate any building programme, setting her up for third-power status.[31]

On 14 December the CID reluctantly authorised the Admiralty's building plan, subject to further efforts to dissuade the Americans from engaging in a naval race, with four initial ships included in the 1921/22

naval estimates the following March.[32] However, by the summer the
Admiralty faced renewed Treasury resistance, provoked partly by
the deteriorating financial climate, but also the prospect of a naval
disarmament conference, proposed by the Americans in early July for
later in the year. The same month, Long's successor, Lord Lee, renewed
the Admiralty case, based on the latest intelligence confirming that twelve
American and eight Japanese Class A ships were on track for completion
by 1925, with specifications far superior to all Royal Navy vessels, save
Hood. While the timing of the conference was politically unfortunate,
it seemed unlikely existing orders would be halted: Britain must not be
left behind, nor could she go naked into the conference.[33] The argument
for negotiating leverage was compelling, and the Cabinet confirmed the
ships should proceed, although some members doubted, correctly as it
transpired, that they would be built.[34]

The four G3 battlecruisers ordered, fittingly, on Trafalgar Day,
21 October 1921, were a plunging design in the finest Fisher tradition,
drawing on the best available intelligence on their rivals. Although called
battlecruisers, the G3s, which were never named, were the first true fast
battleships, a step-change on *Hood*. At 32 knots, they were as fast as
the *Lexington* and *Amagi* battlecruisers, but better protected than the
South Dakota and *Tosa* battleships, with gunpower comparable to all
of them. They were the first capital ships with a tower bridge, with
secondary armament in twin turrets, and with a comprehensive anti-
aircraft armament. About 10 per cent larger than their current Class A
competitors, they were a revolutionary design, at least five years ahead
in balance of qualities and sheer modernity, enabling the Royal Navy to
counter a superior force of the planned American or Japanese ships, and
setting a new baseline for the future. Indeed, as a capital ship design, the
G3 was not surpassed by the best of the new generation twenty years
later.[35] But, inevitably, their quality was expensive. The cost of the four-
ship programme averaged across three fiscal years was about one-fifth
of the overall naval budget, or the interest payable to the United States
for war debt for each year, and two of those years overlapped with the
proposed N3 battleships to follow – hence Treasury insistence that the
whole commitment was unaffordable.[36] In the event, developments in
Washington led to their suspension within weeks, and final cancellation
in February 1922.

In the last eighteen months of the Wilson administration, post-war
political and economic uncertainty, bitter congressional battles over
ratification of Versailles and the League, and lack of presidential direction
following Wilson's illness allowed the naval lobby, led by Benson, to

push naval expansion relentlessly. However, although the resumed 1916 programme had congressional approval, and parity with Britain retained widespread consensus, orders looked excessive, while the depth of anti-British sentiment in some US Navy circles provoked unease. Even before the November 1920 presidential election, pressure therefore mounted in Congress for dialogue on naval arms control to reduce expenditure and produce the peace dividend public opinion expected. This coincided with attitudes in the new administration. President Warren Harding, faced with a deteriorating economy, was focused on domestic issues and uninterested in naval affairs. His Secretary of State, Charles Evan Hughes, who soon dominated naval policy, wanted 'painless parity', happy to dispense with the 1916 ships if Britain conceded parity at a lower level. His price was ending the Anglo-Japanese alliance, to prevent a combined Anglo-Japanese fleet outmatching the United States.[37]

Here, Hughes faced a relatively open door. Britain recognised that in post-war circumstances, renewal of the alliance would inevitably appear directed at the United States, a point underlined by the Dominions at the 1921 Imperial Conference. Choosing Japan over the United States was never credible, nor was Britain willing to provoke a ruinous naval competition she could not win. The Admiralty knew that the US Navy could overtake the Royal Navy and IJN together within a decade, at most. Furthermore, leaving strategic choice aside, by 1921 Foreign Office and Admiralty attitudes to Japan aligned more closely with Hughes's views than he appreciated. Japanese meddling in India, and her aggressive attitude towards China, meant both departments saw Japan somewhere between 'problem' and 'looming threat'. Although in 1921 the Admiralty was confident it could crush the IJN easily in a single-handed war, Chatfield was less sanguine about conducting an offensive war in eastern waters in 1925 against 'the Japanese fleet then existing', and without new Royal Navy ships it would be impossible. Treaty renewal offered reasonable insurance against this threat, but also implied further British arms sales and support, making the IJN a greater danger in the future. By mid 1921, there was, therefore, growing government consensus for a policy of containment, free of alliance baggage, although the Admiralty did not yet exclude a short treaty extension with reduced commitments as temporary insurance, while Britain reinforced naval capability in the Eastern theatre.[38]

The Admiralty quickly recognised that the incoming Harding administration favoured naval dialogue, and by March 1921 began planning for a disarmament conference which ultimately took place in Washington over three months from mid November.[39] During the eight months leading up to the conference, Britain acquired no useful intelligence on real American intentions. Hughes, the driving force on American policy, held his plans so close that the US Navy leadership was little better sighted than their British counterparts. Britain now had no interlocutor equivalent to Wiseman, the Washington embassy offered little, and while the attaché provided better information from his naval contacts, this proved misleading, because they were out of the real policy loop. Although GC&CS was reading both American and Japanese diplomatic traffic, this too revealed little because it could not access the important policy traffic. With the conference in Washington, American decision-makers had no need to brief overseas embassies, including London, on policy developments. Likewise, the Japanese government did not brief its European embassies, and GC&CS could not access cable traffic between Tokyo and Washington. GC&CS intercept was thus restricted to secondary traffic of limited importance. By contrast, the American SIGINT organisation, Herbert Yardley's Black Chamber, read the important Japanese traffic, providing vital insights into their bottom line as negotiations progressed, although not British messages. Britain benefited indirectly from this American intercept of Japanese traffic because, on Japan, British and American goals aligned closely.[40]

Without definitive intelligence of Hughes's intentions, British preparations for the conference reflected their assessment of the balance of political forces in Washington, and extrapolation from the evidence of naval building underway. There seemed little cause for optimism. Hughes's reticence was judged as confusion, and Lloyd George found American preparations amateurish. Lee signalled that Britain was willing to concede formal parity, and to sacrifice the alliance with Japan, subject to satisfactory alternative international security arrangements in the western Pacific. But the Admiralty expected the full 1916 programme to proceed, and security commitments to fall short. It hoped, therefore, to halt American building after the 1916 ships, and to limit Japan to two-thirds of British strength, enabling the Royal Navy to match the IJN, while retaining an adequate fleet in European waters. Britain could then hold to its eight planned new ships, before moving to a steady one-for-one replacement programme.[41]

British expectations of the Washington conference, which opened on 12 November, proved profoundly wrong. But intelligence failure foreshadowed strategic success. In a dramatic opening address, which staggered the British delegation led by Balfour, now Lord President of the Council, Hughes produced a plan, which by the close of the conference in February 1922 satisfied most British objectives. Hankey, present as delegation secretary under Balfour, immediately judged it a 'superb offer'.[42] The United States would scrap all 1916 capital ships not yet commissioned, leaving only *Maryland*, the first of the *Colorado* class. In return, Britain and Japan would also terminate ships under construction, or still fitting-out, including *Mutsu*, the second *Nagato*. Large numbers of older vessels would be scrapped, the majority British, to produce strengths for Britain, the United States and Japan stabilised in the ratio 5:5:3. France and Italy received a ratio of 1.75, while Germany remained subject to more draconian Versailles restrictions. There was a ten-year building holiday for capital ships, and limits placed on future displacement and gun size. Less ambitious limits were agreed for aircraft carriers and cruisers. Japan fought to retain *Mutsu*, and in return the United States kept two more *Colorado*s, while Britain won the right to build two new capital ships, the future *Nelson* class.

The Washington Treaty never lacked critics among its participants. In Britain it was long judged as initiating a naval disarmament process that took inadequate account of Britain's unique global commitments, and fatally weakened her in coping with the multiple threats emerging by the mid 1930s.[43] In reality, Britain did well from Washington. It ended a potentially bitter and expensive Anglo-American naval competition on favourable terms. Arguably, the treaty 'sank the US Navy and restored British maritime supremacy for a decade', the equivalent of a major naval victory.[44] Although the treaty ratio implied capital ship parity with the US Navy, the Royal Navy came away with an advantage in both permitted tonnage (about 6 per cent greater) and numbers (twenty versus eighteen). The US Navy calculated at the end of 1922 that the Royal Navy had gained greater superiority, perhaps 30 per cent, in the effective fighting strength of its capital ship fleet.[45] Once the two *Nelson*s completed in 1927, to a design more modern than any contemporary, along with *Hood*, Britain had the three largest and most powerful warships in the world.[46] She had comfortable superiority over all the European navies combined (most, in any case, friendly) and a 66 per cent margin over Japan, compared to the 50 per cent originally wanted. Moreover, through the 1920s, the Royal Navy won more investment from the Treasury than was required to maintain a one-power standard with the United States as the strongest naval power, a target naval strength reaffirmed by the CID in 1925.[47] By 1930, the ratio of fighting strength between Britain, the United States and Japan, judged across all naval categories and not just capital ships, was closer to 5:4:3.[48]

As anticipated, at Washington, Britain and Japan acceded to American insistence not to extend their alliance. In its place, the United States,

Britain, Japan and France signed a Four-Power Treaty, freezing the status quo in the western Pacific for the next ten years. They promised to respect existing territorial sovereignty, and undertake no military fortification within the defined treaty area. The treaty provided for consultation in case of dispute, but had no enforcement mechanism, or obligation to intervene. A separate Nine-Power Treaty guaranteed the integrity of China and ensured equal commercial access, but again without enforcement arrangements. Ending the Japanese alliance had few immediate adverse consequences. Through the 1920s, the overall Anglo-Japanese relationship and, more specifically, that between the Royal Navy and IJN remained amicable, while the IJN and Japanese naval industry still drew significantly on British technology. Nevertheless, Japan was freed to move against British interests with the Washington deal and would have greater capability to do so. She avoided competitive building, which her weaker economy could sustain less than Britain, let alone the United States, but received a better ratio than her true economic strength merited. The IJN could also concentrate entirely in the Pacific, whereas the Royal Navy and US Navy faced more diverse commitments. Prohibition on new fortified bases in the western Pacific curtailed Britain and the United States from projecting their naval power, effectively ceding regional naval supremacy to Japan. Furthermore, although the Royal Navy left Washington with a better margin over the IJN than it originally sought, the balance of capital ship scrapping meant net strength against Japan still declined.[49]

17

After Washington: Managing Japan and Other Distant Threats 1922–1930

The Washington Treaty defined British naval policy, and therefore naval intelligence requirements, for the next ten years. It significantly eased tensions in the naval relationship with the United States. With parity conceded, the pause in building agreed, a deteriorating economic background pushing both countries towards further naval reductions, and American isolationism gaining force, potential for serious conflict faded. War plans were occasionally dusted off, but remained strictly theoretical, and neither country saw the other as a genuine threat to its security. Nevertheless, fundamental differences over extending the Washington disarmament agenda made the relationship difficult and competitive for most of this period. For Britain, any adverse disarmament development would prejudice her maritime security, and complicate the potential threat from Japan. Intelligence on American thinking was needed to navigate these dangers. By contrast, the European naval powers could exert limited leverage over disarmament, nor during these years did they pose any credible naval threat to Britain, although SIS reporting encouraged a watchful eye on German adherence to the Versailles terms. Despite the Washington cuts, British superiority in both home waters and the Mediterranean was overwhelming.

That left Japan as the only naval power which could potentially threaten British Empire interests and territories. For ten years after Washington, this threat was theoretical, rather than based on intelligence or other evidence of hostile intent. Lack of evidence did not reflect failure to collect intelligence, or accurately assess what was available. During this period, the Tokyo embassy and service attachés retained good access to Japanese decision-makers, and GC&CS diplomatic decrypts provided extensive coverage of bilateral relations, attitudes to further naval disarmament, and to regional policy, especially towards China. It was, rather, because no intent or preparations for an attack on British interests existed in this period or, indeed, for long after. One of the ironies of the interwar period is that while the Royal Navy planned assiduously for war with Japan, the opposite did not apply. The IJN focused entirely on the threat from the US Navy. Not until 1940 did the IJN begin serious planning for war with the British Empire. This absence of hostile Japanese intent was reflected in Foreign Office assessments, until Japanese behaviour towards China in the early 1930s began a reappraisal. In 1925 the CID endorsed the Foreign Office view that aggressive action against the British Empire by Japan within the next ten years was 'not a serious possibility', a judgement that proved sound.[1] Five years later, the Foreign Office still had no reason to qualify its positive assessment, judging bilateral relations 'excellent', while the Japanese attitude to the recent London naval disarmament conference was positive, and her relations with China were improving.[2]

Throughout the 1920s, the Admiralty was more sceptical of Japan's ultimate intentions. It countered the 1925 Foreign Office view by emphasising that Japan had built more cruisers, destroyers and submarines since the war than the rest of the world put together, and the high proportion of government expenditure it devoted to armaments. This building comparison was wrong by a wide margin, while a more specific claim that Japan had laid down more warships since the Washington treaty than other signatories was equally misleading.[3] The Admiralty had good reason to promote the threat from Japan to fend off Treasury cuts and obtain new investment. But it faced a genuine strategic problem in ensuring long-term security for the British Empire's eastern territories, interests and communications, in the face of a naval power with regional superiority, and whose friendship was not guaranteed. The Admiralty was confident that the Royal Navy would ultimately beat the IJN in a single-handed war but, as Beatty stressed, Japan could inflict initial defeats from which it would be difficult to recover.[4] The Admiralty, therefore, sought a risk-based approach to Japan. Lack of current hostile intent towards Britain and low probability of conflict could change, while evolving IJN capability increased its scope to do serious damage. The chiefs of staff agreed that this risk required insurance. In their first review of imperial defence in June 1926, they identified securing the Far East as Britain's top defence priority.[5]

To monitor the IJN through the 1920s, NID still relied primarily on the Tokyo naval attaché. Anglo-Japanese naval relations, while guarded, remained cordial in this period. Until the mid 1930s, the attachés were permitted periodic visits to naval establishments, shipyards and air stations, and sometimes to warships too, often yielding valuable intelligence from visual observation, or comments from friendly IJN escorts.[6] Tracking appropriations debates in the Diet provided detail on order of battle and future building programmes, while the Japanese press and other open sources provided useful details of warship characteristics, despite censorship. Liaison with the American attachés was close, providing two-way collateral for intelligence collected. Well-informed British journalists were helpful too. Malcolm Kennedy, the Reuters correspondent in Japan from 1925 to 1934 before joining GC&CS, had excellent senior IJN contacts.[7] Hector Bywater, resuming his journalist career post-war, reported authoritatively on the IJN, in 1925 publishing his famous book on a future naval war between Japan and the United States. Both British and American attachés found his insights valuable, although he no longer worked for SIS.[8]

NID perceptions of the IJN, and wider Admiralty attitudes to Japan, were also shaped by Japanese procurement of specialist naval expertise and technology. At the end of the war, the IJN identified four key areas where it lagged behind its potential naval competitors: aviation, armour, fire control and submarines. For the first three, it looked to Britain. In October 1920 the Japanese ambassador in London sought an official naval aviation mission to Japan to provide flying training and advice on aviation technology and equipment, including the latest weapons, and on building aircraft carriers. The Foreign Office and new Air Ministry were supportive, but the Admiralty, by now suspicious of IJN ambitions and its exploitative attitude, opposed providing access to an important future capability. However, the prospect of valuable aircraft sales produced a compromise – the despatch of an unofficial aviation mission under Sir William Sempill, a former Royal Air Force officer with experience in the design and testing of Royal Navy aircraft during the war. The Sempill mission, which lasted eighteen months, provided the IJN with a quantum jump in aviation training and technology, catapulting its development by perhaps five years, and was fundamental to making Japan the premier naval air power by the late 1930s. It triggered further links with British aircraft companies through the 1920s, and the arrival of significant numbers of British personnel as advisers and consultants. In February 1923 William Jordan, a former RNAS officer, now employed by Mitsubishi, made the first take-off and landing on the new aircraft carrier *Hosho*.[9]

If the Sempill mission brought the IJN considerable long-term benefit, it also showed NID that in the early 1920s Japanese air capability lagged well behind Britain. In theory, this supported the Foreign Office assessment that aggressive action against Britain was unlikely, but the mission also influenced Admiralty attitudes less positively. Sempill himself passed classified information to IJN officers, including the Japanese naval attaché in London, identified through GC&CS coverage of Japanese communications and provoking a Security Service (MI5) investigation. Although Sempill was probably never a controlled Japanese agent, he only narrowly avoided prosecution for espionage.[10] Quite separately, one of the Air Ministry staff involved in establishing the Sempill mission, Squadron Leader Frederick Rutland, a distinguished former RNAS officer, also offered intelligence to the Japanese attaché, Admiral Seizo Kobayashi, an offer taken up, but again immediately spotted by GC&CS. The Security Service and SIS together monitored this complex case for the next twenty years. Rutland was initially exploited for his aviation expertise and from the mid 1930s to establish a Japanese intelligence network in the United States. The case was important in counter-intelligence terms, but gave NID little insight into evolving IJN capability or plans.[11] However, both cases fed the Admiralty belief that Japan was now potentially an aggressive and hostile power.

Apart from aviation support, Japan procured armour, fire control equipment and optics from British industry until the late 1920s, providing NID with good insights into current IJN equipment and Japanese industrial expertise. In 1921 the Admiralty approved the sale of Vickers armour, knowing it would be used for the abortive *Amagi* battlecruisers, on the basis that it no longer met British specifications.[12] This armour was eventually used in the *Yamato* super battleships of the late 1930s, supplemented with a Japanese-produced variant derived from the original Vickers formula supplied under licence. However, the Admiralty correctly assessed in 1936 that the quality of this Japanese armour was still markedly inferior to the latest British type.[13] In 1924 Barr and Stroud provided a sophisticated fire-control system to Japanese specifications to update the *Kongo*-class battlecruisers. The Admiralty noted that this applied the same principles as the current British system and, despite lacking certain essentials, could support long-range fire out to 30,000m (33,000yds).[14] The same year, the Tokyo attaché obtained photographs demonstrating that the *Nagato*s had a main armament gun elevation of 30°, and other battleships 25°, consistent with this range, which was superior to all British capital ships, except *Hood* and the *Nelson*s under construction.[15] Over the next ten years, the IJN incorporated improvements to the Barr and Stroud system, with help from the Japanese company Aichi, to enhance long-range effectiveness.[16] For submarine technology, and increasingly for optics, Japan turned to Germany. It received seven U-boats, including five of the latest design, as part of its share of reparations paid to the

Allies under Versailles. Study of these boats encouraged Japan to procure further German services in design and construction, including the recruitment of specialists to work in Japan.[17] TR16 alerted SIS to this relationship, and by mid 1923 NID had full details of the cruiser-submarine designs acquired, which the Director of Naval Construction, Sir Eustice D'Eyncourt, assessed were based on the uncompleted German boats *U-183–190*. The naval staff judged that the range of these projected Japanese submarines was a considerable threat both to British trade and reinforcement convoys in the event of an Eastern war.[18] Both British and American attachés subsequently monitored German support from within Japan.[19]

A further development in the mid 1920s influenced long-term intelligence coverage of the IJN. It followed recommendations made by Viscount Jellicoe, as he now was, in his report following a naval mission to Australia in 1919. He proposed a state-of-the-art, shore-based radio intercept and D/F network for the Indian Ocean and Pacific, modelled on British wartime experience. Together with other sources, this would feed an integrated regional empire intelligence organisation, a concept subsequently named the Pacific Naval Intelligence Organisation (PNIO). Post-war financial constraints prevented progress on the construction and staffing of such a project until the mid 1930s. However, the growing Admiralty focus on Japan, and the success achieved by GC&CS on Japanese diplomatic and attaché traffic, including the Sempill and Rutland revelations, encouraged DNI, now Rear Admiral Maurice Fitzmaurice, to recreate a more limited naval SIGINT operation from existing resources. In March 1923 he instructed Commander-in-Chief China to begin ship-borne interception and collection of Japanese naval traffic, and the following year, with Board approval, negotiated cryptanalytical support from GC&CS on naval targets. Under the new arrangement, DNI, in consultation with Director of Plans, defined naval SIGINT policy, the relative importance of foreign navies to be targeted, and an agreed programme of work. Director Signals Division, guided by DNI, provided specialist equipment and training, both ashore and afloat, necessary to collect traffic and enable local traffic analysis and D/F.

GC&CS, therefore, now established a new naval section to conduct cryptanalysis of naval traffic collected under DNI's direction, and provide resulting intelligence to NID. Since Denniston could initially only offer two staff, Fitzmaurice agreed to create a permanent cadre of six Japanese interpreters trained in cryptography, constantly refreshed by two officers always under instruction at GC&CS. NID owned these interpreters, seconding those selected to GC&CS for an initial nine months. Once qualified in basic cryptography, they remained at GC&CS, supporting either naval or diplomatic work, or deployed on SIGINT duty to the China Fleet.[20] This agreement between Denniston and Fitzmaurice, certainly the staffing arrangements, was somewhat convoluted, with scope for ambiguity in future interpretation. However, a crucial point was that GC&CS created a naval section under its direct control, however small its beginning, and in time provided the majority of the staff. Its constitutional status was different from the military and air sections created in 1930 and 1936 respectively. The former, under John Tiltman, was jointly responsible to the Head of GC&CS and Military Intelligence Department with MI providing most of the staff, and the latter, headed by Josh Cooper, was under sole Air Ministry control. Cooper was recruited by GC&CS as a Russian linguist in 1925, and worked briefly on Russian naval traffic in the naval section in 1929. On taking over the new air section, he and others appointed to the unit were transferred to the Air Ministry.[21] These constitutional differences had far-reaching implications when the next war began in 1939, and especially for handling German Enigma intelligence. In 1924, in line with the understanding at GC&CS's founding, the Admiralty anticipated taking back control of the entire naval SIGINT operation and its staff, including the GC&CS section in wartime. Fifteen years later, it found this was neither possible constitutionally, nor desirable operationally.[22]

Despite heading the military section, Tiltman was destined to make a significant contribution to naval requirements over a cryptographic career spanning fifty years. After distinguished war service in the King's Own Scottish Borderers, initially in the ranks, the War Office seconded him to the new GC&CS in 1920, following a short Russian course. Here he came under the influence of Ernst Fetterlein, the former chief cryptanalyst of the Russian Tsarist government, who recognised Tiltman had innate cryptanalytical talent, and set him on a path that made him one of the outstanding cryptographers of his generation, leading to his appointment as GC&CS Chief Cryptographer in 1942. His eclectic approach and love of a challenge enabled him in 1939 to exploit his work on Japanese military systems to achieve the first opening into the primary Japanese naval code of the Second World War, JN25. Subsequently, during the war, he orchestrated successful attacks on the German Lorenz cipher used for strategic teleprinter traffic and the latest Japanese military attaché system, and oversaw important improvements to Royal Navy ciphers. Two other contributions were critically important. He created a short Japanese-language programme that gave Britain a vital edge in the Far East intelligence war, and because he was respected and trusted by the

Americans, he was a central player in cementing an effective Anglo-American cryptographic alliance.[23]

For its first ten years, the GC&CS naval section never comprised more than five officers, including NID-seconded Japanese interpreters, and often less. It was headed by William Clarke, formerly of Room 40. In addition to Japanese, it studied French, Italian, Russian, Spanish and, occasionally, American naval traffic. Although some of the staff were formally classified as cryptographers, in practice the work of the section embraced cryptanalysis, the decryption of target messages, but also translation and analysis, and preparation of the final intelligence report, and there was no absolute distinction over who executed these tasks. Throughout these years, the operation was hampered not just by limited staff, but divided cryptanalytical effort, with some of this work done locally in theatre, as well as in GC&CS. It also suffered because Clarke had an awkward relationship with Denniston and, like him, was a poor manager, who could have deployed his resources better.[24] There was further difficulty ensuring consistent collection against target communications from ship-borne platforms, where frontline support was variable. Adequate intercept training for communications staff was a challenge, especially those required to read Japanese Morse. The time taken getting product back to GC&CS from distant theatres was a further constraint. Nevertheless, by the end of the period there was enough progress to provide a solid basis for future development.

As early as 1924, the three armed services and GC&CS established a Cryptography and Interception Committee, later known as the 'Y' Committee. Chaired by Sinclair, now Chief of SIS and Director GC&CS, this met annually and comprised the three Directors of Intelligence and Signals, with Denniston additionally representing GC&CS. It agreed priorities for interception and collection, and aimed to minimise overlaps, recognising that GC&CS resources were finite, no single service could collect everywhere, and there was benefit in sharing communications. A consensus emerged that the Admiralty had prime responsibility for collection in the Far East, the War Office for the Middle East, where MID had established a major intercept and cryptographic site at Sarafand in Palestine in 1923, Commander-in-Chief India for his area, with Europe and North America covered on a joint basis, although the division was never precise. The 'Y' Committee structure was duplicated in a subcommittee which met more regularly, and included other members such as the GPO, the civilian intelligence agencies, and Special Branch. In 1923, encouraged by Sinclair, the Police Commissioner established a small intercept site at Denmark Hill in London to monitor illegal transmissions from within the

United Kingdom. This remit gradually extended to cover a wide range of diplomatic- and intelligence-related radio transmissions of interest to SIS and MI5, and not covered by collection conducted by the three armed services.[25] Meanwhile, 'Y', or 'Y work', also gradually became widely used cover terms for SIGINT.[26]

In the meantime, the Admiralty encouraged and streamlined support for the shipboard intercept, on which naval collection initially depended. In 1926, to boost output and reduce duplication, fleets and squadrons were given lead responsibility for collection on specific countries: Atlantic – France; Mediterranean – France and Italy; North America and West Indies – USA; China – Japan; East Indies – French and Italian African traffic. The objective was not just traffic for cryptographic study, but information to support traffic analysis, radio procedures, call-signs, frequencies, and overall communications organisation. (Through the interwar period, traffic analysis was still usually referred to as wireless telegraphy intelligence, or WTI.) By now, three years after it was initiated, China Fleet collection was prolific, averaging a thousand Japanese messages per month.[27] The same year, the Admiralty began planning a limited, shore-based intercept network in the Far East, with initial stations at Stonecutters Island in Hong Kong, Esquimalt on the Canadian Pacific coast, and later Kranji in Singapore. The Director of Signals Division involved in this planning was Captain James Somerville, who later played a critical role building the new 'Y' network for the Second World War, before becoming a distinguished commander of the Gibraltar Force (Force H) and Commander-in-Chief Eastern Fleet from 1942. However, financial constraints meant only Esquimalt was completed in the 1920s (largely paid for by Canada), Hong Kong was not operational until 1935, and Singapore not until 1939.[28]

Substantive cryptographic attack on Japanese naval codes began in 1925 under a Royal Australian Navy officer, Paymaster Lieutenant Eric Nave, who was seconded to the Royal Navy China Fleet, and based first in the flagship, the cruiser *Hawkins*, and then in the submarine depot ship *Titania*, specifically to work on breaking coded messages collected by fleet units. Nave qualified as a Japanese interpreter in 1923, with the highest score ever achieved by a naval student. On return to Australia, he worked on Japanese codes alongside his regular duties as a supply officer in the cruiser *Sydney*, sharing the results with the Admiralty. He discovered, as had GC&CS staff working on diplomatic traffic, that Japanese codes were at this time relatively simple. His language skills, codebreaking talent and location in the region made him ideal to lead a more formal cryptographic attack. For the next twenty years, he was one of two main contributors to

Japanese naval codebreaking, the other being Paymaster Captain Harry Shaw, whose interpreter score ranked just behind Nave. Within a year, Nave was reading two of the IJN's standard reporting codes, and at the end of 1927 he reported that the whole of their naval communications system was now understood, a judgement the Admiralty endorsed. DNI, Rear Admiral Barry Domville, Denniston and Clarke therefore agreed he should come to London to continue work on the more complex General Operational Code used for major operational traffic, on which he had already made good progress. Shaw replaced him in the China Fleet, a rotation pattern that continued until the mid 1930s. Within a year, Clarke reported that largely due to Nave the General Code was readable.[29] Nave then became a key player in the attack on Japanese communications during the London Naval Conference, when he concluded that the IJN now saw the US Navy as its primary opponent.[30]

By the early 1930s, ten years on from the decision to re-establish naval SIGINT, there were therefore significant achievements. All the important Japanese naval codes, NID's first priority, were readable, and China Fleet collection and analysis of traffic was progressing. In theory, SIGINT coverage of the IJN looked broadly similar to that available on the German High Seas Fleet at the end of 1914, but with the added advantage that Japanese diplomatic traffic was also read. There was good progress on the other navies on the GC&CS list from NID, including one of Britain's future enemies, Italy. However, important qualifications are required to this promising picture. First, the naval intelligence benefit was potential, not current. Few decrypts, either on Japanese naval traffic, or that of the other navies, yielded immediate value. This partly reflected a perennial limitation of naval SIGINT in peacetime. It offered little coverage of areas the Admiralty most wanted to know about – high-level policy, future building, war plans, weapon performance or fighting efficiency, because these rarely featured in signal traffic. Secondly, SIGINT resources were stretched thin. The collection footprint in the huge Far East theatre was limited compared to North Sea coverage in 1914–18. By the early 1930s, the primary collector was the new submarine depot ship *Medway*, which had replaced *Titania*. This was acceptable when *Medway* was at the fleet base in Hong Kong, which was well-placed geographically for interception, if prone to weather disruption, and traffic collected could be forwarded rapidly to GC&CS by cable. It posed challenges when she deployed elsewhere within the fleet operating area. Thirdly, there was a chronic shortage of staff with the necessary SIGINT expertise. *Medway* had an established, trained, full-time intercept team, although their role in the early 1930s was confined to collection, with little effort on traffic analysis, where the US Navy was then further ahead.[31] Staff skills and availability across the China Fleet cruisers were more variable. Only twenty-two telegraphists in the fleet could read Japanese Morse in 1934.[32] Achieving the planned NID cadre of Japanese interpreters trained in cryptography had proved difficult, with rarely more than one officer doing cryptanalysis on Japanese naval traffic in theatre before the mid 1930s. The cryptography operation was normally based in the flagship, to ensure intelligence was immediately available to the command. Relaying intercepted traffic from *Medway* or other units to the flagship for the cryptographic team to work on was a constant problem, and working conditions were cramped.[33]

D/F capability was also limited before 1935. Until a new station was established at Hong Kong that year, the only shore-based naval D/F site overseas was at Malta in the Mediterranean. However, this lack of shore-based coverage brought what proved a critical benefit, by encouraging the Royal Navy to invest in ship-borne D/F, driven by the need to track the IJN fleet. As a result, through the early 1930s the Royal Navy led the world in deploying D/F at sea, although it only covered medium frequency (MF), with an effective range limited to about one hundred miles, and most navies, including the IJN, were switching to high frequency (HF), which posed new and demanding challenges for D/F.[34] Research into HF/DF began in 1930 under Cecil Horton in the Experimental Department of the Admiralty Signal School. Because of its skywave propagation (the reflection of signals against the ionosphere to give a hopping effect), HF promised much longer D/F ranges, although exploiting the skywave operationally was complex, and required a substantial shore-based network. The first HF/DF shore equipment was only installed in the Far East in 1936 at Hong Kong. Meanwhile, Horton realised that ship-borne HF/DF might be possible, if existing D/F antennae were replaced by rotating frame coils fitted high above the superstructure, and the first experimental sets were installed aboard the cruisers *Berwick* and *Cornwall* in 1935. At the Spithead Coronation Review two years later, the new cruiser *Newcastle* had a set capable of interception up to 22MHz, while no foreign ship present could operate above 1.5MHz. The performance of these early ship-borne sets was limited, but with development they gave the Royal Navy a transformational capability that none of its future enemies believed was conceptually possible, and proved crucial in the Battle of the Atlantic.[35] Over the next three years, HF/DF sets were gradually rolled out to other China Fleet cruisers, and installed ashore at Singapore, and under Australian control at Melbourne, with a further site under construction at Darwin.[36] Even then, with such a limited shore network, initial operational results remained disappointing. An exercise to track the cruiser *Kent* between Hong Kong and Bangkok in early 1939 provided D/F fixes from the three available sites (Hong Kong, Singapore and the Indian Army site at Bombay) with an average fifty-mile error.[37] Overall, therefore, Far East SIGINT before 1935 rested on a fragile base. Recreating a Room 40-style operation for a war with Japan prior to this date was potentially possible, but would require considerable time.

Despite the desire of the 1924–29 Conservative government to reduce defence expenditure, and support further naval disarmament, and Cabinet doubts about the reality of a Japanese threat, the Admiralty was surprisingly successful at using its 'insurance case' to obtain a significant building programme in this period, although the desirability of boosting employment in a faltering economy helped. It even deployed the ten-year rule against the Treasury, arguing readiness for war in the mid 1930s required a steady investment programme. It laid down thirteen heavy 8in gun cruisers (with two more built for Australia), and nineteen large, long-range submarines by mid 1929. Both investments were aimed primarily at Japan.[38] Although, for the cruisers, parity with the United States was a factor, she only laid down ten equivalent 8in ships in this period, compared to Japan's twelve, and began building two years later than Britain.

Japanese forward building plans revealed in Diet budgetary allocations, supplemented by information gleaned by the Tokyo attaché, dictated the start of the British programme, its size and its rate. By January 1923, two months after Japan laid down its first two 8in cruisers (the *Furataka* class), Director of Plans correctly assessed that the Japanese were building four 7000-ton cruisers and four 10,000-ton cruisers with 8in armament, all for completion by 1928. This dictated a Royal Navy requirement for seventeen competitive equivalents, eight to match the IJN in the scouting line and a further nine, calculated by a complex and rather dubious formula, to counter deployment of IJN cruisers against empire trade routes.[39] Despite Treasury resistance, the Admiralty got eleven 10,000-ton 8in armed County-class cruisers, plus two more for Australia, and two smaller 8in *York* class commissioned by 1931. The Counties were the optimum design the Admiralty judged achievable within the Washington treaty cruiser limits of 10,000 tons displacement and 8in gun armament. The first two ships were laid down a month before the first of the IJN *Myoko*s, Japan's initial cruiser class, supposedly built up to full Washington limits. The *Myoko*s and succeeding IJN heavy cruisers were probably a better all-round design, but achieved through cheating. Every IJN class built under treaty limits from the *Myoko*s onward was at least 1000 tons overweight, and often more.[40] NID appears never to have definitively confirmed such cheating, and as late as December 1938 credited the *Myoko*s with 10,000 tons, and the succeeding *Takao* class with 9850 tons.[41] The IJN, therefore, came out of the post-Washington cruiser race with a distinct advantage, as did the Germans at the end of the 1930s.

If, as the Admiralty contested following the Washington treaty, Japan now posed a potential threat to British interests and territories in the Far East, it was necessary to anticipate how this threat would materialise in practice and be countered. Without naval threats closer to home in Europe, evolving a convincing strategy – the ends, ways and means – for this putative Eastern war accordingly became the dominant preoccupation of Admiralty planners from the mid 1920s to the mid 1930s. Their approach rested on three assumptions. First, geography and distance dictated that, apart from the concessions in China, successful Japanese action against Britain could only be prosecuted and sustained by sea. Secondly, the only effective counter to Japanese action was to deploy sufficient naval power to assert maritime control, and ultimately coerce Japan into a satisfactory settlement. Thirdly, sufficient naval power implied deployment of a Royal Navy fleet at least equal, but preferably superior, to the IJN. For political, financial and administrative reasons such a fleet could not be stationed permanently in the East, even with negligible risk in Europe. It would be deployed only when required, but operating on the far side of the world for an extended period required a base, and Singapore was selected. The plans developed to mobilise the major part of the Royal Navy in a crisis, and to deploy it to meet a threat from Japan, became the Singapore Strategy.[42]

During the 1920s, intelligence exerted limited influence over Far East naval planning. Even the Admiralty accepted that conflict was, for the present, unlikely. The intelligence sources already described were adequate to monitor IJN strength, organisation and evolving capability in this decade. The major innovations in IJN tactics and equipment, long-range gunfire and torpedoes, and, above all, maritime air power, only took effect from the mid 1930s. For now, overall Royal Navy strength was sufficient to deploy a fleet comfortably superior to any force the IJN might commit against Britain. NID could have justifiable confidence that surprises in Japanese performance were unlikely. Planning, therefore, focused on identifying the various phases of a conflict, defensive requirements before the main British fleet arrived, logistic requirements for its passage and consolidation at Singapore, and options then for offensive action to apply pressure on Japan. Considerable planning effort, but little investment at this stage, was expended on the defence of Singapore and Hong Kong, where assessments were theoretical, since no Japanese plans existed. Once the British fleet arrived, its role in securing British territory and bases was clear, but thereafter the goals were more challenging. Admiralty planners envisaged gaining control of maritime communications, ideally by destruction of the main enemy fleet. However, with the recent example of the German High Seas Fleet in mind, they recognised the IJN could retreat to its own waters and decline action. Britain would have difficulty attacking the more vital Japanese communications, and could then face a protracted conflict. Drawing further on the German precedent, planners anticipated applying economic pressure through a distant blockade strategy, either to bring Japan to negotiations, or force her to take risks with her fleet.[43]

Japan's vulnerability to economic pressure was initially assumed, rather than studied. However, at the end of the 1920s Plans Division commenced a detailed analysis of Japan's economy and trade patterns, drawing on a wide range of diplomatic, commercial and open sources. Especially important was assistance from the Advisory Committee on Trade Questions in Time of War (ATB Committee). This was a subcommittee of the CID, established in 1923 under Foreign Office chairmanship and with Admiralty representation, to draw lessons from the 1914–19 blockade, and ensure continuity of administrative machinery for applying economic pressure on an enemy. From 1924, it also produced intelligence assessments relevant to economic warfare, completing about fifty by the end of the decade under the supervision of distinct country committees, including Japan.[44] Much information for these assessments came from the Board of Trade and Department of Overseas Trade, but there was significant input on Russia and Germany from SIS, which reopened an economic section (Section VI) in 1926 under Major Desmond Morton. He now became the dominant figure in economic and industrial intelligence for the rest of the interwar period, although he is more frequently portrayed, if rarely accurately, as an important source for Churchill on German rearmament and wider intelligence issues from the mid 1930s.[45]

The Plans Division study had parallels with those carried out by Henry Campbell and Francis Oppenheimer on Germany before the First World War. It concluded that Japanese industry was ill-equipped to cope with the trade disruption resulting from war with the British Empire, and that the most promising target for a naval blockade was the import of strategic raw materials. Japan would make up shortages primarily from the United States and China, so effective British economic pressure depended on cutting those supply lines.[46] Despite much work, translating the theory of Japanese vulnerability into a viable blockade plan was a problem

Admiralty planners never adequately solved. They recognised that a close blockade of the Japanese home islands, including entrances to the Inland Sea, was not feasible until the IJN main fleet was destroyed or neutralised, and presented formidable logistic challenges. However, a distant blockade conducted across the vast reaches of the Pacific, even with American support, was unlikely to work in any reasonable timescale. In examining the distant blockade, planners may not have sufficiently recognised the centrality of WTID and COMINT to the successful execution of the blockade against Germany. Even if a WTID organisation was recreated for a trade war with Japan, there were obvious geographical reasons why Britain could never establish the same dominant control over cable traffic dealing with Japan.[47]

This 1920s planning for a possible war against Japan occurred alongside other important changes in the management of Britain's national security and defence, which affected the use of intelligence. The most significant, in July 1923, was the constitution of the three chiefs of staff, the First Sea Lord, Chief of the Imperial General Staff and Chief of Air Staff, the professional heads of the three armed services, as a formal subcommittee of the CID. The role of this new Chiefs of Staff Committee was to foster a more co-ordinated approach to identifying Britain's overall defence priorities, policy and planning with joint tri-service advice to the prime minister and CID where appropriate. Each chief remained accountable to his own service board, but now had additional responsibility to act collectively, with advice on defence policy as a whole.[48]

From 1927, the chiefs were supported by a Joint Planning Committee. This comprised the Director of Plans in the naval staff, and his equivalent in the army and air staffs. The three directors held the rank of captain, colonel and group captain respectively. They were prestigious posts, and most directors subsequently took senior positions at the level of commander-in-chief or chief of staff. As joint planners, they addressed problems and questions set by the chiefs of staff best tackled on a tri-service basis. They produced joint memoranda, joint papers and, at the most strategic level, major appreciations. These were researched and drafted by officers drawn from the single-service planning staff under each director, who for specific tasks, therefore, became the joint planning staff. The Joint Planning Committee took time to settle down, but by 1935 it was well established. Through the late 1930s, and then through the war, it provided Britain with an integrated strategic planning function not matched in any other country.[49] The joint planners were important users of intelligence at the strategic level. Many of their papers, from the earliest days, contained an element of intelligence assessment since they often advised their chiefs on defence risk, comprising threat (intent and capability), probability of the threat being realised, and its impact. This use of intelligence by the planners further belies the view that assessment was lacking in the pre-war era. Over the first five years of its existence, 1927–1932, two-thirds of Joint Planning Committee meetings focused on Far East issues, indicating defence priorities at the time.[50]

Another development in assessment influenced naval intelligence through the 1930s. In 1929 the Secretaries of State for War and Air, departments not represented on the ATB Committee, persuaded the CID to establish the Industrial Intelligence in Foreign Countries Subcommittee (FCI) to study industrial war potential in foreign countries. Like the ATB, this lacked dedicated research staff, and neither military nor air intelligence staffs had the skills or sources for this new field. Help was therefore sought from Morton and SIS Section VI, leading in 1931 to the establishment of a small distinct research centre, the Industrial Intelligence Centre (IIC). Until 1934, Morton ran the IIC in parallel to Section VI, and it was housed and funded by SIS, despite ambivalence from Sinclair. It boosted SIS's standing when under pressure to deliver value, but imposed extra cost, with resources already tight. In 1934 Sinclair made it an external customer department, although it remained linked to SIS until 1936, when it transferred formally under the Department of Trade.[51] The IIC grew from Morton and one assistant to twenty-five staff by 1938, becoming a vital and well-regarded part of the British intelligence community, and forming an essential core of the new Ministry of Economic Warfare after 1939. The creation of the IIC to assess how the economic power of potentially hostile states translated into military strength was an important intelligence innovation, again not copied by other countries at this time. Although designed to evaluate the war potential of likely enemies, it reflected the enduring centrality of economic blockade in British strategic thinking. It was there to identify vulnerabilities as well as strengths. The IIC was thus a logical evolution from the pre-1914 planning for economic warfare executed by the Admiralty and Hankey through the subsequent wartime operations of the Ministry of Blockade, and the initial ATB work on Japan. Not surprisingly, therefore, Hankey was a strong champion of the IIC until his retirement in 1938.[52]

Although Japan was the dominant Admiralty interest through the 1920s, intelligence during this decade also provided important early warning of a reviving German naval threat. The Versailles treaty prohibited Germany from constructing or acquiring submarines, including for commercial purposes. However, both German shipbuilders and the new Reichsmarine were determined submarine development should continue. The first step was to exploit U-boat expertise and experience commercially, and by 1921, design and consulting services were sold to Japan and Argentina, with negotiations underway in Sweden and Italy. The following year, three German companies, with secret financial help from the navy, established a joint company in Holland, N V Ingenieurskantoor voor Scheepsbouw (IvS), to provide submarine design, consulting and construction services, evading the Allied Control Commission. IvS initially operated covertly in Kiel, after the Dutch authorities refused registration, but by 1925, the Dutch relented and it operated in The Hague until 1945. By the early 1930s, with extensive Reichsmarine support, funding and direction, IvS had designed, provided parts for, and supervised construction of submarines for Japan, Finland, Spain, Sweden and Turkey. The IvS operation enabled the German navy to explore three prototype U-boats – small (250 tons), medium (500 tons) and large (750 tons), the basis for U-boat Types II, VII and IX when official German construction commenced in 1935. IvS research, which also embraced trackless electric torpedoes, enabled the recreation of an effective U-boat arm more quickly than possible otherwise, although parallel covert operations, including tactical research and training under direct German navy control, were important too.[53]

The SIS source TR16 reported regularly and comprehensively on IvS, and other aspects of the covert U-boat programme throughout its existence.[54] This kept NID well-informed, and triggered Foreign Office investigation both unilaterally, and through the Control Commission. Inquiries confirmed that IvS was a 'front', and had acquired control of the Ing Fijenhoord shipyard in Rotterdam with large quantities of U-boat material illegally shipped there after the armistice. The Foreign Office also knew the depth of Finnish complicity.[55] However, for the Foreign Office, IvS never ranked high on the long list of German infringements of Versailles on which, from the late 1920s, there was increasing British government reluctance to tackle Germany robustly. Reasons included the practical difficulty of enforcement after withdrawal of the Control Commissions, desire to avoid damaging European reconciliation, and ensure German co-operation in wider disarmament initiatives, a self-serving view that adequate reduction in German capability had been achieved, and growing guilt that a Carthaginian peace had driven Germany to political extremism.[56] Surprisingly, senior naval staff endorsed these arguments.[57] More specifically, there is little sign that they viewed either U-boat research or IvS construction activity as a serious threat. Even the claim that German personnel were crewing Finnish submarines on trials apparently caused DNI little concern.[58] Perhaps this reflected confidence that TR16 would provide ample warning if research translated into actual creation of a new U-boat force, providing adequate time to respond. Furthermore, the omission of IvS activity from the list of German infringements presented to the Cabinet in July 1933 suggests neither Admiralty nor Foreign Office judged it illegal.

The relaxed Admiralty attitude to a revived U-boat threat also reflected growing confidence in ASDIC as a transformative anti-submarine capability. Its performance, doctrine for tactical employment, and training support had all improved significantly through the 1920s.[59] By 1933, the Royal Navy had commissioned thirty modern ASDIC-equipped fleet destroyers in the previous five years, and was adding a further flotilla every year. Planning was underway to acquire a further two hundred ASDIC sets to equip the reserve fleet in wartime. The naval staff judged that while Germany might soon begin building a new U-boat force, it could not pose a serious threat before the end of the decade, and that ASDIC would constrain its effectiveness in a war with Britain. The belief that ASDIC had countered the submarine threat strengthened through the mid 1930s, although analysis of results in realistic exercise scenarios should have demonstrated that its potential was overestimated.[60] This Admiralty confidence encouraged a deliberate information campaign throughout the decade to promote the power of ASDIC, and induce uncertainty in the German naval leadership over the future value of the U-boat weapon. The effectiveness of this campaign is difficult to disentangle from other influences on German naval policy in the late 1930s, but the idea of ASDIC as a game-changer got considerable traction in senior circles although, importantly, not with Captain Karl Dönitz, the commander of the new U-boat force. Crucially, for all the groundwork done with IvS, between March 1935 and March 1940 Germany completed only sixty-three U-boats, barely one per month, and half of them small and unsuited to open-water operations. This was a deliberate strategic choice, which hardly suggested faith in the U-boat as the decisive naval weapon against Britain.[61] TR16 had a further impact. It was probably his intelligence on IvS, along with separate SIS intelligence on covert German-Russian arms co-operation, which persuaded Sinclair to recreate the SIS economic section, and then to support the IIC.

In 1930, despite a decade of economic retrenchment restraining defence expenditure and American insistence on parity, the Royal Navy remained the world's strongest naval power. It maintained this position at the 1921 Washington Treaty, and over the rest of the decade laid down and completed more warship tonnage than any other navy. Of £1010 million spent by the British government on defence between 1922 and 1930, the Admiralty received over half. British naval strength remained easily equal to the IJN and any single European power, and the Royal Navy was at the cutting edge of most naval capabilities, including air and submarine power. Its merchant marine too was at its peak, and it retained the strongest marine industrial capacity.[62] Contrary to traditional views, Britain retained much of this maritime supremacy and remained an innovative naval power through the 1930s. Nor did it suffer critical failures of naval intelligence in this next decade. There were inevitably gaps, but the Royal Navy leadership maintained an adequate view of the capabilities of naval opponents and plans to deal with them within the political and economic constraints were realistic. It also extended and matured capabilities relevant to naval intelligence initiated in the 1920s. Britain's naval problem in the new decade was the rapid emergence of three powerful naval enemies, across three divergent theatres, before it could mobilise sufficient resources to contain them in a scenario where, as matters turned out, it lacked allies. Against the cataclysm that opened in the late 1930s, it is easy to overlook how benign the global outlook appeared to the Foreign Office in 1930, with the three future Axis enemies, Germany, Japan and Italy, all judged friendly and constructive partners, a view that the chiefs of staff did not challenge in their annual review.[63] Seven years later the world looked different.

Admiral of the Fleet Sir John Fisher in 1915, who was the dominant influence in shaping the Royal Navy, British maritime policy and the naval intelligence infrastructure to support them through the first fifteen years of the twentieth century. (*From a portrait by Reginald Haynes*)

Captain Sir Mansfield Cumming, first Chief of the Secret Service Bureau (SSB), subsequently the Secret Intelligence Service (SIS), 1909–1923, who oversaw important contributions to naval requirements before and during the First World War. (*From a portrait by H F Crowther Smith*)

Hector Bywater, Cumming's top agent on the German naval target from 1910–1914, being entertained at Dresden in 1909 by the United States Consul General Thomas St John Gaffney. St J G, who had employed Hector's brother Ulysses as his deputy, was of Irish origin and virulently anti-British. His extreme pro-German sympathies once war began caused President Woodrow Wilson to demand his resignation in 1915. St J G would have been appalled, therefore, to know that Hector was already in secret contact with the Admiralty. St J G is seated at the centre of the group in profile with his wife standing immediately to his left and Hector seated on his right. (*US Naval War College Archives*)

Captain William Reginald 'Blinker' Hall in 1914, while commanding the battlecruiser *Queen Mary*. He headed British naval intelligence for almost the entire First World War, as Director of the Intelligence Division (DID) from October 1914 until May 1917 and then under the restored title of Director of Naval Intelligence (DNI) from June 1917 until February 1919. He achieved a level of political and strategic influence greater than any predecessor that would never be possible again. (*Public domain*)

Sir Alfred Ewing in 1915. As Director of Naval Education on the outbreak of war, he was asked by the DID, Rear Admiral Henry Oliver, to investigate the interception of German naval communications. Ewing subsequently headed the Admiralty codebreaking operation, Room 40, until late 1916. (*National Portrait Gallery, NPG 80467*)

Failure to exploit intelligence: the German battleship *Thuringen* destroying the British armoured cruiser *Black Prince* during the Jutland night action on 1 June 1916. (*From the painting by Claus Bergen*)

The novelist A E W Mason in 1915. He was aged fifty when recruited by Hall that year and became perhaps his most successful agent, deployed first in Spain and later in Mexico. (*Alamy reproduction of publisher's photograph, 1915*)

Nigel de Grey. Recruited from the Royal Naval Air Service to Room 40 by Hall in 1915, he joined the political section, where he played the primary role in decrypting the Zimmermann telegram, before moving to Rome to establish a joint SIGINT section with the Italians. After spending the interwar period in civilian life, he rejoined the Government Code and Cipher School (GC&CS) in 1939, becoming deputy to the head, Edward Travis, in 1944. (*Churchill Archives Centre*)

Sir William Wiseman, recruited by Cumming in 1915 and appointed SSB representative in New York. From early 1917 he became a close confidant of President Woodrow Wilson's foreign affairs adviser, Colonel Edward House, and enjoyed regular access to the president himself. He thus became a key player in managing Britain's relationship with the United States, including growing tensions over respective naval ambitions and priorities. (*Public domain*)

Alastair Denniston in 1939. Denniston was teaching German at the Royal Naval College, Osborne, in 1914 and was one of Ewing's first recruits to Room 40, where he had a central role throughout the war. He became the first head of GC&CS in 1919 and held this post until 1942. Although a better codebreaker than administrator, the ultimate wartime success of Bletchley Park, and not least its naval contribution, reflected his wise stewardship through the interwar period. (*1939 passport photograph*)

Alfred Dillwyn 'Dilly' Knox joined Room 40 in 1915 from King's College, Cambridge, where he was a Fellow in Classics, one of the first of a steady stream of academics recruited by Ewing, who was also a former Fellow of King's. King's was a prolific source of codebreaking talent for the next thirty years, with Bletchley Park sometimes jokingly referred to as 'Little King's'. Knox remained in GC&CS after the war and was at the heart of British codebreaking, including critical early work on Enigma, until his death in 1943. (*From the sketch by Gilbert Spencer*)

SECRET.

100%. (WRH).

R. $\frac{9}{458}$ c

NAVAL INTELLIGENCE.   ROTTERDAM, 27-6-16. ,
                         Recd.   28-6-16.

Ref: Your telegram 2-6-16 reading:- " Reliable information
urgently required regarding German losses in North Sea
action yesterday."

Following report from "R.16":-

In accordance with instructions received from you on
June 2nd I went at once to BREMEN, travelling from there to
DANZIG, KIEL, ROSTOCK, GEESTEMUNDE, EMDEN and to SANDE near
WILHELMSHAVEN, in order to ascertain the exact German losses
in the North Sea action of May 31st

Following is the result of my investigations:-

On June 3rd I learned that the "PILLAU" was coming to
BREMEN and the "MUNCHEN" was going to Vegesack.

The "PILLAU" arrived at the Weser Werft at 6 am on
June 4th, and I learned from people of this ship, that the
"LUTZOW", "ROSTOCK" and "SEYDLITZ" had also been lost,
although this loss was not acknowledged by the German
Admiralty.   The "SEYDLITZ" had been in tow of the "PILLAU"
but in the outer Weser, the cables had to be cut as the ship
was sinking rapidly.   I have learned afterwards from men
of the "SEYDLITZ" that the ship has been salved since with
the help of the big floating crane of WILHELMSHAVEN, and is
now in dock (floating dock) at this latter port.

When the "DANZIG", which was still in dock, had come out
the "PILLAU" took her place.   She was hit once under the
waterline near the stem and her funnels and superstructure were

---

The first page of the report by the SSB agent TR16 summarising German losses
and damage at the Battle of Jutland. Hall's scrawled comment '100%' is at the top
of the page. (*The National Archives*)

Rear Admiral Sir Hugh Sinclair, successor to Hall as DNI, 1919–1921, and then to Cumming as Chief of SIS, 1923–1939. As 'C', Sinclair also became the director of GC&CS responsible for British codebreaking until it was renamed the Government Communications Headquarters (GCHQ) in 1946. He was thus the dominant figure in the British intelligence community in the interwar period, and a key contributor to naval intelligence requirements. (*Public domain*)

Vice Admiral Sir William James as Deputy Chief of Naval Staff in 1936. Recruited by Hall in 1917 to head an expanded naval SIGINT operation ID25, in succession to Room 40, James advocated an integrated all-source intelligence centre. In 1936, as DCNS, he could finally implement his vision, creating the Admiralty Operational Intelligence Centre (OIC), which transformed the exploitation of naval intelligence through the Second World War. Portrait by Arthur Douglas Wales-Smith. (© *National Maritime Museum, Greenwich, London*)

Vice Admiral John Godfrey, DNI from January 1939 until November 1942. His role was more constrained than that of Hall, but by 1942 he had created a wartime organisation that was supremely effective. This photograph dates from the end of his time as DNI, following his promotion to vice admiral on 15 September 1942. (*Official Royal Navy photograph*)

Sidney Cotton, probably taken in 1941, the maverick pilot, photographer, adventurer and inventor, recruited by SIS in 1939 to conduct covert aerial reconnaissance missions. He provided the innovative thinking that ultimately gave Britain a photographic reconnaissance capability in the Second World War, which rivalled Bletchley Park in the importance of its intelligence contribution. (*Alamy*)

18

Storm Clouds in the East 1930–1939

The rising Axis threat became the primary problem for British naval policy in the 1930s, but threat and policy response were influenced by the naval disarmament process lasting fifteen years from the signing of the Washington Treaty. Intelligence was crucial to British handling of that process through three successive conferences, Geneva in 1927, and London in 1930 and 1936. At these conferences, but especially in London, GC&CS held the geographic advantage in SIGINT collection, through its command of the international cable network which Yardley's Black Chamber enjoyed at Washington in 1921–22. By the first London conference, President Herbert Hoover had abolished the Black Chamber, and British SIGINT dominance was complete.[1] GC&CS read all the significant traffic of the other participants, who read none of Britain's. British intelligence advantage had greatest impact at the first London conference in 1930, the only one to achieve a substantive agreement endorsed by all participants. By contrast, the Geneva conference collapsed owing to irreconcilable differences between Britain and the United States, primarily over cruiser numbers and, to a lesser extent, cruiser specifications. Britain favoured further limitations in principle, and remained content to concede the United States parity. However, because of her trade protection requirements, Britain insisted on a tonnage limit far above what any likely American government would countenance in present circumstances. GC&CS provided good insights into the American position, which only underlined the impossibility of progress.[2] By the opening of the 1936 conference, Britain and the United States had established a common position, but not one Japan would accept, provoking her withdrawal from the naval limitations process and, ultimately, its termination as Britain and the United States resorted to escape clauses in the agreement between the remaining powers, in order to protect their positions against Japan. Once again, GC&CS intelligence was comprehensive, but it contributed little to establishing the common Anglo-American position. It illuminated Japanese intransigence, but without suggesting ways of navigating through it to reach an agreement.

In 1930 GC&CS provided British negotiators with a comprehensive picture of the positions, underlying thinking, and bottom lines of all other major participants. It circulated 397 decrypts, often on complex technical issues, in its special conference series over the three months it lasted from 21 January. The largest number comprised messages from Japan and the United States, but with key contributions on France and Italy too.[3] In addition, there were important decrypts issued in the months leading up to the conference, showing policy formation in Washington and Tokyo, and illuminating divisions between them. This unprecedented coverage allowed the British team to monitor reactions to official meetings and personal contacts, and to cross-check every development, often from multiple sources. It also gave NID occasional insights into specific naval capabilities of other participants.[4] However, this potentially decisive advantage was constrained by the determination of the British prime minister, Ramsay MacDonald, to make substantial concessions to the United States to win its support for liberal internationalism and wider disarmament in Europe. In advance of the conference, he committed unilaterally to earlier scrapping of older British battleships and, more importantly, to the cruiser terms sought by the Americans in 1927, severely weakening Britain's bargaining position. The conference, therefore, opened with Britain and the United States close to a common position, but at the price, from the Admiralty perspective, of weakening British naval security.

The primary challenge for the conference, therefore, became managing the demand from Japan for a 70 per cent or 5:5:3.5 ratio for lighter warships (meaning non-capital ships) and an especially large strength in submarines, against the British and American wish to keep closer to a 5:5:3 ratio. Here, British SIGINT was important in two respects. It helped the chief British negotiator Robert Craigie craft important elements of a compromise with Japan, notably on the tricky issue of heavy cruiser numbers. More important, it facilitated subtle diplomatic manoeuvring to ensure that opposition from the Japanese naval staff did not derail the compromise, which SIGINT confirmed the Japanese government would accept. This was possible because GC&CS covered both traffic from the Japanese foreign ministry to its civilian negotiators, and from the Japanese admiralty to their naval negotiators through their naval attaché network. Through this dual coverage, British negotiators often had a better understanding of the attitudes within the two Japanese teams than they did themselves.[5]

Although British intelligence was important to a successful agreement at London in 1930, the treaty reduced Royal Navy strength and its industrial support, just when it was most needed, while concessions won by Japan further enhanced its regional superiority. Some qualifications are necessary here. In the context of the Great Depression and a benign international environment, with no immediate naval threats on the horizon, some reduction in British naval strength and expenditure was inevitable. Reductions over the next five years were modest and, partly through concessions won at London, Britain maintained a steady annual replacement programme in cruisers, destroyers and submarines during this period. Along with the significant investment in the 1920s, this gave the Royal Navy a core of modern vessels of all types before rearmament began in earnest from 1935. Damage to British naval industry can also be over-stated. Its performance in the late 1930s compares favourably to the years immediately before the First World War.[6] The more important negative consequence of the treaty for both Britain and the United States was the undermining of political stability in Japan. Her endorsement of the treaty partly reflected economic pressures and desire to avoid new naval competition, but also the commitment of Prime Minister Hamaguchi Osachi and his ruling liberal Constitutional Democratic Party to making Japan a co-operative member of the international community. However, opposition from the naval and military lobbies proved tenacious, provoking the attempted assassination of Hamaguchi later in the year.[7] The treaty, therefore, helped encourage the aggressive ultra-nationalism that led to Japan's seizure of Manchuria the following year, the subsequent invasion of China, and eventual confrontation with the Western powers. Given these future developments in the East, MacDonald's concessions to the United States are easily criticised as misplaced idealism. However, these paid off in the longer term. They ended Anglo-American naval rivalry, and the collaboration during the London negotiations began a rapprochement, culminating in the wartime alliance initiated at Placentia Bay in August 1941.[8]

The shift in perception of Japan from co-operative international partner to dangerous threat to British interests in the Far East was rapid, although there were inevitably important differences of emphasis across Whitehall departments. In their sixth annual review in May 1931, the chiefs of staff devoted little space to the Far East, and raised no concerns about Japan.[9] Just ten months later, drawing on a report from their deputies prepared under Hankey's chairmanship, they informed the CID that standing

British forces and their bases in the Far East were exposed and vulnerable. Japan could easily seize Shanghai, Hong Kong and Singapore and range further west, threatening the logistic facilities essential to transfer a Royal Navy fleet to the East. British Empire territories and trade in the East would be open to attack for an extended period. Urgent countermeasures were required.[10] In 1933 the chiefs judged the risks unchanged, with no progress in addressing British deficiencies. They underlined the growing strength of the IJN, including its air power, and the scale of Royal Navy force required to 'meet the IJN at her selected moment'. The Royal Navy would need all its available capital ship and carrier force, and most of its post-London cruisers. The chiefs emphasised the growth of Japanese air power, with equipment and training now 'approaching European standard'.[11] By the end of that year, British planners were considering how this air power would be applied, and options to counter it. Some of their thinking was far-sighted, notably the possibility of dawn strikes by carrier aircraft on bases like Singapore.[12] In their 1934 review, the chiefs further underlined growing IJN strength. Imperial Japanese Naval Air Force (IJNAF) strength had doubled in two years to 675 aircraft, overtaking Britain's maritime air strength, and would reach a thousand by 1940, an estimate that proved about right. Meanwhile, NID correctly assessed that seven out of nine IJN capital ships would be modernised by 1936, equipping them for longer range fire, while providing enhanced protection and new machinery for higher speed.[13]

The chiefs' argument that Japan was steadily improving her naval and overall military strength relative to Britain was valid, as was heightened risk of Japanese ambitions conflicting with British interests in China. However, their analysis also reflected worst-case scenarios designed to procure more defence resources after a long period of retrenchment. The Admiralty was further motivated to underline the threat from Japan to avoid losing out, as the other services pressed for expenditure to counter a new German threat. Throughout the decade the Foreign Office kept a more restrained view of Japanese ambitions, seeing them focused essentially on China. It recognised these might clash with the interests of Britain and the United States, but judged the risks manageable. It doubted Japan would be tempted further south.[14] In 1934 Chatfield, who had become First Sea Lord and chairman of the chiefs of staff the previous year, also doubted Japanese action directed at Britain was imminent. While not complacent, he believed the Royal Navy had time to rearm against both Japan and Germany, and to complete Singapore as a defended base.[15] By 1934, although the incoming Commander-in-Chief Admiral Sir Frederick Dreyer complained about its weakness, the Royal Navy China Fleet was a more powerful permanent force in the region than it was in the 1920s. In particular, its fifteen modern long-range submarines of the 4th Flotilla, based in Hong Kong, represented a serious deterrent to any IJN attack on British territory.[16]

Despite these qualifications, the high-level chiefs of staff assessments of the early 1930s show the Admiralty facing a Japanese naval threat judged broadly comparable to that from the pre-1914 German navy, but with Japan holding the geographic advantage, and other potential threats to British security emerging nearer home. They also belie an enduring view that the Royal Navy consistently underestimated the IJN throughout the decade before the outbreak of war with Japan in 1941. The reality is more complex. British intelligence coverage of the IJN through this period had strengths and weaknesses, but these were not consistent, and evolved over time. In general, NID and Plans Division assessments of current IJN order of battle and fighting capability were accurate and realistic until 1939. Drawing primarily on information from the Tokyo naval and air attachés, they successfully tracked IJN construction and evolution through the two successive multi-year investment programmes, the First Replenishment Plan 1931–36 and Second Replenishment Plan 1934–37.[17] These included the construction of the IJN's first purpose-built fleet carriers, *Hiryu* and *Soryu*, the large cruisers of the *Mogami* and *Tone* classes, substantial numbers of destroyers and long-range submarines, and major modernisation of most capital ships and reconstruction of the earlier fleet carriers *Akagi* and *Kaga*. The long-range threat posed by IJN capital ship modernisation encouraged the Royal Navy to explore tactics to counter it through short-range action and night-fighting.[18] The naval staff later overstated the quality of these IJN modernisations in judging that they provided IJN ships superior to the British rebuilds of the *Renown* and the *Queen Elizabeth*s.[19] Although the importance the Royal Navy attached to IJN battleship modernisation through the 1930s is evident, it apparently gleaned less detail on the IJN carrier reconstructions.[20] In addition to attaché reporting, NID acquired insights into IJN strength during the 1930s from reports by Royal Navy warships during courtesy visits to Japan, although these ceased in 1936, and from contacts in Chinese waters. DIOs in Hong Kong, Shanghai and Singapore also ran a programme of covert photography from British merchant ships.[21]

NID maintained good coverage of the development of Japanese naval air power, its overall strength, and the characteristics and quality of aircraft, helped by the appointment of air attachés to Peking in 1934 and Tokyo the following year. The new attaché in Tokyo, Squadron Leader Roy Chappell, was well qualified to monitor the IJNAF, having spent

three years in Japan as a language student 1925–28 and then training
naval aircrew at Yokosuka in 1930–31, where his star pupil was Minoru
Genda, who later as a captain became chief planner for the Pearl Harbor
attack.[22] Reports from the naval attaché, Captain Guy Vivian, and his
assistant, Lieutenant Commander George Ross, prior to Chappell's
arrival overestimated the speed of the Japanese air build-up in the first
half of the decade, but provided a sound guide to Japanese intent, which
influenced planning for the Royal Navy's new carrier fleet from 1936
under the Defence Requirements Committee rearmament programme.[23]
By the end of 1938, Chappell's breakdown of IJNAF strength, land-based
and seaborne, including frontline aircraft deployed in the carrier fleet, was
accurate and comprehensive. He credited the IJN carriers with a deployed
frontline of 250 aircraft, about 50 per cent greater than the Royal Navy
carriers at this time, and the naval staff recognised some Japanese aircraft
probably had a quality edge too. Chappell assessed that the Mitsubishi
A5M (Claude) Type 96, introduced in 1936, was the best carrier fighter
in the world, outclassing the American Curtiss Hawk during combat in
China. He emphasised the performance of the new land-based navy heavy
bomber, the Type 96 (Nell), noting its exceptionally long range.[24] In late
1939 his successor identified the arrival of the Mitsubishi B5N (Kate)
torpedo bomber, first of the new-generation carrier aircraft deployed by
the IJNAF through the Second World War.[25] By early 1940, DNI credited
the IJNAF with 1230 frontline aircraft, and Director Naval Air Division
accepted the Japanese were probably spending as much as 50 per cent
more on naval air power than the Fleet Air Arm.[26]

There were also far-reaching developments in Far East intelligence
infrastructure, originating from a visit by the DDNI, Captain W E C Tait,
during the winter of 1933/34. Tait made three key, linked, recommendations
which, given the growing Japanese threat underlined by the chiefs of
staff, won agreement in London. They were final establishment of the
Pacific Naval Intelligence Organisation, first suggested in the early
1920s; creation of an onshore inter-service intelligence centre to collate
intelligence throughout the Far East theatre; and expansion of regional
SIGINT directed by a new unit, again operating on a tri-service basis.
These three functions were grouped together under a new organisation,
the Far East Combined Bureau (FECB), which opened in April 1935 at
Hong Kong, under Captain John Waller. Initially, there were five other
officers in the main intelligence centre, two each from navy and army, and
one air force. Harry Shaw led the SIGINT team. Along with three other
naval officer cryptographic interpreters, he was co-located in the main
centre, but also supervised the 'Y' team conducting intercept and D/F at

Stonecutters Island. This comprised eight special communications ratings moved from *Medway* the previous year, subsequently joined by five air force and four army signallers. Shaw also supervised the wider Far East SIGINT collection effort as directed by the 'Y' Subcommittee in London. The D/F element of this became known as the Far East D/F Organisation (FEDO), which fed the shipping plot maintained by the PNIO. Although established on a tri-service basis, the FECB was, throughout its life, Navy-dominated. It was administered by Commander-in-Chief China and later Commander-in-Chief Eastern Fleet, and headed by a Chief of Intelligence Staff (COIS), who was always a Royal Navy captain. This reflected the Admiralty's pre-eminence in Far East defence strategy and planning, the inclusion of the PNIO, an entirely naval operation, and the fact that existing SIGINT resources in the region were naval. Shaw, also a naval officer, effectively served three masters, COIS, Denniston as head of GC&CS, and the 'Y' Subcommittee.[27]

The FECB was visionary for its time – in modern parlance, an all-source, fusion centre – and it established a model for inter-service intelligence collaboration, replicated in different ways elsewhere. This collaborative working and assessment was unique among major powers in 1935, and remained so, long afterwards. Other countries accepted or encouraged a competitive approach between different agencies. Despite the laudable intent, combining the different elements and cultures within FECB into a cohesive whole proved demanding. Perceived naval bias was a constant source of friction, with the other two services resentful that their needs were neither adequately understood, nor resourced, especially in the area of SIGINT, where almost nothing was done on the Japanese air target before mid 1939, and only a little on the Japanese army. The decision to move the organisation to Singapore in early 1939 on account of Hong Kong's perceived vulnerability caused further disruption. FECB, therefore, took time to settle into its primary tasks: provide early warning of Japanese attack; build an accurate Japanese order of battle – naval, land and air; and provide operational intelligence once war broke out.[28] Nevertheless, the outbreak of the Sino-Japanese war in the summer of 1937 provided FECB with new opportunities for intelligence collection. From the autumn, it produced fortnightly updates on the war, and over the next three years gained important, if partial, insights into Japanese capability and fighting effectiveness, through liaison with the Chinese, and direct observation.[29] For NID, this intelligence added usefully to knowledge of IJNAF equipment and performance, and emphasised Japanese strength in amphibious operations. The China coverage helped FECB produce regular set-piece assessments of Japanese capability, and occasional regional strategic overviews. Apart from SIGINT, in March 1940 its sources included SIS, MI and Air Intelligence reports, French, Dutch and Chinese intelligence, diplomatic and consular reports, the Defence Security Organisation, and the naval DIOs.[30]

With a stable and better-staffed collection facility at Stonecutters, the new interception opportunities offered by the war in China, and FECB's assessment resources, Far East SIGINT developed significantly over the second half of the 1930s. By 1939, Stonecutters was linked with additional 'Y' collection and D/F sites at Singapore, Melbourne, Esquimalt and Bombay, and a temporary Royal Australian Navy collection operation targeted at the Japanese Mandates (including the Marianas and Marshalls) from the island of Nauru, 3000 miles northeast of Australia. It was also linked by cable to GC&CS, allowing intercept material and decrypts to pass easily in each direction. Virtually all Japanese naval and diplomatic ciphers and consular traffic were readable in this period. There was a broad division of labour with FECB handling naval decryption, and GC&CS diplomatic, but they collaborated closely in producing reports.[31] Significant progress was also now made for the first time on traffic analysis. Commenting on COIS's annual report for 1939, Commander-in-Chief China Vice Admiral Sir Percy Noble stated that by June that year, helped by the arrival of more HF/DF equipped ships, FECB could track all elements of the Japanese Combined Fleet with reasonable accuracy. This proved invaluable in assessing Japanese intentions on the outbreak of the European war. FECB had also fixed the German pocket battleship *Graf Spee* with four D/F cross-bearings at ranges between 3000 and 5500 miles during her brief foray into the Indian Ocean in November.[32]

Despite this progress, Far East SIGINT remained short of a transformational intelligence capability. Relations between Shaw and COIS were often difficult. Shaw felt SIGINT requirements were poorly understood and under-resourced. By contrast, COIS and China Fleet operational staff found the cryptic Japanese 'signalise', which the SIGINT team produced, of little value in peacetime. It told them nothing about IJN war plans, future investment or fighting efficiency. It was difficult to visualise what this traffic would offer after war broke out.[33] There were several overlapping problems here. The accessible Japanese operational naval traffic did not yield policy and planning insights comparable to revelations often available in diplomatic traffic. However, potential intelligence was also lost, because FECB lacked the understanding, experience and, ultimately, the resources to analyse and assess naval decrypts alongside other information to produce meaningful intelligence. There was no equivalent yet of ID25B, or recognition that it was needed. This reflected a problem inherent in the creation of GC&CS. For the present, it was a cryptanalytical organisation producing raw decrypts, not assessed intelligence. This was less often a problem with diplomatic decrypts, because their status and content were readily understood by most Whitehall customers. By contrast, for naval traffic there was a crucial intermediate step between often meaningless individual decrypts, and usable operational intelligence. It was hardly surprising that FECB did not address this gap, because nor had GC&CS and NID. Fortunately, there were still people who understood the lessons of 1917-18, notably William James, now a vice admiral.[34] In 1935, the same year FECB was founded, he became DCNS, and soon took far-reaching steps to address this problem.

If NID monitoring of current IJN strength was adequate into the late 1930s, its coverage of future investment plans deteriorated from the middle of the decade, coinciding with the start of the Third Replenishment Plan in 1937. It also failed to identify important innovations in equipment and tactics that the IJN was developing and brought to fruition in 1940-41. These failures had important implications for British naval investment and strategic planning, as Japan's invasion of China and increasing alignment with Germany and Italy made a Far East confrontation more likely, and more difficult to manage. They reflected the sharp decline in the access of Western naval attachés, following Japan's withdrawal from the naval limitations treaties in 1936, increased protective security, and a reduction in information available through open sources. They also reflected the limitations of covert sources. With SIGINT unable to contribute much on IJN future plans, SIS failed to fill the gap.

Through the 1930s, SIS sought to cover Japan remotely, first through the head of its China operations, Harry Steptoe, based in Shanghai, and then from 1935 through Charles Drage, a retired lieutenant commander with extensive China Fleet experience, based in Hong Kong. Neither spoke Japanese, or had much understanding of the country, or informed knowledge of the IJN. Both were distracted by pressing requirements on China and Soviet intentions in the Far East. SIS was therefore woefully under-resourced on the difficult Japanese target. Steptoe produced nothing of value on the IJN, and lost the confidence of both NID and Dreyer, who commanded the China Fleet 1933-36. Drage established an agent network primarily composed of Chinese merchants who could visit major Japanese naval bases and shipyards, although he and Steptoe also recruited British businessmen, such as Ernest James in Kobe. These assets took an intelligence brief and reported back, essentially with visual observations, and any information gleaned from Japanese contacts.[35] Few reports were accurate. Details of vessels supposedly observed under construction were invariably incorrect, and accompanying information from Japanese contacts was, at best, second-hand gossip. A report produced in April 1939 covering construction at Yokosuka, Maizuru, Kure and Kawasaki Kobe was wrong in every detail. The only point half-correct was that a 30,000-ton battleship of *Nagato* type was under construction at Kure. There was a battleship here, but it was *Yamato*, and she was more than twice the size. To be fair to SIS, it recognised and was honest to NID about the difficulties it faced, and the limitations of its reporting.[36] This fell far short of that acquired by Trevor Dawson and Hector Bywater on the German navy before 1914, and at no stage, either before the war or during it, did SIS acquire a source on the IJN comparable to TR16. Probably the closest SIS came to such a source was the link established in 1936 to a Japanese army officer serving on the staff of General Count Hisaichi Terauchi, commander of the Taiwan army 1934–36, and later of the Southeast Asia theatre 1941–44. This produced Japanese war plans for attacks on Hong Kong and Singapore. Although the reporting won plaudits from the Admiralty, SIS evidently had doubts about its reliability, and the operation ended.[37]

Despite the inaccuracy of SIS reporting on Japanese building plans, it was consistent enough by spring 1938 to support a consensus within the Tokyo naval attaché community that Japan was building new battleships of around 45,000 tons with 16in armament.[38] This combined intelligence view, along with Japanese evasiveness to Foreign Office inquiries, convinced the British and American governments to invoke the escalator clause of the 1936 limitations treaty and plan their own equivalents – in Britain's case, the four *Lion*-class battleships ordered in 1939.[39] NID also sought other ways of assessing the IJN's future potential. During 1937–38 the head of the Japan section, Commander Hilken, weighed every piece of intelligence on Japanese building, from both covert and overt sources, against what was known of Japanese shipyard capacity and capability.[40] ADNI also sought advice from Morton's IIC.[41] Morton's conclusion was that Japan's maximum simultaneous building capacity was three battleships, two carriers, ten cruisers (large and small), and fifty destroyers/submarines. Furthermore, any yard building a battleship could not undertake another major vessel until it was completed. Weighing all the evidence from these studies, Director of Plans Captain Victor Danckwerts judged that between 1938 and 1942 Japan would probably complete six heavy ships, two battleships, two 'battlecruisers' or 'heavy cruisers', and two carriers, but no other additional cruisers. This led him to project a March 1942 IJN strength which apart from the two 'battlecruisers', in unit terms proved exactly right.[42]

These Admiralty calculations of future IJN strength, along with those of Morton, were influenced by important intelligence from Japanese diplomatic traffic between autumn 1937 and early 1939. This intelligence reflected a significant GC&CS achievement, with wider implications for its long-term capability. Until the early 1930s, GC&CS found Japanese diplomatic systems undemanding, but a new five-character system introduced in 1933 caused difficulty, as did a new attaché system introduced at the same time. It was soon apparent that both were machine-generated. This was GC&CS's first experience of machine ciphers in operational use by a target country, although it had monitored the evolution of commercial cipher machines, including the German Enigma, from the mid 1920s. Hugh Foss, who joined GC&CS in 1924, one of the first direct entrants from university, had even written a paper suggesting how this early Enigma could be broken.[43] The son of a Scottish missionary, and a passionate Scottish dancer all his life, Foss had been brought up in Japan and spoke the language fluently. By the early 1930s he was also one of GC&CS's most able cryptographers. Together with Oliver Strachey and Eric Nave, he now identified vulnerabilities in the new attaché system, and by autumn 1934 they had achieved readability. This experience helped Foss and Strachey attack the diplomatic system. By the end of the same year, they had a way in, but recoveries would be laborious and time-consuming without mechanical help. They sought this from Harold Kenworthy, the chief engineer at the police intercept site at Denmark Hill. In a brilliant piece of innovation, he provided a decryption machine known as the 'J'-machine the following summer, the first of several machines he designed for GC&CS.[44] This was a spectacular entry by GC&CS into the new world of machine cipher attack, and anticipated the successful United States Army attack on the same cipher, which they named Red, by two years.[45] It also foreshadowed the operations against the German Enigma that dominated the next decade, and in which Foss had a starring role, breaking the first complete day of Enigma naval traffic through purely cryptographic attack in November 1940.[46]

The GC&CS coverage of Japanese diplomatic traffic from 1937 to 1939 produced crucial linked insights. It revealed Japanese government awareness that the Chinese war was imposing considerable strain on the Japanese economy and industrial capacity, and that Japan could not risk conflict on additional fronts while it lasted. SIGINT accordingly demonstrated its desire to avoid action in China that might provoke confrontation with the Anglo-Saxon powers, leading to economic reprisals.[47] It also showed that Japan was cultivating Germany and Italy, in the hope of pressing Britain not to support China. This led to the Anti-

Comintern Pact of November 1937, initiating the idea of the Axis, and negotiations for an anti-Soviet military alliance the following year. These negotiations appeared to present Britain with an immediate strategic nightmare of three enemies in widely divergent theatres. However, in probably its most important contribution in the whole interwar period, SIGINT demonstrated this fear was unfounded, at least for the present. In January 1939 Japan refused to endorse the German and Italian proposal extending the anti-Soviet alliance to any third power. Japan informed its partners that its economy relied on access to British and American markets, and it could not afford to alienate these powers.

Apart from these vital revelations of Japanese thinking, the traffic provided unique insights into German and Italian intentions. The Japanese ambassador to Berlin from October 1938 until September 1939, and again from December 1940 until May 1945, Lieutenant General Hiroshi Ōshima, a former military attaché and fluent German speaker, enjoyed a privileged relationship with the chancellor, Adolf Hitler, the foreign minister, Joachim von Ribbentrop, and other Nazi leaders. His exceptional access, influence on policy, and meticulous reporting made his communications with Tokyo an invaluable intelligence source which, with later American help, GC&CS covered through most of his two periods of tenure.[48] Japanese reluctance to damage relations with the Western powers was confirmed in further SIGINT reports through 1939. SIGINT confirmed her effective neutrality following the outbreak of the European war, and her anxiety that vital supplies of raw materials were not disrupted.[49] For Britain, and not least the Admiralty, this intelligence had far-reaching implications.[50] It suggested an early move against British interests in the East was now less likely, allowing the Royal Navy to prioritise the Mediterranean over the Far East. It also underlined Japan's economic limitations, and the Admiralty conviction that, given time, the Royal Navy could out-build the IJN in capital ships and carriers, in a ratio of at least three to two.

While the Admiralty was broadly right up to the end of 1939 on the limits to IJN growth posed by Japan's industrial and shipyard capacity, it got key aspects of the IJN building programme, and the thinking behind it, wrong. First, like the Americans, it completely missed the super-battleship programme. The two 45,000-ton battleships with 16in armament it believed Japan had laid down in 1937 were actually *Yamato* and *Musashi*, displacing 72,000 tons and armed with nine 18.1in guns. Japanese interest in 18in guns was a talking point in the naval attaché community around 1937, and reflected in SIS reporting, but the consensus was that it had not moved beyond a research phase.[51] The IJN anticipated that this highly secret *Yamato* programme would provide a decisive quality advantage to defeat a more numerous American opponent. Secondly, primarily because of SIS reports beginning in 1937, the Admiralty believed the IJN was planning up to four 'battlecruisers' of around 20,000 tons armed with 12in guns.[52] This programme which gripped the Admiralty until the end of 1941 had some underlying substance. From 1934, the IJN genuinely contemplated such ships to replace the *Kongos* but serious design work on the 'B65s' did not begin until 1939 and none were ever laid down.[53] Mirroring also played a part here. Since the French and Germans built such ships, NID was inevitably susceptible to the idea that the IJN would do so too, with SIS then pressed to seek evidence. The enthusiasm with which SIS agents reported the existence of 'battlecruisers' or 'pocket battleships', with specifications similar to Germany, smacks of agents reporting what case officers had told them to look for, and therefore presumably wanted to hear. The 'battlecruiser' fiction also reflected an enduring Royal Navy conviction that during any war with Britain, the IJN would determinedly attack her trade, for which such ships would be eminently suited. In reality, the IJN never planned or pursued such a strategy.

The *Yamato* programme represented a huge industrial commitment, preventing simultaneous construction of other heavy ships. It was not possible to begin the next two ships until mid 1940, and it also limited carrier construction. The IJN laid down only two fleet carriers between mid 1937 and mid 1941 whereas the Royal Navy laid down six. The IJN laid down no cruiser from the beginning of 1936 until mid 1940, the Royal Navy thirty-two. The only major error in Danckwerts' estimate of IJN strength for 1942, therefore, lay in assuming Japan would build four more conventional battleships and battlecruisers, rather than two monsters. The Admiralty's two intelligence failures here did not ultimately matter. Its capital ship and carrier investment programme underway in 1939 took adequate account of what Japan could realistically build, but was more achievable and balanced within available resources, and much more suited to the real needs of modern naval war.

Other intelligence failures on the IJN in the late 1930s were more damaging. The most important were missing the development of the advanced, oxygen-powered, wakeless, long-range Type 93 Long Lance torpedo, deployed from cruisers from 1935 and destroyers from 1940, and the effort the IJNAF was devoting to torpedo attack at long range by its new land-based bombers, such as the Type 96. NID received some early pointers on the Type 93 in 1934, when it was still under development, from the assistant naval attaché Lieutenant Commander George Ross following his visit to the Taura torpedo school. On the specifications Ross had gleaned, NID thought it too large to be a viable destroyer weapon, and the intense secrecy surrounding its subsequent deployment precluded further intelligence, although SIS apparently briefed their Kobe agent, Ernest James, on the requirement.[54]

NID exploited one other source on the IJN in the late 1930s – submarine surveillance. The submarines *Regulus* and *Rainbow*, operating from Hong Kong, each conducted two successive intelligence-gathering patrols in Japanese waters in October and November 1939 respectively. *Regulus'* first patrol focused on the Bungo Channel, the strait separating the islands of Kyushu and Shikoku, giving access to the Inland Sea. It involved significant contact with the IJN Combined Fleet, producing valuable photographic intelligence of major units. Some of these photographs were later found by the Japanese in Singapore following its fall in 1942.[55] *Regulus* spent a week in the Bungo Channel. She sighted the carrier *Ryujo* on 8 October, dived to avoid another carrier the following day, and manoeuvred 'to close the Jap fleet' on 11 October.[56] She covertly observed an IJN exercise, including 'a brand new Japanese carrier', almost certainly *Hiryu*.[57] Simultaneously, the submarine *Perseus* patrolled the Kii Strait south of Osaka Bay, 150 miles to the east. She did not encounter any IJN vessels, and was tasked primarily against suspect German merchant traffic.[58] The Japanese later discovered that *Regulus* had entered Shibushi Bay and Osaka Bay via the Kitan Strait, all producing photographic intelligence, although it is not certain whether these incursions occurred in October or November 1939, or during previous patrols.[59] Such intelligence patrols were apparently frequent in the late 1930s, and foreshadowed a major role of the post-1945 Royal Navy submarine service. They continued until all Royal Navy submarines were withdrawn from the Far East in mid 1940. *Regulus* undertook a further patrol in December 1939, this time to the area around Vladivostok. Primary objectives were to collect intelligence on Russian submarines and their operations, and search for any evidence of Russian submarines being taken over by the German navy, as one intelligence report had suggested.[60] Surviving records of these intelligence operations confirm that the fifteen submarines of the 4th Flotilla were efficient and effective, presenting a major threat to any IJN seaborne invasion forces. Significantly, Japanese and Russian anti-submarine measures were assessed as 'feeble'.[61] Had Royal Navy submarines remained in the Far East after mid 1940, they might have corrected some of the intelligence errors regarding new IJN warships. The substantial US Navy submarine force within their Asiatic Fleet could also have contributed here, but they were never used in this way, and apparently lacked the necessary aggression and risk-taking.[62]

19

The New German Challenge and the Rising Threat from Italy 1933–1938

While the Admiralty perceived the naval threat from Japan as its primary challenge through the 1930s, managing this was greatly complicated from the middle of the decade by the rising threats posed by Germany and Italy. From 1935, the maximum force deployable against any one of the three was automatically determined by the minimum provision required for adequate security against the other two. By that year, both the Director of Plans, Captain Edward King, and the DNI, Rear Admiral Gerald Dickens, expected Germany and Japan to co-operate if either went to war with Britain. If Britain and Germany were at war, DNI expected Japan to act 'ruthlessly' against British interests in the East.[1] By 1938, Germany overtook Japan as Britain's most probable naval enemy, and potentially most dangerous, because of her overall war potential, and the direct threat she posed to the United Kingdom homeland.

The Admiralty recognised by 1937, therefore, that with a growing German threat, and three capital ships unavailable due to simultaneous modernisation, the maximum force available for an Eastern conflict would be significantly inferior to the IJN. This implied a strictly defensive war, with more limited objectives than hitherto. Given the scale of Japan's commitment in China, and her lack of bases before 1940 from which to project an expedition southward, a defensive strategy with a reduced fleet to secure Britain's essential interests remained credible until the end of the decade. However, the prospect of fighting the IJN with inferior forces also drew naval planners towards the less justifiable assumption that the Royal Navy could partly close the gap through greater 'efficiency'. This concept of an efficiency advantage appears to have originated with Chatfield in 1937, and two years later the IJN was more formally rated with 80 per cent of the fighting efficiency of the Royal Navy. Neither the concept, nor the mathematical rating, reflected intelligence assessment. Nor was the idea applied to the Royal Navy's other opponents. A 1935 report by Guy Vivian, the Tokyo attaché, identifying Japanese cultural attitudes that might compromise IJN effectiveness, possibly exerted influence, although there is no evidence of its lasting impact. Equally, the judgement may just have reflected the Royal Navy's ingrained belief that it was superior to all others, an attitude not without foundation in its history, including important successes against superior forces in the Second World War. Overall, the idea of an efficiency advantage, which endured through to 1941, provided false reassurance to some, but its practical impact on naval deployment is doubtful. This was always driven more by available resources.[2]

The new German naval challenge

Developing an intelligence picture of the evolving German naval threat posed different challenges compared to Japan. When Hitler came to power in January 1933, the German navy was smaller than permitted under Versailles limits, less than 10 per cent of the Royal Navy by tonnage, with just five light cruisers and twelve destroyers of post-war design and three Deutschland-class pocket battleships under construction. It would take at least a decade to build a conventional fleet capable of seriously challenging the Royal Navy, and require the German navy to have priority for resources over the other services. An alternative option, achievable more quickly, and potentially more dangerous for Britain, was an asymmetric navy optimised for trade warfare using long-range cruisers, submarines, aircraft and mines. In spring 1934 the German naval staff favoured a force structure of eight Deutschlands, three aircraft carriers and eighteen cruisers.[3]

For the first two years of the Nazi regime, culminating in the Anglo-German Naval Agreement of June 1935, British naval policy towards Germany therefore had three goals: to contain German expansion within a combined total with the IJN that Britain could match; to transition Germany from the resented Versailles restrictions into the international naval limitations framework, without triggering competitive building by France and Italy; and to lure Germany away from the asymmetric option. Chatfield was especially keen to halt the Deutschland programme, comprising ships which, combining heavy armament, high speed and endurance, were ideal for attacking British trade routes.[4] In pursuing these goals, the starting point for the naval staff was that the strength allocated to France under the Washington and London treaties, including a 35 per cent ratio with Britain in capital ships, was the highest acceptable for any European power, consistent with British maritime security. The staff were willing to extend this ratio to Germany and, indeed, judged her justified in pursuing parity with France, but wished to avoid triggering French expansion. The intelligence challenge was, therefore, to establish the true naval policy of the new German government, and to assess when it might credibly reach a 35 per cent level. The rate of German expansion compared to that of Royal Navy modernisation and expansion now being developed under the Defence Requirements Committee was as important as the 35 per cent ceiling itself.[5]

For this intelligence, NID depended on the naval attaché, Captain Gerard Muirhead-Gould, other diplomatic and consular sources, SIS, especially TR16, and some French reporting. The task was complicated because through 1934 the aspirations of the German naval staff under Admiral Erich Raeder, the commander-in-chief of the Kriegsmarine, conflicted with Hitler's own priorities, while the design of battleships 'D' and 'E', the future *Scharnhorst* and *Gneisenau*, the biggest construction project underway, changed drastically to enable them to compete with the new French *Dunkerque*-class battlecruisers. Nevertheless, by early 1935, NID knowledge of German construction, including the true displacement of 'D' and 'E', and the assembly of the first new U-boats, was accurate. Together with insights from Muirhead-Gould on German naval staff thinking, confirming their current focus on parity with France, rather than competition with Britain, this intelligence helped King as Director of Plans conclude that the German navy would not reach one-third of Royal Navy strength before 1942. Here King underestimated future Royal Navy rearmament, and therefore its own real 1942 strength, but with one major exception, his estimates in this first significant forward projection for German navy strength in 1939 and 1942, slightly lower than those of NID, proved about right.[6] King based his assessment on three assumptions to be monitored and tested: that Germany would exchange Versailles for participation in the naval treaty system; that the army and air force would have priority in her rearmament; and that she did not currently intend to build against Britain, her naval priorities instead focusing on securing the Baltic, and countering any threat to her sea communications from France. These assumptions were valid. Until the summer of 1937, the German naval staff judged the prospects of winning a future naval war with Britain as 'hopeless'.[7] King's major error, shared with NID, and puzzling given the flow of intelligence from TR16, was to assume a U-boat strength of only ten in 1939 and twenty in 1942. Even if Germany had ruled out a new submarine trade war against Britain, as King believed, this was a low figure.

King's assessment, backed by Craigie in the Foreign Office, conditioned the British response to the German offer of a bilateral naval agreement. Cabinet willingness to sign this agreement, despite damage to relations with France, and the risk of compromising the forthcoming multi-lateral naval treaty negotiations, reflected confidence in the Admiralty's intelligence judgement of German potential, along with important German concessions. With the exception of special dispensation for submarines, Germany agreed the ratio of 35 per cent would apply to individual warship categories as well as overall global tonnage, thus encouraging the conventional force structure which Britain much preferred. She also agreed that French and Russian building would not alter the ratio, making it easier for Britain to manage French objections. Finally, there was an undertaking to abide by naval treaty qualitative limitations and information-sharing arrangements.

The Admiralty monitored the German expansion programme and its compliance with the agreement carefully. It recognised Germany could cheat, or suddenly terminate the agreement (which Raeder probably always saw as a temporary necessity), which was to last a maximum of five years.[8] In the event, it did both. During 1936 there were important adjustments to King's estimates of German strength the previous year, drawing on two IIC studies, the only ones during 1936–39 which specifically examined German naval production. The first on 'submarine construction' reviewed reporting from TR16, including detailed plans for mass production of U-boats at a rate of seven per month in 'emergency' conditions, which the IIC judged credible.[9] The second, prepared in collaboration with NID, reassessed the German fleets achievable by end 1940 and end 1942 under 'present' and 'maximum' rates of construction. It correctly judged that a 'maximum' rate was probably unachievable owing to financial restrictions, shortage of raw materials, skilled engineering and labour support, and the priority given to land and air rearmament. At present rate of construction, it now expected King's original 1942 fleet to complete by the end of 1940, but with a second carrier, double the destroyer numbers, reflecting the rate established in 1935 with thirteen laid down, and seventy-three U-boats, the 45 per cent ratio for submarines permitted under the naval agreement. As an estimate of total warship tonnage possible, this 1940 projection proved accurate against that actually achieved, although the mix of vessels ultimately built was different. There were 60 per cent more U-boats, reflecting new priorities from 1938, as war with Britain looked more likely, and fewer than half the destroyer numbers, back to King's original figure. The only carrier, *Graf Zeppelin*, was suspended 80 per cent complete, while one of five new cruisers was halted 95 per cent complete, and another sold unfinished to the Soviet Union.[10]

These 1936 IIC/NID estimates contributed to a major Joint Planning Committee paper at the end of the year, which addressed an all-out German offensive against British trade, judged the worst-case naval scenario in a 1939 European war. Its estimate for the scale of attack was accurate, and assessment of how it would be applied, prescient. It assumed the German navy at the end of 1939 would comprise one battleship, two battlecruisers, three *Deutschland*s, one carrier, three 8in cruisers, six 6in cruisers, twenty-eight large modern destroyers, and sixty-six U-boats. Twenty-four U-boats would be the 250-ton small coastal type, and the rest ocean-capable, allowing about ten on station at one time. The paper correctly anticipated a 'combined arms' approach to attacking Britain's trade, with simultaneous deployment of surface raiders and U-boats, with early resort to unrestricted submarine warfare, along with an air and mine offensive directed at ports and coastal shipping.[11] By the time this paper was issued, NID was detecting signs that German naval production was over-extended and through 1937 noted a marked slackening in the building rate.[12] Indeed, only one cruiser and three destroyers were ordered that year. The 1939 German navy was, therefore, somewhat smaller than the Planning Committee anticipated. The battleship (*Bismarck*) and one 8in cruiser (*Prinz Eugen*) were not ready until 1941, and *Graf Zeppelin* never completed. However, projected destroyer and U-boat numbers were about right.

The Anglo-German Naval Agreement was traditionally castigated as a disastrous early act of appeasement by Britain, giving a green light to German rearmament, undermining the Stresa agreement, which had just reaffirmed existing European security structures, damaging relations with France, and displaying astonishing naivety over real German intentions.[13] Later views identified advantages for Britain, notably that the agreement, reflecting Hitler's initial insistence that Britain was not a potential enemy, pushed the German navy into a structure which was sub-optimal for war with Britain in 1939, either in frontline strength or vessels then under construction.[14] Given resources available in the period 1935–39, too much effort went into capital ships and heavy cruisers, where the five additional pocket battleships originally planned by 1939 represented a better investment than the five *Hipper*s, and too little into destroyers and, above all, U-boats. Certainly the superheated steam propulsion fitted to the *Hipper*s was ill-suited to Atlantic trade warfare, proving unreliable in service and lacking adequate range.[15]

This debate overlooks a more important underlying reality. Over the first four years of the Nazi regime, from 1933 to 1936, Germany increased expenditure on naval production by a factor of ten, with about 300,000 tons of warship construction in hand at the end of 1936, compared to 375,000 tons for the Royal Navy. If all German output went to expansion, and all future British output only to replacement, a bold assumption, then in 1936 Germany had a chance of reaching 35 per cent of the Royal Navy by 1940, as the IIC suggested. However, expenditure on naval construction did not, on average, exceed the 1936 figure over the next three years, 1937 to 1939, and Germany only added another 50,000 tons of construction by September 1939, when the British total in build had reached 904,500 tons. Within a year of the naval agreement, the Royal Navy was accelerating out of sight, while Germany struggled to implement its initial construction surge, owing to shortage of shipbuilding capacity and skilled labour, and the technical challenges in manufacturing complex modern warships.[16] King was, therefore, correct that under peacetime constraints, with or without an agreement, Germany would not reach 35 per cent much before 1942. The German slowdown was strikingly apparent in their building declaration for fiscal year 1938, passed to the Admiralty under the agreement three months ahead of the April start date. There were no battleships or carriers, three light cruisers 'M', 'N' and 'O', and thirteen U-boats, of which two cruisers and eight U-boats were delayed 1937 orders. All three cruisers were subsequently cancelled on their slips. This declaration proved accurate and readily checkable. Director of Plans, now Captain Tom Phillips, noted that Germany clearly did not intend 'to force the pace' of construction, confirming they would remain well below their allowance by 1942. Chatfield commented that current estimates of future German strength would need revision downwards.[17]

As evidence of a slackening in the German build rate accumulated through 1937–38, Admiralty fears for the impact of an all-out, combined arms attack on Britain's trade moderated, but the belief, first emphasised by Chatfield, that Germany would use its heavy ships aggressively in the Atlantic at the start of a war with Britain persisted. Although NID never acquired definitive intelligence of German intent, and had to rely on attaché advice and observation of evolving German capability, all Admiralty policy and fleet planning papers from early 1937 reflected this assumption. It stimulated the naval staff to think innovatively about a future war, and hastened adoption of new divisional battle-fleet tactics and the concept of the all-arms, fast task force, or hunting group, of which Force H in the coming war was the supreme example.[18]

Germany could have made better resource choices for a naval war with Britain. Force planning during the years 1935–38 was confused and contradictory, following no structured progression to meet clear strategic requirements, subject instead to the whims of Nazi politics, and conflict over wider defence priorities.[19] The impact of the naval agreement was probably marginal, compared to these internal political, economic and institutional factors encouraging a conventional fleet structure, and prestige warships like the *Bismarck*s and *Hipper*s. That does not make the agreement worthless for Britain, judged from a purely naval perspective. In early 1935 the naval staff did not know the government would authorise an effective two-power rate of building from 1936. The agreement, therefore, provided useful insurance in managing a potential triple threat with a lower building rate. There were some minor gains too. The obligations under the agreement, along with Hitler's wish to avoid antagonising Britain, limited the armament of the *Scharnhorst*s, and possibly the *Bismarck*s, and it probably discouraged the acceleration in U-boat production initiated in May 1938 and subsequent adoption of the 1939 'Z' plan from happening earlier. Whether these relatively slim benefits justified the damage to the Stresa framework is another matter.[20]

In monitoring German navy order of battle, warship and weapon capability and fighting effectiveness between 1935–39 – with one critical exception – intelligence failures were minor compared to those on the IJN in this period, with no prospective surprises comparable to the *Yamato*s, Long Lance, or long-range, land-based torpedo strike. Throughout this period, the Admiralty struggled to reconcile the data the Germans provided under the naval agreement on the *Scharnhorst* battlecruisers, *Bismarck* battleships and *Hipper*-class cruisers with the limited independent NID intelligence available, and its own capital ship design experience. There were doubts whether credible operational speed, range and armour protection were achievable on the claimed displacement, given known armament and independent observed dimensions. There was well-founded suspicion the Germans were significantly understating displacement for all three classes, providing potential superiority over their British equivalents.[21] Assessment of the *Scharnhorst*s was complicated by SIS intelligence correctly reporting that their design allowed for upgrading from 11in to 15in guns. Meanwhile, in March 1937 the Russian ambassador, Ivan Maisky, informed Foreign Secretary Anthony Eden that the Russians had evidence of German cheating, and that the fourth and fifth *Hipper* cruisers, supposedly armed with 6in guns, would be upgraded to 8in.[22] Later that year, the Italian heavy cruiser *Gorizia* docked in Gibraltar for emergency repairs, allowing detailed British measurement, which suggested her real displacement was 10 per cent above the official Italian figure, reinforcing Admiralty suspicion of widespread deception. *Gorizia*'s higher displacement featured in the final pre-war edition of 'particulars of foreign major warships' circulated by NID, but otherwise this publication gave official specifications notified by Axis navies the benefit of the doubt.[23]

Authoritative dimensions of the *Bismarck*s remained a top NID priority until definitive intelligence was acquired from *Bismarck* survivors in 1941. Although two years earlier Godfrey, as DNI, was willing to pay a substantial sum for an SIS informant to provide her plans, the issue mattered less than he believed.[24] *Bismarck* displaced 15 per cent more than her British contemporary, *King George V*, but the latter was conceptually superior, combining 14 per cent greater weight of broadside, much better protection, and only marginally less speed.[25] Despite later criticism from Godfrey, Stanley Goodall, the DNC, correctly judged *Bismarck* an old-fashioned and inefficient design. Furthermore, despite the lack of timely definitive intelligence, Admiralty scepticism over declared German specifications ensured naval planners throughout the late 1930s continued to assume that Germany's new heavy ships would have high speed and large cruising radius optimised for distant raiding.[26]

Meanwhile, intelligence on the U-boat programme was excellent until September 1938, with SIS, through TR16, providing regular updates on numbers under construction and design details for the various classes. This gave NID a reliable check on German declarations under the naval agreement, which remained accurate up to fiscal year 1938. TR16 continued to report until the following summer when he was betrayed through a leak in the SIS station in The Hague, arrested in July, and subsequently executed – a tragic end for an outstanding agent – when he was most needed.[27] NID knew, therefore, that only one U-boat had completed in 1937, that four Type VIIBs and four Type IXs ordered in 1937 were not laid down until the following year, and that in summer 1938 Germany had barely a dozen boats available for operations beyond the North Sea. Of these, only one new 500-ton Type VIIB, the mainstay of the U-boat force until 1941, possessed the range for extended deployment beyond the Western Approaches.[28] TR16's reporting also demonstrated that the new U-boat designs, while robust and reliable, were essentially conservative and standardised to allow rapid production, as anticipated by the 1936 IIC study.[29] Although in 1935–36 TR16 reported interest in developing a large 'cruiser' submarine, optimised for deployment in distant waters, which worried the Admiralty, this concept was never pursued. He probably also alerted NID to the experiments with hydrogen peroxide propulsion overseen by Professor Hellmuth Walter, although it is doubtful this included any specific reference to hydrogen peroxide, or details of the concept. Whatever was mentioned apparently persuaded the Admiralty, correctly as it turned out, that the experiments were not progressing fast enough to present an early threat.[30] Unfortunately, despite these continued inputs from TR16, for reasons explained shortly, NID assessments of U-boat strength went off track for an eighteen-month period beginning in September 1938, leading to a significant overestimate of U-boat strength and production.

TR16's intelligence, alongside the wider picture of evolving German naval policy provided by Muirhead-Gould's successor as naval attaché, Captain Thomas Troubridge, supported a consistent Admiralty assessment through 1937–38 that Germany lacked the U-boat numbers for a sustained mid-Atlantic submarine campaign against British trade before 1940. Instead the Admiralty expected submarine attack to be confined to home waters, defined as an elongated circle extending from the Norwegian coast at Stavanger, north of the Shetland Islands to Rockall, and out to longitude 15° W, before swinging back to the French coast south of Brest. Although by the end of 1938 NID insisted, wrongly, that the Germans had begun deployment to the South Atlantic and Caribbean, the pattern of U-boat operations in the first nine months of the war, with barely twenty ocean-capable boats available, actually closely followed the original home waters prediction. It was German access to the Biscay ports which the Admiralty could not reasonably foresee before 1939 that fundamentally altered the problem of trade defence.

Neither TR16, nor any other source, provided insights into Dönitz's pre-1939 plans for a U-boat war against Britain, specifically the use of extended patrol lines and 'wolf-pack' attacks, conducted under centralised control using long-range radio, to defeat convoying. However, had authoritative intelligence revealed his ideas, they would rightly have been judged aspirational, given the resources he had available, rather than revealing a clear and present danger. Nor would they have seemed especially revelatory. For the popular view that the Royal Navy failed to explore new submarine tactics, and options for countering them in the interwar period is wrong. There were regular convoy exercises with multiple escorts and multiple attacking submarines, and the role of aircraft, land-based and carrier, in an anti-submarine role was studied too. Some of these exercises anticipated U-boat wolf-pack tactics to a remarkable degree. The Royal Navy did not fail to spot the threat of night attack by surfaced submarines, a tactic adopted by its own boats in exercises, and highlighted this in convoy instructions as early as 1934. However, it saw no way of countering the problem prior to the advent of radar.[31] Overall, the Royal Navy correctly predicted both German intent at the strategic level for execution of a trade war, and the methods they would adopt at the tactical level.[32]

The most critical British naval intelligence failure on Germany during the late 1930s has received less attention. This was not identifying the strength and capabilities of the German naval SIGINT organisation, B-Dienst, and its potential to inflict catastrophic damage in a new naval war against Britain. B-Dienst, originally created in the First World War, resumed operations in 1919, and by the early 1930s was re-established as a substantial organisation, targeted primarily on the French and Russian navies, but increasingly the Royal Navy too, with significant successes against all three. By 1935, it had twelve D/F stations covering the North Sea and Baltic, and was planning an additional network for the Mediterranean and Black Sea. Total B-Dienst staff already exceeded the British naval SIGINT effort, and by 1939 it was three times as large. Intermittent study of British communications began in the 1920s, but more systematically from 1932, when the first British naval exercise was observed in its entirety. Investigation continued informally, despite an edict from Hitler barring intelligence operations against Britain while the Anglo-German naval agreement was in force. The five-digit Administrative Code, introduced in 1934 for non-confidential messages, was broken the following year as a result of lax Royal Navy procedures in the Red Sea and the more complex Naval Cipher, used in combination with the Administrative Code for confidential traffic, in 1938, when British exercises in the Atlantic were regularly observed. Anti-submarine operations were monitored at Portland, as were the number of ASDIC-equipped warships. British research into HF/DF was spotted as early as 1932 and Dönitz later alerted to its potential for monitoring U-boat operations at long range from shore-based sites. B-Dienst did not apparently consider the possibility of ship-borne capability until late 1940, but this warning was dismissed as impossible. By the outbreak of war, B-Dienst could read almost all Royal Navy and French navy traffic, and over the first four months of hostilities was processing perhaps a thousand signals per day on the two navies, more than double average British Enigma output when it commenced in 1941. These pre-war German successes against the world's premier maritime power were more impressive for being achieved entirely cryptographically, without access to stolen material. Meanwhile, Britain was reading almost no German traffic.[33]

It is extraordinary that as B-Dienst notched up these achievements in the late 1930s, none of the British personnel involved in the Room 40 successes, now holding high office in the Admiralty or GC&CS, including James, Rear Admiral James Troup, who became DNI in July 1935, Sinclair, Denniston and Clarke, contemplated a comparable German breakthrough, let alone practical steps to investigate. Part of the explanation lies in a wider miscalculation. There was a growing British conviction, dating from the early 1930s, that as the Germans and other potential opponents reflected on the open secret of Britain's naval SIGINT successes during the last war, their response must be radio silence.[34] The British saw less scope, therefore, for offensive SIGINT, an assessment they assumed opponents would mirror. They did not anticipate German exploitation of modern radio technology, combined with secure mechanised cryptographic systems and good intelligence, to execute a new type of U-boat warfare once sufficient resources were available. This failure of imagination was accompanied by complacency over British communications security. This rested not just in misplaced confidence in British hand ciphers, and therefore failure to push the development of Typex, the British equivalent to Enigma, but also that geography would constrain German intercept capability and that Britain's strategic traffic could continue to pass on red-route cables. To be fair, the Germans had their own failures of imagination. They did not contemplate that Enigma could be broken but, equally important, seriously underestimated the potential of British HF/DF capability.[35]

The rising threat from Italy

In parallel with the emerging naval challenge from Germany and the longer standing problem of Japan, from 1935 the Royal Navy faced a third threat from Italy. The Italian navy was equivalent in strength to France, and double that of the 1939 German navy, with about the same tonnage then under construction. Taking account of Italian air power and Italy's geographic position, it was well placed to contest the central Mediterranean, and potentially sever Britain's primary communication route to the East. A curious feature of British naval policy through the 1930s is, therefore, how little attention, including intelligence effort, Italy received in comparison with its two future Axis allies. The Admiralty only seriously contemplated war with Italy from 1935, with the onset of the Abyssinia crisis. Prior to that, as a friend and former ally in the war, its capabilities appeared an open book, easily monitored through the naval attaché in Rome, frequent contacts with the Royal Navy Mediterranean Fleet, and declarations under the naval treaties. Even when Italy became a credible opponent, there were reasons she received lower priority as a threat. So long as the Mediterranean Fleet was in place, it had decisive superiority. If it had to withdraw to counter a threat from Japan, Britain could close both ends of the Mediterranean and rely on France as a counterweight, at least in the western half. Finally, the Royal Navy had a poor opinion of Italian fighting quality, although its overall record here in the coming war proved better than expected.

Although GC&CS naval section read some Italian naval traffic from the late 1920s, the Abyssinian crisis inevitably gave this higher priority, and by the end of 1935, helped by a doubling of staff to twelve, most was successfully covered, despite significant Italian cipher changes. Readability extended to both the secret and general naval ciphers, and one of the naval attaché codes. Overall, this yielded considerable intelligence on fleet dispositions, plans and movements, including during the Munich crisis in autumn 1938, as well as base and coastal defences, although operational exploitation of this haul was variable. Although this excellent SIGINT coverage continued through the outbreak of the Mediterranean war until July 1940, the then Commander-in-Chief Mediterranean Fleet, Admiral Sir Andrew Cunningham, rather surprisingly later asserted that at that time 'intelligence about Italy was sparse'. The naval SIGINT was supplemented by broadly equivalent coverage of the Italian army and air force. There were also some continuing insights into Italian policy from coverage of diplomatic traffic, although the most important material could no longer be accessed, because it went by courier.[36]

The Abyssinian crisis was followed almost immediately by the outbreak of the Spanish civil war in July 1936. Italian and German support for the nationalists, and Royal Navy operations to protect British interests and later conduct non-intervention patrols, ensured continued demand for timely SIGINT, and further reinforcement of Clarke's naval section. A key achievement in 1937 was the breaking by Dilly Knox of the new 'K' Enigma cipher machine used by the Italians and Spanish nationalists, an improved version of the commercial machine studied by Foss in the late 1920s, but less sophisticated than the variants now being used by the German armed forces. Building on Foss's work, Knox invented a cryptanalytical technique called 'rodding', which proved valuable to the subsequent attack on German Enigma. A modified version of this machine used in Spain was introduced by the Italian navy in 1940, and broken by GC&CS in September that year, drawing on their earlier experience, delivering valuable intelligence in early 1941.[37] On two occasions, Italian submarines attacked British destroyers conducting non-intervention international patrols. SIGINT identified *Iride* as the attacker on *Havock* on 31 August 1937, and confirmed that the destroyer had successfully counter-attacked, leaving *Iride*'s crew badly shaken from her depth-charging.[38] During the four years 1936 to 1939, GC&CS produced between forty and seventy Italian naval decrypts per day and, on average, a further one hundred plain-language messages were read at Mediterranean Fleet headquarters in Malta.[39] However British success against Italian diplomatic and naval traffic in this period was balanced by at least equal, and possibly greater, Italian success against British diplomatic and naval codes, the former owing to poor security at the Rome embassy, and the latter stemming from weaknesses in Mediterranean Fleet communications practice during the Abyssinian crisis. The naval attack was rendered more damaging, because by 1939 most Italian achievements were shared with B-Dienst, compounding the damage from the latter's independent attacks on Royal Navy codes.[40]

For most of the 1930s, Italy ranked low in SIS priorities, well behind Germany and Japan.[41] Reporting on the Italian navy prior to 1939 was limited, although a network operating from Austria covered naval activity in Trieste and Genoa from 1935–38, and there was some good political reporting on the intentions of the Italian leader, Benito Mussolini.[42] SIS also acquired an important windfall from its French liaison, passed to NID at the end of August 1939, a copy of the strategic guidance to be followed by the Italian navy in the event of war, recently issued by the Italian ministry of marine.[43] The Spanish civil war did provide NID with an important recruit of its own, Alan Hillgarth, the consul in Majorca, a former naval officer, adventurer, novelist and friend of Churchill. Throughout the conflict, besides supporting and overseeing the evacuation of the British expatriate community, he provided excellent reports to the Foreign Office and Mediterranean Fleet on developments in the Balearics and from his contacts on the mainland, winning plaudits from the Commander-in-Chief, Admiral Sir Dudley Pound, and numerous other senior officers. Two of these naval contacts employed Hillgarth in Britain's coming war. The captain of the battlecruiser *Repulse*, John Godfrey, as DNI from 1939, sent him to Madrid as naval attaché, where he re-established contact with Juan March, while Rear Admiral James Somerville, the future Commander-in-Chief Eastern Fleet, selected him as his intelligence chief in 1943.[44]

The JIC, the OIC and Bletchley Park

The growing threats in Europe triggered two far-reaching initiatives from 1936, influencing the management and assessment of naval intelligence, one at strategic and the other at operational level. The first was the establishment in July of a new subcommittee of the chiefs of staff, the Joint Intelligence Committee (JIC). The creation of the JIC reflected growing recognition by the three armed services heads of intelligence during the early 1930s that more intelligence issues required collaboration. This perception was partly driven by the experience of cross-cutting organisations such as GC&CS, the 'Y' Committee and the IIC, but also new requirements like strategic air targeting.[45] More formal collaboration was also a logical complement to the evolution of the Joint Planning Committee. Here the chiefs of staff agreed that a key function of the new JIC was providing the joint planners with intelligence on subjects where more than one service could contribute. A final factor was the appointment in 1936 of a Minister for Co-ordination of Defence, Sir Thomas Inskip, which added impetus to joint defence policy and planning, and the information to support it. The initial membership of the JIC comprised DDNI, Deputy Director of Intelligence (Air) and the head of the intelligence branch of the general staff. They were supported by the secretary to the Joint Planning Committee, to ensure the work of the two bodies was linked. They met at intervals of two to four weeks, up to the outbreak of war. It was agreed the IIC would support the JIC, and Morton therefore frequently attended meetings too. The Foreign Office, SIS and MI5 were rare attendees, with the first two not sending anyone to a meeting until November 1938.

Until summer 1939, the JIC was a peripheral body with little impact on NID's core interests. The joint planners, who had prime responsibility for tasking it, did not exploit it effectively, and nor did the JIC itself take the initiative in offering assessments on crucial intelligence questions not addressed elsewhere. Its most extensive work in these years covered lessons to be drawn for the future of air warfare from experience in China and Spain. This was useful, but had limited enduring relevance or impact. More positively, it did inculcate a culture of greater sharing and co-operation between the three service intelligence departments. Above all, the concept was right, it could develop, and the war turned it into the finest strategic assessments body in the world.[46]

The second 1936 initiative had more immediate impact on NID. At the end of that year, influenced by experience with intelligence during the Abyssinian crisis, and the developing Royal Navy operations associated with the Spanish civil war, William James as DCNS resurrected the enhanced ID25B he had sought in July 1918. He judged improved 'operational intelligence' for the Admiralty an essential complement to rearmament now underway, and that its availability in wartime required advance preparation. James shared the prevailing opinion that future enemies would be more careful over communications security, and doubted codebreaking would provide the same advantage the Royal Navy enjoyed in 1914–18, although everything possible should still be done to exploit this. However, a key lesson of the war was how much could be achieved by integrating intelligence from other sources, including D/F, traffic analysis, and aerial and submarine reconnaissance. The 'intelligent putting together of little titbits, the sifting of the unimportant from the important' produced 'operational intelligence.'[47] He tasked DNI, now Rear Admiral James Troup, with creating a small pilot unit, exploiting the residual movements section in NID, to experiment with building a composite intelligence picture from multiple sources. (By 1933, the movements section, known as OB4, comprised just one civilian clerk, who kept a limited record of foreign warship movements.[48]) The pilot would also plan the personnel, accommodation and communications to enable rapid creation of a full capability in wartime.[49] This included agreeing the role and location of the GC&CS naval section.[50]

The pilot opened in June 1937 and initially focused on monitoring foreign warships in the western Mediterranean. For its first year it kept the title Movements Section, or NID8, having absorbed OB4. The term Operational Intelligence Section (OIC) came into use around mid 1938. To head it, Troup selected Paymaster Lieutenant Commander Norman Denning. He could not have made a better choice. Denning, usually known from his initials as 'Ned', the son of a small-town Hampshire draper came from a remarkable family. Two of four brothers were killed in the First World War, a third, Tom Denning, became Master of the Rolls and one of the most distinguished judges of the twentieth century, and the last became a lieutenant general. Norman Denning proved a brilliant intelligence officer, exactly the 'astute mind' James wanted, and was in every sense the father of the OIC, as important an intelligence innovation in Britain's coming naval war as Bletchley Park. As Vice Admiral Sir Norman Denning, he later served as the penultimate DNI in 1960, and then Deputy Chief of Defence Staff within the new integrated Defence Intelligence Service in 1964.[51]

By January 1938, Denning, assisted by three clerks, had made progress, drawing on extensive research into Room 40 and ID25 and current GC&CS practice, although struggling with the scale of the task. His first initiative was a database, a card-index system recording and cross-referencing the movements of every warship belonging to Germany, Italy, Japan, France and Spain, drawn from every possible source, overt and covert. Much was gleaned from the DIO network, other naval sources, diplomatic and consular reporting and the international press. The primary covert source was 'Y', although SIS contributed occasionally, especially through TR16 on Germany. 'Y' information comprised plain-language (P/L) and cipher intercepts, with a daily average of 120 of the latter reaching GC&CS naval section, and D/F intercepts passed directly from Flowerdown, Scarborough, Malta and Hong Kong. D/F bearings linked to the originating warship by both commercial and secret call-signs, the latter obtained from GC&CS, were recorded and plotted. Decrypts were available on all the target navies except Germany, on which GC&CS only commenced significant cryptographic effort in mid 1938, reflecting its use of the apparently unbreakable Enigma cipher machine.[52] Because of the lack of German decrypts, D/F of German warships was confined to the Mediterranean – where GC&CS obtained relevant secret call-signs – and its foreign deployments – where P/L intercept was available. Japanese tracking depended on reports passed from FECB. Merchant vessels were only recorded if they were directly associated with warships, although Japanese transports were monitored. All known movements for the target navies were recorded on wall charts, alongside Royal Navy dispositions and movements. By incorporating all warships, surface and submarine, integrating all SIGINT information with other sources, and including British movements, Denning's NID8 pilot was moving towards what James wanted, but never quite achieved with ID25 in 1918. Its roots in Fisher's ideas at the beginning of the century, Rotter's work pre-1914, Room 40 and even WTID, were visible.[53]

However, keeping detailed records on three and a half thousand warships was a huge task for Denning's tiny team. NID8's inability positively to identify 'pirate' Italian submarines like *Iride*, operating in Spanish waters during late summer 1937, demonstrated that merely recording foreign warship deployments outside their home waters was insufficient. A total picture of foreign navy dispositions was essential if specific threats were to be identified and addressed. Movements records also had to be meticulously maintained and current. James's original hope that once operational intelligence had been piloted, the organisation could remain on ice to be stood up on the outbreak of war, was flawed. Considerable peacetime commitment was required to maintain a useful intelligence picture. Without this, it would take months before a wartime NID8 delivered value, and building the initial picture under wartime conditions would be more difficult. Denning's compelling, if unpalatable, message was that more investment in peacetime research on the target navies would deliver better wartime dividends. Monitoring the IJN was especially difficult, since good information was confined to Chinese waters, and fleet dispositions and activities in Japanese home waters were a closed book. SIGINT revealed important IJN organisational changes, but assessing these demanded considerable research effort.[54]

A further problem was the limited number of D/F sites, where understanding of the scale and complexity of the service constructed by 1918 had been lost. In November 1937 a new section, NID9, was established alongside the OIC to co-ordinate 'Y' inputs, initially under a single officer, Commander Humphrey Sandwith. Over the next two years, with robust support from Denning and the head of the new GC&CS German section, Lieutenant Commander Malcolm Saunders, and dogged lobbying of Sinclair, Troup and his successor, John Godfrey, he achieved significant expansion. In addition to Scarborough and Flowerdown, new United Kingdom sites were commissioned at Sunburgh, Cupar, Pembroke, St Albans, Land's End, Sutton Valence and Cooling Marshes. Overseas sites at Bombay, Singapore and Melbourne already authorised were joined by Fremantle, Bermuda, three Canadian sites at Halifax, Montreal and Botwood, and a Middle East site at Ismailia. Most stations, new and existing, obtained modern commercial receivers, many purchased from the United States, and there was a substantial training programme to provide operators. Good telephone and teleprinter communications linking the United Kingdom sites with GC&CS were operational by the Munich crisis, but overseas communications were still inadequate when war broke out.[55]

Another issue not fully resolved until 1941 was how responsibility for SIGINT analysis and assessment should divide between NID8 and GC&CS. Denning believed that effective integration of intelligence and operations ideally required the naval section analysts to be in the Admiralty. He judged that even in 1918, ID25 remained too isolated from the rest of NID, let alone the wider naval staff. Yet the inescapable reality was that key elements of SIGINT, still the most important single source of operational naval intelligence, were now produced geographically separate from the Admiralty by a different organisation outside naval control. In theory, the long-standing plans to bring GC&CS naval section, including its cryptographers, into the Admiralty at the outbreak of war, essentially recreating ID25 in its final form, remained extant, and were supported by Clarke.[56] However, Denniston now opposed separating the naval cryptographers from the rest of GC&CS with its wider expertise and dedicated infrastructure. He wanted to maximise the value of scarce cryptographic resources by keeping them concentrated, but his resistance also reflected a fear that, unless GC&CS retained a monopoly over cryptography, all three services might re-establish dedicated SIGINT agencies on pre-1919 lines, leaving GC&CS with a diplomatic rump, threatening its survival. Yet, if GC&CS remained intact as a cryptographic agency, it could not function effectively without its analysts, nor must it become an ivory tower oblivious to operational needs. Denniston was undoubtedly correct in fighting to keep GC&CS intact, and by early 1938 had won the argument to keep the entire naval section. However, important questions regarding the exploitation of SIGINT by NID8 were left open, with a risk that it would end up wastefully duplicating GC&CS assessment and research. The Munich crisis soon provoked a rethink.

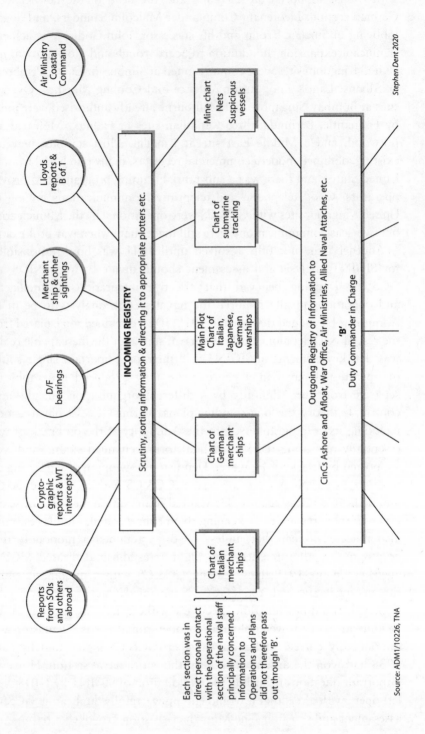

DIAGRAM OF ORGANISATION OF OIC DURING THE MUNICH CRISIS, OCTOBER 1938

Stephen Dent 2020

Reports from SOIs and others abroad

Crypto-graphic reports & WT intercepts

D/F bearings

Merchant ship & other sightings

Lloyds reports & B of T

Air Ministry Coastal Command

INCOMING REGISTRY

Scrutiny, sorting information & directing it to appropriate plotters etc.

Chart of Italian merchant ships

Chart of German merchant ships

Main Plot Chart of Italian, Japanese, German warships

Chart of submarine tracking

Mine chart Nets Suspicious vessels

Each section was in direct personal contact with the operational section of the naval staff principally concerned. Information to Operations and Plans did not therefore pass out through 'B'.

Outgoing Registry of Information to CinCs Ashore and Afloat, War Office, Air Ministries, Allied Naval Attaches, etc.

'B'

Duty Commander in Charge

Source: ADM1/10226, TNA

Despite these challenges, the operational service provided by the small NID8 unit improved steadily through the first half of 1938, as did planning for extra personnel and facilities required in wartime. With support from James, NID8 gained authority to communicate intelligence not only inside the Admiralty and with other government agencies, but directly to frontline commanders and ships at sea. Initially, such communications had to be approved by DNI, but he soon authorised power of direct release.[57] In September the Munich crisis put war mobilisation to the test. The OIC, as NID8 was now formally named, expanded from four to fifty personnel, and was organised as in the accompanying diagram. For the crisis, in addition to the primary plot of Axis warships, it established four additional plots: submarine tracking; German merchant ships; Italian merchant ships; and one for minefields and suspicious vessels. These plots were fed, using dedicated teleprinters, by the sources Denning had established over the previous fifteen months, but now also included Lloyd's and RAF Coastal Command. Each plot was in direct contact with the appropriate operational section of the naval staff, but also contributed to a constantly updated integrated intelligence picture, supervised by a duty commander.[58] However, it is essential to emphasise that, as its name implied, the OIC was an intelligence centre, not an operations centre. It did not manage operations and it did not issue operational orders. The intelligence plots it ran supported and fed, but did not replace, the long-standing operational plots maintained by Operations Division and, following mobilisation, by Trade Division.

GC&CS also implemented mobilisation plans which Sinclair subsequently insisted passed off better than other parts of government.[59] In June he had purchased Bletchley Park in Buckinghamshire, located fifty miles northwest of London, still reasonably accessible but clear of the anticipated bombing, as a war station. The previous year he won Treasury approval for fifty-six additional senior staff and thirty female assistants immediately on the outbreak of war, effectively doubling GC&CS strength. Denniston was accordingly tasked to comb the universities discreetly for recruits, exploiting the academic networks he and Ewing had established twenty years earlier. Many of these were brought into Bletchley alongside existing staff from Broadway during the crisis, partly as a precaution, and partly as an exercise, and received regular training over the remaining year of peace.

This injection of fresh talent was badly needed, because GC&CS was a 'greying institution', too dependent on a 1914–18 generation highly skilled at decrypting codebooks but, with notable exceptions, less suited to attacking the new-generation machine ciphers. The first batch of new recruits included two top-class mathematicians, Alan Turing and Peter Twinn, although it is doubtful that this academic skill was deliberately targeted by Denniston to tackle machine ciphers, as often suggested. Traditionally, GC&CS and its predecessors certainly favoured a background in languages or classics, judging that understanding language patterns and proficiency in multiple languages was well suited to cryptanalysis. However, mathematicians were still recruited before 1937 and only two more, John Jeffries and Gordon Welchman, arrived before the outbreak of war. Two factors encouraged a greater influx after September 1939. The first was the need to trawl more widely for scarce talent, and Denniston's belief that lateral thinking and ability to spot patterns was what mattered most, a reason top chess players were prized. Margaret Rock applied for a post in the Foreign Office as a fluent French and German speaker, but was directed to Bletchley when it was noted that she had a mathematics degree from Bedford College, London, and experience as a statistician. She was then talent-spotted by Dilly Knox to join his research team. The second factor was that once in GC&CS and needing more help urgently under the pressures of wartime, mathematicians recommended others from their academic and social circle. Thus Welchman attracted Stuart Milner-Barry, Hugh Alexander and Joan Clarke (later Murray) from his Cambridge contacts. The mathematicians undoubtedly brought GC&CS new skills and insights, but it is not true that only mathematicians could tackle machine ciphers. In this area Knox, Foss and Tiltman proved fully competitive, as did the young German linguist Mavis Lever (later Batey), who made an outstanding contribution to breaking Italian Enigma before she was twenty. As Welchman advised Joan Clarke, who joined Turing and Twinn in Hut 8 to work on naval Enigma in June 1940, cryptography did not really need mathematics, but mathematicians tended to be good at it.[60] Tiltman took a similar view, seeing cryptography as 'much closer to art than science', which made the 'personal factor so important'.[61]

The Munich crisis not only tested the mobilisation of the OIC and GC&CS, but also the agreed division of naval SIGINT analysis. The latter was not judged a success. Parallel assessment provoked confusion, exacerbated by the inadequate understanding and skills of the incoming OIC reinforcements. Denning found the GC&CS SIGINT summaries unsatisfactory, since it was often insufficiently clear what was fact, and what deduction. He insisted the OIC must not only see final reports issued by GC&CS, but all the raw material, however incomplete, on which they were based. The OIC would respect a GC&CS interpretation, but reserved the right to make its own.[62] Overall, the Munich experience convinced Troup and Denniston that in wartime the naval section would have to split, after all: the cryptographers staying with GC&CS, and the operational analysts doing traffic analysis joining the OIC. This decision was bitterly opposed by William Clarke who, as a passionate advocate of operational intelligence, believed his section should remain intact and move in its entirety to the Admiralty, as envisaged at its founding in 1924. Before this new plan could be implemented, it was shaped by wider organisational changes over the next nine months.[63]

Apart from this demarcation issue, there was consensus within the Admiralty that the OIC had performed well. The reality was more mixed. On the positive side, the OIC accurately located the major German surface units in their home ports or home waters in the last week of September, demonstrating that, as the crisis peaked, the German navy had not moved to an obvious war footing. On the debit side, it struggled to locate a significant proportion of the U-boat force. This was complicated by SIS reports received at the end of August and beginning of September, suggesting up to six boats were deploying to a southern destination with Spain, the Canaries, Spanish Morocco, and even the Far East, listed as candidates. The reports also claimed that at least one U-boat series recently in build had been secretly duplicated, meaning U-boat strength was higher than Germany had declared, or the Admiralty previously assessed.[64] This SIS intelligence caused NID to alert DIOs and, inevitably, apparent sightings of U-boats and even potential U-boat bases flowed into the OIC from merchant ships and dubious consular contacts. Ultimately, the OIC concluded that from September to November around five Type VIIs and possibly four newly completed Type IXs were operating off northwest Africa and Brazil respectively. It judged these deployments originated as exercises, but were then fortuitously placed for attacking key British trade routes had war broken out.[65]

All these reports were false. No U-boat group deployed overseas at this time and, indeed, no U-boat ever operated south of the Gibraltar straits before June 1940, although individual U-boats did deploy to Spanish Atlantic waters in 1938, and sometimes used Cadiz as a base.[66] There was no secret duplication in build, and German U-boat declarations under the naval agreement were accurate. The source of the SIS reports is now unknown. TR16 is a candidate, although there were other agents monitoring warship movements at German ports, including Wilhelmshaven.[67] Godfrey later believed that NID had been the victim of a disinformation campaign conducted by the German intelligence service, the Abwehr, now under the former U-boat officer, Admiral Wilhelm Canaris. Over the winter of 1938/39, the latter, who was opposed to war and sought Hitler's removal, did propagate false rumours of new aggressive moves by Germany designed to stiffen British resistance.[68] However, there is no firm evidence specifically linking him to the U-boat reports. It is more credible that the reports of a 'southern deployment' originated from a proposal put by Dönitz to the German naval high command a few weeks earlier, that one U-boat flotilla should be based permanently overseas, 'to exercise a restraining politico-military influence while peace lasts', and to be ready to strike important enemy lines of communication in war.[69] This proposal was rejected, but it would have been a talking point in U-boat circles during August, and it is possible that the normally reliable TR16 picked up a garbled version. The original SIS reports were restrained, suggesting only five boats were involved, and Spain the most likely destination. It was the OIC that created a more elaborate scenario.

Far from providing comfortable reassurance that the OIC already worked, as Denning and many of the OIC believed, the Munich crisis demonstrated that without better intelligence it would struggle. Its performance on the 'southern' U-boats was a classic example of the intelligence maxim, 'rubbish in, rubbish out'. Even elements of the surface picture should have flagged concern. The OIC knew three light cruisers and ten destroyers were at sea on 29 September, but could only judge it 'possible' that traffic analysis placed them in the Heligoland Bight. James's vision for what could be achieved with the painstaking piecing together of fragments was valid as far as it went, but he underestimated how much the short periods of decryption blackout in 1918 were compensated by an extensive, mature and highly trained D/F system. This did not yet exist in 1938. William Clarke later insisted that GC&CS had fiercely challenged the likelihood of the southern U-boat deployment, finding no evidence of the communications to support it, although as late as March 1939 his German section was still searching for evidence of a 'disguised system' to support such overseas deployments.[70] The OIC should certainly have asked more searching questions. Even if it believed U-boat completions were somewhat higher, it was hardly credible that Dönitz could deploy half his ocean-capable strength on an extended two-month cruise to the South Atlantic – with no previous precedent for any overseas deployment. OIC failings were exacerbated when monitoring in the months following the crisis did not uncover that the U-boat deployments were mistaken. The Type IXs identified by the OIC as candidates for the Brazil force were not commissioned until 1939, but a persistent conviction that Type IXs were completing earlier than expected caused NID to overestimate U-boat strength by about 15 per cent for the next eighteen months.

20

1939: Preparing for War – Godfrey Arrives

The mobilisation of the OIC and GC&CS for the Munich crisis marked a transition point, both for them, and the wider British naval intelligence community. There was no return to pre-crisis staff levels or peacetime patterns of working. The community now began actively preparing for the war most believed was coming, taking advantage of significant new funding released by the Treasury. A new DNI, Rear Admiral John Godfrey, replaced Troup in February 1939, and commenced major organisational changes designed to put NID, not least the OIC, on a war footing.[1]

Like Hall, the 50-year-old Godfrey, tall with an unflinching gaze and misleadingly soft voice, was appointed DNI following command of a battlecruiser, in his case a distinguished three years with *Repulse*, primarily in the Mediterranean Fleet. This brought two powerful professional connections for his forthcoming post. The commander-in-chief throughout his time in the Mediterranean was Admiral Sir Dudley Pound, for whom Godfrey had first worked in Plans Division in the early 1920s, and followed Godfrey to the Admiralty as First Sea Lord in June. His immediate superior for fifteen months in 1937–38, as commander of the battlecruiser squadron, was Vice Admiral Sir Andrew Cunningham, who had then replaced James as DCNS and was effectively in charge of the Admiralty during Godfrey's first months, following the illness of the current First Sea Lord, Admiral of the Fleet Sir Roger Backhouse. Cunningham subsequently relieved Pound in the Mediterranean, and commanded there for most of Godfrey's tenure as DNI. Godfrey was selected by Backhouse on the advice of the Naval Secretary, Rear Admiral Jock Whitworth, but Pound and Cunningham probably exerted considerable influence. He left *Repulse* highly regarded professionally for his leadership, seamanship and operational flair, but Pound also valued and exploited his political and diplomatic skills. The regard was emphasised with the award of a

CB in the 1939 New Year Honours, as with Cumming earlier, a rare distinction for a captain. He was accordingly recommended for flag rank, but specific aspects of his previous career especially fitted him for DNI. He had worked twice in Plans Division, the second time under King as deputy director 1933–35, and, unusually for an officer of his generation, had two postings on the staff of the Royal Naval Staff College Greenwich. His second post there as deputy director gave him exposure to a wide range of external contacts across government, industry and academe. Extensive periods in the Far East, as well as the Mediterranean, fostered a strong global outlook.

Other aspects of Godfrey's personality and background, probably only partly recognised by his superiors, made him a good choice. He had unusually wide interests, many quite different from those favoured by his naval peers, being a connoisseur of art, music, high literature, food and wine. His day cabin in *Repulse* was modelled by Brian O'Rorke, the architect responsible for the Orient liners. A guest recalled the silk coverlet adorning his bunk, from the Forbidden City in Peking, the jade tree abloom with semi-precious flowers on his lacquer dining-table, and the Impressionist pictures on the walls, including sketches by Augustus John, a personal friend.[2] He was also a deep thinker, even a philosopher, gifted with a powerful and original intellect. From his arrival as DNI long into old age, he reflected deeply on the business of intelligence in a way quite alien to Hall. The latter was an intuitive operator, gripped by the game, the manipulation of the pieces on the board to outwit the opposition. He had little appetite for process or structure. Godfrey saw DNI much more from the point of view of creator and manager of a complex organisation, the conductor of the orchestra, bringing disparate talents together to deliver consistent, reliable and high-quality results. His greatest strength was his ability to delegate almost totally to those he trusted.

It was characteristic of Godfrey's commitment to structure, process and rigour that one of his early innovations was to introduce the grading of intelligence reports for reliability and credibility. Reports were graded from 'A' (from a completely reliable source) to 'E' (an unreliable source) and from '1' (a report confirmed by other intelligence) to '5' (an improbable report). So 'A1' indicated a report from a first-rate reliable source, confirmed by other intelligence. 'E2' indicated a bad source, but a probable report. He also introduced strict criteria for differentiating between fact, and inference from the fact or supporting commentary. Variants of this grading system were rapidly adopted by other members of the intelligence community, and with modifications and elaborations it continues to this day. With hindsight, it seems an obvious requirement and, therefore, perhaps an indictment of Godfrey's predecessors that it did not develop earlier.[3]

Godfrey had weaknesses. His intellectualism, combined with remorseless pursuit of the logical and relentless high standards, encouraged pursuit of perfection to the point that it became a vice. In contrast, his eclecticism and vivid imagination sometimes caused problems too. It led him to start 'hares', and insist on pursuing an investigation beyond its likely value. Although capable of great kindness, and the most generous and genial of hosts when he chose, he often appeared cold and forbidding, reflecting underlying reserve and shyness. As his successor, Commodore Edmund Rushbrooke, noted, nobody would describe Godfrey as 'matey'.[4] He lacked Hall's common touch and sense of fun. He found it difficult to throw off the trappings of authority, and his humour was often sardonic and cruel. He not only did not suffer fools, but could be too intolerant of opposing views and, under stress, unleashed a ferocious temper. Most respected him, although not all, but few loved him as they did Hall. Ewen Montagu, head of the Special Intelligence section NID17M and author of the famous Operation Mincemeat in 1943 produced a blunt, but penetrating, assessment: 'He was the world's prize shit, but a genius ... I had enormous admiration for him as an intelligence brain and organiser – the more sincere as I loathed him as a man.'[5] Oddly, while Hall ultimately suffered from his reputation as an intriguer, Godfrey did so by insisting on speaking unvarnished truth, not only to power but to peers, when discretion and compromise might have served him better.[6]

Twenty years stand between Hall's departure and the arrival of Godfrey. His responsibilities as incoming DNI looked much the same, but his inheritance was radically different in three respects. Britain's overall national security structures, and the intelligence community within them, had changed out of all recognition. Godfrey had to contend with a major new service, the RAF, which had hardly impinged on Hall. The Chiefs of Staff Committee, Joint Planners, Joint Intelligence Committee and IIC were new too. Gone were the days when DNI could dominate the SIGINT agenda, extending far into political affairs. Hall had been able to focus almost all his efforts on defeating Germany. By contrast, Godfrey faced a more complex set of challenges spread across the globe, even if Germany again dominated in the short term. Finally, the run-up to war coincided with gathering changes in the intelligence environment. New types of D/F and wide deployment of machine ciphers promised to transform SIGINT, advances in aerial photography would shortly create a new field of imagery intelligence, or IMINT, while radar would give rise to electronic intelligence, or ELINT.

Godfrey later insisted that he did not know much about intelligence when he arrived, and that through the first months of the war, the senior naval staff remained ignorant about 'how to extract, develop, use and keep it'. He witnessed exaggerated faith in the 'efficacy of spies', and insufficient emphasis on the traditional techniques of reconnaissance advocated by James in 1936, basic observation of enemy ports whether by surface craft, submarine or now, crucially, by aerial photography. Understanding of how modern technology applied to intelligence was poor. Even the new DCNS, Vice Admiral Tom Phillips, a term-mate of Godfrey who replaced Cunningham in May 1939, 'with his clever scientific brain', thought of D/F as it had been in 1918. Godfrey 'had to learn first', and then share his knowledge with others.[7] While Godfrey, NID and the wider naval staff were certainly on a steep learning curve through 1939, his previous staff jobs had provided significant exposure to intelligence, and his NID inheritance was not as sparse as he later suggested.

Whatever gaps Godfrey really felt in his knowledge, he used the remaining six months of peace well. He consulted widely, quickly identified the intelligence capabilities essential to NID effectiveness and what was required to support them, began recruiting staff for the expanded organisation he knew would be needed for wartime, and clarified how he would direct this larger operation. Before his formal handover with Troup, he had meetings with Sinclair and his deputy and future successor as 'C', Colonel Stewart Menzies, with Denniston and Travis at GC&CS, with Sir Alexander Cadogan and Sir Warren Fisher, permanent secretaries at the Foreign Office and Treasury respectively, with the main foreign naval attachés in London and his French opposite number in Paris.[8] Troup had already drawn up a shortlist of 150 potential wartime recruits, primarily from the naval retired list.

Hall was quick to offer help and advice, lending Godfrey his London flat, and becoming an essential mentor and model to follow. An early initiative he stimulated, modelled on the *Sayonara* episode, was to encourage Godfrey to despatch a yacht, *Campeador*, under tourist cover, to investigate the possibility of U-boat refuelling facilities in the Canaries.[9] Godfrey noted that although different in character and temperament, he and Hall held the same values, shared a common outlook, and a 'strange similarity of experience'. Furthermore, both achieved for different reasons a position of 'anomalous independence' in the naval staff, both had 'anxiety' about their respective First Sea Lords, both faced hostility from outside the Admiralty, and both had to take responsibility for decisions without help from higher authority. Despite the many changes in the intelligence community and Whitehall, Godfrey evidently saw himself following a Hall tradition, a certain idea of what a DNI should be. Whenever faced with an intractable problem as DNI, he asked himself what Hall would have done. This image of Hall was enhanced by the continuing prominence of Hall disciples: Denniston, Knox, Birch, de Grey and Travis in GC&CS, and Trench and Brandon back as interrogators.[10] At the more practical level, Hall proved invaluable in introducing Godfrey to influential contacts who might also provide recruits. He stressed the importance of a personal assistant in the mould of Claude Serocold, and the Governor of the Bank of England, Sir Montague Norman, delivered the ideal candidate, Ian Fleming, currently a stockbroker and occasional journalist, but in future a novelist and creator of James Bond. The 30-year-old Fleming, recruited over lunch at the Carlton Grill, arrived in July as an RNVR lieutenant, although, like Bond, he was soon promoted to commander, and proved an inspired choice. He lacked the patience or interest for intelligence analysis, which he left to others. He was a supreme fixer who made things happen, a showman and superb networker, with the easy confidence to try selling anything to anyone, adept at working the Admiralty and Whitehall bureaucracy, and producing well-crafted policy and operational papers. He was also a fertile source of ideas, many mad, but some brilliant. He soon represented DNI on key interdepartmental committees and by the end of the year had taken over intelligence planning. Such was the grip he established over every aspect of NID business that when Edmund Rushbrooke succeeded Godfrey in 1942, he rightly judged Fleming indispensable and kept him in place until the end of the war.[11]

Fleming was the most visible example of an extraordinary range of recruits to NID during 1939–40, ranging far beyond Troup's Navy-dominated short list. In came barristers, solicitors, insurance agents, journalists, writers, a historian of fine arts, a marine biologist, and many more, often with little apparent logic to where they were posted. Godfrey claimed that from his arrival as DNI, he was determined that NID should be a decentralised organisation. He would select people with 'the right sort of personality and knowledge' and then, 'as we do at sea', 'thrust responsibility on them even before they were quite ready for it, on the principle that it is only by experiencing responsibility that one can learn to be responsible'. Outsiders from the Sea Lords downwards would deal direct with his experts, not through him. This freed him for 'my rightful duty', to 'organise, sustain and supervise a machine', capable of growing 'from a few dozen to over a thousand individuals'. There was no doubt an element of hindsight here, but the broad intent was visible in some of his earliest moves, notably with the OIC.[12]

Godfrey immediately recognised the OIC's importance, and how much Troup and Denning had achieved from a standing start over two years. Troup had already initiated plans to rehouse it underground in the Admiralty basement, alongside the planned wartime operations and trade war rooms, with their 'executive plots'. Later it moved to the bombproof Admiralty command complex, christened the Citadel, constructed alongside Horse Guards Parade in 1940–41. Meanwhile, the Munich mobilisation had demonstrated that the anticipated wartime OIC had become a large complex organisation and a key requirement identified was for a Deputy Director Intelligence Centre (DDIC), not only to run it effectively, but with the rank, experience and status to ensure its intelligence outputs commanded the confidence of the most senior naval staff, including the First Sea Lord and DCNS.[13] Here, Godfrey selected Rear Admiral Jock Clayton, one of the names on Troup's list of retirees. Clayton was a contemporary, whom Godfrey recalled first meeting as a watch-keeper under James in ID25 in 1917. He proved another outstanding choice, running the OIC with distinction throughout the war. Godfrey described him as a man of 'unruffled calmness', 'impossible to rattle', with 'very shrewd judgement'.[14] One of his staff summarised Clayton as an 'ideal chairman of the board'. He did not seek the limelight, always content to delegate to his able subordinates, and let them make their case at the highest level. But he was always there in support when needed, and with his exceptional intelligence invariably cut through the most tricky problem with the right answer. He lacked the ruthlessness that might otherwise have taken him to the top, and could be too easy-going and tolerant. But his kindly, fatherly temperament and endless wisdom were ideal in knitting together a varied team, naval and civilian, old and young, male and female, often under great stress. He ensured the OIC was not only immensely effective, but a 'happy ship'.[15]

Other key OIC appointments were settled in Godfrey's first weeks. A serving officer, Commander Geoffrey Colpoys, became Clayton's deputy and handled the considerable administrative load, including in due course security arrangements for Ultra, until 1945. Peter Kemp, a leader writer on *The Times*, commissioned as a lieutenant commander, established a specialist D/F plotting section, which he also headed throughout the war, at times providing the only reliable information available to the OIC. Patrick Barrow-Green, ruled unfit for sea duty, took over responsibility for Japan, Italy and Spain, leaving Denning to concentrate on Germany. Perhaps most crucial of all, Godfrey achieved the return of Ernest Thring to run the U-boat plot, bringing his invaluable experience from 1917–18. One of the civilians soon earmarked to assist Thring was a rising barrister, Rodger Winn, who appropriately had initially volunteered himself to NID as an interrogator. In January 1941, when illness obliged Thring to retire, Winn was selected to succeed him, a tribute to his extraordinary aptitude for the work and the respect for his judgement, but also to the willingness of Godfrey, Clayton and others in the naval staff to back talent wherever they found it.[16]

Godfrey also pressed ahead with the establishment of the separate OICs for the Far East and Mediterranean, initiated by Troup. In doing so, he confirmed the emerging view that communications were inadequate to allow the Admiralty OIC to develop a comprehensive intelligence picture for these theatres and transmit it back out to them. Instead, the theatre OICs would have a monopoly over operational intelligence, including traffic analysis, for their respective areas, develop their own picture, and copy essential elements to London.[17] The Far East OIC based in Singapore absorbed and expanded on the Hong Kong-based Pacific Naval Intelligence Organisation. Its development was complicated by debate over the future of the FECB, whose transfer to Singapore was agreed in March, but not completed until the end of August. Progress with accommodation was slow, as was development of adequate D/F infrastructure. The separation of the new OIC and FECB from Commander-in-Chief China and his staff, who remained in Hong Kong until summer 1940, was an added difficulty. It was well into 1940 before performance of the new intelligence organisation reached the barely acceptable.[18] Meanwhile, Troup first discussed a Mediterranean OIC with Pound, as Commander-in-Chief Mediterranean, in December 1938, and Godfrey obtained Board approval the following March to establish it at Malta. It began to function in April, with a peacetime establishment of six officers and five clerks, to be tripled in wartime. To further its operational intelligence remit, GC&CS agreed to supply any broken Italian cipher and code material that could be exploited locally without skilled cryptographic staff. Almost immediately, there were doubts whether Malta was tenable as an OIC site in wartime, and in August it transferred to the Mediterranean Fleet headquarters in Alexandria. At various points during 1938–39 there was tri-service discussion over creating an equivalent to the FECB in the Middle East, but individual service needs proved too distinct, and the idea did not progress.[19]

If by the summer the OIC was adopting the structure and key personnel that served it well through the war, the outlook for good intelligence to feed it was less promising. The naval SIGINT environment Godfrey inherited showed a decline in the quality of sources, and was becoming complicated organisationally. The final peacetime strength of the GC&CS naval section was twenty-seven staff, of whom only five were cryptographers. Through 1939 into the war, the bright spot was continuing excellent coverage of Italian naval traffic, which absorbed eleven staff and most of the cryptographic effort, producing about thirty decrypts daily, although the intelligence value derived from these was variable.[20] However, the more long-standing interwar achievement, reading most IJN traffic, faded from late 1938 as the Japanese introduced new systems. These began with a new, four-character Naval General Operational Code introduced in November 1938, which from 1 June 1939 was confined to important senior officer messages, while most operational traffic switched to a new, five-character Naval General Operational Code, subsequently named by the British and Americans as JN25. John Tiltman, the head of the military section at GC&CS, achieved an early breakthrough on JN25 when, by exploiting his experience with Japanese military attaché ciphers, he broke its additive cipher system. This enabled him to begin identifying the underlying codebook and his first recoveries were flown out to Singapore in September, leaving FECB to lead the subsequent attack on the book under Lieutenant Commander Malcolm Burnett. Progress proved slow, because of its complexity, and regular Japanese security changes. The original codebook, later named JN25A, changed on 1 December 1940 to JN25B, with more frequent changes to the cipher additive system, five during the life of JN25A. While these changes did not require a fresh start, each was a substantial check on progress towards readability, and despite later collaboration with the Americans, no operationally useful JN25 decrypts were achieved before the outbreak of war with Japan in December 1941. Nevertheless, the weaknesses in JN25 construction and use first identified by Tiltman were critical to Allied ability to read significant traffic in early 1942, creating the successes at the Coral Sea and Midway.[21] Meanwhile, in spring 1939 the Japanese also moved diplomatic traffic between Tokyo and their most important posts overseas, including Berlin, London and Washington, on to a sophisticated new cipher machine, arguably more complex than Enigma, which GC&CS could not break and the Americans christened 'Purple'. GC&CS, therefore, lost the critical Ōshima traffic between Berlin and Tokyo, and much else in the final months before the European war broke out, although Ōshima himself was posted back to Japan that September.[22]

Coverage of German naval traffic was dire. From the start of 1939 until the outbreak of war, GC&CS naval section had two officers and three clerks assigned to this target. None had cryptanalytic expertise and no systems were broken. Indeed, no German naval traffic had been read for twenty years. This embryonic German section therefore concentrated on building an overall picture of German naval communications and rudimentary traffic analysis. Following the outbreak of war, when most of the section moved to the OIC to form a traffic analysis section 8G, all that remained in GC&CS was two staff with a card index of German warship call-signs and files of encrypted signals intercepted over the last two years.[23]

However, by the mid 1930s, others in GC&CS — Foss, Strachey, Tiltman and Dilly Knox — were well aware that the German navy, like the army, and probably Luftwaffe too, was using a variant of the commercial Enigma machine for its main communications. Knox investigated German navy Enigma traffic collected in the Mediterranean in 1936–37 in parallel with his work on the Italian 'K' machine. He was helped by papers passed by the French through SIS in 1931 (obtained from their German agent Hans-Thilo Schmidt) which revealed that the Germans had added a 'plugboard', or *stecker*, to the basic machine, further enhancing its security. Although he had ideas to defeat this, he was ultimately stalled after the Germans introduced a new indicator system, the means of establishing an encrypted channel between sender and receiver, on 1 May 1937. Effort continued intermittently over the next eighteen months, encouraged by Knox's breakthrough on the Italian version, and renewed contacts with the French.[24] The last owed much to the close relationship established by the SIS representative in France, Wilfrid 'Biffy' Dunderdale, with Captain Gustave Bertrand, head of the French cryptanalytical department, the Section des Examens. Since 1931, Bertrand had continued to receive valuable intelligence from Schmidt (or Asché as the French called him), which in the absence of apparent British interest he had shared with the Poles. Although GC&CS might have been more proactive in responding to Bertrand's initial approaches, Germany was not a priority in 1931, they were formally barred by ministerial edict from discussing cryptography with the French and, until the Spanish civil war, for geographical reasons they intercepted little Enigma traffic.[25] Dunderdale, the son of a British naval engineer based in Odessa, spoke Russian fluently, as well as French, and was employed by NID as an interpreter during the intervention operations in 1919. His nickname derived from his prowess as a boxer during his naval service. He was a man of great charm and *savoir faire*, much admired later by Ian Fleming, who probably drew on him in creating his James Bond character. Dunderdale had cultivated Bertrand assiduously, despite the meagre interest from GC&CS, and as war loomed with the Munich crisis, this investment paid off. Over the next eighteen months, Bertrand's input, drawing on Schmidt and his relationship with the Poles, gave GC&CS critical new insights.[26] But his relationship with Dunderdale also proved vital in protecting the security of the operation against Enigma throughout the war.

At the end of 1938 Denniston assured Sinclair that Enigma was his top priority, although focus had shifted from the naval variant. GC&CS's 'best brains' were now attacking it at 'its weakest spot which is the machine used by the German army and air force'.[27] Denniston was correct that the naval variant was more challenging. All the variants were now introducing extra rotors for enhanced security, but whereas the army and air force selected three out of five, the navy used three out of eight. The naval machine's eight rotors could be arranged in 336 different ways, compared to just sixty for the army and air force.[28] However, as the new year opened GC&CS did not know what additional modifications the Germans had made, research into the non-naval versions was hampered by a dearth of intercepts, since at this time little non-naval Enigma traffic went by radio, and a trilateral meeting with the Poles, arranged by Bertrand in Paris, yielded nothing new. A vital breakthrough came in late July when the Poles arranged a further meeting at Pyry, outside Warsaw, with Bertrand and a British team comprising Denniston, Knox and Humphrey Sandwith from ID9. Knox was recovering from an operation for stomach cancer and suffering from influenza, but after meeting him in January, the Poles had specially asked for him, and he was determined to go.[29] Sandwith attended, following agreement between Godfrey and Sinclair, revealing their now close relationship.[30] Although Denniston later claimed puzzlement at Sandwith's presence, since he was not a cryptographer, he was there to discuss collaboration with the Poles on 'Y' collection and D/F in the Baltic, a subject Denniston had himself raised with Sandwith the previous month.[31] Sandwith met Waclaw Struszynski, head of D/F in the Polish state telecommunications department. This contact resulted in Struszynski being evacuated to the United Kingdom following the fall of Poland, where he made a critical contribution to the development of ship-borne HF/DF, and thus victory in the Battle of the Atlantic.[32]

More immediately, the Poles provided essential new insights into the wiring of the German Enigma variants used by their army and navy, and revealed the electromechanical devices, or 'bombes', they had devised rapidly to scan tens of thousands of combinations, and thus accelerate the search for the machine settings covering specific periods. They reported that they had read German navy traffic between Berlin and Spanish waters currently for a three-month period in early 1937. On 1 May they were defeated by the same indicator change that had stalled Knox, although they had achieved partial readability for the first few days of May using cribs, suggesting that with greater resources than the Poles had available, further progress on the naval variant might be possible, although it was also clear the Germans were constantly introducing security refinements. The most important single item of information the Poles provided was incredibly simple. They revealed that the Enigma keyboard keys were connected to the entry plate, giving access to the scrambler unit containing the rotors, in simple alphabetical order. Knox was furious that the Poles had made this intuitive leap. He ruefully acknowledged to Denniston that their colleague 'Mrs B. B.' had suggested this solution, but given the enormous number of permutations open to the Germans to increase security, Knox and Foss were convinced they would never do this, and her idea was never tried. If it had been, 'we should be teaching them', ie the Poles.[33]

This aside, the overall Polish revelations were readily understood by Knox from his earlier work, and he and the leading Polish cryptanalyst, Marian Rejewski, established a relationship of mutual respect. The latter later stated that Knox grasped everything 'quick as lightning', and it was evident 'the British really had been working on Enigma', with specialists of a 'different class' from the French.[34] Knox accordingly returned with promising new lines of attack. Indeed, applying the entry plate wiring enabled Peter Twinn to recover the rotor wheel wirings in a couple of hours, which had previously stalled everyone for months, and then to break sample Enigma messages provided by Bertrand from Asché. If Knox and others in the British team had acted on the suggestion by 'Mrs B. B.', and had earlier access to the Asché material, they would have at least matched the Polish achievements, perhaps advancing the successes against German air force and army Enigma in the first half of 1940 by many months. As it was, Denniston and Knox returned unsure they could overcome the latest German changes, let alone future modifications. Furthermore, because the Poles had focused primarily on German army Enigma, had retained some readability of this until December 1938, and had better understanding of the latest changes it incorporated, the attack on this variant retained priority within GC&CS over naval Enigma, just as war began.[35]

With German traffic unreadable, until the outbreak of war and their transfer to the OIC, Clarke's small German team under Malcolm Saunders concentrated on traffic analysis. Denniston later insisted that the wider study of German naval communications began in 1937, after Knox was obliged to abandon Enigma, and that the entire concept of traffic analysis derived from the work of the German team in the two years prior to war.[36] In practice, pre-war analysis focused on identifying and monitoring individual call-signs, and tracking movements through D/F plotting with the limited network then available. Useful supporting intelligence was gleaned from plain-language intercept, and some work was done on mapping the main naval frequencies. Despite valiant efforts, Saunders's team could not give the OIC a comprehensive map of the German navy communications organisation, or predict how it would change in wartime.[37] Nevertheless, important organisational principles were established for intercept and D/F, and research initiated, all of which delivered value later, giving Denniston's claim some validity. If D/F was to be properly targeted and deliver quality results, it was essential it was centrally controlled and closely linked with 'Y'-collection sites supported by a real-time communications infrastructure. Saunders also recognised the importance of co-ordinating D/F with aerial reconnaissance. Research initiated in this period included radio-fingerprinting (RFP), which filmed the type and peculiarities of a transmitter using a cathode ray oscilloscope, and TINA, a similar technique used to identify the Morse characteristics of individual wireless operators. However, it was well into 1940 before these delivered useful operational results. Discussion with the Admiralty Signal School also began in this period over the development of HF/DF, to enable its deployment on smaller warships.[38]

Inability to read any German, and most Japanese, naval traffic was compounded during Godfrey's early months and through the outbreak of war by ongoing debate over the division of responsibility between the OIC and GC&CS. Godfrey later claimed that he rapidly accepted that successful delivery of SIGINT required, 'bringing together its exponents under one roof', and that he accordingly agreed to 'concentrate all our resources at Bletchley Park', with means of rapid and secure dissemination through the OIC to frontline commanders.[39] The model finally achieved was never as clear-cut as Godfrey implied, and the journey towards it neither rapid, nor free from confusion. When the OIC was established in 1937, both James and Clarke assumed that in wartime it would absorb the GC&CS naval section, including its cryptographers, and expand to become the improved 'operationally focused' 1918-style ID25 they had both long advocated. Denniston was insistent that cryptographers must remain at GC&CS, but post-Munich had reluctantly conceded that the rest of naval section, now essentially focused on traffic analysis, should indeed move to the Admiralty. On the outbreak of war, this arrangement was implemented for Saunders's German team, who formed 8G within the OIC, leaving a purely nominal German presence within GC&CS, comprising one officer and one clerk, neither with cryptographic expertise. For Japan, cryptographic work on the naval target devolved to the FECB. Clarke's remaining five Japan staff could contribute nothing useful on operational intelligence for the OIC forming in Singapore, and therefore drifted away to support the Japan diplomatic section. His Italian operational intelligence group was earmarked for the Mediterranean OIC, but ultimately only a single officer transferred. Far from concentrating naval SIGINT at Bletchley Park, the start of the war, therefore, saw the GC&CS naval section reduced to an Italian cryptography and research unit supporting the Alexandria OIC, and its capability on Germany and Japan virtually eradicated.[40]

This outcome was partly due to the sheer difficulty of dividing up the overall SIGINT process, partly to the evolution of the peacetime relationship between the OIC and GC&CS, and partly the differing progress of naval SIGINT on the three Axis enemies, in turn intimately linked with the role of the new overseas OICs and the FECB. It also reflected wider conceptual issues, which perhaps even the ID25 survivors only partially recognised. When James and Clarke originally used the term 'operational intelligence', they generally meant current, or tactical, intelligence, and they also stressed the value of SIGINT without decryption, meaning D/F and traffic analysis, because they anticipated limited use of radio in wartime. This was the thinking that underpinned the origin of the OIC. By early 1939, Denning had a more precise and useful definition of operational intelligence. It was the intelligence which 'immediately affects any naval operation being or about to be undertaken'. The ideal was 'exact knowledge of the whereabouts of enemy warships and associated vessels at any particular time, whether in harbour or at sea, and their present and future intentions'. Denning wanted the GC&CS naval section analysts transferred within the OIC to achieve this and, although he recognised it was not feasible, would have liked the cryptographers too.[41] However, at this point Denning seriously underestimated the complexity of modern cryptography (as did most others in the intelligence community), and his definition also begged the question of who would do the wider long-term research, enabling SIGINT to contribute more strategically. Furthermore, as Clarke certainly appreciated, isolating the cryptographers from the operational context would compromise their effectiveness. Successful cryptography relied on understanding its operational use, on the right targeted collection, and on its intimate relationship with traffic analysis.[42]

Apart from TR16, SIS had at least one established agent regularly reporting German navy movements at Wilhelmshaven during 1939, and several under development. The Wilhelmshaven reports continued after the outbreak of war, suggesting the agent(s) had neutral nationality and were run out of Denmark or Holland.[43] In addition, there were some opportunistic reports on naval requirements, either from liaison services, or the by-product of sources focused elsewhere. SIS's wider political reporting from Munich through the first half of 1939 was also important in guiding the Admiralty on German intentions. It did not provide a complete picture, but was impressive and substantially correct, leaving little doubt that Germany would move against Poland, thereby triggering war with Britain before the end of the year.[44]

Furthermore, Godfrey's early meetings with Sinclair occurred just as SIS was contemplating investment in a new intelligence capability, covert aerial photography. Godfrey saw the value of this as an additional source in peacetime, but also understood that aerial surveillance was now an essential intelligence asset in wartime. Taking his lead from William James's comment in 1937, he soon presented it as the modern equivalent of Nelson's frigates keeping watch off French ports.[45] His early inquiries confirmed that the Royal Navy was effectively barred from conducting land-based reconnaissance under the 1936 agreement establishing the Fleet Air Arm, while RAF capability had atrophied during the interwar period.

The SIS project, supervised by the head of Sinclair's air section, Frederick Winterbotham, began as a joint venture with the French Deuxième Bureau, negotiated through Biffy Dunderdale, and flights commenced over eastern and southern Germany in March 1939, using an American Lockheed 12A procured by SIS. SIS also recruited a pilot, Sidney Cotton, an Australian who had served in the RNAS in the First World War. Cotton, now in his mid forties, was a maverick who combined outstanding flying skills, a genius for invention, a passionate interest in photography, and a love of travel and adventure. His aviation innovations began at the start of his career in the First World War, when he created the one-piece Sidcot flying suit. He was ideally suited to the role of SIS agent, where his talents readily embraced the ability to adopt convincing covers. However, he was never going to fit easily into a conventional military structure and, sadly, once war began, the air force proved incapable of accommodating him, and although he did more than anyone else to put Britain's wartime photographic reconnaissance (PR) capability on the road to outstanding success, his further potential was lost.[46]

Godfrey met Cotton in April, after learning of the proposed flights from Dunderdale, when he visited Paris in January.[47] His interest may have been further spurred by Hall briefing him on the reconnaissance flights planned over German naval bases in November 1918. Cotton vented his frustrations with the French, convincing Godfrey that, with a free hand, he could deliver better results, including on naval targets.

Godfrey accordingly encouraged Sinclair to back independent operations, and contributed funds towards SIS purchase of an additional aircraft for exclusive British use. Cotton modified this to his own specifications, giving it longer range and advanced cameras capable of stereoscopic photography. In early June, at Godfrey's request, he conducted an initial photographic surveillance flight in the new aircraft along the Irish west coast, looking for signs of covert German activity, an updated version of Hall's *Sayonara* escapade. Later in the month he flew out to Malta, from where, over a two-week period, he photographed Italian naval and air sites of interest in Sicily and most Italian Mediterranean islands, before moving on to cover the territories of the Italian empire in north and east Africa, purporting to be scouting new passenger routes for British Imperial Airways. Following this outstanding sortie, he conducted flights over Germany under business cover in August, on one occasion inviting the commandant of Tempelhof airfield for a joyride, operating the concealed cameras in the wings with remarkable sangfroid as they flew together down the Rhine, with his guest oblivious to the real purpose of the outing. The German operation culminated in three flights over Wilhelmshaven to photograph naval targets in the final days before the outbreak of war, confirming, to the relief of the OIC, that most major German warships were still there. Some of those spotted were out of sight of shore and consequently not accessible to SIS ship-watchers.[48]

As a demonstration of the potential contribution aerial photography using the latest techniques could make to naval intelligence requirements, Cotton's achievements under SIS over three months were outstanding. However, set-piece covert flights in peacetime were one thing, constant monitoring of naval targets in the hostile conditions of wartime quite another. SIS and Cotton could not possibly take this on with the tiny resources available to them. Nor, it transpired for quite some while, could the RAF, despite much valuable advice from Cotton.[49]

Given the limitations of reporting from GC&CS and SIS, the performance of the OIC in monitoring German and Italian order of battle and movements in the final six months of peace was variable. From 1 April it presented these in a daily report for the naval staff, also incorporating Spanish and Japanese developments where relevant. It successfully tracked the major German deployment for exercises off western Iberia from mid April to mid May, primarily through traffic analysis, correctly identifying that this included all three pocket battleships, two light cruisers, two destroyer divisions, two submarine depot ships and six U-boats (two Type IX and four Type VIIB). However, existing traffic analysis could not reveal that a primary purpose for the U-boats was to explore Dönitz's ideas for wolf-pack and night surface attack.[50] The cruise of the battlecruiser *Gneisenau* between mid June and mid July, ranging as far south as the Cape Verde Islands, was also accurately covered. Following her return, Denning reported accumulating evidence from his monitoring of warship and merchant movements that the German navy would be on a war footing by mid August.[51] However, crucially, the OIC then missed the contingency deployments for attacks on Atlantic shipping following a British and French declaration of war. The pocket battleship *Graf Spee*, heading for the South Atlantic, and fourteen ocean-capable U-boats sailed on the night of 19 August, all transiting well to the north of United Kingdom waters. *Graf Spee*'s sister, *Deutschland*, and the supply ship *Westerwald* left four days later for a waiting area to the south of Greenland, and four more U-boats sailed before 30 August. These deployments were well-planned with minimal radio traffic, and none were detected, either on departure or during transit, although the OIC did note the disappearance of *Graf Spee*'s supply ship, the naval tanker *Altmark*, after she left Port Arthur in Texas on 19 August. The OIC admitted on 26 August it had little information on U-boat whereabouts, but it believed there were six U-boats in the Atlantic ready to commence operations. It did not suspect a surface-raider at large in the South Atlantic until *Graf Spee* sank her first victim, *Clement*, on 30 September, and the probability of a second raider was not identified until early November. For many weeks after *Clement*, the culprit was believed to be the third pocket battleship, *Admiral Scheer*, which was actually in long refit.[52]

Meanwhile, at the end of June, Godfrey was one of several British officials who met Lieutenant Colonel Gerhard von Schwerin, head of the British section within the intelligence division of the German general staff. Schwerin, tasked to take informal soundings in London to test the strength of the British guarantee to Poland, was introduced by Major General Henry Pownall, Director of Military Operations and Intelligence. He pressed his British interlocutors for a demonstration of British resolve, suggesting despatch of an air striking force to France, a major naval deployment to the Baltic, or the recall of Churchill to government, none of which options appealed to Prime Minister Neville Chamberlain. Von Schwerin later claimed to have departed convinced that Britain would fight, but that he was not believed in Berlin.[53]

Overall, the first six months of Godfrey's tenure leading up to the outbreak of war saw no major new intelligence insights on Britain's three prospective enemies. His achievements in this final period of peace were essentially organisational and structural. NID continued introducing and recreating important capabilities on which it could build, notably the

OIC and its satellites and the D/F network, and there was an increasingly sophisticated wider intelligence community to draw on in support. However, the current flow of intelligence was meagre, and what little there was reduced further on the outbreak of war.

The interwar period in retrospect

If capacity-building rather than intelligence insight marked Godfrey's early months, that is also true of the wider interwar period, both for naval intelligence specifically, and the British intelligence record more generally. The central achievement of these two decades was the creation of a more modern intelligence community with the formation of a single SIGINT agency and the 'Y' structures to support it, the further evolution of SIS, the arrival of interdepartmental organisations: the most important the JIC, but also the IIC and the FECB, and within NID itself, the long-sought OIC. In 1939 most of these new structures had yet to demonstrate their real potential. Within each of the armed services there were lobbies keen to see GC&CS broken up, with cryptography resumed on a single-service basis. The JIC and IIC were still peripheral bodies rather than central to policy-making. Certainly, through the 1930s, this emerging community had not contributed naval intelligence that matched the quality and consistency of that produced on Germany in the five years before 1914.

Nevertheless, the contribution of interwar naval intelligence should not be downplayed too far. The combination of diplomatic and attaché reporting, SIGINT (naval and diplomatic) on Japan and Italy, and SIS insights on Germany, provided the Royal Navy with an adequate picture of the fighting capability of its three potential opponents as of September 1939, if little on the strategy and tactics they would deploy in war. The intelligence picture acquired through these sources guided a Royal Navy rearmament programme, which matched the combined Axis naval output over the period 1935–42, and proved more appropriate to the demands of the coming war. British investment strategy was better than either Germany, which was too slow in committing to U-boats, or Japan, which completely ignored the potential submarine threat to its supply lines until 1943. The same intelligence picture helped Britain navigate the naval limitation process as well as could reasonably be achieved, within the political and economic constraints she faced. She remained the strongest maritime power until 1942, avoided a ruinous competition with the United States, and, by working with her, prevented Japan from building as large a navy as she would have done otherwise, giving the democracies just enough margin to cope in the critical years 1942–43.[54]

PART IV

The Second World War: The Height of the Intelligence Art?

21

Living on Thin Gruel: Winter 1939–1940

Britain's second great naval war of the twentieth century, which began on 3 September 1939 and lasted almost exactly six years, appears superficially to have similarities with the earlier conflict, but there were fundamental differences. It was only briefly an exclusively German war, and for the first year the German navy, constrained by geography and a strength still below that of Britain's ally France, was more a nuisance than the serious challenge it posed in 1914. German air power partly compensated for its naval weakness, enabling her to contest control of the North Sea, and from spring 1940 a wider stretch of inshore waters from mid Norway to Biscay, but in this early period Germany alone could not overcome Britain's wider maritime control. Although the balance of air power contributed, this control was critical in securing Britain against the immediate existential threat of invasion in late summer 1940. Thereafter, as Dönitz had argued since the mid 1930s, Germany's best hope of defeating Britain, as in 1917, lay in breaking her maritime power through a U-boat siege, but deploying greater numbers and modern tactics. However, the slow build-up of the U-boat force, which did not increase at all in the first year of the war, implied a long battle of attrition, assuming Dönitz acquired the resources.

In countering Germany as her most dangerous enemy, British calculations from the beginning of the war were complicated by the risk that Germany would be joined by one or both of her Axis allies, who as major naval powers threatened the security of Britain's wider empire. This global naval challenge was long foreseen, but vastly complicated by the early defeat of France, which gave Germany valuable bases to access the Atlantic, and triggered Italy's entry into the war. Italy was strong enough, with German support, to contest control of the Mediterranean, all of North Africa, and potentially the Middle East. Britain briefly contemplated naval withdrawal from the Mediterranean, but did not do so for three main reasons. It risked extending German control into Spain and northwest Africa, further complicating the defence of Atlantic supply lines, and bringing Turkey into her orbit. Retaining a strong base in the eastern Mediterranean preserved British influence, denied Germany vital resources, above all Middle East oil, and created opportunities to wear Germany down, a key element in British strategic thinking from late 1940, and perhaps collapse Italy. Finally, by 1941 Britain also understood that containing Germany and Italy depended on protecting and mobilising the war potential of her eastern empire, which added about 25 per cent to her fighting power. This goal required control of the Indian Ocean, which in the first months of 1942 was threatened by Japan.

By the end of 1941, therefore, the Royal Navy faced a truly global naval war, more complex, demanding and costly than that of 1914–18, which had focused predominantly on Germany and a theatre largely confined to the North Sea and Western Approaches, with the Dardanelles in 1915 the only major diversion overseas. This global engagement is demonstrated by the fact that half the Royal Navy's losses occurred in the Mediterranean between mid 1940 and mid 1943, and that it deployed a larger fleet to the Indian Ocean in early 1942 than it had in any theatre previously. Its strength, resilience, flexibility and global reach is especially evident in 1942 when, despite being fully engaged in the Battle of the Atlantic, then at its height, and running Arctic convoys to Russia, it successively deployed a significant Eastern Fleet; planned major reinforcements for that fleet; projected a substantial expeditionary force 7000 miles from the United Kingdom to seize Madagascar in May; mounted the immensely complex Pedestal operation at the other end of Africa to relieve Malta, using some of the same forces, just two months later; and finally mobilised 160 warships, including seven carriers, for the Torch landings in November.[1]

A comprehensive account of this global war is beyond the scope of this book, which again focuses solely on how and where British naval intelligence shaped the struggle at sea and the wider war, and the impact it achieved. Although the contribution of naval intelligence in the Second World War has received far more scrutiny than the First, coverage and emphasis has been selective in two important respects. First, it has been strongly biased towards the Atlantic theatre, and above all the U-boat war, with much less attention given to the Mediterranean and, with a few notable exceptions, hardly any to the Eastern theatre. Secondly is the emphasis on, and fascination with, the contribution of Enigma-generated Ultra, leading to an enduring perception that it had dominant influence on British and Allied success. There remains limited awareness of the relatively narrow windows of naval Enigma dominance, or the relative importance of other intelligence sources, such as HF/DF, aerial photographic reconnaissance and, from 1941, prisoner interrogation. Equally important is under-recognition of the impact of German successes in the naval information war in the period 1939–42.

Another issue relevant to the naval intelligence contribution from 1939 requires emphasis. British ambitions for blockade as a weapon against Germany in the new war broadly paralleled those in 1914, but preparations were more extensive and mature, drawing on the interwar bodies established to study aspects of economic warfare. This time a new Ministry of Economic Warfare (MEW) was established immediately, with responsibility for policy, intelligence and action relating to blockade and wider economic attack. The Admiralty was just one Whitehall participant in pre-war blockade planning from the mid 1930s, rather than the central driver it had been before 1914, and it was Desmond Morton's IIC, rather than NID, that formed MEW's initial intelligence capability. However, while blockade plans were ambitious and a panoply of measures – export control, Navicerts, negotiations with neutrals, drawing on experience in 1914–18 – were rapidly instituted, 'activity did not equate with impact'. Implementation was initially hesitant, and the first nine months of the war saw a form of contraband control arguably milder than 1914–15, reflecting the same constraints and pressures. The requirement not to alienate key neutrals like the United States was similar, but the risk of triggering intervention by Italy, Japan, or even the Soviet Union made the politics more difficult while the Nazi-Soviet pact further undermined the effectiveness of any blockade. Germany's conquest of Western Europe by mid 1940, and the entry of Italy into the war, removed many of the constraints on British action, but by giving Germany ready access to resources across the Continent, ensured that, with one critical exception, blockade could never achieve the same impact it had after 1916. The critical exception was the Royal Navy's role in denying Germany the ability to transport oil through the eastern Mediterranean from Romania or the Soviet Union, to access Iraqi oil, or deny Persian oil to Britain. Nevertheless, for all these reasons, blockade in the new war was never the primary preoccupation for the Royal Navy and British naval intelligence that it had been in the First.[2]

NID strength at the Admiralty following mobilisation on 3 September was about two-thirds that at the armistice twenty years earlier, although with GC&CS naval section included, numbers were comparable. The OIC and NID9 absorbed about half this strength. The structure of the remainder of the Admiralty-based division equated broadly to that of 1922. There were still six geographic sections, although with some redistribution of responsibilities. The three most important were NID1, covering Germany and Scandinavia; NID3, covering Italy and the eastern Mediterranean; and NID4, covering Japan and the Far East. Of the others, NID2 covered France and the Low Countries; NID 5, Home Waters and the Americas; and NID11, Russia and the Balkans. NID6 was a relatively new press section; NID7 covered technical intelligence; and NID10 security and British naval codes and ciphers. In addition to the new OICs at Alexandria and Singapore, the 1922 overseas network had expanded slightly, with further intelligence centres at Istanbul, Suez, Freetown and Basra. By mid 1943, changing circumstances added further centres at Algiers, Diego Suarez in Madagascar, Kilindini in Kenya, and Bombay. Feeding the intelligence centres was a network of reporting officers mobilised at the start of the war in three hundred ports across the world. At the end of September, the total staff working directly on naval intelligence requirements in London, at Bletchley Park, the two regional OICs, the overseas intelligence centres, and the 'Y' and D/F sites, home and overseas, but excluding the overseas reporting officers, was at least five hundred.[3]

As foreshadowed in the last chapter, the already limited intelligence available to NID on Germany fell sharply on the outbreak of war. SIGINT, SIS agent coverage and aerial photographic surveillance faced operational and organisational problems that took many months to resolve. Diplomatic and attaché reporting from neutral countries provided some useful background information on naval issues, but little of immediate operational value. The adjustment of the wider intelligence community to the demands of war was hampered by the death of Sinclair from cancer of the spleen. 'First bulletin. Nearly dead,' he famously messaged a friend on the morning of 4 November and died that afternoon. After a hiatus of over three weeks he was succeeded by his deputy, Stewart Menzies. Menzies was Sinclair's own recommendation, but other candidates including Godfrey, other intelligence personnel from the armed forces, and even William Wiseman were considered. Inevitably, Churchill, now back as First Lord, intervened, stressing that it was 'customary' for the post to go to a naval officer, but then unjustifiably criticising Sinclair for permitting a reduction in the intelligence service to the Admiralty in his 'declining years'. This reflected a simplistic comparison between his recollection of SIGINT coverage in 1914, and the present cryptographic 'blank'. Instead of Godfrey, he proffered the eccentric choice of Gerard Muirhead-Gould, the Berlin attaché from 1933–36, with whom he had corresponded over the Anglo-German naval agreement. Alexander Cadogan, who rapidly established Muirhead-Gould was totally unsuited, grumbled that Churchill ought to have plenty to do, without 'butting into other people's business'.[4] Menzies was politically canny, a safe pair of hands with a good grasp of the core business of SIS, and crucially gained the enduring confidence of Churchill when he became prime minister six months later. However, he lacked the inspirational and visionary leadership, and wider strategic insight often displayed by Sinclair and never achieved the same commanding presence in the power centres of Whitehall. He also lacked Sinclair's instinctive management and organisational skills, qualities desperately needed as GC&CS transitioned from a staff of two hundred in September 1939, to the immensely complex operation employing around nine thousand people by 1945.[5]

Before Menzies' appointment was confirmed, Godfrey briefed him on NID's primary requirements two months into the war. These were not just relevant to SIS, but reveal the dominant naval intelligence issues that winter. Top of the list was the whereabouts of the main German warships. Here, Godfrey questioned whether SIGINT would ever deliver the coverage of German movements available in the previous war, and accordingly stressed the importance of establishing agents in the main German bases. SIS had evidently maintained some coverage of Wilhelmshaven following the outbreak of war, apparently from a source in a ship based there, or more likely in a neutral vessel visiting, but the reports were infrequent and proved unreliable. They placed two pocket battleships in Wilhelmshaven on 8 October, when only *Admiral Scheer* was still in German waters, and *Graf Spee* in Wilhelmshaven on 13 October and 20 November, when she was actually raiding in the South Atlantic.[6] Godfrey also underlined the desirability of intelligence, including, ideally, documents, from German naval headquarters, perhaps displaying awareness of the high-level German naval documents acquired in 1914. The next requirement was German shipping movements, warship and merchant, at the entrance to the Baltic and in sight of the Danish, Norwegian and Swedish coasts. Coverage of Swedish iron ore shipments to Germany, vital at this time to her war industries, from the northern Norwegian port of Narvik south through Norwegian coastal waters, was important in facilitating Royal Navy interception. Godfrey claimed that only eight SIS reports had been received since the start of the war on movements through the Baltic entrances, and only three on the Norwegian coastal traffic, although SIS subsequently insisted there had been forty-nine of the latter.

Godfrey's third priority, on which he was under constant pressure from the naval staff, was U-boat construction. NID still did not know whether Germany had embarked on a substantial building programme using the mass-production methods first noted by TR16 in 1936, or was concentrating resources elsewhere. Although Godfrey did not inform Menzies, this lack of intelligence caused NID seriously to overestimate U-boat strength through the winter. This overestimation originated with the late 1938 assessment that some U-boat production runs had been secretly duplicated, leading NID to set strength at sixty-six boats on the outbreak of war, nine more than the reality. Without corrective intelligence, NID felt obliged to assume a dramatic rise in output from the outbreak of war, reflecting the IIC's long-standing assessment of German war mobilisation capacity, numbers of U-boats believed on the stocks in summer 1939, and production at the start of the previous war, with forty-seven U-boats then completed in fourteen months. It therefore initially projected a strength of 129 by end March 1940, later adjusted to 109 by July, before allowing for losses.[7]

Godfrey's fourth priority was the readiness of German naval units, although he recognised this was difficult to cover. Fifth was progress on construction of the battleship *Bismarck* and other major warships on the stocks. Knowing when these would become operational was crucial to planning the Royal Navy's own capital shipbuilding programme. Finally, he wanted intelligence on German mines, especially their new magnetic mine, which was inflicting significant casualties. This last requirement was met without help from SIS, just days after Godfrey wrote to Menzies, when a magnetic mine was recovered intact after it was dropped by a German aircraft in mudflats off Shoeburyness in the Thames Estuary, allowing a detailed examination and development of countermeasures.[8]

As Godfrey implied to Menzies, and Churchill complained in parallel to Cadogan, the initial SIGINT contribution to naval requirements was not promising. As agreed post-Munich, the bulk of GC&CS German section under Saunders moved to the OIC to form 8G, tasked with supplying operational intelligence from traffic analysis. It was also responsible for giving GC&CS regular summaries of the main German operational plot kept by Denning in 8E.[9] Reinforced with German-speaking academic recruits identified pre-war, 8G had a strength of six and worked closely with six D/F plotters, designated 8X. One new 8G arrival, the former travel agent and Olympic sailor Allon Bacon, recruited for his fluent German, was destined, as described later, to have an especially adventurous war.[10] Clarke's residual naval section in GC&CS was left with twenty-five staff, soon almost entirely focused on Italy, although it was still the largest armed forces section.

Meanwhile, Humphrey Sandwith directed the naval 'Y' service, providing an interception and D/F capability to meet naval operational requirements. Formally, as agreed in the 1920s, 'Y' stations and staff were provided by Director Signals Division to meet the requirements of DNI. The combination of secrecy surrounding 'Y work' and limited resources during the interwar period meant Sandwith entered the war running a joint section NID9/DSD9 responsible to two masters. As NID9 he identified DNI's requirements for 'Y' intercept and D/F, heavily influenced by GC&CS naval section, and as DSD9 he then met those requirements, drawing on the resources of Signals Division. In practice, by exploiting the superior status of DNI within the naval staff, for the first three years of the war Sandwith effectively ran a private operation. As DSD9, he recruited and trained his own staff, male and female, and extended, built, equipped and operated his own stations to provide communications intelligence. Even more ambitiously, but crucially, his section initiated a ship-fitting operation to install HF/DF and radio-telephone (R/T) interception equipment and train requisite operators. Inevitably, the ever greater needs of this 'Y' service created tensions within Signals Division, which faced many other demands, and was not privy to DSD9's outputs. Sandwith and Godfrey proved adept at managing these, although as the war progressed, parts of the 'Y' operation were transferred to the conventional Admiralty administrative structures. They proved equally adept at ensuring that various schemes launched by the other two services to reform 'Y' management and delivery did not harm what worked for the navy.

Preserving what worked mattered, because the naval 'Y' service was uniquely effective. Sandwith's personal expertise and leadership were key, but even more important was the collaborative way in which naval SIGINT structures developed during 1939–40. The cryptographer's ideal, and that of the traffic analyst, or D/F plotter, was to receive the maximum number of versions of every enemy transmission from different stations. During the war there were never enough 'Y' receivers to meet all demands, so understanding of requirements, and compromise were essential. At the start, GC&CS staff knew little of communications, and NID staff, including NID9, even less of cryptography. Not the least of Godfrey's achievements was to ensure a remarkably open relationship between the 'Y' service, the OIC and GC&CS naval section. This helped all parties understand what their colleagues needed and why, and stimulated more ideas for getting results than would have happened in a more closed system. There were still recriminations, with every section at times convinced its counterparts were staffed by lunatics. But they usually judged them amiable lunatics, whose aberrations were regarded with amusement rather than anger. This team environment proved crucial both to breaking naval Enigma, and then to exploiting it to advantage.

NID9/DSD9 began the war with a 'Y' operation for intercept and D/F, comprising about fifty receivers spread across twenty stations, home and overseas. The principal 'Y' sites in the United Kingdom remained Scarborough and Flowerdown. The former, starting with twenty receivers of multiple types, specialised in intercepting German traffic, but also controlled a homebased D/F network of seven HF stations and five MF, with the number of these almost doubling by 1942. Scarborough could intercept virtually all German traffic within the Atlantic area. German shore-station transmissions were powerful, ships' messages were invariably repeated by the control station, and usually repeated several times on HF, and in the case of U-boats, by very low frequency (VLF), as well. Flowerdown initially specialised in Italian traffic, but also covered most other targets of interest, notably Japanese, French, Spanish, Portuguese, Swedish and Russian. To provide back-up, smaller intercept stations were commissioned at Chicksands and Cupar in spring 1940. Until the outbreak of war with Italy in June 1940, Malta was the primary 'Y' intercept site in the Mediterranean, but its potential vulnerability resulted in new sites being established at Alexandria and Gibraltar. The Dominions had 'Y' sites at Ottawa, Esquimalt, Melbourne, and Simonstown in South Africa. By 1942 there were further 'Y' sites at Freetown, Kilindini in Kenya, Bermuda, Polarnoe in North Russia, and New Zealand. The overseas D/F stations available to cover the German naval target in its likely areas of operation in 1939 were Halifax, Montreal and Bermuda on the western side of the Atlantic, Gibraltar, and Simonstown in South Africa. By end 1942, the global D/F network overseas under British Empire control had risen to around fifty stations. Despite a significant recruitment and training effort since Munich, the 'Y' network, both home and overseas, remained desperately short of staff, less than two hundred on mobilisation, but increasing to more than a thousand within eighteen months, and 5500 by early 1945.[11]

On the outbreak of war, the German navy ceased using peacetime call-signs and shifted traffic to new frequencies, while plain-language transmissions virtually ceased. Furthermore, it soon became evident that 90 per cent of German radio traffic was encrypted with Enigma, on which GC&CS anticipated no early progress. Whereas the German army only used Enigma down to division level, the navy used it for all but the humblest craft.[12] This widespread Enigma deployment ruled out decryption of German traffic as a major British naval intelligence source, at least for the present, although for the Germans it ultimately proved a vulnerability. Accordingly, 8G struggled to deliver operationally useful results. It began by mapping traffic density against frequencies. With help from D/F, it then identified the location of the main naval shore stations, and by defining the areas where specific frequencies were used, distinguished U-boat from surface-warship transmissions. Over time, this distinction helped illuminate deployment patterns, and it was fundamental to all future traffic analysis work on the German navy. By linking traffic patterns with known operational events, 8G could potentially alert the OIC when similar activity appeared to be underway, but until well into 1940, even with growing support from a reviving GC&CS German naval section, this remained an imperfect science. In addition, 8G began identifying aircraft working with the German navy in this period, and could occasionally warn of their use in impending operations.[13]

In the absence of a break into Enigma, it was assumed that standard D/F was the aspect of SIGINT most likely to deliver operational value, especially in locating and tracking U-boats, even if they were more sparing in their use of radio. By the start of the war, the United Kingdom communications infrastructure was sufficiently mature to allow the home-based D/F stations to be directed and controlled by the primary 'Y' stations at Scarborough and Flowerdown. Scarborough, which led on German operations in the Atlantic, collected bearings from the individual home sites, sometimes up to a dozen within minutes, and telephoned filtered results to the D/F plotting section in the OIC, designated 8X, headed by Peter Kemp. Bearings from overseas D/F sites were signalled directly to the Admiralty, sometimes incurring significant delay. Section 8X operated on a twenty-four-hour basis, and although it supported both Denning's surface plot (8E), and the submarine tracking room (8S), it was collocated with the latter first in the Admiralty basement, and thereafter the Citadel.[14]

Despite the professionalism and ingenuity of the Scarborough and 8X teams, the quality of D/F fixes proved consistently disappointing, and optimistic illusions regarding their accuracy were shattered early in the war. Initially, it was the exception when a fix fell within a fifty-mile radius, but from 1942, sites in Iceland and the Azores, which delivered excellent cross-bearings, brought substantial improvement. So did checking D/F fixes against German U-boat position reports, acquired through decryption in the second half of 1941, although achieving D/F fixes of U-boat single-group short signals and short weather signals was extremely difficult, because they only lasted ten seconds. Overall, despite increased numbers of carefully sited stations, containing carefully calibrated equipment with errors theoretically reduced to half a degree, and later the application of mathematical filtering, expert studies from 1942 demonstrated that a good operator was nine-tenths of the battle. In taking and plotting D/F bearings, skill and experience mattered more than gadgets and quantity. D/F as practised from 1939–45 was therefore more art than science and the art took a long time to learn. Nevertheless, practice of the art did steadily improve and D/F, both land-based and ship-borne, became an essential accompaniment to intelligence from decryption.[15]

On mobilisation, the cream of Denniston's new cryptographic recruits, Turing, Twinn, Jeffries and Welchman, joined a research section led by Knox in the Cottage, an annex to the main house at Bletchley Park, initially to capitalise on the recent Polish gifts from Pyry, and to focus on army and air force Enigma, judged the simplest variants. Over the next nine months, with some further Polish and French assistance, they made substantial progress, breaking settings using hand methods for over one hundred days spread across four different keys, one army (named Green by GC&CS), two air force (Red and Blue), and a special key for the Norwegian campaign, primarily used by the air force (Yellow). In April the first British bombe, designed by Turing and Welchman, became operational. Although this partly exploited Enigma insights shared by the Poles at Pyry, it was conceptually entirely different from their *bomba* machine scanner shown to Denniston and Knox. By now, it was clear that Green could seldom be broken and that the priority for the new bombe should be the primary air force key Red, which covered most of its operational and military traffic. From 22 May, GC&CS broke the Red settings and read its traffic daily and currently, with few interruptions until the end of the war.[16]

These successes triggered reorganisation anticipated by Edward Travis, now Denniston's deputy, the previous November. Encouraged by Welchman, he drew a distinction between Enigma research, and the complex production pipeline required to intercept, decrypt and process traffic, potentially available in industrial quantities, in order to deliver useful intelligence.[17] On the cryptographic side, with no immediate prospect of further progress on the Green army key or naval Enigma, Knox moved to work on, and ultimately break, newly discovered Italian naval Enigma traffic, which used an improved version of the 1937 'K' machine, and then Abwehr Enigma traffic. As described later, both these successes brought important contributions to naval operations. Abwehr traffic not only revealed its naval operations and sources, but became a cornerstone of much of the successful British deception work over the last three years of the war, which often impacted at the strategic level. Meanwhile, the rapidly expanding Red air force cryptographic production effort, along with army attack, moved to Hut 6, one of several newly constructed huts in the Bletchley Park grounds, first under Jeffries, and then Welchman. A second small team, comprising Turing and Twinn and two assistants, established a new naval Enigma attack team in Hut 8. Turing had already played a starring role in the wider Enigma attack, including the design of the bombe, but from early autumn 1939 was gripped by the naval challenge, partly because 'it would be so interesting to break it', and partly because 'no-one else was doing anything about it and I could have it to myself'.[18] He accordingly began (as a spare-time project) picking up where the Poles had left their naval attack in 1937. He replicated their work with cribs on the May traffic, and by the end of the year had a provisional solution to the new indicator system with which, following additional insights from prisoner interrogation, he successfully broke several days of November 1938 traffic, but the current key still defeated him.[19]

Beginning in January 1940, an organisation was also established to process army and air force decrypts emanating first from the Cottage, and then Hut 6. Many of the challenges here were familiar to Denniston and other Room 40 survivors. Decrypts had to be translated, corruptions and ambiguities resolved, and sense made of numerous unfamiliar names, organisations, abbreviations and codewords. This intelligence processing was undertaken by a new inter-service section located in Hut 3. Although it dealt with no naval material, Malcolm Saunders came back from 8G to head it, because he was the only GC&CS officer with requisite experience who was fluent in German. To preserve the security of Enigma decryption, extraordinary security measures were taken, which paralleled those with Room 40 in 1914. In April 1940 there were only thirty people indoctrinated into Enigma outside GC&CS and SIS. Within Bletchley, there were strict internal access controls, and Hut 3 was denied access to Hut 6. Hut 3's exploitation was also kept independent of the GC&CS army and air sections, and it was permitted no direct contact with MI sections or air intelligence, which indeed did not know it existed. Instead, dissemination of intelligence was controlled by SIS, which circulated reports to a limited group of customers, including the OIC in the Admiralty, in carefully sanitised form to suggest they originated from human sources. This arrangement brought tight security, but also replicated the disadvantages of the early Room 40 system. Enigma intelligence could not be linked with other sources, and many of the subject experts in the army and air force best placed to exploit it were denied it.[20]

Although there was very little intelligence from naval Enigma until spring 1941, the system that evolved to handle and develop it, almost from the very start of the war, differed in crucial respects. Several former members of Room 40 were recalled to the GC&CS naval section in September 1939, notably Nigel de Grey, Frank Birch and Herbert Hope, now a retired rear admiral. Clarke wanted Hope to lead the whole naval effort at GC&CS, creating a modern ID25 to feed the OIC. This begged fundamental questions about the relationship between GC&CS and the OIC, but the concept of putting a senior naval officer in charge had merit. If Godfrey and Denniston had found someone similar to Clayton, it could have worked, but Hope now lacked the aptitude and energy, instead briefly replacing Saunders at 8G, after the latter returned to run Hut 3.[21] Birch, who had spent much of the interwar period as a pantomime artist, hence acquiring the nickname 'Widow Twankey', proved more successful at rebuilding a German navy section, following departure of the 8G team to the Admiralty. He took over on 5 September with strict instructions that the task of German section was now entirely 'cryptographic', and 'operational intelligence' not his business.[22] This initially posed challenges, with Denniston casually commenting that all German naval codes were 'unbreakable', a view Birch soon found widely shared.[23] Birch had no cryptographers, and his brief apparently overlapped with Knox's Enigma team, where attack on the military and air force variants had precedence and, initially, nobody could help with naval attack. Furthermore, cryptographic attack, whether on Enigma or other systems, required detailed knowledge of German navy radio networks and practices. But this was now undertaken by 8G, which also had the only pre-war German section staff with any cryptographic experience, and was already investigating simpler German naval air and merchant ship codes. The result was confusion, messy overlaps, and disputes over demarcation for the next nine months, although the underlying truth was that cryptography and traffic analysis were indivisible.

Birch effectively started from scratch and, not surprisingly, later described the cryptographic effort on German naval intercepts in the early months as 'feeble, spasmodic and dispersed'. However, he proved an adept and determined political operator, and by the beginning of 1940, his new team settled in Hut 4 were making progress. With GC&CS the undisputed cryptographic centre, he quickly got their two 8G cryptographers transferred back to him and, supported by new recruits, focused them on reading the 10 per cent of traffic using hand systems. These only occasionally yielded useful intelligence, but were important in understanding the overall German naval communications system, and potentially offered cribs with which to attack Enigma itself. Birch was clear that naval Enigma was the overriding priority, convinced it could be broken 'because it had to be', and his long-standing relationship with Denniston and Knox gave him privileged access to ongoing Enigma research. He soon spotted that he could collaborate with Turing in getting work started on the naval problem. He did not fully understand, and certainly underestimated, the complexities involved, and the challenge of keeping Turing, who was a hopeless communicator and loved diverging down rabbit holes, focused.[24] But he provided Turing with a home in Hut 4, until Hut 8 became available, and the benefit of his team's evolving research on German naval communications, which was essential to effective cryptographic attack. Crucially, he also recognised the importance of bombe capacity, not just to progress the naval attack, but to the whole Enigma operation. With support from Travis, he fought a relentless campaign to get this increased, despite inertia from Denniston and Menzies. Told of all the difficulties in producing bombes – cost, lack of skilled labour and shortage of electrical power, he responded succinctly: 'Tot up the difficulties and balance them against the value to the nation of being able to read current Enigma'.[25]

The close relationship established between Birch and Turing continued after the naval cryptographic team were installed in Hut 8. Although administratively the relationship between Huts 8 and 4 was supposed to parallel that between Huts 6 and 3, in practice they operated as a single unit with free movement and exchange between them. This openness extended in the other direction too. When the first naval Enigma messages were broken over a brief period from May 1940, they were processed by Birch's team in Hut 4 and then passed to the OIC in the same way as non-Enigma intelligence. All German naval SIGINT, whether generated from Enigma, hand systems, or traffic analysis thus travelled down a single integrated production line ending at the OIC. The OIC could not only assess all SIGINT together, knowing exactly what its status was, but also evaluate it alongside intelligence from other sources and then take appropriate action, as James had first anticipated back in 1917 and promoted again twenty years later. Nevertheless, one failing evident in 1917–18 persisted. Enigma and other SIGINT-generated intelligence was exploited freely within the OIC, but otherwise numbers indoctrinated were tightly controlled, and there were strict rules governing action. In particular, the NID geographic sections were not indoctrinated, and until some barriers were broken down later in the war, this meant intelligence not of immediate operational relevance, requiring long-term research, was often wasted.[26]

No formal explanation survives of how the more open naval SIGINT system was permitted. The historical legacy from Room 40 and ID25, the evolution of naval SIGINT between the wars, including the 1924 arrangements underpinning the recreation of a GC&CS naval section, and the 1938–39 debate over the relationship between the OIC and GC&CS, were influential. So was the network of naval personal relationships. The fact that the Admiralty, unlike the other services, executed direct operational command created different needs, and decrypts patently originating from ships at sea could not possibly be presented as agent reports. Whatever the answer, this openness of communication along the naval SIGINT production line had two other consequences over the first six months of 1940. First, as the combined Hut 4 and 8 team extended its research on German naval communications, it overtook 8G in traffic analysis, and ultimately absorbed it. Secondly, it fostered increasing willingness by the OIC and indoctrinated members of NID and the wider naval staff to share operational problems where SIGINT might help. Equally, it encouraged the Bletchley team to explore how naval assets could be used to help the Enigma attack through 'pinch' operations.

On the last point, Denniston advised Godfrey on 10 December that success against naval Enigma was unlikely without 'outside assistance', such as capture of an operational machine with its daily settings intact, and/or relevant operating instructions and cipher material – in other words, a windfall, whether chance or contrived, comparable to those that had delivered the German codebooks in 1914. This advice reflected insistence from Knox's team the previous month that naval Enigma could not be broken without some access to current settings, a conclusion which followed Turing's work on the 1937 indicator changes. Denniston added that prisoner interrogation was also an important potential source, as recently demonstrated with a survivor from *U-35*, but required extreme care to extract relevant intelligence without betraying British knowledge and interests. He suggested deploying a top German-speaking barrister, which Godfrey endorsed, noting that the brutal interrogation methods typically employed by the French were counter-productive.[27] Two months later, before this idea bore fruit, another prisoner, rescued from *U-33* sunk off the Clyde on 12 February 1940, produced a further Enigma contribution, this time involuntarily. He failed to dispose of three Enigma rotors, two exclusive to the naval machine, which were promptly seized from his pocket.[28]

Knowledge of internal wiring of the captured naval rotors reduced the unknowns in the Enigma encryption pathway, and therefore ultimately programming a bombe attack, but did not substitute for the essential acquisition of current settings, and capturing these was not easy. There was a tantalising opportunity when *U-49* was blown to the surface by British destroyers in Norway on 15 April and her crew fled the boat in disorder, allowing the British to retrieve a bag of important classified papers that had been thrown overboard, but not properly weighted. Unfortunately, although valuable, this haul did not include any Enigma material. Commander-in-Chief Home Fleet Admiral Sir Charles Forbes, subsequently advocated more ruthless measures in such scenarios to prevent the crew destroying classified material before a U-boat could be boarded and searched. However, the practicality and wisdom of his instructions is debatable, given that critical items could be destroyed inside the boat, and that it was essential to ensure any Enigma compromise did not leak back to the German command. The first breakthrough came from a less obvious source, also in Norway, later the same month. The destroyer *Griffin* intercepted the small German auxiliary *Polares* disguised as a Dutch trawler, and recovered a significant haul of Enigma cipher material. It is possible that other Enigma material was destroyed or looted by British personnel before it could be properly examined, perhaps enough to have provided a comprehensive breakthrough, but this will never be known for certain.[29] The material available enabled Hut 8 ultimately to read about five hundred naval Enigma messages spread over the six days from 22 to 27 April, the first naval decrypts ever achieved by GC&CS, apart from Turing's test samples from November 1938. Decrypting these messages was a complex operation, requiring considerable intellectual ingenuity and extensive use of the first new British bombe installed at Bletchley on 18 March. The first messages were not broken until 11 May, and the last nearly three months later on 6 August. Much innovative work on exploiting the bombe to achieve these decrypts was done by Joan Clarke after she joined Hut 8 in June.[30]

The time lapse meant few individual decrypts were operationally exploitable. However, by July, with most of the six days of traffic broken, Hut 4 drew on it to produce valuable composite assessments, which also exploited material captured from *U-49* and elsewhere. These included detailed studies of the U-boat and E-boat (the German fast attack craft, or *Schnellboot*) fleets, a review of the status of major surface units, and reports on German naval communications organisation.[31] Given the limitations of the material, these were high-quality contributions, and established the reputation of Hut 4 with the OIC and wider naval staff. Breaking the *Polares* material also confirmed to Turing how the current indicator system worked, how the still-rudimentary bombe could be better programmed, and illuminated the steps needed for a more comprehensive attack. For a variety of reasons, executing that attack stretched beyond the rest of 1940, but the *Polares* success provided confidence that naval Enigma could be broken. It also underlined that its wide deployment, including to vessels ill-equipped to protect it, was a fatal vulnerability. The *Polares* pinch and its resulting decrypts also influenced attitudes within the senior naval staff. Set alongside the growing volume of Red Enigma traffic, it underlined to those in the know how valuable the Bletchley team might be to the naval war, and made them receptive to further pinch proposals.[32]

If the yield from SIS and GC&CS was disappointing, Godfrey's greatest frustration in this first phase of the war was aerial reconnaissance. SIS sanctioned a couple of flights by Cotton on behalf of NID in the first fortnight after the outbreak of war, to photograph naval targets from neutral Holland and Denmark. However, SIS had neither the resources nor the capability to provide effective coverage of the German bases and their approaches in wartime conditions. Constitutionally, strategic reconnaissance was an RAF responsibility, which it was never likely to share, and even if political difficulties could have been overcome, it is doubtful whether another service could have established and operated a parallel capability without RAF support. However, on the outbreak of war the RAF was woefully ill-prepared to meet reconnaissance requirements, lacking the right aircraft, trained aircrew and photographic interpreters and, not least, a credible concept for getting adequate results over well-defended airspace. During the first four months of the war, it conducted eighty-nine missions, mainly with adapted Blenheim light bombers, of which only half produced any usable photographs, and with an unacceptable loss rate of sixteen aircraft. Although the first RAF sortie of the war was a photographic reconnaissance of Wilhelmshaven, only ten of these early reconnaissance missions were conducted for the Admiralty against German naval targets. They were limited to Wilhelmshaven and the Heligoland Bight, half produced no useful intelligence, and they cost three aircraft.[33] The record improved in January, with at least one successful mission to Hamburg, which produced good photographs of *Bismarck* fitting out and suggested she was further advanced than the British *King George V* and could commence trials in the Baltic in the spring.[34]

Despite this gloomy outlook, there was important progress underway in the background. It was partly instigated by the Admiralty, although the Navy saw little return for many months, with results largely down to Cotton. Godfrey lobbied Churchill to persuade the Chief of Air Staff, Air Chief Marshal Sir Cyril Newall, to see Cotton. Newall was sufficiently impressed to bring Cotton into the air force as an acting wing commander, with a remit to establish a special Photographic Development Unit (PDU), based at Heston, from where Cotton had operated for SIS. Cotton believed that to be viable against German defences, photographic reconnaissance must be conducted at high altitude, meaning 30,000ft, three times the maximum the RAF believed could produce usable photographs, by aircraft capable of out-running fighters. To achieve this goal, he had to overcome numerous technical challenges against an RAF hierarchy that, despite Newall's support, was at best doubtful, and at worst downright obstructive. His chosen aircraft was the Spitfire, which had the desired speed and ceiling, and when stripped of all unnecessary weight, adequate range.

However, with the best existing cameras, the scale of photographs was so small at Cotton's chosen altitude that interpretation was difficult. Cotton accordingly turned to a private company, the Aircraft Operating Company, which had pioneered advanced three-dimensional imagery using stereoscopic techniques and the Wild A5 plotting machine, a Swiss device with magnification power sufficient to calculate the dimensions of small objects from extreme altitude. Cotton's contact here was Michael Spender, brother of the poet Stephen, an engineer turned explorer/photographer, who had undertaken expeditions to Greenland and Everest, and had studied stereo-photogrammetric survey in Switzerland. Cotton and Spender were kindred spirits, with a shared love of adventure and disregard for the conventional. Spender now became a second essential player in the creation of British wartime aerial photography, formulating the two main principles on which photographic interpretation was based. He demonstrated that overlapping photographs viewed stereoscopically revealed data that could not be distinguished from a single photograph (a technique the Germans failed to recognise), and that sequential photographs of the same area revealed changes in naval or military movements or in construction that might give preliminary warning of forthcoming capabilities or operations. An early example of the former was the identification in February 1940 of the battleship *Tirpitz* under construction in her graving dock at Wilhelmshaven, while through the summer, sequential photographs enabled Spender to track the German build-up of invasion barges. Spender firmly established the principle, which Godfrey and the OIC already intuitively understood, that regular reconnaissance was necessary for full intelligence.[35]

By January 1940, Cotton and Spender had demonstrated conclusively that the combination of the high-altitude Spitfire and Aircraft Operating Company interpretation could deliver a step-change in aerial photographic surveillance. At that point, the standard RAF flights had photographed 2500 square miles of enemy territory at the cost of over twenty Blenheims. Cotton's PDU had covered 5000 square miles without losing its single Spitfire. This should have led to the immediate incorporation of the PDU and the Aircraft Operating Company into the RAF as a mainstream operational capability and its rapid expansion. Unfortunately, poor leadership, bureaucratic inertia, interdepartmental wrangling, and the distractions of the Norwegian and French campaigns meant it was six months before the PDU ceased to be a development unit nominally under the Director of Air Intelligence and, renamed as the Photographic Reconnaissance Unit (PRU), became a fully fledged operational unit within RAF Coastal Command, with the Aircraft Operating Company, based at Wembley, renamed as the Photographic Interpretation Unit (PIU), established as a branch within it. The latter expanded rapidly, with Spender overseeing training, and recruiting many leading academics. Two of these, David Linton and D P Brachi, made outstanding naval contributions during the next eighteen months to the hunt for the *Bismarck* and U-boat construction respectively.[36]

If Cotton had not been an independent-minded maverick with rare ability to turn unconventional but far-sighted vision into practical reality, he would not have moved the PDU so far so fast. However, his plain speaking, disregard for rank, inability to suffer fools, and inclination to cut corners made him many enemies. He got on well with Godfrey and Ian Fleming, who gave him encouragement and support, and in their frustration over RAF inertia several times considered employing him direct. Unfortunately, Admiralty interventions over the PDU were too often clumsy and naive, arousing RAF hostility, and hindering rather than helping Cotton's progress. In the end, the RAF judged Cotton more trouble than he was worth, and there was no place found for him in the new PRU organisation – a sad outcome, given his enormous contribution to one of the outstanding intelligence successes of the war.[37]

All this meant that through the first half of 1940, and indeed well beyond, the contribution of aerial photographic reconnaissance, or PR as it was now known, remained far below what the Admiralty needed to compensate for the present paucity of SIGINT, and keep adequate track of German movements, order of battle and construction activity. Without these sources, it faced a similar North Sea problem to that anticipated in 1914, as well as raids into the Atlantic. The German navy was now much smaller, but German air power was an important multiplier and, together with the U-boat threat and aggressive mining, had forced the Home Fleet into temporary retreat to the west coast of Scotland, while Scapa Flow defences were upgraded. The PDU's limited resources and the demands of reconnaissance on the Western land front meant the first Spitfire coverage of Wilhelmshaven and Emden, the first time the latter (suspected wrongly of harbouring a submarine base) was covered at all, did not occur until February. At the end of March Godfrey pressed for bi-weekly coverage of the main German bases, a modest requirement, but it was months before this was achieved. During the five months February to June, the PDU achieved just half this target. There was no flight to Kiel until 7 April, when a longer-range Spitfire became available, and this was not repeated before end June.[38] The Admiralty had pressed for coverage of Kiel since January, in order to assess the status of the aircraft carrier *Graf Zeppelin*, which it believed was approaching completion there.

22

The Norwegian Campaign: Still Too Little, Too late

The limitations described in the previous chapter meant that for the first six months of the war, OIC coverage of the whereabouts and movements of German units, surface and submarine, was at best partial and sporadic, and rarely enabled timely action. There was even less reliable intelligence on the German navy's strategic plans or future investment. During this period the best guide to German operational deployment and intent came from ships sunk, or from British, or occasionally neutral, sightings of German warships. RAF Coastal Command tried to maintain aerial surveillance of the Scotland–Norway gap, but shortage of suitable aircraft and the challenge of operating in winter weather left plenty of opportunities for German units to slip through unobserved, as with the 10th Cruiser Squadron in 1914. As already noted, intelligence shed no light on the cruises of *Graf Spee* and *Deutschland*, nor did it contribute to the interception of the former at the River Plate in December. Likewise, it gave no warning of the brief sortie by *Scharnhorst* and *Gneisenau* in late November, when they sank the armed merchant cruiser *Rawalpindi*. Even questioning of her few survivors did not establish the identity of her attackers beyond doubt. Meanwhile, the OIC gained only the roughest guide to U-boat deployments, and there were significant errors, notably the belief there were four U-boats operating in the vicinity of the Cape Verde and Canary Islands in early October.[1]

Intelligence did contribute to a high-profile success in mid February, the interception of *Graf Spee*'s supply ship *Altmark* and release of three hundred prisoners she was carrying. It was an early example of the OIC fulfilling the role James had intended: building a picture from multiple sources, enabling timely action. The OIC lost *Altmark* after she left Texas in late August, and only learnt of her connection with *Graf Spee* from

British prisoners freed from the latter after the River Plate action. Despite considerable efforts to find *Altmark*, she disappeared, until sighted by the British merchant vessel *Helmond*, transiting Norwegian coastal waters northwest of Trondheim, on the afternoon of 14 February. *Helmond* could not identify the German tanker, but was sufficiently suspicious of her status to inform the British naval control officer in Trondheim, who appreciated from previous Admiralty alerts that it was probably *Altmark* escaping homeward, and immediately notified London. Further reports from the naval control officer in Bergen, and the naval attaché in Oslo, Rear Admiral Hector Boyes, both alerted by Norwegian efforts to manage a fraught diplomatic situation, confirmed she was moving south in Norwegian territorial waters. The Admiralty sailed forces to intercept on receipt of the *Helmond* report, and by the evening of 15 February these began searching ahead of *Altmark*'s predicted track, but she was finally located near Stavanger the following afternoon by searching Hudson aircraft of Coastal Command – one example in this period where aerial reconnaissance delivered. Hoping to escape her pursuers, *Altmark* entered Jøssingfjord, where she was boarded from the destroyer *Cossack* that night. Disappointingly, and perhaps surprisingly, the *Altmark* operation did not yield any significant intelligence documents, and certainly no cipher material. It appears the crew were disciplined in destroying all confidential papers.[2]

Three months earlier, Hector Boyes handled the single most important insight into German weapons and sensors, both current and projected, acquired in the first half of the war. It came in early November, as an unsolicited document and sample of an advanced proximity fuze from an unknown source, sent as a one-off windfall to Boyes personally at the Oslo embassy, after the source had first ascertained it would be welcomed. It was accordingly known thereafter as the 'Oslo report'. The author, identified post-war, was Hans Ferdinand Mayer, director of research in the German company Siemens, which was involved in many military projects. His report, initially evaluated by Dr Reginald Jones, an Air Ministry science officer seconded to head the scientific section in SIS, proved controversial, with doubts about its overall credibility and reliability. Many thought it too wide-ranging to derive from a single source, and some parts were patently wrong or implausible, notably that 25,000 to 30,000 Ju 88 bombers would be completed by April 1940. Jones, while accepting the report had errors, was convinced the core contents were accurate. By the end of 1940, there was collateral for important information on radar and radio navigation aids, facilitating British countermeasures, and the proximity fuse stimulated new British research. The report contained the first references to remote-control 'glider' and 'rocket' research at Peenemünde, which became immensely significant later. However, in 1939 the naval references in the report appeared of limited value and doubtful reliability. It stated plausibly that the first German aircraft carrier would be completed in Kiel by April 1940, but lost credibility by incorrectly naming her *Franken*. The long section on torpedoes was largely wrong and muddled. It suggested a remote-control torpedo was already in service, when no such weapon existed, and the first homing torpedo G7eT4 (Falke) introduced in March 1943 had different characteristics. Details of the magnetic warhead currently deployed were broadly accurate, but unexceptional, and NID knew the claim that this warhead had sunk *Royal Oak* in Scapa Flow the previous month was false. However, information on glider bomb research did merit naval attention, foreshadowing the HS 293 and Fritz-X introduced in 1943, the latter blowing apart the Italian battleship *Roma* on passage to surrender, and almost sinking the battleship *Warspite*, off Salerno.[3]

In contrast to the limitations faced by British naval intelligence during these early months, Germany gained significant advantage from her ability to read British and French naval traffic. Decryption was not always fast enough for immediate operational exploitation, but B-Dienst read over 30 per cent of British traffic, enough to gain a clear picture of most British naval movements in the North Sea and north and western approaches, until cipher changes on 26 August 1940 defeated them for a while.[4] This helped ensure Germany's immediate pre-war deployments went undetected, and enabled B-Dienst to alert the naval staff to any subsequent threats to *Graf Spee* and *Deutschland*, although the former ignored a warning that Commodore Henry Harwood's cruiser force, whose composition was accurately identified, was concentrating in South American waters. B-Dienst also assisted Admiral Wilhelm Marschall and the German battlecruisers evade British pursuit following the engagement with *Rawalpindi* on 23 November. Meanwhile, coverage of British communications immediately after the outbreak of war alerted Dönitz to a sharp reduction of merchant traffic in the second half of September while Atlantic convoying was implemented. This persuaded him to withdraw ten U-boats early from his initial August deployment, to prepare them for a concentrated effort against the new convoys in October. B-Dienst continued to provide Dönitz with operational opportunities over the next months, including in February the chance to intercept the battlecruiser *Renown*, carrier *Ark Royal* and damaged cruiser *Exeter*, returning from the River Plate action.[5]

Godfrey, who as DNI was responsible for communications security, was certainly not oblivious to the German SIGINT threat. On the outbreak of war, in concert with the Director of the Signal Division, he established a new section NID10e specifically tasked with monitoring Royal Navy radio communications and looking for vulnerabilities. It was told specifically to examine the threat from traffic analysis. In late November NID10e stressed the potential damage from cipher penetration, but was confident current ciphers were secure if properly used. However, it identified major weaknesses in wider radio practice, demonstrating that British operations were vulnerable to traffic analysis. Here it included compelling examples, showing how it was possible to follow the movements of the cruiser *Achilles*, then part of the search for the South Atlantic raider, subsequently identified as *Graf Spee*. This was a ground-breaking piece of analysis, arousing great interest in GC&CS, and an early visit from Denniston, Travis and Birch. Many of the NID10e ideas were quickly applied by Birch to German section's traffic analysis research, ultimately enhancing their edge over 8G.[6]

In the first six months of the war, before they were reassigned to support the invasion of Norway, U-boats concentrated on attacking British trade in the southwest approaches and North Sea, and primarily targeted independent ships. They were initially subject to complicated restrictions, broadly based on the 1930 Treaty of London Submarine Protocol which Germany had signed in 1936, prohibiting attacks on unarmed vessels unless they refused to stop, or acted suspiciously. These rules were difficult to implement without jeopardising a U-boat's security, and as political incentives for observing them eroded, they were steadily relaxed so that by mid 1940, attacks in the eastern Atlantic, with minor exceptions, were unrestricted. Despite the early constraints in U-boat numbers deployed, their areas of operation, focus on independently sailed ships and the overall losses they inflicted in these six months had parallels with the campaign of March to September 1915. Once again, the strategic impact of this initial attack on British and Allied trade, which cost Dönitz sixteen U-boats, 28 per cent of his opening strength, was negligible. Britain's own loss was less than 0.5 per cent of her shipping stock on the outbreak of war.[7] Dönitz could add significant warship losses to the balance, the partially modernised battleship *Royal Oak* sunk in Scapa Flow, the aircraft carrier *Courageous* in the Western Approaches, and severe damage to the battleship *Nelson*, but in a single-handed war with Germany, these too had little impact on Royal Navy dominance. At about ten merchant ships sunk per U-boat lost, the exchange rate was not promising for either side. For Britain, it meant that, despite the arrival of ASDIC, a small U-boat force could still inflict a loss rate of near 2 million tons a year. As in 1915, it was a stark warning of what a larger force might achieve. Meanwhile, for Dönitz, the U-boats lost included twelve of thirty-one ocean-capable boats deployed. With only eight new boats commissioned, his total strength was down to forty-nine by the end of February, half comprising the small Type II coastal boats, and with further losses to come in Norway, he only recovered his starting point of fifty-seven boats by September, a whole year into the war.[8] Although U-boat production was rising fast by the end of 1940, the figure of forty-eight operational boats in September 1939 was not achieved again until mid 1941. Any decisive impact on Britain's trade appeared a long way off.

Buried within the statistics of this early period was another important message for both sides. Although nearly 95 per cent of merchant ships sunk were independents, Dönitz had also targeted convoys, although several ambitious attempts to execute multi-boat operations here, helped by B-Dienst intelligence, were for various reasons unsuccessful. Command and control arrangements to facilitate multi-boat attacks were still evolving, and some boats were awaiting the necessary radio outfits. Almost all the early convoy attacks were therefore by single boats, only 4.2 per cent of all convoys sailed in the period to end June 1940 suffered any losses, and, from the German viewpoint, the exchange rate was awful with a U-boat lost for every two ships sunk, even though convoys at this stage rarely had more than two escorts.

Important points follow. Britain began investing in anti-submarine escorts at least a year earlier than Germany committed to U-boats, and the early U-boat losses enhanced this logistic advantage. Britain could, therefore, anticipate extending convoy coverage and escort strength faster than Germany could boost its frontline U-boat force which, given the closure of the Dover straits, faced a long, dangerous transit from German bases and reduced time on task. The favourable exchange rate experienced by the British in the early convoy operations also came when the German intelligence advantage was greatest, and the British naval intelligence contribution minimal, underlining the importance of a wider perspective in judging the role of intelligence in the Atlantic battle. Dönitz now resorted to new tactics, but if the strategic balance of the wider war had remained unchanged for the rest of 1940, it is unlikely these measures alone would have brought a decisive shift in Germany's favour.[9]

The ability of NID and the wider naval staff to draw useful conclusions about this initial U-boat campaign, before the German invasion of Norway and France fundamentally altered the strategic context, was inevitably hampered by the dramatic overestimate of U-boat numbers already described. Neither SIS nor aerial photography could provide any corrective intelligence before the true picture emerged in the documents recovered from *U-49* in Norway on 15 April. This revealed that overall U-boat strength was now down to forty-three boats, with twenty-two lost since the start of the war. It also showed that NID had underestimated losses to end February (twelve compared to sixteen). This intelligence enabled NID to recalibrate, and for the rest of the year its assessments were broadly correct. In September it believed strength was seventy compared to the reality of fifty-seven, but its forward projection of 157 by 1 August 1941 was almost exactly right.[10] Other secret documents from *U-49*, rescued from a bag which the escaping German crew did not have time to weight, included grid charts and details of the U-boat deployments to Norway but, as noted earlier, no cipher material.[11]

NID's conservatism over U-boat losses, reflecting Thring's insistence on hard evidence, drawing on experience in the previous war, aroused the ire of Churchill as First Lord, who in relentless pursuit of good news, for both propaganda and political reasons, insisted losses were much higher. This argument, which led to the grossly unfair sacking of Captain Arthur Talbot as Director of Anti-Submarine Warfare, reflected badly on Churchill.[12] Fortunately, Churchill's claim that the U-boat force had been reduced by half in six months did not stop him prioritising anti-submarine forces over the large ship programme in the forthcoming naval estimates for 1940/41. Here he overrode powerful opposition from naval members of the Board of Admiralty, notably Tom Phillips as DCNS, who argued vigorously against delay to the *Lion*-class capital ships. Not for the last time, Churchill got the big picture right, and his influence here helped ensure Britain would retain its logistic advantage as the U-boat campaign evolved.[13]

Germany had no plans to attack Scandinavia in September 1939. Weserübung, her operation to seize Norway and Denmark initiated on 9 April the following year, resulted from a complex interaction of strategic motives, personal agendas and chance events from December onwards. The primary driver was defensive, to pre-empt British and French disruption of iron ore supplies from Sweden via Narvik, or their use of Norway for more extensive operations to support Finland. The perception that Norway might move from neutrality into the Allied camp, either willingly or under coercion, creating a new northern front against Germany, gained influence through the winter with the *Altmark* incident probably decisive in convincing Hitler to act. By this point, the strategic advantages control of Norway would give Germany in attacking British Atlantic trade, strongly promoted by Raeder, gained traction too. German suspicions of British intent, reflecting some good intelligence, were substantially justified, although active Norwegian collaboration in an alliance against her was never likely.[14]

During the five weeks following Hitler's decision on 3 March to proceed with Weserübung, the British political and military leadership received copious warning from authoritative diplomatic sources and SIS, which would have left no doubt of German intent had the intelligence been properly circulated, collated and assessed. Much of the SIS reporting covered indications of German naval preparations.[15] It went initially to NID1 geographic section, but was unfortunately not always copied to the OIC. There were other important specific naval pointers. By 24 March, the OIC noticed that U-boat operations against the trade routes and German minelaying had virtually ceased after the second week of the month. Two days later, the assistant naval attaché for Scandinavia, based in Stockholm, reported a concentration of ships in Kiel, including fast merchantmen with anti-aircraft armament and flying personnel aboard. Fifty vessels had also just arrived in the Baltic through the Kiel Canal. This heavy concentration of shipping at Kiel was confirmed ten days later by the first-ever air reconnaissance over the port, conducted by a Spitfire on 7 April. At the end of March, DNI had informed the naval staff that a German trawler, *Theseus*, was operating as a spy-ship and conducting extensive reconnaissance in Norwegian territorial waters.[16] Shortly afterwards, Boyes in Oslo sent a report, graded A1, that large numbers of troops were concentrating in Rostock. The photographic intelligence over Kiel was accompanied by reports of exceptional naval wireless traffic in the Bight and Jutland areas, and of unprecedented German reconnaissance flights up the Norwegian coast. Simultaneously, the embassy in Copenhagen reported that one German division, accommodated in ten ships, was moving towards Narvik for a landing scheduled for 8 April. This report was shared with Commander-in-Chief Home Fleet Admiral Sir Charles Forbes, but unfortunately with comment from DNI questioning its reliability. Overall, NID believed the flurry of German activity probably reflected deployment of raiders into the Atlantic. This jigsaw of numerous fragmentary signs from multiple sources was precisely the problem that James had created the OIC to solve, but it failed to do so. This reflected inexperience, insufficient staff with the right skills, and poor internal communication within NID, but also reluctance to contemplate the unexpected. Both NID and the wider staff were too focused on British plans, beginning with the mining of Norwegian inshore waters, to consider how the Germans might radically pre-empt them.[17]

The failure to recognise German intent, and the overall scale and ambition of Weserübung, left the Royal Navy poorly deployed to intervene decisively when the Germans were most vulnerable, during their initial landings. Once the Germans were established, geography dictated that they could reinforce successfully, especially with air power, more quickly than Britain and France could mount counter operations. In the naval campaign, Germany maintained its clear intelligence advantage. B-Dienst reading of British traffic, including from units deployed with commanders at sea, and Luftwaffe aerial reconnaissance from captured airfields provided a consistently good picture of British movements. By contrast, Royal Navy commanders struggled to achieve anything similar. SIGINT still offered little. The best D/F fixes rarely improved on a forty-mile radius and coverage north of Bergen was limited. Traffic analysis was immature. The Norwegian campaign Yellow Enigma key produced some intelligence on German naval movements, but little operationally significant.[18] The SIS station commander for Scandinavia, Frank Foley, after successfully fleeing Oslo, provided vital secure communications for London with the Norwegian commander-in-chief, General Otto Ruge, in the immediate post-invasion period, but could contribute nothing useful to the main naval campaign.[19] For information on German surface forces, British commanders therefore depended primarily on sighting reports from British warships and aircraft. Air reconnaissance from bases in the northern United Kingdom, or less often from carriers, was occasional and opportunistic, rather than providing the regular and consistent coverage of the key German-held ports that was needed. The few British aircraft successfully deployed ashore made only a marginal contribution. SIS established an embryonic ship-watching operation near Stavanger in the final weeks of the campaign, but this produced little of value before it was broken up by the Germans.[20]

Nevertheless, it is doubtful whether availability or lack of intelligence affected the strictly naval operations undertaken during the Norwegian campaign, given the constraints of geography and the relative resources the two sides could deploy, where substantial British superiority at sea was matched by German air- and land-force advantage once ashore. German intelligence coverage through B-Dienst could not prevent heavy, arguably unaffordable, German naval losses comprising *Blücher*, one of two heavy cruisers, two of six light cruisers, ten destroyers, almost half its available force, and six U-boats. Its two battlecruisers, *Scharnhorst* and *Gneisenau*, and one of two surviving pocket battleships, *Lützow* (the renamed *Deutschland*), were badly damaged and out of action for six months. Two light cruisers and six destroyers had lesser damage. By the end of June, the German surface navy, reduced to just one heavy cruiser, two light cruisers and four destroyers ready for action, was eliminated as a factor in the naval war for the foreseeable future, as the British leadership rapidly appreciated.[21] Except for *Blücher*, sunk by Norwegian coastal defences, almost all these losses were due to the Royal Navy, and apart from the damage to the battlecruisers, most occurred during or shortly after the initial landings. B-Dienst contributed only marginally to the sole German naval success after mid April, the sinking on 8 June of the carrier *Glorious* and her attendant destroyers by the battlecruisers, following a chance encounter in the North Norwegian Sea, arguably the most serious single loss suffered by the Royal Navy in the first eighteen months of the war.[22]

British naval losses – *Glorious*, two light cruisers (one to navigational accident, not German action), seven destroyers and four submarines, with another three cruisers and eight destroyers damaged, are often presented as broadly equivalent in absolute terms, if less as a proportion of overall strength. This overlooks the fact that many British losses were older and less capable ships than their German equivalents, and replaced by three new fleet carriers, ten cruisers and ten fleet destroyers within a year. However, it is also true that British losses might have been greater if German U-boats had not been gravely hampered by defective torpedoes. NID first learnt that the magnetic torpedo warhead was unreliable in October 1939, from some of the first U-boat prisoners interrogated, but by late 1940 had a comprehensive view of its problems through covert eavesdropping on prisoner-of-war conversations at the Combined Services Detailed Interrogation Centre (CSDIC), where the topic was often discussed 'in considerable detail'.[23] In the event, there was no impact on British control of essential sea areas. With the possible exception of *Glorious* and her escorts, where traffic analysis offered some clues that German heavy units might be at sea, lack of intelligence had little bearing on these losses, which were otherwise mainly incurred during the early counter-attacks at Narvik, or the result of German air attack. Nor, once German landings were underway, is it easy to identify examples where better intelligence would have produced more effective offensive action against German forces, given the constraints of existing British capability.

Intelligence warning relevant to the *Glorious* disaster originated from the 21-year-old Francis Harry Hinsley, a Cambridge undergraduate historian recruited to GC&CS the previous November, where he joined Frank Birch's revived German naval section to work on traffic analysis. He was destined to play as important a role in the evolution of naval SIGINT as Turing, albeit from a different vantage point. Harry Hinsley, as he was always known, the son of an employee of the Walsall Coal Co-operative and a school caretaker, was a striking example of the opportunities the war offered to very talented individuals, however young and modest in background. In 1943 he went to Washington where almost singlehandedly he negotiated the introduction of the UKUSA SIGINT relationship between Britain and the United States, which exists to this day. After the war, he returned to academic life, becoming in due course Vice Chancellor of Cambridge University and primary historian of British intelligence in the Second World War.

Since Birch was barred from 'operational intelligence', Hinsley's avowed purpose was 'cryptographic research', with anything judged operational passed to 8G. However, over the first half of 1940, now installed in Hut 4 with new assistants to help with the additional responsibility of processing the *Polares* decrypts and exploiting direct access to the 'Y' stations, he established a comprehensive picture of German naval communications potentially capable of signposting enemy activity. This initially complemented, but then surpassed, the achievements of 8G, whose knowledge, increasingly isolated from the wider SIGINT effort concentrated at Bletchley, atrophied.[24] Hinsley's initial results with traffic analysis met scepticism in the Admiralty, inevitably exacerbated by turf disputes with 8G, but the delivery of the first *Polares* Enigma decrypts beginning on 11 May raised his profile and credibility. By the end of the month, he was in regular discussion with Clayton and Denning by secure telephone over interpretation of *Polares* material.[25] This developing relationship provided the context for his separate warnings, drawing on traffic indicators during the period 27 May–5 June that a major German operation involving 'heavy ships' appeared underway, probably involving forces deploying northward from the Baltic. The subsequent loss of *Glorious* ensured new respect for his advice.[26]

Hinsley's indicators were less definite than he later implied, and new Admiralty enthusiasm for traffic analysis reflected desire to clutch at any straw that might avoid a repeat, rather than careful analysis of what had happened.[27] The indicators were associated with the preparations and initial deployment for the German Operation Juno, an attack on the Allied convoys running to and from Harstad and Narvik. But Hinsley's team never confirmed the identity of units leaving the Baltic, or a possible destination, other than the Norwegian west coast up to Trondheim, and there were many possible explanations for the radio traffic which ended on 5 June. Supported by useful, if partial, intelligence from B-Dienst, Juno could have inflicted considerable damage, had the German commander, Admiral Wilhelm Marschall, handled his formidable task force with more determination and aggression, but instead the operation was marred by caution, indecision and confused priorities. Although B-Dienst identified two carriers operating in northern waters, they were not specifically targeted and the encounter with *Glorious* came by chance during a sweep westward with the battlecruisers, after Marschall had sent the rest of his force back to Trondheim. An easy victory was undermined by poor tactical handling, leading to the inexcusable torpedoing of *Scharnhorst* by the destroyer *Acasta*. This led indirectly to the subsequent torpedoing of *Gneisenau* by the submarine *Clyde* off Trondheim, after she had returned there with the badly damaged *Scharnhorst*.[28] Ironically, therefore, British intelligence failure in not recognising and addressing the risk posed by Juno triggered a chain of events that put the German battlecruisers out of action for the rest of 1940.

Hinsley was now invited to spend a month with the OIC to brief his knowledge of German naval communications and the techniques of traffic analysis. He was also later sent on several visits to Forbes, and his successor as Commander-in-Chief Home Fleet, Admiral Sir John Tovey. The next nine months were the peak period of traffic analysis, but its contribution to immediate operations, although occasionally useful, proved less than Hinsley hoped and the Admiralty was rightly sceptical of the more extravagant claims it attracted. Nevertheless, by the end of the year, with help from the *Polares* decrypts, captured documents and prisoner interrogation, it gave Hut 4 considerable detail on the distribution of German naval codes and ciphers, and through this the strength, organisation, disposition and habits of its naval forces. It also established Hut 4, with Hinsley to the fore under Birch, as the pre-eminent authority on German naval SIGINT and, increasingly, for long-term intelligence research.[29]

At the end of June 1940 the balance sheet from ten months of naval war against Germany as sole enemy was more complicated than often suggested. Britain's overall strategic position had immeasurably worsened, beyond the bleakest imaginings of 1914–18. Germany now controlled most of Europe and its resources, and from its long western coastline from Norway to Spain could challenge Britain in the Atlantic from multiple points. The entry of Italy, with her substantial navy, into the war as Germany's ally potentially extended Axis control across much of the Mediterranean and North Africa. The Royal Navy had learnt hard lessons about the limits to naval operations within range of land-based air power, although it had also gained valuable experience in multi-role, multi-carrier operations, including the first experiments with radar-directed fighter defence. Yet over these ten months, across the River Plate, the initial U-boat operations and the Norwegian campaign, the Royal Navy had inflicted the equivalent of a major defeat on the small

German navy, exceeding the best hopes of pre-war strategists for a naval offensive against Germany, and easily surpassing the achievements of 1914–15. Britain was also far outstripping Germany in war production most relevant to maritime conflict, with more than twice as much naval tonnage delivered in 1940, and 40 per cent more aircraft, a trend that would continue. Despite her strategic gains, Germany could neither challenge Britain's overall maritime supremacy, nor mount a contested invasion, even across the narrow Channel for the foreseeable future. In August, aware of Germany's naval weakness, Britain had enough naval resources substantially to reinforce the Mediterranean, and take the offensive against Italy.

Overall, intelligence contributed little to the outcome of this first phase of the naval war. There were two major British failures: not progressing photographic reconnaissance more quickly and effectively, and not pulling together the multiple warnings of German action against Norway. In the absence of SIGINT, the first was the only way of adequately monitoring German dispositions and movements. As regards the second, had the Home Fleet deployed in time to intercept German invasion forces at sea, Weserübung would probably have failed, although ironically the damage inflicted on German warships, as opposed to transports, might have been less than they had sustained by the end of the campaign. By the end of June, both these failures were being addressed. The creation of the PRU and PIU at last put PR on a sound organisational footing, even if capability still moved too slowly for the Admiralty. And the failure at Norway provoked a substantial strengthening of the JIC, based on recommendations from Hankey and Godfrey.[30] It now had formal responsibility for monitoring and defining threats, rather than waiting for the service departments to identify topics of interest, and with the growing risk of invasion, it was tasked with obtaining the earliest possible warning of enemy attack. These reforms coincided with improvement to other sources feeding the OIC, the arrival of German air force Red Enigma in quantity, enhancement of the D/F network, and the fruits of the closer relationship with Hut 4.

23

Surviving the Initial German
Onslaught in the West

The fall of France and the related losses suffered by the British expeditionary forces, which overlapped the final phase of the Norwegian campaign, made German invasion of the United Kingdom an immediate risk, and therefore a central focus of naval intelligence until the autumn. However, the loss of France, and German occupation of half its territory, made it harder for Britain to control the sea areas and communications essential both to protect its wider empire and successfully prosecute the war. Apart from the possibility of invasion, the main damage to Britain's naval position lay less in the loss of French naval support than in German access to bases on the French Atlantic coast, which complicated Royal Navy defence of the critical Atlantic trade routes.[1] The primary benefit French bases brought was to the U-boats, which could deploy more quickly and safely from the west coast of France than from Germany, avoiding a long, exposed transit to patrol areas, and increasing effective patrol time by about 30 per cent.[2] But they also helped with surface-raider deployment, whether warship or converted merchant vessel, while French airfields extended the opportunities for air attack on Atlantic and coastal shipping. Britain now also faced a constant risk that Germany or her Axis allies would exploit other French territory against her, whether on the Atlantic coast of Africa, in the Mediterranean, or the Far East.

Countering these new risks to the United Kingdom homeland, and in the Atlantic and Mediterranean, exacerbated by Italy's entry into the war in June, fundamentally changed intelligence needs and tied up significant extra Royal Navy and RAF resources in a way never anticipated pre-war. Nevertheless, by late summer, the Admiralty was cautiously confident that in a war with Germany and Italy it could retain adequate naval control of essential maritime areas for the foreseeable future. The active hostility of France would be an additional commitment, but would still not dangerously weaken British control of essential waters. This confidence reflected accurate appreciation of German naval losses in Norway, the neutralisation of the French fleet, and the naval supremacy established in initial engagements with Italy. It also reflected projections of comparative force levels, using estimates of current strength and anticipated production over the next three years. Here, NID projections for German and Italian naval strength, including German U-boat production, were broadly accurate, although they slightly overstated commissioning of German heavy surface units. U-boat strength was put at seventy U-boats on 1 August, whereas the true figure was fifty-nine, and 157 (or 130 allowing for wastage) by 1 August 1941, when the true figure was 153 on 1 July that year. NID correctly anticipated that only two new battleships, *Bismarck* and *Tirpitz*, would be available before 1942, but assumed incorrectly that there would also be two aircraft carriers and a fourth *Hipper*-class heavy cruiser by the end of 1941. These three were never completed.[3]

The wider strategic and intelligence context through the autumn and winter of 1940/41, against which these naval calculations took place, was partly dictated by an emerging British vision of how the war might be successfully prosecuted and partly assessment of immediate Axis intentions. While the security of the United Kingdom homeland and the defence of the other interests and territory perceived as critical to the future war effort was initially the primary concern, the concept of wearing down Germany through economic attrition using naval blockade, bombing and subversion gained traction in this period as a route to eventual victory, although its credibility ultimately rested on United States support.[4] There was also a key caveat. The new strategic circumstances left no margin for the foreseeable future to deal with any Japanese intervention. At most, a small force, probably comprising a battlecruiser and carrier, might be deployed to deter IJN raider action in the Indian Ocean, and Singapore would be held as a foothold for recovering any losses when stronger forces became available.

The fall of France and risk of invasion

The sheer speed of the French collapse during May and June created an intelligence void for NID, just as it faced the twin challenges of possible invasion, and German use of French bases for Atlantic operations. Since France had been ruled out as a potential enemy for more than thirty years, neither NID nor SIS possessed any covert intelligence-collection capability that would survive German occupation. Not only were they ill-equipped to monitor German intentions and plans, but basic data on French ports and coastal topography was lacking. Most pressing of all was the future of the French fleet, and the prospect of it falling into German hands. To establish French intentions, on 13 June Godfrey despatched Fleming to Paris as an emissary to the French commander-in-chief, Admiral Jean François Darlan. Fleming found Darlan at Tours two days later, where the French ministry of marine had evacuated, and urged him to bring his fleet to Britain. Darlan rejected this proposal, but insisted he would never allow his ships to come under German control, a stance he reiterated in subsequent meetings with the First Lord A V Alexander and Pound. Godfrey had met Darlan in Paris in early 1939, when he assessed him a staunch ally. However, he now passed on a warning to Pound from Lord Tyrrell, the former head of the Foreign Office Political Intelligence Department and ambassador to France in the early 1930s, that Darlan was a 'twister', a judgement broadly confirmed by Darlan's future behaviour.[5] Overall, Fleming spent nearly two weeks in France before finally making his way home via Portugal. The stay was marked by frenetic, often adventurous, activity, but although his link to Darlan was useful, not for the last time much of his effort delivered limited intelligence return for the energy expended.[6] The most authoritative insight into French navy intentions came from their signal traffic, decrypted by GC&CS from 1 July following acquisition of French naval ciphers from the submarine *Narval* after she joined the British at Malta. However, this intelligence was too late to exert much influence over British action against the French fleet at Oran.[7]

Meanwhile, Godfrey took three other important initiatives. Although NID2 continued as a geographic section until September, at the end of May, France, Holland and Belgium were transferred to NID1 German section, as a new sub-section under Lieutenant Commander George Gonin, a reservist who had run a business in Antwerp through the 1930s, and now proved another of Godfrey's inspired recruits. He spoke fluent French, had many useful contacts and proved a natural intelligence officer, over the course of the war becoming master of everything in France that had a bearing on naval requirements. The second initiative endorsed by the JIC and chiefs of staff was to establish a Combined Intelligence Committee (CIC) which met daily under Clayton or his deputy, Geoffrey Colpoys, to collate and circulate across Whitehall all intelligence relevant to possible invasion developments. Other members were Denning and representatives from NID1, Military and Air Intelligence departments.[8]

The final step capitalised on an initiative already underway. The first months of the war, and specifically demands raised by prospective intervention in Norway and Finland, underlined to Godfrey that NID lacked topographic information, and that the Admiralty Geographical Handbook series initiated by Hall was neither complete nor up to date. For example, this series did not include Norway, Iceland, Holland, Belgium, Greece or the Mediterranean islands, all of pressing interest in the new war. In February 1940 he sought help from Professor Kenneth Mason at the Oxford University School of Geography, and commissioned reports on Finland and the Soviet Union. The following month, with the approval of Phillips, he established a small topographic research section, soon designated NID6, to meet growing requirements from Plans Division and others. One of Godfrey's cardinal beliefs, encouraged by Hall, was that somewhere in Britain there was a specialist, on virtually any subject or place, who could help NID. NID6 would operate as a clearing house to apply this principle to topographic expertise and make it digestible to those who needed it. It was headed by Lieutenant Colonel Sam Bassett, Royal Marines, joined by a retired hydrographer, Captain Law, and a new recruit from Oxford, Professor A F (Freddie) Wells, to foster the academic links. Oddly, Wells was not a geographer, but a classicist, and yet, as with many of Godfrey's recruits, he proved a superb choice.[9]

The new section faced an immediate blizzard of demands, starting with Norway, which brutally exposed how poor existing topographic data was in both the Admiralty and the other services. At the end of May, days after Bassett's team was formally constituted as NID6, it was asked to collate every possible piece of information on potential French evacuation sites additional to Dunkirk. Bassett proposed and got authorisation for two specialist reconnaissance parties to conduct instant surveys right along the French north coast, which they completed, with extensive photographs, just ahead of the advancing Germans. One of the first surveys was a beach later used in the 1944 Normandy landings, where these 1940 photographs proved valuable. Simultaneously, NID6 conducted interviews with Royal Mail captains and others who knew the French coast, and with evacuated British and French personnel. France was not the only demand that June, which saw NID6 cope with an extraordinary range of requests including information on the Rhine–Main–Danube Canal, the Canary Islands and Azores, the Zeiss works at Jena, corn-growing areas of Italy, the width of bridges in Iceland on the Reykjavik–Hvalfjord road, oil installations at Huelva and Lisbon, the hydrography and topography of Irish lochs (in case German seaplanes landed), and the height of the breakwater protecting the French fleet at Mers-el-Kébir near Oran.[10]

The lack of topographical information on Norway spurred the chiefs of staff to instruct the JIC to consider measures to improve the service for possible future theatres of war. Rather than establish a new interdepartmental body, it decided to improve tasking of existing service sections, and collaboration and sharing between them. The JIC would set priorities and eliminate duplication. Partly because of Godfrey's driving interest, but also the academic links he had established, the pre-eminence of coastal topography in the circumstances of 1940, and the existing base of information in the Admiralty handbooks, NID6 established a dominant role. It expanded rapidly, and in October moved to Oxford, where it gradually translated into the Inter-Services Topographical Department (ISTD), tasked by the JIC on an inter-service basis, but still administered by NID. As ISTD, its reports became ISIS (Inter-service Information Series) publications. Alongside NID6, a new section NID5 was created in early 1941 to produce updated geographical handbooks, with a unit in Oxford under Mason, and another in Cambridge under James Wordie. Over the rest of the war, the two centres produced fifty-eight volumes, covering every theatre, with input from almost every academic geographer in the United Kingdom, mainly contributed on a voluntary basis. It was probably the largest programme of geographical writing ever attempted. Godfrey specified that the purpose of the books was primarily naval, and designed to give naval commanders comprehensive and digestible information on countries and areas where they were conducting operations. Although the series prioritised the needs of the present war, he anticipated it would have enduring value, providing an essential store of knowledge for the army and RAF and other government departments. He was right about their enduring value. The Iraq handbook published in 1944 was viewed by British military and intelligence officials as still the best overall guide to the country in conducting the operations in 2003, sixty years later.[11]

The most important source of intelligence feeding the CIC on German invasion preparations from June to October was aerial photography. The invasion warning requirement coincided with RAF endorsement of Cotton's methods, and the creation of the PRU, and it was agreed on 10 June that the CIC would direct invasion tasking. Godfrey's influence, and the pressure he exerted through Pound as First Sea Lord and Phillips as VCNS, was probably decisive in getting the PRU off to an effective start and focused on the right priorities, although the ending of military operations in France, and reduced army reconnaissance demands helped. Not only was potential invasion activity monitored but, during June, at the suggestion of NID6, resources were found to photograph key French coastal sites against possible future requirements, before German anti-aircraft defences were in place. Nevertheless, shortage of suitable Spitfires meant adequate coverage of the whole area, from the Gironde estuary in the south to the Baltic and southern Norwegian ports, was not achieved until mid July. From this point, until the picture appeared to change in early September, coverage was sufficiently comprehensive and regular to rule out any threatening concentrations of shipping in the Channel ports, and largely to discount the possibility of surprise attack from more distant embarkation points.[12] Two other sources added significantly to the picture. From end June, German air force Enigma provided some insights into Luftwaffe strength, deployment, readiness, and sometimes operational intentions, although since much traffic was passed by landline these contributions were fragmentary, not comprehensive. It did warn that the Germans were installing long-range guns capable of commanding the Dover straits, a development then monitored closely by the PRU.[13] The other source was the Czech agent A54, the Abwehr officer Paul Thümmel, recruited in 1936, who was now run under the direction of SIS by the Czech intelligence service in exile. He provided fourteen reports between May and December, providing the only insights into German invasion intentions at the strategic level.[14] While these three sources in different ways provided valuable warning indicators, none of them ever revealed the precise timing of a German attack, its overall strength, or how forces would be deployed in detail.[15]

From early September, PRU coverage, ably interpreted by Spender in the PIU, revealed substantial movement of barges westward towards the Channel ports, with the number gathered at Ostend rising from eighteen to 270 over the first week of the month. There was an accompanying movement of merchant vessels towards the Channel from the North Sea and Baltic. The combination of these shipping movements, intensified German air attacks, and conditions of moon and tide persuaded the British leadership to put home forces on immediate alert from 7 September, although two days earlier the CIC was still not convinced preparations for invasion had increased. The German deployment peaked on 14 September, when the CIC identified 1652 barges and fifty-five merchant ships, supported by six destroyers and forty assorted smaller naval escorts, spread across fifteen Channel locations, with by far the largest concentration of shipping and barges at Antwerp, and of warships at Cherbourg. However, unknown to the British, even before this date, the strength of British air opposition had caused Hitler to initiate a series of postponements. By the end of the month it was clear preparations were being scaled down, and in mid October A54 confirmed postponement until early 1941, giving the Admiralty confidence to reallocate destroyers from anti-invasion duty to Atlantic convoy escort.[16]

The developing surface raider threat

Since the anti-invasion PR operation from June onwards included regular coverage of the main German naval bases as far east as Kiel, NID successfully monitored the status of most of Germany's major warships for the rest of 1940. The battleship *Tirpitz* continued under construction at Wilhelmshaven throughout the period, but her sister *Bismarck*, which was further advanced, was observed moving from Hamburg to Kiel in mid September and then further east out of range, in fact to Gotenhafen (modern Gdynia) where, unknown to NID, the heavy cruiser *Prinz Eugen* was also doing her final fitting-out. The battlecruisers *Scharnhorst* and *Gneisenau*, and pocket battleship *Lützow*, all badly damaged in the Norwegian campaign, were regularly photographed under repair at Kiel until late December. *Lützow*'s stern was stripped down to her keel, but damage to the battlecruisers was harder to assess, and at the height of the invasion scare in mid September, NID could not rule out their availability. NID also observed limited progress on the carrier *Graf Zeppelin* at Kiel, and *Prinz Eugen*'s sister, *Seydlitz*, at Bremen. It still judged the latter complete by early September, although in reality work on her had stopped early in the year. The status of *Graf Zeppelin* was a constant Admiralty preoccupation throughout the period 1940–42, reflecting the unique reconnaissance, strike and defensive capability it was judged she would add to any heavy surface-raiding force.[17] Meanwhile, the arrival of the first longer-range Spitfire Ds in late autumn enabled more ambitious flights. Toulon and Marseilles were photographed from the United Kingdom on 2 November, with the former giving NID a valuable check on the status of French warships there, including the battlecruiser *Strasbourg*, and Trondheim and Oslo were covered the same month. Overall, in November and December alone, despite winter conditions, the PRU conducted 236 sorties, the majority on naval targets, with a 70 per cent success rate, and only two aircraft losses. All but five were conducted by Spitfire.[18]

PR had come a long way in twelve months, if still too slow for the Admiralty's liking, making a significant contribution to the priorities first put to Menzies by Godfrey in November 1939, most of which remained extant. However, despite the useful reassurance it provided on German naval and shipping deployment through the second half of 1940, it could not cover everything, and in the present state of the art, despite Spender's best efforts, rarely offered advance warning of naval movements. The limitations of coverage with existing resources became increasingly apparent as the majority of the major German units became operational again at the beginning of 1941. For now, the most pressing gap was in assessing U-boat build-rate. If the methods and, above all, the rate of production were to be accurately calculated, in accordance with Spender's principles, sequential views of U-boat construction yards, ideally at roughly the same time interval, were required. The photographs also had to achieve a quality and definition sufficient to understand the construction process. Aircraft range, flight frequency, camera quality and interpretation skill did not come together adequately to meet these requirements until spring 1941.[19] Two important warship sorties were also missed before the end of 1940. The pocket battleship *Admiral Scheer*, which had disappeared after being photographed at Wilhelmshaven on 20 July, where she had been in refit, sortied on 23 October direct from Gotenhafen, where she had been based while working up, and which was beyond RAF reach. The first OIC knew was when she sank the armed merchant cruiser *Jervis Bay* and five merchant vessels from convoy HX 84 in the Atlantic on 5 November. She then disappeared, with only fleeting hints of her whereabouts, for the South Atlantic and Indian Ocean, finally returning to Kiel via Bergen in April 1941. Meanwhile, on 30 November the heavy cruiser *Hipper* sortied from Brunsbüttel at the mouth of the Elbe, after completing emergency engine repairs at Hamburg down river. Although photographed there by the PRU the previous day, the OIC had no way of knowing the significance of her presence. She too only came to attention when she attempted to attack a heavily escorted troop convoy, 700 miles west of Finisterre, in late December. After incurring some damage, she retreated to Brest, before undertaking another short Atlantic operation in February.[20]

PR also failed to alert NID to a new threat emerging in the spring of 1940, and on which no existing intelligence source shed much light for many months. This was the German deployment of converted merchant vessels as auxiliary commerce-raiders. Although Raeder had shown personal interest in this concept in the late 1930s, and it seemed an obvious option given the success of *Möwe* and *Wolf* in the previous war, it was seven months before the first raider *Atlantis*, subsequently known to the British as Raider C, deployed on 31 March.[21] A further five deployed by mid July. They displaced between 7,500 and 15,000 tons, made skilful use of disguise with changes of appearance and identity, and were generally armed with six concealed 5.9in guns, four or six torpedo tubes, several lighter guns and mines. Five of the six initially headed into the Atlantic, usually through the Denmark Strait, but *Komet* (Raider B), leaving in July, transited north of Russia with Soviet navy assistance into the Bering Strait and the Pacific. The raiders maintained strict radio silence and with aerial reconnaissance preoccupied by commitments to the Norway and France campaigns, none of their sailings were detected.

The Admiralty might have been alerted when *Widder* (Raider D) fought an inconclusive engagement with the submarine *Clyde* off Norway on 13 May, but *Widder* was not unreasonably associated with Norway-related operations. It was, therefore, mid May before the OIC assessed there must be at least one raider at large in the Atlantic, subsequently assessed to have moved on to the Indian Ocean, and mid June before the laying of mines off Auckland pointed to a Pacific raider, as well. Although the OIC did not yet know it, these two identifications were *Atlantis* and *Orion* (Raider A). By late July, the OIC knew there was probably a third raider operating in the South Atlantic after *Thor* (Raider E) was engaged by the British armed merchant cruiser *Alcantara*, 600 miles east of Rio de Janeiro.

Although still unaware there were six raiders deployed and operational across three oceans, the OIC recognised that it faced a distinct and serious problem, with no easy intelligence answers. Because the raiders rarely communicated, SIGINT was little help, and they avoided ports and choke-points where they might be identified. Their policy was slow, incremental gains, preying on individual vessels in distant isolated waters, minimising their chance of meeting patrolling Royal Navy warships, and using a combination of surprise and overwhelming force to prevent distress signals. By the end of the year they sank fifty-four ships, almost 10 per cent of total Allied shipping losses in 1940, and almost four times that inflicted by German warships, including during the Norwegian campaign, without themselves suffering any loss, making them an effective and economical means of attacking trade.

Widder, which proved prone to machinery breakdown, returned successfully to France in October and was replaced by *Kormoran* (Raider G), which deployed via the Denmark Strait in December. Denning responded with a dedicated raider plot under an RNVR sub lieutenant, Patrick Beesly, on which every scrap of evidence relating to raider activity was painstakingly recorded, with regular intelligence summaries then circulated to frontline commanders. This was accompanied by a database of legitimate shipping traffic, enabling the identity of suspect vessels to be quickly checked by intercepting Royal Navy warships. It took many months for Beesly's picture to deliver operational value, although it was greatly helped by intelligence from a British prisoner recovered from a German supply ship. The first major success came in May 1941, when the cruiser *Cornwall* caught and sank *Pinguin* (Raider F), the most successful of all Germany's surface-raiders, in the northwest Indian Ocean. This followed D/F hints suggesting a German unit in the area, and a distress signal transmitted by her final victim, a tanker near the Persian Gulf.[22]

The renewed Atlantic U-boat offensive

Apart from the risk of invasion, the biggest naval threat Britain faced from the middle of the year was the resumed U-boat offensive against Atlantic shipping. During the three months March to May, when the U-boats were withdrawn to support the Norwegian campaign, shipping losses to U-boats fell to 162,388 tons, less than one-fifth of those in the first six months of the war. Over the seven months from 1 June, they approached 2 million tons, double the loss rate to end February, with a broadly similar force deployed in patrol areas. Although the average operational force across these months, of about twenty-five boats, was down one-third from the start of the year, this reduction was compensated by reduced transit time from the French ports, beginning from Lorient in July. British losses were now concentrated in the northwest approaches, reflecting the channelling of traffic to the west-coast ports, especially Liverpool and the Clyde, with about 80 per cent occurring within a radius of 500 miles from Belfast.[23] During this period, and the first quarter of 1941, the U-boats still predominantly targeted independently sailed ships and convoy stragglers, although between August and October there were also significant operations directly against convoys. These months saw the first successful use of wolf-pack tactics, where U-boats exploited surface mobility under radio direction to concentrate and attack at night. They faced limited opposition from escorts, owing to withdrawals for anti-invasion duties, and until the end of August, B-Dienst read British ciphers currently. Nevertheless, although some convoys suffered heavily, the limited U-boat force meant about 80 per cent passed unscathed. Convoys were again heavily targeted from the following March, when new U-boat tactics were initiated.[24]

Through this second half of 1940 and first quarter of 1941, British ability to counter the evolving U-boat threat was shaped primarily by improvements in organisation, increased resources, new technology, notably the fitting of escorts and aircraft with radar and VHF radio telephones, which helped combat night surface attack, along with new tactics and better training. While the operational U-boat force did not increase in these nine months, anti-submarine vessels under British control rose 50 per cent to 350 vessels, and with the redeployment from invasion duty, frontline escort strength in the Atlantic by rather more. In parallel, maritime patrol aircraft strength also increased, including the arrival of long-range American Catalina flying boats. Furthermore, from early 1941, the whole anti-submarine effort was consolidated under Western Approaches Command in a new tailor-made underground headquarters in Liverpool. The new command, under Admiral Sir Percy Noble, drove important changes in policy, escort tactics and training incorporated in *Western Approaches Convoy Instructions*, which emphasised that 'the safe and timely arrival of the convoy at its destination is the primary object of the escort'. These improvements in British anti-submarine direction, strength and capability largely determined why shipping losses in the five months November to March were down 30 per cent on the previous five, although winter weather helped too, as did reduced ability of B-Dienst to read the main British naval cipher from the end of August. By the end of March, with operational availability for its escort force averaging 75 per cent, Britain had about eight operational anti-submarine escorts for every operational U-boat, and average escort strength per convoy was four vessels, double that the previous autumn. This explains German setbacks that month, including the loss of three U-boat 'aces'. The number of new escorts commissioned equalled that of U-boats over the next twelve months. Overall, these organisational and logistic advantages made Britain well-placed to capitalise on new intelligence opportunities.[25]

However, as 1941 opened, the role of intelligence remained limited. On the plus side, the OIC correctly assessed that the Germans could not sustain more than seven to ten boats simultaneously in Atlantic patrol areas, and their estimate of thirty boats lost to date, drawing on Ernest Thring's rigorous analysis of all claimed sinkings, was exactly right. Captured documents like those from *U-49*, and interrogation of prisoners taken from about thirteen boats, had provided a good picture of the current performance, sensors and armament of the different U-boat types, including the problems with torpedoes, although with less insight into future capability. Prisoners were generally reluctant to discuss tactics that might help their enemy although, unusually, in November 1940 a petty officer communicator from *U-32* provided valuable insights into night surface attack tactics, and confirmed there was no pre-arranged co-operation between boats, or radio contact between them. U-boats were instead given any convoy intelligence, and directed when and where to attack by U-boat headquarters, Befehlshaber der Unterseeboote (BdU).[26] Meanwhile, NID assessments of overall U-boat strength and rate of construction, primarily drawn from the same sources, with occasional insights from aerial reconnaissance, had improved across 1940. However, their figure of ninety in commission on 1 March was about 15 per cent below reality, and they badly underestimated output across the rest of the year, on the advice of MEW projecting an addition of ninety in the remaining ten months, whereas the Germans achieved double this figure.[27] New SIS agent networks were beginning to report on the development of the French bases, including the construction of concrete shelters, and the arrival and departure of U-boats. Such movement reports helped the OIC establish deployment patterns, but could not match the precision SIGINT had provided in 1914–18.

The most pressing lack was any consistent and reliable means of locating and tracking U-boats on patrol, good enough to steer convoys clear of danger, or to enable effective prosecution by anti-submarine forces. Naval Enigma remained unbroken, so the only sources available here to the OIC were D/F and traffic analysis. The limitations of D/F bearing accuracy at this stage of the war was compounded by the loss of French sites, producing poorer coverage than in 1916–18, while U-boats were more careful in using radio, keeping wireless silence until they sighted a convoy. Nevertheless, if the immediate outlook for operational intelligence seemed unpromising, there were moves underway capable of transforming Britain's prospects for both the U-boat campaign and the wider naval war.

By early 1941, two developments were enabling NID to direct naval intelligence generally, and any Enigma-generated intelligence specifically, more effectively. The first was the evolution of DNI's central staff, now designated NID17 and located in Room 39. NID17 was part policy and planning cell, and part intelligence clearing house. At this time it comprised a dozen staff, which doubled over the next eighteen months. As with other parts of the wartime NID, most were civilian recruits, including a stockbroker, a schoolmaster, an eminent barrister, an Oxford classics don, an artist and a journalist. The two key figures throughout the war, who shared responsibility for intelligence planning and liaison with external departments and agencies were Fleming, and Commander (later Captain) Charles Drake. Other important members were Lieutenant Commander Ewen Montagu (17M), who arrived in December 1940 to monitor and exploit Abwehr intelligence, including Enigma decrypts of naval interest, and represented DNI on the Double-Cross counter-espionage and deception committee, and Major Lordon (17P), who arrived in July 1941 to supervise Ultra intelligence. The role of 17P in handling Ultra complemented the OIC. The latter was responsible for immediate operational appreciation and action: 17P separately monitored all incoming Ultra intelligence, and prepared a daily summary of important items for DNI and the senior naval staff. It also circulated a version to external departments. Initially, 17P dealt with two hundred decrypts per day, but by the end of 1941 this figure had doubled, and it circulated summaries thrice daily. In July 1942 17M and 17P were split off from NID17 to form a new, self-contained, special intelligence section, NID12. It is customary to describe all SIGINT-generated intelligence from Enigma and related sources during the Second World War as Ultra intelligence. However, Ultra was actually a protective security grading, applied to signals and documents, dictating special handling arrangements and controls over 'action on'. Within the Royal Navy, the content of SIGINT decrypts was always referred to as Special Intelligence, or sometimes 'Z'.[28]

Meanwhile, although it retained the basic structure with which it began the war, the OIC, under Jock Clayton as DDIC, was also evolving.[29] The two most important sections were 8E, German surface craft, under Norman Denning, and 8S, the submarine tracking room, where in January the barrister Rodger Winn took over from Thring. The appointment of a civilian to head such a vital section was unprecedented, but Winn had won the confidence of the entire naval staff over the previous year, and received the backing of Phillips and Pound. It also underlined a point that Godfrey had grasped, and Hall would have endorsed, that naval officers, certainly from the executive branch, did not necessarily make good intelligence officers. The Norwegian campaign convinced Godfrey and Phillips that the role of the OIC was critical, but also persuaded them it was suffering from over-stretch, and a deficit of operational experience. Although badly needed elsewhere, three active service officers of commander rank with recent sea time were therefore appointed as senior watch-keepers, and four additional paymasters were found to add expertise at section level.[30] Not all these naval officers adapted successfully to the intelligence world, but they helped the varied group of civilian incomers navigate their strange new environment and understand the basics of naval operations, and made the OIC an effective twenty-four by seven service. For it was ultimately the eclectic civilians who turned William James's 1936 vision into powerful reality. One of them, the journalist Robin Barrett, wryly speculated that a future Board of Admiralty would surely be aghast to discover that the vital work of the OIC depended on a paymaster lieutenant commander, a lawyer, a geography professor, a female archaeologist, and several accountants, all working under the supervision of a wise and kindly retired senior officer.[31]

Other factors helped the OIC become more effective. In early 1941, together with the Operations and Trade Divisions and the war registry, it moved into the new bombproof underground Citadel at the northwest corner of the Admiralty. There was more space for both the OIC surface and submarine plots and their related facilities, and the D/F plot was collocated with the latter. External communications were much improved, with good teleprinter connections to GC&CS, the D/F stations, and the frontline commands. In February, when Western Approaches Command moved into its new underground headquarters at Derby

House in Liverpool, the OIC submarine plot, with all its intelligence, was duplicated here on a huge wall chart covering the Atlantic, with constant updates by secure telephone.[32] Soon after the move to the Citadel, the previously separate Operations and Trade plots were merged into a single Master Plot, and housed in a large room adjacent to the U-boat tracking room, 8S, with direct access to it, and separated from Denning's sections only by the width of a corridor. The senior command at the Admiralty could now gain a complete picture of the war at sea, including the latest intelligence, by scanning across adjoining rooms.[33] Most important of all, given developments in the coming months, the experience of handling the *Polares* decrypts, and the ups and downs over traffic analysis had fostered a strong integrated relationship between the indoctrinated personnel of the OIC, and Huts 4 and 8. There was now an informal understanding that the Bletchley team did not just produce raw decrypts, but applied their research and expertise to analyse and assess all SIGINT material. Still under Frank Birch, and still often called 'naval section', Hut 4 expanded rapidly, reaching two hundred staff by the end of 1941; 8G surrendered its residual analysis role to Hut 4, and became a SIGINT reception and distribution section for the OIC. The OIC still received raw copies of every decrypt formally processed, but accepted that its role was the operational appreciation of SIGINT, not its production. To improve relations further with Bletchley, in early 1941 Godfrey appointed a senior liaison officer ranked as an assistant director, Captain John (Jasper) Haines. When NID12 was formed a year later, Haines's liaison section, now with about thirty personnel, became NID12a.[34]

The working atmosphere in the Citadel, and the way the OIC interacted with the key operational sections, has been well described by wartime participants. The Master Plot now displayed a comprehensive picture of warship and merchant movements across home waters and the North Atlantic, constantly updated day and night, albeit in sanitised form, with key enemy information from the evolving intelligence picture in the OIC. Each day began with a three-way conference call between the OIC, Coastal Command and Western Approaches, to share the latest intelligence picture and agree any necessary dispositions. This was followed by a meeting, usually in the U-boat tracking room, bringing together ACNS (U-boats and Trade), the Directors of Operations (Home), Trade and Anti-submarine Warfare, together with Clayton, Denning and Winn. ACNS (Foreign) and Director of Operations (Foreign) were also regular attendees. Thereafter, informal contacts across this group were constant throughout the day. In the first half of 1941 the key relationships were between Denning and Captain Ralph Edwards, Director of Operations

(Home), and between Winn and Commander Richard Hall, the head of movements section within Trade Division, and also responsible for managing the Master Plot. Richard was 'a large and genial man', with a face 'fresh and plump', in which a 'majestic nose' recalled the face of his famous father, the redoubtable former DID, 'Blinker'. Hall and Winn worked seamlessly together in one of the 'most cordial partnerships of the war' until 1945, even sharing transport to the Admiralty at seven each morning. Hall gave Winn estimated positions for all merchant ships in the Atlantic from his Master Plot. Winn gave Hall known and suspected U-boat positions. Their motto was 'Never the twain shall meet'. Henry Moore famously told Rear Admiral John Edelsten, when handing over the post of ACNS (U-boats and Trade), 'If those two ever stop bickering, we shall lose the war.'[35]

Overall, therefore, the OIC was poised to exploit better facilities and the growing skill, experience and confidence of its staff, but remained constrained by limited intelligence inputs. Its picture of enemy forces was still partial and sporadic, making prediction of future enemy intent difficult. Already evident in the ongoing U-boat campaign, this was further underlined by the sortie of the battlecruisers *Scharnhorst* and *Gneisenau* between 22 January and 22 March, during which they sank twenty-two ships, totalling 115,622 tons, 25 per cent of the loss to U-boats in the same period. This sortie, and the simultaneous cruise of the pocket battleship *Admiral Scheer* through the South Atlantic and Indian Ocean, which sank 113,223 tons, were the only strategically significant German warship raider operations of the war. In contrast to the previous battlecruiser sorties in November 1939 and June 1940, this time the OIC provided timely warning. Denning circulated an accurate summary of the status of all the main German heavy units on 18 January.[36] Two days later, drawing on Enigma air force decrypts showing the Luftwaffe conducting reconnaissance of ice conditions around Iceland, and unusual radio traffic in the Baltic, he alerted Tovey, the new Commander-in-Chief Home Fleet, that a major fleet operation was imminent. This was two days before the battlecruisers sailed from Kiel under Admiral Günther Lütjens. Tovey therefore deployed to cover the Iceland–Faroes gap, leading to a brief sighting of the German force by the cruiser *Naiad*, in a blinding snowstorm southeast of Iceland. *Naiad* could not definitively identify the enemy vessels, nor was her radar good enough to track them in winter conditions, but confirmation that the battlecruisers had left the Baltic reached the OIC simultaneously from Captain Henry Denham, the naval attaché in Stockholm, drawing on Danish sources. The encounter with *Naiad* persuaded Lütjens temporarily to retreat and head north. B-Dienst, which was again reading British traffic, then enabled him to evade Tovey and successfully transit the Denmark Strait in early February. Thereafter, for most of their cruise, the OIC had little idea of the battlecruisers' whereabouts, demonstrating the difficulty of locating raiders with present sources once they successfully broke into the Atlantic, and the critical importance of better SIGINT and aerial reconnaissance. Both now got renewed Admiralty attention.[37]

The Atlantic in 1941: A Step-change in Intelligence Capability

The breaking of naval Enigma

Breaking several days of April 1940 traffic with the *Polares* captures raised hopes, in both Bletchley and the OIC, that naval Enigma might soon be read regularly and currently, as was the Red air-force system. However, the second half of 1940 produced depressingly few results. Although Turing's team in Hut 8 now knew a lot about the structure of the naval system, and Turing had evolved good potential cryptographic attack strategies, it was soon apparent that further captures, or pinches, of at least some cipher settings were required. In theory, pinches might be unnecessary if settings could be reconstructed by finding a match between a crib (a known or guessed portion of plaintext) and cipher text using a bombe, which electromechanically tested numerous permutations. In practice, finding suitable cribs without more samples of plaintext messages than were yet available was immensely difficult. Cribs were required on a daily basis, ideally at least thirty letters long and accurate down to the last letter. Few ideal cribs ever existed, and without them the bombe time required with this crude approach was prohibitive. Only two were available before the end of 1940, and a bombe run using all the possible rotor orders for the naval machine took almost six times longer than an equivalent run for the Red air-force system. Maintaining current and rapid readability of the latter inevitably had priority. However, if some of the separate indicator settings, the bigram tables, were available, either from a pinch, or by reverse engineering from known daily settings, such as those acquired from *Polares*, a cryptographic process known as Banburismus could partially establish the daily rotor settings, reducing bombe testing time by a factor of ten. In November, using this technique, Hugh Foss, who had temporarily joined Hut 8, recreated enough bigram settings from the *Polares* material to decrypt a further four days of messages in April and May. But this process was too laborious to deliver timely results, and the new decrypts confirmed Hut 8's suspicion that the bigram tables had changed on 1 July, a month later than they previously believed, but rendering Foss's work useless after that date.[1]

In parallel with Hut 8's cryptographic efforts, ideas for further pinches were therefore discussed between GC&CS and NID. On 10 September Hut 4 produced a report on the deployment and activities of German naval units, especially E-boats, in the Channel, drawing on *Polares* material, and suggesting there was scope here for the desired capture.[2] Ian Fleming put a plan to Godfrey two days later. This was Operation Ruthless, which fully lived up to its name. A captured German bomber obtained from the RAF, with a volunteer British crew, preferably, in Fleming's view, 'bachelors', posing as a returning raider from a night sortie, would transmit a distress call on appropriate frequencies before 'crash landing' in the Channel, having attracted a German rescue launch of the type which Hut 4 suggested carried Enigma. The British team would kill the German crew, dump their bodies overboard and return home, hopefully with a haul of Enigma material. Although highly risky, with obvious weaknesses, Ruthless received enthusiastic support from Godfrey and Clayton, along with Birch, still heading Hut 4, and Turing. It was only abandoned when 'Y' coverage indicated there were no longer suitable German craft operating. This caused deep gloom in GC&CS where, according to Birch, on 20 October:

> Turing and Twinn came to me like undertakers cheated of a nice corpse two days ago, all in a stew about the cancellation of Operation Ruthless. The burden of their song was the importance of a pinch. Did the authorities realise that since the Germans did the dirt on their machine on June 1st, there was very little hope, if any, of their deciphering current, or even approximately current, Enigma for months and months and months, if ever?[3]

Ruthless demonstrates, as Fleming reminded Birch, that senior NID staff and indoctrinated members of the wider naval staff understood the importance of a pinch, and were prepared to take significant risks to get it. It also illustrates how Hut 8, Birch's team in Hut 4, the OIC, and DNI and his personal staff were now closely integrated, with complete sharing of information, on the Enigma challenge. However, despite Fleming's assurance that Ruthless was merely suspended, it was over four months before the much desired pinch came – on 4 March 1941, when Enigma settings for February were seized from the German armed trawler *Krebs*, during a commando raid on the Norwegian Lofoten islands. Although this raid had several avowed military objectives, authoritative contemporary witnesses insist that an undisclosed secret priority was the capture of cipher material. If this is true, the importance of the requirement was not sufficiently emphasised to the naval escort commander, Captain Clifford Caslon, in the destroyer *Somali*, who only reluctantly allowed a junior officer to board the damaged *Krebs* and allowed minimum time for a search. Nor did he arrange a thorough search of several captured German merchant vessels before they were destroyed, earning a rebuke from Admiral Tovey.[4]

As with *Polares*, the papers taken from *Krebs* were limited in scope. However, Hut 8 exploited them cryptographically far more quickly, because Turing and his team now knew more about the Enigma system. Hut 4 issued the first decrypt to 8G for the OIC on 12 March, and worked steadily back from the end of February, providing about two hundred decrypts covering the last half of this month by 9 April. At this point, Hut 8 shifted to April traffic and Hut 4 issued its first decrypt from this month, a signal from BdU to *U-75* dated 17 April, five days later on 22 April. This break into April traffic was possible, because Hut 8 successfully exploited the February settings to reconstruct the current bigram tables, facilitating a cryptographic attack using Banburismus plus bombe. About a hundred and fifty decrypts covering the last half of April were issued by 9 May, when Hut 8 began to break into May traffic. It thereafter gave this priority, decrypting more than eight hundred and fifty May signals by the end of the month, by which point the delay between interception and decryption was often down to forty-eight hours. Lack of resources and the priority accorded to the most recent traffic meant March was never broken.[5]

The elapsed time before February and April traffic, and even much of May, could be decrypted meant that only a handful of signals was immediately exploitable operationally. However, the 1250 signals issued across these months still contained a wealth of valuable intelligence. They gave the OIC a superb overview of current U-boat operations, their deployment, how they were controlled by BdU, their tactics, and the sources and quality of their convoy intelligence. There was also significant coverage of the major German surface units. The decrypts disclosed that *Bismarck* and *Prinz Eugen* were working up together in the Baltic during April, and decryption was timely enough for the OIC to know by mid May that their deployment as a joint force was probably imminent. Decryption was not fast enough to give the OIC any help during their subsequent sortie, Operation Rheinübung (Exercise Rhine), beginning on 18 May, although decrypts available immediately afterwards still provided useful information. Meanwhile, May decrypts also showed that *Tirpitz* and *Lützow*, the latter repaired after her damage in the Norwegian campaign, had begun trials early that month, although both were unlikely to be operational for some weeks. There were useful insights into German monitoring of British dispositions at Scapa Flow and Gibraltar. During May, there was an accumulation of intelligence on the location and activities of German supply ships in the Atlantic, partly in readiness for Operation Rhine, which was timely enough to permit countermeasures.[6]

Harry Hinsley also spotted a vital opportunity hidden in the spread of decrypted traffic covering February and the initial days broken for April. This was that the Germans were regularly deploying trawlers, which, crucially, carried Enigma, as weather-reporting ships north of Iceland and in mid Atlantic. On 26 April, four days after the first April results came out, he summarised his research, which also incorporated extensive traffic analysis, and proposed mounting an operation against a carefully chosen vessel to seize its Enigma cipher material. This was a more attractive and realistic opportunity than Ruthless, and with strong backing from DNI's new liaison officer at Bletchley, John Haines, it won speedy endorsement from Godfrey and the senior naval staff, along with considerable resources. This Admiralty commitment was influenced by April decrypts revealing the status of *Bismarck*, *Prinz Eugen* and *Tirpitz* all engaged in work-up and trials in the Baltic. The damage so recently inflicted by *Scharnhorst* and *Gneisenau*, and the prospect of simultaneous Atlantic raids from German and French bases, but also recent successes in the Mediterranean achieved through the breaking of Italian Enigma, ensured investment in better intelligence would not be skimped.

Nine days later, therefore, Tovey's deputy, Vice Admiral Lancelot Holland, left Scapa Flow with three cruisers and five destroyers to search for the chosen target, *München*. She was successfully intercepted north of the Arctic circle on 7 May, and although her crew managed to destroy many of her papers before she was boarded, Haines found the complete Enigma settings for June, along with the weather-signal codebook. This was one of the great intelligence coups of the war, and a brilliant team effort. Its conception by the youthful Hinsley was an outstanding mixture of painstaking research and original insight, concisely and authoritatively presented in an incredibly short timescale. The Admiralty deserve credit for having the imagination and faith to back him, and the subsequent operation was well executed by Holland and Haines, minimising the possibility of compromise to the Germans. Sadly, Holland had less than three weeks to live, being blown up with the battlecruiser *Hood* when back north of Iceland facing the German *Bismarck* on 25 May.[7]

The June settings from *München*, handed over to Peter Twinn on 10 May, were more valuable than the *Krebs* capture because, with the bigram tables already reconstructed, they would enable Hut 8 to read Enigma currently throughout the following month. Furthermore, the weather codebook enabled reconstruction of U-boat short weather signals, generating cribs for bombe menus. Unknown to Twinn, another vital windfall had been acquired the previous day, when a boarding party from the destroyer *Bulldog* ransacked *U-110* after she was forced to the surface and abandoned by her crew in the North Atlantic while attempting to attack a convoy. The haul from Operation Primrose, as this capture was christened, represented the single richest SIGINT prize taken during the whole war. The former 8G officer, Lieutenant Allon Bacon, now installed as Hut 4's travelling expert, was despatched to Scapa Flow to process it and ensure security. The most important item was the current bigram indicator tables which confirmed and completed Hut 8's reconstruction work. Also found were the standard key settings for April and June, the latter duplicating those found in *München*, the special additional settings used for 'Officer Only' signals, together with the operating manual, the codebooks for U-boat short-signal sighting reports and short weather reports, complementing the *München* haul as a vital source of cribs for the future. There were also copies of the standing operational orders for the Atlantic U-boat force, standing orders for U-boats in Lorient, operational charts sufficient to identify the Atlantic grid system used in signals, and details of German swept channels associated with their bases and coastal transit routes. Another document revealed that the Germans believed the British might possess an acoustic homing torpedo. This caused NID to watch for evidence that the Germans were developing such a weapon, and references to 'FAT' torpedoes were spotted in Enigma decrypts later in the year. FAT (*Federapparattorpedo*) proved to be a zigzagging weapon, rather than a homing weapon, but it spurred British countermeasures, which were ready when a true acoustic torpedo appeared in 1943.[8]

Given that Hut 8 had already reconstructed the current bigram tables, the set captured from *U-110* was not crucial to reading May traffic, although they filled some gaps and made it more efficient. The April daily settings also allowed the rapid breaking of another forty signals from that month. Despite some challenges, by the end of the month the combination of Banburismus and bombe-crunching had reduced the delay in breaking signals to forty-eight hours. However, 1 June was transformational. With the current monthly settings and still valid bigram tables, Hut 8 read the traffic for the first half of the month with negligible delay. About 150 signals were decrypted on the first day alone, most reaching the OIC in less than four hours, including one announcing the arrival of *Prinz Eugen* at Brest.[9]

Nevertheless, Hut 8 were not yet out of the woods. The *U-110* bigram tables expired on 15 June. The new ones could be reconstructed using the two weeks' traffic with known daily settings over the last half of the month, but this was a laborious process, and success not guaranteed. Despite more bombe time, with six now available, reading of July traffic would probably involve significant delay, and a blackout, with no settings to resolve it, was possible. Hinsley accordingly identified another weather ship, *Lauenburg*, holding new settings, and Haines convinced the Admiralty to mount a further operation, despite the risk of alerting the Germans. *Lauenburg* was successfully intercepted by another dedicated Home Fleet task force on 28 June, and Allon Bacon, deploying from the destroyer *Jupiter*, duly provided the July daily settings, enabling traffic to be read with minimal delay through that month. This gave Hut 8 a vital window in which to perfect their techniques for breaking what became known as the naval Enigma Home Waters key (which the Germans called Hydra, and the British, Dolphin) without access to further settings, by using a combination of Banburismus, crib and bombe. In finding Dolphin keys, Hut 8 was greatly helped by the German practice of only changing the Enigma rotor mix every second day. This halved the bombe time needed for the second day. Apart from the first six days of August, and 18 and 19 September, Dolphin was read currently, usually within twenty-four to forty-eight hours, for the rest of the war.[10]

Until late 1941, Dolphin was the dominant and all-pervasive German naval Enigma key and the focus, therefore, of Hut 8's entire effort. By the middle of the year, Hut 4 was aware, from intercepted traffic, of at least four other keys in existence. Two were used by warship surface-raiders and auxiliary raiders respectively, and never broken, because they never produced enough traffic to make attack feasible. A third was introduced for the Mediterranean theatre in April, and another for the Baltic, immediately preceding the attack on Russia in late June. Given limited GC&CS resources, these too were not attacked in 1941. However, maintaining the all-important Dolphin coverage still posed challenges. On 29 November the Germans again changed the bigram tables, preventing Banburismus. Decryption remained possible using cribs and bombe-crunching, but this was now less efficient. The tables could be reconstructed using the same methods applied following the *Krebs* capture in March, but this was a lengthy and painstaking process. Knowing that further raids were being planned in Norway, Hut 4 pressed the Admiralty for further pinches. It was accordingly agreed to make the capture of cipher material a subsidiary objective in simultaneous operations mounted against Måløy between Bergen and Trondheim (Archery), and the Lofoten Islands (Anklet) at the end of December. Together these operations – which were planned by Allon Bacon, who drew on intelligence from a Norwegian fisherman, John Sigurdson, and deployed with the Archery force – provided a rich haul of Enigma material, including the desired bigram tables.[11] A more serious problem was foreshadowed in the autumn, when minor divergencies from Dolphin were noted in U-boat traffic. These did not initially cause Hut 8 much difficulty, but they led to a more dramatic security innovation, the introduction of a fourth wheel for U-boat Enigma from 1 February 1942, which created an entirely separate U-boat system (called Triton by the Germans, and Shark by the British), which Hut 8 could not read for ten months.[12]

Most Dolphin signals, like the SKM signals handled by Room 40, were short, invariably no more than twenty words, with abbreviations and technical terms which Hut 4 had to unpack. A typical U-boat signal from October 1941 read:

German write-up (after correcting textual mistakes due to faulty encipherment, transmission or interception):

Von Schulze:
Qu 6852 1 Dampfer,. 1 Tanker wahrscheinlich. Am 15, 10, Tanker Fackel.
Stehe 8967 69 cbm 2 plus 1 Aale SW 3 bis 4 996 mb plus 21
An Bef Ubte

Literal English:

From Schulze:
Sq 8852 1 steamship, 1 tanker probably. One 15/10 tanker torch.
Position 8967, 69 cubic metres, 2 plus 1 eels, SW 3 to 4 996 millibars, plus 21.
To Adm Cmd U/Bs.

Complete translation:

From: Schulze (U 432)
To: Admiral Commanding U-boats
In square 8852 have sunk one steamship (for certain) and one tanker probably. Set one tanker on fire on October 15th.
My present position is square 6967. Have 69 cubic metres of fuel

oil left. Have two (air) and one (electric) torpedoes left. Wind south-west, force 3 to 4. Pressure 996 millibars. Temperature 21 degrees (above freezing point).[13]

The further evolution of aerial PR

Despite the improvements in PR capability and organisation achieved by the end of 1940, the next six months saw growing Admiralty frustration over the quality of service it received, and increasingly bitter recriminations with the Air Ministry. This made a sharp contrast with the highly integrated and collaborative relationship achieved with GC&CS. Phillips as VCNS, writing before the full potential of the *Krebs* Enigma breakthrough was evident, succinctly conveyed Admiralty frustration to Commander-in-Chief Coastal Command Air Chief Marshal Sir Frederick Bowhill on 10 April. Four German heavy ships, *Scharnhorst* and *Gneisenau*, *Admiral Scheer*, and the heavy cruiser *Hipper*, had successfully sortied against British trade and returned to French or German ports during the last five months, without warning from aerial reconnaissance, other than a single report of the battlecruisers returning to Brest one day after a sighting by a Fleet Air Arm aircraft from the carrier *Ark Royal*. Regular coverage of German and German-occupied ports was a critical requirement for the Admiralty which, apart from the failings listed, also lacked any current knowledge of the whereabouts of *Bismarck*, *Tirpitz*, the carrier *Graf Zeppelin*, and the German light cruisers. In the Mediterranean, things were equally bad. Godfrey and Phillips had separately raised concern over lack of coverage of U-boat building yards. Phillips's complaints were neither entirely accurate, nor fair. The RAF had photographed *Hipper* at Brest on 2 January after her abortive engagement with the troop convoy, and from 28 March they mounted sorties at least twice daily there to monitor the battlecruisers. During March, as Godfrey should have advised Phillips, there had also been important progress in U-boat monitoring.[14]

The underlying problem here was not photographic interpretation, where important and far-reaching steps were underway. In January the PIU was rechristened the Central Interpretation Unit (CIU), and although still administered by Coastal Command, with operational control coming under the Assistant Chief of Air Staff (Intelligence) (ACAS (I)), it effectively became an independent tri-service organisation, responsible for interpreting all air photographs from all sources and issuing all resulting intelligence reports. In April it moved from Wembley to Medmenham in Buckinghamshire, where it remained for the rest of the war. By early 1942, it had absorbed all earlier interpretation organisations, including the Bomber Command Damage Assessment organisation, had fourteen separate specialist sections, including several specifically focused on naval interests, and had grown to five hundred staff, with an interpretation school, library and model-making facility.[15]

One of CIU's first major successes was assessment of U-boat construction. Large-scale photographs of Kiel taken on 12 and 13 March 1941 gave CIU much better understanding of the construction process, and specific indicators to look for. On 21 March it issued its first major report on German shipbuilding, based on coverage of all accessible yards and ports. This revealed low activity in surface warship and merchant building, but 'a vast drive in submarine construction which began in the last half of 1940'. In the yards west of Stettin, it counted 118 boats under construction, including a dozen fitting-out. Furthermore, by examining previous photographs taken at Bremen at roughly monthly intervals since the previous August, it estimated current construction time as eight months, enabling forecasting of future frontline strength, including breakdown by type. Three weeks later, excellent photographs of Hamburg identified a further batch of U-boats, raising the total to 144. By September, this had risen to 211, with fifty-three fitting out, although Danzig remained beyond reach.[16] Total boats commissioned in 1941 were 199, compared to fifty in 1940, so this March report potentially represented accurate and transformational intelligence of what was coming, enabling policy and operational countermeasures. However, until the middle of the year, NID was conservative in assessing the impact of this photographic evidence, underestimating the number of boats in service at the end of the year by 15 per cent.[17]

The ultimate cause of Admiralty frustration through much of 1941 was twofold: insufficient PR aircraft to meet growing demands, and inadequate arrangements for prioritising between requirements, especially where service interests competed. Poor relations between the naval and air staffs over aerial reconnaissance were exacerbated by the RAF imposing organisational changes to resolve internal service problems without consulting Admiralty stakeholders, and giving the impression that it prioritised its constitutional control in this area over collaborative problem-solving. The Admiralty did not help by suggesting it would build a supplementary PR organisation under exclusive naval control, employing aircraft purchased from America, and taking on Cotton as a consultant to drive this project forward.[18] This initiative, in which Godfrey and Fleming were prime movers, predictably achieved nothing other than waste time and create more bad blood. Nevertheless, despite many months of bureaucratic warfare, both resources and prioritisation were largely resolved by the end of the year. In August the chiefs of staff agreed there should be a single reconnaissance group in the United Kingdom, No 1 PRU, capable of sustaining twenty-four missions per day, and by December the aircraft, with eight, two-engine, long-range Mosquitos joining fifty Spitfires, were available to achieve this, along with much improved cameras. The Mosquitos were important, since they had the range to cover all the Baltic ports and northern Norway. Meanwhile, better prioritisation was implemented, first by the JIC, and then under a streamlined system controlled by Air Intelligence, but with all stakeholders represented. Over the year, the PRU conducted 1855 successful sorties, compared with 835 in 1940, of which about two-thirds were on naval requirements.[19]

Admiralty requirements for PR were identified by the OIC, which also assessed the operational implications of the resulting CIU reports. Initially, PR was handled by Denning, reflecting the priority given to tracking major fleet units. Following the creation of the CIU, the OIC appointed a liaison officer there, but by the end of 1941 it was apparent that the OIC would benefit from a trained interpreter, and a dedicated photographic intelligence section 8P was established, which did no original interpretation, but assessed and forwarded all naval photographic requirements, and distributed all incoming reports. It also took over photographic records started in 1940 – in time, building up a vast library containing every photograph, card-indexed for easy reference. It thus fulfilled many of the same functions 8G exercised for SIGINT. By the time 8P was created, naval requirements for PR comprised two categories – routine reconnaissance of enemy ports and reconnaissance of special targets. The routine programme involved monitoring sixty ports at stated intervals, from daily to three monthly. Ports and intervals were constantly reviewed, with adjustments as required. Special coverage was only requested for targets neither covered by the routine programme, nor satisfied from 8P's existing records. Interpretation of photographs involved three phases. First phase was done when the aircraft landed at its base. Photographs were instantly developed and urgent results, including pilot comment, passed to 8P by telephone, followed by teleprinter signal. Second phase comprised a detailed activity report summarising all observed events at a target over the previous twenty-four hours. Third phase considered the latest photographs alongside all previous records of the target, identifying significant developments. For the Admiralty, key third-phase work focused particularly on U-boat construction, other shipbuilding, warship and merchant, warship armament and sensor fits, ports and facilities, U-boat shelters, and coastal defences.[20]

The problems in building adequate PR capacity across 1941, and the strained relations between Admiralty and Air Ministry, undoubtedly contributed to one important intelligence and operational failure. This was the slowness in recognising the rapid and extensive German programme in constructing concrete protective E-boat and U-boat shelters at multiple sites on the Belgian and French Atlantic coast. PR identified a site under construction at Ostend as early as January 1941, and SIS reports over the next few months reported preparations underway at many other bases. Given that the Germans had constructed extensive shelters in Belgium in the previous war, NID was slow to focus on the implications of this intelligence, but lack of PR capacity to follow up on SIS warnings meant too little was done until work had reached a point where bombing was ineffective. By early 1942, SIS had delivered detailed plans of the facilities at Brest, St Nazaire, Lorient, La Pallice and Bordeaux, which merely underlined their sophistication and that they were now impervious to attack.[21]

The development of prisoner-of-war intelligence

By early 1941, prisoner-of-war (POW) intelligence added increasing value to the naval intelligence picture, especially on the U-boat force, which provided by far the largest category of naval prisoners. POW interrogation was conducted by the inter-service Combined Services Detailed Interrogation Centre (CSDIC), administered by MI in the War Office, initially based in the Tower of London, but from mid 1940 until 1942 at Cockfosters, Trent Park, Barnet. It was supervised by the three service directors of intelligence, each of whom established a POW section on the outbreak of war, to exercise policy oversight, and manage the dissemination of POW intelligence for their service. Major issues of policy and resources were addressed by the JIC, which then made appropriate recommendations to the chiefs of staff. Godfrey appointed Bernard Trench of Frisian Islands fame, now returned to service with the rank of colonel, to establish the initial POW unit within NID designated NID11. In January 1942 NID11 split into NID1 (PW) and NID3 (PW) for German and Italian prisoners respectively, and collocated in the relevant geographical section. Trench became A/DNI (P/W), exercising overall responsibility for naval POW intelligence home and overseas until 1944.

During the Munich crisis, the CID confirmed that the War Office was responsible for the supervision and administration of all POWs, from whatever service they originated and however they were captured.[22] However, it was Godfrey who initiated interdepartmental discussions in June 1939 on arrangements for interrogation. He did so following discussion in early April with William Brandon, probably at the suggestion of Hall. Brandon briefed him on ID experience in the last war and, importantly, on the joint project undertaken with MI1(a) in 1918.[23] He clearly convinced Godfrey that this model should now be replicated, and the CSDIC concept, and its initial establishment in the Tower immediately war was declared, was agreed at two meetings attended by representatives of the three service intelligence departments, MI5, and the Home Office on 9 June and 21 July. Although the idea of a joint approach to interrogation commanded ready consensus, it was undoubtedly Godfrey who got CSDIC up and running, and established the principles under which it should operate. The choice of Colonel Thomas Kendrick, SIS station commander in Vienna until arrested by the Gestapo in August 1938, to lead CSDIC, which he did successfully throughout the war, probably emerged in discussion between Godfrey and Hugh Sinclair, who was looking for somewhere to place Kendrick. Godfrey also won agreement that the Tower was not suitable as a permanent site for CSDIC, and that the facilities at Trent Park must be deliberately tailored to its requirements, both more extensive and more sophisticated, including concealed microphones fitted in twelve cells for eavesdropping.[24]

From the beginning, encouraged by Godfrey, with first-hand input from Trench and Brandon, the handling and interrogation techniques adopted by CSDIC drew on careful study of experience and best practice established in the previous war, including all the ideas under discussion with MI1(a) at the time of the armistice. CSDIC, therefore, started in September 1939 using what had worked best by November 1918. By 1941, although interrogation facilities and processes remained common to all three services under War Office administration, each service had evolved its own distinct section with specialist expertise. CSDIC also established an offshoot, the Prisoners of War Interrogation Service, PWIS (Home), which provided officers to frontline commands throughout the United Kingdom. Their role was to organise the reception of prisoners and their transfer to CSDIC, to provide advance notice of their identity and unit, and anything volunteered to their captors, but they did not themselves interrogate. Meanwhile, the limited capacity of Trent Park, its perceived vulnerability to bombing, and the distraction caused by air raids, led to the construction of two new purpose-built facilities at Latimer House in Buckinghamshire, and Wilton Park, which became operational in 1942. By then, CSDIC had a thousand staff and could handle nearly four hundred POWs simultaneously. Similar facilities based on the CSDIC model operated in overseas theatres. Godfrey's initiative in summer 1939 had ultimately created an intelligence organisation operating on an industrial scale.[25]

CSDIC used three methods to acquire information: direct interrogation, electronic eavesdropping, and stool pigeons. By 1941, each of these, and the interaction between them, was becoming ever more sophisticated. Successful direct interrogation required the interrogator to have excellent German, the ability to assert his personality over the prisoner, partly by cultivating omniscience, and the skill rapidly to identify those prisoners susceptible to talking, for whatever reason. As in the previous war, omniscience, apparently possessing more knowledge of the German navy and his branch than the prisoner, was highly effective ('knowledge begets knowledge'). So, sometimes, was the cultivation of select prisoners in a relaxed environment, for example, taking U-boat captains out for a meal in London. Physical violence, let alone torture, was never used, mainly because British experience in colonial theatres showed that it was ineffective, but psychological intimidation, playing on a prisoner's fear that he might be handed to the Russians, or shot as a spy, unless he provided evidence of his service work, was considered fair game. If a prisoner was judged to be holding back valuable information, he was placed in a wired cell with another prisoner of similar rank and background, in the hope they confided in each other. In 1941 the Barnet facility had eight such cells, covered by 150 army transcribers. Stool pigeons extended this technique by deliberately raising specific topics with a prisoner. They also played on a prisoner's vulnerabilities, to make him more susceptible to interrogation. Until 1942 naval stool pigeons were almost entirely recruited from the German refugee community, but thereafter many came from prisoner volunteers. By 1944, the number and quality of prisoner 'converts' meant these could extract almost any useful information from any member of the crew of a U-boat within a short period. In December 1939 Godfrey briefly explored the use of drugs, specifically Evipan, to encourage prisoners to talk. There was at least one trial on an NID volunteer. The proposal was challenged on both ethical and legal grounds in both NID and CSDIC, and there were concerns over political accountability. While Godfrey was inclined to overrule these doubts, the opposition ended the idea.[26]

CSDIC naval section, headed initially by Lieutenant Commander Burton Cope, who had also served as an interrogator in the previous war, had three naval officer interrogators and a clerk at the end of 1940, increasing to twenty-five staff by 1944. NID1 (PW) and NID3 (PW) received and processed all prisoner intelligence, but also transmitted specific requirements and background briefing for the interrogators. This background was carefully controlled, so that interrogators had enough information to do their job effectively, but not so much that sensitive sources such as Ultra material risked compromise, or that intelligence they acquired was 'adulterated' by their own extraneous knowledge. The NID (PW) units received any urgent intelligence as an immediate report, if necessary by phone, and eavesdropping reports were issued in a separate SRN (Navy) series. When interrogation of a prisoner or batch of prisoners was complete a full preliminary report was issued by CSDIC, which the NID (PW) sections edited and circulated as a bound copy in the CB 04051 series. The format and presentation of these reports was similar to that in the previous war; 103 reports were issued up to 1944.[27]

The Admiralty's post-war assessment of prisoner intelligence downplayed the value of information acquired before 1942, suggesting it was dominated by accounts of operations too dated to be of value, with little on new capabilities under development. It also emphasised doubts about its reliability, quoting NID refusing to credit that U-boats could dive to 600ft or the armament of *Narvik*-class destroyers.[28] The downplaying is justified by some of the sixteen CB 04051 reports issued in 1939–40, but many of the seventeen 1941 reports provided detail and insights of high value. Notable highlights were reports on U-boat ace Otto Kretschmer's *U-99* issued in April; on the prize crews of *Admiral Scheer* and *Gneisenau* captured in March and issued in July; on *U-110*, issued in July, comprising thirty-seven closely packed pages compounding the damage done by her loss of cipher material and other secret documents; on *Bismarck* the same month; and later in the year, the Atlantic supply ships and the merchant raider *Pinguin*. By September 1941, POW intelligence enabled NID accurately to list most of the U-boats commissioned to date, identifying them by type with the correct German terminology, and with detailed specifications for each. It also knew the Germans were developing supply U-boats, although it did not yet know the type number (Type XIV), or when they would be operational. Meanwhile, the intelligence gleaned on raider operations was important, because it was not available from other sources.[29]

Because prisoner intelligence derived from human sources directly involved in operations, it also offered insight into morale and professional competence, not easily replicated elsewhere. For all his operational success, Kretschmer's 'war weariness' was striking. Revealingly, after the war, he confided that his British interrogators 'were extremely well informed … To them the U-boat service was more than a label; it was a living entity. To us, on the other hand, the enemy was no more than an anonymous mass.' Later in the year, prisoners from *U-570*, *U-501* and

U-111 all revealed starkly declining levels of experience in U-boat crews. As in the previous war, naval prisoners sometimes provided important intelligence on non-naval topics. One of *U-110*'s prisoners had been a political prisoner in Belsen concentration camp, reported extensively on conditions there, and was recruited as the first prisoner stool pigeon.[30]

In November 1941, following thorough inquiries, Godfrey endorsed the overall value of CSDIC intelligence, emphasising its contribution to knowledge of German radar and communications.[31] Ultimately, the power of CSDIC lay in its systematic approach to interrogation and monitoring, exploiting all available techniques and the power of modern technology in effective combination. No other combatant in the Second World war achieved results approaching those of CSDIC from POWs, and the intense security accorded to its work post-war reflected the desire to protect just how successful it had been from future potential enemies.[32]

The development of ship-borne HF/DF

By spring 1941, through traffic analysis, the first breaks into Dolphin, and prisoner interrogation, NID and GC&CS had a good understanding of the overall communications system by which Dönitz controlled his U-boat force from BdU, and which was essential to the group-attack concept he hoped would counter convoying.[33] Boats could only communicate when surfaced, and did so using HF radio, achieving long-range through skywave propagation which bounced signals off the ionosphere. Signal length was minimised, often down to ten seconds, by using short-signal books with designated formats using four-letter groups for sighting reports, fuel states, positions, and weather reports. Dummy short signals were also transmitted to confuse enemy listeners. Apart from rare exceptions where MF signals were transmitted for homing, there was no communication between boats. Instead, U-boat signals relevant to other boats were retransmitted from BdU, along with necessary additional context, intelligence and orders. A network of shore stations maximised the probability of receiving necessarily low-power U-boat transmissions, while outgoing signals were broadcast at high power, with repetition across several frequencies to guarantee receipt. Dönitz recognised that this system was vulnerable to British shore-based D/F, but judged good signal discipline by his boats, keeping transmission time to a minimum, kept the risk of an actionable D/F fix, given the known errors involved, to an acceptable level. This was a reasonable risk–benefit judgement, but Dönitz failed to consider two critical factors, because the Germans judged both impossible. The first was that Enigma would be broken, revealing the content of his messages. The second was that the British would successfully develop an HF/DF system for deployment at sea in anti-submarine escorts, and by this spring they were well on the way towards this goal, with dire consequences for Dönitz's strategy.[34]

By May 1941, the naval staff emphasised the potential of escort-mounted HF/DF against U-boats. If escorts could D/F an accurate bearing of a U-boat transmission at fifteen miles, they had good prospects of forcing the U-boat to submerge, with a 30 per cent chance of subsequent ASDIC contact. Building on its research into ship mounted HF/DF in the late 1930s, the Admiralty Signal Establishment (ASE) produced a trial set mounted in the destroyer *Hesperus* in March 1940. This demonstrated limited capability and, more seriously, it appeared impossible to fit both radar and HF/DF in the same vessel, mainly due to electronic interference between the two, but also top-weight stability problems, and radar took priority. By autumn 1941, the Battle of the Atlantic Committee was convinced of the potential of HF/DF, although it recognised precise ideas for its tactical deployment were still maturing. They were also resigned to fitting radar and HF/DF in different escorts, perhaps in the ratio 6:2. However, earlier in the year, the ASE team had been joined by Polish engineers led by Waclaw Struszynski, whom Humphrey Sandwith had met at Pyry in 1939. Struszynski achieved a series of breakthroughs during the summer, which solved the interference problem, and created an aerial incorporating a 'sense' feature, which provided an indication of signal strength on the correct bearing. His developments were incorporated in a production system known as FH3, first tried out alongside the new Type 271 centimetric radar in an ex-American sloop, *Culver*, in October. By January 1942, twenty-five FH3 sets were at sea in Royal Navy escorts, and by August about seventy. FH3 provided the operator solely with an aural tone to achieve the target bearing. The much improved FH4 used a cathode-ray tube to provide a visual display, and was first used operationally by the destroyer *Leamington* in March 1942. Seaborne HF/DF proved as important to Allied success in the Battle of the Atlantic as the reading of Enigma or employment of radar. It played a critical role in most phases of the campaign from early 1942 onward, and ultimately contributed to a quarter of U-boat losses. It also reached the frontline in time to compensate for the U-boat Enigma blackout which began in February 1942. Britain and her Allies therefore owed much to Struszynski, and also to his father Professor Marceli Struszynski of Warsaw University of Technology, who worked for the Polish resistance, and analysed fuel for the German V2 rocket.[35]

Naval intelligence operations in Sweden and Spain

German control of most of Western Europe from mid 1940 meant the surviving neutrals, Sweden, Spain and Portugal, became an important focus for naval intelligence, with the attachés in Stockholm and Madrid, for different reasons, especially significant. In theory, Sweden offered scope to monitor German operations in Scandinavia and the Baltic, including warship movements from east German ports into the Atlantic. In practice, the new attaché in Stockholm, Captain Henry Denham, who arrived in June 1940, faced a difficult task. Although public opinion favoured Britain, the Swedish armed forces, and especially the navy, were pro-German, doubted Britain's survival, and were disinclined to co-operate, and certainly not with intelligence. Relations further deteriorated after the British temporarily seized four destroyers Sweden had purchased from Italy, while they were transiting the Faroes. Without help from his host country, Denham initially relied on information from neutral attachés, and the Norwegian and Danish exile communities. One early contact, the Danish journalist–explorer Ebbe Munck, developed links to Danish resistance, leading to the creation of a coast-watching network able to report movements through the Great Belt, including the passage of *Scharnhorst* and *Gneisenau* in late January 1941. However, by the end of 1940, Denham had unexpectedly acquired a more valuable source. The Norwegian government in exile maintained a mission in Stockholm, and their military attaché, Colonel Ragnvald Roscher-Lund, was a notable cryptographic expert, who before the war had close links with Sweden's cryptographic unit and the 'C' office, Sweden's secret military intelligence service, including its head, Major Carl Petersen, and his deputy Captain Helmuth (Teddy) Ternberg, who became a close personal friend. Roscher-Lund and Petersen resumed contact and agreed to exchange information on Norway, now Petersen's top priority, to mutual advantage. Roscher-Lund provided information on German troop movements, coastal defences and oil supplies, and Petersen reciprocated, delegating day-to-day management of the relationship to Ternberg, his expert on Germany. Ternberg was virulently anti-German, and the following year conducted the brilliant recruitment of an Abwehr secretary, Erika Wendt, working within the German legation. Partly for this reason and partly through friendship, Ternberg gave Roscher-Lund a wider range of intelligence than Petersen had sanctioned, which he encouraged him to share fully with Denham. Through the spring of 1941, highlights included regular details of German warship and shipping movements, and intelligence suggesting preparations for an early attack on Russia.

Roscher-Lund returned to London in summer 1941 to become overall head of Norwegian intelligence, and the Ternberg relationship lapsed. However, he introduced Denham directly to Petersen, and an intelligence flow continued, albeit not at the same level. Roscher-Lund also facilitated a more important introduction to Colonel Carl Björnstjerna, chief of combined intelligence for the Swedish general staff. Björnstjerna had access to Swedish SIGINT, including decrypts of German military traffic between Berlin and military commands in Norway, which used a cable passing over Swedish territory. This relationship took time to consolidate, but by early 1942, Björnstjerna provided regular high-quality intelligence, primarily from SIGINT, on German naval movements and intentions in Norway, including the deployment of *Tirpitz* and other heavy units against the Russian convoys. These Swedish relationships were complicated, involving motivations which were hard to read and changed over time, and required clandestinity more suited to SIS. However, the SIS station was compromised by operational failures in 1940–41, which therefore drew Denham into activity carrying significant political and operational risk, beyond what the Foreign Office normally permitted to an attaché, even in wartime. Björnstjerna lost his job in autumn 1942, after his relationship with Denham was detected by Swedish security, and Petersen received a severe warning. Denham deserves great credit for creating the opportunities, sustaining them so well, and navigating through the setbacks to avoid a complete break in relations.[36]

Spain's civil war from 1936 made it important to NID, but the victory of the Nationalists led by General Francisco Franco, underpinned by German and Italian support, posed the risk that Spain would now formally ally with Germany, or at least provide covert support. This potential risk was underlined by the extensive German naval deployment in spring 1939, monitored by the OIC, and the conviction U-boats were secretly deploying to the South Atlantic. From the outbreak of war, therefore, assessing Spanish intentions, and specifically any covert supply of U-boats in Spanish ports, was a high priority. Until summer 1939, Spain was covered by the naval attaché in Paris, and casting around for a candidate to open a new post in Madrid, Godfrey remembered Alan Hillgarth, the consul in Majorca, who had impressed him while in command of *Repulse*. Hillgarth was a naval reservist and in March 1939 Pound, as Commander-in-Chief Mediterranean, recommended his immediate promotion to commander – refused by the Admiralty because he had insufficient active service. With Pound's support as incoming First Sea Lord, Godfrey now got him promoted and despatched him to Madrid in August. Over the next four years, Hillgarth dominated British intelligence operations in Spain in a manner without parallel for a naval attaché, before or since, with the possible exception of Gaunt in the United States between 1914–16. This reflected his energy and natural flair for the work, and unrivalled understanding of Spanish politics and culture, never remotely matched by successive SIS representatives, who were beset by operational failings similar to those in Sweden. Hillgarth had two other decisive advantages. He was trusted by, and exerted considerable influence over, the ambassador Sir Samuel Hoare, the former Foreign Secretary, First Lord and SIS officer, who arrived in June 1940, and he enjoyed direct access to Churchill, based on the friendship first established in Majorca.[37]

Hillgarth rapidly re-established contact with Juan March, wooed by Thoroton in 1916, now the richest man in Spain and a key financial sponsor of Franco, but who insisted his sympathies lay with the Allies. Hillgarth encouraged him to visit London, where he saw Godfrey, with two messages. Through his business networks, he could inform the British if U-boats began using Spanish ports, and prevent supplies reaching them. He also suggested a complex plan whereby Britain funded him to buy up German shipping in Spain, for selling on to friendly neutrals to mutual advantage. It was not clear if these propositions were directly linked, but the main beneficiary of the second was undoubtedly March, and the risks of ships falling into the wrong hands significant. The idea rumbled on for some months, encountering major opposition in Whitehall. Under pressure from Godfrey and Fleming, Churchill ordered some funds released for purchase, but the operation then petered out, and most vessels remained in German hands. What did proceed was a major bribery operation whereby, under Hillgarth's direction, up to 10 million US dollars was channelled, through March, over the next two years to senior military officers and members of Franco's inner circle, to keep Spain out of the war.[38]

As he demonstrated in the previous war, March was a ruthless, unscrupulous rogue, adept at playing both sides to his advantage. He was also a malign influence on Spain's well-being over several decades. Hillgarth, Godfrey and Churchill were convinced that in the present conflict, despite pursuing his own financial advantage, he genuinely supported Britain. They were probably too naive. March neither provided adequate intelligence on U-boat operations, as he had promised, nor did he prevent them. From late 1939, the German naval attaché, Captain Kurt Meyer-Döhner, established an elaborate U-boat support operation with Spanish connivance, which allowed at least a dozen boats to resupply at Cadiz, Vigo, El Ferrol and Las Palmas in the Canaries between January 1940 and mid 1942, of which the British had only partial visibility.[39]

In addition, between July 1941 and September 1942, at least twelve blockade-runners reached Bordeaux from the Far East with Spanish support.[40] The Spanish also provided significant support for German air reconnaissance and intelligence operations. March provided only limited and occasional insight into the real balance of thinking in Franco's circle towards co-operation with Germany, with no intelligence on the summit meeting with Hitler at Hendaye in October 1940. Nor is it clear that the bribery operation executed by March had a decisive effect. At most, it probably encouraged its recipients to do what they were already inclined to do, while making both them and March richer.[41]

The fall of France increased the stakes in Spain, raising the prospect that Germany would drive southwest to seize Gibraltar, with or without Spanish support, secure the western Mediterranean, and acquire permanent bases in Spain and on the West African coast, to break the British blockade and support the Atlantic offensive. Throughout the autumn of 1940, the Germans did indeed try hard to draw Spain into the war, with strategic aspirations closely aligned to British fears.[42] However, Franco and his colleagues were unwilling to commit to Germany unless she guaranteed benefits to outweigh the economic damage from subsequent British blockade. Here, Spanish aspirations in North Africa competed with French and Italian interests which Germany was reluctant to confront. Spain was also sceptical British naval power would be easily dislodged from the Mediterranean. As the British recognised, the retention of a powerful fleet in the eastern Mediterranean, in addition to the newly established Force H at Gibraltar, encouraged Spanish caution.[43] Spain understood her dependence on British goodwill for oil and most of her food, and Britain calibrated supplies with great skill, to ensure she had no chance to build up a cushion of stocks.[44]

Through 1940, with SIS initially ineffective, Hillgarth and his able Gibraltarian assistant, Augustus Gomez-Beare, who could pass as a Spaniard, established their own intelligence network, codenamed Secolo, rather as Denham did in Stockholm, to monitor Spanish ports for German activity, either to support U-boats or sabotage British shipping.[45] Hillgarth also acquired a senior Spanish naval source, codename Andros, and contributed to counter-intelligence by purchasing, with SIS agreement, and funding a complete list of Abwehr agents in Spain, from a Spanish security-service source. The embassy doctor was recruited to manage the exfiltration of escapees over the Pyrenees, exploiting his family connections in Vigo.[46] However, until the end of 1942, a dominant theme was the development of contingency plans to meet the consequences of Spain joining the Axis and/or a German invasion, and the probable resulting loss of Gibraltar. These plans, known as Operation Golden Eye, evolved under the direction of Ian Fleming, who preserved the name in his post-war home in Jamaica, and they comprised the deployment of 'stay-behind' networks for intelligence and sabotage. There were two scenarios: Operation Sprinkler to assist the Spanish if they resisted an invasion, and Sconce, if they co-operated. This planning became increasingly complex, with growing conflict between the intelligence objectives, which were the priority for NID and SIS, and sabotage for which the Special Operations Executive (SOE) began enthusiastically training Spanish-speaking groups in the Scottish Highlands. Hoare became increasingly nervous, but was assuaged with assurances that Hillgarth would co-ordinate any SOE activity.

Plans to maintain surveillance of the Gibraltar straits became a distinct industry. Henry Greensleeves, a British businessman in Tangier, was recruited as shadow to Staff Officer Intelligence Gibraltar, and installed in the British consulate to provide an initial NID base if Gibraltar was put out of action.[47] More ambitiously, in mid 1941 Godfrey and Fleming conceived Operation Tracer, which envisaged a small stay-behind team of six personnel, walled up in a chamber high up in the rock of Gibraltar with concealed observation apertures sufficient to command a view over the straits. The team would have supplies for a year, the time it would take the Germans to find them, and they would radio reports to London. Construction began later in the year and was completed with a trained crew earmarked by August 1942.[48] In hindsight, the effort devoted to Golden Eye seems excessive. However, the threat of a German move into Spain was real enough until late 1942, and the consequences of losing Gibraltar severe. Malta would have fallen, placing Britain's whole position in the Mediterranean and Middle East at risk. Ensuring residual intelligence capability justified significant investment.

Just as the British prioritised ability to monitor the Gibraltar straits, so did the Germans. The scale of the German effort was apparent after Oliver Strachey at GC&CS broke the Abwehr hand cipher in December 1940. The resulting decrypts known as ISOS (Intelligence Series Oliver Strachey) were assessed by Ewen Montagu in NID17M. By autumn 1941, they showed that the Germans had a coast-watching operation on both sides of the straits, from Cape Trafalgar to Malaga in the north, and Tangier to Tetouan in the south, comprising at least ten sites, with the most important at Algeciras, opposite Gibraltar. The sites enjoyed Spanish support, two entirely under Spanish control, and the others with German and Italian personnel in Spanish uniform. Algeciras alone transmitted twenty messages per day, which invariably reached Berlin within an hour.

Decrypts also revealed that over the winter of 1941/42, the Germans were installing sophisticated infrared monitoring and night-vision equipment at fourteen different sites, in an operation designated Bodden. During this period, coverage of the Abwehr, and therefore Bodden, was greatly enhanced when Dilly Knox broke two Abwehr Enigma keys, one in December designated ISK (for Knox), and the other in February, designated GGG. By March, Godfrey judged Bodden a serious threat, and advocated action by commando forces or SOE to destroy the network. Samuel Hoare had, surprisingly, already approved an SOE operation to bomb the Tangier site in January, using anti-Franco agents, an attack that had no lasting impact, but Godfrey's proposal was vastly more ambitious. Although Pound initially supported direct action, the chiefs of staff, influenced by Foreign Office advice, ruled against this, fearing that it could provoke Spain to tilt towards the Axis and trigger counter-moves against Gibraltar. Instead, they proposed diplomatic action, which was endorsed by the prime minister and the Foreign Secretary, Sir Anthony Eden. Hoare accordingly demanded the closing down of Bodden directly from Franco. Spanish assurances were duly given in July that the operation had ceased, and decrypts initially appeared to confirm this. However, within a month decrypts showed the Germans resurrecting Bodden on a smaller scale on the southern side of the straits, almost certainly with Spanish connivance. One of their new sites warned of the Pedestal convoy in August, and coverage persisted though Operation Torch, the Allied invasion of North Africa in November. Plans for direct action were revisited, but again turned down in favour of renewed diplomatic protests. These had some effect, as the Spanish became increasingly disinclined to risk Allied displeasure, but they turned a blind eye to vestiges of Bodden, which persisted through 1943, albeit with much reduced capability.[49]

25

The Atlantic in 1941: Intelligence Moves Centre Stage

Intelligence and the German raider force in 1941–42

Effective exploitation by the OIC of the improving intelligence capabilities available during the first half of 1941 was vividly demonstrated during the *Bismarck* sortie, Operation Rhine, again commanded by Lütjens, at the end of May. During the first half of May, Dolphin decrypts showed that *Bismarck* and *Prinz Eugen* continued to work up in the eastern Baltic but as with the battlecruisers earlier in the year, the first indicator of a possible sortie came from German air force Enigma decrypts, revealing reconnaissance of ice conditions in the Denmark Strait, including during the night of 17/18 May. The OIC advised Admiral Tovey, who alerted cruiser patrols north and south of Iceland. At midday on 20 May the *Bismarck* group was sighted in the Kattegat steering northwest, by the Swedish cruiser *Gotland*, whose report was seen by Captain Ternberg – who immediately alerted Roscher-Lund, who called Denham, who signalled the Admiralty at 2058 that evening. Following this report, the OIC asked for air reconnaissance of the Norwegian coast, and No 1 PRU despatched two Spitfires, one of which found and photographed the two German ships in Grimstadfjord, near Bergen, at 1300 the following day, two hours after their arrival. The OIC evidently now asked Hut 4 for any evidence of *Bismarck*'s intentions, because at 1728 that evening Hut 4 summarised decrypted signals relating to *Bismarck* covering the last week of April, the latest available, except one relating to repairs to her crane on 14 May. The most significant references were to the embarkation of 'prize crews' and special charts, the embarkation of 'naval staff', the requirement for cipher material from 16 July, and special communications procedures. One hour later the OIC informed all naval commands that *Bismarck* and *Prinz Eugen* had been sighted at

Bergen earlier in the day, and that 'these ships intend to carry out a raid on trade routes'.[1]

On receipt of the OIC signal, Tovey further strengthened the northern cruiser patrols, and ordered Vice Admiral Holland to take the battlecruiser *Hood* and new battleship *Prince of Wales* to a waiting position southwest of Iceland. For the next two days there was no further intelligence on *Bismarck*'s movements, apart from aerial confirmation late on 22 May that she had left Grimstadfjord, until she was sighted in the Denmark Strait by the cruiser *Suffolk* on the evening of 23 May. The SIS Norwegian station, Skylark B, which had been established by SIS-trained Norwegian exiles in Trondheim in January, also reported the arrival there of three German destroyers. The OIC realised these were part of *Bismarck*'s escort from the Baltic, and had now been detached by Lütjens, offering confirmation that he was headed into the Atlantic. Contrary to claims in various histories of the *Bismarck* operation, there was no reporting on her movements by any other coast-watching SIS agents.[2] *Suffolk* and her sister *Norfolk* successfully tracked the German force with the help of radar for the next thirty hours, through the disastrous engagement with Holland's force, but lost them in the early hours of 25 May, and missed Lütjens' detachment of *Prinz Eugen*.

Both sides now made critical errors. Lütjens, mistakenly believing he was still being shadowed, transmitted three signals in the forenoon of 25 May, including one of half-hour duration at 0852. These transmissions were picked up by numerous British intercept sites, verified as originating from *Bismarck* using RFP and TINA, one of the first major uses of this technique, and carefully plotted by 8X section in the OIC under Peter Kemp. Despite applying corrections, calculated from earlier D/F bearings taken on the German force the previous day, the resulting fix was poor, although it convinced Clayton, Denning and Captain Ralph Edwards, the Director of Operations, that *Bismarck* must be heading for France, rather than continuing raiding operations, or returning direct to Germany. An additional clue was that the previous day, control of *Bismarck*'s communications was observed to shift from Wilhelmshaven to Paris. Unfortunately, Clayton sent Tovey the original D/F bearings rather than the fix in the hope that his ships had achieved their own cross-bearings. The Admiralty bearings were incorrectly plotted by the flagship, giving a position for *Bismarck* 200 miles too far north, and causing Tovey to head in the wrong direction for eight hours. D/F bearings from later transmissions caused both the Admiralty and Tovey briefly to judge *Bismarck* was making for Norway. However, a critical German air force Enigma decrypt received at 1800 on 25 May, responding to an inquiry from

General Hans Jeschonnek, the chief of staff of the German air force, then visiting Athens, confirmed her destination was France. This knowledge, along with the D/F history, enabled a targeted Catalina search, which found *Bismarck* at 1030 next morning, 26 May, triggering the subsequent British moves leading to her destruction next day. Jeschonnek's exchange, motivated purely by personal family concern, beautifully illustrates how gratuitous release of a tiny operational detail to the airwaves, even in a theatre distant from the main action, may bring major consequences.[3]

Overall, despite the D/F saga on 25 May, the pursuit and destruction of *Bismarck* was a textbook example of effective operational exploitation of often fragmentary intelligence from multiple sources, a tribute both to James's vision and Denning's painstaking evolution of the OIC over the last four years. The ultimate accolade came from Tovey, who judged the accuracy and speed of the information passed by the Admiralty 'remarkable', and the balance struck between information and instruction to forces beyond his control 'ideal'.[4] The lessons of Jutland were well learnt. It was also an intelligence success with long-term strategic consequences. The successful cruise of *Scharnhorst* and *Gneisenau* earlier in the year appeared to validate the concept of Atlantic raiding by heavy surface units. The *Bismarck* experience convinced Raeder that improved British ocean surveillance, exploiting better aerial reconnaissance, including coverage from Iceland bases, new radar, and a wider D/F network was fundamentally shifting the balance of advantage. Despite this, he initially judged carefully planned operations remained possible, although it might be necessary to wait for the longer nights and poorer weather of autumn.[5] However, his first step, the deployment of the pocket battleship *Lützow* on 12 June to a forward waiting position in Norway, brought fresh disaster. With Bletchley now reading Dolphin Enigma with minimal delay, decrypts kept the OIC fully informed of her movements, enabling a successful torpedo strike off Egersund early the following morning by RAF Beaufort bombers, with Hut 4 issuing the decrypt of *Lützow's* damage report within four hours of its transmission.[6] She was out of action for eleven months. This classic intelligence-led targeting operation pushed Raeder and Hitler firmly into a defensive mindset. Never again did the Germans seriously contemplate risking a high-value warship for Atlantic raiding.

As increasing quantities of actionable Dolphin Enigma decrypts came on stream, the Admiralty took care, as in the previous war, to protect the source, by using D/F or other explanations as cover, and by careful sanitisation, although greater frankness was permitted where ships had the flag officer's cipher, which was correctly judged sufficiently secure.

From July, further measures were implemented. The prefix Ultra was introduced to denote Special Intelligence, and secure one-time pads, along with stringent security procedures, were issued for traffic carrying it. Nevertheless, balancing desirable action against security remained tricky. This was illustrated in dealing with the network of supply ships deployed by the Germans to support both the *Bismarck* group and U-boat operations, where Dolphin decrypts provided the OIC with a comprehensive picture by the end of May. Of seven ships identified, five were targeted for destruction in early June using D/F as cover, leaving two, *Gedania* and *Gonzenheim*, untouched, on Pound's insistence, in the hope of allaying German suspicion. Unfortunately, these two were also sunk in chance encounters with British warships. Admiralty concern for the security of the Enigma operation was compounded when a further seven supply or weather ships were sunk or captured by mid July, although only one of these, *Lauenburg*, was deliberately targeted. This pattern of sinkings did provoke a major German security inquiry, including close scrutiny of Enigma, but the experts insisted it was unbreakable, a view repeated after Dönitz raised further concerns a few months later. Nevertheless, the British learnt the hard lesson that chance could undermine the best security precautions.[7]

The Germans soon found that the operational advantages of basing heavy units in French ports was matched by their greater exposure to intelligence surveillance and air attack. Once the arrival of the two battlecruisers in Brest was confirmed in late March, they were subject, weather permitting, and contrary to Phillips's complaints, to twice-daily reconnaissance flights at dawn and dusk from St Eval in Cornwall. Between 28 March 1941 and 12 February 1942, 729 sorties were flown, for the loss of nine Spitfires.[8] This surveillance spotted *Gneisenau*'s move on 5 April to the outer harbour, following an initial two-week docking period, facilitating a daring, dawn torpedo attack the following morning by an RAF Beaufort which put her out of action for the rest of the year. Further damage was inflicted in a bombing attack on the night of 9/10 April, when she was back in dock. Since communications regarding the ships in Brest passed by landline, Dolphin traffic revealed little about damage and repairs, while skilful camouflage limited the value of aerial photography. NID was therefore heavily dependent on SIS reporting from French agent networks to monitor the status of the ships, although French access to the ships was limited, with most work done by German personnel.[9] However, an SIS report was crucial in warning that *Scharnhorst*, so far unscathed, would run trials at La Pallice, adjacent to La Rochelle, in late July following lengthy repairs to her boilers. This intelligence enabled RAF bombers to mount an attack there on 24 July, inflicting severe damage. *Scharnhorst* got back to Brest but, like her sister, was now under repair until December. Meanwhile, *Prinz Eugen* was badly damaged on 1 July, exactly a month after her arrival following Operation Rhine.[10]

At the beginning of January 1942, the precise operational status of the three ships in Brest was uncertain. PR showed that *Gneisenau* had finally left dock on 23 December after more than eight months, which NID was confident reflected damage from the two raids in early April. *Scharnhorst* remained in dock, as she had been since the attack at La Pallice, but NID lacked reliable confirmation that she had been damaged there. *Prinz Eugen* was observed leaving dock on 14 December, but had returned a week later, where she remained. The only clue suggesting early resumption of operational status was Dolphin decrypts showing that gun crews from all three ships were conducting firing practice in the Baltic, the battlecruiser personnel in *Admiral Scheer*, and *Prinz Eugen*'s in *Hipper*.[11] However, by the end of the month, evidence of an early move from Brest accumulated. Dolphin, PR and SIS reports showed that the ships were conducting regular night exercises off the port then returning by morning. They also showed increased activity by naval light forces and German air force units along the Channel coast, with significant reinforcement. On 5 February a Dolphin intercept indicated that Vice Admiral Otto Ciliax, admiral commanding battleships, had hoisted his flag in *Scharnhorst*. The Admiralty now assessed a breakout imminent and, although lacking definitive evidence, judged that the ships would probably return to Germany via the Dover strait. They were not aware that Hitler himself was driving the move, wishing to concentrate naval forces to counter a possible British invasion of Norway, but also fearful of the risks in further Atlantic operations. Dispositions were now made to counter a Channel transit, relevant naval and air forces alerted, and extensive mining of likely routes identified in Dolphin decrypts was implemented. However, naval reinforcement was constrained by other pressing commitments, including the need to counter *Tirpitz*, which arrived in Norway in mid January, and the protection of high-value troop convoys. By 11 February, Dolphin had provided details of a new swept passage through the Bight, which removed doubt over German intent, and which the OIC completed plotting that evening, just as the Germans sailed.[12]

The intelligence story of the subsequent German dash through the Channel (Operation Cerberus) displayed extraordinary contrasts. Outstanding success in monitoring German preparations and intent was followed by dismal failure, either in spotting their initial departure, or alerting British commanders that the operation was underway until the

German force was passing Dover, only for intelligence-led intervention in the final phase to offer some redemption. A cascade of individual failings and mishaps in what seemed a well-planned belt-and-braces British alert system enabled the German escape. There were unusual delays in breaking Dolphin traffic, with the crucial days of 10, 11 and 12 February not broken until 15 February. German jamming prevented any departure report radioed from SIS French agents. The duty submarine watching off Brest was out of position, because she had been ordered to attempt an interception in the area where the Germans conducted their nightly exercises. Patrolling radar-equipped shadowing aircraft that night suffered defects. Bad weather and a German smokescreen prevented effective dawn reconnaissance over Brest from finding the ships gone. There was initial British incredulity that the Germans would transit the Dover strait at midday, contributing to slow reaction, compounded by bad weather hampering flying operations. Partial redemption for the sloppy, ineffective British reaction came with the sowing of aerial mines along the latest Dolphin-illuminated route in the Bight. Exploiting captured German charts obtained separately, this mining was extremely accurate. Both battlecruisers were damaged, *Scharnhorst* severely and *Gneisenau* less so, a development soon confirmed by Dolphin. Meticulous planning by the Germans had brought a significant tactical and moral victory, and a blow to British pride. *The Times*, with a degree of overstatement, famously thundered that: 'Vice Admiral Ciliax has succeeded where the Duke of Medina Sidonia failed ... Nothing more mortifying to the pride of sea power has happened in home waters since the seventeenth century'. However, strategically the operation underlined the German retreat from Atlantic surface warfare, and allowed the British Home Fleet to focus on northern waters. More immediate intelligence-driven targeting also ensured German celebration was short-lived. Traffic analysis, followed by an aerial sighting, alerted the OIC on 20 February that *Prinz Eugen* was moving with *Admiral Scheer* from Kiel to Trondheim. Subsequent Dolphin decrypts and SIS reporting revealed their route, enabling interception by the submarine *Trident*, which torpedoed *Prinz Eugen* on the morning of 23 February, putting her out of action for the rest of 1942. Meanwhile, PR identified *Gneisenau* in the floating dock at Kiel, where she was wrecked by an RAF bombing raid on the night of 26/27 February, although not until June did NID assess from PR and reporting from Denham in Stockholm that she had probably been damaged beyond recovery.[13] *Scharnhorst* was also not fully operational until 1943, when she finally redeployed to Norway to counter the new Arctic convoys to Russia.[14]

Intelligence and the U-boat campaign in the second half of 1941

During the second quarter of 1941, despite the initial insights from Dolphin Enigma, including complete readability in June, U-boats sank over 900,000 tons of shipping. In mid June the Joint Planning Committee estimated probable shipping losses for the year at 4.5 million tons, which it judged 'unsustainable'. In reality, losses in the second half of the year dropped dramatically to an overall 750,000 tons, down 50 per cent on the first half, and with a monthly average just one-third of that in the second quarter.[15] There is a well-established and apparently compelling case that this reduction represented a saving of 1.5 million tons of shipping, achieved through the effective exploitation of Dolphin intelligence to divert convoys away from known U-boat concentrations. This calculation compares the actual outcome with an extrapolation from first-half losses, with a 50 per cent addition to reflect the average increase in frontline U-boat strength. It argues, not entirely convincingly, that high losses persisted through June, when Dolphin was read currently, because the OIC required time to digest Dolphin revelations on U-boat operations, and could not exploit the new intelligence effectively before the end of that month. It also claims that the damage inflicted on the few convoys successfully intercepted, notably on eastbound, slow convoys 42 and 44 in September, confirms the overall success of intelligence-driven diversion.[16] At thirty-seven ships, September was the third highest month for convoy losses, and three times the average monthly loss rate across the three years 1940–42.[17]

Nevertheless, much evidence does not readily fit this view that Dolphin-driven diversion was primarily responsible for the striking fall in shipping losses in the second half of 1941, let alone the more specific claim that it saved 1.5 million tons. The main contribution to reduced losses came from ships sailing independently, down by two-thirds, and convoy stragglers, down by half, where Dolphin diversion had little influence, certainly on the former. The obvious explanation for this fall in independent losses is the Admiralty decision to raise the minimum limit for independently routed ships from 13 to 15 knots from the end of June, a move unrelated to the availability of Dolphin intelligence. This transferred about four hundred ships in this bracket, the most vulnerable of the independent category, into convoy, and achieved a permanent fall in independent losses in the middle and eastern Atlantic for the rest of the war.[18] Meanwhile, convoy losses did not fall in the second half of the year. Third-quarter losses were double those of each of the first two quarters, reflecting a sharp rise in U-boat availability. In the final quarter, losses fell back, but only to the level of the first two quarters. This reflected the fall in the frontline U-boat force in the Atlantic from the end of September, as boats began transferring to the Mediterranean, with twenty-six passing through the Gibraltar straits by the end of December. This was about one-third of the then frontline force, although the disruption this transfer caused had a far wider impact on the numbers now immediately available for Atlantic deployment.[19] Furthermore, convoy losses in the second half of 1942, when U-boats again focused their attacks in mid-Atlantic, were proportionately less than those in the equivalent period a year earlier, even though there were 40 per cent more U-boats available for searching, and U-boat Enigma was now unreadable, both making diversion more difficult. Indeed, statistics show that the second half of 1940, not 1941, was the outlier in the pattern of convoy attacks with the then small force of U-boats more productive than at any other point in the war.[20]

Other factors influenced the U-boat campaign in the second half of 1941. The first was U-boat availability and effectiveness in BdU's chosen patrol areas. By mid 1941, BdU's North Atlantic focus had shifted westward, partly in pursuit of a more target-rich environment and partly owing to increased British anti-submarine effectiveness in the northwest approaches, as its air and surface resources increased. This brought the U-boats increased transit time, and the requirement to sweep wider waters, with no prospect of aerial reconnaissance. Both reduced productivity.[21] Increased transit time, compounded by the transfers to the Mediterranean, meant real strength in Atlantic patrol areas was no greater in the final quarter of the year than the first half while, in the new hunting ground, targets, whether independents or convoys, were harder to find, even without any contribution from Dolphin diversion. By mid December, drawing on Dolphin decrypts, the OIC assessed there were only five U-boats in the North Atlantic, although this small number was partly influenced by withdrawals to prepare for an offensive against traffic on the American East Coast (Operation Drumbeat), following the opening of war with the United States.[22] This reduced U-boat availability in the Atlantic in the last quarter of 1941 also initially limited German exploitation of new B-Dienst breaks into British naval ciphers, a modified version of No 2 introduced in September, and No 3, set aside for combined Anglo-American use, introduced in October.[23]

Another limitation on German effectiveness was the United States government decision from September to assume formal responsibility for protecting convoys in the western Atlantic, and the security of Iceland. Coming three months before the United States entered the war, this was a double win for Britain. It meant convoys were relatively secure when under US Navy protection, with Hitler instructing Dönitz to minimise the risk of hostile incidents, and it released Royal Navy and Canadian escorts for reinforcement elsewhere. In October average escort strength for British-controlled convoys accordingly rose from four to six, and they were generally better equipped and experienced.[24]

All this demonstrates that numerous factors shaped the U-boat campaign in the second half of 1941. Within these, Dolphin decrypts made a critical contribution. From mid March they provided the OIC, the naval staff and Western Approaches Command with invaluable insights into every aspect of U-boat operations, which steadily improved as the year progressed. When available in timely fashion, they certainly helped with evasive routing of convoys, but this concept, well-recognised in the previous war, preceded their arrival using other sources, notably D/F, and continued during the long 1942 U-boat Enigma blackout. It is also important not to overlook practical issues in managing diversion. The OIC could rarely take action inside twenty-four hours of a German signal being transmitted, and the operational picture might change substantially in that period. Ocean navigation in the Second World War relied on astronomical observation, which was weather-dependent, and dead reckoning, invariably using hand plotting. In bad weather, position estimates from either side could easily have an error of twenty-five miles, making diversion an uncertain business. Close examination of the statistics across the entire three years 1940–42 suggests Dolphin's role in facilitating diversion in the second half of 1941 was helpful, but not alone decisive in containing shipping losses. However tempting the claim, this was a case where correlation did not imply direct causation.[25]

Meanwhile, the Dolphin decrypts acquired during the second half of 1941 made a contribution to British management of the Battle of the Atlantic that was arguably more important, and certainly more enduring, than current convoy diversion. Just as it had the previous year, Hut 4 exploited Dolphin intelligence to produce assessments that illuminated U-boat policy, tactics and capability. These assessments reflected the growing supremacy of Hut 4 in intelligence research. As Enigma-generated SIGINT became an increasingly important source, so intelligence research within NID became inhibited. The OIC was focused on immediate operational exploitation, and had neither the time nor resources for long-term research. The geographical sections, with NID1 German section the most important, did do research but, apart from their heads of section, were not indoctrinated into SIGINT, so could not use it. It was inevitable that Hut 4 should fill the gap, and it was well-equipped to do so. It not only had the monopoly of SIGINT, with access to air and military decrypts as well as naval, but took custody of all captured naval documents, received all reports of POW interrogations, and was copied on almost every category of information of naval interest. It was also staffed with people, predominantly from an academic background, ideally suited by training and temperament to do this work. The open access across the naval SIGINT domain, pioneered by Birch early in the war, embracing Huts 4 and 8, the OIC, and NID9 now became a huge advantage in promoting high-quality research and assessment.[26] As Dolphin delivered through the summer and autumn of 1941, Hut 4 exploited an ever wider base of intelligence and experience, and its work was outstanding. Its products in this period set a benchmark standard for intelligence assessment that few other parts of the British intelligence community equalled, let alone surpassed, during the war. They included forays into operational research, the application of evidence-based analysis to improve operational decisions. In the naval sphere, GC&CS was no longer just a cryptographic agency producing raw decrypts for others to evaluate. It contributed processed intelligence of the highest value.

The most important single assessment, issued in early November and comprising twenty-five closely packed pages, tackled U-boat methods of 'combined attack on convoys' (Dönitz's wolf-pack concept) over the nine months February to October 1941 inclusive. Drawing, with few exceptions, almost exclusively on German sources, and evidence collected on numerous convoy attacks, it considered circumstances and targets justifying combined attack; 'shadowing' procedure; communications procedures during such attacks; 'loss of contact' procedures by U-boat attackers; and methods of carrying out attacks and policies towards convoy escorts. It also considered the circumstances driving the choice of 'combined attack', the present proficiency achieved, and conclusions to be drawn. Importantly, the assessment argued that the problem of combined attacks would inevitably increase with the growing number of U-boats deployed, and the consequent difficulty of achieving successful convoy evasion. However, not only were U-boat tactics now known, but they followed a stereotyped pattern, which meant countermeasures could be uniformly applied. The most effective countermeasure was to focus on breaking the first contact by a prospective 'shadower'. The shadower should be detected and kept submerged so that it could not communicate, and/or be avoided and deprived of information through frequent and extreme changes of course, preferably with the onset of darkness. The evolution of convoy escort tactics over the next year shows that the intelligence and ideas recorded in this paper were hugely influential. It also drove the development of sensors, notably improved ship-borne HF/DF to target the shadowers.[27]

The beginning of a naval intelligence relationship with the United States

There was a final important development in the eighteen months following the fall of France, which fundamentally influenced the future of British naval intelligence. This was the emergence of a close intelligence relationship with the United States. Through the 1930s, the Anglo-American naval relationship moved steadily from rivalry and suspicion towards cautious friendship, reflecting growing awareness of common interests, especially in dealing with the threat posed by Japan in the Far East. Here, the visit of Captain Royal Ingersoll, the US Navy Director of Plans, to London in January 1938 marked a step-change. It initiated more specific strategic co-operation in the western Pacific, and the principle of sharing sensitive information, causing the Board of Admiralty in May 1938 to authorise release of certain technical information to the US Navy, and agree the Americans would be treated 'exceptionally'. Initially, limited technical exchanges translated into more substantial intelligence-sharing after the outbreak of war the following year.[28]

Consideration of worst-case scenarios following the fall of France, including the intervention of Spain and Japan against Britain, caused Pound, as First Sea Lord, to establish a committee under the retired Admiral Sir Sidney Bailey to determine what naval assistance Britain might seek from the United States. He was also to recommend how an operational partnership should be managed, drawing on experience of the previous war, and what information drawing on war experience could be shared to support a future operational relationship. Godfrey's representations to Bailey were ambitious, advocating a full exchange of intelligence and the appointment of liaison officers within NID and its American equivalent the Office of Naval Intelligence (ONI). He also wanted the Americans pressed to provide naval information relating to France and French possessions overseas, drawing on their Paris attaché and consular network, emphasising that this would reciprocate for the considerable intelligence being provided to the London naval attaché, Captain Alan Kirk, including much material on the IJN.[29] Here, Godfrey underestimated the political and institutional constraints on the American side, while overestimating ONI capability. The intelligence section of Bailey's report completed in early August nevertheless incorporated most of Godfrey's ideas. In particular, an intelligence liaison officer, Captain Arthur Clarke, was despatched to Washington by the end of July with authority to share a vast range of intelligence and operational information.[30]

In parallel with Bailey's deliberations, three other figures important to shaping naval relations, two of them new and one from the past, appeared on the stage. The first new player was a wealthy Canadian businessman, William Stephenson, who on the outbreak of war offered the British government the services of his own private clandestine industrial intelligence organisation, established during the 1930s. Put in touch with SIS, he provided some useful intelligence on Scandinavia and Germany during the winter of 1939/40, but Menzies then judged him ideally suited to open a relationship with the Director of the American Federal Bureau of Investigation (FBI), J Edgar Hoover, exploiting their shared friendship with the boxer Gene Tunney. Like Wiseman, Stephenson had been a notable amateur boxer in his youth. This approach worked and, at Hoover's suggestion, Menzies appointed Stephenson SIS station commander in New York, where he arrived in June. Stephenson's initial brief broadly mirrored that carved out by Hall for Gaunt in 1915. He was to investigate enemy activities, protect British assets and interests from sabotage, and influence American public opinion in Britain's favour. Stephenson pursued these goals with energy and effect, remaining in post for the rest of the war, and creating a huge intelligence and security empire, known from January 1941 as British Security Co-ordination (BSC), extending across the entire Western hemisphere. Although his later memoir embroidered fact with considerable fantasy, Stephenson's real achievements were still remarkable. More than anyone else he laid the foundations of the Anglo-American human intelligence relationship that developed through the war and flourished for the rest of the century.[31]

On arrival, Stephenson exploited several important long-standing American friendships, including the wealthy businessman and confidant of President Franklin Roosevelt, Vincent Astor, who immediately introduced him to another presidential confidant, the lawyer William J Donovan. Roosevelt often used Donovan, who had acquired the nickname 'Wild Bill' while serving in France in 1918, as an international emissary and fact-finder. In mid July, encouraged by his new Navy Secretary Frank Knox, another friend of Donovan, Roosevelt now despatched him to Britain to assess Britain's prospects for survival and provide a check on defeatist reports from the London ambassador, Joseph Kennedy. The British ambassador, Lord Lothian, through diplomatic channels, and Stephenson, through Menzies, ensured Donovan received red-carpet treatment. He saw Churchill, had an audience with King George VI, met Menzies and all the heads of service intelligence, and visited factories and military bases. Donovan spent more time with Godfrey than anyone else, and they got on well. He confirmed that Knox had directed him to establish a close naval relationship, covering technical developments and intelligence. He dined at Godfrey's home and on his last evening they sat up into the early hours reviewing the visit. Donovan confided that Kennedy's defeatism had spread across the rest of the London staff, including Alan Kirk. However, he would advise Roosevelt, as Stephenson soon confirmed, that Britain would hold out and should receive maximum assistance with 'full intelligence co-operation'. He reassured Godfrey that he had been warned the British would prove difficult, patronising and secretive, but found them quite the opposite.

The immediate, albeit marginal, dividend for Godfrey was the opening of a link with his American opposite number, with secure communication and access to reports from American consular officers, especially in French ports. However, at the strategic level, Donovan's advice was probably crucial in convincing Roosevelt to provide fifty old American destroyers, in return for basing rights in the Caribbean at the beginning of September, unlocking other important items of military assistance, and ultimately preparing the way for lend-lease.[32] Meanwhile, as Stephenson established himself in New York, William Wiseman reappeared in London, offering to organise propaganda in the United States. Unfortunately, he could no longer match Stephenson's evident access and influence, while his relentless self-promotion had damaged his credibility with both SIS and the Admiralty, meaning neither was now keen to employ him. He therefore sought the patronage of Lord Halifax, initially Churchill's Foreign Secretary, before being appointed to succeed Lothian in Washington later in the year. Wiseman did not help his prospects by dallying with ideas for a negotiated peace. However, he maintained good relations with Stephenson, who probably found him a useful source, and he did Godfrey one final service in 1941.

Before Donovan returned from London, Roosevelt authorised a further American team under Rear Admiral Robert Ghormley to conduct informal discussions with the British chiefs of staff at the end of August. Ghormley was not empowered to enter agreements, but the visit powerfully reinforced Donovan's assessment that Britain would survive and had a credible war-fighting strategy. It also gave further impetus to intelligence-sharing: in particular, convincing Ghormley's team there was value in a SIGINT exchange.[33] Following initial opposition to SIGINT collaboration from the US Navy SIGINT section OP-20-G, this had to wait until the following February when, as described in a later chapter, an American team visited Bletchley, bearing an important contribution on Japanese diplomatic traffic.[34] With this exception, and an exchange on Japanese naval SIGINT conducted in the Far East, the Americans were easily the main beneficiaries of the naval intelligence trade until their entry into the war in December 1941, with Washington providing little else of value. The United States had no foreign intelligence service, and its naval reporting network outside the Pacific was limited. By contrast, Pound authorised the release of Bailey's report and was, in principle, willing to share any information the Americans sought which lay within the Admiralty's remit. In addition to material channelled through Clarke, NID answered 395 requests for information through the London embassy before the end of 1940. The appointment of Alan Kirk as the US Navy's Director of Intelligence that December, and of a new ambassador to replace Kennedy, John G Winant, with whom Godfrey soon established regular contact, further strengthened relations, but without yielding better intelligence.[35]

Nevertheless, if the flow was one-way, the intelligence relationship also opened doors in Washington, which the British, through Clarke, exploited with considerable skill to gain access to American thinking and, where possible, to influence it. Clarke, who spent a year in Washington from August 1940, is a shadowy figure in British records of this period, and his relations with the senior naval attaché, Rear Admiral Herbert Pott, and Godfrey remain opaque. However, he rapidly became a crucial source on evolving American attitudes and policy, achieving exceptional access to, and the trust of, the notoriously difficult Director of US Navy War Plans, Captain Richmond Kelly Turner. Clarke's success partly reflected his career background, where he had demonstrated equally strong operational and staff skills and had, unusually, also spent four years working for Hankey as assistant naval secretary to the CID through the mid 1930s, with access to the highest levels of British defence planning. But it also reflected exceptional empathy, and ability to lever personal relationships in an unthreatening way. His most important contribution was to alert the British government to the development of the 'Atlantic first' strategy by the Chief of Naval Operations, Admiral Harold 'Betty' Stark, known to history as Plan Dog. Plan Dog was more than a prospective naval strategy. It was, in effect, an overall national security review, which outlined not only the overall strategic risks and choices the United States faced in October 1940, but anticipated its strategy over the next five years.[36]

There were several reasons why the Admiralty led the way in shaping British-American intelligence relations well into 1941. Although the intelligence elements of the exchanges initiated with Ingersoll in 1938 were embryonic, they established a framework and direction that did not yet exist in the other services. The Admiralty also had immediate and pressing requirements to which the Americans could contribute. Through the autumn of 1940, it increasingly saw the US Navy as the primary means of containing the potential threat from Japan, ideally even providing the fleet in Singapore which Britain could no longer supply. More immediately, it hoped the Americans could bring intelligence and resources to the crucial Atlantic theatre, and that reporting from their naval attachés in Berlin and Rome might offer important insights not available otherwise. (By early 1941, Godfrey won agreement that the American attaché in Berlin would copy reports to his colleague in Madrid, where they were shared with Hillgarth for onward transmission to London. British questions were then transmitted in the opposite direction.[37]) From the American perspective, gaining an accurate picture of Britain's naval prospects, the assurance that she would retain command of the sea with minimal risk of her fleet falling into German hands, was essential to their strategic calculations.

This naval intelligence agenda encouraged Godfrey to visit Washington in late May and early June, accompanied by Fleming, which meant both were absent from London for the *Bismarck* operation. His immediate goal was to improve collaboration in the Atlantic U-boat war, reflecting the American decision to establish an extended western Atlantic security zone, where shipping was under its protection. He hoped to persuade the Americans and Canadians to establish variants of the OIC in Washington and Ottawa, with complete sharing between these two centres and London, and significant interchange of staff. A related but wider objective, endorsed by JIC colleagues and the chiefs of staff, was to establish a combined British-United States intelligence organisation. This reflected growing British frustration, underlined by JIC chairman, William Cavendish-Bentinck, that Washington was 'far worse informed' than London, with American intelligence departments 'primitive and rather inexperienced', with 'little contact or collaboration' between them, or across their wider government. Godfrey's colleagues wanted an American variant of the JIC, but Godfrey himself harboured wider ambitions. He hoped to persuade the Americans to go further than co-ordination on the British model, and create a single unified intelligence service, correcting what he saw as the British error of perpetuating four separate organisations (the three service intelligence departments plus SIS and GC&CS). This begged fundamental questions about Godfrey's understanding of how the British intelligence community had evolved, and the attitude of his fellow agency heads, combined with astonishing ignorance and naivety over the politics and culture of American government and its present personalities. It also illuminated prejudices that helped trigger his dismissal the following year.[38]

Predictably, Godfrey made little headway with his ideas for integration, nor was the US Navy yet ready to embrace an OIC. An odd feature of the visit is the absence of reference to Clarke and his insights from Turner.

The omission is striking, because throughout 1941 Turner was engaged in a ferocious dispute with Kirk over the control and distribution of intelligence within the fleet. Nevertheless, there were some achievements. Godfrey gained a better understanding of ONI's organisation and capabilities, including its coverage of Japan and its relationship to OP-20-G, the US Navy cryptographic unit, which came under the Director of Communications. He persuaded Kirk to second officers to NID, which ensured intelligence collaboration following American entry into the war was better than it would otherwise have been. He facilitated additional exchanges of SIGINT material between OP-20-G and GC&CS which, as described later, had begun earlier in the year. These were conducted initially through the Washington embassy, but from August through Stephenson's BSC in New York. Finally, he established an NID outstation in Washington (NID18) under Captain Edward Hastings within the new British Joint Staff Mission under Admiral Sir Charles Little, established following the first formal staff talks with the Americans, known as ABC-1, held earlier in the year. Hastings represented DNI on the new JIC outpost in Washington, established at this time under the former DMI Major General Frederick Beaumont-Nesbitt. This initiated the sharing of strategic assessments between Britain and the United States, as opposed to raw intelligence reports. In the autumn, with the agreement of Menzies and Denniston, Hastings also became liaison officer for GC&CS, and managed the exchange with OP-20-G in collaboration with BSC. Finally, with the help of Wiseman, who exploited a connection with Arthur Sulzberger, the publisher of the *New York Times*, Godfrey met Roosevelt. This enabled him to press the case for a single intelligence overlord, which possibly contributed to the appointment of Donovan as Co-ordinator of Information, and head of what became the United States' first foreign intelligence service, the Office of Strategic Services (OSS). Donovan's appointment was undoubtedly helpful to overall British interests, and strengthened Stephenson's position, but he never achieved much oversight over ONI, or its army equivalent, and his future impact on naval intelligence relations was small.[39]

Despite Godfrey's efforts, in summer 1941 American naval intelligence potential had yet to be mobilised, and ONI was slow even to reciprocate the access its officers enjoyed in London. For the next year, apart from some useful reporting from American observers in Vichy and North Africa, NID received little of value.[40] Meanwhile, British capabilities in the Atlantic and home waters theatres were transformed across that year. The highlights were the mastery of Dolphin and the creation of an effective strategic PR capability. But other areas had advanced too –

prisoner interrogation, ship-borne HF/DF, and SIS monitoring of ports and coastal choke-points. There was strength in depth, and the OIC now had the inputs to make it truly effective. Intelligence had begun the year marginal to most operations. By the end, it was central. The year 1942 would bring new challenges, but meanwhile there had been major intelligence achievements in other theatres too.

26

Towards Global War:
The Mediterranean 1940–1942

Britain's continuing commitment to the eastern Mediterranean and Middle East, following the fall of France, was influenced by two critical factors. First, the need to secure the western boundary of its eastern empire against Axis attack, and protect access to the Indian Ocean and Persian oil. This allowed Britain to generate the full war potential of that empire, deny the Axis vital resources, and later establish direct contact with Russia. Secondly, the influence that Britain's position in the eastern Mediterranean exerted on those neutrals who might turn hostile: Spain, Vichy, Turkey, Russia, and Japan – and especially the prospect of Germany extending its control over the Atlantic coast. The latter point receives little attention, but preoccupied Churchill and the Admiralty leadership for the first half of the war. Tom Phillips told Sir Samuel Hoare, on his appointment as ambassador in Madrid at the end of May 1940, that losing control of this coast might make it impossible to carry on the war.[1]

Although in June the Admiralty suggested withdrawing the Eastern Mediterranean Fleet, in the event of French collapse, to meet the heightened risks in the Atlantic, sealing the western entrance of the Mediterranean, Britain's war leadership endorsed powerful countervailing arguments. Holding Egypt without the fleet might be difficult, Turkey might tilt towards the Axis, and wholesale collapse in Britain's position across the theatre could follow.[2] But the most important arguments related to oil, viewed as a major Axis vulnerability. Britain assessed total German oil receipts (production and imports) for the year beginning 1 June 1940 at 7.5 million tons, although they were about one million tons higher. Secure access from the Black Sea through the eastern Mediterranean to Italy and France could increase German oil imports by 3 million tons per year, about 35 per cent of Germany's projected 1940 supply, through more effective exploitation of Romanian and Russian sources. The Eastern Mediterranean Fleet denied Germany this benefit, and prevented her reaching the Iraq oilfields through Turkey or Syria, while preserving their use for Britain.[3] Germany could not exploit Iraq's oil in the short term if Britain destroyed the infrastructure, but could deny it to Britain, and ultimately threaten the Iranian fields and the refinery at Abadan.[4] This British assessment accurately reflected debates within the German leadership through the second half of 1940, but German aspirations were less coherent than the British assumed.[5] Dislodging Britain from the Middle East would draw resources from a 1941 attack on Russia, to which Hitler was broadly committed from the end of July.[6] German intervention in North Africa or the eastern Mediterranean also risked tensions with Italy, who saw this as her sphere. The German leadership never, therefore, conducted a serious analysis of the strategic benefits, risks, and feasibility of a drive into the Middle East at this time. A partial exception here was the German naval staff, who developed the case for a Mediterranean strategy, put to Hitler by Raeder in September, and again in November. However, Hitler evidently saw the Mediterranean as a distraction from his projected Russia campaign, even though Raeder suggested seizing the Caucasus oilfields from the Middle East, making an attack on Russia in the north unnecessary.[7]

These calculations dictated the desirability of Britain holding a forward position, at a minimum, on the western border of Egypt, although the further west she pushed, the greater her strategic leverage and prospects of collapsing Italy. The military resources mobilised by the eastern empire made this forward position possible. However, these resources were vulnerable if Japan attacked Britain in the East. So were the Indian Ocean communications, on which most of Britain's Middle East effort and the economies of its eastern empire depended. Through 1941, therefore, the challenge for British planners was to balance the maximum possible effort in the Middle East and Mediterranean, an active war theatre, with the minimum deployment to deter Japan from intervening in Southeast Asia or the Indian Ocean. This balance set the context for naval intelligence.

Following Italy's decision not to enter the war alongside Germany in September 1939, British intelligence coverage, primarily from SIGINT, demonstrated through the following winter that early reversal was unlikely. The first warning signs, again from SIGINT, that preparations for intervention might be underway emerged in March 1940, with a build-up of forces in Libya and important changes in Italian naval dispositions. The latter caused Cunningham, now Commander-in-Chief Mediterranean, to seek reinforcements from the Admiralty. The successful German invasion of Norway consolidated the Italian change of heart, with accumulating evidence from mid April that her decision for war was imminent. The OIC started a daily Italian situation report on 18 April, and Cunningham formally moved his staff and the Mediterranean OIC from Malta to Alexandria at the beginning of May. In mid May Cunningham also achieved the temporary loan of a Spitfire from the PDU, to obtain up-to-date photographs of key Italian ports. By the end of the month, the JIC, fulfilling its post-Norway early warning mandate, judged that Italy had definitely decided on war, and the Admiralty identified mid June as the danger period. Italy's formal declaration came on 11 June, but Cunningham authorised initial action against Italian submarines the previous day.[8]

Through May into June, SIGINT coverage of the two main Italian navy codebooks and related ciphers, and one of the naval attaché codebooks, was comprehensive, building on the work of Clarke's team since 1935. Coverage across the other two Italian services in all theatres was also excellent, as was that of diplomatic and consular traffic. In the first month of the war, the Mediterranean OIC exploited SIGINT to great effect: in particular, identifying submarine patrol areas and achieving the destruction or capture of ten boats, 10 per cent of the Italian force, in just over three weeks. This operation was helped by seizing documents from the submarine *Galileo Galilei*, which surrendered in the Red Sea on 19 June, and then the capture of the new general codebook for July from the submarine *Uebi Scebeli* ten days later. SIGINT, D/F and decrypts also helped Cunningham to execute a successful engagement with the Italian battle-fleet off Calabria on 9 July.

This superb SIGINT coverage, enhanced by lax Italian navy signal discipline and procedure, did not last. By the end of July, the Italian navy had changed its high-grade codebooks and additive cipher systems covering all important communications. Further changes, creating multiple new systems, occurred over the next six months, completely baffling GC&CS naval section which, despite now working almost exclusively on Italy, was chronically understaffed, while its liaison with the small cryptographic team in the Mediterranean OIC was poor. The resulting blackout, covering primary operational naval traffic, was never even partially pierced for the rest of the Mediterranean war.[9] However, there were two important compensations. The first was the breaking by Dilly Knox's team in September of an Italian navy Enigma system, based on the 'K' machine successfully attacked in the Spanish civil war. This carried a trickle of important messages, but little useful intelligence before early 1941. The second was GC&CS's rapid breaking of the new Italian air-force systems introduced after the outbreak of war. This helped the Mediterranean OIC monitor Italian air reconnaissance, and provide the fleet with warning of air attacks and advice on evasive routing. It was less helpful at this stage in identifying offensive opportunities.

In conducting their naval operations over the last five months of 1940, Cunningham and the commander of the Gibraltar-based Force H, Vice Admiral Sir James Somerville, were therefore primarily dependent on low-grade naval SIGINT, based on D/F, traffic analysis and some reading of minor codes, limited air reconnaissance resources, and visual sightings. By contrast, the Italian navy retained the coverage of Royal Navy traffic it had achieved in the late 1930s, and enjoyed superior air reconnaissance, providing good insights into British movements, and facilitating substantial reinforcements to Libya with negligible loss. The best the British could expect was warning that enemy forces might be at sea, but without accurate indication of whereabouts or intent. Cunningham did not know, therefore, that almost the entire operational Italian fleet, comprising four battleships, thirteen cruisers, and thirty-nine destroyers, had sailed to intercept him during Operation HATS, the transfer of major Royal Navy reinforcements through the central Mediterranean at the end of August. Nor did Somerville get warning of the Italian fleet's intervention at Cape Spartivento in November, or their sortie to intercept him during his raid on Genoa in February 1941. Although some intelligence on submarine operations was occasionally available from Italian Enigma decrypts, these rarely helped locate submarines, and gave no warning of abortive attacks planned against Gibraltar and Alexandria at the end of October with an innovative submarine-launched weapon, the *Siluro a Lenta Corsa* (SLC), or *maiale*, which the British called the 'chariot', or 'human torpedo'. The Gibraltar operation came closer to success but the British recovered one of three SLCs deployed, alerting them to their existence, and providing design details, which they then copied. Nevertheless, although the rate of Italian submarine losses reduced when the British lost naval SIGINT coverage after July, they remained high. Ten more were sunk between August and December, and seven in the first half of 1941, reducing overall frontline strength by one-third over the first year of war.[10]

Despite initial shortage of aircraft, PR was a more important intelligence asset than SIGINT during the first nine months of the Mediterranean war. Three new Glenn Martin Maryland aircraft procured from the United States, part of a French order taken over by the RAF, were deployed to Malta as 431 Flight in early September. The Maryland was superior in speed and altitude to the Blenheim, and one of these aircraft, piloted by Pilot Officer (later Wing Commander) Adrian Warburton, perhaps the outstanding PR ace of the war, although as much a maverick as Cotton, conducted the surveillance missions critical to the successful Fleet Air Arm attack on Taranto in November, which sank or badly damaged three Italian capital ships. Besides monitoring Italian fleet bases, flights out of Malta and Egypt, where a second PRU base was established at Heliopolis in late 1940, also facilitated the naval bombardment of key Italian ports and bases in North Africa. During 1940–41 the Mediterranean PR units achieved outstanding results, despite a desperate shortage of aircraft. The Maryland supply line proved fragile, and at both Malta and Heliopolis these aircraft were therefore supplemented with a random mix of adapted Beaufighters and Hurricanes. Only in 1942 did the Mediterranean receive PR Spitfires.[11]

The year 1941 began with outstanding British success on land when, in Operation Compass, Lieutenant General Sir Richard O'Connor largely destroyed the Italian army in North Africa, a victory which drew significantly on SIGINT. It started badly at sea, when intelligence from German air force Enigma decrypts, warning of the deployment of a substantial German air force, Fliegerkorps X, to the Mediterranean, failed to reach Cunningham before he was attacked off Malta. The carrier *Illustrious* was badly damaged and the cruiser *Southampton* sunk, the first of many losses to German air power suffered by the Royal Navy across the rest of the year. German intervention in the Mediterranean theatre, with the arrival of Fliegerkorps X, followed by commitment of major land forces in North Africa and Greece, fundamentally changed the strategic situation.[12] It was initially dictated by three motives – to reduce the dangerous pressure on its Italian ally, to secure its southern flank prior to invading Russia, and the opportunity to damage Britain without compromising its main effort in the East. Germany expected its commitment to be low cost and discretionary, but was sucked into a two-and-a-half year war of attrition for control of the North African coast and key Mediterranean sea routes, in which British intelligence exercised increasing influence and imposed a growing price. By late summer 1941, Germany saw the strategic stakes in the Mediterranean much as Britain did. While neither side would lose the war here, the control it provided over Middle East oil, the Persian supply route to Russia, and the Atlantic coast of Spain and West Africa, essential to the Atlantic U-boat war, was vital to winning. By mid 1942, it absorbed perhaps 20 per cent of German fighting power. Too often dismissed as a sideshow, the Mediterranean was in reality a key determinant of the war's outcome.[13]

German intervention brought one important new intelligence source to the Mediterranean theatre, although it took six months before it was fully exploited. This was German air force Enigma. By the end of January, this provided excellent coverage of German air strength, and by the end of March, it had revealed the arrival of land forces in North Africa, and was offering occasional insights into German strategic intent. Crucially, in May it illuminated the supply constraints faced by the German commander, General Erwin Rommel, and the refusal of the German high command to sanction an attack on Tobruk.[14] Secure transfer of Enigma intelligence, or Special Intelligence as it was then known, but later generally abbreviated to Ultra, from GC&CS where it was processed, in a form and timescale which was operationally useful, posed considerable challenges for the army and air force commands in the theatre. For the Navy the problems were less, because German air force Ultra was shared with indoctrinated staff in the Admiralty OIC, and anything relevant to naval operations was then shared with the Alexandria OIC and Mediterranean commanders. From the arrival of Fliegerkorps X, German air force Ultra was an essential and constant element in assessing the air threat to Royal Navy forces in the Mediterranean, but for the first half of 1941 it was also the most important source feeding the wider naval intelligence picture, and informing the conduct of operations.

German air force Ultra made three more specific naval contributions in this period. From April, it provided some intelligence on convoy sailings from Italian ports to Tripoli, although at this time it was rarely specific enough, or delivered fast enough to allow effective interception by the limited Royal Navy and RAF forces operating from Malta. There was, therefore, little more impact on Axis supplies delivered across the central Mediterranean before late summer 1941 than during the previous year. One notable exception was an Admiralty signal to Cunningham on 7 April, alerting him that elements of the German 15th Panzer Division were embarking at Palermo for Tripoli around 9 April. Cunningham deployed four destroyers to Malta, which destroyed an entire convoy of five merchant vessels and three escorting Italian destroyers on 16 April.[15] Its second contribution, both defensive and offensive, was to naval operations during the battle for Crete at the end of May. It helped the Royal Navy limit its exposure to the German air threat, although it could not prevent it taking heavy casualties. Ultra also enabled the Royal Navy to intercept the German convoys bringing troops and heavy equipment by sea, and to prevent any significant seaborne reinforcement. Its final contribution was to naval operations in support of the British intervention in Syria and Lebanon during June, providing important insights into Vichy French naval intentions and movements, including Admiral Darlan's plan to transfer the battlecruiser *Strasbourg* to the eastern Mediterranean under German air force cover.[16]

German air force Ultra also contributed, although only marginally, to the Battle of Matapan at the end of March. This was the first major Royal Navy operation in the Second World War to be based on SIGINT. It forestalled an Italian attack on British convoys to Greece, which promised important strategic success, and gained the Royal Navy its greatest victory at sea in the entire Mediterranean campaign. The primary source here was Italian naval Enigma, broken by Dilly Knox, with considerable help from the 19-year-old Mavis Lever, six months previously. This system had hitherto carried little important traffic, but messages broken on 25 and 26 March strongly suggested an imminent thrust by the Italian navy into the Aegean or eastern Mediterranean. Although the traffic never defined the purpose of the operation, and no SIGINT was available after 27 March, both Cunningham and the Admiralty correctly surmised that the Italians were targeting British convoys to Greece. Cunningham accordingly planned an interception, and on 28 March, after the Italian flagship, the new battleship *Vittorio Veneto*, had been torpedoed by the Fleet Air Arm, his battle-fleet caught and sank three Italian heavy cruisers and two destroyers that night. SIGINT did not guarantee this victory, which owed much to Cunningham's skilful planning and conduct of his fleet, as well as important intelligence contributions from other sources, notably aerial reconnaissance by *Warspite*'s Swordfish aircraft. However, the SIGINT warning made it possible, and saved at least one convoy from probable destruction, as both Cunningham and the Admiralty recognised. Godfrey famously called Bletchley with the message: 'We have won a great victory in the Mediterranean and it is entirely due to Dilly and his girls'. Knox emphasised the contribution of his 'girls', primarily Margaret Rock and Mavis Lever, with characteristic wit – 'Give me a Rock and a Lever and I can move the universe'.[17] He also later penned his own epitaph to Mussolini: 'These have knelled your fall and ruin, but your ears were far away English lassies rustling papers through the sodden Bletchley day.'[18] The Battle of Matapan, achieved for the loss of one British aircraft, is often claimed to have given the Royal Navy enduring moral superiority over its Italian opponent. In the short term, it certainly engendered caution, and dissuaded the Italian main fleet from playing any further part in the Greece and Crete operations. However, the Italian navy was a more determined and formidable opponent, not least in the intelligence war, than often credited by British historians. Although it suffered further reverses in the autumn of 1941, it achieved a series of important successes against the Royal Navy over the six months beginning that December.[19]

In October 1940 one of the many new Italian navy encrypted traffic streams was identified by Clarke's team as belonging to a Swedish machine cipher with similarities to Enigma, the Hagelin C38m. Although it was soon apparent that it carried more traffic than Italian Enigma, six months passed before Knox's research team began an attack, which then produced full and current readability by July, and which lasted with few breaks until the Italian armistice in 1943. Hagelin C38m was a medium-grade cipher, primarily used to carry communications about shipping movements, including all convoys to North Africa, although from mid 1941, when it replaced Italian Enigma for naval traffic, it frequently also carried information on Italian fleet movements. Ironically, from early spring 1941 the Germans had pressed for it to take on North Africa convoy communications, reflecting their belief that, as a machine system, it was more secure than Italian hand cipher systems, which they judged vulnerable. In reality, the reverse was the case.[20]

The break into Hagelin was timely because the contribution of German air force Enigma in the central Mediterranean reduced from early June, when Fliegerkorps X transferred to Greece. Hagelin dramatically increased the ability of British naval and air forces, operating primarily from Malta, to interdict Axis supplies between Italy and North African ports. From July 1941 it provided advance notice of the schedule and composition of convoys, and often details of high-value vessels and cargoes, including independent sailings. Italian use also rose rapidly from six hundred signals per month in August 1941 to four thousand the following July. Its operational exploitation, along with that of other Ultra sources in the Mediterranean, was enhanced by an important innovation in the way high-grade SIGINT was processed, communicated and circulated. Until mid 1941, Ultra intelligence bearing on naval operations went first to the Admiralty OIC, who controlled onward dissemination. It forwarded anything relevant to the Mediterranean to the Alexandria OIC, and thence to Commander-in-Chief Mediterranean, as happened with Matapan. However, it was increasingly clear that Ultra handling was inefficient and uneconomic, owing to the growing volume of traffic, and the overlapping intelligence needs of the three services. An inter-service organisation was therefore established at GC&CS to collate all Ultra intelligence for the Mediterranean and Middle East, and deliver a common set of reports direct from Bletchley to relevant theatre commanders. Transmission involved Special Communication Units (SCUs) equipped with dedicated facilities and Special Liaison Units (SLUs) responsible for secure dissemination. The SCU/SLU system began operating to Cairo on 20 July, to Alexandria from 14 August and to Malta by the end of September. The Admiralty was initially reluctant to cede control of intelligence distribution to GC&CS, but was reassured by the automatic copying of everything to the OIC, the close involvement of the latter in preparing reports, and, above all, by the sheer quality of the daily Ultra intelligence package and its presentation. The great benefit of the new system lay in providing all theatre commanders with a common daily intelligence picture, which inevitably boosted joint service understanding and co-operation. It gave Britain an enormous advantage in the information war.[21]

Over the first half of the year, the proportion of Axis supplies destroyed on passage to North Africa averaged less than 10 per cent, by September it was 30 per cent, and by November over 50 per cent, causing the Italians briefly to suspend traffic.[22] Hagelin intelligence alone was not enough to deliver these results. It required the right forces in the right place to exploit it. Over the last four months of 1941, the British could support a substantial submarine squadron and air group at Malta and, from end October, a surface strike unit, Force K, comprising two light cruisers and two destroyers. Both the air strike units and Force K were equipped with the latest radar for night interdiction, helping the latter despatch an entire convoy of seven ships on 8 November, despite its heavy Italian navy escort. To protect the Hagelin source, Italian ports and convoy routes were subject to regular aerial reconnaissance by the Malta-based Maryland force, comprising ten aircraft by August.[23]

This successful intelligence-driven interdiction operation over the last five months of the year underlined to both sides the value of Malta as an operational base, and brought important strategic consequences. The supply problem it created for the Axis armies in North Africa was probably crucial in turning the British Crusader offensive launched on 18 November from initial stalemate into narrow victory. It also triggered a major Axis response, which brought them temporary regional advantage, but with adverse consequences for other war theatres. The Germans deployed substantial air reinforcements to neutralise Malta, raising the proportion of their overall frontline air strength deployed in the Mediterranean theatre to 20 per cent by the spring, and correspondingly reducing forces available for operations in Russia. In addition, despite strong objections from Dönitz, from late September twenty-six U-boats transferred to the Mediterranean, about one-third of the overall frontline force at the end of the year. Although the U-boats achieved some notable early results, sinking the carrier *Ark Royal*, the battleship *Barham*, and light cruiser *Galatea* before the end of December, it is doubtful whether the benefits during 1942 from this major redeployment matched the impact of losing these resources to the Atlantic campaign, where Britain gained a critical breathing space, just as it lost Enigma cover. Averaged across that year, the Mediterranean U-boat force represented about 15 per cent of overall frontline strength, yet accounted for barely 2 per cent of Allied merchant shipping losses. Furthermore, no U-boat which entered the Mediterranean ever returned.[24]

Nevertheless, as the year turned, the most serious damage to the Royal Navy was inflicted by the Italians. On 19 December, despite fragmentary warnings in Hagelin traffic, a brilliantly conducted SLC human torpedo operation crippled the battleships *Queen Elizabeth* and *Valiant* in Alexandria harbour, putting both out of action for many months. Following the loss of *Barham* and *Ark Royal* in late November, and of the battleship *Prince of Wales* and battlecruiser *Repulse* to the Japanese off Malaya ten days previously, the Italian Alexandria operation was a strategic blow comparable to Taranto. Simultaneously, Force K was largely eliminated after running into an Italian minefield off Tripoli. This prevented it destroying a critical Italian convoy, pinpointed by Hagelin, carrying supplies, which then enabled Rommel to mount a counter-offensive at the end of January. Hagelin hinted at the existence of this minefield in October, but fleet staff possibly discounted the reports owing to the depth of water in the suggested area, and Force K was not warned. These two Italian successes demonstrated that despite the outstanding intelligence value Hagelin provided, it could not substitute for inability to read the high-level Italian naval codes, although at Alexandria the cumulative evidence pointing to a major risk of SLC attack should have dictated stronger harbour defences. In the event, Britain had lost half its available modern capital ship strength in five weeks, and its Mediterranean fleet was reduced to five light cruisers and a handful of destroyers, leaving its maritime control under extreme pressure at both ends of its new, extended, Eastern war theatre.[25]

These British naval losses, combined with the German air and U-boat reinforcements deployed from the end of 1941, fundamentally changed the maritime balance in the central Mediterranean, and opened a battle of attrition focused on Malta, which lasted eight months. For Britain, holding Malta was important, not only to maintain influence over a key strategic area, but also to provide aerial surveillance of the main Axis naval bases, and as an essential staging post for moving aircraft reinforcements to the Middle and Far East theatres. The application of enhanced Axis air power during the first half of 1942 rendered Malta almost useless as a base for British offensive operations, and made it increasingly difficult and costly to bring in minimum essential supplies from either end of the Mediterranean. Nevertheless, Britain deployed enough air reinforcements, with over three hundred Spitfires flown in by successive carrier operations between March and August, first to deter invasion, and then painstakingly to recover local air superiority with nine fighter, seven strike and two reconnaissance squadrons on the island by mid August. This prolonged struggle through the first half of 1942 vividly illustrates the limitations of Ultra. Hagelin intercepts were more prolific, of better quality, and more timely than ever, with more insights into Italian fleet operations. The latter included warning that the battleship *Littorio* and two cruisers had deployed from Taranto against the March convoy to Malta from Alexandria, leading to the engagement known as the Second Battle of Sirte, and sufficient advance notice to prevent a further SLC strike in May, aimed at the floating dock at Alexandria, which the Italians hoped to destroy while it contained *Queen Elizabeth* under repair. However, without secure use of Malta, Britain temporarily lacked the means to exploit its primary contribution of shipping intelligence in order effectively to interdict the main Axis supply lines. During the last five months of 1941, Britain destroyed 36.25 per cent of Axis supplies shipped to North African ports. Over the first five months of 1942, the figure shrank to 5.8 per cent, and the Axis tonnage successfully delivered rose 40 per cent, enabling Rommel to take Tobruk and get within fifty miles of Cairo by June.[26]

Wider Ultra coverage of traffic from the Axis air forces was equally prolific, and illuminated the scale of attack facing Malta and the British convoy routes, but could do little to reduce its impact. Intelligence on how enemy air units were deployed along convoy routes, enemy reconnaissance routines, and the likely armament and tactics of attackers, including Italian air force deployment of the new Motobomba FFF circling torpedo (later developed by the Germans as the LT 350), were all valuable, but the ultimate purpose of Malta convoy operations was inevitably transparent, and evasive routing options limited. The best intelligence could not substitute for the reduced resources in the Mediterranean Fleet in the first half of 1942, or the lack of forward airbases to project cover into the central Mediterranean. The nadir was the failure of two convoys run simultaneously from Gibraltar and Alexandria in June (Harpoon and Vigorous respectively). This combined effort, involving seventeen merchant ships, succeeded in delivering just two from the Harpoon convoy with 18,000 tons of cargo, but no vitally needed oil and aviation fuel. Malta was able to survive another two months, helped by submarine deliveries of aviation spirit, but only by curtailing offensive air activity to a minimum, and temporarily suspending aircraft transit to the East.[27]

The culmination of the struggle for Malta was the Pedestal convoy run from Gibraltar in the second week of August, the largest and most complex operation mounted by the Royal Navy in the war to date. Intelligence, primarily Ultra, provided a clear picture of the threat facing the convoy: 650 Axis aircraft deployed at multiple bases in Sardinia and Sicily, a substantial submarine force (ultimately comprising twenty boats), and large potential surface forces, with motor torpedo boats (MTBs) operating in the Sicilian Narrows, as well as the Italian main fleet. By this time, GC&CS had occasional coverage of the German naval Enigma Porpoise key used in the Mediterranean theatre, as well as comprehensive, almost real-time, coverage from German air force Enigma and Hagelin, and fair cover of Italian air force traffic. German air force Enigma provided good insights into the evolving Axis intelligence picture, and overall air operational planning, but also more strategic appreciations from the German Commander-in-Chief South, Field Marshal Albert Kesselring. For Pedestal, delivery of intelligence updates, including Ultra, were handled by the Admiralty OIC. An intelligence innovation for this operation was the deployment of radio-telephone (R/T) intercept teams (called Headache parties) in several escorts to monitor unencrypted enemy air and MTB radio circuits, and contribute to attack warning. The fourteen merchant ships, with 85,000 tons of supplies, were escorted by a combined force of two battleships, three carriers with seventy-two fighters, seven cruisers and thirty destroyers. A fourth carrier, *Furious*, joined the convoy, initially to fly off forty Spitfire reinforcements. British losses were heavy, but the convoy achieved its strategic purpose. Although only five supply ships got through, their 32,000 tons of general cargo, and 12,000 tons of fuel oil from the sole tanker *Ohio*, restored Malta as a full operational base, capable of deploying submarine and air strike forces under strong fighter protection until November. The planning and execution of this operation, substantially helped by Ultra and aerial surveillance of Italian naval bases from Malta, was a major achievement. Neither the US Navy nor the IJN could have conducted a comparable operation against this level of air attack, and in such a complex multi-threat environment at this time. On the morning of 12 August 117 Italian aircraft and fifty-eight German achieved just one ineffective hit on the carrier *Victorious*. Never before had the Axis air forces used so many aircraft, for so little result.[28]

The impact of Pedestal on the interdiction of Axis supplies to North Africa was immediate. The restored capability of the Malta strike forces coincided with important new insights into the German supply position from Enigma army keys broken from the beginning of August.[29] This revealed that the Axis forces were desperately short of fuel, and also the urgent programme of tanker movements planned to rectify this. The combination of German army and air force Enigma, together with

Italian Hagelin, now allowed British interdiction to apply deliberate target selection, with five tankers destroyed by the end of August. This led directly to Rommel's decision to abandon what proved to be his final planned offensive. The attack on the Axis supply lines tightened steadily over the rest of the year, by the end of November passing the 50 per cent mark achieved a year earlier, but with deliberate targeting delivering greater operational effect. This was crucial to the success of the British land offensive at Alamein, which turned the Mediterranean war permanently in the Allies' favour.[30]

27

The Far East 1939–1942:
An Overlooked Contribution?

Japan's decision to keep out of the war in September 1939 left British naval intelligence initially facing broadly similar requirements to those on Italy. It required warning of any change in Japanese policy, and the form of any subsequent intervention, while continuing to monitor the evolution of IJN strength and order of battle. Where possible, it needed improved intelligence capability to meet these requirements. The fall of France radically changed the intelligence context. It made Japanese intervention more likely, signalled by its early move into northern Indochina, and over the next year the damage Japan could potentially inflict on the British war effort, not least by attacking Indian Ocean communications, steadily increased. Nevertheless, judging Japanese intentions was more difficult than with Italy. Authoritative intelligence was harder to obtain, Japan remained heavily engaged and apparently preoccupied with China well into 1941, and the German invasion of Russia offered her an attractive 'northern option' of intervening against an apparently collapsing traditional enemy. For most of 1941, it was not obvious that Japan would make an aggressive move southward or, if she did, that this implied an immediate attack on Britain. Finally, the attitude of the United States was a fundamental factor in the Far East, in marked contrast to the Mediterranean.

For the Admiralty, the collapse of France and entry of Italy into the war made it impossible for the foreseeable future to deploy a significant fleet to Singapore to counter a threat from Japan, in accordance with pre-war doctrine. Furthermore, the China Fleet was reduced to a token force, and its submarines transferred to the Mediterranean. If Japan intervened, the Force H task force at Gibraltar would move to the Indian Ocean to deter an IJN attack on its vital communications. The defence of Singapore and

Malaya would have to rest on air and land power, and the deterrent effect of the United States on Japanese aggression. Nevertheless, the Admiralty recognised that the IJN was larger and more powerful than the Italian navy, and could not be geographically contained, as the latter was in the Mediterranean. *In extremis*, Indian Ocean communications were more important than the eastern Mediterranean and it would, if necessary, withdraw the Mediterranean Fleet from Alexandria in order to defend them.

In late summer 1941 the prime minister and Admiralty agreed that the vulnerability of the Indian Ocean to Japanese intervention required permanent Royal Navy reinforcement, now rendered possible by the US Navy assuming responsibility for the security of the western Atlantic. At this point, two years into the European war, the British intelligence assessment of the naval threat posed by Japan had strengths, building on its studies through the 1930s, but also important new weaknesses. NID4, the geographic section responsible for Japan, working closely with FECB, maintained a broadly accurate picture of current IJN numerical strength and order of battle, including that of the IJNAF, both ship-borne and land-based.[1] The specifications and performance characteristics credited to warship and aircraft classes were also generally correct. This essentially quantitative view depended primarily on information provided by the Tokyo naval and air attachés, but by mid 1941, SIGINT (traffic analysis and D/F) monitoring provided important collateral for the JJN order of battle, while MEW contributed occasional assessments of Japanese industrial capacity.[2] The military and air attachés in Chungking, and SIS liaisons with the Chinese and French, were also useful sources on the IJNAF, including from late 1940 its deployment in Indochina. There were inevitably some significant errors in the NID picture. The displacement of recently completed carriers was underestimated, overall carrier-deployed air strength was put at 25 per cent below reality (362 compared to 473), and six cruisers of the *Mogami* and *Tone* classes were credited with 6in armament, when they had been upgraded to 8in.[3] However, these errors were minor compared to other gaps in British understanding of IJN fighting capability.

In mid 1941 NID and the JIC not only correctly assessed Japanese numerical air strength (both IJNAF and the Imperial Japanese Army Air Force (IJAAF)), but doubted this would grow significantly over the next two years, judging that production only balanced wastage and re-equipment, taking account of operational losses in China. For the IJNAF, until the end of March 1942 this assessment proved correct. In summer 1941 production of naval aircraft of all types was only 162 per month, and only 10 per cent higher over the first four months of war. It was especially low for more modern combat aircraft, compounded by a paucity of reserves, barely 25 per cent or less of frontline strength.[4] There were only 415 Zero fighters in the frontline at the outbreak of war, and carrier attack aircraft availability was depleting fast, well before the Battle of Midway in June 1942.[5] Overall, British estimates for immediate pre-war Japanese air strength, frontline, reserves and production capacity were better than comparable estimates for pre-war German air strength, and far superior to estimates of German air strength and production during 1940 and the first half of 1941. In 1939 German air force frontline strength was overestimated by 18.5 per cent, while 1940 German aircraft production was overestimated by a minimum of 25 per cent, and at one point by 75 per cent.[6]

By mid 1941, the British intelligence community had accurate performance tables for all Japanese aircraft in use at the outbreak of war, and had identified the exceptional range of naval aircraft, including the new Zero fighter.[7] There was good knowledge of IJNAF aircraft armament, the main types of bomb, and the Type 91 aerial torpedo.[8] Although the latter is often judged superior to the standard Royal Navy 18in Mark XII and XIV Fleet Air Arm torpedoes, specifications, performance and reliability were close. The Type 91 could, in theory, be dropped from 500m (1600ft) altitude, but only 10 per cent functioned correctly at 200m (660ft) and 50 per cent at 100m (330ft). The preferred standard operational drop was from a range of 600–400m at 160–170 knots at a height of 30–50m, little different from the operational performance envelope of the Fleet Air Arm Albacore, although the latter was slower.[9] This intelligence on aircraft and armament was available within Far East Air Headquarters by early autumn 1941.[10]

By August 1941, following the Japanese move into the southern half of Indochina, NID identified eight Japanese airfields there, along with upgrades underway at Saigon and Bien Hoa, two bases used by IJNAF aircraft that December. It also assessed that heavy bombers deploying from Saigon and Soctrang could reach Singapore and the Malacca strait with a normal bomb load.[11] Subsequent reporting confirmed details of the Type 96 IJNAF heavy bomber, correctly estimating it could carry 2200lbs (1000kg) to 950 miles. NID initially doubted Japan could afford to deploy more than 150 land-based aircraft for potential operations against Malaya and the Netherlands East Indies that autumn, but revised this figure sharply upwards by December.[12] Far East Air Headquarters rated the IJNAF high for operational effectiveness, but judged the IJAAF merely mediocre, an assessment shared with FECB and the China Fleet.[13]

While estimates of current IJN strength were reasonably accurate in mid 1941, FECB, and therefore NID, still struggled in reliably assessing IJN building plans.[14] Through 1940, the Admiralty maintained that the IJN would have four new battleships of 35,000–40,000 tons by the end of 1942, up to four additional battlecruisers of around 14,000 tons armed with 12in guns, and assumed the IJN could maintain a rate of three capital ships every two years.[15] NID believed one of the battlecruisers, named *Ibuki*, was on trials by summer 1941. This enduring conviction that battlecruisers were actually under construction encouraged the long-standing Admiralty belief, also held firmly by Churchill, that the IJN would use heavy ships to attack Britain's trade and communications in wartime, especially in the Indian Ocean.

By focusing on industrial capacity and the status of key building slips, an August 1941 FECB report on IJN construction got closer to reality than previous estimates, although important errors persisted.[16] It correctly identified one battleship fitting out (*Yamato*, commissioned that December), and one building at Yokusuka (*Shinano*, the third *Yamato* class, later converted into an aircraft carrier), but misidentified *Musashi*, the second *Yamato* class, fitting out at Nagasaki, and *111*, the fourth *Yamato* on the slip at Kure (never completed), as 12in battlecruisers. It accurately identified three aircraft carriers fitting out: *Shokaku* (commissioned August 1941), *Zuikaku* (commissioned September 1941), and *Taiyo* (also September). Cruisers under construction were put at seven against the reality of four, and seventeen destroyers compared to an official Japanese figure of twelve, although FECB possibly included smaller escort vessels.[17] Unfortunately, the greater realism in this report did not persist. By next March, NID estimates for IJN construction were badly off-track again. Their claim that one new battleship of 40,000 tons was in service, a second imminent, and a further three under construction was consistent with the delivery of the *Yamato* class, but they now anticipated six additional battlecruisers, with two nearing completion, while two carriers were also under construction. The prime minister was rightly sceptical whether Japan had the industrial capacity to support such a programme.[18]

In autumn 1941 NID's tendency to overstate future IJN construction served the useful purpose of reinforcing for the naval staff the clear message from estimates of current IJN order of battle that it was a formidable and dangerous opponent, competitive in numbers and quality with the Royal Navy in most areas of naval capability, except anti-submarine warfare. The previous year Phillips, as VCNS, argued forcefully that the IJN's ten modernised capital ships were 'superior to our own', and that only seven Royal Navy vessels were competitive in an Eastern war.

The new *King George V* class would broadly match anticipated new IJN ships in numbers, but would be out-gunned, without taking account of the four 12in-gunned battlecruisers Japan was building.[19] Royal Navy anxiety over IJN capital ship superiority, especially their long-range fire capability, persisted through most of the war. As late as 1944 NID judged the four older IJN battleships of the *Fuso* and *Ise* classes superior to the modernised *Queen Elizabeth*s, and the *Kongo*-class battlecruisers superior to the modernised *Renown*, although it recognised Royal Navy radar and blind fire could, in practice, make a decisive difference. NID was undoubtedly unfair to both Royal Navy vessels, but reflected an enduring Admiralty view. In reality, there was probably little difference between the two navies in long-range fire under good daytime conditions, but radar gave the Royal Navy a major advantage at night, or in bad weather.[20]

Strangely, this worry over IJN capital ship superiority, so evident in early 1940, did not raise concern about potential superiority in other areas of naval capability, an omission most striking in regard to IJN air power. NID knew the IJN had invested heavily in its air arm since the mid 1930s. Phillips, as Director of Plans, had contributed to the chiefs of staff 1937 Far East appreciation, which provided an accurate assessment of IJNAF strength at that time and, significantly, judged there was then already little difference between IJNAF and RAF or Fleet Air Arm aircraft performance.[21] In February 1940, contemporaneously with Phillips's capital ship comparison, DNI and the Director of the Naval Air Division (DNAD) agreed that, allowing for expenditure on RAF Coastal Command, the IJN was probably still spending 50 per cent more on its air arm than the Royal Navy.[22] They put IJN carrier air arm strength at 450 aircraft, although DNAD questioned (wrongly) whether these were all as modern as their Royal Navy equivalents. Equivalent Fleet Air Arm frontline strength at this point was 264.[23] Cumulative reporting over the next eighteen months, confirming the commissioning of new carriers, re-equipment with new aircraft, and the arrival of land-based units with long-range strike aircraft in Indochina built on this substantial earlier background intelligence.

Senior Royal Navy officers most responsible for meeting the threat from the IJN later cited underestimation of IJN power and effectiveness to explain the disasters that befell the Royal Navy in late 1941 and early 1942. This was inevitably linked with poor intelligence, an excuse more popular with the passage of time. Post-war, Godfrey stated that 'Japan, behind an impenetrable security wall, had built up a fighting machine about whose composition and intentions we knew very little. Both we and the Americans erred and there is hardly anyone entitled to say –

"I told you so."[24] Pound stated: 'we all under-rated the efficiency of the Japanese air forces and certainly did not realise the long ranges at which they could work'.[25] Vice Admiral Sir Henry Moore, Phillips's successor as VCNS, went further: 'we grossly underestimated the power and efficiency of the Japanese naval surface and air forces', adding that 'this may have been due both to lack of intelligence and to faulty assessment of what we had'.[26] Their claims do not withstand scrutiny. These busy officers, focused on a war in Europe, could not reasonably follow the detailed intelligence on the IJN, but as an Eastern confrontation became more likely through 1941 and the naval staff debated reinforcement, they saw sufficient headline assessments from the JIC, NID and the Far East theatre to ask searching questions. It was certainly Godfrey's job to do so. If the IJN had eight carriers, how effective were they? How might they use them, given the luxury of concentration in a single theatre? What lessons might the IJN draw from the Taranto attack? Did the Japanese airbases in Indochina pose the same problem for the Royal Navy it had faced from German and Italian land-based attack in the Mediterranean, notably at Crete? Yet there is no record such questions were ever debated either within the Admiralty or with Commander-in-Chief China Vice Admiral Sir Geoffrey Layton.

This absence of debate on IJN air capability, especially carrier capability, as the Admiralty reviewed the balance of naval forces in the East through 1941 is puzzling. In planning its new Eastern Fleet, the Royal Navy sought equality with the maximum battleship force the IJN might deploy in the South China Sea, but judged a single carrier desirable, rather than essential. The 1937 appreciation, despite few references to carriers compared to capital ships, at least considered the carrier balance, and the deployment of four IJN carriers in a hypothetical 1939 war. This disregard for IJN air power as a critical factor in the Far East naval balance during the second half of 1941 is striking, given the important role that air power, including Royal Navy carrier operations, had already played in both Atlantic and Mediterranean theatres. Throughout this year, Cunningham constantly emphasised the crucial importance of adequate air cover (carrier and land-based) if his fleet was to operate successfully. In November he insisted that operations in the central Mediterranean required a carrier 'stuffed with fighters'. Two carriers were 'better and safer than one', but one was 'essential'.[27]

There were striking analogies between the Mediterranean and South China Sea which the naval staff should have recognised, and explanations for ignoring them are hard to find. One is that none of the Royal Navy's European opponents operated carriers, so it had not faced an air threat beyond the range of land-based aircraft during the war to date. Another was that before Japan moved into southern Indochina, the sheer distance of Japanese airbases rendered the land-based air threat more theoretical than real and immediate. This distance factor perhaps then linked in some Admiralty minds with an expectation that Royal Navy forces operating in the South China Sea would enjoy British or American land-based air support, but recent experience in the Mediterranean showed that with the known balance of forces on each side, this offered little comfort. Finally, the sheer geographical spread of Royal Navy commitments, together with war losses and damage, meant that before 1942 it rarely had more than one carrier available in any theatre of operations and sometimes none, as in the eastern Mediterranean throughout the second half of 1941. With rare exceptions such as Taranto, which achieved a strategic effect comparable to Pearl Harbor, the Royal Navy therefore deployed its carriers in a supportive role, either for local air defence or as a facilitator of fleet action through reconnaissance or attrition, rather than as a decisive weapon in its own right. This perhaps encouraged a mindset within the naval staff that not only was a carrier for the Eastern Fleet discretionary, but that the IJN would follow a similar policy, dividing its carriers not just between Pacific and Southeast Asia theatres, but to support independent hunting groups, rather than concentrating them as a single force. Until 1941, this was a reasonable assumption.[28] Only in January that year did the IJN begin the revolutionary transformation that first grouped its fleet carriers together in the 1st Air Fleet on 1 April and then with extraordinary speed, by the following November, changed their role from tactical support to the battle-fleet to multi-carrier task force, using combined air strike power to project strategic effect at long distance.[29]

The IJN achieved this change in remote locations beyond the reach of British or American intelligence, and without the distraction of fighting a war. The doctrinal innovations occurred alongside, and were facilitated by, a comprehensive aircraft re-equipment programme across the year 1941, again at best only partly visible to the Western powers. The A6M Zero fighter and the latest marks of the Type 97 torpedo bomber and Type 99 dive-bomber were all introduced in the twelve months leading up to the outbreak of war. (Although the Royal Navy and RAF had details of the Zero by mid 1941, they did not appreciate it was designed primarily for carrier deployment.) It was difficult for the Royal Navy or US Navy to spot this revolutionary change. Although by October, FECB SIGINT analysis suggested the three IJN carrier squadrons were now operating as a separate command under the carrier *Akagi*, recognising the implications of this development would have required extraordinary and timely insider intelligence access, and an equivalent military vision of what was possible, driven by similar strategic need.[30] In 1941 both navies faced different challenges and neither had the luxury of concentrating carrier power in a single theatre. It was late 1943 before the US Navy generated equivalent carrier power to the IJN 1st Air Fleet carriers, the Kido Butai, of late 1941.

Along with the RAF, the Royal Navy failed to recognise parallel developments within the land-based components of the IJNAF. Although FECB tracked IJNAF deployments in Indochina effectively in the autumn of 1941, it did not appreciate that with the 11th Air Fleet the IJN had created a land-based equivalent to the carrier-based 1st Air Fleet, which operated as a fully integrated component of the Combined Fleet under the Combined Fleet commander, Admiral Isoruku Yamamoto.[31] This concept not only did not exist in the Royal Navy, where land-based maritime strike was an RAF Coastal Command responsibility, but had no parallel elsewhere in Europe or the United States. Cunningham recognised the requirement, which he advocated in the eastern Mediterranean following the fall of Crete and the loss of his carriers. However, inter-service politics made execution difficult, and it was well into 1942 before something similar was implemented on a smaller scale to the 11th Air Fleet.[32] Thus while intelligence got both IJN aircraft numbers and performance characteristics about right, drawing heavily here on traffic analysis, it failed to recognise that behind these numbers was a highly tuned weapon system dedicated to maritime strike.

This blind spot regarding Japanese naval air power was accompanied by some tendency within British defence and intelligence circles during the period 1939–41 to downplay Japanese military efficiency and effectiveness. It is difficult to judge how much practical effect, if any, this exerted on Royal Navy policy and planning towards the IJN.[33] It possibly encouraged a belief that the IJN was tactically rigid and lacking in innovation, with implications not just for assessment of air and anti-submarine capability (where the experience of the 4th Submarine Flotilla suggested there was justification), but also for missing the development of long-range torpedoes, and the false conviction that the IJN disliked night-fighting.[34] There are two formal references to this downplaying of Japanese capability. In plans prepared for Far East naval reinforcement during the 1939 Tientsin crisis, IJN fighting efficiency was rated at 80 per cent of the Royal Navy.[35] This was evidently endorsed by the Admiralty, but it is not clear where the figure originated, and it probably referred to ability to generate and sustain a fleet at sea, for which there was some substance, rather than to performance in battle.[36] It may have reflected a 1935 report by the Tokyo naval attaché, Guy Vivian, which identified traits in Japanese national characteristics and culture impeding efficiency, and attracted high-level interest in the naval staff.[37] But against this, the subsequent 1937 Far East appreciation insisted that the IJN should be rated equally to the Royal Navy, which accordingly required a capital ship advantage of twelve to nine.

The second reference came in 1941 when successive joint planning staff and JIC assessments rated the Japanese air forces on a par with the Italians.[38] Again, it is not clear where this analogy originated, although it was probably an RAF judgement, based on observation of Japanese forces in China. It possibly encouraged the Royal Navy to be more relaxed than was justified about the air threat to operations in the South China Sea in late 1941, and to pose fewer questions about IJN carrier power. Ironically, while the Italian analogy was intended to be pejorative, the Royal Navy, certainly Cunningham and Somerville, viewed the Italian air force, especially its torpedo bombers, with great respect. Cunningham was unequivocal about the high quality of Italian air performance at sea during the first part of the war, stating that they possessed squadrons 'specially trained for anti-ship work', drawing on 'highly efficient' reconnaissance, which 'seldom failed to find and report our ships'. Bombers then 'invariably arrived in an hour or two', and Italian high-level bombing was 'the best I have ever seen, far better than the German'.[39] Such experience with Italian air performance at sea would surely have tempered any Royal Navy inclination to be complacent about IJNAF aircraft in Indochina, if it had been recognised they were armed with torpedoes, and available intelligence on their range properly absorbed.[40]

Effective assessment of the Japanese naval risk to British interests depended not only on an accurate picture of current IJN fighting capability. It required current knowledge of IJN organisation, the location and movements of its key forces, and, above all, timely warning of hostile intent. This task rested primarily on FECB and by mid 1941, despite limited resources, its intelligence assets could give the Admiralty and local Royal Navy commanders good advice on the probability, scale and timing of an attack.[41] Despite the sharp reduction in Royal Navy forces in the East from 1939, FECB remained accountable to and administered by Commander-in-Chief China, rather than the new overall Commander-in-Chief Far East, Air Chief Marshal Sir Robert Brooke-Popham, and was still commanded by a Royal Navy captain. In the second half of 1941 this was Captain Kenneth Harkness, a gunnery officer not an intelligence specialist, but capable, with a strong operational record, and a good administrator. FECB, therefore, retained its distinct naval bias, and continued to manage the Pacific Naval Intelligence Organisation, which by autumn 1940, along with China Fleet headquarters, had relocated to Singapore from Hong Kong. It still devoted more effort to naval requirements than those of the other services, was more effective here, and collaborated closely with NID, with advantages for naval intelligence distribution and exploitation.[42]

SIGINT remained the biggest contributor to the FECB picture of IJN organisation and movements. By mid 1941, still under Harry Shaw, the FECB SIGINT section comprised three naval, three army, one air force and one civilian officer, with about twenty-five support staff. Shaw's priority was JN25, used by about 75 per cent of intercepted naval traffic, and after the arrival of Tiltman's initial recoveries in autumn 1939 with Malcolm Burnett, this was targeted solely by FECB. Owing to limited resources and the overwhelming priority of European requirements, with the exception of military attaché traffic which ceased to be readable from February 1940, GC&CS made no significant contribution to Japanese naval or military systems for the two years from the end of 1939, when naval section staff working on Japan moved to the diplomatic section.[43] However, although Shaw's team mastered the overall structure of the JN25 system, overcoming problems caused by the Japanese shift to the new JN25B codebook in December 1940, and the frequent changes in additive cipher tables, they never achieved sufficient readability to deliver operational value before the Japanese attack in December 1941.[44] Apart from JN25, Shaw's team did some work on the Flag Office cipher, first identified in November 1938, lesser naval codes such as those used for merchant shipping, low-grade ciphers used by the Japanese consular network, and plain-language intercept. In early 1941 FECB was reading nineteen lower-grade Japanese ciphers. Little of this wider civilian output directly illuminated IJN capabilities and operations, although it provided useful indicators for judging Japanese intentions. The lack of immediate operational value from FECB's cryptographic effort meant that the pre-war tensions over priorities between Shaw and successive COISs continued.[45]

Although it delivered no operational intelligence, the JN25 development work provided better understanding of overall IJN communications to improve traffic analysis, which by 1941 became the dominant means to track IJN organisation, locations and movements. FECB traffic analysis at least matched, and probably surpassed, that achieved by Hut 4 at this time, and drew on the latest techniques, including RFP, which was fitted at the Kranji site in Singapore in early 1941.[46] D/F also contributed, with FEDO now expanded to eight stations, although fixes rarely improved on the fifty-mile radius achieved in 1939.[47] At the end of the year in the run-up to war, FECB successfully tracked both the formation and movements of the IJN southern task force earmarked for the invasion of Malaya, and the Japanese air build-up in Indochina.

Meanwhile, by the end of 1939, GC&CS could no longer decrypt Japanese diplomatic traffic passing between Tokyo and the thirteen missions the Japanese judged most important, which used the new Purple machine cipher, although the Red system, used by many other missions, remained readable. However, from early 1941 Britain benefited from the success of the United States Army Signals Intelligence Service, led by the First World War cryptographer, William Friedman, and created following the closure of Yardley's Black Chamber in 1929, in breaking the Purple cipher from the previous September.[48] The Americans shared this success with GC&CS in February when, following the recommendation of the Ghormley team the previous August, a combined US Army and Navy team, later known as the Sinkov–Rosen mission, named after its Signals Intelligence Service members, Abe Sinkov and Leo Rosen, visited Bletchley and provided a decryption machine, originally destined for the US Navy in Hawaii, to enable the British to read intercepted Purple traffic directly. By spring 1941, the Americans were reading between fifty and seventy-five Japanese diplomatic messages per day. British independent output was somewhat less, largely owing to more limited access to Japanese high-grade traffic, including that linked with their Washington embassy. This Purple windfall caused Denniston to establish a new inter-service Japanese section, which theoretically combined work for all three services with diplomatic requirements, including Purple. In practice, it only did diplomatic and naval work, and nothing on the latter before 1942. The gift of Purple persuaded Denniston that GC&CS should be more forthcoming on Enigma than previously intended. Following consultation with Menzies, the Americans were given a reasonably comprehensive brief on the German Enigma variants and British cryptographic methods deployed to attack them, including sight of a bombe, with indication of where success was being achieved. However, they were not allowed to take notes, and when they returned were asked to restrict details of this briefing to Friedman and Laurance Safford, head of the US Navy cryptographic unit, OP-20-G. Following direction from the prime minister and Menzies, GC&CS emphasised that no Enigma-related intelligence could be shared at this time, and the Americans should not ask for it.[49]

By restoring the crucial insights passing to and from Hiroshi Ōshima, the Japanese ambassador in Berlin, Purple gave the American and British governments valuable insights into Japanese and German leadership thinking and intentions, with seventy-five of his reports to Tokyo decrypted through 1941, and a further 1400 over the rest of the war. Specific naval intelligence insights from Ōshima included details of German blockade-runners, including special U-boats, carrying strategically important materials between Germany and Japan; U-boat deployments in the Indian Ocean from 1942; Japanese interest in establishing a base in Madagascar; the deployment from early 1942 of German heavy warships to Norway against convoys to Russia; and in 1944, important details of the advanced new U-boat types under construction.[50] The combination of Purple decrypts from Ōshima, combined with naval Enigma decrypts, helped the Allies sink twenty-nine of fifty-six cargo-carrying submarines commencing voyages between Germany and Japan. The intelligence product from Purple was called Magic by the Americans, and the decryption machines, likewise, Magic machines.[51] Magic made an important contribution to JIC assessments in 1941, and featured regularly in intercepts sent on a daily basis to the prime minister, especially in the second half of the year.[52] The official post-war summary of SIGINT providing war warning indicators to the British and United States governments in late 1941, including material relevant to Pearl Harbor, found full sharing of Magic, with no evidence that the United States deliberately held any messages back. The only omissions from the British record were some final 'deadline' messages from the last stage of United States-Japanese negotiations in the first week of December.[53] A Purple machine was despatched late in 1941 to FECB.[54] It apparently arrived in Singapore at the end of December in the merchant ship *Sussex*, but never reached FECB, and was presumably destroyed during the chaos of the island's fall. Had it been found by the Japanese, it would not only have compromised the Purple operation, but alerted the Axis to the overall scale of Allied codebreaking, with disastrous consequences.[55]

In parallel with the Purple exchanges, there was a more specific naval element to the Sinkov–Rosen mission, which included two representatives, Robert Weeks and Prescott Currier, from OP-20-G. This naval cryptographic unit originated within the code and signals section in the mid 1920s, taking on the designation OP-20-G in 1935. By 1939 it had around 130 staff, significantly larger than the number then working on naval SIGINT in GC&CS and FECB, and about 300 by end 1941. As a result of the discussions, Godfrey and GC&CS agreed immediately to collaborate with the Americans on Japanese naval codes, and authorised FECB to commence a full exchange the same month with the OP-20-G outstation at Cavite Navy Yard in the Philippines, known as Station Cast, which had lead responsibility for JN25. Both parties brought valuable contributions to the table here, though the British were well ahead, and therefore initially contributed most. By early March, FECB supplied Cast with 'the latest JN25 book, "indicators" and subtractor tables, on all of which the US Navy had no information'. American sources admit that FECB's input, especially an early visit by Malcolm Burnett, was crucial both in starting their effective attack on JN25, and persuading OP-20-G to put more resources into it. For their part, the Americans provided a Japanese merchant ship code, an IJN personnel code, and call-sign data. Burnett also impressed on Shaw the value Cast received from IBM Hollerith tabulating machines, but British counterparts for FECB did not arrive until the autumn. Co-operation between FECB and Station Cast remained close for the rest of 1941, with Singapore controlling the overall JN25 attack, but with complete sharing of all intercepts and decryption results, facilitated by weekly transfers through Clipper flight, and an encrypted radio link using one-time pads. Cast significantly extended FECB access to IJN traffic, because it was better placed geographically to monitor activity around the Japanese home islands, and it was probably better at traffic analysis. Despite this joint effort, progress on the main priority JN25 was slow. By the time the Japanese attacked in December, only about 10 per cent of the latest JN25B codebook had been reconstructed, no message had yet been read currently, and the fragments that had been successfully decrypted yielded no operational intelligence.[56] FECB established a more limited exchange with the Dutch SIGINT unit, Kamer 14, based at Bandung in Java under Colonel Jacobus Verkuyl, which offered additional D/F and traffic analysis capability, but had no significant success against the major Japanese ciphers.[57] Neither Britain nor the United States achieved significant decryption of Japanese army ciphers during 1941.

As through the 1930s, intelligence gleaned from SIGINT had limitations. Magic intercepts only offered occasional and partial indications into Japanese (or German) political and strategic intentions. Without consistent and comprehensive access to JN25 or equivalent Imperial Japanese Army (IJA) systems, SIGINT provided little insight into high-level naval or military planning. It still told the Royal Navy little about the quality of the IJN, its specific weapons systems and its fighting effectiveness, let alone the detailed strategy and tactics it would apply in a war with Britain and its Allies. Nor did it reveal much about IJN building programmes. Human sources were required to access these areas, but the secretive and well-protected Japanese system proved ever more difficult to penetrate either by SIS, or the attachés in Tokyo, although the latter sometimes gained revealing indications of Japanese intent. The naval attaché reported in mid October 1941 that all units of the IJN had mobilised and moved to a war footing.[58]

Without consistent high-level intelligence from human sources, or a substantial breakthrough into JN25, British assessments of how their broadly accurate picture of overall Japanese order of battle would translate into an actual attack on the territory or interests of Britain or its Allies was therefore based on political and military judgement of risk, and warning signs of imminent hostile intent. Risk judgement drew on diplomatic insights from the Tokyo embassy, the current disposition of Japanese forces, geographic and logistic possibility and, not least, existing Japanese military commitments in China. Specific 'warning indicators' listed by FECB in December 1940 primarily comprised troop and transport concentrations, unusual naval movements and concentration of shore-based aircraft, but also evacuation of Japanese nationals and reduction in commercial activity, including commercial shipping.[59] Most of these FECB indicators proved their worth in the immediate run-up to war in late 1941.

From summer 1940 to autumn 1941, the core elements of the risk judgement here, reflected in both London and Singapore, were constant. They were that Japan could easily mobilise a southern expeditionary force of six to ten divisions, had sufficient shipping to lift this from Formosa or Hainan, and could cover this force with most of the IJN's major units and a substantial land-based air force of 350–450 aircraft. The judgement also identified three major constraints facing a Japanese attack on Malaya or the Netherlands East Indies: the challenge of distance, a minimum of 1150 miles from embarkation points to the nearest targets; the possibility of American intervention against long Japanese communication lines; and, above all, the need for advanced airbases to achieve acceptable air cover for an invasion force. An attack relying solely on carrier air cover was judged possible, but inherently risky, and would involve extensive naval activity, likely to be spotted.[60] A key assumption, therefore, underpinning British calculations until the Japanese move into southern Indochina at the end of July 1941, was that the requirement for air cover would lead Japan to a strategy of incremental advance, and thereby provide warning. These perceived constraints on Japan, the idea of incremental advance, and exaggerated faith that Malaya and Singapore could withstand attack at least temporarily created in the minds of the Admiralty and prime minister the idea of a more specific naval risk, that Japan would first weaken Britain through IJN attack on trade and communications in the Indian Ocean. Although never backed by any intelligence, this was the risk constantly highlighted by Churchill through the middle part of 1941.

Such calculations were evident in the comprehensive JIC update published on 1 May 1941[61] and an FECB threat assessment a month earlier on 4 April.[62] FECB stated that the nearest Japanese launch point to Kota Bharu was Hainan. Without prior bases in southern Indochina or Thailand, air cover for an attack on Malaya would have to be ship-borne, with a maximum available force of six carriers and three seaplane carriers capable of delivering seventy-five fighters, 206 strike aircraft and sixty assorted floatplanes. However, with the requisite bases, Japan could deploy a shore-based air force of 200 fighters, 200 light bombers, 150 heavy bombers and 100 reconnaissance aircraft. This estimate correctly anticipated in both numbers and category the combined IJAAF and IJNAF strength deployed against Malaya in December of 564 aircraft with the reinforced IJNAF 22nd Air Fleet contributing thirty-six fighters, ninety-nine heavy bombers and nine reconnaissance aircraft.[63] Far East Air Staff endorsed FECB's assessment, and the inability of a carrier force alone to generate sufficient offensive strength, judging therefore that Japan must control southern Indochina and Thailand, as well as retaining a considerable naval bomber force against American intervention. The occupation, preparation and stocking of Indochina airbases was therefore a critical intelligence indicator, and arrival of the Zero naval fighter a definite sign that Malaya was targeted.[64]

Apart from SIGINT, there were three other important sources of warning: the British consul in Saigon, William Meiklereid, who, unusually for Vichy-administered territory, the French allowed to remain in place; SIS exploitation of former liaison relationships with French intelligence officials in Indochina; and wider independent SIS agent networks in the region. All these provided crucial insights on the Japanese air and troop build-up in southern Indochina during November. Brook-Popham was scathing about SIS performance at the beginning of 1941, soon after his arrival in Malaya, and his criticisms of organisation, low-calibre personnel, and failure to deliver quality strategic insights on Japanese intentions and capability were partly justified.[65] However, in delivering tactical intelligence through the autumn, SIS did better, helped by wider improvements in intelligence organisation through the summer.[66] It tracked the build-up of Japanese forces for their southern operations in detail, and their French liaison source Sectude provided 'ample warning of the attack on Siam and Malaya', including the 'correct date and actual places for landings as well as the strength and movements of the enemy invasion fleet'.[67]

Overall, therefore, by early autumn 1941 the naval intelligence picture of the Japanese threat had strengths and weaknesses. NID and the naval staff had a broadly accurate picture of headline IJN strength in both ships and aircraft, although they had not adequately addressed the implications of known IJNAF strength, and underestimated its effectiveness. They also had accurate assessments of the scale of naval and air attack Japan could deploy against British interests. FECB had a good understanding of IJN organisation, and primarily through SIGINT, but also SIS sources, could track the movement of naval and air units in close to real time. Estimates for IJN new construction and aircraft production had errors, but were closer to reality.

FECB and NID now did well monitoring Japan's naval activity and build-up in Indochina over the three months to early December. At the end of September NID judged that Japan was putting its fleet in a state of readiness.[68] In early October it noted the IJN had completed its annual reorganisation two months ahead of time, and by the end of the month concluded that the IJN was on a 'war footing'.[69] Tracking of Japanese merchant shipping by MEW was also accurate and an additional pointer to likely hostilities.[70] In early October NID, drawing on MEW data, recorded that the number of Japanese merchant vessels at sea, averaging 162 per month during the first half of the year, had declined to just forty since early August.[71] By the middle of the month, MEW reported that normal traffic had virtually ceased, and at the end of October noted possible evacuee ships. NID subsequently stated that the Japanese government had taken control of all shipping on 8 October. The US Navy had similar intelligence on the withdrawal of Japanese merchant shipping, and in early November stated that merchant vessels were being inducted into the IJN 'in alarming numbers'.[72] Monitoring during November and early December of the Japanese air force deployments to southern Indochina and, in collaboration with the Americans, of naval movements was impressive.[73]

By 1 December, FECB had identified 'a special Japanese force' created under the command of Commander-in-Chief Second Fleet Vice Admiral Kondo Nobutake, to undertake operations in the south, probably focused on Thailand, but possibly including a landing on the Kra Isthmus. They estimated the force contained eight 8in cruisers, twelve 6in cruisers, four aircraft carriers, fifty-two destroyers and eighteen submarines. This was an accurate assessment of the IJN southern task force created to support the attacks on the Philippines and Malaya commencing a week later, although FECB initially missed the battlecruisers *Kongo* and *Haruna*, which were also included, and was unaware that the carriers comprised only the light carrier *Ryujo* and seaplane carriers.[74] The identification of the southern task force order of battle, achieved in close co-operation with the Americans using traffic analysis, was an impressive achievement.[75] However, FECB wrongly assessed that the bulk of the Combined Fleet remained in Japan. That was true of the battleships, but the carrier fleet, with two of the *Kongo* battlecruisers, was now heading for Pearl Harbor. NID4's situation report of 1 December also put the full Combined Fleet, including all ten capital ships and four carriers, still in home waters.

Meanwhile, during November, decryption of Purple and Red traffic, and that from the J-19 hand system used for global circulars to all missions, provided important insights into Japanese thinking and intentions at the strategic level. Tokyo advised key overseas posts 'we cannot make any further concessions' and 'the outlook is not bright'.[76] On 25 November GC&CS reported the famous 'Winds Alert' message sent by the ministry of foreign affairs in Tokyo to the chargé d'affaires in London a week earlier. This identified trigger phrases denoting the imminent breaking of diplomatic relations. That for America was: 'Easterly wind, rain'. For Britain, 'Westerly wind, fine'.[77] This 'Winds Alert' message sent in J-19 was first broken by FECB and passed to the Americans on 24 November, the day before it was formally issued in London.[78] FECB and Station Cast subsequently agreed arrangements to maximise chances of capturing an 'Execute' message, which Hong Kong intercepted on the evening of 7 December (6 December in Hawaii).[79] On 28 November the US Army War Plans Division advised the British joint planning staff that negotiations with the Japanese were at the point of breakdown, and offensive action against Thailand, the Netherlands East Indies or the Philippines was possible at any time.[80] A similar message simultaneously reached the Admiralty from the US Navy Chief of Naval Operations, and was relayed to Far East naval commanders the following day.[81] Meanwhile, SIGINT also confirmed that Tokyo was aware that the battleship *Prince of Wales* had reached Cape Town on 19 November, bound for Malaya, a disclosure which the British hoped would have a deterrent effect.[82]

Nevertheless, through November, FECB and the wider British intelligence community, including the JIC, struggled to decide what these developments meant and, specifically, whether the southern build-up was directed at Thailand, rather than Malaya, in line with Japanese 'incrementalism'. The signs pointing to real Japanese intent were cumulative and weighted towards the second half of the month, with the major jump in Japanese air force strength in Indochina only occurring in the final week before their attack. On 28 November Brooke-Popham, drawing on FECB, assessed there were 245 aircraft in Indochina, which Japanese sources confirm was about right.[83] A week later the FECB estimate had risen to 500, again about right.[84] Significantly, the head of

FECB's air section, the former Tokyo air attaché Roy Chappell, recognised that this force included IJNAF units which were torpedo-capable.[85]

The combination of SIGINT and military indicators from FECB, plus important collateral reporting from SIS, along with American warnings, left Britain's war leadership in little doubt by the end of November that the Japanese were headed south, and that the sheer scale of forces allocated made hostilities likely and imminent. This view was underlined in a warning message which on 2 December Menzies instructed Gerald Wilkinson, his SIS representative in Manila, to pass to the Americans in Honolulu.[86] The first days of December brought two further warning pointers specific to the IJN. They changed all naval call-signs on 1 December, significant because the previous change was 1 November, and they normally lasted six months. They also changed the additive cipher for JN25B on 4 December although, in a fatal error, they chose not to change the codebook. JN25B attack was therefore checked while the new additive was dealt with, but it remained vulnerable.[87] What was not foreseeable with existing British sources was the attack on Pearl Harbor and the consequences that flowed from that. Nor was it possible, without a source in the Japanese leadership, to know whether the Japanese would initially consolidate in Thailand, attack the Netherlands East Indies, or strike directly at Malaya. Britain also failed to anticipate a simultaneous attack on the Philippines.[88]

If reading of Japanese intentions was not perfect in these final weeks, it was good enough to persuade the Admiralty to avoid putting its initial Far East reinforcements, comprising *Prince of Wales* and the battlecruiser *Repulse*, subsequently known as Force Z, in an exposed position at Singapore. SIGINT had shown the Japanese knew they were in the Indian Ocean, so any political deterrence effect had been achieved. The Admiralty could have held them at Ceylon, which they reached on 28 November, while the situation clarified. There were three main reasons it did not do so. The US Navy was pressing for a serious Royal Navy commitment to defending the Malay barrier, and Britain could not risk weakening a firm Allied front in the face of Japanese aggression. The British naval leadership was also over-impressed by the scale of planned American air reinforcements for the Philippines, and the protection they could afford to potential Royal Navy operations from Singapore. Finally, because available intelligence did not convey the sheer scale and ambition of Japanese plans, the British judged there was time to review options after war commenced.[89]

With Force Z committed to Singapore, the naval intelligence picture FECB acquired in the final run-up to war, notably on the composition and movements of the IJN southern task force and the deployment of IJNAF units in southern Indochina, and its ongoing SIGINT capabilities, were now poorly exploited by the incoming Commander-in-Chief Eastern Fleet Admiral Sir Tom Phillips and his staff between their arrival in Singapore on 29 November, and the departure of Force Z to attack the Japanese landing forces late on 8 December. Neither Phillips nor his staff visited FECB, nor did he ask for a formal intelligence briefing, although Layton as outgoing Commander-in-Chief China presumably updated him privately. By agreement, Layton remained responsible for FECB until Phillips sailed with Force Z, and he arranged for the RAF to conduct reconnaissance flights, which located the Japanese invasion convoys in the Gulf of Siam on 6 December. However, in an extraordinary omission, Layton did not advise FECB of the deployment of Force Z, who accordingly lacked any context when plain-language intercepts on the morning of 10 December indicated that IJNAF aircraft had sighted British capital ships. Although the failure by Phillips and Layton to make proper use of FECB's knowledge and capabilities is both inexcusable and inexplicable, this did not contribute significantly to the Force Z losses. Phillips had already aborted the operation and, even with full access to everything FECB knew, would have judged he was well beyond the danger radius of effective aerial attack.[90]

Following the loss of Force Z, FECB contributed little value to naval operations before its naval section under Harry Shaw was evacuated from Singapore on 5 January to Colombo in Ceylon, leaving a smaller air and army component behind. Shortly afterwards, the PNIO was also evacuated, and eventually found a new home in Delhi. The IJN focus had temporarily shifted from Malaya to Borneo and the Philippines, the Royal Navy lacked any remaining capability to operate north of Singapore, and the JN25B additive change on 4 December meant there was little chance of significant readability for the rest of that month. Collaboration with Station Cast, now reduced to a tenuous radio link, suffered, while D/F and intercept coverage reduced sharply as sites were lost in Hong Kong and Borneo.[91] The residual FECB team in Singapore left a month later for the Dutch Kamer 14 centre in Bandung, joined by the Cast team evacuated from the Corregidor fortress in Manila Bay, where they had moved after Cavite became vulnerable. Despite this disruption and ineffectiveness, there was one major achievement. Shaw's team at last achieved some current readability of JN25B at the beginning of January, which they resumed on arrival in Colombo, by which time Station Cast had further improved coverage during their final weeks in Corregidor.[92]

Despite many logistic challenges, the FECB team in Colombo, reconstituted as HMS *Anderson*, resumed full SIGINT production in collaboration with Station Cast by the end of January 1942 and, with JN25B traffic perhaps 20 per cent readable by early February, provided more intelligence than ever before. Cast's output from late January, passed to *Anderson* by special encrypted link, increased at 'an amazing rate', stretching the ability of Shaw's team to process its traffic. Over the first quarter of 1942, *Anderson* handled 31,628 Japanese naval intercepts, of which two-thirds were JN25B. The combined effort with Cast through February and into March, despite the hiatus brought by the closing of Corregidor, gradually illuminated IJN operations across the whole southern theatre and beyond. The sheer disparity of forces between the IJN and the Allies in this theatre meant good intelligence could neither avert naval disaster in the Battle of the Java sea at the end of February, nor prevent a damaging psychological blow by carrier aircraft against Darwin. But it did create a more promising opportunity for exploitation from 20 March, when FECB began intercepting JN25B messages referring to a forthcoming operation by an IJN carrier force, accompanied by another force thought to comprise heavy cruisers, which were concentrating at Staring Bay in the Celebes, ready for an operation in the 'D' area (soon recognised as Ceylon) including an air raid against 'DG' (probably Colombo) on 2 April.[93]

On 29 March Admiral Sir James Somerville, the newly arrived Commander-in-Chief Eastern Fleet, assessed the available intelligence with Shaw's team. In addition to JN25B decrypts, this included NID summaries, a daily intelligence bulletin from the US Navy Pacific Fleet Intelligence Organisation, and insights from traffic analysis and D/F. These sources, along with recent JIC assessments, and the precedents of Pearl Harbor and the attack on Darwin in February, showed that the IJN had at least three fleet carriers, three *Kongo*-class battlecruisers, and a substantial cruiser force potentially available for deployment in the Indian Ocean.[94] The force actually deployed under Vice Admiral Chuichi Nagumo was somewhat larger, comprising five carriers with about 275 aircraft, four *Kongo*s, the only occasion on which these operated together, and heavy cruisers *Tone* and *Chikuma*, and it left Staring Bay on 26 March, five days later than believed by *Anderson*.[95] However, in summarising the intelligence picture for the Admiralty, sourced to 'Combined Fleet telegram orders', Somerville accepted Shaw's judgement that the latest JN25B decrypts suggested a smaller force, probably comprising just two carriers, four cruisers, and twelve destroyers, to attack Ceylon about 1 April.[96] *Anderson* not only seriously underestimated the size of the IJN carrier group (five carriers rather than two), but for unexplained reasons misread the attack date, which by mid March IJN commanders had agreed would be 5 April.[97]

Somerville judged his Eastern Fleet, which included two modern carriers, was strong enough to execute a night ambush on the projected IJN force. In theory, with accurate intelligence warning, aerial reconnaissance support from the RAF Catalina force in Ceylon, and reasonable expectation of further SIGINT insights, his prospects here were comparable to those of Cunningham at Matapan exactly a year earlier, or the Americans two months later at Midway. In practice, the serious underestimate of Nagumo's force, the inevitable uncertainties over his approach route, but also poor positioning chosen by Somerville, put his fleet at dangerous risk. Somerville only escaped disaster because Nagumo arrived later than expected, and he chose to refuel his main fleet at Port T, an anchorage established in the Maldives, well away from IJN search areas, rather than Colombo. Still convinced he faced a manageable IJN force, Somerville recklessly persisted with attempts at a night interception after Nagumo was spotted by a searching RAF Catalina, and through a combination of luck, and Japanese negligence, came remarkably close to succeeding. A JN25B intercept late afternoon on 5 April, giving Nagumo's movements the following day, was unfortunately received garbled. Otherwise, when added to reports from his own search aircraft, it might have given Somerville sufficient information to inflict serious damage, or even bring off an improbable victory. However, overall, while the British intelligence was good enough to ensure the survival of Somerville's main fleet, its limitations both before and during Nagumo's raid could not compensate for far superior IJN strength. The losses inflicted by the IJN force, including two heavy cruisers and a carrier, and the prospect of further raids, obliged the Royal Navy Eastern Fleet to retreat west and cede control of the central Indian Ocean at least temporarily, a strategic defeat for the British comparable to that imposed on the Italians at Matapan.[98]

The withdrawal of the Eastern Fleet triggered further changes to naval intelligence organisation in the Eastern theatre, with far-reaching consequences. The perceived vulnerability of Ceylon led to half the FECB SIGINT team at Anderson moving in late April to the new Eastern Fleet base at Kilindini, inland from Mombasa in Kenya. The other half remained to provide essential operational intelligence covering the central and east Indian Ocean area, and seaborne threats to India and Ceylon. In practice, this meant continuing intercept and decryption of JN25B, D/F, and monitoring accessible plain-language traffic.[99] This Anderson 'retard party', building on earlier work, and collaborating closely with its former Station Cast partner now re-established in Melbourne, and their Station Hypo colleagues at the US Navy Pacific Fleet headquarters in Pearl Harbor, made brief but valuable intelligence contributions during the period before the Japanese simultaneously introduced a new JN25 codebook and reciphering tables on 27 May, producing an immediate blackout for both British and American SIGINT teams.

Anderson recognised by mid April that the bulk of the IJN forces deployed in the Indian Ocean were returning to Japan, but also spotted that the carriers *Zuikaku* and *Shokaku* were being redeployed for operations in the southwest Pacific. Subsequent decrypts enabled *Anderson*, in concert with Cast, now established in Melbourne and renamed Belconnen, the small Australian SIGINT operation under Eric Nave,[100] and Hypo in Pearl Harbor to piece together the Japanese plan to invade New Guinea, Operation MO, and facilitate the Allied countermeasures which led to the Battle of the Coral Sea. In parallel, *Anderson* confirmed the IJN was conducting a major redeployment back to Japan, sharply reducing forces in the southern theatre, prior to future operations in the central Pacific, which by early May appeared focused on a target 'AF', which *Anderson* and Corregidor had recognised stood for Midway as early as 7 March.[101] On 20 May Somerville advised the Admiralty that the Americans believed an attack on Midway was looming, and sought any further collateral from British sources.[102] The same day the US Navy listening station in Hawaii intercepted a long JN25B message, which was painstakingly decrypted over the next five days, and proved to be Yamamoto's final operations order for the attack against Midway, and the related diversionary operation in the Aleutians. It is not clear whether Colombo contributed to this decryption, but NID issued full details on 2 June, two days before the main engagement.[103]

The Coral Sea and Midway contributions were the final achievement of what was still recognisable as a remnant of the FECB established in 1935. It had ceased to be a tri-service organisation on leaving Singapore but now, with the JN25B blackout, the Colombo retard party were also withdrawn to Kilindini where they were isolated, ineffective, and therefore soon demoralised. Although in close contact with headquarters Eastern Fleet, they were also separated from the reconstituted PNIO in Delhi. Conditions and facilities were miserable, their ability to intercept traffic centred thousands of miles away the other end of the Indian Ocean was sharply reduced, and communications with Melbourne, Pearl Harbor, Bletchley, Washington and Delhi too tenuous for efficient cryptographic exchange. Far East naval SIGINT, once at the cutting edge, plunged to its nadir, while the Americans, once junior partners on JN25, forged ahead with apparently endless resources, little need for British input and growing disinclination to share. Indeed, for a while the British found themselves treated by OP-20-G on JN25 rather as they had treated the

Poles on Enigma after September 1939. Meanwhile, the decisive American victory at Midway, rendered possible by JN25, effectively ended a major Japanese threat to the Indian Ocean, leading to the rapid rundown of Somerville's fleet. Heavily focused on the Atlantic and the Mediterranean, there was little incentive for NID or Bletchley to give much time to the problems of Kilindini. Any renaissance of Far East naval SIGINT would have to wait.[104]

In explaining Britain's catastrophic early defeats to the IJN – Force Z, the Java Sea and Ceylon – blaming underestimation of the enemy, and especially poor intelligence, later proved easier for senior naval leaders than accepting responsibility for poor strategic or operational decisions, or failure to provide the resources which intelligence suggested were necessary. These explanations also fitted the wider narrative established for the loss of Britain's empire in Southeast Asia. Leaving aside the factors that provoked specific underestimation of the IJNAF, it is hard to support the claims of Moore and Godfrey of wider intelligence failure, given the reality of the record from the mid 1930s to the outbreak of the Eastern war, including the generally excellent record of the JIC, where Godfrey was a key member.[105] Layton, the Far East Naval Commander-in-Chief both before and after Phillips, writing contemporaneously, did not mention intelligence weakness or underestimation, placing blame entirely on inadequate forces, and failure to provide the strength 'we knew to be necessary'.[106] His view was shared by Major General Ian Playfair, Chief of Staff to the American-British-Dutch-Australian (ABDA) joint Far East Command formed in January 1942. The following year, when identifying 'fundamental defects' causing the loss of Malaya, 'not enough forces' came top. He too omitted either poor intelligence or underestimation of the enemy.[107]

There were important gaps in Britain's intelligence picture of the IJN during 1941, but these were less important than the failure properly to understand and exploit what was known, to make appropriate strategic and operational decisions. Once the Japanese were established in strength in Indochina, holding Malaya without a far greater commitment of air power than Britain was willing or able to make was never credible. It followed that, given the known balance of forces, and intelligence warning of Japanese intent in late November, sending Force Z on to Singapore from Ceylon carried significant risk for no immediate benefit. Somerville too got the risk–benefit equation wrong at Ceylon the following April, overestimating both the quality of his intelligence and his capabilities.

However, judging how well the Royal Navy had assessed its IJN opponent by late 1941 also requires perspective on IJN strengths and weaknesses. The IJN's evolution of its air strike capability in 1940–41 was innovative, but based on local concentration of a superbly trained force, rather than overall resource superiority, or any fundamental technical advance in military capability. The IJN, and especially the IJNAF, has been aptly described as 'so highly tempered it was brittle'. Much of its equipment was superb by the standards of 1941 and the competition it immediately faced in the Far East theatre. But, as the British joint planning staff appreciated even before Midway, the commitments it had acquired in its first months of conquest outpaced its industrial, technical, and logistic resources, not least in air power, where the JIC judged production barely matched losses. Furthermore, in exploiting the vital Netherlands East Indies oilfields and other overseas resources it had acquired, Japan faced long sea routes, an acute shortage of shipping, especially tankers, and quite inadequate anti-submarine forces.[108]

The IJN had neither thought about trade protection nor procured relevant capabilities, drawing on Royal Navy lessons in the Atlantic. It began the war with just four dedicated anti-submarine escorts, with no underwater detection equipment available at sea until August 1942, when the Royal Navy was deploying 2100 sonar-equipped ships. Other IJN weaknesses included lack of radar, poor anti-aircraft defence, and indifferent damage control. Aircraft communications were especially deficient, with no VHF voice system until well into 1943, while the HF system, only fitted to strike aircraft and not fighters, was bulky and unreliable. Lack of modern communications imposed severe limitations on strike, reconnaissance and, above all, air defence operations. IJN doctrine was narrowly focused on the concept of a decisive battle with the enemy fleet, where it was 'ingenious, imaginative and beautifully crafted'. But it neglected the wider aspects of maritime power on which Japan depended, and underestimated the limitations of Japan's economic and industrial capacity which threatened rapid obsolescence.[109]

Finally, a judgement of the British naval intelligence contribution in the Eastern theatre from mid 1939 to mid 1942 must underline its role in breaking JN25B. This was a joint effort with the Americans. Whether the Americans would have achieved the breakthrough by early 1942 without British help is impossible to know. But the window of readability, enabling the critical intelligence insights which led to the successes at the Coral Sea and Midway, before the codebook changed at the end of May, was narrow – barely four months. From available evidence, it seems unlikely that Station Cast, which carried the entire American responsibility for JN25B through 1941, would have met that window without British help. In which case, British intelligence deserves some share in two critical turning points of the Pacific campaign, and in the case of Midway, perhaps the whole war.

28

The Atlantic in the Balance 1942–1943

By 1942, NID, now organised as in the accompanying diagram, was a mature and effective organisation, fed by sources of a quality, speed and efficiency unrecognisable from the dark days of the Norwegian campaign and fall of France. At its heart, delivering a constant, almost real-time, operational picture, now with fifteen subsections and about a hundred staff in its bombproof Citadel, with secure communications to Bletchley, Western Approaches and Coastal Command, the OIC was a miniature version of the wider department. The naval intelligence system was not perfect, as Operation Cerberus demonstrated, but seemed well equipped to meet most likely challenges.[1] Nevertheless, the middle years of the war proved far from a comfortable consolidation of existing capabilities. There were new and distinct intelligence problems in every major theatre. In the Atlantic and Arctic, the Royal Navy faced a much expanded U-boat assault, creating difficult intelligence negotiations with the Americans, and a major German effort from Norway against the new supply convoys to Russia. In the Mediterranean, with the securing of Malta following Pedestal and the availability of substantial American resources, the intelligence focus shifted to support for large-scale seaborne assaults on enemy territory, beginning with Torch in North Africa, and then successive operations against the Italian mainland. In the East, the absence of a Japanese threat to the Indian Ocean, following the American victory at Midway, reduced this theatre to a backwater starved of British resources until early 1944. The challenge was to recover the intelligence capabilities which had atrophied following the fall of Singapore and retreat from Ceylon, and to convince the Americans that Britain remained a worthwhile intelligence partner in the Japanese war.

ORGANISATION OF NAVAL INTELLIGENCE DIVISION IN 1943

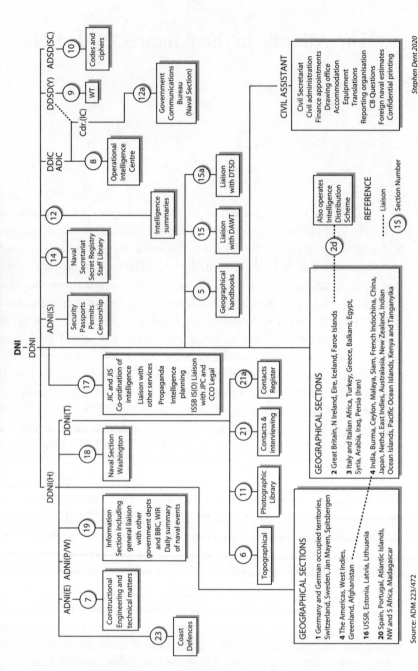

Source: ADM 223/472

Stephen Dent 2020

The loss of U-boat Enigma and its implications

For the Atlantic U-boat war, the intelligence context during 1942 was framed by inability to read Enigma traffic for over ten months, between 1 February and 13 December. This reflected the introduction of a new U-boat Enigma key which used four wheels on the Enigma machine, instead of the previous three. Shark, as the new key was known by the British, was a breakaway from the Dolphin key, and was used by all U-boats except those in Norwegian and Baltic waters, which continued to use Dolphin. Dolphin fortunately also remained the primary key for surface naval forces. The prospect of a breakaway U-boat key had been foreshadowed since April 1941, and Hut 8 had deduced the wiring of the new wheel cryptographically, following a German error when a trial Shark message was repeated on a three-wheel machine. However, achieving successful decryption posed huge problems. Banburismus was no help and the existing three-wheel bombes, even with sixteen available by the end of 1941, were too slow to cope with the twenty-six additional permutations created by the extra wheel for each test setting. Shark was broken for 14 March using the message announcing Dönitz's promotion to admiral, decrypted on Dolphin as a crib. However, it took six bombes seventeen days to break this setting. Two days in February were also broken with opportunistic cribs, but consistent and current readability required regular cribs, and new high-speed, four-wheel bombes. Edward Travis accordingly commissioned development of two prototypes, the first in December 1941, and the second in March 1942. Neither was available until spring 1943, and neither proved reliable. The initial break into Shark, providing current readability for most of the period from 13 December 1942 until end May 1943, came not from four-wheel bombes, but the capture of the U-boat weather short-signal book, and associated indicator tables, from *U-559* in the eastern Mediterranean on 30 October 1942. This book, which sadly cost two lives from the destroyer *Petard*, provided reliable cribs, but Hut 8 also spotted that weather signals were encrypted using Enigma as a three-wheel machine, with the fourth wheel in a neutral position. The three-wheel part of the daily setting could thus be broken with a three-wheel bombe, and finding the starting position of the fourth wheel was then relatively easy. The fact that weather reports were often re-broadcast in German air force Enigma also helped.[2]

The introduction of Shark did not reduce U-boat intelligence to pre-Dolphin days. Newly commissioned U-boats still used Dolphin while working up in the Baltic, giving the OIC a reliable check on the number and type of U-boats entering operational service. Dolphin coverage also often indicated U-boat arrival and departure times from Biscay or

Norwegian bases, and details of Biscay cleared routes. There was the extensive knowledge base of U-boat operations acquired during 1941 and other sources still contributed – D/F, POW, PR and SIS. Nevertheless, with each week that passed, the quality of the OIC picture showed more gaps.[3]

The OIC estimated there were fifty-three U-boats deployed in the Atlantic at the end of January, just before the Dolphin blackout, out of a total operational force of ninety, which increased 50 per cent by end June. Yet the impact of losing Dolphin intelligence on losses in convoys under British control on the main Atlantic routes, during the five months February to June, was negligible. Convoy losses in the first quarter of 1942, at twelve ships, were a third of those in the last quarter of 1941, while the thirty-three ships lost in the second quarter were half those in the third quarter of 1941, and identical to those in the final quarter. The primary reason was a German strategic shift – Operation Drumbeat – whereby almost the entire U-boat effort shifted to targeting independent ships, first off the United States East Coast, and later in the Caribbean and Gulf of Mexico. Drumbeat produced a bonanza for Dönitz. His U-boats sank just over 3 million tons of Allied shipping in American waters west of 40° W between mid December 1941 and end August 1942, a quarter more than all of 1941, and a quarter of all Allied losses to U-boats in the whole of the war. Almost 90 per cent of ships sunk in this period comprised independents. Losses of ships sailing directly under the British or American flag were about equal, around a third each, with most of the rest contracted to Britain.[4] Tanker losses were especially severe with a net reduction in Allied capacity, allowing for new build, of 7 per cent by the end of June, exacerbating the increased transit time required to make good the loss of East Indies and Burma oil supplies to Japan.[5]

Successive OIC assessments, drawing on the final weeks of Dolphin coverage from mid December, revealed the U-boat redeployment to the western Atlantic, but the OIC underestimated its scale, ambition and duration.[6] As the full scope of the Drumbeat campaign became evident, and losses mounted, it posed political, operational and intelligence challenges, which the British struggled to manage. The British were bearing the brunt of the losses, but they were taking place in waters under US Navy control. Inevitably, British naval leaders, with encouragement from Churchill, were inclined to blame the US Navy for not implementing a British-style OIC model for managing the U-boat threat, for failure to introduce convoying and ineffective aerial surveillance, partly reflecting poor co-operation with the US Army Air Forces, with no U-boat sunk by air attack off the American coast until 7 July. It was also easy to blame persistence of peacetime attitudes, such as continued peacetime lighting helpfully illuminating targets against the shoreline. However, the British underestimated the sheer size of the area the Americans had to defend, showed scant understanding of the resource constraints facing the US Navy in a two-ocean war, with major risks facing them in the Pacific, and conveniently ignored other demands facing the American naval forces in the Atlantic theatre, which were a high priority for both countries – above all, safe transport of American troops and equipment to Britain during this period, an objective achieved without loss. Most important of all, the British overlooked that they were neither contributing useful intelligence on Drumbeat, nor explaining why they could not do so.[7] They would have had further cause for humility had they known that by March, the Germans enjoyed almost complete mastery of British Naval Cipher No 3 used for Anglo-American communications. This carried most traffic related to Atlantic convoying, and also shared OIC U-boat disposition signals. The compromise probably had limited impact on Drumbeat itself, with its focus on independent shipping, but it was an important influence on the renewed offensive against mid-Atlantic convoys from the middle of the year. With only occasional gaps, B-Dienst retained current readability of around 80 per cent of traffic on this net until May 1943.[8]

A difficult start to a UK–USA naval intelligence relationship

When Drumbeat began, coinciding with United States entry into the war, British-American SIGINT collaboration had not advanced much beyond the limited sharing initiated by the Sinkov–Rosen visit. In the summer of 1941, following the breaking of Dolphin and the increased US Navy escort role in the western Atlantic, Churchill suggested the Americans should receive some Dolphin intelligence to assist their understanding of the U-boat threat or, at least, that bearing directly on their security. Menzies argued successfully that the security risks in such sharing were too great. He also imposed strict limits on what Denniston was allowed to discuss when he visited Washington in August. He was only to offer the Americans the opportunity to work on Enigma research and development, and barred from mentioning difficulty with bombe capacity, or from inviting American mathematicians to work at Bletchley, and there would be no relaxation on sharing decrypts. American resentment that they were receiving an inadequate return for their help with Purple was fed by GC&CS slowness in responding to further inquiries about the way Enigma worked.[9] The only concession made during the autumn was agreement that Godfrey should send Admiral Stark, as Chief of Naval Operations, regular summaries of U-boat dispositions drawn from Dolphin decrypts, on an exclusive personal basis. Following the outbreak of war, these summaries, which included forewarning of Drumbeat, were accompanied by a wider range of intelligence, drawing on sensitive SIGINT, which Stark was authorised to share with subordinate flag officers, subject to adopting British Ultra security procedures.[10]

Apart from providing forewarning, the U-boat intelligence provided to Stark before the loss of Dolphin was not precise enough to help the Americans prepare for Drumbeat. Thereafter, with Shark unreadable, and little relevant D/F coverage, the British could contribute little on the western Atlantic, beyond crude estimates of U-boat strength deployed.[11] There is an argument that, given the nature of Drumbeat, this lack of intelligence made little difference. Although assigned to specific areas, U-boats did not employ group tactics, but operated independently, selecting targets on an opportunity basis, and with far less use of radio than was customary in convoy operations. Had the Dolphin-type coverage available during the second half of 1941 continued, it would not, therefore, have facilitated evasion or offensive countermeasures.[12] However, there is a compelling alternative view. If Enigma had not been lost, the scale of Drumbeat, including widespread deployment of smaller Type VII boats and new U-tankers, would have become apparent through February. Definitive intelligence that U-boats were operating independently, and details of their assigned target areas, including advance notice of the shift to the Gulf of Mexico and Caribbean, would have been immensely valuable. At a minimum, it would have facilitated safer routing, but also encouraged introduction of convoys, even with minimal escort, or even none at all.[13]

Leaving aside the hypothetical value of continuing U-boat Enigma coverage, the combination of American entry into the war, the aspirations for early Allied offensive operations in Europe, and the Drumbeat crisis made a British policy of limited disclosure regarding its whole Enigma programme hard to sustain. Given the scale of American commitment and the integration of Allied strategy begun at ABC-1, and consolidated at the subsequent leadership summits at Placentia Bay in August, and Washington in January, Ultra intelligence would have to be shared, and some agreement reached on responsibility for future SIGINT requirements. However, during the first months of 1942, pressed by Menzies and Godfrey, the chiefs of staff maintained the position that 'for the time being, our sources of intelligence and most secret methods of acquiring it, should not be divulged to the Americans'.[14] The primary justification was lack of confidence in American security, although desire to maintain British control and leverage over a critical strategic asset played a part. In the specific domain of naval intelligence, Godfrey also felt that the Americans still lacked a credible system for processing and exploiting operationally the information they did have. Without such a system, it would be difficult to share more than headline summaries drawing on Ultra.[15] GC&CS was more open to collaboration, but at this point saw cryptanalytic co-operation as virtually a 'swap' of European for Japanese. The Americans should be persuaded to 'concentrate on Japanese, leaving the German and Italian to us'.[16]

This British-centric position did not survive as the year progressed. By March, both the Admiralty and GC&CS recognised the need to improve SIGINT collaboration, not least to exploit opportunities for joint collection. This led to a joint British-US-Canadian 'Y' meeting in Washington in early April, with Britain represented by Humphrey Sandwith, well qualified to address both intelligence and communications issues, and simultaneous visits by Rodger Winn to promote the OIC model with the US Navy leadership, and John Tiltman to review cryptographic co-operation with OP-20-G. Sandwith saw his purpose as 'educational' as well as 'co-operative'. He described the overall British SIGINT organisation, starting with the 'Y' Committee, the 'Y' collection and D/F organisation, the role of GC&CS, and how it interacted with naval intelligence and operations, emphasising the pivotal position of the OIC. His barely concealed message was that the US and Canadian navies should create similar intelligence centres. The last point was beyond the competence of this meeting, but there were important agreements on technical collaboration and research, including RFP and TINA, and division of responsibility for 'Y' collection and D/F, including proposals for extending the network. By the summer, the Americans had four new HF/DF stations on their east coast, and were piloting a new fully automated Type DAJ receiver in Maine, capable of obtaining an instantaneous bearing on a U-boat transmission.[17]

Winn's visit was a joint initiative of Godfrey and Rear Admiral Robert Ghormley, who had led the American delegation to the chiefs of staff in autumn 1940, and headed the US Navy office in London since the previous year. Ghormley had seen 8S in action and had enthusiastically promoted it in Washington, albeit with little effect. Godfrey, who had advocated the OIC model during his own visit the previous year, believed Winn's specialist expertise and exceptional powers of advocacy would now persuade the US Navy leadership that dealing with Drumbeat required a new approach. Winn, who had studied two years at Yale and Harvard, understood Americans and how to get on with them. As anticipated, Winn found that arrangements for co-ordinating and exploiting U-boat intelligence in both ONI and Command-in-Chief Fleet (COMINCH) headquarters were rudimentary and, less expectedly, that relations between intelligence, represented by ONI, and operations within COMINCH were poor with a 'watertight' division between them. Despite an initially hostile atmosphere emanating from the notoriously Anglophobic Admiral Ernest King, now combining the role of COMINCH and Chief of Naval Operations, and his chief of staff, Rear Admiral R E Edwards, Winn's obvious command of his subject, tenacious lobbying and plain speaking won over both these two, and key members of their staff. When Edwards suggested the Americans would learn their own lessons and could afford to lose ships doing so, Winn famously retorted – 'The trouble is, Admiral, it is not only your bloody ships you are losing: a lot of them are ours!' Edwards, briefly taken aback, laughed and responded – 'Well, maybe you have a point there. Perhaps there is something in what you say. You had better see Admiral King.' King gave Winn a friendly hearing and instructed Edwards to create a tracking room forthwith. Winn then witnessed the speed, drive and resources the Americans applied once they committed. By the time he left Washington, the new Atlantic Section, Operational Intelligence, COMINCH was getting underway, headed by a retired officer, Commander Kenneth Knowles, who proved a perfect counterpart to Winn, and headed the unit for the rest of the war. The relationship between 8S and F21, as it became, was perhaps closer than between any other British and American organisation in any service in any theatre.[18]

Tiltman's visit was primarily focused on coverage of Japan, for which he had now received overall responsibility. In accord with GC&CS's desire for a straight swap, he agreed OP-20-G should lead on JN25, with the American and Australian teams at Melbourne, Pearl Harbor and Colombo (still operational at this point) sending all intercepts and cryptographic results to Washington for assessment. GC&CS would concentrate on the flag officer codes, JN16 and JN49, and assist in tackling the naval attaché cipher introduced in 1939, now known as Coral. In return, the Americans would provide a full review of JN25 recoveries to date. All data and cryptographic results would be shared.[19] Importantly, Tiltman also stressed to Travis, who had now replaced Denniston as head of GC&CS, that since the Americans had a vital interest in U-boat signals traffic now they were at the forefront of the Atlantic war, they were surely entitled to share British Enigma results, or to have a detailed explanation of why traffic could not be read. Without such sharing, US Navy leaders would inevitably insist on OP-20-G attempting to duplicate British Enigma coverage, which was in the interests of neither side. Although this American threat hung over relations through the summer, Tiltman's lobbying brought a shift in the British position on Enigma. In May, Travis promised OP-20-G full design details of the British bombe, and subsequent delivery of a working bombe by September. Travis was also content for the Americans to decrypt traffic intercepted in North America. The British hoped that by sharing decryption techniques and giving OP-20-G a supplementary role, they would discourage duplication and retain overall control of Enigma.[20] However, by the summer, progress on Shark remained stalled, development of the British four-wheel bombes was in trouble, projected demand for bombes to meet all Enigma commitments was outstripping British capacity, while OP-20-G, made suspicious by perceived British prevarication, including failure to deliver the promised bombe, had commissioned its own bombe design, and could potentially call on production resources of which GC&CS could only dream.

British tactics for responding to these developments were now influenced by the urgent need to maintain access to Japanese naval SIGINT. By July 1942, Kilindini was struggling to offer any useful service to Admiral Somerville as Commander-in-Chief Eastern Fleet. Interception was only 50 per cent of that achievable in Colombo or Melbourne, and poor communications left it increasingly isolated from what was supposedly a combined Allied operation. Harry Shaw's team was shaken by news from Edward Hastings in Washington, revealing impressive American results on the latest JN25 version. In mid August, the Japanese, fearing compromise, changed both codebook and additive tables, demonstrating to Kilindini that JN25 was evolving at a speed they could not match. Desperate for intelligence, Somerville despatched Malcolm Burnett to lobby Godfrey and GC&CS. Burnett was an ideal candidate, because he had worked on JN25 at FECB almost from the start, and had also conducted the liaison during 1941 with the American Station Cast team, now mainly installed in Melbourne. From his perspective, Somerville saw a complete lack of co-ordination between the British and American effort, and while open-minded on how co-operation went forward, urged that Washington be given overall direction and a way found to link Kilindini into the American secure SIGINT network linking Melbourne, Honolulu and Washington, thereby unlocking the required intelligence. Unknown to Somerville, Travis had already pressed OP-20-G the previous month to do this, consistent with the arrangements recently negotiated by Tiltman, and the earlier FECB link with Station Cast. Had this happened in mid 1942, instead of partially in 1944 and fully only in 1945, it would have saved incalculable time, labour and friction, but the Americans refused. Although there were practical difficulties, this primarily reflected their perception that Kilindini had little to offer, and resentment that the British were still apparently holding back on Enigma.[21]

To resolve these growing tensions on both Japanese and German targets, Travis and Birch travelled to Washington in September and negotiated a new arrangement, subsequently known as the Holden Agreement after the Director of US Navy Communications, Captain Carl Holden. Detailed implementation of the agreement was then delegated to Hinsley, who arrived in early October.[22] As Somerville had anticipated, and in accord with GC&CS's preferred division of labour, the United States took responsibility for the 'direction and control' of the effort against Japanese naval communications. However, the British conceded more than American primacy. Despite strong objections registered by Burnett on Somerville's behalf at Bletchley before Travis and Birch departed, they agreed to abandon cryptanalysis at Kilindini, retaining only an exploitation unit to read traffic from recoveries supplied by the Americans, and to turn the British-Australian team in Melbourne over to United States control.[23] OP-20-G would send relevant intelligence acquired from Japanese naval communications, and any necessary cryptographic material, to the Admiralty and/or GC&CS, for onward transmission to Kilindini and the Eastern Fleet. 'Relevant' here was defined as intelligence of 'major strategic moves' in any area, and anything bearing on operations in the Indian Ocean. The British, therefore, now agreed to withdraw from active cryptographic work in the whole Eastern theatre, and were effectively left dependent on the Americans in the Indian Ocean. GC&CS would only retain a small Japanese navy intelligence and cryptographic research unit at Bletchley, 'so as not to lose touch with the Japanese problem'. The British soon found that the American interpretation of 'relevant' amounted to very little. In just twelve months, they had fallen from the position of lead partner on JN25 to helpless supplicant.[24]

The British also made major concessions on the German target. They agreed 'in principle to full collaboration upon German submarine and naval cryptanalysis problems, including exchange of intercepted traffic, keys, menus, cribs and other relevant technical information'. Although the agreement text referred to a 'logical division of labor', with the United States exploiting 'better intercept facilities' in the Pacific, and Britain doing the same in the Atlantic, this was far from the trade-off GC&CS had aspired to earlier in the year. Britain conceded the United States complete control over Japan in return for an equal partnership on Germany, and potentially Italy too. To an extent, the outcome acknowledged practical reality. Despite its pre-war successes, Britain now had limited resources for Japan, and for the present, it faced an insurmountable geographic disadvantage. British numbers working on the Japanese naval target in GC&CS naval section and Kilindini combined were 175. Kilindini intercepted about 350 Japanese naval signals per day and Flowerdown another 100. OP-20-G and its overseas sites in Honolulu and Melbourne had ten times as many staff and daily coverage of 2200 intercepts between them.

Nevertheless, Travis and Birch evidently approached the talks determined to avoid any argument over Japan souring collaboration on Germany. They failed, therefore, to impress on OP-20-G that the British contribution on Japan, and specifically from Kilindini, was potentially more valuable than the difference in scale of effort suggested. That autumn, Kilindini broke two important merchant-shipping ciphers, JN40 and JN167, and the navigation warning system JN152. Nor did the British sufficiently appreciate that an agreement with Holden as Director of Naval Communications was restricted to cryptography, and had little sway over either intelligence priorities, or dissemination, which were controlled by ONI and the key overseas commands. Overall, the British obtained an improved supply of Japanese naval intercepts and recoveries, but initially delivered only to Bletchley which, with its present resources, struggled to cope with them, although over the winter a limited, and painfully slow, direct airmail service from OP-20-G to Kilindini was added. The supply of finished intelligence, again solely to Bletchley, proved very poor. In practice, the Americans shared little on the Pacific, and because the Indian Ocean had minimal interest for the US Navy, resource constraints meant little effort went into processing traffic relevant to this theatre. Travis was reluctant to press for a better service. Reasonable proposals to alleviate the situation, advocated by Burnett in January 1943 following a two-month visit to OP-20-G, which the Americans might have accepted, were dismissed by both Travis and Edmund Rushbrooke, who had just succeeded Godfrey as DNI.[25] Kilindini, essentially now dependent on whatever cryptographic and intelligence product GC&CS passed over imperfect communications, gained little if anything from Holden, while Somerville, fobbed off with unconvincing promises of distant improvement, saw scant change in his dismal operational intelligence service, and was left intensely frustrated.[26]

Conceding parity on naval Enigma was harder, given all that had been achieved in the last three years, but here too GC&CS was struggling with capacity constraints, and failure to deliver an effective four-wheel bombe, and Travis now knew OP-20-G could go it alone. The choice was co-operation on equal terms, or risk ultimately falling behind as the Americans applied limitless resources. In contrast to the relationship on Japan, the subsequent combined effort on all aspects of naval Enigma, including Shark, proved very successful, with amicable daily exchanges on work-share, and joint collaboration on cribs, agreed over secure cable communications between OP-20-G and Bletchley. For nine months after Holden, through the initial breaks into Shark, GC&CS led this joint effort, but thereafter greater American resources, and their superior four-wheel bombe design, gave OP-20-G an ever greater role. Two of their experimental bombes began operation in June 1943; by early September six production machines were available; and by the end of the year, seventy-seven. By then, OP-20-G had entirely taken over breaking daily settings of Shark and its derivatives. In early 1944 only three of GC&CS's eighteen four-wheel bombes were operational, and their performance was poor. By this point, OP-20-G had sufficient bombe capacity to divert 45 per cent of its effort to German air force and army Enigma on behalf of Hut 6.[27]

The Atlantic intelligence war in the second half of 1942

Just as traditional opinion holds that Dolphin availability sharply reduced shipping losses in the second half of 1941, it maintains that inability to read Shark was a dominant influence on the progress of Dönitz's renewed offensive against the North Atlantic convoys in the second half of 1942. The picture is, again, more complex. The shift to targeting the major convoy routes reflected anticipation of decisive results in the primary theatre, with the rapidly growing U-boat force, and declining productivity in American waters. Although operational U-boat strength approximately doubled between the two periods, with about 185 boats available by 1 October 1942, the increase in effective operational patrols within the North Atlantic theatre was only about 40 per cent. This reflected a substantial commitment to other theatres with, on average, about forty boats in the second half of 1942 divided evenly between the Mediterranean and Arctic, and one-third of the rest deployed either in South Atlantic or American waters, the latter concentrated now in the Gulf of Mexico. The increased U-boat patrols did not produce a commensurate return in ships sunk, which only rose 14 per cent, although tonnage lost, up 50 per cent, was more proportionate.

Although there were important operational differences between the two periods, there were striking similarities. In the final quarter of 1942, as in the previous year, Dönitz's plans were badly disrupted by Mediterranean commitments, in this case the Allied landings in North Africa under Operation Torch, which reduced the force available to attack the main transatlantic routes by at least half in November and December. This aside, there were also close parallels in the proportion of convoy losses versus independents – about 70 per cent in each case – and the number of convoys losing six ships or more: seven in 1941 and eight in 1942. In both periods, about 50 per cent of U-boats deployed on patrol failed to achieve a single sinking, although the productivity of the remainder was about 25 per cent higher in 1941. Overall, with patrols aborted through defects excluded, 0.9 ships were sunk per U-boat patrol in the North Atlantic theatre in the second half of 1942. After laboriously preparing boats and crews for patrol, a 50 per cent no-score rate posed serious questions for Dönitz's strategy. The fact that losses in the North Atlantic theatre were only 30 per cent of the overall 3.2 million tons lost to U-boats in this six-month period, and that the overall loss rate for convoys was below 2 per cent, is rarely emphasised. In November, when Axis submarines sank 126 Allied ships for 802,160 tons, the highest monthly total of the war, only twenty-nine of these, comprising 166,662 tons, were in the North Atlantic, a low proportion partly explained by U-boat redeployment to meet Torch. Dönitz was never remotely close to breaking the primary North America–United Kingdom lifeline in this period, and by the second half of 1942, Allied, primarily United States, shipbuilding was already comfortably surpassing average global monthly losses by 160,000 tons per month, while net losses for the whole year were only 700,000 tons. Meanwhile, the most striking difference between the periods was in convoys suffering at least one loss, about 30 per cent in 1942, compared to half that the previous year, and U-boat losses in the theatre, thirty-nine in 1942, compared to fourteen in 1941.[28]

These statistics help to illuminate the impact and limitations of intelligence. The Germans attacked about twice the number of convoys in the second half of 1942, compared with the equivalent period a year earlier, but this was not solely due to non-availability of Shark for diversion. They had more boats to search and they were able to read Naval Cipher No 3 'currently and extensively' over the five months July to November.[29] The more important point is that they could neither translate this greater convoy access into a proportionately higher level of sinkings, nor adequately capitalise on their greater deployed strength. Attacking convoys was now less productive, and more costly. There were three major reasons for this failure: more and better trained and equipped escorts, with an average of six per convoy now available; more long-range air support; and growing deployment of the vital new intelligence source, ship-borne HF/DF. OIC and wider Admiralty understanding of the impact of these factors on underlying trends in the Atlantic battle was assisted during 1942 by a new discipline – operational research – which also greatly assisted effective exploitation of available intelligence.

The term 'operational research' originated in the Air Ministry in the late 1930s, and by 1940 its practitioners defined it as the application of evidence-based analysis of past operations to improve the weapons, tactics and strategy in future operations.[30] The Admiralty was slower than the other two services to adopt it, and its application to naval operations only began when Professor Patrick Blackett was appointed chief adviser on operational research in January 1942, and tasked with establishing a small section reporting to ACNS – by this time, Henry Moore. Blackett, often regarded as the 'father' of operational research, began his working life as a Royal Navy officer, and served with distinction through the First World War, before leaving to study physics at Cambridge, becoming one of the outstanding physicists of his generation and winning a Nobel prize in 1948. His interest in operational research developed when he was invited to join Sir Henry Tizard's committee on air defence in the mid 1930s. Following the outbreak of war, he successively advised Fighter Command, Anti-Aircraft Command and Coastal Command, which brought him to the attention of the Admiralty. He also served on the Maud Committee, examining the prospects for an atomic bomb. During 1942–43, Blackett and his team produced nearly one hundred papers for the Admiralty, of which 60 per cent addressed the anti-U-boat campaign. These contributions were hugely valuable in identifying falling U-boat productivity, and underlining the importance of ship-borne HF/DF and air support, both shore-based and from escort carriers, and in optimising escort size and composition. Blackett's work was probably critical in ensuring that the Allied allocation of Very Long Range (VLR) aircraft – starting in autumn 1942 in the face of insatiable demands from the bombing campaign – was just about adequate, if always short of desirable. He provided the rationale for resourcing the major air offensive against transiting U-boats in the Bay of Biscay in the first half of 1943. He also demonstrated that Admiralty assumptions limiting the size of convoys to a preferred forty ships and maximum of sixty were flawed, and that larger convoys would reduce losses. The first convoys of up to one hundred ships sailed in early 1943, and approached two hundred in 1944.[31]

Blackett judged escort-fitted HF/DF to be of 'great importance'. By October 1942, most North Atlantic convoys had at least one escort fitted with the FH3 system. Its great advantage was that a U-boat shadower transmitting on the surface could be detected at ten to fifteen miles using the ground wave, three to four times the range achievable with the latest centimetric radar, with which escorts were increasingly equipped. Furthermore, although HF/DF interception did not provide readability of U-boat signals, an experienced operator, guided by GC&CS intelligence issued through Western Approaches Command, could often identify the type of U-boat transmission: for example, whether it was a first contact report or regular shadowing report. Ship-borne HF/DF was a further valuable source for the OIC but, more important, by running down the HF/DF bearing and forcing a U-boat down within thirty minutes, escorts made it harder for BdU to retain the tactical picture, and for wolf packs to concentrate, exactly the concept that Hut 4 had suggested from its Dolphin-based researches the previous year. Even without this option, as Blackett stressed, HF/DF warning enabled the escort commander to concentrate his escorts on the threatened side of the convoy, and to direct it to evade. The time lapse, usually a minimum of twelve hours, but more often twenty-four, between initial HF/DF warning and a concentrated U-boat attack was also often sufficient to allow VLR aircraft reinforcement. Analysis suggests that, even after Shark became readable in mid December 1942, ship-borne HF/DF was still invariably the decisive factor in determining the outcome of a convoy engagement. Seventy-five years after the Battle of the Atlantic ended, this HF/DF contribution, and its value compared to Enigma decrypts, remains poorly recognised.[32]

The first half of 1943: the crux of the Battle of the Atlantic?

The break into Shark in December coincides with the start of the period long portrayed as the crux of the Battle of the Atlantic, namely the first half of 1943. The period certainly led to a decisive turning point, when Dönitz ordered the withdrawal of the bulk of the North Atlantic U-boat force at the end of May, following a month of miserable results and disastrous losses. Dönitz hoped the withdrawal would be temporary, but for a while contemplated permanent failure.[33] However, this Allied victory contrasts with the long-standing claim, first presented in the British post-war official history, but persisting in popular accounts to this day, that two months earlier, Dönitz had come close to severing the Atlantic lifeline and provoking the Admiralty to contemplate abandoning the convoy system.[34] Such a turnaround, if genuine, poses many questions, not least regarding the role of intelligence, and not surprisingly, many accounts have struggled to present a coherent analysis and explanation of these months.

Some initial perspective is needed. Between 1 December and 1 May, Shark coverage enabled the OIC to monitor the increase in the operational U-boat force from 212 to 240 boats, its peak strength, and its deployment pattern, although it took time to refine the detail.[35] The OIC also observed that the increase in North Atlantic patrols, especially those targeted at the primary transatlantic routes, was proportionately greater, up more than 20 per cent in the first quarter of the year compared to the last quarter of 1942, and with a record eighty-six patrols commencing in April. This increase reflected a 40 per cent decline in patrols to the South Atlantic and Americas, also apparent in Shark traffic. This resource shift raised shipping losses in the North Atlantic theatre to 60 per cent of the global total. However, the overall operational outcomes achieved by this larger force in the theatre during the first quarter of 1943, when Shark coverage was generally available to the Allies, were proportionately remarkably similar to the final quarter of 1942, when Shark was still absent. The number of convoys sailed, about fifteen per month, and which then suffered losses, around 40 per cent, was similar. So was the number losing more than six ships, six in each case. Most important, U-boat productivity, ships sunk per patrol, was almost identical at about 0.75. This was not an encouraging return for the increased effort on the primary Allied route, and buried within the overall statistics was a further productivity warning for Dönitz. The proportion of patrol no-scores was up 5 per cent, and U-boat losses, at thirty-five, were up 40 per cent between the two quarters. The evidence for a productivity problem increased dramatically in April. The eighty-six patrols that month sank only nineteen ships (all in two convoys), reducing output per boat to a pitiful 0.22, and thirty-one U-boats were lost.[36]

Several conclusions emerge from this pattern in the early months of 1943. First, the consistency in operational outcomes for the North Atlantic U-boat force between October and March suggests availability of Shark decrypts did not deliver any immediate transformative advantage, certainly not at the tactical level. The peak in North Atlantic shipping losses came from the U-boat patrols initiated in February, two months after Shark became readable. Secondly, the dramatic losses suffered by three convoys in mid March (HX 229, SC 121 and SC 122) were less significant than they appeared at the time. Other convoys between October and April suffered similar losses and, despite their regrettable human cost, in historical hindsight these March losses were blips on long-term trend lines. Indeed, viewing the U-boat war across the entire eighteen months from January 1942 to mid 1943, a clear pattern emerges. Targeting American and South Atlantic waters in the first half of 1942, predominantly against independents, was highly productive for Dönitz, with over two ships sunk per U-boat patrol. As easy pickings fell away, and he refocused on the North Atlantic convoys, productivity halved during the second half of the year, as Blackett recognised, and thereafter continued to decline steadily, albeit with occasional peaks and troughs, despite the dramatic growth of the U-boat force and the best period of B-Dienst coverage. The battle between December 1942 and May 1943 was not a distinct phase, 'the most prolonged and complex in the history of naval warfare',[37] but part of a continuum.

Pound was sufficiently shocked by the March losses to insist to Admiral King in April that the loss of Shark would increase shipping losses by 50 to 100 per cent. However, he was wrong. Shark was valuable but not critical. More important was that, over three years into the war, the U-boat force lacked any long-range search capability which could complement B-Dienst coverage to find convoys and that when they did attack, as they had to, they were now out-fought with better sensors and weaponry. In this regard, the experience of HX 228, immediately preceding the notorious HX 229, was a better indicator of the true Atlantic balance. Initial intelligence warning here came not from Shark but HF/DF, of which the Germans remained oblivious, and was exploited by a new weapon system, the anti-submarine-equipped escort carrier. Over the subsequent three-day running battle, fifteen U-boats sank only four merchant ships and a destroyer, for two losses of their own. This was a hopeless exchange rate, and the Germans were lucky not to lose more, because the battle foreshadowed the new integration of strong HF/DF and radar-equipped surface escorts with carrier-borne and long-range, shore-based aircraft, as recommended by Blackett. Between September 1942 and February 1943, the number of U-boats lost to air attack in the North Atlantic for the first time matched those lost to surface vessels.[38] With or without Shark, these were the factors that primarily determined falling U-boat productivity, although declining skills levels and morale also contributed. No doubt briefed by Blackett, this productivity trend was understood by Churchill's science adviser, Professor Frederick Lindemann, Lord Cherwell, who succinctly summarised it in a note for the prime minister at the end of July.[39]

Given this wider context, there are other important points bearing on British intelligence coverage. For the first eight months of 1943, Shark readability was subject to delays and gaps. Decryption within twenty-four hours was unusual, and interpreting the disguised geographical positions now deployed in U-boat signals took additional time. On 17 February no traffic had been read for a week, with ten January days also still unbroken. Between 10 March and end June, twenty-two days were either not broken at all, or only after long delay. This included nine days in mid March, following introduction of a new short-signal weather codebook that coincided with the passage of convoys SC 122 and HX 229, which both suffered heavy losses. Even in early August, only a quarter of July traffic was available. These delays made effective evasive routing difficult, and were compounded by the ability of B-Dienst to monitor changes through its reading of Naval Cipher No 3. Although British changes in mid December brought a brief hiatus in German coverage of this

'convoy cipher', as they called it, readability resumed in February and
lasted until June, when it was completely replaced, following conclusive
evidence of its insecurity. During these four months, through some of
the biggest convoy engagements of the war, B-Dienst probably achieved
peak efficiency in processing, and often enabled BdU to react to convoy
diversions more quickly than could Bletchley and the OIC to identified
U-boat concentrations.[40]

Assessing the overall influence of this cryptographic battle, the balance
of advantage between successful convoy interception and evasion is
difficult. Even when intelligence was rapid, relevant and actionable,
the uncertainties introduced by weather, navigation error and limited
detection ranges with 1943 technology made long-range tactical control
by the OIC or BdU demanding. During the four months of maximum
joint readability, February to May 1943, sixty-one convoys sailed on the
North Atlantic routes of which twenty-two (36 per cent) suffered losses.
Of those suffering losses, one-third lost six or more ships, and half, two or
less.[41] In addition, probably 20 per cent of convoys were sighted, but not
attacked, giving an overall interception rate of about 55 per cent.[42] Given
the strength of 1943 convoy escorts, BdU sought concentration against
specific targets rather than blanket coverage – in this period achieving it
for about 20 per cent of convoys. By contrast, with the scale of U-boat
deployment in early 1943, the OIC could not realistically achieve complete
evasion, but sought the maximum possible. Although 45 per cent of
convoys were missed by the Germans, many were never targeted, and
probably at most half benefited from directed evasion. A reasonable
conclusion, therefore, is that Shark coverage helped about 20 per cent of all
convoys evade, while B-Dienst contributed to the interception of a similar
percentage, although there are compelling arguments that in both cases
it was much less.[43] The post-war US Navy claim that B-Dienst reading
of Naval Cipher No 3 directly enabled 70 per cent of successful German
convoy interceptions (as opposed to attacks) in this period certainly seems
much too high.[44] For both sides, these cryptographic contributions were
clearly valuable, but their potential impact was influenced by their other
sources of intelligence, and the operational strength and capability each
could bring to bear.

For the Allies, it is difficult to disentangle the relative intelligence
contribution to convoy protection of Shark decrypts, shore-based D/F,
increased long-range air surveillance and, above all, HF/DF. The D/F
network was now reaching its maximum extent, with fifty stations
covering the North Atlantic area alone, and much more rapid and
accurate processing. D/F fixes often reached an escort commander within

an hour, and therefore a day ahead, at least, of Shark-based intelligence. Meanwhile, the fitting of HF/DF was increasingly prolific, including the more advanced FH4. HF/DF, especially used in conjunction with D/F fixes, was as important an aid to evasion as Shark-influenced direction from the OIC. It was also crucial in maintaining the 20 per cent gap between German convoy detection and translating it into effective attack. There is a compelling case that the greatest German successes, notably to SC 122 and HX 229, occurred when HF/DF coverage or exploitation was, for various reasons, deficient.[45]

In highlighting the limitations of Shark decrypts at the tactical level, its contribution to the Atlantic battle at the wider operational level must not be underestimated. As with Dolphin eighteen months earlier, it provided a wealth of intelligence on the U-boat order of battle, deployment, command and control, successes and failures, and forthcoming new weapons, which directly shaped Allied policy and planning. It helped the Atlantic commanders win more resources, especially aircraft; it was a vital support to the highly productive offensive undertaken against transiting U-boats in the Bay of Biscay from late spring, and against their refuelling network over the summer; and it provided vital warning that Naval Cipher No 3 was compromised.

Nevertheless, it was the increasing effectiveness of the all-arms protective screen supporting all major convoys, rather than Shark-enabled diversion, often still countered by B-Dienst, that rendered the Atlantic arena increasingly unsustainable for the U-boats during April and May. The pattern evident with HX 228 at the beginning of March was regularly repeated, but often with higher U-boat casualties. Only one convoy in these two months, ONS 5 at the beginning of May, suffered heavy casualties, losing thirteen ships, but at ruinous cost to the Germans of nine U-boats, with many more damaged. Taking stock in its weekly situation report for 24 May, the OIC, clearly drawing on Shark decrypts, estimated that twenty-six U-boats had been lost in the month to date, following fifteen in April, making a total of eighty since 1 January. Losses were now outstripping new arrivals to the operational force. It also reported that at least six boats had been lost in the attack on ONS 5, and highlighted growing evidence that 'morale and efficiency are flagging', and that 'growing apprehension is clearly felt of air attack'.[46] Signs of declining morale became notable amongst U-boat prisoners during the first months of 1943, and were more evident as the year progressed. NID1 judged this was not only due to U-boat losses, but the impact of bombing in Germany and at French ports, and general disillusion with the Nazi regime and Germany's prospects, although it cautioned against assuming there was any reduction in fighting spirit while boats were operational at sea.[47] The OIC's initial figure of eighty boats lost in the year was an underestimate by six, and another eighteen were lost by the end of the month. The long-running, steady decline in U-boat productivity had become a rapid descent, and in the last days of May the OIC reported clear signs that U-boats were withdrawing from the transatlantic routes. Meanwhile, decrypted messages from Dönitz himself to all boats at sea, mixing admonishment and encouragement, suggested that BdU recognised prospects for effective offensive operations under present conditions were evaporating.[48] In early June, following a decryption delay, the Admiralty had the text of Dönitz's formal message to the U-boat force issued on 24 May, announcing the suspension of Atlantic operations. For the watchers in Hut 4 and the OIC, the cumulative intelligence of recent weeks left no doubt that the Allies had achieved a decisive victory, confirmed by the loss of only one more ship in convoy up to 18 September. The key question now was whether this victory was permanent.[49]

29

Strategic Pivots: Norway and
North Africa 1942–1943

Norway and the Arctic convoys to Russia

The Admiralty noted an increased German navy commitment to northern Norway from November 1941. This drew primarily on Dolphin coverage, but also German air force Enigma, traffic analysis, and some contributions from PR, submarine surveillance and SIS. Key developments were the establishment of a new operational Northern Waters Command at Tromsø under a flag officer in December and the arrival of significant new naval and air forces. The most important naval development was the formation of a battle group based at Trondheim, comprising the battleship *Tirpitz*, which arrived on 16 January, followed by the pocket battleship *Admiral Scheer* and heavy cruiser *Prinz Eugen*, the latter fresh from the Channel Dash, on 23 February. By the following day, the Admiralty knew from Dolphin that *Prinz Eugen* had been badly damaged by the submarine *Trident* 'with ten metres of her stern blown away', and correctly assessed she would probably have to return to Germany. There were 'tentative' indications that *Scharnhorst* would have joined the battle group had she not been mined, and the Admiralty rightly anticipated that *Scheer*'s sister *Lützow* and *Prinz Eugen*'s sister *Hipper* might arrive in the spring. By the end of February, Dolphin also showed five destroyers at Trondheim and several flotillas of light forces. Since Dolphin continued to be used by Norway-based U-boats after the introduction of Shark, it also revealed nine U-boats deployed between Trondheim and Kirkenes, with five more in transit, and Narvik possibly being prepared as an advance base. Dolphin enabled monitoring of U-boat numbers and dispositions through the summer. In August the OIC assessed there were twenty-one in northern Norway, when the true number was twenty-three. Meanwhile, German air strength in Norway was expected to reach about three hundred aircraft by mid 1942. Although similar to that prior to redeployment for the Russia campaign the previous summer, the intelligence revealed a substantial concentration of new bomber and torpedo carrying aircraft (He 111 and Do 217) at northern airfields and the arrival of FW 200s at Trondheim for long-range reconnaissance.[1]

In early March the Admiralty remained uncertain whether the primary reason for these reinforcements was defensive or offensive. There was growing evidence that the Germans feared further British raids of the Anklet/Archery type on Norway, or even a full-scale invasion, possibly with Russian assistance. However, heavy units based in Norway also posed a constant threat to Atlantic trade routes, with less warning than was probable with deployment from Baltic bases. This posed a considerable strain on the Home Fleet, at a time when it was losing its numerical advantage in heavy units, owing to Mediterranean losses and the requirement to reinforce the Indian Ocean. It was also likely the Germans were building up the capability to interdict the convoys to Russia initiated the previous autumn. By mid year, these would face a scale of threat comparable to Malta convoys in the Mediterranean.[2]

The last assumption proved accurate. Supply convoys via the Arctic route between the United Kingdom or Iceland and Russia, through the Barents Sea to Archangel on the White Sea in summer, and under winter ice conditions to Murmansk in the Kola Inlet, began in August 1941, and over the next forty-five months, 790 ships with nearly 4 million tons of supplies made the outward journey, with 735 returns. For the first six months the operation was uneventful, with ninety-five ships and 281,675 tons of supplies making the outward journey, and sixty-two returning by the end of February, for the loss of one destroyer and one merchantman to U-boats. However, the next twelve months proved the peak period of strain for the Royal Navy in meeting this task. The strategic imperative to help Russia was greatest, the German combined threat – air, surface and submarine – was at its peak, and Royal Navy resources, given its global commitments, most stretched. After deducting early returns, during this year from 1 March 1942, 241 ships made the outward journey in eleven convoys, of which 189 reached Russia, with just over one million tons of supplies, and 209 returned, again in eleven convoys. Although other supply routes to Russia, across the North Pacific and through the Persian Gulf, became increasingly significant through 1942, the Arctic route carried about 90 per cent of weapon shipments up to March 1943, when convoys were suspended for the summer. Since Russian losses in aircraft, tanks and guns far exceeded her domestic production until well into 1943, weapon supplies via the

Arctic were probably critical to her ability to survive the first eighteen months of war.[3]

Protecting the Arctic convoys from the scale and variety of forces the Germans could deploy by spring 1942 against a long, exposed route close to their bases, and offering limited scope for diversion, was a formidable undertaking. From this time, every convoy received a close escort of destroyers and anti-submarine vessels, a supporting force of cruisers, and a distant covering force of battleships and a carrier: in all, often more than forty warships. Even with this commitment, good and timely intelligence was critical in keeping losses to an acceptable level. Apart from the brief contribution of a battleship and two cruisers from the US Navy in the summer, the escort burden fell almost entirely on the Royal Navy, obliging it to divert forces from Western Approaches Command to support the Home Fleet. Despite grudging promises and the significant resources available to them, help from the Soviet naval and air forces to Arctic convoy operations during 1942 proved minimal and unreliable, and only marginally better from 1943.[4]

Throughout this difficult year from 1 March 1942, British knowledge of the overall threat they faced was uniformly excellent. However, exploiting this intelligence tactically in fighting convoys through was more difficult, with each specific German threat posing different challenges. Setting aside the disastrous PQ 17 convoy in early July, losses in the outward convoys during the summer months of long Arctic daylight averaged nearly 25 per cent, and were barely sustainable. Across the whole year, in both directions, half the merchant vessels lost succumbed to air attack, a third to U-boats, only three ships to surface attack, and the remaining five to an unfortunate incursion into a British minefield.[5] Two cruisers, two destroyers, and two smaller escorts were also lost. Intelligence was most successful in countering the U-boat threat. Dolphin ensured the escort forces had a comprehensive picture of U-boat numbers, movements and dispositions, and their operational reports during the convoy passage. Although diversion was rarely possible, aggressive escort measures, exploiting HF/DF and radar, and the latest Atlantic-honed tactics, were highly effective. Despite having a single primary role, which usually permitted ten boats deployed along the convoy routes, and enjoying aerial reconnaissance rarely available in the North Atlantic, with the exception of the ten ships lost from PQ 17 following its dispersal, the Arctic U-boat force sank, on average, substantially less than one ship per convoy in this period, for eight boats lost, a quarter of the total deployed. This was a pitifully small return.[6]

By contrast, intelligence helped less in countering German air force attacks, which did most of the damage. German air force Enigma provided excellent coverage of order of battle and capability, notably the airborne torpedo threat, but its intercepts were rarely timely or precise enough to warn of specific attacks. Lower-grade radio intercepts acquired in the United Kingdom faced similar constraints. A partial solution, developed by NID with Air Intelligence Department, was to deploy specialist Headache teams with the escort commander, as practised with the Malta convoys. Briefed with the best prior intelligence of German air force dispositions, frequencies and call-signs by GC&CS and RAF Cheadle, which specialised in low-grade air interception, these monitored German air force communications locally, and sometimes gained twenty minutes attack warning, beyond what radar achieved.[7]

Although the substantial German surface forces inflicted negligible damage on the convoys, either in this period or later, they exerted by far the greatest influence in framing British strategy. The surface threat was invariably the key determinant in convoy planning, their routes, timing, escort composition and, ultimately, their viability. It was primarily the surface threat that forced the suspension of convoys for two months after PQ 17, and for eight months in the summer of 1943. Consequently, a huge intelligence effort was devoted to monitoring the risk posed by the surface forces, and to identifying opportunities to degrade or destroy key units, above all *Tirpitz*. However, the most comprehensive intelligence monitoring still struggled to cope with fundamental challenges of time and distance, weather, and winter darkness. The key problem was that once the Germans based heavy units at Altenfjord (now known as Altafjord) and related sites at the far northern tip of Norway, they could comfortably reach the main convoy routes in twelve hours of high-speed steaming. Neither Dolphin, which often took more than twenty-four hours to break, nor PR, which faced challenges of range and weather, nor SIS agents in exposed sites with tenuous communications, could guarantee warning. Without warning, a convoy was desperately vulnerable, with a close escort insufficient to hold off heavy attack. Even with warning, positioning British heavy units to provide protection was difficult, given the need to avoid exposing them to air and U-boat attack.

The first German operation against the convoys with their new Norway battle group was conducted by *Tirpitz* and destroyers from Trondheim on 6 March, targeted at the outward-bound PQ 12, following its sighting by German air reconnaissance south of Jan Mayen island. Over the next three days, *Tirpitz* ranged 500 miles north of Trondheim, and only narrowly missed both PQ 12, and the inbound QP 8. She contemplated searching as far east as Bear Island, before retreating to the security of the Norwegian coast. Tovey, still Commander-in-Chief Home Fleet, initially struggled to obtain a clear operational picture. His movements reflected his assessment that *Tirpitz* was conducting an anti-invasion sortie, in the belief that PQ 12 was aimed at a landing in north Norway, rather than bound for Russia. He misinterpreted D/F intercepts, and for the first two days Dolphin did not provide clarity, owing to delays in decryption. The picture cleared late on 8 March, when the OIC began getting decrypts within two or three hours of German transmission, the first time this had happened during a major fleet operation with surface ships. This kept the convoy out of danger, and facilitated two attacks on *Tirpitz*, first by aircraft from the carrier *Victorious*, and then an attempted destroyer ambush when she took cover in Ofotfjord near Narvik, although both failed. Both sides drew important conclusions, with consequences later in the summer. Tovey complained about Admiralty interference, and insufficient clarity and context in providing intelligence. The OIC could have helped him more, but their failings were minor, and reflected inexperience handling real-time intelligence in a fast-moving situation, and Denning learnt quickly. More seriously, while Admiralty interventions were undoubtedly correct on this occasion, it probably encouraged Pound and others towards excessive confidence in intelligence-led direction from the Admiralty. Meanwhile, for the Germans, the attack by *Victorious*'s aircraft underlined the risks inherent in open-ocean operations and the prospect of crippling damage, as *Bismarck* had suffered. Hitler himself was alarmed, and ruled that neither *Tirpitz* nor other prestige units were to sortie, unless the presence of British carriers was definitively ruled out. Never again did German heavy units target convoys west of the Barents Sea.[8]

The German battle group did not intervene against the next four convoy pairs, although destroyers attacked PQ 13 at the end of March, and QP 11 in May, sinking two merchant ships, and contributing to the loss of the cruisers *Trinidad* and *Edinburgh*. However, the arrival of *Hipper* and *Lützow* in Norway, and the subsequent move of the pocket battleships north to Narvik, and warning of a new advance base at Altenfjord near North Cape, raised the threat level and suggested passivity would not last. The reinforcements and additional bases complicated intelligence-monitoring, although by the middle of the year, NID was benefiting from two new sources. Denham's relationship with Björnstjerna had consolidated, and was delivering valuable insights from Swedish cable-tapping, including details of the preparations at Altenfjord.[9] In addition, SIS had made important progress establishing a coast-watching service targeted at German naval and shipping movements. In June there were coastal stations operational at Oslo (codename Beta), Stavanger (Zeta),

Bergen (Theta), Trondheim (Lark, Lark II, Leporis, Scorpion and Virgo), Bodø (Deneb), and Tromsø (Upsilon). The Trondheim stations were established between February and May through outstanding work by Lieutenant Bjørn Rørholt, a member of the earlier Trondheim station, Skylark B, broken up after discovery by German direction-finding in September 1941. Rørholt escaped to Britain, but volunteered to return, at great personal risk, after Theta reported the arrival of *Tirpitz*, and new coverage became urgent. Godfrey endorsed Menzies' proposal that Rørholt receive a DSO, stating that the excellent reporting on German ships at Trondheim was entirely due to him. There were also earlier stations at Florø (Eric), Ålesund (Koppa), betrayed to the Germans in February, and Kristiansand. Most stations had two-way radio communication.

During the course of the war, over a hundred SIS stations were active in Norway, although not simultaneously, and not all on the coast. Some lasted only weeks, but others years. Most were manned by Norwegian exiles, recruited and trained in the United Kingdom, and then returned to Norway. The SIS controlling officer Eric Welsh was keen on 'hermit stations' at isolated sites, where agents, usually in pairs, operated in complete isolation, self-sufficiently for months at a time, 'Eric' in Florø being the first over the winter 1941/42. By mid 1942, the still-limited network had significant achievements to its credit. Theta provided the precise location of *Tirpitz* in a fjord near Trondheim in January, and the following month added to the Dolphin coverage of *Prinz Eugen*'s move along the coast, facilitating the interception by *Trident*. Four stations reported on her subsequent move south to Germany in May for repairs. This enabled an air attack, albeit unsuccessful. The Trondheim group reported regularly on *Tirpitz*, *Scheer* and *Hipper*. The reporting of the SIS coastal stations was a vital supplement to Ultra, and often provided the first intelligence on German naval movements to London.[10]

By early summer, the commitment required to deliver the convoys, and the growing loss rate – 23 per cent for PQ 16 in May – which Tovey judged better than expected, was a dominant concern for the British naval leadership. Pound and Tovey favoured postponing convoys until the darker nights of autumn, but the political and strategic imperative to support Russia, facing a renewed German offensive, was decisive. This was the context against which, on 18 June, Godfrey received one of the most important single intelligence reports of the war, from Denham in Stockholm. Graded A3 (completely reliable, but lacking collateral), this again derived from Björnstjerna, and described German plans under Operation Rösselsprung (Knight's Move) to deal with the next convoy, which would be PQ 17, scheduled to depart at the end of the month.

The two pocket battleships with six destroyers were to position in advance at Altenfjord, with *Tirpitz* and *Hipper* separately moving up to Narvik. Both groups would sortie against the convoy once it had been fixed by aerial reconnaissance, and had passed longitude 5° E, and then conduct a simultaneous attack, supported by aircraft and U-boats, in the vicinity of Bear Island (situated about 300 miles due north of Altenfjord). Oil supplies for the battle group were 'delicate', and reliant on prior deployment of the tanker *Ditmarsch* to Sørøya Sound at the entrance to Altenfjord. Björnstjerna also summarised German air deployment for targeting the convoy, although this element of his report added nothing to Enigma coverage.[11]

When Denham's intelligence reached London, PQ 17, comprising thirty-six merchant ships, predominantly American, and three rescue ships, was already concentrating in Iceland, with departure scheduled for 27 June. Its cargo included 600 tanks, 300 aircraft, and 3500 vehicles. As usual, there was a simultaneous inbound convoy QP 13, this time of similar size, and scheduled to leave Archangel on 26 June. The two convoys, together with their escorts, and the covering forces, which included fourteen submarines (eight British, one French and five Soviet) deployed in a protective screen off the north Norwegian coast, represented the biggest combined operation in the Arctic to date. Although the overall protective forces allocated were the heaviest yet, the German intent to deploy their full battle group, and the prospective use of Altenfjord, posed new risks difficult for British commanders to counter. Because of the air and submarine threat, they could not risk deploying heavy ships east of Bear Island, which meant that over much of the 900-mile stretch and four days' steaming between there and Archangel, the convoys were intensely vulnerable to heavy surface attack. With no real darkness and summer weather, once the Germans successfully intercepted, however valiantly the close escort fought, the prospect of saving their charges and themselves from annihilation was bleak.

Tovey doubted the Germans would risk *Tirpitz* if they believed heavy units of the Home Fleet were covering PQ 17. He also proposed turning PQ 17 around for twelve to eighteen hours if it was threatened, in the hope of luring German forces westward, to bring them in range of a strike from his carrier *Victorious*, or cause them to abandon the operation. The Admiralty vetoed this, fearful that it would, in turn, expose the Home Fleet to heavy air and U-boat attack, and merely extend the period the convoy was exposed. Pound was adamant that sending major units of the Home Fleet into the Barents Sea in high summer in the face of German land-based air power was an unacceptable risk, which even the prize of *Tirpitz* did not justify.[12] The Home Fleet would, therefore, cover the convoy west of Bear Island, but thereafter it must rely on submarine protection, both the screen off Norway, and two boats included in the close escort. Pound, however, also raised the possibility of ordering the convoy to scatter in the face of an imminent surface attack, a prospect Tovey described as 'sheer bloody murder'. Tovey's doubts about the German appetite for risk were valid. Although Denham's opening scene-setter was an accurate summary of German intent, for which there was soon apparent collateral, as often with intelligence there were crucial elements missing. The sortie required Hitler's approval which, in turn, demanded categoric assurance there was no possibility of intervention by British heavy forces and, specifically, a carrier strike. German execution of their intent and the timing of any intervention were, therefore, more constrained than Denham's report suggested. Their plans also evolved to concentrate the whole battle group in Altenfjord, making *Tirpitz* less accessible to Home Fleet interception than if she sortied from Narvik. Both factors now dictated that any convoy interception would occur well to the east of Bear Island, in waters far beyond British support, and that there was minimal prospect of Tovey's turn-back option working.

The stage was therefore set for one of the greatest disasters for the Royal Navy in the war, bringing serious political and strategic consequences, and damage to its reputation that scarred key participants for years. It even provoked a notorious and high-profile libel case a generation later, although, ironically, most of the intelligence essential to a true understanding of events could not then be disclosed. For PQ 17 now became pre-eminently an intelligence-driven story. The contribution of intelligence, primarily Dolphin decrypts, the timing of its availability, the debate over the meaning of each item, and the way operational decisions were taken, has been exhaustively described elsewhere. As with participants at the time, historians have reached different views on whether the crucial decision by Pound on the evening of 4 July, to order the outbound PQ 17, then located 150 miles northeast of Bear Island, to scatter in response to the possibility of imminent interception by the German battle group, was justified.[13]

However, several points deserve more emphasis. The first is the dramatic change in British knowledge of the whereabouts of the German battle group that evening, when Dolphin traffic for the forty-eight hours from noon 3 July became available from Bletchley. Until this moment, the OIC only knew that the battle group had left their respective bases – *Scheer*, and probably *Lützow*, from Narvik, *Tirpitz* and *Hipper* from Trondheim – and were deploying northwards. At 1900 decrypts brought the electrifying news that the whole force, including the *Tirpitz* group, had arrived in Altenfjord at 0900 that morning, and begun refuelling. This intelligence was transformational. Instead of the two groups predicted by Denham, with *Tirpitz* deploying from Narvik, the whole force was now concentrated forward, ready to deploy direct into the Barents Sea. As Pound quickly established, they could have sortied any time from 1200, with PQ 17 only twelve hours' steaming away. Denning made a compelling circumstantial case that the Germans had not yet left Altenfjord, but acknowledged he could not give Pound a guarantee. Pound's critics argue that he gave insufficient weight to Denning's experience and judgement, and did not adequately engage with, or understand, the intelligence detail. That is probably unfair. Given that intelligence had failed to anticipate the German concentration in Altenfjord, it was reasonable for Pound to doubt whether there would be adequate departure warning, especially as radio intercept in Arctic waters was notoriously unreliable. Pound was also aware from Dolphin decrypts that U-boats had the convoy under almost constant surveillance.[14]

Pound's critics have also been better at questioning the manner and timing of his decision, and the poor way it was communicated, than offering convincing alternatives. The other choices were to order the convoy to withdraw westward and fall back on Tovey, or to let it continue, pending further intelligence. Given that Tovey was over 400 miles away, withdrawal was unlikely to save the convoy if an attack was really imminent. If subsequent intelligence revealed it was not, the problem was merely postponed, although fuel shortage would probably mean that temporary withdrawal led inexorably to abandoning the entire PQ 17 operation. By contrast, letting the convoy continue steadily reduced the interception distance for the German battle group, while geographical constraints made later dispersion steadily less effective. In the event, the Germans did not sortie until they had fixed the position of the Home Fleet early on 5 July. Following Hitler's approval, the battle group deployed from Altenfjord later that morning, and would have intercepted the convoy on its original route early the following day, about 150 miles east of North Cape, in overwhelming force. Although intelligence from Dolphin and submarine sightings provided some warning of this delayed sortie, it was fragmentary and imprecise. Decryption delays then meant the British did not know the Germans had abandoned the operation as no longer necessary before the battle group was safely back in Altenfjord. Pound's caution over the limitations of intelligence was, therefore, not unreasonable. Following dispersal, twenty-two of the unprotected PQ 17 ships succumbed to air and U-boat attack. This massacre is often

weighed against other actions in this war, notably the Second Battle of
Sirte, three months before PQ 17, and the Battle of the Barents Sea, six
months afterwards, when the Royal Navy successfully defended convoys
against superior surface attackers, to argue that PQ 17 should have stayed
together. Such parallels downplay the German advantage on this occasion
in air and U-boat surveillance, firepower, and daylight and weather.
Furthermore, judged by overall operational results, Sirte was much less
favourable to the Royal Navy than usually suggested.[15] Comparison with
the better-protected PQ 18 also suggests PQ 17 could still have suffered
half the post-dispersal losses if it had remained intact, and the German
battle group stayed in port. On this basis, Pound's decision to scatter cost
eleven ships, but the cost of meeting the battle group on 6 July might well
have been higher.

The real lesson of PQ 17 lay not in the limitations of intelligence, but
that the escort arrangements east of Bear Island were quite inadequate to
cope with the multiple forces the British knew the Germans could deploy.
This mistake was not repeated with PQ 18, which left Loch Ewe on 2
September, the two-month gap partly dictated by diversion of Home Fleet
assets to the Pedestal convoy to Malta. The close escort was similar to
PQ 17, but for most of the journey it was accompanied by the escort
carrier *Avenger*, for enhanced protection against air attack, and a fighting
group of sixteen fleet destroyers under the cruiser *Scylla*, to deter surface
attack. For the first time, a significant RAF strike and reconnaissance
group was also temporarily deployed to Vaenga in north Russia, with PR
Spitfires providing regular surveillance of the German bases in northern
Norway. By now, after much tortuous negotiation over the summer led
by Allon Bacon, there was also a small British 'Y' team working with the
Russians at Polyarno (now Polyarny), just north of Murmansk. There
was no sharing of Ultra intelligence, but a useful, if limited, intercept,
D/F and traffic analysis dividend. This new PR and SIGINT coverage,
together with Dolphin, enabled the OIC to monitor the deployment of
Scheer, *Hipper* and the light cruiser *Köln* to Altenfjord, and late on 13
September, as PQ 18 approached Bear Island, it advised Rear Admiral
Robert Burnett, the escort commander, that they were at one hour's notice
to sail, but that *Tirpitz* had apparently remained at Narvik. Two days
later, Denham in Stockholm, drawing on SIGINT from Björnstjerna,
confirmed the German intent to deploy the three ships at Altenfjord
against the convoy, but revealed that *Tirpitz* had a defect. A fortnight
later, Björnstjerna reported that *Tirpitz* had bearing trouble and required
a refit. Meanwhile, the Altenfjord group never sortied. The strength of the
escort, and Hitler's insistence on not running risks, dictated cancellation.

However, neither intelligence, including enhanced Headache interception, nor the massive Royal Navy effort deployed, could prevent heavy losses to the convoy from air and U-boat attack during a running battle of attrition lasting more than a week. Although the Germans lost over forty aircraft and four U-boats, they sank thirteen merchant ships, one-third of those that sailed, with the inbound QP 14 losing a further three ships.[16]

Summer 1942 proved the peak period of the German threat to the Arctic convoys. Out of fifty-four merchant ships sunk in the twenty-three outbound convoys between August 1941 and March 1943, forty-six were lost in the three consecutive convoys PQ 16 to PQ 18. Indeed, after PQ 18 no outward-bound merchant ship was lost until 1944, and only five more in all the subsequent twenty-two outbound convoys to the end of the war, although this record is flattered by the eight-month suspension between March and November 1943.[17] The Torch landings in November obliged both sides to divert forces to the Mediterranean. The British, therefore, ran no further outward convoy until December. However, German air force redeployment from northern Norway, revealed in Enigma decrypts, was dramatic, with ninety-nine Ju 88 bombers and sixty Ju 88 torpedo bombers, the whole of the specialist torpedo force, transferred in the first fortnight of November. NID judged that north Norway had been 'almost completely denuded of offensive aircraft', and in mid December it reported there were only some seventy bombers in total, covering the whole area from Oslo to the north Finnish border, and that convoys to and from Russia could now expect minimal air opposition.[18] Most of this decline proved permanent. From 1943, the limited residual air threat was easily countered by covering most convoys with escort carriers. The reduced air threat, and continuing Dolphin coverage of U-boat dispositions, enabled the British to confine losses in the four convoy pairs run between December and February to six inbound ships sunk by U-boats, although winter darkness and bad weather helped too. Dolphin also kept the OIC well informed of German surface dispositions in this period, but it contributed only marginally to a significant British victory, when *Lützow* and *Hipper* and six destroyers sortied from Altenfjord to attack the outward-bound convoy JW 51B on 31 December. Although Burnett, again commanding the covering cruiser force, was advised early on 30 December that the German force was waiting in Altenfjord, subsequent decryption delays meant he did not know that JW 51B had been located by U-boat later the same day, and that the Germans had immediately sailed to intercept. As with the *Tirpitz* sortie the previous March, and with PQ 17, Dolphin proved better at providing strategic context than delivering immediate tactical warning. In the subsequent engagement, known as the Battle of the Barents Sea, fought in bad weather and semi-darkness, each side lost a destroyer, but British aggression and a hit on *Hipper* forced the Germans to withdraw, leaving the convoy unscathed.[19]

This German failure had important political and strategic repercussions within the German leadership, on which intelligence only gave the British a gradual and partial view. Hitler's dissatisfaction with the perceived performance of the Norway battle group triggered his replacement of Raeder by Dönitz, his insistence that the major units be returned to Germany, and instructions that capital ship construction be abandoned in favour of U-boats. Not surprisingly, Dönitz endorsed the emphasis on U-boats, but he convinced Hitler to retain a heavy squadron in Norway to strike at the Russian convoys. NID and the OIC gained no direct intelligence insight into these high-level debates, although they expected Dönitz to pursue a more proactive policy.[20] (NID also reminded its readers that Dönitz had feigned insanity while a POW in 1918 and achieved early repatriation to Germany.) Despite accumulating evidence during the first quarter of 1943 pointing to increased emphasis on U-boat building and development, and to pressures from fuel and manpower shortages, Denning, in an assessment shared with the prime minister, judged that Germany's heavy ships remained an asset which, in the present state of the war, Dönitz would use more aggressively, despite obvious risks. Dolphin coverage showed *Scharnhorst* and *Prinz Eugen*, both now repaired, conducting intensive exercises in the Baltic, with particular emphasis on convoy attacks. Dönitz's most likely strategy was deployment of simultaneous raiding groups into the Atlantic to support the U-boat campaign, comprising a pocket battleship operating in the south, and *Scharnhorst*, together with an 8in cruiser, in the north. *Tirpitz*, following her refit at Trondheim, and any additional available units, potentially including the carrier *Graf Zeppelin*, which PR suggested could be operational by June, would act as a 'containing force' in Norway and continuing threat to the Russian convoys.[21] In the event, *Scharnhorst* successfully evaded British monitoring to deploy to Norway in March, and by early summer was based in Altenfjord with *Tirpitz* and *Lützow*. Although both Dolphin decrypts and SIS reports revealed regular exercises in the fjords, none of the ships deployed into open waters until early September, when *Tirpitz* and *Scharnhorst* conducted a morale-boosting bombardment of Allied weather facilities in Spitzbergen, and *Lützow* returned to Germany. However, their presence, along with an acute shortage of British escort forces, owing to North Atlantic and Mediterranean commitments, was the key factor in the eight-month suspension in Arctic convoys that summer.

It also triggered Operation Source, an attack by 'X'-craft midget submarines on the German ships in their anchorage executed in late September, which inflicted severe damage on *Tirpitz*, putting her out of action for six months. Source was the culmination of a long targeting effort, directed primarily at neutralising *Tirpitz*, which Godfrey had initiated soon after her first arrival in Trondheim in January the previous year. The 'X'-craft option was selected after numerous alternative possibilities, including 'chariots' based on the Italian SLC, aircraft torpedo or bombing, and sabotage by the Special Operations Executive (SOE), proved abortive or ineffective. Source, which involved towing six 'X'-boats by submarine a distance of a thousand miles from Scotland, was immensely complex, and required a prolonged intelligence effort to build a detailed picture of the topography of the fjord and German defences. Ultra, PR from Russian and RAF Spitfires operating from the Russian base at Vaenga, visiting SIS agents, Norwegian resistance reporting through Denham, and ISTD studies all contributed. Although it transpired there were gaps in the picture of the net defences, and news of the Spitzbergen sortie briefly threatened last-minute postponement of the operation, this combined intelligence effort proved just sufficient. Despite much effort, SIS could not establish an agent permanently in Altenfjord until Torstein Raaby was successfully landed by submarine in early September, and established his own communications as Station Ida near Alta two months later. He was too late to report on the defences prior to the attack, but from mid October, initially via Upsilon in Tromsø, and then directly from Ida, he forwarded regular and crucial insights on the damage to *Tirpitz* and the status of repair work. His damage assessments were confirmed by reporting from Ultra and PR, and coded messages in letters from the 'X'-boat crew members taken prisoner. NID was soon aware that the Germans judged it too risky to move *Tirpitz* back to Germany for docking, and that she would therefore be repaired in situ. Although repairs were nominally complete in March 1944, the German naval staff recognised she was unlikely ever again to be fully operational.[22]

The crippling of *Tirpitz* and departure of *Lützow* left *Scharnhorst* and her supporting destroyers to threaten the resumed Arctic convoys, which began with JW 54A in mid November. By then, Enigma decrypts had confirmed that *Scharnhorst* would remain in Altenfjord through the winter, that she and her escorts were maintaining high readiness with frequent exercises in the fjords, and that the German air force was constantly searching the Norwegian sea out to Iceland. Dolphin coverage of *Scharnhorst* specifically was facilitated because she was based in Langfjord, an arm of Altenfjord, whereas the battle group commander remained in *Tirpitz*, twenty-five miles away in Kaafjord at the southern extremity of Altenfjord. *Tirpitz* had landline communications which could not be accessed by Bletchley without Swedish help, now rarely given. Traffic to *Scharnhorst*, however, had to be relayed by radio or couriered by boat, so was often accessible. This window into fleet communications proved crucial.[23]

Careful British planning, winter darkness, bad weather, and limited German air resources nevertheless enabled three outbound convoys and two inbound, comprising a total of seventy-three ships, to transit successfully without loss by 20 December. However, Dolphin decrypts showed that the last outbound convoy, JW 55A had been briefly sighted by a U-boat, causing the *Scharnhorst* group to come to immediate readiness. Admiral Sir Bruce Fraser, Tovey's successor as Commander-in-Chief Home Fleet, correctly judged that, having so far failed to inflict any damage, German commanders would be under pressure to intervene against the next convoy pair and, perhaps anticipating growing British complacency, might take more risks. The relevant convoys were the outbound JW 55B leaving Loch Ewe on 20 December and the inbound RA 55A leaving Kola two days later. As usual, there was a close covering force for both convoys comprising three cruisers under Burnett (Force 1), while Fraser provided heavy support with the battleship *Duke of York* (Force 2) in the Norwegian Sea. By the early hours of Christmas Day, the British knew from successive Ultra reports that the Germans had fixed the outbound JW 55B with aerial sightings, and expected it to pass midway between Altenfjord and Bear Island on Boxing Day morning. They had not yet spotted RA 55A already passing Bear Island, or any heavy British units, but they were conducting an airborne radar search for suspected heavy forces approaching from the southwest. The *Scharnhorst* group was at immediate notice.

There now followed a textbook, intelligence-led operation in which Fraser ambushed and sank *Scharnhorst* on Boxing Day evening, twenty-four hours after she sortied from Altenfjord to intercept JW 55B southeast of Bear Island. The most critical intelligence comprised Ultra decrypts of messages from the German high command, relayed from *Tirpitz* to *Scharnhorst* at her anchorage in Langfjord, which reached Fraser and Burnett at 0230 on the morning of 26 December, reporting that the *Scharnhorst* force (later identified as the battlecruiser and five destroyers) had 'probably sailed' at 1800 the previous evening for Operation Ostfront, and that the Germans had not yet sighted Forces 1 or 2. (Torstein Raaby, located in the small town of Elvebakken near *Tirpitz*, was too far from *Scharnhorst*'s berth to confirm her departure.[24]) Thereafter Ultra contributed little, and the most important intelligence of *Scharnhorst*'s whereabouts came from Burnett's cruisers, which engaged her twice between 0900 and 1300 as she searched vainly for the convoy. There were also valuable supplementary intelligence insights from Headache intercepts, and monitoring of German airborne radar transmissions. Indeed, this engagement, fought largely in darkness and appalling weather, demonstrates how steady improvements in radar performance and its application, and the growing exploitation of electronic intelligence (ELINT) were transforming Royal Navy fighting capability.

Overall, the value of intelligence from all sources during 25 and 26 December was cumulative, covering air and U-boat dispositions and reporting, as well as the *Scharnhorst* group. It enabled Fraser to build a comprehensive picture of the German force's probable movements in relation to the two British convoys and the two separate covering forces, and to position to cut *Scharnhorst* off from her base. It also gave vital insights into German knowledge of British forces and movements. Fraser twice risked breaking radio silence to redirect JW 55B to make German interception more difficult and to reallocate his forces. The Battle of North Cape was the last battleship engagement fought by the Royal Navy, and a small affair compared to the clash of fleets at Jutland a generation earlier, although the scale and complexity of the problems facing Fraser, potentially across three dimensions, were still considerable. In both cases, intelligence made an engagement possible, and then substantially influenced its outcome. Two factors enabled Fraser to penetrate the 'fog of war', and achieve operational success in a way denied to Jellicoe: first, Bletchley and the OIC worked as an integrated team which recognised Fraser's needs, and delivered clear and relevant information immediately it was available; secondly, the careful construction and exploitation of an integrated operational picture, first identified by Fisher, but now evolved into a fine art with the plots kept by the OIC and commanders at sea. At North Cape, in contrast to PQ 17, clear lines of responsibility helped too. Unlike Pound, Cunningham, who had relieved him as First Sea Lord, was temperamentally inclined to delegate maximum authority to his commanders at sea.[25]

Intelligence and Operation Torch

As already mentioned, long before the sinking of *Scharnhorst*, the strategic context for the Arctic convoys, and much else, was fundamentally influenced by Operation Torch, the Allied invasion of northwest Africa in November 1942. Torch was the first British-American, combined all-arms offensive operation at the grand strategic level, it was the most important undertaken before D-Day, and it had consequences that remain underestimated. It required the projection of substantial forces over long, exposed sea routes, where the enemy could deploy significant U-boat numbers, and involved the first large-scale, opposed, amphibious landings conducted by either country since the Dardanelles in 1915. Torch enabled the Allies to secure the southern coast of the Mediterranean, and then most of the Mediterranean itself, opening up a shorter transit route to the East, with substantial shipping savings. It allowed the subsequent invasion of Italy from July 1943, which knocked her out of the war. However, by obliging Germany to redeploy forces it could ill afford, its impact ranged far wider. It was catastrophic for the German air force. The Luftwaffe lost 2400 aircraft in the Mediterranean over the seven months from November 1942 to May 1943, 40 per cent of its overall frontline strength in all theatres at the beginning of November. These Mediterranean losses broadly matched those on the Russian front in the same period, although in some categories, notably fighters, they were higher. The German response to Torch also absorbed large numbers of transport aircraft to build up their forces in Tunisia: 320 Ju 52s were deployed in November and December, of which half were lost by the end of January. The despatch of these precious heavy transport aircraft to the Mediterranean significantly reduced airlift capacity at Stalingrad. By reducing German air power overall, and denuding it of aircraft in north Norway and at Stalingrad, Torch made a direct and lasting contribution to undermining German prospects on the Russian front.[26]

Torch involved simultaneous landings on 8 November by the British within the Mediterranean at Algiers and Oran, and by the Americans on the Atlantic coast of French Morocco. The initial assault forces and their supplies comprised 375 ships in thirteen separate convoys, ten from the United Kingdom, and three direct from the United States. They were covered by 225 warships, of which the Royal Navy provided 160, just over two-thirds. A comprehensive account of the intelligence picture which informed Torch is available elsewhere, and beyond the scope of this book.[27] In overall terms, JIC intelligence estimates of Axis strength immediately available in the western Mediterranean, drawing heavily, but not exclusively, on SIGINT, and the scale of likely Vichy French opposition during the two months prior to Torch, were accurate. The secrecy of the large and complex operation was impeccably monitored and maintained, and deception measures to mislead Axis commanders were effective, ensuring there were no significant reinforcements to the area before the landings. However, in assessing Axis, but primarily German, ability to deploy reinforcements once the landings began, the Allied intelligence judgement proved badly flawed. Within a month of the landings, the German air force was deploying 850 aircraft against Torch forces, instead of the 515 expected by the JIC, and many were operating from Tunisia, which the JIC had discounted as a base for German air operations. Within days, the Germans increased transport aircraft numbers by an astonishing factor of three, and had an armoured division transported and operational in Tunisia by end November, a month before the JIC had judged this feasible. This underestimate of German reinforcement capacity had serious consequences. It meant Allied forces were too weak, and deployed on too narrow a front, to take Tunisia before the Germans could deploy major forces there. It also meant the Allies had, initially, inadequate air and naval forces to interdict Axis reinforcement across the Mediterranean. Ultimately, the securing of North Africa and many of the benefits of Torch were delayed by five months, while the supply and shipping burden to support Allied forces greatly increased.[28]

Despite this mixed record, the specific contribution of naval intelligence was critical in several areas. Managing the U-boat threat was the most important. Throughout the first phase of Torch, Shark remained unbroken. Nevertheless, during the three months before Shark came on line in mid December, by drawing on other sources (PR, Dolphin coverage in the Baltic, agent reports from the French bases, D/F, and contact reports), the OIC picture of overall U-boat numbers deployed, and their broad pattern of distribution, although not precise locations, was still good. In late September the OIC estimated there were 199 U-boats in operational service, with ninety-five currently deployed in the North Atlantic.[29] Rodger Winn judged that if the Germans obtained no prior warning of the Torch operation, they would probably have only two U-boats in the immediate area west of Gibraltar, as the main convoys approached the straits. However, within two days of an alert, BdU could increase numbers to ten, within a week to thirty, and after ten days conceivably fifty, although BdU would have to weigh the benefits of concentrating on Torch, against the inevitable reduction in its attack on Atlantic trade. In addition to the Atlantic threat, Torch could face up to fifty German, Italian and French boats in the western Mediterranean.[30] Even without any redeployment, the OIC judged that with the number of U-boats now deployed in the eastern Atlantic, it would be 'remarkable that any convoy should pass through this area without being intercepted'.[31] The potential risks to the Torch convoys were underlined during October, when Enigma confirmed regular German air force reconnaissance of key United Kingdom ports and Gibraltar, which would probably detect unusual activity.[32]

The Admiralty was obliged, therefore, to provide the Torch convoys with escorts and air support on a lavish scale, and to route them as cautiously as possible, reflecting its best judgement of U-boat concentrations, and keeping out of range of German air reconnaissance. Around 125 anti-submarine vessels, including 100 destroyers, were allocated, primarily diverted from the Gibraltar and Freetown convoys, including complete suspension of the latter. Even so, Pound warned the prime minister that the U-boats might well prove 'extremely menacing' to the 'most valuable convoys ever to leave these shores'.[33] By 2 November, as the Torch convoys closed on Gibraltar, the OIC assessed there were now 228 U-boats operational (an overestimate of sixteen), with ninety-four deployed in the north Atlantic, and seventeen in the Mediterranean (both correct), a pattern little changed over the last month. It noted that a substantial force of U-boats concentrated between the Canaries and Azores had posed a major risk to Torch forces, but had now been concentrated against the final Freetown–United Kingdom convoy SL 125, run before the suspensions on this route, and cost it at least twelve ships.[34] It also advised that Hitler had ordered Mediterranean boats to concentrate against convoys in the western Mediterranean. Although the OIC did not say so, this probably reflected German knowledge of the advance shipping collecting at Gibraltar, and the belief fostered by British deception that this presaged a major Malta convoy.

Remarkably, although the Germans achieved at least five fleeting sightings of the Torch convoys, the main Mediterranean forces, comprising about 340 ships, passed the straits between the evening of 5 November and morning of 7 November unscathed. Dönitz tried to intercept two of the reported convoys, but could not re-establish contact. However, the sightings, the unusual activity at Gibraltar, and Italian reports of heavy British radio traffic persuaded Berlin by 4 November that an amphibious operation in the Mediterranean was imminent, and Dönitz was ordered to despatch an additional seven U-boats to the theatre. New magnetic warhead pistols and a batch of the first FAT torpedoes were also sent to the Mediterranean U-boat bases.[35] The passage of the convoys through the straits was extensively observed, and reported by the Abwehr Bodden network.[36] However, partly due to British deception, and partly their own preconceptions, the Germans remained uncertain of British intent. Multiple SIGINT sources now enabled the British to monitor most, if not all, of the German response in the final three days before the landings. German air force Enigma showed that the Mediterranean theatre commander, Field Marshal Albert Kesselring, still favoured a Malta convoy, although attacks on Sardinia, Sicily or, more likely, in the rear of

Rommel's forces in Libya were considered options. It also showed that on direct orders from Hitler, nine U-boats were deployed on a line between Cartagena and Oran, while air strength in the western Mediterranean was being increased. Abwehr Enigma provided useful supplementary insights into German agent reporting, and the effectiveness of Allied deception operations. GC&CS was also now reading currently the naval Enigma Porpoise key used by German Mediterranean shore authorities and surface ships, although not U-boats, which used Shark as in the Atlantic. A significant Porpoise decrypt on 7 November suggested the Germans were giving increased weight to the Libya option.[37]

German failure correctly to identify Allied objectives, confused and constantly changing orders and, above all, the strength and professionalism of the British anti-submarine escorts and air patrols, with ninety-four dedicated British aircraft operating from Gibraltar and Algiers, rendered the Mediterranean U-boats ineffective against the Torch forces. During the whole of November, they sank only eight ships, including two destroyers, for five losses. This was a pitiful performance, demonstrating how difficult it now was for current U-boat types to penetrate a well-defended convoy. Meanwhile, Dönitz rushed twenty-five U-boats to the areas west of Gibraltar and Morocco in the two weeks following the Torch landings, in addition to the seven despatched through the straits, and a further four sent to the Mediterranean in early December. Like their Mediterranean counterparts, these Atlantic U-boat reinforcements had no significant impact on the Torch operation. In the first fortnight, they sank eleven ships for three losses, an unacceptable exchange rate. Although the U-boat numbers committed to Torch were less than Winn's worst case estimate, he was correct in forecasting a severe impact on Dönitz's wider strategy. Sustaining a minimum of twenty boats west of Gibraltar and providing additional Mediterranean reinforcements, as Berlin insisted, easily absorbed 50 per cent of the North Atlantic force for the rest of the year.[38]

Assessing the impact of Torch on the naval war in early February, the Admiralty claimed a 'field day' against the U-boats. Torch had attracted 'fifty U-boats' (in reality, perhaps thirty-five) into a small area where they faced 100 anti-submarine vessels and a similar number of aircraft. By end December, this U-boat force had sunk 85,000 tons of shipping and three anti-submarine escorts directly committed to Torch, but at the price of ten boats sunk (two more than reality), and many more damaged. The exchange rate was, therefore, 9000 tons of shipping per U-boat sunk (actually about 11,250 tons), compared to an average over the last two years of 50,000 tons. The Admiralty also drew a wider balance sheet.

On the debit side, it estimated that by end December, the loss of Allied shipping directly and indirectly due to Torch, from all causes, was about 360,000 tons. In addition, the disruption caused by Torch had lost the United Kingdom one million tons of imports, and Germany had seized 875,000 tons of shipping in French ports. Against this, the Allies had obtained 500,000 tons of shipping in French North African ports, and the opening of the Mediterranean within the next few months would equate to the acquisition of a further one million tons. Judged in the round, Torch had inflicted a major defeat on the U-boats, while the total dry cargo merchant tonnage available to the Allies was the same as the end of 1941: the 1942 shipping losses had been made good.[39]

Torch also marked the major launch, and first real test, of three specialist NID capabilities, destined to play a steadily growing role over the rest of the war, although they also contributed to the raid on Dieppe three months earlier. The first was the Inter-Service Topographic Department (ISTD) which, as explained earlier, was Godfrey's brainchild, and had evolved from NID6. Although by 1942 it was an inter-service organisation, under the general direction of the JIC, Godfrey retained the decisive influence over day-to-day direction, and it was still funded and administered by the Admiralty. ISTD studies of French North Africa and Spanish Morocco were well underway before the end of 1941, but the scale and complexity of Torch took requirements for intelligence on coastal and beach topography, coast defences, ports and airfields to an entirely new level. Extensive use was made of PR flights from Malta, Gibraltar, and even the United Kingdom, but also two new sources exploiting ideas from the early days of NID6. The first was an appeal launched in 1941, with the help of the BBC, for private photographs of places overseas of potential military interest, which produced eighty thousand replies. The second was the creation of a contacts register of commercial and professional individuals able to provide information on terrain and installations overseas. The Torch ISTD products, including secret target maps, produced overnight by Oxford University Press, received commendations from the overall commander General Dwight Eisenhower, the naval commander Admiral Cunningham, and Pound.[40]

A second capability, closely linked with ITSD, was the Admiralty photographic library, originally created to hold the photographs of the French coast collected under the supervision of NID1 in 1940, but which steadily expanded over the next year. Following the BBC appeal, Godfrey won Board approval for a major expansion, and by the end of 1941, as NID11, it was established in the Isis Hotel in Oxford, with a staff of eighty Wrens. By the time Torch planning commenced, it had become a global photographic resource, drawing pictures of potential military value from all sources except aerial reconnaissance, thus complementing the CIU library. Although funded by the Admiralty and controlled by NID, it had also become a cross-government resource, supporting the other two services and most Whitehall departments, and had established close liaison with counterparts working within Donovan's OSS in the United States.[41]

The final initiative was the creation of a specialist commando assault unit to land with the first wave of invading forces, tasked with rapidly seizing high-grade documents, equipment, and personnel of naval intelligence interest. This unit, 30 Commando, as it was known during Torch (in late 1943 it was renamed 30 Assault Unit or 30AU) was the brainchild of Ian Fleming, an idea he proposed to Godfrey in March 1942, after he observed the Abwehr deploying this concept during German operations in the Balkans the previous year.[42] The idea, which also built on the deployment of Allon Bacon in the Anklet and Archery operations in Norway at the end of 1941, was trialled in the Dieppe raid on 19 August 1942, when Fleming briefed a special unit in No 40 Royal Marine Commando to target the quayside hotel believed to house the local German navy headquarters, and seize items of value, above all cipher material. Unfortunately, Fleming, who was present offshore in the destroyer *Fernie*, had identified the wrong building, and his mission was caught up in the general failure of the Dieppe operation.[43] (A powerful argument has recently been advanced that Fleming's pinch operation was specifically directed at Shark-related material, and that this was the primary justification for the whole Dieppe raid. This claim is unconvincing. It downplays the many well-established goals of the Dieppe operation, and overstates the intelligence objective that had featured in every British raid on the Continent since the start of 1941.[44]) What is clear is that 30 Commando, as a dedicated trained unit, was not operational until Torch. Over the next year, it operated in French North Africa, and subsequently in Sicily, Italy, and elsewhere in the Mediterranean to great effect, acquiring material relating to enemy communications systems, ciphers, radar, and weapons of considerable value. SIGINT-related captures were particularly important, because during this period the Germans introduced new and more complex cipher and signals procedures designed to improve the security of Enigma. The success of the unit depended not only on the speed and surprise of its intervention, but meticulous targeting of specific sites, based on prior intelligence, and careful advance preparation. The most valuable acquisition during Torch was the capture of a modified Abwehr Enigma machine in the German armistice office in Algiers which, following its arrival in Bletchley, enabled Dilly Knox, Margaret Rock and Mavis Lever to break six weeks of previously unread Abwehr traffic.[45]

The dismissal of Godfrey

Godfrey just had time to witness the success of the Torch landings before being replaced as DNI by Commodore Edmund Rushbrooke at the end of November. The change followed his curt dismissal by Pound, two months earlier on 15 September, the same day he was promoted to vice admiral. The ostensible reason was that he had lost the confidence of fellow members of the JIC. Henry Moore, as VCNS tasked by Pound to investigate their complaints, reported that he was 'quite clear that as long as Admiral Godfrey is DNI there cannot be that co-operation amongst the members of the JIC which is important for its proper functioning'.[46] There is no doubt that Godfrey's army and air force counterparts did find him difficult, both in the JIC, and more generally, and pressed their respective chiefs of staff to encourage Pound to make a change. The Foreign Office chairman, Victor Cavendish-Bentinck, confirmed the dissatisfaction within the JIC, and confessed that meetings went more smoothly when Godfrey was absent, although he insisted he personally got on well with him, and admired his ability. His liking and respect for Godfrey were entirely reciprocated, and underlined in a letter Godfrey wrote to Alexander Cadogan in July. After the war, Godfrey emphasised Cavendish-Bentinck's 'agile and subtle mind', and 'real flair for deception plans'.[47]

As already noted, JIC members were not alone in finding Godfrey difficult, and his relentless and uncompromising determination to speak truth to power, as he saw it, was doubtless trying. However, as Cavendish-Bentinck clearly recognised, his cold, pedantic, and sometimes confrontational style was offset by exceptional intellect, grasp of the intelligence business, and almost four years of experience as an intelligence chief, more than any of his colleagues. In professional competence, Cavendish-Bentinck rated Godfrey in all respects superior to others on the committee. Furthermore, intelligence assessment and judgement, especially in wartime, required challenge. Getting the right result mattered more than occasional personality clashes, however uncomfortable, and while Godfrey may have dissented on some issues, there is no evidence that he was a consistent and obstructive outlier. However, he probably displayed impatience more than was wise. In a revealing post-war comment, he noted that 'the JIC could not do much to help the navy', but was a 'partial resolvent of "wishfulness", a vice to which military and air authorities of all countries are addicted'.[48]

Godfrey evidently later believed that specific challenges on his part had irritated the CIGS General Sir Alan Brooke and the Chief of Air Staff (CAS) Air Chief Marshal Sir Charles Portal, and these lay at the root of the JIC problem. He identified his disbelief that Germany possessed a hidden reserve of twenty divisions in 1942; that an invasion of the United Kingdom remained possible; and that India was subject to a co-ordinated German-Japanese pincer operation – views he claimed were strongly held by Brooke – along with his scepticism over the results Bomber Command was achieving against naval targets.[49] This is an over-simplification, but what is true is that through the summer of 1942 the JIC, perhaps for the first time, became an important player in formulating high strategy. Furthermore, in these months the debates over British-American strategy, revolving around prospects for Russia's survival, the need for and feasibility of an early cross-channel invasion, and the risks to the Middle East and India were particularly contentious. In late summer Brooke certainly felt the JIC was over-optimistic about Russia's prospects, and in downplaying an early German descent on the Middle East from the north. Against this context, clashes during JIC presentations to the chiefs of staff between the dominant strategic vision pressed by Brooke, and equally determined intelligence qualifications from Godfrey were inevitable. It is easy to see Brooke preferring a more compliant DNI, who would stick to his naval brief, and Pound, always a passive player in chiefs of staff debates when naval matters were not directly at stake, willing to acquiesce.[50]

Even if Moore and Pound had reached a more balanced appraisal of Godfrey's role and contribution within the JIC, and more generally, changing DNI at this point was reasonable. Godfrey had been in the role nearly four years, longer than any DNI save Hall, a fresh approach as the war moved towards the offensive made sense, and Godfrey himself would probably have appreciated a new challenge, not least at sea. What was not reasonable was the sheer brutality of Pound's treatment. Godfrey was given no proper account of the case against him, no opportunity to offer a defence, and no thanks for his achievements as DNI. He was the only British admiral in the war to receive no honour in recognition of his war service. If Pound had wider complaints about Godfrey's performance, he had never said so, although Godfrey noted an increasing distance in his attitude, and limited apparent interest in what intelligence could offer. Moore's hatchet job on a brother officer, strictly confined to the case for the prosecution, was equally harsh. It is possible that Godfrey's unpopularity in the intelligence community extended to senior levels of the Admiralty, although no convincing case has emerged. By contrast, there was heartfelt appreciation for his contribution from those junior to him both from within NID, but from others across the naval staff and from Bletchley. Ironically, his next post as Flag Officer Commanding Royal Indian Navy was a good one, and required the very qualities of tact and ability to work with other services that Pound and Moore claimed he lacked. Overall, the full circumstances of Godfrey's departure remain opaque.[51]

Edmund Rushbrooke, Godfrey's successor, was DNI through the rest of the war until July 1946, serving in the post, therefore, almost as long as Godfrey. He had a solid professional record, primarily in seagoing appointments, most recently in command of the older carriers *Argus* and *Eagle* (in the latter receiving a CBE, supplementing a DSC won in 1917, for 'bravery and resolution' during a Malta convoy), but was evidently not viewed as an early contender for flag rank. He did, however, have relevant intelligence experience as head of FECB from 1937–39. This and his immediate availability, having been unemployed since June owing to illness and sick leave, and, perhaps, belief that he would bring 'a steady pair of hands' to an organisation running well, seems to have determined his appointment, rather than any perception he had exceptional qualities suited to one of the most important posts in the Admiralty, especially in wartime.[52] The fact that Rushbrooke was the only DNI between 1919 and 1964 not to have or receive flag rank on appointment (he was only promoted rear admiral in July 1945) appears to confirm that he was not viewed as a rising star, and may also imply a deliberate downgrading of the status of the post. Perhaps not surprisingly, therefore, in comparison to Hall or Godfrey, Rushbrooke as DNI is a shadowy figure, who has left scant impression, either positive or negative, on the historical record. He made no major changes in either structure or personnel to the organisation he inherited. Fleming stayed in place – according to some testimony, almost running NID on a daily basis – and certainly free to pursue his special interests like 30AU; the OIC carried on as before under Clayton, so did the likes of Montagu in NID17. Several of Godfrey's 'disciples' claimed in later years that Rushbrooke lacked vision or grip, or even real interest. He, allegedly, claimed that he did not enjoy the job, and had never wanted it.[53] However, none of these witnesses identified specific areas where NID under Rushbrooke failed to perform or deliver. NID from 1943 to 1945 has enjoyed less profile and glamour in popular history, but its intelligence contribution remained impressive.

30

Underpinning Victory in Europe 1944–1945

In the final phase of the war, British naval intelligence faced four main tasks: support for Operation Overlord, the Allied invasion of Normandy; assessing the threat posed by new German weapon systems, especially the new generation U-boats, and their ability to shift the balance of advantage in the Atlantic; the reconstruction of an intelligence capability in the Far East adequate to support operations in Southeast Asia, and the deployment of a substantial British fleet to work alongside the Americans in the Pacific; and, finally, to obtain all useful outstanding intelligence from Germany and Japan following their defeat. Remarkably, the best intelligence on the first two of these requirements came from Japanese, rather than German, sources, and accessing the most important of these jointly with the Americans was a substantial British achievement. There were also more long-standing intelligence requirements that remained extant, notably the operational status of *Tirpitz* in Norway, under repair after Operation Source.

The new U-boats and other German innovative weapons

Given the size of the U-boat force by mid 1943, the Admiralty fully expected the sharp reduction in North Atlantic operations evident from late May to be temporary. However, over the next four months, partly due to the continuing gaps and delays in Shark coverage, but also deliberate German obfuscation, it struggled to assess what future strategy Dönitz anticipated, and how his force might be re-equipped. Important initial insights came in late August, with the first deployment of innovative new German weapons in the Bay of Biscay, and significant SIGINT reports in September, a Purple decrypt in which Japan's Berlin ambassador Hiroshi Ōshima recorded a meeting with Dönitz, and details of new Atlantic convoy operations available from Shark. Dönitz told Ōshima that he planned to resume convoy operations in

October, using new tactics which prioritised attacks on escorts, exploiting improved anti-aircraft guns, torpedoes, and radar warning systems. A new research council would drive further improvements, which he was confident would enable the U-boats to defeat the Allies.[1] The Shark reports confirmed the anti-escort focus, and revealed that this would be executed with the new G7 T5 Zaunkönig acoustic homing torpedo, which the Allies called Gnat, and gave details of the new Hagenuk Wanze radar warning system, and Aphrodite radar decoy balloon. Dönitz advised his boats they could anticipate surprise against complacent and weak escort forces.[2]

The first group of re-equipped boats made their debut against the combined convoy ONS 18/ON 202, comprising sixty-eight merchant ships and twenty-one escorts with strong air support, on 20 September. Based on initial combat reports, Dönitz believed the group had achieved outstanding success, probably sinking fifteen escorts and nine merchant vessels for the loss of two boats, amply justifying the new tactics. Reality was different. Only three escorts and six merchant ships were lost, against three U-boats sunk. Shark decrypts now enabled Hut 4 and the OIC to compare claimed against actual results, and produce a more accurate picture of Zaunkönig performance and its limitations than was possible for the Germans. Furthermore, British countermeasures were underway. As mentioned previously, the prospect of a German homing torpedo had first appeared in the Oslo report, followed from 1941 by regular references in POW interrogations, and Dolphin and Shark reports. Although both lines of reporting frequently confused early versions of Zaunkönig with the different, zigzagging FAT torpedo, the conviction that the Germans were pursuing a homing option, spurred by the Allies' own research into acoustic torpedoes, drove efforts to develop a defence. The result was the Foxer, a noise-making device towed astern of an escort, designed to explode a Zaunkönig harmlessly, which began deployment at sea by mid October – no escort streaming it was ever hit. Ultimately, Zaunkönig was too slow, too sensitive and too unreliable, and attempting a task which few torpedoes twenty-five years later achieved successfully. Meanwhile, neither Wanse nor Aphrodite were effective against the latest British centimetric radar, while the U-boats remained as vulnerable as ever to HF/DF. The sheer strength of the ONS 18/ON 202 escort, and the now-widespread deployment of escort carriers demonstrated that, by late 1943, the Germans faced increasing numerical, as well as technological, superiority. The attack on this convoy was the last occasion they believed they had achieved significant success.[3]

Prior to the arrival of Zaunkönig, another new German naval weapon made its debut in late August against British surface escort groups operating offensively against transiting U-boats in the Bay of Biscay, and caused their temporary withdrawal after the sinking of the sloop *Egret*, and damage to others. This was the Henschel Hs 293 radio-controlled, rocket-powered glide bomb, the first stand-off, air-to-surface, powered weapon to be deployed operationally at sea. The development of the Hs 293 had been foreshadowed in the 1939 Oslo report, and there were occasional references to special aerial weapons from both POW and SIS intelligence during 1941 and 1942. These early reports received limited attention, nor did NID spot the significance of German air force Enigma reports during early summer 1943, suggesting that select air force units were re-equipping with two new weapons, 'Hs 293' and 'FX', for deployment in the Mediterranean. The separate FX (or Fritz-X) weapon was actually used against Allied ships off Sicily in July, but because no damage was done, its novelty went unrecognised. More specific intelligence from German aircrew captured in the Mediterranean in early August, who had participated in trials with the new weapons, did get attention, but it was the end of the month before this was fully assessed alongside the previous Ultra material. This initial assessment recognised that the deployment of two different types of 'glider bomb' was imminent, but no useful warning was issued to the fleet before the Biscay attack, or the first major operation using the FX on 8 September, which sank the Italian battleship *Roma* and damaged *Italia* (previously *Littorio*), both on passage under Royal Navy supervision to surrender. The FX was radio-controlled, but unpowered, with an armour-piercing warhead targeted at battleships and heavy cruisers, whereas the Hs 293 was aimed at light warships and merchant vessels. During September, FXs seriously damaged several Allied warships off Salerno, including the battleship *Warspite* and cruiser *Uganda*.[4]

The appearance of the Hs 293 and FX without prior warning to the fleet provoked an important organisational change in NID. Until now, NID12, the special intelligence section formed in July 1942 from Montagu's 17M and Lordon's 17P, had summarised and sanitised Ultra reports to suggest they derived from human sources, before circulating them to the geographic and technical intelligence sections, which in summer 1943 were still not indoctrinated into Ultra. However, after reviewing the past intelligence on the two glider bombs, NID12 accepted it was not competent to process this type of intelligence to ensure that it achieved the right scientific and technical scrutiny. A new unit, NID7S, was therefore established within NID7, the NID technical section, tasked to provide expert opinion on scientific intelligence from all sources, including Ultra, and then to circulate it to Admiralty departments responsible for weapons research and development, in a form they could understand.[5] The surprise achieved by the glider bombs coincided with accumulating intelligence of other novel German weapons under development, notably jet-powered aircraft, new types of U-boat, pilotless aircraft, and rockets. By late autumn, the last two were judged the most immediate and important threat, because of the advanced state of the programmes, the scale of damage they might inflict on the United Kingdom, and also their ability to impede, or even halt, the planned cross-channel invasion, codename Overlord. In November the JIC therefore created a new subcommittee, codename Bodyline, under the chairmanship of Ian Fleming, to collate and assess all intelligence on German development of rockets, pilotless aircraft, and glider bombs.[6] Although this was driven primarily by the intelligence demands of the emerging weapons, later known as V1 and V2, the inclusion of the glider bombs in the brief ensured they got effective scrutiny from the whole intelligence community. The resulting joint analysis of the Hs 293 and FX attacks during August and September, alongside information acquired from German aircraft abandoned at Foggia later in the autumn, disclosed the radio frequencies with which both weapons were controlled, enabling countermeasures to be developed, and appropriate guidance issued to the fleet.[7] By December, following further changes in its scope and accountability, Bodyline received the more famous designation, Crossbow. Fleming's role in an area of such strategic importance not only promoted naval interests, but demonstrated the recognition he now enjoyed across Whitehall for his skills in intelligence policy and management. It also ensured that innovative weapons and their potential for transformative impact was high on the NID agenda.

NID detected the first tentative pointers to a shift in U-boat construction policy, as opposed to the re-equipping of existing designs with new sensors and weapons, in early autumn. In mid October, drawing on evidence from Ultra decrypts and PR, it noted that only sixteen U-boats had been completed in September, a marked fall from the previous 1943 average monthly output of twenty-five. The OIC also observed a substantial fall in the operational force from a peak of 240 on 1 May, to 185 at the beginning of October.[8] Simultaneously, during the autumn, fragmentary reports from POWs, PR, and Denham's contacts in Stockholm suggested the Germans were developing a new class of small 250-ton U-boats, probably using a novel propulsion system to deliver high speed, although some reports linked this new propulsion system with larger boats in excess of 500 tons. POW intelligence linked the new designs, and especially the propulsion, with Dr Hellmuth Walter, who had come to NID attention in the late 1930s. Meanwhile, in what proved a prophetic indicator,

Denham reported in late December that in several yards U-boats were being broken up on their slips, or launched in an incomplete state, to create space for construction of a new type of boat.[9]

In January the picture was further complicated by the first reports from both POWs and Enigma of experiments with a new device called the *Schnorchel*, a ventilation trunk to allow submerged diesel propulsion. NID7S initially thought the *Schnorchel* was associated with a novel, closed-circuit diesel propulsion system for fully submerged running. However, the concept was not new to the British, since some Dutch submarines which escaped to the United Kingdom in 1940 were *Schnorchel*-fitted, and had demonstrated it was practical.[10] Further assessment, including SIS reports from French bases and analysis of all relevant Ultra references by Hut 4, correctly judged the Germans were probably considering its wider application, to enable U-boats to charge their batteries while running at periscope depth.[11] In early February a detailed PR survey of U-boat building yards, the first since October, demonstrated that Germany was definitely reducing construction of standard U-boat types, with a 26 per cent fall in numbers on the slips and fitting-out.[12] NID was initially uncertain whether this was due to bombing, release of resources for other war priorities, or other factors, but by the end of the month had decided it was instead to allow production of new U-boat types, a view supported by a significant Purple decrypt, in which Ōshima quoted Hitler as saying Germany was developing U-boats with increased speed. Reviewing all the evidence on 28 February, a wider meeting of the naval staff concluded that the Germans were building a substantial fleet of small, high-speed, Walter-boats, using closed-cycle propulsion, primarily as an anti-invasion weapon, probably developing a larger boat with similar characteristics, and also retrofitting existing U-boat types with the *Schnorchel*. By mid March, NID confirmed that Germany had 'practically ceased' to lay down standard U-boat types, and 'had probably decided' to concentrate future building on new types able to defeat current Allied anti-submarine capabilities.[13]

Given the available intelligence and the priority given to potential threats to Overlord, this initial assessment was reasonable, although early British and American technical assessments exaggerated the likely performance of the small Walter-boats, and some bordered on the fanciful.[14] However, although almost all the reports over the winter of 1943/44 were correct as far as they went, they revealed only a small part of Germany's U-boat modernisation programme, and in several respects were badly misleading. Indeed, for all the undoubted Allied success against the U-boats on the Atlantic frontline in 1943, which was substantially intelligence-driven, the poor knowledge of where Dönitz was actually headed with his new programmes, and their current status, was an intelligence failure stretching back more than two years which, had the Germans made different decisions earlier, could have altered the course of the war. Unknown to NID, Walter had pursued his concentrated hydrogen peroxide, subsequently known to the British as high-test peroxide or HTP, propulsion and high-speed design experiments through the early war years, and an 80-ton experimental boat, *V-80*, achieved a submerged speed of 28 knots as early as 1940. By 1942, plans for 250-ton coastal and 600-ton Atlantic boats, incorporating the Walter closed-cycle system and streamlining, capable of delivering transformational speed and submerged endurance, had matured, and contracts for four prototypes of the former and one of the latter were placed in June that year. That September, Raeder and Dönitz convinced Hitler to commit the resources to achieve wholesale transformation of the U-boat fleet to the new designs as soon as possible, with an immediate order for twenty-four, 300-ton coastal boats, subsequently designated Type XVII. This reveals how Raeder and Dönitz viewed prospects for the U-boat war that autumn. They evidently judged that Allied anti-submarine capability and resources were outmatching the existing fleet, and that in order successfully to prosecute the war Germany must take the huge gamble of rapidly building a new-generation fleet, embodying quantum leaps in technology.[15] The intelligence reports reaching NID over the winter of 1943/44 mainly referred to the first two prototype Type XVIIs, *U-792* and *U-793*, which were commissioned in November, subsequently featuring in Enigma reports as U-boats of 'an unusual type' on trials, and two prototype Atlantic boats designated Type XVIII, *U-796* and *U-797*, under construction, but never launched. The latter, at 1600 tons, were much larger versions of the prototype oceangoing vessel ordered in mid 1942, which was also never completed.

What NID did not appreciate, when the naval staff conducted its review at the end of February, was that the Walter HTP programme set in train in autumn 1942 proved too challenging technically, and that by May 1943, Dönitz recognised that neither the coastal Type XVIIs, nor the ocean-capable Type XVIIIs, could be produced in sufficient quantity to influence the outcome of the war. However, Walter proposed an alternative strategy, using the same two basic designs, including their streamlining, but substituting increased battery capacity for HTP tankage, to provide adequate power and endurance for high-speed running, and incorporating the *Schnorchel* to reduce surface vulnerability. If trials of the latter were successful, Walter suggested it could be fitted to all U-boats.[16]

The original Walter programme was therefore cancelled, although trials of the prototypes continued until the end of the war, and the two new 'electro-boats', the 1600-ton Type XXI and 250-ton Type XXIII, were ordered in quantity from autumn 1943. The Type XXI had three times the battery capacity, and at 15.5 knots twice the underwater speed, of the standard Atlantic Type VIIB. Both were constructed in prefabricated sections across multiple sites, and designed for rapid final assembly on the slips. Dönitz hoped to have both boats in service by late spring 1944, but both programmes were heavily delayed by technical and construction failings, and disruption from Allied bombing. Only four Type XXIs and six Type XXIIIs ever entered operational service. In parallel with the initiation of the electro-boats, a proportion of frontline Type VIIs and Type XIs were retrofitted with *Schnorchel*, or snorts, as they were soon known to the British and Americans, but this was beset with technical and safety challenges, and the results were never operationally satisfactory.

Although during March and April 1944, PR confirmed that construction of traditional U-boat types had virtually ceased, there was scant evidence for the expected programme of new Walter anti-invasion submarines, with only a handful of small boats sighted on the slipways or in the Baltic. The first important indicator of future building plans only emerged from PR in the last half of April, when much larger U-boats of a new type, which had clearly been prefabricated elsewhere, were sighted on building slips at Danzig, Bremen and Hamburg. However, beyond the dimensions available from PR, which suggested a displacement in the 1500-ton range, the precise characteristics of these new U-boats remained unknown, while of the expected smaller boats there was still little sign.[17] The first authoritative glimpse into underlying German intentions came from an unexpected direction at the beginning of May.

It followed a breakthrough into the machine cipher used by Japanese naval attachés, known to the Allies as JNA20, or Coral. Introduced in September 1939, Coral used similar operating principles to Purple, but incorporated additions and modifications that made it a more formidable proposition than either Purple or Shark Enigma. It was also used sparingly, and with impeccable security, and in summer 1943 it remained impervious to attack. With American encouragement, GC&CS accordingly gave it new priority. Hut 8, now under Hugh Alexander, had spare capacity, as OP-20-G with their four-wheel bombes moved into the lead on Shark, and commenced a joint attack with the Japanese naval section in Hut 7 under Hugh Foss, taking advantage of a good supply of Japanese traffic intercepted at the major regional SIGINT centre at Sarafand in Palestine. Coral, therefore, received extensive examination from some of the best machine cipher specialists in the world, exploiting all their relevant experience from Enigma. By the end of September, this British team had made real headway, and sent a detailed report to OP-20-G, which the Americans later conceded marked the birth of the successful attack on Coral. Both sides now brought special assets to consolidate this progress, and Foss and Alexander moved to Washington, where they made a major contribution to the final breakthrough, which led to the first messages read on 11 March 1944. The most prolific user of Coral was Vice Admiral Katsuo Abe, who became the senior Japanese naval emissary in Germany in spring 1943, chief of all naval attachés in Europe, and naval representative on the Tripartite Military Commission. Abe's messages on the Coral system to IJN headquarters in Tokyo, of which 5300 were recovered by the end of the war, included reports of the highest value, not only in the naval sphere, but across a wider range of important military and political topics, including issues relevant to Overlord. In addition to illuminating the U-boat programme, including new torpedo developments, early Coral decrypts contained Abe's detailed specifications of the Hs 293 and FX glider bombs, and details of blockade-running operations between German-controlled Atlantic ports and Japan.[18]

The first Coral insight on new U-boats, issued by Hut 4 on 1 May, was a decrypted message from Abe to Tokyo the previous December. This provided broadly accurate headline dimensions and performance data for two new U-boats, which it correctly designated with the type numbers XXI and XXIII. Although it did not specify their propulsion, and referred to them as 'Walter' boats, and Abe admitted to some uncertainties regarding their characteristics, the overall picture conveyed was consistent with that in current PR of building yards and Enigma reports of Baltic trials. It gave NID confidence that neither new type, nor fifty additional midget submarines, ordered, according to Abe, from the Italian firm Caproni, and on which he also reported in detail to Tokyo, would be operational in significant numbers before the autumn.[19] Coral delivered a more definitive view at the end of the month, with a decrypted message from Abe, recording his meeting with Dönitz and senior U-boat staff on 24 April. This gave a comprehensive summary of the specifications of the two boats, and the rationale driving their introduction, and crucial clarification that they were conventionally powered, although equipped with a snort and three times the battery capacity of earlier boats. There was also important confirmation that the boats would not be operational before the autumn. The report resolved most outstanding questions regarding German intent for the new boats and their capability, and it convinced NID12 that the Germans had failed to produce a practical closed-cycle engine. Abe provided regular updates on the characteristics and progress of both boats, including production methods, over the rest of the year.[20]

The Coral intelligence from Abe was exceptionally valuable in illuminating the U-boat programme and other weapon systems, and providing timely reassurance on the submarine threat in the final run-up to Overlord. In January 1945 the Director for Torpedoes and Mining praised the contribution of the Abe decrypts on the T5 torpedo, the HTP torpedo under development which promised to quadruple German torpedo performance, acoustic and magnetic mine sweeps, and small novel weapons such as the two-man, *Seehund* U-boat, emphasising their outstanding relevance, accuracy and reliability, and Abe's grasp of complex technology. The reports had enabled countermeasures against German weapons, and would have a major impact on Japanese naval capability.[21] Like the Purple reports from Ōshima, these Coral reports from Abe were an unusual SIGINT product. They delivered intelligence of a quality and range normally only achieved by the highest-level human penetration agent. It was rare for single decrypts to combine policy and capability insight with impeccable high-level sourcing and strategic impact. Very few naval Enigma decrypts achieved similar impact to the best Coral material quoting Abe, as demonstrated by Enigma's failure to illuminate the new U-boat programmes. So reliable did OP-20-G staff rate Abe's reporting that they christened him 'Honest Abe', in a play on the nickname of President Abraham Lincoln.[22] It was ironic that decrypts of Japanese traffic now delivered the best coverage of German naval policy and capability, when excellent GC&CS coverage of Japan delivered nothing remotely approaching this quality on the IJN in the interwar period. However, the value of Coral should not mask the fact that the Allies had little knowledge of U-boat research and development between the outbreak of war in September 1939 and late 1943, and no clarity on the electro-boats for a further six months. If the Germans had concluded that HTP was a dead end, and adopted the electro-boats in mid 1942 instead of late 1943, then with less economic disruption to the programme from bombing, a significant electro-boat force operational in early 1944, capable of at least temporarily shifting the balance of naval advantage, was possible. Without Coral, with the limitations of Enigma coverage and PR, and no SIS agent comparable to TR16, NID would have been poorly placed to pick this up until too late.

While NID focused on the new U-boat programmes in the first months of 1944, it was also monitoring repairs to *Tirpitz* following Operation Source. It was well-served with regular reports from Torstein Raaby, now established in Elvebakken in the south of Altenfjord, with a job that allowed frequent observation of *Tirpitz* in Kaafjord, supplemented by occasional Enigma insights and PR flights from Vaenga. At the end of January, the OIC judged that repairs to *Tirpitz* would complete by mid March, although she would not be operational for some while afterwards, and badly needed a docking, which required her return to Germany. The prospect of this return, the possibility that she might be risked against a convoy, despite her reduced operational state, and the pressing need to release heavy units of the Home Fleet to the war in the East dictated the desirability of a new attack before she became mobile. The subsequent success of Operation Tungsten, executed by Fleet Air Arm carrier aircraft armed with armour-piercing bombs, which took *Tirpitz* by complete surprise early on the morning of 3 April, putting her out of action for at least four months, required meticulous intelligence preparation. The terrain was demanding for dive-bombing, the layered anti-aircraft defences had to be identified so they could be suppressed by fighters, up-to-date weather reports were crucial, and so was confirmation that *Tirpitz* was still in her anchorage. Raaby, communicating through Station Ida, was the star of this intelligence operation, providing most of the detail on flak locations, radar, and high-tension cables. At considerable risk, he also provided two-hourly weather forecasts. ISTD, drawing on PR coverage, together with Raaby's reports, provided detailed topographical models of the target area. The quality of this target picture, painstakingly put together from multiple sources, far surpassed what had been available at Taranto three and a half years before, and demonstrated how far the Royal Navy had evolved in applying intelligence to operational planning. Despite his exposure, Raaby remained for two months to report on the damage, and to support further attacks if required, before he was withdrawn to receive, like his compatriot Rørholt, a well-earned DSO. Although *Tirpitz* was again patched up by the summer, provoking further British attacks of varying effectiveness until she was finally sunk by RAF heavy bombers in November, Tungsten ended her status as a serious operational threat.[23]

Naval intelligence support to Overlord

Although the potential impact of novel German naval weapons, and the continuing security of the Atlantic and Arctic convoys, were vital issues, the primary focus of NID through the first six months of 1944 was, increasingly, on intelligence to support the invasion of Normandy, Operation Overlord, executed on 6 June and its naval element, Operation Neptune. The genesis of Overlord, stretching back more than two years, and the elaborate intelligence structures and operations developed to support it, has been comprehensively described elsewhere, with Neptune aptly described as a 'never surpassed masterpiece of planning and staff work'.[24] Essentially, the task of Neptune was the safe delivery of the initial Allied assault force through three successive German defensive lines: an offshore screen primarily of U-boats but also E-boats; minefields; and finally the beach defences, the famed Atlantic Wall. The role of intelligence was to illuminate and help the Allies successfully penetrate these lines.

The first, most important, and certainly most enduring naval intelligence input to Overlord was topographical, focused on the third line, the Atlantic Wall: the construction of a comprehensive picture of approaches to landing areas, beaches and their environs, and the immediate German defences. This topographical intelligence determined the decision made in mid 1943 to land in Normandy. As discussed previously, NID1 began collecting intelligence on the coastal areas of France, Belgium and Holland that were militarily significant, and of initial German installations and defences, from June 1940. By the end of that year, collection and assessment were conducted in close collaboration with MI14 in the War Office, and the PIU, soon to become the CIU, and covered the whole coastline from north Norway to the Spanish border. By early 1942, the focus of this effort, now supported by ISTD and the Admiralty photographic library NID11, was shifting from invasion warning, and the support of disruptive British raiding operations, to preparation for when the Allies would mount their own attack on the Continent. From that time, NID1 staff were seconded to a combined intelligence section (CIS), which supported invasion planning, first within the headquarters of Home Forces Command, and then from 1943, with the Chief of Staff to the Supreme Allied Commander Designate (COSSAC).

The first requirement, initiated by NID but supported by MI, was the production of large scale 'chart-maps', covering the coast from Ostend to Cherbourg to a depth of ten miles inland. Produced jointly by the Admiralty Hydrographic Department and War Office Ordnance Survey, these featured coastal waters, coastline and beaches, fixed defences and strongpoints, and anything else of military significance, roads, railways, airfields, communication and radar sites, and fuel and ammunition dumps. To facilitate accurate naval bombardment, it was essential they used an integrated projection system using accurate surveys, which required covert reconnaissance.[25] From spring 1942 until June 1944, the intelligence underpinning these chart-maps and the whole invasion-planning effort was collated in weekly reports under the codename Martian. Martian reports followed a standard format, enabling the intelligence picture to be easily updated on a rolling basis, beginning with a 'strategic survey', then with sections covering 'enemy forces', 'topography and maps', 'transport and industry', 'police and civilians, 'air and naval'. Each weekly report contained attachments comprising aerial photographs, and plans and diagrams based on POW or SIS intelligence. NID and the OIC contributed any new intelligence on enemy naval plans and dispositions that might affect the Allied crossing and force composition.[26]

During the final eight months before D-Day, the best insights into evolving German coastal defences, their troop deployment, assessment of Allied intent, and plans to counter a landing came from decrypts of successive Japanese reports produced by Ambassador Ōshima, the military attaché, Colonel Ito Seiichi, and in the final weeks, following the breaking of Coral, from Abe. Purple decrypts from Ōshima were an invaluable guide to high-level German thinking, drawing on direct access to Hitler himself, and to senior commanders, but Ito complemented him with a massive thirty-two-part account of his extensive tour of the Atlantic Wall in November. However, recovery of the full text of this in the Japanese military attaché cipher was challenging, with about a third available by the end of the year, but some parts not until June.[27] Abe's Coral report on his tour of the northern French coast between 20 and 24 April was the most important of the Japanese insights. Earlier decrypts alerted GC&CS to his departure for France, and 'Y' stations at Freetown, Mauritius, Abbotabad (near the northwest frontier of India), and Brisbane were all tasked to maintain special watch for subsequent traffic. This enabled GC&CS to acquire a complete clean text of his report, sent in thirteen parts by three different routes, by late on 6 May. It was then decrypted and issued in three parts on 8, 9 and 13 May. Abe provided a detailed appraisal of the latest German dispositions and intentions, all the more valuable because he was more critical than either Ōshima or Ito in assessing what he was told. He confirmed that the German commander Field Marshal Rommel intended to destroy a landing as close to the coast as possible, preferably on the beaches, and to ensure communication between airborne and seaborne forces was quickly severed. However, the most important and worrying of his insights was that the Germans now anticipated a major diversionary Allied landing on the Normandy coast, which they therefore planned to reinforce, although diversions in Holland, or even Denmark, were also considered possibilities. There was some collateral for Abe's suggestion that the Germans anticipated a diversion in Normandy, from both German air force Enigma, and from Ōshima. Although this focus on Normandy caused alarm for some days, it was put in more reassuring perspective by the decrypt of an Enigma message from the German

Commander-in-Chief West, Field Marshal Gerd von Runstedt sent on 8 May, which defined the most threatened sector as the whole front from Boulogne to Normandy.[28]

Apart from their role in assessing German coastal defences, NID and the OIC had to monitor the threat posed to the invasion from minelaying, E-boats, other surface forces and, above all, from U-boats. Minefields, both offshore and inshore, were a key part of the German coastal defence system, and their mining effort accelerated considerably from the start of 1944. Identifying the new mined areas was critical to the success of Neptune. SIGINT, from both Enigma and monitoring of R/T transmissions, identified at least twenty-two suspect offshore minelaying operations by E-boats in the Bay of the Seine between January and June, but few of the areas sown could be identified with precision until a fortnight before D-Day. The OIC then exploited an opportunity for which it had been waiting. An Enigma signal decrypted on 20 May warned of an imminent minelaying operation, which enabled the British to lay a successful ambush, severely damaging the German force. Not only did this largely eliminate their capacity for further minelaying in the next few weeks, but it provoked a flood of signals, as the Germans sought to extract their damaged ships from heavily mined areas, disclosing almost all their co-ordinates. Assessing the threat from shallow-water, inshore mining combined with beach obstacles was also problematic until May, when a series of lucky breaks from Enigma decrypts, combined with low-level PR, solved most outstanding questions. This intelligence on inshore defences dictated that the assault should begin at first light shortly after low water on a rising tide. This helped achieve surprise since, as Abe reported, the Germans expected the landings to occur when high water was just before dawn.[29] While the Allies were ultimately relatively successful in exploiting intelligence to neutralise the pre-invasion mining threat, they seriously underestimated German air force ability to conduct a surprisingly effective aerial mining campaign during the six weeks after the invasion. Despite the limited aircraft available, up to four thousand mines, many advanced acoustic and magnetic types, were laid in June and July, which inflicted by far the greatest Allied shipping losses. Other than identifying airfields from which the aircraft operated, intelligence could do little to counter this problem, and for a while the sweeping effort struggled to keep pace, disrupting the logistic build-up. By contrast, Enigma intelligence was successfully exploited to impede German air force efforts to deploy glider bombs, with a pre-emptive attack on their base at Merignac in southern France.[30]

Apart from mining, the E-boat force conducted a higher tempo of operations between January and May, with SIGINT identifying at least forty sorties directed against Channel shipping and, from the spring, armed reconnaissance along the British south coast. Enigma provided good coverage of E-boat order of battle, but during the pre-invasion period it rarely gave advance warning, or indicated the objective of a sortie, and nor did other sources, such as R/T monitoring. The threat the E-boats posed was underlined in the pre-invasion period by a successful surprise attack, with no intelligence warning, on Exercise Tiger, a predominantly American trial landing being conducted at Slapton Sands in Lyme Bay on 28 April, which sank two large landing ships with considerable loss of life, including many engineers. In the two weeks after D-Day, when E-boat operations against the invasion forces were at their peak, Enigma was more helpful in monitoring the status of the fifty boats based at Cherbourg, Le Havre, Boulogne and Ijmuiden, because disruption to landlines forced the Germans to resort to radio, which usually revealed their nightly operational intentions. Although they sank or damaged twenty Allied ships, and more through mining, the intelligence picture was good enough to ensure they were never more than a nuisance, and could not disrupt the Allied build-up. Crucially, Enigma also revealed a major E-boat concentration collected at Le Havre at the end of the first week. This was targeted by Bomber Command, and the concrete E-boat shelters penetrated with tallboy bombs, putting at least a dozen boats out of action, a raid German naval command assessed a 'catastrophe'.[31]

Meanwhile, at the beginning of May NID judged that all Germany's remaining heavy units, except *Tirpitz* and *Gneisenau*, were potentially available to counter Overlord. However, the OIC did not believe heavy ships would be used in the eastern Channel directly against invasion forces, except as a last desperate measure. It was more likely the two pocket battleships *Scheer* and *Lützow* and the heavy cruisers *Prinz Eugen* and *Hipper* would be deployed to northern Norway to threaten a breakout into the Atlantic, and thus divert Allied forces covering the invasion, while the four surviving light cruisers carried out diversionary raids on east-coast convoys. However, all these moves would be subject to requirements in the Baltic, and by the end of the month Enigma and PR coverage showed no sign of any deployment, while *Hipper* and one light cruiser were now in refit and unavailable. In the event, the only attempted intervention post-invasion by surface forces larger than E-boats was by four destroyers operating out of Brest on the night of 8/9 June. Enigma gave ample warning of the sortie, they were successfully intercepted by the 10th Destroyer Flotilla, and two of the German ships were sunk and another badly damaged.[32]

The biggest concern was the U-boat threat, compounded by the prospect of innovative types and weapons. On 29 January BdU was involved in a full-scale invasion alarm, which the OIC monitored through Shark, and found 'amusing and instructive'. The panic was triggered by a German aircraft sighting three hundred supposed landing craft on an easterly heading southwest of Lorient. Although the Germans soon determined the suspect vessels were harmless tunny-fishing boats, the OIC observed that the BdU reaction had been 'vigorous and prompt and characteristic of a pre-determined plan'. Countering an invasion evidently had absolute priority, and all available U-boats would immediately concentrate against it, regardless of risk. Ten days later, Winn produced an appreciation of 'U-boats as a factor in the Second Front'. He assessed there were 175 frontline U-boats, with 130 deployed in the Biscay bases, of which ninety were suitable for Channel operations. In emergency, these could be supplemented by up to seventy-five additional boats drawn from the Arctic and those working up in the Baltic. Although the OIC stuck to these figures in advice given to the JIC three months later on 30 April, these were worst-case assessments, which assumed either that the Germans had significant warning, or were prepared to sacrifice other goals for a counter-invasion strategy for an extended period. By April, there was abundant evidence that such figures were exaggerated, when set against the evolution of German strength and dispositions known from Shark. Over the first four months of the year, Shark decrypts showed overall frontline U-boat strength down by 7 per cent, as construction of standard types petered out, but the reduction in the Biscay bases was more than twice this figure, to the lowest level since July 1942. This was mainly due to a build-up in Norway, reflecting fears of Allied landings there.[33]

Despite these Biscay reductions, from early April the OIC spotted that boats there were being held back from Atlantic deployment, which it correctly assessed as a counter-invasion measure. This insight brought an important strategic benefit to the Allies in the two months before D-Day. It permitted reorganisation of Atlantic convoys to release escorts to protect the Overlord assault area, helped now by the standard use of 100-ship convoys, in accordance with Blackett's advice the previous year. In May the OIC also identified a new 'centre group' of sixteen boats based in south Norway, mainly at Bergen, additional to the Arctic force, which it judged was held there partly as a deterrent to Allied attack, partly as a general operational reserve, but possibly also showed 'cautious reluctance' to have too high a proportion of boats in French ports that might be overrun. Using Enigma-generated intelligence, the south Norway boats were subjected to intense air attack over the next two months, which sank fourteen boats by the end of June, with many more damaged. By 15 May, decrypts showed strength in the Biscay bases down to eighty-seven boats, a third less than the start of the year.[34] More clarity over German intent came in decrypts received on 19 and 20 May, in which Captain U-boats West Hans-Rudolf Rösing informed Naval Group West of his anti-invasion plans in detail. His message would not normally have gone by radio, but Allied bombing and resistance activity had disrupted landlines, producing an intelligence windfall. From this the OIC learnt that forty U-boats would deploy from the Biscay ports, by D+1 at the latest, into the western part of the Channel, probably in two waves. This coincided with the strength the OIC now judged the Germans were keeping at these bases in immediate readiness.

This authoritative intelligence enabled final refinements to Allied plans and gave confidence that force levels were adequate to execute them. These plans envisaged closing off the western entrance to the Channel, and southern boundary of St George's Channel, with 350 aircraft, enough to keep thirty on patrol at one time, and about 275 of 'the best and most experienced' anti-submarine vessels the Allies could muster. These were broadly divided between close protection of the invasion corridors and ten offensive hunting groups, including several escort carriers, down Channel. The Allies now knew that, to reach the invasion corridors, the Germans could deploy a U-boat force no larger than that against the Torch convoys eighteen months earlier, but this faced air and surface anti-submarine forces of three times the size, more experienced and capable, and in more restricted waters. Shark decrypts in the final days showed no evidence of any German alert or fundamental change in dispositions. The OIC believed there were fifty-seven boats in the Biscay ports (compared to a true figure of forty-nine), thirty-four deployed in the Atlantic, and fifty-four in south Norway and the Arctic.[35] There remained two significant gaps in the Allied intelligence picture. Although the OIC was aware U-boats were being fitted with snorts at the Biscay bases, it did not know the number so far equipped, and understanding of snort-boat capability and tactics was still limited. In addition, although the recent Coral intercept quoting Abe on the status of the new U-boats was reassuring, hard intelligence on the threat posed by the small coastal boats, known to be on trials in the Baltic, was also lacking.[36]

Winn described the U-boat response to D-Day as 'prompt, energetic but remarkably confused'.[37] U-boats West followed the plan revealed on 20 May with thirty-six Type VIICs (eight snort-equipped) sailing on the first day, followed by seven further snort-boats in the next few days. The twenty-eight non-snort-boats had negligible prospect of penetrating the outer Allied screen of aircraft and hunting groups, and five boats were sunk and five sufficiently damaged to force them to abort, within ninety-six hours. On 10 June Shark decrypts revealed that BdU had directed that no further non-snort-boats should sail, while those at sea should pull back to hold a defensive line protecting their bases. The decrypts provided enough detail of their locations to enable RAF aircraft to hound U-boats on this patrol line without let-up, forcing Dönitz to order their recall on 13 June. No non-snort-boat sank an Allied ship. The fourteen snort-boats that reached the operational area fared better, albeit under the most gruelling conditions with the primitive system installed in the Type VIICs. Enigma decrypts revealed to the OIC the challenges they faced. It was too risky to snort in daylight, their speed of advance was consequently rarely more than 1.5 knots, and crews were exhausted and suffering from carbon monoxide poisoning. Nevertheless, snorts proved difficult to detect in 1944, either from the air or with surface radar, especially after the weather worsened in mid June, and the better-handled boats kept close inshore, waiting for targets to emerge, and bottoming when threatened by escorts. By the end of June, the OIC had intelligence from both Enigma and interrogation of snort-boat survivors that, despite all the difficulties, they could survive in an intense anti-submarine environment and achieve some success. Overall, the Biscay snort-boats sank three warships and five freighters for three boats lost, an exchange rate the Allies could live with – although it carried a warning for the future. Meanwhile, eleven Type VIIC snort-boats, which had survived the relentless Allied air campaign in Norwegian waters unscathed, sailed to join the D-Day offensive. Seven were lost in transit, while the other four, which reached the western entrance to the Channel from 18 June, sank two ships before withdrawing to Biscay ports. This was the last significant new U-boat attempt to intervene against the landings. That same day, 18 June, a Coral decrypt from Abe recorded his judgement that little could now be expected of either the U-boats, or the E-boats.[38]

The naval intelligence support to the successful execution of the Normandy landings was, with one notable exception, the last major naval intelligence contribution to the naval war with Germany. From now on, the German navy was a fast-waning force. In August the U-boats retreated from their French bases to Norway and, apart from limited Atlantic sorties, concentrated with the residual surface forces on defending the approaches to northern Europe and the Baltic. The OIC continued to worry about the potential impact of the new U-boat types. During October, a flurry of Enigma decrypts, including an address to the Atlantic U-boat force from Dönitz, briefly raised fears that a new campaign was imminent, and could cause sufficient disruption to Allied supply lines to prejudice the ongoing offensive operations in northwest Europe. However, by mid November, there was sufficient intelligence, including authoritative Coral decrypts from Abe, to show that such fears were misplaced, and owing to bombing and dislocation the Germans were struggling to deliver sufficient boats to create a viable operational force before the spring.[39]

The main intelligence focus, therefore, now shifted to supporting the ongoing Royal Navy operations against the Japanese in the east Indian Ocean, and preparations to deploy a major British fleet alongside the Americans in the Pacific. However, there were still two important intelligence coups in the closing days of the German war, one of which helped set the agenda for British naval intelligence over the next fifty years. Following the impressive results achieved by 30 Commando in the Mediterranean in 1943, it was brought back to the United Kingdom in December that year and, under the new name 30 Assault Unit (or 30AU), reorganised and expanded to undertake intelligence collection during Overlord. To improve its tasking, DNI established NID30 in January 1944 to plan the seizure of enemy naval documents and material. It drew on intelligence from multiple sources and technical expertise across the Admiralty to identify key targets. The priorities during Overlord were German developments in torpedoes, mines, minesweeping, centimetric radar, and any novel capabilities for obstructing ports and harbours. To deal with expected German resistance, the combat capability of the 30AU teams was increased, and by November the force had an overall strength of 310 personnel.[40] In the event, there were no spectacular captures either in Normandy, or the subsequent liberation of northern France. However, the operation did establish three important conclusions: that the Germans had a more substantial naval research and development programme on the threshold of delivering important new operational capabilities than NID had appreciated; that they were dispersing research and production facilities; and that they were prioritising the new U-boats, and unconventional weapons such as the *Seehund* midget submarines, human torpedoes, and remote, guided, explosive fast motor boats (the latter two exploiting Italian expertise).[41]

If Normandy proved a disappointment for 30AU, it justified its existence as it accompanied the leading British units into Germany. At the end of April, while pursuing a lead to German naval intelligence records, in collaboration with the Forward Intelligence Unit (FIU) of the US Navy, a 30AU unit led by Lieutenant Commander Sancho Glanville captured the entire German naval archives for the period 1870 to 1945, which had been moved for safe keeping to Tambach Castle in northern

Bavaria. The bulk of the archive, perhaps 500 tons of papers in all, was of historic, rather than current, value, but there was still much of immediate relevance and value relating to new weapons, ongoing research, and German intelligence operations, including important revelations relating to Russia. However, the greatest achievement was the capture at Kiel of Hellmuth Walter, most of his senior staff, and his research facility, the Walterwerke, which was 90 per cent intact. Walter was initially unwilling to co-operate until Dönitz, now Hitler's formal successor, ordered him to disclose everything, probably to ensure the Western Allies benefited rather than the Russians. Thereafter, he gave his British interrogators a full account of his research and the development of the new U-boats, not only the Types XXI and XXIII, but the continuing experiments with the HTP-propelled Type XVIIBs, of which three examples had been completed at the Blohm & Voss shipyard as the war ended. All three had been scuttled, but one boat, *U-1407*, was salvaged and taken to the United Kingdom, and another, *U-1406*, went to the Americans.[42] The Walter revelations set British submarine technology and thinking, and, ultimately, British naval intelligence in a new direction.

31

Redemption in the Far East 1943–1945

The reconstruction of Far East naval intelligence

During 1943, British naval intelligence capability in the Eastern theatre depended almost entirely on SIGINT. PR was basic and confined to the area around Ceylon, and parts of the Bay of Bengal, and East African coast. SIS was developing some coverage into Southeast Asia, but over the next two years, its only contributions of naval interest were occasional coastal and topographical reports. as planning for the invasion of Malaya matured. It never produced much shipping intelligence in the Malay barrier area, and nothing on the IJN or its operations. By contrast, the substantial SIS presence in China, spread across ten stations, did contribute useful, if not essential, naval intelligence. Between 1 December 1944 and 21 January 1945, '21 operational sightings of enemy shipping off the China coast were passed to American naval and air liaison officers for operational action', a sample probably representative of output in the last two years of the war.[1]

For much of 1943, the SIGINT available was compromised by a complex web of 'political' wrangles over effective implementation of the American undertakings on Japan agreed under Holden. By the start of the year, both GC&CS and the Admiralty were frustrated that OP-20-G was failing to deliver the promised intelligence and cryptographic material. There was also growing realisation that Britain was now too dependent on the Americans taking an interest in, and devoting resources to, areas that mattered solely to Britain. Lack of US Navy interest in the Indian Ocean meant many messages relating to it were never decrypted. Dissatisfaction with and suspicion towards OP-20-G was complicated by tensions between Kilindini and Bletchley, and between Admiral Somerville, who remained Commander-in-Chief Eastern Fleet until mid 1944, and the DNI, now Rushbrooke. Kilindini felt it had the best expertise on Japan, and resented being reduced to exploiting keys provided by OP-20-G or GC&CS. Somerville felt he was being denied intelligence, and that an ineffective operation in Bletchley was being expanded at Kilindini's expense.

Malcolm Burnett, who spent the last three months of 1942 working in OP-20-G, where he was well regarded, represented this Kilindini perspective. He judged, probably over-optimistically, that most problems would be solved with a proper British liaison section in OP-20-G, ideally headed by himself, in direct communication with Kilindini. Although, for geographical reasons, Kilindini might not make a contribution towards overseas collection comparable to Melbourne and Pearl Harbor, a British team in OP-20-G would ensure that what it could do was properly exploited. More important, it would spot and process intelligence relevant to Somerville's needs. In Burnett's view, the Japanese naval section at Bletchley (NSIJ), resurrected under Hugh Foss the previous March, was adding little value, and merely acted as a barrier to effective transaction of business. Burnett was too abrasive and forthright in pushing his case, overestimated what he could achieve in OP-20-G, and underestimated the problems in establishing effective and secure communications between Washington and Kilindini, when the Americans were adamant they would not share the electric cipher machine (ECM), used on their own overseas SIGINT circuit, with the British. Nevertheless, he was right about the current limitations of NSIJ, where contemporary witnesses working there confirm it contributed little before mid 1943. Bruce Keith, Foss's deputy, who took over from Harry Shaw as head of Kilindini in February, came to share Burnett's view.[2]

The picture was further complicated, and British access to intelligence further undermined, by the obstructive and unco-operative position adopted by the American Fleet Radio Unit Melbourne (FRUMEL), under Lieutenant Commander Rudi Fabian, which had evolved from the original Station Cast. As agreed at Holden, this had absorbed the Australian naval SIGINT section under Eric Nave. However, Fabian not only had a poisonous personal relationship with Nave but, for a while, proved a major thorn in the side of British-American SIGINT co-operation, indeed viewing all foreign partners through an optic of 'what's yours is mine and what's mine is mine alone'.[3] Another factor was the still-imperfect British understanding of how the US Navy SIGINT centres overseas at Pearl Harbor and FRUMEL interacted with OP-20-G and the major US Navy commands, and with ONI. Finally, although its impact on the naval SIGINT relationship was tangential, GC&CS relations with the US Army during the first half of 1943 were also fraught, primarily owing to arguments over control and access to non-naval Enigma. This led to Alan

Turing initially being barred from certain American facilities when he arrived on a visit in December.

It is not clear why Travis, Birch, and others in GC&CS did not better foresee the problems that would inevitably arise from ceding OP-20-G total control over Japan, or why they resisted establishing the liaison team advocated by Burnett. The liaison team could have been established without granting Kilindini direct access to OP-20-G, although on this point Burnett was not pressing for anything different from the precedents set by FECB and *Anderson*. Rushbrooke certainly struggled to explain the position to Somerville. However, by the spring of 1943, Birch and some others in GC&CS, reflecting pressure from the Admiralty and Somerville over the inadequacies of the post-Holden intelligence service, had to concede that if the Americans would not deliver, it might be necessary to build an independent Japanese capability, good enough to meet British needs without American help. The scale of effort required and the geographical isolation of Kilindini meant this was never a realistic proposition. With all its commitments in Europe, GC&CS lacked the capacity to support a two-hemisphere naval war on the same terms as OP-20-G. However, there was a concerted effort to build up capacity at both Bletchley and Kilindini through the summer. Fortunately, the summer also brought a gradual shift in American attitudes. This was probably owing to a combination of British lobbying at senior Admiralty and political level, as well as by GC&CS, growing recognition by OP-20-G that Kilindini, despite its limitations, could bring them value, the close relationship established on Enigma, and the prospect of the Kilindini operation transferring back to Colombo, a move that took place in September. Impetus from both the political leadership and the joint chiefs of staff for improved intelligence co-operation, which spurred the far-reaching UKUSA agreement between GC&CS and the US Army, probably also helped.[4]

The positive shift from OP-20-G led to a new extension agreement to Holden, when Rear Admiral Joseph Redman, Director of US Navy Communications, and Commander Joseph Wenger, the head of OP-20-G, visited Bletchley in July 1943. From the British perspective, this brought three important benefits. There was agreement on a substantial upgrade in communications between OP-20-G and GC&CS. From November, traffic passed between OP-20-G and BSC in New York over a Western Union landline teletype, and thence to GC&CS by both radio and landline. The Americans recognised that the new *Anderson* site at Colombo had an important SIGINT-collection role, in addition to acting as an intelligence distribution point. They accordingly agreed a direct exchange of recoveries and special intelligence between FRUMEL and Colombo when it reopened.

This promised to restore Colombo to the status and communications it had enjoyed between January and May 1942. Meanwhile, the atmosphere in FRUMEL, including relations between Australian and American personnel, improved noticeably over the summer when Fabian was replaced by Lieutenant Commander J S Holtwick. Finally, GC&CS would 'pay special attention' to machine ciphers, for which the Americans acknowledged British experience was especially suited. This led directly to the British work on Coral described earlier.[5]

Despite these positive developments, turning Colombo into an effective SIGINT centre proved demanding. When Holtwick visited in December, two months after the move from Kilindini, he judged that by the spring, Colombo would still only deliver a fraction of the operational intelligence required by Commander-in-Chief Eastern Fleet, and struggle to process traffic it was intercepting for at least six months. Although the Colombo team included some of the most capable SIGINT experts Holtwick had encountered anywhere, the operation was starved of both personnel and equipment. The one bright spot was the potential for collection. The sixty receivers currently in place intercepted a daily average of 1800 messages (almost double the Honolulu average at the start of 1943[6]) with another sixty on the way, and a further ten each for substations at Calcutta and the Cocos Islands, providing capacity to reach four thousand messages per day. However, the ability to process this take was a long way off.[7] Malcolm Saunders, the former head of 8G and Hut 3, who toured all the US Navy SIGINT centres in late 1943, and Burnett, now based at Colombo, were similarly realistic about the effort required. They believed Colombo had the potential to be as productive as the US Navy site at Honolulu, which Saunders judged an ideal model, within a year, and to provide the same quality of intelligence service to Commander-in-Chief Eastern Fleet as his American counterpart Commander-in-Chief Pacific received. But achieving this required a radical change of mindset, and to accord the Far East war the same priority as Europe.[8] The demands on *Anderson* would also expand hugely when Admiral Lord Louis Mountbatten, the Supreme Allied Commander for Southeast Asia appointed in autumn 1943, moved his headquarters to Kandy in Ceylon in mid 1944.

There was another important development for Far East intelligence in the summer of 1943. As noted earlier, Somerville had met and developed a high regard for Alan Hillgarth during the Spanish civil war. His respect for Hillgarth's talents as a political and intelligence operator were further strengthened while he commanded Force H from July 1940 until December 1941.[9] When in London in May 1943, he accordingly asked Rushbrooke if Hillgarth could be released from Madrid to become Chief of Intelligence Staff Eastern Fleet. Rushbrooke agreed and Hillgarth left Madrid in October for leave and briefings in London, before departing for Colombo in mid December.[10] More than anyone else, Hillgarth was now responsible for developing the intelligence organisation to support naval operations in the Eastern theatre for the rest of the war. In November 1944, following the creation of the British Pacific Fleet, he became Chief of British Naval Intelligence Eastern Theatre, acting as both Chief of Intelligence Staff East Indies Fleet and Chief of Intelligence Staff Pacific Fleet. Cunningham, as First Sea Lord, queried whether this was too large a task for one individual, but Rushbrooke insisted the appointment should stand.[11]

Hillgarth's arrival coincided with developments that drove a need for better intelligence, and raised the importance to the Allies, as well as the British, of Colombo as a potential SIGINT centre. In January 1944 Somerville received significant reinforcements, the battleships *Queen Elizabeth* and *Valiant*, the battlecruiser *Renown*, and carrier *Illustrious*, foreshadowing the deployment of the bulk of the Royal Navy's fighting strength to the Eastern theatre over the rest of the year. Somerville could now conduct offensive operations in the east Indian Ocean. The US Navy also now had a major asset able to strike north into the Netherlands East Indies, Rear Admiral Ralph Christie's thirty Southwest Pacific submarines, operating out of Fremantle in Western Australia, which in the first two months of the year sank 325,000 tons of Japanese shipping. (In August nine British submarines and one Dutch of the 8th Flotilla, together with their depot ship *Maidstone*, moved from Trincomalee to join Christie's command at Fremantle.[12]) While effective offensive operations required good intelligence, the most pressing requirement for both Somerville and Christie in early 1944 was the status and intentions of the major part of the remaining Japanese fleet, which Australian-generated SIGINT, initially from D/F and traffic analysis rather than decrypts, showed had relocated to Singapore in February. If this fleet sortied into the Indian Ocean, which the Americans thought the Japanese were contemplating, it would outmatch Somerville's reinforced Eastern Fleet, and could attack either Ceylon or Fremantle, although the air strength now deployed at the former would be a major deterrent. Somerville initially planned to move his fleet west to Port T in the Maldives, but by March, further SIGINT decrypts on IJN dispositions suggested there were no preparations consistent with an early operation, and that the move to Singapore was to keep the main fleet units out of reach of the Americans. Proximity to Sumatra oil supplies was a further factor.[13]

Anderson's SIGINT capability was crucial to supporting these offensive and defensive needs, and Colombo was also now the closest centre from which to monitor the primary IJN force for most of 1944. It was well placed, not only to collect traffic for decryption but, together with the outstations in the Bay of Bengal, for D/F and traffic analysis. This enhanced importance encouraged further agreements between GC&CS and OP-20-G, leading to communications upgrades, the most significant being the 1944 BRUSA Agreement, negotiated almost single-handedly by Harry Hinsley (still only just twenty-five years old) in January. This agreement did not give the British full access to the OP-20-G ECM circuit used for transmission of SIGINT material between centres, but created a parallel BRUSA circuit, using much of the ECM infrastructure, but with a different combined cipher machine (CCM). BRUSA had to overcome further political, capacity and technical constraints before it was fully effective, but as 1944 progressed, it enabled an ever closer, if never complete, exchange of intelligence and cryptographic material across an integrated circuit, comprising OP-20-G in Washington (NEGAT), GC&CS (SKOOL), Pearl Harbor (FRUPAC), Melbourne (FRUMEL) and Colombo (FRUEF). In late 1944 Radio Analysis Group Forward (RAGFOR) in Guam was added. As Saunders and Holtwick anticipated, staffing and equipping *Anderson* was a protracted process, but it reached a strength of 1280 by the end of 1944. By then, there were 550 staff working on Japan in Bletchley, primarily in NSIJ, so overall GC&CS was devoting about 25 per cent of its capacity to the Japanese target. The BRUSA agreement did not alter the OP-20-G primacy on Japan agreed at Holden. Over the final eighteen months of the war, OP-20-G continued directing and co-ordinating all Allied tasks, with GC&CS free to contribute suggestions, although the latter insisted that tasking of *Anderson* was normally done via Bletchley, rather than direct from Washington. Although Somerville continued a determined campaign for *Anderson* to have greater autonomy, with freedom to conduct its own relations with Washington, Bletchley, with full Admiralty support, was determined that *Anderson* should remain an outstation of GC&CS, not OP-20-G. *Anderson* also remained primarily a site focused on collection and intelligence processing and distribution, rather than cryptanalysis which, with rare exceptions, was centred on Bletchley.[14]

The arrangements for sharing Japanese naval SIGINT were a sobering lesson in the limits of British power. GC&CS felt it received a poor return for its generous sharing of European naval SIGINT, above all Enigma, and its early work on JN25, and resented being treated as a 'poor relation'. The American attitude was often selfish, and at times brutal. However, the underlying reality was that the British needed the US Navy in the Atlantic and Mediterranean, while, by contrast, the US Navy saw little need for British help in dealing with Japan, certainly in the primary Pacific theatre. For OP-20-G, in covering Japan between mid 1942 and early 1944 GC&CS was a supplicant and a burden. For the last eighteen months of the war, Britain had more to offer, but the balance remained profoundly unequal. The further east the Royal Navy deployed, the more it needed American SIGINT support, while the contribution GC&CS could offer in return was useful, not essential, although over time American perceptions of its value did increase. In March 1945 Redman, not noted for his pro-British stance, stated that *Anderson* had a definite and valuable role, providing contributions to both intelligence and cryptanalysis, although principally in the former. American refusal to share its ECM network frustrated GC&CS, but this was an inevitable consequence of the sheer imbalance in the intelligence contribution on Japan, and GC&CS was slow to appreciate the backwardness of British communications, and the extra burden imposed on the Americans in servicing British needs. Furthermore, while the Americans were sometimes harsh in their treatment, they could be extraordinarily generous, notably in their intelligence support to the British Pacific Fleet.[15]

Intelligence support for the British Pacific Fleet

For the Royal Navy in the Indian Ocean, most of 1944 was a work-up period for the steadily expanding Eastern Fleet. Between April and October, it executed eight increasingly ambitious carrier strikes on Southeast Asia targets, two accompanied by shore bombardments by battleships. At the beginning of this period, most ships involved lacked training and experience, had not operated together, and lacked awareness of the logistic challenges posed by the long-range operations they now faced. Few of the carrier staff or aircrew were either battle-hardened, or experienced in planning complex multi-carrier operations. By the end of the year, when the Eastern Fleet divided into the British Pacific Fleet, destined to join the Americans in the central theatre, and the East Indies Fleet, remaining in the Indian Ocean, it had become a highly professional force. Intelligence too had progressed. At the start of the period, SIGINT, primarily American-supplied, was the only significant source, apart from limited contributions from British and American submarine surveillance. The first offensive strikes in April and May – against oil facilities at Sabang, northeast of Sumatra, and the port of Surabaya in Java respectively – in which the American carrier *Saratoga* joined *Illustrious*, were conducted with minimal targeting intelligence, other than outdated information from Dutch naval sources. However, operating with *Saratoga* delivered crucial intelligence lessons which the British took to heart. One was the importance of instant debriefing of strike leaders and aircrew by trained intelligence officers following a raid. Another was the value of carrier-based PR aircraft. Delivery of detailed photographs from American Hellcats recording damage inflicted was an eye-opener to the British command. Somerville promptly asked for Fleet Air Arm Hellcats to be modified, and twelve duly arrived in September in 888 Squadron, aboard the escort carrier *Rajah*.[16]

The British Pacific Fleet (BPF) was officially formed in late November, and over the next two months, its core component, the 1st Aircraft Carrier Squadron, under Vice Admiral Sir Philip Vian, comprising the fleet carriers *Indomitable, Illustrious, Victorious* and *Indefatigable*, with nearly 250 aircraft, conducted four successive attacks on the Japanese oil refineries in Sumatra. Admiral Chester Nimitz, Commander-in-Chief of the US Navy Pacific Fleet, wanted Bruce Fraser, the new BPF commander, to target the refineries, because they were strategically significant, potentially capable of delivering 3 million tons of oil per year, and a significant part of Japan's supply, including 75 per cent of its aviation fuel, but also to confirm the BPF could operate on equal terms with the US Navy in the Pacific. The refineries at Pangkalan Brandan in northern Sumatra, and Palembang in the southeast, were complicated facilities spread over a wide area, difficult to approach and well-defended, especially Palembang, which could draw on air support from Singapore and Java. In August an attack on the Sumatra facilities by the new US Air Force B-29 heavy bombers based in China, but staging through Ceylon, did little damage. The carrier operations had similarities to Tungsten, which Fraser had overseen as Home Fleet commander, and in which *Victorious* had also participated, but the targets were more complex and the Royal Navy force larger.

Planning and execution of the successive attacks was thus a formidable test. As with the operations earlier in the year, there was no advance PR. Prior target intelligence depended on detailed briefing from Royal Dutch Shell and Standard oil personnel who had worked at the refineries pre-war, and on SIGINT for the location of fighters and anti-aircraft defences. American intelligence also emphasised the new threat the British task force could face from kamikaze attack. An additional source now available was the newly complete geographic handbook for the Netherlands East Indies from NID5, which helped in planning the air strike force approach route, and NID6 produced target maps. As with Tungsten, detailed models were constructed to aid target planning and briefing. The main intelligence shortcoming was failure to foresee the use of defensive barrage balloons, which hampered the first of the two Palembang strikes. Although, there was no advance PR, six of the newly arrived Hellcats of 888 PR Squadron were embarked for the first time in *Indomitable*, and conducted immediate and excellent post-strike surveys, but also reconnoitred and photographed suspected enemy airfields and other targets. The four attacks also developed and refined the capability of the 'Y' teams embarked in the carriers to conduct D/F and traffic analysis of enemy air activity. Overall, the second of the northern attacks, which reduced output at Pangkalan Brandon by one-third, and the two primary strikes at Palembang (Operations Meridian I and II), were highly successful. Combined production at Palembang was barely a third of potential at the end of May, more than four months after the attack, and was never restored before Japan's surrender. It was the BPF's greatest single contribution to the defeat of Japan, and ensured that employment of carrier forces to attack enemy economic infrastructure, and the requirement for intelligence to support this, would be an enduring theme of post-war British naval policy.[17]

The British desire to deploy a major fleet to the Pacific provoked controversy, both within the British war leadership and with the Americans. There was a compelling case, pressed by Churchill and Southeast Asia Command under Mountbatten, that Britain should concentrate on securing the Indian Ocean and the reconquest of Southeast Asia by advance through Burma and landings in Malaya. The counter-argument, advocated by the chiefs of staff, which Churchill ultimately accepted, was partly political, and partly strategic. To renew its defence obligations to Australia and New Zealand, and exert any influence over terms for ending the war with Japan, and the future of the Far East region, Britain must participate directly and substantially in the primary war theatre. However, the chiefs were also looking beyond the war to maintaining the strongest possible partnership with the United States, in order to secure Britain's long-term strategic position. There was also a more specific naval motive. To remain a serious naval power, the Royal Navy must master the full range of modern maritime warfare, including the projection of carrier power at long-range. Fraser interpreted his mission as joining with the US Navy 'in their most advanced operations against Japan'. His deputy, Vice Admiral Bernard Rawlings, expected 'the invaluable experience of participating in naval air operations on this grand scale will be of lasting benefit to the British navy'. The Royal Navy had, therefore, to demonstrate that it could work alongside the US Navy on equal terms in the most demanding environment. Churchill was not the only opponent to British participation. Admiral King fought tenaciously against it and, when forced to concede by President Roosevelt, insisted that British ships should expect no help from the Americans.[18]

King's attitude, and the long-standing problems Britain had experienced gaining adequate access to Japanese SIGINT, did not appear to bode well for the intelligence support the BPF required in the new theatre. However, the solution, agreed at a British-American intelligence conference at Nimitz's headquarters at Pearl Harbor between 19 and 21 December 1944, proved both logical and generous. Fraser separately agreed with Nimitz that the frontline component of the BPF would operate as a task force (Task Force 57) under Rawlings, within the US Fifth Fleet, commanded by Admiral Raymond Spruance. TF57 would be allocated specific tasks by Spruance, providing as much tactical independence as possible, within the overall strategic directive set by Nimitz, and with the approval of Fraser. Nimitz's intelligence staff initially proposed that Rawlings should receive the same intelligence material from the Joint Intelligence Centre Pacific Ocean Area (JICPOA) at Nimitz's headquarters as any equivalent American task force. This meant minimal access to Ultra material. However, Nimitz approved a more generous package. Rawlings would receive the Ultra-generated weekly intelligence summaries, giving the latest Japanese order of battle and deployment, together with Ultra-based mining charts. This would give Rawlings the same service as Spruance and other fleet commanders. Nimitz was not prepared to provide access to daily raw decrypts as shared on the OP-20-G network, not least because he correctly doubted the BPF had sufficient capacity to process them, but he assured Fraser that he took responsibility to ensure the BPF at sea received 'all the intelligence it required'. Furthermore, BPF headquarters in Sydney had access to Ultra through FRUMEL. This generosity from the top was all the more impressive, because it required significant extra work for the Americans in providing the BPF with the necessary encrypted communication systems and communication liaison teams to operate them, and a substantial backlog of historic intelligence material of all types. The primary task of Hillgarth's evolving intelligence organisation was now to ensure that the huge quantities of American intelligence which began arriving were passed efficiently to all units who needed it, and that they had the capacity to exploit it.[19]

The BPF intelligence headquarters was established in Sydney in January, with the intention that it would move closer to the front line in the spring. However, this idea was abandoned, posing considerable logistic challenges in distributing intelligence material to fleet units, given the vast distances involved, and JICPOA was asked to dispatch intelligence direct to the fleet instead of via Sydney. Commander L C S Sheppard, who had led the intelligence negotiations at Pearl Harbor, went there as liaison officer. Meanwhile, an OIC was now established at Sydney under Commander C S Holmes, which absorbed the PNIO at Delhi and, using NID8 as a model, comprised four main sections: a warship section to monitor IJN and Allied surface units; an enemy merchant ship section which generated targeting intelligence for Royal Navy submarines, primarily in the east Indian Ocean and Malay barrier area; a submarine section to plot enemy and Allied submarines across the whole Eastern theatre, and keep abreast of all anti-submarine intelligence; and finally, an air section to keep an air order of battle. Running in parallel was a Strategic Intelligence Centre (SIC), which performed similar functions to NID17 and NID12. Both sections made substantial use of Ultra, primarily the American summaries, to provide tailored appreciations for BPF commanders, but also drew on British-generated material from Colombo. BPF commanders were also sent some raw decrypts, if they were directly relevant to BPF operations, and also some exclusive political intelligence.[20]

Frontline BPF units were deployed continuously at sea for much longer than was normal for the Royal Navy in the Atlantic and Mediterranean. This, along with the distance from base support, posed problems for intelligence management. All ships, but especially flag units and carriers, had to carry more background information, and be more self-supporting in collecting and interpreting intelligence. Intelligence staff at sea therefore had to be considerably strengthened, not only to cope with the sheer quantity of material, but the specific demands of ship-borne 'Y' (D/F and traffic analysis, and R/T intercept directed at enemy air activity) and photographic interpretation to support targeting and damage assessment. They also had to meet rapid changes in operational priorities. Even during its first major operation (Iceberg I), supporting Fifth Fleet neutralisation of Japanese airbases in the Sakashima Gunto Islands, TF 57 was invited at short notice to switch to attacking airfields in northern Formosa. The British intelligence organisation initially struggled to cope with the new demands, and especially in finding sufficient trained personnel. Following Iceberg I, Vice Admiral Vian, commanding the carrier strike group under Rawlings, was particularly concerned by the lack of training and experience in his embarked 'Y' team, limitations in their equipment fit, and inadequate prior briefing on Japanese communications, although similar weaknesses in photographic interpretation were probably more pressing. The Americans generously loaned air intelligence officers, and the Australian air force and army, photographic interpreters, while more British staff were trained. However, British commanders and intelligence staff learnt fast, responded flexibly and effectively, if not always efficiently, to overcome such problems, and at no point during its five months of operations did the BPF fail to meet its tasking through failings in its intelligence system. The British contribution in the Pacific was not essential to the Americans, but it was valued and won their respect. This was important to the future intelligence relationship between the two navies. The British may have been largely dependent on American intelligence support, but they had proved in the attacks on the Sumatra oil facilities, and in the operations undertaken by the BPF that they could put it to good use.[21]

There were other specific British achievements against the IJN in 1945. The Royal Navy sank three of the six IJN heavy cruisers still operational on 1 January 1945: *Haguro* in a textbook destroyer attack in the Malacca Strait on 16 May; *Ashigara* by the submarine *Trenchant* in the Banka Strait on 8 June; and *Takao* by 'X'-craft attack in Singapore on 31 July. Prior intelligence contributed in different ways to these successes – a JN25 decrypt supported by subsequent submarine surveillance in the case of *Haguro*; an earlier American submarine sighting in the case of *Ashigara*; and PR over Singapore. The same day as the attack on *Takao*, the midget *XE-4* cut the Japanese telegraphic cables at Saigon linking it with Singapore and Hong Kong, an operation reminiscent of German U-boat cable-cutting in the First World War. This obliged the Japanese to revert to radio, making their traffic vulnerable to interception, although the ending of hostilities with the dropping of the A-bombs a week later meant there was no intelligence value. The *XE-4* attack proved the last act in Britain's intelligence war.[22]

The Second World War in retrospect

At the end of his magisterial study of the Second World War at sea, the official naval historian, Stephen Roskill, assessed overall Royal Navy performance.[23] This view appeared some years before his colleague Arthur Marder published his conclusions on the first great conflict of the twentieth century, which were described earlier. Roskill judged that whereas Britain had fought the earlier war deploying a continental strategy, in this later war, Britain reverted to its traditional concept of using maritime power to create the conditions necessary for the downfall of its enemies. His implication that Britain had used its strengths more effectively, and achieved its ends at less human cost, was an attractive argument for a naval historian, although he recognised that this maritime strategy was forced on Britain by its expulsion from the Continent. His argument had some merit. Britain did use maritime power to protect the United Kingdom and other key strategic points from invasion; to wear

Germany down by stretching its forces in the Mediterranean; to constrain its war potential by denying it Middle East oil; to deliver supplies to help keep Russia in the war; and to mobilise the war resources of the wider empire. But there were closer parallels with the earlier war than Roskill acknowledged. In 1914–18 British maritime power had still been essential to success through ensuring delivery of overseas supplies to the Allies and denying them to Germany, with the blockade ultimately a vital accompaniment to the Western Front. Nor could Britain escape a major land commitment in 1944. Blockade was less effective against Germany in the second war, but Britain pursued the economic warfare long favoured by the Admiralty through area bombing instead, expending huge resources here, and incurring a proportionate casualty rate to aircrew far higher than at the Somme. Furthermore, judgements over strategy demand recognition that in both wars Britain operated as part of an alliance which constrained its choices. In the second war, by autumn 1942 it was becoming the junior partner to the United States, and its relative naval power was fast declining.

Roskill, as a former Royal Navy officer with war service in the Admiralty, knew more about the role of intelligence in writing his history than did Marder, but was permitted little reference to it, and certainly not to Ultra. The omission of much intelligence detail in his account seems less important now than it did for at least thirty years after the existence of Ultra was revealed to the public in 1974. For if the role of British naval intelligence in the First World War has been underestimated, in some respects its impact from 1939–45 has been overestimated. By the end of 1914, British naval intelligence gained decisive information advantage over Germany, which it never lost during the next four years. By contrast, it brought negligible benefit in the naval war against Germany for eighteen months from 3 September 1939, and only fleeting advantage against Italy when she entered the war in June 1940. Indeed, it was Germany and Italy who both held an intelligence edge in this period, although neither had the maritime resources to exploit it effectively against the stronger Royal Navy. That does not mean there were no British achievements. During this time, British capability in SIGINT, PR, POW interrogation, and topography made enormous strides in collection, assessment, and secure distribution to operational users. These were tri-service capabilities, but the Admiralty played a major role in driving each of them forward, and with the OIC it had the organisation best equipped to apply and integrate their intelligence outputs to operational advantage. By mid 1941, therefore, there was a system and structure to meet naval intelligence requirements at every level of war, from strategic to tactical, and potentially on a mass scale. Over the next year, the United States replicated much of this organisation, albeit with far greater resources. Meanwhile, German and Italian capabilities and organisation failed to develop.

This evolving British naval intelligence system played some part in almost every British success at sea, beginning with Taranto at the end of 1940. It provided crucial indicators of enemy intent at Matapan, against PQ 17, and for the last sortie of *Scharnhorst*, or revealed opportunities, such as the targeting of *Lützow* in mid 1941, or mining the route of the German battlecruisers during their dash through the Channel. Such indicators were usually fragmentary rather than comprehensive but, in general, the British system, with the OIC at its heart, provided commanders with a better operational picture than that available to their enemies. The single most important and enduring contributor was the stream of Ultra decrypts, acquired through intercepting the communications of all three Axis powers, beginning with the decisive break into Dolphin Enigma in May 1941, although PR ran Ultra a close second. Delays in processing, gaps in coverage, and enemy SIGINT successes meant that, as during the previous war, Ultra was more useful at the strategic and operational level than the tactical. It was invaluable, especially when combined with timely PR, to building and maintaining a picture of enemy naval and maritime air strength and deployment, and identifying likely enemy objectives. It was a force multiplier, enabling Britain, then the Allies to apply their forces to counter threats and exploit opportunities with more assurance and precision.

Ultra was less critical to the Atlantic U-boat war than traditional accounts claim. During the peak period from mid 1940 to mid 1943, it was only available for 40 per cent of the time. The battle was ultimately decided more by relative economic resources, logistics, comparative advantage in technology, including ship-borne sensors, than shore-based SIGINT, where for long periods the balance was surprisingly even. The initial U-boat advantage in night surface attack was overcome by radar, escort numbers, and later HF/DF. U-boat numbers and, until the very end of the war, improvements in their fighting capability always lagged behind the Allies, and the snort-equipped Type VIIs of 1944 could not adequately counter Allied air power. The specific contribution of Ultra from Dolphin Enigma to saving shipping in the second half of 1941 is overstated. Although it helped facilitate convoy evasion, it was most valuable in building understanding of the wolf-pack control system, and the potential of ship-borne HF/DF to counter it. The parallel break into the Italian Hagelin system, which receives less attention, was probably more important in transforming Britain's prospects in 1941. By enabling the Royal Navy to cut Axis supply lines, it not only stabilised Britain's position in North Africa, but forced Germany to divert substantial air and U-boat resources to the Mediterranean, with negative consequences for its effort in the Atlantic and Russia, a compelling example where Roskill's maritime strategy achieved decisive effect. Yet even here, as the first months of 1942 demonstrated, good intelligence was no use without the operational forces to exploit it.[24]

Ironically, British naval intelligence gained its greatest strategic edge, certainly in the Atlantic and Mediterranean, but even potentially in the Far East, at the end of 1941, just when American entry into the war, with the promise of its vast resources made its contribution less critical. Furthermore, for much of 1942 the U-boat shift to Shark, the sharp decline in SIGINT coverage in the East following the Japanese advances, and improved B-Dienst coverage reduced the intelligence advantage, while naval losses in the Mediterranean and Eastern theatres made it harder to exploit intelligence effectively. Thereafter, intelligence helped the Allies deploy their naval forces more efficiently, but the progress of the naval war in all theatres was increasingly determined by the sheer preponderance of Allied, and primarily American, naval resources. Britain was also increasingly dependent on the United States for much of the most important naval Ultra production. As noted previously, the single area where intelligence early warning was most important, the development of the new U-boats, was where it was weakest.

Despite the qualifications above, the overall contribution of intelligence to Britain's war at sea was still outstanding. The scale and diversity of outputs delivered by SIGINT and PR in 1945, compared to the limited capabilities of 1939, represented an extraordinary achievement. So was their integration with intelligence from other sources through the OIC and the JIC system to deliver a service to commanders at sea, which was not matched in its entirety by any other country, even the United States, which suffered from far greater inter-service rivalry. Much of the organisation which achieved this was John Godfrey's creation, even if he received limited recognition outside NID. By 1945, there were perhaps fifteen thousand people working on naval requirements across the wider intelligence community, about three times the number at the end of the previous war. The SIGINT and imagery operations that naval needs had driven forward had each become large complex industries. The DNI, his counterparts in the other services, and the civilian agency heads now had to adapt their community to the demands of a new world order.

Commander Ian Fleming in 1942. Recruited by Godfrey as his personal assistant in May 1939, he retained the position under Edmund Rushbrooke. He was thus at the centre of naval intelligence policy, planning and organisation, and a key player in the wider Whitehall intelligence community throughout the war. He later used this experience to create the fictional James Bond. (*Official Royal Navy photograph*)

Frank Birch, another of Ewing's King's recruits, who reached Room 40 in late 1915 following service in the Royal Navy Volunteer Reserve, including the Dardanelles. After a distinguished contribution to Room 40 and helping to write its classified post-war history, he pursued his enduring passion for theatrical comedy. In 1939 Denniston and Knox coaxed him back to Bletchley Park,

where he took over the tiny residual naval section with the tricky task of directing the brilliant but unpredictable Alan Turing (also from King's). After writing the official history of British SIGINT up to 1945, he returned to the theatre. Here he is acting with Sid James in the 1953 film comedy *Will Any Gentleman*. (*Courtesy Bletchley Park magazine, issue no 4*)

Mavis Lever (later Batey), recruited to Bletchley Park in 1940 at the age of nineteen while studying German at University College London. She joined Dilly Knox's team and made a key contribution to the breaking of Italian navy Enigma, providing crucial intelligence which led to the Royal Navy victory at the Battle of Matapan in March 1941. (*Public domain*)

Hugh Foss, one of the first direct entry recruits to GC&CS in the early 1920s. A key player in early work on Enigma, he broke the first complete day of naval traffic using purely cryptographic methods in November 1940. Earlier, in 1934, he had broken the first machine cipher introduced by the Japanese for their naval attachés and had a key role in breaking the more advanced Coral system in 1943–44. (*Public domain*)

John Tiltman, the former Indian Army officer who was at the cutting edge of cryptography, first for the British and later the Americans, for almost sixty years. He made the first crucial breaks into the new JN25 code introduced by the Imperial Japanese Navy in 1939 and played a critical part in initiating the wartime British-American SIGINT relationship that then evolved into UKUSA in 1946. (*Public domain*)

Room 39 wartime morning meeting. An impression drawn by Godfrey's private secretary, Ted Merrett, in 1945. Godfrey is the tall figure silhouetted on the right. (*Donald McLachlan collection*)

Commander Rodger Winn, a barrister in civilian life and later a distinguished judge, who was the presiding genius of the OIC submarine tracking room from 1941–45. (*Donald McLachlan collection*)

Captain Alan Hillgarth, the adventurer, novelist and consul in Majorca during the Spanish civil war, despatched by Godfrey to be naval attaché in Madrid in the summer of 1939. For the next four years, he supervised all British intelligence operations in Spain to great effect, before moving to become Chief of Intelligence Staff in the Far East theatre at the end of 1943. (*Courtesy Hillgarth family*)

By 1942, aerial photography was a crucial naval intelligence source. This picture, probably taken by a PRU Spitfire, shows the German battlecruiser *Scharnhorst* (white arrow bottom right) under repair at Kiel in June 1942 following her escape through the Channel. (*United States Naval History and Heritage Command, NH 97506*)

Intelligence success: the sinking of *Scharnhorst* in the Barents Sea, 26 December 1943. Painting by Charles Pears. (© *National Maritime Museum, Greenwich, London, presented by the War Artists Advisory Committee, 1947*)

Rear Admiral Edmund Rushbrooke, who succeeded Godfrey as DNI in November 1942 and held the post until July 1946. With him is Joyce Cameron, secretary to DNI throughout the war. (*Donald McLachlan collection*)

Vice Admiral Katsuo Abe visiting Bergen in January 1944, in the company of the German Commander-in-Chief Western Norway, Admiral Otto von Schrader. Abe unwittingly became one of the best Allied intelligence sources in the last eighteen months of the war, through the interception of his Coral communications system. (*Suddeutsch Zeitung archives*)

From left to right, Harry Hinsley, Edward Travis and John Tiltman in Washington for UKUSA talks, November 1945. (*The National Archives*)

Rear Admiral Norman Denning on his appointment as the last DNI in 1958. As a commander, he oversaw the development of the OIC under the direction of William James from mid 1937 and directed the enemy surface operations plot throughout the war. (*Admiralty photograph*)

HMS *Courageous*, the first SSN specifically committed to special intelligence collection, from her completion in late 1971. (*MOD photograph*)

United States National Reconnaissance Organisation KH-7 Gambit satellite photograph of the Moscow anti-ballistic missile system under development in June 1967. Key: A – transmitter complex; B – woodland cleared in front of northwest phased array; C – receiver complex; D – support area. This is representative of the intelligence which persuaded British ministers to begin contemplating an upgrade to the Polaris system. (*Imagery released to the United States Geographical Survey and research by Martin J F Fowler*)

The British Chevaline package fitted to its Polaris missiles in order to penetrate the Moscow ABM system. Visible are the two hardened re-entry bodies each containing a slightly larger warhead than the three 200-kiloton warheads fitted in the original British front end. One of the re-entry bodies is mounted in a penetration aid carrier, effectively a mini-spacecraft containing multiple decoys to confuse the ABM radar system. (*Reproduced from AWE archive photograph*)

Soviet Delta III-class SSBN photographed in northern waters in 1982. The introduction of the Delta class, with their long-range missiles capable of launch from under the ice, helped trigger a shift in Soviet maritime strategy in the early 1980s. (*Alamy*)

PART V

The Cold War: Leveraging Strategic Advantage

32

1945–1960: Mixed Results in the
Early Cold War

Post-war restructuring of the intelligence community

By the end of 1944, even though the end of the war with Japan, if not
Germany, was judged still a year away, the British intelligence community
had given much thought to post-war intelligence needs. The vehicle for
examining this future was the JIC. This reflected the steady rise in its
status across five years of war. Formally, it remained a subcommittee of
the chiefs of staff, but under the strong, Foreign Office chairmanship of
William Cavendish-Bentinck, it had achieved increasing independence,
moving from a relatively obscure and distrusted position in 1939, to one of
influence and respect extending well beyond the military sphere. Its readers
now ranged across Whitehall from the prime minister downward, and
included key overseas embassies, as well as military commands. SIS, MI5
and MEW were established members, alongside the three service directors
of intelligence, and there was a dedicated JIC staff to draft assessments.
During the war the JIC held 391 meetings, produced 729 assessments,
most over five pages long, 5295 secretariat minutes, and numerous daily
and weekly intelligence summaries. Torch had demonstrated its ability to
provide the comprehensive intelligence picture, created from all available
sources, which was essential to effective joint operations. Its subsequent
contributions to the landings in Italy, the threat from novel German
weapons and, above all, to Overlord had entrenched its centrality and
importance. However, it was now not only responsible for 'co-ordinating
the product of the various collectors of intelligence' into 'agreed advice on
enemy intentions'. It was also responsible for 'watching, directing and to
some extent controlling the British intelligence organisation throughout
the world', to ensure that intelligence delivery was economical 'in time,

effort and manpower', without 'overlapping'. It directly supervised the work of several inter-service intelligence organisations, notably the CIU, CSDIC, ISTD, the Intelligence Section (Operations) (IS(O)), and the Inter-Service Security Board (ISSB).[1]

In developing its post-war proposals, the JIC reflected a consensus across the defence and security community that the prospect of sharp reductions in the armed services made it essential to maintain a strong intelligence capability. Intelligence was not a substitute for military strength, and did not alone win battles, but it provided warning in an uncertain world and, if absent or faulty, battles might easily be lost. Drastic cuts, which were perceived to have crippled intelligence in the interwar period, should not, therefore, be repeated. Rushbrooke, as DNI, believed the war had shown that a good intelligence organisation combined continuity and long-term study with ability to respond flexibly to unforeseen events.[2] However, the JIC was also clear that the wartime organisation was not a suitable model for peacetime. It was 'largely improvised', 'complicated and uneconomical', with too much duplication. With support from the chiefs of staff and the Cabinet Secretary, Sir Edward Bridges, the JIC established three key principles: that Britain's future intelligence community must be centrally directed; that its collecting agencies must cover the world; and that collating and assessment staff should work on an inter-service basis. These principles drove key organisational developments over the period 1944–48 that shaped the future structure of the intelligence community, and set the new context for naval intelligence within it.

The first and most important development, an initiative driven forward by Cavendish-Bentinck with considerable help from Ian Fleming, was the creation of a Joint Intelligence Bureau (JIB), which commenced work in August 1945 under Major General Sir Kenneth Strong, former intelligence chief to the Supreme Allied Commander, General Dwight Eisenhower. The JIB's primary role was to focus on 'economic intelligence for defence purposes', including the trade, raw materials, fuel, power, industrial production and shipbuilding of potential enemies. It was also responsible for logistic and topographical intelligence, including ports, airfields, static defence systems and telecommunications, and for collating intelligence from open sources. It therefore absorbed and preserved most of the functions of the wartime MEW, ISTD, IS(O), elements of the CIU, and even parts of the ISSB brief. The pre-war IIC was clearly part of its heritage, as were the early ideas for integrating armed service intelligence, first suggested by Sir Alfred Mond in 1922. The JIC was clear that a key theme guiding the JIB's work should be the effective exploitation of open-source intelligence (OSINT). This reflected the pre-war experience of the

IIC in obtaining valuable insights from German publications, but also the successful public trawl for personal photographs undertaken during the war. Emphasising OSINT demonstrated that the JIC understood the importance of exploiting all possible sources for national intelligence, and that secrecy did not necessarily match importance. The JIB was also significant in marking the start of a journey which would end with the full integration of the armed service intelligence agencies twenty years later.[3]

These JIC developments were accompanied by a pre-emptive strike by the Foreign Office permanent secretary, Sir Alexander Cadogan, to settle the post-war status of SIS, SOE and GC&CS. In October 1943 he commissioned a report from Sir Nevile Bland, ambassador to the Dutch government in exile. Bland, working closely with Cavendish-Bentinck, argued that human intelligence would become more important in the post-war world, and that SIS was the cheapest form of insurance in peacetime against defeat in war. However, to be effective, it must be focused on the right priorities, and staffed with talented people, given credible official or business cover from which to operate. He also insisted there should be no return to the starvation funding of the interwar years. Crucially, he recommended that both SIS and GC&CS remained under the direct supervision of the Foreign Secretary, that no other secret organisation should operate abroad unless under SIS direction, and that the wartime practice of seconding a senior Foreign Office official to liaise with 'C' and ensure accountability should continue. This report was a powerful endorsement of SIS's value and set the template for its post-war status. It reasserted the principle of Foreign Office political control, ensuring that, despite the demands of wartime, it would not become an agency solely dedicated to defence requirements. By insisting on Foreign Office supervision of intelligence operations overseas, and an SIS monopoly in executing them, it also ensured that SOE would merge into SIS, a move forcefully backed by Cavendish-Bentinck, and that the independent wartime intelligence initiatives, exemplified by Hillgarth in Spain, and Denham in Sweden would cease. Any secret agents meeting naval requirements would now be handled exclusively by SIS.[4]

Meanwhile, senior figures in GC&CS, notably Gordon Welchman, Harry Hinsley, Hugh Foss and Edward Crankshaw, the latter responsible for wartime relations with the Soviet Union, were ambitious for the future of SIGINT, which they saw as the crowning glory of British intelligence in the war. In size and complexity, GC&CS certainly dwarfed the other agencies, with 8902 core staff at the end of the war, a far cry from the 200 who gathered at Bletchley in September 1939. In a surprise reappearance, William Clarke, of Jutland fame, was put in charge of post-war planning in January 1945, and saw the key challenge as ensuring that SIGINT did not revert to the essentially diplomatic focus which had dominated from 1919 until well into the 1930s. Despite the internal ambitions, the crucial decision regarding GC&CS's future was again implemented by Cavendish-Bentinck who got the JIC, the chiefs of staff, and Foreign Secretary to agree that, while remaining under the overall direction of 'C', it should be a separate organisation, distinct from SIS, with its own budget from the secret vote. By VJ-Day, Edward Travis was free to negotiate GC&CS's future directly with the Treasury. There was no specific date marking either the formal separation from SIS, or the adoption of a new name, Government Communications Headquarters (GCHQ), which had been used as an occasional cover name for GC&CS since the late 1930s, but had largely taken over by the end of 1946. 'C's continuing 'direction' was exercised through his chairmanship of the London Signals Intelligence Board, the successor to the 'Y' Committee, which agreed SIGINT strategic tasking, and negotiated the contribution to collection from the armed services and by handling relations with the Foreign Secretary over political oversight. In practice, from 1945 the JIC increasingly defined the new GCHQ's tasking, while Travis and his successor gained direct access to the Foreign Secretary. However the last vestige of SIS oversight only ceased in 1956 when the incoming 'C', Dick White, relinquished his role on the London Signals Board to the Director of GCHQ, Eric Jones. Although Travis had to accept dramatic staff reductions, down to 1010 by 1946, he insisted that preserving and fostering quality was more important than quantity, and that he had negotiated a good deal with the Treasury. He was also clear his top priority was enhancing coverage of the Soviet Union.[5]

The post-war status of SIS and GCHQ was important to the future of naval intelligence because they were the primary national collectors of secret intelligence, but also because NID and Royal Navy warships would support both agencies in accessing naval targets. This support was occasional and modest for SIS, but frequent and critically important for GCHQ. Furthermore, both agencies were fundamental to fostering an effective post-war relationship with the American intelligence agencies, and leveraging the vastly greater American collection capability through the coming Cold War. This post-war British-American intelligence relationship took time to settle down, not least because the American community took longer to reorganise than did the British. Bill Donovan's OSS, broadly analogous to a combination of SIS and SOE, was wound up in late 1945, and its capabilities dispersed mainly to the War Department. Two years later, it was substantially recreated as the Central Intelligence

Agency (CIA). From its origins, CIA was not only much larger but had a far more wide-ranging role than SIS. Like SIS, it collected secret intelligence from human sources overseas and conducted covert operations, albeit on a much larger scale. Unlike SIS, it also had an assessment and analytical wing, which not only evaluated its own material, but produced integrated national intelligence assessments, analogous to those of the JIC. Finally, it had a substantial operation focused on strategic technical collection. It therefore overlapped significantly with areas that in Britain fell to the JIC, the new JIB, and the service intelligence directorates, including covert PR operations undertaken by the RAF. In the specific area of naval intelligence, during the first part of the Cold War there was a broad division of labour between CIA and the US Navy ONI over analysis and assessment. CIA focused on technical analysis of naval weapon systems and naval shipbuilding. By contrast, intelligence research on Soviet naval operations was conducted almost exclusively by ONI.[6]

British-American SIGINT collaboration had made a huge contribution to British naval intelligence requirements during the war, and it would continue to do so as attention turned to potential new threats, especially from Russia. The framework for post-war collaboration was negotiated at the beginning of 1946, and incorporated in a new BRUSA agreement signed in Washington on 5 March 1946. The initial priorities and their implementation, including procedures to ensure the security of SIGINT collection and distribution, were then worked out at a subsequent inaugural conference in London between 11 and 27 March. The agreement was formally between the London Signals Intelligence Board (LSIB) on the British side, chaired by Stewart Menzies as 'C', and the State–Army–Navy Communication Intelligence Board (STANCIB), led by Brigadier General W P Corderman, on the American side. Given the awkward politics, tensions, frequent distrust and growing aggressive American assertiveness that had often characterised the wartime relationship, the scope of this agreement, and the speed with which it was concluded, was remarkable. It was also notable for bringing not just the US Army and US Navy together to the same table, but the State Department as well. The headline wartime agreements had all been reached on a single-service basis.[7]

Given that Britain and the United States were now neither at war, nor formally yet committed to any alliance against common enemies, the depth and range of collaboration agreed during the London conference, with many familiar figures to the fore, including Travis, Tiltman, Hastings and Hinsley representing GCHQ, and Joseph Wenger leading for the US Navy, was striking. Furthermore, both the agreement and subsequent discussions reflected greater equality between the parties than was evident in the last period of the war. This was because Britain brought some powerful cards to the table. It could exploit its close intelligence partnerships with the Dominions, who were not participants in the agreement, but were not to be treated as 'third parties', either. These relationships, Britain's global network of military bases, and her own proximity to the main potential enemy meant she offered significant resources and geographic assets. The new GCHQ's expertise in machine ciphers was also valued by the Americans, and they recognised that Britain was ahead in the exploitation of the important new field of electronic intelligence (ELINT), the study of electronic emissions not used for communication, such as radar. Britain would gain leverage from a further advantage over the next ten to fifteen years, an often greater political willingness to accept risk in executing covert intelligence collection. The UKUSA relationship would constantly evolve over the rest of the century, with important early updates in 1948, 1951 and 1956, the latter to recognise the fusing of the American SIGINT effort into a new single agency, the National Security Agency (NSA), but 1946 established an unprecedented intelligence partnership for both sides.[8]

First assessments of the Soviet naval threat

The JIC took its first comprehensive look at Russia's post-war intentions in December 1944. It expected Russian policy to be dominated by the requirement for maximum security from new threats. Russia would be prepared to collaborate with Britain and the United States if they recognised her security needs, including the requirement for a strategic buffer zone under her influence in Eastern Europe, and the JIC did not, therefore, anticipate an aggressive policy of territorial expansion in the short term. However, if Russia judged collaboration was failing, she would be tempted to push further into Europe, stir up trouble in the Middle East and India and, if war seemed imminent, contemplate a pre-emptive strike at Middle East oil. Looking specifically at Russia's post-war naval policy, the JIC expected her to resume the ambitions for an oceangoing navy, which had been abandoned in 1941, with her primary fleet located in northern waters, and defensive forces, composed of lighter craft and submarines, in the Baltic, Black Sea and Far East, but backed by strong, land-based air forces.[9] In its next major assessment, fifteen months later, the JIC saw some hardening of Russian attitudes and greater determination to create a zone of 'satellite states' subservient to her interests in Eastern Europe, and to extend her influence over Turkey and Iran. There were also growing points of tension with the Western powers. However, although she would pursue her security interests determinedly, the JIC did not expect Russia to seek or, indeed, risk direct military confrontation.[10]

This March 1946 assessment reaffirmed Russia's intent to build a large modern navy and mercantile marine, commensurate with her status as a first-class power. Primary motives were security, ensuring control of her Arctic waters, the eastern Baltic, Black Sea and her Pacific coast, but also desire to use sea power to promote her global influence. The reconstruction of an oceangoing navy after the heavy war losses would be a difficult task, especially in producing heavy ships, where experience was limited. Nevertheless, Russia had 210 submarines, including ten ex-German, and was more proficient in this sphere than any other, if still inexperienced in attack tactics. She had demonstrated the ability to execute a rapid submarine-building programme, and German experience with prefabricated methods could give her a formidable force in a comparatively short period.[11]

NID produced a more comprehensive, and more downbeat assessment of the Russian navy that October, which was extensively reviewed by the naval staff over the next year. The most formidable units in the surface fleet were the six modern cruisers armed with 7.1in guns, and there were about thirty modern destroyers. NID judged that neither this surface force, nor the small naval air force, posed much threat to the British or American navies. However, as had the JIC, it emphasised the strength of the submarine force with its 200 boats. The Russians had an excellent oceangoing boat in the 1700-ton 'K' class, an efficient medium boat, the *Schtchuka* class, roughly equivalent to the German Type VII, and a less effective 'M'-class coastal boat. They were known to have acquired several intact Type XXI and Type XXIII German boats, along with several Type VIIBs and Cs. They had probably acquired most plans for all the new German boats, including the Walter HTP-powered Type XXVI. However, NID did not believe they could reproduce a German boat, or a new class of their own suitable for large-scale production, before 1949. Furthermore, damage to key shipyards would probably rule out any significant new output of existing types before then, either. This assessment of future building prospects proved accurate. The only submarines completed before 1950 were six 'K' class, trapped in Leningrad during the war in an incomplete state. The first submarines of post-war design, designated by the North Atlantic Treaty Organisation (NATO) as the Zulu and Whiskey classes, did not arrive until 1951.

Drawing on its observations during the Arctic convoy operations, NID was also dismissive of the current fighting capability of the existing Russian submarine force. They lacked modern fire-control systems, and their tactics were amateurish. Unless evasive tactics had improved in the last year, they would have little chance against Royal Navy escort groups. NID acknowledged the Russians would, no doubt, benefit from captured German equipment, and be able to exploit German knowledge and experience more generally, but this would take time. They would need considerable training before becoming a serious threat to British trade. In addition to benefiting from German equipment and experience, the Russians had received wide exposure to British and American naval capabilities during the war. They had been supplied with most ASDIC and radar sets, although not the most modern, Hedgehog and Foxer. They had also had a comprehensive view of British convoy tactics, although it was doubtful they had the skills to apply this independently. Russian naval air capability, essentially an arm of the Red Army air force, was assessed as primitive. They had little experience of maritime search, anti-submarine work, convoy escort, or co-operation with surface forces. Overall, NID judged the Russians well below the standard of the British and American navies. In a war, their surface ships would probably be confined to coastal support of the Red Army. Their submarine force would undoubtedly operate against Western shipping, using German techniques practised in the late war, but less efficiently.[12]

Although the naval staff accepted this NID assessment, they assumed their Russian counterparts would judge a submarine attack on seaborne trade as their most effective option in a maritime war with the Western powers. Their submarine strength and capability would improve, and might overtake British capacity to provide effective convoy defence. It was necessary, therefore, to consider 'offensive measures' to contain or reduce the threat, including attacks on submarine bases, communication facilities and production centres. The development of 'weapons of mass destruction' offered potential for such attacks at source, since sufficient conventional air power might not be available. However, offensive mining and deploying submarines to blockade enemy bases should also be examined.[13]

By mid 1948, the prospects of a collaborative relationship with the Soviet Union were fast evaporating. The aggressive assertion of control over Eastern Europe and apparent intent to extend this to Greece, Turkey and Iran, disregard for agreements reached at Yalta and Potsdam, and the blockade of Berlin commenced in July that year translated the British-American assessment of the Soviet Union from difficult partner to immediate potential enemy. The Cold War was underway and for the next forty years, with rare exceptions, British naval policy, planning and intelligence was focused on the Soviet threat. By spring 1949, naval planners made four basic assumptions: Russia was the only credible maritime enemy for the foreseeable future; war with Russia would only be undertaken in alliance with the United States; British capability would be severely constrained by economic factors; and the primary naval tasks were the defence of sea communications, the United Kingdom homeland, and the Middle East.

During 1948–49, NID reviewed its assessment of the Soviet navy which, together with initial contributions from the JIB, underpinned the judgements of the JIC. In a wide-ranging study of Soviet economic and industrial potential in September 1948, the JIB stated that all available evidence suggested the Soviet navy intended to focus on building submarines and fast surface vessels, no larger than light cruisers. NID agreed that the primary threat came from the submarine force, and the following summer it estimated there were about 160 oceangoing boats, a figure 25 per cent higher than it calculated in 1946. This compared with the German strength of twenty-six ocean-capable boats in 1939, and therefore provided 'tremendous capability'. By contrast, the surface fleet remained small, with little evidence of new construction, and none suggesting units larger than cruisers. There were, however, signs that reconstruction of shipyards was proceeding rapidly. The following year, NID thought the professional efficiency of the Soviet navy was rising steadily, with considerable effort focused on developing modern, high-speed submarines, with plans for mass production. Oceangoing submarine numbers had now risen to 181, with capacity to produce fifty per year.[14]

Early Cold War intelligence-collection capabilities

To validate these early post-war assessments, and to monitor the development and expansion of the Soviet fleet, NID depended on limited overt information, insights from the Moscow-based British, American and neutral naval attachés, the interrogation of returning German POWs and deportees who had been held by the Russians, some of whom became SIS agents, some SIGINT, and contributions from covert aerial photographic reconnaissance. Although the access of the attachés was strictly controlled, and Soviet security tight, as with Japan in the late 1930s, much valuable intelligence could be gleaned from observation during authorised visits to bases such as Leningrad, from pooling information between colleagues, and even from official minders.

Following the German surrender and the division of Germany into Allied zones of occupation, British intelligence-collection in Germany became a vast industry, as it did for the other occupying powers. The British Control Commission, which administered the British occupation zone until the Federal Republic of Germany was established in 1949, rapidly established an Intelligence Division jointly staffed from the three service intelligence directorates, the JIB and SIS. It soon had branches dedicated to security and counter-intelligence, political and military collection, scientific and technical intelligence and analysis. From the naval perspective, effort initially focused on collecting everything possible on Germany's wartime projects, building on the work of 30AU. However, the priority steadily shifted to exploiting the opportunities Germany offered to collect on the Soviet Union. The period 1945–55 has aptly been called 'the years of the Germans'.

During this decade, the Intelligence Division screened up to 400,000 returning German POWs, and interrogated a high proportion. In 1949 NID judged this POW intelligence of 'great value'. Intelligence Division also ran a programme, Dragon Return, to identify German scientists, technicians and engineers deported to the Soviet Union from 1945, who were subsequently allowed to return to the Soviet zone, later the German Democratic Republic, and to entice them to West Germany with attractive settlement packages, including job offers. One 'Dragon-returner' provided valuable insights into Soviet inquiries into acoustic torpedo technology. The Soviets left a few former defence research centres, including some working on naval requirements in their zone, rather than moving them east, leaving them vulnerable to British targeting. A parallel British operation, called Matchbox, attempted to deprive the Russians of Germans in their zone who might enhance their defence technology capability, by luring them to the West. The Admiralty sponsored the transfer of the whole technical department of the Dresden-based company Brückner-Kanis, which specialised in the high-speed turbines relevant to novel U-boats and torpedoes. Automated machine tools were another target for removal. POW and Dragon-return intelligence was a key source on Soviet defence research and technology well into the 1950s. It provided a good overview, both of Soviet research lines during the war, and also the areas of German technology they judged to have most value for the future. Britain thus gained valuable insights into Soviet programmes relating to the nuclear, missile, aircraft, radar and chemical weapon fields. The German sources also provided much background information, which helped COMINT and ELINT targeting, and future aerial photography programmes. The overall contribution to specific naval requirements is hard to establish, but it probably provided a good overview of the status of most naval bases and dockyards, and some details of specific warship and weapon characteristics and capabilities.[15]

The scale and extent of British aerial intelligence collection in the late 1940s and early 1950s is also difficult to quantify. Under UKUSA, British and American 'ferret' aircraft collected SIGINT, both COMINT and ELINT, along the periphery of the Soviet Union, with the British initially leading the way on ELINT. The ferrets, with all British flights subject to close political control, deliberately tried to provoke radio chatter for collection, and radar coverage to illuminate so that it could be mapped. From the mid 1950s, they also intercepted telemetry from Soviet missile tests. These aerial SIGINT operations included naval targets in the Barents Sea and Kola area, Baltic, Black Sea, Caspian and Far East. Northern waters got primary attention in the second half of the decade with British Washington, Canberra and Comet aircraft flying out of Norway, and ranging as far as Novaya Zemlya, which had become the main Soviet nuclear test site. British flights caused the Norwegians some anxiety, since they judged the pilots took unnecessary risks in flying directly towards the Soviet coast to test radar reaction.[16] In parallel to this UKUSA SIGINT flight programme, the RAF and US Air Force negotiated a separate agreement during 1948, to cover the joint collection and exchange of targeting intelligence on the Soviet Union, including through covert photography. By this time, the wartime CIU had been renamed the Joint Air Photographic Intelligence Centre, which became the Joint Air Reconnaissance Intelligence Centre (JARIC) in 1953. In 1956 it moved from Medmenham to Brampton in Huntingdon. For much of the period from the signing of the 1948 agreement until the arrival of the American U2 high-altitude reconnaissance aircraft in 1956, the political restrictions on American overflights of the Soviet Union, other than in the Far East, were often tighter than those imposed on the RAF. The British were, therefore, more equal partners than the balance of resources implied, and could undertake some tasks denied to the US Air Force.

From early 1948, British aircraft – initially, modified Spitfire XIXs, which could comfortably fly up to 40,000ft, and Mosquitoes, but after 1951 the new Canberra jets – conducted PR flights from Germany, Crete, Cyprus, Iraq and Iran. Sorties were targeted at Soviet naval units on the rare occasions they ventured out of home waters in the early post-war years, such as the move of two new *Sverdlov* cruisers from the Baltic to the Northern Fleet in December 1951, the first opportunity to obtain photographs of these vessels.[17] Sorties were also occasionally flown to investigate reports of Soviet vessels basing in countries allied or sympathetic to the Soviet Union, such as the possibility of submarines in Valona Bay in Albania in March 1950.[18] Both categories of flight were subject to specific political clearance. Sorties were also regularly flown along the perimeters of Soviet and Soviet-bloc territory and coasts, to gain oblique photographic coverage of immediate border areas, including an extensive survey of the southern shore of the Caspian in late 1948. In

November 1952 the DNI, now Rear Admiral Anthony Buzzard, sought Norwegian approval for Canberra aircraft to stage through Bodø and conduct reconnaissance 'towards north-western Russia', presumably targeted at the northern naval bases, and for a separate series of ELINT flights, which would remain in Norwegian territory. It appears the Canberra operation was refused.[19]

However, there were certainly some specially sanctioned deeper British overflights of the Soviet Union in the early 1950s, the most ambitious being the coverage in early 1953 of the primary Soviet missile research centre at Kapustin Yar, forty-five miles east of Stalingrad (later Volgograd), by a modified Canberra PR3, deploying from Germany and landing in Iran. (The first indication of the importance of Kapustin Yar came from Lieutenant Colonel Grigori Tokaev, who defected to the British in Germany in October 1947.[20]) Coming just fourteen years after Sydney Cotton first pioneered high-altitude covert reconnaissance, this long-range flight at close to 50,000ft, over hostile territory with an alert air defence system, was a remarkable achievement. Partly because the aircraft was almost shot down, it was judged so sensitive that the British did not brief the Americans for nearly a year. In 1952, and again in 1954, RAF pilots using American RB-45C aircraft conducted multi-aircraft night sorties (Operation Jiu-Jitsu) to radar-map key Soviet sites, including Moscow, a task which President Eisenhower had refused to sanction. The Soviet Union was not the only target. During the Korean war Spitfire XIXs operating from Hong Kong conducted flights over China.[21]

These early British contributions to joint aerial reconnaissance led to Britain becoming a formal partner in the CIA U2 high-altitude reconnaissance programme (Project Aquatone, later Chalice) from 1958–60, a relationship designated Project Oldster, and negotiated with SIS assistance between CIA and the RAF Director of Air Intelligence. The idea was for Britain to share the political and operational risks in overflying the Soviet Union by undertaking flights entirely under British control and, thus, from CIA's viewpoint, increase a sortie rate constrained by President Eisenhower's extreme caution. (He authorised only one flight in each of the years 1958 and 1959 and two in 1960, with the second meeting disaster.) Oldster was approved in principle by the prime minister, Harold Macmillan, and Eisenhower on 27 August 1958, and the operational plan two months later. Britain not only provided four RAF pilots, but took formal ownership of the aircraft before each flight, and was entirely responsible for its political approval and execution. In the event, there were only two British overflights, both staged from Peshawar, Pakistan, on 6 December 1959 covering Kapustin Yar, and on 5 February

1960 covering the Intercontinental Ballistic Missile (ICBM) test range at Tyuratam in Kazakhstan, before all overflights were terminated, following the shooting down of American pilot Gary Powers' aircraft on 1 May. In addition to their two overflights, which CIA judged to have achieved 'excellent' results, Britain conducted five peripheral ELINT flights along the Soviet border, and seventeen sorties over the Middle East. In the eighteen months up to the fateful Powers flight, the British conducted 20 per cent of U2 sorties over all areas, and two of only five successful overflights of the Soviet Union between 1 January 1958 and the loss of Powers' aircraft.[22]

This British participation brought JARIC complete access to U2-generated intelligence from mid 1958, and much of that acquired on the Soviet Union over the previous two years as well. Furthermore, because the U2 was a CIA programme, the British commitment built credit that released a wider range of CIA intelligence, including naval material, that might not have happened otherwise. Although naval requirements suffered throughout the U2 programme, from the higher priority placed on covering nuclear, ballistic missile and strategic bomber sites, most of which were located in the southwest sector of the Soviet Union, the early missions still delivered a significant yield of naval intelligence. The first-ever U2 flight over Soviet territory on 4 July 1956 focused on the naval shipyards at Leningrad, important to the submarine programme, and specifically sought evidence that a nuclear boat might be under construction. The first Soviet nuclear boat, *Leninsky Komsomol*, was under construction at this time, but at Severodvinsk, twenty miles west of Archangel, not Leningrad. Subsequent flights on 9 and 10 July covered Riga in the Baltic, and Odessa and Sebastopol in the Black Sea, but it was a further fifteen months before it was possible, in successive flights on 11 and 13 October 1957, first to conduct electronic surveillance of an exercise in the Barents Sea, and then to photograph the northern naval bases at Polyarny, Murmansk and Severomorsk.[23] The Norwegians, who were not forewarned, anxiously followed both flights on radar, and the fruitless efforts of Soviet MiG-17 fighters to intercept.[24]

The primary justification for the second (photographic) mission was to establish whether submarines were being configured to deliver a nuclear armed missile against the United States. Early variants of the SS-N-3 Shaddock missile to be launched from a Zulu- or Whiskey-class submarine were being fitted and tested at this time but, as with nuclear construction, at Severodvinsk on the White Sea, further to the east.[25] Severodvinsk could easily be reached by a U2 launched from Norway, but the Norwegians were not prepared to permit overflights, although they would allow ELINT flights outside Soviet airspace. CIA flew flights into the Kara Sea (flying north round Novaya Zemlya) and Baltic from Bodø in October/November 1958, and the British sought approval for a U2 flight along the Kola coast in early 1959, but this was not carried out.[26] Without the use of Norway, Severodvinsk could not be reached from other U2 bases without a long, exposed transit across much of the Soviet Union. This option finally received reluctant presidential approval for the final sortie on 1 May 1960. Powers' flight plan began in Peshawar, took him north across the entire Soviet Union, and envisaged covering all the northern naval bases, including the first ever overflight of Severodvinsk before landing at Bodø in Norway, but he never reached them.[27]

Despite the failure to cover Severodvinsk, the overall CIA assessment of U2 programme intelligence nevertheless insisted that it provided 'a large amount of information on naval installations and order of battle', and was 'particularly useful in confirming naval order of battle in the Murmansk and Black Sea areas'.[28] The British-American collaboration through the 1950s in imagery intelligence (IMINT), as the product of covert PR was now known, had far-reaching consequences. It established a partnership which continued to deliver the British intelligence community exceptional access to American-generated imagery, including on important naval targets, even when Britain ceased to have the capability to offer much in return.

As the 1950s opened, some of these intelligence-collection capabilities remained in the future, but meanwhile the Royal Navy faced a growing prospect of early conflict with the Soviet navy, exacerbated by the outbreak of the Korean War. The priority was to counter the submarine threat which, despite fragmentary coverage, NID perceived to be growing in quantity and quality. To attack British trade and communications, Soviet submarines had to sortie from their Baltic or northern bases. Given their proximity to the United Kingdom, the exits to the Baltic could be more easily controlled by mining and aerial surveillance than those through the Barents Sea. Attention, therefore, focused on the deployment of British submarines outside the Soviet Arctic bases, both to provide early warning of war preparations, and to interdict Soviet boats once hostilities began. Given this operational imperative, and the related need to improve intelligence on Soviet naval capability, it is surprising that the Admiralty deployed no submarine into the Barents Sea until autumn 1952. This delay in investigating the Soviet navy's primary operating area was in striking contrast to the effort committed to aerial intelligence collection from early 1948, which often involved significant political and operational risk. The delay is even more surprising, given that the US Navy had deployed the submarine *Cochino*, equipped with British SIGINT equipment fitted in Portsmouth, on a covert intelligence collection mission into the Barents Sea as early as August 1949. Admittedly, this mission ended in disaster. *Cochino* was abandoned, following a severe battery fire as she began her return journey, although her crew were rescued by the accompanying submarine *Tusk*. It was many years before the Americans returned. This experience may, therefore, have provoked Admiralty caution, and it also took time, post-war, to equip British submarines with snort apparatus, and acquire the experience to conduct the long, covert snort transits necessary to conduct Barents Sea patrols without detection.[29]

The first covert entry into the Barents Sea was conducted in September 1952 by the submarine *Alcide*, commanded by Lieutenant Commander Jimmy Launders, although it was not the first occasion Royal Navy submarines had conducted surveillance in Russian waters. That distinction fell to *Regulus* and her sister boats off Vladivostok in 1939. In February 1945, while commanding *Venturer*, Launders had sunk *U-864* in Norwegian waters, to this day the only successful attack conducted on another submarine with both boats submerged. The objectives for this patrol, Operation Admaston, were to remain undetected, to investigate communications reception, including that of radio-fixing aids for navigation, and sonar conditions – and generally to assess the viability of a long, fully submerged patrol under wartime conditions. Although there was considerable experience of submarine operations in the Barents Sea from wartime patrols conducted in support of the Arctic convoys, those boats were not snort-equipped, and had not covered the eastern part of the sea. *Alcide* was to record and report on return all Soviet traffic – naval and merchant – sighted, but intelligence collection was a secondary objective on this patrol. The area to be covered during Admaston was ambitious. *Alcide* was to pass north of Novaya Zemlya at the eastern end of the Barents Sea, and pass into the Kara Sea. Novaya Zemlya would shortly become the primary Soviet nuclear test site, with construction of facilities beginning in 1954, although it is unlikely NID knew this. Admaston achieved little benefit, primarily because a damaged fuel tank, compounded by failure to carry adequate fuel reserves, for which Launders was subsequently reprimanded, caused the patrol to be aborted before attempting to pass Novaya Zemlya and thus reach its primary target area. The patrol illuminated potential difficulties with communications and navigation, but provided limited insight on the operational environment to guide future patrols, and no useful intelligence. The DNI, now Rear Admiral Anthony Buzzard, expressed disappointment, and stressed the need for repeat operations since 'knowledge of this area is not otherwise covered'. The following February, the Admiralty sought political approval to cover a Soviet fleet exercise in the Barents Sea, but this was refused by the prime minister after he was independently advised, probably by Lord Cherwell, that the submarine was unlikely to avoid detection. This made an interesting contrast with his willingness to authorise the simultaneous Kapustin Yar Canberra overflight. Admaston was not, therefore, repeated for two years.[30]

To demonstrate that Barents Sea reconnaissance without detection was viable, and thus persuade the prime minister to change his mind, Captain Arthur 'Baldy' Hezlet, Chief of Staff to Flag Officer Submarines, and himself a distinguished future holder of the post, arranged for the submarine *Totem* to conduct Operation Cravat in March 1954. *Totem*, commanded by Lieutenant Commander John Coote, was one of eight wartime 'T'-class submarines reconstructed in the early 1950s to bring them up to a Type XXI level of performance significantly superior to 'A'-class boats, such as *Alcide*. To equip her for intelligence collection, she was also specially fitted with state-of-the-art COMINT and ELINT equipment. Cravat involved *Totem* conducting covert surveillance, without prior warning, of the Home and Mediterranean fleets, which had gathered at Gibraltar for spring exercises. Over a ten-day period, *Totem* successfully collected what the Admiralty subsequently acknowledged was a frightening amount of high-quality intelligence, both photographic and electronic, and all without detection, despite the regular presence of some of the Royal Navy's best anti-submarine vessels. Hezlet argued that *Totem* had proved that 'a corresponding probe among Soviet forces was a justifiable risk, unlikely to create an embarrassing international incident'. His case was strengthened when, in early June, the submarines *Trenchant* and *Sentinel* successfully trailed a new *Sverdlov*-class cruiser and her accompanying destroyers in the eastern Mediterranean, collecting what DNI judged 'valuable' intelligence, both photographic and recordings of their acoustic characteristics and sonar transmissions. Meanwhile, DNI, now Rear Admiral John Inglis, emphasised the ever-growing threat posed by the Soviet submarine force. Production was steadily increasing, with fifty-four oceangoing boats completed in 1953, and capacity for seventy-four by the end of 1954. There were also signs the submarine fleet was being organised for global operations.[31] DNI overstated actual submarine production in 1953 by about one-third, but production in 1955 did exceed seventy boats, so overall his building estimates were reasonable. However, NID estimates of overall Soviet submarine strength, placed at 422 boats that summer, were grossly exaggerated.[32] Effective frontline strength was well below three hundred, including small coastal boats, and there were at most seventy Whiskeys and Zulus of post-war design. The combined case of a growing threat, backed by evidence that valuable intelligence could be acquired at minimal risk, proved sufficient for Churchill to authorise *Totem* to conduct Operation Defiant, the Royal Navy's first dedicated, covert intelligence mission in the Barents Sea.[33]

Operation Defiant established a pattern for covert intelligence patrols in the Barents Sea, conducted by the submarines *Totem, Turpin, Tabard, Taciturn* and *Tiptoe*, all 'T' conversions, during the remainder of the decade. Apart from a pause in the second half of 1956, there were normally two patrols per year. There were also some patrols into the Baltic. Typically, patrols lasted six weeks and involved a submerged snort transit to and from the operational area, allowing around four weeks on task. Despite their reconstruction, conditions in the 'T' boats were primitive, and just maintaining operational effectiveness in the harsh Arctic environment, far from any friendly support, was a huge endurance test. Commanding officers had to balance carefully necessary aggression to get useful intelligence, with sufficient caution to minimise risk of detection. Following the pattern established with the Cravat trial, the intelligence collected comprised COMINT, ELINT, including missile telemetry, acoustic intelligence (ACINT), and photographic. DNI set the overall intelligence priorities, but the COMINT and ELINT collection and processing was directed by GCHQ, with the submarines essentially providing a naval collection platform equivalent to the aircraft platforms provided by the RAF since 1948. By autumn 1954, Defiant and succeeding patrols benefited from new intelligence-support capabilities. To undertake COMINT and ELINT collection against the new Cold War enemy, the Royal Navy created communications specialists, the Coder Special Branch, whose recruits undertook intensive Russian language training on a joint-service basis, followed by specialist collection courses. Coder specialists, along with dedicated collection equipment, were embarked for all patrols. They also manned a specialist naval listening post at Kiel, scanning the Baltic. Meanwhile, the Admiralty Research Laboratory (ARL) at Teddington established a specialist section, later known as 'A' Group, to support the collection and analysis of high-grade acoustic intelligence on behalf of NID from its dedicated collection units. In the 1960s a separate Joint Acoustic Analysis Centre (JAAC) was also established at Teddington, with distinct sections supporting the Royal Navy and RAF respectively. JAAC provided more general acoustic support to frontline operational maritime units. Its analysis of acoustic data collected across the whole frontline also produced important intelligence, but it combined this analytical role with wider responsibilities for advice on all passive sonar systems, training and operational standards, and the publishing of guidance and reference material.[34]

The 'T'-boat patrols between 1954 and 1960 provided NID with considerable insight into the capabilities and intentions of the Soviet naval enemy it would face in wartime. Given that, in this period, the Soviet navy rarely ventured outside its immediate home waters, they offered almost the only opportunity to study many of its ships at all. The boats covertly observed all classes of warship in the Northern Fleet, along with their sensors and weapons, giving particular priority to new ships introduced, the final *Sverdlov* cruisers built at Severodvinsk, *Skoryy* and Kotlin destroyers, their successors, the Kildins and Krupnys, the first to be armed with surface-to-surface missiles, Petya frigates, and the Zulu-, Whiskey-, Foxtrot- and Golf-class submarines. Importantly, they provided the only reliable, if still fragmentary, intelligence on emerging, submarine-launched missile programmes, both through photography of missile-equipped boats, and intercepted telemetry from missile tests. The first ballistic missile launch from a submarine by any navy was the test firing of an R11 Scud by a surfaced Zulu boat at the Kola test range in September 1955, and four modified Zulus, each with two missiles with nuclear warheads, were deployed in the Northern Fleet by the end of 1957. However, although the US Navy anticipated the imminent emergence of a submarine missile threat to the United States homeland from the mid 1950s onward, triggering the priority placed on U2 surveillance of the accessible northern bases in autumn 1957, it is doubtful any of the Zulus ever deployed into the Atlantic. The Golfs, initially carrying three R11s in the fin, and later the longer-range, nuclear-tipped D2, only appeared at the end of the decade. In parallel, testing of the P5 Shaddock cruise missile began on a Whiskey-class boat in 1957, and several were operational by 1960. The British patrols also monitored tactical exercises, and sometimes practice weapon-firing. On several occasions, boats were counter-detected and experienced aggressive anti-submarine hunting and live depth-charging, designed to force them to the surface, or worse. HMS *Totem* was caught during Coote's second patrol in early 1955, suffering significant damage to her casing and fin. Nevertheless, Coote insisted that his two patrols had demonstrated the Soviets' 'demonstrable weakness in anti-submarine warfare', and that British naval policies should be adjusted to exploit this.[35]

However, there were limitations to what these early British intelligence patrols could provide. Time on task was little more than two months per year, and the diesel-electric 'T'-boats' limited mobility restricted the area that could be covered. Acquisition of any intelligence on the highest priority targets, such as missile-equipped submarines, was therefore a rare and chance event. Nor could such patrols adequately illuminate the scale and priorities of future Soviet naval construction and their underlying intent, notably the distinct shift towards nuclear submarine construction from 1956, with the first November-class attack boat operational by early 1959, and a further four boats, along with eight Hotel-class ballistic missile boats, building at Severodvinsk by the end of that year.

New strands in the British-American naval intelligence relationship

In April 1955 Coote was appointed assistant naval attaché in Washington, responsible for liaison with the US Navy submarine force, and specifically for sharing NID reports on the Barents Sea patrols. Although American boats had been increasingly proactive in intelligence-gathering against Soviet Pacific bases since the Korean War, the US Navy was, at this point, content for the British to cover the Barents, leading to an informal division of labour. The same year, under an officer-exchange programme initiated between the two navies, a Royal Navy submarine officer joined the US Navy's Submarine Development Squadron 2 (later 12) at New London, Connecticut. This unit, created in 1949, was originally tasked with solving the problem of using submarines 'to detect and destroy enemy submarines', although its brief gradually widened to embrace all areas of submarine operations. The Royal Navy presence here continued for the rest of the Cold War, and beyond. These important new strands in the British-American intelligence relationship were further strengthened in August the following year, when Coote was invited to join a two-month intelligence patrol, conducted by the American submarine *Stickleback*, similar in capability to *Totem*, off the Soviet Pacific submarine base at Petropavlovsk in the Kamchatka peninsula. Coote was surprised by the scale of the American Pacific submarine collection effort, which had been underway since 1952, with up to six submarines sometimes deployed simultaneously. While generally impressed with the American performance and results, Coote judged them behind in SIGINT collection and recording. The patrol also reinforced his low opinion of Soviet anti-submarine performance.[36]

During the winter of 1955/56, the strengthening naval intelligence relationship, fuelled on the British side by the product of the new Barents Sea patrols, but also the wider contributions from GCHQ and strategic aerial reconnaissance, helped foster British access to American naval capabilities of lasting importance. These were nuclear submarine propulsion and submarine-launched cruise and ballistic missiles. Following initial research, the Admiralty accurately assessed the potential of a nuclear-powered submarine as early as 1950, and judged that a submarine reactor could be developed for trial deployment in seven or eight years. Importantly, it also judged it inevitable that the Soviets would pursue this option, posing a dangerous threat to British maritime communications.[37] Nevertheless, British ambitions to pursue nuclear propulsion suffered during the early 1950s from insufficient design resources, given the higher priority given to the nuclear weapons and civil nuclear programmes, but also technological wrong turns. By the end of 1955, the Admiralty knew that with a first boat, *Nautilus*, operational, another building, and three more about to be laid down, the US Navy was far ahead, and feared the Russians were not much behind.

The last assumption did not reflect any hard intelligence, but was a logical deduction from the probable status of wider Soviet nuclear research and capability, and possibly fed too by German returnees, who also reported limited Soviet interest in HTP propulsion. Otherwise, neither SIS nor CIA ever acquired reliable intelligence from human sources on the Soviet nuclear submarine programme prior to 1959. SIS had no credible source with relevant access. CIA had a high-grade source, the military intelligence (GRU) officer Lieutenant Colonel Pyotr Popov, who provided occasional intelligence on naval topics from his conversations with naval officers. Unfortunately, such second-hand reporting was rarely sufficiently reliable. A mid-1957 CIA report from Popov quoted a naval officer the previous autumn stating that submarine and surface vessels with nuclear propulsion were under construction (which was correct), and that a nuclear submarine was in operation (which was incorrect – the first boat was still ten months from launching at this time). A year later, in September 1958, CIA still lacked definitive intelligence on Soviet nuclear submarine completions, reporting (again probably from Popov) that a Soviet naval officer had travelled to Leningrad the previous year for acceptance tests on one of a series of submarines under construction. There were no nuclear submarines building at Leningrad and the first November-class boat did not begin trials at Severodvinsk until June 1958.[38]

Despite the technical and financial challenges, by the end of 1956 the Admiralty was committed to building a nuclear attack submarine with Treasury approval, and by January 1958, there was a detailed programme to deliver *Dreadnought* by 1963. The Admiralty was clear that the nuclear submarine represented a 'revolutionary advance in naval warfare', underpinned by witnessing the performance of *Nautilus* in the NATO exercise, Rum Tub, the previous autumn, which demonstrated conclusively that the threat she posed could only adequately be countered by another nuclear submarine. Significantly, the Admiralty also recognised that a key secondary role for the nuclear boat was peacetime 'Cold War intelligence operations'.[39] In theory, in 1958 Britain possessed all the necessary indigenous nuclear and shipbuilding skills to construct a nuclear submarine, demonstrated by the completion of *Valiant* in 1966 to an entirely British design, powered by a British reactor. *Valiant* was then markedly superior to contemporary Russian boats, although not as good as the latest American ones. US Navy support was, nevertheless, important in several respects. It helped the Royal Navy appreciate the scale of transformation in naval capability the nuclear submarine represented, and that its potential far exceeded a Type XXI with unlimited endurance. American experience showed that a successful boat required not only viable nuclear propulsion, but a new hull form, propeller, sensors and, potentially, weapons. It also demonstrated that designing, building and operating nuclear submarines required a revolution in management, standards and procedures. Britain hoped to exploit this expertise and gain access to American nuclear fuel, given its own limited supplies, but gained rather more. It was offered, and accepted, an entire American nuclear propulsion system, which was incorporated in *Dreadnought*, effectively making her a one-off 'pilot' nuclear submarine commissioned in 1963, the original Admiralty target, three years before *Valiant*. Overall, this comprised a hugely generous transfer of intelligence and technology. Although its real impact has been much debated, it probably saved Britain two or three years and significant money in executing its nuclear submarine programme, and was equally important in generating technical and tactical operating skills.[40]

The motives behind this transfer have also been much debated. The value placed on the British intelligence contribution, and desire to see it continue, was a factor. So were personalities, and notably the personal relationships between Lord Louis Mountbatten, who became First Sea Lord in 1955, and his American opposite number, Admiral Arleigh Burke, and the fanatical eccentric architect of the US Navy nuclear submarine programme, Rear Admiral Hyman Rickover. Although Mountbatten exploited these links with considerable skill, there were wider strategic factors in play too. The Royal Navy contribution in the eastern Atlantic remained very important to the United States, as did access to the United Kingdom as a base, including potentially for nuclear submarines. In addition, once it was clear to the US Navy that Britain was committed to producing nuclear boats and possessed the capability to do so, there was probably a desire to prevent her wasting scarce defence resources repeating everything the Americans had already done. This argument applied in the nuclear weapon exchanges that were taking place in parallel.

Just as Coote was reporting on the *Stickleback* mission in October 1956, intelligence relations with the Americans came under strain from two separate events, an intelligence disaster in Portsmouth harbour the previous spring, and the Anglo-French invasion of Egypt to recover the Suez Canal. The Portsmouth disaster reflected failings in intelligence management, exposed when an SIS attempt to photograph the hull and underwater fittings of the Soviet *Sverdlov*-class cruiser *Ordzhonikidze*, which had brought the Soviet premier Nikolai Bulganin and First Secretary Nikita Khrushchev on a state visit to the United Kingdom, went badly wrong. Deploying frogmen for a covert underwater survey of Russian warships accessible in British or other friendly waters was not unusual by the mid 1950s. The Russians did the same against British ships visiting their ports, and viewed such action as inevitable. There was a standing 'high-priority' Admiralty requirement for 'information about the underwater noise characteristics of Russian warships', relevant to the effectiveness of certain Royal Navy torpedoes and mines, which NID sought SIS help to meet, when possible. Political approval to survey the newly completed *Sverdlov* when she attended the 1953 Coronation naval review at Spithead was refused, but Prime Minister Anthony Eden was less categoric towards an Admiralty request for SIS to survey *Sverdlov* when she made a subsequent courtesy visit to Portsmouth in October 1955. His stipulation that no action should be taken which 'involves the remotest risk of detection' was interpreted as acquiescence by the Admiralty, and SIS duly deployed the retired naval diver Commander Lionel 'Buster' Crabb to conduct the operation, which produced 'useful results'. However, when the Foreign Office, on behalf of the Admiralty, sought approval for a repeat operation, designated Claret, during the state visit, Eden was categoric that nothing should be done 'on this occasion', and his refusal was formally conveyed to both departments on 12 April. Unfortunately, confusion between the Foreign Office and Admiralty over who had ultimate responsibility for Claret, along with key personnel absences, meant nobody informed SIS that the operation was prohibited. This failure was compounded by an earlier misunderstanding between SIS and the Foreign Office, which led SIS to believe that Claret had been authorised.[41]

Confident it had a green light, SIS duly deployed Crabb to dive beneath *Ordzhonikidze* and he entered the water at 0700 on 19 April, the day after her arrival. He was never seen again until his headless body was washed up near Chichester a year later. What happened beneath the cruiser will never be known for certain, but he probably either succumbed to a medical condition (his fitness was poor), or a catastrophic equipment failure. Crabb's tragic end, and his likely role, might have escaped press and political attention, but for failures of SIS tradecraft, which included both Crabb and his SIS supervisor booking into a local Portsmouth hotel using their own names and addresses. Press suspicion was then aroused when police Special Branch removed the page from the hotel register. The visiting Russian admiral let slip to his British counterpart that a frogman had been sighted near *Ordzhonikidze* at the time of Crabb's dive, but he promised there would be no formal complaint, and kept his word until speculation broke in the media, and the Soviet embassy not unreasonably sought an 'explanation'. Whitehall attempts to execute a cover-up, and delay in informing ministers exactly what had happened, with Eden – incredibly – not aware until 4 May, were as abject as the chaotic handling of the Claret clearance process. Bridges patently struggled to explain, let alone defend, the performance of the relevant departments before a furious Eden, who rightly dismissed much of his explanation as 'ridiculous'. Eden's fury in the face of acute embarrassment to his government was not assuaged by Bridges' claim that no single official was responsible![42]

The Claret fiasco undermined Eden's confidence in the intelligence community, and he instructed Bridges to suspend a wide range of intelligence operations, pending a review into their conduct and approval. He held SIS primarily responsible, and replaced Sir John Sinclair, who had succeeded Menzies as chief in 1953, with the more able Sir Dick White, who moved across from heading the Security Service. White created a markedly more professional service over the next ten years, delivering significant contributions to naval requirements. The operational suspensions included the Barents Sea patrols, and flights from the newly arrived U2 out of British airfields. The U2 detachment earmarked for Lakenheath was moved to Wiesbaden in Germany. Use of the 'blanket approval', which had previously governed short-notice aerial SIGINT operations, including those against Soviet naval deployments, also ceased.[43] Although the clearance system failed for Claret, and Bridges' review confirmed that lines of accountability for some intelligence operations required tightening, it did not reveal major unauthorised activity. Despite some popular claims to the contrary, intelligence collection in the early 1950s was under firm political control.

The British-French attack on Egypt at the end of October 1956, to recover control of the Suez Canal following its nationalisation the previous July by the Egyptian government of President Gamal Abdel Nasser, was potentially more damaging. It briefly threatened the whole British intelligence relationship with the United States, with some areas of co-operation and the supply of American material suspended. However, the combination of Soviet sabre-rattling in response to the British-French operation, and their parallel action to crush the Hungarian uprising required a united Western front, and ensured the damage was contained. Following Eden's resignation, and replacement as prime minister by Harold Macmillan at the beginning of 1957, normal relations rapidly resumed.

Although the Suez operation was politically disastrous for Britain, the naval contribution was well-planned and executed, and drew on sound intelligence. There were three specific naval intelligence challenges: the threat posed by the Egyptian navy and air force, which had received substantial quantities of Soviet bloc equipment; targeting information for the carrier air groups, which were responsible for a significant proportion of the initial air campaign; and topographical intelligence for the landing zones. Since British forces had only completed their withdrawal from the Canal Zone in March, knowledge of the Egyptian order of battle and the location of key military facilities, especially airfields, and key infrastructure targets was up to date, and PR from Canberras operating from Cyprus filled most gaps. The Egyptian navy, which comprised ten assorted destroyers and frigates, and twenty torpedo boats, posed little challenge to a combined British-French fleet, which included seven carriers, and the only early worry was the possible arrival of three submarines, which PR ruled out. The air force which included 110 Soviet bloc-supplied MiG-15 jet fighters and forty-nine Il-28 light bombers, with the possibility of some more advanced MiG-17s, was a bigger concern, with the MiG-15s superior in performance to the Fleet Air Arm fighters.[44] However, at the beginning of the crisis on 3 August the JIC judged that the Navy and air force would not be able to operate their new equipment effectively until the end of the year, and faced major technical, maintenance and logistic challenges.[45] Naval preparations also benefited from considerable work by the JIB on updating Egypt's topography, which had been driven by the potential Soviet threat to the Middle East region.[46] Despite the theoretical advantage enjoyed by the MiG-15s, and tight political restrictions, the performance of the British carriers was impressive. They conducted twice as many strike sorties as the RAF, sank six torpedo boats, destroyed 139 of 250 aircraft and 150 armoured vehicles in low-level attacks. The amphibious landings were also achieved efficiently, with minimal loss.[47]

Meanwhile, although the intelligence-gathering patrol in the Barents Sea planned for autumn 1956, Operation Pontiac, was cancelled in accordance with Eden's post-Claret directive, the impact of this was reduced by the need to deploy two submarines in November, *Tabard* and *Artful*, to provide early warning of any Northern Fleet movement associated with the tensions provoked by the Hungarian uprising.

The First Lord, Lord Hailsham, approved this deployment, Operation Nightjar, on his own authority, on the basis that the purpose was not specifically intelligence-gathering, and on condition that the submarines did not get closer to the Russian coast than fifty miles. Both patrols were uneventful, with minimal detection of Soviet warships. However, despite this modified British presence, the cancellation of Pontiac caused the Americans to initiate their own Barents Sea intelligence operations, beginning the following spring. Although they wanted Coote's advice on operating conditions, they initially asked him not to brief either Flag Officer Submarines or DNI, a condition Coote refused to accept, forcing the Americans to concede that they were informed. The British naval staff in Washington judged that the Americans not only intended to plug a temporary British gap, but to make a long-term commitment. This reflected the value of the intelligence the British had provided to date, and the evidence from their patrols that the risk of detection was low, enabling the US Navy to press for political clearance. The British now feared that with Eden's suspension continuing, their role would be usurped. Fortunately, Eden's replacement by Macmillan in January 1957 brought a change of policy. Not only were British patrols resumed, but the spring saw the initiation of a joint programme of co-ordinated deployments with the Americans that continued throughout the Cold War. The Americans called this the Special Naval Collection Programme (SNCP), initially with the codeword Holystone. SNCP was soon adopted by the British too, within the small group of indoctrinated personnel. By 1960, the Americans were deploying nuclear boats, and towards the end of that year one of these, *Skipjack*, allegedly pressed in close to the entrance of the channel to Severomorsk and Murmansk.[48]

It was ironic that the Claret debacle, arising from an operation that would probably have added little new intelligence to that gleaned from *Sverdlov* the previous October, diverted attention from a valuable pointer to future Soviet naval policy, delivered by Khrushchev himself in a speech to a senior naval audience at Greenwich on 20 April. He stated that, although his British hosts had praised the quality of *Ordzhonikidze*, the ship and its armament were outdated. The future lay in guided missile submarines, which would give the Soviet Union the capability for 'defensive' attacks on the United States. A month later, this message was underlined in the Soviet military publication, *Krasnaya Zvezda* (*Red Star*), which stated that: 'Submarines, having atomic propulsion and guided missiles as basic armaments, can perform at great distances from their bases and secretly strike blows not only against ships but also against land targets deep in enemy territory'. These public messages were influenced by the ideas of Admiral Sergey Gorshkov, appointed commander-in-chief by Khrushchev at the beginning of the year, although his motives and those of his patron were probably not entirely aligned. Nor were Khrushchev's ideas yet fully formed. However, several important themes were developing. Although the Soviet navy would retain traditional roles long recognised by the Admiralty – defending its home waters, interdicting enemy sea communications, and supporting the seaward flank of land operations – its mission would now expand to include strategic defence against seaborne nuclear attack, and conducting its own nuclear missile attacks against enemy territory. Submarines would become core strategic weapons, while small missile-equipped surface ships, backed by long-range aircraft, could counter much larger, conventionally armed warships. Like Jacky Fisher fifty years earlier, Khrushchev was searching for a more effective navy, but also a cheaper one.

The first signs of these changes began appearing in 1958, a year when, working in close concert with Gorshkov, Khrushchev committed to implementing a vast nuclear submarine programme, based on seventy boats armed with nuclear ballistic missiles (SSBN), sixty with anti-ship cruise missiles (SSGN), and fifty torpedo-armed attack boats (SSN). About half this planned force was commissioned by 1970, an average construction rate of eight boats per year. In parallel, there would be new surface ships, often fitted with gas turbine propulsion, armed with surface-to-surface and surface-to-air missile systems, and deploying much improved anti-submarine sensors and weapons. There would also be considerable emphasis on missile-armed, fast patrol boats. Meanwhile, pre-1955 surface-ship construction programmes, notably the *Sverdlov*s, virtually halted, with a dramatic fall in naval expenditure between 1955 and 1957 as policy adjusted. The Greenwich speech, therefore, foreshadowed radical and imminent shifts in Soviet naval thinking and investment which, coming just a year after the US Navy had launched its first nuclear submarine, and some months before it defined the first concept of a solid-fuel, submarine-launched, ballistic missile, were remarkably visionary. It was a striking example of how sometimes the best intelligence lies in plain sight.[49]

Apart from one fleeting reference gleaned from Popov in June 1957, neither SIS nor CIA could immediately offer any intelligence to illuminate this shift in Soviet naval policy.[50] SIS not only failed to acquire any useful Soviet naval source in the late 1950s, but the Admiralty suffered serious damage from two successful Soviet intelligence penetrations. The first was the clerk, Harry Houghton, recruited by Polish intelligence in 1951 when working for the British naval attaché in Warsaw, and subsequently passed on to the KGB when he returned to Britain to work in the Admiralty Underwater Detection Establishment at Portland. He had limited access himself, but in 1959 began an affair with a fellow clerk, Ethel Gee, and persuaded her to pass him top-secret material, the most significant being details of the new 2001 sonar system being designed for *Dreadnought* and future British nuclear submarines. Houghton was detected through information provided by the Polish intelligence officer Michael Goleniewski, who defected to the United States in 1960. The second was John Vassall, also an Admiralty clerk, who was recruited in a blackmail operation while on a posting to the British embassy in Moscow in 1955, and worked continuously as a KGB agent, until exposed by another defector to the United States, the KGB officer Anatoli Golitsyn, in 1962.[51] However, the defection of a senior naval officer to the United States in June 1959 brought compensation for these Soviet successes.[52] This was Captain Nikolai Artamonov, a man of high intellect, professionalism and great charm, the youngest-ever destroyer commander in the Soviet navy, and destined for high rank. He made a daring escape with his Polish girlfriend across the Baltic from Gdynia to Sweden in a commandeered naval launch. Artamonov proved an intelligence goldmine for CIA and ONI, not least for his knowledge of naval nuclear missile development and deployment, and much of his material was shared with NID through SIS.[53] This included a detailed account of the Northern Fleet and its bases, including the role of Severodvinsk in nuclear submarine construction.[54]

Despite the limitations of late 1950s submarine collection, the lack of U2 coverage against naval targets and the absence of high-quality human sources, with Artamonov a notable exception, by early 1960, the JIC and CIA had a broadly consistent view of Soviet naval policy and capability, which was close to reality. Both recognised the new emphasis on defence against seaborne nuclear attack by Western forces from either carriers or, potentially, from ballistic-missile-equipped submarines, and the offensive deployment of Soviet submarines for strategic nuclear attack. Both stressed the centrality of submarines to the new Soviet navy, with about 420 now in commission. Both judged that a few SSNs were in commission at the end of 1959, although CIA doubted any were yet operational, and that strength would reach about thirty nuclear boats by mid 1964, with about one-third missile-launching types. CIA correctly assessed that the Soviets could achieve an annual building rate of eight nuclear boats by 1961. Both assessed there were four converted Zulu-class submarines and six new Golfs, capable of launching ballistic missiles with a maximum range of 350 miles, although the number and specification of those in the latter class was not yet certain. The JIC correctly anticipated that the

Soviets would pursue intensive research into long-range, solid-fuel missiles capable of submerged launch, with deployment likely in the time bracket 1965–70. It also judged that both new submarines and surface vessels were being equipped with improved sonar, exploiting lower frequencies and higher power, although it thought the British-American lead in sonar technology was about ten years. However, reflecting a preoccupation that would endure throughout the Cold War, the JIC thought the Soviets would devote major effort to 'non-acoustic' options, such as the radioactive traces left by nuclear boats, and wake detection. There was also evidence of research into sound absorption cladding for submarines.[55]

Both organisations emphasised the addition of destroyers armed with surface-to-surface missiles, which the JIC was confident would now displace the large cruisers. CIA put missile range at forty miles, but the JIC believed it was at least double that, allowing a Soviet force commander much greater tactical flexibility and hitting power, although better sensors were required fully to exploit this. The missiles could be used against carriers, but there was insufficient intelligence yet to clarify their primary task. Both organisations saw a considerable improvement in anti-submarine capability with the new sonars, multiple rocket weapons and helicopters although, for the present, weapon performance here far outstripped sensors. Finally, the two organisations had a similar breakdown of Soviet naval air power and distribution. Both saw the primary threat coming from TU16 Badger medium bombers armed with air-to-surface missiles, although the JIC was the more convinced the missiles were already operational. These early 1960 assessments left many details about Soviet naval capability, and some important questions about policy and intentions unresolved, but the British and Americans were shortly to receive a huge intelligence windfall, probably the most important of the Cold War, that did much to answer them.[56]

Looking back across the 1950s, there is, nevertheless, a curious disjunction between the effort devoted to naval intelligence collection against Britain's primary potential enemy, and the broadly accurate picture of Soviet capability and intent it produced, and decisions regarding Royal Navy force structure and future procurement. Through much of the decade, the Admiralty struggled to define a convincing role for the Navy in a war shaped by early and devastating nuclear conflict. The Navy was also the prime target for cuts, as the government prioritised the airborne nuclear deterrent, and a continental army commitment in Germany. Radical ideas promoted by Duncan Sandys during tenures as Minister of Supply 1951–54 and Minister of Defence 1957–59, including abolition of the Fleet Air Arm and RAF Fighter Command, and replacement of manned aircraft by missiles, went beyond anything contemplated by either Britain or comparable military powers across the rest of the twentieth century. Against this background, successive First Sea Lords, primarily Mountbatten, did remarkably well, ensuring the Royal Navy ended the decade with a balanced fleet, including heavy aircraft carriers and important modern weapon systems coming on stream, notably the Buccaneer strike aircraft, guided missile destroyers and SSNs. However, there is a compelling case that this 'balanced fleet' was shaped more by skilful political manoeuvring by Mountbatten, and by technological opportunity, than deep analysis of the future Soviet threat. It is remarkable how little intelligence informed the major policy debates of the era. By contrast, Mountbatten was adept at stressing the importance the Americans attached to Britain retaining a full range of naval capabilities and the role of the Navy, including the carriers, in meeting unpredictable global commitments, where the different cases of Korea and Suez were helpful. The overall result was a navy that met Britain's commitments in the peacekeeping and limited conflict commitments she faced, mainly in Eastern theatres in the 1960s, but less well-suited to the challenges posed by the emerging Soviet navy.[57]

33

The 1960s: A Time of Transition

Transformational intelligence sources

At the opening of the 1960s, British naval intelligence acquired two exceptional new intelligence sources which transformed the quality of its assessments of current and future Soviet strength and capability, but equally important, understanding of its policies and strategic priorities. The first was access to the product from two American satellite intelligence programmes, Grab and its successor, Poppy, which collected SIGINT, primarily ELINT, and Corona, which provided IMINT. The first Grab satellite, with a SIGINT package designed by the Naval Research Laboratory that drew on submarine-deployed ELINT systems, launched in June 1960, and the first Corona satellite two months later. The first Corona mission provided 3000ft of film, more than the entire U2 programme to date, covering 1.65 million square miles of Soviet territory, and President Eisenhower saw the first photographs on 25 August. The scale and sensitivity of this new intelligence capability led Eisenhower to approve the creation of a new civilian intelligence agency, the National Reconnaissance Organisation (NRO), with CIA, the US Air Force and US Navy all stakeholders. This decision was confirmed by the incoming administration of President John F Kennedy, and the NRO was formally established on 6 September 1961. The Corona programme lasted throughout the 1960s, and when it was replaced in 1972 it had completed 145 missions, taking 800,000 images. In summer 1962 the NRO also took over responsibility for the overhead SIGINT programme from the Naval Research Laboratory, after the latter had completed a second Grab mission, launched in June 1961, and began developing the follow-on system, Poppy. Both the Naval Research Laboratory and NRO passed the SIGINT take to NSA for exploitation, and much of it was then shared with GCHQ. NSA, inevitably, also became a key partner in improving collection capability. Meanwhile, for imagery, NRO now became JARIC's most important partner.[1]

The priorities for satellite imagery, identified by the US intelligence community in August 1960, were intercontinental and intermediate-range ballistic missile (ICBM and IRBM) sites, submarine-launched missiles, long-range bomber airfields, and nuclear sites. Severodvinsk, Murmansk, Severomorsk, Kildin and Polyarny were all, therefore, priority targets, but it was emphasised that initially the ICBM target transcended all others. The key target of Severodvinsk, which had never been covered by the U2s, was not, therefore, photographed until June 1961. There were subsequent passes here in May 1962, June 1963 and summer 1964. By that point, CIA was confident Severodvinsk was the largest producer of nuclear submarines, covering all three classes, November SSNs, Echo SSGNs and Hotel SSBNs, and that the only other nuclear yard was Komsomolsk Amur in the Far East, which only produced Echo boats.[2] Satellite naval ELINT collection from the Grab and Poppy missions was initially a useful, if not critical, supplement to other SIGINT platforms, but as the scope and sophistication of the systems expanded through the decade, it contributed substantially to a growing ocean-surveillance capability.

The second transformational source was human, the 42-year-old Soviet military intelligence officer, Colonel Oleg Penkovsky. Following various attempts to signal his wish to collaborate with Western intelligence, eventually attracting the interest of both SIS and CIA, he finally made contact with a joint team from both services on 20 April 1961 in the Mount Royal Hotel, near Marble Arch, London, while accompanying a Soviet trade delegation to the United Kingdom. Over the next eighteen months, until his arrest in Moscow on 22 October 1962, he delivered a vast treasure trove of high-grade intelligence, contained in over one hundred hours of recorded debriefings during overseas visits, and eight thousand photographed pages of sensitive documents, either passed in meetings or in clandestine contacts in Moscow. He was the highest-ranking Soviet officer to work for the West up to that time, and provided the first authoritative views of the development of Soviet military capability and strategy, and the composition of its military establishment. A detailed history of the case, including Penkovsky's motivation, the reasons for his exceptional access, which partly reflected powerful patrons in the Soviet military hierarchy, how he was run, and why it was a joint SIS/CIA operation throughout, is available elsewhere, and beyond the scope of this book, which concentrates solely on his naval contributions.[3]

Accounts of the Penkovsky case mainly focus on his insights into Soviet missile capability, the rationale behind Khrushchev's deployment to Cuba, and his attitude to American counter-moves. However, the intelligence he provided on the Soviet navy was extensive and important. In addition to details of naval order of battle, the status and development of the nuclear submarine fleet and submarine-launched ballistic missiles, he provided copies of most articles written over the period 1960–62 for the top secret *Special Collection of Articles of the Journal Military Thought*. The *Special Collection*, first produced in 1960, was a highly unusual initiative for the Soviet Union. It provided an ad hoc forum for airing frank, controversial and far-ranging views by senior officers, but expressed on a purely personal basis. Circulation was confined to the level of army and fleet commanders, and contributors were drawn from a small circle of the military elite. The articles by naval contributors explored perceptions of the Western naval threat, current and future Soviet naval capability and its capacity to respond, the strategy underpinning Soviet naval deployment, and emerging doctrine. Because of the long lead times required to develop and deploy new ships and systems, discussions conducted within the journal regarding their performance and purpose remained relevant for the rest of the decade and beyond. For British and American analysts, developments first observed in the early 1970s could often be directly related to, and explained by, the intelligence Penkovsky had supplied ten years previously.[4]

Special Collection articles illuminated British and American perceptions of the Soviet naval threat in two important respects. First, they confirmed Khrushchev's commitment to the defence policy first hinted at in his 1956 Greenwich speech. His premise was that any conflict with the West over vital interests would quickly escalate into an all-out nuclear exchange, removing the prospect of any significant conventional land battle in Western Europe, and therefore rendering expenditure on large, sophisticated, conventional land forces pointless. This led Khrushchev to a policy of minimal but effective nuclear deterrence and war-fighting, financed by sharp reductions in conventional capabilities, which would also bring the important bonus of more resources for civil investment and consumer goods. In the short to medium term, this policy (popularly termed by some American analysts as 'more rubble for the rouble') relied heavily on convincing the United States and its key allies that Soviet nuclear strength was much greater than it actually was. Here, the combination of Penkovsky's intelligence on the real status of Soviet nuclear and missile programmes, backed by the new Corona and Grab satellite surveillance, exposed Soviet inferiority. Importantly, the *Special Collection* showed that the majority of the Soviet military leadership saw serious risks in Khrushchev's policy, were strongly opposed to downgrading conventional forces, and believed the Soviet Union must invest in a wide range of capabilities to meet future threats and opportunities.

Against this sharp policy debate, the *Special Collection* showed how senior Soviet naval officers viewed naval priorities, and the capabilities required to meet them. It clarified that the present short-range, submarine-launched, ballistic missiles associated with the Golfs would be targeted at naval bases and ports, rather than cities or inland military targets, but it was silent on whether a more strategic submarine system would be developed. For the immediate future, the *Special Collection* emphasised two main missions, anti-carrier and anti-Polaris. Polaris was the US Navy's submarine-borne ballistic missile, the first capable of submerged launch, initially with a range of 1400 miles, which became operational in late 1960. For *Special Collection* contributors, the American attack carrier still remained the primary threat in the early 1960s. Cruise missiles, delivered by aircraft or submarine, were identified as the primary anti-carrier weapon. This clarified the role of the SS-N-3 Shaddock missile and the new Echo-class nuclear submarine, and the Kennel and Kipper air-launched cruise missiles associated with the Tu-16 Badger bomber, confirming therefore the assumptions suggested by the JIC in its assessment of February 1960. The *Special Collection* insights into anti-carrier tactics and weapons proved invaluable as the Soviets began testing these in exercises in the Norwegian Sea through the mid 1960s.

However, the *Special Collection* expected the Polaris submarine to replace the US Navy carrier force as the primary maritime threat well before 1971. Senior naval contributors thought the SSN would probably prove the best counter to Polaris boats although, as of 1962, they were uncertain how specialised the requirement would prove, and whether deploying multi-role nuclear boats was feasible. They also believed aircraft and surface vessels had a crucial 'stalking' role. One reference anticipated the anti-submarine role of the *Moskva*-class helicopter carriers commissioned from 1967. Contributors also advocated specialist anti-submarine warfare (ASW) cruisers and destroyers, with improved sonars and anti-submarine weapons, but also armed with strong surface–air missile (SAM) armament to protect them while hunting Polaris far out at sea. The joint ASW/SAM concept was evident in the *Moskva*s, but also other new warship classes appearing later in the decade, notably the Krestas and Karas.[5]

Penkovsky's naval intelligence, primarily covering submarine-launched ballistic missiles and the *Special Collection* insights, along with the first results from Corona satellite imagery, was reflected in JIC assessments from the beginning of 1962, but the accuracy of its conclusions varied.

By April, the JIC assessed there were eleven new Hotel-class SSBNs operational, each armed with three ballistic missiles, joining five November-class SSNs. It now expected sixty nuclear boats to complete in the next five years, with about two-thirds missile-armed, a substantial and unconvincing uplift on its estimate of two years earlier. There were also thirty-one conventional missile boats in commission, six Zulus with two missiles each, one with a single, and twenty-four Golfs with three. The JIC therefore counted 118 submarine-launched ballistic missiles in total, all with an estimated 300-mile range and expected a figure of 200-plus in 1966, depending on building rate. In reality, the present force was somewhat smaller, with only eight Hotels and twenty-three Golfs ever completed, and there would be no further SSBNs, until the much more advanced and capable Yankee class began commissioning in late 1967. The JIC (correctly) did not believe the Soviet navy yet had a submerged launch capability, or a ballistic missile with range above 300 miles but, rightly, still thought both capabilities were probably under development. In fact, the fitting of the 600-mile D-4 system to the Golfs and Hotels was already getting underway. The JIC also correctly noted a submarine-launched cruise missile in development, with a range of 200 miles. (This was a variant of the SS-N-3 Shaddock deployed with some Whiskeys and the new Echo-class nuclear boats.) The JIC reaffirmed that advances were underway in ASW. The advent of Polaris was driving Soviet effort in this field, and they were making strenuous efforts to develop countermeasures. They had not yet produced an effective SSN, but this must be a key goal. New sonar was being fitted to both nuclear and conventional submarines. Meanwhile, the JIC expected naval air force Tu-16 Badger strength to double to about 400 aircraft, armed with air-to-surface missiles by 1966, with the longer-range Kipper missile replacing the Kennel. However, it badly overestimated the growth of the cruise missile-armed destroyers, expecting the Krupny force to quadruple by 1966 when, in reality, construction had halted at the present eight, and was now switching to ASW vessels.[6]

In 1964 the JIC updated its assessment of the role of the Soviet navy in all-out war. It reflected the latest information on evolving Soviet strength, but also the influence of the thinking disclosed in the *Special Collection*. It identified three primary tasks for the Soviet navy in a general war: offensive operations by its SSBNs; anti-Polaris; and countering carrier strike. The current limitations of the Soviet SSBNs, still centred on the conventional Golfs with limited range and payload, meant they could not be deployed permanently off the United States, or used on hard targets. They would, therefore, be sailed in time of tension as a second strike force, primarily against American coastal targets, but possibly also against British targets to circumvent the ballistic missile early warning system. Although preventing Western carriers achieving a position to launch nuclear strikes remained critical, the JIC thought that locating and destroying Polaris with every available means now took priority. However, the Soviets must recognise that the wide area available for launching offered them little prospect of significant success.[7]

The JIC also underlined the growing Soviet capability for worldwide operations.[8] Early signs that the Soviet navy was preparing for more distant operations were evident by 1959. Submarines had deployed as far as latitude 50° N with a tanker in support, and two submarines with a tanker and support ship had transited from Murmansk to the Far East. The naval staff perceived this as a navy 'spreading its wings' to gain experience, particularly with the long-range conduct of submarine operations. Indeed, it mirrored the pattern adopted by Dönitz in 1938–39. In October 1959 the incoming First Sea Lord Admiral Sir Charles Lambe agreed with Arleigh Burke that it was, therefore, desirable to implement an extended surveillance capability in the South Atlantic and Indian Ocean. The following April, the incoming DNI, the redoubtable Norman Denning, now a vice admiral, presented proposals agreed with the RAF to achieve this, but implementation stalled with political constraints on aerial surveillance that followed the downing of Powers' U2 aircraft.[9] Four years later, the JIC noted greatly increased Soviet activity outside its home waters, including regular exercises, about forty long-range submarine patrols annually, a SIGINT surveillance network comprised of thirty 'auxiliary gatherers of intelligence' (AGIs), mainly former trawlers, and an extensive oceanographic research programme. However, the JIC also emphasised Soviet shortcomings. Many ships still had limited endurance, there was insufficient afloat logistic support essential for sustained operations, and no ship-borne air capability, except helicopters.[10]

From 1962 through the rest of the decade, the Soviet Northern and Baltic fleets conducted a major exercise in the Norwegian Sea each summer, which invariably tested tactics to counter a NATO carrier strike fleet. These exercises were the most advanced undertaken by the Soviet navy, and the deployments grew steadily longer and more ambitious. The Baltic Fleet usually took the part of NATO, sometimes deploying through the Channel, with the Northern Fleet assuming its wartime interception task. The exercises accordingly offered a unique opportunity to assess developing Soviet capability and tactics, and an extensive NATO surveillance effort was mounted each year under Royal Navy control, reflecting its responsibility for the eastern Atlantic area.

This surveillance involved aircraft for shadowing, and photographic and ELINT collection; intruder operations by submarine; and surface vessels equipped for SIGINT recording. It was recognised that submarines promised the best intelligence results, since Soviet forces would inevitably restrict communications or electronic transmissions if they believed they were under observation. However, submarine collection was constrained until the late 1960s, because nuclear boats were rarely available, and conventional boats lacked sufficient mobility. An early lesson was that, with Soviet submarines able to use the whole 200-mile gap between Norway and Bear Island even in winter, establishing an effective submarine barrier to intercept them with conventional boats equipped with existing sonar was extremely difficult. Intelligence collection against these exercises remained under close political control, invariably requiring prime ministerial approval.[11]

These forward Soviet deployments, along with the intelligence insights gained in the early 1960s, underlined the requirement for improved wide-area ocean surveillance. This was especially pressing in dealing with the different elements of the prospective Soviet nuclear submarine threat, ballistic missile against land targets, cruise missile against the carrier fleet, and SSN against Polaris. During the 1950s, both the British and Americans established research programmes to achieve longer-range submarine detection using shore-based, submarine-mounted and aircraft-deployed sonar systems. Together with Norway and Canada, both also invested significantly in oceanography, and monitored Soviet work in this area.[12] They shared most of their results, although both were more restrictive with third parties. In pursuing the shore-based option, both countries laid long hydrophone arrays on the seabed, tuned to exploit passively the recently discovered deep-water sound channels which trapped and focused low-frequency sound waves, including, potentially, those emanating from submarines. However, they used different techniques to process and analyse the anticipated submarine-generated sound signals. The British system, Corsair, developed by ARL, adopted concepts from radio astronomy to correlate weak signals from widely dispersed antennae covering a wide frequency band. Although Corsair was initially promising, and in a 1952 trial detected a snorting submarine at over a hundred miles, it proved disappointing in realistic operational conditions, even against relatively noisy Second World War boats. During trials with the British *Porpoise*-class boats introduced in 1957, they proved so quiet, radiating only 3 per cent of the noise of previous types while snorting, that the best Corsair range was barely ten miles. Since it was assumed Soviet boats would ultimately achieve comparable performance, Corsair would not deliver the wide-area performance wanted, and it was abandoned in 1957. For a while, ARL saw active sonar as a more promising answer to long-range submarine detection, and active capability was accordingly a key feature in the 2001 sonar, which equipped all British nuclear boats until the 1980s. However, the Corsair research was not wasted. Its processing techniques, when matched with an evolution of the superior hydrophones developed during the war, underpinned highly successful, hull-mounted arrays for long-range passive detection, fitted in British submarines from the late 1950s and the towed submarine arrays, which transformed detection potential twenty years later.[13]

The American system Jezebel exploited narrowband processing, soon called Low-Frequency Analysis and Ranging (LOFAR), to identify discrete signals radiated, and proved more effective. It ultimately transformed the potential of passive sonar, and was the basis for the whole new field of acoustic intelligence. The great advantage of LOFAR was that it filtered out most of the noise generated by a submarine, to focus on specific components of submarine machinery generating specific low frequencies, or 'tonals', where sound levels were highest compared to background noise. These might be those generated by particular parts of a diesel engine or, later, the main coolant pumps of a nuclear reactor. By focusing narrowly where noise levels were greatest, LOFAR provided much greater range, and as it developed, ever-improving classification of target identity, ultimately not just submarine class, but sometimes individual boats within the class. However, these advantages came at the price of poorer bearing discrimination, and little feel for the range of the target. Research and development for Jezebel was co-ordinated by Bell Laboratories, and the first experimental array was laid, with British support, at Eleuthera in the Bahamas in 1951. Within a year, the results convinced the US Navy to implement, under Project Caesar, an extensive network along the United States East Coast covering the western Atlantic, now under the classified name Sound Surveillance System (SOSUS). Arrays were positioned along the continental shelf in a wide semicircle from Barbados to Nova Scotia, each connected by underwater cable to a processing site ashore. The first stations were commissioned in 1954. By the end of the decade there were twelve Atlantic stations, including two in Canada, and seven covering a separate Pacific network. The operational concept was that SOSUS would provide warning of Soviet submarines approaching the American coast, especially the feared missile boats. Cross-bearings from different arrays could provide a general location of the hostile boat, allowing ASW forces then to be cued to intercept. SOSUS frequency coverage was originally targeted at snorting Soviet diesels and, influenced by their experience with Corsair, British experts were sceptical of its effectiveness as these got quieter. However, SOSUS potential against nuclear boats, where it ultimately performed best, was demonstrated when it tracked the new Polaris submarine *George Washington* in 1961, on passage from the United States to the United Kingdom. Partly because the western Atlantic arrays had poor reception beyond the mid-Atlantic ridge, and partly because there were few Soviet deployments into the Atlantic prior to 1960, there were no detections of Soviet submarines until summer 1962, when they achieved distant contacts with a snorting diesel boat and a transiting nuclear boat northwest of Iceland. A Foxtrot was also detected during the Cuban missile crisis that October. In 1965 further SOSUS arrays were constructed in the Norwegian Sea northeast of the Iceland–Faroes Gap, and brought ashore to a new processing station at Keflavik. These soon proved their value, with detections against the second-generation Soviet nuclear boats from 1968, and a key role in locating the American SSN *Scorpion*, lost in an accident near the Azores the same year.[14]

The success of the Norwegian Sea array convinced the US Navy that SOSUS should be extended to the eastern Atlantic, and this created an opportunity for British participation. From the US Navy perspective, Britain was an essential partner for geographic reasons, because of its NATO command responsibilities (although it always emphasised that SOSUS-sharing was a bilateral, not NATO, arrangement), for its overall ASW expertise, and as an operator of nuclear submarines, including Polaris. They also wanted a reserve terminal for the Norwegian array should Keflavik become politically untenable. They accordingly approached the British in 1968 with proposals for constructing a new eastern Atlantic array, capable of covering most of this sea area, linked to a regional evaluation centre in the United Kingdom, which would also be fed in parallel to Keflavik from an upgraded North Atlantic array in the Norwegian Sea. For the British, there were compelling benefits. The eastern Atlantic array would add 'considerably' to knowledge of Soviet navy dispositions, especially the nature and deployment of the submarine-launched ballistic missile force, which was increasing in size, and being equipped with second-generation nuclear submarines, but also submarines transiting to and from the Mediterranean. It would enable the tracking of individual submarines, their marking in times of tension, and prosecution in wartime. The case presented to ministers also stressed that in the western Atlantic, American and Canadian long-range maritime patrol aircraft were almost entirely tasked to prosecute SOSUS contacts, and their acoustic sensors were admirably suited to this task. The capabilities of the new RAF Nimrod aircraft would enable it to adopt the same role in wartime, but prosecution in peacetime would initially be more cautious, to avoid alerting the Soviets to the existence of the new SOSUS system. Surprisingly, the case did not mention what became a primary benefit of SOSUS – the protection of British Polaris submarines by warning of Soviet boats in their vicinity. Nor did it stress the opportunities for British SOSUS-facilitated intelligence collection, which also became an important development from the mid 1970s. The project, known as Backscratch, was approved in early 1971, and the new system, controlled from a centre at RAF Brawdy in Wales, became operational in 1974. Given the scale of the intelligence benefit, the financial cost to the British, of £1.5 million for construction of the centre, about 20 per cent of a frigate, and a contribution to running expenditure, was negligible.[15]

In parallel to the evolution of SOSUS through the 1950s and 1960s, there were important developments in Norway, which was superbly placed geographically to monitor Soviet deployment in northern waters and the main exit route into the Atlantic. The Norwegian Defence Research Establishment began conducting oceanographic research directed at ASW in collaboration with the British and Americans in 1951, but by the late 1950s it had extended this to long-range sonar, with a research station in Andøya, an island eighty miles southwest of Tromsø, aimed at monitoring submarine traffic passing through the gap between here and Jan Mayen island, some 450 miles to the west. This project was initially called Bridge, and comprised a hydrophone antenna offshore at a depth of 1000m (3300ft); experiments with separate antennae hung from moored buoys; and digital signal processing which was conceptually similar to the British Corsair. As with Corsair, the Norwegians found that their aspiration – to 'bridge' all the way to Jan Mayen and locate submarines with precision – was too ambitious. However, by 1960, the US Navy joined Bridge as a partner, and its scope was extended with the laying of additional hydrophone arrays, and provision of the SOSUS LOFAR technology, the first time it was shared with a foreign partner. These new measures, with processing that combined correlation elements similar to Corsair with American narrow-band analysis, delivered good results, and the performance of the system was discreetly validated by using American and Norwegian maritime patrol aircraft to investigate Bridge contacts during the major Soviet summer exercise of 1963. Following this, Bridge became operational, and an assessment the following summer showed that twenty Soviet diesel and four nuclear submarines had been detected over the previous twelve months, with one tracked for eighty-six hours. ONI in Washington judged Bridge to have provided the best submarine-tracking to date. The two Bridge partners now assessed it could provide reliable early warning of submarine deployment into the Atlantic, good location data, and important intelligence on acoustic signatures, especially of new submarine types. It also showed considerable potential to reach eastward into the Barents Sea.[16]

In 1965 the US Navy proposed that since Bridge produced 'extremely important' and often 'unique' material on 'operational characteristics of Soviet submarines, their tactics and transit routes', which were of 'exceptional interest' to the United Kingdom, especially in the vicinity of the British Isles, Bridge intelligence should now be passed to the British. This led to a formal trilateral agreement on the sharing of Bridge and SOSUS intelligence to ensure ASW surveillance of the Norwegian Sea, christened Canasta. The agreement also indoctrinated the British and Norwegians into the construction of the SOSUS array northeast of the Iceland–Faroes gap, and the regional centre at Keflavik. It also contained the important caveat that there would be no exchange of intelligence about the movements of each country's own submarines, unless required for safety reasons. The capability of Bridge prior to the Iceland–Faroes array was evident in a 1966 assessment of coverage between mid June and mid August the previous year. Thirty-six contacts were identified, usually with time, position, direction, signature characteristics, and whether the contact was new. There were nine Soviet surface vessels, ten nuclear submarines and fifteen Soviet diesels. The two remaining contacts were British submarines, one certain and one possible. From 1967, there were substantial upgrades and extensions to the Bridge/Canasta operation, mainly financed by the US Navy, with more advanced processing in a new purpose-built centre in Andøya, and new arrays, including one off Finnmark, which covered the exit from the Barents Sea. A consequence was that the operation became more closely integrated with the expanding SOSUS system.[17]

During the 1950s and 1960s, Britain and the United States collaborated with Norway in another area of naval intelligence collection. Norway had the world's fourth largest merchant fleet, which was highly active in trade with the Communist bloc. Its ships called at important Soviet and bloc ports, providing considerable opportunity to observe and photograph objects of intelligence interest, and even conduct limited SIGINT collection, both in the ports themselves, and along the approach routes. By the late 1950s, the Norwegian intelligence service was actively managing and exploiting this opportunity, recruiting and briefing dedicated agents in ships and providing specialist cameras. It also posted representatives to foreign ports as far afield as Singapore and Hong Kong. The Kola peninsula and White Sea were inevitably the primary interest, especially Murmansk and

Archangel. Between 1955 and 1960, Norwegian intelligence produced about 250 reports per year, about 150 film strips and occasional cine film. Reporting was not confined to Norwegian vessels, but drew on British and German shipping operating in the Barents and Baltic Seas, as well. Nor was it confined to northern Europe, but was extensive in Asia, responding to British and American interest in China, as well as the Soviet Far East. Through the 1960s, the Norwegian effort increased considerably with the annual yield of film strips up to 3000–8000. The highest priority was the shipyards building nuclear submarines, Severodvinsk and Leningrad, but also focused on nuclear facilities, such as the Novaya Zemlya sites. Despite the extension of satellite surveillance, ground-level photography remained highly prized throughout this decade and beyond, for the unique perspectives it could add.[18]

For this reason, NID, with the support of SIS, also ran a collection programme focused primarily on the Barents Sea, exploiting long-range trawlers which regularly fished those waters. There is, perhaps inevitably, some discrepancy between surviving official records of this operation and the later memories of participants. However, there is broad consensus that a formal collection operation, under the codeword Hornbeam, began in the early 1960s centred on Hull, and ran for the remainder of the decade. SIS deployed a retired naval officer, Commander John Brookes, to Hull, and he recruited certain trawler skippers, probably on the recommendation of the company employing them. The skippers were given an intelligence briefing, which included a recognition manual for Soviet warships, and equipped with high-specification cameras and telescopes. They were tasked to photograph any warships or other vessels of interest they encountered during their normal fishing activities. In consultation with skippers, their mates and radio operators were also sometimes briefed, the latter listening and recording traffic on specific frequencies. With rare exceptions, they were instructed not to deviate from their normal fishing pattern, and certainly not to venture into Soviet territorial waters. They were also given security instructions on disposing compromising items in weighted bags if they were boarded, something that never occurred during the life of Hornbeam. In addition to trawler skippers, a few junior serving Royal Navy officers joined trawlers for sea experience, and were then tasked to participate in intelligence collection on the same basis, but these secondments steadily declined over the decade. The value of the intelligence produced from this voluntary collaboration and the naval secondees, which was collected and passed back to SIS through Brookes, is hard to assess from available evidence. It is clear from participants that there were often good-quality photographs taken of warships, including submarines, in close proximity. One describes fishing off Kildin Island at the mouth of the Kola inlet in 1967, watching warships gather together at the entrance on his radar, and then capturing photographs of the brand-new helicopter carrier *Moskva* on her trials.[19]

Apart from the standard Hornbeam effort, there were five more specific intelligence operations using trawlers. The trawler *Arctic Galliard* was specially chartered, using Brookes as intermediary, for a voyage in each of three summers over 1965–67 for SIGINT collection, with a Royal Navy liaison officer and coder specials embarked. The vessel positioned to meet intelligence needs, rather than fishing, with the skipper compensated for any losses. These operations were evidently conducted for GCHQ, but the results were judged disappointing. In the early 1970s there were two operations using the trawlers *Invincible* and *Lord Nelson*, which sought unsuccessfully to recover a Soviet missile known to have landed in international waters following a test-firing. For many years, there was a persistent belief that the modern trawler *Gaul*, sunk with all hands in 1974, was involved in intelligence-gathering, and that this played a part in her loss. The records are clear there was no such intelligence connection, and that Hornbeam was over by 1970 at the latest.[20]

The end of NID and the creation of the Defence Intelligence Staff

While British naval intelligence considered the implications raised by changing Soviet naval capability and policy in the early 1960s, it faced three other immediate challenges: the reform and modernisation of defence intelligence; the Royal Navy acquiring responsibility for the British strategic nuclear deterrent; and the prospect of war against a significant naval opponent in the Far East. The reform of defence intelligence which brought the three service intelligence departments together in a new integrated Defence Intelligence Staff (DIS) on 1 April 1964 was a logical consequence of the wider reorganisation of defence which began in the mid 1950s. This led to the abolition of the individual service ministries and their merging with parts of the Ministry of Aviation/Supply in a unified Ministry of Defence, with a central defence staff. The primary motivations were the need for economy, and more effective use of scarce defence resources through taking a holistic view of Britain's defence needs, rather than summing the separate resource demands of the three services. It reflected recognition dating back to the 1930s that defence was an ever more integrated business. The creation of the chiefs of staff committee, the joint planning staff and the appointment of a Minister for Defence Co-ordination in 1936, and the introduction of an integrated Ministry of Supply after the war, were steps on the way. Unification nevertheless met stiff resistance, and achieving it by 1964 reflected the driving determination of Macmillan and Mountbatten, who became the overarching Chief of the Defence Staff (CDS) in 1959.

Mountbatten's case for integrating defence intelligence was unambiguous. Service, economic and scientific intelligence were 'clearly inter-related', and should be 'much more closely integrated', with service intelligence departments and JIB forming a single agency, accountable to the CDS and Secretary of State. This would deliver a more effective intelligence operation, better focused on the right threats and priorities, along with substantial efficiency savings. Others were less convinced. Although, in theory, the precedent of the JIB, generally judged a success, suggested a single service could deliver considerable benefits, for each chief of staff the loss of their own dedicated intelligence department was an especially neuralgic issue. There was a genuine fear that essential specialist service expertise and understanding would be diluted or lost, but also underlying recognition that 'intelligence is power', meaning CDS would gain in strength and authority at their expense. Mountbatten had the political support to overcome the chiefs' opposition, but it was strong enough to ensure that intelligence integration was both a staged process, and ended some way short of his ambition. The initial DIS organisation brought the three service departments and JIB, together with about a thousand staff, under a single Director General Intelligence (DGI), Kenneth Strong, who moved into the post from heading the JIB. He was supported by a Deputy Chief of Defence Staff (Intelligence) (DCDS (I)), Norman Denning, who moved from DNI, and was, perhaps fittingly, therefore the last full term holder of the post in the line that began with William Hall in 1887.[21] Both were strong supporters of the Mountbatten vision. They oversaw four directorates: Service Intelligence created from merging the three service departments; Economic Intelligence, and Scientific and Technical Intelligence, both largely formed out of the JIB; and a new Management and Support directorate. Under the overall Director of Service Intelligence, the three service departments initially retained their distinct identity under their own individual service head, albeit at lower rank, and continued as before, subject to adopting common hybrid designations. Thus NID4 covering the Far East became DI(NI)2 where 'NI' signified 'naval intelligence', while the OIC became DI(NI)3 for NATO, and DI(NI)10 for rest of the world. Cynics at the time suggested this merely perpetuated the existing system, but embedded new layers of bureaucracy at substantial increased cost.[22]

Mountbatten was determined this initial merger would be merely a first step, and in Strong and Denning, with powerful backing from the forceful and effective Denis Healey as Defence Secretary in the incoming 1964 Labour government, he had powerful advocates for further integration. There was also relentless pressure from the Treasury for savings. In March 1965, as DIS completed its first year, Strong and Denning argued that the merger had produced a more effective intelligence organisation, while saving seventy-five posts. However, they well knew that within the all-important Directorate of Service Intelligence, change had so far been cosmetic. It remained organised on service rather than functional lines, staff looked to their own service head within the directorate, put their own service priorities first and, importantly, believed their career prospects were decided by their own service, not DIS. There was also a pervasive and persistent belief that intelligence was a single-service business. The leadership of the three services evidently hoped that 'co-location' rather than 'integration' would suffice, and life would continue much as before. Strong and Denning were emphatic that co-location was not sufficient, and belief in the primacy of single-service intelligence misguided. Most intelligence sources contributed to all three services, and few modern requirements could be adequately addressed on a single-service basis. A joint approach was required, as the last war had amply demonstrated, and as the new joint commands overseas wanted. New demands, both geographic and functional, were also emerging to reinforce the need for collaboration. Real integration would produce greater efficiency in using scarce intelligence skills and common services, but without it, DGI could never brigade his resources to optimum effect. Overall, the benefits of further integration were considerable and could be achieved without compromising single-service needs. Healey broadly accepted this view, and was willing to face down continued resistance from the chiefs, but accepted advice that completely breaking down service structures in favour of an organisation built on functional lines was too radical at this stage. There was, therefore, a compromise. The management of the Directorate of Service Intelligence was streamlined and restructured on a functional basis, but single-service sections remained at a lower level, especially those covering the Warsaw Pact.[23]

The creation of DIS underlined important points regarding the wider British intelligence community relevant to naval requirements. It emphasised that although the three services each ran important collection operations, good defence intelligence depended on high-quality evaluation and assessment, drawing on open as well as covert sources, and this was a central role of the new organisation. DIS was therefore distinct from SIS and GCHQ, which were both pre-eminently collection agencies. Furthermore, apart from the small Foreign Office Research Department,

DIS possessed the only sources of deep analytical expertise within government. This inevitably led to DIS being asked to tackle intelligence issues outside the defence sphere, a proportion assessed at 20 per cent in 1967.[24] It also triggered further reforms to the JIC system. In 1947 the JIC was upgraded from subcommittee to full committee of the chiefs of staff, and ten years later brought into the Cabinet committee structure, with its requirements ultimately set by the Cabinet and individual ministers, rather than the chiefs. Although it also gained a larger secretariat in 1957, most JIC assessments were still drafted by staff from member departments as an addition to their normal departmental duties. In 1968 the Cabinet Secretary, Sir Burke Trend, achieved two important reforms. He established a permanent assessments staff, composed from secondees from member departments, primarily the Foreign Office and Ministry of Defence, under a Chief of Assessments, and separately, a senior intelligence co-ordinator to supervise intelligence policy and expenditure, with Dick White appointed the first incumbent.[25] In promoting these reforms, Trend stressed that the British intelligence model was different from that of the United States. The latter had pursued the 'professionalisation' of intelligence, with experts on every imaginable subject, technically impeccable, but often politically irrelevant or misleading. They also had a structure and culture of institutional and intellectual independence based on competitive analysis. The British model was leaner, reflecting limited resources, but had two considerable strengths. It was based on a 'joint clearing-house' approach for pooling the best information and reaching a consensual assessment of what it meant. It also enabled the intelligence machine and policy-making, while structurally distinct, to react against each other, ensuring intelligence assessments were policy-relevant, and that the intelligence community shared responsibility for advice to ministers.[26]

The influence of intelligence on British Polaris

As the Admiralty grappled with defence integration in the early 1960s, it faced a second major challenge, posing new intelligence problems, that became a primary preoccupation for the rest of the decade and, indeed, for the remainder of the Cold War. This followed the government decision that the future British nuclear deterrent would comprise the submarine-launched ballistic missile system Polaris, which the Americans agreed to supply, at the Nassau meeting between Prime Minister Harold Macmillan and President Kennedy in December 1962. The journey to British Polaris began seven years earlier in late 1955, when Arleigh Burke told Mountbatten that he had created a Special Projects Office under Rear

Admiral 'Red' Raborn to create a ballistic missile system capable not just of submarine launch, but from underwater. At this stage, the US Navy anticipated a joint project with the US Army to develop the liquid fuel Jupiter missile. It was a further year before the prospect of combining a solid-fuel missile with a new lighter more compact warhead caused the navy to break away and pursue its own project so, strictly speaking, Polaris dates from late 1956. Mountbatten was quick to grasp the revolutionary potential of Polaris and, as with nuclear propulsion, Burke was generous with his briefings. In May 1958 he offered to accommodate a Royal Navy officer in the Special Projects Office, providing Britain, therefore, with remarkable access to, and intelligence on, one of the most sensitive American defence projects.[27] In November 1958 Mountbatten circulated the Minister of Defence (Duncan Sandys) and his fellow chiefs of staff detailed specifications of both the missile and the first submarine to carry it, *George Washington*, which had just been laid down. He stressed that the Polaris submarine was entirely self-sufficient, and could fire with complete freedom of mobility from anywhere within the range bracket of the missiles, which the Americans now expected eventually to reach 2300 miles. The missile could not be jammed and was accurate within two miles. The launching submarine was virtually undetectable, and therefore invulnerable, dispensing with the need for a complex and expensive defence system. By contrast, the defensive task facing the enemy was almost impossible. If the Polaris system was deployed by Britain, it would remove the temptation for an enemy to conduct a surprise attack, because the principal target (the deterrent) would no longer be there, and retribution was certain.[28]

Mountbatten's arguments in favour of Polaris were compelling, and the next two years, fed by further intelligence from liaison with the Special Projects Office, saw a broad consensus across the British defence community that Polaris was the best long-term solution to the requirement for an independent nuclear deterrent. However, as the 1960s began, there were many factors that weighed against Polaris in the short term, and some emerged to cast doubt on the long term too. There were existing proposals for meeting nuclear delivery through to 1970, which had their own momentum. The RAF saw strategic nuclear delivery as central to its role, and was determined to retain it. By contrast, for the Royal Navy, Polaris was still unproven, and with *Dreadnought* three years from completion, it had no experience operating nuclear submarines. It also feared that taking on the deterrent would mean sharp reductions in the conventional fleet. Meanwhile, there was a wide-ranging debate underway within government over Britain's objectives in remaining a nuclear power, the meaning and credibility of 'independent' deterrence, and what counted as sufficient force. Finally, despite Arleigh Burke's enthusiasm and support for British participation in Polaris, he was not the United States government decision-maker. It seemed that if Polaris was supplied at all, this might be subject to American-imposed political constraints, involving its commitment to a NATO multilateral force that Britain would find difficult or unacceptable. The Americans were, however, exceptionally prepared to supply the air-launched ballistic missile Skybolt, currently under development, on the basis that this extended the life of an existing British capability, the V-bombers, rather than creating a new one. Britain therefore adopted this option. It secured an 'independent' deterrent up to 1970, at much cheaper cost than buying Polaris immediately, assuming that was possible, but did not rule out its future purchase. The subsequent American cancellation of Skybolt left the Macmillan government acutely exposed politically, with Polaris now the only viable option. Macmillan's great achievement was to secure its supply at Nassau on acceptable political terms, and subsequently to negotiate a favourable sales agreement, securing long-term technology transfer and support at surprisingly low cost.[29]

Although the Admiralty had done some work examining what would be involved in constructing and operating a Polaris force, as part of various government studies into future deterrent options, the Nassau agreement posed huge challenges. Instead of a hypothetical option for the future, it faced an immediate and immensely complex programme to construct and commission a force of SSBNs, deploying technology of which it had no experience, against a deadline that by today's standards would be viewed as impossible, with the first boat due to be operational in just over five years. Many of the work strands in this programme involved difficult intelligence judgements, on which NID staff, addressing the first requirements as they merged into DIS, again lacked prior experience. Key early decisions where intelligence exerted important influence were the number of missiles to be permanently deployed at sea, which determined the overall size of the force required, and whether to adopt the already-in-service A2 variant, or the more advanced, longer-range A3 variant still under development.

The desirability of minimising risk and extra cost, in a tight schedule, dictated that the British submarines should adopt the American missile compartment with its sixteen missiles. The number of submarines was then a balance between the political and military goal to be achieved, and cost. The naval staff advised that four boats was the minimum to guarantee one constantly on patrol through the lifetime of the force, but that five, providing two constantly on patrol, were required to meet the national targeting requirements previously established for a successor to the V-bomber force, which implied destruction of fifteen to twenty Soviet cities. However, through 1963, as the size of force was debated, intelligence that the Soviet Union was investing in an anti-ballistic missile (ABM) capability steadily accumulated, and introduced a further factor into the decision. By the end of that year, the British and American intelligence picture, drawn from satellite observation, SIGINT, and some observation by respective military attachés, remained fragmentary. Nevertheless, in February 1964 the JIB (still at this stage responsible for scientific and technical intelligence) judged that it would be wise to assume that a Soviet ABM system would be effective against Polaris A3 from mid 1968, when the first boat went on patrol. Two boats constantly at sea would not only double the number of missiles fired, but enable their launching from two widely separated geographical points, greatly complicating the task of an ABM defence. Ultimately, much hinged on a political assessment of the level of assurance needed for an independent national nuclear deterrent, in the remote circumstance that Britain somehow faced the Soviet Union and an ABM system alone. This assurance had to be balanced against the extra cost of a fifth boat, but also the resilience it provided in the event of an accident causing temporary or permanent loss of a boat. If the primary purpose of the Polaris force was to make a nuclear contribution to NATO, and independent use judged almost inconceivable, then the value of a fifth boat was marginal, especially as the naval staff hoped a four-boat force could provide a second at sea about two-thirds of the time (a calculation that proved wildly optimistic).[30]

The consensus across the defence community and among responsible ministers on this issue between 1963–65 was finely balanced. The outgoing Conservative government tilted reluctantly to five boats, and the incoming 1964 Labour government reversed it to four. This reflected acceptance that this was the minimum viable force, increased desire to minimise costs, but also greater ambivalence towards the possibility of Britain ever deploying its force alone. The choice of the A3 was easier. The ABM intelligence was an important factor swaying the decision, since the A3 allowed a more advanced warhead with penetration aids. However, its greater range (950 miles more than the A2) was also a major advantage, and once it was established that the Americans would upgrade their whole fleet to this variant, it was desirable for Britain to ensure long-term missile supply at minimal cost.[31]

Although these initial decisions regarding submarine numbers and missile type had profound implications for the effectiveness and vulnerability of the force over a lifetime which turned out to be twenty-six years, in reaching them little account was taken of how Soviet anti-submarine capability might evolve to threaten the force. This absence is especially surprising, given that the decisions coincided with the arrival of Penkovsky's *Special Collection* intelligence, stressing the priority the Soviet navy attached to anti-Polaris operations. The A3 range advantage over the A2 increased the potential Polaris patrol areas available in the Atlantic, otherwise confined to the Norwegian Sea, by a factor of three, and enabled continued coverage of most potential targets in the Soviet Union during a transit into the Mediterranean. It also enabled many Soviet targets to be reached from the Indian Ocean, where deployment was seriously, if surprisingly, contemplated for a period in the mid 1960s.[32] These patrol options vastly increased the security of the force, by enabling boats to operate much further from Soviet home waters, and by extending the areas an enemy had to search, yet this factor apparently exerted little influence over the choice of missile. Likewise, the ASW threat did not feature significantly in the debate over a fifth submarine.[33] Yet a second submarine always at sea added substantially to the resilience of the force in the event of one boat being detected. This lack of early focus on the ASW threat probably reflected both lack of knowledge in 1963 on current Soviet out-of-area ASW capability, and how it might develop, especially in regard to their new SSNs, but also the Royal Navy's own lack of nuclear submarine operating experience.

However, intelligence did shape other decisions, and exerted more influence once detailed operational planning started. The choice of Faslane on the Clyde as Polaris base took account of the difficulties faced by hostile submarines or other forces in conducting surveillance in the approach areas, and the opportunities offered by different exit routes.[34] Once the A3 decision was made, knowledge of Soviet transit and deployment patterns influenced selection of proposed patrol areas. The requirement for Polaris boats to have options for obtaining a precise update of their position covertly spurred a major hydrographic programme to produce highly detailed classified charts for navigation by bottom contour fixing. By late 1967, six months before the first Polaris operational patrol, DIS acknowledged the priority the Soviets placed on countering Polaris, and the potential role played by their SSNs, and the British naval staff produced a reasonably realistic scenario for how the Soviets might implement such an anti-Polaris operation.[35]

In the winter of 1964/65 the political judgement that the guaranteed launch of one boatload of missiles, capable of destroying Moscow, Leningrad and five additional cities, was sufficient insurance against a remote hypothetical 'supreme national interest' emergency (in the Nassau language) could be viewed as credible, as well as politically expedient. However, as the intelligence on Soviet ABM capability evolved further, through the second half of the 1960s, it posed increasing questions for the continuing credibility of the proposed British Polaris force through the next decade. To answer these questions, the British were heavily dependent on the Americans for both intelligence, and insights into options for countering the ABM threat, which invariably drew on testing and modelling which only the Americans could undertake. Assessment of the threat was complicated, not just by gaps in the intelligence, but limited expertise within the British intelligence and nuclear communities on the complex issues involved. The same applied to countermeasures, where the Americans were slow to reveal a comprehensive view of the options, so that working these out from disclosures across different parts of the British-American defence, intelligence and nuclear exchange network became a distinct intelligence challenge in itself. All of this arguably justified Mountbatten's case that an integrated DIS was essential to tackle the big new problems of the Cold War. By early 1965, through their liaison with the Polaris Special Projects Office, the British knew that the Americans were planning to convert the majority of their Polaris submarines to take a more advanced and heavier missile, the Poseidon C3, offering improvements in accuracy, payload, and penetration ability.[36] By the following year, they knew that the Americans saw Poseidon as a large part of the answer to the ABM problem by fitting it with a multiple independent re-entry vehicle (MIRV) system, capable of deploying multiple warheads against different targets. Despite the attractions of preserving commonality with the Americans, the Labour government ruled this out on political, technical and cost grounds.

Nevertheless, the Americans at this stage also planned improvements to their residual Polaris force, which were of definite relevance and interest, and from early 1967, they were increasingly generous in identifying the measures for improving the ability of Polaris to penetrate an ABM system. Essentially, these comprised various combinations of missile and warhead re-entry body-hardening against X-ray damage, from high-altitude nuclear explosions, and multiple decoys to swamp the defensive radar picture. Although the British defence and intelligence community still struggled to construct a comprehensive intelligence picture of the ABM problem, by 1969 there was a broad consensus emerging that substantial improvements were required to keep the British Polaris force credible against the system the Soviets were expected to deploy through the 1970s. British expert opinion was coalescing around an improved version of the American penetration system called Antelope, which was prepared for their residual non-Poseidon Polaris force, but ultimately not fitted. The British-designed Super Antelope was assessed to improve Polaris penetrability by a factor of fifteen, almost twice as much as the basic Antelope, ensuring the continuing effectiveness of Polaris into the 1980s at a capital cost of around £65m, about the same as overall capital expenditure on Polaris the previous fiscal year.[37] There were important dissenters to this view, notably the government's chief scientific adviser, Professor Solly Zuckerman, who, drawing on CIA assessments, argued that the scale and effectiveness of the Soviet system was exaggerated, and also saw no prospect of British Polaris being deployed in isolation. In addition to disputes over ABM effectiveness, there was also the emerging prospect of an ABM limitations agreement between the United States and the Soviet Union, which might drastically reduce the threat. Zuckerman provided some valuable insights into American intelligence assessments and evolving policy, but not all his claims were accurate, and he was guilty of the same partisanship he complained about in others, thereby undermining his case.[38]

At the high political level, Zuckerman's influence was also tempered by the advice of the Cabinet Secretary, Sir Burke Trend. He had produced a masterly summary of the arguments for and against Polaris as an independent British deterrent, for Prime Minister Harold Wilson in December 1967.[39] Despite its careful balance, it was one of the clearest and most compelling cases in favour ever produced. Crucially, Burke emphasised in beautifully concise terms the case for Polaris improvement. It would leave the British independent threat to the Soviet Union, and therefore its credibility, only marginally reduced, even if the present Soviet ABM plans were completed, and extended to cover the whole of western Russia. The Soviet Union would then have to increase their defences tenfold to reduce the British threat to below ten cities. This was an easy calculus for ministers to understand. In the immediate term, Trend's case helped ensure the risk of Polaris being cancelled, even at this late stage, was removed. In the longer term, his argument for improvement probably weighed heavily with Wilson, Healey as Defence Secretary, and Michael Stewart as Foreign Secretary, although apparently not with Roy Jenkins, as Chancellor of the Exchequer.[40]

Continuing doubts over ultimate Soviet ABM scope and intent, the insurance offered by a second boatload of missiles at sea, albeit for part of the time, the ability to sidestep the initial ABM radars with careful choice of submarine patrol areas, and residual political ambivalence over the need for an assured independent capability encouraged Labour ministers to defer final decisions on Polaris improvement before they lost office in 1970. However, despite Zuckerman's lobbying, a complex mix of political and military factors, and institutional pressure, was now injecting momentum towards an anti-ABM programme at the advanced end of the range of options, based on a worst-case intelligence picture. Wiser American voices warned British counterparts they were taking on challenges that would test their capabilities to the limit. As 1970 got underway, with an election in prospect, two things were badly needed. The first was a fundamental review of all the available ABM intelligence, including prospects for a limitations agreement, and recent hints that Soviet deployment might be stalling. The second was a clear government position on precisely what goals Britain's strategic nuclear force had to meet. These could then feed a clear naval staff requirement, and the options to meet it. Either the basic and already semi-proven Antelope or, even at this late stage, building a fifth submarine might have emerged as better options.[41] The naval staff had indeed resurfaced the arguments for a fifth submarine, in the context of both the ABM and new ASW threats in mid 1969.[42]

Intelligence and Indonesian Confrontation

The intelligence problems associated with the acquisition of Polaris partially overlapped and, through the deployment proposals for the Indian Ocean, were marginally influenced by a limited war in the Far East with Indonesia from 1963 to 1966, although neither side ever acknowledged formal hostilities, and it was referred to, at the time and since, as the Indonesian Confrontation, or *Konfrontasi*. The catalyst was the amalgamation in September 1963 of the separate territories of Malaya, Singapore and British Borneo to form the Federation of Malaysia. By 1963, these territories were all self-governing, although Britain retained varying responsibility for their defence and external affairs. The Federation was encouraged and sponsored by Britain to promote the long-term stability and security of the territories, reduce the risk of Communist subversion, ensure continued use of the vital British military base at Singapore, and ultimately help Britain preserve influence in the region, at reduced cost and liability. However, Indonesia, under President Sukarno, saw the Federation as an artificial construct designed to perpetuate British imperialism, and forestall its claims to the Borneo territories. Sukarno's attitude was conditioned by an increasingly anti-Western stance from the late 1950s, which brought steadily closer links with the Soviet Union and China. By 1963, Indonesia had received more Soviet military aid than any country, save Cuba. The combination of aggressive nationalism and anti-Western ideology, encouraged by the influential Indonesian Communist Party, persuaded Sukarno to mount a costly, but ultimately successful, campaign to gain control of Netherlands New Guinea in 1962. Against this background, from early 1963 Sukarno pursued a strategy to destabilise the Malaysia project through a campaign of subversion and infiltration, initially with deniable irregular insurgent units, but later regular Indonesian army units. Borneo was initially the main focus for infiltration, but western Malaya also soon became a target.

In meeting Indonesian aggression, British strategy was to minimise the damage inflicted by infiltration, and wear down Indonesian resources and political will, while managing the risk of escalation, to avoid alienating international opinion or a scale of Indonesian military commitment that required an unacceptable level of British reinforcement to defeat it.[43] Britain had an excellent picture of Indonesian naval capability as Confrontation began. This came from the defence attachés in the embassy in Jakarta (which remained open throughout the conflict), supported by regular visits from naval staff in Singapore, SIS and GCHQ coverage, and covert RAF reconnaissance flights.[44] The six submarines of the 7th Submarine Division based in Singapore also conducted intelligence-gathering patrols against Indonesian naval targets, and in support of GCHQ SIGINT, as they did on any visiting Soviet vessels in the region, and on Chinese targets.[45] Once the Confrontation was underway, the intercepted communications of the Indonesian embassy in London also proved a valuable source on Indonesian policy and strategic intent. On paper, the Indonesian naval order of battle, composed mainly of Soviet-supplied warships and aircraft, appeared significant and relatively modern. It included a cruiser, the former *Ordzhonikidze*, of Commander Crabb fame, transferred in 1962, thirteen destroyers/frigates (increasing to eighteen by late 1965), twelve Whiskey-class submarines, of which perhaps six were operational, four Komar-class fast patrol boats (twelve by 1965), each armed with two SS-N-2 Styx missiles. There were numerous smaller craft, and a considerable mining capability. The air force also had modern Soviet aircraft, including about twenty Tu-16 Badgers, armed with air-launched Kennel missiles, and MiG-19 and MiG-21 fighters. In theory, these forces could support more ambitious land attacks against Malaysia, and DIS recognised that, if shrewdly used, drawing on about 150 Soviet naval advisers, the Komars and submarines posed a potential threat to British sea communications, and to Malaysian commerce.[46] However, British intelligence assessments consistently judged that Indonesian fighting efficiency was low, reflecting lack of training, and poor maintenance and support. DIS doubted the SS-N-2s were usable without direct Soviet participation in firing them, which was unlikely, while the submarines would be restricted to simple mining operations, or occasional attacks on merchant ships, and vulnerable to British countermeasures. Serviceability for the Badgers and MiGs was, at best, 50 per cent, and use of the Kennels without direct Soviet assistance was again unlikely. The Royal Navy Far East Fleet, usually with two strike carriers, and comprising a balanced force of around eighty warships by 1964, about one-third of overall Royal Navy strength, and RAF strike forces at Singapore, including V-bombers in the conventional role, were a major deterrent to Indonesian adventurism. The JIC judged that Indonesian military commanders knew that any major intervention with conventional forces would be ineffective, lead to heavy losses, and meet a devastating British response.[47]

Once the Confrontation began, intelligence from the same sources as those pre-hostilities remained effective in monitoring Indonesian deployment and additions to its order of battle. With ministerial approval, air reconnaissance was more extensive, keeping a constant check on airfields and naval bases.[48] Ironically, many of the airfields featured were those receiving attention during Operation Meridian twenty years earlier. Good tactical intelligence, primarily from SIGINT, but also prisoner interrogation, enabled Royal Navy patrols significantly to reduce Indonesian efforts to infiltrate across the Malacca Straits into western Malaya from mid 1964. At the strategic level, intelligence was generally good enough to guide commanders on wider Indonesian naval dispositions and the possibility of intervention, and therefore in managing the risk of escalation. Theatre commanders, the chiefs of staff and ministers were acutely aware that if deterrence failed, major reinforcement in the Far East would be necessary, with dire repercussions for commitments elsewhere.[49]

However, strategic intelligence assessments did not always sufficiently allow for unpredictability or miscalculation in Indonesian decision-making. The most serious risk of naval escalation came during the Sunda Strait crisis in September 1964, stemming from the Indonesian claim of sovereignty over the entire waters of the Sunda and Lombok straits, the main passages through the Indonesian archipelago. From the late 1950s, Indonesia demanded prior approval of all warship movements through the two straits, but this was resisted by the United States, Britain and the Commonwealth, who rejected Indonesian sovereignty claims, and insisted on the right of innocent passage. The 1964 crisis was triggered by the transit of the British carrier *Victorious* and her escorts through the Sunda Straits in late August to visit Fremantle in Australia. In accordance with standing British policy, the Jakarta embassy notified the Indonesian government, but did not seek permission. While such transits were not unusual, the deployment of a carrier group immediately following the first major Indonesian raids on western Malaya risked interpretation as deliberately provocative, and led to a firm response. Indonesia first demanded more formal notification in future, then indicated that passage for *Victorious* on her return in mid September would be refused, and put her forces on alert. This posed Britain with a dilemma. Diverting the *Victorious* force would involve considerable loss of face, when expressing political will and determination was a key factor in winning the Confrontation. This initially produced a bullish attitude in Whitehall, and willingness to accept military action, encouraged by intelligence suggesting Indonesian nervousness over British intent. However, theatre commanders were more cautious, stressing the potential risks to the force from combined all-arms attack in restricted waters. Balancing these factors provoked sharp divisions between Singapore and London, and between different Whitehall departments, with tensions increased by the Indonesian announcement of 'naval exercises' in the strait. It had been decided that destroyers alone would transit the strait, while *Victorious* diverted north of Sumatra, when the Indonesians offered their own compromise. They had no objection if, owing to the Sunda naval exercises, the British force transited the Lombok Strait instead, an offer the British accepted. There has been much debate over who won from this episode. Each side claimed victory but, in reality, both made significant concessions rather than risk a descent into war, where neither could guarantee adequate benefits to balance the possible losses.[50]

Special collection in the Barents Sea

Meanwhile, in northern waters on the other side of the world, the British-American SNCP patrols continued in the Barents Sea throughout the 1960s. Until 1968, the Royal Navy still conducted these with conventional submarines, although usually now with the new *Porpoise-* and *Oberon-*class boats, which were much superior to the 'T' class. By contrast, the US Navy almost always deployed SSNs. Their greater mobility, and the presence of American boats on station perhaps six times as long as British in a given year, meant that the Americans now dominated the intelligence partnership here in this period, although British tactical skills and risk appetite still produced surprisingly good results. ELINT, especially collection of missile telemetry, became increasingly important across this decade with most naval ballistic and cruise missile tests now conducted from the Nenoksa (also Nyonoksa) test site twenty miles northwest of Severodvinsk.[51] On several occasions, British submarines conducting surveillance in northern waters in this period were counter-detected by

Soviet vessels, hunted effectively and forced to surface. In early 1963, after *Sealion* took refuge in Norwegian waters, the Admiralty admitted to Norwegian intelligence that she had been surprised by a Soviet helicopter while collecting ELINT when monitoring a Soviet exercise off Kildin island. They promised to share the information collected.[52] In summer 1965 *Opportune* was acquired by two *Skoriy*-class destroyers she was shadowing in the North Norwegian Sea, and prosecuted aggressively for over thirty hours.[53]

In 1968 the Royal Navy began deploying SSNs to the Barents Sea, initially using the first two boats of entirely British design, *Valiant* and *Warspite*, since *Dreadnought* was judged too noisy. From this point onward, for the rest of the Cold War British SSNs conducted at least two patrols per year with one submarine in the SSN fleet, and later two, always 'specially fitted' with tailored and sometimes experimental sensors and recording equipment for the SNCP task.[54] Although always under national command, these patrols were now part of an integrated programme supervised and co-ordinated by the US Navy, and there was often an American liaison officer embarked. The greater mobility and endurance of the SSNs, their speed for shifting between areas or for following fast-moving targets or for evasion, and their more sophisticated sonar made them ideal collection platforms, and with no requirement to snort, they were at less risk from counter-detection. They could deploy techniques, such as the underwater look on a moving target, which were difficult or impossible for a conventional boat. They also had the space to accommodate often more than twenty specialist intelligence personnel for a patrol.[55]

The British SSNs began operating at a crucial time just as capabilities foreshadowed in the *Special Collection* intelligence of the early 1960s, such as Kresta cruisers and the *Moskva*-class helicopter carriers to support long-range ASW operations, were arriving on the scene. They also coincided with the appearance of the far more capable second-generation Soviet nuclear submarines, the Yankee SSBNs, broadly comparable to *George Washington* and A1 Polaris, Victor-class SSNs, and the formidable Charlie, the first SSGN able to deploy an anti-surface missile from underwater. In May 1968 the Americans knew from satellite imagery, subsequently shared with the British, that the first Yankee would shortly become operational, and no less than fifteen others were under construction.[56] The role of the SNCP boats was critical in establishing the characteristics and capability of these new-generation surface warships and submarines. Their targets were not only more accessible, but many activities, such as missile- and torpedo-firings, were only carried out in the secure waters of the Barents Sea, or equivalent areas adjacent to the Soviet Far East bases. Collecting acoustic intelligence on the new nuclear boats and assessing the threat posed by the Victor SSNs against the Western SSBN force was especially important. At the start of 1968, DIS judged that the Soviets had started well behind the West in the SSN field, but the new generation would be 'very good'. The Victor could achieve 30 knots, dive to 1600ft, a depth unreachable by the British Mark 24 torpedo under development, was considerably quieter, and equipped with much better sonar than the November.[57]

The deployment of the British SSNs in the Barents Sea restored full parity with the Americans in the quality, if not the quantity, of intelligence collected here, and ensured that as the 1970s opened, the naval intelligence exchange remained as strong as ever. The influence of the British SNCP contribution extended beyond the relationship between DI3 Navy and ONI. It was valued by the United States Defence Intelligence Agency (DIA) (established in 1961 to provide strategic direction and co-ordination to the individual service agencies) and the CIA Directorate of Intelligence, while GCHQ analysis of the COMINT and ELINT collected was important to NSA.[58] It undoubtedly helped ensure continued access to American intelligence sources, like Corona, that the British did not possess. When Britain faced decisions over Polaris improvement, this wider access to American knowledge was crucial. The importance of Corona to the naval intelligence picture in the late 1960s was illustrated in a detailed CIA survey of Yankee SSBN construction in October 1968, which assessed that three were now in service, another four fitting out, and that numbers would reach thirty-five by mid 1973, with about two-thirds committed to the Northern Fleet.[59] Corona intelligence also showed that by the late 1960s, Leningrad and Gorkiy, inland east of Moscow, had joined Severodvinsk and Komsomolsk in the far east in building nuclear submarines, with definite signs that Leningrad was constructing a new type. This was soon identified as the Victor-class SSN.[60]

This intelligence dividend, and its direct relevance to the nuclear deterrent, ensured the continuing approval and support of the prime minister, and foreign and defence secretaries for the SNCP operation. The naval and DIS leadership were shrewd in managing ministers. They were scrupulous in setting out the case for the patrols and detailed presentations, frequently including the prime minister himself, provided intelligence highlights on return. Naval leaders had evidently absorbed Macmillan's comment when approving RAF SIGINT collection on behalf of the Admiralty in 1958 – 'Sometime, it would be interesting to know what – if any – use all these operations are'.[61] The small group of indoctrinated ministers, therefore, remained surprisingly robust in weighing benefits against risks, even when things went wrong, including a near-disaster when the SSN *Warspite* collided with an Echo II SSGN while trailing it in October 1968. *Warspite* suffered significant damage and was initially patched up in Loch Ewe to suggest this was due to hitting an 'iceberg', before undergoing permanent repair at Barrow. It was not the last such incident.[62]

Overall, British naval intelligence was reasonably successful during the 1960s in monitoring the evolution of its primary Soviet opponent, and in managing other threats like Indonesia. However, the political and defence context underpinning the naval intelligence effort changed profoundly across the decade. In 1960 the Royal Navy remained a significant global force, with nearly half its frontline strength deployed in the Mediterranean, Persian Gulf and Far East. By 1970, changing geopolitical circumstances and economic retrenchment meant it would soon be focused almost entirely on the North Atlantic. If Harold Wilson's vision for deploying Polaris in the Indian Ocean looked somewhat fanciful in 1965, five years later it appeared ridiculous. There were other key trends too. The Soviet naval threat to transatlantic communications and NATO reinforcement remained important, but it was the maturing of the SSBN that now set the agenda. Both sides were determined to reduce the threat from enemy SSBNs, while protecting their own. For Britain, protecting its nuclear deterrent and maintaining its effectiveness was now its top naval intelligence priority. The arrival of its new SSNs had underlined how the SNCP programme was central to this, and that it was one area where Britain enjoyed greatest comparative intelligence advantage. The five additional SSNs building by end 1969 offered scope to extend this intelligence role in new ways. Exploiting such advantage mattered if Britain was to continue benefiting from American intelligence that it now had little hope of collecting itself.

34

The 1970s: The Rise of Submarine Intelligence

As the 1970s opened, both the British and American intelligence communities reviewed the Soviet naval threat, and drawing on broadly shared, but primarily American, sources, reached similar conclusions. These reviews reflected on changes over the previous decade, as well as looking forward. They agreed that some long-established goals of Soviet naval strategy, defence of the homeland against seaborne attack, interdiction of enemy maritime communications, and support for own land operations had not altered across the 1960s. However, important new goals were now apparent, notably provision of a maritime strategic nuclear strike capability, primarily directed at the United States, and the promotion of global political influence, with a substantial permanent naval presence in the Mediterranean, and regular appearances in the Caribbean and Indian Ocean. There were also important shifts in emphasis and execution within these over-arching goals, with a more offensive approach both to ASW directed at countering Polaris, and to counter-carrier operations. The focus on taking the offensive with more forward deployment in the North Atlantic, and the capability for longer-range global operations was evident in new construction, where there was also a notable shift towards improving quality, rather than just increasing numbers, a trend especially evident in the new-generation submarines. Finally, both communities saw a steady improvement in the Soviet navy's fighting efficiency. Although Soviet commanders displayed a certain rigidity and lack of initiative, and were hampered by a large proportion of conscripts, their ability to conduct increasingly complex operations was not to be underestimated.[1]

The Soviet nuclear submarine threat moves centre stage
British assessments, which were heavily influenced by CIA and DIA data and analysis, emphasised the priority the Soviet navy was now giving

to nuclear submarine construction. Building capacity had expanded significantly, with Leningrad and Gorkiy now established as additional nuclear shipyards, and production by 1970 was about double that of the early 1960s, with a new boat launched on average every three weeks. DIS estimated that the nuclear submarine programme absorbed about three-quarters of naval investment, with about half devoted to the new Yankee-class SSBNs, and the other half divided about equally between new SSN and SSGN classes. These construction calculations were mainly based on satellite imagery. DIS concluded that the Soviet navy was becoming a predominantly nuclear submarine force, and it expected this pattern to continue. The new nuclear submarine classes combined high-speed and deep-diving performance with improved low-frequency active and passive sonar, and were much quieter. A large number of new classes had appeared simultaneously, six in two years, and the pace of development suggested yet another new generation could arrive during this decade. With the exception of the Yankee, all of these new classes had anti-submarine potential, and there had been a notable increase in submarine-versus-submarine exercises. DIS thought the present gap between Western and Soviet sonar capability would probably narrow within the next few years, and if Soviet progress continued at the present pace, there might be no gap at all by 1980, giving the Soviet submarine force potential qualitative, as well as quantitative, superiority.[2]

Within the surface navy, the trend was towards powerful multi-role vessels like the Kresta II cruisers, which illustrated the Soviet intent to combine offensive firepower while improving survivability in the open ocean. DIS believed they were, accordingly, armed with new shorter-range, surface strike missiles, which no longer required external targeting information, powerful surface-to-air missile armament to facilitate survival outside the range of fighter protection, and a comprehensive package of electronic warfare (EW) and ASW sensors and weapons, including a helicopter. These ships fitted the new concept of task forces operating well forward for attacking carrier groups, or Polaris hunting. Despite the priority given to the nuclear submarine fleet, numbers of guided missile cruisers and destroyers were predicted to double by 1975. The naval air force was also expanding, and receiving better aircraft, such as the Badger G, equipped with new Kelt air-to-surface missiles. Important targets like the strike fleet could be attacked by up to one hundred aircraft, with successive waves of six to eight launching twelve to sixteen Kelts from eighty to a hundred miles, co-ordinated with submarine-launched cruise missiles. Only in airborne ASW capability were the Soviets noticeably still behind the major Western navies.[3]

Both British and American assessments stressed the increased priority given to countering Polaris. They judged that Soviet naval leaders were satisfied they had solved the problem posed by the US Navy carrier strike fleet, and the nuclear threat it posed to the homeland. They now had the intelligence systems to provide early warning of its approach and fix it accurately, and the means to deal with it through the combination of long-range reconnaissance and strike aircraft, cruise missile- and torpedo-armed submarines, and missile-armed surface vessels. The same confidence did not extend to the Western SSBN threat. British and American assessments agreed that this was now the highest-priority task facing the Soviet navy and, although they were confident it did not yet have a credible solution, it was pursuing every aspect of ASW warfare to find one. For the Americans, the possibility of the Soviets making enough ASW progress to render Polaris vulnerable was an intelligence issue that ranked alongside the ability of NATO holding the central front, without immediate resort to tactical nuclear weapons.[4]

CIA assessments shared with the British expected the Soviets to adopt three measures in wartime against Polaris submarines: destroying their bases; attempting to detect and trail submarines on leaving their base, and destroy them before they reached their operating area; and deploying ASW task forces to locate and destroy submarines in their predicted launching areas.[5] All three elements were currently being exercised. Soviet SSBNs had not yet deployed in range of Polaris bases in the United States but Golf- and Hotel-class boats had operated in areas from where they could reach overseas bases, including the Holy Loch in Scotland. AGIs regularly conducted surveillance off Polaris bases overseas, and had attempted to direct their SSNs into a trail on an outgoing SSBN. They had also deployed harassing tactics against SSBNs entering or leaving. In April 1973 an AGI aggressively pursued the British SSBN *Repulse* when she left the Clyde, apparently intent on ramming her.[6] In November 1974 the SSBN *James Madison* collided with a Soviet SSN waiting to take up trail off the approaches to the Clyde.[7] Meanwhile, all major new surface units were ASW-capable, with improved sensors and weapons, and were engaging in increasingly complex exercises, which were moving into the open ocean. The most important new ASW ship was the *Moskva*-class helicopter carrier, equipped with fifteen Hormone helicopters with new dipping sonar. They also had advanced hull-mounted and variable depth sonars, stand-off ASW weapons, and surface-to-air missile systems for protection. They were evidently designed as the core of ASW task forces to hunt Polaris. CIA saw all these recent Soviet advances in ASW reflecting decisions taken in the late 1950s, and foreshadowed in Penkovsky's intelligence almost ten years earlier.

Reflecting this intelligence as well as their own, the British naval staff were equally focused on SSBN vulnerability, and DIS agreed that the Polaris problem had led to greater emphasis on ASW across every branch of the Soviet navy. In autumn 1969 a permanent working group, in which Denis Healey took a personal interest, was established to monitor this. In addition to the threats identified by the Americans, the group was tasked to consider the risk of mining, especially in the Clyde approaches to the Polaris bases, detection by satellite and seabed-mounted sensors, and the possibility of deploying infrared sensors to detect the 'thermal scars' left by a nuclear submarine. The biggest problem was judged to come from the new Victor SSN, which was known to have new low-frequency active sonars. Its passive capability was harder to assess, and partly depended on self-noise reduction, which was still being evaluated, but it was likely both the Victor and Charlie SSGN had a significantly longer-range passive search capability than their predecessors, possibly combined with frequency analysis equipment. Although this improved sonar capability potentially increased the risk to Western SSBNs on patrol, the sea areas involved were vast, and the Soviet SSN numbers required for an effective search, without intelligence of specific locations, would be prohibitive, given the need to cover the Mediterranean, north Pacific, and potentially north Indian Ocean, as well as the Atlantic. For the foreseeable future, the risk of detection on patrol would therefore be limited to chance encounters: the probability of these was low, and if a Soviet SSN did get into a successful trail, its duration would be short. To help assess this risk, it was hoped the Americans would agree to deploy an SSN to exercise with a British SSBN and attempt a trail. Meanwhile, measures were underway to improve the sonar performance of the British SSBNs, the installation of a GRP dome over the 2001 transducer array to reduce flow noise being the most promising. There was also a wider programme to reduce radiated noise from the machinery spaces, including the reactor pumps.[8]

Balancing the threat posed by Polaris and its Poseidon successor, the JIC saw the arrival of the Yankee SSBN, which had begun operational patrols in the Atlantic in mid 1969, providing a fundamental transformation in Soviet nuclear strike capability. With one boat completing every six to eight weeks, the JIC expected the force to comprise thirty-five by the end of 1972, and easily to match total Western SSBN numbers by 1975. However, DIS stressed that for the next few years, despite this growing equality in numbers, their impact would be reduced by shorter missile range, estimated at only 1100 miles, and consequently longer transit time to reach patrol areas, meaning time on station was presently only about thirty days out of a sixty-day patrol. DIS assessed that at the end of 1970 there were usually two Yankees on patrol in the Atlantic, although it was puzzled that the patrol areas used so far were outside missile range of North American targets. In fact, the range of the initial version of the SS-N-6 fitted to the Yankee was about one-third greater than DIS and its American counterparts believed. However, DIS did know through ELINT that a new 3000-mile missile was also under development, which would significantly enhance the credibility and flexibility of the Soviet SSBN force, although the launching platform for the new missile was not yet certain.[9]

While DIS assumed the Victor was primarily aimed at targeting SSBNs, the rationale for, and capability, of the contemporary Charlie-class SSGN initially posed questions on which only the SNCP programme could gradually shed light. The Charlie brought the benefit of Victor-type performance, and carried eight new SS-N-7 Starbright missiles, initially believed to have an optimum range of seventeen miles and maximum of thirty, which proved about right. At the end of 1970, when two boats were believed operational, DIS was not sure if the missiles could be launched submerged, but judged this likely. While this was an obvious advantage, and made the Charlie harder to detect, DIS was puzzled as to why the Soviets had settled for a much shorter missile range than the SS-N-3 carried by the earlier Juliets and Echoes, even though the missile flight envelope was similar. Although the shorter range removed the possibility or need for mid-course correction, as required with the SS-N-3, it was also not clear how the Charlie would establish the range or classification of its target, given the known limitations of even the latest Soviet sonar. It later became clear that the SS-N-7 was a stopgap missile, derived from the SS-N-2 Styx and fitted because of major development problems with the intended missile, the more advanced and long-range SS-N-9 Siren, which entered submarine service in the late 1970s. The Soviets apparently hoped to overcome the Charlie's sensor limitations with targeting data from satellites. However, the results here were poor, undermining the Charlie's effectiveness. Partly for this reason, relatively few were built, with only twelve operational by mid 1975, half the numbers DIS expected in 1970, and only five more equipped with the new SS-N-9 by the end of the decade. While the Charlie ultimately proved less dangerous than the British and Americans feared, it had two important consequences. It encouraged them both to invest in passive sonar for their surface ASW forces (to avoid disclosing valuable targeting data with active transmissions), and it stimulated a noise-reduction programme for future ship classes.[10]

By late 1970, DIS had identified another potential new SSN class, designated the Alfa. It acknowledged knowing little about it, and its information probably derived entirely from the Americans. CIA first spotted the Alfa at the Sudomekh shipyard at Leningrad, soon after its launching in April 1969, although it is not clear if this initial sighting came from satellite coverage, or a visiting naval attaché walking the Neva river. Intense satellite study over the next eighteen months, before she was moved by inland waterway to the Northern Fleet bases for trials, raised questions that took a decade to resolve. Satellite imagery soon established that the Alfa was probably nuclear-powered and streamlined for high speed but, with an estimated displacement of 2600 tons, was smaller than any nuclear boat produced by any country to date. Subsequent analysis raised the possibility that she represented a revolutionary combination of a titanium alloy hull, a novel, high-power nuclear plant, possibly liquid metal-cooled, and significant automation permitting a smaller crew. This assessment was broadly accurate, but it required many years of further painstaking intelligence work before it was accepted by senior naval staff on either side of the Atlantic. In 1971 CIA expected nine Alfas to complete by 1975, but the first boat suffered a serious reactor accident in 1972, and was scrapped the following year. This delayed the programme, with a second boat only completed in 1977, and three others by the end of the decade. DIS then expected five in service by the end of 1981. The Alfas continued to suffer from poor reliability, and only rarely deployed operationally, although when they did they could prove formidable opponents, as the British SSN *Spartan* discovered in July 1980, when she was counter-detected and pursued at high speed. The Soviet persistence with the class, despite severe technical difficulties and considerable cost, suggested they still anticipated important benefits. Ultimately, the intelligence which illuminated the Alfa story had two consequences. It convinced the British and American naval intelligence communities that the Soviet navy would embrace radical and unconventional concepts, and incur considerable risk to achieve decisive advantage over their Western counterparts. By 1980, DIS assessed the Soviets had largely solved the Alfa's technical problems, were determined to capitalise on its deep diving in excess of 2000ft and 40-knot speed, and would either produce an improved version or a new class exploiting its technology which showed 'remarkable advances' and would challenge Western ASW capability. The Soviet intent here and the struggle to understand it had obvious parallels with Dönitz's pursuit of revolutionary step change in 1942–43. The Alfa also persuaded the British and Americans that better torpedoes were urgently needed, to address the Soviet emphasis on speed and deep diving in their future submarines. For the British, this ultimately led to the Spearfish programme.[11]

By the end of 1973, DIS could answer some of the questions outstanding at the beginning of the decade. The priority the Soviet navy attached to strategic nuclear strike against the United States through its SSBN programme, and to countering Polaris and its successor Poseidon, was steadily more apparent. At this point over thirty Yankees were known to be operational, but a potentially transformational development was the appearance of the Delta class, which carried twelve of the longer range SS-N-8 missiles spotted under development in 1970. DIS believed the first Delta was operational, and expected at least thirty to be completed by the end of the decade, a figure consistent with the Strategic Arms Limitation agreement recently concluded with the United States. This estimate proved accurate, with thirty-two commissioned by the end of 1979. The SS-N-8 was now correctly assessed to have a range of 4000 miles, 60 per cent more than Polaris A3 and Poseidon, and a distance the United States would not match until the first Trident missile was deployed in 1979. DIS noted that it could therefore cover all of North America, all of NATO Europe and much of China, including Peking, from a position in the North Norwegian Sea, just two days' passage from its base in the Kola.[12]

Along with the Delta, DIS noted the arrival of a modified Victor, later designated Victor II, 20ft longer than the first boats. With increased building capacity available, DIS now expected the operational Victor force to be above twenty by 1975, 25 per cent more than expected in 1970, an estimate that was again accurate. From its first appearance, DIS consistently judged the Victor the best potential ASW vehicle, but over the five years from early 1969 to late 1973, there were striking revisions in its assessment of its sonar capability. Although it recognised the Victor's low-frequency set marked a step-change in performance compared to earlier boats, DIS was initially confident British boats retained a significant sonar advantage. However, in late 1972, drawing on 'new intelligence' it 'reassessed' the threat posed by the Victor and Charlie (the latter in its anti-submarine role) to British SSBNs. It now rated detection capability (usually in the range 8–10,000yds) to be 'about equal' on both sides. This comparatively short range meant the risk of detection for an SSBN in open-ocean patrol areas remained very low, and it would still be difficult for a Soviet SSN to turn detection into a firm target classification, let alone a trail against a well-handled SSBN. The planned introduction of towed arrays for the SSBNs would also restore an advantage.[13] (The towed array was a long line of hydrophones contained in a neutrally buoyant cable towed behind a submarine, where they were free from self-noise.) It is not clear where this 'new intelligence' came from, but it may have reflected recent experience in the Barents Sea, where the new special-fit SSN *Courageous* completed a first patrol in early October.[14] It was certainly not the Americans who, in a contemporary CIA assessment of Soviet ASW capability, stated that Soviet passive-detection ranges were half those of American nuclear boats, a judgement that was amply confirmed over the next few years, and which DIS soon endorsed.[15]

The intent to deploy Victors against Western SSBNs was demonstrated when SSNs of this class loitered in the outer Clyde exercise areas, northwest of the North Channel separating Ireland from southwest Scotland, on four occasions in 1973–74. They were evidently assessing the feasibility of trailing an SSBN leaving the Clyde bases.[16] The first incident began on 19 January 1973, with the chance detection of a Victor by an RAF Nimrod maritime patrol aircraft on a training flight. Nimrod contact was re-established five days later, leading to the most extensive tracking of a hostile SSN yet undertaken by the RAF, involving twenty-four sorties and expenditure of 1400 Jezebel sonobuoys. Sonobuoy detection range averaged fifteen to twenty miles, and showed the Victor conducting small area searches at a speed under 7 knots, before transiting to a new area at 15 knots. On 27 January the SSN *Conqueror* deployed under orders from the First Sea Lord to 'sweep the Russian from our waters'. *Conqueror* was successful in detecting the Victor and, despite dangerous manoeuvring by the latter, managed to lure it away. Overall, the incident yielded much useful intelligence on *Victor* performance and tactics. It confirmed that although it was, indeed, a far more capable boat than its predecessors, it remained vulnerable to aerial detection and tracking by sonobuoy and, crucially, that Royal Navy SSNs, and therefore SSBNs, still retained an important passive sonar advantage.[17]

Meanwhile, by late 1973 DIS saw the emphasis on long-range ASW confirmed by developments in the surface fleet, with the appearance of the new Kara-class cruiser, which packed a considerable anti-submarine punch, with a sonar suite identical to the *Moskva* helicopter carriers. The variable-depth sonar included in the Kara was also being retrofitted in some Kashin-class destroyers. DIS had also observed more sophisticated ASW training during 1973, notably an out-of-area exercise in the Norwegian Sea, involving two Kresta IIs and a Kashin in co-operation with Bear F long-range ASW aircraft. Significantly, DIS was now inclined to believed that the missile tubes fitted in the Kara and Kresta II classes, previously believed to be for the SS-N-10 surface-to-surface missile, but which had never been observed being loaded, unloaded, stockpiled or fired, were actually for a different long-range anti-submarine weapon spotted under development in the Black Sea and designated by NATO, SS-NX-14 or Silex.[18] This link with SS-NX-14 derived from CIA interpretation of satellite imagery of the ASW missile test facility at Feodosiya in the Crimea.[19] CIA later saw the confusion between SS-N-10 and SS-NX-14 as a major intelligence blunder by Western intelligence analysts, which had far-reaching consequences in understanding Soviet naval policy. Whereas the major surface warships laid down in the first half of the 1960s, the Kashin, Kynda and Kresta I classes, were prioritised for an anti-surface role aimed at the US Navy carrier force, their successors, the Kresta II, Kara and Krivak frigate were ASW vessels targeted at the Western SSBNs, as Penkovsky's *Special Collection* articles anticipated. The Soviets had always publicly designated the latest group as ASW ships, but British-American intelligence did not finally accept this until 1975, because of the initially mistaken belief that their primary missile armament was directed at surface targets. This failure to recognise the ASW priority driving Soviet construction even extended to the aircraft carrier *Kiev*, when she appeared in 1976. Western analysts initially saw her as a first step towards a conventional strike carrier capability for global power projection, whereas for the Soviets *Kiev* was primarily an ASW ship.[20]

Despite this picture of steady improvement in Soviet naval strength, operational capability, and potential fighting effectiveness, and its apparent determination to adopt a more offensive posture, both DIS and its American counterparts registered important qualifications. At the end of 1973, DIS saw Soviet surface ASW as still a 'plodding' business, even as it got more realistic. Co-ordinated ASW close to home could be good, but in the open ocean their chances against a nuclear submarine ranged from poor to zero. In contrast to its claim of 'sonar parity' the previous year, it stated that in the few encounters with Soviet SSNs outside their home waters, they had demonstrated aggression, but their tactics were primitive and their detection capability limited. American assessments of Soviet ASW became noticeably more disparaging over the first part of the decade. CIA's 1972 assessment of Soviet ASW judged that their capability fell 'far short of the minimum requirements for protection of the surface navy', and represented 'an almost negligible threat' to the US Navy SSBN fleet. This was owing to the lack of an ocean surveillance system and inadequate sensors. CIA saw little evidence that the undoubted commitment to an offensive against Western SSBNs was being put into practice. In particular, SSNs were still deployed rarely outside home waters, and then predominantly in protection of their own SSBN force. Observation to date showed that the Soviets had neither the suitable submarines, nor the tactics effectively to trail the quieter Western boats.[21]

New intelligence-collection capabilities

This early 1970s naval intelligence picture relied heavily on American-provided satellite intelligence, both imagery and ELINT derived from Poppy, from SNCP collection in the Barents Sea, and close observation of Soviet out-of-area exercises. Satellite imagery had improved steadily across the 1960s. The Corona programme, which lasted into the 1970s, soon evolved into a search capability designed to image large areas looking for new targets. In the mid 1960s it was complemented by a new satellite, Gambit, designed to study identified targets in detail, with 2–3ft ground resolution, about ten times better than Corona could achieve. It was Gambit imagery, therefore, which enabled DIS to monitor the Soviet navy construction programme, and especially its nuclear boats, with such precision. It was also a vital contributor to monitoring the Soviet ABM system, and therefore informing the debate on Polaris improvement. Meanwhile, from 1972, Corona was replaced by a much larger and more capable search satellite called Hexagon, a programme which lasted until the mid 1980s and comprised nineteen flights. While Corona returned 2.1 million feet of film in its 145 flights, a single Hexagon satellite carried 300,000ft of film, its resolution matched Gambit, and it could sweep an area 370 miles wide. Despite its discrimination, Hexagon was still a search system, and Gambit was still required for detailed target surveillance. Like Corona, neither was yet a real-time system. Film had to be returned to ground by capsules which were then recovered by aircraft. Nevertheless, the sheer quantity of material that Gambit and Hexagon produced completely swamped the available interpretation capacity, leading to strict prioritisation. This also meant that the sharing of imagery with JARIC was not entirely altruistic. JARIC provided vital additional interpretation capacity, and often found things the Americans missed. The 1960s also saw the first experiments with radar satellite reconnaissance, although as the 1970s opened, the results from this were still poor, and delivered little operational value.[22]

Meanwhile, the British contribution to the Barents Sea SNCP programme of two patrols each year, providing about 20 per cent of the joint coverage with the Americans, became steadily more effective with the deployment of the newer SSNs, *Courageous* from 1972, and from the middle of the decade, second-generation boats – *Swiftsure*, followed by *Superb*. The growing size of the SSN fleet allowed these boats to become more specialist intelligence collectors, with more elaborate equipment fits, catering for photography, SIGINT and ACINT. By 1977, it was policy always to have two SSNs simultaneously equipped for the role.[23] Almost every new Soviet warship class and naval weapon, including submarine-launched ballistic missiles, made its first appearance in the Barents Sea, and it was also the primary area for exercising new tactics. Every piece of intelligence collected was, therefore, exhaustively analysed for clues to Soviet capability and practice. In addition to the SNCP SSNs, there was always one *Oberon*-class conventional boat fitted with equivalent special-fit equipment for intelligence collection, primarily in the Baltic. Apart from the dedicated SNCP submarines, most other operational SSNs and SSKs were employed on covert surveillance operations for an average of at least a month each year. SSKs were particularly suitable for surveillance of Soviet AGIs, including those covering SSBN movements and covert scrutiny of vessels involved in oceanographical research. They also conducted operations in shallow waters difficult for the larger SSNs to access.[24] Co-operation with the Americans was underpinned by a high-level memorandum of understanding, agreed between the two navies in April 1973, which covered the sharing of threat forecasts and collaboration in ASW scientific and technical research, and operational evaluation.[25]

Overall, the British SNCP patrols, and the access they facilitated to a wide range of American sources, provided an outstanding picture of evolving Soviet naval capability through the 1970s and 1980s. They were Britain's single most important defence intelligence contribution in the second half of the Cold War, and a major contributor to GCHQ's defence intelligence effort. They helped ensure that Britain benefited from the results of another highly sensitive American operation that began in 1971 and lasted for ten years. This was Operation Ivy Bells, the covert tapping, using the specially adapted submarine *Halibut*, of the Soviet communications cable linking the naval base at Petropavlovsk on the Kamchatka peninsula in the Far East (where John Coote had joined a patrol in 1956) across the Sea of Okhotsk with the base at Magadan on the mainland.[26]

Apart from their contribution to the SNCP programme, the British brought other collection assets to the relationship with the Americans, which became increasingly important from the mid 1960s onward. Together with Canada, GCHQ and NSA ran a network of intercept sites, including several in the United Kingdom, similar to that in the Second World War, to monitor Soviet naval communications across the whole North Atlantic area. This had considerable success breaking into the developing Soviet ocean surveillance system, which drew in intelligence from deployed warships, including submarines, AGIs and merchant vessels. It also exploited weaknesses in the highly effective, but also rigid and inflexible, Soviet navy command and control system to achieve real-time intercepts of Soviet units. This COMINT attack was greatly helped by intelligence supplied to CIA through most of the 1970s by a Polish colonel, Ryszard Kuklinski, who liaised with Moscow on war planning. He provided a comprehensive account of the communications networks through which the Soviet general staff controlled Warsaw Pact forces, including the precise location of underground bunkers used by top commanders and political leaders in wartime. Crucially, he provided interpretation for what satellites had previously been able to 'see' and 'hear', but not 'comprehend'.[27]

Another important British asset was the SIGINT and radar facilities at the British sovereign bases in Cyprus. The SIGINT sites at Ayios Nikolaos and in the Troodos mountains comprised GCHQ's biggest operation overseas, and were ideal for collecting COMINT and ELINT in the Mediterranean, the Black Sea, and across the southern Soviet Union, including the missile test sites at Kapustin Yar and Tyuratam. From 1962 joint British-American projects, designated Sandra and Cobra Shoe, created an innovative over-the-horizon, long-range radar capability installed high on Mount Olympus in Cyprus, which contributed to ballistic missile early warning, but could also monitor the Soviet test sites.[28] These Cyprus facilities provided valuable intelligence on the growing Soviet naval presence in the Mediterranean, including the potential threat to Western SSBNs operating there, and naval research and development in the Crimean bases. Coverage of Kapustin Yar and Tyuratam yielded little on naval ballistic missile development, which was centred in the far north, but it added to the British balance in the wider intelligence exchange. By the early 1970s, both GCHQ and NSA were running collection operations from the British and American embassies in Moscow, primarily directed at Soviet leadership communications. The results were variable, but there were some valuable strategic insights relevant to the naval domain.[29] More important was the work the two agencies undertook in this decade in mapping, and then gaining access to, parts of the Soviet communications network dealing with defence procurement. This provided important insights into long-term naval building and acquisition plans.[30] It is striking that CIA had notice of the large Typhoon SSBN and the SS-N-20 missile it was to carry in June 1977, when their respective launch and flight testing were still two years away.[31]

In contrast to these technical sources, although SIS achieved important penetrations of the Soviet system during the decade from 1970, these sources contributed little intelligence on naval requirements, and certainly nothing comparable to the insights from Penkovsky. CIA did better, gaining valuable documents from clandestine sources covering

Soviet naval strategy, operations and tactics from the late 1960s and through the 1970s, including renewed access to the secret version of the military journal *Military Thought*. A significant contributor was Dimitry Polyakov, an officer of the Soviet military intelligence service, the GRU, who worked for the CIA from the early 1960s until about 1980, by which time he was a general. His intelligence included considerable insights into Soviet communication networks, including those relevant to naval operations. This reporting made a vital contribution to successive National Intelligence Evaluations, most of which were shared with the United Kingdom, as was much of the original reporting.[32] Although the secret version of *Military Thought* was a level below the *Special Collection* provided by Penkovsky, it still offered important policy insights, including a 1968 article by Rear Admiral N Gonchar, a submarine specialist, on 'The Location and Destruction of Polaris Submarines', which CIA acquired in 1973.[33] The Soviets also had successes, recruiting Sub Lieutenant David Bingham in early 1970 after he offered his services while serving in the frigate *Rothesay*. Over eighteen months, he passed a considerable quantity of classified material to the GRU, of which probably the most important item was a copy of the secret Fleet Operational and Tactical Instructions.[34] Although the Bingham case was useful to the Soviets, it was trivial compared to the penetration of the US Navy which began when the warrant officer, John Walker, offered his services in 1967, and lasted nearly twenty years. The devastating consequences are described in the next chapter.

The important evolutions in Soviet naval policy and strategy which intelligence illuminated in the early 1970s drove a British response, both in countering the new threats, and setting priorities for future intelligence collection, which evolved over the rest of the decade. This was most evident in the submarine area, where the Soviets had now posed three distinct problems. First, their growing SSBN force, which represented not only an assured strategic nuclear second-strike capability, but a major proportion of their overall nuclear strength, and which the arrival of the Delta and its SS-N-8 missile potentially made less susceptible to Western counteraction. Secondly, the threat posed by their growing SSN force to Western SSBNs, especially if there was a breakthrough in sonar effectiveness or non-acoustic sensors. Finally, the threat posed to NATO strike and amphibious forces, and lines of communication, partly by the same SSNs, but more by the SSGN force, and especially the Charlie, where the Soviets were five years ahead of the West in submerged-launch cruise missiles, with the possibility of better types on the way. These specific submarine problems had to be set within the wider effort the Soviets were making to assert and exploit maritime influence. Their deployment of SSBNs and active peacetime searching for Western SSBNs using surface task forces, as well as SSNs, potentially blurred the boundary between peace and war, moving NATO towards a state of permanent confrontation.

The British response reflected its responsibility for the NATO Eastern Atlantic (EASTLANT) and Channel (ACCAN) areas, where it exercised command and provided two-thirds of the submarine and ASW forces. Planning and execution of surveillance in peacetime and periods of tension in these areas, and meeting the initial maritime attack in war, therefore fell primarily to the United Kingdom. The goal in peacetime was to acquire deep understanding of evolving Soviet capability, deployment patterns, operational practice and tactics. The means adopted through the mid 1970s was to focus surveillance across the main Soviet deployment routes, exploiting their need to pass through geographic choke-points to reach the Atlantic, either northwest of Iceland, where they were bounded by the ice, or through the Iceland–Faroes or Faroes–Shetland gaps. The SOSUS coverage provided by the new Norwegian and east Atlantic arrays, along with localisation provided by long-range maritime patrol aircraft, would cover the gaps, and enable SSNs to be vectored into an intercept position from where they could detect and move into a trail. The British naval staff recognised that Soviet perceptions of British naval capability were formed in peacetime. Covert surveillance and shadowing through trailing not only built an authoritative picture of Soviet operational practice and intent, but asserted superiority, and conveyed a permanent sense of menace, thus contributing to deterrence. Regular shadowing also provided the essential knowledge to enable escalation to permanent 'marking' of hostile units in time of tension.[35]

When the policy was being developed in the mid 1970s, it may possibly have credited the Soviets with a more aggressive posture towards Western SSBNs than was yet the case. CIA assessed that the Soviets lacked the capability at this time for any widespread surveillance of Western SSBNs in their patrol areas, let alone consistent marking. They had no effective ocean surveillance system, and they must recognise that their SSNs lacked the sensors and skills for prolonged trailing. The Victor was probably adequate for overt trailing of a non-evading submarine with active sonar, which might encourage their occasional deployment off Polaris bases in an attempt to intimidate or embarrass the West, but this seemed a risky proposition for limited return. CIA also thought it possible the Soviets might view any wider attempt to trail and mark Western SSBNs, leading to reprisals against their own boats, as provocative and destabilising. Overall, recognising that the West had geographic and, for the present, technical advantages, they were likely to be cautious.[36]

Trailing for intelligence collection, progressing to marking in time of tension, ready for immediate attack in wartime, represented a decisive shift in the ASW battle away from the area immediately surrounding a surface force so familiar in the Second World War. It required the wider British submarine service rapidly to absorb lessons from the Barents Sea operations, and it marked a complete break with the traditional static submarine patrol area in a fixed box. To be effective, it required centralised direction of the British attack submarine force (the conventional SSKs as well as the SSNs) to achieve the desired aided intercepts, close collaboration with RAF long-range maritime patrol aircraft, good operational intelligence, and improvements in sonar, communications and navigation. All of these elements posed challenges which took time to resolve. Much was done in the period 1974–77, but it became clear that the 'area of probability' for a Soviet submarine provided by SOSUS, even when backed by localisation from a searching maritime patrol aircraft, was rarely enough reliably to vector an SSN using its hull-mounted passive broadband sonar into an effective trail against the latest generation Soviet boats.[37] Something more was needed.

The answer was the towed array sonar – 'a long flexible snake-like body containing a number of hydrophones' which could be 400yds (365m) long, towed up to 2000yds (1800m) behind the submarine by a cable. The array was thus clear of the noise generated by the towing submarine, and was specifically designed to acquire the discrete narrowband frequencies generated by a target submarine. The signals captured by the array were processed and presented using techniques similar to those developed with Jezebel and SOSUS. They produced an accurate target classification and approximate bearing, which improved as range decreased. In many respects, the towed array was a submarine-borne version of SOSUS, which the US Navy pioneered and began installing in its SSBNs from the mid 1960s. This was one secret they seem to have kept from the British for some years, although the latter began their own research at ARL Teddington by 1971. ARL produced an experimental array known as sonar 2024, which was installed in two British SSNs in 1977 and proved highly effective. In parallel, a limited number of American arrays, designated type 2023 by the British, were purchased for installation in the SSBNs during their second refits, the first becoming operational in *Resolution* in 1976. By July 1978, the British naval staff judged that the operational value of the towed array was 'beyond question', and planned to install a much improved version of sonar 2024 across the whole submarine fleet.[38]

In meeting the objective to monitor and mark the Soviet submarine fleet and protect the SSBN force, the towed array was transformational. Detection ranges of the latest generation Soviet nuclear boats improved by a factor of ten, and one hundred miles on a fast-transiting Victor was not uncommon, although far less for a slow-moving, well-handled SSBN. The array, therefore, substantially solved the problem of localising and finding a target identified by SOSUS. There were still drawbacks with the early versions. They constrained submarine mobility, required time to stabilise and produce information after a change of course, and they lacked all-round coverage. They were not initially integrated with the submarine action information system, and exploiting the data the arrays produced to establish the course, speed and range of a contact, especially if it was regularly manoeuvring, was immensely challenging. Bearings from the early arrays were not accurate enough to produce a definitive torpedo-firing solution, which still required the submarine to close the target until it achieved contact with its more accurate hull-mounted sonar. Nevertheless, through 1977 the first 2024 towed arrays deployed in SSNs promised a major improvement in the eastern Atlantic intelligence picture, with several multi-day trails on Soviet boats. Meanwhile, the 2023 installed in *Resolution* greatly extended the intelligence view provided by SOSUS, and helped her evade potential threats with greater confidence. The full potential of towed arrays was confirmed in the autumn of 1978, when the SSN *Sovereign* conducted Operation Agile Eagle, involving probably the longest Western trail of a Soviet submarine in the entire Cold War. Intelligence from SOSUS and maritime patrol aircraft enabled *Sovereign* to establish contact with a Soviet Delta-class SSBN on 6 October, 650 miles west of Cape Finisterre. Between then and 1 December, *Sovereign* followed the Delta almost to the equator and then back to the Barents Sea, covering more than 10,000 miles, and was in continuous contact for all but a handful of days. The operation yielded a vast amount of intelligence on the conduct of a Soviet SSBN patrol, with a considerable impact on British standing with the US Navy and wider US intelligence community. It also taught valuable lessons on the management of such operations, but substantially vindicated the vision for monitoring Soviet activity, developed five years earlier.[39]

The submarine's unique capabilities as a covert collection platform, the growing reach of its sensors and, in the case of the SSN, its outstanding mobility and endurance made it the dominant naval intelligence asset through this decade. Nevertheless, submarine numbers were limited against the forces the Soviets increasingly deployed in the EASTLANT area. Even at the end of the decade, after allowing for refits and work-ups, and essential trials and training, there were rarely more than six SSNs, and a similar number of *Oberon-* and *Porpoise-*class SSKs, immediately available for frontline operations. The contribution of the RAF maritime patrol aircraft and of the surface Navy to maintain adequate surveillance of Soviet deployments was, therefore, important. The potential of the Nimrod aircraft, first introduced in 1969, was demonstrated during the hunt for the Victor off the Clyde in 1973. Over the decade it received new radar, electronic surveillance sensors, and acoustic processing for the latest sonobuoys, which made it an even more formidable submarine hunter and long-range maritime reconnaissance aircraft. There were also three specialist SIGINT Nimrod R1s which could be tasked on maritime collection.

Britain had deployed both aircraft and surface warships to monitor major Soviet exercises and other significant movements throughout the 1960s, and this pattern continued in the next decade. Unlike their submarine counterparts, during the 1970s surface warships were rarely given any specialist collection equipment or personnel, even when covering major exercises. Some of their equipment, notably the standard electronic warning sensor for detecting and recording radar transmissions, was also obsolescent. Shadowing rules for surface warships (and aircraft) were much stricter. All these factors limited the quality of photographic and SIGINT material, although it could still be useful. However, constant observation, sometimes over several days, could also yield information hard to obtain by other means. Surface shadowers gained a good impression of overall Soviet capability, not just weapon systems and sensors, but crew discipline, operating procedures, general seamanship and efficiency, morale, and how well ships operated together. For this reason, British commanders devoted significant resources, deploying six frigates over several weeks for the major Soviet global exercise Okean 75 in the spring of 1975.[40]

From the early 1970s, the Royal Navy also deployed patrol vessels, under Operation Musketry, to track, shadow, and generally make life more difficult for the Soviet AGIs loitering off Malin Head in Northern Ireland, to spot submarine movements, and especially SSBNs, in and out of the Clyde. In 1974 it purchased a tug, *Wakeful*, specifically for this purpose. *Wakeful* conducted regular patrols to provide warning of AGI whereabouts, build up a picture of their movements, and ensure any incursions into United Kingdom territorial waters were firmly dealt with. As Irish Republican Army terrorism gathered pace in the 1970s, the Royal Navy also mounted surveillance looking for gun-runners, either from the Republic of Ireland to the north, or from further afield. In a few cases, submarines were deployed for covert observation and insertion of special forces, an updated version of Hall's activities with *Sayonara* in 1915.[41]

Polaris upgrade and the road to Chevaline

Meanwhile, the Conservative government of Edward Heath took office in June 1970, with the debate over Polaris improvement unresolved. Within a month, his new Defence Secretary, Lord Carrington, well-informed on Polaris from his tenure as First Lord in the early 1960s, provided a stark warning that the British force would become ineffective as an independent national deterrent from the mid 1970s. Intelligence provided 'incontrovertible evidence' of the establishment of a complex Russian ABM system centred on Moscow. This currently had gaps in its radar cover, which allowed a British SSBN to continue threatening Moscow, Leningrad, and about seven other cities from the southern part of the available North Atlantic patrol areas. However, within five years the initial ABM system could potentially extend to provide some defence for all major cities in western Russia within Polaris range, including Moscow and Leningrad, against a submarine firing from either the Atlantic or the Mediterranean. With this ABM extension, even if the Russians kept to the present sixty-four Galosh ABM missile launchers, there would be only a 5 per cent chance of getting one missile load out of thirty-two from two boats through to the well-defended central area containing Moscow and thirty other cities. Alternatively, an attack on ten more peripheral cities might destroy one, or at most three. The deterrent capability of the present four-boat British force would thus be eliminated, and the addition of a fifth submarine to provide two constantly on patrol would make little difference. Carrington stressed there were options involving warhead hardening and decoys to keep Polaris effective, but only by immediately commencing a project definition study of the most promising of these, Super-Antelope. Without this, Polaris would lose credibility with the Russians, there would be loss of confidence within the Polaris force itself, and the Americans would become less inclined to share sensitive nuclear- and missile-related information. Britain would also have less to offer in the prospective dialogue on nuclear matters Heath hoped to initiate with the French. More positively, Carrington reported that the risk of SSBNs on patrol being detected or trailed was negligible. However, from 1974, this risk, while remaining 'very small', could increase owing to advances in Soviet detection methods, especially submarine sonar, to become significant when only one boat was deployed. Countermeasures were being addressed, including improved sonar, noise reduction and new evasion tactics.[42]

Although Carrington's primary purpose was to initiate the Super-Antelope study at a cost of £4m, which Heath approved, his submission also formally established the wider parameters under which Polaris improvement was justified and executed over the rest of the decade. It obliged British decision-makers to reaffirm the need for, and minimum requirements of, independent deterrence, and the assurance therefore required against the maximum probable ABM system. It also established momentum in favour of Super-Antelope, which ultimately proved compelling. Zuckerman, still government science adviser, insisted that Carrington had presented a worst-case analysis of Soviet intent and capability, which ignored the impact of a Soviet-American ABM limitations agreement. He reasonably stressed there were important gaps in the intelligence picture, and divided views in the United States on the effectiveness of the Soviet ABM system, but he could not argue against studies to keep British options open.[43]

Reaching a final decision on the way ahead took more than three years and the ultimate choice, as already illustrated during the discussions in the previous Wilson administration, reflected a complex mix of political, intelligence, technical and cost judgements. As Zuckerman stressed, the signing of an ABM treaty between the United States and Soviet Union in May 1972 was important in framing these judgements. This limited ABM deployment to a maximum of 100 missiles at the capital and one other site in each country, subsequently reduced to one site each in 1974. However, Zuckerman and other critics of independent deterrence did not anticipate that its impact on British thinking would be double-edged. It greatly reduced the scale of the ABM problem, and meant that an expensive Polaris improvement programme was, arguably, only required in order to threaten Moscow. Britain could, in theory, continue to target Leningrad, and perhaps ten other major cities, with its present capability. However, the more limited ABM system also made the current preferred national targeting package laid down by the JIC in 1962, and reaffirmed in 1971, to threaten destruction of five major cities, including Moscow, an achievable goal with an option like Super-Antelope. The term 'Moscow criterion' for this package probably dates from chiefs of staff discussion in November 1971.[44]

The full advice of the chiefs on national targeting has never been released, but the goal sought by the JIC and approved by ministers (who probably never saw precise target lists[45]) was a 'high probability of inflicting unacceptable damage on the Soviet Union'. Although intelligence could, in theory, help to illuminate what Soviet leaders judged unacceptable, and the specific value they placed on Moscow, there is no evidence such reporting existed or exerted influence during the 1970s. Defining such damage was therefore a judgement, but 'unacceptability' could still be measured through comparison with any potential gain from Soviet aggression, or its effect on Soviet ability subsequently to compete with 'other superpowers' (a term in the 1970s mainly applicable to the United States, although from the Soviet perspective the threat from China was also a growing concern) after a nuclear exchange with Britain. What the chiefs considered 'unacceptable damage' can be judged from their discussion on the future of the United Kingdom nuclear deterrent in August 1979, when they were offered four options in the report completed on this issue by the then-chairman of the JIC, Sir Anthony Duff, and the Chief Defence Scientific Adviser, Professor Sir Ronald Mason, the previous December.[46] (Duff, the son of an admiral, had been a distinguished submarine commander in the Second World War.) These were:

- Option 1: Disruption of the main government organs of the Soviet state;
- Option 2: Breakdown level damage to several cities including Moscow;
- Option 3a: Breakdown level damage to a significantly larger number of cities than Option 2 but excluding Moscow or others covered by an ABM defence;
- Option 3b: Grave but not necessarily breakdown level damage to thirty major targets outside ABM coverage.

Although Duff and Mason felt that any of these options was unacceptable, the chiefs were not convinced. The Soviet Union had sustained over twenty million casualties in the Second World War, and inflicted about the same on itself between 1930 and 1950, giving a measure of the price it might be willing to pay in a future war. It followed that Option 3b might not always be sufficient to guarantee deterring the Soviet Union from the perceived advantage of knocking out the United Kingdom. On the other hand, Option 1, the loss of government control along with great collateral damage, leaving the Soviet Union completely vulnerable to the United States or even China, would be viewed as unacceptable in almost all conceivable circumstances. The chiefs accepted that Options 2 and 3a would be unacceptable in most circumstances, but felt the absence of Moscow in 3a lowered the deterrence threshold significantly. They viewed Moscow as uniquely important to the Soviet leadership as their capital, as a decision-making and administrative focal point, and the largest centre of population. Its destruction might not cause total breakdown if the leadership was able to locate elsewhere before an attack, but its loss would cause considerable disruption and might threaten the cohesion of the country, a view the events of 1989–90 arguably supported. Furthermore, an attack on Moscow would inevitably attenuate ABM defences, leaving the Soviets more vulnerable to further strikes from any opponent. The chiefs therefore ranked the options from 1 to 3a with only Option 1 meeting deterrence in all circumstances.[47]

It can be assumed that the same thinking underpinned a JIC assessment that the Heath government accepted in November 1972, that:

the destruction of the Moscow area alone would be regarded by the Russians as an unacceptable price to pay for anything they might hope to gain by a nuclear attack on the United Kingdom and that our deterrent will therefore remain credible so long as it is capable of destroying Moscow'.[48]

The JIC probably also saw continuing Soviet commitment to ABM defence of Moscow through the treaty negotiations then underway as underlining its special status and, therefore, British need to penetrate it. This view of Moscow as an essential target, affirmed at both ends of the 1970s, built on a consistent theme in British thinking, stretching back as far as 1949, that their limited nuclear capability had to focus ruthlessly on the destruction of 'Soviet state power'. In briefing ministers on the case for renewing the strategic deterrent in January 1982, the then Chief of the Defence Staff Admiral of the Fleet Sir Terence Lewin advised them that Moscow had been a target when the V-bomber force became active in 1957, thereby confirming that the 1972 JIC report merely reiterated long-standing policy.[49] Indeed, it is tempting to see the brutal calculus of city destruction stretching back to Ottley's long-ago promise to see grass growing in the streets of Hamburg.[50]

Along with the JIC view on the overriding importance of Moscow as a target, Heath's small ministerial decision group were given an updated assessment of the Moscow ABM system, following the treaty agreed with the Americans. The Russians were not only permitted up to 100 launchers, but allowed to extend their radar arcs to cover all areas of the Atlantic and Mediterranean within missile range of Moscow. Intelligence, which drew almost entirely on American-provided satellite intelligence and ELINT, suggested their cover would extend over the whole North Atlantic by 1974–75, from which date they could defeat even three boatloads of missiles (the theoretical maximum of the British force) fired at Moscow from this area. There were no current plans to extend radar cover to the

Mediterranean, and British SSBNs could continue to reach Moscow from there. However, the Mediterranean posed severe operational constraints, and although intelligence would provide about three years' warning, the Russians would probably close this flank by the end of the decade. It followed that to maintain a credible national targeting capability against Moscow, it was necessary to upgrade, a recommendation ministers now formally endorsed.[51]

In reaching this decision, it is doubtful whether most ministers involved in nuclear decision-making, either in the Heath government or its successors, ever saw Polaris improvement as a straight choice between meeting the Moscow criterion or settling for a reduced target package. There were always other factors. The view that deterrence relied on maximising doubt in the enemy mind, and that Britain should seek as much credibility as was affordable within existing political constraints, was persuasive. So was concern that, without improvement, Polaris would inevitably degrade over time, especially if the Soviets introduced ABM enhancements, either permitted under the present treaty, or following its renunciation in the future. Burke Trend questioned the purpose of accepting a second-rate deterrent, suggesting the real choice was abandonment or upgrade.[52] Ministers of both the Heath government and its Labour successors were aware that Polaris improvement was intimately linked with its long-term replacement. In 1972 the Ministry of Defence thought a successor would be required by 1994 at the latest, and that seventeen years were required from decision to proceed to having the full force operational. The longer the existing force remained credible, the greater the room for manoeuvre in planning any successor. For both political and financial reasons, 'improvement' was an attractive alternative to the awkward issue of 'replacement' through most of the 1970s.[53] Keeping long-term options open also made it desirable to maintain national capability at the cutting edge of nuclear weapons research. The political and military impact of the Moscow ABM system was also complex. Sir Michael Quinlan, who oversaw Polaris improvement as deputy secretary (policy and programmes) in the Ministry of Defence from 1977–81 later insisted that because the Soviet ABM system was exo-atmospheric, it defended much more than Moscow, in practice covering an area measured in tens of thousands of square miles, the precise size dependent on the incoming missile trajectories. The argument was thus only partly about Moscow. It was whether in assessing the threat from British Polaris, the Soviet Union should count on this wider sanctuary space, and how far that diminished British credibility.[54] Finally, the term 'Moscow criterion' is potentially misleading, since it could embrace both Options 1 and 2 described above, and the former was much more demanding than the latter, requiring double the number of warheads.[55] It is therefore unlikely a single boatload of Polaris missiles, however effectively upgraded, could ever achieve Option 1.

While refinement of Super-Antelope proceeded between 1970–72, Poseidon with American-transferred MIRV technology, but British warheads, also remained potentially on the table, as did a fifth submarine. Although the latter would improve the resilience of the SSBN force, including against Soviet advances in ASW, it was ruled out by the end of 1972, because it would not be available before 1980, meaning it would only complete half its useful life before the other four boats expired but, above all, because it would not alone solve the 'Moscow' problem, given the probability that, by then, ABM radar would extend to the Mediterranean. Meanwhile, the political problems with purchasing Poseidon increased. Heath feared that visibly reaffirming the unique British-American strategic relationship would be received badly in France, compromising his overriding goal of joining the European Community. There were also growing doubts whether the United States Congress would approve the sale, in case it undermined current arms limitation negotiations with the Soviet Union. Partly to overcome congressional concerns, two new options emerged in discussion with the United States. These were a combination of the Poseidon missile and a re-entry vehicle based on Super-Antelope technology known as Hybrid/STAG, and a variant of an idea aired in the late 1960s, which combined Poseidon and MIRV technology, but substituted decoys for most of the multiple warheads, known as Option M.

There was a strong consensus for Hybrid/STAG in the Ministry of Defence. Using Poseidon kept Britain aligned with the United States, as the Royal Navy always wanted and ensured long-term missile supply, while limiting the political hazards in acquiring MIRV-related technology. Importantly, a Super-Antelope variant combined with Poseidon had at least 20 per cent more range than with Polaris, which increased the available Atlantic patrol areas by nearly 50 per cent, thereby reducing vulnerability to anticipated improvements in Soviet ASW. There was also sufficient payload reserve to include enhancements to counter any endo-atmospheric terminal defence capability incorporated in the Moscow ABM system. By contrast, there would be little scope to develop Super-Antelope plus Polaris against terminal defence.[56]

The ultimate decision in favour of Super-Antelope plus Polaris on 30 October 1973 was swayed more by politics and cost than intelligence.[57] Presenting a Poseidon purchase domestically looked increasingly difficult, the Heath government's relations with the administration of President Richard Nixon deteriorated badly that autumn, primarily over the Yom Kippur War, even leading the Americans to sever some intelligence supply. It was judged that Super-Antelope would adequately meet the Moscow criterion, involved less technical risk, would be available sooner, and cost significantly less than the alternatives over the period 1973–78, although not the full lifetime of the present SSBN force. In the autumn of 1973, with the Middle East oil crisis underway, short-term cost mattered. Super-Antelope also preserved advanced British defence expertise, and thereby helped contain dependence on the United States for the nuclear deterrent. A factor which probably exerted more influence, on Heath specifically, was that choosing Super-Antelope made it easier to keep open potential collaboration with France on a long-term Polaris successor, whereas any Poseidon purchase would imply Britain remained wedded to its 'nuclear alliance' with the United States.[58]

These arguments in favour of Super-Antelope were balanced by two intelligence warnings. First, during 1973, new American studies of available ABM intelligence suggested the Soviets had several practical options to deliver a 'sprint' missile terminal defence capability, or to improve radar discrimination against decoys, either of which would drastically reduce the effectiveness of Super-Antelope. However, they agreed with British analysts that there was no current intelligence revealing intent to do this. Such options were hypothetical possibilities, unlikely before 1980 at the earliest, and the Soviets would face doubts over their real value. By January 1974, the JIC judged an effective terminal defence unlikely.[59] The position had not changed significantly five years later, when the Defence Secretary Fred Mulley updated his colleagues on ABM developments. Intelligence showed continuing research on efforts to improve both the existing Galosh system, and produce a terminal defence missile, but neither posed an early threat to the Super-Antelope package.[60]

Secondly, the Americans underlined the importance of sea room in managing SSBN vulnerability. This was an abiding concern for the British naval staff as the Super-Antelope programme progressed through the 1970s. Combining Super-Antelope with Poseidon produced a 20 per cent range advantage compared to Polaris, but it only maintained the existing A3 range of 2450 miles with the original British warhead package. It followed that the Super-Antelope/Polaris package would produce a 50 per cent reduction in sea room. Calculations done for the naval staff in 1972, probably by the Polaris Performance Analysis Group (PPAG)[61] which was established in 1968 to monitor the deployed performance of the Polaris system, suggested this would increase the chances of a British

SSBN being detected in the 1980s by a factor of four. If the range reduction was 10 per cent greater, a distinct risk with the Super-Antelope weight projections in 1972, the probability of detection would rise by a factor of ten, reflecting a further drastic reduction in sea room, compared to that available with the standard A3 range. From 1980, this would imply a detection, on average, once per year which would be unacceptable.[62] It is not clear how PPAG reached this assessment. They could extrapolate Soviet sonar performance in 1980 from current exercises between SSBNs and British and American SSNs, but assessing the level of ASW effort the Soviets might credibly deploy then in SSBN patrol areas involved huge unknowns. Nor could PPAG in 1972 take account of the combined impact of SOSUS and towed arrays, which fundamentally improved SSBN security from the mid 1970s.

Technically, Super-Antelope, renamed Chevaline in 1974, was an outstanding success. When its deployment in two submarines was eventually complete in 1983, it met its designed goal of providing credible penetration assurance against the Moscow ABM system, sufficient to achieve Option 2, although not Option 1 in the national criteria, for the rest of the Cold War. An American National Intelligence Evaluation published in October the previous year stated that, although the Moscow ABM system was being upgraded, it was still only capable of a limited, single-layer defence, confined to intercepting re-entry vehicles outside the atmosphere. It could probably counter a small attack without penetration aids and decoys, but anything larger would exhaust the available interceptors. There was an active ABM research programme, and the Soviets had the capability to deploy a more ambitious and extensive system by the late 1980s if they abrogated the ABM treaty, but there was no intelligence that they intended to do so.[63]

However, Chevaline took four years longer than anticipated in 1973, and cost twice as much in real terms. By 1983, its costs were about the same as all the remaining capital and running costs for Polaris over its twenty-year life to that time, and over its peak period from 1974–80, Chevaline absorbed about 2.3 per cent of the overall defence budget. These figures require perspective. The overall costs of the nuclear deterrent in these six years was 3.7 per cent of the defence budget, compared to twice this in the late 1960s. In discussing a successor to Polaris in 1979, the chiefs of staff stated that the United Kingdom independent deterrent was the 'foundation' upon which its defence policy stood, and justified 6–7 per cent of the defence budget.[64] Critics of Chevaline, both at the time and later, argued that ordering a fifth submarine, or settling for basic Antelope by 1970, would have delivered adequate assurance at far less cost. Others, notably David Owen, the Foreign Secretary from 1977–79, disputed the need to target Moscow.[65] Critics also point out that the Chief of the Defence Staff, Field Marshal Sir Michael Carver, had to advise ministers at the end of 1975 that the latest intelligence confirmed what Carrington had predicted in 1970, that British targeting of Moscow from Atlantic patrol areas was now ineffective, pending the introduction of Chevaline.[66] If Britain accepted a gap in the Moscow criterion for seven years, why not make it permanent? On this specific point, as with most others in the deterrent debate, matters were not so clear-cut. The Russians did not complete ABM radar cover against Mediterranean firing in this period, and Britain could and did occasionally deploy an SSBN to this area. Overall, a case can be made for most of these policy alternatives from the critics and, as this chapter shows, most (along with many others) were actively considered. However, ministers, officials and military leaders made the best judgements they could, within difficult political and economic constraints, and on the best available intelligence at the time.

There were no major naval intelligence challenges for Britain outside the NATO area during the 1970s on the scale of Indonesian confrontation. By 1973, Britain had ended its permanent military presence in the Far East and the Gulf, and by 1979 its Malta bases had closed too. Indeed, as the decade progressed, apart from limited forays into the Mediterranean, it appeared increasingly unlikely that the Royal Navy would ever again contemplate major operations outside the North Atlantic. Naval intelligence capability outside the core NATO area accordingly began to atrophy. The substantial and growing Soviet presence in the Mediterranean, both surface units and submarines, was an attractive target for covert collection, not least because it was easier to access than the Barents Sea or the Baltic, and both SSNs and conventional boats were, accordingly, regularly deployed. The requirement to operate a British SSBN there on an occasional basis also generated a demand for up-to-date intelligence.[67]

Meanwhile, there was one precautionary intelligence-led deployment outside the NATO area at the end of 1977, which seemed a minor distraction from more pressing priorities at the time, but attracted considerable attention just over four years later. During the year, there were exploratory talks between Britain and Argentina over the future of the Falkland Islands, a British dependency to which Argentina claimed sovereignty. By the autumn, the Foreign Secretary, David Owen, expected the talks to break down, and asked the JIC to assess the risk of Argentinian hostile action. The JIC drew on significant SIGINT and SIS intelligence, as well as diplomatic reporting, including an important warning passed to the naval attaché, Captain Daniel Leggatt, by a senior Argentinian naval officer. It emphasised an aggressive stance being adopted by Admiral Emilio Massera, the commander-in-chief of the Argentinian navy and a member of the ruling military junta. The JIC did not consider a full-blown invasion likely, but judged that action against British shipping, occupation of some of the Falklands dependent territories, or even small-scale raiding was possible. In response, a task force, comprising two frigates with supporting supply vessels, and the SSN *Dreadnought* were despatched as a precautionary measure under Operation Journeyman. The surface force remained at a distance, but *Dreadnought*, which had stored for war, closed the islands and conducted a covert reconnaissance of the surrounding waters over a five-day period, but found nothing unusual. New intelligence suggested the risks of Argentine aggression had diminished, and the force was withdrawn. There has been much debate over whether the Argentines were discreetly advised of the deployment on SIS or other channels, so that it exercised a deliberate deterrent effect, rather than remaining a purely precautionary and intelligence-gathering operation. SIS action is unlikely, given Owen's insistence that the deployment was to be kept secret, to avoid giving the Argentines the impression of bad faith and intransigence while talks were ongoing. It is possible that Leggatt, on his own initiative, advised his Argentinian source of the presence of an SSN but if he did, it is not clear this exerted any influence on Argentinian attitudes.[68]

The 1970s were a difficult decade for Britain, which was beset by economic difficulties, chronic industrial unrest, and a gloomy sense of national decline, factors from which the Royal Navy was not immune. Yet, despite these problems, by exploiting the potential of the submarine service and GCHQ, and the leverage this provided with the Americans, its picture of Soviet naval strength and capability at the end of the decade was stronger than at any previous point in the Cold War. The JIC recognised the priority the Soviets had given to submarine development, and especially its SSBN force, where DIS had accurately assessed the characteristics of the latest Delta class, with their long-range missiles which could be launched from close to their bases, and expected forty-five to be operational by 1985. The JIC anticipated that the appearance of the Victor III in 1979 foreshadowed new SSN classes, which intelligence showed were under construction, and which, through improved noise reduction, would sharply reduce the lead the West still enjoyed in passive sonar detection. Following an analysis of recent encounters, DIS had assessed that British nuclear submarines still outranged their Soviet competitors by a factor of two or three. The gap would close further if the Soviets introduced towed arrays and made progress with non-acoustic sensors, as seemed possible, in the early 1980s. (In fact, by 1980, the first experimental towed array was deployed with the Victor III, although neither the British nor the Americans appreciated this for a further three years. It is more doubtful whether the Soviets acquired the narrowband processing techniques to exploit a towed array effectively during this decade.) The JIC noted a distinct drop in detection of Soviet SSNs outside their home waters since 1976, which it judged probably reflected noise reduction, but also better operating skills and exploitation of the huge effort the Soviets had put into oceanographic research. Deployments which had been observed appeared to be focusing more on suspected SSBN patrol areas out to the west of Ireland. British analysts were also now clear that although the twenty-nine major Soviet surface combatants completed since the early 1970s, including the carrier *Kiev*, had a significant anti-surface and anti-air capability, their primary purpose was ASW directed at countering Western SSBNs. The JIC emphasised the increased offensive power of the Soviet naval air force, with the arrival of the Backfire bomber, which could cover the whole EASTLANT area without refuelling, and steady improvement in the quality of airborne ASW assets.[69]

The JIC noted that the rapid growth of the Soviet navy through the 1970s had produced some visible signs of strain. With a high proportion of conscripts, it was struggling to meet the demands of rapidly advancing technology, especially in the nuclear submarine sector. Training was narrowly focused and retention levels low, leading to a lack of experience. Low ship-usage rates and low levels of routine training had been seen in surface ships deployed overseas, raising doubts about sustained operational effectiveness. However, in a clear reference to Barents Sea observation, the JIC stated that it also conducted its exercises and fired its weapons to good effect, and its ultimate readiness to act was not in doubt. The range and quality of new weaponry and sensors, air, surface and submarine, now in service was formidable but, in a hint at SIGINT coverage of defence acquisition, it added that research and development on naval missiles continued to expand, with major programmes underway for both nuclear submarines, and the *Kirov*-class missile-armed cruisers under construction. Finally, the JIC underlined the improvement in command and control arrangements, and the growing maturity of the Soviet ocean surveillance system, drawing on inputs from deployed naval forces, AGIs, ELINT and radar surveillance satellites and its merchant fleet, which could now often deliver real-time positional fixes on Western forces.[70]

There were significant differences of emphasis in British and American assessments developing at this time, which became more pronounced in the first part of the 1980s. The Americans were more confident the West retained a decisive lead in ASW, especially through the narrowband processing techniques associated with SOSUS and towed arrays, a judgement that proved misplaced. By contrast, the British over-stated Soviet progress with ocean surveillance. The British recognised that Soviet war priorities focused on countering Western SSBNs and the US Navy carrier strike fleets, and that this had driven much of their recent building effort, but they also saw a long-term commitment to creating a navy capable of global power projection. They also believed that in wartime the Soviets would deploy major attack submarine forces south of the Iceland–Shetland line to disrupt NATO reinforcement across the Atlantic, with seventy nuclear boats available in the EASTLANT area alone by 1985. The Americans were less convinced of the strength of the global focus, or the commitment to attacking transatlantic communications, although American views were complicated by some sharp divisions across their intelligence community. However, both countries were missing something more important in their assessments. While the Soviets were, for various reasons, on the threshold of greater equality in ASW, they were also intent on shifting to a radically different, and initially more defensive, naval strategy. Both countries also underestimated the impact of the growing economic problems facing the Soviet Union, and the constraints this would impose on the Soviet navy in the 1980s.[71]

The 1980s: The Final Soviet Challenge

British naval intelligence began the 1980s firmly focused on the Soviet naval threat, and predominantly within the EASTLANT area, where the Royal Navy was now almost exclusively based. There were no permanent forces in the Mediterranean, and even temporary deployments there were more rare. From the mid 1970s, a balanced task force, including an SSN, had visited the Indian Ocean and Far East every two years or so, and the incoming Conservative government aspired to conduct such operations more frequently. Nevertheless contemporary commentators, probably rightly, saw this more as a desire to retain old links, broaden experience and boost morale, rather than demonstrating any serious commitment to lasting global power projection. The Royal Navy had become an EASTLANT ASW force, and this was reflected in DIS priorities, with coverage of the rest of the world reduced to, at best, a watching brief, a limitation which posed challenges when the Falklands War erupted in 1982.

Emerging reappraisals of Soviet naval strategy

While inadequate coverage of non-Soviet threats was a weakness, DIS and the naval leadership were also slow to examine critically what recent intelligence meant for Soviet naval intent at the strategic level. Reviewing Soviet maritime policy in October 1981, the JIC reaffirmed the key Soviet goals identified in British and American assessments over the last twenty years: 'strategic offence' through effective deployment of its SSBN fleet; 'strategic defence' of the homeland against Western SSBNs and carrier strike; interdiction of NATO sea communications to prevent reinforcement and resupply of Europe; and support for Soviet land operations. The emphasis given to these goals reflected intelligence on Soviet strategic thinking from the *Military Thought* articles shared by CIA through the

1970s, but also interpretation of Soviet construction policy and their conduct of major exercises. The JIC calculated that over the past five years the Soviet navy had also acquired greater strength and capability to execute these goals. Principal surface combatants had increased by about one-quarter and nuclear submarines by one-third in this period. Along with increased numbers, new sensors and weapons, such as the 500km-range SS-NX-19 missile fitted in the new Oscar-class SSGN and *Kirov*-class cruiser, and a quietening programme for nuclear submarines, had provided an accompanying rise in quality. In 1976 Western navies dominated the Soviets tactically. Now they were matched in most areas, and surpassed in some. New Soviet designs showed originality which owed little to Western influence, and was more than a reaction to Western capabilities. The JIC judged that this enhanced strength would translate into a more forward and offensive strategy in wartime. The Soviets would seek freedom of action in the Barents, Norwegian and North seas and the northeast Atlantic, at an early stage. Increased submarine deployment into the Atlantic prior to hostilities was probable, both to interdict American strike forces at long range, and enable attacks on reinforcement shipping. Once northern waters were secure, these interdiction operations would be pursued with increasing intensity. The Soviet navy aimed to operate against NATO forces worldwide, and its capability to do so was increasing with strengthened forces in the Mediterranean and Indian Ocean.[1]

This JIC view was a logical progression from previous assessments, and much of its analysis of emerging Soviet capability was accurate and perceptive. However, in judging how the Soviets would use this capability, it diverged from developing American thinking. The American intelligence community and the US Navy leadership, unsurprisingly, shared the British view of the main Soviet naval goals, since both countries drew on the same source base. However, by 1981, their interpretation of how the Soviets would prioritise and execute these tasks was different. They judged that the top Soviet priority was the protection and support of its SSBN fleet, 'withholding' it as a second strike force against both strategic and theatre targets. They noted that only one-third of the available operational force was normally at sea, with the rest kept at high readiness for deployment at short notice in time of tension. This standby force, comprising a high proportion of long-range Deltas, would deploy in predominantly northern waters, behind an 'echeloned' defence in depth. In the NATO area, this echeloned defence (illustrated in the accompanying map) aimed to control an inner zone north of 70° N, comprising the Kara, Barents, north Norwegian and Greenland seas as a safe operating area for SSBNs. The Northern Fleet also planned to deny NATO forces significant access to the area between 70° N and the Greenland–Iceland–Shetland line. Virtually all major surface combatants and combat aircraft, and three-quarters of the SSNs and SSGNs in the Northern Fleet would be allocated to secure these two defensive zones, with SSNs often acting as direct escort to SSBNs. While part of this echeloned defence would be exclusively focused on SSBN protection, more forward units deployed in the outer sea denial zone, and especially along the Greenland–Iceland–Shetland line, would also contribute to defence of the Soviet homeland from attacks by the American carrier strike fleet, or submarine-launched cruise missile.[2]

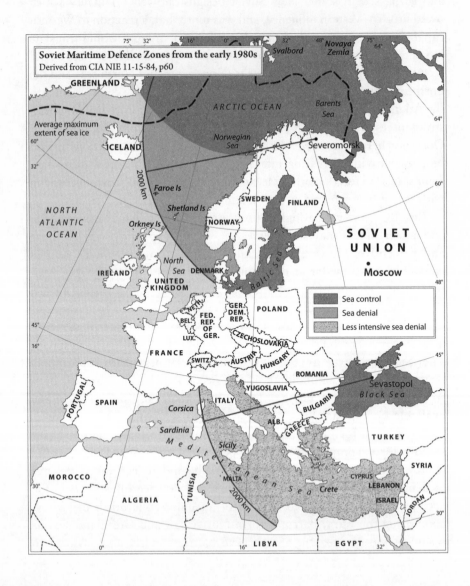

Soviet Maritime Defence Zones from the early 1980s
Derived from CIA NIE 11-15-84, p60

The Americans agreed that defence against Western SSBNs remained a fundamental Soviet navy task, but judged the Soviets currently perceived a wide gap between the importance of the goal, and their ability to execute it with current forces. While Soviet doctrine suggested they would now have no qualms about attacking Western SSBNs in the conventional phase of hostilities, they probably recognised they had minimal chance of achieving a detection, or conducting a trail, in the open ocean. The US Navy deployment of Trident missiles, which with their greater range vastly extended the ocean space to be searched, compounded the Soviet problem. Anti-SSBN operations would, therefore, focus on choke-points and approaches to SSBN bases, exploiting cueing from AGI intelligence where possible. Some of the best Soviet ASW SSNs would tackle this task, but their numbers would be small, compared to those allocated to SSBN protection in the north. Against this background, the Americans judged that the interdiction of NATO sea lines of communication was now a 'less urgent' task for the Soviet navy. The Soviets now believed Warsaw Pact forces would defeat NATO in central Europe, or that war would escalate to a theatre nuclear exchange before NATO seaborne supply and reinforcement became a critical factor. They would, therefore, allocate only a few forces, primarily SSKs, to this task at the start of hostilities.

The confidence with which the Americans reached their assessment that Soviet naval policy now comprised a defensive 'withholding strategy', focused on protecting their SSBN force, was striking. It reflected examination by the civilian Center for Naval Analyses (CNA) of published Soviet material over the last decade, including articles by Admiral Gorshkov, and input from CIA, drawing on the classified *Military Thought* material. The CIA source of the *Military Thought* articles probably provided wider background on naval planning, and CIA also had a source reporting on submarine construction by the early 1980s.[3] SIGINT would have provided some insights too. Nevertheless, prior to 1980 the Soviet adoption of a withholding strategy, promoted by CNA, was viewed within ONI and other parts of the American intelligence community as an interesting theory unsupported by hard intelligence. What changed in mid 1980 was the arrival of new, highly sensitive intelligence, confined to a small group in ONI and the US Navy leadership, and probably only partly shared with the British. One contributor to this intelligence was probably a new underwater cable-tapping operation conducted by a joint US Navy/NSA/CIA team. The original Ivy Bells operation in the Sea of Okhotsk produced valuable intelligence throughout the 1970s, but ended after it was betrayed to the Soviets by an NSA employee Ronald Pelton, who offered his services to the Soviet embassy in Washington in early 1980. However, the previous year, the US Navy submarine *Parche* achieved an even more valuable tap on the Barents Sea cable connecting Severodvinsk with Northern Fleet headquarters at Murmansk, an operation which, fortunately, Pelton did not know about. This tap delivered valuable intelligence for the rest of the Cold War. However, it was not the only new high-grade source at this time. For several years in the early 1980s, CIA successfully tapped the underground communication lines between the Krasnaya Pakhra nuclear weapons research institute in the closed city of Troitsk and the Soviet ministry of defence, yielding a treasure trove of intelligence in an operation designated CKTAW. There were other technical operations of similar quality.[4]

The US Navy and the wider American intelligence community may not have shared all their raw intelligence with the British, but they did share their finished assessments and their general thinking. The British knew there had been a fierce debate between different American agencies over the level of Soviet commitment to Atlantic supply line interdiction since early 1979, as the withholding concept gained traction, but this did not apparently stimulate equivalent questioning over Soviet strategy in London.[5] When the British Defence Secretary John Nott visited Norfolk, Virginia, in March 1981 for a briefing from the NATO Supreme Allied Commander Atlantic, Admiral Harry Train, he was not only impressed by the American picture of shifting Soviet naval strategy, but found the quality of American analysis and presentation superior to anything he had received from the naval staff in London.[6] It accordingly influenced the major defence review then underway, which was published in late June. It provided Nott – who faced the requirement to reduce conventional defence expenditure, partly to create space for the Trident nuclear deterrent replacement programme – with convenient justification for cuts in the Royal Navy's surface fleet. If there was a reduced threat to the main reinforcement routes through the EASTLANT area, then forces earmarked for traditional convoy-type defence in wartime could be cut to achieve long-term savings, but also to provide more resources for ASW defence of the Greenland–Iceland–Shetland line, predominantly by submarines and aircraft.

Nott, therefore, planned to cut the surface fleet by one-third within five years, but to enhance the long-term SSN programme, provide new SSKs, and strengthen the Nimrod long-range maritime patrol force. The immediate cuts announced in 1981 were less: one of the three new *Invincible*-class light carriers, a 15 per cent reduction in destroyers and frigates, and early phasing out of the two amphibious assault ships, but the intent to prioritise future investment on submarines and aircraft to secure EASTLANT's northern flank was clear. It would be misleading to suggest the naval component of the 1981 review was intelligence-driven. It would be several years before the JIC fully embraced the 'withholding strategy'. The overriding driver was financial, and without the American intelligence dimension, given the Cold War and NATO context at the time, and Britain's priorities within it, the Navy would still have suffered as the least bad option. However, the American assessment undoubtedly gave Nott the confidence to cut further than was wise, or ultimately proved sustainable. That said, the American intelligence picture of the evolving Soviet naval threat, which was broadly confirmed over the rest of the decade, made the case for a strategic adjustment in Royal Navy priorities compelling. Inevitably, the cuts in the surface fleet faced fierce resistance from the Navy, which felt it had been targeted to protect the other services. However, the naval staff led by the First Sea Lord, Admiral Sir Henry Leach, made its case poorly, and failed adequately to address the substantive issues. The review acquired further notoriety the following year, when the Falklands War allowed Leach to reinforce his position. This slowed the pace of reduction, but it made no sense to refashion the Navy on the basis of an exceptional case, and the Navy that emerged by 1990 was not far from that envisaged by Nott ten years earlier.[7]

It is not clear why DIS and the British naval staff were slow to endorse the American view that the overriding priority the Soviets gave to the security of northern waters meant that the bulk of the Northern Fleet would remain north of the Greenland–Shetland line, permitting little effort against transatlantic supply lines. There were areas of agreement. The British accepted that an increased element of the Soviet SSN force would be deployed in protecting SSBNs. As early as January 1981, the British SSN *Spartan* gained independent intelligence confirmation for this aspect of the operational pattern described by the Americans, when she observed a Victor checking for hostile trailing of, or 'delousing', two Delta SSBNs outbound on patrol off Bear Island. She then followed the Deltas, moving in tandem northwest into the Greenland Sea, where they headed under the ice.[8] The British also thought that only a 'limited proportion' of Soviet submarine forces could be deployed against Western SSBNs transiting from their bases, although they overstated the numbers that would be credible, given other commitments. In October 1982 they judged the Soviets could still deploy three SSNs, four SSGNs and eight SSKs for operations against SSBNs and other targets in waters around the United Kingdom. This included mining before and after hostilities began.

This represented 10 per cent of the available Northern Fleet SSN force, and 20 percent of its SSGN and SSK force.[9]

However, even in 1985, acceptance by the British intelligence community of the American assessment remained qualified. It agreed that Soviet SSBNs were increasingly operating in Arctic waters, with the new Typhoon, and probably the Delta IV, designed to shelter under the ice before breaking through in order to fire. It also acknowledged that substantial elements of the Northern Fleet would be deployed on SSBN protection and countering the threat from US Navy carrier strike and cruise missile forces. But the British still believed interdiction of transatlantic communications was an essential Soviet goal. To sustain the NATO central front, they expected one million service personnel, 9 million tons of equipment and 14 million tons of oil to cross the Atlantic in the opening weeks of war.[10] These British qualifications arose partly because they lacked some of the raw intelligence available to the Americans, which disposed them, therefore, to keep a more open mind. They were also convinced that Soviet ideology, the ambitions regularly voiced by Gorshkov, and observed naval construction over the last ten years all pointed to continuing intent to build a superpower navy capable of challenging the Western naval powers globally on equal terms, and even winning a conventional war against them without resorting to nuclear weapons. It was not evident to the British why this goal would be postponed or downgraded, unless the Soviet Union faced economic constraints, of which there was no observed evidence through the early 1980s.[11]

Another important factor influenced British attitudes to this debate over Soviet strategy through the early 1980s. During the period 1979–82, the British saw a greater risk than did the Americans that the Soviets could achieve an early breakthrough in ASW capability exploiting conventional passive sonar improvement, where it became clear the Victor III had made great strides, but possibly also with non-acoustic sensors, where DIS had seen Soviet progress with wake detection under trial conditions.[12] In 1978 the British judged the second generation Soviet SSNs and SSGNs, such as the Victor II and Charlie II, to be ten years behind their *Swiftsure* class in noise reduction, giving most British SSNs a minimum of twice the detection range with hull-mounted sonar.[13] By 1982, the Victor III was demonstrating that it could operate on close to equal terms with hull-mounted sonar, although not yet with a towed array, and there were more advanced boats such as the Oscar-class SSGN and the Sierra- and Akula-class SSNs, all of which promised a step-change in capability, coming on stream.[14] Meanwhile, the new Typhoon-class SSBN, on which the British SNCP submarine *Superb* acquired excellent intelligence during her trials in 1982, was clearly designed to operate under the ice, and quiet enough to do so without SSN protection. For the British, therefore, the Soviet withholding of their SSBNs in northern bastions, and their ability to conduct aggressive forward operations in the wider Atlantic, exploiting new boats and sensors, were not necessarily mutually exclusive propositions.

The British were correct about the Soviet ambition to innovate, but they overestimated the speed with which they could introduce and build submarines to designs genuinely competitive with their Western counterparts. A detailed American satellite survey issued in June 1983 illustrated the quality of imagery now available to the British and American intelligence communities. It showed that nuclear submarine production the previous year was unusually low, with only six new boats completed, compared to the usual average of nine. It also suggested this lower pace of construction would continue, or even decrease further. Only two of the 1982 completions were new designs – one Typhoon (the second to be completed) and one Oscar, and two, of three, Victor IIIs were built at Komsomolsk for the Pacific Fleet. The first Typhoon had completed sea trials during the year, including launch of sixteen of the new SS-NX-20 missiles, and at the end of 1982 was undergoing operational work-up. Four further Typhoons were building in the construction halls at Severodvinsk. One Delta III had completed in 1982, the fourteenth in the class, transferring to its operational base in December, and three more remained under construction in the halls. The Oscar observed was the second in the class and still fitting out at the end of the year. No others were currently seen under construction. The three Victor IIIs completed brought the total in this class to eighteen, and production continued. No Alfas were launched during 1982, but an Alfa, or possibly a follow-on class, was observed under construction at both Severodvinsk and Sudomekh.[15]

The British also overestimated the possibilities for a breakthrough with non-acoustic sensors capable of wide area detection. The American judgement in early 1979 that none of the options the Soviets were pursuing, including thermal effects, wake detection, radio-isotope traces or electromagnetic radiation, would deliver early operational value ultimately proved correct.[16] Nevertheless, British assessments of the scale of Soviet research in these areas did help persuade American agencies that a breakthrough was conceptually possible, and that close monitoring was needed. While non-acoustic research did not give the Soviets the ocean search capability they wanted, it did help them with noise reduction and submarine performance. Investigation of wake and flow effects resulted in innovative hull designs, the coating of hulls with anechoic tiles, and better propellers, although the latter were also the result of advanced milling machines procured illegally through the Japanese company Toshiba. In pursuit of speed, they also looked at the ejection of synthetic polymers from the bow to reduce hull turbulence.[17]

Through 1985, despite residual differences on the scale of Soviet intervention south of Greenland–Shetland, the British and American intelligence communities were moving towards consensus on recent developments in Soviet capability and the outlook for the 1990s. Both agreed the submarine force remained the most important element of the Soviet navy, and that from the late 1970s its latest boats had successfully pioneered characteristics which addressed traditional weaknesses, and were fast eroding the long-standing Western advantage in ASW. The key trends were reduced noise and enhanced sonar performance, exemplified in the Victor III; high speed and deep diving, represented in the improved Alfa, with its novel power plant and titanium hull; survivability against conventional weapon hits through the use of double hull design and advanced hull material; and better weapons – advanced torpedoes, more accurate and longer-range ballistic missiles, and the introduction of improved cruise missiles. Both communities agreed that, operationally, the latest SSBNs, the Typhoon and most of the Deltas, would now deploy in protected 'bastions' close to or under the icefields, where they were safe from attack by Western air and surface forces, but could still reach almost all significant Western targets. The latest SS-N-20 missile carried by the Typhoon had the accuracy and fire control to hit hard targets. Although SSBNs under the ice could still be reached by Western SSNs, the challenges these faced, from defending Soviet SSNs, difficult sonar conditions, and in overcoming double-hull protection, were formidable. Both communities also agreed that the next Soviet priority was securing northern waters against the American strike fleet.[18]

By 1985, the British and Americans also had their first sight of a third generation of Soviet nuclear submarines incorporating these new advances. Three different SSN types had appeared the previous year, the Mike and Sierra joining the Northern Fleet, and the first Akula in the Pacific. These SSNs followed two Oscar-class SSGNs, apparently a successor to the Charlie, commissioned earlier in the decade. Both intelligence communities were puzzled by the simultaneous arrival of three new SSN designs, and debated how this would affect the speed with which new classes were produced. The JIC was wary of assuming that each new boat would be followed by quantity production. It noted a growing pattern of Soviet ventures into new categories of warship, which were not then pursued. Recent examples included the *Berezina* replenishment vessel, apparently the first of a series to support distant operations, which remained single, and the *Ivan Rogov* amphibious ships, which had stopped at two and been little employed. By contrast, CIA seemed surprisingly confident that the Soviets would focus on both the Sierras and Akulas, producing about twenty of each by the mid 1990s, while limiting the Mike class to a further four or five units and ending production by 1989. It also expected the Oscar force to reach six by the end of the decade. It is possible that this detailed intelligence, which extended to the likely weapon fit for each class, derived from either Barents Sea cable-tapping, or separate penetration of the Soviet acquisition system. CIA, nevertheless, thought that the production of multiple submarine types, all apparently with complex new nuclear power plants and most with titanium hull material, which was difficult to fabricate, presented a considerable challenge. Although productive capacity had increased with new shipyards at Gorkiy and Komsomolsk, the Victor III programme was still running, as was steady construction of the large, complex Typhoon and Delta IV SSBNs. CIA, therefore, judged that delivering the demanding new SSN classes at a rate comparable to the late 1970s might be beyond the reach of Soviet shipbuilders. These doubts proved justified. Only one more Sierra, four Akulas and four more Oscars were completed by the end of the decade, while the Mike never went into series production, and the single boat was lost in an accident in 1989. Judged on a unit basis, nuclear submarine output in the second half of the 1980s was less than half that of a decade earlier.[19]

In 1985 confirmation of declining Soviet submarine productivity lay in the future. Meanwhile, for both the British and Americans, early assessment of the new classes commissioned in 1984 suggested they were comparable to most Western boats in quietness and sonar performance, but superior in speed, diving depth and survivability. It followed that if they did arrive in significant numbers, the threat picture could evolve in important ways by the early 1990s. The prospect of quiet Western submarines against equally quiet Soviet boats would greatly complicate operations near or under the ice. Engagements were likely to be short range, with speed and weapon reliability as important as stealth. Active sonar might again become an important option. It was also possible that the new, quieter Delta IV and Typhoon SSBNs would require less support under the ice, releasing SSNs for deployment elsewhere. Controlling the waters north of the Greenland–Shetland line would remain a Soviet priority, but the new SSNs, with a flexible mix of weapons including cruise missiles, greatly increased Soviet options for exercising effective sea denial to Western forces. The release of the more capable, new-generation boats from SSBN protection duties would also permit their deployment in groups of two or three on long-range sorties into the wider Atlantic, deliberately to destabilise Western SSBN operations. It would also allow significant effort against transatlantic communications.[20]

Intelligence and the renewal of the nuclear deterrent: the selection of Trident D5

As it grappled with challenges posed by evolving Soviet maritime strategy and capability, British naval intelligence faced two more distinct demands in the early 1980s: the renewal of the nuclear deterrent, and the Falklands war with Argentina. The process which led Britain to decide that its nuclear deterrent should be renewed, to select the Trident D5 submarine-launched ballistic missile as the preferred option, and to negotiate its provision with the Americans, began with the review by Anthony Duff and Ronald Mason under the Labour government of James Callaghan, referred to in the last chapter. The terms of the Duff–Mason study, as it became known, agreed by Callaghan on 30 January 1978, directed them to consider the politico-military requirement; criteria for deterrence; operational and technical characteristics; international developments; options; and resources and comparative costs.[21] The study was complete by the end of that year. It argued that if the political case for a continuing British deterrent was confirmed, then it must be capable of inflicting damage unacceptable to the Soviet leadership, must be immune to surprise attack, and must penetrate any likely Soviet defences from the mid 1990s well into the next century. It concluded that only a submarine-launched ballistic missile system provided the required combination of immunity and penetration.

Intelligence influenced the Duff–Mason analysis in broadly the same areas as it had during the Chevaline debate, but it had to shape judgements about the future threat environment even further ahead. The conclusion that a submarine-based system offered greater immunity than any air or land-based alternative was easy to reach. The level of submarine immunity then rested on detection advantage, sea room, which determined the area an enemy had to search, and redundancy, and the size of the guaranteed force. In 1978 intelligence suggested the British advantage in hull-mounted sonar was eroding, but more than compensated by the arrival of the towed array. However, to guard against any future Soviet ASW breakthrough, Duff–Mason suggested the minimum missile range to ensure adequate sea room should be 3000 miles, and that a five-boat force, providing two on permanent patrol, was desirable, to provide insurance in case of detection and subsequent loss to enemy action.[22] Assessing the ballistic missile force required to meet British national deterrence criteria against the ABM defences the Soviets could deploy in the 1990s, and beyond, was harder. Much depended on whether the Soviets remained within the current ABM treaty. If they did, and there was no intelligence to suggest otherwise, meeting the Moscow criterion meant assessing the worst-case ABM upgrade the Soviets might achieve with evolving technology under treaty terms. For this assessment, Duff and Mason were heavily dependent on American imagery, which was detailed on the Moscow system, and ELINT from NSA/GCHQ.[23] Although they were confident in their picture of current ABM capability and its prospects, based on 'sensitive sources over many years', there were still limitations. Intelligence could provide reasonable assurance on developments out to the early 1990s, but thereafter the outlook was more speculative, especially in regard to a possible Soviet breakout from the treaty. Duff–Mason concluded that a Chevaline-type system did not offer adequate assurance against a 1990s ABM defence, and a MIRV system was required. Furthermore, even if Britain acquired the present Trident C4 MIRV system, two boatloads of missiles would be needed to meet national criteria above Option 3a (see Chapter 34), which implied a five-boat force, and even this would not guarantee achieving Option 1, which required double the warheads needed for any other option.[24]

The Duff–Mason report assessed that Soviet air defences in 1978 had limited capability against cruise missiles. However, there were no overriding technical obstacles to developing defences against projected American cruise missiles, which were all fairly slow, and Soviet systems with potent anti-cruise missile capability in the 1990s were feasible. Arms control limits on cruise missile defences could not be assumed, and Soviet defences would be geared to a maximum United States attack. If the Soviets deployed large numbers of modern surface-to-air missiles, fighters with lookdown shoot-down capability, and airborne early warning radar (all achievable by 1990), a British cruise missile attack could expect 80 per cent losses. This meant at least three hundred missiles must be fired to meet the least demanding damage criterion. Overall, for the United Kingdom, a cruise missile deterrent was far more defence-sensitive than a ballistic missile option, and the problems in providing credible launch platforms, and the necessary navigational support, were almost insurmountable.[25]

For two reasons, the Duff–Mason report probably received more searching scrutiny from Callaghan's small nuclear ministerial group in December 1978 than from ministers of the succeeding Conservative government led by Margaret Thatcher. First, Labour ministers were acutely aware of the opposition within their party to a Polaris successor, and there was ambivalence even within Callaghan's carefully chosen group. Secondly, Denis Healey, now Chancellor of the Exchequer, and David Owen as Foreign Secretary had defence expertise, and the intellectual self-confidence to challenge every assumption.[26] Owen, in particular, was deeply opposed to the Moscow criterion, and strongly in favour of a more minimalist deterrent, based on cruise missiles carried by SSNs.[27] Callaghan himself was evidently disposed to back the Duff–Mason recommendations supported by shrewd briefing from Cabinet Secretary Sir John Hunt. Like Trend, Hunt was a master at steering his prime minister towards his own preferred outcome, in this case Trident, while professing studied neutrality. His quiet demolition of Owen's 'bargain-basement' deterrent was masterly, although Michael Quinlan was even harsher on Owen, describing his arguments as 'unexceptional' and 'superficial'.[28] Despite the various reservations, Callaghan's group agreed he should sound out President Jimmy Carter on United States' willingness potentially to supply American systems, including Trident. Callaghan raised the issue at the Guadeloupe summit of Western leaders in January 1979, and received an immediately favourable response.[29]

Margaret Thatcher's first government entered office in May 1979, with a firm political commitment to renew the deterrent, and ministers considered the options to achieve this the following December. Callaghan had authorised the release of the Duff–Mason report, which had been updated by Mason following consultations in Washington, and reviewed by the chiefs of staff.[30] The intelligence view on the penetration problem had not changed, and the Ministry of Defence recommendation was clear that only the Trident C4 MIRV would adequately meet the desired damage criteria, and provide an essential hedge against future Soviet ABM improvements. If this was accepted, the other key decision was five boats or four. The case for five rested on ability to deliver the national criteria above Option 3a, but also improved immunity where the ASW intelligence case had developed further in the last year. Not entirely accurately, the Cabinet Secretary, now Sir Robert Armstrong, advised Mrs Thatcher that cancelling the fifth Polaris submarine in 1965 had proved 'an expensive mistake', since it would have avoided the need for Chevaline.[31]

The latest DIS ASW threat assessment, which drew on advice from PPAG, stated that the Soviets were devoting 'massive resources' to this area, in both acoustic and non-acoustic fields. There was no sign that this would produce an imminent breakthrough to make the seas 'translucent', and the pattern of past slow, incremental, improvement in ASW detection was likely to continue. However, despite a current lead in British acoustic ASW, the chances of a Soviet submarine locating and trailing an SSBN, and to achieve an attack when ordered, were gradually increasing. A preliminary assessment indicated that with just one British Trident C4 SSBN on patrol, a sustained Soviet search could, by the 1990s, achieve one detection per year. However, with two SSBNs on patrol, the prospect of simultaneous detection was less than once in thirty years. The Soviets would certainly appreciate that their prospects of taking out two boats at sea were remote, but with only one boat, the risk of the United Kingdom losing its entire retaliatory force was clearly much higher.[32]

The benefits, risks and costs in the choice of a Trident C4 system were debated within the British leadership as its purchase was explored with the United States through 1980. However, the case was fundamentally altered in 1981 by the decision of the incoming administration of President Ronald Reagan to proceed with rapid development and acquisition of the more advanced Trident D5. This had much longer range than the C4 (about 7500 miles compared to 4600), was more accurate and had a larger payload. Crucially, from a British viewpoint, the Americans now intended to have the D5 in service by 1989 and phase out the C4 by 1998. With the first British boat planned to enter service in 1994, if Britain stayed with the C4, it risked having sole responsibility for its support, maintenance and testing, with all the associated costs, for twenty years. As Lewin, the Chief of the Defence Staff stressed to ministers, the penalties of 'uniqueness' had been demonstrated with Polaris and Chevaline, and were considerable. The benefits of 'commonality' with the Americans were probably, therefore, decisive in persuading the Thatcher government to procure the D5, despite its greater cost. However, Lewin stressed other advantages. The greater payload and accuracy of the D5 enabled a single boatload of missiles to meet all the national targeting criteria, while its range vastly increased the available sea room. The sea room available with the D5 was twice that of the C4, and about ten times that of Polaris fitted with Chevaline. A D5-equipped SSBN could comfortably reach any target in the Soviet Union west of the Urals, from any point in the Atlantic north of the equator. The intelligence risks relating to penetration and immunity inherent in the C4 largely fell away, as did the requirement for a fifth submarine.[33]

The Falklands War

On 4 March 1982 the full Cabinet endorsed the decision that the future nuclear deterrent should comprise a four-boat force, equipped with the Trident D5. Four weeks later, British naval intelligence, which for a decade had focused almost exclusively on the Soviet threat, was diverted to a new and unexpected target, following Argentina's invasion of the Falkland Islands. The result, Operation Corporate, was not the largest military campaign conducted by Britain in the post-1945 period, but the projection of an amphibious force 7000 miles from the nearest available naval base, to recover territory in the face of substantial land-based air power, was the most complex and carried the highest military risk. Corporate was pre-eminently a naval operation: it involved the first sustained use of a full range of modern naval weapons and sensors, including missiles and SSNs, in a hot war at sea, and effective naval intelligence support substantially influenced British success. Yet, in intelligence terms, it also marked the end of an era. The geographical remoteness of the conflict zone restricted the intelligence assets that could be deployed. For the Royal Navy theatre commander, Rear Admiral Sandy Woodward, the intelligence experience was probably closer to his predecessors in the Second World War than with the conflicts of the 1990s, when global surveillance, instant communications and precision weaponry had become ubiquitous.

The reasons a conflict long in the making, but clearly heading for a decisive impasse, led to an attack that still took the British government and intelligence community by surprise have been summarised elsewhere.[34] For years, Britain used diplomacy to avoid two unpalatable options – either making concessions to Argentina on sovereignty, against the wishes of the islanders and powerful political lobbies in the United Kingdom, or making sufficient defence and economic investment in the islands to deter Argentine aggression. By late 1981, the Foreign Office recognised that Argentine patience was running out and that they would apply increasing pressure to force British concessions. However, the experience of previous periods of tension persuaded the British that Argentina would follow a standard escalation route. It would begin by withdrawing mainland services to the islands, and then steadily ratchet up economic action to a full blockade. Any early military moves would be essentially symbolic, and probably confined to flag-planting on outlying dependent territories. This was the judgement of the last full pre-invasion JIC assessment in July 1981, and nine months later it still conditioned expectations across Whitehall.

Because they were wedded to this pattern of Argentine behaviour, which diplomatic SIGINT from GCHQ and occasional SIS reports tended to reinforce, rather than challenge, neither the Foreign Office nor the JIC sufficiently questioned whether the new military junta, under General Leopoldo Galtieri, which took power in December 1981, might adopt a different strategy. The British ambassador in Buenos Aires had already warned that a policy based on diplomatic prevarication was losing credibility, and now emphasised that Falklands policy was increasingly defined by the hard-line commander-in-chief of the navy, Admiral Anaya. There was also a more specific intelligence failure. In mid January, the new regime circulated a national security directive, which explicitly stated that using military force to achieve its Falklands objective was now an option, and plans should be ready by mid May. No hint of this reached the British, since it required a high level penetration of the military, which SIS did not have.[35] Against this background, both sides miscalculated through March, following an unauthorised landing by Argentine personnel in South Georgia, ostensibly for commercial reasons but, in reality, part of a strategy to gain a presence in the Falklands dependent territories. The British badly misread the dynamics within the ruling Argentinian military junta, and failed to recognise their willingness, under growing domestic political and economic pressure, to exploit the Falklands as a distraction and shift from a gradualist strategy to a sudden strike. The Argentinians underestimated British political will, and were unprepared for a military response. Intelligence warning, primarily from SIGINT, that Argentine attitudes were becoming more dangerous caused the British to begin deploying SSNs as a deterrent force five days before the invasion took place, and before the Argentine junta took its final decision, but this was far too late to have any impact.[36]

There is a widespread view that following the Argentine invasion on 2 April, Britain began planning its response almost bereft of useful intelligence, and heavily reliant on open sources such as *Jane's*.[37] For frontline units in the first days, and even for Woodward, the task force commander, as his signal to Commander-in-Chief Fleet Admiral Sir John Fieldhouse attested while he was heading south from Gibraltar on 5 April, it was broadly true.[38] However, the view is also misleading, because it downplays important existing coverage of Argentina, and the extraordinary ability of the wider British intelligence community rapidly to surge and exploit its global assets and partners. Argentina was certainly a low priority for DIS in 1982, with one desk officer (DI4A2) covering all of Latin America. However, DI4A2 had the support of a naval attaché in Buenos Aires, Captain Julian Mitchell, and a military attaché, Colonel Stephen Love, and with their help completed an updated 'form-at-a-glance' assessment of the Argentinian forces by the end of 1981.[39] Despite the growing tensions over the Falklands, British-Argentine naval relations were historically close, providing Mitchell with good access and contacts. He also obtained valuable intelligence, including on the deployment of the Argentine fleet, immediately prior to the invasion from his American colleague, who drew on a US Navy officer seconded to the Argentine navy.[40] Meanwhile, earlier in March, Love speculated on Argentine intentions in terms that were remarkably prescient.[41] In addition to the attachés, there was an SIS station in Buenos Aires, producing some reporting on the Argentine leadership and military, although not at the highest levels, and GCHQ had considerable coverage of Argentine diplomatic and military traffic. It was GCHQ coverage that revealed by 31 March that invasion was imminent.[42] Finally, there was the Royal Navy ice patrol ship *Endurance*, which was deployed in the South Atlantic during the southern hemisphere summer. Although primarily tasked on scientific and hydrographic work, she provided a visible naval presence in the Falklands region, and carried a limited armament of two missile-equipped helicopters. She also had an important intelligence role in monitoring unauthorised Argentine activity around the Falklands and the outlying dependencies, reporting on unusual naval movements, and any significant developments in naval capability. For this, she had a SIGINT intercept suite and a team of Spanish-speaking coder specials. Her planned withdrawal following Nott's 1981 defence review was viewed by the Argentinians as a sign of weakening British commitment to the Falklands, but she remained present, and was a key player in the events of 1982.[43]

These sources underpinned an assessment approved by DCDS(I), Lieutenant General Sir James Glover, on 5 April, three days after the invasion, on the capability of the Argentine armed forces to defend the South Atlantic and the Falklands Islands against the British task force. Given the speed with which it was produced, it inevitably got some details wrong, but as a basis for initial planning, it gave a reasonably accurate picture of the Argentine order of battle and its fighting effectiveness, and Argentina's overall strengths and weaknesses in defending the islands. It judged the main naval threat came from the single carrier *Veinticinco de Mayo* operating A4 Skyhawks, eight Exocet-equipped escorts, with a total stock of thirty-six missiles (the French soon confirmed the true figure was thirty-nine), and two modern German-supplied Type 209 submarines. It concluded that although the British task force might suffer 'some damage', it was 'more than a match' for the Argentine navy and air force, and that Argentine communications with the Falklands were vulnerable to attack. It nevertheless recognised that their occupation force would be difficult to dislodge, if allowed to reinforce without interruption.[44] In judging the risk to the task force, this first assessment got two important things wrong. It discounted the likelihood that the Argentine navy had yet acquired air-launched AM39 Exocet missiles for its five new Super

Étendard aircraft, and it underestimated the strength of the Mirage force, its next most capable aircraft, by 30 per cent.

These errors were corrected just over a week later in an updated assessment of the air threat, drawing on new intelligence from the Americans and the French.[45] The best French intelligence was provided by Pierre Marion, the head of France's external intelligence service, the Direction Générale de la Sécurité Extérieure (DGSE), to the SIS station commander in Paris, Alexis Forter. DGSE had an officer working with the Dassault team commissioning the Super Étendards and their Exocets at the Espora naval air base. Marion and his staff confirmed that five air-launched Exocets had been supplied, and could be made operational on the Super Étendard by late April. They also reported that the Argentinians planned to deploy the aircraft operationally at Rio Grande in the extreme south, and that the Super Étendard was capable of being refuelled by Argentina's two C-130 tanker aircraft, although there was no evidence this had yet been practised. The Dassault team did not believe *Veinticinco de Mayo* could launch the Super Étendard with a viable operational load, but the Americans were less certain. DGSE also provided considerable intelligence on the numbers, status and deployment of other French-supplied aircraft, including the impact of spares shortages, and on their associated weapon stocks, and the location and capability of the main Argentine airbases. Although there have been frequent suggestions that the Dassault team gave unauthorised assistance to the Argentinians in integrating the Super Étendard with their Exocets, the latest evidence suggests this is unlikely.[46] As the primary supplier of non-French equipment, the Americans could, and did, fill most other pressing gaps in British knowledge, and provided important wider insights into Argentine leadership, professional skills, both operational and technical, and their overall experience and training. These American inputs came from both their service intelligence departments and from CIA. While making good use of the new French and American intelligence, DIS nevertheless applied sensible adjustments to gauge Argentine aircraft sortie rate and combat effectiveness over the Falklands, which proved broadly accurate.[47] By mid April, the intelligence baseline was good enough to answer most of the initial questions Woodward had posed to Fieldhouse on 5 April, and provide a sound basis for future operations. Indeed, Captain David Hart-Dyke, commanding the destroyer *Coventry*, described the intelligence picture by this time as outstanding, with apparently 'nothing we did not know'.[48]

From mid April, naval intelligence priorities were the deployment of and threat posed by the Argentine navy as British forces moved south;

Argentine activity within the exclusion zone the British had established around the Falklands, including reinforcement and supply operations; Argentine defences at South Georgia, which the British planned to recapture as early as possible; and attempts to acquire key military supplies from overseas – above all, additional air-launched Exocets. These naval requirements existed alongside, and were partly shaped by, a wider intelligence picture, as Britain sought every means to maximise international support for its position. Maintaining that support, including the supply of vital military equipment and intelligence assistance, required the war to be fought within carefully judged political and legal constraints. These complexities underlined the value of the JIC, which presented the British War Cabinet with a daily integrated consensus summary of key developments and their implications.[49]

The key British-controlled intelligence sources available to meet the immediate naval needs from mid April, as the British moved south to enforce the exclusion zone, were GCHQ SIGINT, submarine surveillance with three SSNs (*Spartan*, *Splendid* and *Conqueror*) in the Falklands area by 18 April, and aerial surveillance mounted from Ascension Island. All these had limitations. GCHQ collected and read Argentine naval traffic throughout the war, but coverage was never comprehensive, with often a delay of several hours between interception and dissemination of useful intelligence. Strategic SIGINT usually proved sufficient to warn fleet headquarters in Northwood, and Woodward in the flagship *Hermes*, of significant Argentine naval movements, both surface and submarine, and their likely intent, but given gaps and time lags, it was a valuable guide to conducting operations, rather than a precise answer to every threat.[50] The SSNs did valuable initial reconnaissance of the Port Stanley area and South Georgia, but with only three available, further inshore tasking required careful selection.[51] Meanwhile, even with towed arrays, they were not well-suited to wide-area, surface surveillance of the exclusion zone, and their overriding priority was detecting, marking and intercepting major Argentine naval sorties. From 12 April, Nimrod aircraft commenced flying surveillance patrols southward from Ascension, and after being fitted for in-flight refuelling, with extensive tanker support they could potentially reach as far as the Falklands area. At least one sortie reached the vicinity of the Falklands before 23 April, because significant ELINT had been collected on Argentine radar transmissions on the islands by this date. Victor aircraft also conducted radar reconnaissance of South Georgia in the days before its capture on 25 April. However, while Nimrods were invaluable in protecting the route south from Ascension throughout the war, flying more than 150 sorties, with some flights lasting nineteen hours, the refuelling effort required to extend their range beyond 2000 miles from Ascension was prohibitive.[52] Overall, therefore, prior to the arrival of the task force, capability for wide-area search, or to clarify specific SIGINT-generated leads, was thin, and the small carrier air groups and other task force assets would only partially fill it.

Two other sources might have helped address this surveillance gap, but ultimately the contribution of both was modest. The first was American satellite coverage. There was no regular visual or radar satellite surveillance of the South Atlantic when the crisis started, so any coverage required redirection of satellites from other priority tasks. On the few occasions this was done, winter weather and cloud cover limited the results. The British official history suggests the American imagery contribution was confined to a few passes over South Georgia in mid April, which provided the British with useful confirmation that the Argentine occupation force was very small.[53] The Chief of the General Staff, General Sir Edwin Bramall, later claimed that satellite imagery was important in late May in showing there was no significant Argentine opposition confronting the San Carlos bridgehead.[54] Although this is possible, the inability of special forces planners to obtain any useful imagery during the first half of May, when planning their attack on the Rio Grande air base, casts doubt on the claim.[55] The most authoritative sources available all agree that the imagery service was limited and of low quality, and that the need for film recovery from the Hexagon system involved considerable time lags. NSA SIGINT coverage of Argentina and South America was conducted jointly with GCHQ under UKUSA arrangements, with the product automatically shared. However, it seems NSA did facilitate some additional coverage by re-tasking SIGINT satellites to supplement GCHQ's primary collection site at Ascension Island. This would also have facilitated better and easier ELINT collection on Argentine radars, both in the Falkland Islands and on the mainland. CIA records suggest that its reporting passed once the conflict was underway probably added little to British assessments, and there were more constraints on sharing information drawn from human sources than within the SIGINT relationship.[56] Probably the most important contribution the Americans made to British intelligence capability was the provision of satellite communications facilities, which vastly improved the timely transmission of information to and from the task force, especially the SSNs.

The second option was support from Chile, which had its own territorial dispute with Argentina, a government under General Augusto Pinochet well-disposed to Britain, and with long-standing defence links, including regular British arms sales. However, there were political constraints on both sides – British concern over Chilean human rights, and Chile's desire not to move too far from Latin-American solidarity or provoke Argentine attack, which made achieving assistance difficult. The British chiefs of staff wanted to base Nimrods, and possibly Canberra PR9 reconnaissance aircraft at a southern airfield, which would substantially help maritime surveillance across the whole South Atlantic operational area, and with the Canberras provide regular coverage of the Falklands themselves. After long, tortuous negotiations, a Nimrod supported by a VC10 tanker was briefly based at San Felix, a remote island off the coast opposite Valparaiso, and three long sorties were flown round the southern tip of Argentina between 9 and 17 May, with limited, but still useful, results, before Chilean nervousness brought the operation to a close. More important was an arrangement negotiated whereby the Chileans passed details of Argentine air movements from their southern airbases by satellite communications link direct to the task force, thus providing some attack warning. There were also exchanges on the Argentine order of battle, which addressed some British gaps, including news of the despatch of a Roland surface–air missile system to the Falklands in late April.[57]

The strengths and weaknesses of British intelligence were evident in the only major engagement between the Argentine navy and the British task force, which led to the sinking of the Argentine cruiser *Belgrano* by the SSN *Conqueror* on 2 May. Following the start of British operations against the Falklands themselves the previous day, including attacks on the airfield at Port Stanley, GCHQ intercepts revealed that the bulk of the Argentine fleet was at sea in two groups, one centred on *Veinticinco de Mayo* to the north of the islands, and the other on *Belgrano* to the south. The intercepts gave the composition of the groups and, importantly, their intent to execute a pincer attack on the task force early on 2 May. However, they provided little detail on the precise Argentine locations and movements, and none in real time. Supporting intelligence from the task force's own sensors, including a Sea Harrier despatched towards the northern group, was imprecise, and the carrier was never definitively located. The seriousness of the known threat, combined with the uncertainties over overall Argentine locations and movements, led inexorably to Woodward proposing, and London approving, an attack on the southern *Belgrano* group, which was being trailed by *Conqueror*.[58] SIGINT had a critical influence on decisions taken on 2 May, and played a central role in the conspiracy theories that surrounded the *Belgrano* affair for years afterwards. Yet the underlying reality is that, for all the intervening advances in modern sensors and communications, Woodward's problem off the Falklands was broadly similar to that of Cunningham at Matapan, or Fraser at North Cape forty years earlier. As with those engagements, SIGINT had provided a superb insight into enemy intent, and it was accompanied by considerable knowledge of enemy capability. But knowing what the enemy wanted to do was not the same as knowing where he was now. Intelligence only gave Woodward a part of the picture, as it did his predecessors. Like them, he had to balance opportunities and risks with imperfect knowledge. The sinking of *Belgrano* also brought a similar strategic effect to Matapan. It underlined to the Argentine navy how vulnerable their warships were to SSN attack, and they never again ventured far from Argentine territorial waters. Their caution was justified. As the war progressed, British understanding of Argentine communications developed, and SSN numbers increased to five, SIGINT-led targeting of SSNs made any naval move a high risk proposition.

Following the withdrawal of the Argentine navy, with some notable exceptions, the focus of intelligence requirements became more tactical, and the balance of collection shifted to the task force's own assets and sensors, and to special forces reconnaissance parties deployed ashore. The passivity of the Argentine navy enabled the SSNs increasingly to focus on the unexpected but valuable role of air raid early warning. By positioning off the Argentine coast, close to the flight paths of attacking aircraft heading to the Falklands, the SSNs could pick the raiders up visually through periscope watch, or by intercepting their radar transmissions, and using satellite communications transmit an instant alert direct to the task force. This was a new variant of the traditional submarine surveillance role off an enemy base, and despite an odd juxtaposition of rather primitive sensors and state-of-the-art communications, it was highly effective, often giving the task force at least thirty minutes warning of an incoming raid, and sometimes even its probable composition. Between 17 May and 10 July, *Valiant*, primarily located off the Rio Grande naval airbase, home to both the Super Étendards and navy Skyhawks, reported 263 enemy aircraft contacts, earning heartfelt congratulations from Woodward. The SSNs, therefore, partially filled the long-range surveillance gap the task force faced from the beginning of the campaign.[59] In addition to the SSNs, the destroyer *Coventry*, which had recently received an advanced ELINT fit for a forthcoming mission in the Barents Sea, monitored Argentine air communications to great effect during the crucial period from the British landing at San Carlos until she was sunk on 25 May.[60] The recapture of South Georgia also initiated exploitation of the traditional source of prisoner-of-war interrogation. Questioning of the captured crew of the submarine *Santa Fe* produced useful intelligence on the status of the more important Type 209s and their torpedo armament.[61] Intelligence did not play a major part in the two strategic decisions taken in the first ten days of May: to proceed with a full-scale amphibious landing to recover the islands (Operation Sutton) rather than following a 'wear-down' strategy based on blockade and harassment; and the choice of San Carlos as the landing site. The first reflected the judgement that as winter advanced, the capabilities of the task force could degrade faster than the Argentine garrison, and that Britain's diplomatic advantage might also erode over time. The second was dictated by geography, an area offering shelter from the elements and air attack, logistics, accessibility to the main objectives, and lack of immediate opposition forces to counter a landing.[62]

The single area where intelligence external to the task force exerted most influence over the second half of the war was in countering the Exocet threat. There were two strands to this: preventing Argentina acquiring additional missiles from willing state suppliers; and facilitating an operation to destroy the Super Étendards, their missiles and crews at Rio Grande. The first strand was managed by SIS, following a tip-off from DGSE, that the head of the Argentine naval purchasing commission in Paris, Captain Carlos Corti, had been tasked with considerable funding to procure extra missiles. GCHQ monitored Corti's communications, and SIS distracted him with false offers from various fictitious sellers. It is doubtful Corti was ever close to finding a credible source of Exocets, but the SIS operation provided essential assurance the threat was contained. The priority given to countering the Exocet threat was underlined by the risks the military leadership, and ultimately the War Cabinet, were prepared to contemplate in neutralising the Rio Grande force. With Vulcan bombing ruled out for both political and logistic reasons, special forces developed two linked operations: the first, known as Plum Duff, for reconnaissance, followed possibly by an opportunistic strike; and the second, Mikado, for an all-out attack, deploying some fifty personnel by Hercules transport. However, both operations suffered from a lack of the most basic intelligence on Rio Grande, its immediate defences and the surrounding environment, and the plans were consequently badly flawed. Indeed, they were an object lesson in the dangers of prioritising daring and fighting skill over well-informed preparation. The Plum Duff party was inserted by Sea King helicopter launched on a one-way trip from the carrier *Invincible* on 17 May, but the operation was aborted after the commander judged it compromised, and the team exited through Chile, where the Sea King was abandoned and burnt. Mikado was cancelled.[63]

The New Maritime Strategy and the final phase of the Cold War

The Falklands war caused the Royal Navy to learn, or relearn, important lessons, which influenced both the design and procurement of new ships, weapons and sensors, but also its doctrine and tactics. It raised its profile and reputation, which ensured there was political support for new investment, preserving and even enhancing key capabilities such as the *Invincible*-class carriers and the amphibious fleet, and moderating the pace of surface fleet reductions set in the 1981 Nott review. However, it is ultimately difficult to disentangle the real influence of the Falklands war from the much bigger impact on the Royal Navy brought by the end of the Cold War just eight years later. For the rest of the 1980s, the Royal Navy remained predominantly an EASTLANT ASW force, and new investment reflected that. However, there is a compelling argument that the Falklands encouraged thinking, and some significant shifts in capability, that culminated in the proposals of the Labour government of 1997 to transition from an ASW force towards a global expeditionary Navy based around two large carriers. The impact on naval intelligence was mixed. The geographical remoteness of the conflict had denied the task force many of the sources routinely available in the EASTLANT area, where priorities and the nature of the enemy were also different. In that respect, the intelligence read across was limited, although the difficulty the task force faced locating just one operational Type 209 submarine perhaps carried a powerful warning. However, the war did underline the need to pay more attention to threats outside the NATO area, and to improve global warning. GCHQ, SIS and DIS all, therefore, received some additional funding to meet this need.

By the mid 1980s, the British intelligence community and naval leadership had accepted most of the American analysis that the Soviet navy had adopted a defensive strategy, focused on securing the waters north of the Greenland–Shetland line, and protecting its SSBNs in Arctic bastions. Its concern that the Americans risked downplaying a continuing Soviet threat to Atlantic communications, and to Western SSBNs, from its new quiet SSNs was gradually overcome by the logic underpinning the US Navy response to the Soviet strategy, which evolved through the first half of the 1980s, driven in part by the substantial new naval investment, 'the 600-ship navy', initiated under the Reagan administration. This American response, the New Maritime Strategy, was essentially an offensive riposte designed to reinforce Soviet defensiveness and keep them off-balance. As summarised in the over-arching National Security Strategy of the United States, published in January 1987, by asserting maritime superiority, the United States and its allies aimed 'to tie down Soviet naval forces in defensive posture protecting Soviet ballistic missile submarines and the seaward approaches to the Soviet homeland and thereby to minimise the wartime threat to the reinforcement and resupply of Europe by sea'.[64] Underpinning this broad statement of intent, the Maritime Strategy set three principal goals: destroying as many Soviet SSBNs as possible, thus reducing the strategic nuclear threat to the United States; launching strikes on Soviet targets from US Navy carriers; and tying down the Soviet fleet in static defensive operations in the far north, and thereby preventing it causing mischief elsewhere. In other words, by threatening the SSBN bastions and the Soviet homeland, the US Navy would discourage any Soviet deployment into the wider Atlantic. In particular, prioritising the targeting of SSBNs would force the Soviet navy to divert increasing numbers of their most capable SSNs to protect them, preventing their deployment on offensive missions. A specific concern here was the threat posed by the very quiet Akula, with its new SS-N-21 Sampson cruise missile.[65]

The credibility of this strategy depended primarily on American naval power, but Britain brought important supporting forces to the table, especially with its growing fleet of SSNs, and securing the Atlantic through forward defence was a concept it was willing to endorse, and help the United States promote in NATO.[66] In the last half of the 1980s and final phase of the Cold War, the Royal Navy, therefore, adopted two main roles in the New Maritime Strategy. Its SSNs would join the American submarine force in targeting the Soviet SSBN bastions near and under the ice, while its surface fleet would form ASW task forces, led by the *Invincible*-class carriers, to protect the American strike fleet as it moved northward. If the British SSNs were to operate effectively in the Arctic in wartime, they required experience of the environment in peacetime, along with the best possible picture of exactly how and where the Soviets were deploying.

Here, the British gained from important advances in American maritime intelligence surveillance over the previous decade. During the 1970s, the US Navy had established a worldwide Ocean Surveillance Information System (OSIS) which drew together intelligence from all sources – COMINT, ELINT, ACINT and IMINT – and from multiple platforms, satellites, shore-based SIGINT stations, aircraft, surface warships and submarines, to produce a composite picture of the location and movement of Soviet naval units. Essentially, this was an updated and vastly more sophisticated version of the wartime OIC and, like the OIC, it monitored own forces and merchant traffic too. It was, therefore, the ultimate culmination of Fisher's long-ago vision of the integrated War Room. By 1980, relevant parts of the national-level global OSIS picture were replicated in Fleet Ocean Surveillance Information Centers (FOSICs), including Royal Navy Fleet Headquarters at Northwood, and on a smaller scale to force commanders at sea. While the vision for OSIS and most of its major capabilities were American, Britain hosted key facilities, including the SOSUS regional centre at Brawdy, but also contributed important intelligence, notably through GCHQ.

OSIS stimulated the introduction of new intelligence sensors during the 1980s, from which the Royal Navy benefited. The SOSUS arrays were extended and upgraded and supplemented by Rapidly Deployable Surveillance System (RDSS) units, dropped to the ocean floor at short notice to produce semi-permanent mini-SOSUS arrays, and civilian-manned Surveillance Towed Array Sensor System (SURTASS) ships equipped with very long and wide aperture towed arrays, which were deployed in northern waters. In parallel, the new Royal Navy task forces deploying into the north Norwegian Sea deployed increasing numbers of towed array-equipped frigates. Technical improvements were matched by new operational approaches such as reverse cueing, where aircraft or ship contacts with a Soviet submarine were passed to SOSUS for review and investigation. These new ACINT capabilities combined to form an Integrated Undersea Surveillance System (IUSS), capable of tracking Soviet submarines over a much wider area and with greater precision than before, with data uplinked via satellite link to the OSIS system. The scope of this intelligence was demonstrated in the spring of 1987 when the Soviets deployed five Victor IIIs into the eastern Atlantic in a determined and aggressive operation, evidently aimed at finding Western SSBNs. Despite the greater quietness of the Victor IIIs, SOSUS picked them up on rounding North Cape, and most of the group was tracked continuously, using every available platform and sensor – satellite, air, surface and submarine – over the next ninety days as they conducted a long, circular sweep west of Ireland, then across the Atlantic to the United States East Coast, before heading back north. The following year the SSN *Torbay* received no less than 798 intelligence signals during a thirty-day patrol in the north Norwegian Sea, involving multiple successful detections and trails of Soviet boats.[67]

Another key element of OSIS, in which Britain was also integrated, was a shore-based HF/DF network known as Bullseye, an updated version of the British-American network of the Second World War. In the 1970s the US Navy introduced what was effectively a sea-based version of Bullseye, for deployment in select warships, known as Outboard. It offered a high-precision, over-the-horizon intercept and D/F system, capable of acquiring, recording and analysing signals across a vast frequency range, covering not just radar, but voice and data transmissions of all types, and again up-linking the results to OSIS, or passing them to other units. At its best, it provided a force commander with a long-range picture of both enemy dispositions and considerable insight into his intent. Six Royal Navy Type 22 frigates completed between 1983–90 were equipped with Outboard, as were the *Invincible*-class carriers, and other units followed later. Outboard brought a step-change, not only to detection capability in wartime directly relevant to forward operations in the Norwegian Sea, but to intelligence collection by Royal Navy vessels tasked with shadowing operations in peacetime.[68]

These intelligence advances through the 1980s were tempered by the revelation in 1985 that the Soviets had been penetrating the US Navy communications system since 1967, with the espionage ring established by Chief Warrant Officer John Walker, who, when he offered his services to the KGB, was a communications watch officer on the staff of Commander Submarine Forces in the Atlantic (COMSUBLANT) in Norfolk, Virginia. Over those eighteen years, Walker and his associates passed a vast amount of communications and cryptographic data, giving access to strategic plans, intelligence assessments, day-to-day operations, and technical capability. It gave the Soviets a deep understanding of their naval strengths and weaknesses compared to the Americans and other Western powers, especially how far behind they were in ASW, and the acute vulnerability of their SSBNs, where they must concentrate to compensate or catch up, and even how they might achieve an eventual lead. The Soviet shift to their defensive strategy in northern waters, the dramatic performance improvements in their third-generation nuclear submarines, and the greater skill shown in their deployment and tactics from the late 1970s owed much to Walker's intelligence.[69]

While the naval intelligence story of the 1980s is dominated by this shift in Soviet strategy, and success in closing the Western lead in ASW technology, another issue requires emphasis. In the first half of the 1980s, the combined total of SSNs and SSGNs completed by the Soviet navy (close to five boats per year) exactly equalled the combined total of American and British SSNs completed in the same period. In 1985 the British and American intelligence communities were confident that this production rate would continue over the next ten years and that output would be dominated by the new Akulas and Sierras, which they judged broadly competitive with Western boats. CIA expected twenty 'high quality' (post-Victor III) SSNs in commission by 1990.[70] In the event, Soviet SSN output in the second half of the 1980s was more than 50 per cent down on the first half. Only eight boats were completed, half the American-British SSN total in this period, and three were Victor IIIs, following a reopening of the Victor production line. Indeed, the final Victor III was laid down in 1990, underlining their dependence on a tried and tested design to maintain force numbers. There was an important message here, still under-appreciated by British and American intelligence as the Cold War drew to a close. The Soviets could develop submarines that matched Western levels of performance, but they could not reproduce these complex technology packages fast enough to be truly competitive. For all the anxiety raised in the Western navies by the Akula, which proved almost undetectable to SOSUS, there was only one, along with two Sierras, operational in the Northern Fleet in 1989. If war had come in the late 1980s, the Americans and British could have surged thirty modern SSNs to hunt Northern Fleet SSBNs, but the Soviets would have struggled to mobilise ten boats of Victor III, or later, classes with a performance adequate to oppose them. Similar signs of strain were evident in the production of major surface warships. *Admiral Kuznetsov*, the first large aircraft carrier, took two years longer to complete than CIA expected in 1985. The fourth *Kiev*-class carrier completed in 1987 required double the construction time of the first, finished in 1975. The pattern for the *Slava*-class cruisers over the same period was similar. Overall, by the late 1980s the Soviet shipbuilding and naval defence industries were struggling to cope with the demands imposed by advanced technology requirements. The 'mills of sea power', predominantly American, but with the Royal Navy contributing valuable support, were grinding the foundations of Gorshkov's navy, and helping to end the last great challenge to Britain's security in the twentieth century.

The Cold War period in retrospect

The story of the Royal Navy from 1945 to the end of the Cold War is usually presented as one of declining size and relevance, an epilogue to a proud maritime history neatly symbolised by the disappearance of the Admiralty, and hardly deserving, therefore, the attention of a Marder or Roskill.[71] Just as impressions of the First World War are shaped by the Western Front, so those of the Cold War are influenced more by the military confrontation on the dividing line in Germany, or comparisons of the nuclear balance, than developments at sea, even though that is where both sides ultimately placed much of their strategic nuclear strike forces. The declinist picture inevitably extends to British naval intelligence, which after the perceived glory days of Bletchley Park disappears from public view. Apart from the Falklands and some details of Cold War submarine operations which have emerged in recent years, Cold War intelligence histories give little indication that it mattered.

The final section of this book brings a different perspective. The role of the Royal Navy did steadily reduce from global naval power to EASTLANT ASW force, and the focus of naval intelligence narrowed with it. However, the defence of EASTLANT, primarily a British responsibility, was critically important to the integrity and effectiveness of NATO and, in the last resort, directly to the national security of the United Kingdom. Good intelligence was a force multiplier, and it remained essential. If Britain had not achieved such powerful intelligence capabilities by the end of the Second World War, it might have accepted greater intelligence dependence on the United States. However, it saw the maintenance of high-quality global intelligence as a crucial first line of defence, and rapidly came to appreciate that it also brought benefits from its closest ally that it might not have acquired otherwise. Through the UKUSA agreement, collaboration on aerial reconnaissance, and submarine special collection, Britain achieved a deep and enduring relationship on naval matters across the United States intelligence community, which it levered to huge strategic effect. It brought access to nuclear submarine technologies, the means to create and sustain a submarine-launched nuclear deterrent capable of penetrating the most advanced Soviet defences, and participation in a range of naval intelligence programmes and operations, especially in the ASW sector, on almost equal terms. The creation of the British SSN force, which reached its zenith in the late 1980s, was a huge national achievement, comparable with the dreadnought fleet seventy-five years earlier. But what made the SSNs an effective capability able to take on and beat the best of the Soviet navy was the access Britain won to the powerful American OSIS system. This was a worthy successor to Room 40, Bletchley and the OIC, and marks a fitting end-point to the story of British naval intelligence through the twentieth century.

Conclusion

The ultimate purpose of British naval intelligence, and the sources and techniques that developed to sustain it across the twentieth century, was to improve knowledge and understanding in order to counter naval threats to the security and wellbeing of Britain and its empire, and to obtain maritime, and sometimes wider political or strategic, advantage. In size, complexity and technical reach, it would be hard to over-state the gulf between the intelligence capabilities existing at the end of the Cold War and the embryonic intelligence structures that existed in the Napoleonic wars two hundred years earlier. Yet the essential enduring role and purpose would seem entirely familiar to William Pitt, Horatio Nelson or Evan Nepean, even if they might not have phrased it in quite the same terms. They well understood that intelligence enabled better use of scarce resources and guided the application of power. The extent to which British naval intelligence achieved its core purpose has been assessed at the end of each of the five periods into which this book is divided, but there are some wider points which deserve emphasis.

It is sometimes said that intelligence is only useful if it achieves identifiable change in strategic goals, or specific policy or operational outcomes. There is usually an accompanying implication that most intelligence activity is at best wasteful, and at worst pointless. Indeed, it has recently been suggested that just 'one thousandth of 1 per cent of material garnered from secret sources of all the belligerents in the Second World War contributed to changing battlefield outcomes'.[1] This conception of intelligence, as comprising rare nuggets of pure gold in a sea of dross, does not fit easily with the contribution and experience of intelligence described in this book. Intelligence can indeed provide those nuggets, especially in wartime – those crucial and timely insights into enemy intent or capability, with the Coral decrypts from Vice Admiral

Abe a classic example. However, most of the time it is closer to that cumulative process of knowledge and understanding described by William James, the 'intelligent putting together of little titbits, the sifting of the unimportant from the important', well-illustrated during the *Bismarck* sortie, Operation Rhine.[2] For policy-makers and decision-takers, it comes with recognised limitations that wiser recipients keep in mind. It is almost always incomplete, often fragmentary, and some things are not knowable. Even the best intelligence invariably only illuminates and influences one part of a complex picture.[3]

As stressed in the Introduction, intelligence is best perceived as information, subject to discrimination, protection and, above all, assessment and judgement, whether exercised at the high level of the JIC or in the OIC. Viewed in this way, intelligence spans a huge range of sources, human and technical, terrestrial and space-based, from the most open to the most sensitive and closely guarded, which all interact together. Furthermore, there is no direct, and certainly no guaranteed, correlation between sensitivity and value. A striking revelation in this book is how often good intelligence insights came from relatively open sources, whether from the reporting of the naval attachés on Germany before 1914; and on Germany and Japan in the 1930s; from Khrushchev's speech at Greenwich in April 1956; or the later published naval writings in the Soviet Union, which revealed their shift to a defensive strategy in the 1970s. Excessive focus on, even fascination with, more sensitive or exotic intelligence sources risks overstating their impact and neglecting less well-known sources, judged equally or more important by those engaged in policy or operations at the time. This book has shown how difficult it is to disentangle the real impact of Ultra in the Battle of the Atlantic from multiple other intelligence sources – radar, HF/DF, aerial PR and prisoners of war – and the comparative fighting resources that each side was able to deploy in each phase of the campaign. The British exploitation of Italian Hagelin to interdict Axis supply lines to North Africa, provoking significant redeployment of U-boats to the Mediterranean, probably had as much impact as Enigma-generated Ultra diversion in reducing Atlantic shipping losses in the second half of 1941, while HF/DF was at least as important as the contribution of Ultra at the tactical level during the convoy battles of 1942–43. Yet Enigma was earlier important in highlighting the potential of HF/DF, thereby underlining how complex the story is. It follows that presenting intelligence as the 'missing dimension' of twentieth-century history needs qualification.[4] Sometimes the revelation of previously hidden intelligence, with Enigma the classic example, does, indeed, radically change historical perception, but its real impact still needs careful appraisal, and often equally important and influential intelligence exists in plain sight.

Intelligence is also inextricably linked with the availability and exercise of power. It cannot compensate for its lack, as the Royal Navy found both in the central Mediterranean and in confronting the Japanese onslaught at the turn of 1941. Yet the balance of power is not static. Britain lost control of the central Mediterranean for nine months from December 1941, but it had sufficient forces to exploit the same sources of intelligence successfully, both before and after that period. Good intelligence coverage of the IJN could not save Singapore, but the Americans subsequently deployed British work on JN25 to great effect, which neatly demonstrates how investment in intelligence may bring value impossible to foresee. Even when excellent intelligence and the power to use it combine, its value may be compromised by failure of assessment and communication, as during the night action at Jutland. Alternatively, superb intelligence and masterly exploitation may be rendered marginal, because it merely reinforces something that was going to happen anyway, as with the Zimmermann telegram and the American decision to enter the First World War.

Finally, a key theme in this book is that British naval intelligence during the period it covers, as with most categories of intelligence at any time, was not something that existed in isolation. While it often shaped strategy and policy and operational outcomes, it was also itself shaped by them, and the context within which they interacted together was forever evolving. Burke Trend in 1968 was thinking of the British system when he emphasised the value of intelligence and policy-making interacting to produce intelligence assessments that were policy-relevant. But he expressed a wider universal truth, which is as applicable to the operational as the policy domain. That explains why, in the end, this book is as much an overview of British naval policy, strategy and high-level operations through the twentieth century as it is a history of intelligence. They were always interwoven, and it is impossible to write usefully about one without considering the others.

Notes

Introduction

1 John le Carré, *Tinker Tailor Soldier Spy* (Sceptre edition, 2011), p407. 2 Matthew S Seligmann summarises recent historiography here in his introduction to Navy Records Society, Vol 161, *The Naval Route to the Abyss: The Anglo-German Naval Race 1895–1914* (Ashgate Publishing, 2015), xv. 3 Peter Hennessy and James Jinks, *The Silent Deep: The Royal Navy Submarine Service since 1945* (London: Allen Lane, 2015); Anthony R Wells, *A Tale of Two Navies: Geopolitics, Technology, and Strategy in the United States Navy and the Royal Navy, 1960–2015* (Annapolis: Naval Institute Press, 2015). 4 The index to Max Hastings' intelligence work on the Second World War, *The Secret War: Spies, Codes and Guerrillas 1939–1945* (London: William Collins, 2015) contains no references to 'naval intelligence', 'NID', or 'Operational Intelligence Centre (OIC)'. 5 For example, Professor F H (Harry) Hinsley's view of NID in the interwar period in *British Intelligence in the Second World War*, Vol 1 (HMSO, 1979), pp10–11. 6 Keith Jeffery, *MI6: The History of the Secret Intelligence Service, 1909–1949* (Bloomsbury, 2010). 7 John Lomas obituary, *The Times*, 29 November 2019. 8 Hugh Sebag-Montefiore, *Enigma: The Battle for the Code* (London: Phoenix, 2001), p138. 9 Patrick Beesly, *Room 40: British Naval Intelligence 1914–1918* (OUP, 1984). 10 Patrick Beesly, *Very Special Intelligence: The Story of the Admiralty's Operational Intelligence Centre 1939–1945* (Chatham Publishing, 1977). 11 For discussion of the definitions of 'intelligence', see Michael Warner, 'Wanted: A definition of "intelligence"' in *Secret Intelligence: A Reader*, ed Christopher Andrew, Richard J Aldrich and Wesley Wark (Abingdon, Oxon: Routledge, 2009). The *Review of Intelligence on Weapons of Mass Destruction* produced by Lord Butler in 2004 (HC 898, HM Stationery Office, London) has a valuable description of 'The Nature and Use of Intelligence' in its opening chapter. 12 Butler, 'The Limitations of Intelligence', Ch 1.7.

Chapter 1 Beginnings 1800–1882

1 Steven Maffeo, *Most Secret and Confidential: Intelligence in the Age of Nelson* (Annapolis: Naval Institute Press, 2012), Ch 2. 2 Christopher Andrew, *Secret Service: The Making of the British Intelligence Community* (London: William Heinemann, 1985), p2; Maffeo, Ch 1. 3 Roger Knight, *Britain Against Napoleon: The Organisation of Victory, 1793–1815* (Allen Lane, 2013), pp130–1; Christopher Andrew, *The Secret World: A History of Intelligence* (Allen Lane, 2018), Ch 16. 4 Maffeo, Ch 1. 5 Ibid. 6 Roger Knight, pp6–8 and Ch 5; Michael Duffy, 'British Intelligence and the Breakout of the French Atlantic Fleet from Brest in 1799', *Intelligence and National Security*, 22:5 (2007), pp602–3. 7 Roger Knight, pp6–7. 8 Roger Knight, pp128–9; Nicholas Rodger, *The Command of the Ocean: A Naval History of Britain, 1649–1815* (London: Allen Lane, 2004), p428. 9 Jane Knight, 'Nelson and the Eastern Mediterranean 1803–5', *MM*, 91:2 (May 2005), pp195–215. 10 Colin White, '"A Man of Business": Nelson as Commander in Chief Mediterranean, May 1803–January 1805', *MM*, 91:2 (May 2005), pp175–94. 11 Roger Knight, p7. 12 Roger Knight, pp123–4; Duffy, 'British Intelligence and the Breakout of the French Atlantic Fleet', pp602–3. Professor N A M Rodger has stressed that Admiralty archives covering naval intelligence in this period are extensive but under-explored, 'Review of *Most Secret and Confidential: Intelligence in the*

Age of Nelson by Steven Maffeo', *War in History*, 8:3 (2001). **13** Roger Knight, pp144–8; Michael Duffy, 'British Naval Intelligence and Bonaparte's Egyptian Expedition of 1798', *MM*, 84:3 (August 1998), pp278–90. Knight describes the British intelligence performance over the Egypt expedition as the 'biggest blunder of the French Revolutionary War', which seems over-critical. For the map of Aboukir, Tom Malcomson, 'An Aid to Nelson's Victory? A Description of the Harbour of Aboukir, 1798', *MM*, 84:3 (August 1998), pp291–7. Also, John Keegan, *Intelligence in War: Knowledge of the Enemy from Napoleon to Al-Qaeda* (Vintage Digital, 2010), Ch 2. **14** Jane Knight, 'Nelson and the Eastern Mediterranean 1803–5'; Colin White, '"A Man of Business": Nelson as Commander in Chief Mediterranean, May 1803–January 1805'. **15** Rodger, pp438–9. **16** Rodger, p532. **17** Rodger, pp535–6. **18** Huw Davies, 'Naval Intelligence Support to the British Army in the Peninsular War', *Journal of the Society for Army Historical Research*, 86:345 (2008); Roger Knight, p428. **19** Duffy, 'British Intelligence and the Breakout of the French Atlantic Fleet', p615. **20** Roger Knight, pp137–41. **21** Keegan, Ch 2. **22** www.measuringworth.com. **23** Paul M Kennedy, *The Rise and Fall of the Great Powers* (London: Unwin Hyman, 1988), p151. **24** Rodger, *Command of the Ocean*. **25** Andrew Lambert, 'Preparing for the Long Peace: The Reconstruction of the Royal Navy 1815–1830', *MM*, 82:1 (February 1996), pp41–54. **26** Paul M Kennedy, *The Rise and Fall of British Naval Mastery* (Basingstoke: MacMillan, 1983), pp172–3. **27** C I Hamilton, *The Anglo-French Naval Rivalry, 1840–1870* (New York and Oxford: OUP, 1993). **28** Ben Wilson, *Empire of the Deep: The Rise and Fall of the British Navy* (London: Weidenfeld & Nicolson, 2013), pp492–3. **29** Andrew, *Secret Service*, pp5–6. **30** Matthew Allen, 'The Foreign Intelligence Commission and the Origins of the Naval Intelligence Department of the Admiralty', *MM*, 81:1 (February 1995), pp65–78. **31** 'Espionage in time of peace', paper for Director of Military Operations by Lieutenant Colonel J E Edmonds, MO5, January 1909, KV 1/2, TNA. **32** Memorandum by Henry Corry, Secretary to the Admiralty, on the 'Relative State of the English and French Naval Forces', dated 29 July 1858, Milne papers, MLN/142/2, NMM. Navy Records Society, Vol 147, *Milne Papers, Vol 1 1820–1859*, ed John Beeler (UK: Ashgate, 2004). **33** Paul M Kennedy, 'Imperial Cable Communications and Strategy, 1870–1914', *English Historical Review*, 86:341 (October 1971), pp728–52. **34** Stephen Twigge, Edward Hampshire, and Graham Macklin, *British Intelligence: Secrets, Spies and Sources* (National Archives, Kew, 2008), pp135–6. **35** Roger Morris, '200 Years of Admiralty Charts and Surveys', *MM*, 82:4 (November 1996), pp420–35. **36** 'List of the Chief Ports on the Federal Coast of the United States showing the Shipping, Population, Dockyards and Defences as far as known …', dated 15 December 1861, Milne papers MLN/114/8, item 450, Navy Records Society, Vol 162, *The Milne Papers, Vol 2 1860–1862*, ed John Beeler (UK: Ashgate Publishing, 2015). The document was apparently composed by the Hydrographer John Washington, who, in the absence of a naval staff at the Admiralty, sometimes acted unofficially in that capacity. **37** Roger Parkinson, 'The Origins of the Naval Defence Act of 1889 and the New Navalism of the 1890s' (unpublished doctoral thesis, University of Exeter, 2004), p44. The Hydrographer here was Sir Bartholomew Sulivan who had surveyed the Baltic during the Crimean War. **38** Colonel Edward Claremont mentioned in the Milne papers cited at fn 32 was probably the first military attaché. Claremont's valuable naval reporting in 1858 drawn on by Corry probably persuaded the Admiralty to deploy its own attaché to Paris. **39** Matthew S Seligmann, *Spies in Uniform: British Military and Naval Intelligence on the Eve of the First World War* (Oxford: OUP, 2006). **40** Kennedy, *The Rise and Fall of British Naval Mastery*, p200. **41** N A M Rodger, 'The Dark Ages of the Admiralty, 1869–85', *MM*, Part 1, 61:4 (1975), pp331–344; Part 2, 62:1 (1976), pp33–46; Part 3, 62:2 (1976), pp121–8. **42** Roger Parkinson, unpublished doctoral thesis, pp37–43. **43** Matthew Allen, 'The Foreign Intelligence Commission and the Origins of the Naval Intelligence Department of the Admiralty', *MM*, 81:1 (February 1995), pp65–78. **44** Bryan Ranft, 'The protection of British seaborne trade and the development of systematic planning for war, 1860–1906', in *Technical Change and British Naval Policy 1860–1906*, ed Bryan Ranft (London: Hodder and Stoughton, 1977), p2. **45** Parkinson, pp64–7. **46** Charles Morgan, 'Naval Intelligence 1939–1945', NID internal history, 'Origins', p3, ADM 223/464, TNA; Allen, p67. **47** Minute by Key, dated 28 November 1881, Intelligence records, Box 1, Naval Historical Branch (NHB). **48** Minute by Captain

Tryon, dated 29 August 1882; Minute by Lord Northbrook, dated 30 August 1882; Report of Departmental Committee on collecting and recording Naval Information, dated 1 November 1882; Foreign Intelligence Committee Report, dated 24 March 1885; all in Intelligence records, Box 1, NHB. Allen, pp67–8; Robert E Mullins, 'Sharpening the Trident: The Decisions of 1889 and the Creation of Modern Seapower' (unpublished doctoral thesis, King's College, University of London, 2000), pp72–5. **49** Admiralty letter to Treasury from H Campbell-Bannerman, dated 26 February 1884, Intelligence records, Box 1, NHB. **50** Appointment of Commander W H Hall RN, minutes by Tryon of 30 October and Key of 31 October 1882, Intelligence records, Box 1, NHB. **51** Admiralty letter to the Treasury of 26 February 1884. **52** Rodger, 'Dark Ages', Part 3, p125. **53** Robert E Mullins, 'Sharpening the Trident: The Decisions of 1889 and the Creation of Modern Seapower' (unpublished doctoral thesis, King's College, University of London, 2000), pp73–4.

Chapter 2 The Creation of a Naval Intelligence Department 1882–1905
1 'The Naval Staff of the Admiralty: Its Work and Development', BR 1875, pp27–8, ADM 234/434, TNA. **2** Rodger, 'The Dark Ages of the Admiralty', Part 3, p124–5. **3** Allen, p70. **4** ADM 231/1, TNA. **5** ADM 231/2, TNA. **6** Andrew, *Secret Service*, p13. **7** Allen, p69. **8** Parkinson, pp82–3. **9** For example, Vice Admiral Aube, French Minister of Marine 1886–7, published the articles, 'L'avenir de la Marine Francais' and 'La Guerre Maritime et les Ports Militaire de la France' in the periodical *Revue de deux Mondé*, Parkinson, p154. **10** Lord Northbrook's 1885 Response to William T Stead's Criticisms of Naval Preparedness in the *Pall Mall Gazette*, ed John Beeler, Ch 7 in Navy Records Society, Vol 164, *The Naval Miscellany Vol 8*, ed Brian Vale (UK: Routledge, 2017). For Beeler's foreword, pp295–302; Northbrook's memorandum, pp303–46; French building programme and British response, pp314–26. **11** Mullins, pp45–7. **12** Northbrook memorandum, Navy Records Society, Vol 164, reference to Foreign Intelligence Committee and Hall, p330. **13** Northbrook memorandum, Navy Records Society, Vol 164, Beeler's commentary pp295–8. **14** Mullins, pp74–7. **15** M S Partridge, 'The Royal Navy and the End of the Close Blockade, 1885–1905: A Revolution in Naval Strategy?', *MM*, 75:2, p21. **16** Partridge describes the 1885 exercise and the conclusions drawn at p122. **17** War Office to Admiralty, 15 February 1886, ADM 1/6942, TNA. **18** Above two paragraphs, Mullins, pp45–50 and Parkinson, pp153–5. **19** Admiralty Library Pamphlets, Vol 825, Report by Captain Lewis Beaumont in 1881 on Russian Fleets and Dockyards, quoted by Parkinson, p83. **20** Mullins, pp40–5 and Parkinson, pp83–4. **21** Mullins, pp77–8. **22** David Morgan-Owen, *The Fear of Invasion: Strategy, Politics and British War Planning, 1880–1914* (OUP, 2017), pp22–3. **23** Above three paragraphs primarily from Mullins, pp78–81. **24** Allen, p74. **25** NID Report for 1887, Appendix 2, pp5–6, ADM 231/12, TNA. **26** BR 1875, p37. **27** Naval Intelligence Department, Report of the Work of the Department during the Year 1887, February 1888, ADM 231/12, TNA, **28** 'Comparison of the Fleets of England, France and Russia in 1890', revised version of Naval Intelligence Department Report No 149, May 1888, ADM 231/12, TNA. **29** Ibid; Mullins, pp87–90. **30** Parkinson, p248; Eric Grove, 'The Battleship is dead; Long live the battleship. HMS Dreadnought and the limits of technological innovation', *MM*, 93:4, 415–27, p42. **31** Cm 7953, *A Strong Britain in an Age of Uncertainty: The National Security Strategy* (London: HMSO, 2010). **32** Mullins, pp50–1. **33** Partridge summarises Colomb's thinking on blockade at pp120–1. **34** Partridge, pp123–5. **35** The paragraphs above draw on Mullins, pp93–122, and Parkinson, pp143–64. **36** N A M Rodger, 'Anglo-German Naval Rivalry, 1860–1914', in *Jutland: World War I's Greatest Naval Battle*, ed Michael Epkenhans, Jörg Hillmann and Frank Nagler (University Press of Kentucky, 2014). **37** Parkinson, p236. **38** Rodger, 'Anglo-German Naval Rivalry'. **39** Parkinson, pp285–6. **40** Arthur J Marder, *The Anatomy of British Sea Power: A History of British Naval Policy in the Pre-Dreadnought Era 1880–1905* (London, Frank Cass & Co, 1964), pp338–40, quoting NID report 537 of April 1899. **41** Parkinson, p277, quoting memorandum by Senior Naval Lord on new works 1895–6, ADM 116/878, TNA. **42** Parkinson, pp278–80. **43** Marder, *Anatomy of Sea Power*, pp112–3. **44** Marder, *Anatomy of Sea Power*, pp578–80, quoting DNI memorandum on naval policy dated 28 October 1896. **45** NID 10388/21, 'Naval Intelligence Organisation – Abroad', ADM 116/1842, TNA. **46** Custance minute, 10 September 1900, ADM 1/7472, TNA. **47** Parkinson,

p235. **48** For the above two paragraphs, Matthew S Seligmann, 'Britain's Great Security Mirage: The Royal Navy and the Franco-Russian Naval Threat, 1898–1906', *Journal of Strategic Studies*, 35:6 (December 2012), pp861–86. **49** There were two attachés in Tokyo on the outbreak of war, Captains E C Troubridge and A D Ricardo. They were initially joined by Captain W C Pakenham, followed later by Captains T Jackson and J Hutchinson. By the end of the war, Jackson, a future DNI, and Hutchinson had taken over the attaché positions. Meanwhile, Captain C J Eyres was sent to join the Russian fleet but got marooned in Vladivostok, achieving little. **50** The initial attaché reports circulated are in ADM 233/44, TNA. These were amplified in Admiralty reference books issued as four volumes from 1904 to 1908 under the title 'The Russo-Japanese War: Reports from the Naval Attachés': Vol 1, NID 755, December 1904, BR 807; Vol 2, NID 772, July 1905, BR 801; Vol 3, NID 783, January 1906, BR 807; Vol 4, NID 807, August 1907, BR 803.There were two further publications: 'Reports on Technical Subjects', NID 835, June 1908, BR 808; and 'Maritime Operations in the Russo-Japanese War' by Julian Corbett and Rear Admiral Sir Edmund Slade, ID 944, January 1914, BR 805. Copies of the BR publications are in the Caird Library, NMM. **51** For a comprehensive account of British coverage of the war: Philip Towle, 'The evaluation of the experience of the Russo-Japanese War', in *Technical Change and British Naval Policy 1860–1939*, ed Bryan Ranft (London: Hodder and Stoughton, 1977). For the impact of mining, Richard Dunley, *Britain and the Mine, 1900–1915: Culture, Strategy and International Law* (Palgrave Macmillan, 2018), pp62–3. **52** 'The Building Programme of the British Navy', 15 February 1906, p14, ADM 1/7933, TNA. **53** The title First Naval Lord for the professional head of the Royal Navy changed to First Sea Lord with Fisher's appointment in October 1904. **54** BR 1875, pp40, 42. **55** 'Naval Intelligence Department, Distribution of Work', April 1907, ADM 231/50, TNA. **56** Matthew S Seligmann, *Spies in Uniform: British Military and Naval Intelligence on the Eve of the First World War* (Oxford: OUP, 2006), Introduction. **57** John W M Chapman, 'Russia, Germany and Anglo-Japanese Intelligence Cooperation, 1898–1906', in *Russia: War, Peace and Diplomacy: Essays in honour of John Erickson*, ed Ljubica and Mark Erickson (Weidenfeld and Nicolson, 2004), p47. **58** Lord Hankey, *The Supreme Command 1914–1918* (London: George Allen & Unwin, 1961), Vol 1, pp12, 16–18, 39–43. Roskill states that as Mediterranean Fleet Intelligence Officer Hankey recruited the Bishop of Gibraltar as an agent and sent his deputy Captain Gilbert Drage RMLI on an intelligence-gathering mission in the Black Sea. S W Roskill, *Hankey: Man of Secrets* (London, Collins 1970–1974), Vol 1, p81. **59** List of Reports issued and printed by the Naval Intelligence Department, January 1908, ADM 231/50, TNA. **60** List of Annual Publications, Newspapers and Periodicals supplied to the Naval Intelligence Department (1907), ADM 231/50, TNA. **61** Chapman, pp43–4. The British-owned Eastern Telegraph Company was the largest cable company in the world and dominated traffic between Europe, India and the Far East. The agreement with Eastern apparently began as a local arrangement with Cottrell. However, Fisher consolidated and extended the relationship at a meeting with the chairman of Eastern, Sir John Wolfe-Barry, in 1902. At this time Syra was handling 2500 messages per day. **62** Richard Dunley, '"Not Intended to Act as Spies": The Consular Intelligence Service in Denmark and Germany 1906–14', *International History Review*, 37:3 (2015), pp482–3; his blog, 'Caviar is for battleships: Intelligence and the late Victorian Navy', blog.nationalarchives. gov.uk/blog/caviar-battleships, dated 16 April 2018; Jan Morris, *Fisher's Face* (Viking Press, 1995), pp109–10; Chapman, p45. **63** Dunley, 'Not Intended to Act as Spies', p483 and 'Caviar is for battleships'. **64** Norman Friedman, *Network-Centric Warfare: How Navies Learned to Fight Smarter through Three World Wars* (Naval Institute Press, 2009), pp3–4, and *Fighting the Great War at Sea*, Ch 5. 'Network-Centric Warfare' fills many books and documents but boils down to bringing information rapidly from multiple sources in multiple locations to produce a composite picture shared between commanders to enable rapid joint action. **65** 'Naval Intelligence Organisation – Abroad', ADM 116/1842. Also Matthew S Seligmann, *The Royal Navy and the German Threat, 1901–1914: Admiralty Plans to Protect British Trade in a War against Germany* (OUP, 2012), Ch 6. **66** Richmond to Julian Corbett, 20 November 1904, quoted by Nicholas A Lambert, 'Strategic Command and Control for Manoeuvre Warfare: Creation of the Royal Navy's "War Room" System, 1905–1915', *Journal of Military History*, 69:2 (2005), pp361–410. **67** Hankey, *The Supreme Command 1914–1918*, Vol 1, p23.

Chapter 3 Defining a Rising German Threat 1905–1909

1 Arthur J Marder, *From the Dreadnought to Scapa Flow, Vol 1, The Road to War, 1904–1914* (OUP, 1961), but also his earlier work, *The Anatomy of British Sea Power: A History of British Naval Policy in the Pre-Dreadnought Era, 1880–1905* (New York, 1940). 2 Notably, Jon Tetsuro Sumida, *In Defence of Naval Supremacy: Finance, Technology and British Naval Policy 1889–1914* (London, 1989), and Nicholas A Lambert, *Sir John Fisher's Naval Revolution* (University of South Carolina Press, 2002). 3 Nicholas A Lambert, *Planning Armageddon: British Economic Warfare and the First World War* (Harvard University Press, 2012). 4 Seligmann, *The Royal Navy and the German Threat, 1901–1914*; Shawn T Grimes, *Strategy and War Planning in the British Navy, 1887–1918* (Boydell Press, 2012); and David Morgan-Owen, 'A Revolution in Naval Affairs? Technology, Strategy and British Naval Policy in the "Fisher Era"', *Journal of Strategic Studies*, 38:7 (2015), pp944–65. 5 The historiography here is summarised by Matthew Seligmann in his 'Introduction' to Navy Records Society, Vol 161, *The Naval Route to the Abyss: The Anglo-German Naval Race 1895–1914*, ed with Frank Nagler and Michael Epkenhans (UK: Ashgate Publishing, 2015); and by Christopher M Bell in 'Contested Waters: The Royal Navy in the Fisher Era', *War in History*, 23:1 (2016), pp115–26. 6 Professor N A M Rodger's review of *The Royal Navy and the German Threat, 1914–1918: Admiralty Plans to Protect British Trade in a War against Germany*, by Matthew S Seligmann, *International Journal of Maritime History*, 24:2 (2012). 7 Seligmann comes closest in *Spies in Uniform*, but this focuses primarily on the contribution of the naval attachés and NID. It does not discuss the contribution of the Secret Service Bureau in detail. Likewise, historians covering the SSB generally provide a partial picture of its naval coverage and do not address the wider naval intelligence contribution in NID and elsewhere. 8 Matthew S Seligmann, *Spies in Uniform*. 9 Nicholas A Lambert, 'Transformation and Technology in the Fisher Era: The Impact of the Communications Revolution', *Journal of Strategic Studies*, 27:2 (2004), pp272–97. 10 Jon Tetsuro Sumida, 'A Matter of Timing: The Royal Navy and the Tactics of Decisive Battle, 1912–1916', *Journal of Military History*, 67:1 (2003), pp85–136. 11 Rear Admiral Reginald Hall, *A Clear Case of Genius: Room 40's Code-breaking Pioneer*, original unpublished autobiography from 1926–1933, ed Philip Vickers (The History Press, 2017), Ch 1. 12 'Memorandum by the State Secretary of the Imperial Navy Office, Rear Admiral Tirpitz, June 1897', NRS, Vol 161, Item 4, p42. 13 'Rear Admiral Tirpitz. Notes on his Report to the Sovereign on the Amendment to the Navy Law, to be given on 28 September 1899', NRS Vol 161, Item 7, p57, and Introduction, p11. Also, Lawrence Sondhaus, *The Great War at Sea: A Naval History of the First World War* (Cambridge University Press, 2014), Ch 1. 14 Matthew S Seligmann, 'Switching Horses: The Admiralty's Recognition of the Threat from Germany, 1900–1905', *International History Review*, 30:2 (June 2008), pp239–58. 15 Fashoda in southern Sudan became the focus of a territorial dispute between Britain and France as each sought to expand its influence in East Africa. 16 'Memorandum by Custance, 19 December 1901', NRS Vol 161, Item 20, p115. 17 'Minute by Custance on unknown docket of unknown date, 14 September 1901', NRS Vol 161, Item 21a, p116. 18 Grimes, p51. 19 'Minute by Lord Selborne, 27 September 1901', NRS Vol 161, Item 21c, p117. 20 'Selborne, "The Navy Estimates and the Chancellor of the Exchequer's Memorandum on the Growth of Expenditure", 16 November 1901', 'Selborne's Conundrums', and 'Lascelles to Lansdowne, 25 April 1902', NRS Vol 161, Item 24, p119, Item 28b, p122, and Item 28c, p123. 21 Seligmann, 'Switching Horses', pp246–7. 22 Shawn T Grimes, 'War Planning and Strategic Development in the Royal Navy 1887–1918 (unpublished doctoral thesis, King's College, University of London, 2004), pp52–6. 23 'Naval Intelligence Department. "Germany, Naval Manoeuvres, 1903"', NRS Vol 161, Item 39, pp145–6. 24 'Selborne, "Navy Estimates, 1903–1904", 10 October 1902', NRS Vol 161, Item 34, p137. 25 Morgan-Owen, *Fear of Invasion*, p135. 26 'H O Arnold-Forster, "Notes on a Visit to Kiel and Wilhelmshaven, August 1902, and General Remarks on the German Navy and Naval Establishments", 15 September 1902', NRS Vol 161, Item 33, pp132–7. 27 Seligmann, 'Switching Horses', pp247–8. 28 Keith Wilson, 'Directions of Travel: The Earl of Selborne, the Cabinet and the Threat from Germany, 1900–1904', *International History Review*, 30:2 (2008), pp268–9. 29 Chapman, p53, fn 39; Grimes, p57. 30 Chapman, p52. 31 Grimes, p62. 32 'Selborne, 'Memorandum on the Situation

created by the Building of Four German Steamers for the Atlantic Trade of 23 Knots and Upwards', 1 July 1902', NRS Vol 161, Item 31, p126. **33** Matthew S Seligmann, *The Royal Navy and the German Threat 1901–1914: Admiralty Plans to protect British Trade in a war with Germany* (OUP, 2012), Ch 2. **34** Seligmann, ibid, Ch 1. **35** Seligmann, 'Britain's Great Security Mirage', p880. **36** 'Selborne, 'Memorandum respecting additional Problems to be dealt with and Questions to be taken up', sent to Sir John Fisher, 9 June 1904', NRS Vol 161, Item 41, p148. **37** N A M Rodger, in 'Anglo-German Naval Rivalry', and Nicholas A Lambert, in 'Transformation and Technology in the Fisher Era', pp272–97. Both argue that Fisher was relaxed about the German threat, at least during the first half of his tenure as First Sea Lord and perhaps longer, and that it had limited influence on his modernisation agenda. **38** Grimes, p66. **39** 'Memorandum by Battenberg, 7 November 1904', NRS Vol 161, Item 43, pp152–3; Mullins, p67. **40** Morgan-Owen, *Fear of Invasion*, p140. **41** 'Minute by Selborne, 21 November 1904', NRS Vol 161, Item 45, p154. **42** Figures extrapolated from Sumida, *In Search of Naval Supremacy*, Appendix, Tables 1 and 3; www. measuringworth.com; and *The Growth of Public Expenditure in the United Kingdom*, ed Alan Peacock and Jack Wiseman (Princeton University Press, 1961). It appears that Sumida's figures for overall UK government expenditure in his Table 1 are not correct. **43** Sumida, *In Search of Naval Supremacy*; Lambert, *Sir John Fisher's Naval Revolution*. **44** 'Ottley, "Effect on the Naval Situation of the Acquisition by Germany of Sea-Ports upon the Coast of Morocco", 6 July 1905', NRS Vol 161, Item 68, pp246–7. **45** 'Unsigned memorandum (Ottley) on "British intervention in the event of France being suddenly attacked by Germany", July 1905', NRS Vol 161, Item 69, pp247–8. **46** Grimes, pp66–87. **47** Morgan-Owen, *Fear of Invasion*, pp152–3. **48** Dunley, 'Not Intended to Act as Spies', pp483–92. **49** Marder, *FDSF*, Vol I, pp341–4. **50** 'List of Papers of the Committee of Imperial Defence', CAB 38/29, TNA. **51** Norman Friedman, *The British Battleship 1906–1946* (Barnsley: Seaforth Publishing, 2015), p69. **52** Summary of report by US Navy Inspector of Gunnery, Lieutenant Commander William Sims, included at pp16–18 of a paper by DNI Captain C Ottley, 7 January 1907, 'The Strategic Aspect of our Building Programme, 1907', ADM 1/7933, TNA. Later in his career, as a vice admiral, Sims would command the US Navy forces operating with Britain in the European theatre in 1917–18. **53** Friedman, ibid, pp76–7 and notes 6 and 7; Marder, *FDSF*, Vol 1, p57. **54** Matthew S Seligmann, 'The Anglo-German Naval Race, 1898–1914', in *Arms Races in International Politics: From the Nineteenth to the Twenty-First Century*, ed Thomas Mahnken, Joseph Maiolo and David Stevenson (OUP, 2016), pp27–9. **55** The source most frequently quoted is the Committee on Designs, established by Fisher, at its first meeting on 5 January 1905. See NRS Vol 102, *The Fisher Papers, Vol I*, ed P K Kemp (Spottiswoode, Ballantyne & Co, 1960), p219. **56** Richard Hough, *Dreadnought: A History of the Modern Battleship* (London: Michael Joseph, 1965), p9. **57** Hough, ibid, pp12, 34–8. **58** Hough, ibid, pp23–4. **59** 'Naval Necessities', Jackson paper, NRS Vol 106, *The Fisher Papers, Vol 2*, ed P K Kemp (Spottiswoode, Ballantyne & Co, 1964), p263. **60** 'The Building Programme of the British Navy', 15 February 1906, ADM 1/7933, TNA. **61** Matthew S Seligmann, *The Royal Navy and the German Threat 1901–1914*, Ch 3, and Stephen Cobb, *Preparing for Blockade 1885–1914: Naval Contingency for Economic Warfare* (Ashgate Publishing, 2013), pp184–8, provide detailed accounts. **62** Seligmann, 'Switching Horses', pp253–4. **63** For example: 'Sunday 2nd December 1905' and ' Mercantile Cruisers', papers B and C respectively in Naval Necessities IV, NRS Vol 161, Items 72a and 72b, p250–1. **64** For evidence relating to the role of the *Invincibles* in countering German merchant raiders, Seligmann, *The Royal Navy and the German Threat*, Ch 4. **65** 'Admiralty, "Memorandum on the Protection of Ocean Trade in Wartime", October 1903', NRS Vol 161, Item 38, pp143–4. **66** 'The Building Programme of the British Navy', Appendix, p40. **67** Sumida, *In Search of Naval Supremacy*, and Lambert, *Sir John Fisher's Naval Revolution*. **68** Friedman, *Fighting the Great War at Sea*, Ch 5. **69** Nicholas Black, *The British Naval Staff in the First World War* (Woodbridge: Boydell Press, 2009), pp41–2. **70** Nicholas A Lambert, 'Strategic Command and Control for Maneuver Warfare: Creation of the Royal Navy's War Room System, 1905–1915', *Journal of Military History*, 69: 2 (April 2005), p374; A J L Blond, 'Technology and Tradition: Wireless Telegraphy and the Royal Navy 1895–1920' (unpublished and uncompleted doctoral thesis, University of Lancaster, 1993), pp107–8. **71** Blond, pp112–3. **72** Letter from Inglefield to Campbell, 14

November 1907, ADM 137/2864, TNA. Also BR 1875, p44; Blond, pp369–70. **73** War staff paper, 'Admiralty Responsibilities Regarding National Commerce in War', 30 October 1913, pp6–7, ADM 137/2864, TNA. **74** Seligmann, *The Royal Navy and the German Threat*, Ch 6. **75** BR 1875, p46. **76** Seligmann, *The Royal Navy and the German Threat*, Ch 6. **77** 'Naval Intelligence Organisation – Abroad', ADM 116/1842. For wartime work of the Shanghai centre, 'Notes on Work of Naval Intelligence Centre Shanghai', Hall papers, 2/1, CCA. For the initial home-based network, 'Naval Intelligence Organisation – Home', ADM 116/1842. These centres began with sixty staff. **78** Ibid. **79** War staff paper 'Admiralty Responsibilities Regarding National Commerce in War', pp2–3; Seligmann, Ch 6. **80** Javier Ponce Marrero, 'Logistics for Commerce War in the Atlantic during the First World War: The German *Etappe* System in Action' *MM*, 92:4 (2006), pp455–64. **81** BR 1875, pp59–62 and 'Organisation for War Room Work, ADM 1/8272, TNA. **82** The paragraphs above draw substantially on Nicholas A Lambert, 'Strategic Command and Control for Maneuver Warfare'. **83** James Goldrick, 'The need for a New Naval History of the First World War', Corbett Paper No 7, King's College, London, November 2011, pp8–10. **84** James Goldrick, *Before Jutland: The Naval War in Northern European Waters, August 1914–February 1915* (Annapolis USA: Naval Institute Press, 2015), p49. **85** Lambert, 'Strategic Command and Control', pp384–5. **86** BR 1875, p61. By contrast, Commander Herbert Hope, who joined NID as a watch-keeper on the outbreak of war, stated that there was very little quality information available for updating the plot and that he was often underemployed. W F Clarke, History of Room 40 OB, appendix, HW 3/3, TNA. **87** Goldrick, pp48–9; Friedman, *Network-Centric Warfare*, pp6–12, and *Fighting the Great War at Sea*, Ch 5. Under the 'broadcast' system, messages transmitted by the Admiralty, or eventually subordinate commanders, did not require a reply from addressees. Signals were numbered sequentially and repeated several times. Addressees could therefore easily spot if they were missing traffic. The 'broadcast' concept was the mainstay of communication with Royal Navy submarines throughout the twentieth century. **88** Ottley, 'The Strategic Aspect of our Building Programme, 1907', pp11–19. **89** 'Captain Philip Dumas, 'German Ships Laid Down', November 1907', NRS Vol 161, Item 82, pp268–9. **90** Matthew S Seligmann, 'Intelligence Information and the 1909 Naval Scare: The Secret Foundations of a Public Panic', *War in History*, 17:1 (2010), pp42–3. **91** Mulliner letter to General Haddon, MGO War Office, 11 May 1906, ADM 116/3340, TNA. **92** 'Minute by Edmond Slade, 15 July 1908', NRS Vol 116, Item 108b, pp362–3. For the agent in the Krupps works, Dunley, 'Not Intended to Act as Spies', p492. **93** The traditional account of the 'naval scare' and still one of the best is by Marder in *FDSF*, Vol 1, pp151–71. A modern account focusing mainly on the intelligence dimension is Seligmann's 'Intelligence Information and the 1909 Naval Scare'. **94** 'Digest entry for the (now missing) docket "British Consul, 14 October 1908"', NRS Vol 161, Item 109a, p363. **95** Seligmann, 'Intelligence Information and the 1909 Naval Scare', p56, quoting Michael Epkenhans, *Tirpitz: Architect of the German High Seas Fleet* (Washington, 2008), p42. **96** 'Minute by Slade, 21 October 1908', NRS Vol 161, Item 109b, p363. **97** 'H Conyers Surtees, MA Constantinople 66/08, 18 December 1908', NRS Vol 116, Item 111, pp368–70. **98** Seligmann, 'Intelligence Information and the 1909 Naval Scare', pp49–51. **99** Secret reports by Commander Sir Trevor Dawson to the Admiralty 1906–14, Misc 73/Item 1098, IWM. The cover page to these reports notes that they were produced – 'As a result of visits made to the continent at the request of the First Lord of the Admiralty and as collected through special agencies'. McKenna's private papers contain the reports produced by Dawson during his tenure as First Lord. These show that Dawson addressed his reports, often with a covering letter, directly to McKenna up to the latter's departure in September 1911. McKenna, 3/31, CCA. **100** Fisher note to Churchill dated 2 March 1915, Roskill papers, 3/18 Part 2, CCA. **101** 'Note by Sir Charles Ottley, 24 February 1909' and 'Note by Sir Charles Ottley, 8 March 1909', NRS Vol 116, Items 113 and 114, pp372–4. **102** '"Germany" in Reports on Foreign Naval Affairs, 1908–9 (NID 871, April 1909)', NRS Vol 161, Item 116, pp377–8. **103** McKenna papers, 3/31, CCA, especially Board of Admiralty paper setting out their agreement on 'acceleration' and McKenna's note for the Cabinet 'A Reply to Mr Churchill's Note on Navy Estimates 1909–1910'. **104** McKenna papers, 3/19, CCA, and Seligmann, 'Intelligence Information and the 1909 Naval Scare', p53. **105** At the outbreak of war in August 1914, British dreadnought strength until

November was nineteen battleships, dropping to eighteen after the loss of *Audacious*, and eight battlecruisers. Germany had fifteen battleships and five battlecruisers, dropping to four after the transfer of *Goeben* to Turkey. Marder, *FDSF*, Vol 1, Appendix. See Quintin Barry, *The War in the North Sea: The Royal Navy and the Imperial German Navy 1914–1918* (Helion & Co, 2016), p74, for a summary of the narrowness of the British margin at this time.

Chapter 4 The Beginning of an Intelligence Community 1909–1914

1 Andrew, *Secret Service*, p50. **2** Temple worked as personal staff officer to Bethell at the end of 1909, but also ran some agents which he passed to Commander Mansfield Cumming, head of the new Secret Service Bureau formed that autumn. Alan Judd, *The Quest for C: Mansfield Cumming and the Founding of the Secret Service* (London: Harper Collins, 1999), pp118, 125–6, 131. He continued working for NID throughout the First World War. Black, *Naval Staff*, References, p331. **3** Regnart worked for NID until 1913 when he transferred to the new Secret Service Bureau to open its first overseas station in Brussels. This was not a success and he returned to the mainstream Royal Marines the following year. Between 1909–13 he worked closely with Cumming in running agent operations as the SSB got off the ground and is regularly mentioned in Cumming's diary. Judd, *Quest for C*, References, p497. **4** Dunley, 'Not Intended to Act as Spies', pp492–5. **5** Ibid, pp496–7. **6** For reconnaissance trips by serving officers, conducted by the War Office as well as NID, Judd, *Quest for C*, pp134–5. **7** Admiral Sir William James, *The Eyes of the Navy: A Biographical Study of Admiral Sir Reginald Hall* (London: Methuen, 1955), pp7–8, and Hall autobiography, Ch 1. **8** Hough, p27. **9** James, p8. **10** ADM 137/1013, TNA. **11** Hector C Bywater and H C Ferraby, *Strange Intelligence: Memoirs of Naval Secret Service* (Biteback Publishing, 2015), Ch 8. The original version was published by Constable in 1934. **12** 'Secret Service in the Event of a European War', HD 3/124, TNA. This paper is undated and unsigned but its context suggests it was prepared during 1903. **13** Nicholas P Hiley, 'The Failure of British Espionage against Germany, 1907–1914', *Historical Journal*, 26: 4 (December 1983), pp869–73; and Christopher Andrew, *The Defence of the Realm: The Authorised History of MI5* (London, Allen Lane, 2009), pp8–10. **14** Melville's personal memoir written in December 1917 is in KV 1/8, TNA. It describes how he joined the War Office in December 1903 and gives a selective account of his subsequent work in MO5, and then from 1909 the Counter-Espionage Bureau which became MI5. The memoir concentrates almost exclusively on his defensive security work, with little about his offensive intelligence work overseas. **15** Andrew, *Defence of the Realm*, pp5–6. **16** Payments to these agents appear in the monthly accounts forwarded by Edmonds to the Foreign Office for secret vote funding in HD 3/136 and HD 3/137, TNA. Melville, Long and Byzewski received monthly payments throughout 1908–9, Verrue from autumn 1908, Bywater from early 1909, part funded by NID, and Christmas slightly later. They appear under the designations: M, L, B, V/U, HC and K respectively. Bywater's initials were H C, standing for Hector Charles. For valuable background, Judd, *Quest for C*, Ch 4, and Michael Smith, *Six: A History of Britain's Secret Intelligence Service*, Part 1: Murder and Mayhem 1909–1939 (London: Dialogue, Biteback, 2010), Ch 1. **17** Dunley, 'Not Intended to Act as Spies', p491; Hiley, 'Failure of British Espionage against Germany', pp872–3. **18** Inglefield letter to Vincent Baddeley, private secretary to the First Lord, 19 October 1909, ADM 116/940B, TNA. **19** Smith, *Six*, Ch 2. **20** Andrew, *Secret Service*, pp49–51, and Philip H J Davies, *MI6 and the Machinery of Spying* (Abingdon, Oxon: Frank Cass, 2004), Ch 2. **21** Hiley, p873. **22** Smith, *Six*, Ch 1. **23** Minutes from DMO (Ewart) to Chief of the General Staff, Field Marshal Sir William Nicholson, 31 December 1908 and 12 January 1909, enclosing paper from Lieutenant Colonel James Edmonds, KV 1/2, TNA. The Chief of the General Staff became Chief of the Imperial General Staff in November 1909. **24** 'Foreign Espionage, Terms of Reference', 25 March 1909, Report on the Proceedings of a Sub Committee of the Committee of Imperial Defence appointed to consider the Question of Foreign Espionage in the United Kingdom, CAB 16/8, TNA. **25** Report on the Proceedings of CID Sub Committee appointed to consider the Question of Foreign Espionage in the United Kingdom, iv. **26** 'Conclusions of the Sub-Committee requested to consider how a secret service bureau could be established in Great Britain', CAB 16/232, TNA. Also Keith Jeffery, *MI6: The History of the Secret Intelligence Service 1909–1949* (London: Bloomsbury, 2010), pp6–7. **27** Judd, *Quest for C*, p104. **28** Ibid. **29** Hiley, p876. **30** Report on the Proceedings of CID Sub Committee appointed to consider the Question of Foreign Espionage in the United Kingdom, iii–vi. The complete conclusions and recommendations are at vi. Apart from the establishment of the SSB, these were the strengthening of the Official Secrets Act 1889 and relations between the SSB and other government departments including the Post Office and Customs. **31** For Cumming's background, selection by Bethell as the first 'C', his suitability for the role and his personal qualities, the indispensable source is Judd, *Quest for C*. Gill Bennett contributes important insights in *Churchill's Man of Mystery: Desmond Morton and the World of Intelligence* (Abingdon, Oxon: Routledge, 2007), Ch 3, 'SIS in 1919'. Cumming's naval service record is in ADM 196/39/377, TNA. **32** For a detailed account, Jeffery, *MI6*, pp8–17; Andrew, *The Defence of the Realm*, pp21–8. **33** Judd, *Quest for C*, p87. **34** For Macdonogh's career and qualities, Judd, *Quest for C*, pp88–92. **35** See accounts and correspondence, including submissions to the Foreign Secretary, Sir Edward Grey, in FO 1093/25, FO 1093/29 and FO 1093/30, all in TNA. **36** Smith, *Six*, Ch 1. **37** Judd, *Quest for C*, pp137–40. **38** Dawson is probably the individual referred to as 'FRS' in Cumming's diary, Judd, *Quest for C*, pp126–7, 140–3. The description of FRS's reporting fits with Dawson's reports file at the IWM and the cover to the file suggests Dawson had contact with the SSB. **39** Text in Judd, *Quest for C*, pp136–7. **40** Smith, *Six*, Ch 2. **41** Michael Epkenhans, 'Technology, Shipbuilding and Future Combat in Germany, 1880–1914', in *Technology and Naval Combat in the Twentieth Century and Beyond*, ed Phillips Payson O'Brien (Routledge, 2001), sourced to Epkenhans, *Die Wilhelminische Flottenrustung 1908–1914: Weltmachtstreben, Industrieller Fortschritt, Soziale Integration (Beitrage Zur Militargeschichte)* (Walter de Gruyter, 1991), pp 256–65. **42** Detailed accounts of the Schultz affair and Hipsich's recruitment are in Smith, *MI6*, Ch 2; Judd, *Quest for C*, pp217–21; and some background in Andrew, *Secret Service*, pp78–9. **43** Schultz's story is told by Ian Sumner in his short biography *Despise it Not: A Hull Man Spies on the Kaiser's Germany* (Highgate Publications, 2002). **44** By 1914, under the War Room organisation planned on mobilisation, Section A tracked British warship movements, home and abroad except flotillas, Section B covered flotillas, Section C covered intercepted wireless messages, Section D colliers, oilers and auxiliaries, E1 foreign warships, and E2 foreign merchant ships. Section C was never established. On the outbreak of war, E1 became 'Enemy ships of war' and E2 section covered 'Enemy merchant ships and raiders'. Unlike the other sections, they were staffed from ID (the successor to NID) and were soon located separately from the other sections. BR 1875, p61 and fn 2. **45** Admiral of the Fleet Sir Henry Oliver, Recollections 1901–1939, Vol 2, p89, OLV/12, NMM. Rotter's service record is in ADM 196/82/335 and ADM 196/172/14, both TNA. For his initial part in SIGINT, www.gchq.gov.uk/features/birth-signals-intelligence. **46** For example SSB report S663, 3 May 1913, stated that preparatory work on the new battlecruiser *Ersatz Hertha*, later named *Hindenburg*, was going slowly. She was officially supposed to be laid down on 1 June but this was likely to be delayed to end July at the earliest. In fact she was not laid down until 1 October. ADM 137/3880, TNA. **47** ADM 137/4354, TNA. Also Seligmann, *The Royal Navy and the German Threat*, Ch 2. **48** The intelligence reporting dating from April 1911, much evidently originating from the SSB, is in ADM 137/4354, TNA. Churchill emphasised the threat, quoting a potential force of forty German merchant raiders, at the 122nd meeting of the CID on 6 February 1913 (Item VI, 'Maintenance of overseas commerce in time of war'), CAB 38/23, TNA. For the War College exercise and impact on Trade Division, 'Richard Webb, Memorandum on Possible Losses to British Commerce in an Anglo-German War', 28 May 1914, NRS Vol 161, Item 152, pp 475–6. There is an earlier paper by Webb 'Proposed Scheme of Commerce Protection and Work of Trade Branch of War Staff', autumn 1913, in the papers of Admiral Sir Herbert Richmond, RIC/14/3, NMM. This quotes thirty-eight prospective raiders already carrying armament aboard, of which twenty-seven operated in the Atlantic. For the July 1914 conference, Matthew S Seligmann, 'A Service Ready for Total War? The State of the Royal Navy in July 1914', *English Historical Review*, 133:560 (February 2018), pp16–17. **49** Footnote 41. **50** The three-figure numbers for SSB reports shown in the surviving Rotter records show that about 540 SSB reports were issued over the 31 months from the beginning of 1912 to the outbreak of war on 4 August 1914. It is conceivable these numbers refer only to the reports SSB issued to NID. However, it is unlikely SSB could have generated this number of reports on Admiralty requirements in this period. It is more probable the numbers refer to the totality of SSB output. SSB did not introduce the term 'CX' to indicate SSB (and subsequently SIS) reports until the end of 1914. Phil Tomaselli, *Tracing your Secret Service Ancestors* (Barnsley: Pen & Sword, 2009), Ch 4. **51** ADM 137/3905, TNA. **52** Judd, *Quest for C*, Appendix 1, drawing on Cumming's diary. **53** William H Honan, *Bywater: The Man who invented the Pacific War* (London: Macdonald & Co, 1990), especially Chs 1 and 2, provides much background on Bywater's early life and pre-1914 work for SSB. Another vital source, which Honan appears to have missed, is Bywater's application to the Home Office in June 1926 to resume British citizenship which is in HO 45/12328, TNA. Bywater's Home Office interview provides important corrections to Honan's account, notably his acquisition of United States citizenship and the dates of his time in Germany. **54** The two letters from Fisher to Churchill as recently appointed First Lord are dated 6 and 30 December 1911 and are included in Randolph S Churchill, *Winston S Churchill*, Vol 2 Companion, Part 2, 1907–1911 (Heinemann, 1969), pp1351–2 and 1364–6 respectively. Although Fisher refers to a 'splendid spy' in Germany in the first letter and 'first class spy' in the second, it is clear from the context that the term 'spy' here refers to a journalist source of the *Navy League Journal* rather than a British government agent. If Fisher had previously recommended Bywater to Slade or Bethell, it is unlikely he knew of his subsequent recruitment by the SSB or he would not have referred to him in this way. Both letters encourage Churchill to get more detail on the 'spy' from Alan Burgoyne, whom Fisher evidently rated highly, describing him as knowing more about the Navy than the rest of the House of Commons put together. Burgoyne was a successful businessman and a Conservative MP from 1910–22 and 1924–29. He was also the author of several naval books. **55** Memorandum of Interview, HO 45/12328. Honan, pp30, 41, suggests Bywater was based in England from late 1910, following marriage to a Yorkshire girl, Emma Robinson, and made visits to Germany under journalist cover for SSB. The interview report states that he remained based in Germany until June 1914, when he returned to Britain for leave and was still there when war broke out. **56** Memorandum of Interview with Bywater and record of separate interview conducted by Sergeant Flynn with Bywater's parents, 23 July 1926, also in HO 45/12328. Bywater's American passport not only gave a false place of birth, Boston, but also made his date of birth 21 October 1882, exactly two years earlier than the real date. This was because compulsory registration of births did not begin in Massachussetts until 1883. **57** Hector C Bywater and H C Ferraby, *Strange Intelligence: Memoirs of Naval Secret Service*. According to Honan, p31, Bywater told his son that the experiences attributed to a third person in this book were actually Bywater's own. A later book on wartime intelligence by Bywater alone, *Their Secret Purposes: Dramas and Mysteries of the Naval War* (London: Constable, 1932), describes the wartime exploits of one or more secret agents, but is probably entirely fictional. **58** Assessing the reliability of Bywater's autobiography is complicated, because he was fed some information by the wartime DNI Captain Reginald Hall, who also wrote a foreword to the second edition. Hall was motivated to use Bywater as a channel for publicising naval intelligence successes after the Admiralty refused to let him publish his own account. Robert M Grant, *The U-boat Hunters: Codebreakers, Divers and the Defeat of the U-boats 1914–1918* (Periscope Publishing, 2003), p13. **59** 'Estimate of SS Expenditure for the months of February and March 1912', FO 1093/29, TNA. **60** Jeffery, *MI6*, pp34–5. As noted later, after the outbreak of war, Bywater continued to work for the SSB and NID, including at least two visits to the United States on their behalf. After the war he resumed his career as journalist and author, writing regularly for the *Daily Telegraph*, among other outlets, and publishing several books. By 1924, some of his reporting on British naval affairs had provoked serious security concerns. An MI5 report on his British citizenship application in 1926 stated that he had committed two breaches of the Official Secrets Act and had been formally reprimanded by the Secretary of the Admiralty. He was also denied access to all Royal Navy ships and establishments. MI5 had not known that Bywater was British by birth or that his American passport was false. They were unaware that the SSB had endorsed his American application although they did confirm he had worked for them. MI5 report dated 24 June 1926, HO 45/12328. Bywater is mainly now remembered for his fictional work, *The Great Pacific War* published in 1925, which prophesied a future naval war between the United States and Japan and anticipated a surprise Japanese attack on Pearl Harbor. **61** Judd, p142. **62** Navy Records Society Vol 113, *The Naval Air Service, Vol 1 1908–1918*, ed S W

Roskill (Spottiswoode, Ballantyne & Co, 1969), item 17, 'Airship Policy. Extracts from Report by the Technical Sub-Committee of the Standing Sub-Committee of the CID, 30 July 1912', pp45–55. 63 Admiralty attempts to acquire a Zeppelin Mercedes engine through commercial channels had not succeeded by June 1913. NRS Vol 113, item 31, 'Extracts from the first Annual Report of the Air Committee on the Progress of the Royal Flying Corps, 7 June 1913', paragraph 96, p103. 64 For example, Berlin Embassy report No 396 of 5 September 1912 and 'Report on Zeppelin 'E IV' of April 1913, both in AIR 1/2492, TNA. 65 NRS Vol 113, items 22, 25, 26, 27 and 30; James Wyllie and Michael McKinley, *Codebreakers: The Secret Intelligence Unit that changed the course of the First World War* (Ebury Press, 2015), Ch 8; Andrew, *Secret Service*, pp79–80; and 'John Herbert Spottiswoode: Zeppelin spy?' at www.crossandcockade.com/forum_posts.asp. 66 Goldrick, *Before Jutland*, pp166, 190, 236–42. 67 For background, including on Erskine, Dunley, 'Not Intended to Act as Spies', pp487, 495–6. 68 Smith, *Six*, Ch 2, Judd, *Quest for C*, pp256, 265–6; Jeffery, *MI6*, p27. There are several references to the operation in FO 1093/29, TNA. A secret minute submitted to Sir Arthur Nicholson and approved by the Foreign Secretary dated 13 February 1913 refers to an Admiralty scheme to obtain intelligence in northern Europe approved the previous November at a cost of £1200 per annum. The operation is also listed in the Estimate of Secret Service Expenditure 1 April 1913 – 31 March 1914 under Norway with a budget of £1200. 69 Nicholas P Hiley, 'The strategic origins of room 40', *Intelligence and National Security*, 2:2 (1987), p253. 70 'Report on Cable Censorship during the Great War (1914–1919)', pp9–11, DEFE 1/130, TNA. 71 Ibid, pp253–5. 72 John Ferris, 'Before 'Room 40': The British Empire and signals intelligence, 1898–1914', *Journal of Strategic Studies*, 12:4 (1989), pp431–57. 73 NID Report 785, dated May 1906, 'Wireless Telegraphy: British and Foreign', ADM 231/50, TNA. 74 Nigel West, *The Sigint Secrets: The Signals Intelligence War, 1900 to Today* (New York: William Morrow and Company, 1986), p41. 75 Ferris, p443. 76 Black, *Naval Staff*, p78. 77 There are conflicting accounts of this purchase. Oliver states at pp95–6 of his Recollections, Vol 2, that he authorised purchase, probably in early 1914, from a contact in Brussels for £1200 split 50:50 with the French. Although he does not say so, the context implies that the SSB handled the purchase. John Ferris also claims the codebook was purchased by early 1914. 'Before Room 40', p443. Alastair Denniston, the future head of GC&CS, stated that it was acquired by the SSB and was given to Alfred Ewing when he began work on German ciphers shortly after the outbreak of war. Presumably at that point it was still judged authentic. Oliver implies it was authentic but rendered invalid by German changes at the start of the war. Robin Denniston, *Thirty Secret Years: A G Denniston's work in Signals Intelligence 1914–1944* (UK: Polperro Heritage Press, 2007), p29. 78 www.gchq.gov.uk/features/birth-signals-intelligence. 79 John R Ferris, *Intelligence and Strategy* (London, Routledge: 2005), p140. Ferris suggests cipher machines had been under investigation since 1906. Neither service found a satisfactory solution, but Ferris argues that they deserve credit for making so thorough an investigation at such an early stage. 80 'Adoption of Mechanical Cryptography in the Navy', June 1914, ADM 1/8380/144, TNA. Also, Ferris, 'Before Room 40', p445. 81 BR 1875, pp60, 64. 82 'Germany, Historical, Naval Radio Intelligence, Report No 1', paragraph 6, IR 95443, United States Office of Naval Intelligence, 31 TS 51, dated 21 August 1951. 83 Ibid, pp443–6.

Chapter 5 Trafalgar or Economic Warfare 1912–1914

1 'War Plans Provisional 0020, Part 1 General Instructions', 25 November 1912, ADM 116/3412, TNA; Goldrick, pp61–2. 2 Matthew S Seligmann, 'Failing to Prepare for the Great War? The Absence of Grand Strategy in British War Planning before 1914', *War in History*, 24:4 (2017), pp419–20. 3 David Morgan-Owen, 'Cooked up in the Dinner Hour?: Sir Arthur Wilson's War Plan Reconsidered', *English Historical Review*, 130:545 (August 2015), pp889–91, and Seligmann, 'Failing to Prepare for the Great War', pp425–6. 4 Goldrick, p61. 5 Matthew S Seligmann, 'A Service Ready for Total War?', pp18–19. 6 For a full discussion, Seligmann, 'A Service Ready for Total War?'. 7 Grimes, *Strategy and War Planning*, p42. The flotilla defence strategy is the central theme of Lambert, *Sir John Fisher's Naval Revolution*. 8 Dunley, 'Not Intended to Act as Spies', pp489–90; NRS, Vol 106, *The Fisher Papers, Vol 2*, ed P K Kemp (Spottiswoode, Ballantyne & Co, 1964), p353. 9 For a full account, Judd, pp178–94, 237–8. 10 Bywater's detailed account is given in Bywater and

Ferraby, Ch 10. Oliver refers to the vice consul's reporting at p92 of his Recollections, Vol 2. According to Oliver, the consul was briefly arrested by the Germans on the outbreak of war, although they failed to find anything incriminating. He was then sacked by the Foreign Office for losing his cipher! **11** Goldrick, *Before Jutland*, p243. **12** Dunley, *Britain and the Mine*, pp136–8, 173. **13** Morgan-Owen, 'Cooked up in the Dinner Hour?', pp886–8, fn 112, quoting Grimes. **14** Grimes, pp154–65. **15** Seligmann, *Spies in Uniform*, Ch 3. **16** 'Unsigned memorandum (Ottley) on "British Intervention in the Event of France being suddenly attacked by Germany", July 1905', NRS Vol 161, item 69, pp247–8. **17** NRS, Vol 106, p353. **18** Ibid, 'War Plans', Parts 2 and 3, pp346–83. Also, Avner Offer, *The First World War: An Agrarian Interpretation* (OUP, 1991), pp235–6. **19** 'Unsigned minute, numbered M.0171/07, attached to a printed copy of Philip Dumas, Germany Naval Attaché Report No.3/07, 29 January 1907', NRS Vol 161, item 78, pp257–61. The case for Ottley as the author is in the footnote at p257. **20** Offer, pp 239–42. **21** Marder, *FDSF*, Vol 1, p379, quoting letter from Ottley to McKenna, 5 December 1908. Ottley used similar language two years earlier in a note to Vincent Baddeley, the private secretary to the First Lord. 'Charles Ottley to Vincent Baddeley', 16 November 1906, NRS Vol 161, item 77, pp255–6. Ottley was paraphrasing the historian, Alfred Mahan, in *The Influence of Sea Power upon History 1660–1783* (1890), when describing Cromwell's blockade of the Dutch ports in 1652. **22** 'Report and Proceedings of a Sub-Committee of the Committee of Imperial Defence on The Military Needs of the Empire 1909', CAB 16/5, TNA, and Offer, pp242–3. **23** Rodger, *Command of the Ocean*, pp551–60. **24** Goldrick, *Before Jutland*, pp61–3. **25** Marder, *FDSF*, Vol 1, p381. **26** 'Minute by Slade, M0604/08, NID445', early May 1908 and 'Admiralty, RS NID Berlin 19/08', early May 1908, NRS Vol 161, items 106a and 106b, pp356–7. **27** 'Dumas, NARS Germany 64/08', 20 May 1908, NRS Vol 161, item 106, pp357–9. **28** Sir Francis Oppenheimer, *Stranger Within: Autobiographical Pages* (Faber & Faber, 1960). The strength of the ministerial relationships is demonstrated by the fact that, when Oppenheimer arrived back from Germany on the day war broke out, Isaacs took him straight in to brief Lloyd George. **29** Letter and report from Consul General Sir Francis Oppenheimer to Sir Edward Grey, dated 28 September 1909, ADM 116/940B, TNA. Also Kieran West, 'Intelligence and the Development of British Grand Strategy in the First World War' (unpublished doctoral thesis, University of Cambridge, 2011), pp115–20. **30** Oppenheimer claimed this paper 'had evoked encomiums more flattering than any that had gone before'. Eyre Crowe, the future Foreign Office permanent undersecretary, then head of the German department, was especially complimentary. *Stranger Within*, p193. **31** Grimes, pp192–5. **32** Bethell proposal to merge Trade Division with War Division, p9 of his paper for First Sea Lord, dated 15 May 1909, 'Proposals for carrying out the duties of a General Staff and Reorganisation of the Naval Intelligence Department', ADM 1/8047, TNA. **33** *Stranger Within*, p217. **34** Ibid, p199. Oppenheimer does not say who approached him, but his use of the term 'secret service' suggests the SSB. It is unlikely Cumming would have taken the initiative without a recommendation. Bethell seems the likely candidate. Oppenheimer believed he must remain scrupulously above suspicion, or his excellent German sources would dry up. **35** Report of the Sub-committee of the CID on Trading with the Enemy dated 30 July 1912, CAB 17/89. TNA. **36** CID, Minutes of the 120th Meeting, December 6 1912, CAB 38/22/42, TNA. **37** Lambert, *Planning Armageddon*, pp178–9. **38** Matthew Seligmann commentary, NRS Vol 161, p419. **39** John Ferris, 'Pragmatic hegemony and British economic warfare, 1900–1918', in *Britain's War at Sea 1914–1918*, ed Greg Kennedy (Routledge, 2016). **40** 'War Plans', December 1912, Part 1, pp3–4, ADM 116/3412. **41** Ferris, 'Pragmatic hegemony and British economic warfare, 1900–1918'. **42** Matthew S Seligmann, 'The Renaissance of Pre-First World War Naval History', *Journal of Strategic Studies*, 36:3 (2012), pp472–7; John W Coogan, 'The Short War Illusion Resurrected: The Myth of Economic Warfare as the British Schlieffen Plan', *Journal of Strategic Studies*, 38:7 (2015), pp1053–4. **43** Report on 'Trading with the Enemy', pp23–6. **44** *Stranger Within*, p218. **45** Offer, Ch 23, and Hew Strachan, *The First World War, Vol 1 To Arms* (OUP, 2001), pp1015–49. **46** Christopher Bell, *Churchill and Seapower* (Oxford University Press, 2012), Ch 1; Grimes, pp178–9. **47** Matthew S Seligmann, 'Failing to Prepare for the Great War? The Absence of Grand Strategy in British War Planning before 1914'. **48** Callaghan to Admiralty, 28 August 1913, ADM 137/1936, TNA. **49** Ferris, 'Pragmatic hegemony and British economic warfare, 1900–1918'. **50** Note from Bethell to First Sea Lord, 15 May 1909, covering paper 'Proposals for carrying out the duties of a General Staff and Reorganisation of the Naval Intelligence Department', ADM 1/8047, TNA. **51** BR 1875, pp48–9. **52** Wilson's arguments against a naval staff are provided in two papers 'Naval War Staff' and 'Proposals for carrying out the duties of a General Staff and Reorganisation of the Naval Intelligence Department', undated but probably originating late 1909, ADM 1/8047, TNA. **53** Marder, *FDSF*, Vol 1, pp88–104, 186–203. **54** Wilson note for CID 'Naval War Staff', 30 October 1911, CAB 1/42, TNA. Also Marder, *FDSF*, Vol 1, pp255–8. **55** BR 1875, pp52–4; Black, *Naval Staff*, p58; and Oliver, Recollections, Vol 2, p89. **56** BR 1875, p53. **57** Grimes, pp171–4. **58** M/NID 2359/14, 30 September 1914, ADM 137/1906, TNA. **59** Court of Inquiry extracts included at pp351–62 of Navy Records Society, Vol 115, *Policy and Operations in the Mediterranean 1912–1914*, ed E R S Lumby (William Clowes and Sons, 1970). **60** ID No 973, ADM 137/4799, TNA. **61** Bywater and Ferraby, Ch 8. **62** Keith Jeffery, *MI6*, pp35–6. **63** NRS Vol 113, *The Naval Air Service, Vol 1 1908–1918*, item 59, 'Memorandum for the War Council by Mr Churchill, First Lord, and Report on the Anti-Aircraft Defence of London by Captain Murray F Sueter, Director Air Department, both 1 January 1915', pp188–90, and item 60, 'Extracts from "Secretary's Notes of a Meeting of the War Council" held on 7 January 1915', pp190–2. Churchill (item 59) and Fisher (item 60) both refer to this intelligence. **64** By 1 January, the implications of an attack on London had been fully assessed by Sueter, which suggests the intelligence probably arrived during the last half of December. German planning for airship attacks on the British mainland was well advanced by December, and the first attack on an east-coast target was attempted on the night of 13 January. This was abandoned due to bad weather and the first bombs were dropped a week later on Great Yarmouth and Kings Lynn. Douglas H Robinson, *The Zeppelin in Combat: A History of the German Naval Airship Division, 1912–1918* (Schiffer Publishing edn, 1994). **65** John Ferris, 'Airbandit: C3I and Strategic Air Defence during the First Battle of Britain', in *Strategy and Intelligence: British Policy during the First World War*, ed Michael Dockrill and David French (London: Hambledon Press, 1996), pp26–7 and fn 13, 14 and 15. The testimony to the American naval attaché is not conclusive. The Germans were still unaware of the success of Room 40, and throughout the war ascribed apparent British foreknowledge of German movements to 'secret agents'. Ferris also notes that there is an NID report (No 086 undated) with Lloyd George's papers (E/8/5, House of Lords Record Office), which comprises an authentic copy of Admiral Reinhard Scheer's official despatch to the Kaiser on the Battle of Jutland, issued on 4 July 1916. Ferris states that the date Lloyd George received this report is unknown, but that it is in the section of his papers usually confined to documents received during the war. He further states that Scheer's report was not available for official British access until years after the war and nor was it published in English or German in Lloyd George's lifetime. He therefore suggests that the document was acquired by British intelligence from a source in Germany at some point during the war. This is possible, but unlikely given the complete absence of any reference to such an intelligence coup anywhere else. A document of this importance with major strategic implications would surely have left a trail. Ferris's assertion that Scheer's report was not available until years after the war is also not correct. Copies, along with other Jutland material, including Vice Admiral Franz von Hipper's report, were recovered from German ships at Scapa Flow in 1919. This material was still topical enough to merit circulation, including to the prime minister. It is probable, therefore, that this is the origin of NID 086. The recovery from Scapa Flow is referred to in an extract from the Board of Admiralty minutes of 28 February 1920 in CAB 45/269, Part 1, TNA. The relevant originals of Scheer's reports are probably those in ADM 137/4805 and 4806, TNA. **66** Jeffery, *MI6*, p332. **67** For full discussion of the impact of this intelligence within the Grand Fleet, Matthew S Seligmann, 'A German Preference for a Medium-Range Battle? British Assumptions about German Naval Gunnery, 1914–1915', *War in History*, 19:1 (2012), pp33–48; John Brooks, 'Preparing for Armageddon: Gunnery Practices and Exercises in the Grand Fleet prior to Jutland', *Journal of Strategic Studies*, 38:7 (2015), pp1006–23. **68** Admiral Viscount John Jellicoe of Scapa, *The Grand Fleet 1914–16* (London: Cassell & Co, 1919), pp62–3. **69** West thesis, pp16–18. **70** Black, *Naval Staff*, p58. **71** Sir Trevor Dawson's final report dated September 1914 provided an accurate summary of the expected commissioning dates of the German capital ships currently in build, although in the event wartime re-prioritisation meant delivery of the first two *Baden*-class battleships and the battlecruiser *Hindenburg* slipped by around a year to mid 1917. Misc73/Item 1098, IWM. **72** 'Germany, War Vessels', ID No 896, 1914, Jellicoe papers Vol 15, Add MS 49003, BL. This report is undated, but the context and content suggest its circulation probably coincided with the outbreak of war. **73** Hiley, 'The Failure of British Espionage against Germany, pp887–8. **74** 'Jellicoe to Churchill with marginal comments by Churchill, 14 July 1914', NRS, Vol 161, item 153b, pp478–83. **75** First Lord note for the Cabinet on 'Fuel', 30 January 1914, p 2, CAB 1/42, TNA. **76** First Lord note on 'Practice Ammunition', February 1914, CAB 1/42. **77** K I McCallum, 'A Little Neglect: Defective Shell in the Royal Navy', *Journal of Naval Engineering*, 34:2 (1993). Also Ian Johnston and Ian Buxton, *The Battleship Builders: Constructing and Arming British Capital Ships* (Barnsley: Seaforth, 2013), pp203–4. **78** For details of pre-war German naval intelligence operations against Britain, Andrew, *The Defence of the Realm*, pp38–52. **79** Judd, *Quest for C*, pp257–8. By contrast, Macdonogh did not receive his CB until 1915 and Kell not until 1918. **80** West, p18.

Chapter 6 Room 40 and the Foundation of Modern SIGINT
1 Fisher to Jellicoe, 9 April 1915, Jellicoe Papers, Add MS 49007, ff 9–10, BL. **2** Marrero, 'Logistics for Commerce War in the Atlantic during the First World War: The German *Etappe* System in Action'. **3** 'Report on the Opening of the War', 1 November 1914, Appendix, p17, CAB 38/28/51, TNA. **4** Jellicoe to Beatty, 23 March 1915, Jellicoe Papers, Add MS 49008, ff 27–8, BL. **5** Andrew Lambert, '"The Possibility of Ultimate Action in the Baltic": The Royal Navy at War, 1914–1916', in *Jutland, World War I's Greatest Naval Battle*, ed Michael Epkenhans, Jörg Hillmann and Frank Nagler (University Press of Kentucky, 2015). **6** Report of the Standing Sub Committee of the Committee of Imperial Defence, Submarine Cable Communications in Time of War, 11 December 1911, CAB 38/19/56, TNA. **7** Jonathan Reed Winkler, 'Information Warfare in World War I', *Journal of Military History*, 73:3 (July 2009), pp849–52; Patrick Beesly, *Room 40: British Naval Intelligence 1914–1918* (OUP, 1984), p2. **8** Even early in the war there were surprising successes here. On 30 November 1914 the British Consul General at Genoa forwarded an intercepted letter dated 3 November from the German military attaché in the United States, Major Franz von Papen, to the General Staff. KV 2/519, TNA. **9** Blond, p283; Hiley, 'Strategic origins of Room 40', pp258–9; Winkler, pp851–3. **10** Winkler, pp855–65. For cable-cutting by U-boats, Grant, *The U-boat Hunters*, pp16–17. **11** Oliver, Recollections, Vol 2, p102. Ewing's account of his recruitment was included in his address to the Edinburgh Philosophical Institution in December 1927, R V Jones, 'Alfred Ewing and "Room 40"', *Notes and Records of the Royal Society of London*, 34:1 (July 1979), pp65–90. Oliver states their lunch was the day after war broke out, whereas Ewing dates the conversation on the afternoon of the 4th. Admiral Sir William James later claimed that Ewing narrowly escaped prosecution under the Official Secrets Act for revealing the activities of Room 40 in this lecture. *Naval Review*, 1 (1966), providing a transcript of James's speech at the Haldane Dinner, Edinburgh University, in November 1964. As regards radio expertise, Ewing had patented an 'electro-magnetic wave detector' and addressed the Royal Society in 1904 on electric oscillations occurring during radio transmissions. West, *Sigint Secrets*, p59. **12** For Ewing's initial brief from Oliver, Hiley, 'Strategic origins'. James confirms that Ewing's initial focus was the messages from high-power German stations to their overseas colonies, *Eyes of the Navy*, p28. **13** W F Clarke's history of Room 40, Ch 8, HW 3/3, TNA. **14** Hiley, 'Strategic origins', p256; Strachan, p508. **15** ADM 223/638, TNA. **16** Robin Denniston, *Thirty Secret Years: A G Denniston's work in Signals Intelligence 1914–1944* (UK: Polperro Heritage Press, 2007), pp28–9. **17** John Ferris, 'The road to Bletchley Park: The British experience with Signals Intelligence, 1892–1945', *Intelligence and National Security*, 17:1, p60. **18** James Bruce, '"A shadowy entity": M.I.1(b) and British Communications Intelligence, 1914–1922', *Intelligence and National Security*, 32:3 (2017), pp315–16; MO5(e) summary probably written spring 1915, ADM 223/767, TNA; Hiley, 'Strategic origins', pp260–2. **19** Beesly describes the difference between a 'code' and a 'cipher', and how codebooks were constructed and deployed at this time in Ch 3 of *Room 40*. Also Paul Gannon, *Inside Room 40: The Codebreakers of World War I* (Ian Allen Publishing, 2010), Ch 4. **20** Josef H Straczek, 'The Origins and Development of Royal Australian Navy Signals Intelligence in an Era of Imperial Defence 1914–1945' (unpublished doctoral thesis,

University of New South Wales, 2008), pp26–43. Beesly states wrongly that the Australians waited a month before notifying the Admiralty of the *Hobart* capture. **21** The initial Russian offer to share material from *Magdeburg* was communicated by the British ambassador, Sir George Buchanan, in a telegram from Petrograd on 6 September. This mentioned a codebook, two ciphers and squared naval charts. The Russians suggested these be transported in a Royal Navy warship and the cruiser *Theseus* was despatched to Archangel on 30 September. These dates are different to those quoted by Beesly at pp5–6 of his *Room 40*. The exchanges of telegrams between the Admiralty and Petrograd are in FO 800/74, TNA. **22** Beesly, *Room 40*, pp3–7; Denniston, p36. **23** Jones, 'Alfred Ewing and "Room 40"', p70. **24** The most authoritative account of Clarke's approach to Ewing and the events leading to the Hunstanton trial is Hippisley's note 'The Start of Room 40 OB' in HW 3/5, TNA. This was sent to W F Clarke (not to be confused with Russell Clarke) on 31 January 1955, when W F Clarke was researching the records of Room 40. Some details in Hippisley's account (which is clear despite being written after a gap of forty years) conflict with those provided by Beesly, pp13–15, and Denniston, p30. There are also minutes covering the Hunstanton trial by Kettlewell and Ewing, both 21 October 1914, in ADM 116/1301, TNA. Biographical background on Hippisley in the website blogs.mhs.ox.ac.uk/innovatingcombat/hippisley, although minor details of the Hunstanton episode conflict with Hippisley's 1955 account. **25** 'List of documents regarding the German Navy', recovered from SMS *Magdeburg*, attached to letter from Admiral A Rusin to Admiral Sir John Jellicoe, 14 September 1914, Jellicoe papers, Vol 47, Add MS 49035, p111, BL **26** Clarke, Room 40, Ch 2, p3, Ch 4, pp2–3, where Clarke stresses Rotter's pioneering work. Also, Beesly, pp14–15, 22–25. Beesly provides useful information on SKM structure and weaknesses. Neither he nor Clarke emphasise the importance of the cipher tables provided by the Russians in guiding Rotter to a solution. **27** 'Germany, Historical, Naval Radio Intelligence, Report No 1', paragraphs 7 and 8, IR 95443, United States Office of Naval Intelligence, 31 TS 51, 21 August 1951. **28** Hall later insisted that from the beginning of the war all wireless intercept sites came under the direct and exclusive control of ID. Hall paper, 'Wireless Intelligence in the Mediterranean', April 1918, ADM 137/4699, TNA. **29** Black, *Naval Staff*, pp78–9, 93; Clarke, Room 40, chapter 8; Jones, p70, and letter from W Bradfield, Marconi General Manager, dated 19 September 1914, probably to Ewing, giving details of Marconi coverage of German transmissions, ADM 223/768, TNA. **30** Hippisley, 'The Start of Room 40 OB'. Hippisley used Marconi sites at the Lizard and Ballybunion (in Kerry, Ireland) and Post Office sites at Hunstanton and Slough. Also, Hiley, 'Strategic origins', pp262–6; Beesly, pp14–15; Denniston, pp31–2. **31** Frank Birch, *The Official History of British Sigint 1914–1945*, Vol 1, Part 1, ed John Jackson (Military Press, 2004), pp3–5. **32** Sir Alfred Ewing, 'Some Special War Work', Lecture to the Edinburgh Philosophical Institution, 13 December 1927, in R V Jones, 'Alfred Ewing and Room 40', *Royal Society*, 34:1 (1979), p76. **33** Denniston, p36; Beesly, p43. **34** Beesly, *Room 40*, pp15–16. **35** Bruce, M.I.1(b), p 317; Peter Freeman, 'MI1(b) and the origins of British diplomatic cryptanalysis', *Intelligence and National Security*, 22:2 (2007); Daniel Larsen, 'British codebreaking and American diplomatic telegrams, 1914–1915', *Intelligence and National Security*, 32:2 (2017), pp256–63; Denniston, pp32–3. Denniston probably overstates the damage done by the end of joint working. **36** Both these notes are in HW 3/4, TNA. Also, Beesly, *Room 40*, pp16–17. **37** Pencil notes, Denniston papers, 1/2, CCA. **38** BR 1875, Appendix K1, p143. **39** ADM 196/90/43, TNA. **40** Beesly, pp17–18. **41** Clarke, Room 40; Hope, Appendix, pp2–3. **42** Oliver, 'Notes about Room 40 and Sir Alfred Ewing in the 1914–18 War', OLV/8, NMM; Beesly, *Room 40*, p134. **43** Saul Kelly, 'Room 47: The Persian Prelude to the Zimmermann Telegram', *Cryptologia*, 37:1 (2013), pp14–18. **44** Clarke, Room 40, Ch 3, p3. **45** Andrew, *Secret Service*, pp106–7. **46** Andrew, *The Secret World*, Ch 24. **47** Beesly, *Room 40*, p123. **48** Jones, 'Alfred Ewing and "Room 40"', pp78–80. For Jutland see reference in First Sea Lord, Henry Jackson, letter to Jellicoe of 1 June 1916, Jellicoe papers, Add MS 49009, f 96r, BL. **49** Ewing to Hall, 7 October 1915, ADM 223/772, and letters to Ewing from Sir William Slingo, Engineer-in-Chief Post Office, 11 May 1916, and Marconi, 4 June 1916, ADM 223/768, all TNA. **50** Beesly, *Room 40*, pp133–4. This view, probably derived from William James and W F Clarke, has been widely repeated. **51** Memo, 'Political Branch of Room 40', by George Young, ADM 223/773, TNA. **52** Graham Greene to Ewing, 28 September 1916, ADM 223/768, TNA. **53** R T

Glazebrook, 'James Alfred Ewing 1855–1935', *Obituary Notices of Fellows of the Royal Society*, 1: 4 (December 1935), pp475–92. Marder, the first historian to include Room 40 within a comprehensive account of the 1914–1918 naval war, described Ewing as 'the brilliant head of Room 40 until 1917'. *FDSF, Vol 2, The War Years: To the Eve of Jutland 1914–1916*, p133. **54** Oliver letter to the Admiralty, 7 March 1919, OLV/8, NMM. **55** Oliver states that, during his brief spell as Naval Secretary in November 1914, he was instructed to offer Wilson the post of chief of staff in place of Vice Admiral Sir Doveton Sturdee, when the latter was given command of the South Atlantic task force despatched after the defeat at Coronel. Wilson insisted he was too out of date to take on this post and would only come to the Admiralty as an adviser. Recollections, Vol 2, p116. **56** Beesly, *Room 40*, p17. **57** F H Hinsley, with E E Thomas, C F G Ransom and R C Knight, *British Intelligence in the Second World War. Its Influence on Strategy and Operations*, 3 vols (London: HMSO, 1977–1984), Vol 1, pp138–9. **58** Goldrick, *Before Jutland*, pp186–7. **59** Jason Hines, 'Sins of Omission and Commission: A Reassessment of the Role of Intelligence in the Battle of Jutland', *Journal of Military History*, 72:4 (2008), p1130. **60** Minute by Oliver to Balfour, 'Remarks on the Question of supplying fuller information to the C-in-C', dated 8 November 1916, HW 3/1, TNA. **61** Keith Bird and Jason Hines, 'In the Shadow of Ultra: A Reappraisal of German Naval Communications Intelligence in 1914–1918', *The Northern Mariner*, 18:2 (2018), pp97–117; 'German Codes and Ciphers', June 1921, pp44–5, HW 3/1, TNA; 'Germany, Historical, Naval Radio Intelligence, Report No 1', paragraphs 7–11, IR 95443, United States Office of Naval Intelligence, 31 TS 51, 21 August 1951; Ferris, *Intelligence and Strategy*, p141, and 'The Road to Bletchley Park', p62. **62** Violet Bonham Carter, *Winston Churchill as I knew him* (London: Eyre & Spottiswoode, 1965), pp367–9; David Stafford, *Churchill and Secret Service* (UK: Overlook Press, 1997), p76, quoting Asquith's letter to Venetia Stanley, 21 December 1914. For Asquith's cavalier attitude, Andrew, *The Secret World*, Ch 24. **63** Jellicoe papers, Add MS 49009, BL. Also Ferris, 'The Road to Bletchley Park', p61.

Chapter 7 The Initial Exploitation of Modern SIGINT

1 It is not possible from surviving records to estimate how many intercepted German signals reached Room 40 from the intercept stations on a daily basis. Ewing claimed that later in the war the number of incoming messages addressed to 'Ewing Admiralty' reached two thousand per day. That seems too high, set against a maximum output of SIGINT reports issued in 1917–18 of about two hundred per day. Jones, 'Alfred Ewing and "Room 40"', p69. **2** Clarke, Room 40, appendix, 'Narrative of Captain Hope'. **3** For examples, ADM 137/3956 and ADM 137/3957, TNA. **4** Oliver, Recollections, Vol 2, p103. **5** William F Clarke and Frank Birch, 'A Contribution to the History of German Naval Warfare 1914–1918', Vol 1, Introduction, pp36–7, HW 7/1, TNA. **6** W F Clarke quotes 54,000 issued between October 1914 and end June 1918 in Room 40, Epilogue. If output by then was 2000–2500 per month, an overall figure of 65,000 is reasonable. The Jutland figure is from the Jutland intercepts in ADM 137/4710, TNA. **7** Estimates taken from the numbered intercepts in ADM 137/3956 and ADM 137/3957 and the lists relating to Scarborough and Dogger Bank in ADM 137/4067, all in TNA. **8** Jutland intercepts, ADM 137/4710, TNA. **9** ADM 137/4067. **10** Ibid. **11** Barry, *The War in the North Sea*, p83, quoting Raeder's autobiography. **12** W F Clarke paper, 'Operational Intelligence', pp3–5, HW 3/1, TNA. **13** For comparison, in mid 1918, officers employed on cable censorship were each handling about 150 messages per day, and earlier in the war, perhaps double that figure. 'Report on Cable Censorship during the Great War (1914–1919)', pp92–3, DEFE 1/130. **14** Oliver, Recollections, Vol 2, pp189–90. **15** Ibid, p156. **16** Oliver states that secure communications were available, connected to the buoys to which flagships moored, up to the moment of slipping. Recollections, Vol 2, p125. **17** ATs issued between 1400 and 1815 on 23 January 1915, ADM 137/203, TNA. **18** ATs of 1310 (U-boats) and 1540 (destroyers) of 24 January, ADM 137/203. These drew on intercepts listed for 24 January at times 1124, 1325 and 1434 in ADM 137/4067. **19** Ewing, 'Some Special War Work', p84. **20** For a discussion of 'at sea dissemination' and source protection, see Hines, 'Sins of Omission and Commission', pp1130–4. **21** Grant, *U-boat Hunters*, p30, quoting Peter Wright, *Spycatcher*, pp10–13. **22** 'Direction Finding', Denniston papers, 1/2, CCA; Beesly, pp69–70; Black, pp78–9, 154–5; Hines, 'Sins of Omission and Commission', pp1121–2. **23** Hippisley,

'The Start of Room 40 OB'. **24** Admiralty letter to the Treasury dated 3 October 1915, ADM 116/1454, TNA. **25** *Naval Review*, 1 (1966), providing a transcript of James's speech at the Haldane Dinner, Edinburgh University, in November 1964, and Beesly, p70. For Hall's insistence he retained strategic direction, 'Wireless Intelligence in the Mediterranean', April 1918, ADM 137/4699. **26** Clark and Birch, Vol 1, p37. **27** Beesly, p70. **28** For a layman's description of traffic analysis, Hinsley, *British Intelligence in the Second World War*, Vol 1, pp20–1. **29** Beesly, Ch 2; David Ramsay, *'Blinker' Hall: Spymaster: The Man who brought America into World War I* (Stroud, Gloucester: Spellmount, 2008), p162; Andrew Gordon, *The Rules of the Game: Jutland and British Naval Command* (London: John Murray, 1996), p508. **30** Clark and Birch, Vol 1, p38; Clarke, Room 40, appendix, 'Narrative of Captain Hope'. **31** 'Extracts from Jellicoe's proposed revised version of a new Appendix to "The Grand Fleet" (Add MSS 49040, ff 5–146)', NRS Vol 111, *The Jellicoe Papers Vol 2*, ed A Temple Patterson (London: Spottiswoode, Ballantyne & Co, 1968), item 144, pp425–6. Jellicoe expected the new battleship *Bayern* to be present, along with the new battlecruiser *Hindenburg*, and eight, rather than six, pre-dreadnoughts. *Bayern* was not commissioned until mid July, and *Hindenburg* not until May 1917. Also Marder, *FDSF, Vol 3, Jutland and After*, p95 and fn 1, and Friedman, *Fighting the Great War at Sea*, Ch 7. Friedman notes that in February 1916 ID reported that the battlecruisers *Derfflinger*, *Lützow* and *Hindenburg* were all operational. In reality, *Lützow* was not operational until May, just before Jutland. ID also wrongly suggested all three might have six 15in guns rather than eight 12in. **32** NRS Vol 128, *The Beatty Papers*, Vol 1 1902–1918, ed Brian Ranft (Scolar Press, 1989), items 145–8, pp282–95. **33** W F Clark recorded by Roskill in *Admiral of the Fleet Earl Beatty: The Last Naval Hero* (New York: Athenaum, 1981), pp152–3; Jackson, letter of 14 July 1916, Jellicoe papers, Add MS 49009, f 109r, BL. **34** Ibid, p31. **35** BR 1875, pp65–6. **36** Memo from James to Deputy First Sea Lord, 30 October 1917, HW 3/1, TNA; Marder, *FDSF, Vol 4, Year of Crisis*, p 267. **37** Ferris, 'The Road to Bletchley Park', p61. **38** Clarke, Room 40, Hope appendix, p5. **39** Clarke and Birch, Introduction, pp31–9. **40** 'Rough outline for memoirs', Hall papers, 1/4, CCA. Hall probably started sketching his memoirs in the late 1920s, but serious planning only began in 1932, with the help of the author Ralph Strauss. Although, through literary agent James Pinker & Son, he obtained a publishing contract, the Admiralty refused to allow him to publish (Admiralty letter M 02133/33 of 4 August 1933), a decision he accepted. Some completed chapters were then destroyed, but seven early draft chapters survive, out of the possible total of about forty. Five of the surviving chapters (1, 2, 3, 5 and 6) come from the opening section of the planned book, and their content can be tracked in the 'rough outline'. A sixth chapter, actually 7, titled 'Lord Fisher and Mr Churchill' is drawn from several chapter sections originally projected. The only survivor from later in the book is Ch 25 (originally 29) 'The Zimmermann Telegram and America's Entry into the War'. These surviving chapters are with the Hall papers at CCA, but have recently been published under the title *A Clear Case of Genius: Room 40's Code-breaking Pioneer, Admiral Sir Reginald 'Blinker' Hall*, ed Philip Vickers, with a foreword by Nigel West (The History Press, 2017). **41** Gannon, *Inside Room 40*, pp100–1; Beesly, pp90–4. **42** For German figures, Lawrence Sondhaus, *The Great War at Sea*, Ch 5. For Admiralty figures, 'Summary of Naval Situation', Table F, p 14, CAB 24/2/10, TNA. **43** Beesly, pp90–4; Gannon, p104; Oliver, Recollections, Vol 2, p156. **44** E1 Atlantic U-boat reports from March 1916 to April 1917, ADM 137/3920, TNA; BR1875, pp61–2. **45** For E1 U-boat tracking at this time, 'Some recollections of my time in NID Section E1 during the First World War', papers of Captain E W C Thring, IWM 71/30/1. **46** Robert M Grant, *U-boats Destroyed: The Effect of Anti-Submarine Warfare 1914–1918* (Periscope Publishing, 2002); www.uboat.net/wwi/fates/losses. **47** Jellicoe to Admiral Sir Henry Jackson (successor to Fisher as First Sea Lord from May 1915), dated 24 June 1915, Jellicoe Papers ed A Temple Patterson, NRS Vol 108 (Spottiswoode, Ballantyne & Co, 1966), Item 144. **48** Marder, *FDSF*, Vol 2, pp329–41. **49** E1 Mediterranean U-boat reports, ADM 137/3919, TNA. **50** Navy Records Society, Vol 137, *The Defeat of the Enemy Attack on Shipping, 1939–1945*, ed Eric J Grove (UK: Ashgate Publishing, 1997), Plan 1. **51** Hankey, *The Supreme Command 1914–1918*, Vol 2, p489; Sondhaus, Ch 5. **52** Goldrick, *Before Jutland*, p89. **53** Marder, *FDSF, Vol 4, Year of Crisis*, p52. **54** The Military Intelligence Directorate was recreated in December 1915 and MO5(e) was transferred to it at the same time. 'History of MI1B', p3, undated but probably written in the early 1920s, HW 7/35, TNA. 55 Hankey diary extract for 1 February 1916 quoted in Roskill, *Man of Secrets*, p247. 56 Hall autobiography, Ch 25. Hall claimed that ID had advance warning of the timing of the Verdun offensive from a staff officer in Berlin. 57 Paul G Halpern, *The Naval War in the Mediterranean: 1914–1918* (Routledge, 2017 edn), table 6.1, p194. 58 For U-boats at sea, Marder, *FDSF*, Vol 5, p118; for shipping losses, Marder, *FDSF*, Vol 4, pp102, 182, 277. 59 Marder, *FDSF*, Vol 4, p64. 60 Black, *Naval Staff*, pp166–9. 61 Ferris, 'Airbandit: C3I and Strategic Air Defence during the First Battle of Britain'; Beesly, *Room 40*, pp141–2. 62 Beesly, *Room 40*, pp78–9. 63 'Photographic Reconnaissance by the Royal Air Force in the war of 1939–45', p13, AIR 41/6, TNA. 64 Straczek, pp42–3; Beesly, pp74–5. 65 Marder, *FDSF*, Vol 2, pp371–2; Beesly, *Room 40*, p145. 66 Marder, *FDSF*, Vol 4, pp99–101; Beesly, *Room 40*, p275. For TR16's contribution, Henry Landau, *The Spy Net: The Greatest Intelligence Operations of the First World War* (Biteback Publishing edn, 2013), pp180–6. 67 Beesly, *Room 40*, p28. 68 Ibid, pp80–3. 69 Christopher Bell, *Churchill and the Dardanelles* (OUP, 2017), pp129–30. 70 Ramsay, p82. 71 Matthew Seligmann shows that this document reached the Admiralty sometime between August and November 1914. This date range fits with *Magdeburg*, but not *S-119*, 'A German Preference for a Medium-Range Battle? British Assumptions about German Naval Gunnery, 1914–1915', *War in History*, 19:1 (2012), p44 and fn39. 72 Navy Records Society, Vol 108, *The Jellicoe Papers, Vol 1 1893–1916*, ed A Temple Patterson (Spottiswoode, Ballantyne & Co, 1966), 'Jellicoe to Beatty', 12 December, item 80, p105. This letter refers to receiving 'important information on the conduct of the High Seas Fleet in action'. 73 The three numbered ID reports together with one copy of the 'Manoeuvring Instructions' are in ADM 186/17, TNA. There is also a copy of the 'Manoeuvring Instructions' in the Jellicoe papers, Vol 16, Add MS 49035, f 70, BL. Items (ii) and (iii) are included in a list of documents recovered from *Magdeburg* included in the Jellicoe papers, 'List of Documents regarding the German Navy', Vol 47, Add MS 49035, p111. 74 Ch 5, fn71. 75 For example: 'German Naval Manoeuvre carried out in March 1913', document received in February 1915, translated by Rotter, ADM 137/3869, TNA; CB 1279, 'German Battlecruiser "Derfflinger": Hull, Fittings, &tc', December 1916, German Material Organisation Etc, March 1916–March 1919, Admiralty Library.

Chapter 8 The Hall Tradition
1 Hall service record, ADM 196/88/106, TNA. 2 'Rough Notes', 10 January 1936, Hall papers, 2/1, CCA. 3 'The Hall Tradition', papers of Vice Admiral John Godfrey, MLBE 1/2, CCA. 4 As recorded by Compton Mackenzie in his autobiography, *My Life and Times – Octave Five 1915–1923* (Chatto and Windus, 1966), p113. 5 Quoted by James, *Eyes of the Navy*, xvii. 6 Herbert O Yardley, *The American Black Chamber* (USA: Amereon, 1996 reprint of 1931 edn), pp148–9. 7 Andrew, *Secret Service*, p117. 8 'The Hall Tradition'. 9 Ibid. The best portrait of Hall remains that by William James in *The Eyes of the Navy*. It has significant errors and is too partisan in Hall's favour, but benefits from first-hand experience of Hall and Room 40. David Ramsay's more recent *'Blinker' Hall: Spymaster: The Man who brought America into World War I* (Stroud, Gloucester: Spellmount, 2008) is workmanlike but also has errors and lacks sufficient objectivity. In addition to these sources, this section draws on Beesly, pp36–8 and Judd, pp294–6. 10 Andrew, *Secret Service*, pp306–8; Gill Bennett, *The Zinoviev Letter: The Conspiracy that Never Dies* (OUP, 2018), pp132, 248, 252. 11 Daniel Larsen, 'British signals intelligence and the 1916 Easter Rising in Ireland', *Intelligence and National Security*, 33:1 (2018), pp48–66. 12 Jacob Rosen, 'Captain Reginald Hall and the Balfour Declaration', *Middle Eastern Studies*, 24:1 (1988), pp56–67. 13 Daniel Larsen, 'British Intelligence and the 1916 Mediation Mission of Colonel Edward M House', *Intelligence and National Security*, 25:5 (October 2010), pp685–7. 14 Accounts differ as to whether all three travelled and participated in negotiations. Most sources agree that Eady was present, but disagree on whether he was accompanied by Whittall or Fitzmaurice, or both. It is conceivable that Fitzmaurice was already in the area, since Fisher thought he had recently been based in Sofia. 15 Hall edited autobiography, Ch 7; Ramsay, pp75–81; Captain G R G Allen, 'A Ghost from Gallipoli', *Journal of the Royal United Services Institution* (May 1963); letter by Admiral W M James, *Journal of the Royal United Services Institution* (November 1963); Robert Rhodes James, *Gallipoli* (Pimlico,

1999); Judd, pp304–5. **16** Letter from Vice Admiral Sir Sackville Carden to Admiralty Secretary, 11 February 1915, covering comparative assessment of Dardanelles defences, ADM 137/1089, TNA. The latest British assessment, 'Turkey Coast Defences' was NID 838. **17** West thesis, p91. His Ch 4 provides an excellent overview of Dardanelles intelligence and planning. **18** Admiral Sir Henry Jackson, 'Note on forcing the passages of the Dardanelles and Bosporus by the Allied Fleets, in order to destroy the Turko-German squadron, and threaten Constantinople without Military Co-operation', 5 January 1915, ADM 137/1089. **19** Ramsay, pp78–80. **20** For this paragraph, Bell, *Churchill and the Dardanelles*, esp pp259–64. **21** CB 1515 (19), The Technical History and Index, The Geographical Work of the Naval Intelligence Division, Naval Staff, 1915–1919, Naval History Branch; Hugh Clout, and Cyril Gosme, 'The Naval Intelligence Handbooks: a monument in geographical writing', *Progress in Human Geography*, 27:2 (2003), pp154–5; Erik Goldstein, 'Hertford House: The Naval Intelligence Geographical Section and Peace Conference Planning, 1917–1919', *MM*, 72:1 (1986), Notes. **22** Thring to A/DID, 22 July 1915, Papers of Captain E W C Thring, IWM. **23** Jeffery, *MI6*, pp58, 61. **24** Ibid, pp49–55. **25** David French, 'Failures of Intelligence: The Retreat to the Hindenburg Line and the March 1918 Offensive', in *Strategy and Intelligence: British Policy during the First World War*, ed Michael Dockrill and David French (London: Hambledon Press, 1996), pp73–4; Jeffery, *MI6*, pp91–2. **26** Jeffery, *MI6*, pp 47–9; Jim Beach, *Haig's Intelligence* (Cambridge University Press, 2015), pp127–8. **27** Judd, pp295–6. **28** Hankey, 'The Origins and Development of the SIS', pp2–3, CAB 63/192, TNA. **29** Beach, *Haig's Intelligence*, p128. For background on Tinsley, Judd, *Quest for C*, pp336, 408; Frans Kluiters, 'R B Tinsley: A Biographical Note', www.nisa-intelligence.nl, January 2004. **30** DNI special telegrams, ADM 223/759, TNA. **31** Stagg is listed along with Brandon within ID in Room 39BI in both March and September 1915. By February 1916, Stagg had left ID and Brandon had moved to join Captain Bernard Trench Royal Marines in the ID Interrogation Unit, Room 32BIII. Black, *Naval Staff*, lists pp256, 260, 265. **32** Smith, *Six*, Ch 7. Stagg's service record is in ADM 196/49/267 and ADM 196/143/502, both TNA. Smith suggests Stagg transferred to the SSB in late 1914. However, Judd, p317, quoting Cumming's diary, states it was September 1915. Stagg, who joined ID in October 1914, also remains listed in the Admiralty phone book until September 1915, Black, *Naval Staff*, appendix B, p260. If he worked for Cumming before September 1915, as he evidently did, it must therefore have been on a visiting basis. **33** One of Christmas's reports, dated 25 April 1915, survives in the Fisher papers. It included progress of the battlecruiser *Lützow* and battleship *Prinzregent Luitpold*, damage to *Seydlitz* and *Derfflinger* at the Dogger Bank and numbers of submarines under construction. E1 section rightly doubted the accuracy of some details. Fisher papers, 5/27, CCA. **34** Jeffery, *MI6*, pp87–8. **35** For this clash and other background on Stagg, Michael Clemmesen, 'On the Effects of Knavery: From a London Working Lunch to the Danish Summer 1916 War Scare', *From war and peace*, Danish Military History Commission, No 1 (2015). **36** Smith, *Six*, Ch 7. D15's Jutland report, CX 183, is in ADM 223/637, TNA. **37** Tel Nicolson to Lowther, Copenhagen, 10 May 1916, FO 211/381, TNA. **38** Jeffery, *MI6*, p88. **39** CX 106 of 20 September 1915 from Copenhagen and report from 'C' dated 8 August, both KV 2/6/2, TNA. **40** Mason was an MP for the single term 1906–10, but this would have brought him to Churchill's notice, while as a prominent supporter of the Navy League he would have been well known to Fisher. **41** Judd, pp302–3. **42** AT to British Consul Punta Arenas on instructions of First Sea Lord, dated 29 January 1915, ADM 137/203, TNA. This was a repeat of an earlier telegram dated 6 January to which Milward did not reply, suggesting it never reached him. **43** Cumming's diary states that his agent set off on 11 February. For this, and evidence that he helped locate *Dresden*, Judd, pp302–3. For *Glasgow*'s decryption of the vital HVB signal, Beesly, p78. An excellent blog describes the three-month hunt for *Dresden* and the contribution made by expatriate supporters on both sides at: boredhistorian.blogspot.co.uk/2015/02/the-hunt-for-sms-dresden. Hall listed the hunt for *Dresden* as an 'intelligence failure' under Ch 17 in the draft outline of his memoirs, although he provided no detail. 'Rough outline of memoirs', Hall papers, 1/4, CCA. **44** It is conceivable that O'Caffrey was the source for the projected mass Zeppelin raid on London mentioned at the end of Ch 5. However, surviving documents covering O'Caffrey's intelligence suggest it is unlikely, and that the source lay elsewhere. For the background to the London raid, NRS Vol 113, item 59, 'Memorandum for the War Council by Mr Churchill, First Lord, and Report on the Anti-Aircraft Defence of London by Captain Murray F Sueter, Director Air Department, both dated 1 January 1915', pp188–90, and item 60, 'Extracts from "Secretary's Notes of a Meeting of the War Council" held on 7 January 1915', pp190–2. 45 AIR 1/562/16/15/64, TNA. 46 Smith, *Six*, Ch 5, describes O'Caffrey's intelligence career. Judd, *Quest for C*, p350, notes that he featured regularly in Cumming's diary, and his role providing aviation intelligence for the Admiralty is recorded by Jeffery in *MI6*, pp71–2. O'Caffrey's family background, pre-war experience, and key elements of his wartime service are in his application for naturalisation in HO 144/3470, TNA. His initial offer of service and dealings with the RNAS and Naval Air Department prior to the handover to Cumming are recorded in AIR 1/305/15/226/157, TNA. This has letters of appreciation for the raid on Evere. 47 One of the best accounts of TR16 and how he was run by the Rotterdam station from 1915–18 was provided by the SSB officer Henry Landau who served in Rotterdam in this period and knew TR16 under the nickname 'The Dane'. *The Spy Net: The Greatest Intelligence Operations of the First World War*, pp180–6. 48 ADM 223/637, TNA. 49 Jeffery, *MI6*, p84. 50 Decipher telegram from Findlay (Christiania) of 30 October 1914 and copy of letter from Findlay dated 29 October to Sir Edward Grey, KV 2/6, TNA. It is clear from these and other papers in KV 2/6 that Christensen walked into the British legation and offered information. Findlay not only promised Christensen the exorbitant sum of £5000 but, perhaps unwisely, gave him a written undertaking to this effect. For whatever reason, soon after his second round of meetings with Findlay between November and January, Christensen stepped back from his betrayal. Either he made a full confession to Casement or, more likely, insisted that he had been kidnapped by the British and forced to supply further information – thus explaining Findlay's letter, which Casement promptly published in the German press with the help of his German backers as an example of ruthless British perfidy. Prior to the release of security service records in the KV 2 series, the Casement version had considerable traction with some Irish and German historians. 51 Findlay letter to Sir Arthur Nicolson, dated 4 December 1914, enclosing copies of Casement letters to supporters in America, Father Gerald Coughlan, Patrick Devlin and Joe Macgarrity, Findlay telegrams to Nicolson dated 27 December, 29 December, 3 and 4 January, all in KV 2/6. 52 Hall autobiography, Ch 5. 53 Hall, Ch 5. There is an intelligence report, probably from the *Sayonara* operation with the MO5(g) 'Casement' papers. It records a possible U-boat sighting and attempts to link this with Sinn Fein sympathisers in the locality. It demonstrates how fragmentary and marginal the product probably was. DID to Captain Frank Hall (MO5(g)) dated 3 February 1915, KV 2/6, TNA. The Admiralty could find no surviving papers on the *Sayonara* operation when Hall was researching his autobiography. Letter from Vice Admiral Sir Dudley Pound, dated 24 October 1932, Hall papers, 1/3, CCA. 54 Beesly, *Room 40*, pp185–6; Ramsay, pp130–2; Andrew, *Secret Service*, p115. An example of intelligence from internal Irish sources is 'Revolutionary Movement', dated 26 December 1914, from James O'Mahoney, Royal Irish Constabulary, KV 2/6. 55 Findlay's telegram to Nicolson of 29 December was copied to the prime minister and all senior colleagues. 56 Hall, Ch 5. 57 Ramsay, pp138–9; Beesly, p186, 190. 58 Jeffery, *MI6*, pp122–3. 59 Philip Vickers, *Finding Thoroton: The Royal Marine who ran British Naval Intelligence in World War One*, Royal Marines Historical Society, Special Publication No 40 (2013), pp69–76. 60 Ramsay, p141; Andrew, *Secret Service*, p119. 61 Vickers, Ch 11; Andrew, *Secret Service*, pp116–17. 62 Both operations are described by Beesly, *Room 40*, pp191–202, and Ramsay, pp247–53. Beesly drew heavily on Lloyd Hirst's first-hand account, which has some additional detail especially on the wider biological campaign. 'Admiralty Room 40B and the "Erri Berro"', McLachlan/Beesly papers, MLBE 5/1, CCA. *Erri Berro* was the name of the schooner hired by the Germans to transport the wolfram to the U-boat rendezvous.

Chapter 9 Hall's Intelligence War in the United States 1915–1916

1 Richard Popplewell, *Intelligence and Imperial Defence: British Intelligence and the Defence of the Indian Empire 1904–1924* (Frank Cass, 1995), pp150–60, 237–8. 2 Thomas F Troy, 'The Gaunt-Wiseman Affair: British Intelligence in New York in 1915', *International Journal of Intelligence and CounterIntelligence*, 16:3 (2003), pp442–3. 3 Diaries of Edward Mandell House, Vol 4, Yale University Library. House is perhaps best viewed as a quasi-national security adviser, a post that did not then exist. He had more influence over, and was much

more trusted by, Wilson in foreign policy than Lansing. This explains the appeal of a communication route to the British government separate from State Department. 4 Gaunt's memoir, *The Yield of the Years: A Story of Adventure Afloat and Ashore* (Hutchinson & Co, 1940), gives some feel for the man and his exploits, although it is necessary to aim off for considerable embellishment. Gaunt's description of himself as 'Naval Attaché and Chief of the British Intelligence Service in the United States 1914–1918' certainly overstates his role. Also Beesly, *Room 40*, pp228–9. For Gaunt's relationship with House, Daniel Larsen, 'British Intelligence and the 1916 Mediation Mission of Colonel Edward M House', *Intelligence and National Security*, 25:5 (October 2010), pp 682–704. 5 Memorandum of Interview with Bywater, HO 45/12328; Honan, p45; Bywater, *Strange Intelligence*, Ch 16, where the references to a 'German speaking ID man' are almost certainly Bywater himself. 6 Beesly, *Room 40*, pp69–84; Ramsay, pp125–30; Barbara W Tuchman, *The Zimmermann Telegram* (First Ballantine Books Edition, 1979), pp69–72; Brendan McNally, 'E V Voska: The US Army Captain who founded Czechoslovakia', Defence Media Network (26 September 2017). 7 Gaunt, Sir Guy Reginald Archer (1869–1953), by Sally O'Neill, entry in *Australian Dictionary of National Biography*, Vol 8, 1981. 8 Samuel D Kleinman, 'State's Spies: The Bureau of Secret Intelligence and the Development of State Department Bureaucracy in the First World War' (unpublished honours thesis, Department of History, University of Georgetown, 2016), pp37–40. 9 Justus D Doenecke, *Nothing Less than War: A New History of America's Entry into World War I* (University Press of Kentucky, 2011), pp300–5. Wilson quote to Page from Adam Tooze, *The Deluge: The Great War and the Remaking of Global Order 1916–1931* (London: Allen Lane, 2014), Ch 1. 10 The nickname 'Dark Invader' derives from Rintelen's later memoir – Franz von Kleist Rintelen, *The Dark Invader* (London: Lovat Dickson, 1933). 11 Kleinman, p41, quoting memoirs of Secretary of State Robert Lansing. 12 Rintelen effectively admitted his responsibility for 'Black Tom' during dinner with Hall on 21 December 1926. 'Memorandum by Mr Peaslee of statements of Admiral Hall regarding Mr Rintelen's recent visit to London', dated 27 December 1926, Hall papers, 1/3, CCA. 13 Testimony of German agent, Horst von der Goltz, provided to British security officials 5 February 1916, KV 2/519; Popplewell, pp238–9, 242–3; Doenecke, pp130–2. 14 Thomas Boghardt, *The Zimmermann Telegram: Intelligence, Diplomacy and America's Entry into World War I* (Annapolis USA: Naval Institute Press, 2012), p112. 15 Ibid, p112. 16 David Kahn, 'Edward Bell and his Zimmermann telegram memoranda', *Intelligence and National Security*, 14:3 (1999), pp143–59,. 17 Kleinman, pp61–3; Eric Setzekorn, 'The Office of Naval Intelligence in the First World War: Diverse Threats, Divergent Responses', *Studies in Intelligence*, 61:2 (June 2017). MacDougall's biography is on the Arlington Cemetery website. 18 The Counselor was a post within State formally created by Congress to provide the Secretary with legal advice. The Counselor was also effectively the Secretary's deputy. Kleinman, p32. 19 For the founding of BSI and its key personnel, Kleinman, pp52–6. For the conduct of foreign policy in the Wilson era and House's role, Kleinman, pp84–8. 20 Kleinman, p76; Boghardt, pp109–10. 21 Bell note on British personalities, undated, Hall papers, 2/1, CCA. 22 Tuchman, *The Zimmermann Telegram*, p83. 23 Beesly, *Room 40*, pp231–2. 24 Andrew, *The Secret World*, Ch 24. 25 Daniel Larsen, 'British signals intelligence and the 1916 Easter Rising in Ireland'. 26 John Maclaren, and Nicholas Hiley, 'Nearer the Truth: The search for Alexander Szek', *Intelligence and National Security*, 4:4 (1989), pp813–26. 27 Saul Kelly, 'Room 47: The Persian Prelude to the Zimmermann Telegram'. This comprehensive and authoritative account produced in 2013 examines all the evidence now available on the Persian captures, as well as summarising their treatment, and the reasons for it, in the previous historiography stretching over some ninety years. 28 Pencil notes, Denniston papers, 1/2, CCA. 29 Kelly, pp45–8. 30 Young, 'Political Branch of Room 40', ADM 223/773; Peter Donovan and John Mack, *Codebreaking in the Pacific* (New York: Springer International, 2014), p18. 31 'Political Branch of Room 40'. 32 Larsen, 'British signals intelligence and the 1916 Easter Rising', pp54–5. 33 Hall autobiography, Ch 25; Freeman, 'MI1(b) and the origins of British diplomatic cryptanalysis', p213; Larsen, 'British signals intelligence and the 1916 Easter Rising', pp55–6. Hankey apparently learned of the 'roundabout' and Room 40's ability to read German diplomatic communications with their Washington embassy from Balfour on 25 August 1916. Hankey diary entry quoted in Roskill, *Man of Secrets*, Vol 1, p295. 34 Larsen, 'British signals intelligence and the 1916 Easter Rising', p56. 35 The

'History of MI1B' written in the early 1920s suggests that all three American diplomatic codebooks together with 'several re-ciphering tables used with them' had been solved by the end of 1915. HW 7/35. 36 Beach states that after 1914 MI1(b) made little direct contribution to intelligence on the German army for the rest of the war. *Haig's Intelligence*, p156. However, the 'History of MI1B' shows that this is not correct. MI1(b) made a significant SIGINT contribution on the Western Front in 1917–18 as well as to operations in the Near East theatre. 37 'History of MI1B'. 38 For examples of exchanges between Denniston and Crocker, HW 3/186, TNA. Also 'History of MI1B'; Freeman, MI1(b); Larsen, 'British codebreaking and American diplomatic telegrams, 1914–1915'. 39 'History of the Cryptographic and Wireless Intelligence Organisation', HW 3/39, TNA; Ferris, 'Airbandit: C3I and Strategic Air Defence during the First Battle of Britain', p35. 40 Pencil note, drawing on input from Dilly Knox, attached to letter (also in pencil), dated 19 December 1927, from W F Clarke, formerly Room 40, but by then head of the naval section in GC&CS, to Sir Oswyn Murray, Admiralty permanent secretary. HW 3/182, TNA. 41 Larsen, 'British signals intelligence and the 1916 Easter Rising' provides a detailed analysis. The breaking of the *Satzbuch* is described in 'Political Branch of Room 40', ADM 223/773. Beesly, *Room 40*, pp186–8, provides useful corroboration and some additional detail. 42 MO5(g) was renamed MI5 in January 1916. 43 The interrogation records are in KV 2/8, TNA. 44 Daniel Larsen, 'British Intelligence and the 1916 Mediation Mission of Colonel Edward M House', *Intelligence and National Security*, 25:5 (October 2010), p686, quoting various sources. 45 Larsen, 'British signals intelligence and the 1916 Easter Rising'. 46 Larsen, 'British Intelligence and the 1916 Mediation Mission of Colonel Edward M House'. 47 Quoted in Michael S Goodman, *The Official History of the Joint Intelligence Committee, Vol 1, From the Approach of the Second World War to the Suez Crisis* (Abingdon, Oxon: Routledge, 2014), p14. 48 Christopher Andrew, *The Defence of the Realm: The Authorised History of MI5* (London, Allen Lane, 2009), pp87–90; Beesly, *Room 40*, pp187–8; James, *Eyes of the Navy*, pp114–15. James implies Hall confessed to him his role in leaking the diaries and James evidently felt uncomfortable about it. There has been endless historical debate, of variable quality and too often coloured by partisan viewpoints, over whether the diaries were genuine. Forgery would compound Hall's offence. Andrew regards the forensic evidence that the diaries are genuine as convincing, and rightly argues that a forgery on the scale required and against a tight timescale would be impossible, even with KGB-level resources. He could have added that forgery would mean that either the full multi-volume diary was created in 1916, inconceivable in wartime, or most of the forgery was done post-war to validate earlier forged extracts. Yet such post-war effort would surely have been viewed as quite pointless. Casement was dead and the diaries could be claimed as 'lost'. Finally, forgery would have involved too many people not to leak at some point.

Chapter 10 Jutland: Intelligence Limitations Exposed

1 Friedman, *Network-Centric Warfare*, pp39–41, and *Fighting the Great War at Sea*, Ch 4. 2 These figures assumed the battleship *Bayern* and battlecruiser *Lützow* were operational. *Lützow* had finally become operational in March after lengthy main-engine problems. *Bayern* was complete, but did not formally commission until September. 3 This belief was based on a judgement of Scheer's personality, rather than any hard intelligence. 4 Oliver minute M 02315, dated 5 April 1916, ADM 137/1165, TNA; Black, *Naval Staff*, pp148–54. 5 Friedman, *Fighting the Great War at Sea*, Ch 7. 6 Marder, *FDSF, Vol 2, To the Eve of Jutland*, p444. 7 Ibid, pp430–5. 8 Hope account, ADM 137/4168, TNA. 9 Decrypt No 20274 dated 30 May 1916, ADM 137/4710, TNA. 10 Marder, *FDSF, Vol 3, Jutland and After*, p40. 11 This was the view of the Room 40 cryptographer William Clarke expressed in 1939. W F Clarke lecture (probably to the naval staff course) 'Operational Intelligence', 3 January 1939, p5, HW 3/1, TNA. Also Hope summary of Jutland intercepts, ADM 137/4067, TNA. 12 Werner Rahn, The Battle of Jutland from the German Perspective', in *Jutland: World War I's Greatest Naval Battle*, ed Michael Epkenhans, Jörg Hillmann and Frank Nagler (University Press of Kentucky, 2015). Scheer's original plan involved a bombardment operation against Sunderland. 13 Hope war diary, ADM 137/4168, TNA. 14 Hope summary of Jutland intercepts. 15 Jackson was still a captain. He was promoted to rear admiral on 9 June 1916. 16 Marder, *FDSF, Vol 3, Jutland and After*, pp45–7; Beesly, *Room*

40, p155; Andrew Gordon, pp72–3. **17** Jason Hines, 'Sins of Omission and Commission: A Reassessment of the Role of Intelligence in the Battle of Jutland', *Journal of Military History*, 72:4 (2008), pp1127–9. **18** Black, *Naval Staff*, pp161–3. **19** The First Sea Lord's letter to Jellicoe of 1 June shows that he was an active participant in all Admiralty decisions of 31 May. **20** Rahn, 'The Battle of Jutland from the German Perspective'; Marder, *FDSF, Vol 3, Jutland and After*, pp39–40. Marder sets out Scheer's reasons for downplaying the significance of the U-boat sightings. **21** Hines, ibid. **22** Gordon, pp415–16, for a detailed analysis and refutation of Marder's claim that this signal lost Jellicoe an hour or two of daylight in which to engage the High Seas Fleet. **23** Details and timing of positions as intercepted by Room 40 from Hines, p1151, and Jellicoe's reaction p1136. Room 40 positions compared with the track chart in the official post-war record prepared by Captain John Harper, 'Battle of Jutland: Battlecruiser Action Second Phase, 3.40–5pm', Harper 5, www.jutland1916.com. **24** For Jellicoe's view, NRS Volume 111, item 144, pp422–3. **25** Marder, *FDSF, Vol 3, Jutland and After*, pp93–100; Gordon, pp421–5, and map, p423. **26** In finding a way through astern of the Grand Fleet, Scheer may have been helped by German intercepts of British signals. See Jellicoe's letter to the official naval historian Sir Julian Corbett dated 17 September 1922, CAB 45/269, TNA. **27** The mined areas are shown by Marder in *FDSF*, Vol 3, Chart 1. The most northerly were the lines sown by *Abdiel* to guard the Horns Reef route on Jellicoe's instructions earlier in the day. These *Abdiel* lines were sown due south of Horns Reef at latitude 55° 10' N and are best viewed on Track Chart 35 (source Groos), www.jutland1916. com. **28** Marder, *FDSF*, Vol 3, Chart 15, and Track chart No 35 (source Groos), www. jutland1916.com. **29** Marder, *FDSF*, Vol 3, pp178–81; Gordon, pp484–9. **30** For Jellicoe's view of both the 2100 and 2241 Admiralty signals, NRS Vol 111, item 144, pp435–6. **31** Details of Room 40 intercepts and subsequent handling provided by W F Clarke to Admiral Sir Frederick Dreyer in July 1955, Dreyer papers, 6/4, CCA. **32** Hope summary of Jutland intercepts, ADM 137/4067. **33** The listed intercepts are drawn from the Hope summary. About two-thirds appear in Clarke's 1955 list given to Dreyer and he also provided the times of receipt in Operations Division. See also Hines, pp1151–2. **34** Hines, pp1146–8, puts most weight on this factor. Also, First Sea Lord letter to Jellicoe of 1 June. **35** First Sea Lord letter to Jellicoe of 1 June. **36** Marder, *FDSF*, Vol 3, pp175–6. Roskill endorsed Marder's judgement in his Beatty biography, pp181–2. **37** Quoted in Marder, *FDSF*, Vol 3, p175, and Nicholas Jellicoe, *Jutland: The Unfinished Battle* (Seaforth Publishing, 2016), p228. However, one of the best insights into Jellicoe's thinking regarding Scheer's return options and his reaction to Admiralty and other intelligence is his post-war letter to Sir Julian Corbett, 6 August 1922, CAB 45/269, TNA. **38** Marder's analysis, *FDSF*, Vol 3, pp181–2, is hard to better. John Brooks takes a similar view in 'The Battle of Jutland: "an unpalatable result"', in *Jutland, History and the First World War*, ed David Morgan-Owen, Corbett Paper No 18 (King's College, London, 2017). **39** The final German losses were *Lützow, Pommern*, four light cruisers (*Rostock, Elbing, Frauenlob, Wiesbaden*) and five destroyers (*S-35, V-4, V-27, V-29* and *V-48*). Marder, *FDSF*, Vol 3, p249. **40** First Sea Lord letter to Jellicoe of 1 June. **41** Hankey, *Supreme Command*, Vol 2, p492. **42** CX 183 of 19 June, ADM 223/637. Smith, Ch 7, rightly states that D15's list of damaged ships included three that had not been hit and two that had not taken part. However, he is perhaps overcritical of the report, which contained much of value. **43** 'Naval Intelligence', report from 'R16', 27 June, ADM 223/637; Jeffery, *MI6*, pp84–5. **44** Hankey, *Supreme Command*, Vol 2, p492; Marder, *FDSF*, Vol 3, pp253–5. **45** Ferris, 'The road to Bletchley Park', pp61–2. **46** Black, *Naval Staff*, pp264–5; BR 1875, Appendix P. **47** Jeffery, *MI6*, p68.

Chapter 11 Blockade: The Under-recognised Intelligence Triumph
1 Tooze, *The Deluge*, Ch 1. **2** Marder, *FDSF*, Vol 3, pp256–8 and fn 27. **3** Ibid, pp285–96. **4** Marder, *FDSF*, Vol 5, p156, quoting James's letter (as DCNS) written to the First Sea Lord, 12 March 1936. **5** Marder, *FDSF*, Vol 3, pp296–305; James Goldrick, *After Jutland: The Naval War in Northern European Waters, June 1916–November 1918* (Annapolis: Naval Institute Press, 2018), Ch 5 and pp110–12. **6** Marder, *FDSF*, Vol 3, pp305–7; Goldrick, *After Jutland*, pp108–12. **7** Beatty to Hankey, 23 October 1918, 'Naval Terms of an Armistice', Notes, paragraph 6, CAB 24/68/7, TNA. **8** For analysis of the strategic naval situation from

the end of 1916, 'British Naval Policy', 1 July 1917, CAB 24/18/73, TNA. 9 'Development of the Blockade', appendix to Director of Plans paper on 'Freedom of the Seas', 2 December 1918, p 24, ADM 1/8545/312, TNA. 10 Webb, 'Report on the work of the Naval Patrols (Home Waters)', 13 May 1915, ADM 137/2909, TNA. 11 Hall emphasised this balance at the end of 1916, summarising key war supplies from each neutral. NRS Vol 111, Item 24, Jellicoe secret enclosure sent to Beatty on 30 December 1916 containing a section on 'Neutrals' prepared by ID, p131. 12 The above two paragraphs draw on Ch 1 of the Admiralty staff history produced in 1920 by Lieutenant Commander W E Arnold-Forster, 'The Economic Blockade 1914–1919', or CB 1554 in ADM 186/603, TNA; Eric W Osborne, *Britain's Blockade of Germany, 1914–1919* (London: Frank Cass, 2004), Chs 4 and 5; Ferris, 'Pragmatic hegemony and British economic warfare, 1900–1918'; Greg Kennedy, 'The North Atlantic Triangle and the blockade, 1914–1915', *Journal of Transatlantic Studies*, 6:1 (2008), pp22–33. 13 'Development of the Blockade', p26. 14 Ferris, 'Pragmatic hegemony'. 15 CB 1554, pp138–9, Greg Kennedy, 'Intelligence and the Blockade, 1914–1917: A Study in Administration, Friction and Command', *Intelligence and National Security*, 22:5 (2007), p706. 16 'The N.E.T. Index', ADM 1/8408/1, TNA. 17 CB 1554, p139, and 'Conference at Trade Clearing House on 13 March 1916', ADM 137/2735, TNA. 18 Kennedy, 'The North Atlantic Triangle', p29. 19 Nicholas Lambert, *Planning Armageddon*, Chs 8 and 9; Kennedy, 'Intelligence and the Blockade, 1914–1917', pp702–5. 20 Jeffery, *MI6*, pp60, 94–7. 21 Eg Webb letter to Hankey dated 28 May 1915, and Webb 'Note on Mr Cohen's Letter to the First Sea Lord', 9 June 1915, both ADM 137/2735, TNA. Also, Osborne, Ch 5. 22 Memorandum for the prime minister by Edwin Montagu, 21 July 1915, CAB 17/22, TNA. 23 CB 1554, p139–40; Kennedy, 'Intelligence and the Blockade, 1914–1917', pp704–5. 24 'Report on Cable Censorship during the Great War (1914–1919)', pp9–11, 99, DEFE 1/130; Andrew, *Defence of the Realm*, pp63–4; Black, *Naval Staff*, p253. 25 'The Coordination of the War Arrangements for Trade Restrictions, &c', Note by CID Secretary, 13 January 1915, CAB 42/1/15, TNA; Lambert, *Planning Armageddon*, pp345–9. 26 Hall autobiography, Ch 4; Andrew, *Defence of the Realm*, pp63–4; Lambert, *Planning Armageddon*, p376. 27 Black, *Naval Staff*, Figure 4.1, p109, shows that T11 section was established by March 1915. Prior to the war, Harris was a shipping insurance expert, well connected to Lloyd's. He was also a Conservative Member of Parliament throughout the period 1900–1918. He was a naval reservist before the war. This together with his shipping expertise makes his appointment to Trade Division logical, but connections with NID before the war are possible. He was certainly able, became a highly regarded expert on all blockade issues, and was an undersecretary in the new Ministry of Blockade in 1916. Lambert, *Planning Armageddon*, pp351–2. 28 Andrew, *Defence of the Realm*, p64. 29 Black, *Naval Staff*, Figure 4.1, p109. 30 For sample issues, FO 371/2679, TNA. 31 Kennedy, 'Intelligence and the Blockade', p708. 32 CB 1554, p140; Kennedy, 'Intelligence and the Blockade, 1914–1917', p707; 'Conference at Trade Clearing House on 13 March 1916', ADM 137/2735. 33 Kennedy, p714. Max Müller was the best source on conditions in Germany throughout the first half of the war and reported monthly to the Foreign Office. 'The General Review of the War', para 16, CAB 24/2/46, TNA. 34 Memorandum on attitudes within the United States prepared for Canadian prime minister, Robert Bordern, and copied by him on 28 January 1916 to Andrew Bonar Law, Colonial Secretary and leader of the Conservative Party, CAB 42/8/9, TNA. 35 CB 1554, p8; Ferris, 'Pragmatic Hegemony'; Kennedy, 'The North Atlantic Triangle', pp29–30. 36 Kennedy, 'Intelligence and the Blockade', p710. 37 CID, Minutes of 120th Meeting, 6 December 1912, p8, CAB 38/22/42, TNA. 38 This strengthening is illustrated in Webb's memorandum of 8 June 1916 and Cecil's subsequent comments of 17 June, both ADM 137/2737, TNA. 39 CB 1554, pp142–6; John Ferris, 'Issues in British and American Signals Intelligence, 1919–1932', *National Security Agency, Center for Cryptologic History*, Special Series I, Vol 11 (2016), p8. 40 CB 1554, pp148–52. 41 Ibid, pp9–10. 42 CB 1554, Table p152. 43 'Memorandum for C-in-C Grand Fleet', by DID, 1 November 1917, ADM 137/1373, TNA. 44 Director of Plans paper, dated 3 December 1918, 'Development of the Blockade', ADM 1/8545/312, TNA. 45 The above three paragraphs also draw on Ferris, 'Pragmatic hegemony'; 'The road to Bletchley Park', pp62–3; Kennedy, 'Intelligence and the Blockade, 1914–1917', pp716–17. 46 ID had at least fifty officers on its strength by end 1916 and Room 40 about the same. Taking account of support staff and staff in other sections, such as Trade Division, employed on intelligence duties, a total figure of two hundred working directly on intelligence in the Admiralty is reasonable. BR 1875, Appendix B. **47** Osborne, Ch 6. **48** The most authoritative synthesis of various GDP calculations is by Tobias A Jopp. 'Firms and the German war economy: Warmongers for the sake of profit?', in *The Economics of the Great War: A Centennial Perspective*, ed Stephen Broadberry and Mark Harrison (London: Centre for Economic Policy Research, 2018), Table 1, p87. Jopp shows that Britain was the only combatant whose GDP rose over the first half of the war, up 8 per cent by 1916. Albrecht Ritschl provides a range of comparable figures for Germany from different sources in 'The pity of peace: Germany's economy at war, 1914–1918 and beyond', in *The Economics of World War I*, ed Stephen Broadberry (Cambridge University Press, 2009), Table 2.1, p44. **49** Ritschl, Table 2.13, p58; Strachan, *The First World War*, pp212–15. **50** 'The Economic Position of Germany', memorandum by WTID, 30 October 1916, CAB 24/2/44, TNA. **51** Eg Berlin telegram 4530 of 7 November 1916, Office of the Historian, Department of State. **52** 'Hankey's Memorandum', 8 December 1916, CAB 42/19/2, TNA. This memorandum was evidently prepared as a personal note for Lloyd George, who had succeeded Asquith the previous day, although Hankey anticipated it would probably be shared with the new War Committee of senior ministers. The heading and content of the memorandum confirm that it was drafted on 7/8 December, but it has been misfiled by the National Archives with September 1916 papers of the CAB 42 (War Committee and successors) papers. This seems to have happened because there is a short note from Hankey attached at the front referring to a separate paper sent to Asquith on 2 September that year.

Chapter 12　Counter-Blockade: Struggling with the U-boat Threat

1 'Excerpts from a German Conference concerning Unrestricted Submarine Warfare', 31 August 1916, from Official German Documents relating to the World War, www.gwpda. org. **2** HW 7/19, TNA. **3** Tel 4375 from Ambassador Gerard, 25 September 1916. Original with Office of the Historian, US State Department. **4** Tels 4412 of 1 October and 4436 of 6 October, both from Grew (chargé). Original, Office of Historian, US State. **5** Tel 4439 from Grew (chargé), 7 October 1916. Original, Office of Historian, US State. **6** HW 7/17, TNA. **7** Boghardt, *The Zimmermann Telegram*, pp35–7. **8** Max von Montgelas, 1860–1938, was military attaché in Peking 1901–02, and commander of the 4th Bavarian division at the start of the war. He retired from the army in 1915 and became official adviser to the Reichstag committee of inquiry on the outbreak of the war. He was an official adviser at the Versailles negotiations. He was in occasional contact with several American and British diplomats and intelligence officers in Switzerland, where his brother was serving in the German Legation, through 1918. His objective was to persuade the Allies to open talks with 'moderate' parties in Germany. He was never a controlled agent, but did provide some useful intelligence insights. Probably the most valuable, delivered to the American diplomat George Hersey on 1 March 1918, was warning of a major forthcoming German offensive to knock France out of the war, and renewed U-boat operations to prevent American reinforcements reaching Europe. Hersey's report was intercepted by MI1(b) and is in HW 7/22, TNA. **9** Hall autobiography, Ch 25. The following year Balfour, by then Foreign Secretary, asked Hall for a briefing on German peace manoeuvres during 1916. Hall's response included a summary of the Bethmann-Hollweg telegram, underlining its impact when received. Hall letter to Balfour, 7 October 1917, HW 7/22, TNA. **10** 'Information as regards Enemy Submarines', 23 January 1917, ADM 137/4699, TNA. **11** U-boat intercept entries in Captain Hope's Diary, February–December 1916, ADM 137/4169, TNA; Beesly, *Room 40*, pp254–5. **12** CB 01412, 'Germany Naval Construction', ID report issued January 1918, in 'German Material Organisation Etc March 1916–March 1919', Admiralty Library. Table D, 'Submarines: Additions and Deductions from the outbreak of war up to December 1917', pp20–1, and Table E, 'Submarine Construction'. Also 'Remarks on Output and Losses of Enemy Submarines', undated but probably January 1918 from the content and context of associated papers, ADM 137/1937, TNA. **13** In particular, the work of Robert Grant. His best assessment of monthly U-boat losses appears to be that in *U-boat Hunters*, 'Revised List of German Submarines Sunk or Interned', pp136–45, which updates that in *U-boat Intelligence*, pp175–83. **14** Output figures from Dr Graham Watson, *Organisation of the Imperial German Navy 1914–1918*, tables for 'U-boats by type and entry into service' and 'Strength of the U-boat Arm', www. naval-history.net. **15** Hall autobiography, Ch 25. **16** Ibid. For more detail of the sources exploited by the Germans, Holger H Herwig, 'Total Rhetoric, Limited War: Germany's U-boat Campaign 1917–1918', *Journal of Military and Strategic Studies, University of Calgary*, 1:1 (1998). **17** Jackson letter to Jellicoe, 19 October 1916, Jellicoe papers, ADD MS 49009, f 132r. **18** NRS Vol 111, Item 24, Jellicoe secret enclosure sent to Beatty on 30 December 1916 containing section on 'Neutrals' prepared by ID, pp134–5. **19** Ferris, 'The Road to Bletchley Park', p64. **20** Dirk Steffen, 'The Holtzendorff Memorandum of 22 December 1916 and Germany's Declaration of Unrestricted U-Boat Warfare', *Journal of Military History*, 68:1 (2004). There is a full translation of Holtzendorff's memorandum and excerpts of the 9 January conference translated and edited by Steffan at www.gwpda.org. **21** For Mediterranean statistics, Halpern, tables 7.3, 7.4 and 9.1. **22** Marder, *FDSF*, Vol 3, pp320–4; Sondhaus, *The Great War at Sea*, Ch 7; Grant, *U-boat Intelligence*, p177. **23** Watson gives an overall strength of 153 for the start of the unrestricted U-boat campaign on 1 February 1917. Scheer in his memoirs has 134 deployed on the frontline at this date (fifty-seven in the North Sea, eight in the Baltic, thirty-eight in Flanders and thirty-one in the Mediterranean). Admiral Reinhard Scheer, *Germany's High Seas Fleet in the World War* (London: Cassell & Co, 1920), p261. **24** Marder, *FDSF*, Vol 3, pp323, 332. Balfour's famously detached attitude to life was epitomised by the remark attributed to him: 'Nothing matters very much and few things matter at all'. **25** NRS Vol 111, 'Jellicoe's increasing anxiety about the submarine menace', item 11, pp87–93; Marder, *FDSF*, Vol 3, p331. **26** 'The General Review of the War', memorandum by the Secretary of the War Committee, 31 October 1916, paras 18–23, CAB 24/2/46; 'Merchant Shipping', memorandum by the President of the Board of Trade, 24 October 1916, CAB 24/2/42. Both TNA. **27** For comparative figures on Mediterranean losses due to U-boats, Halpern, tables 6.2, 7.2 and 7.3. **28** Jellicoe's concept here eventually reached fruition as the Squid mortar system of the Second World War, which then evolved into the Mortar Mark 10, widely deployed in Royal Navy service from the mid 1950s until late 1980s. However, such a weapon was of little use until the invention of ASDIC, or active sonar, first deployed in the early 1920s. **29** Minutes of the 127th Meeting of the War Committee, 2 November 1916, CAB 42/23/3, TNA. In addition to Jellicoe, the naval attendees were Balfour, Henry Jackson, Oliver and Webb. Asquith, as prime minister, was in the chair. **30** Record of anti-submarine conference on 3 November, ADM 137/1211, TNA. Oliver subsequently provided a more wide-ranging and thoughtful assessment of current anti-submarine measures in a minute written a week later on 10 November. Convoy was not specifically addressed in these exchanges, but Oliver noted that when high-value targets were escorted they were rarely attacked. **31** 'Combined Strategy in connection with Submarines', 16 November 1916, CAB 24/2/51, TNA. **32** 'Minutes of the 135th meeting of the War Committee', 20 November 1916, CAB 42/23/3; draft note from Asquith to the Chief of the Imperial General Staff, 21 November 1916, CAB 42/25/4. Both TNA. **33** Hankey memorandum, 8 December 1916, CAB 42/19/2, TNA. **34** Office memorandum establishing new Anti-Submarine Division, 16 December 1916, ADM 137/1211. Its control over anti-submarine forces was significantly extended on 8 February 1917. BR 1875, pp74–5. **35** J Allan C Macfarlane, 'A Naval Travesty: The Dismissal of Admiral Sir John Jellicoe, 1917' (unpublished doctoral thesis, University of St Andrews, 2014), pp52–3. **36** Marder, *FDSF*, Vol 4, p96. **37** Captain Hope's U-boat summaries, ADM 137/4170, TNA. **38** Grant, *The U-boat Hunters*, p20. **39** NRS Vol 117, *The Keyes Papers, Volume 1 1914–1918*, ed Paul G Halpern (William Clowes, 1972); 'Minute by Keyes – Proposed Net Barrage across Straits of Dover', item 196, 19 October 1917, pp 416–17; 'Interim Report of the Channel Barrage Committee', item 198, 29 November 1917, pp 419–20. **40** Grant, *U-boat Intelligence*, p83. **41** For the role of SIGINT, Beesly, *Room 40*, pp267–8. For mining policy and its effectiveness, James Goldrick, 'Anti-access for Sea Control: The British Mining Campaign in World War I', *US Naval Institute Naval History Magazine*, 32:5 (October 2018); Marder, *FDSF*, Vol 4, pp83–5. For the increased effectiveness of the Dover barrage and a detailed breakdown of U-boat losses, NRS, Vol 137, Ch 1, 'Some Lessons of the First World War', p13, and Plans 1 and 4, and www.uboat.net. In addition to the single loss to a British submarine in 1916, a further two U-boats were lost to Q-ships and submarines operating in tandem. **42** Friedman, *The Great War at Sea*, Ch 12. **43** Holtzendorff memorandum of 22 December 1916, www.gwpda.org. **44** Macfarlane, pp56–7. **45** Macfarlane, pp55–7.

46 Beesly, *Room 40*, pp255–6. **47** Friedman, *The Great War at Sea*, Ch 12. **48** Macfarlane, pp58–62. **49** NRS Vol 137, Plan 4. In theory, convoy concentrated escorts where U-boats were, converting it therefore from a defensive to offensive measure, the convoy becoming fatal bait. However, in 1917–18, unlike the Second World War, this effect was limited, because escorts lacked the ability to detect and kill U-boats. Friedman, *Fighting the Great War at Sea*, Ch 12. **50** 'Forecast of increase in losses of merchant shipping', 28 January 1917, attachment to War Cabinet paper 'Shipbuilding Programme to 1918', CAB 1/23, TNA; Marder, *FDSF*, Vol 4, pp102–3, 182. **51** 'British Tonnage – Losses and Gains', letter and attachment from John Anderson, Secretary of Department of Controller of Shipping, to Hankey, 6 February 1917, CAB 1/23. **52** Mediterranean statistics from Halpern, tables 7.4 and 9.1. **53** 'Additional German vessels probable by January 1919', 28 January 1917, attachment to War Cabinet paper, 'Shipbuilding Programme to 1918', CAB 1/23; and 'Report of Allied Naval Conference, 23 and 24 January', prime minister's opening remarks, p7, CAB 24/6/72, TNA. **54** War Cabinet 57th Meeting, 8 February 1917, p3, CAB 23/1/57, TNA; Hankey, *Supreme Command*, Vol 2, p641. **55** 'Development of the Blockade', pp28–9, ADM 1/8545/312. **56** Holger H Herwig, 'Total Rhetoric, Limited War: Germany's U-boat Campaign 1917–1918', *Journal of Military and Strategic Studies, University of Calgary*, 1:1 (1998). **57** P E Dewey, 'Food Production and Policy in the United Kingdom, 1914–1918', *Transactions of the Royal Historical Society*, Vol 30 (1980), pp71–89, esp Table VI, p88. **58** I am grateful to Professor Eric Grove for this point. **59** 'Naval Policy in relation to Mercantile Shipping Losses from Submarine Warfare, and the Effect on the Strategical Situation', dated 21 February 1917, CAB 24/6/60, TNA. **60** 'Review of the Naval Situation', 24 March 1917, CAB 24/8/78, TNA. Jellicoe's prediction for shipping losses was about right. Losses over the first six months of the unrestricted campaign were 3,825,255 tons, averaging 637,542 per month. He was also right that deployed U-boat numbers would increase. These rose through the summer from an average of thirty-six in February to forty-six in September. Marder, *FDSF*, Vol 4, pp52–3, 102, 182, 277. **61** Jellicoe's report to the War Cabinet on submarine output is 'Submarine Construction, Etc', 24 March 1917, CAB 24/8/83, TNA. The original TR16 report is 'Naval Intelligence from H16', sent from Rotterdam 16 March 1917. Other reports came from Rotterdam on 20 January, 15 February, 19 April (containing the figures for current strength and losses) and 18 May. All are in ADM 223/637. Smith, *MI6*, Ch 7, suggests the substitution of '3' for '1' in the April report. In 1916, 108 U-boats were built, ninety-three in 1917, and eighty in 1918, Marder, *FDSF*, Vol 5, p118, U-boat Statistics, quoting various authoritative sources. For U-boat orders in 1917, Marder, *FDSF*, Vol 4, p53. Watson gives U-boat strength on 31 March as 150. Grant's figure for losses up to the end of March is fifty-eight. **62** 'The Submarine Menace and Food Supply', First Sea Lord note, 22 April, CAB 24/11/19, TNA. **63** This system is described in Jellicoe's paper for the War Cabinet of 21 February, CAB 24/6/60. **64** Marder, *FDSF*, Vol 4, pp69–88; Beesly, *Room 40*, pp252–4. **65** 'The Submarine Menace and Food Supply', CAB 24/11/19, and separate note by First Sea Lord dated 18 April, CAB 24/10/99, TNA. **66** Marder, *FDSF*, Vol 3, pp269–70; Roskill, Beatty, p194. **67** Balfour letter to Jellicoe of 14 November 1916, Clarke 1, CCA. **68** Beesly, *Room 40*, pp177–8. **69** Clarke and Birch, Vol 1, p32. **70** 'Submarine Service: General Information', pp507–9 of bound volume designated ADM 137/1906, TNA. This assessment is undated but it mentions that *U-63* is 'now on her way to the Mediterranean', which dates its origin to the last week of October 1916. **71** One of these documents was CB 01228, 'German Navigational Instructions for Submarines (Channel and SE Coast of England)', issued by ID July 1916, in 'German Material Organisation Etc March 1916–March 1919', Admiralty Library. Its French origin is demonstrated by the 'Note by French Translator' at iv. **72** Robert M Grant, *U-boat Intelligence: Admiralty Intelligence Division and the Defeat of the U-boats 1914–1918* (Periscope Publishing, 2002), pp60–1. **73** For a summary of *UC-12* intelligence, M 03046, 'Report of German submarine 'UC 12' blown up of Taranto on 16th March 1916', ADM 137/3876, TNA. **74** For prisoner intelligence, NID 6504, 'Information obtained from prisoners from German submarine "UC 5"', ADM 137/3876; Grant, *U-boat Intelligence*, p13; *The U-boat Hunters*, pp47–50. **75** William Schliehauf, *Jutland: The Naval Staff Appreciation* (Seaforth, 2016), Interception of German Signals, Ch 11; Marder, *FDSF*, Vol 4, pp264–8. **76** Hankey, *Supreme Command*, Vol 2, p649, quoting diary entry for 29 April 1917. **77** Hankey, *Supreme Command*, Vol 2, pp645–7. **78** Figures for U-boat losses made an impression on both Lloyd George and Hankey. Lloyd George told the Spanish ambassador on 16 February that five U-boats had been destroyed or captured in the last week. London to Madrid intercept, dated 17 February, HW 7/21, TNA. Hankey's diary of 8 February recorded that 'we seem to be sinking a good many submarines' although, he added, 'they are sinking a terrible lot of ships'. *Supreme Command*, Vol 2, p645. In reality, only two U-boats were sunk in the first half of February. Grant, *U-boat Intelligence*, p177. 79 War Cabinet 97th Meeting, 15 March 1917, Appendix 1, Note from Captain Richard Webb, CAB 23/2/15, TNA. 80 Hankey, *Supreme Command*, Vol 2, pp641–50. 81 Quoted by Nick Lloyd, *Passchendaele: A New History* (Viking, UK: 2017), pp30–3. 82 House diary entry for 31 January 1917. 83 House diary entries for 22 and 29 March. 84 John Bruce Lockhart, 'Sir William Wiseman Bart – agent of influence', *RUSI Journal*, 134:2 (1989), 63–7, p64. 85 Kleinman, pp74–6. 86 Auchinloss's diary for 29 May records Wiseman having a recent private meeting with Wilson. Kleinman, p76. By contrast, Christopher Andrew places their first meeting on 26 June. *For the President's Eyes Only: Secret Intelligence and the American Presidency from Washington to Bush* (New York: Harper Collins, 1995), p48. Bruce Lockhart, p65, suggests Wiseman had several private sessions with Wilson before the end of 1916, although that seems unlikely. He also records the Northcliffe quote, p67. The depth of Wiseman's relationship with Wilson by the beginning of 1918 is displayed in the Balfour papers. Vol 59, Add MS 49741, f 1–161b, BL. 87 Balfour comment on Wiseman note to Sir Eric Drummond dated 27 April 1918, Add MS 49741. 88 Andrew, *For the President's Eyes Only*, pp38–9. 89 House diary entries December to April; Jeffery, *MI6*, pp110–20; Richard Spence, 'Englishmen in New York: The SIS American Station, 1915–21', *Intelligence and National Security*, 19:3 (2004), pp511–37; Thomas F Troy, 'The Gaunt-Wiseman Affair: British Intelligence in New York in 1915', *International Journal of Intelligence and CounterIntelligence*, 16:3 (2003), pp442–61. 90 The quality and depth of their relationship, embracing frank discussion of grand strategy, the whole sweep of Anglo-American relations and political gossip covering both nations is demonstrated in House's diary entry for 14 September 1917, when they spent two days together. 91 Jeffery describes Wiseman as the most successful 'agent of influence' in the first forty years of SIS. This is incorrect. Wiseman was an SSB officer not an agent, and House was not an agent under SSB control, either. Rather, he was a confidential contact, aware that Wiseman had special status with the British government, and accordingly a useful channel and sounding board. Wiseman could influence House but not direct him. *MI6*, p113. 92 The most comprehensive modern account is Thomas Boghardt, *The Zimmermann Telegram: Intelligence, Diplomacy and America's Entry into World War I*. This draws on but supersedes and corrects the famous account by Barbara Tuchman first published in 1958, *The Zimmermann Telegram* (First Ballantine Books edn, 1979). Hall's role is explored in detail by his biographer David Ramsay, *'Blinker' Hall, Spymaster: The Man who brought America into the War*. The accounts of Boghardt and Ramsay are supplemented by Kelly, 'Persian Prelude', and Peter Freeman, 'The Zimmermann Telegram Revisited: A Reconciliation of the Primary Sources', *Cryptologia*, 30:2 (2006), pp98–150. 93 Hall's main account is Ch 25 of his autobiography. There are some additional glosses from Hall in the notes on his draft written by Ralph Strauss and included in the Hall papers, 1/4 in CCA, and in his later book written with Amos Peaslee, *Three Wars with Germany* (London: Putnam's, 1944). De Grey's account, written 31 October 1945, is in HW 3/177, TNA. 94 Boghardt, pp96–7. A copy of the first decrypt is in HW 3/187, TNA. 95 NRS Vol 111, 'Jellicoe to Beatty (Beatty MSS)', 25 January 1917, item 28, p 140. Beatty acknowledged in a reply two days later. Jellicoe papers, Add MS 49008, f 234r, BL. There were other telegrams between Berlin and Washington in the second half of January referring to the date for commencing unrestricted submarine warfare, most of which were also intercepted by Room 40. However, it is not clear whether any of these were decrypted sufficiently quickly and clearly to be the source of Jellicoe's 25 January comment. 96 De Grey's account, 'Zimmermann Telegram: Footnote to Friedman's Account', 31 October 1945, although subsequently shown to be deliberately misleading on the role played by different codebooks and the routing of the telegram, suggests Hall phoned for a meeting with Balfour on Thursday, 18 January, which probably therefore took place early the week of 22 January at the latest. HW 3/177, TNA. Hall's autobiography, Ch 25, lends circumstantial support to de Grey's account of his 18 January discussion with Hall, but again cannot be totally relied on. The account of Assistant Paymaster Lloyd Hirst, who was responsible for Mexico in ID at this time and briefed by Hall on the telegram, also suggests an early meeting with Balfour. 'Comments on the Zimmermann Telegram', McLachlan/Beesly papers, MLBE 5/1, CCA. The fact that on 20 February Balfour authorised Hall to handle communication of the Zimmermann telegram to the Americans as he saw fit (Balfour comment on R H Campbell minute quoted in Hall autobiography, Ch 25) rather implies that Hall had prior discussion with Balfour on the telegram and probably more than once. Hirst describes Kraft's recruitment and deployment in the German embassy. MLBE 5/1. **97** For a summary of the latest research demonstrating that the telegram took a single route between Berlin and Washington, and the reasons for the previous confusion over the years, Kelly, 'Persian Prelude'. However, the belief that multiple routes were deployed, including the Swedish 'roundabout', persists, being repeated by Christopher Andrew in *The Secret World*, Ch 24, as recently as 2018. **98** For a comparison of the various versions, Boghardt, Ch 7. **99** HW 3/181, TNA. **100** Text of US ambassador Page telegram to State Department, 24 February, and quoted in Hall autobiography, Ch 25. Page's telegram and subsequent exchanges with State Department, as intercepted by MI1(b) are also in HW 3/179, TNA. **101** Noted by Ralph Strauss when working with Hall on his abortive autobiography. Strauss note, 29 November 1932, HALL 1/4, CCA. **102** Hall autobiography, Ch 25. **103** Ramsay, Ch 12; Boghardt, Ch 8. **104** Balfour comment on Foreign Office minutes from Campbell and Hardinge, dated 20 February, quoted in Hall autobiography, Ch 25. **105** House diary entries for 25 and 28 February, which demonstrate Polk in charge of dealing with the Zimmermann telegram, and 20 March where House states that Lansing did not know how the telegram had been obtained, other than that it came through the London embassy. House went on to record that it had in fact been 'caught', 'deciphered' and 'given to us' by Admiral Hall. On 24 March House stated that he had agreed with Lansing that it was best to say as little as possible about the origin of the telegram. Diaries from Yale Library. **106** HW 3/179, TNA. **107** House diary for 8 November 1917. **108** For analysis of the impact of the Zimmermann telegram on opinion in Congress, press and public attitudes, and on Wilson, Boghardt, Chs 10, 11, 12 and conclusion. **109** Ramsay, pp253–7. **110** Lloyd Hirst note on Kraft, Mclachlan/Beesly papers, MLBE 5/1, CCA, refers to the first pointer to Ixtapalapa. The most comprehensive account of the affair is given by Ramsay, pp258–9. See also Beesly, *Room 40*, pp241–2; Andrew, *Secret Service*, pp119–20; Boghardt, *The Zimmermann Telegram*, pp219–20.

Chapter 13 The Emergence of Operational Intelligence 1917–1918
1 124th and 125th meetings of the War Cabinet in CAB 23/2/42 and CAB 23/2/43 respectively, both TNA. **2** War Cabinet 126th meeting, 25 April 1917, CAB 23/2/44, TNA. **3** 'The Submarine Menace and Food Supply', note from the First Sea Lord, 22 April 1917, CAB 24/11/19, TNA. **4** Roskill, *Beatty*, pp210, 220; Marder, *FDSF*, Vol 4, pp157–9; BR 1875, pp76–7. **5** War Cabinet 124th meeting, p3, CAB 23/2/42. **6** MI1(b) intercepts of London–Washington telegrams, 17 and 18 April, HW 3/179, TNA. **7** Minutes by Webb, dated 26 December 1916 and Duff, 26 April 1917, ADM 137/1322, TNA; Marder, *FDSF*, Vol 4, pp115–36; Hankey, *Supreme Command*, Vol 2, p647. **8** NRS Vol 137, *Defeat of the enemy attack on shipping*, Vol 1b, Table 1. **9** Jellicoe note to First Lord, dated 27 April 1917, ADM 1/8480/36, TNA. **10** 'Naval Policy in relation to Mercantile Shipping Losses from Submarine Warfare', CAB 24/6/60; 'A General Review of the Naval Situation', 24 March 1917, CAB 24/8/78, TNA. **11** 'A General Review of the Naval Situation', 24 March 1917, CAB 24/8/78. For the supposed advantage enjoyed by German battlecruisers, 'Battlecruiser Strength', 2 August 1917, CAB 24/24/61, TNA. For the SIGINT blackout in May, Clarke, History of Room 40 OB, Ch 5, HW 3/3; NRS Vol 3, Item 46, Jellicoe letter to Beatty of 1 May, p162, Item 48, letter of 10 May, p163, and Item 54, letter of 8 June, p168. **12** For discussion of offensive operations during the summer, NRS Vol 111, Item 83, 'Notes of a Conference held on board HMS Queen Elizabeth, 24th August 1917', pp 200–1, and Item 86, 'Report of a Naval Conference of Powers united against Germany, September 4th and 5th 1917', pp203–4. For the November operation, Marder, *FDSF*, Vol 4, pp299–311; Goldrick, *After Jutland*, pp211–18. **13** Jellicoe paper, 'Shipbuilding Programme for 1918', dated 31 January 1917, and Controller of Shipping 'Naval Shipbuilding and the Mercantile Marine Position', dated 5 February 1917, both CAB 1/23, TNA. **14** For a detailed analysis of the availability of

destroyer escorts at this time, Marder, *FDSF*, Vol 4, pp122–6. **15** Hankey, *Supreme Command*, Vol 2, p679. **16** Most modern accounts of the debate before the Passchendaele offensive have either offered nothing new on the naval dimension or neglected it entirely. Gary Sheffield perhaps provides the best summary in *The Chief: Douglas Haig and the British Army* (Aurum Press, 2012). Innes McCartney addresses the possible implications that lack of SIGINT coverage of the Flanders U-boats had on the Passchendaele debate in 'The Archaeology of First World War U-boat Losses in the English Channel and its Impact on the Historical Record', *MM*, 105:2 (2019), 183–201, pp196–99. Nick Lloyd, *Passchendaele*, p71, merely notes that Jellicoe's influence on the decision to approve Third Ypres remains contentious. Andrew Wiest's more specialist work, *Passchendaele and the Royal Navy* (New York: Greenwood Press, 1995), emphasises that Jellicoe was not particularly worried about the number of U-boats based at Ostend and Zeebrugge, but rather the dangers that continued German occupation of the Belgian coast posed to crucial lines of communication. That appears unduly to play down his overriding pessimism about Britain's prospects. **17** A J P Taylor famously claimed that on 30 March Lloyd George 'took command – the only occasion in British history when a prime minister has directed a great department of state in the teeth of the minister responsible for it'. 'The board of Admiralty acknowledged defeat and produced a scheme for convoy…', *English History 1914–1945* (OUP, 1965), p123. **18** James Goldrick, *After Jutland: The Naval War in Northern European Waters, June 1916–November 1918* (Annapolis: Naval Institute Press, 2018), p161. **19** 'Note by the Prime Minister of his Conference at the Admiralty, April 30th 1917', CAB 24/12/4, TNA. **20** BR 1875, Chs 15–17; Black, *Naval Staff*, Chs 6 and 7. For the January 1918 structure, Black, Figure 7.2, p230. Black places more emphasis on the role of Jellicoe than Lloyd George in initiating these changes. Lloyd George's official record drafted the day of the meeting and the summary in BR 1875 suggest his intervention was crucial. **21** Hall letter to Beatty dated 18 May 1917, ADM 223/768, TNA. Hall stated here that Hope had 'broken down' from overwork and had been sent on leave. James was known throughout the navy as 'Bubbles' because, as a child, his portrait was painted by his grandfather, Sir John Millais, blowing soap bubbles. Beesly, *Room 40*, fn p35. **22** Black, *Naval Staff*, pp269, 280. 'X' Room is listed under DID for May 1917 but by February 1918 is listed under DASD. **23** BR 1875, pp60–1. **24** 'Positions of submarines', 5 October 1917, HW 3/9, TNA. **25** BR 1875, pp79–81; Clarke and Birch, Vol 1, p32; C I Hamilton, *The Making of the Modern Admiralty: British Naval Policy-making, 1805–1927* (CUP, 2011), Appendix 2, p320; Marder, *FDSF*, Vol 4, pp267–8. For 'X' Room staff, see Black, *Naval Staff*, pp269, 280, 290, 301. **26** 'Proposal re Naval Intelligence', 4 January 1918, HW 3/9, TNA. **27** BR 1875, p95. **28** Memo from James to Deputy First Sea Lord, 30 October 1917, HW 3/1, TNA. **29** NRS Vol 137, Ch 1, 'Some Lessons of the First World War', pp3–13; Marder, *FDSF*, Vol 5, pp85–97; Jan S Breemer, 'Defeating the U-boat: Inventing Anti-submarine Warfare', *US Naval War College Newport Papers*, No 36 (August 2010), pp62–4. The difficulty a U-boat faced in dealing with convoy escorts was well described by Vice Admiral Sims. 'Naval Conference of Powers united against Germany, September 4 and 5, 1917', CAB 24/28/11, TNA. **30** Breemer, pp62–4. For a description of 'X' Room evasive routing, BR 1875, p81. **31** List of SSB reports, especially items 66–70, in ADM 223/637. **32** For the comprehensive account, CB 01453, '1917 Mutiny in the German Fleet', June 1918, ADM 137/3060, TNA. **33** ID report 'Mutiny on board German Men-of-War', 12 October 1917, and Hall's covering minute, ADM 137/3849, TNA. *U-45* and *UC-55* were sunk on 12 and 29 September respectively. Hall referred to the mutiny in a note to the First Lord on 11 October, but it had evidently been discussed previously, HW 7/22, TNA. Geddes then briefed the War Cabinet the following day, drawing attention to a report from Christiania. CAB 23/4/22, TNA. Hankey saw it as a significant development during his breakfast meeting with the prime minister on 15 October, CAB 1/42, TNA. Beatty referred to it in a letter to his wife on 13 October. NRS Vol 128, Item 248, p452. Also Henry Newbolt, *Naval Operations* Vol 5, Ch I.14; Marder, *FDSF*, Vol 4, p287; Sondhaus, *Great War at Sea*, Ch 9. **34** Lloyd, *Passchendaele: A New History*, pp30–33, 82–3, 141. **35** For a detailed analysis, David Stevenson, 'The Failure of Peace by Negotiation in 1917', *Historical Journal*, 34:1 (1991), pp65–86. **36** MI1(b) intercepts between Brussels and Madrid in early September, HW 7/22. **37** Hall letter to Balfour of 7 November 1917, HW 7/22. **38** Hall minutes to First Lord dated 8, 9, 10, 12 and 22 November. HW 7/22. **39** FO telegram of 8 October

1917, CAB 23/16/3, TNA. **40** Marder, *FDSF*, Vol 5, pp177–8. **41** Report to First Lord of 24 October 1917, HW 7/22. **42** Black, *Naval Staff*, pp206–7. For shipping loss figures used in calculations, Marder, *FDSF*, Vol 4, pp102, 182, 277. **43** NRS Vol 137, Ch 1, pp3–13. **44** Black, *Naval Staff*, pp203–13. **45** Ferris, 'The road to Bletchley Park', p65. **46** Marder, *FDSF*, Vol 5, p84. **47** NRS Vol 137, Plan for Operation ZO and Remarks by the Sea Lords', item 220, pp 460–78. **48** 'Photographic Reconnaissance by the Royal Air Force in the war of 1939–45', pp13–14, AIR 41/6. **49** Marder, *FDSF*, Vol 5, pp60–4; Extract from 'Der Krieg in der Nordsee' Vol 7, German Official Naval History of the War at Sea 1914–1918, Roskill papers, ROSK 3/18, CCA. **50** Several sources confirm that Trench and Brandon were interrogators from 1916. Black has them listed together under Hall in ID in Room B 32III in February 1916 and May 1917 and then in 3 AnxII in February 1918. By early 1916 Ennals and Bagot were listed next door to Trench and Brandon in Room 31BIII. Cope joined ID in October 1915. Ennals, Bagot and Cope were all qualified German interpreters. *Naval Staff*, pp40, 264–5, 269, 276. Trench arrived in ID in August 1915 and probably immediately started work as an interrogator. Brandon was in charge of E1 from December 1914, based in Room 39 BI, until moving to join Trench at some point before February 1916. *Naval Staff*, pp256, 260. **51** Vice Admiral John Godfrey, 'The Hall Tradition', p5, McLachlan/Beesly papers, MLBE 1/2, CCA. **52** Grant, *U-boat Intelligence*, pp21–3; Ramsay, *Hall*, p232. For insights into 'omniscience' and 'empathy' in regard to U-boat prisoners, Donald McLachlan, *Room 39: Naval Intelligence in Action 1939–45* (Weidenfeld and Nicolson, 1968), pp165–8. For interrogation techniques in the Second World War, Hinsley, Vol 1, pp282–3, and for Trench's use of stool pigeons in this conflict, Andrew, *Secret Service*, p81, quoting S W Roskill, who had interviewed Trench while researching *The War at Sea*. **53** 'The Story of MI19', Historical Background, Section 1, paragraphs (i) to (iii), WO 208/4970, TNA. **54** This murder claim was disputed by other prisoners. 'Mutiny on board German Men-of-War', ADM 137/3849. **55** 'Interrogation of Survivors of Submarines (UC Boats)', ADM 137/3876, and 'Interrogation of Survivors of Submarines, U-Boats', ADM 137/3872, both TNA. **56** Admiralty secret letter M 05200 of 4 June 1918 to C-in-C Grand Fleet and others, ADM 137/1937, TNA; and, Marder, *FDSF*, Vol 5, pp82–3. **57** CB 01288, February 1917, CB 01316, May 1917, and CB 01335, July 1917, ADM 137/3060. Also ADM 137/3877. Both TNA. **58** NID 15391, 2 October 1917, 'Written record of the Conference with Captains of Submarines on 17.1.17', NID 15478, dated 6 October 1917, 'Enemy Mines in the German Bight, 20 June 1917', NID 15544, 10 October 1917, 'Escort Services for Submarines in the German Bight', all in ADM 137/3866, TNA. Also CB 01376, 'German Submarine Orders', issued November 1917, providing extracts drawn from version issued to submarines on 23 September 1916, from 'German Material Organisation Etc March 1916–March 1919', Admiralty Library. **59** Grant, *U-boat Intelligence*, pp113–116. Grant acknowledges that it is impossible to prove that one of the earlier mines laid by *UC-42* in June destroyed *UC-44*. It is possible she set off one of her own mines during the laying operation, as happened to other boats. **60** Dr Innes McCartney, 'The "Tin Openers" – Myth and Reality: Intelligence from U-boat Wrecks during World War I', *Proceedings of the Twenty-Fourth Annual Historical Diving Conference, Poole, 2014* (Historical Diving Society, 2014). **61** Ibid. **62** Naval Weekly Appreciation 1, 27 May 1917, CAB 24/14/94, TNA. **63** Naval Weekly Appreciation 2, 3 June 1917, CAB 24/15/73, TNA. **64** Naval Weekly Appreciation 19, 30 September 1917, CAB 24/28/20 and Naval Weekly Appreciation 33, 5 January 1918, CAB 24/39/17, both TNA. Of the battlecruisers, *Mackensen* was launched in April 1917, but was still a year away from completion at the armistice. *Graf Spee* was launched in September 1917, but no further advanced. Goldrick, *After Jutland*, p231. **65** Naval Weekly Appreciation 39, 16 February, CAB 24/42/101, TNA. **66** Mediterranean statistics from Halpern, tables 6.2, 7.2, 7.3, 7.4, 9.1 and 10.1. **67** Clarke and Birch, *History of Naval SIGINT*, Vol 1, pp33–5, HW 7/1. De Grey's posting to Italy is noted by W F Clarke in his paper '40 OB', Clarke papers, CLKE 3, CCA. **68** Hall, 'Report on Intelligence Organisation in the Mediterranean', 4 April 1918, pp4–6, ADM 137/4699, TNA. **69** Grant, *U-boat Intelligence*, pp136–7. **70** Halpern, p293, states that Hall visited in early 1917, as does Beesly, p263. There is no record of any 1917 visit, and for the first four months of that year Hall was definitely in London, preoccupied with managing the Zimmermann telegram and the United States entry into the war. In 1942 Hall's successor as DNI, John Godfrey, confirmed that the only DNI visit to the Mediterranean during the previous war was in early 1918. NID 005858A/42, 'NID Policy', 7 November 1942, Godfrey papers, GOD/37, NMM. The references to a 1917 visit are therefore wrong. **71** The limitations of Mediterranean D/F before summer 1918 are summarised by Grant, *U-boat Intelligence*, pp132–9. **72** Grant, *U-boat Intelligence*, p133. **73** Halpern, p393, and Beesly, p264, suggest there were many more British sites. Hippisley, 'The Start of Room 40 OB', confirms that the British collection sites were at Malta, Otranto and Ancona. HW 3/5. **74** Hall, 'Report on Intelligence Organisation in the Mediterranean'; Clarke and Birch, *History of Naval SIGINT*, Vol 1, pp33–5. **75** Halpern, tables 11.1 and 12.1.

Chapter 14 1918: Last Acts and *Finis Germaniae*

1 Norway and Sweden supplied iron ore, pyrites, specialised steels, nitrates, zinc and aluminium, all vital to production of munitions and other war materials. Marder, *FDSF*, Vol 4, p251. **2** Memo from James to Deputy First Sea Lord, dated 30 October 1917, HW 3/1. For *U-70*, Grant, *U-boat Intelligence*, pp77–8. For the Scandinavian convoy action, Marder, *FDSF*, Vol 4, pp294–9. **3** NRS Vol 111, Item 89, 'Memorandum on Admiralty Organisation, with attached chart, by Sir Eric Geddes, 10 September 1917', pp211–18, and chart p216. **4** Minute to DID, probably from First Sea Lord, dated 9 November 1917, and other related papers, HW 3/9, TNA. **5** NRS Volume 128, Beatty Papers Vol 1, item 251, 'Notes on visit of Director of Intelligence Division to Beatty', 19 December 1917, pp454–6. **6** Clarke and Birch, Vol 1, p32. **7** Clarke and Birch, Vol 1, p8. **8** Marder, *FDSF*, Vol 5, pp131–8. **9** Ibid, pp143–56; Goldrick, *After Jutland*, pp250–7. Also James letter to Roskill dated 7 April 1968, ROSK 3/18, CCA. **10** James letter to Roskill of 7 April 1968. **11** Goldrick, pp256, 258. **12** 'Battlecruiser Position and Shipbuilding Programme', 31 August 1918, CAB 24/62/75, TNA; Naval Records Society, Vol 130, *Anglo-American Naval Relations 1917–1919*, ed Michael Simpson (Scolar Press, 1991), 'Memorandum of a Conference held at the Navy Department to discuss the Naval Situation', 8 October 1918, item 402, pp529–32. *Mackensen* was armed with eight 35cm (13.8in) guns compared to the eight 12in of *Hindenburg* and *Derfflinger*. **13** Minutes from ADNI(E), 4 June 1918, and Captain Dudley Pound, DOD(H) of 6 June, HW 3/9. **14** The improved intelligence engagement with Beatty is demonstrated in the letter to him from Rear Admiral Sir Sydney Fremantle, by then DCNS, on 29 October 1918. NRS Vol 128, Beatty Papers Vol 1, item 285, pp558–9. **15** The change back to DNI was announced in Office Memo 95, dated 5 April 1918, 'Intelligence 1918', p78, ADM 137/1630, TNA. However, it seems the formal change probably occurred on 1 June. There are references to Hall as DID and James as ADID(E) during May, but by 4 June James had become ADNI(E). **16** First Sea Lord minute to Hall dated 5 July 1918, HW 3/9. **17** James memo dated June 1918, probably to DCNS, HW 3/1, TNA. Clarke and Birch, Vol 1, pp39, 47–8. **18** Hinsley, Vol 1, p21. **19** NRS Vol 130, Admiralty Plans Division Memorandum, 6 May 1918, 'Proposed Measures to be taken if Enemy Battlecruisers enter Atlantic', item 259, pp344–5; Benson to Sims, 2 July 1918, item 262, p347; Sims to Benson, 3 August 1918, item 263, pp348–9; Sims to Bailey, 20 August 1918, item 265, pp349–51; Opnav to Sims, 3 September 1918, item 266, pp352–3; 'Instructions as to Action to be taken in regard to North Atlantic convoys in the event of a Raid in the North Atlantic by an Enemy Battlecruiser', 4 November 1918, item 269, pp356–8. **20** Tobias R Philbin, 'Admiral Hipper as Naval Commander' (unpublished doctoral thesis, King's College, University of London, 1975), pp193–7. **21** 'Some Important Aspects of the Naval Situation and Submarine Campaign', 25 September 1918, CAB 24/64/86, TNA; NRS Vol 130, 'Memorandum of a Conference held at the Navy Department to discuss the Naval Situation', 8 October 1918, item 402, pp529–32. **22** Marder, *FDSF*, Vol 5, pp107–8; Gary Weir, 'Naval Strategy and Industrial Mobilisation at the Twelfth Hour', *MM*, 77:3 (1991), pp275–87. **23** ID figures had 167 U-boats lost during the war up to 31 August with 299 built. 'Some Important Aspects of the Naval Situation and Submarine Campaign', appendix A. Actual figures were 161 lost and 308 built so the Admiralty underestimated headline strength by 15. Marder, *FDSF*, Vol 5, p118. ID had fifty-two losses during the first eight months of 1918 while the actual figure was fifty-four. **24** Statistics from Marder, *FDSF*, Vol 5, p118. **25** Goldrick, *After Jutland*, p273. **26** AT (S) 707 of 23 October 1918, ADM 137/964, TNA. **27** Marder, *FDSF*, Vol 5, pp171–2; NRS Vol 128, Wemyss to Beatty, 19 October 1918, item 284, pp557–

8, and Fremantle to Beatty, 29 October 1918, item 285, pp558–9. **28** AT(S) 955 of 29
October, 978 of 30 October and 080 of 2 November, ADM 137/964. **29** DNI tel to NA
Copenhagen, 28 October 1918, ADM 223/759, TNA. **30** ID25A War Diary, decrypts 1158
and 1731 of 4 November, ADM 137/4184, TNA. **31** ID25A War Diary, ADM 137/4184;
NRS Vol 130, Wemyss to Beatty, 5 November 1918, item 286, pp559–61; Beesly, *Room 40*,
pp295–8. **32** ID25A War Diary, ADM 137/4184; Beesly, *Room 40*, pp298–9. **33** Beatty
referred to 'considerable discontent' at Kiel in a letter to his wife on 22 September. NRS
Vol 128, item 281, p554. **34** Sumner, *Despise it Not*, pp46–52; Landau, *The Spy Net*,
pp235–42. **35** Marder, *FDSF*, Vol 5, pp298–9. **36** Andrew's global overview of intelligence
history, *The Secret World*, published in 2018, makes no reference to WTID. Beesly mentions
it once when he credits Hall (inaccurately) with its founding. *Room 40*, p128. **37** Ferris,
'Issues in British and American Signals Intelligence, 1919–1932', p1. **38** BR 1875, Appendix
P, lists 140 officers within the naval staff working for 'Intelligence' in November 1918. Black
lists eighty-one by name in NID in August that year, *Naval Staff*, pp295–8, but this list omits
almost all of ID25. However, James states that ID25 strength was seventy-four officers and
thirty-three 'ladies' in June 1918. James memorandum, HW 3/1. Adding this to the Black total
gives about 150 officers, close to BR 1875. **39** The twenty-six overseas intelligence centres
are listed in 'Naval Intelligence Organisation Abroad', and the thirty home centres in 'Naval
Intelligence Organisation – Home', both in NID 10388/21 undated but late 1921, ADM
116/1842, TNA. By 1918 the overseas centres employed 169 staff and those at home about
150. **40** Marder, *FDSF*, Vol 5, p322.

Chapter 15 Post-war Retrenchment and Restructuring
1 Vice Admiral John Godfrey memoirs; Hinsley, Vol 1, pp10–11; Andrew, *Secret Service*, p341;
Ralph Bennett, *Behind the Battle: Intelligence in the War with Germany, 1939–1945* (Pimlico,
1999), pp19–20. Their view is broadly endorsed in Charles Morgan's official history 'Naval
Intelligence 1939–1942', Ch 2, pp7–9, ADM 223/464. **2** 'Proposed Scheme for Reduction
after the War', DNI minute, 16 November 1918, ADM 116/1842, TNA. **3** 'Memorandum
No 1, Naval Intelligence Organisation Inside the Admiralty', ADM 1/8623/64, TNA; BR 1875,
appendix P. **4** 'Relative Strength of Navies', Admiralty Memorandum for the War Cabinet,
7 May 1919, CAB 24/79/29, TNA. **5** ADM 116/1842. **6** DNI minute, 1 September 1918,
and subsequent papers, ADM 1/8532/214, TNA. **7** 'Naval Intelligence Organisation', ADM
1/8623/64, including chart of 'worldwide naval organisation'. **8** Hinsley, Vol 1, pp9–10 and
fn 6; Anthony Wells, 'Studies in British Naval Intelligence 1880–1945' (unpublished doctoral
thesis, University of London, 1972), p99 and fn 1. Hinsley states that 'in 1918 there was a
considerable body of opinion, supported by the Foreign Office, in favour of abolishing the
posts of DNI and DDNI. His main source was apparently Wells who possibly misinterpreted
the role of a committee chaired by Rear Admiral J C Ley which examined ID's home-based
organisation in early 1918. Ley's brief was limited, none of his conclusions were controversial
and all were endorsed by Hall. He certainly made no comment on the status of DID or ID's
overall status. Wells, however, links the committee's deliberations with the change in Hall's
title in June that year suggesting that 'at one stage in 1918 the titles DNI and DDNI were
abolished but were soon revived on 5 April 1918'. The roles were never abolished. As stated
in the previous chapter the titles 'DID' and 'DDID' were merely changed back to the pre-1914
'DNI' and 'DDNI'. **9** For the debate over Hall's departure: William James, *The Sky was
always Blue* (London: Methuen & Co, 1951), p112; Beesly, *Room 40*, pp303–7; Ramsay,
pp282–9; Boghardt, *Zimmermann Telegram*, pp234–7. Andrew frequently refers to Hall's
willingness to manipulate intelligence, but does not provide precise sources and omits the
MI1(b) dimension. *For the President's Eyes Only*, Ch 2. **10** Jeffery, *MI6*, p169. There are
conflicting accounts for how the nickname 'Quex' originated. Jeffery, *MI6*, p170, states it was
bestowed on him as a young man, deriving from Arthur Pinero's play *The Gay Lord Quex*, in
which the hero is described as the 'wickedest man in London'. It reflected Sinclair's reputation
as a womaniser and bon viveur. Beesly, *Room 40*, p304, fn 1, claims it reflected his nasal way
of talking which suggested the quacking of a duck. **11** Cabinet conclusions, 17 February
1922, CAB 23/29/11, TNA, and Office of the Cabinet letters to First Lord, 16 and 23 March

1922, ADM 1/8623/64. **12** Cabinet conclusions, 10 May 1922, CAB 23/30/4, TNA. **13** BR 1875, Appendix 'O'. In 1922 there were six divisions reporting to DCNS: Intelligence, Plans, Operations, Trade, Training and Staff and Local Defence. Local Defence was abolished in 1923 and Trade in 1928, while in 1923 Training and Staff was incorporated with the divisions reporting to ACNS. **14** 'General scheme of Organisation inside the Admiralty', 1922, ADM 1/8623/64, TNA. **15** Hinsley, Vol 1, pp10–11; for Richmond comment, Ch 2, p40. **16** For an account of the technical assessment process, Joseph Maiolo, '"I believe the Hun is cheating": British Admiralty technical intelligence and the German Navy, 1936–39', *Intelligence and National Security*, 11:1 (1996), pp33–6. Although this article focuses primarily on the mid 1930s, the process was in place in the early 1920s. **17** War Cabinet 519, 24 January 1919, item 4, CAB 23/9/6, TNA. Curzon acted for Balfour while the latter was in Paris attending the Peace Conference. He succeeded Balfour formally in October. **18** Long's submission to the War Cabinet, GT 6665 'The Secret Service', 16 January 1919, is in CAB 24/73/65, while that of the Home Secretary, Edward Shortt, GT 6690, 23 January, is in CAB 24/73/90, both TNA. Also, Jeffery, *MI6*, pp145–6. **19** Minutes of conference on 29 April 1919 to consider new Code and Cipher Department, ADM 1/8637/55, TNA. The record and recommendation of the 27 February interdepartmental committee meeting and supporting papers are attached. DNI's minute to the First Lord of 28 March, also ADM 1/8637/55, provides the case for locating in the Admiralty. There are copies of most papers in HW 3/34, TNA. **20** David Kahn, *Seizing the Enigma: The Race to Break the German U-boat Codes* (Frontline Books version, 2012), Ch 6. **21** Michael Smith, *The Emperor's Codes: Bletchley Park's role in breaking Japan's secret ciphers* (London, Bantam Press, 2000), pp16–17, 43–4. **22** Denniston, 'History of GC&CS 1919–1939', 2 December 1944, pp 1–3, 19, Denniston papers, DENN 1/4, CCA; Birch and de Grey comments on Dennistion history, January 1948, HW 3/33, TNA; W F Clarke, 'The Years Between, November 11th 1918 – September 1939', Clarke papers, CLKE 3, CCA; Jeffery, *MI6*, pp209–11. **23** W F Clarke, 'GC&CS: Its foundation and development with special reference to its Naval side', Chs 1 and 2, 4 January 1945, Clarke papers, CLKE 3, CCA. **24** Denniston, 'History of GC&CS 1919–1939', pp6–10. **25** HW 12, TNA **26** ADM 1/8637/55. **27** Jeffery, *MI6*, p211. **28** HW 12. **29** For an overview of the founding of GC&CS and influence of MI1(b), Peter Freeman, 'MI1(b) and the origins of British diplomatic cryptanalysis', pp218–23. **30** Ferris, 'The Road to Bletchley Park', p67, and '"Now that the Milk is Spilt": Appeasement and the Archive on Intelligence', *Diplomacy and Statecraft*, 19:3 (2008), pp551–3. For GC&CS strength, Denniston, *Thirty Secret Years*, p90. **31** Andrew, *Defence of the Realm*, pp106–9. **32** Jeffery, *MI6*, p142. **33** 'Report of Secret Service Committee', February 1919, paragraph 7, CAB 24/76/67, TNA. **34** Jeffery, pp152–68; Bennett, *Desmond Morton*, Ch 4, 'SIS in 1923'. **35** Ferris, 'Now that the Milk is Spilt', p541. **36** Jeffery, pp 168–71; Judd, *Quest for C*, p469. **37** Jeffery, *MI6*, p209. **38** Ibid, pp162–8. **39** Ladislas Farago, *The Game of the Foxes: British and German intelligence operations and personalities which changed the course of the Second World War* (London: Hodder and Stoughton, 1971), pp117–18; Judd, *Quest for C*, p338. **40** Joseph Maiolo, 'I believe the Hun is cheating', p47. **41** Jeffery, *MI6*, pp248–55. **42** Max Everest-Phillips, 'Colin Davidson's British Indian Intelligence Operations in Japan 1915–23 and the Demise of the Anglo-Japanese Alliance', *Intelligence and National Security*, 24:5 (2009), pp 674–99. **43** Jeffery, *MI6*, pp255–263; Smith, *MI6*, Ch 20. **44** Judd, *Quest for C*, pp423–7. **45** Jeffery, *MI6*, p175. **46** Ibid, pp172–8; Judd, pp426–7; Augustus Agar, *Footprints in the Sea* (London: Evans bros, 1959), Ch 6, and *Baltic Episode* (London: Hodder & Stoughton, 1963), Ch 1. The latter provides a vivid first-hand account of all the operations, including a good portrait of Cumming. **47** NRS Vol 132, First Sea Lord memorandum for Cabinet, 4 November 1919, 'Proposal to maintain a Naval Force in the Baltic during Winter 1919–20', item 31, pp80–1. **48** NRS Vol 132: Beatty to Long, memorandum forwarded to Lloyd George, 6 January 1920, 'Caspian Situation', item 34, pp85–6; 'Report of Cabinet conference on oil supply and control of Caspian', 18 January 1920, item 36, pp87–8; Naval Staff memorandum, 5 August 1920, 'Black Sea: Possible Naval Operations against the Bolsheviks', item 42, p98. **49** Andrew, *Defence of the Realm*, pp162–3. **50** NRS Vol 132, Beatty to Lloyd George, 29 August 1920, item 43, pp99–100.

Chapter 16 New Naval Rivals and the Road to the 1921 Washington Conference

1 John Ferris, 'Armaments and allies: the Anglo-Japanese strategic relationship 1911–1921', in *The Anglo-Japanese Alliance, 1902–1922*, ed Phillips Payson O'Brien (RoutledgeCurzon, 2004); Friedman, *The British Battleship*, p149. 2 Ferris, ibid, pp251–2; Arthur J Marder, *Old Friends, New Enemies: the Royal Navy and the Imperial Japanese Navy, 1936–1945* (London and New York: Oxford University Press, 1981–1990), *Vol 1 Strategic Illusions 1936–1941* (1981), p5; Memorandum by the First Lord of the Admiralty, 'The Japanese as Naval Allies', 17 June 1921, CAB 24/125/57, TNA. 3 Admiral of the Fleet Lord Chatfield, *The Navy and Defence* (London: William Heinemann, 1942), p195. Chatfield was Fourth Sea Lord 1919–20, Assistant Chief of Naval Staff 1920–22, and Controller and Third Sea Lord 1925–28. 4 Christopher M Bell, 'Thinking the Unthinkable: British and American Naval Strategies for an Anglo-American War, 1918–1931', *International History Review*, 19:4 (November 1997), pp789–808 and *The Royal Navy, Seapower and Strategy between the Wars* (Basingstoke, UK: Macmillan Press Ltd, 2000), Ch 2. 5 First Lord memorandum, 'Future Naval Programme', 25 March 1919, and First Sea Lord memorandum, 'Future Naval Programme, Strength of British Fleet in the Future', 24 March 1919, both ADM 167/58, TNA. 6 War Cabinet 537, 28 February 1919, 'The Naval Clause', CAB 23/9/24, TNA; NRS Vol 130, Admiralty memorandum for War Cabinet, GT 6979 'The Battlecruiser Programme', 13 March 1919, CAB 24/76/80, TNA. 7 For an excellent overview, NRS Vol 130, Michael Simpson's 'Introduction' to Part 9, pp477–94. 8 Edward Eugene Beiriger, 'Building a Navy "Second to None": The US Naval Act of 1916, American Attitudes toward Great Britain, and the First World War', *British Journal for Military History*, 3:3 (2017). 9 NRS Vol 130, Planning Committee Office of Naval Operations, 'Building Policy', 7 October 1918, item 409, pp539–41. 10 Friedman, *The British Battleship*, p189; NRS Vol 130, 'Third Sea Lord to Gaunt', 13 February 1918, item 385, p501, and US Navy Department memorandum, 'British and American Naval Strength', probably early 1919, item 434, paragraph 5, pp576–7. 11 NRS Vol 130, Memorandum by Wemyss, 17 October 1918, 'An Enquiry into the Meaning and Effect of the Demand for "Freedom of the Seas"', item 414, pp548–51. 12 House Diaries, Vol 6, 28 October 1918. 13 House Diaries, Vol 6, 4 November 1918. 14 D of P paper, 'British Imperial Naval Bases in the Pacific', and related minutes, ADM 1/8570/287, TNA; NRS Vol 130, US Planning Section, London early 1919, 'Building Program', item 435, pp577–83; Phillips Payson O'Brien, *British and American Naval Power: Politics and Policy, 1900–1936* (Westport, Connecticut: Praeger, 1998), pp137–9. 15 NRS Vol 130, 'Memorandum by Benson on Anglo-American Talks on Naval Building at the Paris Peace Conference, March 1919', Washington 16 May 1921, item 446, pp597–9; Jerry W Jones, 'The Naval Battle of Paris', *US Naval War College Review*, 62:2 (2009). 16 CAB 24/76/80. 17 'British Policy as regards the American Naval Programme', 14 March 1919, CAB 24/76/88, TNA. 18 House diary, 30 and 31 March 1919. 19 House diary, 8, 9 and 10 April 1919. 20 War Cabinet 516A, 15 August 1919, CAB 23/15/31, and Admiralty memorandum for the War Cabinet, 'Post-war Naval Policy', 12 August 1919, CAB 24/86/78, both TNA. O'Brien, *British and American Naval Power*, p150. 21 NRS Vol 155, *Anglo-American Naval Relations 1919–1939*, ed Michael Simpson (Ashgate, 2010), memorandum by First Lord, 'Naval Policy and Expenditure', 24 October 1919, item 5, pp19–20. 22 'Naval Situation in the Far East', 31 October 1919, CAB 24/92/55, and 'Post-war Naval Policy' Appendix 2 'Japanese Navy', CAB 24/86/78, both TNA; Ferris, 'Anglo-Japanese strategic relationship', p257. 23 Memorandum by the First Lord, 'Naval Policy and Construction' CAB 24/115/77, and memorandum by First Lord, 'Naval Policy and Shipbuilding', 31 January 1921, CAB 24/119/19, both TNA. 24 Nevertheless, the Japanese were still ordering large quantities of armour plate from Britain at the end of 1920. Admiralty memorandum, 'Naval Construction', 10 December 1920, CAB 24/116/78, TNA. 25 'Tables of Comparative Strength', CAB 24/115/77. 26 Friedman, *The British Battleship*, fn 16, pp393–4. 27 'Tables of Comparative Strength', CAB 24/115/77. 28 Friedman, *The British Battleship*, p212. 29 Ibid, fn 16, pp393–4. 30 David C Evans and Mark R Peattie, *Kaigun: Strategy, Tactics and Technology in the Imperial Japanese Navy* (Annapolis, USA: Naval Institute Press, 1997), pp174–5. 31 Memorandum by the First Lord, 'Naval Policy and

Shipbuilding', 31 January 1921, CAB 24/119/19, TNA. **32** O'Brien, *British and American Naval Power*, pp153–4. **33** Memorandum by the First Lord, 'The Government's Naval Policy', 15 July 1921, CAB 24/126/38, TNA. Separate tables on US Navy and IJN ships under construction summarised the latest intelligence on their specifications. **34** Cabinet 60 (21), 20 July 1921, CAB 23/26/15, TNA. **35** Friedman, *The British Battleship*, pp210–13; R A Burt, *British Battleships 1919–1945* (Barnsley: Seaforth Publishing, 2014), pp335–37. **36** Table 'Expenditure in Financial Years', CAB 24/115/77. **37** O'Brien, *British and American Naval Power*, pp155–60. **38** First Lord memorandum, 'Anglo-Japanese Alliance', 21 May 1921, CAB 24/123/65, TNA; Ferris, 'Anglo-Japanese strategic relationship'; Phillips Payson O'Brien, 'Britain and the end of the Anglo-Japanese Alliance', in *The Anglo-Japanese Alliance, 1902–1922*, ed Phillips Payson O'Brien, pp269, 272–5, 279. **39** D of P minute, 7 March 1921, ADM 116/3447, TNA. **40** John Ferris, 'Issues in British and American Signals Intelligence, 1919–1932', pp43–5; Andrew, *The Secret World*, Ch 26. **41** O'Brien, *British and American Naval Power*, pp164–5, and 'Britain and the end of the Anglo-Japanese Alliance', p279. **42** NRS Vol 155, 'Hankey to his wife', 13 November 1921, item 21, p41. **43** For example, Correlli Barnett, *Engage the Enemy More Closely* (London: Hodder and Stoughton, 1991), pp21–2. **44** Ferris, 'Anglo-Japanese strategic relationship', p258. Ferris's view here contrasts sharply with the majority opinion of British historians for some fifty years after the Second World War, which judged the Washington Treaty a disaster for Britain's naval prospects. **45** NRS Vol 155, US Navy General Board to the Secretary of the Navy, 29 November 1922, item 37, pp53–4. **46** Barnett, *Engage the Enemy More Closely*, p24, describes the *Nelson*s as a 'flawed compromise design'. The ships, which drew heavily on the G3 design, but recast to meet the new displacement limit of 35,000 tons, had their faults, but all battleships involved difficult trade-offs between gunpower, protection and speed. The *Nelson*s had the heaviest armament in the world until 1941, most experts agree they were also the best protected until the new generation capital ships of the early 1940s, and they were 2 knots faster than any of the remaining American battleships, although not the two Japanese *Nagato*s. **47** Prime minister note, 'Naval Policy', 3 April 1925, CAB 24/172/96, TNA. **48** O'Brien, *British and American Naval Power*, pp166–74. **49** Ferris, 'Anglo-Japanese strategic relationship', pp258–60.

Chapter 17 After Washington: Managing Japan and Other Distant Threats 1922–1930
1 Prime minister note, 'Naval Policy', 3 April 1925. **2** COS 235, 'Imperial Defence Policy', papers prepared for use of chiefs of staff in their fifth annual review, 1930, CAB 53/21/4, TNA. **3** First Lord memorandum, 'Political Outlook in the Far East, 5 March 1925, CAB 24/172/39, TNA. The memorandum referred to the 'incontrovertible fact' that Japan had built more cruisers, destroyers and submarines since the war than the rest of the world together. In reality, Japan had completed fourteen cruisers, forty-nine destroyers and forty submarines. In contrast, Britain had completed thirteen, twenty-two and thirty, while American figures were nine cruisers, sixty-five submarines and over two hundred destroyers. The more specific claim for ships laid down since Washington was in the Naval Staff paper attached to the memorandum. Here the only Japanese lead was in destroyers. **4** CID 193rd meeting, 5 January 1925, CAB 2/4, TNA. **5** COS 41, 'Review of Imperial Defence, 1926', 22 June 1926, CAB 53/12/10, TNA. **6** Rear Admiral G C Ross unpublished autobiography, pp236–7, IWM. **7** Captain Malcolm Duncan Kennedy, Diaries 1917–1946, Library, University of Sheffield. **8** Thomas G Mahnken, 'Gazing at the sun: The Office of Naval Intelligence and Japanese naval innovation, 1918–1941', *Intelligence and National Security*, 11:3 (1996), pp427–8. **9** Mark R Peattie, *Sunburst: The Rise of Japanese Naval Air Power, 1909–1941* (Annapolis: Naval Institute Press, 2001), pp18–20; John Ferris, 'A British "unofficial" aviation mission and Japanese naval developments, 1919–1929', *Journal of Strategic Studies*, 5:3 (1982), pp416–39. **10** KV 2/871, TNA. **11** Max Everest-Phillips, 'Reassessing pre-war Japanese Espionage: The Rutland naval spy case and the Japanese intelligence threat before Pearl Harbor', *Intelligence and National Security*, 21:2 (2006), pp258–85; Rutland's security service file is KV 2/328–332. The beginning of the case is summarised in 'Notes on the Case of Squadron Leader Rutland, RAF', undated but probably

mid 1924, KV 2/328, TNA. **12** Douglas Ford, 'US Naval Intelligence and the Imperial Japanese Fleet during the Washington Treaty Era, c 1922–36', *MM*, 93:3 (2007), 281–306, p289. **13** Ferris, 'Anglo-Japanese Strategic Relationship', p260; Controller's minute, 26 September 1936, ADM 116/3382, TNA. **14** Minutes by Director of Ordnance and Director Gunnery Division, December 1924, ADM 1/8655/13, TNA. **15** Ford, 'US Naval Intelligence and the Imperial Japanese Fleet', p287 and fn 50. **16** Evans and Peattie, *Kaigun*, p251. **17** Ibid, p215. **18** Admiralty minutes of July/August 1923 and summaries of intelligence reports, ADM 1/8636/40, TNA. **19** Mahnken, 'Gazing at the sun', p428. **20** DNI memorandum, 'Naval Special Intelligence, 16 November 1927, HW 3/1, TNA. **21** Birch, Vol 1, Part 1, p20. **22** Christopher Smith, *The Hidden History of Bletchley Park: A Social and Organisational History, 1939–1945* (Basingstoke: Palgrave Macmillan, 2015), Ch 1. **23** Ralph Erskine and Peter Freeman, 'Brigadier John Tiltman: One of Britain's Finest Cryptologists', *Cryptologia*, 27:4 (2003), pp289–318; John F Clabby, 'Brigadier John Tiltman: A Giant among Cryptanalysts' (Center for Cryptologic History, National Security Agency, 2007). **24** 'Naval Section 1927–1939', 'Mr Bodsworth's Account', undated but probably immediately post-war, HW 3/1, TNA. **25** H C Kenworthy, 'A Brief History of Events relating to the Growth of the Y Service', 11 June 1957, HW 3/81, TNA. **26** Denniston, History of GC&CS 1919–1939, pp19–20, DENN 1/4, CCA; Birch and de Grey comments on Denniston history, HW 3/33; Hinsley, Vol 1, pp23–4. **27** Straczek, 'Origins and Development', pp67–8. **28** Straczek, 'Origins and Development', pp75–7; Donovan and Mack, p37; Captain Tait's report, 'Interception and Cryptography', April 1934, HW 67/1, TNA. The latter is clear there was no land-based intercept in the Far East area in 1934. There is broad agreement that Esquimalt was under construction by 1925. **29** 'HMS Anderson and Special Intelligence in the Far East', NID Vol 42, ADM 223/297, TNA; GC&CS messages, 18 and 30 April 1928, HW 67/1, TNA; Straczek, 'Origins and Development', Ch 2; Smith, *The Emperor's Codes*, pp21–30. **30** Donovan and Mack, p38. **31** 'The Origination and Evolution of Radio Traffic Analysis: The Period between the Wars', *Cryptologic Quarterly*, 6:1 (Spring 1987), www.nsa. gov. **32** Birch, Vol 1, Part 1, p13. **33** Tait report 'Interception and Cryptography', HW 67/1; 'HMS Anderson and Special Intelligence in the Far East', NID Vol 42, ADM 223/297; Clarke, 'GC&CS: Its foundation and development with special reference to the Naval side', Ch 3, 7 January 1945, HW 3/1; Straczek, 'Origins and Development', p83. **34** 'D/F in the Far East in relationship to Procedure Y', undated but 1933, HW 67/1, TNA. **35** For Horton's role, F A Kingsley, *Radar: The Development of Equipments for the Royal Navy 1939–45* (Macmillan, 1995), xxv; 'Tribute: Cecil Horton: Father of British Naval Radar' by Basil Lythall; Norman Friedman, *British Cruisers: Two World Wars and After* (Barnsley: Seaforth, 2012), pp12, 80 and Ch 8; 'Ship-borne Y Operations in the Far East', p1, HW 8/100, TNA. **36** 'Annual Report on Pacific Naval Intelligence Organisation 1938', HW 67/1. **37** Straczek, 'Origins and Development', p102 including map. **38** Naval staff papers 1923–24, ADM 1/8672/227, TNA; Christopher Bell, *Churchill and Seapower* (Oxford University Press, 2012), Ch 4, for political arguments. **39** Plans Division note, 'Reasons why it is necessary to build 17 – 10,000 ton Light Cruisers as soon as possible', 3 January 1923, ADM 1/8672/227. **40** David K Brown, *Nelson to Vanguard: Warship Design and Development 1923–1945* (Seaforth Publishing, 2012 edn), Ch 4. **41** Forecast of Comparative Royal Navy and IJN Strength, 31 March 1939, December 1938, ADM 116/4393, TNA. **42** Andrew Boyd, *The Royal Navy in Eastern Waters: Linchpin of Victory 1935–1942* (Barnsley: Seaforth, 2017), pp55–6. **43** Christopher M Bell, *The Royal Navy, Seapower and Strategy between the Wars* (Basingstoke, UK: Macmillan Press, 2000), Ch 3, and 'The Royal Navy, war planning, and intelligence assessments of Japan', in *Intelligence and Statecraft: Use and Limits of Intelligence in International Security*, ed Peter Jackson and Jennifer Siegel (Westport, CT, USA: Praeger, 2005). **44** CAB 47/1–4, TNA. **45** Hinsley, Vol 1, p30; Gill Bennett, *Desmond Morton*, Ch 7; CAB 47, TNA. **46** ATB 89, 'Japan: Dependence on Overseas Trade and the Possibilities of the Exercise of Naval Pressure on Such Trade', CAB 47/4. **47** Bell, *Royal Navy, Seapower and Strategy*, pp76–7. **48** CP 346 (23), Co-ordination of the Defence Forces, 27 July 1923, CAB 24/161/46, TNA. **49** Boyd, *The Royal Navy in Eastern Waters*, pp51–2. **50** JP Minutes Nos 1–100, CAB 55/1/1, TNA. **51** Jeffery, *MI6*, pp313–14. 52 Wesley Wark, *The Ultimate Enemy: British Intelligence and Nazi Germany, 1933–1939* (USA: Cornell University Press, 1985), pp155–60. 53 Gunther Hessler, *The U-Boat War in the Atlantic*, official Admiralty history ed Bob Carruthers (Barnsley: Pen & Sword, 2013), Vol 1, Appendix 1; Eberhard Rössler, *The U-Boat: The evolution and technical history of German submarines* (Cassell & Co, 2001 edn), pp88–90; Williamson R Murray and Allan Millett, *Military Innovation in the Interwar Period* (Cambridge University Press, 1996), p232; Clay Blair, *Hitler's U-boat War, The Hunters 1939–1942* (London: Weidenfeld & Nicolson, 1997), pp31–2, 40–5. 54 DNI minute, 8 August 1933, ADM 116/2945, TNA; Joseph Maiolo, 'Deception and intelligence Failure: Anglo-German preparations for U-boat warfare in the 1930s', *Journal of Strategic Studies*, 22:4 (1999), 55–76, p59. 55 Donald Stoker, *Britain, France and the Naval Arms Trade in the Baltic 1919–1939: Grand Strategy and Failure* (Frank Cass, 2003), pp140–50. 56 CP 184 (33), 'Indications of Germany's Disregard of Part V of the Versailles Treaty', 14 July 1933, CAB 24/242/34, and CP 82 (34), 'Germany's Illegal Rearmament and its Effect on British Policy', 21 March 1934, CAB 24/248/18, both TNA; Tim Bouverie, *Appeasing Hitler: Chamberlain, Churchill and the Road to War* (London: Bodley Head, 2019), Ch 3. 57 For example, minute by Head of M, 25 January 1932, and subsequent minutes by DNI and D of P, ADM 116/2945. 58 DNI minute, 8 August 1933. 59 George Franklin, *Britain's Anti-Submarine Capability 1919–1939* (London: Routledge, 2003). 60 George Franklin, 'A Breakdown in Communication: Britain's Over Estimation of ASDIC's Capabilities in the 1930s', *MM*, 84:2 (1998), pp204–14. 61 Maiolo, 'Deception and intelligence Failure'. 62 John Ferris, '"It is our business in the Navy to command the Seas": The Last Decade of British Maritime Supremacy, 1919–1929', in *Far Flung Lines – Essays on Imperial Defence in honour of Donald Mackenzie Schurman*, ed Greg Kennedy and Keith Neilson (London: Frank Cass, 1997), pp124–5. 63 COS 235, 'Imperial Defence Policy', papers prepared for use of chiefs of staff in their fifth annual review, 1930, CAB 53/21/4.

Chapter 18 Storm Clouds in the East 1930–1939

1 Andrew, *The Secret World*, Ch 26. 2 Ferris, 'Issues in British and American Signals Intelligence 1919–1932', Part 3, p45; For details of respective British and American positions, NRS Vol 155, Part 2, The Geneva Conference, pp57–90. 3 'Decrypts of intercepted diplomatic communications: International Naval Conference for Fleet Reduction', HW 12/126, TNA. 4 For example, Naval Conference decrypt 177 of 10 March, covering Japanese Admiralty telegram No 49 of 4 March 1930, HW 12/126. 5 Ferris, 'Issues in British and American Signals Intelligence 1919–1932', Part 3, pp45–56. 6 Orest Babij, 'The Royal Navy and the Defence of the British Empire 1928–1934', in *Far Flung Lines – Essays on Imperial Defence in Honour of Donald Mackenzie Schurman*, ed Greg Kennedy and Keith Neilson (London: Frank Cass, 1997); John H Maurer and Christopher M Bell, *At the Crossroads between Peace and War: The London Naval Conference of 1930* (Annapolis, USA: Naval Institute Press, 2014), pp34–5, 75, 240–50; Ferris, 'It is our business in the Navy to command the Seas'. 7 Eri Hotta, *Japan 1941, Countdown to Infamy* (New York: Knopf Publishing, 2013), Ch 4. 8 Maurer and Bell, *At the Crossroads*, p4. 9 COS 271, 'Imperial Defence Policy: Sixth Annual Review (1931)', 29 May 1931, CAB 53/22, TNA. 10 COS 296, 'The Situation in the Far East', 3 March 1932, CAB 53/22. 11 COS 310, 'Imperial Defence Policy, Annual Review (1933)', 12 October 1933, CAB 53/23, TNA. 12 COS 314, 14 October 1933, and COS 317, 11 January 1934, both CAB 53/23. 13 COS 357, 'Annual Review of Imperial Defence 1934', 30 November 1934, CAB 53/24, TNA. 14 CID 1111-B, 'The Policy of Japan', 27 May, 1933, CAB 4/22, TNA; COS 368, 16 March 1935, 'The Situation in the Far East', CAB 53/24, TNA. 15 Chatfield letters to Admiral Sir Frederick Dreyer, Commander-in-Chief China Fleet, 2 February and 7 August 1934, CHT/4/4, NMM. 16 James Goldrick, 'Buying Time: British Submarine Capability in the Far East, 1919–1940', *Global War Studies*, 11:3 (2014), pp33–50. 17 Japanese Monograph JM 145, 'Outline of Naval Armaments and Preparations for War, Part I'. 18 CB 3001/36, 'Progress in Naval Gunnery' 1936, pp95–9, ADM 186/338, TNA; Jon Tetsuro Sumida, '"The Best Laid Plans": The Development of British Battlefleet Tactics, 1919–1942', *International History Review*, 14:4 (1992), 681–700, pp687–8.

For IJN work on 'outranging', Evans and Peatty, *Kaigun*, pp250–66. **19** DCNS note to First Sea Lord and First Lord, 6 February 1940, ADM 205/5, TNA. **20** CID paper 1366-B, 'Comparison of the Strength Of Great Britain with that of certain other Nations as at January 1938', Appendix 1, CAB 24/273, TNA, listed two out of three IJN carriers as 'modernised'. These were *Akagi* and *Kaga*, with the newly completed *Soryu* the third. The Royal Navy apparently missed the scale of these modernisations, as it listed the ships with their original displacement of 27,000 tons until at least 1941, whereas it increased by about 30 per cent in each case. *Akagi* and *Kaga* were completely reconstructed between 1934–35 and 1935–38 respectively, finishing at 36,500 and 38,200 tons. Peattie, Appendix 4. The light carrier *Ryujo* was also reconstructed in this period. None of the older Royal Navy carriers received comparable investment. **21** Arthur Marder, *Old Friends, New Enemies*, Vol 1, pp345, 355–6. **22** Chappell letters to Arthur Marder, 23 November and 6 December 1978, Arthur J Marder papers, MS-F02, Special Collections and Archives, UC Irvine Libraries, Irvine California. **23** Director of Plans paper PD 05739/36 'Carrier Construction', undated but clearly summer 1936, and related minutes, ADM 116/3376, TNA. **24** 'Japan: Annual Report, 1938', including Appendix A, Air Strength and Distribution Tables, FO 371/23570; AI2 (c) note, 6 May 1937, AIR 40/2218, TNA. This had an overall IJNAF strength of 46.5 squadrons with 780 frontline operational aircraft and a further 394 at immediate readiness. It quoted a frontline carrier air strength of 250 (seventy-eight fighters, 118 torpedo bombers and fifty-four dive-bombers). The most accessible authoritative Japanese record of IJNAF strength across the 1930s is provided in Japanese Monographs 145 and 149, 'Outline of Naval Armaments and Preparations for War', Parts 1 and 2. IJNAF strength at the end of 1936 when the Second Replenishment Plan completed was thirty-nine squadrons. The Third Replenishment Plan commencing 1937 planned fifty-three squadrons, including 600 ship-borne aircraft by end 1941, JM 149, pp7–8 and appendix 2. By end 1938, the plan was at the halfway point, so the British figure was in the right order. British deployed carrier air strength the following year (1939) was 169 (129 torpedo strike reconnaissance, thirty fighters), 'State of Fleet Air Arm 4 September 1939', ADM 116/3722, TNA. **25** 'Japan: Annual Report, 1939', FO 371/24743; Note on 'Naval Air Display: Haneda Airport', 5 November 1939, AIR 40/2218; both TNA. **26** NID 3515/39, DNI 19 February 1940 and DNAD 20 February 1940, ADM 116/5757, TNA. **27** Anthony Best, *British Intelligence and the Japanese Challenge in Asia 1914–1941* (London: Palgrave Macmillan, 2002); Tait report, Ch 3, 'Interception and Cryptography', 2 April 1934, 'Annual Report of PNIO 1936', 'Procedure Y', and 'Annual Report of PNIO 1938', all HW 67/1, TNA; NID Vol 40, 'Far East and Pacific Intelligence History', 'The Far East Combined Bureau', and NID Vol 42, 'HMS Anderson and Special Intelligence in the Far East', both ADM 223/297, TNA. **28** 'The Far East Combined Bureau', ADM 223/297; Nigel de Grey's History of Air SIGINT, Ch IX, HW 3/102, TNA. **29** Best, pp133–5, 139–41. **30** NID 001262/40, 'The Far East Combined Intelligence Bureau, Singapore', 30 March 1940, ADM 223/495, TNA. **31** For example, GC&CS 070237, 29 December 1937, HW 12/222, TNA. **32** NID Vol 40, 'Far East and Pacific I History', p12, ADM 223/297, TNA. **33** 'HMS Anderson and Special Intelligence'. **34** William Clarke addressed this problem in a 1939 lecture probably to a senior officers' course. 'Operational Intelligence', 3 January 1939, HW 3/1. See also his notes to Director GC&CS, undated but probably soon after 1945, HW 3/33. Both TNA. **35** Jeffery, *MI6*, pp262–6. For Ernest James, Rear Admiral G C Ross unpublished autobiography, pp249–50, IWM and Keiko Tamura, 'Engagement with Japan: How Westerners lived in Kobe before and after World War II', presentation at National Library of Australia, November 2002, www.nia.gov.au. **36** SIS note 'Japanese Naval Shipbuilding', 17 April 1939, covering report of major naval construction currently underway, ADM 223/885, TNA. **37** CX 37300, 25 May 1937, and subsequent minutes from DNI of 2 June 1937 and Director of Plans of 10 June, ADM 223/495, TNA. **38** John Prados, *Combined Fleet Decoded: The Secret History of American Intelligence and the Japanese Navy in World War II* (New York: Random House, 1995), pp21–2. **39** Plans Division paper '1938 Programme Capital Ships', 10 May 1938, Director of Plans minuting, 31 January 1938, and DNI minutes dated 22 December 1937, file PD 06563/37, all ADM 116/3735; Director of Plans PD 06823/38, 16 May 1938, ADM 116/3382, all TNA. **40** NID report 'Japanese Warship Construction', November 1938, ADM 116/5757, TNA. **41** Morton to ADNI, ICF/430, 13 November 1937, and Morton to Seal of 13 February 1940 quoting conclusions in ICF/448 of 20 December 1938, ADM 116/5757. **42** Director of Plans minute, 1 December 1938, ADM 116/5757. **43** Foss account, in Ralph Erskine and Michael Smith, *The Bletchley Park Codebreakers: How Ultra shortened the War and led to the birth of the computer* (Biteback Publishing, 2011), Ch 3. **44** Kenworthy, 'A Brief History of Events relating to the Growth of the Y Service', Ch 6. **45** Smith, *Emperor's Codes*, pp34–5, 44–7. **46** Hugh Alexander, 'Cryptographic History of Work on the German Naval Enigma', p26, HW 25/1, TNA. **47** GC&CS 070132, 14 December 1937, HW 12/222. **48** Carl Boyd, *Hitler's Japanese Confidant: General Ōshima Hiroshi and Magic Intelligence 1941–1945* (USA: University of Kansas, 1993); GC&CS reports 073432, 24 January 1939, 073458, 26 January, and 073505, 28 January, HW 12/235, TNA. **49** GC&CS reports 075727, 8 September 1939, and 076006, 21 September, HW 12/243, TNA. **50** Foreign Office minuting of February and March 1939, FO 371/22944, TNA; Best, *British Intelligence and the Japanese Challenge*, pp148–51; Ferris, 'The Road to Bletchley Park', pp68–9. **51** Prados, pp22–4. **52** DNI minute, 22 December 1937, PD 06563/37, ADM 116/3735, TNA; SIS report 'Japanese Naval Shipbuilding', dated 17 April 1939, ADM 223/885, TNA; Diary entry of DNC Sir Stanley Goodall dated 3 March 1939: 'First Sea Lord (Backhouse) talking about *Hood*. Believes Japan building 12in battlecruisers. I said that was an argument against laying up *Hood*', quoted by D K Brown, *Nelson to Vanguard*, Ch 9, fn 12. **53** Evans and Peatty, *Kaigun*, p294; William H Garzke and Robert O Dulin, *Battleships: Axis and Neutral Battleships in World War II* (Annapolis: Naval Institute Press, 1985), p86. **54** Rear Admiral G C Ross unpublished autobiography, pp237, 249–50, IWM; Best, *British Intelligence and the Japanese Challenge*, pp118–19; Maiolo, 'I believe the Hun is cheating', p33. For an account of Long Lance development, Evans and Peattie, *Kaigun*, pp266–72. **55** Marder, *Old Friends, New Enemies*, Vol 1, p356. Marder believed the patrol occurred in October 1940, a year later than the true date. By autumn 1940, *Regulus* was in the Mediterranean. **56** Log of HMS *Regulus*, October 1939, ADM 173/15986, TNA. It has not been possible to identify the relevant patrol report. **57** Alistair Mars, *Submarines at War 1939–1945*, pp57–8. His Chs 3 and 4 give a wider account of British submarine operations in the Far East in the late 1930s. **58** Private papers of Commander J H Bartlett, HMS *Perseus* March 1939 – July 1940, p10, Item 1459, IWM. **59** Marder. **60** HMS *Regulus*, 'Report of Proceedings for Vladivostok Patrol No 1', 4 January 1940, ADM 199/1833, TNA. **61** Mars, Chs 3 and 4; Goldrick, 'Buying Time'. **62** Captain John F Connell, *Submarine Operational Effectiveness in the 20th Century, Part Two (1939–1945)*, Ch 3 (British submarines) and Ch 8 (American submarines).

Chapter 19 The New German Challenge and the Rising Threat from Italy 1933–1938
1 Director of Plans minute, 20 March 1935, enclosing papers for the Joint Planning Committee, and DNI minute, 26 March 1935, ADM 1/27413, TNA. **2** Boyd, *The Royal Navy in Eastern Waters*, pp66–7, 251–3. **3** Wilhelm Deist et al, *Germany and the Second World War, Vol 1, The Build-up of German Aggression* (OUP, 2015 edn), pp460–1. **4** Joseph Maiolo, 'The Knock-out blow against the Import System: Admiralty Expectations of Nazi Germany's Naval Strategy, 1934–9', *Institute of Historical Research*, 72:178 (June 1999), p209. **5** Plans Division, 'Notes on German Naval Strength', 27 May 1935, ADM 116/3373, TNA; Joseph A Maiolo, 'Admiralty War Planning, Armaments, Diplomacy, and Intelligence Perceptions of German Sea Power and their influence on British Foreign and Defence Policy 1933–1939' (unpublished doctoral thesis, Department of International History, London School of Economics and Political Science, 1996). **6** Plans Division letter to Joint Planning Committee covering estimate of German naval forces for 1939 and 1942, 9 January 1935, ADM 116/3373. **7** Klaus A Maier et al, *Germany and the Second World War*, Vol 2, *Germany's initial conquests in Europe* (OUP, 2015 edn), II.II, Bernd Stegemann, 'Germany's Second Attempt to become a Naval Power', pp60–1. **8** Deist, *Germany and the Second World War*, Vol 1, p464. **9** ICF/118, 'Submarine Construction', 8 April 1936, CAB 104/29, TNA. **10** CID 1252-B, 'German Naval Construction', 22 July 1936, CAB 48/4, TNA. **11** COS 535 (JP), 15 December 1936, 'The Protection of Seaborne Trade, part 1, War

with Germany', CAB 53/29, TNA; Maiolo, 'The Knock-out blow against the Import System', pp212–13; Boyd, *The Royal Navy in Eastern Waters*, pp51–2. **12** Maiolo thesis, pp94–5. **13** A view convincingly reaffirmed by Tim Bouverie in *Appeasing Hitler*, pp70–2. **14** Maiolo thesis, Ch 1; Clare M Scammell, 'The Royal Navy and the strategic origins of the Anglo-German naval agreement of 1935', *Journal of Strategic Studies*, 20:2 (1997), pp92–118. **15** Maier and Stegemann, *Germany and the Second World War*, Vol 2, pp60–1. **16** Deist *Germany and the Second World War*, Vol 1, pp457–8 and Table III.ii.4; Adam Tooze, 'Quantifying Armaments Production in the Third Reich 1933–1945', unpublished paper, www.adamtooze.com, June 2006. **17** Phillips's minute, 17 March 1938, covering 'Notification of the German Government in accordance with Part III of the Anglo-German Naval Treaty, 1937', ADM 116/3699, TNA. **18** Maiolo, 'The Knock-out blow against the Import System', pp216–18. **19** Deist, *Germany and the Second World War*, Vol 1, p471. **20** For U-boat plans, Hessler, Vol 1, Appendix 1. **21** Maiolo, 'I believe the Hun is cheating', pp36–46; Hinsley, Vol 1, Appendix 4. **22** Ibid, pp40–1; 'Anglo-Soviet Naval Armaments Diplomacy before the Second World War', *English Historical Review*, 123:501 (2008), p376 and fn 88. **23** 'Particulars of Foreign Major War Vessels', CB 1815, April 1939, ADM 239/46, TNA. **24** 'Bismarck and Tirpitz, tonnage, draught and endurance', 18 July 1948, GOD/92, and 'Afterthoughts', p161, GOD/175, both Godfrey papers, National Maritime Museum. **25** Friedman, *The British Battleship*, pp317–19. **26** Maiolo, 'I believe the Hun is cheating', p45; 'War with Germany', July 1938, CAB 55/12, TNA. **27** Jeffery, *MI6*, pp299–300; Farago, pp115–19. **28** Clay Blair, *The Hunters 1939–1941*, p43, Plate 4. **29** DNI minute, 22 July 1937, with details of secret reports, ADM 1/9074, TNA. **30** Maiolo, 'I believe the Hun is cheating', pp47–53. **31** George Franklin, 'The origins of the Royal Navy's vulnerability to surfaced night U-boat attack 1939–40', *MM*, 90:1 (2004), pp73–84. **32** *Britain's Anti-Submarine Capability 1919–1939*, Ch 7 and Conclusion. **33** NID Monograph No 18 by R T Barrett, 'German Success against British Codes and Ciphers', *c*1947, ADM 223/469, TNA; Marcus Faulkner, 'The *Kriegsmarine*, Signals Intelligence and the Development of *B-Dienst* before the Second World War', *Intelligence and National Security*, 25:4 (2010), pp521–46. **34** 'Report of W/T and V/S Organisation Committee 1930', pp8–9, ADM 1/8740/69, TNA. **35** Ferris, *Road to Bletchley Park*, pp71–2. **36** Clarke, GC&CS Naval Section history, Ch 4, W Bodsworth account, Naval Section 1937–1939, 'Report on work of the Italian Section (Naval) GC&CS for period September 18th to October 9th', all in HW 3/1; Hinsley, Vol 1, pp199–200; Ferris, 'Now the Milk is Spilt', pp551–2. **37** Mavis Batey, 'Dilly Knox – A Reminiscence of this Pioneer Enigma Cryptanalyst', *Cryptologia*, 32:2 (2008), 104–30, pp108–10; Hinsley, Vol 1, p210. **38** Franklin, *Britain's Anti-Submarine Capability*, p180. **39** Memorandum, 5 January 1939, and GC&CS Naval Section to ID8 undated, ADM 223/482, TNA. **40** David Alvarez, 'Left in the Dust: Italian Signals Intelligence, 1915–1943', *International Journal of Intelligence and CounterIntelligence*, 14:3 (2001), pp393–5; Ferris, 'Now the Milk is Spilt', p559. **41** Ferris, 'Now that the Milk is Spilt', pp547–8; Smith, *MI6*, Ch 20. **42** Jeffery, *MI6*, pp286–9. **43** 'Ministry of Marine, Conduct of War in the Mediterranean', 25 June 1939, under DNI note, 30 August 1939, ADM 223/488, TNA; Hinsley, Vol 1, p204. **44** Duff Hart-Davis, *Man of War: The Secret Life of Captain Alan Hillgarth* (London: Century, 2012), Ch 8. **45** CID 1208B, 'Central Machinery for Co-ordination of Intelligence', 20 January 1936, CAB 48/4, TNA. **46** Goodman, *JIC History*, Vol 1, Chs 1 and 2; Hinsley, Vol 1, pp34–43; Percy Cradock, *Know Your Enemy: How the Joint Intelligence Committee saw the World*, (London: John Murray, 2002), pp7–10. **47** DCNS memoranda, 'Operational Intelligence', 8 December 1936 and 11 February 1937, ADM 223/286, TNA. **48** Morgan, NID History 1939–1942, p9, ADM 223/464. **49** DCNS minute, 1 February 1937, ADM 223/286. **50** DNI letter to Sinclair, 9 December 1936 and undated W F Clarke manuscript note, ADM 223/268. **51** Charles Hamilton, 'The Character and Organisation of the Admiralty Operational Intelligence Centre during the Second World War', *War in History*, 7: 3 (2000), pp295–324; Hinsley, Vol 1, p12; Patrick Beesly, *Very Special Intelligence: The Story of the Admiralty's Operational Intelligence Centre 1939–1945* (Chatham Publishing edition, 2006), pp11–12. **52** Clarke, GC&CS Naval Section history, 1945, Ch 5, HW 3/1, TNA. **53** Denning report, 'Movement Section of NID', 25 January 1938, ADM 223/286. **54** Ibid. **55** 'Before September 1939: NID Revives', ADM 223/469, TNA; Morgan, NID History, pp131–2; Saunders letter to Forster, 26 November 1945, HW 3/134, TNA. **56** Clarke, 'Naval Cryptography in Wartime', 5 February 1937, ADM 223/286. **57** Beesly, *Very Special Intelligence*, p15. **58** 'Operational Intelligence Centre: Expansion in the Emergency of September 1938', ADM 223/482, TNA; DNI letter to Rushbrooke, 18 October 1938, ADM 1/10226, TNA. **59** Jeffery, *MI6*, pp319–20. **60** Ibid, pp317–20; Denniston, *Thirty Secret Years*, p97; Smith, *Hidden History of Bletchley Park*, Ch 2; Ferris, *Road to Bletchley Park*, pp72–4; F H Hinsley and Alan Stripp, *Code Breakers: The Inside Story of Bletchley Park* (Oxford University Press, 1993), Joan Murray's account of Hut 8, Ch 14. **61** Batey, Introduction, xviii. **62** Hamilton, p306. **63** Birch, Vol 1, Part 1, pp23–4; Beesly, *Very Special Intelligence*, pp12–15. **64** 'Rumours of German Submarine Activities in the South Atlantic prior to September 1939 – U-boats in excess of treaty allowance and duplication of numbers', undated but written by Godfrey in 1948, Godfrey papers, GOD/37, NMM. **65** For the OIC performance in the Munich crisis, CB 04019, 'German Naval Activities during the Czecho-Slovakian Crisis, September 1938', ADM 223/483, TNA. Morgan's NID History, 'NID8', p11, records the conviction that this was a successful intelligence performance. **66** Interrogation report, 'Erich May, W/T Petty Officer of U35', 5 December 1939, HW 8/21, TNA; NRS Vol 137, Plan 16 (1). **67** Jeffery, *MI6*, p310. **68** Bouverie, pp314, 318. **69** Karl Dönitz, *Memoirs: Ten Years and Twenty Days* (Frontline Books edn, 2012), Ch 4. **70** 'Post-war Organisation: The place of Cryptoanalysis and Traffic Analysis in the Intelligence Organisation as a whole', 4 April 1945, Clarke papers, CLKE 3, CCA; 'German Naval Section, GC&CS: Functions', 10 March 1939, HW 3/1.

Chapter 20 1939: Preparing for War – Godfrey Arrives

1 Godfrey spent his first two weeks as DNI in the rank of captain before being advanced early to rear admiral with effect from 22 February. Naval memoirs, Vol 5, Ch 1, GOD/170, NMM. **2** Joy Packer, *Deep as the Sea* (Eyre Methuen, 1976). **3** 'Organisation of the Naval Intelligence Division in Wartime', p12, 'Grading of Intelligence', 1 August 1939, Godfrey papers, GOD 36, NMM. **4** Letter to Donald McLachlan, 2 March 1968, Rushbrooke papers, IWM. **5** Quoted by Ben Macintyre, *Operation Mincemeat* (London: Bloomsbury Publishing, 2010), p81. **6** Patrick Beesly, *Very Special Admiral: The Life of Admiral J H Godfrey* (London: Hamish Hamilton, 1980), foreword by S W Roskill, and pp83–5; Hamilton, pp316–17. **7** Godfrey memoirs, Vol 5, Ch 7, pp32–3, and Ch 18, pp121–2, GOD/170. **8** Beesly, *Very Special Admiral*, pp102–3. **9** Godfrey monograph, 'Methods', November 1947, p3, ADM 223/475, TNA. **10** 'The Hall Tradition', McLachlan/Beesly papers, MLBE 1/2, CCA. **11** Godfrey memoirs, Vol 5, Ch 2, pp8–9; McLachlan, *Room 39*, pp8–9; Nicholas Rankin, *Ian Fleming's Commandos: The Story of 30 Assault Unit in WWII* (London: Faber & Faber, 2011), Ch 2. **12** 'NID Policy', 7 November 1942, Godfrey papers, GOD/37, NMM; McLachlan, *Room 39*, Ch 3. **13** 'Operational Intelligence Centre: Expansion in the Emergency of September 1938'. **14** Godfrey memoirs, Vol 5, Ch 2, p11. **15** Beesly, *Very Special Intelligence*, p254. **16** Ibid, pp16–21. **17** Hamilton, pp307–8. **18** Troup letter to Rushbrooke, 18 October 1938, ADM 1/10226; PNIO Annual Report 1938 and War Office meeting on transfer of FECB, 16 March 1939, HW 67/1; Birch History, Vol 1, Part 1, pp16–18. **19** Birch History, Vol 1, pp18–19. **20** Clarke, 'GC&CS: Foundation and Development with special relevance to Naval side', Ch 6, HW 3/1; Note for Frank Birch by Nigel de Grey headed 'Miscellaneous papers 3 September 1939', 17 March 1950. De Grey worked briefly in the Italian section on the outbreak of war. HW 8/21. **21** Paymaster Captain Shaw letter to GC&CS, 7 July 1939, HW 67/1, TNA; Birch History, Vol 1, Part 1, pp16–17; Donovan and Mack, Ch 9; Erskine and Freeman, 'Brigadier John Tiltman', p296; Clabby, 'Brigadier John Tiltman', pp17–18; Smith, *Emperor's Codes*, pp58–60. **22** Boyd, *Hitler's Japanese Confidant*, p13; Prados, pp163–5. **23** 'Introductory Note', probably by Frank Birch immediately post-war, HW 8/21, TNA. **24** Batey, 'Dilly Knox', p114; Denniston, History of GC&CS 1919–1939, 2 December 1944, Denniston papers, DENN 1/4, CCA. **25** Hinsley, Vol 1, Appendix 1, and Vol 3, Part 2, Appendix

30. 26 Jeffery, *MI6*, pp199–200, 293–4. 27 Ferris, *Road to Bletchley Park*, p73. 28 The most authoritative description of the naval Enigma expressed in layman's terms is A P Mahon's account in 'The History of Hut Eight', Ch 1 'The Machine and the Traffic', written in June 1945, HW 25/2, TNA. Mahon succeeded Turing as head of Hut 8 in 1944. 29 Batey, 'Dilly Knox', p116. 30 Patrick Beesly, 'Who was the Third Man at Pyry?', *Cryptologia*, 11:2 (1987), pp78–80. 31 Denniston to Sandwith, 8 June 1939, HW 3/1, TNA. 32 P G Redgment, 'High Frequency Direction Finding in the Royal Navy: Development of Equipment for Use against U-boats Part 1', *Journal of Naval Science*, 8:1 (1982), ADM 206/189, TNA. 33 Ralph Erskine, 'The Poles reveal their Secrets: Alistair Denniston's Account of the July 1939 Meeting at Pyry', *Cryptologia*, 30:4 (2006), 294–305, p296. 'Mrs B. B.' has never been identified. 34 Batey, 'Dilly Knox', pp116–18. 35 Ibid; Denniston account of Pyry meeting, 11 May 1948, HW 25/12, TNA; Birch History, Vol 1, pp19–22; Alexander, History of German Naval Enigma, p18; Gordon Welchman, 'From Polish Bomba to British Bombe: The birth of ultra', *Intelligence and National Security*, 1:1 (1986), 71–110, pp93–8; Hinsley, Vol 1, Appendix 1; Smith, *Codebreakers*, Ch 3 Introduction. 36 History of GC&CS between the Wars, 2 December 1944, p13, Denniston papers, DENN 1/4. 37 'History of ID8G August 1939–December 1942', p4, HW 3/134, TNA. 38 'German Naval Section, GC&CS: Functions', 10 March 1939, HW 3/1; 'Report of RFP and TINA', 28 May 1940, HW 41/387, TNA. 39 Godfrey memoirs, Vol 8, 'Afterthoughts', Ch 5, pp33–4, GOD/175. 40 Birch History, Vol 1, pp23–4, 33–4. 41 Denning note, 'Operational Intelligence', early 1939, Denning papers, DEN 8/2, NMM. 42 Morgan, NID History, p15. 43 NID daily reports from March to September 1939 regularly refer to visual sightings at Wilhelmshaven. ADM 223/79, TNA. 44 Bennett, *Desmond Morton*, Ch 9. 45 Ch 8, fn 4. 46 Taylor Downing, *Spies in the Sky: The Secret Battle for Aerial Intelligence in World War II* (London: Little Brown, 2011), Ch 1. 47 Jeffery, *MI6*, p291. 48 Hinsley, Vol 1, Appendix 2; Jeffery, *MI6*, p323; for Godfrey's involvement, Morgan, NID History, 'Photographic Reconnaissance', pp273–4, ADM 223/464. 49 Downing, Chs 1 and 2. 50 NID 'Daily Reports', ADM 223/79; Dönitz, *Ten Years and Twenty Days*, Ch 3. 51 Denning report, 25 July 1939, McLachlan/ Beesly papers, MLBE 1/10, CCA. 52 NID 'Daily Reports', ADM 223/79 and ADM 223/80; Morgan, NID History, pp222–3; NRS Vol 137, p54; Hessler, Vol 1, Ch 1. 53 'German General Staff Mission to London, June 1939', GOD/37, NMM: Bouverie, Ch 20. 54 For comparative naval investment, Boyd, *The Royal Navy in Eastern Waters*, Annex. For an assessment of the naval limitations process, see commentaries by Michael Simpson in NRS Vol 155, *Anglo-American Naval Relations, 1919–1939* (UK: Ashgate Publishing, 2010).

Chapter 21 Living on Thin Gruel: Winter 1939–1940
1 For the importance of the Mediterranean and Indian Ocean, Boyd, *Royal Navy in Eastern Waters*, pp398–9 and Conclusion. For proportion of Royal Navy losses suffered in the Mediterranean, 'Admiralty Notes on the Mediterranean Effort 1939–1945', CAB 106/615, TNA. 2 William N Medlicott, *The Economic Blockade*, Vol 1 (London, HMSO, 1952), pp40–44, 415–16; Desmond Morton Bennett, Ch 10. 3 Morgan, NID History, p12; Organisation of Naval Intelligence Division in Wartime, August 1939, GOD/36; 'Development and Organisation of the Naval Intelligence Division', April 1944, ADM 223/472, TNA; Birch History, Vol 1, p52. 4 Jeffery, *MI6*, pp328–31. 5 Ibid, pp734–48. 6 OIC Daily Reports, ADM 223/80, TNA; For description of the source, SIS reports dated 12 January 1940, ADM 223/884, TNA. 7 'Truth, Reality and Publicity', 'Number of U-boats (E and OE)', GOD/37, NMM. 8 Above three paragraphs from Jeffery, *MI6*, pp335–7. 9 'Organisation of Admiralty OIC', 28 September 1939, HW 8/21. 10 Biography, www.bletchleypark.org. uk; Hugh Sebag-Montefiore, 2017 article for the *Newcastle Journal*. 11 Birch History, Vol 1 (Part 1), pp32, 52–6, 164–7; 'The Naval Y Service in Wartime 1939–1945', HW 8/98, TNA; NRS Vol 144, *The Battle of the Atlantic and Signals Intelligence: U-boat Tracking Papers, 1941–1947*, ed David Syrett (UK: Ashgate Publishing, 2002), 'NID(9) Wireless Intelligence', item 170, pp368–80. 12 Birch History, Vol 1 (Part 1), p157. 13 Ibid, p35: Saunders letter to Denniston, 22 December 1939, HW 8/21; 'History of ID8G August 1939–December 1942', Part I, HW 3/134. 14 NRS Vol 144, 'The D/F plotting section of the OIC', probably 1946–7,

item 171. **15** Birch, Vol 1 (Part 1), p170; 'The Naval Y Service in Wartime 1939–1945', HW 8/98, TNA; NRS Vol 144, 'HF/DF organisation 1939–1945', probably 1946–7, item 172; Ralph Erskine, Afterword in Beesly, *Very Special Intelligence*. **16** Andrew Hodges, *Alan Turing: The Enigma of Intelligence* (London: Unwin Hyman Ltd, 1985), p161; Welchman, 'From Polish Bomba to British Bombe', pp79–80, 94–5; Hinsley, Vol 1, pp108–9 and Appendix 1; Hinsley and Stripp, *Code Breakers*, pp91–2; Hinsley, 'The Influence of ULTRA in the Second World War' (University of Cambridge Lecture, 19 October 1993). **17** Travis note to Denniston, 18 November 1939, HW 14/2, TNA; Welchman, 'From Polish Bomba to British Bombe', pp73–5. **18** Alexander, 'History of German Naval Enigma', pp19–20. **19** Mahon History, p21; Alexander History, p23; Birch, Vol 1 (Part 1), p42. Mahon and Alexander both identify the prisoner source as 'Funkmaat Meyer'. His key revelations concerned abbreviated signals and that numbers were spelt out rather than given as numerals. However, there is no obvious candidate with the name 'Meyer' at this time and it is probable 'Meyer' is a misspelling of Funkmaat Erich May, a survivor of *U-35* which was sunk on 29 November. He was interrogated by Saunders of 8G on 5 December. Interrogation report, 'Erich May, W/T Petty Officer of U35', 5 December; all HW 8/21. 'Funkmaat' means 'radio operator'. **20** Birch History, Vol 1, pp41–2. **21** Clarke, Naval Section history, Ch 6. **22** Birch, 'Introductory Note', HW 8/21; Birch History, Vol 1, p34. **23** Mahon History, p14. **24** Mahon, p24. **25** Birch History, Vol 1, pp34, 157; 'History of ID8G August 1939–December 1942', Part 1; Ralph Erskine and Michael Smith, *Codebreakers*, Ch 11. **26** Birch History, Vol 1, pp42–4. **27** Denniston letter to DNI, 10 December 1939; Godfrey reply, 16 December; Interrogation report, 'Erich May. **28** Kahn, *Seizing the Enigma*, Ch 8. **29** Birch History, Vol 1, pp42–3. **30** ADM 223/620, TNA. Although this file contains two hundred Enigma related 'Z' messages issued by Hut 4 between 11 May and mid September, this number does not relate to individual decrypts. Many messages, especially the early ones, contained multiple decrypts, eg No 1 had twenty-one, No 2, five and No 3, seventeen. Some messages were also 'assessments' drawing on Enigma material. Hut 4 only began issuing every decrypt as a distinct 'Z' numbered message the following year. Also, Ralph Erskine, 'The First Naval Enigma Decrypts of World War II', *Cryptologia*, 21:1 (1997), pp42–6. **31** Z reports 25, 65, 151, 154 and 178, ADM 223/620. **32** John Wright, 'The Turing Bombe Victory and the first naval Enigma decrypts', *Cryptologia*, 41:4 (2017), pp295–328; Alexander, History of German Naval Enigma, pp24–6; Hugh Sebag-Montefiore, *Enigma: The Battle for the Code* (London: Weidenfeld and Nicolson, 2000), pp81–8; Blair, *The Hunters 1939–1941*, pp152–3. **33** Downing, Ch 2; Hinsley, Vol 1, p104; 'Photographic Reconnaissance by the Royal Air Force in the war of 1939–45', Appendix X, AIR 41/6; OIC Daily reports, ADM 223/80. **34** First Lord minute, 'Photographs of Bismarck', 28 January 1940, ADM 1/10617, TNA. **35** W G V Balchin, 'United Kingdom Geographers in the Second World War: A Report', *Geographic Journal*, 153:2 (July 1987), 159–180, pp171–3. **36** Hinsley, Vol 1, pp104, 171–2; Balchin, p172–3; Downing, Ch 2. **37** Downing, Chs 2 and 3; Morgan, NID History, pp274–8. **38** 'Photographic Reconnaissance by the Royal Air Force in the war of 1939–45', Appendix XXVI, AIR 41/6; Downing, Chs 2 and 3; Hinsley, Vol 1, p104.

Chapter 22 The Norwegian Campaign: Still Too Little, Too Late

1 OIC Daily Reports, ADM 223/80 and 223/81; Beesly, *Very Special Intelligence*, Ch 2. **2** Geirr Haarr, *The Gathering Storm: The Naval War in Northern Europe, September 1939–April 1940* (Barnsley: Seaforth Publishing, 2013), Ch 23. **3** R V Jones describes the delivery of the report and initial reactions in *Most Secret War: British Scientific Intelligence 1939–1945* (London: Hamish Hamilton, 1978), Ch 8. His post-war assessment of its value, drafted in 1946, is in AIR 40/2572, TNA. Hinsley provides the full text in Vol 1, p100 and Appendix 5. **4** Frank Birch, *The Official History of British Sigint 1914–1945*, Vol 1, Part 2 and Vol 2, ed John Jackson (Military Press, 2007), Diagram No 47, p251. **5** Hessler, Vol 1, Ch 1; Beesly, *Very Special Intelligence*, Ch 2. **6** 'Preliminary report on W/T traffic and Strategic Security', 28 November 1939, ADM 223/505, TNA; 'History of ID8G', pp22–4. **7** W K Hancock and M M Gowing, *The British War Economy* (London: HMSO, 1949), Table 3 (c), p80. **8** 'Truth, Reality and Publicity', 'Number of U-boats (E and OE)', GOD/37. **9** NRS

Vol 137, pp55–6, Appendix 2 p251 (with amendments, xlix), and Plan 16 (1); Captain G E Colpoys, 'Admiralty use of Special Intelligence in Naval Operations', HW 8/47, TNA; Hessler, Vol 1, Ch 1. **10** NID figures in 'Future Strategy', WP 362, 4 September 1940, CAB 66/11/42, TNA. German figures in Horst Boog and others, *Germany and the Second World War*, (OUP, 2001), Vol 6, table III.iii.i, p348. **11** Blair, *The Hunters 1939–1941*, pp152–3. **12** 'Truth, Reality and Publicity', 'Number of U-boats (E and OE)', GOD/37. **13** 'Naval Programme 1940–41', especially paragraph 9, WP (40) 53, 2 March 1940, CAB 66/5/33. For Churchill's previous exchanges in early February with DCNS and the Controller, ADM 205/5. Both TNA. **14** Geirr Haarr, *The German Invasion of Norway, April 1940* (Barnsley: Seaforth Publishing, 2011), Ch 2. **15** Hankey letter to Sir Horace Wilson, 29 April 1940, CAB 127/375, TNA. **16** Tony Insall, *Secret Alliances: Special Operations and Intelligence in Norway 1940–1945 – The British Perspective* (London: Biteback Publishing, 2019), pp83–4. **17** Hinsley, Vol 1, pp115–25. **18** Ibid, p141; Birch, Vol 1 (Part 1). **19** Jeffery, *MI6*, pp373–4. **20** Insall, p41. **21** Geirr Haarr, *The Battle for Norway, April – June 1940* (Barnsley, Seaforth Publishing, 2010), Ch 14; Maier, *Germany and the Second World War*, Vol 2, pp218–19. **22** Haarr, *Battle for Norway*, Ch 13. **23** Interrogation reports for *U27* and *U42*, both October 1939, ADM 186/805, TNA; CSDIC Survey 3 September – 31 December 1940, WO 208/3455, TNA. **24** Birch, Vol 1 (Part 1), p85. **25** ADM 223/620, TNA. **26** Hinsley to Beesly, 16 November 1975, McLachlan/Beesly Papers, MLBE 2/12, CCA; Hinsley, Vol 1, pp141–2. **27** J D Brown, AD (H) NSD, 'The Loss of the Glorious, Ardent and Acasta, 8 June 1940', NHB Portsmouth. **28** Haarr, *Battle for Norway*, Ch 13. **29** Birch, Vol 1 (Part 1), pp85–6: F H Hinsley and Alan Stripp, *Code Breakers: The Inside Story of Bletchley Park* (Oxford University Press, 1993), Ch 10; Sebag-Montefiore, *Enigma*, Ch 12. **30** Goodman, *JIC History*, Vol 1, pp72–7.

Chapter 23 Surviving the Initial German Onslaught in the West
1 David Brown, *The Road to Oran: Anglo-French Naval Relations September 1939–July 1940* (London: Frank Cass, 2004). **2** Dönitz, *Ten Years and Twenty Days*, Ch 8. **3** 'Future Strategy', W.P. 362 of 4 September, CAB 66/11/42, TNA; Horst Boog and others, *Germany and the Second World War*, Vol 6, Table III.iii.i, p348. **4** 'Future Strategy'; Brian Farrell, *The Basis and Making of Grand Strategy – Was there a Plan?* (UK: Edwin Mellen Press, 1998), pp21–3. **5** Godfrey memoirs, Vol 5, 1939–1942, pp119–20, GOD/170, NMM; Beesly, *Very Special Admiral*, p159. **6** Rankin, Ch 5; Andrew Lycett, *Ian Fleming* (London: Weidenfeld & Nicolson, 1995), Ch 4. **7** Hinsley, Vol 1, pp152–4. **8** Morgan, NID History, pp34–7. **9** Balchin, 'United Kingdom Geographers in the Second World War', pp169–71; Godfrey, *Afterthoughts*, pp134–5. **10** McLachlan, *Room 39*, p300. **11** ADM 223/90, TNA; Clout and Gosme, 'The Naval Intelligence Handbooks: a monument in geographical writing'; Hinsley, Vol 1, pp161, 292; Balchin, pp170–1. **12** Hinsley, Vol 1, pp170–6; Morgan, NID History, pp277–8; 'Photographic Reconnaissance by the Royal Air Force in the war of 1939–45', pp217–36. **13** Ibid and Hinsley, pp176–82. **14** Jeffery, *MI6*, pp399–401. **15** Hinsley, p186. **16** Morgan, NID History, pp37–45; OIC Daily Reports, ADM 223/83, TNA; Hinsley, pp184–90: Jeffery, p401. **17** Marcus Faulkner and Christopher Bell, *Decision in the Atlantic: The Allies and the Longest Campaign of the Second World War* (Andarta Books, University of Kentucky, 2019), Ch 7. **18** 'Photographic Reconnaissance by the Royal Air Force in the war of 1939–45', pp237–8, 261, 268–70; OIC Daily Reports, ADM 223/83. **19** Ibid, pp262–3. **20** Morgan, NID History, pp226–7; Hinsley, Vol 1, p332. **21** Captain Thomas Troubridge note, 'Admiral Raeder on Cruiser Warfare', 23 September 1939, Denning papers, DEN 8/2, NMM. **22** Morgan, NID History, p224, 229–30; NRS Vol 137, Ch 25, p218; McLachlan, *Room 39*, pp275–82; S W Roskill, *War at Sea*, Vol 3, *The Offensive*, Part 2 (London: HMSO, 1961), Appendix ZZ. **23** Blair, Vol 1, Appendix 18; NRS Vol 137, Plan 16 (2). **24** NRS Vol 137, Ch 10 and Plan 8; Colpoys, 'Admiralty use of Special Intelligence in Naval Operations', Illustration No 4; Eric Grove, '"The Battle of the Atlantic": A Legend Deconstructed', *MM*, 105:3 (August 2019), pp336–9. **25** Marc Milner, *Battle of the Atlantic* (Stroud: The History Press, 2011), Chs 2 and 3; NRS Vol 137, Appendix 5, Table 11, Plans 7 and 10. **26** NID 003979/40, 'Information Concerning German U-boat Tactics', 9 November

1940, ADM 223/85, TNA. **27** NID1, 27 February 1941, ADM 223/84, TNA; Hinsley, Vol 1, pp333–4. **28** Godfrey memoirs 1939–1942, pp173–7, GOD 170, NMM; Morgan NID History, pp137–57; Hinsley, Vol 2, Appendix 2, Part 1; Beesly, *Very Special Intelligence*, p100. **29** Birch, Vol 1 (Part 1), tables, pp52, 93. **30** VCNS minute, 11 July 1940, ADM 223/286, TNA. **31** Hamilton, OIC, p310–11. **32** 'Admiralty use of Special Intelligence' pp12–13, HW 8/47. **33** Beesly, *Very Special Intelligence*, pp164–5. **34** Ibid, p309–10; NID 004766/42, 'Current Developments in NID', ADM 223/472. **35** McLachlan, Ch 5; Beesly, *Very Special Intelligence*, pp164–72. **36** 'Operation of German Warships winter 1940/1941 up to 18th January', Denning papers, DEN 8/2, NMM. **37** Donald P Steury, 'Naval Intelligence, the Atlantic Campaign and the Sinking of the Bismarck: A Study in the Integration of Intelligence into the Conduct of Naval Warfare', *Journal of Contemporary History*, 22:2 (April 1987), Intelligence Services during the Second World War, 209–233, pp214–22.

Chapter 24 The Atlantic in 1941: A Step-change in Intelligence Capability
1 Alexander, History of German Naval Enigma, Ch 2; Mahon, History of Hut 8, Ch 2c. **2** Z report No 191, 10 September 1940, ADM 223/620. **3** Morgan, NID History, pp263–4. **4** Hinsley, Vol 1, p337 and Mahon, History of Hut 8, Ch 2c state that cipher capture was a priority agreed between GC&CS and NID. For events on the ground, Sebag-Montefiore, *Enigma*, pp132–6. **5** DEFE 3/1, TNA; Mahon, 'History of Hut 8, Ch 2c; Ralph Erskine, 'Naval Enigma: A Missing Link', *International Journal of Intelligence and Counter Intelligence*, 3:4 (1989), 493–508, p497. **6** DEFE 3/1. **7** Ibid; Hinsley, Vol 1, p337 and Appendix 12 (i); Sebag-Montefiore, *Enigma*, Ch 12; Kahn, *Seizing the Enigma*, Ch 12. **8** ADM 223/343, TNA; Hinsley, Vol 1, pp337–8; Hinsley, Vol 2, Appendix 10; Birch, Vol 1 (Part 1), p158; Sebag-Montefiore, Ch 13; Kahn, Ch 13; Beesly, *Very Special Intelligence*, p97 and Erskine's Afterword. **9** DEFE 3/1 and 3/2 TNA; NRS Vol 144, 'Availability of special intelligence', item 1, p29; Kahn, Ch 13. **10** Hinsley, Vol 1, pp337–8 and Appendix 12 (ii); Sebag-Montefiore, Ch 14; Kahn, Ch 14; Birch, Vol 1, p158; Erskine, Afterword in Beesly, *Very Special Intelligence*. **11** Sebag-Montefiore, *Enigma*, pp218–28. **12** Birch, Vol 1 (Part 1), p158; Beesly, *Very Special Intelligence*, pp64–5. **13** Birch, Vol 1 (Part 2) and Vol 2, pp229–30. **14** Morgan, NID History, p281; 'Photographic Reconnaissance by the Royal Air Force in the war of 1939–45', pp261–6. **15** Hinsley, Vol 1, pp279, 281, and Vol 2, pp34–6; Balchin, pp172–3. **16** 'Photographic Reconnaissance by the Royal Air Force in the war of 1939–45', pp262–6. **17** DNI minute, 27 March, and NID1 minute, 16 June 1941, ADM 223/84. **18** NID 003580/41, 13 September 1941, ADM 223/475. **19** Hinsley, Vol 1, pp281–2, and Vol 2, pp36–8; Morgan, NID History, pp282–7. **20** 'Photographic Reconnaissance', ADM 223/84. **21** Morgan, NID History, pp243–4. **22** 'The Story of MI19', Section 2, paragraph (i), WO 208/4970. **23** Godfrey to Vernon Kell, 19 April 1939, KV 4/302, TNA. **24** Godfrey minutes of 18 and 21 July 1939, ADM 1/10579, TNA. **25** Hinsley, Vol 1, pp282–3, and Vol 2, pp32–4; Falko Bell, '"One of our Most Valuable Sources of Intelligence": British Intelligence and the Prisoner of War System in 1944', *Intelligence and National Security*, 31:4 (2016), pp556–78; Kent Fedorowich, 'Axis prisoners of war as sources for British military intelligence, 1939–42', *Intelligence and National Security*, 14:2 (1999), 156–178, pp159–60; Helen Fry, *Spymaster: The Secret Life of Kendrick* (London: Thistle Publishing, 2015). **26** DNI minute, 12 December 1939, and NID Section XIV comment, 9 January 1940, ADM 223/475. **27** Charles Mitchell, 'The German Prisoners of War Interrogation Section in NID during the 1939–45 war', November 1947, and Lieutenant Commander Colin McFadyean, 'Prisoner of War Interrogation 1939–1945', both ADM 223/475, TNA; Lieutenant Commander D B Welbourn RNVR memoir, IWM; Helen Fry, *The London Cage: The Secret History of Britain's World War II Interrogation Centre* (Yale University Press, 2017), pp88–90. **28** Ibid; Hinsley, Vol 2, pp33–4. **29** ADM 186/805 and 186/806, TNA; CSDIC Six Monthly Surveys, WO 208/4970; Welbourn memoir; Hinsley, Vol 2, Appendix 10; Blair, *Hunters*, p586; McLachlan, *Room 39*, Ch 8. **30** Ibid. **31** DNI minute, 1 November 1941, ADM 223/475. **32** Falko Bell, 'One of our most Valuable Sources', pp557–8, 571. **33** NRS Vol 137, Appendix 10, 'Report of Committee on the

Winter Campaign of 1941–1942 in the Battle of the Atlantic, dated 6th May 1941', 'The Tactical Problem', p346. 34 Redgment, 'High Frequency Direction Finding in the Royal Navy: Development of Equipment for use against U-boats, Part 1', ADM 206/189; Erskine, Afterword in Beesly, *Very Special Intelligence*. 35 NRS Vol 137, Appendix 10, p350; Battle of Atlantic Committee meetings, 9 September and 18 November 1941, ADM 205/23, TNA; Redgment, Part 1; Blair, *Hitler's U-boat War, The Hunted 1942–1945* (London: Weidenfeld & Nicolson, 1999), Appendix 8; Derek Howse, *Radar at Sea: The Royal Navy in World War II* (Palgrave Macmillan, 1993), pp142–7; Ralph Erskine, 'High Frequency Direction Finding', in *Military Communications from Ancient Times to the 21st Century*, ed C H Sterling (ABC-CLIO, 2007), pp215–17. 36 Denham war diary, December 1946, ADM 223/489, TNA; Morgan, NID History, pp73–6; C G McKay and Bengt Beckman, *Swedish Signal Intelligence 1900–1945* (London: Routledge, 2014), pp225–8, 238–9; Jeffery, *MI6*, pp376–8. 37 Hart-Davis, *Man of War*, Ch 9; Jeffery, *MI6*, pp402–8. 38 David Stafford, *Churchill and Secret Service* (UK: Overlook Press, 1997), pp236–8; Macintyre, *Operation Mincemeat*, Ch 11. 39 Charles Burdick, '"Moro": The Resupply of German Submarines in Spain, 1939–1942', *Central European History*, 3:3 (1970), pp256–84; Morgan, NID History, pp88, 91–2; Hillgarth to DNI, 13 April 1940, ADM 223/490, TNA. 40 Morgan, NID History, p91. 41 For details of Spanish support to the Axis and a critical view of March, Paul Preston, *A People Betrayed: A History of Corruption, Political Incompetence and Social Division in Modern Spain* (William Collins, 2020), especially Ch 12. 42 Führer Directive No 18 of 12 November 1940, www.ww2db.com; Halder Diaries, Vol 4 Part 2, US Army Archives, Fort Leavenworth. 43 Michael Simpson, 'Force H and British Strategy in the Western Mediterranean 1939–42', *MM*, 83:1 (1997), pp62–7. 44 Gerhard Schreiber and Bernd Stegemann, *Germany and the Second World War: Vol 3: The Mediterranean, South-East Europe and North Africa 1939–1941* (UK English edn: Clarendon Press, 1998), pp145–52, 187–93. 45 Jeffery, *MI6*, pp403–4. 46 Hart-Davis, Ch 9; Macintyre, *Mincemeat*, Ch 11. 47 Morgan, NID History, p87. 48 Mark Simmons, *Ian Fleming and Operation Goldeneye: Spies, Scoundrels and Envoys keeping Spain out of World War II* (Oxford: Casemate Publishing, 2018), Chs 8 and 9. 49 Hinsley, Vol 2, Appendix 15; Ralph Erskine, '"Eavesdropping on 'Bodden'": ISOS v the Abwehr in the straits of Gibraltar', *Intelligence and National Security*, 12:3 (1997), pp110–29.

Chapter 25 The Atlantic in 1941: Intelligence Moves Centre Stage

1 Hinsley, Vol 1, pp340–1; ZTP/619, 1728 21 May, DEFE 3/1, TNA. 2 Insall, *Secret Alliances*, pp24–5, 143–4. The agent most frequently quoted as reporting on *Bismarck* is Viggo Axelsen. Axelsen did work for SOE but was not involved in the *Bismarck* operation. 3 McLachlan, *Room 39*, pp153–4; Hinsley, Vol 1, pp342–5. For Jeschonnek, CX/JQ 993, 26 May, HW 5/16, TNA. 4 Admiral Sir John Tovey despatch on Bismarck operation, 5 July 1941, para 93, ADM 234/509, TNA. 5 Report of the Commander in Chief, Navy, to the Führer on 6 June 1941, at the Berghof, Annex 2, KBismarck.com. 6 ZTP 2701 and 2831, DEFE 3/3, and 2950 and 2963, DEFE 3/4, both TNA. Hinsley, Vol 2, pp164–5. 7 Special Intelligence summary No 2, 11 July 1941, ADM 223/92, TNA; Colpoys, 'Admiralty use of Special Intelligence', pp15–19; Hinsley, Vol 1, pp345–6; Kahn, *Seizing Enigma*, Ch 16. 8 *Proceedings of the Royal Air Force Historical Society*, 10 (1991), pp22–3; Hinsley, Vol 2, p179. 9 Jeffery, *MI6*, p393. 10 Hinsley, Vol 2, p180. 11 Special Intelligence summary no 56, 12 January 1942, ADM 223/92. 12 Colpoys, 'Admiralty use of Special Intelligence', pp84–93; Hinsley, Vol 2, pp181–3. 13 DNI to First Sea Lord, 11 June 1942, ADM 205/14, TNA. 14 Special Intelligence summaries 93 and 94, 12 and 15 February 1942, ADM 223/92; Hinsley, Vol 2, pp183–8, 201. 15 JP 444, 14 June 1941, 'Draft Future Strategy: Review', CAB 79/12, TNA; Blair, *The Hunters*, Appendix 18. 16 Hinsley, Vol 2, pp169–71. 17 Blair, *The Hunters*, pp361–7; NRS Vol 37, Tables 12 (ii) and 13. 18 NRS Vol 137, Table 10 for rise in numbers convoyed between two halves of 1941, and Plans 16 (2) – 16 (5) for pattern of independent losses. 19 NRS Vol 137, Plan 7; Blair, *The Hunters*, p403. 20 NRS Vol 137, Tables 10 and 13 and Plans 7, 16 (2) and 16 (5); Birch, Vol 1 (Part 2) and Vol 2, Diagram no 47. 21 W J R Gardner, *Decoding History: The Battle of the Atlantic and Ultra* (Annapolis: Naval Institute

Press, 2000), pp169–70. **22** OIC U-boat Situation reports for 15 and 22 December, ADM 223/92, TNA. **23** R T Barrett, 'German success against British codes and ciphers', probably 1946–7, ADM 223/469, TNA; Birch, Vol 1 (Part 2) and Vol 2, Diagram no 47. **24** NRS Vol 137, Table 11. **25** Gardner, pp175–7. **26** Birch, Vol 1 (Part 2) and Vol 2, pp209–11. **27** 'U-boat methods of combined attack on convoys from February 1st to October 31st 1941', 10 November 1941, ADM 223/1, TNA; NRS Vol 144, item 18. **28** Boyd, *Royal Navy in Eastern Waters*, pp175–7. **29** DNI minute, 19 July 1940, ADM 223/85. **30** Bailey report, Section VII, ADM 199/1159; Notes of conversation between Captain A G Clarke and Rear Admiral Ghormley and Rear Admiral Ingersoll USN, 31 July 1940, ADM 223/491. Both TNA. **31** Jeffery, *MI6*, pp439–55; Andrew, *For the President's Eyes Only*, p101. **32** Godfrey memoirs 1939–1942, pp128–134, GOD/170, NMM; Jeffery, pp441–3; Andrew, pp93–5. **33** COS (40) 285th Meeting, 29 August 1940, and 289th Meeting, 31 August, CAB 79/6, TNA. For future intelligence relationship, 289th, p9. **34** Ralph Erskine, 'The Holden agreement on naval Sigint: The first BRUSA?', *Intelligence and National Security*, 14:2 (1999), 187–97, p187. **35** Alan Harris Bath, *Tracking the Axis Enemy: The Triumph of Anglo-American Naval Intelligence* (USA: Kansas University Press, 1998), pp34–9; Hinsley, Vol 1, pp312–13. **36** Boyd, *The Royal Navy in Eastern Waters*, pp188–92. For background on Clarke, James R Leutze, *Bargaining for Supremacy: Anglo-American Naval Collaboration, 1937–1941* (USA: University of North Carolina Press, 1977), pp136–8, 186–8, 198–9. **37** Godfrey, 'Methods', pp6–7, ADM 223/475. **38** Goodman, *JIC History*, Vol 1, pp100–1; Bath, pp58–63; Beesly, *Very Special Admiral*, pp180–4. **39** JIC, 17th Meeting 1941, 17 June, CAB 81/88, TNA; Godfrey memoirs 1939–1942, pp133–7; Bath, pp61–4; Robert Louis Benson, *A History of US Communications during World War II: Policy and Administration* (Center for Cryptologic History, US National Security Agency, 1997), p21; Hinsley, Vol 1, p314. **40** NID2 minute, 10 August 1942, ADM 223/491.

Chapter 26 Towards Global War: The Mediterranean 1940–1942

1 McLachlan, *Room 39*, p194, quoting Hoare's memoir. **2** COS (40) 469 of 17 June, 'Military Implications of the Withdrawal of the Eastern Mediterranean Fleet', CAB 80/13, and Director of Plans' paper with naval arguments for withdrawal attached to minutes of Chiefs of Staff 183rd meeting, 17 June 1940, CAB 79/5; COS (40) 521 of 3 July, 'Military Policy in Egypt and the Middle East', CAB 80/14, all TNA. **3** Gabriel Gorodetsky, *Grand Delusion: Stalin and the German Invasion of Russia* (Yale University Press, 1999), pp13, 58–9. **4** Michael Howard, *The Mediterranean Strategy in the Second World War* (London: Greenhill Books, 1993), p10; Harold E Raugh, *Wavell in the Middle East 1939–1941* (London: Brassey's, 1993), pp61–3. **5** Gerhard Schreiber and others, *Germany and the Second World War: Vol 3: The Mediterranean, South-East Europe and North Africa 1939–1941*, Section 3, 'The Strategic Dilemma of the Summer and Autumn of 1940: An Alternative or Interim Strategy?'. **6** *Germany and the Second World War: Vol 3*, p133. **7** *Germany and the Second World War: Vol 3*, pp212–35; German Naval History Series, 'Axis Naval Policy and Operations in the Mediterranean 1939 – 1943', by Vice Admiral Eberhard Weichold, German Admiral in Rome 1940–1943, para 62, ADM 199/2518, TNA. **8** Hinsley, Vol 1, pp198–205. **9** Clarke, History, Ch 6, HW 3/16, TNA; Birch, Vol 1 (Part 1), pp69–71 and (Part 2) and Vol 2, pp5–7, 195–6. **10** Hinsley, Vol 1, pp208–12; Birch, Vol 1 (Part 2) and Vol 2, pp194–5. For SLCs, Jack Greene and Alessandro Massignani, *The Naval War in the Mediterranean 1940–1943* (UK: Chatham Publishing, 2002), pp16–17, 95–6. **11** Tony Spooner, *Warburton's War: The Life of Maverick Ace Adrian Warburton* (Manchester: Crecy Publishing, 2003), Chs 2 and 3; Downing, Ch 8. **12** Hinsley, Vol 1, pp382–6. **13** Boyd, *The Royal Navy in Eastern Waters*, pp136–8. **14** Hinsley, Vol 1, pp396–7. **15** Ibid, pp400–1. **16** Ibid, pp421–7. **17** Bletchley Park magazine, issue no 4, p43. **18** Colpoys, 'Admiralty use of Special Intelligence', pp307–18, HW 8/47; Hinsley, Vol 1, pp404–6; Mavis Batey, *Dilly: The Man who broke Enigmas* (Biteback Publishing, 2017), Ch 9; John Winton, *Cunningham: The Greatest Admiral since Nelson* (London: John Murray, 1998), Chs 9–11. **19** Vincent P O'Hara, *Six Victories: North Africa, Malta, and the Mediterranean Convoy War, November 1941–March 1942* (Annapolis: Naval Institute Press, 2019). **20** Clarke History, Ch 6, HW 3/16; Birch, Part

2 and Vol 2, pp195, 235; Hinsley, Vol 2, pp22, 28.   **21** Colpoys, 'Admiralty use of Special Intelligence', pp319–21, HW 8/47; Hinsley, Vol 1, pp283–7 and Appendix 13.   **22** Colpoys, 'Admiralty use of Special Intelligence', p323; Major General I S O Playfair, *The Mediterranean and Middle East, Vol 2, The Germans Come to the Help of their Ally* (1956), pp58, 280–1; Mark E Stille, 'The Influence of British Operational Intelligence on the War at Sea in the Mediterranean June 1940 – November 1942', Naval War College paper (1994).   **23** Greene and Massignani, Ch 14.   **24** Blair, *Hunters*, pp395–404; NRS Vol 137, Table 21; Hessler, Vol 1, Ch 3.   **25** Hinsley, Vol 2, pp324, 329; O'Hara, *Six Victories*, Ch 6; Winton, *Cunningham*, Ch 16; Richard Ollard, *Fisher and Cunningham: A study of the personalities of the Churchill era* (London: Constable and Company, 1991), p123.   **26** Colpoys, 'Admiralty use of Special Intelligence', Appendix A, p323; HW 8/47.   **27** Hinsley, Vol 2, pp346–50.   **28** Milan Vego, 'Major Convoy Operation to Malta, 10–15 August 1942 (Operation Pedestal)', *US Naval War College Review*, 63:1 (Winter 2010); Greene and Massignani, Ch 19; for R/T intercept, Hinsley, Vol 2, pp194–5.   **29** Hinsley, Vol 2, pp411–12.   **30** Birch, Vol 1 (Part 2) and Vol 2, pp236–8; Hinsley, Vol 2, pp419–25.

Chapter 27   The Far East 1939–1942: An Overlooked Contribution?
1 NID4 minute, 26 August, PREM 3/252/4; JIC (41) 175 of 1 May, CAB 81/101; WIR No 74, 8 August 1941, ADM 223/151; Air Ministry Weekly Intelligence Summary No 120, 17 December 1941, AIR 22/75. All references TNA. For comparison with post-war records, JM 160, Naval Production – Immediate Preparations for War 1940–41, p35 and Chart 6, p37, and S W Roskill, *War at Sea Vol 2, The Period of Balance* (London: HMSO, 1956), Appendix L.   **2** For SIGINT, FECB Intelligence Summary, 31 July 1941, 'D/F and WT Subjects', 'Disposition of Japanese Forces', HW 4/26, TNA.   **3** NID4 quoted 10,000 tons for *Hiryu* and *Soryu*, and 7000 tons for *Ryujo*. True figures, Peattie, *Sunburst*, Appendix 4, were: *Hiryu* 17,300; *Soryu* 15,900; and *Ryujo* 10,600. Official Japanese figure for embarked carrier complement at the outbreak of war in December, JM 160, Chart 6, p37. For cruiser armament, Evans and Peattie, *Kaigun*, Ch 8.   **4** Ismay to prime minister, 7 March 1942, PREM 3/252/3, TNA, and JM 160, Chart 6.   **5** JM 160, Chart 6 and Japanese Monograph 172, Naval Production 1942–44, Chart 4, pp50–1; Peattie, p166.   **6** Hinsley, *British Intelligence*, Vol 1, p75, for pre-war German estimates, and pp227–8 for 1940 estimates.   **7** 'Performance Tables, Japanese Army and Naval Air Services', under Air Ministry (A.I.2.©), 20 May 1941, AIR 40/241, TNA. A.I.2.© also circulated accurate assessments of the three primary IJN carrier aircraft, Zero fighter, Type 97 torpedo bomber, and Type 99 dive-bomber, on 13 December 1941, drawing on data available in the intelligence community including NID for some months, AIR 40/33 and AIR 40/35, both TNA. Details of Zero also in 'Japanese Service Aircraft' issued by the General Staff in India at the time of Pearl Harbor, A D Harvey, 'Army Air Force and Navy Air Force: Japanese Aviation and the opening phase of the war in the Far East', *War in History*, 6:2 (1999), 174–204, p178.   **8** WIS No 120, 17 December.   **9** Type 91 performance data, US Strategic Bombing Survey, Military Analysis Division, Japanese Air Weapons, pp55–6, and operational deployment, USSBS, NAV No 77, Operations of 22nd Air Flotilla in Malaya.   **10** Group Captain Lawrence Darvall, senior Air Staff Officer Far East, informed Commander-in-Chief Air Chief Marshal Sir Robert Brooke-Popham, around September 1941, that Japanese light bombers could carry 1000lbs to 800 miles and heavy bombers 4000lbs to 600–1000 miles, AIR 23/1970, TNA.   **11** WIR No 76, 2 August 1941, ADM 223/151, TNA.   **12** WIR, No 77, 29 August, ADM 223/151, TNA.   **13** Despatch of Air Vice Marshal Sir Paul Maltby on Air Operations in Malaya and NEI 1941–1942, paragraphs 68 and 104, Supplement to London Gazette 26 February 1948, CAB 106/86, TNA.   **14** Commander Hilken review, ADM 116/5757, TNA.   **15** 'Comparison of British and Japanese Fleets', 12 March 1940, CAB 66/6/25, TNA.   **16** FECB Intelligence Summary, 'Japan: Warship Construction Programme', Index No: 911, 1 August 1941, ADM 223/347, TNA. This was shared with DNI.   **17** Japanese figures, JM 160, p35.   **18** First Lord note for prime minister, 16 March 1942, PREM 3/324/14, TNA.   **19** Phillips to Pound and Churchill, 6 February 1940, ADM 205/5, TNA; W.P. (40) 95, 'Comparison of British and Japanese Fleets', 12 March 1940; Data contributing to W.P. (40) 95 in 'British Equivalent to Japanese

Capital Ships', attached to Director of Plans minute, 26 February 1940, ADM 116/5757, TNA; 'Future Strategy', paragraph 25, CAB 66/11/42, TNA. **20** Director of Gunnery and Anti-Aircraft Warfare Division of Naval Staff to First Sea Lord, 13 March 1942, ADM 205/13, TNA; DNI minute, 11 March 1944, 'Comparison of British and Japanese capital ships in South East Asia', ADM 223/495, TNA; Evans and Peattie, pp250–63 and footnote 69, p595. **21** 'Far East Appreciation 1937', p84, CAB 53/31, TNA. **22** DNI minute NID 3515/39 of 19 February 1940, ADM 116/5757, TNA. **23** Admiralty History of Naval Aviation 1919–1945, Vol 2, Appendix 7, ADM 234/374, TNA. **24** Godfrey, 'Afterthoughts', ADM 223/619, TNA. **25** Marder, *Old Friends, New Enemies*, Vol 1, p491, quoting personal letter dated February 1942. **26** Marder, *Old Friends, New Enemies*, Vol 1, p352, quoting letter to Marder in 1976. **27** Cunningham signals to Admiralty, 25 April, 29 April, 27 May, 2 June, and 2 November. Cunningham Papers, ADD MS 52567, British Library. Cunningham's views on the centrality of carriers in modern naval warfare were shared by Somerville at Force H and Admiral Sir John Tovey as Commander-in-Chief Home Fleet. **28** Peattie, pp147–53. **29** Jonathan Parshall and Michael Wenger, 'Pearl Harbour's Overlooked Answer', *Naval History Magazine*, 25:6 (December 2011). **30** For FECB analysis, 'Far East D/F Organisation, Periodical Analysis', 16 October 1941, Part III, Aircraft Carrier squadrons, paragraph 8, HW 4/26. **31** Peattie, pp147–53. **32** Cunningham, *A Sailor's Odyssey*, p396. **33** Davis to Roskill, 16 April 1975, ROSK 4/79, CCA, Cambridge. **34** Commander-in-Chief Eastern Fleet signal 1227z to Admiralty, 13 February 1942, ADM 223/867, TNA. Layton's view was incorporated in WIR No 102 of 20 February, ADM 223/153, TNA, stating that pre-war impressions were confirmed by wartime experience. Also, Marder, *Old Friends, New Enemies*, Vol 2, p45. **35** COS 931, 'Situation in the Far East', paragraph 10, CAB 53/50, TNA; Director of Plans paper, 4 August 1939, 'The Situation if Japan intervened when we are already at war with Germany and Italy', ADM 1/9767, TNA. **36** Evans and Peattie, Ch 11, esp pp401–5. **37** ADM 116/3862, TNA; Marder, *Old Friends, New Enemies*, Vol 1, pp346–52. **38** COS (41) 13th meeting of 8 January 1941 and attached papers, CAB 79/8, TNA. **39** Cunningham, *A Sailor's Odyssey*, pp258–9. **40** James J Sadkovich, 'Understanding Defeat: Reappraising Italy's Role in World War II', *Journal of Contemporary History*, 24:1 (January 1989), pp27–61. **41** Ong Chit Chung, Ch 8, esp pp215–20; John Ferris, '"Consistent with an Intention": The Far East Combined Bureau and the Outbreak of the Pacific War, 1940–41, *Intelligence and National Security*, 27:1 (February 2012), pp5–26; Marder, *Old Friends, New Enemies*, Vol 1, pp355–62. **42** Beesly, *Very Special Admiral*, pp202–3. Relevant SIS reporting was passed to FECB but the JIC recommended in May 1941 that an SIS representative 'should become a member'. Minutes of 14th JIC Meeting 1941, CAB 81/88, TNA. **43** Birch, Vol 1 (Part 2) and Vol 2, pp34–5. **44** Draft history of FECB, pp7–9, HW 50/88, TNA; Donovan and Mack, Ch 9; Frederick D Parker, *Pearl Harbor Revisited: US Navy Communications Intelligence 1924–1941*, pp22–3; Captain Duane L Whitlock, 'The Silent War against the Japanese Navy', *US Naval War College Review*, 48: 4 (Autumn 1995). All official British (and American) records seem clear that there was no operational intelligence, ie full decryption of key signals, before the end of 1941. **45** Birch, Vol 1 (Part 2) and Vol 2, pp34–6. **46** Straczek, p114; Ferris, 'The Far East Combined Bureau and the Pacific War', pp15–16. Pfennigwerth, pp140–1, also has a description of RFP. **47** Lieutenant Commander E P G Sandwith, who joined FECB in August 1941, was critical of D/F, claiming bearings were often inaccurate and call-sign identification out of date. Monograph, 'Loss of Singapore, February 1942 and its Lessons for NID', p3, Godfrey papers, GOD/92, NMM. Also, paper for Marder by Lieutenant Commander S W Francis, May 1979, Marder Papers, MS-F02, Special Collections and Archives, University of California Irvine Libraries, Irvine, California. **48** Donovan and Mack, pp52, 96–7. **49** Birch, Vol 1 (Part 2) and Vol 2, pp35–8; GCHQ's post-war assessment of 'war warning' intelligence, HW 50/52, TNA; Benson, *US Communications during World War II*, p19, drawing on NSA records; David Sherman, 'The First Americans: The 1941 US Codebreaking Visit to Bletchley Park', National Security Agency Center for Cryptologic History (2016); Michael Smith, *Emperor's Codes*, Ch 6; Stephen Budiansky, 'Bletchley Park and the Birth of a Very Special Relationship', in Erskine and Smith, *Bletchley Park Codebreakers*. **50** Smith, *Emperor's Codes*, pp86–8; Hastings,

The Secret War, Ch 15, Part 2; Alan Stripp, *Codebreaker in the Far East* (OUP, 1995), pp86–8; Boyd, *Hitler's Japanese Confidant*, pp48–50, 54–6. **51** Magic intercepts during 1941 in five volume 'Magic Background of Pearl Harbor' published by US Department of Defence in 1978. British intercepts of Japanese Purple messages from July to December 1941, HW 12/266–HW 12/271, TNA. **52** HW/1, TNA. **53** HW 50/52, TNA. **54** Benson, *US Communications during World War II*, p20. **55** Ralph Erskine, 'When a Purple Machine went missing: How Japan nearly discovered America's greatest secret', *Intelligence and National Security*, 12:3 (1997), pp185–9; Straczek, p259; Smith, *Emperor's Codes*, pp105–6. **56** Post-war GCHQ summary of 'war warning' intelligence, HW 50/52, TNA; NID Vol 42, 'Far East and Pacific III, Special Collaboration of British and US Radio Intelligence', ADM 223/297, TNA; 'History of Far East Sigint', HW 4/25; Burnett letter to GC&CS, 19 January 1943, providing history of British-US collaboration on Japan, ADM 223/496, TNA; Donovan and Mack, pp58–64, and Ch 9.14; Birch, Vol 1 (Part 2) and Vol 2, p39; Erskine and Smith, *Bletchley Park Codebreakers*, Chs 8, 10 and 13, Table 10.1; Smith, *Emperor's Codes*, p80; Parker, *Pearl Harbor Revisited*, pp37–8; Benson, *US Communications during World War II*, pp4, 7, 20. **57** Donovan and Mack, p44. **58** Craigie 2017 to FO of 17 October, FO 371/27964, TNA; Jeffery, *MI6*, pp262–6; Ralph Lee Defalco III, 'Blind to the Sun: US Intelligence Failures Before the War with Japan', *International Journal of Intelligence and Counter-Intelligence*, 16:1 (2003), pp95–107. **59** FECB Intelligence Summary No 1822, 'Warning of attack by Japan', December 1940, WO 208/888, TNA. **60** FECB 1822, p4. **61** JIC (41) 175 of 1 May, 'Japan's Future Strategy'. **62** AIR 23/1865, TNA. **63** JM 107, Malaya Invasion Naval Operations, Office of US Military History, p6. **64** August comments, AIR 23/1865, TNA. **65** Commander-in-Chief Far East to Air Ministry for Chiefs of Staff, 6 January 1941, WO 193/920, TNA. **66** War Office to Commander-in-Chief Far East of 7 June 1941, WO 193/607, TNA. **67** For Meiklereid, Martin Thomas, 'Disaster Foreseen? France and the Fall of Singapore', in *Sixty Years On: The Fall of Singapore Revisited*, ed Brian Farrell and Sandy Hunter (Singapore: Eastern Universities Press, 2003), p83. For examples of his reporting: Ong Chit Chung, *Operation Matador*, pp219, 224, 227, 229. For intelligence from Sectude, Jeffery, *MI6*, pp574–5. SIS claimed in March 1942 to have issued twenty-one reports on Japan's 'preparations for southward move' during the week 30 November – 7 December alone. **68** WIR No 81 of 26 September, ADM 223/151, TNA. **69** NID4 report, 7 October 1941, 'Disposition of Japanese Fleet', FO 371/27964, TNA; ADM 223/152, TNA. **70** MEW produced weekly reports on Japanese Shipping Intelligence under reference T 33/57/Z. Examples in FO 371/27964. Ferris, 'Consistent with Intention', p25, drawing on FECB sources, states that FECB traffic analysis showed that, by early November, all Japanese merchant traffic had withdrawn northward, suggesting danger at the end of the month. This triggered air searches which found the Japanese invasion convoys. Although FECB contributed to shipping intelligence, the process was directed by MEW and drew on many other sources, eg Lloyd's. MEW reports were circulated to the Foreign Office, Admiralty and Ministry of War Transport. **71** NID4 Note 4/20, 8 October, FO 371/27964. **72** Whitlock, 'The Silent War against the Japanese Navy'. **73** Douglas Ford, 'Climbing the Learning Curve: British Intelligence on Japanese Strategy and Military Capabilities during the Second World War in Asia and the Pacific, July 1937 to August 1945' (unpublished doctoral thesis, London School of Economics and Political Science, 2002), Ch 1, is less positive on British assessment of these warning indicators. Also Ferris, 'Consistent with Intention', compared with Ong Chit Chung, *Operation Matador*, Ch 8. The latter emphasises the range and diversity of inputs feeding the intelligence picture through October and November. By end October it was clear something was probable in the southern theatre but definitive warning signs only triggered in the last half of November. The British system did well picking these up. WO 208/1080, TNA, has representative reports at this time, including American sources via BAD. **74** NID 4/23 – 'Naval Situation in the Far East: Situation up to 1 December', WO 208/1080, TNA, and Hillgarth and Barrett memorandum, 'History of the Far East and Pacific War', 'Pearl Harbor and the Loss of Prince of Wales and Repulse', ADM 223/494, TNA. For composition of the Southern Force, Roskill, *War at Sea*, Vol 2, Appendix L. **75** For American input, Smith, *Emperor's Codes*, p96. **76** GC&CS report 095151, HW 12/270, TNA. **77** GC&CS report 098127, HW 12/270 and NID 00429 of 25 November,

ADM 223/321, both TNA. **78** Robert J Hanyok and David P Mowry, 'West Wind Clear: Cryptology and the Winds Message Controversy – A Documentary History', Center for Cryptologic History (US National Security Agency, 2008), pp23–5. **79** GCHQ post-war official history of HMS *Anderson*, HW 50/52, TNA. **80** Caesar 560 from Joint Military Staff in Washington of 28 November, CAB 122/73, TNA. **81** AT to Commander-in-Chief China, 29 November, ADM 199/1477, TNA. **82** GC&CS report 098017, 22 November 1941. A second intercept, 098052, issued the following day. HW 12/270, TNA. Also NID report 00421 of 23 November, ADM 223/321, TNA. For deterrence, First Sea Lord minute to Prime Minister, 18 November, ADM 205/10, TNA. **83** JM 107, p2, has 225. **84** Ong Chit Chung, p229, for more detail on British estimates and sources. **85** Chappell letters to Harkness (COIS Singapore), 14 October 1978, and Marder, 6 December 1978, Marder papers. **86** Jeffery, *MI6*, pp576–7; Henry C Clausen, *Pearl Harbor: Final Judgement* (USA: Da Capo Press, 2001), pp113–14. **87** Donovan and Mack, p85. **88** For other perspectives, Ford, 'Climbing the Learning Curve', Ch 1; Ferris, 'Consistent with an Intention', p26; Richard Aldrich, *Intelligence and the War against Japan: Britain, America, and the Politics of Secret Service* (Cambridge University Press, 2000), Ch 4. **89** Boyd, *The Royal Navy in Eastern Waters*, Ch 7. **90** For the issues raised in this paragraph, Boyd, *The Royal Navy in Eastern Waters*, Ch 7. For FECB plain-language intercept, Birch, Vol 1 (Part 2) and Vol 2, p40. **91** Burnett letter to GC&CS, 19 January 1943, ADM 223/496. **92** Birch, Vol 1 (Part 2) and Vol 2, p40–2; History of HMS *Anderson*, Ch 4, p5, HW 4/25, and 'Organisation and Evolution of Japanese Naval Sigint Part VI, Production and Use of Sigint in the Early Part of the War, December 1941–1942', p6, HW 50/59, both TNA. Also, Smith, *Emperor's Codes*, pp104–5; Frederick Parker, *A Priceless Advantage: US Navy Communications and the Battles of Coral Sea, Midway and the Aleutians* (Center for Cryptologic History, US Navy Security Agency, 1993), p20; Prados, *Combined Fleet Decoded*, p215. **93** 'Organisation and Evolution of Japanese Naval Sigint Part VI', HW 50/59, TNA; Birch, Vol 1 (Part 2) and Vol 2, p41; Straczek, p283. **94** NRS Vol 134, The Somerville Papers, 'Pocket Diary, 1942', 29 March 1942, item 229 (Scolar Press, 1995); NID L.C. Report No 136 of 1 March 1942, ADM 205/13, WIRs No 105 of 13 March and 106 of 20 March, ADM 223/153, JIC (42) 70 (O) of 3 March, 'Defence of Ceylon', CAB 79/19, all TNA; Prados, p274; Parker, *A Priceless Advantage*, p12; John B Lundstrom, *The First South Pacific Campaign* (Annapolis, USA: Naval Institute Press, 2014), Ch 9. **95** JM 113, p65, for breakdown of the IJN force; Blog in website www.combinedfleet.com, 'Operation C' under 'Battles' forum, initiated 1 December 2008 by Rob Stuart, quoting Japanese Carrier Group records, provides air group total of 273 plus carrier allocations. **96** Commander-in-Chief Eastern Fleet Zymotic signal 0626Z (probably 1226 Ceylon time) to Admiralty, 29 March 1941, ADM 223/867, TNA. 'Zymotic' indicated sensitive SIGINT material. **97** JM 113, p64 and 68; Discussion between Cabinet Office and Japanese historians, Tokyo September 1966, 'Ceylon', CAB 106/180, TNA. **98** Boyd, *The Royal Navy in Eastern Waters*, Ch 8. **99** Birch, Vol 1 (Part 2) and Vol 2, pp41–2. **100** Nave returned to Australia in May 1940 to head a new Australian SIGINT organisation, the Special Intelligence Bureau. Straczek, pp186–7, 206–19; Pfennigwerth, *Man of Intelligence*, Ch 8. **101** NID report 00866A, 19 April 1942, drawing on JN25B intercepts, ADM 223/322, TNA; WIRs 111 of 24 April, 112 of 1 May, 113 of 8 May and 116 of 29 May, all ADM 223/154, TNA; Smith, *Emperor's Codes*, Ch 11. **102** C-in-C Eastern Fleet Zymotic, 20 May, ADM 223/867, TNA. **103** NID 00976, 2 June 1942, ADM 223/322, TNA; Smith, *Emperor's Codes*, Ch 11. **104** Birch Vol 1 (Part 2) and Vol 2, Ch 18. **105** Patrick Beesly, Godfrey's biographer, refuted Godfrey's negative assessment of intelligence on the IJN, *Very Special Admiral*, pp201–4. Goodman, *JIC History*, Vol 1, p106, states that, when reviewing JIC reporting during 1941, Godfrey concluded that 'the War Cabinet and Chiefs of Staff were fully and accurately advised as to Japanese intentions and preparations'. This is sourced to NID paper 'JIC Appreciations in 1941 of Japanese Intentions' in ADM 223/494, which does indeed reach this judgement, endorsing the separate assessment conducted in early 1942 by DMI. However, this paper was written post-war by Captain Alan Hillgarth in 1945–46 when Godfrey was long gone. It did not necessarily reflect Godfrey's personal assessment, with no certainty he even saw it. **106** Vice Admiral Sir Geoffrey Layton, 'Remarks on the operations in Malaya and the Defence of Singapore', ADM 199/1472A,

TNA. **107** 'Some Personal Reflections on the Malayan Campaign July 1941–January 1942', CAB 106/193, TNA. **108** JP (42) 537, 30 May 1942, 'Appreciation of the War Against Japan', CAB 79/21, TNA; JIC (42) 231, 15 June 1942, 'Japanese Air Situation', CAB 79/21, TNA. For official Japanese production data, JM 172 and for aircraft loss figures, NAV No 50, USSBS No 202. **109** H P Willmott, *Empires in the Balance*, pp82–3, and *The Second World War in the Far East* (London: Cassell, 1999), p71. Osamu Tagaya, *Imperial Japanese Aviator* (Osprey, 2003), takes a similar view of the air communications; Alan Zimm, *The Attack on Pearl Harbor*, Ch 4.

Chapter 28 The Atlantic in the Balance 1942–1943

1 Beesly, *Very Special Intelligence*, p101; Hamilton, 'The Admiralty OIC', Section I. **2** Hinsley, Vol 2, Appendix 19; Birch, Vol 1 (Part 2) and Vol 2, pp191–4, and Diagram 45; Sebag-Montefiore, *Enigma*, Ch 20. **3** Hinsley, Vol 2, pp230–2. **4** NRS Vol 137, Table 13; Blair, *The Hunters*, Appendix 18; www.uboat.net, monthly statistics. **5** Boyd, *The Royal Navy in Eastern Waters*, p361. **6** NRS Vol 139, *The Battle of the Atlantic and Signals Intelligence: U-boat Situations and Trends, 1941–1945*, ed David Syrett (Ashgate, 1998), U-boat Situation reports, items 1–6. **7** Blair, *The Hunters*, pp521–7, 691–4. **8** Barrett, 'German success against British codes and ciphers', ADM 223/469. **9** Budiansky, 'Bletchley Park and the Birth of a Very Special Relationship'; Sebag-Montefiore, *Enigma*, Ch 20. **10** NRS Vol 144, 'DNI to Captain Edward Hastings', 23 January 1942, item 22, p77. **11** NRS Vol 139, U-boat Situation reports December 1941 to June 1942, items 1–28. **12** Hinsley, Vol 2, p229. **13** Blair, *The Hunters*, pp693–4. **14** JIC (41) 40th meeting, 30 November 1941, item 2, CAB 81/88, TNA. **15** Hinsley, Vol 2, pp55–6. **16** Birch, Vol 1 (Part 2) and Vol 2, pp261–2. **17** NRS Vol 144, 'Final report: British-Canadian-American radio intelligence discussions, Washington DC', 6–17 April 1942, item 27; Hinsley, Vol 2, p56; Bath, pp75–6; Birch, Vol 1 (Part 2) and Vol 2, p261; Blair, *The Hunters*, pp556–7. **18** NRS, Vol 144, 'Commander Rodger Winn's report on a visit to Washington', 3 June 1942, item 28; Beesly, *Very Special Intelligence*, pp107–10; Bath, pp76–8. **19** Smith, *Emperor's Codes*, pp124–5. **20** Erskine and Freeman, 'Brigadier John Tiltman', p308; Clabby, 'Brigadier John Tiltman', pp35–40. **21** C-in-C Eastern Fleet letter, 28 August 1942, ADM 223/496, TNA; Birch, Vol 1 (Part 2) and Vol 2, pp262–4. **22** Bradley F Smith, *The Ultra-Magic Deals and the Most Secret Special Relationship 1940–1946* (UK: Airlife Publishing, 1993), pp127–9. **23** 'Remarks by Burnett on his visits to London and Washington in connection with Japanese special intelligence', 7 April 1943, ADM 223/496. **24** Erskine, 'The Holden agreement on naval sigint', including appendix with Holden text; Birch, Vol 1 (Part 2) and Vol 2, pp263–4. **25** Rushbrooke to Somerville, 31 January 1943, and Burnett letter to GC&CS, 19 January 1943, both ADM 223/496. **26** Ralph Erskine, 'The 1944 Naval BRUSA Agreement and its Aftermath', *Cryptologia*, 30:1 (2006), pp1–22; Smith, *Emperor's Codes*, pp147–56. **27** Erskine, Afterword in Beesly, *Very Special Intelligence*; Budiansky, 'Bletchley Park and the Birth of a Very Special Relationship'; Hinsley, Vol 2, p57 and fn p752; Kahn, *Seizing the Enigma*, Ch 19. **28** Blair, *The Hunters*, Appendix 2, 3 and 4; and *The Hunted*, pp47–9 and 134–5, Plate 1, Appendix 2,3, 4, 5 and 6; NRS Vol 137, Table 13; First Lord note to prime minister, 10 February 1943, ADM 205/27, TNA. **29** Birch, Vol 1 (Part 2) and Vol 2, p252. **30** 'Operational Research in War', 29 October 1945, and 'The Origins of Operational Research in the Armed Forces of the United Kingdom', undated but mid 1941, both ADM 219/629, TNA. **31** 'Notes for Lecture on Science and the U-boat War', DNOR May 1943, ADM 219/629; M W Kirby, *Operational Research in War and Peace: The British Experience from the 1930s to the 1970s* (London: Imperial College Press, 2003), pp111–15. **32** For 'operational research', 'Notes for Lecture on Science and the U-boat War', DNOR May 1943, ADM 219/629; For average escort strength, NRS Vol 137, Table 11. For HF/DF capability, Howse, *Radar at Sea* pp142–7; for HF/DF examples, Blair, *The Hunters*, pp655, 662–3, 667, and *The Hunted*, pp42, 130–1. For the overall impact of HF/DF, Jurgen Rohwer, *Critical Convoy Battles of WWII: Crisis in the North Atlantic, March 1943* (Stackpole edn, 2015), Chs 3 and 14. **33** Dönitz, *Ten Years and Twenty Days*, Ch 18. **34** Roskill, *War at Sea*, Vol 2, Ch 14; Jonathan Dimbleby, *The Battle of the Atlantic: How the Allies Won the War* (Penguin, 2015), Ch 19. **35** NRS Vol 139, U-boat Situation, Week ending 5/7/43. **36** Blair,

The Hunted, pp48, 135, 169, Plate 13 and Appendix 2. **37** Hinsley, Vol 2, p549. **38** David Syrett, 'On the Threshold of Victory: Communications Intelligence and the Battle for Convoy HX-228, 7–12 March 1943', *Northern Mariner*, 3 (July 2000), pp49–55. **39** This paragraph also draws on Gardner, *Decoding History*, Ch 9. It dissents from Hinsley, Vol 2, pp548–9. Lord Cherwell's note to the prime minister, 24 July 1943, is in ADM 205/27, TNA. **40** NRS Vol 139, weekly U-boat situation reports; Hinsley, Vol 2, pp551–6, 570–1 and Appendix 19; Colpoys, Ch 15. **41** Blair, *The Hunted*, Appendix 3. **42** Gardner, *Decoding History*, Table 9.2, p187. **43** Romney B Duffey, 'Submarine warfare and intelligence in the Atlantic and Pacific in the Second World War: comparisons and lessons learned for two opponents', *Journal for Maritime Research*, 19:2 (2017), pp143–67. **44** NRS Vol 139, Introduction, xxiv. **45** Rohwer, *Critical Convoy Battles*, Ch 14. **46** NRS Vol 139, U-boat Situation, week ending 24/5/43. **47** NID UC reports 318. 2 April 1943, and 361, 10 August 1943, ADM 223/120. **48** ZTPGU/14191 of 24/5/43, ZTPGU/14246 of 26/5/43, and ZTPGU/14382 of 6/6/43, all DEFE 3/719, TNA. **49** Beesly, *Very Special Intelligence*, pp183–4.

Chapter 29 Strategic Pivots: Norway and North Africa 1942–1943

1 OIC SI/96, 16 February 1942, ADM 223/92, and OIC SI/110, 3 March 1942, ADM 223/93, both TNA; Hinsley, Vol 2, pp199–201; Blair, *The Hunters*, Appendix 5. **2** Ibid. **3** Colpoys, Ch 10, HW 8/47; Roskill, *The War at Sea*, Vol 3, Part 3, Appendix R; T H Vail Motter, *US Official History of the US Army in World War II, The Middle East Theatre, The Persian Corridor and Aid to Russia* (US Army Center of Military History, Library of Congress, 1952), Appendix A. For further comment on aid to Russia and its significance and the impact of the different routes, Boyd, *The Royal Navy in Eastern Waters*, pp362–3, 485. **4** Joseph Francis Ryan, 'The Royal Navy and Soviet Seapower, 1930–1950: Intelligence, Naval Co-operation and Antagonism' (unpublished doctoral thesis, University of Hull, 1996), Chs 11 and 12. **5** Colpoys, Ch 10. **6** NRS Vol 139, U-boat Situation Reports, 4/5/42, 29/6/42, 14/9/42 and 25/1/43; Blair, *The Hunters*, Appendix 5 and *The Hunted*, Appendix 6; Hinsley, Vol 2, pp203–4. **7** Hinsley, Vol 2, p204. **8** Colpoys, pp123–8; Hinsley, Vol 2, pp205–10, 213; Beesly, *Very Special Intelligence*, pp128–30. **9** Beesly, *Very Special Intelligence*, p130. **10** Insall, *Secret Alliances*, Ch 8. For Rørholt, Godfrey minute on 'C' recommendation, 30 May 1942, ADM 223/475, TNA. **11** Morgan, NID History, pp77–81; Beesly, *Very Special Intelligence*, pp131–2; Hinsley, Vol 2, p213. For special intelligence on German air strength in Norway, SI 170, 26 April 1942, ADM 223/93. **12** Pound note for First Lord, 10 July 1942, ADM 205/14. **13** Roskill, *The War at Sea*, Vol 2, Ch 5; Hinsley, Vol 2, pp214–23 and list of Ultra signals Appendix 11; Patrick Beesly, 'Convoy PQ 17: A study of intelligence and decision-making', *Intelligence and National Security*, 5:2 (1990), pp292–322; Milan Vego, 'The Destruction of Convoy PQ 17, 27 June–10 July 1942', *US Naval War College Review*, 69:3 (Summer 2016); Robin Brodhurst, *Churchill's Anchor: The Biography of Admiral of the Fleet Sir Dudley Pound OM, GCB, GCVO* (UK: Leo Cooper, 2000), Ch 14. David Irving's *The Destruction of Convoy PQ 17*, first published by Cassell & Co in 1968, is controversial and was subject to a famous libel action in 1970. Successive editions up to 2005 incorporated intelligence material, especially Ultra, not previously accessible. Irving interviewed many key participants, so it contains much information not available elsewhere. **14** Colpoys, pp129–34. **15** O'Hara, *Six Victories*, pp250–4. **16** Correlli Barnett, *Engage the Enemy More Closely* (London: Hodder and Stoughton, 1991), pp722–8; Hinsley, Vol 2, pp225–6. For Polyarno SIGINT, R T Barrett, 'USSR Y Collaboration: A Solitary Success', probably 1946–47, ADM 223/496, TNA. **17** Colpoys, p136. **18** SI 433, 19 November 1942, SI448, 30 November 1942, and SI 459, 10 December 1942, ADM 223/470, TNA. **19** Hinsley, Vol 2, pp528–9; Colpoys, pp137–8. **20** NID UC Report 292, 31 January 1943, ADM 223/120, TNA. **21** Denning, 'The Future Use of German Heavy Surface Craft', 22 February, 1943, Denning papers, DENN 8/2, NMM; and reply to prime minister's M 141/3, 'Significance of recent German naval changes in high personnel', ADM 205/27, TNA. For *Graf Zeppelin*, NID UC Report 293, 4 February 1943, ADM 223/120. **22** For an account of Operation Source, Patrick Bishop, *Target Tirpitz: X-craft, Agents and Dambusters – The Epic Quest to destroy Hitler's Mightiest Warship* (Harper Press, 2012), Chs 13–15. For intelligence background: Hinsley, Vol 3 Part 1, pp258–62; Insall, *Secret Alliances*, Ch 11. For intelligence on the damage: NID 405, 'German Battleship "Tirpitz"', 8 December 1943, and NID 893, 'Midget Attack on Tirpitz', 6 February 1944, and NID monograph 'Tirpitz', all in ADM 223/470. 23 Beesly, *Very Special Intelligence*, pp208, 210. 24 Insall, p227. 25 Colpoys, Ch 8; Hinsley, Vol 3, Part 1, pp262–9 and Appendix 14; Barnett, *Engage the Enemy More Closely*, pp739–44. 26 Williamson Murray, *The Luftwaffe 1933–1945: Strategy for Defeat* (London: Brassey's, 1996), pp159–66 and Tables 30 and 31; Joel S A Hayward, *Stopped at Stalingrad: The Luftwaffe and Hitler's Defeat in the East 1942–1943* (University Press of Kansas, 1998). 27 Hinsley, Vol 2, Ch 24. 28 Ibid; JIC (42) 304 (0) (Final), 7 August 1942, CAB 81/109, TNA. 29 NRS Vol 139, U-boat Trends, week ending 28/9/42, item 41. 30 Beesly, *Very Special Intelligence*, p149. 31 NRS Vol 139, U-boat Trends, week ending 12/10/42, item 43. 32 Hinsley, Vol 2, p476. 33 Roskill, *War at Sea*, Vol 2, p317. 34 NRS Vol 139, U-boat Trends, Weeks ending 12/10/42, 26/10/42 and 2/11/42, items 43, 45 and 46. Roskill, *War at Sea*, Vol 2, Ch 13; Hinsley, Vol 2, pp476–8. 35 Blair, *The Hunted*, pp88–117. 36 Erskine, 'Eavesdropping on "Bodden"' pp118–21. 37 Hinsley, Vol 2, pp475–82. 38 Blair, *The Hunted*, pp88–117. 39 Director of Plans note, 10 February 1943, covering papers by Director of Trade Division and Director of Anti-Submarine Warfare, ADM 223/470. 40 C W R Lamplough NID letter, 13 December 1941, and note 'Geographic handbooks and inter-service topographical department', both ADM 223/90; Hinsley, Vol 2, pp482–3. 41 NID 004766/42, 'Current Developments in NID', 12 September 1942, ADM 223/472, TNA. 42 Fleming minute, 20 March 1942, and '30 Assault Unit – Brief history, results obtained and proposals for future organisation', ADM 223/500, TNA. 43 Hinsley, Vol 2, Appendix 13, p704; Nicholas Rankin, *Ian Fleming's Commandos: The Story of 30 Assault Unit in WWII* (London: Faber & Faber, 2011), Ch 1. 44 David O'Keefe, *One Day in August: The Untold Story Behind Canada's Tragedy at Dieppe* (Knopf Canada, 2013). 45 Hinsley, Vol 3, Part 1, pp468–9; Rankin, Ch 8. 46 Pound minutes to First Lord and DNI, both 16 September 1942, ADM 205/20, TNA. 47 Beesly, *Very Special Admiral*, pp225, 230, quoting Cavendish-Bentinck; Godfrey memoirs, Vol 5, p102, GOD/170, NMM. 48 Godfrey memoirs, Vol 5, p102. 49 NID Monograph no 1, 'Joint Intelligence Committee and Joint Intelligence Staff', Godfrey papers, GOD/69, NMM; Godfrey memoirs, Vol V, pp106–8, and Vol VIII, pp162–3, GOD/170 and GOD/175, NMM. Beesly, *Very Special Admiral*, pp232–3. 50 Andrew Roberts, *Masters and Commanders: The Military Geniuses who led the West to Victory in World War II* (London: Allen Lane, 2008), Chs 7–10; Hinsley, Vol 2, pp93–104. 51 Beesly, *Very Special Admiral*, Ch 11. 52 Personal record, ADM 196/55/188, TNA. 53 Rankin, pp141–2.

Chapter 30 Underpinning Victory in Europe 1944–1945

1 Hinsley, Vol 3, Part 1, p221. 2 ZTPGU/16880 issued 13/9/43, ZTPGU/16990 issued 20/9/43 and ZTPGU/16961 issued 20/9/43, DEFE 3/721, TNA. 3 Blair, *The Hunted*, pp420–6; Hinsley, Vol 3, Part 1, pp222–3. 4 Hinsley, Vol 3, Part 1, pp337–442. 5 Ibid, p340 and Appendix 1, Part B. 6 Goodman, *JIC History*, Vol 1, p135; Hinsley, Vol 3, Part 1, pp46–8 and 411 fn. 7 Hinsley, Vol 3, Part 1, p341. 8 Ibid, p240; NRS Vol 139, U-boat Situation, 4/10/43. 9 NID UC reports 401, 29 November 1943, and 413, 5 January 1944, ADM 223/120; Hinsley, Vol 3, Part 1, pp240–3. 10 Donald B Welbourn and Tim Crichton, 'The Schnorchel: A Short-Lived Engineering Solution to Scientific Developments', *Transactions of the Newcomen Society*, 78:2 (2008), p295. 11 NID UC report 432, 24 February 1944, ADM 223/120. 12 NID UC report 427, 15 February 1944, ADM 223/120. 13 NID UC report 450, 15 March 1944, ADM 223/120; Hinsley, Vol 3, Part 1, pp240–3. 14 NRS Vol 144, 'Underwater internal combustion propulsion in U-boats', 3 February 1944, item 118, and 'Memorandum by Commander Kenneth A Knowles', 3 March 1944, item 121. 15 Blair, *The Hunted*, pp10–12; Hinsley, Vol 3, Part 1, p239. 16 Walter letter to Dönitz, 19 May 1943, reproduced in Welbourn and Crichton, 'The Schnorchel', pp297–8. 17 NID UC report 472, 1 May 1944, ADM 223/120; Hinsley, Vol 3, Part 1, pp243–5. 18 Smith, *Emperor's Codes*, pp218–20; Prados, *Combined Fleet Decoded*, p439; Hinsley, Vol 3, Part 1, p341; Naval Section Historical Memorandum No A.I.b. (4), Japanese Naval Attaché Machine Party (Translation), probably 1945–46, HW 8/52, TNA. 19 NID12 SI/Tech/001, 17 April

1944, and SI/Tech/002, 18 May 1944, both ADM 223/43, TNA; NRS Vol 144, 'New Types of German U-boats', 18 May 1944, item 129; Hinsley, Vol 3, Part 1, p244. 20 NID12 SI/Tech/003, 30 May 1944, SI/Tech/004, 23 August 1944, and SI/Tech/005, 8 October 1944, all ADM 223/43; NID UC report 495, 7 June 1944; Hinsley, Vol 3, Part 1, pp244–5 and Appendix 11. 21 DTM note, 8 January 1945, ADM 223/632, TNA. 22 David Kenyon, *Bletchley Park and D-Day: The Untold Story of How the Battle for Normandy Was Won* (Newhaven USA and London: Yale University Press, 2019), Ch 2. 23 Hinsley, Vol 3, Part 1, pp272–6 and Appendix 13; Insall, *Secret Alliances*, pp321–6 and Appendix. 24 Hinsley, Vol 3, Part 2, Chs 43 and 44; Barnett, *Engage the Enemy More Closely*, Chs 24 and 25. 25 'Operation Neptune: The part taken by NID', ADM 223/287, TNA. 26 Hinsley, Vol 3, Part 2, pp10–14 and Appendix 2. 27 Ibid, p18 and fn and Appendix 5. 28 Ibid, pp58–9 and Appendices 7 and 8; Boyd, *Hitler's Japanese Confidant*, pp120–5; Smith, *Emperor's Codes*, pp224–5. 29 'The Use of Special Intelligence in connection with Operation Neptune, January 1944 – September 1944', ADM 223/287; Hinsley, Vol 3, Part 2, pp91–4. 30 Hinsley, Vol 3, Part 2, pp165–8. 31 'Use of Special Intelligence in connection with Operation Neptune', ADM 223/287; Hinsley, Vol 3, Part 2, pp56 and 162–5. 32 Barnett, pp830–1. 33 NRS Vol 139, U-boat situation reports, 3/1/44, 28/2/44, 10/4/44 and 24/4/44; Hinsley, Vol 3, Part 2, pp95–7; Beesly, *Very Special Intelligence*, pp240–1. 34 NRS Vol 139, U-boat situation report, 15/5/44; Blair, *The Hunted*, pp589–96. 35 NRS Vol 139, U-boat situation reports, 22/5/44 and 5/6/44; Hinsley, Vol 3, Part 2, pp97–9; Milner, *Battle of the Atlantic*, Ch 8. For true figure of U-boats in Biscay bases on 4 June, Blair, *The Hunted*, Plate 9. 36 NRS Vol 139, U-boat situation report, 5/6/44; Blair, *The Hunted*, p574. 37 NRS Vol 139, U-boat situation report, 12/6/44. 38 NRS Vol 139, U-boat situation, 19/6/44 and 26/6/44; Blair, *The Hunted*, pp579–92; Milner, Ch 8; Hinsley, Vol 3, Part 2, p156. 39 Ibid, pp474–87. 40 '30 Assault Unit – Brief history, results obtained and proposals for future organisation', ADM 223/500; Hinsley, Vol 3, Part 1, pp468–70. 41 Rankin, Chs 12–14. 42 Ibid; David Kohnen, 'Seizing German Naval Intelligence from the Archives 1870–1945', *Global War Studies*: 12:1 (2015), pp133–71; Peter Hennessy and James Jinks, *The Silent Deep: The Royal Navy Submarine Service since 1945* (London: Allen Lane, 2015), pp50–2.

Chapter 31 Redemption in the Far East 1943–1945

1 Jeffery, *MI6*, pp594–5. 2 'Organisation of Special Intelligence for Use of Commander-in-Chief Eastern Fleet', 2 April 1943, ADM 223/496, TNA; Ralph Erskine, 'The 1944 Naval BRUSA Agreement and its Aftermath', *Cryptologia*, 30:1 (2006), pp1–22; Smith, *Emperor's Codes*, Chs 12; Aldrich, *Intelligence and the War against Japan*, pp237–40; Hinsley and Stripp, *Codebreakers*, Ch 27. 3 Straczek, pp276–9. 4 Rushbrooke to Somerville, 31 January 1943, and 'Organisation of Special Intelligence for Use of Commander-in-Chief Eastern Fleet', 2 April 1943, both ADM 223/496, TNA; Birch, Vol 1, Part 2 and Vol 2, pp163–5; Smith, *Emperor's Codes*, Chs 12 and 16. 5 Benson, *US Communications during World War II*, p119–20; Smith, *Emperor's Codes*, Chs 12 and 16. 6 Burnett report, 'Collaboration of British and US Radio Intelligence', 19 January 1943, ADM 223/496. 7 'Extract from the report of Commander Holtwick USN on his visit to the Colombo Unit, 2nd December 1943', ADM 223/496, TNA. 8 Lieutenant Commander M G Saunders, 'Report on visit to US and other Signals Intelligence Centres', 15 December 1943, and 'Signals Intelligence Unit Colombo', from the context probably by Burnett about December 1943, both ADM 223/496. 9 Naval Records Society, Vol 134, *The Somerville Papers*, ed Michael Simpson (Scolar Press, 1995), pp16, 17, 23, 52, 150, 154, 161, 164, 170, 171, 249, 266, 303. 10 Hart-Davis, *Man of War*, Chs 11 and 12. 11 C-in-C Eastern Fleet signal, 20 November 1944, and First Sea Lord to DNI, 21 November 1944, both ADM 223/495. 12 Michael Wilson, *A Submariners' War: The Indian Ocean 1939–45* (UK: Spellmount Ltd, 2008), p176. 13 NRS Vol 134, items 361, 363, 365; Straczek, pp320–2. 14 'HMS Anderson and Special Intelligence in the Far East', Erskine, 'The 1944 Naval BRUSA Agreement', pp4–8; HW 4/24; Benson, *US Communications during World War II*, p121. 15 Erskine, 'The 1944 Naval BRUSA Agreement', pp13–14. 16 David Hobbs, *The British Pacific Fleet: The Royal Navy's Most Powerful Strike Force* (Barnsley: Seaforth Publishing, 2011), Ch 3. 17 Hobbs, Ch 4. 18 Jon Robb-Webb, 'Anglo-American

Naval Intelligence Cooperation in the Pacific, 1944–45', *Intelligence and National Security*, 22:5 (November 2007), 767–786, pp768–9; Barnett, *Engage the Enemy More Closely*, pp873–7. **19** 'Report on the Intelligence Organisation of the British Pacific Fleet in the War against Japan', 10 July 1946, ADM 223/496; SOI BPF to Hillgarth (CBNIET), 20 December 1944, ADM 223/495, both TNA; Robb-Webb, 'Anglo-American Naval Intelligence Cooperation in the Pacific', pp775–7. **20** 'BPF Intelligence Organisation', ADM 223/495; 'Report on the Intelligence Organisation of the British Pacific Fleet in the War against Japan', ADM 223/496; Robb-Webb, pp778–80. **21** 'Report on the Intelligence Organisation of the British Pacific Fleet in the War against Japan', ADM 223/496; 'Operation Iceberg – "Y" Party Report, 27 April 1945', ADM 223/495; Robb-Webb, pp779–84; Hobbs, Ch 6. **22** Iain Ballantyne, *The Deadly Trade: A History of Submarine Warfare from Archimedes to the Present*, (London: W&N, 2018), Chs 40 and 41. Strictly speaking, *Takao* was terminally disabled rather than formally sunk. **23** Roskill, *War at Sea*, Vol 3, Part 2, Ch 29. **24** John R Ferris and Evan Mawdsley, *The Cambridge History of the Second World War, Vol 1, Fighting the War* (Cambridge University Press, 2015), Ch 22, 'Intelligence', by John Ferris.

Chapter 32 1945–1960: Mixed Results in the Early Cold War
1 JIC (44) 86 (O), 'The British Intelligence Organisation', 3 March 1944, CAB 81/121, TNA; Goodman, Chs 3–5; Richard J Aldrich, Rory Cormac and Michael S Goodman, *Spying on the World: The Declassified Documents of the Joint Intelligence Committee, 1936–2013* (Edinburgh University Press, 2014), Ch 4. **2** 'Development and Organisation of the Naval Intelligence Division', April 1944, preface, iv, ADM 223/472. **3** 'The Intelligence Machine', 10 January 1945, CAB 163/6, and JIC (45) 265 (O) 'Post-War Organisation of Intelligence', 7 September 1945, CAB 81/130, both TNA; Huw Dylan, 'The Joint Intelligence Bureau: (Not So) Secret Intelligence for the Post-War World', *Intelligence and National Security*, 27:1 (2012), pp27–45; Goodman, pp162–8. **4** Jeffery, *MI6*, pp599–610. **5** Richard Aldrich, *GCHQ: The Uncensored Story of Britain's Most Secret Intelligence Agency* (London: William Collins Edition, 2019), pp59–67, 134. **6** Michael S Goodman, 'The Foundations of Anglo-American Intelligence Sharing', *Studies in Intelligence*, 59:2 (June 2015); 'Soviet Navy: Intelligence and Analysis during the Cold War', CIA Historical Review Program, CIA Digital Library, Ch 1, p8. **7** 'British-US Communication Intelligence Agreement', 5 March 1946, and 'Minutes of Inauguration Meeting of US-British Signals Intelligence Technical Conference', 11 March 1946, both at www.nsa.gov/news-features/declassified-documents/ukusa. **8** 'Appendices to US-British Communications Intelligence Agreement', 15–26 July 1948; 'Appendices to BRUSA Agreement', 26 June 1951, and 'UKUSA Agreement', 10 October 1956, at: www.nsa.gov/news-features/declassified-documents/ukusa. Also Aldrich, *GCHQ*, Chs 5 and 6. **9** JIC (44) 467 (O), 'Russia's Strategic Interests and Intentions from the Point of View of her Security', 18 December 1944, CAB 81/126, TNA. **10** JIC (46) 1 (O), 'Russia's Strategic Interests and Intentions', 1 March 1946, CAB 81/132, TNA. **11** Ibid, Annex, Part 2, pp9–10. **12** NID16 'Russian Naval Tactics', 10 October 1946, ADM 1/20030, TNA. **13** 'Countermeasures to Russian Naval Threat', September 1947, ADM 1/20030. **14** Ryan, 'The Royal Navy and Soviet Seapower, pp207–10; Aldrich, Cormac and Goodman, Ch 9. **15** For a detailed account and assessment of this post-war German collection, Paul Maddrell, 'Britain's Exploitation of Occupied Germany for Scientific and Technical Intelligence on the Soviet Union' (unpublished doctoral thesis, University of Cambridge, 1998). **16** Olav Riste, *The Norwegian Intelligence Service 1945–1970* (Routledge edn, 2013), Ch 4. **17** Admiralty minute, 22 December 1951, and prime minister reply next day, AIR 19/1107, TNA. **18** Note to prime minister, 17 March 1950, and opinion from Attorney General, 20 March 1950, AIR 19/1107. **19** Riste, Ch 4. **20** Maddrell, p103. **21** For Jiu-Jitsu, Kevin O'Daly, 'Living in the Shadows: Britain and the USSR's nuclear weapon delivery systems 1949–62' (unpublished doctoral thesis, University of Westminster, 2016), pp122–7; for Kapustin Yar, Gregory W Pedlow and Donald E Welzebach, *The CIA and the U2 Program 1954–1974* (History Staff Center for the Study of Intelligence, CIA release 2013, National Security Archive, George Washington University), pp23–4. Also, Huw Dylan, *Defence Intelligence and the Cold War: Britain's Joint Intelligence Bureau 1945–1964* (OUP, 2014),

p42; Richard Aldrich, *Espionage, security and intelligence in Britain 1945–1970* (Manchester University Press, 1998), Ch 7. **22** CIA 'History of the Office of Special Activities (OSA) from Inception to 1969', 1 April 1969, Ch 13 and Annex 120, CIA U2 Missions Flown, www.governmentattic.org; Pedlow and Welzebach, Chs 3 and 4. **23** Pedlow and Welzebach, Ch 3. **24** Riste, Ch 4. **25** 'Justification for Photographic Coverage of two Highest Priority Targets: Severomorsk and Molotovsk', 7 October 1957, CIA Digital Library Electronic Reading Room; Hennessy and Jinks, *Silent Deep*, p154. **26** Riste, Ch 4; CIA 'History of the Office of Special Activities (OSA) from Inception to 1969', 1 April 1969, Annex 120, CIA U2 Missions Flown, www.governmentattic.org. **27** CIA 'History of the Office of Special Activities', Ch 14; Pedlow and Welzebach, Ch 4. **28** CIA 'History of the Office of Special Activities', Ch 19; www.governmentattic.org. **29** Hennessy and Jinks, *Silent Deep*, pp83–5, 94–6; Aldrich, *GCHQ*, pp107–9. **30** Captain 3rd Submarine Squadron report on Operation Admaston, 21 November 1952, and subsequent Admiralty comments including from DNI, ADM 1/27784, TNA; Hennessy and Jinks, *Silent Deep*, pp96–7. **31** DNI to First Sea Lord, 26 July 1954, ADM 205/97, TNA. **32** First Lord to Birch, Ministry of Defence, 3 August 1954, ADM 205/97. **33** Hennessy and Jinks, pp97–105. **34** 'Anti-Submarine Warfare: Review of Scientific Intelligence Organisations', February 1974, DEFE 31/139, TNA. **35** Hennessy and Jinks, pp105–8, 115–26, 153–4; Lieutenant Commander A D Roake, 'Cold War Warrior', *Naval Review*, 4 (1994). **36** Vice Admiral R Elkins to First Sea Lord, 16 October 1956, ADM 205/110; Hennessy and Jinks, pp109, 139; Dan Conley and Richard Woodman, *Cold War Command: The Dramatic Story of a Nuclear Submariner* (Barnsley: Seaforth, 2014), Ch 13. **37** Admiralty memorandum, 'Nuclear Fuel Submarines', 5 June 1950, DEFE 7/2055, TNA. **38** 'Conversion of Soviet Naval Vessels to Nuclear Propulsion and Rocket Weapons' and 'Operational Status of Atomic Submarine', 20 June 1957, and 'Soviet Government Acceptance of a Series Production Atomic Submarine in 1957', 23 September 1958, CIA reports, CIA Digital Library. **39** First Lord to Prime Minister, 12 September 1957, DEFE 7/2162, and Admiralty memorandum, 'The Nuclear Powered Submarine', 14 January 1958, DEFE 7/2055, both TNA. **40** Admiralty memorandum, 'Assistance Required to Develop Nuclear Submarine Propulsion' and 'Admiral Rickover', 30 January 1958, both DEFE 7/2055; Hennessy and Jinks, Ch 3. **41** Cabinet Secretary, Sir Edward Bridges, 'Report of an Enquiry on an Intelligence Operation against Russian Warships', 18 May 1956, NHB Portsmouth: Michael S Goodman, 'Covering up Spying in the "Buster Crabb" Affair: A Note', *The International History Review*, 30:1 (December 2008), pp768–84. **42** Ibid. **43** First Lord to Foreign Secretary and Minister of Defence, 14 June 1957, Appendix, paragraphs 6 and 7, ADM 1/29320, TNA. **44** Tim Benbow, 'The Impact of Air Power on Navies: The United Kingdom, 1945–1957' (unpublished doctoral thesis, University of Oxford, 1999), pp238–9. **45** JIC 56 (80) 'Egyptian Nationalisation of the Suez Canal Company', 3 August 1956, CAB 158/25, TNA. **46** Dylan, *Defence Intelligence and the Cold War*, pp52–3. **47** Benbow, pp244–7. **48** For Operation Nightjar, ADM 1/28939; for initiation of American Barents patrols, Elkins to First Sea Lord, 1 December 1956, ADM 205/110. Also, Hennessy and Jinks, pp110–15; Sherry Sontag and Christopher Drew, *Blind Man's Buff: The Untold Story of Cold War Submarine Espionage* (London: Hutchinson, 1999), p42. **49** 'Soviet Navy: Intelligence and Analysis in the Cold War', CIA Digital Library, Ch 2, p12; 'Soviet Naval Strategy and its Effect on the Development of Naval Forces, 1953–63', 22 October 1963, CIA Office of Research and Reports, CIA Digital Library; Memoirs of Nikita Khrushchev, Vol 3 (Pennsylvania State University edition, 2007), pp75–6; Hennessy and Jinks, p169. **50** 'Conversion of Soviet Naval Vessels to Nuclear Propulsion and Rocket Weapons', CIA Library. **51** Andrew, *Defence of the Realm*, pp484–8, 492–3. **52** 'Defection of Captain Artamonov', JIC (60) 47th Meeting, 15 September 1960, CAB 159/34, TNA. **53** 'Of Moles and Molehunters: A Review of Counter-intelligence Literature, 1977–92', An Intelligence Monograph, CIA Center for the Study of Intelligence, October 1993, pp30–2, CIA Library. **54** 'Northern Fleet units, including missile base near Severomorsk' and 'Atomic submarine construction at Severodvinsk' etc, 1 September 1959, CIA report, CIA Digital Library. **55** JIC (60) 6 (Final), 24 February 1960, 'The Employment of the Soviet Navy and Soviet Air Forces in the Maritime Role at the outbreak of Global War–1960–64',

CAB 158/39, and JIC (60) 85, 'Trends in Soviet Research and Development for the Next 7–10 Years', 19 December 1960, CAB 158/41, both TNA, and CIA National Intelligence Estimate 11–4–59, 9 February 1960, 'Main Trends in Soviet Capabilities and Policies, 1959–64', pp31, 53–4 and 60–3, CIA Digital Library. 56 Ibid. 57 G C Peden, *Arms, Economics and British Strategy: From Dreadnoughts to Hydrogen Bombs* (Cambridge University Press, 2007), Chs 5 and 6; Eric Grove, 'The Royal Navy and the guided missile', in Richard Harding, *The Royal Navy, 1930–2000, Innovation and Defence* (London and New York: Frank Cass, 2004).

Chapter 33 The 1960s: A Time of Transition

1 'The National Reconnaissance Office at 50 Years: A Brief History', 'Corona Fact Sheet' and 'Raising the Periscope: Grab and Poppy: America's Early Elint Satellites', all History and Studies, NRO website. 2 'Severodvinsk Naval Base and Shipyard 402', November 1964, Corona: America's First Satellite Program, CIA History Staff 1995, pp43–9, 253–9, CIA Digital Library. 3 The most authoritative source comprises the numerous original records released over the last thirty years by CIA and available in digital form through the CIA Digital Library. Useful items here include: 'Meeting No 1'; 'Penkovskiy Operation, Parts 3 and 4'; 'Penkovskiy Review 1963'; and 'Penkovskiy Case 1963'. Gordon Brooke-Shepherd's *The Storm Birds: Soviet Post-War Defectors* (London: Weidenfeld and Nicolson, 1988), Chs 9 and 10, provides a useful and broadly accurate summary of the case, especially Penkovsky's initial approaches. 4 'Soviet Navy: Intelligence and Analysis in the Cold War', p13, CIA Digital Library; Len Parkinson, 'Penkovskiy's Legacy and Strategic Research', in *CIA Studies in Intelligence*, 16:2 (Spring 1972), pp1–19, CIA Digital Library. 5 Parkinson, 'Penkovskiy's Legacy'. 6 'Intelligence Digest for Technical Departments', JIC (62) 5, 2 January 1962, CAB 158/45, and 'The Soviet Missile Threat up to the end of 1966', JIC (62) 28, 20 March 1962, and separate 'Note by the Secretary', 11 April 1962, all TNA. 7 JIC (64) 4, 'Employment of Soviet Forces in the event of General War up to the end of 1968', 24 February 1964, CAB 158/51, TNA. 8 JIC (63) 78, 'Soviet Maritime Policy', 18 February 1964, CAB 158/50, TNA. 9 DNI minutes, 10 May 1960 and 8 April 1961 and related papers, ADM 1/27860, TNA; Mason Redfearn and Richard Aldrich, 'The Perfect Cover: British Intelligence, the Soviet Fleet and Distant Water Trawler Operations, 1963–1974', *Intelligence and National Security*, 12:3 (1997), 166–77, pp166–71. 10 JIC (63) 78. 11 Flag Officer Scotland and Northern Ireland, 'Operation Bargold', 28 September 1963, and related naval staff comments including DNI, ADM 1/29149, and Defence Secretary to Prime Minister, 'British Surveillance Effort against the Soviet Northern Fleet's Summer Exercise 1967', 3 November 1966, DEFE 13/499, both TNA. 12 Samuel Alexander Robinson, 'Between the devil and the deep blue sea: Ocean Science and the British Cold War State' (unpublished doctoral thesis, University of Manchester, 2015); Riste, Ch 8. 13 www.arl.teddington.org.uk>arl_corsair; David Parry, 'The History of British Submarine Sonars', www.rnsubs.co.uk/articles. 14 www.iusscaa.org>history; www.public.navy.mil>subfor>cus>pages>mission; www.navy.mil/navy data/cno/n87/usw/issue-25/sosus2. Also, Norman Friedman, 'Electronics and the Royal Navy', in Harding, *The Royal Navy, 1930–2000, Innovation and Defence*. 15 Head of Naval Home Division MOD submission, 10 November 1970, and Chief of Defence Staff to Secretary of State, 'Participation by UK in US SOSUS Projects', 15 December 1970, both AIR 20/12879, TNA. Also Hennessy and Jinks, *Silent Deep*, pp324–9. 16 Riste, Ch 8. 17 Ibid. 18 Riste, Ch 4. 19 'Report of the Re-Opened Investigation into the Loss of the FV Gaul', London, Stationery Office, 2004, pp134–41; Redfearn and Aldrich, 'The Perfect Cover: British Intelligence, the Soviet Fleet and Distant Water Trawler Operations, 1963–1974', pp171–7. 20 Ibid. 21 Rear Admiral Patrick Graham held the title DNI in parallel for a transitional year from spring 1964. 22 Pete Davies, 'Estimating Soviet Power: The Creation of Britain's Defence Intelligence Staff 1960–65', *Intelligence and National Security*, 26:6 (2011), pp818–41; Philip H J Davies, *Intelligence and Government in Britain and the United States: A Comparative Perspective, Vol 2, Evolution of the UK Community* (Praeger, 2012), pp24–9, 182–3. 23 Ibid. Also, 'Future of the Defence Intelligence Staff', 2nd Permanent Secretary minute and paper for Secretary of State, 4 March 1965, DEFE 13/923, TNA. 24 DGI to Secretary of State, 20 September 1967, DEFE 13/923. 25 Percy Cradock, *Know Your*

Enemy: How the Joint Intelligence Committee saw the World (London: John Murray, 2002), Ch 15. **26** Davies, p215. **27** Hennessy and Jinks, *Silent Deep*, pp200–4. **28** First Sea Lord to Minister of Defence, 'Polaris', 10 November 1958, DEFE 7/2162, TNA. **29** Matthew Jones, *The Official History of the UK Strategic Nuclear Deterrent: Vol I: From the V-Bomber Era to the Arrival of Polaris, 1945–1964* (Abingdon, Oxon: Routledge, 2017), Chs 4–10. **30** Ibid, pp458–66, 513–20. **31** MOD memorandum, 'Size of the British Polaris Force', 19 November 1964, DEFE 13/350, TNA; Jones, *Official History Vol 1*, pp413–18, 435–46. **32** First Sea Lord to Defence Secretary, 'Polaris Submarines – Deployment East of Suez' with attachment, 13 January 1965, 'Support Facilities for Polaris Submarines East of Suez' with annexes, 1 July 1965, Chief of Defence Staff to Defence Secretary, 'Deployment of Polaris Submarines East of Suez, 21 January 1966, DEFE 13/350, TNA. Also Defence Secretary to prime minister, 5 June 1968, PREM 13/2493, TNA. **33** MOD memorandum of 19 November 1964. **34** Hennessy and Jinks, *Silent Deep*, pp224–5. **35** 'SSN Working Party, Interim Report', 19 December 1967, and Scenario 1, and DI3 Navy report, 'Background Information on the Soviet Navy', 1 December 1967, both DEFE 13/949, TNA. **36** Chief Polaris Executive note, 'Poseidon', 19 January 1965, and subsequent note for prime minister, 22 January 1965, DEFE 13/350, TNA. **37** Jones, Vol 2, pp210–17, 406–15, 456–64. For the CIA view, 'Soviet Strategic Air and Missile Defenses', NIE 11-3-68, 31 October 1968, CIA Digital Library. **38** Zuckerman minutes to prime minister, 'Sentinel Anti-Missile System', 21 October 1968, SZ/0330 of 6 December 1968, and 'Atomic Weapons Establishments', 19 December 1968, PREM 13/2493. **39** Cabinet Secretary to prime minister, 'Nuclear Policy', 1 December 1967, PREM 13/2493. **40** Jones, Vol 2, Chs 9 and 12. **41** Jones, Vol 2, pp503–9 and Postcript. **42** 'Polaris Policy Committee: The future of the UK Strategic Deterrent', 26 August 1969, and 'Polaris Policy Committee: The Case for building a Fifth Polaris Submarine', 21 November 1969, both DEFE 24/510, TNA. **43** Christopher Tuck, *Confrontation, Strategy and War Termination: Britain's Conflict with Indonesia* (Abingdon, Oxon: Routledge, 2016). **44** COS 313/63, 'Planning to Meet Threats to the Borneo Territories', 18 September 1963, Annex and Appendix A, DEFE 5/143, TNA. **45** Hennessy and Jinks, *Silent Deep*, pp285–9; Foreign Office to prime minister in support of intelligence-gathering operation by submarine Ambush, 8 January 1965, DEFE 13/405, TNA. **46** JIC (63) 78, 'Soviet Maritime Policy', 18 February 1964, paragraph 16, CAB 158/50, TNA. **47** COS 313/63; also, COS 329/63, 'Requirements to counter increasing Indonesian action short of overt hostilities against Sabah and Sarawak', 27 September 1963, DEFE 5/143; JIC (63) 89, 'Likelihood of Indonesian Air Attack on Malaysia', 26 November 1963, CAB 158/50, and JIC (67) 37, 'The Outlook for Indonesia up to the end of 1970', 12 June 1967, pp21–25, PREM 13/2718, both TNA. **48** Photographic reconnaissance of two airfields in Sumatra', 5 January 1965, 'Photographic reconnaissance of the Medan area in Sumatra', 28 April 1965, and 'Photographic reconnaissance of targets in Eastern Indonesia', 5 May 1965, all in DEFE 13/405. **49** DGI to Defence Secretary, 'Intelligence and Confrontation', 22 June 1966, DEFE 13/476, TNA; Tuck, *Confrontation, Strategy and War Termination*, especially Ch 5; David Easter, 'British Intelligence and Propaganda during the "Confrontation", 1963–1966', *Intelligence and National Security*, 16:2 (2001), pp83–102. **50** Toh Boon Kwan, 'Brinksmanship and Deterrence Success during the Anglo-Indonesian Sunda Straits Crisis, 1964–1966', *Journal of South-East Asian Studies*, 36:3 (2005), pp399–417; Easter, 'British Intelligence and Propaganda during the "Confrontation", 1963–1966'. **51** 'President's Intelligence Checklist', 12 June 1962, 'Missile Test Center Nenoksa', 1 June 1966, and 'Cruise Missile Launch Center Nenoksa', 7 June 1967, all CIA Digital Library. **52** Hennessy and Jinks, *Silent Deep*, pp277–85; Riste, Ch 11. **53** MOD letter to prime minister, 6 December 1965, DEFE 13/498, TNA. **54** Director of Naval Plans, 'Future Policy for Special Fit', 9 May 1977, DEFE 69/653, TNA. **55** Michael Pitkeathly and David Wixon, *Submarine Courageous: Cold War Warrior: The Life and Times of a Nuclear Submarine* (HMS Courageous Society, 2010), pp37, 55, 71, 91–3. **56** 'President's Daily Brief', 8 May 1968, CIA Digital Library. **57** DI3 Navy, 'Background Information on the Soviet Navy', 1 December 1967, DEFE 13/949. **58** DCDS(I) note, 25 January 1972, 'The Mechanics of Establishing a Co-operative Project between DIS, UK Naval Staff, UK Scientific Staff, USN,

US Naval Intelligence, Defence Intelligence Agency, Central Intelligence Agency and Dr Foster's Presidential Committee to determine the State of Soviet ASW' and, 'Intelligence Cooperation with the US on ASW', 7 March 1972, both DEFE 31/139, TNA.　59 'The Soviet Y-Class Submarine Construction Program', October 1968, CIA Digital Library.　60 'Leningrad enters Nuclear Submarine Program with new Attack Class', May 1968, CIA Digital Library.　61 PM Private Secretary to Air Ministry, 27 June 1958, ADM 1/29320, TNA.　62 For full accounts of the *Warspite* episode: Hennessy and Jinks, *Silent Deep*, pp310-13; Iain Ballantyne, *Hunter Killers: The Dramatic Untold Story of the Royal Navy's Most Secret Service* (London: Orion, 2014), Chs 22-25.

Chapter 34　The 1970s: The Rise of Submarine Intelligence
1 JIC (A) (71) 21, 'Soviet Maritime Policy', 30 July 1971, CAB 186/9, TNA; 'Soviet and East European General Purpose Forces', NEI 11-14-69, 4 December 1969 and CIA Contribution to NIE 11-14-69, August 1969, both CIA Digital Library.　2 JIC (A) (71) 21 and 'Minutes of Anti-Submarine Warfare Conference', 20 January 1971, pp8-13, DEFE 69/726, TNA. The influence of CIA is evident by comparing data in these British assessments with the CIA 'Intelligence Handbook', 'Soviet Submarines', December 1969, CIA Digital Library.　3 Ibid.　4 Memorandum for the Director, NEI 11-14-69, 13 November 1969, CIA Digital Library.　5 Ibid.　6 Ballantyne, *Hunter Killers*, Ch 33.　7 Brent Scowcroft message to Henry Kissinger, 3 November 1974, LOC-HAC-262-2-14-3, CIA Digital Library.　8 Director of Naval Warfare memorandum, 'SSBN Invulnerability', 22 July 1969; 'Polaris Policy Committee: SSBN Invulnerability Working Group', 21 November 1969; Defence Secretary memorandum, 28 November 1969; and Chief Adviser (Projects and Research) to Defence Secretary, 26 November 1969, all DEFE 24/510, TNA.　9 JIC (A) (71) 21; 'Minutes of Anti-Submarine Warfare Conference', 1971, pp8-13.　10 Ibid. Also, Owen R Cote, 'The Third Battle: Innovation in the US Navy's Silent Cold War Struggle with Soviet Submarines', *US Naval War College Newport Papers*, 16 (2003), pp60-3.　11 CIA report 'Construction and Investment at Admiralty Shipyard', March 1970, p3; CIA Intelligence Memorandum, 'The Soviet Attack Submarine Force: Evolution and Operations', September 1971, pp17-18; Gerhardt Thamm, 'Unravelling a Cold War Mystery: The Alfa SSN: Challenging Paradigms, Finding New Truths 1969-79', *Studies in Intelligence*, 37:3 (Fall 1993); all in CIA Digital Library. Also, COS 8th Meeting, 25 March 1980, paragraph 9, DEFE 32/26, and DI74 report, 'The Alfa Class SSN: Recent Developments and the Future', 24 October 1980, DEFE 19/356, both TNA. For the *Spartan* incident, Hennessy and Jinks, *Silent Deep*, pp520-3.　12 'Minutes of Anti-Submarine Warfare Conference', 1973, pp149-53, DEFE 629/727, TNA.　13 'Russian ASW Capability', Annex B, 'Strategic Nuclear Options' paper, 2 November 1972, PREM 15/1359, TNA.　14 Pitkeathly and Wixon, *Submarine Courageous*, pp71-2.　15 Intelligence Report, Soviet Anti-Submarine Warfare: Current Capabilities and Priorities, September 1972, CIA Digital Library, pp25-6.　16 JIC (79) 2, 'The Increasing Capability of the Soviet General Purpose Maritime Forces', 28 March 1979, main report, paragraph 15, CAB 186/28, TNA.　17 'Minutes of Anti-Submarine Warfare Conference', 1973, pp156-71; Hennessy and Jinks, *Silent Deep*, pp342-6.　18 'Minutes of Anti-Submarine Warfare Conference', 1973, pp149-53.　19 'Feodosiya Probable ASW Checkout Facility and Feodosiya Naval Missile Test Facility, November 1979, CIA Digital Library.　20 CIA 'Soviet Navy: Intelligence and Analysis during the Cold War', p27.　21 'Minutes of Anti-Submarine Warfare Conference', 1973, pp149-55; CIA Directorate of Science and Technology Intelligence Report, 'Soviet Anti-Submarine Warfare: Current Capabilities and Priorities', September 1972, CIA Digital Library.　22 'The National Reconnaissance Office at 50 Years', pp15-19; 'Critical to US Security: The Gambit and Hexagon Satellite Reconnaissance Systems', History and Studies, NRO website.　23 Hennessy and Jinks, *Silent Deep*, pp351-2; Wells, *A Tale of Two Navies*, pp115-16; Director of Plans to ACNS (OR), 'Future Policy for Special Fit', 9 May 1977, DEFE 69/653, TNA.　24 'The SSK – Replacement of the Oberon Class', paragraphs 9-13, attached to ACNS (OR) letter, 8 May 1978, DEFE 24/1391, TNA.　25 Memorandum of Understanding between Director ASW US Navy and VCNS on exchange of ASW information, signed 26 April and 5 May 1973, DEFE 31/139.　26 Sontag

and Drew, *Blind Man's Buff*, Ch 8. **27** Wells, *A Tale of Two Navies*, p119; Gordon S Barrass, *The Great Cold War: A Journey through the Hall of Mirrors* (USA: Stanford University Press, 2009), pp394–5; D J Willison (DIS) to J O H Burrough (GCHQ), 11 April 1974, 'Intelligence on Soviet ASW', DEFE 31/139; 'Sea Air Warfare Committee – Operational Concept for Anti-Submarine Warfare', 29 June 1978, paragraphs 10 and 11, DEFE 13/1357, TNA. **28** Jeffrey T Richelson, *The US Intelligence Community* (7th edn, Westview Press, 2015), p278; Aldrich, *GCHQ*, pp305–6; D/DSTI/123/12. Also, 'Orfordness' note, paragraph 9, 21 May 1973, DEFE 31/155, and Royal Aircraft Establishment, 'Zinnia: An Ionospheric Reflection Radar, February 1962, AVIA 6/17569, both TNA. **29** Barrass, p392; Aldrich, pp266–7. **30** Wells, *A Tale of Two Navies*, pp116–17; Barrass, p396; COS 9th Meeting, 5 March 1979, paragraph 3, DEFE 32/26, TNA. **31** 'Soviet Program to Develop a New Large SLBM/SSBN', June 1977, CIA Digital Library. **32** CIA 'Soviet Navy: Intelligence and Analysis during the Cold War', pp17–18. **33** 'Military Thought (USSR): The Location and Destruction of Polaris Submarines', 22 May 1973, CIA Digital Library. **34** Stephen Twigge, Edward Hampshire and Graham Macklin, *British Intelligence: Secrets, Spies and Sources* (London: Bloomsbury Academic, 2008), pp161–4. **35** 'Sea Air Warfare Committee: Operational Concept for Anti-Submarine Warfare', 29 June 1978, DEFE 13/1357, TNA; 'Minutes of Anti-Submarine Warfare Conference', 1973, pp222–7. Also Commander Richard Sharpe quoted in Pitkeathly and Wixon, *Submarine Courageous*, p124. **36** CIA 'Soviet Anti-Submarine Warfare', 1972, pp49–50; CIA Intelligence memorandum, 'The Soviet Attack Submarine Force: Evolution and Operations', September 1971, pp33–4. **37** Hennessy and Jinks, *Silent Deep*, pp374–5. **38** 'Towed Arrays for Submarines – Sonar 2026', 18 July 1978, DEFE 13/1357, TNA; Parry, 'History of British Submarine Sonars'; Pitkeathly and Wixon, *Submarine Courageous*, pp244–5. **39** Hennessy and Jinks, *Silent Deep*, pp375–83. **40** Edward Hampshire, 'From Malin Head to "Okean 75": shadowing and intelligence operations by Royal Navy surface ships 1975–1985', *Intelligence and National Security*, 33:5 (2018), pp659–74. **41** Ibid; Hennessy and Jinks, pp360–1. **42** Defence Secretary to prime minister, 'Improvement of the Polaris System', 16 July 1970, PREM 15/1359, TNA. **43** Zuckerman to prime minister, 17 July 1970, PREM 15/1359. **44** COS 41st Meeting 1971, 'Strategic Nuclear Deterrent', 30 November 1971, DEFE 32/21, TNA. **45** Jones, Vol 2, pp544–5. **46** For a good summary of the Duff/Mason report, Hennessy and Jinks, *Silent Deep*, pp472–82. **47** COS 22nd Meeting 1979, 'The Future of the UK Nuclear Deterrent', 21 August 1979, Attachment, 'The Politico-Military Requirement', paragraphs 10–12, DEFE 32/26, TNA. **48** Cabinet Secretary to prime minister, 10 November 1972, PREM 15/1359. **49** CDS 'Draft Speaking Notes', 8 January 1982, DEFE 24/2123, TNA. **50** Kristan Stoddart, 'Maintaining the "Moscow Criterion": British Strategic Nuclear Targeting 1974–1979', *Journal of Strategic Studies*, 31:6 (2008), pp897–924; Rodric Braithwaite, *Armageddon and Paranoia: The Nuclear Confrontation* (London: Profile Books, 2017), Ch 8. **51** Ibid and Defence Secretary to prime minister, 'Strategic Nuclear Policy' plus attachments, 6 November 1972, PREM 15/1359. Also, Helen Parr, 'The British Decision to Upgrade Polaris, 1970–4', *Contemporary European History*, 22:2 (May 2013), pp253–74; Stoddart, 'Maintaining the 'Moscow Criterion', pp900–2, 905–6. **52** Cabinet secretary to prime minister, 17 April 1972, PREM 15/1359. **53** Defence Secretary, 'Strategic Nuclear Policy' plus attachments, 6 November 1972. **54** Catherine Haddon, 'Union Jacks and Red Stars on Them: UK Intelligence, the Soviet Nuclear Threat and British Nuclear Weapons Policy, 1945–1970' (unpublished doctoral thesis, Queen Mary College, University of London, 2008), pp289–90. **55** Confidential Annex to COS 22nd meeting, 21 August 1979, 'The Future of the UK Nuclear Deterrent', Attachment 2, paragraph 18, DEFE 32/26, TNA. **56** 'Strategic Nuclear Options', 2 November 1972, PREM 15/1359; CDS to Defence Secretary, 'Options for Improving the Polaris Force', 12 April 1973, DEFE 13/1293, TNA. **57** 'Defence Expenditure', Minutes of a meeting held at 10 Downing Street on 30 October 1973, and Cabinet Secretary to prime minister, 29 October, PREM 15/2038, TNA. **58** Cabinet Secretary to prime minister, 'The Nuclear Deterrent: Polaris Improvements', 11 June 1973, PREM 15/1360, and 'The Nuclear Deterrent', 11 September 1973, PREM 15/2038, both TNA; Cabinet Secretary, 'Strategic Nuclear Options', 10 November 1972; Chancellor to prime minister, 'Defence Expenditure',

10 September 1973, PREM 15/2038; Parr, 'Decision to Upgrade Polaris'. **59** 'Polaris Improvements: Further Consultation with the US', 8 June 1973, PREM 15/1360, Defence Secretary to prime minister, 7 January and Cabinet Secretary to prime minister, 10 January 1974, both in PREM 15/2038, all TNA. **60** Defence Secretary to prime minister, 'Chevaline', 18 January 1979, PREM 16/1978, TNA. **61** For PPAG and its terms of reference, 'The Management of the BNMBS', 8 March 1968, ADM 331/15, TNA. **62** Plot of missile range against number of trails per annum in 1980s and separate range chart overlaying North-East Atlantic, undated but probably late 1972, DEFE 13/1293, TNA. For subsequent First Sea Lord comments on the 'sea room' issue: Chevaline Steering Committee, 5 April 1976, paragraph 2B, and 'Chevaline', Record of meeting in Defence Secretary's Office 27 May 1976, paragraph 3, both also DEFE 13/1293. **63** NEI 11-13-82, 'Soviet Ballistic Missile Defense', 13 October 1982, pp7, 16, 27, CIA Digital Library. **64** Frank Cooper to Defence Secretary, 'Chevaline: Meeting with Prime Minister', 25 June 1976, DEFE 13/1039, TNA; COS 22nd Meeting, 21 August 1979, 'The Future of the UK Nuclear Deterrent', DEFE 68/406; Lawrence Freedman, *Britain and Nuclear Weapons* (Basingstoke: Macmillan, 1980), Appendix 3. **65** David Owen, *Nuclear Papers* (Liverpool University Press, 2009), Documents 2 and 3, pp97–104. **66** J F Mayne note, 'Meeting British National Criteria for Strategic Deterrence', 27 November 1975, covering CDS Minute 1141/5, 10 November 1975, DEFE 13/1039; Kristin Stoddart, 'Maintaining the "Moscow Criterion": British Strategic Nuclear Targeting 1974–1979', *Journal of Strategic Studies*, 31:6 (2008), 897–924, pp904–5. **67** Hennessy and Jinks, *Silent Deep*, pp355–7; Pitkeathly and Wixon, *Submarine Courageous*, p136. **68** Freedman, Lawrence, *The Official History of the Falklands Campaign* (London: Routledge, 2005), Vol 1, *The Origins of the Falklands War*, Ch 8; Hennessy and Jinks, *Silent Deep*, pp388–93; Aaron Donaghy, *The British Government and the Falkland Islands 1974– 79* (Palgrave Macmillan, 2014), p181; *Naval Review*, 71:4 (October 1983), p334. **69** JIC (79) 2, 'The Increasing Capability of the Soviet General Purpose Maritime Forces', 28 March 1979, CAB 186/28, and JIC (80) 13, 'Soviet Military Expenditure 1970–1979 and the Outlook for the 1980s', 15 May 1980, CAB 186/30, both TNA. Also, 'Sea Air Warfare Committee – Operational Concept for Anti-Submarine Warfare', 29 June 1978, paragraphs 7–12, DEFE 13/1357. **70** Ibid. **71** NIE 11-14-79, 'Warsaw Pact Forces Opposite NATO', Vol II, Key Judgements and Chs 2C, 4D and 6; DIS paper, 'Soviet Maritime Policy', 8 May 1981, DEFE 19/356, TNA; Cote, 'The Third Battle', Ch 4.

Chapter 35 The 1980s: The Final Soviet Challenge

1 JIC (81) 12, 'Soviet Maritime Policy', 5 October 1981, CAB 186/32, TNA. **2** NIE 11-15-82, 'Soviet Naval Strategy and Programs through the 1990s', 19 October 1982, CIA Digital Library. **3** 'Submarine Projects at …', 10 October 1984, CIA Digital Library. **4** John B Hattendorf, 'The Evolution of the US Navy's Maritime Strategy, 1977–1986', *US Naval War College Newport Papers,* 19 (2004), pp29–31; Christopher A Ford and David A Rosenberg, 'The Naval Intelligence Underpinnings of Reagan's Maritime Strategy', *Journal of Strategic Studies,* 28:2 (April 2005), 379–409, pp381–90; Hennessy and Jinks, *Silent Deep*, pp530–2; Sontag and Drew, *Blind Man's Buff*, Chs 10 and 11. **5** NIE 11-14-79, 'Warsaw Pact Forces Opposite NATO', 31 January 1979, Part 2, Section 2, paragraphs 145–9. **6** Hennessy and Jinks, pp532–5. **7** 'The United Kingdom Defence Programme: The Way Forward', Cmnd 8288, June 1988 (London, HMSO); Clive Whitmore, notes 'Defence Programme', 19 May and 8 June 1981, Defence Secretary note, 'Defence Programme', 2 June 1981, especially paragraph 16 and Appendix A, and First Sea Lord to prime minister, 18 May 1981, all in PREM 19/416, TNA; Charles Moore, *Margaret Thatcher: The Authorised Biography* (London: Allen Lane, 2013–19), *Vol 1: Not for Turning,* pp660–1; Hennessy and Jinks, pp532–5. **8** Ballantyne, *Hunter Killers*, Ch 57; Conley and Woodman, *Cold War Command,* Ch 12. **9** JIC (82) 14, 'The Soviet Military Capability to attack the United Kingdom Base', 29 October 1982, paragraph 19 and Annex C, CAB 186/34, TNA. **10** JIC (85) 7, 'Soviet Naval Policy', 19 July 1985, CAB 186/39, and 'Defence Staff Briefing to SACLANT', 11 February 1986, DEFE 31/325, both TNA. **11** DIS paper, 'Soviet Maritime Policy', 8 May 1981, DEFE 19/356; JIC (83) 5, 'The Soviet Global Perception', 5 September 1983, paragraph

34 and Annex E, CAB 186/36, and JIC (85) 1, 'Soviet Defence Policy and Strategy', 1 February 1985, especially paragraphs 52–5, both TNA.   **12** JIC (79) 2, CAB 186/28; COS 9th Meeting, 5 March 1979, paragraph 6, DEFE 32/26; Wells, *Tale of Two Navies*, p117.   **13** 'Sea Air Warfare Committee – Operational Concept for Anti-Submarine Warfare', 29 June 1978, paragraphs 11a and b, DEFE 13/1357.   **14** Wells, pp117–18; Hennessy and Jinks, *Silent Deep*, pp547–8, 564–8. **15** Imagery Report, 'Soviet Submarine Construction Program During 1982', June 1983, CIA Digital Library.   **16** NIE 11-14-79, Part 2, Section 6, paragraph 88.   **17** Wells, *Tale of Two Navies*, Ch 6.   **18** JIC (85) 7; SNIE 11-20-84, 'Soviet Submarine Warfare Trends', March 1985, CIA Digital Library.   **19** Ibid; also, NIE 11-15-84, 'Soviet Naval Strategy and Programs through the 1990s', March 1985, pp31–2, CIA Digital Library. **20** Anthony Wells, 'Soviet Submarine Prospects 1985–2000', *Submarine Review* (January 1986). **21** PM Private Secretary to Cabinet Secretary, 30 January 1978, PREM 16/1564, TNA.   **22** 'Future of the Nuclear Deterrent: Part III, System Options', paragraph 15, DEFE 68/406, TNA.   **23** 'SAL-Related Activities Summary Report', December 1979, pp14–16, CIA Digital Library.   **24** 'Future of the Nuclear Deterrent: Part III, System Options', paragraphs 19–24; Confidential Annex to COS 22nd meeting, 21 August 1979, 'The Future of the UK Nuclear Deterrent', Attachment 2, DEFE 32/26.   **25** 'Future of the Nuclear Deterrent: Part III, System Options', paragraphs 12, 13 and 25–30.   **26** Meeting record, 'Future of the British Deterrent', 22 December 1978, and 'Nuclear Defence Policy', Note of a Meeting, 2 January 1979, PREM 16/1978, TNA.   **27** Foreign Secretary to prime minister, 19 December 1978, PREM 16/1978.   **28** Cabinet Secretary to prime minister, 'Future of the British Deterrent', 20 December 1978, PREM 16/1978; Hennessy and Jinks, *Silent Deep*, p483.   **29** 'Prime Minister's conversation with President Carter: 3.30pm, 5 January, at Guadeloupe', PREM 16/1978.   **30** COS 22nd meeting, 29 August, 1979.   **31** Cabinet Secretary to prime minister, 'Future of the Strategic Deterrent (Misc 7)', 4 December 1979, PREM 19/159, TNA.   **32** 'Successor System: The Case for Five Ballistic Missile Firing Submarines (SSBN)', paragraph 8, undated but late 1979, DEFE 25/325, TNA. **33** 'Draft Speaking Notes for CDS' for MISC 7 meeting, 8 January 1982, DEFE 24/2123; Hennessy and Jinks, *Silent Deep*, pp499–503.   **34** Lawrence Freedman, *The Official History of the Falklands Campaign* (London: Routledge, 2005), *Vol 1 The Origins of the Falklands War*, Ch 20 – Conclusion.   **35** Freedman, Vol 1, Ch 15.   **36** Ibid, Chs 16–18.   **37** Freedman, *Vol 2, War and Diplomacy*, Ch 5.   **38** Hennessy and Jinks, *Silent Deep*, p404.   **39** DI4 letter to Mitchell, 12 May 1981, DEFE 31/207, TNA; Freedman, Vol 1, Ch 15.   **40** Buenos Aires to MODUK, 'South Georgia: Argentine Navy Deployment', 31 March 1982, DEFE 31/207.   **41** Defence attaché letter to Governor of Falklands, 'The Argentine Threat to the Falkland Islands', 2 March 1982, DEFE 31/227, TNA.   **42** For a summary of GCHQ and SIS intelligence and its limitations, the Falklands Islands Review chaired by Lord Franks, January 1983, HMSO.   **43** Freedman, Vol 1, pp57–63, 141–8, 163–5; Aldrich, *GCHQ*, p369.   **44** DCDS(I) 'Capabilities of the Argentine Armed Forces', 5 April 1982, DEFE 31/227.   **45** DCDS(I) 'Assessment of Argentine Air Power', 14 April 1982, DEFE 68/622, TNA.   **46** Ewen Southby-Tailyour, *Exocet Falklands: The Untold Story of Special Forces Operations* (Barnsley: Pen & Sword, 2014), Ch 3.   **47** DCDS(I) 'Assessment of Argentine Air Power', 14 April 1982.   **48** David Hart-Dyke, *Four Weeks in May: A Captain's Story of War at Sea* (Atlantic Books, 2007), pp29–30.   **49** Aldrich, Cormac and Goodman, *Spying on the World*, Ch 17.   **50** Freedman, Vol 2, Ch 21.   **51** Hennessy and Jinks, *Silent Deep*, pp405, 408.   **52** Freedman, Vol 2, Ch 16; Director of Air Staff, Commanders Briefing, 'Operation Corporate', September 1982, DEFE 31/227. For ELINT collection, 'Air Defence of the Falkland Islands', 23 April 1982, paragraph 3a, DEFE 68/622, TNA.   **53** Freedman, Vol 2, Ch 16.   **54** Quoted in Andrew Dorman, Michael D Kandiah, and Gillian Staerck, 'The Falklands War', Centre for Contemporary British History, Oral History Programme (2005), p50.   **55** Southby-Tailyour, *Exocet Falklands*, Ch 7.   **56** For example, DDI 3334-82, 'What's Next in the Falklands? – (Part II) The Defensive Perspective', 21 April 1982, CIA Digital Library.   **57** Freedman, Vol 2, Ch 27. For the Roland, 'Air Defence of the Falkland Islands', 23 April 1982, paragraph 4d, DEFE 68/622.   **58** Ibid, Ch 21.   **59** Hennessy and Jinks, *Silent Deep*, pp446–9.   **60** Hart-Dyke, *Four Weeks in May*, pp63–4.   **61** CTF 317 to

Ascension from *Tidespring*, 121833Z May 82, DEFE 70/940, TNA. **62** Freedman, Vol 2, Ch 31. **63** Ibid, pp370–2: Southby-Tailyour, *Exocet Falklands*; Nigel West, *The Secret War for the Falklands: The SAS, MI6, and the War Whitehall nearly lost* (Sphere edition, 2007). **64** 'National Security Strategy of the United States', January 1987, pp29–30. **65** Ford and Rosenberg, 'The Naval Intelligence Underpinnings of Reagan's Maritime Strategy', p394. **66** Hennessy and Jinks, *Silent Deep*, pp553–6. **67** Ford and Rosenberg, pp396–8; Hennessy and Jinks, *Silent Deep*, pp564–8, 573–4; John Howard, 'Fixed Sonar Systems: The History and Future of the Underwater Silent Sentinel', *Submarine Review* (April 2011). **68** Hampshire, 'From Malin Head to "Okean 75"', pp662–4; Jim Ring, *We Come Unseen: The Untold History of Britain's Cold War Submariners* (London: John Murray, 2001), pp240–3. **69** Hennessy and Jinks, *Silent Deep*, pp548–50; Wells, *Tale of Two Navies*, pp128–9. **70** SNIE 11-20-84, 'Soviet Submarine Warfare Trends', March 1985, pp6, 13, CIA Digital Library. **71** Andrew Lambert, *Seapower States: Maritime Culture, Continental Empires and the Conflict that made the Modern World* (Yale University Press, 2018), pp307–10; Kennedy, *Rise and Fall*, Ch 12; Ben Wilson, *Empire of the Deep: The Rise and Fall of the British Navy* (London: Weidenfeld & Nicolson, 2013), Part 15. An important exception to the 'declinist' view is Eric Grove's *Vanguard to Trident: British Naval Policy Since World War II* (Annapolis, Naval Institute Press, 1987).

Conclusion

1 Hastings, *The Secret War*, Introduction. **2** Ch 19 and fn 47. **3** For a valuable and insightful discussion of this whole topic: Ferris, 'Intelligence', *Cambridge History of the Second World War*, Vol 1, Ch 22. **4** Andrew, *The Secret World*, Conclusion.

Bibliography

Primary sources

The National Archives

Cabinet Office papers
CAB 1: Miscellaneous Records 1866–1949
CAB 2: Committee of Imperial Defence and Standing Defence Sub Committee: Minutes 1902–1939
CAB 16: Committee of Imperial Defence, Ad Hoc Sub Committees: Minutes, Memoranda and Reports 1905–1939
CAB 23: War Cabinet and Cabinet Minutes 1916–1939
CAB 24: War Cabinet and Cabinet Memoranda (GT, CP and G War Series) 1915–1939
CAB 30: Washington (Disarmament) Conference, Minutes and Memoranda
CAB 37: Photographic Copies of Cabinet Papers 1880–1916
CAB 38: Committee of Imperial Defence: Photographic Copies of Minutes and Memoranda 1888–1916
CAB 42: War Council and Successors: Photographic Copies of Minutes and Papers
CAB 53: Chiefs of Staff Minutes and Memoranda 1923–1939
CAB 55: Joint Planning Committee Minutes and Memoranda 1923–1939
CAB 65: War Cabinet and Cabinet Minutes (WM and CM Series) 1939–1942
CAB 66: War Cabinet and Cabinet Memoranda (WP and CP Series) 1939–1942
CAB 69: Defence Committee Operations Minutes and Papers 1940–1942
CAB 70: Defence Committee Supply 1941–1942
CAB 79: Chiefs of Staff Minutes 1940–1942
CAB 80: Chiefs of Staff Memoranda (O) 1940–1942
CAB 81: JIC Minutes and Reports 1941–1942
CAB 84: Joint Planning Committee Papers 1940–1942
CAB 88: Combined Chiefs of Staff Meetings 1942
CAB 99: US and UK Summit Conferences 1941–1942
CAB 105: War Cabinet and Cabinet Office Telegrams.
CAB 106: Historical Section: Archivist and Librarian Files
CAB 119: Joint Planning Staff: Correspondence and Papers
CAB 120: Minister of Defence Secretariat Records
CAB 121: Special Secret Information Centre: Files
CAB 122: Records of British Joint Staff and Joint Services Missions Washington
CAB 146: Historical Section, Enemy Documents Section: Files and Papers
CAB 158: Ministry of Defence and Cabinet Office: Central Intelligence Machinery: Joint Intelligence Sub-Committee, later Committee: Memoranda
CAB 159: Ministry of Defence and Cabinet Office: Central Intelligence Machinery: Joint Intelligence Sub-Committee, later Committee: Minutes
CAB 186: Central Intelligence Machinery: Joint Intelligence Committee Memoranda
Premier files
PREM 1: Prime Minister's Office: Correspondence and papers 1916–1940

PREM 3: Prime Minister's Office: Operational correspondence 1937–1946
PREM 4: Prime Minister's Office: Confidential correspondence 1934–1946
PREM 11: Prime Minister's Office: Correspondence and Papers 1951–1964
PREM 13: Prime Minister's Office: Correspondence and Papers 1964–1970
PREM 15: Prime Minister's Office: Correspondence and Papers 1970–1974
PREM 16: Prime Minister's Office: Correspondence and Papers 1974–1979
PREM 19: Prime Minister's Office: Correspondence and Papers 1979–1997

Foreign Office records
FO 371: Political Developments: General correspondence from 1906–1966

Intelligence records
HW 1: Government Code and Cipher School: Signals Intelligence passed to the Prime Minister, messages and correspondence
HW 3: Government Code and Cipher School and predecessors: Personal Papers, Unofficial Histories, Foreign Office X Files and Miscellaneous Records
HW 4: Government Code and Cipher School: Far East Combined Bureau, Signals Intelligence Centre in the Far East (HMS *Anderson*): Records
HW 5: Government Code and Cipher School: German Section: Reports of German Army and Air Force High Grade Machine Decrypts
HW 7: Room 40 and Successors: World War I Official Histories 1914–1923
HW 8: Government Code and Cipher School: Naval Section: Reports, Working Aids and Correspondence
HW 12: Government Code and Cipher School: Diplomatic Section and predecessors: Decrypts of intercepted diplomatic communications (BJ Series)
HW 14: Government Code and Cipher School: Directorate: Second World War Policy Papers
HW 41: Government Code and Cipher School: Services Field Signals Intelligence Units: Reports of Intercepted Signals and Histories of Field Signals Intelligence Units
HW 43: Government Code and Cipher School: Histories of British Sigint
HW 50: Government Code and Cipher School: Records relating to the writing of the history of British signals intelligence in the Second World War
KV 1: The Security Service: First World War Historical Reports and Other Papers 1908–1939
KV 2: The Security Service: Personal (PF Series) Files 1913–1983
KV 3: The Security Service: Subject (SF Series) Files 1905–1978
KV 4: The Security Service: Policy (Pol F Series) Files
HD 3: Foreign Office: Permanent Under Secretary's Department: Correspondence and Papers 1742–1909

Records of the fighting services

Admiralty
ADM 1: Admiralty: Correspondence and Papers
ADM 116: Admiralty: Record Office: Cases
ADM 137: Admiralty: Historical Section: Records used for Official History, First World War 1860–1937
ADM 167: Board of Admiralty: Minutes and Memoranda
ADM 173: Admiralty: Submarine Logs
ADM 178: Admiralty: Naval Courts Martial Cases, Boards of Enquiry Reports, and other papers
ADM 199: Admiralty: War History Cases and Papers, Second World War
ADM 205: Admiralty: Office of the First Sea Lord, correspondence and papers
ADM 223: Admiralty: Naval Intelligence Division and Operational Intelligence Centre: Intelligence Reports and Papers
ADM 234: Admiralty: Reference Books (BR Series)
ADM 331: Admiralty and Ministry of Defence: Organisation and Methods Department
War Office
WO 193: Directorate of Military Operations and Plans: Planning and Intelligence
WO 208: Records of Directorate of Military Intelligence 1940–1942
WO 216: Office of the Chief of the Imperial General Staff: Papers

Air Ministry
AIR 2: Air Ministry records comprising policy, case and committee reports
AIR 8: Records of the Chief of Air Staff

AIR 14: Bomber Command operational and technical matters.

AIR 19: Air Ministry and Ministry of Defence, Air Department, Private Office Papers

AIR 20: Papers accumulated by the Air Historical Branch

AIR 22: Air Intelligence Summaries

AIR 23: Royal Air Force Overseas Commands

AIR 40: Air Ministry: Directorate of Intelligence: reports and papers

AIR 41: Air Ministry and Ministry of Defence: Air Historical Branch: Narratives and Monographs.

Ministry of Defence

DEFE 3: Admiralty: Operational Intelligence Centre: Intelligence from Intercepted German, Italian and Japanese Radio Communications, WWII

DEFE 5: Ministry of Defence: Chiefs of Staff Committee: Memoranda

DEFE 7: Ministry of Defence prior to 1964: Registered Files (General Series)

DEFE 13: Ministry of Defence: Private Office: Registered Files (All Ministers)

DEFE 19: Ministry of Defence: Central Defence Scientific Staff

DEFE 24: Ministry of Defence: Defence Secretariat Branches and Predecessors

DEFE 25: Ministry of Defence: Chief of Defence Staff Series

DEFE 31: Ministry of Defence: Defence Intelligence Staff: Director General of Intelligence, later Chief of Defence Intelligence.

DEFE 32: Ministry of Defence: Chiefs of Staff Committee: Secretary's Standard Files

DEFE 68: Ministry of Defence: Central Staffs

DEFE 69: Ministry of Defence (Navy): Registered Files and Branch Folders

DEFE 70: Ministry of Defence (Army): Registered Files

Published official records

United Kingdom

Navy Records Society

Vol 102, *The Fisher Papers, Vol I*, ed P K Kemp (Spottiswoode, Ballantyne & Co, 1960)

Vol 106, *The Fisher Papers, Vol II*, ed P K Kemp (Spottiswoode, Ballantyne & Co, 1964)

Vol 108, *The Jellicoe Papers, Vol I 1893–1916*, ed A Temple Patterson (Spottiswoode, Ballantyne & Co, 1966)

Vol 111, *The Jellicoe Papers, Vol II 1916–1935*, ed A Temple Patterson (Spottiswoode, Ballantyne & Co, 1968)

Vol 113, *The Naval Air Service, Vol I 1908–1918*, ed S W Roskill (Spottiswoode, Ballantyne & Co, 1969)

Vol 115, *Policy and Operations in the Mediterranean 1912–1914*, ed E R S Lumby (William Clowes and Sons, 1970)

Vol 117, *The Keyes Papers, Vol I 1914–1918*, ed Paul G Halpern (William Clowes, 1972)

Vol 121, *The Keyes Papers, Vol II 1919–1938*, ed Paul G Halpern (William Clowes, 1980)

Vol 126, *The Royal Navy in the Mediterranean 1915–1918*, ed Paul G Halpern (George Allen and Unwin, 1980)

Vol 130, *Anglo-American Naval Relations 1917–1919*, ed Michael Simpson (Scolar Press, 1991)

Vol 131, *British Naval Documents 1204–1960*, ed John B Hattendorf, R J B Knight, A W H Pearsall, N A M Rodger and Geoffrey Till (Scolar Press, 1993)

Vol 128, *The Beatty Papers, Vol I 1902–1918*, ed B Ranft (Scolar Press, 1989)

Vol 132, *The Beatty Papers, Vol II 1916–1927*, ed B Ranft (Scolar Press, 1993)

Vol 134, *The Somerville Papers*, ed Michael Simpson (Scolar Press, 1995)

Vol 136, *The Collective Naval Defence of the Empire 1900–1940*, ed Nicholas Tracy (Ashgate Publishing, 1997)

Vol 137, *The Defeat of the Enemy Attack on Shipping, 1939–1945*, ed Eric J Grove (Ashgate Publishing, 1997)

Vol 139, *The Battle of the Atlantic and Signals Intelligence: U-boat Situations and Trends, 1941–1945*, ed David Syrett (Ashgate Publishing, 1998)

Vol 140, *The Cunningham papers, Selections from the Private and Official Correspondence, Vol 1, The Mediterranean Fleet, 1939–1942*, ed Michael Simpson (Ashgate Publishing, 1999)

Vol 142, *The Submarine Service 1900–1918*, ed N A Lambert (Ashgate Publishing, 2001)

Vol 144, *The Battle of the Atlantic and Signals Intelligence: U-boat Tracking Papers, 1941–1947*, ed David Syrett (Ashgate Publishing, 2002)

Vol 145, *The Maritime Blockade of Germany in the Great War: The Northern Patrol 1914–1918*, ed John D Grainger (Ashgate Publishing, 2003)

Vol 147, *The Milne Papers, Vol 1 1820–1859*, ed John Beeler (Ashgate Publishing, 2004)

Vol 149, *Sea Power and the Control of Trade: Belligerent Rights from the Russian War to the Beira Patrol, 1854–1970*, ed Nicholas Tracy (Ashgate Publishing, 2005)

Vol 150, *The Cunningham papers, Selections from the Private and Official Correspondence, Vol 2, The Triumph of Allied Sea Power, 1942–1946*, ed Michael Simpson (Ashgate Publishing, 2006)

Vol 152, *Naval Intelligence from Germany: The Reports of the British Naval Attachés in Berlin, 1906–1914*, ed Matthew S Seligmann (Ashgate Publishing, 2007)

Vol 155, *Anglo-American Naval Relations, 1919–1939*, ed Michael Simpson (Ashgate Publishing, 2010)

Vol 158, *The Mediterranean Fleet 1919–1929*, ed Paul Halpern (Ashgate Publishing, 2011)

Vol 159, *The Fleet Air Arm in the Second World War, Vol 1, 1939–1941*, ed Ben Jones (Ashgate Publishing, 2012)

Vol 161, *The Naval Route to the Abyss: The Anglo-German Naval Race 1895–1914*, ed Matthew S Seligmann, Frank Nagler and Michael Epkenhans (Ashgate Publishing, 2015)

Vol 162, *The Milne Papers, Vol II 1860–1862*, ed John Beeler (Ashgate Publishing, 2015)

Vol 164, *The Naval Miscellany Vol VIII*, ed Brian Vale (Routledge, 2017)

United States

Franklin D Roosevelt Presidential Library

US Congress, Joint Committee on the Investigation of the Pearl Harbor Attack, *Report* (Washington DC: US Government Printing Office, 1946)

US Congress, Joint Committee on the Investigation of the Pearl Harbor Attack, *Hearings before the Joint Committee*, Vols 1–39 (Washington, DC: US Government Printing Office, 1946)

The 'Magic' Background to Pearl Harbor, Vols 1–8 (US Department of Defence, 1977)

US Strategic Bombing Survey (Pacific), Naval Analysis Division, *Interrogation of Japanese Officials*, OPNAV-P-03-100

Military History Section Headquarters, US Army Forces Far East, *Japanese Monographs*, distributed by the Office of the Chief of Military History, Department of the Army, 1946 – 1960. Most of these monographs can be accessed at: www.ibiblio.org/hyperwar/Japan/Monos/index.html; and, www.milspecmanuals.com

Reports of General MacArthur: Japanese Operations in the Southwest Pacific Area, Vol II, Part I. Compiled from Japanese Demobilisation Bureau Records. (US Centre for Military History, 1994 edition)

Private papers

Alexander, Viscount A V, Churchill College, Cambridge

Beesly, Patrick, Churchill College, Cambridge

Chatfield, Admiral of the Fleet, Lord, National Maritime Museum, Greenwich

Clarke, William Francis, Churchill College, Cambridge

Cunningham, Admiral of the Fleet Viscount of Hyndhope, British Library

Davis, Admiral Sir William, Churchill College, Cambridge

Dawson, Sir Trevor, Secret reports to the Admiralty 1906–14, Imperial War Museum.

Denning, Vice Admiral Sir Norman, National Maritime Museum.

Denniston, Alistair G, Churchill College, Cambridge

Doig, Captain D H, Royal Naval Museum Library, Portsmouth

Drax, Admiral Sir Reginald P E, Churchill College, Cambridge

Dreyer, Admiral Sir Frederick, Churchill College, Cambridge

Fisher, Admiral of the Fleet, John Arbuthnot, 1st Baron, Churchill College, Cambridge

Godfrey, Vice Admiral J H, National Maritime Museum

Grimsdale, Major General G E, Personal Memoir, Imperial War Museum

Hall, Rear Admiral Sir Reginald, Churchill College, Cambridge

House, Colonel Edward Mandell, Yale University Library

Jellicoe, Admiral of the Fleet Earl, British Library

Kennedy, Captain Malcolm Duncan, Diaries 1917–1946, Library, University of Sheffield.

Layton, Admiral Sir Geoffrey, British Library

McKenna, Reginald, Churchill College, Cambridge

Marder, Professor Arthur J, University of California Irvine Libraries, Special Collections

Oliver, Admiral of the Fleet Sir Henry, National Maritime Museum

Richmond, Admiral Sir Herbert, National Maritime Museum

Roskill, Captain S W, Churchill College, Cambridge

Ross, Rear Admiral G C, Imperial War Museum

Rushbrooke, Rear Admiral Edmund, Imperial War Museum

Somerville, Admiral of the Fleet Sir James, Churchill College, Cambridge

Published memoirs

Agar, Augustus, *Footprints in the Sea* (London: Evans Bros, 1959)

Alanbrooke, Field Marshal Lord, ed Alex Danchev and Daniel Todman, *War Diaries 1939–1945* (London: Weidenfeld and Nicolson, 2001)

Bywater, Hector C and H C Ferraby, *Strange Intelligence: Memoirs of Naval Secret Service* (London: Constable & Co, 1931)

Chatfield, Admiral of the Fleet Lord, *The Navy and Defence* (London: William Heinemann, 1942–1947): *Vol 1: The Navy and Defence* (1942); *Vol 2: It Might Happen Again* (1947)

Churchill, Winston S, *The Second World War* (London: Cassell, 1948–1954): *The Gathering Storm* (1948); *Their Finest Hour* (1949); *The Grand Alliance* (1950); *The Hinge of Fate* (1951)

Cunningham, Admiral of the Fleet Viscount of Hyndhope, *A Sailor's Odyssey* (London: Hutchinson, 1957)

Dönitz, Admiral Karl, *Memoirs: Ten Years and Twenty Days* (Frontline Books edn, 2012)

Hall, Rear Admiral Reginald, *A Clear Case of Genius: Room 40's Code-breaking Pioneer*, original unpublished autobiography from 1926–1933, ed Philip Vickers (The History Press, 2017)

Hankey, Lord, *The Supreme Command 1914–1918* (London: George Allen & Unwin, 1961)

Ismay, General the Lord, *Memoirs* (London: William Heinemann, 1960)

James, Admiral Sir William, *The Sky was always Blue* (London: Methuen & Co, 1951)

Jellicoe, Admiral Viscount John of Scapa, *The Grand Fleet 1914–16* (London: Cassell & Co, 1919)

Kennedy, Major General Sir John, *The Business of War: The War Narrative of Major General Sir John Kennedy* (London: Hutchinson, 1957)

Oppenheimer, Sir Francis, *Stranger Within: Autobiographical Pages* (Faber & Faber, 1960)

Pownall, Lieutenant General Sir Henry, *Chief of Staff: The Diaries of Lieutenant General Sir Henry Pownall, Vol 2 1940–44*, ed Brian Bond (London: Leo Cooper, 1974)

Scheer, Admiral Reinhard, *Germany's High Seas Fleet in the World War* (London: Cassell & Co, 1920)

Slessor, Marshal of the Royal Air Force Sir John, *The Central Blue: Recollections and Reflections by Marshal of the Royal Air Force Sir John Slessor* (London: Cassell & Co, 1956)

Tirpitz, Grand Admiral Alfred von, *My Memoirs* (New York: Dodd, Mead & Co, 1920)

Published official books

Naval Intelligence Division, *Iraq and the Persian Gulf (Geographical Handbook Series)* (reprint of 1942 publication by Kegan Paul, 2005)

Secondary works

Books

Aldrich, Richard J, *Espionage, security and intelligence in Britain 1945–1970* (Manchester University Press, 1998)

——, *Intelligence and the War against Japan: Britain, America, and the Politics of Secret Service* (Cambridge University Press, 2000)

——, *GCHQ: The Uncensored Story of Britain's Most Secret Intelligence Agency* (London: William Collins edn, 2019)

Aldrich, Richard J, Rory Cormac and Michael S Goodman, *Spying on the World: The Declassified Documents of the Joint Intelligence Committee, 1936–2013* (Edinburgh University Press, 2014)

Aldrich, Richard J, and Rory Cormac, *The Black Door: Spies, Secret Intelligence and British Prime Ministers* (London: William Collins, 2016)

Andrew, Christopher, *Secret Service: The Making of the British Intelligence Community* (London: William Heinemann, 1985)

——, *For the President's Eyes Only: Secret Intelligence and the American Presidency from Washington to Bush* (New York: Harper Collins, 1995)

——, *The Defence of the Realm: The Authorised History of MI5* (London, Allen Lane, 2009)

——, *The Secret World: A History of Intelligence* (Allen Lane, 2018)

Andrew, Christopher, with Richard Aldrich and Wesley K Wark, *Secret Intelligence: A Reader* (Abingdon, Oxon: Routledge, 2009)

Ballantyne, Iain, *Hunter Killers: The Dramatic Untold Story of the Royal Navy's Most Secret Service* (London: Orion, 2014)

——, *The Deadly Trade: A History of Submarine Warfare from Archimedes to the Present* (London: W&N, 2018)

Barnett, Correlli, *The Collapse of British Power* (Eyre Methuen, 1972)

——, *The Audit of War: The Illusion and Reality of Britain as a Great Nation* (Basingstoke: Macmillan, 1986)

——, *Engage the Enemy More Closely* (London: Hodder and Stoughton, 1991)

Barrass, Gordon S, *The Great Cold War: A Journey through the Hall of Mirrors* (USA: Stanford University Press, 2009)

Barry, Quintin, *The War in the North Sea: The Royal Navy and the Imperial German Navy 1914–1918* (Helion & Co, 2016)

Batey, Mavis, *Dilly: The Man who broke Enigmas* (Biteback Publishing, 2017)

Bath, Alan Harris, *Tracking the Axis Enemy: The Triumph of Anglo-American Naval Intelligence* (USA: Kansas University Press, 1998)

Beach, Jim, *Haig's Intelligence* (Cambridge University Press, 2015)

Beesly, Patrick, *Very Special Admiral: The Life of Admiral J H Godfrey* (London: Hamish Hamilton, 1980)

——, *Room 40: British Naval Intelligence 1914–1918* (OUP, 1984)

——, *Very Special Intelligence: The Story of the Admiralty's Operational Intelligence Centre 1939–1945* (Chatham Publishing edn, 2006)

Beevor, Anthony, *The Second World War* (London: Weidenfeld and Nicolson, 2012)

Bell, Christopher M, *The Royal Navy, Seapower and Strategy between the Wars* (Basingstoke, UK: Macmillan Press, 2000)

——, *Churchill and Seapower* (Oxford University Press, 2012)

——, *Churchill and the Dardanelles* (Oxford University Press, 2017)

Bennett, G H, *The Royal Navy in the Age of Austerity: Naval and Foreign Policy under Lloyd George* (London: Bloomsbury Academic, 2016)

Bennett, Gill, *Churchill's Man of Mystery: Desmond Morton and the World of Intelligence* (Abingdon, Oxon: Routledge, 2007)

——, *The Zinoviev Letter: The Conspiracy that Never Dies* (OUP, 2018)

Bennett, Ralph, *Behind the Battle: Intelligence in the War with Germany, 1939–1945* (Pimlico, 1999)

Benson, Robert L, *A History of US Communications Intelligence in World War II: Policy and Administration* (USA: Center for Cryptological History, National Security Agency, 1997)

Best, Anthony, *British Intelligence and the Japanese Challenge in Asia 1914–1941* (London: Palgrave Macmillan, 2002)

Birch, Frank, *The Official History of British Sigint 1914–1945*, Vol 1, Part 1, ed John Jackson (Military Press, 2004)

——, *The Official History of British Sigint 1914–1945*, Vol 1, Part 2 and Vol 2, ed John Jackson (Military Press, 2007)

Black, Jeremy, *The Politics of World War Two* (London: Social Affairs Unit, 2009)

Black, Nicholas, *The British Naval Staff in the First World War* (Woodbridge: Boydell Press, 2009)

Blair, Clay, *Hitler's U-boat War, The Hunters 1939–1942* (London: Weidenfeld & Nicolson, 1997)

——, *Hitler's U-boat War, The Hunted 1942–1945* (London: Weidenfeld & Nicolson, 1999)

Boghardt, Thomas, *The Zimmermann Telegram: Intelligence, Diplomacy and America's Entry into World War I* (Annapolis USA: Naval Institute Press, 2012)

Bonham Carter, Violet, *Winston Churchill as I knew him* (London: Eyre & Spottiswoode, 1965)

Boog, Horst, Werner Rahn and Bernd Wegner, *Germany and the Second World War, Vol VI, The Global War* (OUP, 2001)

Bouverie, Tim, *Appeasing Hitler: Chamberlain, Churchill and the Road to War* (London: Bodley Head, 2019)

Boyd, Andrew, *The Royal Navy in Eastern Waters: Linchpin of Victory 1935–1942* (Barnsley: Seaforth, 2017)

Boyd, Carl, *Hitler's Japanese Confidant: General Ōshima Hiroshi and Magic Intelligence 1941–1945* (USA: University of Kansas, 1993)

Braithwaite, Rodric, *Armageddon and Paranoia: The Nuclear Confrontation* (London: Profile Books, 2017)

Brodhurst, Robin, *Churchill's Anchor: The Biography of Admiral of the Fleet Sir Dudley Pound OM, GCB, GCVO* (UK: Leo Cooper, 2000)

Brooke-Shepherd, Gordon, *The Storm Birds: Soviet Post-War Defectors* (London: Weidenfeld and Nicolson, 1988)

Brooks, John, *Dreadnought Gunnery and the Battle of Jutland: The Question of Fire Control* (London: Routledge, 2005)

——, *The Battle of Jutland* (Cambridge Military Histories) (CUP, 2016)

Brown, David K, *Nelson to Vanguard: Warship Design and Development 1923–1945* (Seaforth Publishing, 2012 edn)

Budiansky, Stephen, *Battle of Wits: The Complete Story of Codebreaking in World War II* (London: Viking, 2000)

Burt, R A, *British Battleships 1919–1945* (Barnsley: Seaforth Publishing, 2014)

Butler, Professor J R M, *Grand Strategy Vol II: September 1939–June 1941* (London: HMSO, 1957)

——, *Grand Strategy Vol III: June 1941–August 1942, Part II* (London: HMSO, 1964)

Bywater, Hector C, and H C Ferraby, *Strange Intelligence: Memoirs of Naval Secret Service* (Biteback Publishing, 2015)

Carruthers, Bob, *The U-Boat War in the Atlantic*, ed version of 3 vol official Admiralty history by Gunther Hessler (Barnsley: Pen & Sword, 2013)

Churchill, Randolph S, *Winston S Churchill: Young Statesman 1901–1914* (Houghton, 1967)

——, *Winston S Churchill*, Vol II Companion, Part 2, 1908–1911 (Heinemann, 1969)

Clausen, Henry C, and Bruce Lee, *Pearl Harbor: Final Judgement* (USA: Da Capo Press, 2001)

Clayton, Tim, *Sea Wolves: The Extraordinary Story of Britain's WWII Submarines* (Little Brown, 2011)

Cobb, Stephen, *Preparing for Blockade 1885–1914: Naval Contingency for Economic Warfare* (Ashgate Publishing, 2013)

Conley, Dan, and Richard Woodman, *Cold War Command: The Dramatic Story of a Nuclear Submariner* (Barnsley: Seaforth, 2014)

Corbett, Sir Julian S, and Henry Newbolt, *History of the Great War: Naval Operations*, 5 vols (London: Longmans Green & Co, 1920–1931)

Corera, Gordon, *Intercept: The Secret History of Computers and Spies* (Weidenfeld & Nicolson, 2015)

Cradock, Percy, *Know Your Enemy: How the Joint Intelligence Committee saw the World* (London: John Murray, 2002)

Davies, Philip H J, *MI6 and the Machinery of Spying* (Abingdon, Oxon: Frank Cass, 2004)

——, *Intelligence and Government in Britain and the United States: A Comparative Perspective, Vol 2, Evolution of the UK Community* (Praeger, 2012)

Deacon, Richard, *The Silent War: A History of Western Naval Intelligence* (London: Grafton Books, revised edn, 1988)

Dear, I C B; and M R D Foot, *The Oxford Companion to World War II*, paperback edn (Oxford University Press, 2001)

Deist, Wilhelm, and others, *Germany and the Second World War, Vol I, The Build-up of German Aggression* (OUP, 2015 edn)

Denniston, Robin, *Thirty Secret Years: A G Denniston's work in Signals Intelligence 1914–1944* (UK: Polperro Heritage Press, 2007)

Dimbleby, Jonathan, *The Battle of the Atlantic: How the Allies Won the War* (Penguin, 2015)

Doenecke, Justus D, *Nothing Less than War: A New History of America's Entry into World War I* (University Press of Kentucky, 2011)

Donaghy, Aaron, *The British Government and the Falkland Islands 1974–79* (Palgrave Macmillan, 2014)

Donovan, Peter, and John Mack, *Codebreaking in the Pacific* (New York: Springer International, 2014)

Downing, Taylor, *Spies in the Sky: The Secret Battle for Aerial Intelligence in World War II* (London: Little Brown, 2011)

Dunley, Richard, *Britain and the Mine, 1900–1915: Culture, Strategy and International Law* (Palgrave Macmillan, 2018)

Dunn, Steve R, *Blockade: Cruiser Warfare and the Starvation of Germany in World War One* (Barnsley: Seaforth, 2016)

Dylan, Huw, *Defence Intelligence and the Cold War: Britain's Joint Intelligence Bureau 1945–1964* (OUP, 2014)

Edgerton, David, *Warfare State: Britain, 1920–1970* (Cambridge University Press, 2006)

——, *Britain's War Machine: Weapons, Resources and Experts in the Second World War* (London: Allen Lane, 2011)

Erskine, Ralph, and Michael Smith, *The Bletchley Park Codebreakers: How Ultra shortened the War and led to the birth of the computer* (Biteback Publishing, 2011)

Evans, David C, and Mark R Peattie, *Kaigun: Strategy, Tactics and Technology in the Imperial Japanese Navy* (Annapolis, USA: Naval Institute Press, 1997)

Evans, Richard J, *The Third Reich at War* (London: Penguin, 2009)

Farago, Ladislas, *The Game of the Foxes: British and German intelligence operations and personalities which changed the course of the Second World War* (London: Hodder and Stoughton, 1971)

Farrell, Brian, *The Basis and Making of Grand Strategy – Was there a Plan?* (UK: Edwin Mellen Press, 1998)

Farrell, Brian, and Sandy Hunter, *Sixty Years On: The Fall of Singapore Revisited* (Singapore: Eastern Universities Press, 2003)

Faulkner, Marcus, and Christopher Bell, *Decision in the Atlantic: The Allies and the Longest Campaign of the Second World War* (Andarta Books, University of Kentucky, 2019)

Ferris, John R, *Intelligence and Strategy* (London, Routledge: 2005)

Ferris, John R, and Evan Mawdsley, *The Cambridge History of the Second World War, Vol 1, Fighting the War* (Cambridge University Press, 2015)

Ford, Douglas, *Britain's Secret War Against Japan 1937–1945* (Abingdon, UK: Routledge, 2006)

Franklin, George, *Britain's Anti-Submarine Capability 1919–1939* (London: Routledge, 2003)

Freedman, Lawrence, *Britain and Nuclear Weapons* (Basingstoke: Macmillan, 1980)

——, *The Official History of the Falklands Campaign* (London: Routledge, 2005):*Vol I The Origins of the Falklands War; Vol II War and Diplomacy*

Friedman, Norman, *Network-Centric Warfare: How Navies Learned to Fight Smarter through Three World Wars* (Naval Institute Press, 2009)

——, *British Cruisers: Two World Wars and After* (Barnsley: Seaforth, 2012)

——, *Fighting the Great War at Sea: Strategy, Tactics and Technology* (Seaforth Publishing, 2014)

——, *The British Battleship 1906–1946* (Barnsley: Seaforth Publishing, 2015).

Fry, Helen, *Spymaster: The Secret Life of Kendrick* (London: Thistle Publishing, 2015)

——, *The London Cage: The Secret History of Britain's World War II Interrogation Centre* (Yale University Press, 2017)

Gannon, Paul, *Inside Room 40: The Codebreakers of World War I* (Ian Allen Publishing, 2010)

Gardner, W J R, *Decoding History: The Battle of the Atlantic and Ultra* (Annapolis: Naval Institute Press, 2000)

Gibbs, Professor N H, *Grand Strategy*, Vol I (HMSO, 1976)

Gilbert, Martin, *Winston S Churchill, Vol VI, Finest Hour 1939–1941* and *Vol VII, Road to Victory 1941–1945* (London: William Heinemann, 1983 and 1986)

——, *The Churchill War Papers, Vol 3, The ever-widening war* (London: William Heinemann, 2000)

Goldrick, James, *Before Jutland: The Naval War in Northern European Waters, August 1914–February 1915* (Annapolis USA: Naval Institute Press, 2015)

——, *After Jutland: The Naval War in Northern European Waters, June 1916–November 1918* (Annapolis: Naval Institute Press, 2018)

Goodman, Michael S, *The Official History of the Joint Intelligence Committee: Vol I, From the Approach of the Second World War to the Suez Crisis* (Abingdon, Oxon: Routledge, 2014)

Gordon, Andrew, *The Rules of the Game: Jutland and British Naval Command* (London: John Murray, 1996)

Gough, Barry, *Historical Dreadnoughts: Arthur Marder, Stephen Roskill and Battles for Naval History* (Barnsley UK: Seaforth Publishing, 2010)

Grant, Robert M, *U-boats Destroyed: The Effect of Anti-Submarine Warfare 1914–1918* (Periscope Publishing, 2002)

——, *U-boat Intelligence: Admiralty Intelligence Division and the Defeat of the U-boats 1914–1918* (Periscope Publishing, 2002)

——, *The U-boat Hunters: Codebreakers, Divers and the Defeat of the U-boats 1914–1918* (Periscope Publishing, 2003)

Greenberg, Joel, *Alistair Denniston: Code-breaking from Room 40 to Berkeley Street and the Birth of GCHQ* (Frontline Books edn, 2017)

Greene, Jack, and Alessandro Massignani, *The Naval War in the Mediterranean 1940–1943* (UK: Chatham Publishing, 2002)

Grieves, Keith, *Sir Eric Geddes: Business and Government in War and Peace* (Manchester University Press, 1989)

Grimes, Shawn T, *Strategy and War Planning in the British Navy, 1887–1918* (Boydell Press, 2012)

Grove, Eric, *Vanguard to Trident: British Naval Policy Since World War II* (Annapolis, Naval Institute Press, 1987)

——, *The Royal Navy* (Basingstoke, UK, Palgrave Macmillan, 2005)

Gwyer, J M A, *Grand Strategy Vol III: June 1941–August 1942, Part I* (London: HMSO, 1964)

Haarr, Geirr H, *The Battle for Norway, April – June 1940* (Barnsley, Seaforth Publishing, 2010)

——, *The German Invasion of Norway, April 1940* (Barnsley: Seaforth Publishing, 2011)

——, *The Gathering Storm: The Naval War in Northern Europe, September 1939–April 1940* (Barnsley: Seaforth Publishing, 2013)

Halpern, Paul G, *The Naval War in the Mediterranean: 1914–1918* (Routledge, 2017 edn)

Hamilton, C I, *The Anglo-French Naval Rivalry, 1840–1870* (New York and Oxford: OUP, 1993)

——, *The Making of the Modern Admiralty: British Naval Policy-making, 1805–1927* (Cambridge University Press, 2011)

Hancock, W K, and M M Gowing, *The British War Economy* (British Official History Civil Series) (London: HMSO, 1949)

Harding, Richard, *The Royal Navy, 1930–2000, Innovation and Defence* (London and New York: Frank Cass, 2004)

Hart-Davis, Duff, *Man of War: The Secret Life of Captain Alan Hillgarth* (London: Century, 2012)

Hart-Dyke, David, *Four Weeks in May: A Captain's Story of War at Sea* (Atlantic Books, 2007)

Hastings, Max, *All Hell Let Loose: The World at War 1939–45* (London: Harper Press, 2011)

——, *The Secret War: Spies, Codes and Guerrillas 1939–1945* (London: William Collins, 2015)

Hennessy, Peter, and James Jinks, *The Silent Deep: The Royal Navy Submarine Service since 1945* (London: Allen Lane, 2015)

Herwig, Holger H, *The First World War: Germany and Austria–Hungary 1914–1918* (2nd edn, Bloomsbury Academic, 2014)

Hinsley, F H, with E E Thomas, C F G Ransom and R C Knight, *British Intelligence in the Second World War. Its Influence on Strategy and Operations*, 3 vols (London: HMSO, 1977–1984)

Hinsley, F H, and Alan Stripp, *Code Breakers: The Inside Story of Bletchley Park* (Oxford University Press, 1993)

Hobbs, David, *The British Pacific Fleet: The Royal Navy's Most Powerful Strike Force* (Barnsley: Seaforth Publishing, 2011)

Hodges, Andrew, *Alan Turing: The Enigma of Intelligence* (London: Unwin Hyman, 1985)

Honan, William H, *Bywater: The Man who invented the Pacific War* (London: Macdonald & Co, 1990)

Hore, Peter, *Dreadnought to Daring: 100 Years of Comment, Controversy and Debate in The Naval Review* (Barnsley: Seaforth Publishing, 2012)

Hotta, Eri, *Japan 1941, Countdown to Infamy* (New York: Knopf Publishing, 2013)

Hough, Richard, *Dreadnought: A History of the Modern Battleship* (London: Michael Joseph, 1965)

Howard, Michael, *The Mediterranean Strategy in the Second World War* (London: Greenhill Books, 1993)

Howse, Derek, *Radar at Sea: The Royal Navy in World War II* (Palgrave Macmillan, 1993)

Insall, Tony, *Secret Alliances: Special Operations and Intelligence in Norway 1940–1945 – The British Perspective* (London: Biteback Publishing, 2019)

Irving, David, *The Destruction of Convoy PQ17* (Focal Point Edition, 2005)

James, Admiral Sir William, *The Sky was always Blue* (London: Methuen & Co, 1951)

——, *The Eyes of the Navy: A Biographical Study of Admiral Sir Reginald Hall* (London: Methuen, 1955)

Jeffery, Keith, *MI6: The History of the Secret Intelligence Service 1909–1949* (London: Bloomsbury, 2010)

Jellicoe, Nicholas, *Jutland: The Unfinished Battle* (Seaforth Publishing, 2016)

Jones, Matthew, *The Official History of the UK Strategic Nuclear Deterrent Vol I: From the V-Bomber Era to the Arrival of Polaris, 1945–1964* (Abingdon, Oxon: Routledge, 2017)

——, *The Official History of the UK Strategic Nuclear Deterrent Vol II: The Labour Government and the Polaris Programme, 1964–1970* (Abingdon, Oxon: Routledge, 2017)

Jones, R V, *Most Secret War: British Scientific Intelligence 1939–1945* (London: Hamish Hamilton, 1978)

Judd, Alan, *The Quest for C: Mansfield Cumming and the Founding of the Secret Service* (London: Harper Collins, 1999)

Kahn, David, *The Code-Breakers: The Comprehensive History of Secret Communication from Ancient Times to the Internet* (New York: Scribner, 1996 edition)

——, *Seizing the Enigma: The Race to Break the German U-boat Codes* (Frontline Books edn, 2012).

Keegan, John, *Intelligence in War: Knowledge of the Enemy from Napoleon to Al-Qaeda* (Vintage Digital, 2010)

Kennedy, Greg, *Anglo-American Strategic Relations in the Far East 1933–1939* (London: Frank Cass, 2002)

——, *Britain's War at Sea 1914–1918: The war they thought and the war they fought* (Routledge, 2016)

Kennedy, Paul M, *The Rise and Fall of British Naval Mastery* (London: Allen Lane, 1976)

——, *The Rise and Fall of the Great Powers* (London: Unwin Hyman, 1988)

——, *Engineers of Victory: The Problem Solvers Who Turned the Tide in the Second World War* (London: Allen Lane, 2013)

Kenyon, David, *Bletchley Park and D-Day: The Untold Story of How the Battle for Normandy Was Won* (Newhaven USA and London: Yale University Press, 2019)

Kershaw, Ian, *Fateful Choices: Ten Decisions That Changed The World* (London: Penguin Group, 2007)

Kingsley, F A, *Radar: The Development of Equipments for the Royal Navy 1939–45* (Macmillan, 1995)

Kirby, M W, *Operational Research in War and Peace: The British Experience from the 1930s to the 1970s* (London: Imperial College Press, 2003)

Kiszely, John, *Anatomy of a Campaign: The British Fiasco in Norway, 1940* (CUP, 2017)

Knight, Roger, *Britain Against Napoleon: The Organisation of Victory, 1793–1815* (Allen Lane, 2013).

Kotani, Ken, *Japanese Intelligence in World War II* (Oxford, UK: Osprey Publishing, 2009)

Kroener, Bernhard R, Rolf Dieter Muller and Hans Umbreit, *Germany and the Second World War: Vol V: Organisation and Mobilisation in the German Sphere of Power: Part 1: Wartime Administration, Economy and Manpower Resources 1939–1941*, English edn (UK: Clarendon Press, 2006)

——, *Germany and the Second World War: Vol V: Organisation and Mobilisation in the German Sphere of Power: Part 2: Wartime Administration, Economy and Manpower Resources 1942–1944/45*, English edn (UK: Clarendon Press, 2006)

Lambert, Andrew, *Seapower States: Maritime Culture, Continental Empires and the Conflict that made the Modern World* (Yale University Press, 2018

Lambert, Nicholas A, *Sir John Fisher's Naval Revolution* (University of South Carolina Press, 2002).

——, *Planning Armageddon: British Economic Warfare and the First World War* (Harvard University press, 2012)

Landau, Henry, *The Spy Net: The Greatest Intelligence Operations of the First World War* (Biteback Publishing edn, 2013)

Leutze, James R, *Bargaining for Supremacy: Anglo-American Naval Collaboration, 1937–1941* (USA: University of North Carolina Press, 1977)

Lloyd, Nick, *Passchendaele: A New History* (UK: Viking, 2017)

Lukacs, John, *The Legacy of the Second World War* (New Haven, USA and London: Yale University Press, 2010).

Lycett, Andrew, *Ian Fleming* (London: Weidenfeld & Nicolson, 1995)

Macintyre, Ben, *Operation Mincemeat* (London: Bloomsbury Publishing, 2010)

MacIntyre, Captain Donald, *Fighting Admiral: The Life of Admiral of the Fleet Sir James Somerville* (London: Evans brothers, 1961)

McKay, C G, and Bengt Beckman, *Swedish Signal Intelligence 1900–1945* (London: Routledge, 2014)

McLachlan, Donald, *Room 39, Naval Intelligence in Action 1939–45* (London: Weidenfeld and Nicolson, 1968)

Maffeo, Steven, *Most Secret and Confidential: Intelligence in the Age of Nelson*, (Annapolis: Naval Institute Press, 2012)

Maier, Klaus A, and others, *Germany and the Second World War, Vol II, Germany's initial conquests in Europe* (OUP, 2015 edn)

Maiolo, Joe, *Cry Havoc: The Arms Race and the Second World War 1931–1941* (London: John Murray, 2011)

Marder, Arthur J, *The Anatomy of British Sea Power: A History of British Naval Policy in the Pre-Dreadnought Era 1880–1905* (London, Frank Cass & Co, 1964)

——, *From the Dreadnought to Scapa Flow* (Seaforth Publishing edn, 2013–14): *Vol I, The Road to War 1904–1914; Vol II, The War Years: To the Eve of Jutland 1914–1916; Vol III, Jutland and After: May to December 1916; Vol IV, 1917: The Year of Crisis; Vol V, Victory and Aftermath: 1918–1919*

——, *From the Dardanelles to Oran: Studies of the Royal Navy in War and Peace, 1915–1940* (London: Oxford University Press, 1974)

——, *Old Friends, New Enemies: the Royal Navy and the Imperial Japanese Navy, 1936-1945* (London and New York: Oxford University Press, 1981–1990): *Vol 1 Strategic Illusions 1936–1941* (1981); *Vol 2 The Pacific War 1942–1945* (1990)

Mars, Alastair, *Submarines at War 1939–1945* (UK: William Kimber, 1971)

Maurer, John H, and Christopher M Bell, *At the Crossroads between Peace and War: The London Naval Conference of 1930* (Annapolis, USA: Naval Institute Press, 2014)

Medlicott, William N, *The Economic Blockade* (London, HMSO, Vol 1 1952, Vol 2 1959)

Millett, Allan, and Williamson R Murray, *Military Innovation in the Interwar Period* (Cambridge University Press, 1996)

——, *A War To Be Won: Fighting the Second World War* (USA: Harvard University Press, 2000)

——, *Military Effectiveness, Vol 2, The Interwar Period* (Cambridge University Press, 2010)

Milner, Marc, *Battle of the Atlantic* (Stroud: The History Press, 2011)

Montagu, Ewen, *Beyond Top Secret U: The Inside Story of WWII Intelligence* (Endeavour Press Ltd edition, 2016)

Moore, Charles, *Margaret Thatcher: The Authorised Biography* (London: Allen Lane, 2013–19): *Vol 1 Not for Turning*; *Vol 2 Everything She Wants*

Morgan-Owen, David, *The Fear of Invasion: Strategy, Politics and British War Planning, 1880–1914* (OUP, 2017)

Morison, Samuel Eliot, *The Two Ocean War* (USA: Little, Brown & Co, 1963)

Morris, Jan, *Fisher's Face* (Viking Press, 1995)

Murfett, Malcolm, *Fool Proof Relations: The Search for Anglo-American Naval Cooperation during the Chamberlain Years 1937–1940* (Singapore University Press: 1984)

——, *The First Sea Lords: From Fisher to Mountbatten* (Westport CT, USA: Praeger, 1995)

——, *Naval Warfare 1919–1945: An operational history of the volatile war at sea* (Oxford: Routledge, 2009)

O'Brien, Phillips Payson, *British and American Naval Power: Politics and Policy, 1900–1936* (Westport, CT, USA: Praeger, 1998)

——, *The Anglo-Japanese Alliance, 1902–1922* (RoutledgeCurzon, 2004)

——, *How the War was Won: Air-Sea Power and Allied Victory in World War II* (Cambridge University Press, 2015)

O'Connell, John F, *Submarine Operational Effectiveness in the 20th Century: Part Two 1939–1945* (USA: iUniverse Inc, 2011)

Offer, Avner, *The First World War: An Agrarian Interpretation* (OUP, 1991)

O'Hara, Vincent P, *Six Victories: North Africa, Malta, and the Mediterranean Convoy War, November 1941–March 1942* (Annapolis: Naval Institute Press, 2019)

O'Keefe, David, *One Day in August: The Untold Story Behind Canada's Tragedy at Dieppe* (Knopf Canada, 2013)

Oliver, David H, *German Naval Strategy,1856–1888: Forerunners to Tirpitz* (Routledge, 2012)

Ollard, Richard, *Fisher and Cunningham: A study of the personalities of the Churchill era* (London: Constable and Company, 1991)

Ong, Chit Chung, *Operation Matador: World War II: Britain's attempt to foil the Japanese invasion of Malaya and Singapore* (London: Times Academic Press, 1997)

Osborne, Eric W, *Britain's Blockade of Germany, 1914–1919* (London: Frank Cass, 2004)

Overy, Richard, *Why the Allies Won* (London: Pimlico, 2006)

Owen, David, *Nuclear Papers* (Liverpool University Press, 2009)

Packer, Joy, *Deep as the Sea* (Eyre Methuen, 1976)

Peattie, Mark R, *Sunburst: The Rise of Japanese Naval Air Power, 1909–1941* (Annapolis: Naval Institute Press, 2001)

Peden, G C, *Arms, Economics and British Strategy: From Dreadnoughts to Hydrogen Bombs* (Cambridge University Press, 2007)

Pedlow, Gregory W, and Donald E Welzebach, *The CIA and the U2 Program 1954–1974* (History Staff Center for the Study of Intelligence, Central Intelligence Agency, 1998)

Pfennigwerth, Ian, *A Man of Intelligence: The Life of Captain Eric Nave, Australian Codebreaker Extraordinary* (Rosenberg Publishing, 2006)

Pitkeathly, Michael, and David Wixon, *Submarine Courageous: Cold War Warrior: The Life and Times of a Nuclear Submarine* (HMS *Courageous* Society, 2010)

Playfair, Major General I S O, *The Mediterranean and Middle East* (HMSO, 1954): *Vol 1 The Early Successes against Italy* (1954); *Vol 2 The Germans Come to the Help of their Ally* (1956)

Popplewell, Richard, *Intelligence and Imperial Defence: British Intelligence and the Defence of the Indian Empire 1904–1924* (Frank Cass, 1995)

Porch, Douglas, *The Path to Victory; The Mediterranean Theatre in World War II* (New York: Farrar, Straus and Giroux, 2004)

Prados, John, *Combined Fleet Decoded: The Secret History of American Intelligence and the Japanese Navy in World War II* (New York: Random House, 1995)

Prange, Gordon W, *Miracle at Midway* (USA: McGraw-Hill Book Co, 1982)

Preston, Paul, *A People Betrayed: A History of Corruption, Political Incompetence and Social Division in Modern Spain* (William Collins, 2020)

Ramsay, David, *'Blinker' Hall: Spymaster: The Man who brought America into World War I* (Stroud, Gloucester: Spellmount, 2008)

Rankin, Nicholas, *Ian Fleming's Commandos: The Story of 30 Assault Unit in WWII* (London: Faber & Faber, 2011)

Redford, Duncan, *A History of the Royal Navy, World War II* (London: I B Tauris, 2014)

Reynolds, David, *The Creation of the Anglo-American Alliance 1937–41: A Study in Competitive Co-operation* (Europe Publications, 1981)

——, *From Munich to Pearl Harbor: Roosevelt's America and the Origins of the Second World War* (Chicago: Ivan Dee, 2001)

——, *In Command of History: Churchill Fighting and Writing the Second World War* (London: Allen Lane, 2004)

Richelson, Jeffrey T, *The US Intelligence Community* (7th edn, Westview Press, 2015)

Ring, Jim, *We Come Unseen: The Untold History of Britain's Cold War Submariners* (London: John Murray, 2001)

Riste, Olav, *The Norwegian Intelligence Service 1945–1970* (Routledge edn, 2013)

Robb-Webb, Jon, *The British Pacific Fleet Experience and Legacy, 1944–50* (UK: Ashgate, 2013)

Roberts, Andrew, *The Holy Fox: A Life of Lord Halifax* (London: Weidenfeld and Nicolson, 1991)

——, *Masters and Commanders: The Military Geniuses who led the West to Victory in World War II* (London: Allen Lane, 2008)

——, *The Storm of War: A New History of the Second World War* (London: Allen Lane, 2009)

Robinson, Douglas H, *The Zeppelin in Combat: A History of the German Naval Airship Division, 1912–1918* (Schiffer edn, 1994)

Rodger, N A M, *The Command of the Ocean: A Naval History of Britain, 1649–1815* (London: Allen Lane, 2004)

Rohwer, Jurgen, *Critical Convoy Battles of WWII: Crisis in the North Atlantic, March 1943* (Stackpole edn, 2015)

Roskill, S W, *The War at Sea* (London: HMSO, 1954–1961): Vol 1 *The Defensive* (1954); Vol 2 *The Period of Balance* (1956); Vol 3 *The Offensive* (1961)

——, *The Navy At War 1939–1945* (London: Collins, 1960)

——, *Naval Policy Between the Wars* (London: Collins, 1968–1976): Vol 1 *The Period of Anglo-American Antagonism, 1919–1929* (1968); Vol 2 *The Period of Reluctant Rearmament, 1930–1939* (1976)

——, *Hankey: Man of Secrets* (London, Collins 1970–1974): Vol 1 *1877–1918*; Vol 2 *1919–1931*; Vol 3 *1931–1963*

——, *Churchill and the Admirals* (London: Collins, 1977)

——, *Naval Policy between the Wars* (National Maritime Museum, Maritime Monograph 29, 1978)

——, *Admiral of the Fleet Earl Beatty: The Last Naval Hero* (New York: Atheneum, 1981)

Rössler, Eberhard, *The U-Boat: The evolution and technical history of German submarines* (Cassell & Co, 2001 edn)

Salerno, Reynolds M, *Vital Crossroads: Mediterranean Origins of the Second World War, 1935–1940* (New York: Cornell University Press, 2002)

Schliehauf, William, *Jutland: The Naval Staff Appreciation* (Seaforth, 2016)

Schreiber, Gerhardt, and Bernd Stegemann, *Germany and the Second World War: Vol 3: The Mediterranean, South-East Europe and North Africa 1939–1941*, English edn (UK: Clarendon Press, 1998)

Sebag-Montefiore, Hugh, *Enigma: The Battle for the Code* (London: Weidenfeld and Nicolson, 2000)

Seligmann, Matthew S, *Spies in Uniform: British Military and Naval Intelligence on the Eve of the First World War* (Oxford: OUP, 2006)

——, *The Royal Navy and the German Threat 1901–1914: Admiralty Plans to protect British Trade in a war with Germany* (OUP, 2012)

Sheffield, Gary, *The Chief: Douglas Haig and the British Army* (Aurum Press, 2012)

Simmons, Mark, *Ian Fleming and Operation Goldeneye: Spies, Scoundrels and Envoys keeping Spain out of World War II* (Oxford: Casemate Publishing, 2018)

Smith, Bradley F, *The Ultra-Magic Deals and the Most Secret Special Relationship 1940–1946* (UK: Airlife Publishing, 1993)

Smith, Christopher, *The Hidden History of Bletchley Park: A Social and Organisational History, 1939–1945* (Basingstoke: Palgrave Macmillan, 2015)

Smith, Michael, *The Emperor's Codes: Bletchley Park's role in breaking Japan's secret ciphers* (London, Bantam Press, 2000)

——, *Six: A History of Britain's Secret Intelligence Service, Part 1: Murder and Mayhem 1909–1939* (London: Dialogue, Biteback, 2010)

Sondhaus, Lawrence, *The Great War at Sea: A Naval History of the First World War* (Cambridge University Press, 2014)

Sontag, Sherry, and Christopher Drew, *Blind Man's Buff: The Untold Story of Cold War Submarine Espionage* (London: Hutchinson, 1999)

Southby-Tailyour, Ewen, *Exocet Falklands: The Untold Story of Special Forces Operations* (Barnsley: Pen & Sword, 2014)

Soybell, Phyllis L, *A Necessary Relationship: The Development of Anglo-American Co-operation in Naval Intelligence* (USA: Praeger, 2005)

Spooner, Tony, *Warburton's War: The Life of Maverick Ace Adrian Warburton* (Manchester: Crecy Publishing, 2003)

Stafford, David, *Churchill and Secret Service* (UK: Overlook Press, 1997)

Stoker, Donald, *Britain, France and the Naval Arms Trade in the Baltic 1919–1939: Grand Strategy and Failure* (Frank Cass, 2003)

Stoler, Mark, *Allies in War: Britain and America Against the Axis Powers 1940–1945* (London: Hodder Education, 2005)

Strachan, Hew, *The First World War, Vol 1 To Arms* (OUP, 2001)

Stripp, Alan, *Codebreaker in the Far East* (OUP, 1995)

Sumida, Jon Tetsuro, *In Defence of Naval Supremacy: Finance, Technology and British Naval Policy 1889–1914* (Annapolis, USA: Naval Institute Press, 2014 (reissue))

Sumner, Ian, *Despise it Not: A Hull Man Spies on the Kaiser's Germany* (Highgate Publications, 2002)

Taylor, A J P, *English History 1914–1945* (OUP, 1965)

Terraine, John, *Business in Great Waters: The U-Boat Wars 1916–1945* (Barnsley: Pen & Sword, 2009)

Thorne, Christopher, *Allies of a Kind: The United States, Britain and the War Against Japan, 1937–1945* (London: Hamish Hamilton, 1978)

Tomaselli, Phil, *Tracing your Secret Service Ancestors* (Barnsley: Pen & Sword, 2009)

Tombs, Robert, *The English and Their History* (Allen Lane, 2014)

Tooze, Adam, *The Wages of Destruction: The Making and Breaking of the Nazi Economy* (London: Allen Lane, 2006)

——, *The Deluge: The Great War and the Remaking of Global Order 1916–1931* (London: Allen Lane, 2014)

Toye, Richard, *Churchill's Empire: The World that Made Him and the World He Made* (London: Macmillan, 2010)

Tuchman, Barbara W, *The Zimmermann Telegram* (First Ballantine Books Edition, 1979)

Tuck, Christopher, *Confrontation, Strategy and War Termination: Britain's Conflict with Indonesia* (Abingdon, Oxon: Routledge, 2016)

Twigge, Stephen, Edward Hampshire and Graham Macklin, *British Intelligence: Secrets, Spies and Sources* (National Archives, Kew, 2008)

Vickers, Philip, *Finding Thoroton: The Royal Marine who ran British Naval Intelligence in World War One* (Royal Marines Historical Society, Special Publication No 40, 2013)

——, *A Clear Case of Genius: Room 40's Code-breaking Pioneer: Admiral Sir Reginald 'Blinker' Hall* (Stroud, UK: The History Press, 2017)

Wark, Wesley, *The Ultimate Enemy: British Intelligence and Nazi Germany, 1933–1939* (USA: Cornell University Press, 1985)

West, Nigel, *The Sigint Secrets: The Signals Intelligence War, 1900 to Today* (New York: William Morrow and Company, 1986)

——, *The Secret War for the Falklands: The SAS, MI6, and the War Whitehall nearly lost* (Sphere edition, 2007)

Willmott, H P, *Empires in the Balance: Japanese and Allied Pacific Strategies to April 1942* (Annapolis USA: Naval Institute Press, 1982)

——, *The Barrier and the Javelin: Japanese and Allied Pacific Strategies February to June 1942* (Annapolis USA: Naval Institute Press, 1983)

——, *Grave of a Dozen Schemes: British Naval Planning and the War Against Japan 1943–1945* (UK: Airlife Publishing, 1996)

Wilson, Ben, *Empire of the Deep: The Rise and Fall of the British Navy* (London: Weidenfeld & Nicolson, 2013)

Wilson, Michael, *A Submariners' War: The Indian Ocean 1939–45* (UK: Spellmount, 2008)

Winton, John, *Ultra in the Pacific: how breaking Japanese codes and ciphers affected naval operations against Japan 1941–1945* (Annapolis USA, Naval Institute Press, 1993)

——, *Cunningham: The Greatest Admiral since Nelson* (London: John Murray, 1998)

Woodburn-Kirby, S, *The War against Japan:* (London, HMSO, 1957–60): Vol 1 *The Loss of Singapore* (1957); Vol 2 *India's Most Dangerous Hour* (1958)

——, *Singapore: The Chain of Disaster* (London: Cassell, 1971)

Worth, Roland H, *Secret Allies in the Pacific: covert intelligence and codebreaking between the United States, Great Britain and other nations prior to Pearl Harbor* (North Carolina, USA: McFarland & Co, 2001)

Wyllie, James, and Michael McKinley, *Codebreakers: The Secret Intelligence Unit that changed the course of the First World War* (Ebury Press, 2015)

Yardley, Herbert O, *The American Black Chamber* (USA: Amereon, 1996 reprint of 1931 edn)

Articles and monographs

Allen, G R G, 'A Ghost from Gallipoli', *Journal of the Royal United Service Institution*, 108 (May 1963), 137

Allen, Matthew, 'Rear Admiral Reginald Custance: Director of Naval Intelligence 1899–1902', *Mariner's Mirror*, 78:1 (February 1992), 61–75

——, 'The Foreign Intelligence Commission and the Origins of the Naval Intelligence Department of the Admiralty', *Mariner's Mirror*, 81:1 (February 1995), 65–78

Alvarez, David, 'Left in the Dust: Italian Signals Intelligence, 1915–1943', *International Journal of Intelligence and CounterIntelligence*, 14:3 (2001), 388–408

Babij, Orest, 'The Royal Navy and the Defence of the British Empire 1928–1934', in *Far Flung Lines – Essays on Imperial Defence in Honour of Donald Mackenzie Schurman*, ed Greg Kennedy and Keith Neilson (London: Frank Cass, 1997)

Balchin, W G V, 'United Kingdom Geographers in the Second World War: A Report', *Geographic Journal*, 153:2 (July 1987), 159–80

Barnett, Correlli, 'The Influence of History upon Sea Power: The Royal Navy in the Second World War', in *Naval Power in the Twentieth Century*, ed N A M Rodger (Basingstoke: Macmillan, 1996)

Batey, Mavis, 'Dilly Knox – A Reminiscence of this Pioneer Enigma Cryptanalyst', *Cryptologia*, 32:2 (2008), 104–30

Baugh, Daniel A, 'Confusions and Constraints: The Navy and British Defence Planning 1919–39', in *Naval Power in the Twentieth Century*, ed N A M Rodger (Basingstoke: Macmillan, 1996)

Beesly, Patrick, 'Who was the Third Man at Pyry?', *Cryptologia*, 11:2 (1987), 78–80

——, 'Convoy PQ 17: A study of intelligence and decision-making', *Intelligence and National Security*, 5:2 (1990), 292–322

——, 'Godfrey, Vice Admiral John Henry (1888–1971)', *Dictionary of National Biography* (OUP, 2004)

Beiriger, Edward Eugene, 'Building a Navy "Second to None": The US Naval Act of 1916, American Attitudes toward Great Britain, and the First World War', *British Journal for Military History*, 3:3 (2017)

Bell, Christopher M, 'Thinking the Unthinkable: British and American Naval Strategies for an Anglo-American War, 1918–1931', *International History Review*, 19:4 (November 1997), 789–808

——, 'The "Singapore Strategy" and the Deterrence of Japan: Winston Churchill, the Admiralty and the Dispatch of Force Z', *English Historical Review*, 116:467 (June 2001), 604–64

——, 'The Royal Navy, war planning, and intelligence assessments of Japan', in *Intelligence and Statecraft: Use and Limits of Intelligence in International Security*, ed Peter Jackson and Jennifer Siegel (Westport, CT, USA: Praeger, 2005)

——, 'Contested Waters: The Royal Navy in the Fisher Era', *War in History*, 23:1 (2016), 115–26

Bell, Falko, '"One of our Most Valuable Sources of Intelligence": British Intelligence and the Prisoner of War System in 1944', *Intelligence and National Security*, 31:4 (2016), 556–78

Best, Anthony, 'This probably overvalued military power: British Intelligence and Whitehall's view of Japan', *Intelligence and National Security*, 12:3 (1997), 67–94

——, 'Intelligence, diplomacy and the Japanese threat to British interests, 1914–1941', *Intelligence and National Security*, 17:1 (2002)

Bird, Keith, and Jason Hines, 'In the Shadow of Ultra: A Reappraisal of German Naval Communications Intelligence in 1914–1918', *Northern Mariner*, 18:2 (2018), 97–117

Breemer, Jan S, 'Defeating the U-boat: Inventing Anti-submarine Warfare', *US Naval War College Newport Papers*, 36 (August 2010)

Brooks, John, 'Preparing for Armageddon: Gunnery Practices and Exercises in the Grand Fleet prior to Jutland', *Journal of Strategic Studies*, 38:7 (2015), 1006–23

——, 'The Battle of Jutland: "an unpalatable result"', in *Jutland, History and the First World War*, ed David Morgan-Owen, Corbett Paper No 18 (King's College, London, 2017)

Bruce, James, '"A shadowy entity": M.I.1(b) and British Communications Intelligence, 1914–1922', *Intelligence and National Security*, 32:3 (2017), 313–32

Burdick, Charles, '"Moro": The Resupply of German Submarines in Spain, 1939–1942', *Central European History*, 3:3 (1970), 256–84

Chapman, John W M, 'Russia, Germany and Anglo-Japanese Intelligence Co-operation, 1898–1906', in *Russia: War, Peace and Diplomacy: Essays in honour of John Erickson*, ed Ljubica and Mark Erickson (Weidenfeld and Nicolson, 2004)

Clabby, John F, 'Brigadier John Tiltman: A Giant among Cryptanalysts' (Center for Cryptologic History, National Security Agency, 2007)

Clemmesen, Michael, 'On the Effects of Knavery: From a London Working Lunch to the Danish Summer 1916 War Scare', *From war and peace*, Danish Military History Commission, No 1 (2015)

Clout, Hugh, and Cyril Gosme, 'The Naval Intelligence Handbooks: a monument in geographical writing', *Progress in Human Geography*, 27:2 (2003), 153–73

Cobb, Stephen W A, 'Evasion or Enforcement – the complexity of the Blockade revisited: the *bona fides* of the Lavino Company across three continents in 1916', *British Journal for Military History*, 3:3 (2017)

Coogan, John W, 'The Short War Illusion Resurrected: The Myth of Economic Warfare as the British Schlieffen Plan', *Journal of Strategic Studies*, 38:7 (2015), 1045–64

Cote, Owen R, 'The Third Battle: Innovation in the US Navy's Silent Cold War Struggle with Soviet Submarines', *US Naval War College Newport Papers*, 16 (2003)

Davies, Huw, 'Naval Intelligence Support to the British Army in the Peninsular War', *Journal of the Society for Army Historical Research*, 86:345 (2008)

Davies, Pete, 'Estimating Soviet Power: The Creation of Britain's Defence Intelligence Staff 1960–65', *Intelligence and National Security*, 26:6 (2011), 818–41

Defalco III, Ralph Lee, 'Blind to the Sun: US Intelligence Failures before the War with Japan', *International Journal of Intelligence and Counter-Intelligence*, 16 (2003), 95–107

Dewey, P E, 'Food Production and Policy in the United Kingdom, 1914–1918', *Transactions of the Royal Historical Society*, 30 (1980), 71–89

Dockrill, Michael, 'The Foreign Office Political Intelligence Department and Germany in 1918', in *Strategy and Intelligence: British Policy during the First World War*, ed Michael Dockrill and David French (London: Hambledon Press, 1996)

Dorman, Andrew, Michael D Kandiah and Gillian Staerck, 'The Falklands War', Centre for Contemporary British History, Oral History Programme (2005)

Duffey, Romney B, 'Submarine warfare and intelligence in the Atlantic and Pacific in the Second World War: comparisons and lessons learned for two opponents', *Journal for Maritime Research*, 19:2 (2017), 143–67

Duffy, Michael, 'British Naval Intelligence and Bonaparte's Egyptian Expedition of 1798', *Mariner's Mirror*, 84:3 (August 1998), 278–90

——, 'British Intelligence and the Breakout of the French Atlantic Fleet from Brest in 1799', *Intelligence and National Security*, 22:5 (2007), 601–18

Dunley, Richard, '"Not Intended to Act as Spies": The Consular Intelligence Service in Denmark and Germany 1906–14', *International History Review*, 37:3 (2015), 481–502

Dylan, Huw, 'The Joint Intelligence Bureau: (Not So) Secret Intelligence for the Post-War World', *Intelligence and National Security*, 27:1 (2012), 27–45

Easter, David, 'British Intelligence and Propaganda during the "Confrontation", 1963–1966', *Intelligence and National Security*, 16:2 (2001), 83–102

——, 'GCHQ and British External Policy in the 1960s', *Intelligence and National Security*, 23:5 (2008), 681–706

Erskine, Ralph, 'Naval Enigma: A Missing Link', *International Journal of Intelligence and Counter Intelligence*, 3:4 (1989), 493–508

——, 'The First Naval Enigma Decrypts of World War II', *Cryptologia*, 21:1 (1997), 42–46

——, 'Eavesdropping on "Bodden": ISOS v the Abwehr in the straits of Gibraltar', *Intelligence and National Security*, 12:3 (1997), 110–29

——, 'When a Purple Machine went missing: How Japan nearly discovered America's greatest secret', *Intelligence and National Security*, 12:3 (1997), 185–9

——, 'The Holden agreement on naval sigint: The first BRUSA?', *Intelligence and National Security*, 14:2 (1999), 187–97

——, 'The Poles reveal their Secrets: Alistair Denniston's Account of the July 1939 Meeting at Pyry', *Cryptologia*, 30:4 (2006), 294–305

——, 'The 1944 Naval BRUSA Agreement and its Aftermath', *Cryptologia*, 30:1 (2006), 1–22

Erskine, Ralph, and Peter Freeman, 'Brigadier John Tiltman: One of Britain's Finest Cryptologists', *Cryptologia*, 27:4 (2003), 289–318

Everest-Phillips, Max, 'Reassessing pre-war Japanese Espionage: The Rutland naval spy case and the Japanese intelligence threat before Pearl Harbor', *Intelligence and National Security*, 21:2 (2006), 258–85

——, 'Colin Davidson's British Indian Intelligence Operations in Japan 1915–23 and the Demise of the Anglo-Japanese Alliance', *Intelligence and National Security*, 24:5 (2009), 674–69

Faulkner, Marcus, 'The Kriegsmarine, Signals Intelligence and the Development of B-Dienst before the Second World War', *Intelligence and National Security*, 25:4 (2010), 521–46

Fedorowich, Kent, 'Axis prisoners of war as sources for British military intelligence, 1939–42', *Intelligence and National Security*, 14:2 (1999), 156–78

Ferris, John, 'A British "unofficial" aviation mission and Japanese naval developments, 1919–1929', *Journal of Strategic Studies*, 5:3 (1982), 416–39

——, 'Before "Room 40": The British Empire and signals intelligence, 1898–1914', *Journal of Strategic Studies*, 12:4 1989), 431–57

——, '"Worthy of Some Better Enemy?" The British Assessment of the Imperial Japanese Army, 1919–1941, and the Fall of Singapore', *Canadian Journal of History*, 28 (August 1993)

——, 'Airbandit: C3I and Strategic Air Defence during the First Battle of Britain', in *Strategy and Intelligence: British Policy during the First World War*, ed Michael Dockrill and David French (London: Hambledon Press, 1996)

——, '"It is our business in the Navy to command the Seas": The Last Decade of British Maritime Supremacy, 1919–1929', in *Far Flung Lines – Essays on Imperial Defence in honour of Donald Mackenzie Schurman*, ed Greg Kennedy and Keith Neilson (London: Frank Cass, 1997)

——, 'The road to Bletchley Park: the British experience with Signals Intelligence, 1892–1945', *Intelligence and National Security*, 17:1 (March 2002), 53–84

——, 'Armaments and allies: the Anglo-Japanese strategic relationship 1911–1921', in *The Anglo-Japanese Alliance, 1902–1922*, ed Phillips Payson O'Brien (RoutledgeCurzon, 2004)

——, '"Now that the Milk is Spilt": Appeasement and the Archive on Intelligence', *Diplomacy and Statecraft*, 19:3 (2008), 527–65

——, '"Consistent with an Intention": The Far East Combined Bureau and the Outbreak of the Pacific War, 1940–41', *Intelligence and National Security*, 27:1 (February 2012), 5–26

——, 'The Fulcrum of Power: Britain, Japan and the Asia-Pacific Region: 1880–1945', in *Maritime Strategy and National Security in Japan and Britain*, ed Alessio Patalano (Leiden: Koninklijke Brill NV, 2012)

——, 'Pragmatic hegemony and British economic warfare, 1900–1918', in *Britain's War at Sea 1914–1918*, ed Greg Kennedy (Routledge, 2016)

——, 'Issues in British and American Signals Intelligence, 1919–1932', National Security Agency, Center for Cryptologic History, Special Series I, Vol 11 (2016)

Ford, Christopher A, and Rosenberg, David A, 'The Naval Intelligence Underpinnings of Reagan's Maritime Strategy', *Journal of Strategic Studies*, 28:2 (April 2005), 379–409

Ford, Douglas, 'British Naval Policy and the War against Japan 1937–1945: Distorted Doctrine, Insufficient Resources, or Inadequate Intelligence', *International Journal of Naval History*, 4: 1 (April 2005)

——, 'US Naval Intelligence and the Imperial Japanese Fleet during the Washington Treaty Era, c1922–36', *Mariner's Mirror*, 93:3 (2007), 281–306

——, 'A Statement of Hopes? The effectiveness of US and British naval war plans against Japan, 1920–1941', *Mariner's Mirror*, 101:1 (February 2015), 63–80

Franklin, G D, 'A Breakdown in Communication: Britain's Over Estimation of ASDIC's Capabilities in the 1930s', *Mariner's Mirror*, 84:2 (1998), 204–14

——, 'The origins of the Royal Navy's vulnerability to surfaced night U-boat attack 1939–40', *Mariner's Mirror*, 90:1 (February 2004), 73–84

Freeman, Peter, 'MI1(b) and the origins of British diplomatic cryptanalysis', *Intelligence and National Security*, 22:2 (2007), 206–28

French, David, 'Failures of Intelligence: The Retreat to the Hindenburg Line and the March 1918 Offensive', in *Strategy and Intelligence: British Policy during the First World War*, ed Michael Dockrill and David French (London: Hambledon Press, 1996)

Glazebrook, R T, 'James Alfred Ewing 1855–1935', *Obituary Notices of Fellows of the Royal Society*, 1: 4 (December 1935), 475–92

Goldrick, James, 'The need for a New Naval History of the First World War', Corbett Paper No 7 (King's College, London, November 2011)

——, 'Buying Time: British Submarine Capability in the Far East, 1919–1940', *Global War Studies*, 11:3 (2014), 3–50

——, 'Anti-access for Sea Control: The British Mining Campaign in World War I', *US Naval Institute Naval History Magazine*, 32: 5 (October 2018)

Goldstein, Erik, 'Hertford House: The Naval Intelligence Geographical Section and Peace Conference Planning, 1917–1919', *Mariner's Mirror*, 72:1 (1986), Notes

Goodman, Michael S, 'Covering up Spying in the "Buster Crabb" Affair: A Note', *International History Review*, 30:1 (December 2008), 768–84

——, 'Learning to Walk: The Origins of the UK's Joint Intelligence Committee', *International Journal of Intelligence and CounterIntelligence*, 21:1 (2008), 40–56

——, 'The Foundations of Anglo-American Intelligence Sharing', *Studies in Intelligence*, 59:2 (June 2015)

Gordon, Andrew, 'The Admiralty and Imperial Overstretch 1902–1940', *Journal of Strategic Studies*, 17:1 (1994), 63–85

Grove, Eric, 'A War Fleet built for Peace: British Naval Rearmament in the 1930s and the dilemma of Deterrence versus Defence', *US Naval War College Review*, 44:2 (Spring 1991)

——, 'The battleship is dead; Long live the battleship. HMS *Dreadnought* and the limits of technological innovation', *Mariner's Mirror*, 93:4 (2007), 415–27.

——, '"The Battle of the Atlantic": A Legend Deconstructed', *Mariner's Mirror*, 105:3 (August 2019), 336–9

Hackmann, Willem D, 'Sonar Research and Naval Warfare 1914–1954: A Case Study of Twentieth-Century Establishment Science', *Historical Studies in the Physical and Biological Sciences*, 16:1 (1986), 83–110

Haggie, Paul, 'The Royal Navy and War Planning in the Fisher Era', *Journal of Contemporary History*, 8:3 (July 1973), 113–31

Hamilton, Charles Iain, 'The Character and Organisation of the Admiralty Operational Intelligence Centre during the Second World War', *War in History*, 7:3 (2000), 295–324

Hammant, Thomas R, 'The Magdeburg Incident: The Russian View', *Cryptologia*, 24:4 (2000), 333–8

Hampshire, Edward, 'From Malin Head to "Okean 75": shadowing and intelligence operations by Royal Navy surface ships 1975–1985', *Intelligence and National Security*, 33:5 (2018), 659–74

Hanyok, Robert J, and David P Mowry, 'West Wind Clear: Cryptology and the Winds Message Controversy – A Documentary History', Center for Cryptologic History, US National Security Agency (2008)

Harrison, E D R, 'British Radio Security and Intelligence, 1939–43', *English Historical Review*, 124:506 (February 2009), 53–93

Hattendorf, John B, 'The Evolution of the US Navy's Maritime Strategy, 1977–1986', *US Naval War College Newport Papers*, 19 (2004)

Hattendorf, John B, and Peter M Swartz, 'US Naval Strategy in the 1980s: Selected Documents', *US Naval War College Newport Papers*, 33 (2008)

Herman, Michael, 'What Difference Did It Make?', *Intelligence and National Security*, 26:6 (2011), 886–901

Herwig, Holger H, 'Total Rhetoric, Limited War: Germany's U-boat Campaign 1917–1918', *Journal of Military and Strategic Studies, University of Calgary*, 1:1 (1998)

Hiley, Nicholas P, 'The Failure of British Espionage against Germany, 1907–1914', *Historical Journal*, 26:4 (December 1983), 867–89

——, 'The strategic origins of room 40', *Intelligence and National Security*, 2:2 (1987), 245–73

Hines, Jason, 'Sins of Omission and Commission: A Reassessment of the Role of Intelligence in the Battle of Jutland', *Journal of Military History*, 72:4 (2008)

Hinsley, F H, 'British Intelligence in the Second World War: An Overview', *Cryptologia*, 14:1 (1990), 1–10

——, 'The Influence of ULTRA in the Second World War', University of Cambridge lecture (19 October 1993)

Hoerber, Thomas, 'Psychology and Reasoning in the Anglo-German Naval Agreement, 1935–1939', *Historical Journal*, 52:1 (March 2009), 153–74

Horner, D M, 'Australian Estimates of the Japanese Threat, 1905–1941', in *Estimating Foreign Military Power*, ed Philip Towle (London: Croom Helm, 1982)

Howard, John, 'Fixed Sonar Systems: The History and Future of the Underwater Silent Sentinel', *Submarine Review* (April 2011)

James, W M, 'A Ghost from Gallipoli', *Journal of the Royal United Service Institution*, 108 (November 1963), 373

Janicki, David A, 'The British Blockade during World War I: The Weapon of Deprivation', *Inquiries Journal*, 6:6 (2014), 1–5

Jones, Jerry W, 'The Naval Battle of Paris', *US Naval War College Review*, 62:2 (2009)

Jones, R V, 'Alfred Ewing and "Room 40"', *Notes and Records of the Royal Society of London*, 34:1 (July 1979), 65–90

Jopp, Tobias A, 'Firms and the German war economy: Warmongers for the sake of profit?', in *The Economics of the Great War: A Centennial Perspective*, ed Stephen Broadberry and Mark Harrison (London: Centre for Economic Policy Research, 2018)

Kahn, David, 'Codebreaking in World Wars I and II: The Major Successes and Failures: Their Causes and their Effects', *Historical Journal*, 23:3 (Sep 1980), 617–39

——, 'Edward Bell and his Zimmermann telegram memoranda', *Intelligence and National Security*, 14:3 (1999), 143–59

Kelly, Saul, 'Room 47: The Persian Prelude to the Zimmermann Telegram', *Cryptologia*, 37:1 (2013), 11–50

Kemp, Peter, 'Chatfield, Admiral of the Fleet Lord Alfred Ernle Montacute (1873–1967)', *Dictionary of National Biography* (OUP, 2004)

Kennedy, Greg, 'What Worth the Americans? The British Strategic Foreign Policy-Making Elite's View of American Maritime Power in the Far East, 1933–1941', in *British Naval Strategy East of Suez, 1900–2000*, ed Greg Kennedy (UK: Frank Cass, 2005)

——, 'Intelligence and the Blockade, 1914–1917: A Study in Administration, Friction and Command', *Intelligence and National Security*, 22:5 (2007)

——, 'Strategy and Power: The Royal Navy, the Foreign Office and the Blockade, 1914–17', *Defence Studies*, 8:2 (2008), 190–206

——, 'The North Atlantic Triangle and the blockade, 1914–1915', *Journal of Transatlantic Studies*, 6:1 (2008), 22–33

——, 'Anglo-American Strategic Relations and Intelligence Assessments of Japanese Airpower 1934–1941', *Journal of Military History*, 7:4 (July 2010), 737–73

Kennedy, Paul M, 'Imperial Cable Communications and Strategy, 1870–1914', *English Historical Review*, 86:341 (October 1971), 728–52

Kluiters, Frans, 'R B Tinsley: A Biographical Note', www.nisa-intelligence.nl (January 2004)

Knight, Jane, 'Nelson and the Eastern Mediterranean 1803–5', *Mariner's Mirror*, 91:2 (May 2005), 195–215

Kohnen, David, 'Seizing German Naval Intelligence from the Archives 1870–1945', *Global War Studies*, 12:1 (2015), 133–71

Kwan, Toh Boon, 'Brinksmanship and Deterrence Success during the Anglo-Indonesian Sunda Straits Crisis, 1964–1966', *Journal of South-East Asian Studies*, 36:3 (2005), 399–417

Lambert, Andrew, 'Preparing for the Long Peace: The Reconstruction of the Royal Navy 1815–1830', *Mariner's Mirror*, 82:1 (February 1996), 41–54

——, '"The Possibility of Ultimate Action in the Baltic": The Royal Navy at War, 1914–1916', in *Jutland, World War I's Greatest Naval Battle*, ed Michael Epkenhans, Jörg Hillmann and Frank Nagler (University Press of Kentucky, 2015)

Lambert, Nicholas, 'British Naval Policy: 1913–1914: Financial Limitation and Strategic Revolution', *Journal of Modern History*, 67:3 (September 1995), 595–626

——, 'Transformation and Technology in the Fisher Era: The Impact of the Communications Revolution', *Journal of Strategic Studies*, 27:2 (2004), 272–97

——, 'Strategic Command and Control for Manoeuvre Warfare: Creation of the Royal Navy's War Room System, 1905–1915', *Journal of Military History*, 69:2 (April 2005), 361–410

Larsen, Daniel, 'British Intelligence and the 1916 Mediation Mission of Colonel Edward M House', *Intelligence and National Security*, 25:5 (October 2010), 682–704

——, 'The First Intelligence Prime Minister: David Lloyd George (1916–1922)', UK Cabinet Office (February 2013)

——, 'Intelligence in the First World War: The State of the Field', *Intelligence and National Security*, 29:2 (2014), 282–302

——, 'British codebreaking and American diplomatic telegrams, 1914–1915', *Intelligence and National Security*, 32:2 (2017), 256–63

——, 'British signals intelligence and the 1916 Easter Rising in Ireland', *Intelligence and National Security*, 33:1 (2018), 48–66

Lockhart, John Bruce, 'Sir William Wiseman Bart – agent of influence', *RUSI Journal*, 134:2 (1989), 63–7

Lundeberg, Philip K, 'The German Naval Critique of the U-boat Campaign 1915–1918', *Military Affairs*, 27:3 (1963)

McCallum, K I, 'A Little Neglect: Defective Shell in the Royal Navy', *Journal of Naval Engineering*, 34:2 (1993)

McCartney, Innes, 'The "Tin Openers" – Myth and Reality: Intelligence from U-boat Wrecks during World War I', *Proceedings of the Twenty-Fourth Annual Historical Diving Conference, Poole, 2014* (Historical Diving Society, 2014)

——, 'The Archaeology of First World War U-boat Losses in the English Channel and its Impact on the Historical Record', *Mariner's Mirror*, 105:2 (2019), 183–201

Maclaren, John, and Nicholas Hiley, 'Nearer the Truth: The search for Alexander Szek', *Intelligence and National Security*, 4:4 (1989), 813–26

McLaughlin, Stephen, 'Battlelines and Fast Wings: Battlefleet Tactics in the Royal Navy, 1900–1914', *Journal of Strategic Studies*, 38:7 (2015), 985–1005

Mahnken, Thomas G, 'Gazing at the sun: The Office of Naval Intelligence and Japanese naval innovation, 1918–1941', *Intelligence and National Security*, 11:3 (1996), 424–46

Maiolo, Joseph, '"I believe the Hun is cheating": British Admiralty technical intelligence and the German navy, 1936–39', *Intelligence and National Security*, 11:1 (1996), 32–58

——, 'Deception and Intelligence Failure: Anglo-German preparations for U-boat warfare in the 1930s', *Journal of Strategic Studies*, 22:4 (1999), 55–76

——, 'The Knock-out Blow against the Import System: Admiralty Expectations of Nazi Germany's Naval Strategy, 1934–9', *Institute of Historical Research*, 72:178 (June 1999)

——, 'Anglo-Soviet Naval Armaments Diplomacy before the Second World War', *English Historical Review*, 123:501 (2008), 351–78

——, 'Did the Royal Navy Decline between the two World Wars?', *RUSI Journal*, 159:4 (August/ September 2014), 18–24

Malcomson, Tom, 'An Aid to Nelson's Victory? A Description of the Harbour of Aboukir, 1798', *Mariner's Mirror*, 84:3 (August 1998), 291–7

Marrero, Javier Ponce, 'Logistics for Commerce War in the Atlantic during the First World War: The German *Etappe* System in Action', *Mariner's Mirror*, 92:4 (2006), 455–64

Morgan-Owen, David, 'A Revolution in Naval Affairs? Technology, Strategy and British Naval Policy in the "Fisher Era"', *Journal of Strategic Studies*, 38:7 (2015), 944–65

——, 'Cooked up in the Dinner Hour?: Sir Arthur Wilson's War Plan Reconsidered', *English Historical Review*, 80:545 (August 2015)

Morris, Roger, '200 Years of Admiralty Charts and Surveys', *Mariner's Mirror*, 82:4 (November 1996), 420–35

Murfett, Malcolm H, 'Phillips, Admiral Sir Tom Spencer Vaughan (1888–1941)', *Dictionary of National Biography* (OUP, 2004)

Neilson, Keith, 'The Defence Requirements Sub-Committee, British Strategic Foreign Policy, Neville Chamberlain and the Path to Appeasement', *English Historical Review*, 118:477 (June 2003), 651–84

——, '"Unbroken Thread": Japan, Maritime Power and British Imperial Defence, 1920–32', in *British Naval Strategy East of Suez 1900–2000*, ed Greg Kennedy (UK: Frank Cass, 2005)

O'Brien, Phillips Payson, 'The Titan Refreshed: Imperial Overstretch and the British Navy before the First World War', *Past & Present*, 172 (August 2001), 146–69

——, 'Britain and the end of the Anglo-Japanese Alliance', in *The Anglo-Japanese Alliance, 1902–1922*, ed Phillips Payson O'Brien (RoutledgeCurzon, 2004)

Offer, Avner, 'British Naval Plans and the Coming of the Great War', *Past and Present*, 107 (May 1985), 204–26

——, 'Morality and Admiralty: "Jacky" Fisher, Economic Warfare and the Laws of War', *Journal of Contemporary History*, 23:1 (January 1988), 99–118

Parker, Frederick D, 'Pearl Harbor Revisited: US Navy Communications Intelligence 1924–1941', *Center for Cryptologic History* (US National Security Agency, 1993)

——, 'A Priceless Advantage: US Navy Communications Intelligence and the Battles of Coral Sea, Midway and the Aleutians', *Center for Cryptologic History* (US National Security Agency, 1993)

Parr, Helen, 'The British Decision to Upgrade Polaris, 1970–4', *Contemporary European History*, 22:2 (May 2013), 253–74

Parry, David, 'The History of British Submarine Sonars', www.rnsubs.co.uk/articles

Partridge, M S, 'The Royal Navy and the End of the Close Blockade, 1885–1905: A Revolution in Naval Strategy?', *Mariner's Mirror*, 75:2, 119–36

Peden, G C, 'The Burden of Imperial Defence and the Continental Commitment Reconsidered', *Historical Journal*, 27: 2 (1984), 405–23

Pratt, Lawrence, 'The Anglo-American Naval Conversations on the Far East of January 1938', *International Affairs (Royal Institute of International Affairs 1944–)*, 47:4 (1971), 745–63

Rahn, Werner, 'German Naval Strategy and Armament, 1919–39', in *Technology and Naval Combat in the Twentieth Century and Beyond*, ed Phillips Payson O'Brien (London: Routledge, 2007)

——, 'The Battle of Jutland from the German Perspective', in *Jutland: World War I's Greatest Naval Battle*, ed Michael Epkenhans, Jörg Hillmann and Frank Nagler (University Press of Kentucky, 2015)

Ranft, Bryan, 'The protection of British seaborne trade and the development of systematic planning for war, 1860–1906', in *Technical Change and British Naval Policy 1860–1906*, ed Bryan Ranft (London: Hodder and Stoughton, 1977)

Redfearn, Mason, and Richard Aldrich, 'The Perfect Cover: British Intelligence, the Soviet Fleet and Distant Water Trawler Operations, 1963–1974', *Intelligence and National Security*, 12:3 (1997), 166–77

Redgment, P G, 'High-Frequency Direction Finding in the Royal Navy – Development of Anti-U-Boat Equipment, 1941–45', in *The Applications of Radar and other Electronic Systems in the Royal Navy in World War 2*, ed F A Kingsley (Palgrave Macmillan, 1995)

Ripsman, Norrin M, and Jack S Levy, 'Wishful Thinking or Buying Time? The Logic of British Appeasement in the 1930s', *International Security*, 33:2 (Fall 2008), 148–81

Ritschl, Albrecht, 'The pity of peace: Germany's economy at war, 1914–1918 and beyond', in *The Economics of World War I*, ed Stephen Broadberry (Cambridge University Press, 2009)

Robb-Webb, Jon, 'Anglo-American Naval Intelligence Co-operation in the Pacific, 1944–45', *Intelligence and National Security*, 22: 5 (November 2007), 767–86

Robson, Maria, 'Signals in the sea: the value of Ultra intelligence in the Mediterranean in World War II', *Journal of Intelligence History*, 13:2 (2014), 176–88

Rodger, N A M, 'The Dark Ages of the Admiralty, 1869–85', *Mariner's Mirror*, Part I 61:4 (1975), 331–344; Part II 62:1 (1976), 33–46; Part III 62:2 (1976), 121–8

——, 'The Royal Navy in the Era of the World Wars: Was it fit for purpose?', *Mariner's Mirror*, 97:1 (February 2011), 272–84

——, 'Anglo-German Naval Rivalry, 1860–1914', in *Jutland: World War I's Greatest Naval Battle*, ed Michael Epkenhans, Jörg Hillmann and Frank Nagler (University Press of Kentucky, 2014)

Rosen, Jacob, 'Captain Reginald Hall and the Balfour Declaration', *Middle Eastern Studies*, 24:1 (January 1988), 56–67

Sadkovich, James J, 'Understanding Defeat: Reappraising Italy's Role in World War II', *Journal of Contemporary History*, 24:1 (January 1989), 27–61

Sarantakes, Nicholas E, 'One Last Crusade: The British Pacific Fleet and its Impact on the Anglo-American Alliance', *English Historical Review*, 121:491 (April 2006), 429–66

Scammell, Clare M, 'The Royal Navy and the strategic origins of the Anglo-German naval agreement of 1935', *Journal of Strategic Studies*, 20:2 (1997), 92–118

Seligmann, Matthew S, 'New Weapons for New Targets: Sir John Fisher, the Threat from Germany, and the building of HMS "Dreadnought" and HMS "Invincible", 1902–1907', *International History Review*, 30:2 (June 2008), 303–31

——, 'Switching Horses: The Admiralty's Recognition of the Threat from Germany, 1900–1905', *International History Review*, 30:2 (June 2008), 239–58

——, 'Intelligence Information and the 1909 Naval Scare: The Secret Foundations of a Public Panic', *War in History*, 17:1 (2010), 37–59

——, 'Britain's Great Security Mirage: The Royal Navy and the Franco-Russian Naval Threat, 1898–1906', *Journal of Strategic Studies*, 35:6 (2012), 861–86

——, 'A German Preference for a Medium-Range Battle? British Assumptions about German Naval Gunnery, 1914–1915', *War in History*, 19:1 (2012), 33–48

——, 'The Renaissance of Pre-First World War Naval History', *Journal of Strategic Studies*, 36:3 (2012), 454–79

——, 'Naval History by Conspiracy Theory: The British Admiralty before the First World War and the Methodology of Revisionism', *Journal of Strategic Studies*, 38:7 (2015), 966–84

——, 'Failing to Prepare for the Great War? The Absence of Grand Strategy in British War Planning before 1914', *War in History*, 24:4 (2017), 414–37

——, 'The Anglo-German Naval Race, 1898–1914', in *Arms Races in International Politics: From the Nineteenth to the Twenty-First Century*, ed Thomas Mahnken, Joseph Maiolo and David Stevenson (OUP, 2016)

——, 'A Service Ready for Total War? The State of the Royal Navy in July 1914', *English Historical Review*, 133:560 (February 2018)

Setzekorn, Eric, 'The Office of Naval Intelligence in the First World War: Diverse Threats, Divergent Responses', *Studies in Intelligence*, 61:2 (June 2017)

Sherman, David, 'The First Americans: The 1941 US Codebreaking Visit to Bletchley Park' (National Security Agency Center for Cryptologic History, 2016)

Simpson, Michael, 'Force H and British Strategy in the Western Mediterranean 1939–42', *Mariner's Mirror*, 83:1 (1997), 62–75

Siney, Marion C, 'British Official Histories of the Blockade of the Central Powers during the First World War', *American Historical Review*, 68:2 (January 1963), 392–401

Sloan, Geoff, 'Dartmouth, Sir Mansfield Cumming and the origins of the British intelligence community', *Intelligence and National Security*, 22:2 (August 2007), 298–305

Spence, Richard, 'Englishmen in New York: The SIS American Station, 1915–21', *Intelligence and National Security*, 19:3 (2004), 511–37

Steffen, Dirk, 'The Holtzendorff Memorandum of 22 December 1916 and Germany's Declaration of Unrestricted U-boat Warfare', *Journal of Military History*, 68:1 (January 2004), 215–24

Steury, Donald P, 'Naval Intelligence, the Atlantic Campaign and the Sinking of the Bismarck: A Study in the Integration of Intelligence into the Conduct of Naval Warfare', *Journal of Contemporary History*, Intelligence Services during the Second World War, 22:2 (April 1987), 209–33

Stevenson, David, 'The Failure of Peace by Negotiation in 1917', *Historical Journal*, 34:1 (1991), 65–86

Stille, Mark E, 'The Influence of British Operational Intelligence on the War at Sea in the Mediterranean June 1940 – November 1942', Naval War College paper (1994)

Stoddart, Kristan, 'Maintaining the "Moscow Criterion": British Strategic Nuclear Targeting 1974–1979', *Journal of Strategic Studies*, 31:6 (2008), 897–924

Sumida, Jon Tetsuro, '"The Best Laid Plans": The Development of British Battlefleet Tactics, 1919–1942', *International History Review*, 14:4 (1992), 681–700

——, 'A Matter of Timing: The Royal Navy and the Tactics of Decisive Battle, 1912–1916', *Journal of Military History*, 67:1 (2003), 85–136

——, 'Geography, Technology, and British Naval Strategy in the Dreadnought Era', *US Naval War College Review*, 59:3 (Summer 2006)

——, 'British Naval Procurement and Technological Change, 1919–1939', in *Technology and Naval Combat in the Twentieth Century and Beyond*, ed Phillips Payson O'Brien (London: Routledge, 2007)

——, 'Expectation, Adaptation and Resignation: British Battlefleet Tactical Planning, August 1914–April 1916', *US Naval War College Review*, 60:3 (Summer 2007)

Syrett, David, 'On the Threshold of Victory: Communications Intelligence and the Battle for Convoy HX-228, 7–12 March 1943', *Northern Mariner*, 3 (July 2000), 49–55

Tooze, Adam, 'Quantifying Armaments Production in the Third Reich 1933–1945', unpublished paper, www.adamtooze.com (June 2006)

Towle, Philip, 'The evaluation of the experience of the Russo-Japanese War', in *Technical Change and British Naval Policy 1860–1939*, ed Bryan Ranft (London: Hodder and Stoughton, 1977)

Troy, Thomas F, 'The Gaunt-Wiseman Affair: British Intelligence in New York in 1915', *International Journal of Intelligence and CounterIntelligence*, 16:3 (2003), 442–61

Tully, Anthony, and Lu Yu, 'A Question of Estimates: How Faulty Intelligence Drove Scouting at the Battle of Midway', *US Naval War College Review*, 68:2 (Spring 2015)

Vego, Milan, 'Major Convoy Operation to Malta, 10–15 August 1942 (Operation Pedestal)', *US Naval War College Review*, 63:1 (Winter 2010)

——, 'The Destruction of Convoy PQ 17, 27 June–10 July 1942', *US Naval War College Review*, 69:3 (Summer 2016)

Wark, Wesley K, 'In Search of a Suitable Japan: British Naval Intelligence in the Pacific before the Second World War', *Intelligence and National Security*, 1:2 (1986), 189–211

——, 'Baltic myths and submarine bogies: British naval intelligence and Nazi Germany 1933–1939', *Journal of Strategic Studies*, 6:1 (1983), 60–81

Weir, Gary, 'Naval Strategy and Industrial Mobilisation at the Twelfth Hour', *Mariner's Mirror*, 77:3 (1991), 275–87

Welbourn, Donald B, and Tim Crichton, 'The Schnorchel: A Short-Lived Engineering Solution to Scientific Developments', *Transactions of the Newcomen Society*, 78:2 (2008), 293–315

Welchman, Gordon, 'From Polish Bomba to British Bombe: The birth of ultra', *Intelligence and National Security*, 1:1 (1986), 71–110

Wells, Anthony, 'Soviet Submarine Prospects 1985–2000', *Submarine Review* (January 1986)

White, Colin, '"A Man of Business": Nelson as Commander in Chief Mediterranean, May 1803–January 1805', *Mariner's Mirror*, 91:2 (May 2005), 175–94

Whitlock, Captain Duane L, 'The Silent War against the Japanese Navy', *US Naval War College Review*, 48:4 (Autumn 1995), 43

Wilford, Timothy, 'Watching the North Pacific: British and Commonwealth Intelligence before Pearl Harbor', *Intelligence and National Security*, 17:4 (2002), 131–64

——, 'Decoding Pearl Harbor: USN Cryptanalysis and the Challenge of JN25B in 1941', *Northern Mariner*, 12:1 (January 2002), 17–37

Wilson, Keith, 'Directions of Travel: The Earl of Selborne, the Cabinet and the Threat from Germany, 1900–1904', *International History Review*, 30:2 (2008), 259–72

Winkler, Jonathan Reed, 'Information Warfare in World War I', *Journal of Military History*, 73:3 (July 2009), 845–67

Wright, John, 'The Turing Bombe Victory and the first naval Enigma decrypts', *Cryptologia*, 41:4 (2017), 295–328

Unpublished theses

Bell, Falko, 'Wissen ist menschlich. Der Stellenwert der Human Intelligence in der Britischen Kriegsführung 1939–1945' (unpublished doctoral thesis, University of Glasgow, 2014)

Benbow, Tim, 'The Impact of Air Power on Navies: The United Kingdom, 1945–1957' (unpublished doctoral thesis, University of Oxford, 1999)

Blond, A J L, 'Technology and Tradition: Wireless Telegraphy and the Royal Navy 1895–1920' (unpublished and uncompleted doctoral thesis, University of Lancaster, 1993)

Buckey, Christopher M, 'Forging the Shaft of the Spear of Victory: The Creation of the Home Fleet in the Pre-war Era, 1900–1914' (unpublished doctoral thesis, University of Salford, 2013)

Easter, David, 'British defence policy in South-East Asia and the "Confrontation" 1960–66' (unpublished doctoral thesis, London School of Economics and Political Science, 1998)

Ford, Douglas Eric, 'Climbing the Learning Curve: British Intelligence on Japanese Strategy and Military Capabilities during the Second World War in Asia and the Pacific, July 1937 to August 1945' (unpublished doctoral thesis, London School of Economics and Political Science, 2002)

Grimes, Shawn T, 'War Planning and Strategic Development in the Royal Navy 1887–1918' (unpublished doctoral thesis, King's College, University of London, 2004)

Haddon, Catherine, 'Union Jacks and Red Stars on Them: UK Intelligence, the Soviet Nuclear Threat and British Nuclear Weapons Policy, 1945–1970' (unpublished doctoral thesis, Queen Mary College, University of London, 2008)

Hall, Christopher, 'Britain, America and the Search for Comprehensive Naval Limitation, 1927–1936' (unpublished doctoral thesis, University of Oxford, 1982)

Kleinman, Samuel D, 'State's Spies: The Bureau of Secret Intelligence and the Development of State Department Bureaucracy in the First World War' (unpublished honours thesis, Department of History, University of Georgetown, 2016)

Macfarlane, J Allan C, 'A Naval Travesty: The Dismissal of Admiral Sir John Jellicoe, 1917' (unpublished doctoral thesis, University of St Andrews, 2014)

Maddrell, Paul, 'Britain's Exploitation of Occupied Germany for Scientific and Technical Intelligence on the Soviet Union' (unpublished doctoral thesis, University of Cambridge, 1998)

Maiolo, Joseph A, 'Admiralty War Planning, Armaments, Diplomacy, and Intelligence Perceptions of German Sea Power and their influence on British Foreign and Defence Policy 1933–1939' (unpublished doctoral thesis, Department of International History, London School of Economics and Political Science, 1996)

Millar, Russell D, 'The Development of Anglo-American Naval Strategy in the Period of the Second World War, 1938–1941' (unpublished doctoral thesis, King's College, University of London, 1988)

Mullins, Robert E, 'Sharpening the Trident: The Decisions of 1889 and the Creation of Modern Seapower' (unpublished doctoral thesis, King's College, University of London, 2000)

Murfett, Malcolm H, 'Anglo-American Relations in the Period of the Chamberlain Premiership May 1937–May 1940: The Relationship between Naval Strategy and Foreign Policy' (unpublished doctoral thesis, University of Oxford, 1980)

O'Daly, Kevin, 'Living in the Shadows: Britain and the USSR's nuclear weapon delivery systems 1949–62' (unpublished doctoral thesis, University of Westminster, 2016)

Parkinson, Roger, 'The Origins of the Naval Defence Act of 1889 and the New Navalism of the 1890s' (unpublished doctoral thesis, University of Exeter, 2004)

Philbin, Tobias R, 'Admiral Hipper as Naval Commander' (unpublished doctoral thesis, King's College, University of London, 1975)

Robb-Webb, Jonathan J, 'The British Pacific Fleet Experience and Legacy: A Levels of Warfare Analysis' (unpublished doctoral thesis, University of London, 2006)

Robinson, Samuel Alexander, 'Between the devil and the deep blue sea: Ocean Science and the British Cold War State' (unpublished doctoral thesis, University of Manchester, 2015)

Ryan, Joseph Francis, 'The Royal Navy and Soviet Seapower, 1930–1950: Intelligence, Naval Co-operation and Antagonism' (unpublished doctoral thesis, University of Hull, 1996)

Straczek, Josef H, 'The Origins and Development of Royal Australian Navy Signals Intelligence in an Era of Imperial Defence 1914–1945' (unpublished doctoral thesis, University of New South Wales, 2008)

Weir, Philip Anthony, 'The Development of Naval Air Warfare by the Royal Navy and Fleet Air Arm between the two World Wars' (unpublished doctoral thesis, University of Exeter, 2006)

Wells, Anthony Roland, 'Studies in British Naval Intelligence 1880–1945' (unpublished doctoral thesis, University of London, 1972)

West, Kieran, 'Intelligence and the Development of British Grand Strategy in the First World War' (unpublished doctoral thesis, University of Cambridge, 2011)

Websites

The following have provided valuable information and in some cases access to primary documents. Where appropriate they are referenced in the footnotes.

forum.axishistory.com Forum primarily devoted to the military operations and capabilities of the Axis states but much Allied material too. Covers all major war theatres.

www.britishempireatwar.org Forum for scholars interested in all aspects of the British Empire's war history.

www.cia.gov/library/readingroom Contains a treasure trove of original CIA and other United States Government intelligence documents officially released.

www.combinedfleet.com Editor Jonathan Parshall. Contains useful reference material and comment on all aspects of the IJN and its operations during the Second World War.

www.cryptocellar.org Managed by Frode Weierud. Contains much historical material on twentieth-century cryptography but primarily Second World War.

www.ellsbury.com Contains much historical background on Enigma, including the full texts of Hugh Alexander, 'Cryptographic History of Work on the German Naval Enigma', and A P Mahon, 'History of Hut Eight'.

www.fleetairarmarchive.net Excellent source of material on the Fleet Air Arm.

www.gwpda.org Contains a useful collection of primary documents relating to the First World War.

www.history.army.mil Website for the US Army Center of Military History. Contains a range of US Army publications and some documents in digital form relevant to the Second World War. Includes a full digital collection of the US Army's Official History of the Second World War.

www.ibiblio.org/hyperwar Contains a useful selection of digitised original political, military and diplomatic documents relating to the Second World War. Includes some digitised official histories including volumes from the British Official History series.

www.intellit.muskingum.edu Editor J Ransom Clark. This is an excellent bibliography of published works on intelligence history.

www.jacar.go.jp/english Japan Centre for Asian Historical records. Operated by the National Archives of Japan and provides digital access to a wide range of Japanese official documents relating to the Second World War originating with the cabinet, ministry of foreign affairs, army and navy. It facilitates searching in English, but the documents themselves remain in the original Japanese.

www.j-aircraft.com Primarily a site devoted to IJNAF and IJAAF aircraft capability, deployment and operations. However, it includes much information on wider naval operations in the Eastern and Pacific theatres complementing that in www.combinedfleet.com.

www.jutland1916.com Comprehensive website marking the centenary of the Battle of Jutland sponsored by distinguished naval historians, providing much valuable information including authoritative track charts.

www.measuringworth.com Contains useful statistical data on the UK and US economies from 1800.

www.milspecmanuals.com Contains a large range of digitised military and intelligence documents relating to the Second World War. The emphasis is primarily on American sources.

Especially useful for sourcing Japanese monographs and similar material. Includes a good searchable database.

www.naval-history.net Provides a substantial collection of digitised original documents and naval history books across the whole twentieth century.

www.navweaps.com Naval technology section has useful papers on technical topics, eg naval weaponry of all types, armoured flight decks and the Royal Navy High Altitude Control System (HACS) for anti-aircraft defence.

www.navypedia.org Reference site providing construction data and basic order of battle of the main naval powers in the twentieth century.

www.nsa.gov/about/cryptologic_heritage/center_crypt The historical section in the US National Security Agency website. Contains publications relating to the Second World War which can be downloaded in pdf format.

www.pacificwrecks.com Database contains much valuable information on all naval and air forces involved in the Pacific war.

www.secretintelligencefiles.com Provides details of British government secret intelligence and foreign policy files, mainly sourced from The National Archives, from 1873 to 1953, with the majority in the 1930s and 1940s.

www.uboat.net Website dedicated to U-boat operations in both World Wars. Includes specifications, individual boat histories and causes of loss.

www.unithistories.com Database providing a breakdown of individual units and biographical details of key individuals involved in the Second World War. Useful for checking appointments held by Royal Navy officers.

www.worldnavalships.com/forums Searchable database and vast series of blogs covering every aspect of naval capabilities and operations in the Second World War.

www.ww2db.com Database with useful reference material relating to the Second World War including copies of original documents.

Index